THE OXFORD ENCYCLOPEDIA OF
BUDDHISM

EDITORIAL BOARD

Editors in Chief
Richard K. Payne
Institute of Buddhist Studies, Emeritus

Georgios T. Halkias
University of Hong Kong

Associate Editors
Anne M. Blackburn
Cornell University

Robert Linrothe
Northwestern University

Scott A. Mitchell
Institute of Buddhist Studies

Francesca Tarocco
Ca' Foscari University of Venice and NYU Shanghai

Vesna A. Wallace
University of California, Santa Barbara

THE OXFORD ENCYCLOPEDIA OF
BUDDHISM

Richard K. Payne
Georgios T. Halkias
EDITORS IN CHIEF

VOLUME 2
G–P

OXFORD
UNIVERSITY PRESS

OXFORD
UNIVERSITY PRESS

Oxford University Press is a department of the University of Oxford.
It furthers the University's objective of excellence in research, scholarship,
and education by publishing worldwide. Oxford is a registered trade mark of
Oxford University Press in the UK and in certain other countries.

Published in the United States of America by Oxford University Press
198 Madison Avenue, New York, NY 10016, United States of America.

Library of Congress Cataloging-in-Publication Data

Names: Payne, Richard K., editor. | Halkias, Georgios, 1967– editor.
Title: The Oxford encyclopedia of Buddhism / Richard K. Payne,
Georgios T. Halkias, Editors in Chief.
Description: New York : Oxford University Press, 2023. |
Includes bibliographical references and index. | Contents: Vol 1 — Vol 2 — Vol 3
Identifiers: LCCN 2023019480 (print) | LCCN 2023019481 (ebook) |
ISBN 9780190256890 (set) | ISBN 9780190605995 (vol. 1 ; hardback) |
ISBN 9780190606008 (vol. 2 ; hardback) | ISBN 9780197746073 (vol. 3 ; hardback) |
ISBN 9780190668433 (ebk)
Subjects: LCSH: Buddhism—Encyclopedias.
Classification: LCC BQ128 .O94 2023 (print) | LCC BQ128 (ebook) |
DDC 294.303—dc23/eng/20230509
LC record available at https://lccn.loc.gov/2023019480
LC ebook record available at https://lccn.loc.gov/2023019481

MIX
Paper from
responsible sources
FSC® C008955

Sheridan Books, Inc., United States of America

About the *Oxford Research Encyclopedia of Religion*

The Oxford Encyclopedia of Buddhism is published as part of the *Oxford Research Encyclopedia of Religion*, a dynamic and scholarly digital resource. This online collection of overview articles provides in-depth, foundational essays on both core and emerging topics in religion. All articles are commissioned under the editorial leadership of international experts of the highest caliber and are vetted through rigorous peer review. A living reference work, the online publication is updatable and enriched with crosslinking and multimedia features. The essays are intended for scholars, practitioners, and university-level readers, including advanced undergraduates, graduate students, and researchers.

Oxford Research Encyclopedia of Religion
Editor in Chief: John Barton, University of Oxford

Selected print titles from the *Oxford Encyclopedia of Religion* series:

The Oxford Encyclopedia of Martin Luther
Edited by Derek R. Nelson and Paul R. Hinlicky

The Oxford Encyclopedia of Religion in America
Edited by John Corrigan

Contents

List of Articles ix

Thematic and Geographical Outlines xiii

Preface (vol. 1) xxi

Introduction (vol. 1) xxiii

Acknowledgments (vol. 1) xxix

THE OXFORD ENCYCLOPEDIA OF BUDDHISM

Directory of Contributors (vol. 3) 2757

Index (vol. 3) 2765

List of Articles

A

Abhidharmakośabhāṣya (Treasury of Metaphysics with Self-Commentary)
Abhisamayālaṃkāra (Ornament for Clear Realization)
American Buddhism during World War II Imprisonment
Amoghavajra
Art, Architecture, and National Memory-Making
Avalokiteśvara: The Bodhisattva of Compassion

B

Bodhisattvabhūmi (The Bodhisattva Stages)
The Body of the Buddha
The Bön Tradition of Dzogchen
Buddhaghosa
Buddhism and Bioethics
Buddhism and Biography
Buddhism and Globalization
Buddhism and Healing in China
Buddhism and Media
Buddhism and Medicine in India
Buddhism and Medicine in Japan
Buddhism and Medicine in Premodern Japan
Buddhism and Print Culture in China
Buddhism and Shinto
Buddhism and the Environment
Buddhism in Colonial Contexts
Buddhism in Film
Buddhisms in Diaspora: The Canadian Context of Chinese Buddhism
Buddhist Art and Architecture in Tibet
Buddhist Chaplaincy

Buddhist Cosmology
Buddhist Geography and Regionalism
Buddhist Meditation and Contemplation
Buddhist Philosophy as Philosophy
Buddhist Wall Paintings
Buddhist Wizards (*Vidhyadhāra/Weizzā/Weikza*): Contemporary Burma/Myanmar
Buddhist Wizards (*Vidhyadhāra/Weizzā/Weikza*): Origins and History

C

Candrakīrti's Middle Way Philosophy
Canon and Commentary in the Earliest Buddhist Manuscripts
Chan Literature
Chöd: A Tibetan Buddhist Practice

D

D. T. Suzuki: A Biography
D. T. Suzuki: Ideas and Influences
Debate in the Tibetan Tradition
Debate Traditions in Premodern Japan
Domestic Dharma in Japan
Dunhuang Art
Dunhuang Texts
Dzogchen

E

Early History of the Drukpa Kagyü School
Early Modern European Encounters with Buddhism
The Economics of Buddhism
Engaged Buddhism
Epigraphy and the Study of Buddhism: South Asia's Northern Corridor
Esoteric Buddhism in Southeast Asia
Ethics and Buddhism

F

Filial Piety in Chinese Buddhism
Fo Guang Shan
Four Noble Truths
From Manuscript to Print in South and Southeast Asia

G

Gelukpa
Global Buddhism
Global Theravada Buddhism: Asian Foundations
Global Theravada: Transmission beyond Asia
Globalizing Tantric Buddhism
Guardian/Protector Deities in Tibetan Buddhism

H

History of Buddhisms in China: The Nanbeicho Period (Late 4th Century to the Sui Dynasty)
Homa: Tantric Fire Ritual
Hsing Yun
Huineng
Humanistic Buddhism (Rensheng Fojiao 人生佛教 / Renjian Fojiao 人間佛教)

I

Imaging the Buddha in South Asia
The Imamura Families and the Making of American Buddhism
Intention in the Pali Suttas and Abhidharma

J

Japanese Buddhisms in Diaspora
Jātaka
Jebtsundamba Khutugtus of Mongolia

K

The Kadampa: A Formative Movement of Tibetan Buddhism
Kālacakra-Maṇḍala: Symbolism and Construction

L

Longchenpa

M

Madhyamaka
Mahāmudrā in India and Tibet
Mañjuśrī
Maritime Buddhism
Marpa Lotsawa Chökyi Lodrö
Mipam
Monastic Education in Contemporary Asia
Mongolian Buddhism in the Democratic Period
Mongolian Buddhism in the Early 20th Century
Mongolian Buddhism in the Yuan Period
Muslim–Buddhist Relations and Buddhism in Muslim Sources until the Mongol Period

N

Nāgārjuna
Naikan: A Meditation Method and Psychotherapy
Narratives of Buddhist Relics and Images
Nechung: A Tibetan Buddhist Oracle
Nichiren

P

Patronage of Buddhist Monasteries in Eastern India, 600–1300 CE
Perfections (Six and Ten) of Bodhisattvas in Buddhist Literature
The Philosophical Works and Influence of Dignāga and Dharmakīrti
Pilgrimage in Buddhist Tibet
Pilgrimage in China
Practices of Protection in the Pali World
Prajñāpāramitā and Khmer Esoteric Buddhism in the 10th to 13th centuries
Psychological Interpreters of Buddhism
Pure Land Buddhism in Tibetan Contexts

Q

Queering Buddhist Traditions

R

The Reincarnation System in Central Asian Buddhism
Rennyo
Ryōgen

S

The Sangha as an Institution
Śāntideva's Introduction to the Practices of Awakening (*Bodhicaryāvatāra*)
Sarvāstivāda Abhidharma
Secular Buddhism
Sheng Yen
Shingon
The Six Nara Schools
Sōka Gakkai
Southeast Asian Refugees in North America
Sri Lanka's Sinhala Buddhist Guardian Deities: Satara Varan Devi
The Study of Visual Culture in South and Southeast Asian Buddhism

T

Taixu
Tantra and the Tantric Traditions of Hinduism and Buddhism
Tantric Buddhism in Japan: Kukai and Saicho

Tantric Buddhism in Japan: Shingon, Tendai, and the Esotericization of Japanese Buddhisms
Tantric Revival in China
Theravāda Buddhism
Thích Nhất Hạnh in the Context of the Modern Development of Vietnamese Buddhism
Three Turnings of the Wheel of Doctrine (Dharma-Cakra)
Tibetan Book of the Dead (*Bardo Thödol*)
Tibetan Buddhism and the Gesar Epic
Tibetan Buddhist Power Objects
Tibetan Medicine and Its Buddhist Contexts
Tibetan Visionary Buddhism
Transmission of Buddhist Media and Texts
Tri Songdetsen
Tsangpa Gyare (1161–1211), Founder of the Drukpa Kagyü School
Tzu Chi

V

The Vajrakīla Tantras
Vinaya Rules for Monks and Nuns
Visualization/Contemplation Sutras (Guan Jing)

W

Western Buddhism and Race

X

Xuyun

Z

Zhentong (Other-Emptiness)

Thematic and Geographical Outlines

Over its two-and-a-half-millennia-long history Buddhism has developed a profusion of literary sources in several languages, reflecting an astounding variety of lineages, institutions, doctrines, practices, and teachers. As an academic field of study, it is changing and expanding in ways that make the image of a closed and comprehensive encyclopedia a mirage—an ever-enticing, ever-receding goal. Being aware of this, *The Oxford Encyclopedia of Buddhism* seeks to address the current needs of students, researchers, and scholars of Buddhism by surveying the richness of the tradition and the different fields of expertise that have emerged in the 21st century. The volume shows what a research encyclopedia of Buddhism is today: an ongoing organic development of nodes and networks of knowledge; an open-ended project accelerated by technological advancements in the fields of digital information. It inaugurates a promising beginning without a defining end.

The following thematic clusters are intended to facilitate use of this network, giving the user access to entries that may otherwise be difficult to locate in the alphabetic organization of the body of the work itself. As such, it includes well-established categories that the user may be expecting, and ones that are less familiar. As mentioned above, the field is continuously developing, and therefore it does not sort neatly into exclusive categories. Consequently, we have created two outlines—one thematic and one geographic. Additionally, while there are a total of 139 articles constituting this print version, several entries appear under more than one heading. This reflects the overall goal of this research encyclopedia. Rather than presuming to impose some conceptual framework onto the field, our goal has been to represent currently developing topics to facilitate the growth of Buddhist studies.

THEMATIC OUTLINE

ART, ARCHITECTURE, AND SYMBOLIC MOTIFS

Art, Architecture, and National Memory-Making
Buddhist Art and Architecture in Tibet
Buddhism in Film
Buddhist Wall Paintings
Dunhuang Art
Epigraphy and the Study of Buddhism: South Asia's Northern Corridor
From Manuscript to Print in South and Southeast Asia
Imaging the Buddha in South Asia
Kālacakra-Maṇḍala: Symbolism and Construction
Patronage of Buddhist Monasteries in Eastern India, 600–1300 CE
Prajñāpāramitā and Khmer Esoteric Buddhism in the 10th to 13th centuries
The Study of Visual Culture in South and Southeast Asian Buddhism

BUDDHAS, BODHISATTVAS, GUARDIANS, AND DEITIES

Avalokiteśvara: The Bodhisattva of Compassion
The Body of the Buddha
Buddhist Wizards (*Vidhyadhāra/Weizzā/Weikza*): Contemporary Burma/Myanmar
Buddhist Wizards (*Vidhyadhāra/Weizzā/Weikza*): Origins and History
Guardian/Protector Deities in Tibetan Buddhism
Mañjuśrī
Prajñāpāramitā and Khmer Esoteric Buddhism in the 10th to 13th centuries
Sri Lanka's Sinhala Buddhist Guardian Deities: Satara Varan Devi

HISTORICAL AND HISTORIOGRAPHIC STUDIES

Buddhism and Shinto
Buddhism in Colonial Contexts
Buddhisms in Diaspora: The Canadian Context of Chinese Buddhism
Buddhist Geography and Regionalism
Early Modern European Encounters with Buddhism
Global Buddhism
Globalizing Tantric Buddhism
History of Buddhisms in China: The Nanbeicho Period (Late 4th Century to the Sui Dynasty)
Japanese Buddhisms in Diaspora
Maritime Buddhism
Mongolian Buddhism in the Early 20th Century
Mongolian Buddhism in the Democratic Period
Mongolian Buddhism in the Yuan Period
Three Turnings of the Wheel of Doctrine (Dharma-Cakra)

PHILOSOPHICAL AND DOCTRINAL STUDIES

Buddhist Cosmology
Buddhist Philosophy as Philosophy
Dzogchen
Four Noble Truths
Intention in the Pali Suttas and Abhidharma
Madhyamaka
Mahāmudrā in India and Tibet
Perfections (Six and Ten) of Bodhisattvas in Buddhist Literature
The Philosophical Works and Influence of Dignāga and Dharmakīrti
The Reincarnation System in Central Asian Buddhism
Sarvāstivāda Abhidharma
Theravada Buddhism

Three Turnings of the Wheel of Doctrine (Dharma-Cakra)
Vinaya Rules for Monks and Nuns
Zhentong (Other-Emptiness)

RITUALS, CONTEMPLATIVE PRACTICES, AND APPLICATIONS

The Bön Tradition of Dzogchen
Buddhist Chaplaincy
Buddhist Meditation and Contemplation
Chöd: A Tibetan Buddhist Practice
Debate in the Tibetan Tradition
Debate Traditions in Premodern Japan
Dzogchen
Filial Piety in Chinese Buddhism
Homa: Tantric Fire Ritual
Kālacakra-Maṇḍala: Symbolism and Construction
Mahāmudrā in India and Tibet
Naikan: A Meditation Method and Psychotherapy
Nechung: A Tibetan Buddhist Oracle
Pilgrimage in Buddhist Tibet
Pilgrimage in China
Practices of Protection in the Pali World
Śāntideva's Introduction to the Practices of Awakening (*Bodhicaryāvatāra*)
Tibetan Buddhist Power Objects
Tibetan Visionary Buddhism

SCHOOLS, TRADITIONS, AND LINEAGES

The Bön Tradition of Dzogchen
Chan Literature
Chöd: A Tibetan Buddhist Practice
Dzogchen
Early History of the Drukpa Kagyü School
Esoteric Buddhism in Southeast Asia
Fo Guang Shan
Gelukpa
Global Theravada Buddhism: Asian Foundations
Global Theravada: Transmission beyond Asia
Globalizing Tantric Buddhism
Humanistic Buddhism (Rensheng Fojiao 人生佛教 / Renjian Fojiao 人間佛教)
Japanese Buddhisms in Diaspora
Jebtsundamba Khutugtus of Mongolia
The Kadampa: A Formative Movement of Tibetan Buddhism
Mongolian Buddhism in the Democratic Period
Pure Land Buddhism in Tibetan Contexts
Sarvāstivāda Abhidharma
Secular Buddhism
Shingon
The Six Nara Schools
Soka Gakkai
Tantra and the Tantric Traditions of Hinduism and Buddhism
Tantric Buddhism in Japan: Kukai and Saicho
Tantric Buddhism in Japan: Shingon, Tendai, and the Esotericization of Japanese Buddhisms
Tantric Revival in China
Theravada Buddhism
Tibetan Visionary Buddhism
Zhentong (Other-Emptiness)

SOCIAL, CULTURAL, AND INTELLECTUAL ISSUES

American Buddhism during World War II Imprisonment
Art, Architecture, and National Memory-Making
Buddhism and Bioethics
Buddhism and Biography
Buddhism and Globalization
Buddhism and Healing in China
Buddhism and Media

Buddhism and Print Culture in China
Buddhism and the Environment
Buddhism and Medicine in India
Buddhism and Medicine in Japan
Buddhism and Medicine in Premodern Japan
Buddhism in Colonial Contexts
Buddhism in Film
Buddhist Chaplaincy
Buddhist Geography and Regionalism
Muslim–Buddhist Relations and Buddhism in Muslim Sources until the Mongol Period
Domestic Dharma in Japan
The Economics of Buddhism
Engaged Buddhism
Ethics and Buddhism
Monastic Education in Contemporary Asia
Narratives of Buddhist Relics and Images
Patronage of Buddhist Monasteries in Eastern India, 600–1300 CE
Psychological Interpreters of Buddhism
Queering Buddhist Traditions
The Sangha as an Institution
Secular Buddhism
Southeast Asian Refugees in North America
The Study of Visual Culture in South and Southeast Asian Buddhism
Tibetan Medicine and Its Buddhist Contexts
Transmission of Buddhist Media and Texts
Western Buddhism and Race

TEACHERS AND HISTORICAL FIGURES

Amoghavajra
Buddhaghosa
Buddhist Wizards (*Vidhyadhāra/Weizzā/Weikza*): Origins and History
Buddhist Wizards (*Vidhyadhāra/Weizzā/Weikza*): Contemporary Burma/Myanmar
Candrakīrti's Middle Way Philosophy
D. T. Suzuki: A Biography
D. T. Suzuki: Ideas and Influences
Hsing Yun
Huineng
Jebtsundamba Khutugtus of Mongolia
Longchenpa
Marpa Lotsawa Chökyi Lodrö
Mipam
Nāgārjuna
Nichiren
Rennyo
Ryōgen
Taixu
Tantric Buddhism in Japan: Kukai and Saicho
The Body of the Buddha
The Philosophical Works and Influence of Dignāga and Dharmakīrti
The Imamura Families and the Making of American Buddhism
Thích Nhất Hạnh in the Context of the Modern Development of Vietnamese Buddhism
Tri Songdetsen
Tsangpa Gyare (1161–1211), Founder of the Drukpa Kagyü School
Tzu Chi
Xuyun

TEXTS AND PHILOLOGICAL STUDIES

Abhidharmakośabhāṣya (Treasury of Metaphysics with Self-Commentary)
Abhisamayālaṃkāra (Ornament for Clear Realization)
Bodhisattvabhūmi (The Bodhisattva Stages)
Canon and Commentary in the Earliest Buddhist Manuscripts
Chan Literature
Dunhuang Texts
Epigraphy and the Study of Buddhism: South Asia's Northern Corridor
From Manuscript to Print in South and Southeast Asia
Jātaka
The Vajrakīla Tantras
Tibetan Book of the Dead (*Bardo Thödol*)

Tibetan Buddhism and the Gesar Epic
Visualization/Contemplation Sutras (Guan Jing)

GEOGRAPHICAL OUTLINE

EAST ASIA

Amoghavajra
Buddhism and Healing in China
Buddhism and Medicine in Japan
Buddhism and Medicine in Premodern Japan
Buddhism and Print Culture in China
Buddhism and Shinto
Candrakīrti's Middle Way Philosophy
Chan Literature
D. T. Suzuki: A Biography
D. T. Suzuki: Ideas and Influences
Debate Traditions in Premodern Japan
Domestic Dharma in Japan
Filial Piety in Chinese Buddhism
Fo Guang Shan
History of Buddhisms in China: The Nanbeicho Period (Late 4th Century to the Sui Dynasty)
Hsing Yun
Huineng
Humanistic Buddhism (Rensheng Fojiao 人生佛教 / Renjian Fojiao 人間佛教)
Monastic Education in Contemporary Asia
Naikan: A Meditation Method and Psychotherapy
Nichiren
Pilgrimage in China
Rennyo
Ryōgen
Shingon
The Six Nara Schools
Sōka Gakkai
Taixu
Tantric Buddhism in Japan: Kukai and Saicho
Tantric Buddhism in Japan: Shingon, Tendai, and the Esotericization of Japanese Buddhisms
Tantric Revival in China
Thích Nhất Hạnh in the Context of the Modern Development of Vietnamese Buddhism
Tzu Chi
Visualization/Contemplation Sutras (Guan Jing)
Xuyun

EUROPE AND THE AMERICAS

American Buddhism during World War II Imprisonment
Buddhisms in Diaspora: The Canadian Context of Chinese Buddhism
Early Modern European Encounters with Buddhism
Southeast Asian Refugees in North America
The Imamura Families and the Making of American Buddhism
Western Buddhism and Race

INNER ASIA

Abhidharmakośabhāṣya (Treasury of Metaphysics with Self-Commentary)
Abhisamayālaṃkāra (Ornament for Clear Realization)
Bodhisattvabhūmi (The Bodhisattva Stages)
The Bön Tradition of Dzogchen
Buddhist Art and Architecture in Tibet
Buddhist Wall Paintings
Chöd: A Tibetan Buddhist Practice
Debate in the Tibetan Tradition
Dunhuang Art
Dunhuang Texts
Dzogchen
Early History of the Drukpa Kagyü School
Gelukpa
Guardian/Protector Deities in Tibetan Buddhism

Jebtsundamba Khutugtus of Mongolia
Kālacakra-Maṇḍala: Symbolism and Construction
Longchenpa
Mahāmudrā in India and Tibet
Mipam
Monastic Education in Contemporary Asia
Mongolian Buddhism in the Democratic Period
Mongolian Buddhism in the Early 20th Century
Mongolian Buddhism in the Yuan Period
Nechung: A Tibetan Buddhist Oracle
Pilgrimage in Buddhist Tibet
Pure Land Buddhism in Tibetan Contexts
The Sangha as an Institution
Soka Gakkai
The Kadampa: A Formative Movement of Tibetan Buddhism
Marpa Lotsawa Chökyi Lodrö
The Vajrakīla Tantras
Tibetan Book of the Dead (*Bardo Thödol*)
Tibetan Buddhism and the Gesar Epic
Tibetan Buddhist Power Objects
Tibetan Medicine and Its Buddhist Contexts
Tibetan Visionary Buddhism
Tri Songdetsen
Tsangpa Gyare (1161–1211), Founder of the Drukpa Kagyü School
Zhentong (Other-Emptiness)

SOUTH ASIA

Abhidharmakośabhāṣya (Treasury of Metaphysics with Self-Commentary)
Abhisamayālaṃkāra (Ornament for Clear Realization)
Bodhisattvabhūmi (The Bodhisattva Stages)
Buddhaghosa
Buddhism and Medicine in India
Muslim–Buddhist Relations and Buddhism in Muslim Sources until the Mongol Period
Epigraphy and the Study of Buddhism: South Asia's Northern Corridor
Esoteric Buddhism in Southeast Asia
Prajñāpāramitā and Khmer Esoteric Buddhism in the 10th to 13th centuries
From Manuscript to Print in South and Southeast Asia
Imaging the Buddha in South Asia
Jātaka
Kālacakra-Maṇḍala: Symbolism and Construction
Mahāmudrā in India and Tibet
Monastic Education in Contemporary Asia
Nāgārjuna
Patronage of Buddhist Monasteries in Eastern India, 600–1300 CE
Practices of Protection in the Pali World
Sarvāstivāda Abhidharma
Sri Lanka's Sinhala Buddhist Guardian Deities: Satara Varan Devi

SOUTHEAST ASIA

Buddhist Wizards (*Vidhyadhāra/Weizzā/Weikza*): Contemporary Burma/Myanmar
Buddhist Wizards (*Vidhyadhāra/Weizzā/Weikza*): Origins and History
Esoteric Buddhism in Southeast Asia
Prajñāpāramitā and Khmer Esoteric Buddhism in the 10th to 13th centuries
Practices of Protection in the Pali World
The Study of Visual Culture in South and Southeast Asian Buddhism

TRANS-REGIONAL

Art, Architecture, and National Memory-Making
Avalokiteśvara: The Bodhisattva of Compassion
The Body of the Buddha
Buddhism and Bioethics
Buddhism and Biography
Buddhism and Globalization
Buddhism and Media
Buddhism and the Environment

Buddhist Cosmology
Buddhist Geography and Regionalism
Buddhism in Colonial Contexts
Buddhism in Film
Buddhist Chaplaincy
Buddhist Meditation and Contemplation
Buddhist Philosophy as Philosophy
Canon and Commentary in the Earliest Buddhist Manuscripts
The Economics of Buddhism
Engaged Buddhism
Ethics and Buddhism
Four Noble Truths
Global Buddhism
Global Theravada Buddhism: Asian Foundations
Global Theravada: Transmission beyond Asia
Globalizing Tantric Buddhism
Homa: Tantric Fire Ritual
Intention in the Pali Suttas and Abhidharma
Japanese Buddhisms in Diaspora
Madhyamaka
Mañjuśrī
Maritime Buddhism
Nāgārjuna
Narratives of Buddhist Relics and Images
Perfections (Six and Ten) of Bodhisattvas in Buddhist Literature
The Philosophical Works and Influence of Dignāga and Dharmakīrti
Psychological Interpreters of Buddhism
Queering Buddhist Traditions
The Reincarnation System in Central Asian Buddhism
Secular Buddhism
Tantra and the Tantric Traditions of Hinduism and Buddhism
Theravada Buddhism
Three Turnings of the Wheel of Doctrine (Dharma-Cakra)
Transmission of Buddhist Media and Texts
Vinaya Rules for Monks and Nuns

G

GELUKPA

GELUKPA, FOLLOWERS OF THE SYSTEM OF VIRTUE

Gelukpa (*dge lugs pa*) in Tibetan literally means "Followers of the System of Virtue" and refers to a person associated with the Geluk (*dge lugs*) school of Tibetan Buddhism, a tradition integrating the study and practice of Buddhist *sutras* and tantras as propagated by Tsongkhapa Losang Drakpa (*tsong kha pa blo bzang grags pa*, 1357–1419) and his principal disciples.[1] Beginning with Tsongkhapa and his followers, the tradition was initially referred to as Gandenpa (*dga' ldan pa*), "those of Ganden monastery," based on the founding of Riwo Ganden (*ri bo dga' ldan*) Monastery in 1409. In addition to being known as "the tradition of Ganden" (*dga' ldan pa'i lugs*), their system is referred to in the early writings of the founding figures as "the tradition of the virtuous ones" (*dge ldan ring lugs*) because of their strict adherence to monastic law (*vinaya*) and ethical virtue (*śīla*). The term Geluk (*dge lugs*), popularized only after the 17th century, may be an abbreviation from one of these latter phrases, and the suffix "*pa*" signifies one who belongs to this tradition. Throughout history, the Geluk tradition has also been distinguished from other Tibetan religious groups by the term "yellow hat tradition" (*zhwa ser po*). This nomenclature has historical precedence in the attire that was adopted by 10th-century Tibetan figures who re-established the Vinaya in central Tibet at the beginning of the second propagation (*phyi dar*) of Buddhism in Tibetan history. The wearing of the yellow hat became associated with the Kadampa (*bka' gdams pa*) traditions for their rigor in adherence to monastic ordination rules. Tsongkhapa claimed this legacy of strict adherence to monastic law and the wearing of yellow hats of the Kadam tradition.[2] Be that as it may, the designation became popular, particularly after the 18th century, in European and Chinese languages as a marker of sectarian difference, which has no equivalent within Tibetan traditions. As such, the term "Yellow Hat school" should be avoided. The followers of Tsongkhapa also became known as the New Kadam school (*bka' gdams gsar ma*) based on following teachings derived from Kadam traditions that placed emphasis on "new" or later traditions (*gsar ma*) of esoteric Buddhist literature translated during the post-11th-century dissemination period of Buddhism into Tibet.[3] Implicit in this polemic classification is the understanding that Geluk traditions do not accept esoteric Buddhist literature, or tantras, translated into Tibetan before the 10th century.

Founding Figures. The beginnings and foundation of the Geluk (*dge lugs*) tradition are found in the life and works of Tsongkhapa Losang Drakpa (1357–1419), one of the most profoundly influential and innovative scholar/practitioners in the history of Tibetan Buddhism. An erudite and thoroughly trained scholar, Tsongkhapa was also an accomplished practitioner who blended together theory and practice, emphasizing both monastic discipline and the techniques of esoteric Buddhist meditation.

Tsongkhapa was a prolific author and commentator who wrote slightly over 300 works in 18 volumes. His works would shape the thought and practice of his immediate disciples and the subsequent Geluk tradition up to the present day. In 1397, after years of arduous study and meditation retreats, Tsongkhapa had a breakthrough experience at the age of 40. He composed major works and began to gain a number of followers. Tsongkhapa's major treatises—such as the *Great Stages on the Path to Awakening* (*Lam rim chen mo*) completed in 1401, his masterpiece of Buddhist hermeneutics, the *Essence of True Eloquence* (*Legs bshad snying po*) in 1407; the *Ocean of Reasoning* (*Rigs pa'i rgya mtsho*), a commentary on Nāgārjuna's *Fundamental Wisdom of the Middle* composed in 1408; and his last major work, the *Illumination of the Thought* (*Dgongs pa rab gsal*), a commentary on Candrakīrti's *Entering the Middle Way* (*Madhyamakāvatāra*) completed in 1418—are fundamental to the understanding of Gelukpa doctrine and practice.

Tsongkhapa also performed "four great deeds" that shaped the practices of his followers, the developing Gelukpa tradition, as well as the broader Tibetan Buddhist culture. The four great deeds are the refurbishing of the Maitreya image at Dzingchi (*'dzing ji*, 1395), the teaching of monastic discipline (*vinaya*) at Namtsé Deng (*gnam rtse ldeng*, 1400), establishing the Great Prayer Festival in Lhasa (1409), and the founding of Ganden (*dga' ldan*) Monastery (1409). A charismatic teacher, Tsongkhapa attracted numerous faithful and talented disciples who were dedicated to following and developing his system of study and practice. Disciples such as Tokden Jampal gyatso (1356–1428), Gyeltsap Darma Rinchen (*rgyal tshab dar ma rin chen*, 1364–1432; also known as Gyeltsap Jé), Dülzinpa (*dul 'dzin grags pa rgyal mtshan*, 1374–1434), Khedrup Gelek Palsang (*mkhas grub dge legs dpal bzang*, 1385–1438; also known as Khedrup Jé), Jamyang Chöjé Tashi Palden (*'jam dbyangs chos rje bkra shis dpal ldan*, 1379–1440), Jamchen Chöjé Shākya Yeshe (*Byams chen chos rje shākya ye shes*, 1354–1435),

Sherap Sengé (*shes rab seng ge*, 1383–1445), and Gendün Drup Pal Sangpo (*dge 'dun grub dpal bzang po*, 1391–1474) were among the forefront of Tsongkhapa's hundreds of disciples.

When Tsongkhapa was establishing the Ganden ("Land of Joy") Monastery in 1409, 40 kilometers northeast of Lhasa, he delegated Gyeltsap Jé and Dülzinpa to supervise its construction. After the founding of Ganden, with Tsongkhapa's encouragement, Jamyang Chöjé Tashi Palden founded Drepung (*'bras spungs*, "rice heap") Monastery 10 kilometers west of Lhasa in 1416. Jamchen Chöje Shākya Yeshe, a long-serving attendant to Tsongkhpa, founded Sera (*se ra*, "wild rose") Monastery located 3 kilometers north of Lhasa in 1419. Although some scholars have claimed that Tsongkhapa and his earliest disciples did not consider themselves a new school apart from the Sakya (*sa skya*) tradition, Tsongkhapa's encouragement to his early disciples to establish new monastic institutions emphasizing his system of study and practice indicates that the early Gandenpas did see themselves as developing a new tradition.[4] The three monasteries of Ganden, Drepung, and Sera became known as the "three seats of learning" (*gdan sa gsum*) and developed into intellectual and political centers of hegemonic power and influence within the later Geluk system of monasticism. A factor contributing to the Geluk tradition's rise to power and popularity was that no other Tibetan Buddhist school had such large monasteries in proximity to Lhasa, with its potential aristocratic patrons and resources..

Before Tsongkhapa died in 1419, he gave his yellow paṇḍita hat, robes, and cape to Gyeltsap Jé as an indication that he was to succeed Tsongkhapa. Gyeltsap Jé, a former Sakya (*sa skya*) monk and senior disciple of Tsongkhapa, became Tsongkhapa's successor as abbot of Ganden Monastery after Tsongkhapa's death. Gyeltsap Jé took on this responsibility at the age of 56 and held the position for 13 years, teaching and solidifying the scholarly curriculum at Ganden. A year before he died, Gyeltsap Jé met with Khedrup Jé, choosing him as successor to the abbatial throne of Ganden. Khedrup Jé, a brilliant scholar skilled in the art of polemics, had a close personal relationship with Tsongkhapa and came to be known as his "sole inner disciple" (*nang thugs kyi sras gcig*). Khedrup Jé was enthroned at Ganden in 1431 and consolidated the identity of the nascent Ganden school, emphasizing strictly doctrinal loyalty to Tsongkhapa's writings and composing sharp rebuttals to any criticism of his master's system of thought and practice.[5] The doctrinal orthodoxy created by Khedrub Jé in the theory and practice of both exoteric and esoteric Buddhism was unprecedented in the history of Tibetan Buddhism.[6] Khedrup Jé died at age 53 at Ganden after solidifying the followers of Ganden as a distinct, self-conscious, tradition of Tibetan Buddhism. Over time, Tsongkhapa and his two most prominent followers, Gyeltsap and Khedrup, became known as "The Trio of the Precious Master and (his two chief) Disciples" (*rje yab sras gsum*).

The Development of Monastic Institutions. Before his death in 1419, Tsongkhapa gave lectures on the *Guhyasamājatantra* to several disciples and among them, Sherap Sengé (*shes rab seng ge*, 1383–1445) agreed to uphold and perpetuate these esoteric Buddhist teachings. In 1432 in the Sé (*sras*) district of Tsang (*gtsang*), Sherap Sengé founded a tantric college called the Ségyü dratsang (*sras rgyud grwa tshang*), the first monastery dedicated to Tsongkhapa's esoteric Buddhist teachings. In 1433, Sherap Sengé established Gyumé dratsang (*rgyud smad grwa tshang*), the Lower Tantric College, south of Lhasa. This was the first of two monastic colleges that perpetuated Geluk esoteric Buddhist teachings and practice. A second college, Gyutö dratsang (*rgyud stod grwa tshang*), the Upper Tantric College, was established in 1475 by Sherap Sengé's disciple Kunga dondrub (*kun dga' don grub*, 1419–1486). The terms "lower" and "upper" are in reference to the geographical location of the colleges and have no other implications. Monks from Ganden, Drepung, and Sera could go on to receive advanced training in the esoteric Buddhist systems of Geluk focus at these colleges, namely, the *Guhyasamājatantra*, *Cakrasaṃvaratantra*, and *Vajrabhairavatantra*.

Gendün Drup (*dge 'dun grub*, 1391–1474), a junior disciple who met Tsongkhapa in 1415, became a distinguished scholar, teacher, and astute administrator. In 1433, Gendün Drup became the abbot of the Rikhu (*ri khud*) Monastery; in 1438, he built a large residence at Jang Monastery (*byang*), becoming a notable figure in central Tibet. In 1447, he founded the first major Gelukpa monastery outside of central Tibet, Tashilhünpo (*bkra shis lhun po*), also known as Shigatsé (*gzhis ka rtse*) in Tsang. Gendün Drup, following in the tradition of Tsongkhapa, established an annual Great Prayer Festival at Tashilhünpo in 1474, helping to establish Geluk influence in south central Tibet. He would posthumously be recognized as the First Dalai Lama.

A devoted couple of Buddhist laypersons who had been disciples of Gendün Drup had a son who was recognized as his reincarnation in 1475. The young boy would become known as Gendün Gyatso (1475–1542), posthumously known as the Second Dalai Lama.[7] The tülku system of incarnate lamas was not widely accepted in the Geluk tradition at the time. Gendün Gyatso was enthroned at Tashilhünpo in 1487, but owing to tensions, he left for Drepung in 1494. During this time, the Gelukpa in the Lhasa region were suppressed by the Ringpung (*ring spungs*) administration, who backed the Karma Kagyüpa tradition. The Gelukpa were also not allowed to participate in the Great Prayer Festival in Lhasa.

Meanwhile, Gendün Gyatso went on to become abbot of Tashilhünpo in 1512 and abbot of Drepung in 1517. Also in 1517, the Ringpung withdrew their forces from the Lhasa region, five years after the death of the ruler Dönyö Dorje (1462–1512). Backed by the Phakmodru ruler, Ngawang Tashi Drakpa (r. 1499–1560), Gendün Gyatso reclaimed Geluk administration of the Great Prayer Festival as well as the return of the Lhasa region to Geluk control. In the same year, the Phakmodru ruler donated his residence in Drepung to the household estate (*labrang*) of Gendün Gyatso. Gendün Gyatso renamed the residence Ganden Phodrang (*dga' ldan pho brang*). This residence would become synonymous with the Tibetan government under the Fifth Dalai Lama. In 1528, Gendün Gyatso became the abbot of Sera. In 1541, Gendün Gyatso also founded Ngari Dratsang (*mnga' ris grwa tshang*) in response to the growing support for Geluk teachings of the kings of Guge (*gu ge*) in Ngari. Gendün Gyatso increased the influence of the Geluk tradition from western-area Ngari to the Kham in the east.

In the 15th and 16th centuries, Geluk monastic colleges within the great seats of learning of Ganden, Drepung, and Sera were formed. The spread of monastic institutions, networks of affiliated monasteries, and the development of systems fed monks and resources into the great seats of learning. Jetsun Chökyi Gyaltsen (*rje btsun chos kyi rgyal mtshan*, 1469–1546) served as the 12th abbot of Sera and authored monastic textbooks, or *yikcha* (*yig cha*), for Sera Je and Jangtsé college of Ganden. Chökyi Gyaltsen also wrote critiques against scholars in other traditions, such as Shākya Chokden (1428–1507), Gorampa Sönam Senge (1429–1489), and the Eighth Karmapa Mikyö Dorjé (1507–1554), defending the system of Tsongkhapa.[8] Another important Gelukpa figure during this time was Paṇchen Sönam Drakpa (*bsod namas grags pa*, 1478–1554), who was a principal disciple of Gendün Gyatso. One of the foremost scholars of his era, Paṇchen Sönam Drakpa served as abbot of Drepung and then became the 15th Ganden tripa in 1535. He wrote monastic textbooks for the Loseling (*blo gsal gling*) college of Drepung and Ganden Shartsé (*shar rtse*) college. The political and religious work and writings of Chökyi Gyaltsen and Sönam Drakpa brought more doctrinal unity to the Gelukpa tradition in their influence upon Ganden, Drepung, and Sera.

The Age of Dalai Lamas. In 1546, Sönam Gyatso (*rgyal ba bsod nams rgya mtsho*, 1543–1588), the initial incarnate in the line to actually hold the title "Dalai Lama," was officially recognized by the Nedong (*sne'u gdong*) rulers and enthroned at Drepung. Sönam Gyatso was under the care of Paṇchen Sönam Drakpa at Drepung. Sönam Drakpa gave the young incarnation lay vows (*upāsaka*) and then novice monk vows as well as his monastic name. Sönam Gyatso traveled throughout central Tibet and visited many monasteries as an advocate for the Geluk tradition. His missionary work further consolidated the Geluk tradition. Sönam Gyatso also instigated the construction of Kumbum (*sku 'bum*) Monastery in Amdo on his travels to Mongolia in 1577. Sönam Gyatso was responsible for the cultural bonds that formed between the Tibetans and Mongolians in the late 16th century.

The Mongols patronized Sönam Gyatso and he entered into a patron-priest, or *yönchö* (*yon mchod*), relationship when he met the Mongolian leader Altan Khan in 1578. Receiving the title "Dalai Lama" in this meeting, Sönam Gyatso returned to Tibet as the third among this lineage of Geluk incarnates (*sprul sku*). Sönam Gyatso was the foremost missionary and traveler among historical Dalai Lamas. After the death of Altan Khan, Sönam Gyatso spent several years giving Buddhist teachings and founding monasteries before dying while traveling in Mongolia in 1588.

Yönten Gyatso (*yon tan rgya mtsho*, 1589–1617), the fourth incarnation of the Dalai Lama, was recognized among royalty of the Tümed Mongols. He was the only non-Tibetan Dalai Lama and his recognition brought further cohesion to the relations between the Mongols and the Gelukpa school. Though recognized as a young boy, Yönten Gyatso did not arrive in central Tibet until 1602. He was tutored and ordained by the abbot of Tashilhünpo, Losang Chökyi Gyeltsen (*blo bzang chos kyi rgyal mtshan*, 1570–1662), who would go on to be recognized as the first (or, according to an alternative count, fourth) Paṇ chen Lama. The successive line of Paṇ chen Lama incarnates would gain political power second only to the line of Dalai Lamas. The recognition of a royal Mongolian as the Fourth Dalai Lama had a positive economic effect for the resources of the Gelukpa as this gave rise to a stream of Mongolian pilgrims to the Lhasa area. After the death of the Fourth Dalai Lama, a Tsang ruler who was a patron of the Karma Kagyüpa began applying pressure to diminish Gelukpa power in central Tibet. The tensions between the Tsangpa and central Tibet were paralleled as a rivalry between the Karma Kagyüpa and the Gelukpa. The conflict and tension between Gelukpa monasteries, supported by Mongols, and the Karma Kagyü order had reached a critical juncture with the ascent of the Fifth Dalai Lama.

Ngawang Losang Gyatso (*ngag dbang blo bzang rgya mtsho*, 1617–1682), later known as the Great Fifth, was chosen from among several rival candidates. He was born into a noble family with connection to royalty in the Yarlung valley and recognized as the Fifth Dalai Lama in 1622 by a team of Geluk hierarchs, including Losang Chökyi Gyeltsen. The Fifth Dalai Lama would also receive his novice vows in 1625 and his full monastic vows in 1638 from Losang Chökyi Gyeltsen. During the time period when the Fifth Dalai Lama was being enthroned and educated, the Gelukpa continued to be persecuted by the rulers of Tsang. The Fifth Dalai Lama, building upon the priest-patron (*yönchö*) models of his predecessors, the Third and Fourth Dalai Lamas, formed an alliance with the Qoshot Mongols. In alliance with the Qoshot Mongol leader Gushri Khan (1582–1655), the Fifth Dalai Lama, along with supporters in Lhasa, defeated the ruler of Tsang in central Tibet in 1642. The 13 Tibetan myriarchies were given over to the Fifth Dalai Lama, who, along with his regent Sönam Chöphel (*bsod nams chos 'phel*), assumed undisputed sovereignty over state resources for furthering Gelukpa economic and political power. For the first time, the executive powers of the head of state aligned with the prestige and cultural capital of an incarnate lama.

The Fifth Dalai Lama institutionalized the cultural belief that the lineage of Dalai Lamas constituted incarnations of the bodhisattva of compassion, Avalokiteśvara (Tib. *spyan ras gzigs*), and the Fifth Dalai Lama constructed the Potala (*po ta la*) Palace on an ancient hill site (*dmar po ri*, "red hill") in Lhasa, naming it after the residence of Avalokiteśvara, the *Potalaka*. The Fifth Dalai Lama also associated himself with the reigns of the great religious kings (*chos rgyal*) Songtsen Gampo, Trisong detsen, and Ralpacan.[9] The residence of the Dalai Lamas, the Ganden Phodrang, was relocated to the Potala and became the seat of government under the Dalai Lamas. The Ganden Phodrang regime would last from 1642 to 1959. The Fifth Dalai Lama forged a unique political system with a relationship between religion and secular (*chos srid gnyis ldan*). During his reign, monastic Buddhist hierarchs became more involved in offices of Tibetan government.

The Fifth Dalai Lama promoted the Great Prayer Festival for political purposes, increasing its length to 22 days and increasing the power of the Geluk monastics who managed he festival.[10] He more broadly implemented the use of monastic constitutions (*bca' yig*) to standardize the procedures of monastic life.[11] He forcibly converted non-Geluk monasteries into Geluk institutions in the west and in the east of Tibet.[12] The Fifth Dalai Lama also traveled to the Manchu imperial court in Beijing in 1653 at the invitation of the Qing emperor, Shun Zhi (1639–1661). In brief, "consolidation of religious authority supported by strategic alliance with Mongolian factions... were keys to the ascendancy of the Geluk school in Tibet."[13]

Desi Sanggyé Gyatso (*sde srid sangs rgyas rgya mtsho*, 1653–1705) became regent in 1678 and the designated ruler of Tibet. He initiated refinements in law and education and staunchly supported the extension of Gelukpa monasticism, greatly increasing the number of monasteries and monks.[14] In 1700, Jamyang Zhepa Dorjé Ngawang Tsondrü (*'jam dbyangs bzhad pa'i rdo rje ngag dbang brtson 'grus*, 1648–1722) was appointed abbot of Drepung Gomang (*sgo mang*) and Lhazang Khan became chief of Mongol forces in Tibet. After Sanggyé Gyatso was executed by Mongolian forces in 1705, Jamyang Zhepa moved to the northeastern Tibet region of Amdo (*a mdo*) and founded Labrang Tashikyil (*bla brang bkra shis 'khyil*) in 1709. With over 48 temples and 3,000 monks, Labrang became one of the largest Gelukpa monasteries outside of central Tibet. Labrang contributed to the consolidation of Geluk power in the Amdo region and served as a vital network to Geluk authorities in central Tibet.

The Sixth Dalai Lama, Tsangyang Gyatso (*tshangs dbyang rgya mtsho*, 1683–1706), did not fulfill his duties as a monk and became famous for his poetry and fondness for worldly pleasures as a layperson, eventually dying while traveling to the Chinese capital after having been removed from office. The Seventh Dalai Lama, Kalzang Gyatso (*skal bzang rgya mtsho*, 1708–1757), born in Lithang (*li thang*), was forced to be educated at Kumbum (*sku 'bum*) because of turmoil in central Tibet. He would assume authority only in 1751, ruling with a cabinet (*bka' shag*) of four ministers. A generation of scholars from the Amdo region who were Gelukpa in sectarian affiliation, but who had allegiances to the Qing rulers, were active at this time as well. These included the polymath historian Sumpa Khenpo Yeshé Paljor (*sum pa mkhan po ye shes dpal 'byor*, 1704–1787) as well as the doxographers Changkya Rölpai Dorjé (lcang skya rol pa'i rdo rje, 1717–1786) and the third Thuken (T. *thu'u bkwan*, Ch. *tuguan*) *hutuqtu* Losang Chökyi Nyima (*blo bzang chos kyi nyi ma*, 1737–1802).

The Thirteenth Dalai Lama, Thubten Gyatso (*thub bstan rgya mtsho*, 1876–1933), assumed office in 1895 when Tibetans were encountering forces of British, Russian, and Han Chinese imperialism. As described by later Tibetan historians, the "Great Thirteenth" displayed remarkable political and diplomatic skills as he guided Tibet through surrounding geopolitical instability. The Thirteenth Dalai Lama tried to implement modernization measures after 1913 but ran up against the conservative patriarchal land-owning aristocracy as well as the religiously conservative leadership of the three major Gelukpa monasteries. Adherence to Buddhist monastic tradition led to the cessation of modernization efforts in the mid-1920s while conservative monastic values were reinforced and dominated by Gelukpa interests.

After the death of the Thirteenth Dalai Lama, Tibet remained isolated from the developments of modernity and from the Europe-based colonial forces that influenced the formations of modern Buddhism. Tibet also endured internal dissension and weak leadership during this time. Gelukpa orthodoxy sought to reassert its hegemony, particularly in reaction to the Rimé (*ris med*) "impartial" movement in eastern Tibet. A charismatic Gelukpa teacher during this period was Jampa Tenzin Trinley (*byams pa bstan 'dzin 'phrin las*), alias Phabongkhapa Dechen Nyingpo (*pha bong kha pa bde chen snying po*, 1878–1941), who promoted Gelukpa exclusivism. At the same time, two incarnate monks, Reting Rinpoché Thubten Jampel Yeshé Gyaltshan (*rwa sgreng rin po che thub bstan 'jam dpal ye shes rgyal mtshan*, 1911–1947) and Taktra Rinpoché Ngawang Sungrab (*stag brag rin po che ngag dbang gsung rab*, 1874–1952), fought over power and control during the regency period leading up to ascent to office of the Fourteenth Dalai Lama. Gendun Chopel (*dge 'dun chos 'phel*, 1905–1951), an innovative and controversial author who was critical of Gelukpa authorities, traveled throughout South Asia and was imprisoned in Lhasa upon his return in 1946 for political reasons.

During its ascendancy in governmental authority and power, the Geluk system of monasticism, in part through its administrative organization and institution-building techniques, was able to establish influence throughout Tibet, constructing new monasteries and renewing old ones. Over time, the Gelukpas developed an elaborate institutional hierarchy and administrative bureaucratic apparatus that interconnected regional monasteries with the four Geluk monastic seats in central Tibet. The school gradually spread as a cultural force of Tibetan Buddhism from central Tibet across the Tibetan plateau and into Mongolia as well as regions of inner and East Asia.

The Gelukpa continued to gain renown politically for its establishment of the Ganden Podrang (*dga' ldan pho brang*) government in 1642 under the rulership of successive Dalai Lamas (*dā la'i bla ma*) until 1959. After the fourteenth and present Dalai Lama, Tenzin Gyatso (*bstan 'dzin rgya mtsho*, b. 1935), escaped from the Chinese communist invasion of Tibet in 1959, communities of refugee Geluk members (as well as non-Geluk Tibetans) re-established monasteries, nunneries, and colleges primarily in India and Nepal. Smaller versions of the three main monastic universities have been re-established in South India with over 10,000 monks. Gelukpa teachers also gathered international followers, including Geshé Rabten (1920–1986), the charismatic Lama Thubten Yeshé (*thub bstan ye shes*, 1935–1984), and Geshé Lhundub Sopa (*lhun grub bzod pa*, 1923–2014), the first Tibetan to be a tenured professor at an American university. The Dalai Lama brought international attention to the Tibetan cause and Tibetan Buddhism when he was awarded the Nobel Prize for Peace in 1989. Although Geluk monastic communities still exist in the traditional geographical areas of Tibet, they do not resemble the pre-1959 institutions. Outside of traditional Tibetan cultural regions, the Dalai Lama and eminent Gelukpa spiritual teachers continue to teach and publish, and Gelukpa-based Tibetan Buddhist religious centers have been established in India, Europe, and North America.

REVIEW OF LITERATURE

In the early 21st century, there is still not a book-length study in English dedicated solely to the history and doctrines of the Gelukpa as one may find for Nyingma (*rnying ma*) or Sakya (*sa skya*) traditions.[15] Nevertheless, there are numerous studies that provide general historical information on the Gelukpa order as well as specific studies on the founder Tsongkhapa, hagiographies of Gelukpa holy persons, and monographs focused on specific topics within Gelukpa scholastic traditions. The brief selection of works that follow centers upon historical overviews of the Geluk order; works that focus on Tsongkhapa, the Dalai Lamas, or doxography, for instance, are not discussed.

Historical Overviews. Giuseppe Tucci provides an early (though now dated) overview of the Geluk tradition in his *Tibetan Painted Scrolls*.[16] W. D. Shakabpa (1907–1989), a former finance minister of the government of Tibet before the invasion of the communist Chinese, provides a historical overview of the Geluk tradition in his *Tibet: A Political History*.[17] Snellgrove and Richardson outline salient characteristics of the Geluk tradition in *A Cultural History of Tibet*.[18] E. Gene Smith's volume, *Among Tibetan Texts*, in its coverage of Tibetan history and literature, provides informative biographical overviews of four major Geluk scholars: the First Paṇ chen Lama, Lcang skya Rol pa'i rdo rje, Thu'u bkwan Blo bzang chos kyi nyi ma, and Ye shes rgyal mtshan.[19] John Powers's comprehensive overview of Tibetan Buddhist practice and culture contains a chapter on the Gelukpa that furnishes an introduction to the history and practices found in the tradition.[20] Roberto Vitali analyzes the history of the Geluk pa tradition in western Tibet.[21] Gray Tuttle and Kurtis R. Schaeffer's reader contains selections of not readily accessible research essays that discuss the Geluk tradition from the analytical lens of Tibetan studies.[22] Schaeffer, Matthew Kapstein, and Tuttle furnish a comprehensive collection of Tibetan historical sources, and Part 4 of the volume documents the rise and growth of the Geluk tradition.[23] An important study on developments in modern Tibetan history, Peter Schwieger's *The Dalai Lama and the Emperor of China: A Political History of the Tibetan Institution of Reincarnation*, outlines the institution of the Dalai Lama's relationship with China during the 17th to 19th centuries, providing a historical analysis of the development of incarnate lamas (*sprul sku*) in the Geluk tradition.[24] Brenton Sullivan's *Building a Religious Empire: Tibetan Buddhism, Bureaucracy, and the Rise of the Gelukpa* examines institutional structures and source materials, such as monastic "constitutions" (*bca' yig*), in an attempt to explain the Geluk school's rise to dominance in Tibet and the frontiers of China and Mongolia.[25] Cabezón and Dorjee trace the history of the great monastery of Sera from its founding in Tibet to its struggles and renaissance in exile and along the way provide a vibrant account of monastic life in the Gelukpa order.[26] George Dreyfus furnishes an overview of the Gelukpa monastic curriculum while providing an autobiographical account of the first Westerner to receive a Geshé (*dge bshes*) degree.[27] In *The Life of My Teacher*, the present Dalai Lama gives a vivid biographical portrait of Thupten Lungtok Namgyal Trinlé (*thub bstan lung rtogs bstan 'dzin 'phrin las*, 1903–1983), the Sixth Ling Rinpoché, who was the longest Ganden Tripa throne holder in Geluk history and senior tutor to the Fourteenth Dalai Lama.[28]

PRIMARY SOURCES

A great number of Tibetan sources on the history, doctrines, and practices of the Gelukpa tradition may be accessed online at the togs Buddhist Digital Archives by the Buddhist Digital Resource Center (https://library.bdrc.io/). Original Tibetan sources are continually being scanned and uploaded on an ongoing basis. The following primary sources are of specific relevance to the Gelukpa tradition:

Dkon mchog 'jigs med dbang po (1728–1791). "dGe ldan chos 'byung nor bu'i phreng ba rtsom 'phro." *gSung 'bum dkon mchog 'jigs med dbang po (bla brang par ma)*, vol. 5, Ngawang Gelek Demo, 1971, pp. 540–709. Buddhist Digital Resource Center (BDRC), purl.bdrc.io/resource/MW1KG9560_0C16E0. [BDRC bdr:MW1KG9560_0C16E0]

Do rgya dbang drag rdo rje. 2013. *dGe lugs pa'i grub mtha' spyi bshad*. Bod ljongs mi dmangs dpe skrun khang. Buddhist Digital Resource Center (BDRC), purl.bdrc.io/resource/MW1AC6. [BDRC bdr:MW1AC6]

kLong rdol bla ma ngag dbang blo bzang. "bKa' gdams pa dang dge lugs pa'i bla ma rags rim gyi gsung 'bum mtshan tho (ra)." *gSung 'bum ngag dbang blo bzang*, pp. 1301–430. Buddhist Digital Resource Center (BDRC), purl.bdrc.io/resource/MW87_233946. [BDRC bdr:MW87_233946]

Las chen kun dga' rgyal mtshan (1432–1506). *bKa' gdams chos 'byung gsal ba'i sgron me*. Par gzhi dang po, Bod ljongs mi dmangs dpe skrun khang, 2003. Buddhist Digital Resource Center (BDRC), purl.bdrc.io/resource/MW26009. [BDRC bdr:MW26009]

mKhar nag lo tsā ba dpal 'byor rgya mtsho (Seventeenth century). *mKhar nag chos 'byung*. Par gzhi dang po, Ser gtsug nang bstan dpe rnying 'tshol bsdu phyogs sgrig khang, 2016. Buddhist Digital Resource Center (BDRC), purl.bdrc.io/resource/MW1KG25150. [BDRC bdr:MW1KG25150]

Paṇchen Sonam Drakpa (1478–1554). *bKa' gdams gsar rnying gi chos 'byung yid kyi mdzes rgyan* (bod ljongs bod yig dpe rnying dpe skrun khang). Bod ljongs bod yig dpe rnying dpe skrun khang, 2001. Buddhist Digital Resource Center (BDRC), purl.bdrc.io/resource/MW1GS91831. [BDRC bdr:MW1GS91831]

sDe srid sangs rgyas rgya mtsho (1653–1705). *dGa' ldan chos 'byung bai ḍurya ser po*. Krung go'i bod rig pa dpe skrun khang, 1989. Buddhist Digital Resource Center (BDRC), purl.bdrc.io/resource/MW3CN3209. [BDRC bdr:MW3CN3209]

Ser byes tre hor lha rams dge bshes tshul dga'. *Ser byes chos 'byung legs bshad rta bdun bdag po'i 'od zer*. Sera Jey Library And Computer Center, 2009. Buddhist Digital Resource Center (BDRC), purl.bdrc.io/resource/MW1KG2757. [BDRC bdr:MW1KG2757]

Shis tshang tshul khrims. 2012. *Ri bo dge lugs pa'i grub mtha'i byung ba brjod pa*. Par gzhi dang po par thengs dang po, (shis tshang tshul khrims). Buddhist Digital Resource Center (BDRC), purl.bdrc.io/resource/MW2KG209985. [BDRC bdr:MW2KG209985]

Tā la'i bla ma 05 ngag dbang blo bzang rgya mtsho. *dGe lugs pa'i skyes chen 'ga'i lo rgyus dpyad gzhi zur bkol*. Buddhist Digital Resource Center (BDRC), purl.bdrc.io/resource/MW1KG9304. [BDRC bdr:MW1KG9304]

Tshe mchog gling yongs 'dzin ye shes rgyal mtshan. *Lam rim bla ma brgyud pa'i rnam thar*. Ngawang Gelek Demo, 1970–1972. Buddhist Digital Resource Center (BDRC), purl.bdrc.io/resource/MW986. [BDRC bdr:MW986]

"Zhar byung ri bo dge lugs pa'i byung ba." *'Bras spungs chos 'byung*, Steiner, 1974, pp. 328–341. Buddhist Digital Resource Center (BDRC), purl.bdrc.io/resource/MW2CZ8087_B3F25E. [BDRC bdr:MW2CZ8087_B3F25E]

DIGITAL MATERIALS

The Buddhist Digital Archives (https://library.bdrc.io/).
The Treasury of Lives (https://treasuryoflives.org/).
The Tibetan & Himalayan Library (https://www.thlib.org/index.php).
Himalayan Art Resources (https://www.himalayanart.org/).
Asian Classics Input Project (https://asianclassics.org/).

FURTHER READING

Apple, James B. "Maitreya's Tuṣita Heaven as a Pure Land in Gelukpa Forms of Tibetan Buddhism." In *Pure Lands in Asian Texts and Contexts: An Anthology*. Edited by Georgios T. Halkias and Richard K. Payne, 188–222. Honolulu: University of Hawai'i Press, 2019.

Ary, Elijah S. *Authorized Lives: Biography and the Early Formation of Geluk identity*. Somerville, MA: Wisdom Publications, 2015.

Blo-bzang-ye-shes-bstan-'dzin-rgya-mtsho, Sharpa Tulku, and Bstan-'dzin-rgya-mtsho. *The Magical Play of Illusion: The Autobiography of Trijang Rinpoché*. Somerville, MA: Wisdom Publications, 2018.

Brauen, Martin. *The Dalai Lamas: A Visual History*. Zürich: Ethnographic Museum of the University of Zürich, 2005.

Bstan-'dzin-rgya-mtsho, and Gavin Kilty. *The Life of My Teacher: A Biography of Kyabje "Ling Rinpoché*. Somerville, MA: Wisdom Publications, 2017.

Cabezón, José Ignacio, and Penpa Dorjee. *Sera Monastery*. Somerville, MA: Wisdom Publications, 2019.

Dreyfus, Georges. *The Sound of Two Hands Clapping: The Education of a Tibetan Buddhist Monk*. Berkeley: University of California Press, 2003.

Dreyfus, Georges. "An Introduction to Drepung's Colleges," The Drepung Monastery Project, 2006. https://www.thlib.org/places/monasteries/drepung/intro.php#!essay=/dreyfus/drepung/colleges/.

Hopkins, Jeffrey. *Maps of the Profound: Jam-yang-shay-ba's Great Exposition of Buddhist and Non-Buddhist Views on the Nature of Reality*. Ithaca, NY: Snow Lion, 2003.

Jackson, Roger R. *Mind Seeing Mind: Mahāmudrā and the Geluk Tradition of Tibetan Buddhism*. Somerville, MA: Wisdom Publications, 2019.

Jinpa, Thupten. *Tsongkhapa: A Buddha in the Land of Snows*. Boulder, CO: Shambhala, 2019.

Mills, Martin A. *Identity, Ritual and State in Tibetan Buddhism: The Foundations of Authority in Gelukpa Monasticism*. London: RoutledgeCurzon, 2003.

Nyima, Thuken Losang Chokyi. *The Crystal Mirror of Philosophical Systems: A Tibetan Study of Asian Religious Thought.* Translated by Geshe Lhundrup Sopa. Edited by Roger R. Jackson. Boston: Wisdom Publications, 2009.

Schaeffer, Kurtis R., Matthew Kapstein, and Gray Tuttle. *Sources of Tibetan Tradition.* New York: Columbia University Press, 2013.

Schwieger, Peter. *The Dalai Lama and the Emperor of China: A Political History of the Tibetan Institution of Reincarnation.* New York: Columbia University Press, 2015.

Shakabpa, Tsepon. *One Hundred Thousand Moons: An Advanced Political History of Tibet,* 2 vols. Translated by Derek Maher. Leiden and Boston: Brill, 2009 and 2010.

Sullivan, Brenton. *Building a Religious Empire: Tibetan Buddhism, Bureaucracy, and the Rise of the Gelukpa.* Philadelphia: University of Pennsylvania Press, 2021.

Thurman, Robert A. F., ed. *Life and Teachings of Tsongkhapa.* Somerville, MA: Wisdom Publications, 2018.

Tuttle, Gray, and Kurtis R. Schaeffer. *The Tibetan History Reader.* New York: Columbia University Press, 2013.

Van Schaik, Sam. *Tibet: A History.* New Haven, CT: Yale University Press, 2011.

Willis, Janice Dean. *Enlightened Beings: Life Stories from the Ganden Oral Tradition.* Boston: Wisdom Publications, 1995.

NOTES

1. *Bod rgya tshig mdzod chen mo,* p. 454: *rje tsong kha pa blo bzang grags pa yab sras kyis srol btod dar rgyas 'dzin pa'i mdo sngags bshad sgrub zung 'brel gyi ring lugs 'dzin mkhan rjes 'brang dang bcas pa/.*
2. Dung dkar blo bzang 'phrin las (1927–1997), *Grub mtha'i skor gyi rnam bshad. Chos lugs grub mtha' khag gi gzhi rtsa'i shes yon mdzub mo ri ston/grub mtha'i mdzub ston.* Par gzhi dang po. Issue 495. Ser gtsug nang bstan dpe rnying 'tshol bsdu phyogs sgrig khang: Lha sa, 2016, p. 575.
3. Dung dkar blo bzang 'phrin las (1927–1997), *Grub mtha'i skor gyi rnam bshad,* 2016, pp. 577–580. The distinction between "Old traditions" (*rnying ma*) and "New traditions" (*gsar ma*) is a highly polemical distinction in Tibetan Buddhist history; and see Kadri Raudsepp, "*Rnying ma* and *Gsar ma*: First Appearances of the Terms during the Early *Phyi Dar* (Later Spread of the Doctrine)," *Revue d'Études Tibétaines* 22 (2012): 25–46. Though not widely known in Euro-North American scholarship, the classification also presumes a distinction between Kadampas who accepted old traditions, *bka' gdams rnying ma,* and those who followed new traditions, *bka' gdams gsar ma.* See, for example, Mkhan po blo gros don yod, 2005, "bKa' gdams rnying ma dang gsar ma'i ring lugs bshad pa." *Dus 'khor chos 'byung indra nī la'i phra tshom,* 'Bo dkar nges don chos 'khor gling gi bla spyi spar bskrun zhus, 2005, pp. 224–229. Buddhist Digital Resource Center (BDRC), purl.bdrc.io/resource/MW00EGS1016994_9892FD. [BDRC bdr:MW00EGS1016994_9892FD].
4. José Cabezón and Penpa Dorjee, *Sera Monastery* (Somerville, MA: Wisdom Publications, 2019), 140–141; Thupten Jinpa, *Tsongkhapa: A Buddha in the Land of Snows* (Boulder, CO: Shambhala, 2019), 349–350.
5. Jinpa, *Tsongkhapa,* 354–355.
6. Rachel M. McCleary and Leonard W. J. van der Kujip, "The Market Approach to the Rise of the Geluk School, 1419–1642," *The Journal of Asian Studies* 69, no. 1 (2010): 162; and cf. Elijah S. Ary, *Authorized Lives: Biography and the Early Formation of Geluk Identity* (Somerville, MA: Wisdom Publications, 2015).
7. See Ary, *Authorized Lives,* 76–78; Cabezón and Dorjee, *Sera Monastery,* 181–183, 193–194; Matthew T. Kapstein, *The Tibetans* (Malden, MA: Blackwell, 2006), 129–131; and Peter Schwieger, *The Dalai Lama and the Emperor of China: A Political History of the Tibetan Institution of Reincarnation* (New York: Columbia University Press, 2015), 25–29.

8. Cabezón and Dorjee, *Sera Monastery*, 184–186; Ary, *Authorized Lives*, 67–102.
9. Yumiko Ishihama, "On the Dissemination of the Belief in the Dalai Lama as a Manifestation of the Bodhisattva Avalokitesvara," *Acta Asiatica* 64 (1993): 38–56; Ishihama (2015). Ishihama, Yumiko, "The Dalai Lama as the cakravarti-Rāja as Manifested by the Bodhisattva Avalokiteśvara," *Cahiers d'Extrême-Asie* 24 (2015): 169–188.
10. George Dreyfus 2006, "An Introduction to Drepung's Colleges," The Drepung Monastery Project.
11. Brenton Sullivan, *Building a Religious Empire: Tibetan Buddhism, Bureaucracy, and the Rise of the Gelukpa* (Philadelphia: University of Pennsylvania Press, 2021).
12. Cabezón and Dorjee, *Sera Monastery*, 310; and Sullivan, *Building a Religious Empire*, 141–142.
13. McCleary and van der Kujip, "The Market Approach", 173.
14. Kapstein, *Tibetans*, 142.
15. For the Nyingma tradition, for example, see Dudjom Rinpoche and Gyurme Dorje, *The Nyingma School of Tibetan Buddhism: Its Fundamentals and History by Dudjom Rinpoche, Jikdrel Yeshe Dorje*, trans. and ed. Gyurme Dorje and Matthew Kapstein (Boston: Wisdom Publications, 1991) and for the Sakya, see Tenpé Gyaltsen Dhongthog and Sam Van Schaik, *The Sakya School of Tibetan Buddhism: A History* (Somerville, MA: Wisdom Publications, 2016).
16. Giuseppe Tucci, *Tibetan Painted Scrolls* (Rome: Libreria dello Stato, 1949).
17. Wangchuk Deden Shakabpa, *Tibet: A Political History* (London: Yale University Press, 1967).
18. David Llewellyn Snellgrove and Hugh Edward Richardson, *A Cultural History of Tibet* (New York: F. A. Praeger, 1968).
19. Ellis Gene Smith and Kurtis R. Schaeffer, ed., *Among Tibetan Texts: History and Literature of the Himalayan Plateau* (Boston: Wisdom Publications, 2001).
20. John Powers, *Introduction to Tibetan Buddhism*, 2nd ed. (Ithaca, NY: Snow Lion Publications, 2007).
21. Roberto Vitali, *The Dge-lugs-pa in Gu-ge and the Western Himalaya (Early 15th–Late 17th Century)* (Dharamsala, HP: Amnye Machen Institute, 2012).
22. Gray Tuttle and Kurtis R. Schaeffer, *The Tibetan History Reader* (New York: Columbia University Press, 2013).
23. Kurtis R. Schaeffer, Matthew Kapstein, and Gray Tuttle, *Sources of Tibetan Tradition* (New York: Columbia University Press, 2013).
24. Schwieger, *The Dalai Lama and the Emperor of China.*
25. Sullivan, *Building a Religious Empire.*
26. Cabezón and Dorjee, *Sera Monastery.*
27. Georges B. J. Dreyfus, *The Sound of Two Hands Clapping: The Education of a Tibetan Buddhist Monk* (Berkeley: University of California Press, 2003).
28. Bstan-'dzin-rgya-mtsho and Gavin Kilty, trans., *The Life of My Teacher: A Biography of Ling Rinpoché* (Somerville, MA: Wisdom Publications, 2017).

James B. Apple

GLOBAL BUDDHISM

INTRODUCTION

Buddhism has been a mobile religion, crossing mountains, desserts, and seas and spreading into faraway cultures long before the early 21st century. In the earliest collection of the religion's texts, the Pali Canon, the Buddha calls on his disciples to wander around and propagate the Buddhist Dharma.[1] Consequently, through their travels on the land and sea trade routes, itinerant monastics, together with merchants, have spread Buddhism to many corners of the Asian continent. The Chinese monk Xuanzang's (602–664) seventeen-year overland journey from China to India and back is perhaps the most famous example of Buddhist mobility in history. During two and a half millennia, Buddhist teachings and practices have spread across many parts of Asia and in this process have diversified into complex sets of local traditions with their many branches and ramifications.

Since the early 19th century, marked by increased global integration, Buddhism's dispersion was further accelerated. In a relatively short period of time, Buddhism has expanded its historical influence sphere and developed over significant parts of the globe. Big intra-Buddhist conferences with delegations from dozens of countries, Buddhist-inspired mindfulness practices in Australian health care facilities, Hispanic and African American adherents of Soka Gakkai chanting Nam-Myoho-Renge-Kyo in a US coastal city, Thai translations of the Dalai Lama's books in a bookstore in Bangkok, or Taiwanese Buddhist charity organizations serving the poor in southern Africa are just some examples of an endless list of how Buddhism is practiced under the conditions of globalization.

Globalization is a contested term of recent provenance. The term has appeared only during the last decades of the 20th century and, from the 1990s on, became increasingly popular. Although the usage of the term is somewhat ambiguous in regard to its content and also the time span to which it refers, it decidedly expresses a new awareness of the global as a spatial category. This new awareness became widespread only after the end of the Cold War; from the 1990s on, multinational corporations, nongovernmental organizations (NGOs), mass tourism to overseas destinations, and transnational migrants have increasingly created linkages on a global scale. Many scholars argue that the 21st-century state of intensified global integration is nothing new; in many ways it is the outcome of earlier historical processes. They thus date the beginnings of globalization back to the colonial era. From the 15th century on, the colonial projects of Europe facilitated increased contact and interaction between different regions of the world. These developments had significant repercussions for the fields of the economy, politics, culture, but also religion, not only in the colonized but also in the colonizing regions of the world. Colonialism was not only characterized by the unequal power equilibrium between Europe and the rest of the world, it also facilitated an unprecedented exchange of ideas, people, and goods. The enhanced integration of the globe brought with it a new degree of standardization, but also new forms of fragmentation. European military expansion and trade caused, for example, the dissemination of European units of measurement and the development of international law, but it also brought about the global prevalence of the modern nation-state over the earlier plurality of spatial units.

Globalization is often understood to be a process that primarily concerns the fields of politics and economics. Within this thread of thought, it describes a process where newly emerging global forces impose themselves on smaller-scale spatial units such as the local. A common example of this perspective, which is sometimes called globalization from the top, is the tension between an uninhibited global economy and the sovereign nation-state. Researchers who look at the global from this perspective, for example, analyze the emergence of a global market, the impact of transnational corporations on national labor laws, or the entanglements of global commodity chains. Other scholars examine global processes that play out in different fields and on different levels of society. They examine issues such as the work of NGOs, the flows of transnational migration, the effects of mass tourism, the dispersion of global media spheres, and so on. In spite of their different angles, both perspectives stress the importance of technological progress and the resulting advancements in travel and communication for the increased integration of the globe.

While the initial focus of globalization studies was often on politics and the economy, over time the relationship between religion and globalization has also become a subject of scholarly attention. The understanding of religion as a universal human experience expressed in a distinct social unit that is clearly separated from others, such as the political or the economic, and as something that appears in all societies of the globe, is in fact itself an outcome of the early stages of globalization. The discourse of world religions, and Buddhism as one among them, had replaced earlier 18th- and 19th-century developmental schemas characterized by speculations on the origin of religion.[2] Buddhism had an important role within the development of this discourse. The European discovery of Buddhism through textual reconstruction construed Buddhism as another transnational universal religion alongside Christianity. It thereby caused European scholars to develop the concept of world religions.[3] The new Western concept was then globally diffused as a byproduct of colonialism. During this process, it has produced a plethora of neologisms in non-European languages. As a result, many of the existing traditions of the world have remodeled themselves through the negotiation of the concept of religion in its 19th-century Protestant meaning. A well-researched example for this process is the case of 19th-century Japan. Faced with the threat of Western aggression, Japanese initiated measures in order to thoroughly modernize their country. The goal was to reconstruct Japan as a modern nation-state. To achieve this goal, Japan imported European concepts and practices linked to Western notions of modernity. Japanese, for example, adapted notions of the secular, of science, but also religion and superstition, which had emerged out of the particularities of European history, to their own local contexts. They did not completely abandon their own traditions within this process, but instead reordered the space of their native institutions, discourses, and practices within society through the application of the labels of Western modernity.[4] Subsequently, the new concepts traveled from Japan to other places in Asia such as, for example, China, where they initiated similar processes. These developments had lasting impacts on the religious landscape of the globe. Many native traditions, including Buddhism, renegotiated their space within society by taking the Christian-secular model as a point of reference.[5]

Buddhist traditions of Asia were reconstructed in accordance to the modern concept of religion, including some and excluding other elements. An important factor was the relation to the newly emerging nation-state. The historical Buddhism that was often linked to village life in rural society had to reinvent itself as a productive force that contributes to the modernizing nation. Reconstructing Buddhism as a modern religion also led to the idea of Buddhism being one particular religion in a global system of religions. Subsequently, on an intra-Buddhist level, it caused a heightened mutual awareness and exchange between the different locally fixed Buddhist traditions in Asia. As with the concept of religion, the term Buddhism as a generic concept for the different threads of traditions that developed out of the teachings of the buddha is a Western neologism, and its worldwide dispersion the result of globalization in its early, colonial stage.[6] Thus, modern institutional forms and understandings of Buddhism are themselves, to a degree, manifestations of globalization. Due to the unequal power equilibrium between the colonizing states and those places that had been colonized, the influence of Europe and the West on this development is undeniable. However, it is important to stress the agency of non-Western Buddhist elites within this process. Buddhist elites in Asia did not just passively accept foreign notions of religion but actively negotiated and applied these categories to their own local contexts. The relationship between Buddhism and globalization is thus a complex and multifaceted one that is concurrently shaped by various processes of standardization and pluralization. Buddhism as one religion among others in a global system of religions is linked to a new global framework of reference points: the nation-state, the secular, the religious, superstition, and so on. Asian Buddhists had to position themselves to these new concepts in one way or another, yet at the same time, through these negotiating processes and enhanced contact between the different Asian Buddhist traditions, the many forms of Buddhism have also become more and more pluralistic. Thus, instead of understanding globalization as a homogenizing process in which the world is standardized after a Western model, taking into consideration the global developments of Buddhism since the early 19th century shows globalization as a process that is shaped by a multitude of globalization projects from a plethora of actors that act from a huge variety of spaces.

GLOBAL RECONFIGURATIONS OF BUDDHISM IN THE COLONIAL ERA

As the period of European colonialism produced the conditions for contemporary globalization, it was a foundational time for the relationship between globalization and Buddhism. From the 15th century onward, European powers had expanded their influence and power around the globe, thereby linking the different parts of the world on a historically unprecedented scale. Although trade and military expansion were the main driving forces of the colonial projects of the European powers, religion too played its role. Christianity, in its Catholic and Protestant forms, set an important model for religious globalization. Missionaries traveled the colonial routes to spread their faith to all parts of the world. Jesuit missionaries, for example, arrived in Japan as early as in the 16th century. From the 19th century on, it was particularly Protestant missionaries who produced the reference points for Buddhists in the colonial and semicolonial countries of Asia. Not only did they encourage people to convert to Protestant Christianity, they also presented their religion as the paradigm modern model religion. This specific presentation of Protestant Christianity produced lasting effects on the Buddhist worlds in Asia.

A famous example for the impact that the encounter of Asian Buddhism and Protestant Christianity under the conditions of European colonialism had produced is the work and life of Anagārika Dharmapāla (1864–1933). Dharmapāla was a Sri Lankan Buddhist reformer and global missionary. Born into a wealthy merchant family, he became influenced by the Theosophical Society and would become a key figure in the modern Sinhalese Buddhist reform movement. He was the founder of the Maha Bodhi Society and spent a good part of his life in India to revive Buddhism in its place of origin. He also traveled to Japan, Burma, Thailand, Europe, and the United States to propagate Buddhism und promote the establishment of a pan-Buddhist movement. The encounter of Sri Lanka with British colonialism caused the development of a local printing culture, introduced Western-style education, and led to the emergence of a middle class. All these developments had a profound impact on Buddhism. Yet it was particularly the contact with Protestant missionaries that influenced modern Singhalese Buddhists. Modernist Buddhists in Sri Lanka began to sing Buddhist carols, they established Buddhist associations formed after the Young Men's Christian Association (YMCA), and ran Buddhist Sunday schools. These are the reasons why Gananath Obeyesekere so famously dubbed the movement "Protestant Buddhism."

The newly emerging middle class in Sri Lanka constitutes an important factor for the development of this new Buddhism. New understandings of what it meant to be religious for modern Sri Lankan Buddhists were in many ways based on British Victorian values and stand in contradiction with the earthier village religiosity. Another important aspect related to this dynamic is a new appreciation for the role of the laity. Buddhism was untied from the communal ways of village life and instead became linked to the private sphere of the individual. New possibilities for lay Buddhists to act as preachers were created. Dharmapāla himself chose to become a monastic only at the end of his life, after many years of teaching. Yet not only was the role of laity transformed in this process, new roles for Buddhist clerics as teachers or officiators of weddings were also created. Arguably the most impactful outcome for the global development of modern Buddhism was the increased interest of the lay Buddhists in meditation. Meditation had in the past been reserved for a small group of monastics. Opening meditation for the laity would become one of the core characteristics (arguably the only one) of modern Buddhism.

Another important idea that shapes the global discourse on Buddhism even today, particularly but not exclusively in its Western variants, is the idea of Buddhism as an atheist philosophy. The idea that Buddhism is at its core an atheist philosophy originates from European orientalist studies. European scholars, such as Eugène Burnouf (1801–1851), or Thomas William (1843–1922) and Caroline Augusta Rhys Davids (1857–1942), had little regard for Buddhism as it was practiced by Asians on the ground. Based on textual studies, they portrayed Buddhism as a rationalist tradition without ritual and magic. When Christian missionaries attacked Buddhism for supposedly being backward and superstitious, Buddhist reformers appropriated the orientalist discourse and argued that because of the absence of a creator god and the doctrine of cause and condition, it is Buddhism rather than Christianity that is in accordance with modern science. They thus contended that it is their religion that is the most suitable for modernity.[7] Sri Lankan Buddhists were not the only ones who applied orientalist scholarship to their own means. The same line of reasoning was popular within Buddhist circles of other Asian countries.

An important change that resulted from the encounter between the Buddhist traditions in Asia and European colonialism is the modification of Buddhism as a modern religion that contributes to the development of the nation-state. It is therefore not a surprise that modernizers such as Dharmapāla were also involved in the nationalist movements of their time. In China, this approach is well represented by the monastic reformer Taixu (1890–1947). Taixu was an important figure in the reformation of Chinese Buddhism. He promoted the modernization of Buddhism through his commitment to modern monastic education and the reformation of the sangha.[8] He was also a political activist and utopian thinker who merged socialist, anarchist, and later nationalist theory with Chinese Buddhist doctrine and practice. Taixu criticized the Buddhism of the past as escapist and overly concerned with death and ghosts. Instead, he promoted a Buddhism that affirms the relevance of worldly matters and contributed to society.[9] However, it is important to add that the changes facilitated by the new times also affected the conservative factions of the sangha. Conservative Chinese Buddhists too had to adapt in order to secure the space of their religion in a modernizing Chinese society. Chinese Buddhists of all backgrounds in the first half of the 20th century thus founded orphanages and schools, established presses and journals, and became involved in the anti-Japanese resistance.[10]

Yet besides their nationalist agenda, Buddhists such as Dharmapāla and Taixu were also committed to the development of a transnational pan-Buddhist movement. As did Dharmapāla, Taixu traveled overseas, including to Japan, South and Southeast Asia, and even to Europe and the United States, to advocate for Buddhist ecumenism and to promote his religion globally.[11] He also sent some of his students to study in the southern or Theravāda tradition.[12] And just as Dharmapāla had founded a society for the resuscitation of Buddhism in India, Taixu had ambitions to establish a World Buddhist Association.[13] Although the two would never met in person, Taixu became a member of Dharmapāla's Maha Bodhi Society.

The example of the two Buddhist reformers, one from East and the other from South Asia, shows that many of the tenets of Buddhism as it is practiced today—Buddhism as rational and in accordance with modern science, the promotion of lay meditation, Buddhist social engagement, pan-Buddhist visions, and so on—have all emerged out of the encounter between Asian Buddhist elites and Western colonialism. Yet the relationship between them was not one-way. The colonial engagements of the European powers had also caused the emergence of orientalist scholarship, such as the philology of Asian languages but also Buddhist studies, in the universities back home. This also facilitated a Buddhist influence on European thinking. The most famous example is likely the German philosopher Arthur Schopenhauer (1788–1860) and his main opus *The World as Will and Representation*.[14] Maybe even more influential, especially in the long run, was the Theosophical Society. The society not only influenced Asian Buddhists such as Dharmapāla, but has also shaped the perception of Asian religiosity and Buddhism in the West even today. Through measures such as the first Parliament of Religions, held in 1893 in Chicago—the first global interfaith meeting between Eastern and Western spiritual leaders—the Theosophical Society introduced Buddhism to a broader Western audience.[15]

GLOBAL SPREAD OF NATIONAL ASIAN TRADITIONS

The Buddhist traditions in Asia that were reconstructed as modern national religions did not confine themselves to their spaces of origin but also traveled to new places. The main channel for the global dissemination of Asian Buddhism in the 20th century was migration. Colonial-era Chinese migration linked the southern coastal provinces of China to, for example, maritime Southeast Asia, and thereby facilitated the rise of vibrant Chinese Buddhist communities in the region. Most of the early Chinese migrants who had migrated to countries such as Malaysia or Indonesia practiced a syncretic mixture of Buddhism, Taoism, and folk religion, all underpinned with Confucian discourses and practices. These religiosities dealt less with complicated Buddhist doctrine and instead directly responded to daily life issues. The religious diversity in maritime Southeast Asia was further enhanced through the encounter of overseas Chinese with the Theravāda Buddhist traditions of Southeast Asia. Later, in the late

19th and early 20th centuries, the transformations Buddhism went through in China also produced their effects in the diaspora. Monastics from China arrived in Southeast Asia and began to promote institutional Buddhism in accordance with modernist ideas but also Chinese Mahāyāna doctrinal orthodoxy.

The early efforts were continued by a later wave of modernist monks. Monastics such as Chuk Mor (1913–2002), Yen Pei (1917–1996), and Ashin Jinarakkhita (1923–2002) arrived in Indonesia, Malaysia, and Singapore in the second half of the 20th century. As did their predecessors, they distanced themselves from the religious syncretism of the past. To promote scripture-based orthodoxy they founded new Buddhist institutions that are influential even today. In accordance with Asian Buddhist modernism, they also promoted Buddhism as a religion that is committed to the building of the modern nation-state. Although the modernizers had a Chinese Mahāyāna background, they contributed to the development of a localized form of Chinese Buddhism, applying Mandarin Chinese, southern Chinese dialects, and Southeast Asian languages to Buddhist liturgy and scriptures.[16]

While the majority of ethnic Chinese during the colonial era migrated to Southeast Asia, some went to places as far as South Africa or the United States. The gold rush in mid-19th-century California, for example, inspired Chinese migrants to cross the Pacific. As of 1870, 60,000 Chinese lived in the United States, the majority of them on the West Coast. However, because of discriminatory practices from white American mainstream society, many Chinese were forced to move further east to find employment in the construction of the transcontinental railroad. Only very few historic remnants have survived the times, yet it seems safe to assume that similar to the situation in maritime Southeast Asia, the religious practices of the early Chinese migrants consisted of a mixture of Daoist, Buddhist, and folk religious practices.[17] The discriminations that the Chinese migrants had to endure would not decrease. In 1882, the American government issued the Chinese Exclusion Act, prohibiting all immigration of Chinese laborers. This ended Chinese migration to the United States and also brought the transmission of Chinese Buddhism to American soil to a temporary halt.

Chinese migrants were not the only ones who contributed to the global spread of Buddhism in the 19th century. Because of a labor agreement between US businesses and the Japanese government, people from Japan also began to migrate to Hawaii and the US West Coast. The Japanese who left their country to work in the agricultural sector mostly came from prefectures that predominantly practiced the Jodo Shinshu school of Japanese Buddhism. Accordingly, the first Japanese Buddhist priest who arrived in Hawaii in 1889 belonged to this school. However, other Japanese Buddhist schools, such as Jodoshu, followed shortly, and, after the turn to the 20th century, practitioners of Nichiren, Soto Zen, and Shingon all crossed the Pacific. Yet the largest of the schools in Hawaii even today is Jodo Shinshu. Jodo Shinshu was also the first to move to the American mainland. Shin Buddhists successfully adapted to the new environment by making adjustments to fit the North American Protestant landscape.[18]

Although Japanese were not affected by the Chinese Exclusion Act, they too were facing discrimination from mainstream society and were eventually excluded from continued migration to the United States. The Gentlemen's Agreement of 1907 and the Immigration Act of 1924 effectively banned all immigration from Asia. As a result, Japanese migrants went south to Mexico, Brazil, Chile, and Argentina. Brazil, for example, became an important destination for Japanese migration. After World War II, Japanese clerics migrated to Brazil.

Consequently, Japanese Buddhist schools and organizations, such as Soto Zen, Nichiren Honmon Butsuryu Shu, Jodo Shinshu, and Soka Gakkai, all developed a strong presence in Brazil.[19]

The situation for Japanese Americans, and thus Japanese Buddhism, in the United States became even more difficult after the attack on Pearl Harbor. As a reaction to the incident, President Franklin D. Roosevelt (1882–1945) issued Executive Order 9066, which allowed the military to remove all persons of Japanese descent from the coastal areas and incarcerate them in internment camps. Although all people of Japanese descent were targeted by the discriminatory law, Buddhists aroused particular suspicion. Buddhism was perceived as a security threat and essentially un-American. To be American meant to be Christian.[20] Japanese Buddhists continued to practice their religion in the camps. In 1944, Shin Buddhists at the Topaz War Relocation Center in Utah renamed their organization the Buddhist Churches of America. The decision was one of several efforts to negotiate discrimination from the white Protestant mainstream. Out of the same concern, Japanese American Buddhists altered the architecture of their temples and Buddhist liturgy to resemble the Protestant American model. Japanese Buddhist's activities continued to focus on the Japanese American community after the war, but they also increasingly began to be involved in cross-ethnic outreach. Some temples tried to target a non–Japanese American audience through the publication of English-language Buddhist periodicals but also by teaching meditation.

The second half of the 20th century saw Asian Buddhist traditions outside of Asia proliferate and thrive. The post–World War II era was dominated by the Cold War between the United States and the Soviet Union. The US government implemented the strategy of "containment" in order to prevent Soviet influence from spreading in Asia. It therefore enhanced its ties with many Asian countries, but also promoted the emergence of domestic area studies. Both operations led to increased interaction between the two world regions. This had an impact on the development of Buddhism outside of Asia. Subsequent changes in migration policies in countries such as the United States, Canada, and Australia further accelerated this process. The Hart–Celler Act of 1965 stopped the discriminatory practices that had prevented nonwhites from immigrating to the United States. As a result, Taiwanese, Chinese, Koreans, Vietnamese, Cambodians, Thais, Tibetans, Indians, and so on arrived. The new generation of migrants had a significantly higher socioeconomic background than their predecessors and brought with them Buddhism as it was practiced in 20th-century Asia.

Taiwanese were among the earliest of the new Asian migrants. Taiwan had become the new center of Chinese Buddhism after the establishment of the People's Republic of China (PRC). Early reform Buddhist movements that were only supported by a small minority in China had transformed into Buddhist mass organizations in Taiwan. Following the modern migration routes, Buddhist organizations such as Tzu Chi and Fo Guang Shan applied modern forms of organization and management to promote their socially engaged Buddhism all over the globe. These groups not only aimed to spread Buddhism among the overseas Taiwanese population, but among ethnic Chinese of all national origins, and also, albeit to a lesser degree, among non-Chinese.[21]

The Buddhist tradition that may be most visible globally is Tibetan Buddhism. The annexation of Tibet by the PRC had a significant impact on Tibetan Buddhism, not only within Tibet but also on a global scale. In the 1959 Tibetan uprising against the occupation, the fourteenth

Dalai Lama (b. 1940) fled to India, where he lives today as a refugee. He would become the most famous Buddhist worldwide, being revered by Buddhists of all backgrounds and even non-Buddhists. Other Tibetan clerics who had fled Tibet moved to European countries and the United States. In contrast to the Taiwanese Buddhists who provided religious services to ethnic Chinese communities overseas, the Tibetan lamas in the West had no large overseas communities to tend. As a result, they became very influential in the global development of non-Asian Buddhism. Small groups gathered around a handful of individual teachers developed, over time, into big transnational networks. Global patronage played an important role within this process, making possible the establishment of new and the maintenance of existing monasteries in Asia. Western celebrities, as well as generous Taiwanese Buddhists, constituted (and constitute) important new sources of support for the globalization of Tibetan Buddhism.[22]

As with Mahāyāna Buddhism, the political transformations of the second half of the 20th century and the new migration policies in the West also facilitated the global spread of the Theravāda traditions from South and Southeast Asia. The globalization of Thai Buddhism, for example, was shaped by the growth of Thai migrant communities abroad, but also by missionary efforts sponsored by the monastic orders and the Thai government through the Ministry of Education and the Office of National Buddhism under the Ministry of Culture.[23] In Sweden, Thai Buddhists represent the largest Buddhist migrant group and Thai Buddhism is the fastest growing form of Buddhism.[24] Similar to the Thais, Theravāda Buddhists from Sri Lanka migrated to the United States from the 1960s on. In contrast, Southeast Asian Buddhists from places such as Vietnam or Cambodia came as refugees having no ties with the large organizations from their home countries.[25] Once they had settled, they established small-scale individual temples. Among the Vietnamese refugees who left their country first, there were many Sino-Vietnamese. In the diaspora, some of them reconnected with their Chinese roots and became involved in Taiwanese Mahāyāna temples. Fo Guang Shan's main temple in North America, Hsi Lai Temple, located in a nonintegrated city just outside of Los Angeles, for example, maintains a big Sino-Vietnamese following. Although most of these examples have focused on the United States, similar developments took place in Oceania, South America, in the countries of Western Europe, but also in South Africa.

GLOBAL SPREAD OF BUDDHISM AMONG NON-ASIANS

Another important aspect of the globalization of Buddhism is the spread of discourses and practices linked to the tradition among non-Asians. Europeans encountered Buddhism long before it was introduced to a bigger audience, through the writings of Arthur Schopenhauer and the Theosophical Society. Among the first Europeans who learned about Buddhism were Catholic missionaries. The Italian Jesuit Matteo Ricci (1552–1610) went to China in the 16th century. In order to better promote Catholic Christianity in China, Ricci thought it would be advantageous to adapt to the local religious landscape. One of his measures to do so was by wearing Chinese Buddhist attire. However, after realizing the dominant role of Confucianism within Chinese society, he switched his alliance to Confucianism. He began to dress as a Confucian scholar and even defended Confucian orthodoxy against a supposedly corrupted Buddhism. Despite this troublesome beginning, the relationship between Catholicism and Buddhism would become more multifaceted over time and reports on Buddhism sent home by Jesuit missionaries were an important intellectual resource that shaped the perception of Buddhism in Europe. The German romanticist Friedrich Schlegel (1772–1829) was among the first European scholars who studied Buddhism, although he, as did his contemporaries, subsumed it into the belief systems of Hinduism. The 19th century saw the emergence of European orientalist and philological studies on Buddhism. The studies by European scholars, such as Eugène Burnouf or Thomas William and Caroline Augusta Rhys Davids, centered on the founder of Buddhism, Gautama Siddhartha, and aimed to reconstruct Buddhism on a basis of textual studies. The scholarly interest in Buddhism also facilitated attempts to practice Buddhism as a religion. After the turn of the century, Buddhist societies were first established in Germany and the United Kingdom.[26] In the 19th century in the United States, European Romanticism similarly was one of the roots of emerging interest in Buddhism. American transcendentalists such as Emerson, Thoreau, and Wordsworth were fascinated by Asian religiosities and integrated Buddhist ideas into their philosophies.[27]

In the 20th century, German Jesuit Hugo Makibi Enomiya-Lassalle (1898–1990) became one of the foremost proponents of incorporating Japanese Zen Buddhist meditation practice into Catholicism. Lassalle was sent to Japan by his order in 1929. In 1935 he moved to Hiroshima, where he developed an interest in Japanese Buddhism. He survived the American bombing of the city and, after the Second Vatican Council in 1965, became an active promoter of Zen meditation in Europe. He founded a Christian Zen meditation center in Germany and led many Zen meditation retreats all over the continent.[28]

Japanese Zen became popular in the United States too. The work of Japanese Daisetsu Teitaro Suzuki (1870–1966) played an important role within this process. Together with his teacher Soyen Shaku (1860–1919), Suzuki had participated in the World's Parliament of Religions in 1893. Later in his life, he widely traveled in the United States and Europe, lectured and published extensively on Buddhism and Zen, and became an important representative of Zen in the United States in the 1950s. After the war, a group of writers, the so-called Beat generation, developed an interest in Zen and Asian religiosity. Authors such as Alan Watts (1915–1973) and Gary Snyder (b. 1930) incorporated aspects of Buddhism into their writings, thereby facilitating American popular interest in the religion. However, the reception of Zen Buddhism of this period did not develop into firm institutional structures. This only changed with the arrival of the Japanese Soto monk Shunryū Suzuki (1904–1971) to the United States in the late 1950s. Suzuki founded the San Francisco Zen Center in 1962, which would become a very important site for the spread of Zen Buddhism among non-Asian Americans. A book of his teachings, *Zen Mind, Beginner's Mind,* became one of the most popular texts on Zen and Buddhism in the West.[29]

From the 1960s on, Buddhism slowly became increasingly popular in the countries of the West. Economic recovery after the war in Europe, the pluralization of Western societies, and the emergence of counterculture movements from the 1960s on all produced the conditions for a heightened interest in Buddhism. At the same time, US containment policy led to US military presence and economic assistance in Asia. The time saw increased travel, volunteerism, and tourism of Westerners to Asia. Many of the Westerners who traveled to Asia were influenced by the newly emerging countercultural movements of the 1960s. The American meditation teacher Jack Kornfield, for example, traveled to Thailand with the Peace Corps. Others went to Southeast Asia as tourists and backpackers. In Southeast Asia, they encountered influential modernist Buddhist teachers such as Mahasy Sayadaw (1904–1982) or Satya Narayan Goenka (1924–2013). Their modernist approaches to Theravāda, which modified Buddhist meditation to make it suitable for laypeople, would become important for the development of the US Vipassana or insight meditation movement. The emphasis on lay practice and meditation at the expense of other aspects of the Buddhist teachings made modernist Theravāda very adaptable to different cultural settings. Some American mediation teachers removed the Buddhist label to an even greater degree than their Asian teachers. This turned out to be very successful, and today Buddhist-derived practices such as mindfulness are promoted all over the globe, often in the context of health care and clinical psychology and without any recognizable link to Buddhism.[30] On the other side of the spectrum of Theravāda modernism were reformist Theravāda movements that held on to the role of monasticism. These groups too would become influential in the West. In the late 1970s, for example, the Thai Forest Tradition, probably most widely known through Ajahn Chah, was first transmitted to the United Kingdom. Today the tradition is practiced in many countries over the globe and has attracted many non-Asians to become monastics. The British monk Ajahn Brahm, for example, was ordained in Thailand at the age of twenty-three and subsequently spent nine years training under Ajahn Chah. He later settled in Australia where he founded a monastery. He often gives dharma talks on the monastery's YouTube channel and regularly travels the world to teach meditation classes. Yet another form of Buddhism that has gained popularity in the West is socially engaged Buddhism. Socially engaged Buddhism developed out of the modernist national Buddhist reform movements in Asia and was later popularized in the West by Thich Nhat Hanh.[31] In European and American contexts, socially engaged Buddhists often align themselves with progressive causes such as environmentalism, pacifism, or gender equality.[32]

Yet the Buddhist tradition that is probably best known in the West is Tibetan Buddhism. The publications of Heinrich Harrer (1912–2006), an Austrian mountaineer and former member of Nazi Party paramilitary organization the Schutzstaffel (SS), who had spent time in India and Tibet from 1939 to 1951, for example, played an important role in introducing Tibetan Buddhism and culture to a German-speaking audience after the war. During his stay in Tibet, Harrer got to know and even befriended the young Fourteenth Dalai Lama. His book *Seven Years in Tibet* gives account of his time in Tibet. It was first published in 1952 and later translated into twenty-three languages.[33] In the 1990s it was even turned into a Hollywood movie. Yet the person most influential in promoting Tibetan Buddhism on a global level is, of course, the Dalai Lama himself. After his escape from occupied Tibet, he traveled the world and has spoken on a broad range of issues. These issues include, along with various Tibetan Buddhist teachings, the welfare of Tibetans, the environment, economics, women's rights, nonviolence, interfaith dialogue, Buddhism, and science. He even received the Nobel Peace Prize in 1989 and is popular with Buddhists of many backgrounds as well as with non-Buddhists. Another representative of Tibetan Buddhism in the West is the Shambhala International organization founded by controversial Buddhist leader Chögyam Trungpa (1939–1987). Shambhala International promotes a mixture of Tibetan Buddhist practices, Japanese Buddhist-influenced arts, Western arts, and psychotherapy. Chögyam Trungpa has even founded a Buddhist university in the United States, and Shambhala International has great influence through its various publications, which include the US Buddhist periodical *Lion's Roar*.

Postwar Western Buddhism is often linked to the so-called baby boomer generation, a term used to describe a person who was born between 1946 and 1964. Those who were attracted to Buddhism were often white, educated, and belonged to the middle class. The Buddhism they practiced differed significantly from the Buddhism practiced by their Asian contemporaries. Some scholars have characterized the Buddhism practiced by non-Asian Westerners as meditation-focused, rationalized, romantic, and individualistic. This was sometimes juxtaposed with the image of a "traditional" and community-oriented Buddhism practiced by immigrants. Since 2010, this supposed bifurcation of a Buddhism practiced by Asians and non-Asians has become increasingly problematized. The image of a bifurcated Buddhism does not acknowledge the complexity of the Buddhism practiced by Asians outside of Asia or issues related to second and later generations of immigration. Since the 1990s, Buddhism practiced by non-Asian Westerners too became increasingly complex. Concomitantly, a younger generation of Buddhists and Buddhist scholars began to critically examine the Buddhism of the baby boomer generation with regard to issues related to class, race, and ethnicity.[34]

Yet what earlier and later forms of non-Asian Buddhism in the West have in common is their strong focus on meditation. Due to the global dominance of the United States and the global spread of the English language, US Buddhism is probably the most influential of the forms of Buddhism that have developed within non-Asian countries. Through their publications and the global travel of American teachers, non–Asian American Buddhist discourses and practices shape the development of non-Asian Buddhism worldwide, including in the African continent. Here, it is most influential, albeit still on a very small degree, among white South Africans. At the same time, Buddhist organizations from Asia, such as Fo Guang Shan from Taiwan, Soka Gakkai from Japan, or Theravāda Buddhists from Sri Lanka, that adept a more proactive approach to spreading their Buddhist traditions have reached a modest level of success in attracting local Black Africans.[35] However, it is important to add that, numerically, non-Asian Buddhists still represent a minority compared to the Buddhists in Asia and the global Asian diasporas. The number of non-Asian Buddhists, however defined, is relatively small. At the same time, Buddhism has a strong media presence and a strong appeal even to non-Buddhists. Orientalist depictions of the Asian monk, for example, have become staples of mass media and popular culture in non-Asian countries.[36] In contrast to other religions, such as Islam, for example, Buddhism generates a global image that appears attractive even to non-adherents. It is therefore no surprise that buddha images and other images linked to Buddhism—such as pictures of Buddhist temples, lush lotus flowers, or serene mediators—are applied in many, often commercial, contexts.

NEW MODES OF INNER-ASIAN BUDDHIST EXCHANGE

Increased global integration has not only facilitated the spread of Buddhism to localities that historically were not Buddhist. It has also facilitated intensified intra-Buddhist contact and exchange within Asia. These interactions continuously impact the development of the national traditions all over Asia. The early pan-Buddhist ambitions harbored by Dharmapāla or Taixu have, over time, transformed into transnationally oriented institutions that continually foster intra-Buddhist cooperation. Pan-Buddhist organizations and mega conferences, such as the World Fellowship of Buddhists founded 1950 in Sri Lanka, the World Buddhist Forum in

China, or the World Buddhist Summits that have taken place in Japan, Thailand, Cambodia, and Sri Lanka, connect Asian Buddhist institutions of different traditions and national backgrounds. Other pan-Buddhist organizations again are centered on specific issues. The Sakyadhita International Association of Buddhist Women, for example, was founded in 1987 and holds biannual conferences in different Asian localities, bringing together monastic and lay Buddhist women from all over the world and all backgrounds.[37] Besides constituting a forum for intrareligious dialogue, big pan-Buddhist conferences also may serve the political goals of the country that organizes them. For the government of the PRC, Buddhism constitutes a resource to project soft power in its diplomacy. The World Buddhist Forum, for example, receives the support of the highest level of government in the PRC. For the Chinese Communist Party, Buddhist cross-strait cooperation constitutes a resource to achieve its goal of national unification with Taiwan.[38]

The reinvigoration of Buddhism in the PRC is one of the most outstanding developments starting in the end of the 20th century within the Buddhist scene in Asia. Since the end of the Cultural Revolution, numerous Buddhist temples have been rebuilt and people have again begun to be ordained as Buddhist monastics. Chinese Mahāyāna today has about 15,000 Buddhist sites and 100,000 monastics.[39] Temples such as the Longquan Temple in the outskirts of Beijing follow the example of the big Taiwanese organizations and are developing a global presence. Chinese Mahāyāna is not the only Buddhist tradition practiced in China. Other traditions such as Theravāda or Tibetan Buddhism too are increasingly popular, not only within the ethnic minority communities they are practiced historically, but also among Han Chinese. Tibetan Buddhism, for example, has gained popularity particularly in China's moneyed and middle classes.[40]

New flows of inner-Asian migration have changed the Buddhist landscape of many countries. This becomes apparent if the example of Southeast Asian migration to Taiwan is considered. There is a large Vietnamese diaspora that exists in Taiwan, many of whom are Buddhists. Vietnamese move to Taiwan to find work, to marry, or to receive education. Taiwan has several universities run by Buddhist organizations, with Buddhist studies programs that attract monastics from other Asian countries, including Vietnam. In addition, there are many Buddhist seminaries that also attract overseas monastics. Some of the Vietnamese students of these institutions provide religious services for the Vietnamese community in Taiwan. Others help out at rituals that are conducted at Taiwanese temples, which struggle to find monastics because less and less Taiwanese choose to become ordained into the Buddhist sangha.

A proactive agenda to spread the Buddhist Dharma is another important channel for the dissemination of Buddhism under the conditions of globalization. Theravāda Buddhist traditions such Sri Lankan Buddhism have also developed a presence in Taiwan. Sri Lankan Buddhist monastics do not come to the country to care for a diaspora community but to proselytize among the Taiwanese. The Sri Lankan monk Bodagama Chandima (b. 1957), for example, founded the Theravāda Samadhi Education Association in Taipei in 1999. Bodagama Chandima is a transnational Buddhist missionary, who frequently travels between Sri Lanka, Taiwan, India, and Malaysia, among other countries. Not only does he maintain connections with other Sri Lankan Buddhist transnational networks such as the Maha Bodhi Society in India, but also with Chinese Malaysian Buddhist groups. He is, for example, involved in the construction and operation of a new Buddhist university in Sri Lanka, the Nagananda

International Institute for Buddhist Studies. The university has received support and financial aid for its founding from the popular Chinese monk Chin Kung (b. 1927).[41]

One important factor in producing the conditions for increased contact and exchange between Buddhists of different national and traditional origins in Asia is the emergence of a globally minded Asian middle class. Asian Buddhist traditions, particularly in their modernist variants that distance themselves from folk Buddhism, resonate with the members of the middle and upper classes. Not only do members of these segments of society have the educational background to study the diversity of Asian Buddhist traditions, they can also afford domestic and inner-Asian religious tourism. Pilgrimages and religious festivals have always shaped Buddhist mobility, yet what is new is the degree of commercialization. In Buddhist countries, Buddhist theme parks, museums, and monuments have emerged everywhere, attracting a persistent flow of visitors. Many are not linked to a particular Buddhist tradition but are capitalist enterprises that aim to attract the general public. Others are linked to a particular temple or order, but also target an audience of Buddhists of all backgrounds as well as non-Buddhists. People visit these sites for religious as well as recreational motives.[42]

Amalgamations of religion and tourism in Asia are not exclusively aimed toward Asians. Meditation tourism to places such as Thailand attracts both Westerners and also people from other Asian countries, such as China. They travel to Thailand to practice meditation in retreat centers specifically built for this purpose. Meditation is here partly dissociated from the local Buddhist contexts and often marketed through orientalist imagery. The example shows how Asian Buddhists deploy the visual Orientalism that has developed in Western popular culture for their own purposes. These encounters between Thai Buddhist temples and international lay meditators have facilitated new globalization projects. They lead to the development of transnational lay Buddhist lineages, but also create loose networks of Thai teachers who are invited overseas.[43]

Intra-Buddhist interactions also influence on how Buddhism is practiced on a monastic level. This applies in particular to gender relations in Buddhism. The biggest impact so far generated by the cooperation of Buddhists of different Asian traditions relates to the issue of bhikkhunī ordination. In some Asian Buddhist traditions, the full female monastic, or bhikkhunī, ordination had died out centuries ago, while in others full ordination of bhikkhunīs has never existed. Since the 1980s, cross-traditional cooperation of monastics from different countries has facilitated the full ordination of women in these traditions. In 1998, the Taiwanese order Fo Guang Shan organized an international ordination ceremony in Bodhgaya. Among the participants were 134 women from nineteen countries. Buddhist monastics from Theravāda, Mahāyāna, and Vajrayana all came together to make the ordination possible and ensure its validity according to Buddhist orthodoxy. Male and female monastics from Taiwan, Hong Kong, Malaysia, Sri Lanka, Nepal, Thailand, India, the United Kingdom, Cambodia, Burma, and Tibet served as preceptors. The nuns who received ordination belonged to the Chinese Mahāyāna, the Theravāda, and the Tibetan tradition.[44] In 2009, the Thai Forest Tradition Monastery, headed by Ajahn Brahm in Perth, Western Australia, organized a bhikkhunī ordination ceremony for four nuns. However, in more conservative Buddhist circles bhikkhunī ordination is still controversial; after the ordination Ajahn Brahm was, for example, officially expelled from the Ajahn Chah sangha. But what is important for the scope of this article is that the events, which were not the only ones of their kind, exemplify a new degree of transnational and cross-tradition cooperation within the Buddhist world, and the impacts that are thereby produced. Global integration of the world has created new linkages based on gender that cross customary affiliations based on traditions such as Mahāyāna and Theravāda or on national origin.

Buddhists have also begun to rally together for global causes. The issue that has most consensus among Buddhists is probably environmentalism. Many environmental problems are caused by excessive consumerism and, thus, from a Buddhist perspective, linked to Buddhist core concerns such as the erasure of ignorance and cravings. Other Buddhists, such as the Taiwanese female monastic and university professor Chao Hui, go a step further and apply Buddhist ethics to a whole range of contemporary issues. Chao Hui has voiced a progressive standpoint on a whole range of topics, including gender equality, same-sex relationships, organ transplant, surrogate mothers, stem-cell research, euthanasia, the death penalty, environmental protection, and animal rights. Furthermore, Chao Hui has also officiated at lesbian and gay weddings.[45]

CONCLUSION

The relationship between Buddhism and globalization is a complex and multifaceted one. By approaching the increased global integration of the world through the lens of Buddhism, it becomes clear that globalization does not simply correspond with a standardized Western model but is instead a multidirectional process generated by a multitude of actors. The global dissemination of terms such as religion and Buddhism as generic concepts is the outcome of earlier colonial stages of globalization. But it would be wrong to assume that Buddhism in its diversity, as it developed during the last hundred and more years, is just a passive object of global forces and dynamics. Buddhists from all backgrounds and traditions are themselves agents who actively take part in the globalization of the world. A multitude of Buddhists—ranging from members of pan-Buddhist organizations or transnationally active Buddhist orders, missionaries, and also individual Buddhists such as tourists, migrants, businessmen and women, and so on—all take part in the globalization of Buddhism and the world. Many of them have an Asian background; others are ethnic Europeans, Africans, and so on. Buddhism as it is practiced today is a producer of globalization while it is at the same time a product of globalization.

Although the relationship between Buddhism and globalization plays out differently at different times and places, certain key issues are foundational. Of particular importance has been the emergence of a global middle class, together with the proliferation of modern education and an increase in literacy worldwide. As result, Buddhists worldwide differentiate their tradition from earlier blendings with folk and village religiosity. This has caused an enhanced interest in Buddhist doctrine, Buddhist modes of contributing to modernizing society, and a general re-evaluation of the role of the Buddhist laity. Individual practices of religious cultivation, particularly meditation, have moved to the religion's center. Protestant Christianity has acted as an important point of reference within this process. Protestant Christianity has functioned as a model to emulate and to compete with, but also as a sparring partner and an opponent to distance oneself from. It has facilitated the idea of Buddhism as a modern religion that contributes to the nation-state, but also the idea of Buddhism as an atheist philosophy and the equation of Buddhism with meditation. Buddhist missionaries such as Dharmapāla and Taixu have followed the example of Protestant missionaries and have propagated the Dharma in places without a local Buddhist tradition or where the tradition has died out. Migration, media, the Internet, and tourism have, over time, become ever more important channels of the global transmission of Buddhism. A plurality of Buddhist traditions has been firmly established in many non-Asian countries and Buddhism has further diversified in the countries of Asia. Inner Buddhist exchange and contact have generated conditions for the revival of the bhikkhunī ordination in traditions where it has ceased to exist or introduced this in traditions in which it never previously existed. All these dynamics play out differently in different localities and are formulated in relation to their specific local contexts, but all reflect the enhanced degree of Buddhist mobility under the condition of globalization.

DISCUSSION OF THE LITERATURE

The study of Buddhism's relationship with globalization is situated within the broader context of religion and globalization. On a more comprehensive theoretical level, the issue is primarily approached from a sociological perspective. Here, globalization has replaced secularization as the sociological framework for contemporary religious developments. Sociologist Roland Robertson argues that the social sciences were established at a particular point of globalization, the late 19th and early 20th centuries, characterized by the emergence of the nation-state as the main organizational and administrative unit. Since the end of the 20th century, however, there has been a shift from secularization to globalization as the theoretical framework for sociological research in general and sociological research on religion in particular. Concurrently, religions increasingly adapt to this perspective and integrate positions on global issues such as environmentalism into their theologies.[46] In a later publication, Robertson suggested the notion of "glocalization" as a refinement to the concept of globalization. Originally developed in Japanese business models in the late 1980s, the concept of "glocalization" emphasizes the heterogenizing dynamics of globalization. Thus, instead of perceiving globalization as a process of standardization that increases uniformity, Robertson argues that it involves the incorporation but also creation of locality.[47] Within the sociological study of religion in the context of globalization, Peter Beyer's work is foundational. His book-length study *Religion and Globalization* was published as early as 1994 and he has continued to publish on the issue during the following decades. Beyer is highly influenced by Luhmanian system theory. He analyses the global expansion of the religious system through case studies that focus on the formation processes of religion in different regions and cultures of the modern world.[48]

Martin Baumann has incorporated the global angle specifically to his study of Buddhism. Baumann suggests subdividing the historical development of Buddhism into four different eras: canonical, traditionalist, modernist, and global. According to Baumann, global Buddhism includes the latest developments within the cumulative traditions of Buddhism. The examples he provides for his category of global Buddhism include the controversial Danish lama Ole Nydahl, Chögyam Trungpa's Shambhala Training, and the Insight Meditation Society. Baumann argues that global Buddhism, which he also calls postmodern Buddhism, secularizes and psychologizes modernist forms of Buddhism.[49]

Another approach to theorizing on religion and globalization is to orient scholarly attention to the category of space. Based on a case study of Cuban immigrants in Miami, Thomas Tweed has developed a theory of religion that considers how religions find places to settle as well as move across space. In order to capture these dynamics, Tweed argues for applying aquatic metaphors to the study of religion.[50] Tweed has also specified his theory for the study of Buddhism. He states five axioms for the translocative study of Buddhism. The first one is to follow the flow of people, artifacts, institutions, practices, and so on, but also to notice how apparently fixed things, such as temple constructions, are changing over time. Second, he stresses the importance of including all people involved in Buddhism in one's examination, from religious leaders to ordinary devotees to children. But it is not only people one should pay attention to; Tweed calls on scholars to examine all components of religion through the application of all one's senses—sight, smell, taste, touch, and hearing. The fourth axiom is particularly concerned with globalization in that it urges the scholar to not just look at Buddhism by placing it into a particular nation-state or continent but to reframe the study of Buddhism by considering a variety of scales. Finally, Tweed emphasizes the importance of examining how power dynamics shape the global trajectory of Buddhist flows.[51]

Most research on Buddhism and globalization does not consider the issue from a comprehensive theoretical angle but instead focuses on particular case studies. There are two academic journals that publish many articles on the issue, *Contemporary Buddhism* and the *Journal of Global Buddhism,* the latter published online. An abundance of research exists in religious and area studies that examines the modernization of national Asian Buddhist traditions and looks at how they are influenced by and involved in the global flows of colonial modernity. Historical research in the institutional context of area studies has produced important insights in the development of modern Asian Buddhist traditions under the influence of European colonialism. As a result, there exist many studies that look at the modern development of national traditions in countries such as Sri Lanka, India, China, Korea, Burma, and so on.[52] Other studies apply an ethnographic approach to analyze more contemporary developments in Asia. They examine the activities of big transnationally active Buddhist organizations, but also consider how these traditions reorganize themselves by adapting to global capitalism and consumer culture.[53]

Research on Buddhism in countries where Buddhism only took hold during the last two centuries—the countries of the Americas, of Oceania, of Europe, and of Africa—constitutes another subfield of the study of Buddhism and globalization. Within this field of scholarship, the main focus lies on the United States. Scholars have here primarily analyzed forms of Buddhism that are practiced by Euro-Americans.[54] In addition, a smaller number of similar studies considering the development of Buddhism in Latin America, Canada, Europe, Australia, New Zealand, and Africa exist.[55] In the early 21st century, studies on Buddhism outside of Asia increasingly reflect on the global embeddedness of Western Buddhism, but also discuss issues related to Buddhism and race, or the dynamics of transmission, change, and translation.[56]

Furthermore, there exists an expanding body of scholarship on Asian Buddhism that places diverse national traditions in a global context by considering transcontinental or inner-Asian transnationalism, migration, or tourism. Scholars have written on modern and contemporary Asian Buddhist missionary work and are looking at how different Asian traditions from the colonial era on have tried to spread their religion beyond their historical borders.[57] The global outlook of Japanese Buddhism constitutes an important and well-researched subtopic of Buddhism and globalization.[58] Many scholars have considered the case of the Soka Gakkai movement.[59] Studies examine the accommodation of Soka Gakkai in countries all over the globe, including the United States, Canada, Mexico, Cuba, Brazil, Southeast Asia, the United Kingdom, Austria, and Germany.[60] The Buddhist transnationalism of modernist Taiwanese Buddhist organizations too has received some substantial scholarly attention. By examining regional developments in the United States, Canada, Malaysia, and the PRC, scholars have analyzed the nature of the global networks of Tzu Chi or Fo Guang Shan.[61]

Much research examines the global spread of Buddhism through migration. Many studies exist, for example, on the transmission of Asian Buddhist traditions to the United States, such as Japanese Shin or Cambodian Buddhism.[62] Other studies look at Japanese Buddhism and migration in Latin America, or Vietnamese Buddhism in countries such as Canada or Germany.[63] While most studies examine how Asian Buddhists practice their religion after they have moved to Western countries, some scholars have looked at the reception and practice of Western Buddhism in Asia.[64] Other studies on Asian migrants and Buddhism include non-Western places, such as Africa, and the dynamics of Buddhist dispersion linked to inner-Asian migration.[65] Important driving forces that produce contemporary inner-Asian Buddhist entanglements besides migration are tourism and pilgrimage. Scholars have produced edited volumes on many aspects on Buddhist tourism in Asia and the role of Buddhist pilgrimage sites such as Bodh Gaya, the place where the historical Buddha supposedly reached enlightenment within the context of the Indian nation-state or the flows of globalization.[66]

DIGITAL MATERIALS

Journal of Global Buddhism (http://www.globalbuddhism.org/jgb/index.php/jgb/).

FURTHER READING

Bruntz, Courtney, and Brooke Schedneck, eds. *Buddhist Tourism in Asia*. Honolulu: University of Hawaii Press, 2020.

Cadge, Wendy. *Heartwood: The First Generation of Theravada Buddhism in America*. Chicago: University of Chicago Press, 2005.

Josephson, Jason Ānanda. *The Invention of Religion in Japan*. Chicago and London: University of Chicago Press, 2012.

Juergensmeyer, Mark, ed. *Global Religions: An Introduction*. Oxford and New York: Oxford University Press, 2003.

Learman, Linda, ed. *Buddhist Missionaries in the Era of Globalization*. Honolulu: University of Hawaii Press, 2005.

Masuzawa, Tomoko. *The Invention of World Religions: Or, How European Universalism Was Preserved in the Language of Pluralism*. Chicago: University of Chicago Press, 2005.

McMahan, David L., ed. *Buddhism in the Modern World*. New York: Routledge, 2012.

Mitchell, Scott A., and Natalie E. F. Quli, eds. *Buddhism beyond Borders: New Perspectives on Buddhism in the United States*. Albany, NY: SUNY Press, 2016.

Prebish, Charles S., and Martin Baumann, eds. *Westward Dharma: Buddhism beyond Asia.* Berkeley: University of California Press, 2002.

Tweed, Thomas A. "Theory and Method in the Study of Buddhism: Toward 'Translocative' Analysis." In *Buddhism beyond Borders: New Perspectives on Buddhism in the United States.* Edited by Scott A. Mitchell and Natalie E. F. Quli, 3–20. Albany, NY: SUNY Press, 2016.

Wong, Diana, and Peggy Levitt. "Travelling Faiths and Migrant Religions: The Case of Circulating Models of Da'wa among the Tablighi Jamaat and Foguangshan in Malaysia." *Global Networks* 14, no. 3 (2014): 348–362.

NOTES

1. Linda Learman, "Introduction," in *Buddhist Missionaries in the Era of Globalization,* ed. Linda Learman (Honolulu: University of Hawaii Press, 2005), 5.
2. Tomoko Masuzawa, *The Invention of World Religions: Or, How European Universalism Was Preserved in the Language of Pluralism* (Chicago: University of Chicago Press, 2005), 12.
3. Masazuwa, *The Invention of World Religions,* 138–144.
4. Jason Ānanda Josephson, *The Invention of Religion in Japan* (Chicago and London: University of Chicago Press, 2012), 255–259.
5. Vincent Goossaert and David A. Palmer, *The Religious Question in Modern China* (Chicago: University of Chicago Press, 2011), 68.
6. Gananath Obeyesekere, "Buddhism," in *Global Religions: An Introduction,* ed. Mark Juergensmeyer (Oxford and New York: Oxford University Press, 2003), 64.
7. Richard Francis Gombrich and Gananath Obeyesekere, *Buddhism Transformed: Religious Change in Sri Lanka* (Princeton, NJ: Princeton University Press, 1988), 202–240.
8. The community of monks and nuns.
9. Don Alvin Pittman, *Toward a Modern Chinese Buddhism: Taixu's Reforms* (Honolulu: University of Hawaii Press, 2001); and Justin Ritzinger, *Anarchy in the Pure Land: Reinventing the Cult of Maitreya in Modern Chinese Buddhism* (New York: Oxford University Press, 2017).
10. Goossaert and Palmer, *The Religious Question in Modern China,* 82.
11. Pittman, *Toward a Modern Chinese Buddhism,* 118–129.
12. Justin R. Ritzinger, "Original Buddhism and Its Discontents: The Chinese Buddhist Exchange Monks and the Search for the Pure Dharma in Ceylon," *Journal of Chinese Religions* 44, no. 2 (2016): 149–173.
13. Pittman, *Toward a Modern Chinese Buddhism,* 106.
14. Arthur Schopenhauer, *Die Welt als Wille und Vorstellung: I und II* (Munich: Deutscher Taschenbuch Verlagsgesellschaft, 2011).
15. Obeyesekere, "Buddhism," 67–69.
16. Jack Meng-Tat Chia, *Monks in Motion: Buddhism and Modernity across the South China Sea* (New York: Oxford University Press, 2020), 237, 241.
17. Stuart Chandler, "Chinese Buddhism in America: Identity and Practice," in *The Faces of Buddhism in America,* ed. Charles S. Prebish and Kenneth K. Tanaka (Berkeley: University of California Press, 1998), 16.
18. Elisabetta Porcu, "Contemporary Japanese Buddhist Traditions," in *Oxford Handbook of Contemporary Buddhism,* ed. Michael K. Jerryson (New York: Oxford University Press, 2016), 133.
19. Porcu, "Contemporary Japanese Buddhist Traditions," 134.
20. Dunkan Ryukan Williams, *American Sutra: A Story of Faith and Freedom in the Second World War* (Cambridge, MA: Harvard University Press, 2019), 4–5.
21. Chien-yu Julia Huang, "The Compassion Relief Diaspora," in *Buddhist Missionaries,* ed. Learman, 185–201; Stuart Chandler, "Spreading Buddha's Light: The Internationalization of Foguang Shan," in *Buddhist*

Missionaries, ed. Learman, 162–184; Jens Reinke, "Sacred Secularities: Ritual and Social Engagement in a Global Buddhist China," *Religions* 9, no. 11 (2018): 1–12.
22. Abraham Zablocki, "Contemporary Tibetan Buddhism," in *Oxford Handbook of Contemporary Buddhism*, ed. Jerryson, 153–154.
23. Pattana Kitiarsa, "Missionary Intent and Monastic Networks: Thai Buddhism as a Transnational Religion," *Sojourn: Journal of Social Issues in Southeast Asia* 25, no. 1 (2010): 109–132.
24. Katarina Plank, "The Sacred Foodscapes of Thai Buddhist Temples in Sweden," *Scripta Instituti Donneriani Aboensis* 26 (2015): 203.
25. Wendy Cadge, *Heartwood: The First Generation of Theravada Buddhism in America* (Chicago: University of Chicago Press, 2005).
26. Martin Baumann, "Buddhism in Europe: Past, Present, Prospects," in *Westward Dharma: Buddhism beyond Asia*, ed. Charles S. Prebish and Martin Baumann (Berkeley: University of California Press, 2002), 88.
27. Arthur Versluis, *American Transcendentalism and Asian Religions* (Oxford: Oxford University Press, 1993), 3.
28. Ursula Baatz, "Hugo M. Enomiya-Lassalle: Zen-Enlightenment and Christianity," in *A Companion to Jesuit Mysticism*, ed. Robert A. Maryks (Leiden, The Netherlands: Brill, 2017), 335–357.
29. Shunryū Suzuki, *Zen Mind, Beginner's Mind* (Berkeley, CA: Shambhala, 2020).
30. Jeff Wilson, *Mindful America: The Mutual Transformation of Buddhist Meditation and American Culture* (New York: Oxford University Press, 2014).
31. Jessica L. Main and Lai Rongdao, "Reformulating 'Socially Engaged Buddhism' as an Analytical Category," *The Eastern Buddhist* 44 (2013): 1–34.
32. Christopher S. Queen and Sallie B. King, eds., *Engaged Buddhism: Buddhist Liberation Movements in Asia* (Albany: State University of New York Press, 1996); Christopher S. Queen, *Engaged Buddhism in the West* (Boston: Wisdom, 2000); and Sallie B. King, *Socially Engaged Buddhism* (Honolulu: University of Hawaii Press, 2009).
33. Heinrich Harrer, *Sieben Jahre in Tibet: Mein Leben am Hofe des Dalai Lama* (Berlin: Ullstein Verlag, 2004).
34. Ann Gleig, *American Dharma: Buddhism beyond Modernity* (New Haven, CT: Yale University Press, 2019), 249–280.
35. Michel Clasquin, "Buddhism in Africa," in *Oxford Handbook of Contemporary Buddhism*, ed. Jerryson, 349–365; and Jens Reinke, "The Buddha in Bronkhorstspruit: The Transnational Spread of the Taiwanese Buddhist Order Fo Guang Shan to South Africa," *Contemporary Buddhism* 3, no. 2 (2020): 1–18.
36. Jane Naomi Iwamura, *Virtual Orientalism: Asian Religions and American Popular Culture* (New York: Oxford University Press, 2011).
37. Mavis L. Fenn and Kay Koppedrayer, "Sakyadhita: A Transnational Gathering Place for Buddhist Women," *Journal of Global Buddhism* 9 (2008): 45–79; and Anna Halafoff and Praveena Rajkobal, "Sakyadhita International: Gender Equity in Ultramodern Buddhism," *Feminist Theology* 23, no. 2 (2015): 111–127.
38. André Laliberté, "Buddhism under Jiang, Hu, and Xi: The Politics of Incorporation," in *Buddhism after Mao: Negotiations, Continuities, and Reinventions*, ed. Zhe Ji, Gareth Fisher, and André Laliberté (Honolulu: University of Hawaii Press, 2019), 37.
39. Zhe Ji, "Chinese Buddhism as a Social Force: Reality and Potential of Thirty Years of Revival," *Chinese Sociological Review* 45, no. 2 (2012): 14.
40. Dan Smyer Yu, *The Spread of Tibetan Buddhism in China: Charisma, Money, Enlightenment* (New York: Routledge, 2014).

41. Wei-Yi Cheng, "Transnational Buddhism and Ritual Performance in Taiwan," *Contemporary Buddhism* 38 (2020): 5.
42. Justin McDaniel, *Architects of Buddhist Leisure: Socially Disengaged Buddhism in Asia's Museums, Monuments, and Amusement Parks* (Honolulu: University of Hawaii Press, 2017), 7.
43. Brooke Schedneck, *Thailand's International Meditation Centers: Tourism and the Global Commodification of Religious Practices* (London: Routledge, 2017), 168–176.
44. Yuzhen Li, "Ordination, Legitimacy, and Sisterhood: The International Full Ordination Ceremony in Bodhgaya," in *Innovative Buddhist Women: Swimming against the Stream*, ed. Karma L. Tsomo (Richmond, UK: Curzon Press, 2000), 175–180.
45. Hsiao-Lan Hu, "Buddhism and Sexual Orientation," in *Oxford Handbook of Contemporary Buddhism*, ed. Jerryson, 663–664.
46. Roland Robertson, "Religion and the Global Field," *Social Compass* 41, no. 1 (1994): 121–135, esp. 132–133.
47. Roland Robertson, "Globalisation or Glocalisation?" *Journal of International Communication* 18, no. 2 (2012): 191–208.
48. Peter Beyer, *Religion and Globalization: Theory, Culture and Society* (London: SAGE, 1994); Peter Beyer, *Religions in Global Society* (London: Routledge, 2006); Peter Beyer and Lori G. Beaman, *Religion, Globalization and Culture* (Leiden, The Netherlands, and Boston: Brill, 2007); and Peter Beyer, *Religion in the Context of Globalization: Essays on Concept, Form, and Political Implication* (New York: Routledge, 2013).
49. Martin Baumann, "Global Buddhism: Developmental Periods, Regional Histories, and a New Analytical Perspective," *Journal of Global Buddhism* 2 (2015): 31–32.
50. Thomas A. Tweed, *Crossing and Dwelling: A Theory of Religion* (Cambridge, MA, and London: Harvard University Press, 2006).
51. Thomas A. Tweed, "Theory and Method in the Study of Buddhism: Toward 'Translocative' Analysis," in *Buddhism beyond Borders: New Perspectives on Buddhism in the United States*, ed. Scott A. Mitchell and Natalie E. F. Quli (Albany, NY: SUNY Press, 2016), 13–15.
52. Anne M. Blackburn, *Locations of Buddhism: Colonialism and Modernity in Sri Lanka* (Chicago: University of Chicago Press, 2010); Johannes Beltz and Surendra Jondhale, eds., *Reconstructing the World: B. R. Ambedkar and Buddhism in India* (New Delhi: Oxford University Press, 2004); Ritzinger, *Anarchy in the Pure Land*; Jin Y. Park, *Makers of Modern Korean Buddhism* (Albany: State University of New York Press, 2010); Alicia Marie Turner, *Saving Buddhism: The Impermanence of Religion in Colonial Burma* (Honolulu: University of Hawaii Press, 2014); and Juliane Schober, *Modern Buddhist Conjunctures in Myanmar: Cultural Narratives, Colonial Legacies, and Civil Society* (Honolulu: University of Hawaii Press, 2011).
53. Stuart Chandler, *Establishing a Pure Land on Earth: The Foguang Buddhist Perspective on Modernization and Globalization* (Honolulu: University of Hawaii Press, 2004); and Rachelle M. Scott, *Nirvana for Sale? Buddhism, Wealth, and the Dhammakāya Temple in Contemporary Thailand* (Albany, NY: SUNY Press, 2009).
54. Thomas A. Tweed, *The American Encounter with Buddhism, 1844–1912: Victorian Culture and the Limits of Dissent* (Chapel Hill: University of North Carolina Press, 2000); Richard Hughes Seager, *Buddhism in America* (New York: Columbia University Press, 2012); Charles S. Prebish, *Luminous Passage: The Practice and Study of Buddhism in America* (Berkeley: University of California Press, 1999); Prebish and Baumann, eds., *Westward Dharma*; and Prebish and Tanaka, eds., *The Faces of Buddhism.*
55. Cristina Rocha, *Zen in Brazil: The Quest for Cosmopolitan Modernity* (Honolulu: University of Hawaii Press, 2006); Victor S. Hori, John S. Harding, and Alexander D. Soucy, eds., *Flowers on the Rock: Global and Local Buddhisms in Canada* (Montreal: McGill–Queen's University Press, 2014); Laurence Cox,

"European Buddhist Traditions," in *Oxford Handbook of Contemporary Buddhism*, ed. Jerryson, 332–345; Michelle Barker and Cristina Rocha, *Buddhism in Australia: Traditions in Change* (London: Routledge, 2011); Sally McAra, *Land of Beautiful Vision: Making a Buddhist Sacred Place in New Zealand* (Honolulu: University of Hawaii Press, 2007); Michel Clasquin and Jacobus S. Krüger, eds., *Buddhism and Africa* (Pretoria: University of South Africa Press, 1999); Michel Clasquin, "Buddhism in South Africa," in *Westward Dharma*, ed. Prebish and Baumann, 152–162; and Clasquin, "Buddhism in Africa."

56. Scott A. Mitchell, *Buddhism in America: Global Religion, Local Contexts* (London: Bloomsbury Academic, 2016); Mitchell and Quli, eds., *Buddhism beyond Borders*; Joseph Cheah, *Race and Religion in American Buddhism: White Supremacy and Immigrant Adaptation*, Academy Series (Oxford and New York: Oxford University Press, 2011); and Abraham Zablocki, Jay L. Garfield, and Nalini Bhushan, eds., *TransBuddhism: Transmission, Translation, Transformation* (Amherst: University of Massachusetts Press, 2009).
57. Learman, *Buddhist Missionaries*.
58. Michihiro Ama, *Immigrants to the Pure Land: The Modernization, Acculturation, and Globalization of Shin Buddhism, 1898–1941* (Honolulu: University of Hawaii Press, 2011); and Regina Yoshie Matsue, "The Glocalization Process of Shin Buddhism in Brasilia," *Journal of Religion in Japan* 3 (2014): 226–246.
59. Richard Hughes Seager, *Encountering the Dharma: Daisaku Ikeda, Soka Gakkai, and the Globalization of Buddhist Humanism* (Berkeley and London: University of California Press, 2006); Peter B. Clarke, "'Success' and 'Failure': Japanese New Religions Abroad," in *Japanese New Religions: In Global Perspective*, ed. Peter B. Clarke (Richmond, UK: Curzon Press, 2000), 272–311; and Brian Bocking, "Of Priests, Protests and Protestant Buddhists: The Case of Soka Gakkai International," in *Japanese New Religions in the West*, ed. Peter B. Clarke and Jeffrey Somers Sandgate (Folkestone, UK: Japan Library, 1994), 117–131.
60. Phillip E. Hammond and David W. Machacek, *Soka Gakkai in America: Accommodation and Conversion* (Oxford: Oxford University Press, 1999); Daniel A. Métraux, *The Soka Gakkai Buddhist Movement in Quebec: The Lotus and the Fleur de Lys* (Lewiston, NY: Edwin Mellen Press, 1997); Ōkubo Masayuki, "The Acceptance of Nichiren Shōshū Sōka Gakkai in Mexico," *Japanese Journal of Religious Studies* 18 (1991): 189–211; Girardo Rodriguez Plasencia, "Sōka Gakkai in Cuba," *Journal of Religion in Japan* 3 (2014): 198–225; Peter B. Clarke, "Globalization and the Pursuit of a Shared Understanding of the Absolute: The Case of Soka Gakkai in Brazil," in *Buddhist Missionaries*, ed. Learman, 123–139; John Clammer, "The Happiness-Making Machine: Soka Gakkai and Japanese Cultural Presence in Singapore," in *Japan in Singapore: Cultural Occurrences and Cultural Flows*, ed. Eyal Ben-Ari and John Clammer (Richmond, UK: Curzon Press, 2000), 175–193; Daniel A. Métraux, *The International Expansion of a Modern Buddhist Movement: The Soka Gakkai in Southeast Asia and Australia* (Lanham, MD: University Press of America, 2001); Bryan R. Wilson and Karel Dobbelaere, *A Time to Chant: The Sōka Gakkai Buddhists in Britain* (Oxford: Clarendon Press, 1994); Lukas Pokorny, "'A Grand Stage for Kōsen Rufu in the Future': Sōka Gakkai in Austria, 1961–1981," in *Religion in Austria*, ed. Hans Gerald Hödl and Lukas Pokorny (Vienna: Praesens, 2015), 1–47; and Sanda Ionescu, "Adapt or Perish: The Story of Soka Gakkai in Germany," in *Japanese New Religions*, ed. Clarke, 182–197.
61. Huang Weishan, "Buddhists in Action: Transnational Migration and Religious Cosmopolitanism," *Encounters* 4 (2011): 215–239; Yan Ho-don, "Social Entrepreneurship of the Buddhist Tzu Chi Movement," *American Journal of Entrepreneurship* 1 (2012): 37–56; Jonathan H. Lee, "Tzu Chi Compassion Society's Peace Work in America," *Journal of the International Association of Buddhist Universities* 3 (2012): 145–164; Jonathan H. Lee and Hsun Chang, "Globalization or Transnationalism? Analysis of Buddhist Compassion Relief Tzu Chi Foundation's Expansion and Development," *Chinese America: History & Perspectives* 1 (2013): 9–22; André Laliberté and Manuel Litalien, "The Tzu Chi Merit Society from Taiwan to Canada," in *Wild Geese: Buddhism in Canada*, ed. John S. Harding, Victor Sogen Hori, and Alexander Soucy (Montreal: McGill-Queen's University Press, 2010), 295–320;

Chien-yu Julia Huang, "Buddhism and Its Trust Networks between Taiwan, Malaysia, and the United States," *The Eastern Buddhist* 44, no. 2 (2013): 59–76; Chien-yu Julia Huang, "From Diasporic to Ecumenical: The Buddhist Tzu Chi (Ciji) Movement in Malaysia," in *Proselytizing and the Limits of Religious Pluralism in Contemporary Asia*, ed. Juliana Finucane (New York: Springer, 2013); André Laliberté, "'Love Transcends Borders' or 'Blood Is Thicker Than Water': The Charity Work of the Buddhist Tzu Chi Foundation in the People's Republic of China," *European Journal of East Asian Studies* 2 (2003): 243–262; André Laliberté, "Buddhist Charities and China's Social Policy," *Archives de Sciences Sociales des Religions* 158 (2012): 95–117; André Laliberté, "The Growth of a Taiwanese Buddhist Association in China: Soft Power and Institutional Learning," *China Information* 27 (2013): 81–105; Huang, "The Compassion Relief Diaspora"; Gareth Fisher, "Globalizing Buddhists from Margins to Center: Mobile Charisma in the Tzu Chi Movement," *Inter-Asia Cultural Studies* 11 (2010): 451–456; and Chandler, *Establishing a Pure Land on Earth*; Chandler, "Spreading Buddha's Light"; and Reinke, "Sacred Secularities."

62. Ama, *Immigrants to the Pure Land*; and Carol A. Mortland, *Cambodian Buddhism in the United States* (Albany: State University of New York Press, 2017).
63. Frank Usarski and Rafael Shoji, "Japanese New Religions in Latin America," in *Encyclopedia of Latin American Religions*, ed. Henri P. P. Gooren (Cham, Switzerland: Springer, 2019), 10; Alexander Soucy, "The Buddha and the Birch Tree: The Great Pine Forest Monastery and the Localization of Vietnamese Buddhism to Canada," *Contemporary Buddhism* 15 (2014): 373–393; Martin Baumann, *Deutsche Buddhisten: Geschichte und Gemeinschaften* (Marburg, Germany: Diagonal-Verlag, 1995); Martin Baumann, *Migration, Religion, Integration: Buddhistische Vietnamesen und hinduistische Tamilen in Deutschland* (Marburg, Germany: Diagonal-Verlag, 2000); and Olaf Beuchling, *Vom Mekong an die Elbe: Buddhistisches Klosterleben in der vietnamesischen Diaspora* (Hamburg, Germany: Abera, 2013).
64. Ryan B. Joo, "Countercurrents from the West: 'Blue-Eyed' Zen Masters, Vipassanā Meditation, and Buddhist Psychotherapy in Contemporary Korea," *Journal of the American Academy of Religion* 79, no. 3 (2011): 614–638.
65. Reinke, "The Buddha in Bronkhorstspruit"; Diana Wong and Peggy Levitt, "Travelling Faiths and Migrant Religions: The Case of Circulating Models of Da'wa among the Tablighi Jamaat and Foguangshan in Malaysia," *Global Networks* 14, no. 3 (2014): 348–362; and Cheng, "Transnational Buddhism."
66. Courtney Bruntz and Brooke Schedneck, eds., *Buddhist Tourism in Asia*, Contemporary Buddhism (Honolulu: University of Hawaii Press, 2020); David Geary, "Destination Enlightenment: Branding Buddhism and Spiritual Tourism in Bodhgaya, Bihar," *Anthropology Today* 24, no. 3 (2008): 11–14; David Geary, "Rebuilding the Navel of the Earth: Buddhist Pilgrimage and Transnational Religious Networks," *Modern Asian Studies* 48, no. 3 (2014): 645–692; and Toni Huber, *The Holy Land Reborn: Pilgrimage and the Tibetan Reinvention of Buddhist India*, Buddhism and Modernity (Chicago: University of Chicago Press, 2008).

Jens Reinke

GLOBAL THERAVADA BUDDHISM: ASIAN FOUNDATIONS

PRECOLONIAL SPREAD

The development of Theravada Buddhism and the political and social development of Sri Lanka and Southeast Asia are entwined and mutually influential. To understand Theravada in the 21st century, we need to understand its evolution within the historical and ever-evolving sociopolitical context. There were no "countries" as we understand them, that is, firm geographic boundaries demarcating a nation-state, prior to the colonial period. The common pattern was a mandala system. Radiating out from a center of power (a king or leader) was a series of circles of influence that would owe allegiance and pay tribute to one or more centers of power.[1] Allegiances shifted, disputes arose, boundaries shifted. Commonly used terms today such as "Southeast Asia," are relatively modern.

From the beginning Buddhism was aligned with kingship. One of the Buddhist missions sent by King Ashoka arrived on the island of Lanka. King Devanampiyatissa (250–210 BCE) established Buddhism on the island through the construction of the Mahavihara Monastery and by planting a seedling from the Bodhi tree.[2] Over time, three different teaching lineages emerged at three different monasteries. In the 12th century, King Parakkama Bahu I carried out an intensive "purification" of the sangha that set the stage for two major developments. First, the teaching lineage of the Mahavihara was established as the standard understanding of Buddhist doctrine and practice. As Buddhism spread, the Mahavihara lineage influenced the development of Buddhism throughout the region. The second development was the placement of the sangha under state control through the creation of a *sangharaja* (head of the sangha), who ruled over the sangha with the assistance of two officials of the king.[3] Mahavihara influence and reforms that brought the sangha increasingly under administrative control of the king/state were to be repeated in each emerging kingdom that arose in the precolonial era.

The Pagan dynasty formed the core of what is now Myanmar and is remembered as a "golden era"—strong, prosperous, and a center of Buddhist scholarship.[4] Kings adopted the tradition of the *cakkavattin*, the "righteous ruler."[5] While the king's power was absolute, it was often moderated by the influence of Buddhist monk-ministers.[6] After the Pagan dynasty was destroyed (at the end of the 13th century), it was not until the middle of the 18th century that a new kingdom at Ava rose, becoming a major regional power.[7] Ava was annexed in 1866 by the British as the colony of Burma, a name subsequently adopted at independence (1948) and changed in 1989 to Myanmar.[8] Steinberg notes that until the colonial period, there was no institution more important than the Theravada sangha.[9]

This pattern of Buddhist-king alliances and influence of the Mahavihara lineage continued as the Tai-speaking peoples migrated south.[10] They adopted Buddhism, and during the rule of the Sukhothai kings (13th–15th centuries) the Buddhism of the Mahavihara lineage became dominant.[11] The other powerful Sukhothai Kingdom was Lan Na. Lan Na was famous for its Buddhist scholarship and as a center for the spread of Buddhism.[12] It was followed by the Kingdom of Ayutthaya (14th–18th centuries), known as Siam by its neighbors. Ayutthaya also provided lavish support for Buddhism.[13] After the destruction of Ayutthaya, in 1767, by the Ava kingdom, the empire was rebuilt and the dynastic line of the Siamese/Thai monarchy began.[14] Siam (never formally colonized) became a constitutional monarchy in 1932, and Thailand in 1939.

The Khmer empire (9th–13th centuries) was centered at Angkor and represented the height of Khmer power.[15] The founder of the kingdom, Jayavarman II (r. 802–850 CE), was established as a *cakkavartin* (righteous ruler). After the invasion by Ayutthaya (Siam) in the 15th century, the Mahavihara lineage was adopted at court. As a weaker kingdom, the Khmer were in danger of losing territory to both Ayutthaya (Siam) and Dai Viet. Siam had considerable influence in the region, but a strong Dai Viet began to assert its power.[16] During Dai Viet occupation Buddhism received little support. When the Vietnamese left in 1846, Buddhism was restored. In 1863, prior to his coronation, King Norodom signed a treaty of protection with the French, likely due to fears of further encroachment by Siam. This began the French colonial period, from 1863 to 1953.[17] The Khmer Kingdom became Cambodia. It gained its independence in 1953.

The Tai people continued their migration south from Nanzhao (founded 729, fell 902) and were positioned between the Mon and Khmer mandalas.[18] When the Mongols destroyed the Pagan dynasty (13th century), the Tai took advantage of Khmer weakness to found Lan Na (capital Chiang Mai) and Sukhothai to the south. In the mid-14th century, the first kingdoms arose—the Tai-Siam mandala of Ayutthaya (1351), which eventually absorbed Sukhothai (1438), and the Tai-Lao of Lan Xang (1353).[19]

The Kingdom of Lan Xang (1353) was a center of Buddhist scholarship.[20] After a long period of chaos, and a brief period of calm when King Surinyavongsa took the throne (1637), battles for succession ensued. Dai Viet and Siamese involvement resulted in the division of the kingdom into three (Luang Prabang, Lan Na, and Viang Chan), all subsequently absorbed into the Siamese mandala.[21] The French, Siamese, and Dai Viet competed for territory, which led to the creation of French Indochina: Cochinchina (Nam Ky, a French colony), Annam, Tonkin, Kampuchea, and what was left of Lan Xang (Laos), which became a French protectorate (1893–1945; 1946–1953).[22] Laos gained independence in 1949.

Throughout this period of turmoil and shifting allegiances, Buddhism continued to grow, and the sangha became increasingly powerful through its influence on the various kings and courts in the region. The king and sangha were mutually legitimizing: the sangha acted as advisors to the king and, in return, the king made donations to the sangha. Regarding the general population, the sangha were teachers of Buddhist morality, performers of ritual, educators, and providers of a "field of merit" for the laity. Giving to the sangha provided the laity with spiritual benefit (in this life) and the hope of a better rebirth. The *sangharaja* (head of the sangha) provided the link between the political and religious segments of society.

Colonial Period. Loss of the traditional triad of king, sangha, and people, the imposition of Western colonial education, economic and administrative systems, and the introduction of aggressive Christian missionaries had severe consequences for the Ceylonese, Burmese, Cambodians, Laotians, and even the noncolonized Siamese.

British colonization from the 19th to mid-20th century had the greatest impact on Ceylon and Burma. The removal of the Kandyan king in 1815 solidified British control over the entire island and disrupted the fundamental political and social foundation of Buddhist society: king, sangha, and people. The Kandyan Convention (1815) stipulated that Buddhism would continue to play its traditional role in society including receiving financial support, but pressure from Christian missionaries saw that support vanish. The king also appointed the heads of temples. When the British no longer authorized these Acts of Appointment, the internal administration of the sangha was severely disrupted.[23] The sangha also lost its prominence in education. Christian schools were established, and English became a means to upper mobility.

The loss of the Burmese king was even more destabilizing as, unlike the Kandyan king who had challenges from various chiefs, the Burmese king wielded absolute power that extended into every area of Burmese society.[24] When the British took complete control of Burma (1855) and deposed the king, there was no administrative system in place. The position of *dhamma-raja* (head of the sangha) was abolished, and the sangha lost its internal administration.

The loss of these kings required the laity and the sangha to fill the political and administrative void. Many Buddhists believed that colonization was evidence of the decline of the dhamma (teaching and practice) due to lax morality, both institutionally (sangha) and personally. Morality became a priority. Internal and external reform of the sangha was instituted to restore its purity. Encouraged by monks such as Burmese monk Ledi Sayadaw, laypeople began to meditate and study; they took over some temple organization, and formed associations to advance the Buddhist cause. Buddhism needed to be protected from the Christian missionaries, and the country returned to its precolonial roots. The theme of restoring the moral universe including proper governance of king, sangha, and the people, runs throughout the colonial period and shapes the Buddhist response to modernism, resistance to colonial rule, and the development of Buddhist nationalism.[25]

Modernism, Resistance, and Nationalism. Modernism required a re-examination of traditional ways of working, studying, social organization and governance, and communal and personal identity. Reforms were made or rejected according to expectations of reforming and purifying the sangha, restoring the dhamma as the basis of society, and, if not a righteous ruler, then a system of righteous governance rather than colonial subjugation.

Modernism, broadly characterized, was marked by science, technology, rationalism, the rise of nation-states, urbanization, and bureaucracy. In religion, it was marked by the demythologizing and psychologizing of religious narratives, the application of critical theory to textual studies, and the discounting of amulets, spells, and traditional practices deemed "superstitious."[26]

In Ceylon, aspects of Buddhist modernism began in the 18th century and were connected to the reorganization of the sangha and the development of a standardized educational system for monastics. There was a focus on manuscripts, their Pali commentaries, and Sinhala preaching guides. This "textual community" included both monastics and laypeople and was made possible by wealthy patrons and royal funds.[27] The primary instigator of these reforms was Valivita Saranankara, the founder of the Siyam Nikaya (1753).[28] The spread of the Siyam Nikaya outside of Ceylon and the introduction of standardized monastic education created Buddhist networks across Asia, and these were crucial in resisting colonial and missionary pressures. High-ranking monks such as Hikkaduve Sumangala (1826–1911) fostered relations between the colonial rulers, the populace, and Western scholars. Contacts with temples and courts in Asia provided some leverage with the British. Monastic education, preaching, and editing of Pali texts continued, and monks and laity used the new print technology to produce pamphlets.[29]

As colonialism was a consequence of the decline of the dhamma due to a decline in Buddhist morality, protecting the *sasana* (doctrine and practice) from further decline became a personal moral and communal responsibility. In Burma, lay associations began as a means for raising donations for the sangha and as study groups that sponsored preachers and educational events.[30] Most of these groups were founded by Ledi Sayadaw (1846–1923). He introduced *abhidhamma* (philosophy) study and *vipassana* (insight meditation) practice for the laity. This style of meditation is the root of the modern insight meditation movement. Ledi

Sayadaw gave talks and published books written in an accessible style to increase awareness of Buddhist philosophy.[31] As Turner notes, "In this sense, *sasana* was both the means and the product of a continuous process of reform and reimagining."[32] Burmese Buddhist associations fostered a sense of moral community and communal belonging.[33] At the local level, Buddhist networks helped people to adapt to aspects of modernism such as urbanization. When urbanization compelled people to move to cities, they were able to maintain family ties through temple networks.[34]

Most people experienced modernism as an aspect of colonization.[35] In Ceylon, plantations replaced small peasant farmers, forced labor was used to build roads for these plantations, and commercial producers were exempt from paddy and rice taxes. Related industries were also dominated by Europeans.[36] This created poverty and landlessness. When people refused to work on the coffee plantations, the British brought in laborers from South Asia.[37] There was little interaction between the Sinhalese and the South Indian Tamils, as the Tamils lived on the plantations.[38]

Ceylonese notions of "identity" changed. Nira Wickramasinghe states that, prior to 1824, the identities "Sinhala" and "Tamil" were more fluid, but the process of several British censuses narrowed categories, and "identity" came to be seen as fixed. Belonging to a recognized group became the basis for entitlements and rights.[39] These categories, often multiplying, fostered intergroup competition and tension. The question of "identity" was an important aspect of the development of Buddhist nationalism. Michael Roberts points out that the early phase of nationalism was "Ceylonese nationalism," "an ecumenical all-island nationalism which embraced all island peoples in expressing an opposition to British rule or its specifics."[40] However, while a majority population, Sinhalese Buddhists felt like ethnic and religious minorities under attack. What had begun as Ceylonese nationalism became Sinhalese Buddhist nationalism that excluded not only the British and Christianity but came to exclude other religions, ethnic groups, and "foreigners."

Anagarika Dhammapala is often identified as the leader of Sinhalese Buddhist nationalism. As Michael Roberts, Steven Kemper, and Stephen Prothero have shown, Dharmapala was complex.[41] His self-identity was that of a celibate renouncer (*brahmacarya*) on the path to becoming a buddha (bodhisattva). He traveled extensively and was important in establishing Ceylonese Buddhism in the West.

Dhammapala also wanted to raise the Sinhalese from the economic, social, and moral degeneration that resulted from colonialism and a lack of moral cultivation.[42] He launched several economic and social projects, some successful and some not, including the establishment of the Sanghamitta Monastery for women and the publication of Mahabodhi and other publications.[43] He launched speaking tours, in which he sought to reform the Sinhalese through castigating them for their moral decline and their acceptance of their treatment by "foreigners." His language was vitriolic.[44] His vision of a Sinhalese Buddhist kingdom that excluded all others as foreigners, and his diatribes against other religions and ethnicities, made him ideal for appropriation by the violent elements in the Buddhist nationalist movement.[45]

One of the texts Dhammapala used was the *Mahavamsa*. The *Mahavamsa* is the textual underpinning for Buddhist nationalism.[46] Composed in the 6th century, the *Mahavamsa* provides a particular view of parts of Sri Lankan history. In the *Mahavamsa*, Dhammapala saw a great and righteous kingdom, a *dhammadipa* ("island of dhamma"), destroyed by the British who cut down forests to plant tea, destroyed jobs, and introduced alcohol and drugs eroding the morality of the people.[47] He wanted them to reclaim their Sinhalese identity and restore Ceylon to an island of dhamma ruled in the ancient manner: king, sangha, and people.

Dharmapala was not the only Sinhalese Buddhist nationalist of his time, and he appears to have had no wish to be a political leader. Yet, his use of the myth of Dutugamunu may have "kindled the fires of violence."[48] Buddhist nationalists often refer to the *Mahavamsa* narrative of King Dutthagamani (161–137 BCE), who rode into battle with a Buddhist relic in his spear against the Tamil King Elara. Concerned about the *kammic* consequences, his monastic advisors tell him he should not be concerned. Most opponents had not taken the Refuges or the five precepts, and his success brought honor to the Buddha's teaching.[49] Nationalists have argued that Sri Laṅka is a Sinhalese Buddhist island and violence against non-Buddhists is justified as a means of protection—what Bartholomeusz refers to as a "just-war" theory.[50] The concern that Buddhism is under threat from other religions (Muslims, Christians) and ethnic groups (Tamils) comes, in part, from colonization and, in part, from the pressures of creating a modern, multicultural nation-state. The predominant Buddhist nationalist organization is the Budo Bala Sena (BBS, Army of Buddhist Power), established by Galangoda A. Gnanasara in 2013.[51] With the end of the civil war in 2009, the BBS turned their attention from Tamils to the Muslim and Christian communities. They accused Muslims of rape and forced conversion, and Christians of using development projects and aid to manipulate conversions. Mikael Gravers notes that they have also instigated and participated in riots.[52] While BBS represents a small number, it has some public support and "is widely considered to be connected with former President Mahinda Rajapakse" and the military.[53] Pressure by the sangha on the government may be the modern version of king, sangha, and people.

In Burma, while the notion of a moral community in defense of Buddhism has been a constant, the nature of the Buddhist associations began to change around 1920. With the Montagu–Chelmsford Reforms (Government of India Act, 1919), the British offered reforms that would lead to Indian self-government under British supervision.[54] The Burmese were not included in these reforms, and agitation for similar reforms began. Younger members of the Young Men's Buddhist Association pushed for a nationalist focus and confrontation. Buddhist associations became Burmese associations. Buddhism became part of a national identity and a means toward nationalist ends.[55]

Ethnicity also became an element of Buddhist identity. Burma is a multiethnic state. During colonial times, the British populated the Burmese army primarily with Indian and ethnic minorities (Karen, Chin, and Kachin). Further, minority areas were only indirectly administered by the British.[56] This led to the perception that the minorities were being favored over the Burman majority.[57] There is also the belief that Burman culture is being attacked by foreigners.[58]

The Rohingya, a Muslim population in the Rakhine province, are not considered to be citizens of Burma because they were not listed as one of the pre-1824 original ethnic groups granted citizenship.[59] They are considered by the Burmese to be illegal immigrants from Bangladesh. As "foreigners" and Muslims, they have been subject to a series of riots, and since 2016, there has been destruction of villages and allegations of human rights violations.[60] The most outspoken monk is U Wirathu, the leader of the 969 anti-Muslim group, recently renamed as Ma Ba Tha (Association to Protect Buddhist Race, Language, and Religion).[61]

In both Ceylon and Burma, colonization led to a hardening of ethnic and religious distinctions and a narrowing of what it means to be a "citizen." Political organizing and voting tend to be along ethnic and religious lines.

Although Siam was never directly colonized, it was affected by the British and French colonization that surrounded it and the criticism of Christian missionaries. It also played an important role in anticolonial movements through its participation in Buddhist networks, formed to support Buddhism and independence movements. As in Ceylon and Burma, there was a sense that the sangha was declining, becoming morally corrupt with lax educational standards and monks who practiced magic and fortune-telling. The reforms of the 19th and 20th centuries were intended to return the sangha to the ideal triad of sangha, king, and people.[62]

Following the historical pattern of kings, a series of reforms in the late 19th and early 20th century brought Buddhism increasingly under state control. Prince Mongkut (later King Rama IV, 1804–1868) established a new monastic lineage, Dhammayutika (Thommayut). He considered this new lineage more disciplined and orthodox, and it conformed to his sense of what the sangha should be.[63] The first Sangha Act of 1902 centralized administrative control of all the sanghas, standardized textbooks, and set exams. The textbook material presented a modernist view of Buddhism.[64] Buddhist monks in monasteries were to be a "service to the nation." After Siam became a constitutional monarchy (1932), the state continued to incorporate Buddhism into the state structure. The state vision was that monastery activities should be practical, socially engaged, and active in rural areas.[65] Buddhism became part of nation building.

The population of Thailand is 90 percent Buddhist. In the southern three provinces, the population is 85 percent Malay Muslim. This area was part of a southern Thai kingdom (Langkasuka), followed by an Islamic kingdom (Patani). Attempts to attain independence or negotiate with the Thai government broke down, and in 2004 martial law was imposed after violence erupted.[66] A category of military monks was established. These men are both soldiers and ordained monks, and they live in the temples. As with Burma and Sri Lanka, these military monks are seen as necessary to protect Buddhism. Buddhism represents morality and order and the heritage of Langkasuka.[67]

French Colonization in Cambodia and Laos. Cambodia became a French protectorate in 1863 and a French colony in 1889. Just prior to this (1885), the Dhammayutika Nikaya (Thommayut) was introduced from Thailand (1854) to aid in reforming the sangha. In 1880, King Norodom instructed the patriarchs of the two Nikayas to restructure the sangha. There were deep divisions in the Mahanikaya between those who saw the Thommayut as a divisive Thai imposition (traditionalists) and those who were open to the rationalist reform (modernists).[68] The French, concerned about the number of monks and the possibility of insurrection, inserted themselves into the monastic administration. An official registration process was instituted, and provincial head monks were approved in consultation with the Ministry of Religious Affairs. Certain practices were forbidden—martial arts, astrology, and producing protective amulets, for example.[69] The French gradually transformed the education system. They added secular subjects—such as arithmetic, history, and biology—standardized teacher training, and introduced a state educational system, eroding monastic influence. The monastic Ecole superieure de Pali, especially for Buddhist monastic education, also saw its curriculum expanded to include secular subjects.[70] In effect, the French took the place of the king.

When the French left in 1953, there was a protracted period of political struggle that ended with the Khmer Rouge taking control of Cambodia in 1975 under Pol Pot, who was removed in 1979.[71] Pol Pot felt that it was Buddhism and the sangha that prevented the creation of a communist state. During the period of the Khmer Rouge almost two million Cambodians were killed, more than half a million were forced to flee their homes to refugee camps in Thailand, and the sangha was almost destroyed.[72] Many of those refugees settled in North America. The trauma inflicted upon them deeply affected their ability to settle and integrate in their new homes.[73] Amanda Kent indicates that for those Cambodians who remained, there is still a lack of security, access to food, health care, jobs, and impartial institutions. The changes made during the peace process of the 1990s, liberalization of the economy, democratization, and an influx of aid have created new inequalities and exacerbated old ones. Cambodians seek safety through rebuilding the sangha and the containment of power through Buddhist virtues (*sel*), sacred boundaries (*sim*), and the saffron robe of the monk.[74]

French colonization produced similar effects in Laos. Ananda Wickremeratne provides a concise description of these effects: bifurcation of society through the creation of an elite inclined toward Western mores, capitalism, and liberalism; this, in turn, provided openings for Marxist-Leninist ideologies. By the time the French left in 1953 there was a sustained struggle between the Royal Pathet Lao, who advocated democratic forms of government and economic liberalism, and the Pathet Lao, who favored literalist interpretations of Marxist-Leninist doctrine. By the time the Pathet Lao took control in 1975, Buddhism was severely weakened and, while Buddhism was integrated within the Marxist-Leninist system, when disputes arose, Buddhism had to give way.[75] Between 1975 and 1980, over four hundred thousand Laotians crossed the border into Thai refugee camps.[76] Many of these refugees also moved to North America and have had difficulties resettling.

The *Bhikkhuni Sangha*. The theme that threads through the history of women in the Buddhist tradition, especially for nuns, is one of opportunity and ambiguity. The order of nuns (*bhikkhuni sangha*) was established in India about five years after that of the *bhikkhu sangha*. The religious life provided an option for women who did not want to follow the traditional life of daughter, wife, and widow.[77] From the beginning, there has been ambiguity about the role of women in the sangha. In *Cullavagga X*, the Buddha is clearly reluctant to establish an order of nuns when asked by Mahaprajapati.[78] Ananda intervenes on her behalf. He asks if women can attain "perfection" (enlightenment). When assured by the Buddha that they can, Ananda argues that since women have the capacity for enlightenment, they should have the same opportunity to pursue it. The Buddha agrees but imposes eight extra rules on the *bhikkhuni sangha*. These rules place the *bhikkhuni sangha* in a subordinate position within the monastic hierarchy. While the text affirms the spiritual capacity of women, it also maintains their lower social status. Women's lower social status disadvantages nuns. They may be respected as monastics, but donations to them are believed to produce less merit than gifts to monks. This may be one reason why the *bhikkhuni* order died out in India before that of the *bhikkhu*.[79]

In 11th-century Lanka, both the male and female sangha died out. The *bhikkhu* lineage was reinstituted from the Pagan but there appears to have been no move to reinstate the *bhikkhuni sangha* until the colonial era.[80] Women embraced the religious life as part of the Buddhist reform, anticolonial movement. Many took robes and the ten precepts (novice ordination) and began to preach publicly. Known as *dasa sil matas* (ten precept mothers), they included upper-class women. Interest in restoring the *bhikkhuni sangha* dissolved after independence.[81] There were no further moves to reinstate full ordination for women (*upasampada*) until the late 1980s and early 1990s, although the Sri Lankan Ministry of Buddhist Affairs improved their conditions by registering them and providing some financial support for their education.[82] By 1986, a national organization of dasa *sil matas* had been formed. Some representatives were among the first to take full ordination.

Little is known about the *bhikkhuni sangha* in precolonial Burma. It is generally accepted that there were nuns in Burma until about the 13th century. Whether these were fully ordained *bhikkhuni* or *tilashin* (novice nuns) or whether both were present is unclear.[83] There were several unsuccessful attempts to revive the order in the 1930s, 1950s, and 1970s.[84] In the 1980s a process began to incorporate all monastics, including the *tilashin* (novice nuns), into a state registration system, issuing them an identification card that safeguarded their status.

The female ordination does not appear to have reached Thailand. There were unsuccessful attempts to establish full ordination for Thai women in 1932 and 2009 in Australia.[85] Harris notes the presence of *bhikkhuni* in Cambodia, but by the late 13th century they appear to be gone.[86] The *ṭun ji* (5–10 precept nuns) have often been dismissed as old women with low status who do menial chores for the monks.[87] Elizabeth Guthrie noted that the *ṭun ji* at Wat Mangalavan do assist in maintaining the *wat*; they are not domestic servants. The nuns at Wat Mangalavan live near the *wat*, eat with the *bhikkhu* and *samanera* (novice monks), and travel after the rains retreat for pilgrimage and to study with teachers. While some are poor, others are supported by families.[88]

Like the precept nuns of Cambodia, the *maekhao* (8–10 precept nuns) of Laos are subject to the common stereotype that they are simply old widows or younger women who have failed in life.[89] Yet, many practice *vipassana* (insight meditation) and provide village women with instruction in dhamma, meditation, languages, and personal issues. They receive no financial support from the government as monks do, but attract support from the laity, primarily women, and Tsomo notes several cases in which support was provided by a former husband.[90] Although limited in number, some have also engaged in development projects.[91]

Full Ordination* (Upasampada) *and Its Controversies. The themes of the Buddhist response to modernism, decline of the dhamma, resistance to colonialism, and Buddhist nationalism are all echoed in the controversies surrounding the reinstitution of the *bhikkhuni sangha* with the additional aspect of gender. In the latter part of the 20th century, there was a new movement to reinstate the *bhikkhuni sangha*. Initial support came from Asian monks working outside of Asia and Western-educated women. The monks wished to strengthen Theravada in the West and re-establish the fourfold sangha of monks, nuns, and male and female lay supporters.[92] The education Asian *bhikkhuni's* would receive would provide them with positive career choices, higher social status, and the ability to serve the community as educators and spiritual leaders.[93]

The first modern full ordination was held at Hsi Lai temple in California in 1988, with the assistance of Chinese nuns, Theravada monks, and the support of Sakyadhita.[94] Sakyadhita (Daughters of the Buddha) was founded in 1987 by a group of prominent nuns and laywomen.[95]

Now the Sakyadhita International Association of Buddhist Women, the organization's website states that its aims include "to work for gender equity in Buddhist education, training, institutional structures, and ordination."[96]

The revival of the *bhikkhuni sangha* is highly contested and entwined with issues concerning colonial legacy, Western values and ideals, internal sangha politics, and technical matters and interpretations of the Pali Vinaya (Rules of Monastic Discipline). Since the deposing of the Burmese and Kandyan kings, the sangha, with lay support, is considered the glue that holds Buddhist societies together. The remaining king, the King of Thailand, appoints the members of the Sangha Supreme Council.[97] Tradition holds that the dhamma (teachings and practice) will exist if the *vinaya* (monastic discipline) is upheld. Issues regarding monastic rules, then, are tied to concerns about the decline of the dhamma. Senior monks of the Sri Lankan Sangha reject reordination on several grounds. The Pali Vinaya (Monastic Code) requires ten fully ordained senior nuns to administer the full ordination. The order died out by the 13th century, so there is no quorum of *bhikkhuni*. Ordination is impossible. Further, the monastic code used was the Dharmagupta Vinaya, not the Theravada. Finally, they reject modern ordinations as not authentically Theravada because they were administered by Mahayana nuns.

Supporters of the revival argue that the Dharmagupta Vinaya is closely related to the Theravada and originated in India. As well, the nuns ordained in 1998 at Bodhgaya were ordained again at Dambulla by Sri Lankan *bhikkhus* and *bhikkhunis* according to the rules of the Theravada Vinaya.[98]

Resistance to the reinstitution of the *bhikkhuni sangha* also reflects a concern about the role played by Western, liberal, and feminist women in the movement.[99] Colonization not only brought new methods of agriculture, manufacturing, and business, it brought liberal values. Values such as rationality, equality, human rights, and feminism were justified as bringing civilization and modernity to the colonized. Antoinette Burton points out that British feminists assumed their superiority to, and need to raise up, Indian women. This also engenders the idea that what is "European" is universal.[100] Nirmala Salgado and Hiroko Kawanami (among others) find colonial attitudes reflected in the work of Western scholars and activists working toward the revival of full ordination. Western scholars see the lives of renunciants as "lacking" and a "problem" to be solved by the adoption of gender equity. They envision an ideal, universalized renunciant, an ideal to which all can and *should* aspire. The result is to silence the voices of those whose experience and understanding are different.[101]

Hiroko Kawanami points out that while ideals of Western liberalism appear liberal and universal, they are secular and do not consider the needs of faith-based communities that value duty and humility.[102] There is a different understanding of society. As in the narrative of the founding of the *bhikkhuni* order, soteriological equality is affirmed, but social distinction is maintained.[103] Society is viewed as a community of interdependent hierarchical relationships. There are different roles, duties, and obligations according to age, gender, and status. It is within that structure that nuns "assume(s) different domains of power."[104]

Many nuns in Burma, Sri Lanka, and Thailand consider the language of individual rights to be inappropriate.[105] They, implicitly and sometimes explicitly, consider "rights" language a foreign imposition, and maintain that those who use it do so for personal gain or are being "political."[106]

Susanne Mrozik welcomes Salgado's critique of scholarly narratives that assume *dasa sil matas* are an oppressed group and narratives "that turn nuns into imperialist curative projects." She notes that Salgado's work draws attention to the broad range of practice among *dasa sil matas*, their daily practices and concerns, as these issues are often eclipsed by the focus on the ordination issue.[107] Salgado's analysis of the role played by Western, liberal, feminist women has not, however, gone unchallenged. Mrozik and Karma Lekshe Tsomo note that the ideal of a fully ordained *bhikkhuni* is not a specifically liberal feminist ideal, but is presented as the ideal in monastic regulations, and full ordination was instituted by the Buddha.[108] Tsomo argues that this analysis ignores the contributions of women such as Bhikkhuni Kusama and Ranjani de Silva, and takes insufficient account of the agency of Asian nuns. Regarding accusations that those who support the reinstitution of the *bhikkhuni sangha* do so for personal gain, Tsomo argues that such accusations are often leveled at those who seek resources, education, and social justice in order to discourage renunciants from seeking the "knowledge and requisites they need to live healthy renunciant lives."[109]

In Sri Lanka, full ordination has been adopted by Buddhist nationalists. Kirama Wimalajothi, following Dharmapala (1864–1933), established the Dekanduwala Bhikkhuni Training Centre. He sees restoration of the full ordination as part of a nationalist platform to protect against "anti-Buddhist challenges" from "foreign influences"—Christianity and Islam. Cofounder of the BBS, with whom he broke in 2014, he echoes the theme of the decline of the *sasana* (doctrine and practice) and believes that *bhikkhuni* would be especially helpful in rural areas where the monks are very lax, and that *bhikkhuni* can better serve women and prevent them from converting.[110]

Issues of authenticity and authority cause tensions between groups that support full ordination, and within the sangha. Inamaluwe Sumangala, another controversial Sri Lankan monk, has argued that for the *bhikkhuni sangha* to be fully restored there must be indigenous ordinations.[111]

He established a *bhikkhuni* training center at Dambulla and, with the assistance of the nuns ordained at Sarnath in 1996, the nuns ordained at Bodhgaya in 1998 were ordained with the Theravada Vinaya. A rift subsequently arose over monastic seniority (1996 or 1998 ordinations).

Sumangala claimed that the 1998 ordination was authoritative (Theravada), while the 1996 ordination was Mahayana. Sumangala dismisses as "inauthentic" all ordinations other than those at Dambulla. As Salgado points out, this amounts to a claim that only the Dambulla temple can decide what is or is not an authentic Theravada *bhikkhuni* ordination. The heads of all three Nikayas, spearheaded by the Asigiriya monks of the Siyam Nikaya, with whom Sumangala had ongoing conflicts since 1985, made their disapproval of a *bhikkhuni sangha*, and of his behavior, public.[112]

Regardless of one's position on the restoration of full ordination and the *bhikkhuni sangha*, in effect there are two *bhikkhuni sangha*: one in Thailand, estimated at less than three hundred by Ven. Dhammananda, all of whom were ordained abroad, and one in Sri Lanka estimated to be between one thousand and two thousand.[113] This does not mean that all issues have been solved or that controversies have all been settled. Tensions remain, and new issues will continue to arise. Some women do wish to become *bhikkhuni* despite opposition, some do not, and some are uncertain.[114] Their reasons for choosing either are varied and complicated.

LITERATURE REVIEW

The context within which early scholars worked was a colonial one influenced by the Enlightenment, Darwin, and industrialization. The British, in particular, had a vast empire that, by the end of the 19th century, covered almost a quarter of the world's landmass and over a quarter of its population.[115] The primary goal was resource extraction, justified, in part, by a stated desire to govern and to bring "civilization" to the colonies. Buddhist scholarship was guided by the questions that interested Western scholars. They were interested in rationality and texts rather than lived religion. Within the volumes of texts available, their concern was for the texts of the Pali canon, most notably those that were felt to be "early" and "original," without the trappings of later accretions. Some texts were held to reveal aspects of the historical Buddha, his thought, and the development of the early sangha. Judith Snodgrass provides an excellent example of how this worked regarding two of the foremost translators of the time and the Pali Text Society they founded.[116] In an excellent editorial Kate Crosby discusses the second wave of Buddhist scholars who, along with social anthropologists, continued to ask the same types of questions without examining the social context within which texts were found meaningful, and generally ignoring texts in the vernacular or oral traditions.[117] Following Charles Hallisey, Crosby notes that this is natural as we tend to internalize our mentors, but postcolonial studies, gender studies, and subaltern studies have created more self-critical scholars who pay attention to whose stories we hear.[118] Scholars from a variety of fields—history, sociology, and textual studies—have benefitted from access to these analytic tools.[119] Sociological and political studies over the past several decades take Buddhism into account when examining Asian power structures and the role that Buddhism played in establishing and disrupting these structures, the roots of Buddhist nationalism and violence, the origins of "prosperity Buddhism," and the revival of meditation methods other than *vipassana*.[120] Quli reminds us that "tradition" is always in movement, being contested, augmented, and revived. So too, is Buddhist studies.[121]

PRIMARY SOURCES

Translations of some Pali texts by various translators are available in print and digitally. The largest number are published by the Pali Text Society, which was founded in 1881 by Pali scholar Thomas Rhys Davids. The translation of *Cullavagga X* used here is I. B. Horner's translation, "Cullavagga X," in *The Book of Discipline (Vinaya-Piṭaka)*, Vol. 5 (Oxford: Pali Text Society, [1952] 1988), 352–393.

A popular website, Access to Insight, also provides a wide list of Buddhist texts by various translators.

Another website is Sutta Central, which includes translations from the Chinese and Tibetan, as well as Pali.

A search on book websites should bring up translations by K. R. Norman (1925–2020), Maurice O. Connell Walshe (1911–1998), and Naṇamoli Bhikkhu (1905–1960) to more recent translators such as Bhikkhu Bodhi, Ajahn Ṭhanissaro, and Bhikkhu Sujato.

DIGITAL MATERIALS

There are many scholarly online journals. Several are open access, and where a particular article or journal is not, access is usually obtainable through a university or large library.

Journal of the International Association of Buddhist Studies (https://journals.ub.uni-heidelberg.de/index.php/jiabs/index).

Buddhist Studies Review (https://journals.equinoxpub.com/index.php/BSR).
Contemporary Buddhism (https://www.tandfonline.com/toc/rcbh20/current).
Journal of Global Buddhism (http://www.globalbuddhism.org/jgb/index.php/jgb/).
Journal of Buddhist Ethics (https://blogs.dickinson.edu/buddhistethics/).
The Ho Center for Buddhist Studies (Stanford School of Humanities) at Stanford University has a selected list of films and documentaries (https://buddhiststudies.stanford.edu/resourcesonline-resources/list-selected-buddhist-films).
The Alliance for Bhikkhunis (https://www.bhikkhuni.net/) who support the *bhikkhuni sangha* maintain a website in English that provides links to other sites, a library, and a directory to monasteries worldwide, among other things.

FURTHER READING

Blackburn, Anne M. *Locations of Buddhism: Colonialism and Modernity in Sri Lanka*. Chicago and London: University of Chicago Press, 2009.
Cheng, Wei-Yi. *Buddhist Nuns in Taiwan and Sri Lanka: A Critique of the Feminist Perspective*. London and New York: Routledge, 2007.
Church, Peter. *A Short History of South-East Asia*. Singapore: John Wiley & Sons, 2017.
Falk, Monica Lindberg. *Making Fields of Merit: Buddhist Female Ascetics and Gendered Orders in Thailand*. Copenhagen: NIAS Press, 2007.
Gravers, Mikael. "Anti-Muslim Buddhist Nationalism in Burma and Sri Lanka." *Contemporary Buddhism* 16, no. 1 (2015): 1–27. https://doi.org/10.1080/14639947.2015.1008090.
Harris, Ian. *Cambodian Buddhism: History and Practice*. Honolulu: University of Hawai'i Press, 2005.
Kawanami, Hiroko. "The Bhikkhuni Ordination Debate: Global Aspirations, Local Concerns, with Special Emphasis on the Views of the Monastic Community in Burma." *Buddhist Studies Review* 24, no. 2 (2007): 226–244. https://journals.equinoxpub.com/index.php/BSR/article/viewArticle/4097.
Kemper, Steven. *Rescued from the Nation: Anagarika Dharmapala and the Buddhist World*. Chicago and London: University of Chicago Press, 2015.
Kent, Alexandra. "Peace, Power and Pagodas in Present-Day Cambodia." *Contemporary Buddhism* 9, no. 1 (2008): 77–97. https://doi.org/10.1080/14639940802312717.
Lehrer, Tyler. "Mobilizing Gendered Piety in Sri Lanka's Contemporary *Bhikkhuni* Ordination Dispute." *Buddhist Studies Review* 36, no. 1 (2019): 99–121. https://doi.org/10.1558/bsrv.35050.
Mrozik, Susanne. "Sri Lankan Buddhist Nuns: Complicating the Debate over Ordination." *Feminist Studies in Religion* 36, no. 1 (Spring 2020): 33–49. https://doi.org/10.2979/jfemistudreli.36.1.05.
Salgado, Nirmala S. *Buddhist Nuns and Gendered Practice: In Search of the Female Renunciant*. Oxford: Oxford University Press, 2013.
Schober, Juliane, and Steven Collins, eds. *Theravada Buddhist Encounters with Modernity*. London: Routledge, 2017.
Stuart-Fox, Martin. *A History of Laos*. Cambridge, UK: Cambridge University Press, 1997.
Turner, Alicia. *Saving Buddhism: The Impermanence of Religion in Colonial Burma*. Honolulu: University of Hawai'i Press, 2014.

NOTES

1. David I. Steinberg, *Burma/Myanmar: What Everyone Needs to Know* (Oxford and New York: Oxford University Press, 2010), 17–18 [Kindle edition].
2. Andrew Skilton, *A Concise History of Buddhism* (Cambridge, UK: Windhorse Publications, 1997), 145–146.

3. Richard F. Gombrich, *Theravada Buddhism: A Social History from Ancient Benares to Modern Colombo* (London and New York: Routledge & Kegan Paul, 1988), 117.
4. Maung Htin Aung et al., "Myanmar," *Encyclopedia Britannica*, September 14, 2020; and Peter Church, *A Short History of South-East Asia*, 6th ed. (Singapore: John Wiley & Sons, 2017), 120.
5. Steinberg, *Burma/Myanmar*, 17.
6. Steinberg, *Burma/Myanmar*, 19.
7. Church, *A Short History*, 109.
8. Maung Htin Aung et al., "Myanmar," *Encyclopedia Britannica*, September 14, 2020.
9. Steinberg, *Burma/Myanmar*, 23.
10. George Campbell and Gareth King, *The Concise Compendium of the World's Languages* (London: Routledge, 2018), 718; and "Tai vs Thai 2," *Languagehat*, October 19, 2003.
11. James Hafner et al., "Thailand," *Encyclopedia Britannica*, January 17, 2021; and Rachelle M. Scott, "Contemporary Thai Buddhism," in *The Oxford Handbook of Contemporary Buddhism*, ed. Michael Jerryson (Oxford: Oxford University Press, 2017), 197–198.
12. Hafner et al., "Thailand."
13. Scott, "Contemporary Thai Buddhism," 197–198.
14. Church, *A Short History*, 183.
15. Ashley Thompson, "Contemporary Cambodian Traditions: Seen from the Past," in Jerryson, *The Oxford Handbook of Contemporary Buddhism*, 239.
16. Ian Harris, *Cambodian Buddhism: History and Practice* (Honolulu: University of Hawai'i Press, 2005), 43.
17. Harris, *Cambodian Buddhism*, 105, 106.
18. Editors of Encyclopedia Britannica, "Nanzhao," *Encyclopedia Britannica*, May 29, 2012; and Martin Stuart-Fox, *A History of Laos* (Cambridge, UK: Cambridge University Press, 1997), 8.
19. Stuart-Fox, *A History*, 9.
20. Church, *A Short History*, 77; Stuart-Fox, *A History*, 13; and Ananda Wickremeratne, "Buddhism in Cambodia and Laos," *Encyclopedia of Buddhism*, ed. Damien Keown and Charles S. Prebish (London and New York: Routledge, 2007), 191–194, 194.
21. Stuart-Fox, *A History*, 12–13.
22. Martin Stuart-Fox, "The French in Laos, 1887–1945," *Modern Asian Studies* 29, no. 1 (1995): 111; Wickremeratne, "Cambodia and Laos," 194; and "Laos Profile-Timeline," *BBC News*, January 9, 2018.
23. Gombrich, *Theravada Buddhism*, 129–130.
24. Steinberg, *Burma/Myanmar*, 18–19.
25. Matthew J. Walton, "Burmese Buddhist Politics," *Oxford Handbooks Online*, October 2015, presents a review of scholarly positions regarding the extent to which the classical model affects current affairs.
26. Sharon L. Synder, "Modernity," *Encyclopedia Britannica*, May 20, 2016.
27. Anne M. Blackburn, *Buddhist Learning and Textual Practice in Eighteenth-Century Lankan Monastic Culture* (Princeton, NJ: Princeton University Press, 2001), 5–19.
28. Blackburn, *Buddhist Learning*, 46.
29. Anne M. Blackburn, *Locations of Buddhism: Colonialism and Modernity in Sri Lanka* (Chicago and London: University of Chicago Press, 2009), 200.
30. Alicia Turner, *Saving Buddhism: The Impermanence of Religion in Colonial Burma* (Honolulu: University of Hawai'i Press, 2014), 40–43.
31. Eric Braun, *The Birth of Insight: Meditation, Modern Buddhism, and the Burmese Monk Ledi Sayadaw* (Chicago: University of Chicago Press, 2013), 4–5.
32. Turner, *Saving Buddhism*, 5.
33. Turner, *Saving Buddhism*, 136–137.
34. Blackburn, *Locations of Buddhism*, x–xi.

35. Juliane Schober and Steven Collins, "Theravada Buddhist Civilizations and Their Modern Formations," in *Theravada Buddhist Encounters with Modernity*, ed. Juliane Schober and Steven Collins (Abingdon and New York: Routledge, 2018), 8.
36. P. V. J. Jayasekera, *Confrontations with Colonialism: Resistance, Revivalism, and Reform under British Rule in Sri Lanka, 1796–1920*, Vol. 1 (Colombo, Sri Lanka: Vijitha Yapa Publications, 2017), 42, 57; and Chandra Richard de Silva, Review of "Confrontations with Colonialism: Resistance, Revivalism, and Reform under British Rule in Sri Lanka, 1796–1920 (Vol. 1) by P. V. J. Jayasekera," *Sri Lankan Journal of Social Sciences* 41, no. 1 (2018): 65–66.
37. James Wilson, "Reappropriation, Resistance, and British Autocracy in Sri Lanka, 1820–1850," *Cambridge Historical Journal* 60, no. 1 (2017): 55; and Nira Wickramasinghe, *Sri Lanka in the Modern Age: A History* (New York: Oxford University Press, 2014), 50–52.
38. Wickramasinghe, *Sri Lanka in the Modern Age*, 52–53.
39. Wickramasinghe, *Sri Lanka in the Modern Age*, 62–66.
40. Michael Roberts, "Himself and Project. A Serial Autobiography. Our Journey with a Zealot, Anagarika Dharmapala," *Social Analysis* 44, no. 1 (April 2000): 114.
41. Stephen Kemper, *Rescued from the Nation: Anagarika Dharmapala and the Buddhist World* (Chicago and London: University of Chicago Press, 2015); Michael Roberts, "For Humanity. For the Sinhalese. Dharmapala as Crusading Bosat," *Journal of Asian Studies* 56, no. 4 (1997): 1006–1032; Roberts, "Himself and Project"; and Stephen Prothero, "Henry Steel Olcott and 'Protestant Buddhism,'" *Journal of the American Academy of Religion* 63, no. 2 (1995): 281–302.
42. Roberts, "For Humanity," 1025; and Roberts, "Himself and Project," 117.
43. Tessa Bartholomeusz, *Women under the Bo Tree* (Cambridge, UK: Cambridge University Press, 1994), Chapters 3 and 4, 44–91; and Roberts, "Himself and Project," 132.
44. Roberts, "For Humanity," 1024–1026.
45. Kemper, *Rescued from the Nation*, 40; Prothero, "Henry Steel Olcott," 297; Gananath Obeyesekere, "Buddhism and Conscience: An Exploratory Essay," *Daedalus* 120, no. 3 (1991): 219–239, 238; and Roberts, "For Humanity," 1008–1009.
46. Gombrich, *Theravada Buddhism*, 103–104.
47. Peter Schalk, "Semantic Transformations of the *Dhammadipa*," in *Buddhism, Conflict and Violence in Modern Sri Lanka*, ed. Mahinda Deegalle (London and New York: Routledge, 2006), 86–92. This chapter challenges that translation; and Harshana Rambukwella, "Anagarika Dharmapala," in *The Politics and Poetics of Authenticity: A Cultural Geneology of Sinhala Nationalism*, ed. Harshana Rambukwella (London: UCL Press, 2018), 48–72, 55–56, 60–61.
48. Kemper, *Rescued from the Nation*, 40; and Prothero, "Henry Steel Olcott," 297.
49. Gombrich, *Theravada Buddhism*, 104.
50. Tessa Bartholomeusz, *In Defense of Dharma: Just-War Ideology in Buddhist Sri Lanka* (London and New York: RoutledgeCurzon, 2002).
51. Mikael Gravers, "Anti-Muslim Buddhist Nationalism in Burma and Sri Lanka," *Contemporary Buddhism* 16, no. 1 (2015): 1–27.
52. Gravers, "Anti-Muslim Buddhist Nationalism," 16.
53. Gravers, "Anti-Muslim Buddhist Nationalism," 16.
54. Durba Ghosh, "The Reforms of 1919: Montagu-Chelmsford, the Rowlatt Act, Jails Commission, and the Royal Amnesty," in *Gentlemanly Terrorists: Political Violence and the Colonial State in India, 1919–1947*, ed. Durba Ghosh (Cambridge, UK: Cambridge University Press, 2017), 28.
55. Turner, *Saving Buddhism*, 138–139.
56. Steinberg, *Burma/Myanmar*, 28–29.
57. Steinberg, *Burma/Myanmar*, 28–29.

58. Steinberg, *Burma/Myanmar*, 156.
59. Gravers, "Anti-Muslim Buddhist Nationalism," 3.
60. United Nations Office for the Coordination of Humanitarian Affairs, "Rohingya Refugee Crisis," *OCHA: United Nations*, August 29, 2018.
61. Gravers, "Anti-Muslim Buddhist Nationalism," 13–14; see also Associated Press, "Firebrand Monk Surrenders to Police Days before Myanmar Vote," *abcNews*, November 2, 2020; and Hannah Ellis-Petersen, "Myanmar Police Hunt 'Buddhist bin Laden' over Suu Kyi Comments," *The Guardian*, May 29, 2019.
62. McDaniel, "Buddhism in Thailand," 104.
63. Scott, "Contemporary Thai Buddhism," 200; and McDaniel, "Buddhism in Thailand," 103–104.
64. Scott, "Contemporary Thai Buddhism," 201.
65. McDaniel, "Buddhism in Thailand," 107–108.
66. Michael K. Jerryson, "Buddhism, Conflict, and Peace Building," in Jerryson, *The Oxford Handbook of Contemporary Buddhism*, 554; Michael K. Jerryson, "Militarizing Buddhism: Violence in Southern Thailand," in *Buddhist Warfare*, ed. Michael K. Jerryson and Mark Juergensmeyer (New York: Oxford University Press, 2010), 179–209; and Michael K. Jerryson, *Buddhist Fury: Religion and Violence in Southern Thailand* (New York: Oxford University Press, 2011).
67. Jerryson, "Buddhism, Conflict," 554.
68. Harris, *Cambodian Buddhism*, 108–110.
69. Harris, *Cambodian Buddhism*, 112.
70. Harris, *Cambodian Buddhism*, 125–128.
71. Wickremeratne, "Cambodia and Laos," 193.
72. Carol A. Mortland, *Cambodian Buddhism in the United States* (Albany: State University of New York Press, 2017), 19–25.
73. Janet McLellan, *Cambodian Refugees in Canada* (Toronto: University of Toronto Press, 2009), xi.
74. Alexandra Kent, "Peace, Power and Pagodas in Present-Day Cambodia," *Contemporary Buddhism* 9, no. 1 (2008): 78–80.
75. Wickremeratne, "Cambodia and Laos," 194.
76. Marybeth White, "That Luang: The Journey and Relocation of Lao Buddhism in Canada," in *Wild Geese: Buddhism in Canada*, ed. John S. Harding, Victor Sogen Hori, and Alexander Soucy (Montreal and Kingston: McGill–Queen's University Press, 2010), 169–170.
77. Mavis L. Fenn, "Dhammadinna and Jayanta," in *Flowers on the Rock: Global and Local Buddhisms in Canada*, ed. John S. Harding, Victor Sogen Hori, and Alexander Soucy (Montreal and Kingston: McGill–Queen's University Press, 2014), 313–332, esp. 314–315.
78. "Cullavagga X," in *The Book of Discipline (Vinaya-Piṭaka)*, Vol. 5, trans. B. Horner (Oxford: Pali Text Society, [1952] 1988), 352–358.
79. Nancy Falk, "The Case of the Vanishing Nuns: The Fruits of Ambivalence in Ancient Indian Buddhism," in *Unspoken Worlds: Women's Religious Lives in Non-Western Cultures*, ed. Nancy Falk and Rita Gross (San Francisco: Harper & Row, 1980).
80. H. R. Perera, "Buddhism in Sri Lanka: A Short History," *Access to Insight (BCBS Edition)*, December 1, 2013; and Bartholomeusz, *Women*, 20–22.
81. Bartholomeusz, *Women*, 27, 94, 97, 101, 126–127.
82. Nirmala S. Salgado, *Buddhist Nuns and Gendered Practice: In Search of the Female Renunciant* (Oxford: Oxford University Press, 2013), 136.
83. Hiroko Kawanami, "The Bhikkhuni Ordination Debate: Global Aspirations, Local Concerns, with Special Emphasis on the Views of the Monastic Community in Burma," *Buddhist Studies Review* 24, no. 2 (2007): 229.

84. Kawanami, "The *Bhikkhuni* Ordination Debate," 230.
85. Chatsumarn Kabilsingh, *Thai Women in Buddhism* (Berkeley, CA: Parallax Press, 1991), 45–48; and "Ajahn Brahm Excommunicated for Performing Bhikkhuni Ordination in Australia," *The Buddhist Channel*, November 5, 2009.
86. Harris, *Cambodian Buddhism*, 23, 25.
87. Harris, *Cambodian Buddhism*, 74.
88. Elizabeth Guthrie, "Khmer Buddhism, Female Asceticism, and Salvation," in *History, Buddhism, and New Religious Movements in Cambodia*, ed. John Marston and Elizabeth Guthrie (Honolulu: University of Hawai'i Press, 2004), 133–137, 138–140, 148.
89. Tsomo, "Lao Buddhist Women," 96.
90. Tsomo, "Lao Buddhist Women," 97–99.
91. Patrice Ladwig, "Applying Dhamma to Contemporary Society: Socially-Engaged Buddhism and Development Work in the Lao PDR," *Juth Pakai* 7 (October 2006): 16–27; and Toung Eh Synuanchanh, "A Case Study of Buddhism for Development Project at Ban Bungsanthueng, Nongbok District, Khammouane Province," MIC (Master of International Communication), Unitec Institute of Technology, 2018.
92. Bartholomeusz, *Women*, 186–194; and Bhikkhu Bodhi, "The Revival of the Bhikkhuni Ordination," in *Dignity and Discipline: Reviving Full Ordination for Nuns*, ed. Thea Mohr and Jampa Tsedron (Boston: Wisdom, 2010), 99–142, esp. 110–111.
93. Kabilsingh, *Thai Women in Buddhism*, 85.
94. Mavis L. Fenn, "Buddhist Women, Anthropological Approaches to," in *Encyclopedia of Buddhism*, ed. Damien Keown and Charles S. Prebish (New York and Toronto: Routledge, 2007), 443.
95. "Brief History of Sakyadhita," *Sakyadhita: International Association of Buddhist Women*, accessed December 12, 2019.
96. "Sakyadhita International Association of Buddhist Women: Aims and Achievements," *Sakyadhita: International Association of Buddhist Women*, accessed December 12, 2019.
97. "King to Appoint, Oversee New Sangha Council," *The Nation Thailand*, July 5, 2018.
98. Susanne Mrozik, "Sri Lankan Buddhist Nuns: Complicating the Debate over Ordination," *Journal of Feminist Studies in Religion* 36, no. 1 (2020): 33–49, esp. 36.
99. For example, see Salgado, *Buddhist Nuns and Gendered Practice*; Kawanami, "The *Bhikkhuni* Ordination Debate"; Lisa J. Battaglia, "Becoming *Bhikkhuni? Mae Chis* and the Global Women's Ordination Movement," *Journal of Buddhist Ethics* 22 (2015): 25–62; Steven Collins and Justin McDaniel, "Buddhist 'Nuns' (*Mae Chi*) and the Teaching of Pali in Contemporary Thailand," *Modern Asian Studies* 44, no. 6 (2010): 1373–1408; Wei-Yi Cheng, *Buddhist Nuns in Taiwan and Sri Lanka: A Critique of Feminist Perspective* (London and New York: Routledge, 2007), Chapter 1, 1–10; Vanessa R. Sasson, "Politics of Higher Ordination for Women in Sri Lanka: Discussions with *Silmatas*," *Journal for the Study of Religion* 20, no. 1 (2007): 57–71, esp. 59; and Kay Koppedrayer and Mavis L. Fenn, "Sakyadhita: Buddhist Women in a Transnational Forum," *Canadian Journal of Buddhist Studies* 2 (2006): 143–179.
100. Salgado, *Buddhist Nuns and Gendered Practice*, 3–4; see also Tomoko Masuzawa, *The Invention of Religion: Or, How European Universalism Was Preserved in the Language of Pluralism* (Chicago: University of Chicago Press, 2005); and Antoinette Burton, *Burdens of History: British Feminists, Indian Women, and Imperial Culture, 1865–1915* (Chapel Hill, NC: University of North Carolina Press, 1994), 9–10 [Kindle edition].
101. Salgado, *Buddhist Nuns and Gendered Practice*, 3–5, 212–213, 221–224.
102. Kawanami, "The *Bhikkhuni* Ordination Debate," 238, 242–243.
103. Susanne Mrozik, "A Robed Revolution: The Contemporary Buddhist Nun's (Bhikṣuṇī) Movement," *Religion Compass* 3, no. 3 (2009): 360–378, esp. 364, following Charles Hallisey, "Buddhism," in *The Life of Virtue*, ed. Jacob Neusner (Belmont, CA: Wadsworth/Thomson Learning, 2001), 113.
104. Kate Crosby, *Theravada Buddhism: Continuity, Diversity, and Identity* (Malden, MA: Wiley Blackwell, 2014), 285–288, esp. 285; and Battaglia, "Becoming *Bhikkhuni?*," 47.

105. Battaglia, "Becoming *Bhikkhuni?*," 41.
106. Battaglia, "Becoming *Bhikkhuni?*, 46; Collins and McDaniel, "Buddhist Nuns," 1399; Kawanami, "The *Bhikkhuni* Ordination Debate," 241; Salgado, *Buddhist Nuns and Gendered Practice*; Mrozik, "Sri Lankan Buddhist Nuns," 37; and Monica Lindberg Falk, *Making Merit: Buddhist Female Ascetics and Gendered Orders in Thailand* (Copenhagen: NIAS, 2007), 10.
107. Mrozik, "Sri Lankan Buddhist Nuns," 44.
108. Mrozik, "Sri Lankan Buddhist Nuns," 44; and Lekshe Lekshe Tsomo, Review of "*Buddhist Nuns and Gendered Practice: In Search of the Female Renunciant* by Nirmala S. Salgado (Oxford and New York: Oxford University Press, 2013)," *Journal of Global Buddhism* 16 (2015): 1–7.
109. Tsomo, Review of "*Buddhist Nuns*," 4.
110. Tyler Lehrer, "Mobilizing Gendered Piety in Sri Lanka's Contemporary *Bhikkhuni* Ordination Dispute," *Buddhist Studies Review* 36, no. 1 (2019): 99–121, esp. 110–111.
111. Nirmala Salgado, "Unity and Diversity among Buddhist Nuns in Sri Lanka," in *Innovative Buddhist Women: Swimming against the Stream*, ed. Karma Lekshe Tsomo (Surrey: Curzon, 2000), 37–38.
112. Salgado, *Buddhist Nuns and Gendered Practice*, 169–181, esp. 171; see also Kawanami, "The *Bhikkhuni* Ordination Debate," 228.
113. Isobel Van Hagen, "Thailand's Bhikkhunis Want Recognition and Respect," *Atlas Obscura*, December 17, 2020; and Tsomo, Review of "*Buddhist Nuns*," 4; and Susanne Mrozik, "'We Love Our Nuns': Affective Dimensions of the Sri Lankan Bhikkhuni Revival," *Journal of Buddhist Ethics* 21 (2014): 58.
114. Saroj Pathirana, "Sri Lanka's Bhikkhuni Nuns and Their Fight for Identity Papers," *BBC Sinhala Service*, December 22, 2019.
115. "Dominance and Dominions," *Encyclopedia Britannica*, revised by Adam Augustyn April 6, 2010.
116. Judith Snodgrass, "Defining Modern Buddhism: Mr. and Mrs. Rhys Davids and the Pali Text Society," *Comparative Studies of South Asia, Africa and the Middle East* 27, no. 1 (2007): 186–202.
117. Standard works in Buddhist Studies: Gombrich, *Theravada Buddhism*; Richard F. Gombrich, *Precept and Practice: Traditional Buddhism in the Rural Highlands of Ceylon* (Oxford: Clarendon Press, 1971); Melford E. Spiro, *Buddhism and Society: A Great Tradition and Its Burmese Vicissitudes*, 2nd exp. ed. (Berkeley: University of California Press, 1982); and Gananath Obeyesekere, "The Great Tradition and the Little in the Perspective of Sinhalese Buddhism," *Journal of Asian Studies* 22, no. 2 (1963): 159–163.
118. Charles Hallisey, "Roads Taken and Not Taken in the Study of Theravada Buddhism," in *Curators of the Buddha: The Study of Buddhism under Colonialism*, ed. Donald S. Lopez Jr. (Chicago: University of Chicago Press, 1995); and Kate Crosby, "Changing the Landscape of Theravada Studies," *Contemporary Buddhism* 9, no. 1 (2008): 1–6.
119. Examples: Turner, *Saving Buddhism*; Blackburn, *Locations of Buddhism*; Burton, *Burdens of History*; and Wickramamasinghe, *Sri Lanka in the Modern Age*.
120. Gravers, "Anti-Muslim Buddhist Nationalism"; Jerryson, "Buddhism, Conflict," 554; Jerryson, "Militarizing Buddhism," 179–209; Jerryson, *Buddhist Fury*; Niklas Foxeus, "Possessed for Success: Prosperity Buddhism and the Cult of the Guardians of the Treasure Trove in Upper Burma," *Contemporary Buddhism* 18, no. 1 (2017): 108–139; Kate Crosby, "The Impact of the Science–Religion Bifurcation on the Landscape of Modern Theravada Meditation," in *Buddhist Encounters with Modernity*, ed. Juliane Schober and Steven Collins (London and New York: Routledge, 2017); and Kate Crosby, *Esoteric Theravada: The Story of the Forgotten Meditation Tradition of Southeast Asia* (Boulder, CO: Shambhala Publications, 2020).
121. Nathalie E. Quli, "Western Self, Asian Other: Modernity, Authenticity, and Nostalgia for 'Tradition' in Buddhist Studies," *Journal of Buddhist Ethics* 16 (2009): 1–38.

Mavis L. Fenn

GLOBAL THERAVADA: TRANSMISSION BEYOND ASIA

HERITAGE BUDDHISM

Immigration and Refugees. Due to restrictions on immigration, until the 1960s and 1970s there was no significant immigration from Asian Theravada Buddhist countries to either Europe or North America. Because of the variety of languages, national histories, and contextual issues, research on Buddhism in individual European countries is relatively sparse.[1] The first groups to arrive were highly educated professionals fluent in English. In the United States, these were Sri Lankans, Thais, and Burmese.[2] In Sweden and Norway, a major source of Thai immigration has been through Thai women who have married and come with their husbands.[3] Cambodians and Laotians came to the United States, Canada, Europe, and Australia as refugees, and there have been surges of Burmese refugees starting after the military coup in 1962 and most recently in 2021 after a popular uprising.[4]

Resettlement: Centrality of the Temple. The traditional focus of Buddhist life in South and Southeast Asia is the temple. It is the center of community life, ritual practices, religious teaching, preaching, and guidance. Building a temple in the diaspora is a means of rebuilding community, ensuring religious and cultural preservation, and passing the tradition to subsequent generations. Penny . . . notes that religion is an important component of self- and . . . religious tradition *and* provides resources for resettlement.[5] That resettlement begins with building a Buddhist temple.

Temples come in many forms. There are traditional temples built in Asian architectural styles and temples created in modified houses, warehouses, former churches, and schools. Proportionately, purpose-built temples are in the minority. The cost of land, building, and services is high. Traditional temples may face considerable community resistance due to aesthetic concerns, resistance over parking and space usage, or simple racism. Such was the case with Wat Lao Veluwanaram, the only traditional Laotian temple in Canada.[6] In Britain, of fifty-nine Theravada buildings identified by Starkey and Tomlin, there were only two traditional temples, the Birmingham Buddhist Vihara (Burmese) and Wat Buddhapadipa (Thai).[7]

House temples face similar challenges. Immigrant and refugee populations are small and often separated by long distances. This has been especially true for refugees who were often required to spread out across the country.[8] Costs of purchase, remodeling, and maintaining such temples are high. Ethnically or geographically diverse groups often share meeting space or temple space until individual groups can afford their own culturally specific temple.[9] That is, although a temple may be known as Sri Lankan, American Buddhists from Cambodia or Laos may attend as well as some nonheritage Buddhists. Those without a temple raise money to periodically bring a monk to their community to hold ceremonies.[10]

One of the challenges faced by house temples is space. Communities buy what they can afford, but as communities grow, they need more space. Temples may relocate like "growing families"; Wat Dhammaram in Chicago (1976) moved three times.[11] Problems with zoning permits, services, and community resistance may repeat each time a move occurs. Because many temples are in suburban or industrial areas, it means a longer commute for the laity, lower attendance, and more difficulty hosting visiting monks in member households.

The generation of new temples in America is not simply due to a growing population but also because of schisms and offshoots of established temples.[12] The San Jose Buddhist Vihara, subsequently the Dharmapala Institute, generated two additional temples, one as the result of a dispute (Buddhi Vihara in Santa Clara) and the other (Berkeley Buddhist Vihara) due to a long commute for some members.[13] At the Mahavihara temple in Toronto, Canada, monks argued for providing services that fit a contemporary setting (*intelligent adaptation*), while many of the laity wanted cultural preservation to be the focus. The monks and their supporters ended up founding a new temple.[14]

The two temples have long reconciled, and the new West End Buddhist Temple and Meditation Centre operates more as a "healthy" offshoot institution, setting itself apart by engaging in social services, cultural entertainment in seniors' homes, and helping new immigrants.[15] Two more new temples have been established, one that focuses on meditation and spiritual awakening (Mahamevnawa) and one that focuses on social and educational services in Sri Lanka (Buddhist Mission Centre). By providing options, some balance is found between cultural preservation and intelligent adaptation.

As the style, size, and location of temples were adapted to new sociopolitical–economic contexts, so too were relationships between the laity, the monks, and the broader community.

Adaptation: Monks and the Laity. The primary focus of heritage temples is to provide for the needs of diaspora communities, and these needs (rituals, ceremonies, dhamma preaching, and guidance) are performed by the monks.[16] Just as temple architecture was forced to adapt to new constraints, the relationship between monks and laity has altered in the diaspora due to the new sociopolitical–economic context. In North America, for example, religious organizations must have a board of directors made up of community representatives. This provides the laity more authority in temple affairs, including monastic behavior.

The relationship between the monks and laity is a symbiotic one. The monks provide for the religious needs of the laity, and the laity provide economic support for the monks, generating religious merit that provides status and recognition within the community and karmic benefit for the next life. Jeffrey Samuels also notes that for many, *hita* (happiness) in the heart and mind of the donor is intimately tied to the idea of making merit.[17] Monks are expected to keep strict adherence to the Vinaya, the monastic code of discipline. This adherence ensures their worthiness to receive support and the integrity of the lay merit derived from it.

However, the Vinaya rules are reflective of rural village culture and can be problematic in an urban industrial culture. While both laity and monks may realize that adaptations in Vinaya are required due to distance, long working hours, and the need to move certain ceremonies and rituals to weekends, they often disagree about which adaptations are appropriate.[18] Laity in all traditions tend to be conservative, as following the Vinaya ensures monastic purity, protecting both the dhamma and lay merit.[19] They fear that adapting the rules could be a slippery slope, eroding the monastic-led core of Buddhism and leading to its dissolution.[20]

The Vinaya rules at issue are driving, using money, work, preparation of food, and contact with women. Temples vary in the degree to which they are willing to adapt, but most adaptations are made on the grounds of practical necessity.[21] The Sri Lankan temples in Quli's study, while uncomfortable with it, accepted driving as an adaptation of practical necessity.[22] Driving may be to do errands for the temple, and so a temple credit card may be used.[23] For the same reason, monks may do some general repairs to the temple.[24] Due to weather, especially in the north, hats, boots, jackets, and sweaters have been allowed.[25]

There have also been adaptations to the monastic rules regarding food. Traditionally, monks do an alms round in the morning (*piṇḍapāta*), or food is cooked and brought to the temple for the before-noon meal. This is often not possible because there may be no laypeople living in the area or they are at work. Therefore, providing for the monks may include frozen food or takeout, or food preparation may be assigned to families or groups.[26] The Burmese Dhammananda Monastery has a Burmese *thilashin* (nun) as cook and housekeeper.[27]

The question of contact with women is more complicated and contentious. Monks are not to touch a woman, be touched by a woman, or be alone with one. When referring to American Cambodian Buddhists, Mortland notes that this rule was heavily monitored by the laity. Non-Buddhist women in Khmer contexts were instructed not to touch the monks, and sometimes they were diverted from contact. When the rule is violated, the monk is required to do purification rituals.[28] Some Cambodian monks do not believe that unintentional touches by women in the context of hospital or clinic visits or airport check-ins are a concern.[29]

Theravada monks do not shake hands, a common cultural ritual in North America. Quli notes that two Sri Lankan monks in her study did feel that it was acceptable to touch women when tying *pirit* (blessing) bracelets, and one of Paul Numrich's informants predicted monks will "slowly adopt the practices of shaking hands and hugging women as normal, cultural expressions of courtesy and friendship."[30] The rigorous lay scrutiny of monastic behavior is difficult for the monks, who some lay people expect to follow the rules as they did before emigrating, an expectation many monks find unrealistic.[31] As in the Toronto Mahavihara temple community, the laity's greater power and the demands of a new context may lead to disagreements about the temple's primary purpose.

Adaptation: Future Generations and Integration. The question of cultural preservation or intelligent adaptation is relevant to the challenge of keeping youth interested in the temple and Buddhist traditions. Transmission from one generation to the next is complicated.[32] Language is a problem if the temple monk does not speak English, and there are no English translations of the *suttas*.[33] Youth want rituals explained and tend to identify with the reformist version of Buddhism.[34] Having read or taken academic courses, they become uncomfortable with the cultural baggage, and superstitious practices, attributed to American Asian Buddhists by the non-Buddhist, white, and primarily Christian surrounding culture.[35] Temples have responded to these challenges in a variety of ways, from summer camps, services in English, heritage language classes, chanting classes, and the domestic setting.[36] English-speaking monks with knowledge of North American culture often act as a bridge between generations and are effective communicators of the tradition.[37] Through their experience of their parents' practice, their own exploration of Buddhism, and their awareness of the dominant culture that surrounds them, young Asian American Buddhists "forge Buddhist identities influenced by—yet distinct from—those of their parents."[38]

Having knowledge of both their heritage culture and that of their new home, Buddhist youth may be instrumental in the integration process, although temples may have different levels of participation with the broader community, from minimal contact to partly or fully integrated temples. Some laypeople see the temple as a place for cultural preservation and a safe haven from outside pressures, "without need for explanation to outsiders."[39] Other temples offer meditation and chanting classes, lectures, and invitations to ritual events such as *Wesak* for non-Buddhists in their community.[40] The first American Theravada temple in the United States was the Washington Buddhist Vihara.[41] It was founded by both heritage and nonheritage supporters, funds were raised in Sri Lanka and the United States, and the location was purchased from the Thai government in 1967.[42] The services are in English, and the vihara is supported by both heritage and nonheritage members. As well, Jiemin Bao's study of a mixed American Thai temple in Silicon Valley shows an ethnically, racially, intergenerationally diverse community in which temple members interact on all levels and demonstrate a flexibility in practice and operation of the temple. While the level of integration in Wat Thai appears greater than at other temples, it may mark a new direction of development.[43]

Refugees and Racism. Communities of refugees face even more challenges adapting to new contexts than immigrants with more agency. Refugees have been forced from their homes due to threatened or real violence and usually come to a new country with emotional trauma and few financial or material resources. Burmese, Cambodian, and Laotian refugees arrived in the United States and Canada with few, if any, family contacts, often after living in refugee camps for months or years. The camps are largely run by Christian organizations that are also involved in refugee settlement. Some refugees feel pressure to convert, others convert from gratitude.[44] As Janet McLellan points out regarding the Cambodian refugees who settled in Toronto, Ontario, monks provide culturally appropriate ways of dealing with issues of trauma through memorial rituals and other practices.[45] The Cambodian genocide hampered the community's ability to heal, re-establish community, and integrate into a new system.[46] Laotian refugees also faced a multitude of problems: they were largely rural, had little education, and were not fluent in English or French.[47] In Canada, sponsorship of monks was further hampered because the prohibition against handling money caused them to be considered unemployed by the government and not good candidates for immigration.[48] Refugees were often required to spread out across the country.[49] However, the fear that Buddhism would die out in Cambodia and Laos fueled their determination to build temples and restore their communities.[50] The first concern was to be able to perform ceremonies, especially for the dead, and these refugees have often attended Thai or Lao temples where a Khmer-speaking monk is available.[51] Whereas most temples are situated in houses or remodeled halls, some communities have been able to build traditional Cambodian temples. The traditional temple stands as evidence of their worth as a group, a demonstration that they belong, and it "inspires in them a sense of being Khmer and Buddhist and encourages them in their spiritual lives."[52] As well as the Washington temple, Wat Buddhikarma (1993), there are other traditional temples across the United States.[53]

Between 1979 and 1981, about 105,000 Laotians came to the United States from refugee camps in Thailand.[54] During the 1980s, they became geographically spread out across the country and founded Lao Buddhist temples throughout America.[55] The Laotians who settled in Iberia Parish, Louisiana, created Lane Xang village, a traditional Lao temple surrounded by a residential area (1987). The temple serves as a religious and cultural center for American Laotian Buddhists in southwest Louisiana.[56]

Between 1979 and 1980, Canada received 10,000 refugees from Laos, and from 1980 to 1992 Canada received 18,000 Cambodian refugees. It took some time before these communities amassed sufficient funds to support a monk and build a temple. Both had low social capital and faced significant resistance from local non-Asian communities arising from ethnic and religious prejudice.[57] Marybeth White details the difficulty the Laotian community had in dealing with the surrounding community and the legal and bylaw issues that arose.[58] Both temples were eventually built: Wat Khmer in Toronto (1995) and Wat Lao Veluwanaram (1997), the only traditional Laotian temple in Canada, in Caledon, Ontario.[59] Traditional temples are sometimes more accepted when they are seen as producing revenue as tourist sites or as lending an air of cosmopolitanism to an area.[60]

Still, racism against Asian Americans persists.[61] Violent attacks and overt harassment have increased significantly in the United States and elsewhere since the beginning of the COVID-19 pandemic, but there has long been a more subtle strain of bias. It exists in the question, "Where are you 'really' from?" It exists in long-standing American stereotypes of the yellow peril, which reflected white concerns that Chinese workers would take their jobs in the mid 1880s, and in the model-minority myth.[62] Covert racism can also be found where zoning laws and complaints of noise and traffic are made only when Asian temples are concerned.[63] Both overt and covert racism puts all American Asians, regardless of country or ethnic background, into one group and sees them as perpetual foreigners, not eligible for the mythical melting pot.[64]

Australia and Canada have adopted multiculturalism as official policy. The two pillars of multiculturalism are identity and participation.[65] In theory, the ability to maintain one's religious and cultural identity mitigates the stress and problems associated with integration and provides a sense of stability.[66] While collective identity is protected by law, it must accommodate Canadian law, which was established within a predominantly white, British, French, and Christian context (excluding Indigenous voices).[67] Expansion of Canadian identity to be more inclusive has often been socially difficult and litigious. Although Canadian attitudes to immigration are primarily positive, there has been a downward trend.[68] The author of a 2015 study that identified over one hundred right-wing groups in Canada said, "The current crop of far-right activists uses the term *cultural nationalism* as a way of muting the impact and minimizing the issue of race" (emphasis mine).[69] Hate crimes against visible minorities and ethnicities in Canada increased in 2018–2019, even before the misplaced anger stemming from the COVID-19 pandemic.[70]

NONHERITAGE BUDDHISM

Scholars and Teachers. The economic, social, and political context of the 19th to mid-20th century was one shaped by modernism, the European Enlightenment, social Darwinism, and colonization.[71] European and American scholars of religion applied the values of rationality and science to the study of religious texts, aiming to strip the mythology from what they believed to be the authentic teachings of Jesus or the buddha. Ritual was dismissed as superstitious. Social Darwinism contributed to the notion that white Euro-Americans were at the top of the evolutionary ladder, and the colonization of other countries civilized them by introducing new technologies, agricultural management, and Enlightenment values. These ideas underlay scholarly decisions about what aspects of Buddhism were authentic and worthwhile and what could be discarded. Scholars were interested in canonical texts, texts as history, texts as philosophy, and ethics.

Scholars such as T. W. Rhys Davids (1843–1922) and the Pali Text Society (PTS, 1881) played a major role in shaping and disseminating nonheritage Buddhism. They were interested only in canonical and philosophical texts.[72] They took a strictly philological approach to translation, while their Asian collaborators took an inclusive approach that included various sources, such as traditional commentaries, as guides to understanding. Snodgrass notes that Asian Buddhists had trouble "being heard" in the society.[73] Rhys-Davids and the PTS promoted this rational, philosophical Buddhism with the strong implication that this, not the lived Buddhism of Sri Lanka and Southeast Asia, was *real* Buddhism. The stereotypes created by these categories continue to impact relationships between heritage and nonheritage Buddhists in the 21st century.

Colonial scholarship on Buddhism laid the foundation for the new field of Buddhist studies in universities outside Asia and shaped nonheritage understanding of Buddhism. When Euro-Americans traveled to Asia in the 1970s, they often studied meditation, which could be taught as a discrete practice more easily than other aspects of lay and monastic Buddhism that were integrated into society. Meditation became the primary practice for nonheritage Buddhists. Initially, efforts to establish a stable nonheritage Buddhism community in Europe faltered.[74] The lectures and pamphlets offered by lay societies were ineffective. The Asian model of monastic life also faced challenges. When a monastery was established in Hampstead (1978), it struggled to survive. The people who came to the monastery came for meditation and did not think of themselves as a community. There was financial support but no ritual giving (*dāna*) that cements the bond between laity and monks.[75] Ajahn Chah of the Thai forest tradition, who had trained many Euro Americans in Thailand, rejuvenated the monastery by instituting daily alms rounds and facilitated bonds between laypeople over time. He appointed his senior student, Ajahn Sumedo, a nonheritage monk, as abbot.[76] Ajahn Sumedo was also the first abbot of Amaravati Monastery (1980) built in Hertfordshire on land granted by the English Sangha Trust, fueled by gifts of work and money from laity and generous donations from the Thai government.[77] Thai forest monasteries outside Asia focus on monastic practice, have retreat centers for the public and a calendar of events, and are supported by donations from heritage and nonheritage laypersons.[78] Amaravati networks with Thai forest monasteries in Canada and the United States, Europe, and New Zealand. As with heritage Buddhist traditions, adaptations were made. Temporary ordination was combined with the path of a novice monk, and *dāna* is encouraged without the concept of merit.[79] The Thai forest lineage does not allow for full *bhikkhunī* ordination (*upasampadā*). Amaravati has an order for women called *sīladharā* (upholders of virtue). Women take the ten precepts and follow rules taken from the male novice ordination. They are referred to as nuns, and their routine is like that of the monks.[80] While the Sīladharā Order is an adaptation within the Thai forest tradition that allows a role for women, it is considered inadequate by those who believe the restoration of a full *bhikkunī saṅgha* is necessary to complete the fourfold saṅgha (monks, nuns, male and female laity).

In 2011, Ayya Santacitta and Ayya Anandabodhi left the Sīladharā Order and took full ordination at Spirit Rock Meditation Center in the United States, and then they established Aloka Vihara Forest Monastery in California.[81]

Vipassana, Insight Meditation, and Mindfulness. Spirit Rock Meditation Center (1988), formerly Insight Meditation West (1984), where the founders of Aloka Vihara Forest

Monastery took full ordination, was established by Jack Kornfield. Kornfield is one of the founders of the first meditation group to be established in the United States, the Insight Meditation Society (IMS), founded in Barre, Massachusetts (1975). Spirit Rock added influences from therapeutic practices such as psychotherapy and other spiritual practices to the *vipassana* foundation of IMS.[82] The founders of IMS—Joseph Goldstein, Jack Kornfield, Sharon Salzberg, and Jacqueline Schwartz (later Mandell)—all had extensive training in Asia and were grounded in Theravada Buddhism.[83] The meditation they teach is *vipassana,* called insight meditation in America.

Vipassana groups in the United States generally trace their lineage to the Burmese tradition through Mahasi Sayadaw, the Thai forest tradition of Ajahn Chah or S. N. Goenka.[84] Some *vipassana* groups maintain their attachment to their Burmese, Thai, or Sri Lankan roots, whereas others do not.[85] Insight meditation (*vipassana*) is usually presented without any historical or religious context and is described as a technique to produce psychological healing and awareness derived from techniques taught by the buddha.[86]

This reframing is a good example of what Cheah refers to as *cultural articulation,* a way of representing a religious tradition from one culture through ideas and practices familiar and meaningful in another.[87] Mindfulness represents the latest adaptation of *vipassana,* to the modern, individualist, and capitalist American culture.

Jeff Wilson provides a thorough history of the transformation of insight meditation into mindfulness.[88] Buddhist cosmology was psychologized, and monasticism, religious elements, and the Asian context were removed.[89] Once mindfulness became individual, secular, and non-Asian, it was recontextualized within American religious history, metaphysical religion, spirituality, and liberal religion.[90]

Without the monastic focus and cultural context of its original setting, mindfulness becomes a means to deal with the difficulties of life and their psychological effects. It is a means of living authentically and improving one's overall well-being.[91] Jon Kabat-Zinn's Mindfulness-Based Stress Reduction Program (MBSR) placed mindfulness within the clinical context. Various programs using MBSR and MBCT (Mindfulness-Based Cognitive Therapy) are widely used in the United States, Canada, and Europe in secular treatment programs for coping with pain, stress, and illness.[92]

Secular Buddhism and Technology. Modernist constructions of Buddhism as a technique or way of life without dogmas have made it compatible with other religious traditions and secular culture.[93] McMahon and Baumann discuss the development of more consciously secular hybrid models such as the Springwater Center for Meditative Inquiry and Retreats founded by Toni Packer (1927–2013) and Triratna (formerly FWBO, Friends of the Western Buddhist Order).[94] According to the Secular Buddhist Association, secular Buddhism takes a practical and humanistic view of doctrine and practice in Buddhism.[95] It understands the buddha as a human being and the four noble truths as an "accurate, empirical description" of life.[96] Regardless of the form that secular Buddhist groups may take, secular Buddhists either find no evidence for or consider irrelevant the doctrine of rebirth or supernatural elements.[97]

The generations that have grown up with digital technology take online Buddhist practice in cybercommunities as a given.[98] Gleig identifies five common themes: technology as a means to enhance current practice, the legitimation of all aspects of life (including virtual) as potential sites of enlightenment, a pragmatic and experiential approach that uses and personalizes all teachings and practices designed to end suffering, the disruption of traditional forms of Buddhist hierarchy and a democratization of practice, and a pluralistic/nonsectarian approach to Buddhist traditions and other systems of knowledge.[99] Hybrid groups, such as those founded by Noah Levine, Meditate.io (formerly Buddhist Geeks), and the Center for Pragmatic Dharma, provide a wider variety of options in an increasingly diverse society.[100]

Buddhism, Inclusivity, and Backlash. There are a variety of ways to be Buddhist and to practice Buddhism—too many, some would argue. Retraditionalization is found across Buddhist traditions, a response to modernist constructions of Buddhism. Critiques of modernism come from both heritage and nonheritage teachers, indicating that "not all westerners desire a thoroughly modernized version of Buddhism."[101] A tension also exists between those who believe Buddhism is a personal, internal spiritual journey and those who believe that Buddhists must be engaged in social issues.[102] These two tensions are manifest when issues of diversity, equity, and inclusion (DEI) arise.

Cheah points out that race is a social fact that affects daily life.[103] As more Asian Americans and Black, Indigenous, and People of Color (BIPOC) join previously all- or predominantly white Insight Meditation groups, issues regarding racialized inclusion and exclusion arise.[104] Some BIPOC and LGBTQ2S+ people have established their own saṅghas or POC affiliation groups as a means of dealing with racialized exclusion and to find their life experience reflected in the teaching.[105] In a study published in 2019, Hase, Meadows, and Budge identified interpersonal and institutional barriers to inclusion experienced by POC, including a notable failure of leadership and what coping mechanisms racialized Buddhists employ.[106] Various meditation centers, including Spirit Rock Meditation Center and Insight Meditation Society, have instituted programs to increase DEI.[107] These initiatives may be seen as the most recent example of adaptation and change within nonheritage meditative communities.

The call for DEI initiatives has been followed by a backlash against engaged Buddhism. As McMahon notes, engaged Buddhism expands the five precepts to address systemic suffering in the world.[108] Some believe that Buddhism deals only with individual suffering and the application of Buddhism to social issues makes it political. Ann Gleig and Brenna Artinger note that Buddhism has become a site in the culture wars, ongoing clashes between conservatives and progressives in society at large. Terms such as *politically correct, postmodern identity politics,* and *cultural Marxism,* used in opposition to Buddhist DEI initiatives, are indicative of right-wing rhetoric.[109]

These responses reflect both a resistance to social change and a desire to return to an often unspecified tradition. Quli reminds us that no tradition is static: "As an invention of the present projecting itself onto the past, tradition is always in movement, being contested, forgotten, remembered, reinvented, augmented, abandoned, revived, and above all, *lived.*"[110]

Bhikkhunī Saṅgha. Quli's comment about tradition is reflective of the history of efforts to revive the Theravada *bhikkhunī saṅgha,* which died out in South and Southeast Asia between the 11th and 13th centuries and does not appear to have reached Thailand. Since then, women have been able to take a novice ordination but not full ordination (*upasampadā*). There were periodic attempts that ended in failure. The first modern full ordination was held at the Hsi Lai Temple (California) in 1988. While full ordination is generally accepted in Europe and North America, its legitimacy is contested in South and Southeast Asia.

In the 1970s and 1980s, many European and American women traveled to Asia, and some wanted to ordain as nuns in the Theravada tradition. Initial support for reinstitution of the *bhikkhunī saṅgha* came from heritage monks working outside of Asia such as Henepola Gunaratna (1927–) and Havanpola Ratanasara (1920–2000), who believed that without full ordination (*upasampadā*), Theravada growth would be hindered outside Asia.[111]

Sakyadhita (1987), now Sakyadhita International (SI), was formed with the express purpose of improving the lives of Buddhist women and working for the reinstitution of the *bhikkhunī saṅgha* where it no longer existed. The founding members were both monastic and lay. SI is an activist organization and the core of a movement whose aims include "to work for gender equity in Buddhist education, training, institutional structures, and ordination."[112] They believe that restoring the order of nuns is necessary to improve the lives of Buddhist women. It confers higher social status, more respect, and more donations than those given to nuns who have taken only the novice ordination (ten precepts) or limited precepts (five through eight). Bhikkhuni Dhammananda argues that ordination will raise Thai women from poverty and sex trafficking through education, both secular and Buddhist, which will allow them to serve the community as educators and spiritual leaders.[113]

Restoration of the *bhikkhunī saṅgha* is controversial for technical and cultural reasons as well as in its implications for practice. The order of nuns disappeared around the 13th century in Sri Lanka and Burma and never reached Thailand. In a tradition that values lineage, there is no quorum of senior nuns to administer the full ordination. The Vinaya used at Hsi Lai (Dharmagupta) is not the Theravada (Pali Vinaya), and it was administered by Mahayana monks and nuns.[114] Supporters of reinstitution assert the need to restore the fourfold saṅgha (monks, nuns, laymen, and laywomen) and that the Dharmagupta Vinaya is a related Vinaya and thus legitimate when administered by senior monks and nuns.[115]

Reinstituting the full ordination (*upasampadā*) is also culturally controversial. The term *gender equity* is part of liberal feminist discourse and encompasses Enlightenment values such as individual rights. Battaglia notes that this language ignores Thai cultural context, one of duty within a web of social relations.[116] The lack of interest or resistance to full ordination by Thai nuns or Sri Lankan nuns has sometimes been dismissed as patriarchal socialization or a clouded perspective that mutes their agency.[117] Many are simply not interested in ordination. They see their lives as *mae chi* (precept nuns) as freer than nuns who are bound by the 311 Vinaya rules, institutionalization, and supervision by the *bhikkhu saṅgha*, the monks. This view is shared by several Thai *mae chi* who are Pali scholars or meditation teachers or work in the areas of social and psychological work.[118]

Writing within the Sri Lankan context, Nirmala Salgado has been critical of Sakyadhita International and the 2007 Hamburg conference on the *bhikṣuṇī (bhikkhunī)* Vinaya and ordination lineages.[119] She argues that liberal feminist terms carry assumptions about the meanings of *nun* and *renunciant* that may not be understood locally; they create an ideal that does not resonate with renunciant women. The language does not align with their notion of empowerment and is reminiscent of orientalist attitudes during the British colonial period.[120]

Susanne Mrozik welcomes Salgado's critique of scholarly narratives that assume female renunciants are an oppressed group and narratives "that turn nuns into imperialist curative projects." However, she and Karma Lekshe Tsomo point out that the ideal of a fully ordained *bhikkhunī* is presented as an ideal in monastic regulations and that full ordination was instituted by the Buddha.[121] Tsomo also responds to Salgado's critique citing, in part, the improvement in the lives of nuns since 1987, the numbers of nuns that have received *upasampadā* since then, the views of nuns that are contrary to those noted by Salgado, and the fact that the initial push for ordination at the first Sakyadhita conference came from Sri Lankan Buddhist women, not Euro-American women.[122]

While there were efforts in Burma to reinstate the order from the 1930s into the 1970s, they failed. Hiroko Kawanami notes that Burma is very conservative and that Burmese nuns (*thilashin*) believe that it is not possible to revive full ordination.[123] Burmese nuns were integrated into the government administrative system in the 1980s and are elected to township councils. They are scholar-nuns and heads of monastic schools and are responsible for the education and training of new nuns, and they follow a code like that in the *Bhikkhunī-vibhanga*.[124] It is not surprising that many feel they do not need, and might be disadvantaged by, a revived *bhikkhunī saṅgha*.

Reinstitution of the *bhikkhunī saṅgha* threatens confusion of monastic seniority roles. Seniority, determined by date of ordination, regulates monastic life: seating, alms, decision-making, and respect. It is also hierarchical: monk, nun, novice, renunciants (*dasa sil mātās, mae chi*, and *thilashin*), and laity. If a junior *dasa sil mātā* becomes a *bhikkhunī*, she becomes senior to her *dasa sil mātā* teacher. In a culture of respect, junior to senior, this can be confusing and painful.[125]

In terms of practice, heritage nuns and nonheritage nuns share some common problems: financial support and education.[126] In both cases, the problems are cultural. Seeger notes of Thai *mae chi* that while educational opportunities and financial support have increased, and they are gaining in respect among the laity, these conditions are still dependent on their home temple.[127] Women's status is less than men's, and so *dāna* produces less merit for the laity. In 2007, the Alliance for Bhikkhunis, a nonprofit lay organization based in the United States, was established to help Theravada nuns worldwide.[128] Many Euro-Americans are not familiar with the monastic system and assume that nonheritage nuns are supported by their "denomination." Such is not the case. Many nonheritage nuns live in Europe and North America but must travel to Asia for important teachings, initiations, and rituals and pay for travel and accommodation. Raising funds may be difficult for a nun with a small support base.[129] Some nonheritage nuns work at various occupations to support themselves. As the number of heritage and nonheritage nuns grows, these issues will become increasingly important.

The issue of the restoration of the *bhikkhunī saṅgha* lays bare the complexity and challenges that are a part of adaptation and change. Religious traditions vary across the Buddhist spectrum, and within traditions, individuals disagree. Finally, the dialogue is entwined with the effects of colonialism and resentment at the intrusion of foreign ideas.

LITERATURE REVIEW

Scholarly literature on Buddhism is, like tradition, an ongoing process of reflection sometimes sparked by self-questioning and sometimes by critiques from others.[130] Early writings on Buddhism were rooted in a Euro-American, colonial mentality that set assumptions about what texts, practices, and people were authentically Buddhist. In an editorial preface to a special issue of *Contemporary Buddhism*, Kate Crosby outlines some of the consequences this had for Theravada studies: creation of a canon within the canon, ignoring the social context within which texts acquired meaning, and the conflation of Theravada with early Buddhism.[131] Earlier assumptions continue to be present, but critiques of Orientalism and self-critical scholarship that combines linguistic, historical, social, and analytical skills have expanded our knowledge and understanding of Theravada considerably.[132]

But the colonial mentality lingers in the typologies used to describe and distinguish between heritage and nonheritage Buddhism. This terminology continues to be contested. Because these terms are drawn from a Euro-American, Christian theological context, as is the term *religion* itself, they are narrowly conceived.[133] Typologies are structured categories, and religious traditions are organic and changing. There has been vigorous debate about the typologies used in Buddhist studies to distinguish between heritage and nonheritage Buddhists. The two Buddhisms (ethnic/convert) typology has been the most contested.[134] Two useful articles are those by Paul Numrich and Wakoh Shannon Hickey. Both articles provide an in-depth history of the debate, a critique of various positions, and suggestions for moving forward in terms of language. Numrich argues that this distinction still has value.[135] Hickey acknowledges its descriptive value regarding the needs of the two communities, the lack of interaction between them, and the race-based difference in power. Her primary focus, however, is on how the various typologies used in Buddhist studies reflect white privilege and an essentialist view of race.[136] Quli deals with how orientalist thought, combined with this terminology, affects notions of authenticity and authority in a predominantly white insight community.[137] The study by Hase, Meadows, and Budge explores how this plays out in terms of racialized exclusion in primarily white meditation groups with suggestions for how to remedy the situation.[138] Race and racialization have not generally been a factor of analysis in religious studies, although it is an important social and institutional factor in American society. Cheah states, "The study of Asian American Buddhists in the United States must take into account race/racism and white privilege and supremacy, which are part and parcel of their religious experiences."[139] Andeana McNicholl provides a good review article on scholarship of Buddhism and race in the United States.[140] Asian American authors such as Joseph Cheah, Jiemin Bao, and Chenxing Han directly address these issues in their studies.[141] Chenxing Han's article, "We're Not Who You Think We Are," provides insight into how terminology and preconceptions turn into stereotypes and exclusion.[142] Funie Hsu provides a critical discussion of secular mindfulness in public schools within the context of neoliberalism and the dynamics of race.[143]

Developments in American meditation-based convert Buddhism need to be placed within a wider cultural context if we are to deepen our understanding of the seemingly chaotic and often contradictory trends seen in the 21st century. The concluding chapter of Gleig's *American Dharma* provides some context and analyzes the potential and limitations of various terminologies put forward to encompass these new trends.[144] The broader context is the cultural shift from modernity to postmodernity, with the relationship between the two contested. She follows sociologist David Lyon in seeing postmodernity as a reshaping of modernity rather than replacing it.[145] She uses *postmodern* and *postmodernity* to indicate the effects of the societal shifts—economic, sociocultural, and intellectual—as Western society transitions from a modern industrial to a postmodern, postindustrial age. These effects—interrogation of modernism, rejection of metanarratives, revaluation of previously devalued religious communities and their practices, embracing of difference, diversity, and hybridity—pose a challenge to assimilative modern liberalism.[146] These effects are present, to varying degrees, within predominantly white, meditation-based, nonheritage Buddhist groups.

DIGITAL MATERIALS

Numerous digital resources are available for contemporary Buddhism, both popular and academic:

Journal of Global Buddhism (http://www.globalbuddhism.org/).
Contemporary Buddhism (https://www.tandfonline.com/toc/rcbh20/current).
The Journal of Buddhist Ethics (https://blogs.dickinson.edu/buddhistethics/).
The Canadian Journal of Buddhist Studies (https://thecjbs.org/).
The Buddhist Studies Review (https://journals.equinoxpub.com/BSR/index).
The New Books Network (podcasts): New Books on Buddhism (https://newbooksnetwork.com/category/religion-faith/buddhist-studies).
Tricycle (https://tricycle.org/).
The Lion's Roar/Buddhadharma (https://www.lionsroar.com/).
Sakyadhita International (https://sakyadhita.org/).

FURTHER READING

Bankston, Carl L., III. "Bayou Lotus: Theravada Buddhism in Southwestern Louisiana." *Sociological Spectrum* 17, no. 4 (1997): 453–472, 454. https://doi.org/10.1080/02732173.1997.9982178.

Bao, Jiemin. *Creating a Buddhist Community: A Thai Temple in Silicon Valley*. Philadelphia: Temple University Press, 2015. Kindle ed.

Barua, Deba. Mitra. *Seeding Buddhism with Multiculturalism: The Transmission of Sri Lankan Buddhism in Toronto*. Montreal and Kingston: McGill–Queen's University Press, 2019.

Baumann, Martin. "Global Buddhism: Development Periods, Regional Histories, and a New Analytical Perspective." *Journal of Global Buddhism* 2 (2001): 1–43.

Cadge, Wendy. *Heartwood: The First Generation of Theravada Buddhism in America*. Chicago and London: University of Chicago Press, 2005.

Cheah, Joseph. *Race and Religion in American Buddhism: White Supremacy and Immigrant Adaptation*. Oxford: Oxford University Press, 2011.

Cox, Lawrence. *Buddhism and Ireland: From the Celts to the Counter-Culture and Beyond*. Sheffeld, UK: Equinox, 2013.

Gleig, Ann. *American Dharma: Buddhism beyond Modernity* (New Haven, CT, and London: Yale University Press, 2019).

Gleig, Ann, and Brenna Grace Artinger. "#Buddhist Culture Wars: BuddhaBros, Alt-Right Dharma, and Snowflake Saṅghas." *Journal of Global Buddhism* 22, no. 1 (2021): 19–48. https://www.globalbuddhism.org/jgb/index.php/jgb/article/view/357.

Han, Chenxing. *Be the Refuge: Raising the Voices of Asian American Buddhists*. Berkeley, CA: North Atlantic Books, 2021.

Harding, John S., Victor Sōgen Hori, and Alexander Soucy, eds. *Flowers on the Rock: Global and Local Buddhisms in Canada*. Montreal and Kingston: McGill–Queen's University Press, 2014.

Hase, Craig N., James C. Meadows, and Stephanie L. Budge. "Inclusion and Exclusion in the White Space: An Investigation of the Experiences of People of Color in a Primarily White American Meditation

Community." *Journal of Global Buddhism* 20 (2019): 1–18. https://www.globalbuddhism.org/jgb/index.php/jgb/article/view/270.

Hsu, Funie. "What Is the Sound of One Invisible Hand Clapping? Neoliberalism, the Invisibility of Asian and Asian American Buddhists, and Secular Mindfulness in Education." In *Handbook of Mindfulness. Mindfulness in Behavioral Health*. Edited by R. Purser, D. Forbes, and A. Burke, 369–381. Cham, Switzerland: Springer, 2016. https://link.springer.com/chapter/10.1007/978-3-319-44019-4_24.

Jerryson, Michael, ed. *The Oxford Handbook of Contemporary Buddhism*. New York: Oxford University Press, 2017.

Kemper, Steven. *Rescued by the Nation: Anagarika Dharmapala and the Buddhist World*. Chicago: University of Chicago Press, 2015.

McLellan, Janet. *Cambodian Refugees in Ontario: Resettlement, Religion, and Identity*. Buffalo, NY: University of Toronto Press, 2009.

McMahon, David L. *The Making of Buddhist Modernism*. New York: Oxford University Press, 2008. Google Play ed.

Mortland, Carol. *Cambodian Buddhism in America*. Albany, NY: SUNY, 2017. Google Play edition.

Prothero, Stephen. *The White Buddhist: The Asian Odyssey of Henry Steel Olcott*. Bloomington: Indiana University Press, 2011.

Quli, Natalie Fisk, "On Authenticity: Scholarship, the Insight Movement, and White Authority." In *Methods in Buddhist Studies: Essays in Honor of Richard K. Payne*. Edited by Scott A. Mitchell and Natalie Fisk Quli, 154–172. London and New York: Bloomsbury Academic, 2019.

Rocha, Cristina, and Michelle Barker, eds. *Buddhism in Australia: Traditions in Change,"* London and New York: Routledge, 2011.

Salgado, Nirmala S. *Buddhist Nuns and Gendered Practice: In Search of the Female Renunciant*. Oxford and New York: Oxford University Press, 2013.

Seager, Richard Hughes. *The World's Parliament of Religions: The East/West Encounter, Chicago, 1893*. Bloomington and Indianapolis: Indiana University Press, 1995.

Tsomo, Karma Lekshe, "Buddhist Nuns and Gendered Practice: In Search of the Female Renunciant." *Journal of Global Buddhism* 16 (2015): 1–7, 4–5. http://www.globalbuddhism.org/jgb/index.php/jgb/issue/view/5Buddhist.

Turner, Alicia, Laurence Cox, and Brian Bocking, *The Irish Buddhist*. New York: Oxford University Press, 2020. Kindle ed.

Van Esterick, Penny. *Taking Refuge: Lao Buddhists in North America*. Tempe: SAS Arizona State University, 2003.

Wilson, Jeff. *Mindful America: The Mutual Transformation of Buddhist Meditation and American Culture*. Oxford and New York: Oxford University Press, 2014.

NOTES

1. Laurence Cox, "European Buddhist Traditions," in *The Oxford Handbook of Contemporary Buddhism*, ed. Michael Jerryson (Oxford: University Press, 2017): 332–349, 335; Laurence Cox, *Buddhism and Ireland: From the Celts to the Counter-Culture and Beyond* (Sheffield, UK: Equinox, 2013); Jørn Borup, "Who Are These Buddhists and How Many of Them Are There?," *Journal of Contemporary Buddhism* 31, no. 1 (2015): 85–100; and Jørn Borup, "Buddhism in Denmark," *Journal of Global Buddhism* 9 (2008): 32.
2. Nathalie E. F. Quli, "Laicization in Four Sri Lankan Temple in Northern California" (Dissertation, Faculty of the Graduate Theological Union, August 2010.8–2010.9); Wendy Cadge, *Heartwood: The First Generation of Theravada Buddhism in America* (Chicago and London: University of Chicago Press, 2005),

14; and Joseph Cheah, *Race and Religion in American Buddhism: White Supremacy and Immigrant Adaptation* (Oxford: Oxford University Press, 2011), 82.
3. Katarina Plank, "The Sacred Foodscapes of Thai Buddhist Temples in Sweden," *Religion and Food* 26 (2015): 201–224, 203.
4. Scott Mitchell, "Theravada Traditions," in *Buddhism in America: Global Religion, Local Contexts* (London and New York, 2016), 89–110, 97; and "Desperate Burmese Refugees Flee to Thailand and India to Escape Crisis," *The Guardian*, June 2, 2021.
5. Penny Van Esterick, *Taking Refuge: Lao Buddhists in North America* (Tempe: SAS Arizona State University, 2003), 5.
6. Marybeth White, "Lao Buddhism," in *Wild Geese: Buddhism in Canada*, ed. John S. Harding, Victor Sōgen Hori, and Alexander Soucy (Montreal and Kingston: McGill–Queen's University Press, 2010), 168–187, 175.
7. Caroline Starkey and Emma Tomalin, "Building Buddhism in England: The Flourishing of a Minority Faith Heritage," *Contemporary Buddhism* 17, no. 2 (2016), 326–356, 334.
8. Mitchell, "Theravada Traditions," 99–100.
9. Deba Mitra Barua, *Seeding Buddhism with Multiculturalism: The Transmission of Sri Lankan Buddhism in Toronto* (Montreal and Kingston: McGill–Queen's University Press, 2019), 36; Starkey and Tomalin, "Building Buddhism in England," 334.
10. Plank, Katarina, "The Sacred Foodscapes," *Religion and Food* 26 (2015), 201–224, 203, 205.
11. Paul David Numrich, *Old Wisdom in the New World: Americanization in Two Immigrant Theravada Buddhist Temples* (Knoxville: University of Tennessee Press, 1996), 3, 6.
12. Quli, "Laicization," 122; Cadge, *Heartwood*, 20; and Numrich, *Old Wisdom in the New World*, xxi.
13. Quli, "Laicization," 125.
14. Barua, *Seeding Buddhism*, 46.
15. Barua, *Seeding Buddhism*, 46–47.
16. Ceri Peach and Richard Gale, "Muslims, Hindus, and Sikhs in the New Religious Landscape of England," *Geographical Review* 93, no. 4: 469–490, 482–486; Starkey and Tomalin, "Building Buddhism," 334; and Borup, "Buddhism in Denmark," 28.
17. Jeffrey Samuels, "Is Merit in the Milk Powder? Pursuing *PUÑÑA* in Contemporary Sri Lanka," *Contemporary Buddhism* 9, no. 1 (2008): 123–147, 127.
18. Carol A. Mortland, *Cambodian Buddhism in America* (Albany, NY: SUNY, 2017), 140–143, 134–136. Google Play ed.; and Barua, *Seeding Buddhism*, 44–45.
19. Quli, "Laicization," 172–173.
20. Mortland, *Cambodian Buddhism*, 22–24; and Hiroko Kawanami, "The *Bhikkhunī* Ordination Debate: Global Aspirations, Local Concerns, with Special Emphasis on the Views of the Monastic Community in Burma," *Buddhist Studies Review* 24, no. 2 (2007): 226–244.
21. Mortland, *Cambodian Buddhism*, 136–139.
22. Quli, "Laicization," 176, 177; and Cheah, *Race and Religion*, 110–111.
23. Mortland, *Cambodian Buddhism*, 125.
24. Mortland, *Cambodian Buddhism*, 139–141.
25. Mortland, *Cambodian Buddhism*, 136–139.
26. Mortland, *Cambodian Buddhism*, 181–184.
27. Cheah, *Race and Religion*, 110–111.
28. Mortland, *Cambodian Buddhism*, 132–134
29. Mortland, *Cambodian Buddhism*, 132–134.
30. Quli, "Laicization," 177; Paul David Numrich, "Vinaya in Theravada Temples in the United States," *Journal of Buddhist Ethics* 1 (1994): 28–32, 27–28; and Quli, "Laicization," 177–178.

31. Walpola Piyananda, "The Difficulties of a Monk," The Pluralism Project; Quli, "Laicization," 179; and Barua, *Seeding Buddhism*, 44–45.
32. Richard Hughes Seager, *The World's Parliament of Religions: The East/West Encounter, Chicago, 1893* (Bloomington and Indianapolis: Indiana University Press, 1995), 157.
33. Chenxing Han, *Be the Refuge: Raising the Voices of Asian American Buddhists* (Berkeley, CA: North Atlantic Books, 2021), 71.
34. Han, *Be the Refuge*, 81–82.
35. Han, *Be the Refuge*, 82.
36. Cheah, *Race and Religion*, 102–109; and Mortland, *Cambodian Buddhism*, 59–61.
37. Barua, *Seeding Buddhism*, 145, 146.
38. Han, *Be the Refuge*, 80.
39. Quli, "Laicization," 251.
40. Mahinda Deegallee, "Promoting Buddhism in the UK: Sri Saddhatissa International Buddhist Centre's Contribution to British Buddhism," in *Dharma to the UK: A Centennial Celebration of Buddhist Legacy*, ed. Mahinda Deegalle (London: World Buddhist Foundation, 2008), 180–230; See also the websites for "Irish Sangha Trust,"; MYTOWN; The Rattanadipa Thai Buddhist Centre Baan Phra.
41. Cadge, *Heartwood*, 19.
42. Cadge, *Heartwood*, 25; Pattana Kitiarsa, "Missionary Intent and Monastic Networks: Thai Buddhism as a Transnational Religion," *Sojourn: Journal of Social Issues in Southeast Asia* 25, no. 1 (2010): 109.
43. Jiemin Bao, *Creating a Buddhist Community: A Thai Temple in Silicon Valley* (Philadelphia: Temple University Press, 2015). Kindle ed.
44. Van Esterick, *Taking Refuge*, 20–22.
45. Janet McLellan, "Buddhism in the Greater Toronto Area: The Politics of Recognition," in *Buddhism in Canada*, ed. Bruce Matthews (London and New York: Routledge, 2006), 85–105, 93; and see also Shiva Vasi, "Adaptation and Continuity in Cambodian Buddhist Temples: Implications for Service Delivery and Community Development," in *Buddhism in Australia: Traditions in Change*, ed. Cristina Rocha and Michelle Barker (London and New York: Routledge, 2011), 98–99.
46. McLellan, "Greater Toronto," *Buddhism in Canada*, 94.
47. Janet McLellan, *Cambodian Refugees in Ontario: Resettlement, Religion, and Identity* (Buffalo, NY: University of Toronto Press, 2009), 45; McLellan, "Greater Toronto," 95; White, "Lao Buddhism," 168–187, 172; and see also Louis-Jacques Dorais, trans. Eileen Reardon, *The Cambodians, Laotians and Vietnamese in Canada*, The Canadian Historical Association, Canada's Ethnic Group Series, Booklet 28, 8–9.
48. White, "Lao Buddhism," 173.
49. Mitchell, "Theravada Traditions," 99–100.
50. Mortland, *Cambodian Buddhism*, 89–92.
51. Mortland, *Cambodian Buddhism*, 96–98.
52. Mortland, *Cambodian Buddhism*, 118–120.
53. Mortland, *Cambodian Buddhism*, 117–119; and Mortland, *Cambodian Buddhism*, 120–121.
54. Carl L. Bankston, "Bayou Lotus: Theravada Buddhism in Southwestern Louisiana," *Sociological Spectrum* 17, no. 4 (1997): 453–472, 462; and Ruben G. Rumbaut, "Vietnamese, Laotians and Cambodian Americans," *Asian Americans: Contemporary Trends and Issues*, ed. Pyong Gap Min (Thousand Oaks, CA: Sage, 1995): 230–267, 239.
55. Carl L. Bankston III and Danielle Antoinette Hidalgo, "Temple and Society in the New World: Theravada Buddhism and Social Order in North America," in *North American Buddhists in Social Context*, ed. Paul David Numrich (Leiden, The Netherlands: Brill, 2008), 51–87, 64; and listings for "Wat Lao Worldwide Can Be Found at Wat Lao in the USA."
56. Bankston, "Bayou Lotus," 464.

57. McLellan, "Greater Toronto," 96.
58. Marybeth White, "Lao Buddhism in Toronto: A Case Study of Community Relations," in *Buddhism in Canada*, ed. Bruce Matthews (London and New York: Routledge, 2006), 105–120; and White, "Lao Buddhism," 168–187.
59. White, "Lao Buddhism," 175.
60. Sally McAra, "Buddifying Australia: Multicultural Capital and Buddhist Material Culture in Rural Victoria," in *Buddhism in Australia: Traditions in Change*, ed. Cristina Rocha and Michelle Barker (London and New York: Routledge, 2011), 69.
61. Adeana McNicholl, "Buddhism and Race in the United States," *Religion Compass* 15 no. 8 (August 2021): e12412. Provides a thorough overview.
62. "More Than 9,000 Anti-Asian Incidents Have Been Reported since the Pandemic Began,"NPR (National) August 12, 2021; Cheah, *Race and Religion*, 132; Han, Be the Refuge, 66; Cheah, *Race and Religion*, 81–82; and Cheah, *Race and Religion*, 86–87.
63. Cheah, *Race and Religion*, 88.
64. Cheah, *Race and Religion*, 12, 132–134; and also see Cheah, Joseph. "US Buddhist Traditions." in *The Oxford Handbook of Contemporary Buddhism*, ed. Michael Jerryson (OUP, 2016), 316-331, 329–330.
65. Mavis L. Fenn, "Buddhism," in *World Religions: Canadian Perspectives, Eastern Traditions*, ed. Doris R. Jakobsh and M. Darrol Bryant (Toronto: Nelson Education: 2013), 198; and Deba Mitra Barua and Mavis L. Fenn, "Community," in *The Buddhist World*, ed. John Powers (London and New York: Routledge, 2015), 386.
66. Janet McLellan, *Many Petals of the Lotus: Five Asian Buddhist Communities in Toronto* (Toronto: University of Toronto Press, 1999), 6, 192.
67. McLellan, *Many Petals*, 193.
68. Government of Canada, *Evaluation of the Multiculturalism Program 2011–12 to 2016–17* (Ottawa: Evaluation Services Directorate, March 29, 2018), 3;
69. Cy Gonick and Andrea Levy, "Barbara Perry on the Far Right in Canada," *Canadian* Dimension 51, no. 4 (Autumn–Winter 2017), cited in *Evaluation*, 3.
70. Greg Moreau, "Police-Reported Hate Crime in Canada 2019 (Canadian Centre for Justice and Community Safety Statistics)," *Statistics Canada* Catalogue no. 85-002-X (March 2021), 1.
71. Judith Snodgrass, "Defining Modern Buddhism: Mr. and Mrs. Rhys Davids and the Pali Text Society," in *Comparative Studies of South Asia, Africa and the Middle East* 27, no. 1 (2007): 186–202, 187.
72. Martin Baumann, "Buddhism in Europe: Past, Present, Prospects," in *Westward Dharma: Buddhism Beyond Asia*, ed. Charles S. Prebish and Martin Baumann (Berkeley: University of California Press, 2002), 85–106, 86.
73. Snodgrass, "Defining Modern Buddhism," 195–196.
74. Cox, "European Buddhist Traditions," 335.
75. Sandra Bell, "Being Creative with Tradition: Rooting Theravada Buddhism in Britain," *Journal of Global Buddhism* 1 (2000): 1–23, 12, 16–17.
76. Bell, "Being Creative," 13–15.
77. Bell, "Being Creative," 16, 17; and Kitiarsa, "Missionary Intent and Monastic Networks," 109.
78. Amaravati: History of the Monastery.
79. Bell, "Being Creative," 18–19; Bell, "Being Creative," 20; and Sandra Bell, "British Theravada Buddhism: Otherworldly Theories, and the Theory of Exchange," *Journal of Contemporary Religion* 13, no. 2 (1998): 149–170; and for North America, see Jeff Wilson, "Buddhism without Merit: Theorizing Buddhist Religio-Economic Activity in the Contemporary World," *Journal of Global Buddhism* 20 (2019): 87–104.
80. Bell, "Being Creative," 18.
81. Aloka Vihara Forest Monastery: History, Saranaloka Foundation.
82. Cadge, *Heartwood*, 35.

83. Cadge, *Heartwood*, 28–29; Jacqueline Mandell, "Portland Teacher Back to IMS for 40-Year Reunion," *NW Dharma News* 29, no. 3 (Fall 2016).
84. Cadge, *Heartwood*, 35.
85. David Bubna-Litic and Winton Higgins, "The Emergence of Secular Insight Practice in Australia," *Journal of Global Buddhism* 8 (2007): 157–173, 157–160; Bubna-Litic and Winton Higgins, "The Emergence of Secular Insight Practice in Australia," in *Buddhism in Australia: Traditions in Change*, ed. Cristina Rocha and Michelle Barker (Routledge, 2011), 23–25.
86. Cadge, *Heartwood*, 193; and Richard Hughes Seager, *Buddhism in America* (New York: Columbia University Press, 1999), 148.
87. Cheah, *Race and Religion*, 60; and Cheah, "US Buddhist Traditions," 322.
88. Jeff Wilson, *Mindful America: The Mutual Transformation of Buddhist Meditation and American Culture* (Oxford and New York: Oxford University Press, 2014).
89. Wilson, *Mindful America*, 46, 49, 54–55, 61–64.
90. Wilson, *Mindful America*, 192–194.
91. Jon Kabat-Zinn, *Coming to Our Senses: Healing Ourselves and the World through Mindfulness* (New York: Hyperion, 2005), 128; Wilson, *Mindful America*, 108–109; and David L. McMahon, *The Making of Buddhist Modernism* (New York: Oxford University Press, 2008), 261–263. Google Play ed.
92. Cox, *Buddhism and Ireland*, 372; and Katarina Plank, "Mindful Medicine: The Growing Trend of Mindfulness-Based Therapies in the Swedish Health Care System," *Finnish Journal of Ethnicity and Migration* 5, no. 2 (2010): 47–55.
93. McMahon, *The Making*, 254–256.
94. McMahon, *Buddhist Modernism*, 254–256; and see also Stephen Batchelor, *Buddhism without Beliefs: A Contemporary Guide to Awakening* (New York: Riverhead Books, 1997), 15–16.
95. Ann Gleig, *American Dharma: Buddhism beyond Modernity* (New Haven, CT, and London: Yale University Press, 2019), 270–271.
96. "Secular Buddhist Association: About: Guiding Principles," Secular Buddhist Association.
97. Gleig, *American Dharma*, 271, 272.
98. Charles S. Prebish, "The Cybersaṅgha: Buddhism on the Internet," in *Religion Online: Finding Faith on the Internet*, ed. Lorne L. Dawson and Douglas E. Cowan (New York and London: Routledge, 2004), 137–151; Louise Connelly, "Virtual Buddhism," in *The Changing World Religion Map: Changing Places, Identities, Practices and Politics*, ed. Stanley D. Brunn (Cham, Switzerland: Springer, 2015), 3869–3882, 204.1 "Introduction"; and Gleig, *American Dharma*, 5.
99. Gleig, *American Dharma*, 188–191. See her analysis of Buddhist geeks (now Meditate i.o), Ann Gleig, "From Buddhist Hippies to Buddhist Geeks: The Emergence of Buddhist Postmoderrnism," *Journal of Buddhist Ethics* 15 (2014): 15–33.
100. "Against the Stream Closes Doors as Investigation Finds Misconduct by Founder Noah Levine," *Tricycle* (August 27, 2018); "Refuge Recovery Splits,," Buddha Buzz Weekly: *Tricycle* (July 3, 2019); Dharma Punx NYC; "Against the Stream Meditation Center: Upcoming Classes and Retreats"; and Vincent Horn,"Making Meditation Modular," Medium.com.
101. McMahon, *The Making*, 256–261.
102. McMahon, *The Making*, 35–37.
103. Cheah, "Buddhism, Race, and Ethnicity," in *The Oxford Handbook of Contemporary Buddhism*, ed. Michael Jerryson (OUP, 2016), 650–661, 655.
104. McNicholl, "Buddhism and Race in the United States" ; and Ann Gleig, "Buddhists and Racial Justice: A History," *Tricycle* (Trike Daily), July 24, 2020.
105. For example, "Gay Buddhist Sangha: About Us, and BIPOC Sangha, Insight Meditation Society"; Craig N. Hase, James C. Meadows, and Stephanie L. Budge, "Inclusion and Exclusion in the White Space: An Investigation of the Experiences of People of Color in a Primarily White American Meditation Community," *Journal of Global Buddhism* 20 (2019): 1–8, 7.

106. Hase, Meadows, and Budge, "Inclusion and Exclusion," 1.
107. Hase, Meadows, and Budge, "Inclusion and Exclusion," 14–15.
108. McMahon, *The Making*, 261–263.
109. Ann Gleig and Brenna Grace Artinger, "The #Buddhist Culture Wars: BuddhaBros, Alt-Right Dharma, and Snowflake Saṅghas," *Journal of Global Buddhism* 22, no. 1 (2021): 19–48, 19. Responses to writing on racism and abuse in Buddhism can be vitriolic: "Why Are White Buddhists So Angry?" and "Late Night Phone Alerts and Other Intrusions," Shiloh Project.
110. Nathalie E. F. Quli, "Western Self, Asian Other: Modernity, Authenticity, and Nostalgia for 'Tradition' in Buddhist Studies," *Journal of Buddhist Ethics* 16 (2009): 1–38, 10.
111. Tessa J. Bartholemeusz, *Women under the Bō Tree: Buddhist Nuns in Sri Lanka* (Cambridge, UK: Cambridge University Press, 1994), 186–189.
112. "Sakyadhita International Association of Buddhist Women."
113. Chatsumarn Kabilsingh, *Thai Women in Buddhism* (Berkeley, CA: Parallax Press, 1991), 85.
114. Steven Collins and Justin McDaniel, "Buddhist 'Nuns' (Mae Chi) and the Teaching of Pali in Contemporary Thailand," *Modern Asian Studies* 44, no. 6 (2010), 1373–1408, 1392n46.
115. Susanne Mrozik, "Sri Lankan Buddhist Nuns: Complicating the Debate over Ordination," *Journal of Feminist Studies in Religion* 36, no. 1 (2020): 33–49, 36.
116. Lisa J. Battaglia, "Becoming *Bhikkhunī*? *Mae Chis* and the Global Women's Ordination Movement," *Journal of Buddhist Ethics* 22 (2015): 25–62, 40–42.
117. Battaglia, "Becoming *Bhikkhunī*," 38.
118. Battaglia, "Becoming *Bhikkhunī*," 52; and Collins and McDaniel, "Buddhist 'Nuns'," 1385.
119. Thea Mohr and Jampa Tsedron, eds., *Dignity and Discipline: Reviving Full Ordination for Buddhist Nuns* (Boston: Wisdom, 2010).
120. Antoinette Burton, *Burdens of History: British Feminists, Indian Women, and Imperial Culture, 1865–32* (Chapel Hill and London: University of North Carolina Press, 1994), 101; Nirmala S. Salgado, *Buddhist Nuns and Gendered Practice: In Search of the Female Renunciant* (Oxford and New York: Oxford University Press, 2013), 3–4.
121. Mrozik, "Buddhist Nuns," 44; Karma Lekshe Tsomo, "Review of *Buddhist Nuns and Gendered Practice: In Search of the Female Renunciant*, Nirmala S. Salgado (Oxford and New York: Oxford University Press, 2013)," *Journal of Global Buddhism* 16 (2015): 1–7.
122. Tsomo, *Buddhist Nuns*, 4–5.
123. Kawanami, "*Bhikkhunī* Ordination Debate: Global Aspirations, Local Concerns, with Special Emphasis on the Views of the Monastic Community in Burma Burma," *Buddhist Studies Review* 24, no. 2 (2007): 226–244, 229, 230, 237; and Elizabeth J. Harris, "Internal and External Authority among Lay Buddhist Women in Contemporary Sri Lanka," *Scottish Journal of Religious Studies* 18, no. 1 (1995): 51–75.
124. Kawanami, "*Bhikkhunī* Ordination Debate," 239.
125. Mrozik, "Buddhist Nuns," 37, 46; and Salgado, *Buddhist Nuns*, 153–161, 153, 159.
126. Fenn, "Buddhism," in *World Religions: Canadian Perspectives (Eastern Traditions)*," ed. Doris Jakobsh (Toronto: Nelson Education, 2013), 199.
127. Martin Seeger, "The Changing Roles of Thai Women: Obscuring Identity and increasing Charisma," *Religion Compass* 3, no. 5 (2009): 806–822, 809.
128. "Mission," Alliance for Bhikkhunis.
129. Alliance of Non-Himalayan Nuns, Dongyu Gatsal Ling Initiatives.
130. Charles Hallisey, "Roads Taken and Not Taken in the Study of Theravada Buddhism," in *Curators of the Buddha: The Study of Buddhism Under Colonialism*, ed. Donald S. Lopez Jr. (Chicago: University of Chicago Press, 1995).
131. Kate Crosby, "Changing the Landscape of Theravada Studies," *Contemporary Buddhism* 9, no. 1 (2008): 1–6.

132. Edward W. Said, *Orientalism*, 25th anniversary ed. (London: Penguin Books, 2007); Tomoko Masuzawa, "World Religions," in *Encyclopedia of Religion*, ed. Lindsay Jones, 2nd ed. (New York: MacMillan References U.S.A., 2005); Salgado, *Buddhist Nuns*; and Juliane Schober and Steven Collins, eds., *Theravada Buddhist Encounters with Modernity* (London and New York: Routledge, 2018).
133. Masuzawa, "World Religions"; and Salgado, *Buddhist Nuns*."
134. Charles S. Prebish, *American Buddhism* (North Scituate, MA: Duxbury Press, 1979), 51–52; "Two Buddhisms Reconsidered," *Buddhist Studies Review* 10, no. 2 (1993): 187–206; Charles S. Prebish, *Luminous Passage: The Practice and Study of Buddhism in America* (Berkeley: University of California Press, 1999), 57–63; Charles S. Prebish and Kenneth K. Tanaka, eds., *The Faces of Buddhism in America* (Berkeley: University of California Press, 1998); Jan Nattier, "Who Is a Buddhist? Charting the Landscape of Buddhist America," in *The Faces of Buddhism in America*, ed. Charles S. Prebish and Kenneth K. Tanaka (Berkeley: University of California Press, 1998), 183–196, 188–190; Rick Fields, "Divided Dharma; White Buddhists, Ethnic Buddhists, and Racism," in *The Faces of Buddhism in America*, ed. Charles S. Prebish and Kenneth K. Tanaka (Berkeley: University of California Press, 1998), 196–206; and Cheah, *Race and Religion*, 7.
135. Paul David Numrich, "Two Buddhisms Further Considered ," *Contemporary Buddhism* 4, no 1: 55–78.
136. Wakoh Shannon Hickey, "Two Buddhisms, Three Buddhisms, and Racism," *Journal of Global Buddhism* 11 (2010): 1–25. Revised in Scott A Mitchell and Natalie E. F. Quli, eds., *Buddhism beyond Borders: Perspectives in the United States of America* (Albany: State University of New York, 2015), 35–57; and see also, Han, *Be the Refuge*, esp. 147.
137. Natalie Fisk Quli, "On Authenticity: Scholarship, the Insight Movement, and White Authority," in *Methods in Buddhist Studies: Essays in Honor of Richard K. Payne*, ed. Scott A. Mitchell and Natalie Fisk Quli (London and New York: Bloomsbury Academic, 2019), 154–172.
138. Hase, Craig Nicholas, James C. Meadows, and Stephanie L. Budge, "Inclusion and Exclusion,"*Global Buddhism* 20 (2019): 1–18.
139. Cheah, "US Buddhist Traditions," 326.
140. Adeana McNicholl, "Buddhism and Race in the United States," *Religion Compass* 15, no.8 (August 2021): 1–13.
141. Joseph Cheah, "Buddhism, Race, and Ethnicity," in *The Oxford Handbook of Contemporary Buddhism*, ed. Michael Jerryson (OUP, 2016); and Chenzing Han, *Be the Refuge*; "Contesting 'Conversion' and 'Reversion' among Young Adult Asian American Buddhists," *Religions* 10 (2019): 261; "Diverse Practices and Flexible Beliefs Among Young Adult Asian American Buddhists," *Journal of Global Buddhism* 18 (2017): 1–24; "We're Not Who You Think We Are," *Asian American Policy Review* 29 (Spring 2019): 71–78, 94; Funie Hsu, "What Is the Sound of One Invisible Hand Clapping? Neoliberalism, the Invisibility of Asian and Asian American Buddhists, and Secular Mindfulness in Education," in *Handbook of Mindfulness. Mindfulness in Behavioral Health*, ed. Ronald E. Purser, David Forbes, and Adam Burke (Cham, Switzerland: Springer, 2016), 369–381; Funie Hsu|, "We've Been Here All Along," *Lion's Roar*, March 17, 2021; Jiemin Bao, *Marital Arts: Gender, Sexuality, and Identity Among the Chinese Diaspora* (Honolulu: University of Hawaii Press, 2004); and Jiemin Bao, "Merit-Making Capitalism: Re-territorializing Thai Buddhism in Silicon Valley, California," *Journal of Asian American Studies* 8, no. 2 (2005): 115–142.
142. Han, "We're Not Who You Think We Are," 71–78.
143. Hsu, "What Is the Sound of One Invisible Hand Clapping?," 369–381.
144. Gleig, *American Buddhism*, 281–304, originally published in the spring 2016 issue of *Buddhadharma: The Practitioner's Quarterly*.
145. David Lyon, *Jesus in Disneyland: Religion in Postmodern Times* (Cambridge, UK: Polity Press, 2000), 7; and Gleig, *American Dharma*, 8.
146. Gleig, *American Buddhism*, 289.

Mavis L. Fenn

GLOBALIZING TANTRIC BUDDHISM

INTRODUCTION

The historical spread of Buddhism can best be described as the extension of the nodes and strands of a network. "Globalization" is used here to identify the fact that over the last two centuries those networks have extended across the globe, bringing diverse communities in different countries into closer and more frequent contact than was previously possible. Thomas J. Csordas points out that globalization can also mean economic globalization, with religion being simply one commodity now traded internationally like any other. He argues, however, that it "is more productive to understand globalization from the outset as a multidimensional process, with religion, popular culture, politics, and economics as necessarily coeval and intimately intertwined, as they are in the lives of actors responsible for bringing about globalization in the first place."[1] Citing the work of Peter Berger, Linda Learman highlights "four cultural dimensions of the worldwide communication and economic integration called 'globalization': the cultures of international business, of the Western intelligentsia, of American popular tastes and values, and of Evangelical and Pentecostal Protestantism."[2] She then goes on to point out multidirectional flows, including Buddhist groups, that "are examples of transnational and cross-cultural movements resulting from and shaped by globalization but also making use of it."[3] Understanding the dynamics of Buddhism in the age of globalization requires a perspective different from the static conception of different kinds of Buddhism defined either by modern nation-states or by sectarian identity.

Thomas Tweed has argued that shifting the scholarly perspective to what he calls "translocative history" leads the historian to trace "non-linear" and "multidirectional cultural flows across multiple locales and reimagined historical periods."[4] Elsewhere Tweed notes that reimagining histories is not only an intellectual project, but also one with political implications. "Historical narratives, then, never are 'just' history. There always is a great deal at stake for narrators and readers, always much to gain and lose in power and meaning."[5] The familiar categories of nation-state and sect are not simply the ones in current use, but are entrenched in textbooks, syllabi, academic titles, departmental structures, institutional statements of purpose, categories used by funding agencies, and so on. Taken as simply the "natural" way to organize our thinking about Buddhism, they are hegemonic.

Globalization and modernization are two aspects of the same set of processes that have been reshaping the world for over two centuries. Globalization is sometimes contrasted nostalgically with an imagined past in which there was a natural integrity of religion and society. For example, following Anthony Giddens's work on modernization, Hans Kippenberg has claimed that

> the dynamic of modernity cut the old connection between space and time. All [religious] traditions became an object of radical examination and lost their usual embedding in space and time. This "alienation" meant that worldviews and norms that had once been valid only in certain geographical spaces and at certain times were now available beyond regions and beyond time. The global disembedding of all traditions was accompanied by a global reflection on modernization.[6]

This clearly articulates the links between globalization and modernization, and it employs the modern conception of religious traditions as distinct entities, separable from a sociocultural context. At the same time, it is necessary to question the implicit assumption that there is some kind of "naturally" embedded condition for traditions, an understanding that implies stability as the normal condition of religious traditions. Clearly in some cases dislocation and disruption have been violent and involuntary, such as the economically motivated diasporas of Chinese and Japanese laborers in the 19th and early 20th centuries and the flight of Tibetans—including the Dalai Lama—from the invasion of Tibet by China in 1959.[7] Conversely, however, other instances have been voluntary, as in the travels of missionaries and pilgrims. Considered broadly, the history of religion can be interpreted equally well under two different rubrics. Either the history of religion is marked by virtually constant movement, dislocation, and disruption, or it is marked by stability and permanence. Each interpretive framework is possible, each emphasizing and uncovering different moments and sequences of events. Either rubric implies a state of normalcy, in which the events not fitting that pattern are what stand out as requiring explanation.

GLOBALIZING BUDDHISM

The imperialistic structures of direct governance that were built up in the 19th century have fractured and collapsed throughout the 20th century and been replaced by economic and cultural imperialist structures of dominance. One of the consequences of these transformations has been the globalization of Buddhism. Peter Bishop describes one instance of globalization, revealing the complexity of the Western reception of Tibetan Buddhism. "The story of the Western reaction to Tibet and its religion is far wider than the limited circle of Buddhologists and Tibetologists. It embraces the concerns of imperialism, psychotherapy, science, theosophy and alternative religions, psychadelics [*sic*], adventure travel, explorations, mountaineering and the ecology movement."[8]

Until the middle of the 20th century, Buddhism was largely imported by cultural elites or as part of the culture of workers brought from China and Japan to work in the construction of the railroad system or in agriculture.[9] Around the middle of the 20th century, however, these patterns changed dramatically as postcolonial conditions created an influx of previously colonized peoples into the countries of their former colonizers, and as a cultural transformation within Europe and the Americas followed in the decades of recovery after World War II. Martin Baumann notes that since the middle of the 20th century "Buddhist groups and centers have flourished and multiplied to an extent never before observed during Buddhism's 150 years of dissemination outside of Asia."[10]

Shingon Buddhism and Tibetan Buddhism are followed here as significant strands of the network that continues to expand under globalization. While neither of these is exclusively tantric in nature, they are two of the traditions that have globalized tantric Buddhist praxes. These are not, of course, equivalent categories. While Shingon is the name of a specific Japanese sect of tantric Buddhism, Tibetan Buddhism designates a geopolitical, ethnic, and linguistic category. Burkhard Scherer adds the category of identity, explaining that "contemporary Tibetan Buddhism can be seen as a patchwork of disparate yet linked religious identities and observances resulting from the multi-layered process of change, which started with the communist Chinese occupation of Tibet in the 1950s."[11] Following the Chinese occupation of the country of Tibet, the category has become complex for Buddhist studies, requiring greater specificity—is it being used to identify a geography, a political entity, a society, a culture, a language, a religious tradition? In contrast, when used by converts and adherents who are not ethnically Tibetan, "Tibetan Buddhist" is clearly a marker of religious identity.[12]

SHINGON MISSION: UNITED STATES AND BRAZIL

Like many of the Japanese Buddhist organizations in the United States, the Shingon Mission was established as a consequence of economically motivated outmigration from Japan beginning toward the end of the 19th century.[13] Reforms by the Meiji government (1868–1912) resulted in many peasants losing their land and going abroad to work as laborers. Effectively ethnic churches, these served the first generation of immigrants and their descendants, who are known as issei, nisei, and sansei, that is, first, second, and third generations. Since most Japanese were involved in agriculture, many churches were rural as well as ethnically based. The exceptions, located in urban centers with large Japanese communities, such as Los Angeles and Sacramento, have survived political storms and demographic tides. However, many smaller temples—both rural and urban—have not.

In Los Angeles, the Koyasan Buddhist Temple was established as a fellowship of adherents devoted to Kūkai, an *O Daishi kyokai*, in 1912 by Reverend Shutai Aoyama.[14] He had originally gone to San Francisco in 1909, intending to provide religious services to the immigrant Japanese community. But after arriving, he fell ill and medical costs used up his resources. He then worked as a laborer until arriving in Los Angeles, where with the assistance of members of the local Japanese community he was able to establish the Kūkai fellowship. The name was changed to Koyasan Beikoku Betsuin of Los Angeles (*betsuin* indicating a direct branch temple) in 1935, when it was given official recognition by Kongōbuji, head temple of the Chūin ryū lineage of Shingon, located on Kōyasan. The church continued to grow and eventually moved to a new location at 342 East First Street, Los Angeles. A year and a half later came Japan's attack on Pearl Harbor, and Japanese individuals—whether citizens of the United States or not—were relocated to camps away from the coast.[15]

It would be more than three years before temple members were able to return to their homes and re-establish the temple. Los Angeles County officials then announced that having been used to store members' property for the duration of the incarceration, the temple had lost its religious function and therefore owed property taxes of $5,000.[16] A decade later the temple was finally able to pay off this debt, ironically with donations coming from members who had received reparations payments from the US government.[17] In 2012, the temple celebrated its centennial, under the direction of now Bishop Emeritus Taisen Miyata.[18] The Koyasan Buddhist Temple remains an active part of the Japanese American Buddhist community in the greater Los Angeles area and is one of the members of the Los Angeles Buddhist Temple Federation.[19] However, not all Shingon temples survived through the 20th century.

Elizabeth Eastman has noted the apparent contradiction between the rising popular interest in Buddhism during the last third of the 20th century and the decline—and indeed extinction—of many immigrant temples of long standing. Her research into her own family's involvement with the Oregon Koyasan Shinnoin Temple was "a search to rediscover a lost community and to find out why it failed to flourish in America's inclusive religious environment."[20]

Shinnoin was founded in 1951 by a splinter group from the Henjoji Temple in Portland, which itself dated from 1946. Eastman's great-grandparents were active in establishing the new temple, which had its prime during the 1950s, 1960s, and 1970s, when there were "as many as a hundred people at its rituals and celebrations."[21] Eastman identifies several issues involved in the decline of Shinnoin. In addition to economic strains created by the temple being dependent on donations alone because it had no endowment, generational transmission was not actively pursued. Second- and third-generation children of members were not involved in temple activities, except to provide assistance with celebrations and other events. Not developing an English program for services also contributed to the failure of generational transmission. Priests "were always sent directly from Japan and spoke very little English, but since the majority of members were *issei* [first generation, i.e., native speakers] they didn't see this as a problem."[22] However, this kept the second- and third-generation children of the membership who were not native speakers of Japanese at a distance. "The situation was essentially a vicious spiral in which there weren't enough youth to justify special programming and no special programming to interest youth."[23]

As with many of the Japanese immigrant temples, the temple served as a way of maintaining cultural identity. While this had been important for the first generation, it became increasingly dysfunctional, hindering the ability of the temple organization to adapt to a wider audience when the time came that the first-generation membership was shrinking due to old age and death.[24] Ownership of Shinnoin's building had never been formally transferred to the temple body, and so when the temple closed, the building reverted to its original private owners.

The temple from which Shinnoin split, Henjoji (Daihonzan Henjyoji Temple), located in downtown Portland, remains active as of 2021.[25] Reverend Kosho Finch is currently the temple's head of ministry. Previously, Reverend Finch had been responsible for Hosshinji, another temple in the Portland area, but with his responsibilities at Henjoji, development of that temple has been postponed. Indicative of the temple's expansive intent, the Foundation for Shingon Buddhism provides an umbrella organization, including an affiliate chapter of Hosshinji in Honolulu. Under Reverend Finch's leadership, Henjoji was working to expand membership and to renovate its current building. That building itself dates from the 1890s and became the temple's home in 1951.[26] The changes evidenced by the history of Shingon in the Portland area—decline and dissolution of Shinnoin, and efforts to rebuild a temple community at Henjoji—are also evident in the Shingon Mission in Brazil.[27]

Historically, Brazil experienced two periods of immigration from Japan, one before World War II and the second between 1952 and 1965.[28] Reverend Shinba arrived in Brazil in 1934, founding a temple that was at first independent but later became a branch of the Kōyasan lineage of Shingon, that is, Chūin-ryū. At the time of his research (2003), Rafael Shoji reports that there were six Shingon temples in Brazil, the headquarters temple being Koyasan Koyaji in São Paulo. Shoji notes that "the risk of extinction exists in the majority of these temples, because the immigrants and priests are very old and many descendants are not interested in the continuity of temple activities."[29] This is the same kind of dynamic that Eastman notes had led to the decline and eventual disappearance of Shinnoin in Portland.

By contrast, Shoji highlights one temple that is quite active. Located in Suzano outside São Paulo, it is known as the "Church Shingonshu Kongoji." The adherents of this temple contrast sharply with the stereotypic image of convert Buddhists in the United States. While the latter are typically upper middle class and highly educated, most of Church Shingonshu Kongoji's adherents are lower to middle class. Generally interested in the worldly benefits that Shingon can provide—spiritual curing of karmic problems—they have little interest in meditation or Buddhist thought.

Shoji explains that both a lack of information about Shingon in Portuguese and the long-standing tendency toward syncretism in Brazil contribute to a willingness on the part of adherents to blend Shingon with other religious traditions. "As a result, the practice of Shingon with other Brazilian or New Age religions through resemblance and juxtaposition, is not understood as mutually exclusive. On the contrary, a magical worldview is the common ground of these practices, illustrating a combination that characterizes syncretism in its more strict sense."[30] A similar connection is made in some modern Chinese tantric groups with the practices of feng shui, or with 19th-century European esoterism.

TWO SOURCES OF CHINA'S TANTRIC REBIRTH MOVEMENT

Tantric Buddhism in its Tibetan form was introduced to China during the Yuan dynasty (Mongol, 1280 to 1368 CE).[31] Through the next two dynasties, Ming (1368–1644) and Qing (1636–1912), contact with Tibet continued via centers of study and practice. They were, however, "mainly visited by Tibetan and Mongolian monks and laymen, and, even if the Imperial Court showed at times interest in them, nonetheless their influence on the Chinese Buddhist world was irrelevant."[32] The Qing Dynasty continued to propagate the Tibetan form for political reasons as part of the dynasty's imposition of a "political hierarchical structure in the triangular interrelationship between the Qing, Tibet, and Mongolia."[33] Despite dynastic support, Tibetan forms of Buddhism never became a significant influence outside the Tibetan and Mongolian cultural areas, although during the Qing, as well as the Republic (1912–1949) era, some Chinese intellectuals did begin to study tantric Buddhism.[34] Especially at the end of the Republican era, interest in Buddhism in general increased.[35] Similarly, tantric Buddhism was reintroduced to mainland China from Japan during the Republican era. Though this had little lasting impact in mainland China, it did provide a basis for later developments in Taiwan, as will be discussed.[36]

These developments at the beginning of the 20th century are part of a more general "Buddhist rebirth movement" in early modern China. Martino Dibeltulo traces the origins of this reform movement, and the recovery of tantric Buddhism, to "the aftermath of the destruction of Buddhist images, scriptures, and temples that occurred in southeast China at the time of the Opium Wars" (1839–1842 and 1856–1860).[37] During the Republican era there were groups who focused on reviving not just Chinese Buddhism more generally, but also tantric Buddhism specifically.[38] This interest in re-establishing the Chinese school of tantric Buddhism was not infrequently promoted as a way to reclaim the glory of Tang era esoteric Buddhism

(Tangmi). Those involved in these efforts turned to two sources, Japan and Tibet, as either retaining Tang era tantra in the case of Japan or as holding a more developed form in the case of Tibet.

Looking to Shingon. Dibeltulo identifies 1880 as the year in which Chinese interest in re-establishing tantric Buddhism began.[39] In that year Yang Wenhui visited London and then began a correspondence with Nanjō Bunyū, who became an advisor to Yang. Nanjō introduced Yang to philology and to the idea of a scientific approach to the history of Buddhism. One consequence was that Yang translated the *Hasshū-kōyō* by Gyōnen (1240–1321), which presents the eight principal Buddhist schools of Japan when it was written in 1268.[40] One of the eight schools that Gyōnen discusses is Shingon. "During the Republican Period, Gyōnen's compelling account of *Mizong* ['esoteric Buddhism,' tantra] inspired in Yang Wenhui's students the quest of this tradition."[41]

Contact between Chinese Buddhists interested in re-establishing tantric Buddhism and the Shingon tradition in Japan moved to a new level in the 1920s. A key issue, beyond making information about Japanese tantric Buddhism (*mikkyō*) available in Chinese translation, was the transmission of initiations, *abhiṣekas,* that had been discontinued in China. In order to assure proper transmission, Taixu sent one of his disciples, Dayong, to Kōyasan. Being himself an ordained monk, and having received tantric initiations while on Kōyasan, after returning from Japan Dayong began to give initiations in 1924.[42] Dayong later died during an expedition to Lhasa to pursue Tibetan tantric Buddhism, but his disciple, Fazun (1902–1980), "would become the greatest translator of Buddhist scriptures from Tibetan into Chinese."[43] At the end of the 20th century the tantric rebirth movement in Taiwan again turned to Japanese tantric Buddhism with much the same rationale as previously on the mainland: reclaiming the Tang era tradition of Chinese tantra.

One consequence of Japanese influence throughout East Asia from the end of the 19th into the first half of the 20th century was the spread of specific conceptions of institutionalization. As Cody Bahir explains,

> Buddhist sectarian consciousness in the Sinosphere has been greatly influenced by relatively rigid Japanese Buddhist denominational boundaries that solidified during the Tokugawa Period (1603–1868). These boundaries are articulated *via* the terms "school" (*zong*) and "lineage" (*liu*). Often "school" represents an over-arching denominational identity that consists of multiple "lineages."[44]

Bahir argues that despite "the fact that the well-demarcated boundaries that this framework offers have never reflected common perception and are in fact a product of East Asian appropriations of Western religious boundaries, they have shaped both religionist and scholarly understandings of Buddhist sectarianism."[45] Jimmy Yu has pointed out that the processes of globalization that brought Western Christian missionaries to Japan introduced modern European conceptions of what constitutes a religion, that is, as a "discrete universal category of human endeavor, separable from science and politics."[46] The term used for religion "was initially a Japanese neologism crafted during this time and was used to express a Western idea that had not existed in East Asian discourses before—an idea that referred to the post-Reformation sense of systems of doctrine organized as churches separate from the state."[47] This post-Reformation conception of religion then combined with Japanese conceptions of sectarian identity. This hybridized concept in turn influenced the Taiwanese movements being considered here.

One of the contemporary sects of the tantric rebirth movement that is oriented toward Japanese tantric Buddhism is the Mantra School Bright Lineage (MSBL) in Taiwan.[48] The sect is very eclectic, drawing together influences of Western esotericism from the late 19th century, as well as Shingon rituals. As with the interest in tantric Buddhism in late-19th-century China, the rationale behind Wuguang's creation of the MSBL sect is the reclamation of Tang dynasty Zhenyan. In other words, the MSBL is presented as a continuation of the lost medieval Chinese tradition, conceived as having been preserved in Japanese Shingon, rather than as a branch of Shingon. "Since Zhenyan's orthodox initiation chain disappeared from China after it had been transmitted to Japan by Kūkai, Chinese devotees had to venture outside the confines of Chinese Buddhism if they wanted to study orthodox forms of esoteric Buddhism."[49]

One of the Tibetan masters to propagate Tibetan Buddhism in China during the tantric rebirth movement was Gangkar Rinpoche (1893–1957), a Karma Kagyu master. His disciple, Elder Gongga (1903–1997), left China in 1958 and moved to Taiwan where she worked to spread the teachings and practices of her lineage. The founder of MSBL, Wuguang (1918–2000), was briefly her disciple in 1960, but he soon broke his affiliation with her. Seeking his own dharma transmission, he went to Kōyasan in 1971, where he received ordination as a Shingon *ācārya* (Jpn. *ajari*).[50] With this authority he began initiating his own disciples himself in Taiwan, rather than sending them to Kōyasan for ordination. This led to a breach with the Shingon authorities, such that MSBL ordinands are not recognized by Kōyasan.[51] The importance of lineal authority led Wuguang to develop a number of intersemiotic connections intended to link MSBL directly to Chinese Zhenyan, rather than to the lineage as deriving through Japan. This strategy "was executed by employing pre-existing techniques that are widely used to legitimate Buddhist sectarian identity and authority."[52]

The tantric rebirth movement led from Taixu, through the Tibetan Karma Kagyu master Gangkar Rinpoche coming to China, to his disciple Elder Gonggan, who moved to Taiwan, and then to Wuguang. However, instead of following the Tibetan strain of authority, Wuguang turned to Japan. This set of nodes and strands led to a different outcome with one of Wuguang's own initiates, Guru Chesheng, who founded the Zhenyan Samantabhadra Lineage.

Looking to Tibet. The second of the two strains of the tantric rebirth movement turned to Tibet as a source of teachings and practices. Europeans and Americans are not the only ones to be fascinated by Tibetan Buddhism. Since the time of the Manchus, who not only made the Gelug sect the politically predominant form in Tibet itself but also installed a large contingent of Gelug monks in what is known today as "the Lama temple" to serve as their own religious functionaries, Tibetan Buddhism has been present in Beijing. Visiting Beijing at the beginning of the 21st century, I found the Lama temple to be one of the most crowded, not only with ethnic Tibetans and other minorities, but also with many Han Chinese, as well as European and American tourists. Much of what was being sold in the stalls outside the temple was either of Tibetan origin or at least inspired by Tibetan motifs. Later, in several shops we found many Tibetan curios for sale, items such as small statues of Tara. This fascination with Tibetan

Buddhism is found in expatriate Chinese communities in Asia and the West as well.[53] According to Khenpo Sodargye and Dan Smyer Yü, "Tibetan Buddhism is one of the fastest growing religions among Chinese in the twenty-first century."[54] John Powers notes, however, that "in contemporary China, there is no more sensitive topic than Tibet."[55] Although there are many negative stereotypes of Tibet and Tibetans that circulate in Chinese society, at the same time the Chinese *imaginaire* of Tibetan Buddhism is both an object of fascination and a source of authority.

In contemporary Chinese global society, several sects claim descent through the Tibetan side of the tantric rebirth movement. These include Black Sect esoteric Buddhism, the True Buddha School, Yogi Chen, and the Zhenyan Samantabhadra Lineage.

Black Sect Esoteric Buddhism. This group claims to be founded on the basis of Bon, by which they mean a pre-Buddhist indigenous Tibetan tradition. The claim is that the Bon tradition stretches back 18,000 years and is the first stage of the development of Black Sect esoteric Buddhism.[56] Through intervening stages, the fourth stage arrived when Grandmaster Lin Yun brought the sect to the West. When Grandmaster Lin Yun passed away in 2010, his successor Khadro Crystal Chu Rinpoche brought the sect into its fifth stage of development. Indicative of the syncretic character of the sect, and similar to the kind of syncretism discussed by Shoji in Brazil, much of the focus of Black Sect esoteric Buddhism is on feng shui. The sect provides feng shui consultations, paraphernalia from its "feng shui shop," and feng shui trainings.

True Buddha School. Headquartered in Seattle at the Ling Shen Ching Tze Temple, the True Buddha School claims descent through Tibetan Buddhism. Specifically, Grand Master Lu Sheng-Yen (also known as Living Buddha Lian-Sheng) claims to have "attained the highest fruition in all four orders" of Tibetan Buddhism—Dzogchen (Nyingma), Mahāmudrā and the Six Yogas of Naropa (Kagyu), Great Completion (Sakya), and Yamantaka (Gelug).[57] His teachings are described as "a potent and life transforming mixture of Taoist, Sutrayana and Tantrayana practices, empowering His disciples to transform their life's issues into positivity on the path toward enlightenment."[58]

Lian Shen claims that he is the emanation of Padmakumara (Lotus Bodhisattva), and the sect's website explains that "actually, the body of Living Buddha Lian-shen is that of Buddha Amitabha, his speech that of Bodhisattva Maitreya, his mind that of Buddha Shakyamuni, and his hands those of Vajrapani. Therefore, as Padmasambhava had predicted, Living Buddha Lian-shen is the Vajra Emanation of the Body, Mind, and Speech of all Buddhas and Bodhisattvas."[59] The reference to Padmasambhava signifies that, while Lian Shen acknowledges having five human tantric masters, "the most direct teachings he has received are the Tantric Dharma Practices transmitted to him by Padmasambhava."[60] This claim to authority effectively jumps over any intervening system of initiatory legitimation to claim direct authority from Padmasambhava. Indicative of the international scope of the school, and the use of new technologies, remote empowerments are now considered normal.[61] "The Empowerments for Initiation, Four Preliminary Practices, Padmakumara Vajra Yoga, Personal Deity Yoga, and Karma Yoga can be obtained through remote empowerment."[62] Higher initiations, "Dharma Protector (or Wrathful Deity) Yoga," however, require a personal meeting with the guru. Similarly, the Mantra School Bright Lineage discussed above employs remote empowerments as well.[63]

Yogi Chen. Yogi Chen (1906–1987), who also looked to Tibet, can be seen as representative of the effect of the tantric rebirth movement on an individual practitioner. Yogi Chen's life story reveals the complexity of the networks of 20th-century globalizing Buddhism.[64] His autobiography is structured into the four categories used in Tibetan life-writing works: outer, inner, secret, and most secret.[65] Not only is his autobiography structured in this traditional fashion, but he interprets his life experiences in parallel with doctrinal understandings. Speaking in the third person, he recounts a miraculous birth, saying that the "young Chen was born covered by an unbroken placenta and so undefiled by the mother blood." He says that he had an auspicious dent in his forehead, located where we would call the "third eye." His mother developed a second pair of breasts, and he took nourishment from all four. Despite these auspicious signs, his early life was marked by discord and violence in the family. Additionally, in the course of his childhood, several of his siblings died, as did his grandfather, and thus he knew the first Noble Truth, suffering, from personal experience.

The inner biography tells of his education, and of meeting Venerable Taixu, who was a "key figure in supporting Tibetan Buddhism in China."[66] Taixu was instrumental in the formation of the tantric rebirth movement, as well as being considered the founder of humanistic Buddhism.[67] In his secret biography, Yogi Chen tells us that the "Dakini of Heruka" told him to go to Sichuan (the Kham region of traditional Tibet) in order to receive teachings. Over the course of five years in the Tibetan cultural region of China and in Tibet as such he received several empowerments and teachings from various schools of Tibetan Buddhism. In closing his most secret biography, he says he regrets that he has not completed the four conditions of an ideal Buddhist, and he gives a poem structured around the four parts of his autobiography:

> Outwardly we must appear poor and be content with little.
> Inwardly, flourishes the Bodhicitta.
> Secretly, we must have a lot of great joy, in third initiation.
> And Most Secretly, the Chan Liberated attitude.[68]

He relocated to Kalimpong in 1947, where he stayed until 1974, then moved to the United States, developing a following in the Berkeley, Oakland, and Emeryville area of California. The global network connecting China, Tibet, and India eventually brought his version of Tibetan tantric Buddhism filtered through Chinese cultural categories to the immigrant Chinese communities of the greater San Francisco Bay Area.

Zhenyan Samantabhadra Lineage. This school was established by Guru Chesheng (b. 1938), who was himself initiated by Wuguang of the Mantra School Bright Lineage discussed above. While this initially placed him on the Japanese side of the tantric rebirth movement, Chesheng moved to establish his own lineage, independent from Wuguang's MSBL. Because of the problematics of MSBL claims to legitimacy, this additional breach meant even greater issues for Chesheng. While one aspect of his authority derives from his initiation by Wuguang, Chesheng also emphasizes links to Tibetan tantric Buddhism. As Bahir explains,

> in order to prominently display this additional Tibetan inheritance, Chesheng has incorporated aspects from Elder Gongga's teachings into the orthopraxis, symbolism, liturgy

and even history of the Samantabhadra Sect. Thus, the weakness of the chain that links Chesheng to Tang dynasty Zhenyan has been strengthened by the presence of another, the Tibetan Karma Kagyü school.[69]

One source of legitimation is a set of dreams that Chesheng reports, dreams in which he is shown that although he did not receive dharma transmission directly from Elder Gongga, he is in fact her dharma heir. The dream sequence originates with a buddha, moves to a set of patriarchs, and concludes with Elder Gongga giving Chesheng the scroll on which his authority is recorded. Because Chesheng was presented a scroll in the last part of his dream sequence Bahir interprets these dreams as at least analogous to Tibetan *terma*, that is, texts that were hidden by earlier teachers and only later revealed to qualified recipients. "This chain of communication renders Chesheng a transmission holder of the Karma Kagyü school of Tibetan Buddhism and a Dharma-heir of Elder Gongga."[70] Significant cultural practices move through the nodes and strands of the network, even beyond the direct transmission of initiations or doctrinal teachings.

GLOBAL TIBET

Mark Juergensmeyer has outlined three kinds of religious globalization: "diasporas, transnational religions, and the religions of plural societies."[71] Much of Tibetan Buddhism now on the global stage originates in diaspora, although it has moved in the last half century to become a transnational religion. Stephen C. Berkwitz explains that some "one million Tibetans were internally displaced during the Chinese expansion into Tibet between 1949 and 1959, and tens of thousands of them left Tibet for India, Nepal, and Bhutan to escape political and religious persecution."[72] The category "Tibetan Buddhism" is a modern formation of scholarly and journalistic discourse. And, although it is widely used, "Tibetan Buddhism" is too vague a term to be useful for substantive analysis of the globalization of tantric traditions per se. Individual sectarian forms that have successfully maintained and propagated tantric praxes on the global horizon, however, are instances of a "negotiated transnational religious organization," in Peggy Levitt's terminology.[73] Levitt describes such organizations as flexible and decentralized, which requires them to negotiate "with respect to authority, organization, and ritual. There is generally no one leader or administrative hierarchy to set policy and dictate how things are done. A more diverse, dilute set of partnerships emerges that are malleable and shift over time."[74]

The Foundation for the Preservation of the Mahayana Tradition (FPMT) is an instance of an "extended transnational religious organization." Although not headquartered in Tibet, FPMT does operate to "broaden and deepen a global religious system that is already powerful and legitimate."[75]

FPMT: Foundation for the Preservation of the Mahayana Tradition. One of the institutional consequences of globalization is the creation of the "transnational enterprise."[76] The Foundation for the Preservation of the Mahayana Tradition is one such transnational enterprise, comprised of an international network, categorized into centers, projects, and services.[77] It was initiated in 1975 by two Gelug monks, Lama Thubten Yeshe (1935–1984) and Lama Thubten Zopa.

Hugh Urban has characterized the way that Hindu tantra has been appropriated in the West as "largely as a form of spiritual hedonism."[78] Urban has also emphasized that "tantra is a highly variable and shifting category, whose meaning may differ depending on the particular historical moment, cultural milieu, and political context."[79] Glenys Eddy picks up on this latter point, that tantra "cannot be viewed as a unitary religious phenomenon," in order to emphasize that the tantric praxis of the FPMT is organized in a form that, contrary to Urban's generalization, cannot be characterized as a form of spiritual hedonism.[80] Based on a study of the practices of one FPMT center, the Vajrayana Institute in Sydney, Australia, Eddy points to the way in which tantric practice is nested within a larger Mahāyāna context. Particularly, two sets of teachings are emphasized at the Vajrayana Institute.[81] The first is the six perfections of the bodhisattva: generosity (*dāna*), morality (*śīla*), patience (*kṣānti*), courage (*vīrya*), meditation (*dhyāna*), and insight (*prajñā*). The second set is described as the "three principal aspects of the path: renunciation, bodhicitta, and wisdom–realizing–emptiness."[82] Eddy points out that with the exception of three of the modules of the eighteen-month-long introductory course, "FPMT does not hold teachings or courses specifically on Tantra."[83] Those modules are intentionally general enough so as to not provide details about tantric practices. Indeed, within the community membership, "the Tantric practitioners do not make themselves obvious."[84]

The international scope of the FPMT is reflected in the construction projects that it has launched. One of the projects initiated by Lama Thubten Zopa, head of FPMT, that would place FPMT prominently, and literally, on the landscape of Australia is the "Great Stupa of Universal Compassion."[85] A similar project promoted by FPMT, the construction of an image of Maitreya over 500 feet tall in Kushinagar, has, however, "made little progress over the past forty years."[86] More recently the thirty-nine-foot-tall Mahabodhi stupa being built in the Santa Cruz Mountains in California's central coast has made significant progress. This is part of a vision of building 100,000 large stupas around the world.[87] Because of the benefits that stupa construction is understood to provide, protection for California's coast from earthquakes in the case of the Mahabodhi stupa, these are considered part of the FPMT's charitable undertakings.[88] In addition to building stupas and monasteries, the foundation provides support for monks and nuns, liberating animals, supporting the elderly, and educational projects.[89]

FPMT is an example of the extended transnational religious organizations that have been the main institutional vehicles for propagating Tibetan tantric Buddhism globally. There are several other such organizations and networks that also function in this fashion. Here several individual teachers representing a variety of Tibetan lineages will be mentioned, as well as the widespread practice of Dzogchen. While each organization includes a variety of activities and projects, this section focuses on the tantric dimensions of each, rather than attempting to give a full picture of the institution.

Tenzin Gyatso, His Holiness the Fourteenth Dalai Lama: Tantra in Global Gelug. The Fourteenth Dalai Lama, Tenzin Gyatso (b. 1935), is perhaps the most widely recognized Buddhist figure on the world mediascape. His flight from Lhasa to India following the Chinese incursion into Tibet in 1959 is not only the stuff of legend but serves as a marker for the modern globalization of Tibetan tantra. In previous centuries the connections between Tibet and both China and Mongolia may be taken as earlier instances of globalization, but this article focuses on the modern, postcolonial era.

The Government of Tibet in Exile established headquarters in Dharamsala, India, and began to provide services to the Tibetan community in exile. In addition to a variety of charitable, cultural, and educational endeavors, some 200 monasteries and nunneries were re-founded outside Tibet. The major training monasteries, Ganden, Drepung, and Sera, were relocated in Karnataka in South India.[90] The Dalai Lama ritually prepared for the construction of Sera Monastery at Bylakuppe with a Kālacakra initiation in 1971.[91] The Dalai Lama's personal monastery, Namgyal, "is the foremost institution of the Kālacakra teachings, being responsible for creating the intricate sand mandala and providing other ritual support at each initiation that His Holiness gives."[92] Internationally, the Dalai Lama has given several trainings and initiations that are tantric in character, and he has published several works on these topics. These include, for example, the Kālacakra initiation in 1981 at Deer Park, near Madison, Wisconsin,[93] as well as the 2004 initiation in Toronto, to be discussed below as an instance of global contestation of tantric practices. His publications include many books on tantra, including a three-volume commentary on Tsongkhapa's *Great Exposition of Secret Mantra,* as well as works on the tantric meditative traditions of Dzogchen and Mahāmudrā.[94]

Correlated with the Dalai Lama's high profile is the extensive influence of the Gelug school. Particularly influential in this regard has been Robert Thurman, of Columbia University, who was, for example, instrumental in the campaign for the Dalai Lama to receive the Nobel Peace Prize. The American Institute of Buddhist Studies (AIBS), which is affiliated with Columbia University and its Center for Buddhist Studies, has undertaken an ambitious program of translating the Tengyur (*bstan gyur,* a section of the Tibetan Buddhist Canon).[95] This project has led to the publication of several important tantric texts in both translation and critical editions, and also commentaries on tantras.[96]

Dzongsar Khyentse: Rimé Movement and Tantra. Some of the influential figures in contemporary global Tibetan tantra may be understood as propagating a nonsectarian or intersectarian approach to Tibetan Buddhism that inspired the Rimé (*ris med,* lit. "unbiased") movement. The intention of the movement, which originated in eastern Tibet in the 19th century, was to revitalize tantric lineage traditions that had lost prominence in Tibet in order to promote greater freedom and openness between sectarian traditions. The tantric practices were collected by figures such as Jamyang Khyentse Wangpo (1820–1892), who inspired the movement, and Jamgon Kongtrul (1813–1899), and five later incarnations (*tulku, sprul sku*) continue the lineage.[97] The tantric dimension of the Rimé movement continues today with figures such as Dzongsar Khyentse.

"84,000: Translating the Words of the Buddha," established by Dzongsar Khyentse, is another translation project that, like the AIBS, makes tantric texts (along with sutras and commentaries) available in English translation. This project was initiated following a meeting of translators in 2009, which had been funded by the Khyentse Foundation. The goal of translating the entire Tibetan canon, both Kangyur and Tengyur, is projected forward for a hundred years, and 2020 marked the ten-year anniversary of the project. As of this anniversary, thirty-two tantric texts had been published in English translation.[98] As with other publication projects that make tantric texts available, these are marked by a warning, which in this case states:

> Readers are reminded that according to Vajrayāna Buddhist tradition there are restrictions and commitments concerning tantra.

> Practitioners who are not sure if they should read translations in this section are advised to consult the authorities of their lineage.
>
> The responsibility for reading these texts or sharing them with others—and hence the consequences—lies in the hands of readers.[99]

The Khyentse Foundation has also initiated the Kumarajiva Project, the goal of which is to translate Tibetan canonic materials into Chinese, supplementing the materials already available in that language. Related to the globalization of Tibetan tantra, the Kumarajiva Project website explains that 65 percent of the tantras in the Kangyur do not have Chinese equivalents, while 98 percent of the tantric commentaries in the Tengyur "have not yet been translated into Chinese."[100] Another project of the Khyentse Foundation is the Khyentse Vision Project, which is planning to translate all of the works of Jamyang Khyentse Wangpo, the majority of which are tantric texts.[101] An important contribution to the globalization of tantric Buddhism has been Dzongsar Khyentse's attempts to clarify the practice of pure vision in relation to scandals.

As seemingly throughout contemporary Buddhism, there have been scandals related to tantric teachers. For the Tibetan tantric tradition, this is complicated by the uniquely important role of the guru–disciple relationship in the Tibetan tradition—one that is not duplicated in other tantric Buddhist traditions. Students are told that they are to consider the guru a buddha, and above reproach. In *Finding Rest in the Nature of Mind,* Longchenpa advises the reader that "fortunate disciples"

> are ever mindful
> Of their teachers' qualities.
> They never think that they have defects,
> And if perchance they see them,
> They will take them for good qualities.
> Sincerely they tell themselves, "The master has no defects—
> This is just my own perception."
> They thus confess their error and,
> Resolving to refrain from it,
> They implement the antidotes.[102]

This is an instance of the practice of "pure view" (*dag snang*) in which the student practices experiencing the world as a buddha would.

Cultural conflicts have resulted when teachers engage in activities considered by their Western students to be unethical according to modern secular values.[103] There have been a number of recent scandals within the Tibetan Buddhist world, the most high profile of which was in relation to the now deceased Sogyal Rinpoche. Dzongsar Khyentse had already attempted to address misconceptions regarding pure vision practices in the book *The Guru Drinks Bourbon?,* and specifically in response to the scandal he also wrote a lengthy post regarding the allegations made against Sogyal Rinpoche.[104] This is a complex issue at the social and personal interface of preconceptions regarding religious practice and devotion based in Western culture and those of Tibetan culture. As such, it is not unreasonable to expect it to continue as a source of contention for the foreseeable future.

Chogyam Trungpa: Secularized Tantra. Chogyam Trungpa (1939–1987) was both charismatic and controversial, and highly successful at creating a transnational enterprise. Holder of both Kagyu and Nyingma lineages, he fled Tibet in 1959, around the same time as the Dalai Lama, undertaking an arduous journey lasting three months. He first came to the West in 1963, having received a scholarship to study comparative religions at St. Antony's College, Oxford. Beginning from 1967, he established centers first in Scotland (Samye Ling), Cape Breton, Nova Scotia (Gampo Abbey), Colorado, and Vermont. As of 2007, there were "over 150 centers worldwide, as well as a number of retreat centers and a monastery," Gampo Abbey in Nova Scotia.[105]

In medieval India, tantric Buddhist *mahāsiddhas* were known for transgressive behavior and ecstatic poetry.[106] These figures are central to the tantric Mahāmudrā lineages within the Kagyu, Gelug, and Sakya traditions. Congruent with the *mahāsiddha* traditions, Trungpa promoted the idea of "crazy wisdom"—a total spontaneity and freedom from social conventions that results from awakening.[107] Trungpa created a nonmonastic and modernized version of Vajrayāna Buddhism, one that seems to have wide global appeal.

Trungpa's early death, together with a series of scandals, created a difficult time for the organization.[108] Most recently, Trungpa's son, Sakyong Mipham, was at the center of major scandal involving multiple women claiming sexual assault. Sakyong removed himself from his leadership position in 2018. As noted by Lynn P. Eldershaw, "the death of the charismatic founding leader has long been identified as a time of instability in a new religious movement, having the potential to provoke disruption, factionalism, dispersal, or even collapse of a movement."[109] In Eldershaw's analysis, however, it was a strong sense of collective identity that held the movement together and indeed allowed it to continue to prosper. She defines collective identity as "a conscious construction that assembles elements of a movement's beliefs and activities into a unified whole to convey to the world 'who we are.' "[110] As of 2021, the Shambhala organization, which Trungpa founded, offers several different kinds of trainings. These constitute a graded, progressive path of training, which culminates in an opportunity for the practitioner to commit to a life of "basic goodness" by taking the "Shambhala vow."[111] This evidences a shift in the Shambhala community toward more traditional forms of Tibetan Buddhism.

Dzogchen and Tibetan Yoga. In addition to these three further examples of transnational organizations, the adaptation of tantric teachings in the present is evident by the widespread interest in both Mahāmudrā and Dzogchen. In contrast to tantric *sadhanas*, which involve more elaborate sets of ritualized actions, both can be practiced as individual, silent meditation. In other words, they fit well with familiar kinds of meditation practices, from insight to Zen.

Dzogchen is associated with the Nyingma tradition but also has teachings found in several other Tibetan traditions. Nyingma Dzogchen teachers include Tsewang Dongyal, teacher for the Padmasambhava Buddhist Center in New York, which lists two more centers in New York, four in Florida, one each in Oregon, Puerto Rico, California, and Illinois, two in Tennessee, and, internationally, three centers in India and three centers in Russia.[112] The Padmasambhava Buddhist Center seems to present a fairly traditional version of Nyingma Dzogchen. Another Nyingma teacher who offers Dzogchen training is Orgyen Chowang. He established the Pristine Mind Foundation in California and began offering Dzogchen training in 2021.[113]

Another important proponent of Dzogchen is Namkhai Norbu (1938–2018). Invited to Italy in 1960 by Guiseppe Tucci, he taught at Naples Eastern University (1964–1992) and began teaching Tibetan yoga (*yantra yoga*, Tib. *tsalung trulkhor*) in 1971, and Dzogchen in 1976. Starting with a small group of students in Italy, what is now known as the International Dzogchen Community has centers in more than forty countries.[114] In addition to Dzogchen the International Dzogchen Community also continues Namkhai Norbu's teaching of different dance practices and Yantra Yoga.[115] The website says of Dzogchen that the "fundamental practice consist[s] of reaching a deep knowledge of oneself and one's essential existence through the various experiences of daily life. For this reason, Dzogchen is particularly well suited to the needs of modern society."[116]

Tibet also saw the development of Bon Dzogchen, a tradition represented in the West today by Tenzin Wangyal and his Ligmincha International, which lists three practice centers in the United States, two in Mexico, two in Europe, and one in India. Another international organization is the Himalayan Bön Foundation, headquartered in Colorado. It was established by Khenpo Tenpa Yungdrung, under the guidance of Yongdzin Lopön Tenzin Namdak.[117] The training program focuses on A Khrid Dzogchen, which employs meditation on the syllable A.[118]

The Bon lineage of the Himalayan Bön Foundation traces to the Triten Norbutse Monastery, originally established in Tibet in the 14th century. As with the other monasteries discussed above, it was refounded following the exile. Having been refounded in 1987, it is now located in Kathmandu, Nepal. A recent project of the foundation is the TISE School, located in Silguri, India, initiated in 2018. This is an elementary school serving students from the Himalayan region and focusing especially on reaching "orphans, children from economically marginalized families and remote rural communities."[119]

The style of representation of Dzogchen in the West is for the most part as an individual meditative practice, compatible with lay life in a modern society. The style of Tibetan yoga (referred to here as *tsalung tummo*) as taught at Namdroling Monastery is quite different from the style of hatha yoga now widely practiced for body enhancement in the West. Namdroling was established in Karnataka, South India, in 1963 by Palyul Padma Norbu, as the second seat of Palyul Monastery in Tibet.[120] Palyul is considered one of the six "mother" monasteries of the Nyingma tradition in Tibet, established in 1665 in Dege. Namdroling is perhaps the largest center of Nyingma today, having registered more than 9,000 monks and nuns since its establishment. The website lists five affiliate Dharma Centers in Canada, one each in Hong Kong, Indonesia, Macau, Philippines, and Singapore, three each in India and Nepal, two in Malaysia, seven in Taiwan, and nine in the United States.

The website does not promote yoga training for nonmonastics, but at least one lay Westerner has taken month-long trainings in Tibetan yoga there. "Since 1973, Namdroling monks, nuns and Tibetan refugees have quietly been practicing *Sky Dharma* (*gNam chos*), the set of contemplative manuals revealed by Namchö Mingyur Dorje (*gNam chos mi 'gyur rdo rje*; 1645–1667) in Tibet."[121] In contrast to the common emphasis on simply observing the present moment, "Tibetan yoga is specific, clear, and unwavering in the ways that it *directs the mind*." And, instead of emphasizing relaxation and stretching, as is common to some Westernized forms of postural yoga, Tibetan yoga as taught at Namdroling "involves a significant amount of jumping and landing in a seated position (lotus or half-lotus), which can be hard on the knees and not relaxing." The author raises the question as to why Tibetan yoga is not as well-known as other forms of yoga and suggests that this is because it is embedded in a tantric context and "is one among many of Tibetan Buddhism's secret practices that require preliminary practice and initiation."

CONTESTATION

It is perhaps tempting to think of the globalization of tantric Buddhism as a steady, even spread outward from premodern centers—like some maps one sees with arrows indicating unilinear geographic movement. Globalization, however, has led to different kinds of contestation. Indicative of this is the conflict between MSBL and the Shingon authorities described above. Three additional instances provide examples of globalization as contestation, one a controversy centering on a tantric Buddhist deity, the second between Buddhist groups in Nepal, and the third between Tibetan Buddhists and evangelical Christians.

Dorje Shugden Controversy. The spread of tantric Buddhism in the last half of the 20th century was largely a consequence of the Tibetan diaspora. The availability of living teachers and traditions, together with the charismatic quality of the Dalai Lama's leadership and Kerouac-inspired travel through South Asia, led to a great upsurge in interest in Tibetan Buddhism. And a significant subset of those who were interested went on to become practitioners or scholars or both. In general, the narrative of this history has cast it in a positive light as increasing religious diversity and the successful transplantation of Tibetan religious traditions into new homes.[122] What is known as the Dorje Shugden controversy, however, has shown how the globalization of Tibetan Buddhism has led to the involvement of non-Tibetans in disputes, recasting the terms of the conflict in ways foreign to Tibetan culture.

In a foundational study of Dorje Shugden, Georges Dreyfus provides an overview of the complex history of Dorje Shugden and the figure's origin in an intrasectarian conflict at the time of the Fifth Dalai Lama. While Dorje Shugden originated as a "minor spirit coming from an obscure location in Central Tibet [in the 20th century he] has become the center of a raging controversy that has cost the lives of several Ge-luk monks and continues to threaten the unity of the Ge-luk tradition."[123] Dreyfus's careful historical analysis untangles two different stories that have led to a modern conflict with tragic consequences.

One story is that of Drak-ba Gyel-tsen, an important figure in 17th-century Tibet who came into conflict with the Fifth Dalai Lama over the Fifth's affinity for Nyingma practices. Drak-ba Gyel-tsen's sudden death was attributed to the Dalai Lama, and in 20th-century retellings Drak-ba Gyel-tsen is transformed into the wrathful figure Dorje Shugden. This interpretation was promoted in the first half of the 20th century by Pabongka (1878–1941), who compiled a collection of tales in which Dorje Shugden employs violence as a means to protect Gelug orthodoxy from heterodoxies such as the Fifth's involvement with Nyingma praxis. Known colloquially as "the Yellow Book," this collection became a source of conflict in the early years of the diaspora, when the Fourteenth Dalai Lama was working to create a unified sense of Tibetan Buddhist identity, one involving all the different lineages, not just the Gelug.

According to Jeannine Chandler, this conflict would have remained largely internal to the Tibetan community were it not for the fact that by the end of the 20th century, the conflict came to be played out on an international stage in the glare of the global media. In response to the divisive potential of the Shugden cult, associated with a Gelug exclusivity, the Dalai Lama eventually prohibited its practice.[124]

By that time, however, both "pro-Shugden" and "anti-Shugen" lamas had international followings. The involvement of Westerners in the conflict transformed it in several ways. Although in "traditional Tibetan society this issue regarding Shugden would have been a private matter (confined to a small group of religious elite), since Westerners have become involved, the international press has begun to pay more attention to the controversy, and the Internet has become a primary forum for debating the issue."[125] Westerners inserting themselves into the controversy are, in Chandler's analysis, engaged in what she has called "conspicuous compassion," taking the traditional guru–disciple relation to extremes of unquestioning devotion and blind adherence.

In a broader examination of such conflicts and other scandals in contemporary Buddhism, John Makransky has provided additional nuance. In his analysis, attempts to modernize Buddhism create situations in which old issues are given new life—and new relevance. In interaction with different religious cultures, doctrinal concepts have become constellated in new ways. One exemplary instance is a doctrinal issue key to Tibetan tantric traditions, that of "pure vision" (*dag snang*, i.e., the practitioner's view of his/her lama as a fully awakened buddha).[126] As indicated by Chandler, since pure vision teaching is now on an international stage, interpreting this teaching has become central to discussions about the immoral or abusive behavior of some teachers. Should such behavior be attributed to the human aspect of the teacher—distinguished from her/his status as a buddha? Or is such behavior actually an instance of skillful means (*upaya*) that the practitioner needs in order to transcend her/his own limitations? Makransky has pointed out that the tension between these two interpretations is not simply between the Tibetan community and the international community of converts to Tibetan Buddhism, but rather between two interpretations—each of which is held by both Tibetans and converts.[127] He has emphasized the importance of this nuance, noting that

> it is not the case that one perspective corresponds to western converts and the other to Tibetans themselves. Rather, each perspective is upheld both by some Tibetan teachers and by some Western converts. In other words, the "conflict," is not Westerners vs. Tibetans; it is "exclusivist" Tibetans and western converts vs. "inclusivist" Tibetans and western converts.[128]

The perspective that Makransky identifies as "inclusivist" is attempting to incorporate aspects of modern culture into Buddhist practice, which corresponds to the modernizing trends that have been part of Buddhism internationally since the latter part of the 19th century. The ideology of the "exclusive" view emphasizes the preservation of traditional forms over adaptation to modern forms. Importantly, Makransky also shows that the Tibetan categories have been generalized as part of the international Buddhist discourse, as, for instance, the misbehavior of certain Zen teachers is now treated under the same rubrics.

In the case of Dorje Shugden, involvement by non-Tibetan actors has itself created a backlash, in which Tibetans have asserted the autonomous right of Tibetans to determine Tibetan matters without interference from outsiders—no matter how strongly self-identified those outsiders may be with Tibetan Buddhist lineages. Such involvement has reframed the conflict in terms of Western values of democracy and freedom, changing the conflict fundamentally.[129] More recently, however, it seems that Shugden adherents have given up their previous practice of engaging in public protests against the Dalai Lama.[130]

Traditional Newar Buddhism and Modernist Theravāda Buddhism. The Newars in the Kathmandu valley of Nepal constitute "the last remaining Mahayana South Asia Buddhists."[131] While having disappeared from the rest of the subcontinent, the Newar tradition has retained its characteristic tantric quality into the 21st century. The tradition is maintained by two castes of priests, one of which, the Vajracharya, act as "priests for others," and Shakyas, who "tend to be artisans by profession."[132] Globalization, however, has led both to the decline of the Newar tradition and to a challenge by Theravādin-oriented modernists. Like many young people in the West who do not see a religious life as worth pursuing, so also Newar youth value more prestigious and higher-paying careers, such as medicine and engineering. This has created a "vicious circle by which only boys who are unable to forge any other career enter the priesthood.... Therefore, the laity respect Vajracharya priests less and less, which ensures that only those who have no alternative enter the priesthood."[133] Thus, it is recognized that Newar Buddhism "is in decline and that in the 1980s it appeared to be facing a severe and possibly terminal crisis."[134] In addition, beginning in the 1920s under the modernizing influence of Anagārika Dharmapāla (1864–1933), "the revivalist, modernizing form of Theravada pushed by Dharmapala's Maha Bodhi Society" made inroads into Nepal.[135]

Levine and Gellner describe traditional Newar Buddhism in terms of seven characteristics. There are numerous rituals of varying complexity that serve social and instrumental ends, frequent feasts marked by sanctioned consumption of meat and alcohol, and a hierarchical organization; both literacy and religious instruction is limited to high-caste males; tantric initiation is restricted to high castes; it maintains an elaborate pantheon; and membership in the lineage of the specialists who maintain the tradition and perform the rituals is hereditary.[136] In contrast, the modernist Theravāda that has made major inroads into Nepal is characterized by few rituals, usually of a commemorative nature, a focus on Śākyamuni, monastic ordination that is open to all males, and a resistance to any practices of possession and magic.[137]

Traditional Newar Buddhist practitioners have in turn made efforts to revitalize their tradition. These efforts have included re-establishing transmissions from Tibet; providing additional ritual training; reviving rituals that had lapsed, including performances in Lumbini, symbolically important because it is the Buddha's birthplace; public lectures on Mahāyāna teachings; and translating key Sanskrit and Tibetan texts into Nepal Bhasha, the language of the Newars.[138] Individual members of the tradition, such as Naresh Bajracarya, have also actively participated in international academic events.[139] Like the influence of the Maha Bodhi Society's style of modernist Buddhism from India, the attempts to revitalize Newar Buddhism by drawing on Tibetan connections and ritual activities in Lumbini demonstrate the effects of globalization.

Contesting the Kālacakra Mandala. The global visibility of the Dalai Lama has led to competing interpretations of the goal and significance of the Kālacakra initiations that he has offered in several locations around the world, generally offered for world peace.[140] Laura Harrington has called attention to the response to the Kālacakra initiations on the part of evangelical Christians, a group that has also become global.[141]

The Spiritual Warfare and Spiritual Mapping movements have resisted the Dalai Lama and particularly the Kālacakra initiations. This modern Gnostic worldview of the forces of righteousness in spiritual conflict with those of darkness sees all forms of religiosity other than modern evangelical Christianity as part of a grand satanic force motivated by opposition to the truth of the Risen Christ. Thus, the social interest in occultism and Eastern religions seen in the 1960s and 1970s is understood in this view as the rise of satanic forces that needed to be resisted.

In 2004, as part of the "Kalachakra for World Peace" program held in Toronto and lasting eleven days, a sand mandala was constructed. Sand mandala are popular with many people who find the construction process fascinating. Almost equally fascinating is the final destruction of the mandala, signifying the emptiness of all entities. In Toronto the sand was poured into Lake Ontario, conveying the blessings of the deities of the mandala into the waters.

A very different perspective was held by a Pentecostal Christian minister who led "a team in a chain of prayer sessions around the perimeter of the Lake to prevent the Tibetan spirits that would be poured into the waters from being dispersed into the adjacent lands."[142] The conception involved is as literally territorial as it sounds. The Neo-Pentecostal movement of Spiritual Mapping is global and seeks to break the strongholds "of a hierarchy of invisible, demonic spirits that hold specific geographical centers and ethnic populations in their grip."[143] Rather than considering the exorcism of the mandala from either the perspective of the history of Buddhism in the West, or the history of Christian interaction with Buddhism, Harrington suggests that it is "the by-product of the simultaneous globalizations of Tibetan Buddhism and Evangelicalism with the human rights discourse that emerged in late twentieth century America."[144]

The emergence of Tibetan Buddhism as a part of global society coincided with the rise of an expanding discourse of human rights, including the "rights of indigenous minorities."[145] This discourse then provided a grounding for claims to political autonomy for Tibetan peoples and freedom of Tibet from Chinese occupation. Assisting this project was the representation of Tibetan Buddhism as a form of Buddhist modernism, rational and sophisticated philosophical teachings of personal self-development. In contrast, Spiritual Mapping understands Tibetan Buddhism to be a vehicle for the territorial conquest of the West by demonic spiritual forces. From this perspective, the Dalai Lama is not a force for world peace deserving of a Nobel Prize, but rather a "powerful adept with dominion over a wide range of Tibetan spirits."[146]

As Harrington summarizes,

> the Tibetan–Evangelical encounter is both by-product and critique of globalism. Insofar as Tibetan Buddhism is equated with so-called justice globalism, Spiritual Mapping may fruitfully be contextualized within broader fundamentalist critiques of globalization as an unfettered assault of liberal or secular values. As such, it may be more accurate to characterize our protagonists as competing "alter-globalization" projects—alternatives to the dominant neo-liberal vision of an integrated world based on free-market principles.[147]

CONCLUSION

The globalization of tantric Buddhism comprises the extension of the pattern of nodes and strands that have always characterized Buddhism generally as a translocal tradition. The network metaphor holds the tension between local praxes and the discourse of a globally distributed

Buddhism. A purely local focus obscures the connections that exist between locales. The representation of a unitary Buddhism distributed globally marginalizes forms that do not fit neatly with the modern idea that Buddhism is a religion, separate from but equal to other world religions. Having largely been molded to meet the expectations of what it means to be a religion, Buddhist modernism is perhaps the easiest match to the preconceptions about a religion as having a specific founder with a reformist message, a sacred text, and an individual program of self-development, whether conceived as salvation from sin or awakening from ignorance.

As mentioned at the outset, tantric Buddhists in many locales are not only affected by globalization but also take advantage of the opportunities it offers. New transnational organizations, such as FPMT and MSBL, have been created on a landscape already populated by the international system of the foreign missions of Shingon and other sects that are part of the Japanese diaspora.

In addition to greater ease of transportation and communication, tantric Buddhists have encountered both Western intelligentsia and neo-Pentecostal groups such as Spiritual Warfare. Places that used to be remote, such as Nepal, Ladakh, and Buryat Mongolia, were previously parts of networks connecting to Tibet. In the 21st century, however, they are interconnected much more widely, so that other global interactions are part of their translocal reality.

REVIEW OF LITERATURE

Globalization has largely replaced theories of modernization, which tended to presume a correlation between modernization and secularization. Globalization studies began with contemporary capitalism but expanded to cultural dynamics, including religious ones. Thomas J. Csordas summarizes current issues and rejects subsuming religion under a neoliberal interpretation of it as a commodity, as per rational choice theories.[148]

Linda Learman focuses on the globalization of Buddhism, specifically missionary forms in the late 19th and 20th centuries.[149] She cites Jonathan Walters's critique of the trope that Buddhism has always been a missionizing religion. Walters argues that this trope "is an Anglo-American construct that has been maintained only by silencing the premodern Buddhists who paradoxically are depicted as agents."[150] The projection of modern, Western constructs onto the history of contemporary Buddhism affects our understanding of the globalization of tantra. Globalization reinforces a shift within Buddhist studies toward understanding Buddhism as a living tradition. Late-19th-century religious studies focused on "origins" and gave "original Buddhism" an ideologically definitive function for understanding the tradition.

From the last quarter of the 19th century, the Buddhist revitalization movement created modern Chinese forms of tantric Buddhism by drawing on Tibetan and Japanese sources. Martino Dibeltulo's dissertation focuses on tantric streams from Tibet employed to revitalize Chinese tantra.[151] Ester Bianchi's study examines both Tibetan and Japanese tantric influences.[152] Expatriate forms have been studied extensively by Cody Bahir, whose research details the ways in which Japanese Shingon has been drawn on in the creation of new sects of Chinese tantric Buddhism.[153] The ongoing globalization of tantric Buddhism involves the many dimensions of contemporary relations between China and Tibet, which have been studied by John Powers.[154]

Japanese emigration in the latter part of the 19th century led Shingon priests to Hawai'i, California, and thereafter Brazil.[155] Elizabeth Eastman describes the social dynamics of the decline and closure of one Shingon temple in the Portland, Oregon, area.[156] Richard K. Payne's study of the Shingon Mission in the United States discusses the invisibility of immigrant Buddhism.[157] Similar issues have been explored by Rafael Shoji in his study of Shingon in Brazil.[158]

Gray Tuttle argues that Tibetan lamas in exile have been active agents not only in propagating Buddhism, but also politically.[159] The globalization of tantric Buddhism has not gone uncontested. The controversy over Dorje Shugden, modernizing Theravadin entry into Nepal, and fundamentalist Christian resistance to the Dalai Lama are all instances of the complexity of the present global place of tantric Buddhism.[160]

FURTHER READING

While the study of global Buddhism is well established, the study of the globalization of tantric Buddhism is a more limited field of inquiry. There are, therefore, a limited number of relevant publications available, and theoretical understandings are naturally derivative of the study of global Buddhism.

Bahir, Cody. "Reenchanting Buddhism via Modernizing Magic: Guru Wuguang of Taiwan's Philosophy and Science of 'Superstition.'" PhD diss., Leiden University, 2017.

Baumann, Martin. "Global Buddhism: Developmental Periods, Regional Histories, and a New Analytical Perspective." *Journal of Global Buddhism* 2 (2001): 1–43.

Bianchi, Ester. "The Tantric Rebirth Movement in Modern China: Esoteric Buddhism Re-vivified by the Japanese and Tibetan Traditions." *Acta Orientalia Academiae Scientiarum Hung* 57, no. 1 (2004): 31–54.

Csordas, Thomas J., ed. *Transnational Transcendence: Essays on Religion and Globalization.* Berkeley, Los Angeles, and London: University of California Press, 2009 (see especially the introduction).

Dibeltulo, Martino. "The Revival of Tantrism: Tibetan Buddhism and Modern China." PhD diss., University of Michigan, 2015.

Learman, Linda, ed. *Buddhist Missionaries in the Era of Globalization.* Honolulu: University of Hawai'i Press, 2005 (see especially the introduction and chapters 4 and 9).

Scherer, Burkhard. "Interpreting the Diamond Way: Contemporary Convert Buddhism in Transition." *Journal of Global Buddhism* 10 (2009): 17–48.

NOTES

1. Thomas J. Csordas, "Introduction: Modalities of Transnational Transcendence," in *Transnational Transcendence: Essays on Religion and Globalization,* ed. Thomas J. Csordas (Berkeley, Los Angeles, and London: University of California Press, 2009), 1–29, 3.
2. Linda Learman, "Introduction," in *Buddhist Missionaries in the Era of Globalization,* ed. Linda Learman (Honolulu: University of Hawai'i Press, 2005), 1–21, 1; see Peter Berger, "Four Faces of Global Culture," *The National Interest* 49 (Fall 1997): 23–29.
3. Learman, "Introduction," 1.
4. Thomas A. Tweed, "American Occultism and Japanese Buddhism: Albert J. Edmunds, D. T. Suzuki, and Translocative History," *Japanese Journal of Religious Studies* 32, no. 2 (2005): 249–281, 273. For an example of such a perspectival shift and discussion of its importance, see Laurie F. Maffly-Kipp, "Eastward Ho! American Religion from the Perspective of the Pacific Rim," in *Retelling U.S. Religious History,* ed. Thomas A. Tweed (Berkeley, Los Angeles, and London: University of California Press, 1997), 127–148.

5. Thomas A. Tweed, "Introduction: Narrating U.S. Religious History," in *Retelling U.S. Religious History*, ed. Thomas A. Tweed (Berkeley, Los Angeles, and London: University of California Press, 1997), 1–23, 2.
6. Hans G. Kippenberg, *Discovering Religious History in the Modern Age*, trans. Barbara Harshaw (Princeton, NJ, and Oxford: Princeton University Press, 2002), 192. Kippenberg is here drawing on the work of Anthony Giddens, *The Consequences of Modernity* (Stanford, CA: Stanford University Press, 1990).
7. John Nelson, "Diasporic Buddhisms and Convert Communities," in *The Oxford Handbook of Contemporary Buddhism*, ed. Michael Jerryson (Oxford and New York: Oxford University Press, 2017), 381–397, 382–385.
8. Peter Bishop, *Dreams of Power: Tibetan Buddhism and the Western Imagination* (London: Athlone Press, 1993), 13.
9. Martin Baumann has used the terminology of "pull" to describe the dynamics of German interest in Buddhism in the 18th and 19th centuries, which sought out Buddhism as an alternative to Christianity. Martin Baumann, "Culture Contact and Valuation: Early German Buddhists and the Creation of a 'Buddhism in Protestant Shape'," *Numen* 44 (1997): 270–295, 274. Pull can be contrasted with the dynamics of "push," which characterizes the increase of immigrant Buddhists beginning in the mid-20th century, who for political and economic reasons moved to Euro-American societies.
10. Martin Baumann, "Global Buddhism: Developmental Periods, Regional Histories, and a New Analytical Perspective," *Journal of Global Buddhism* 2 (2001): 1–43, 2.
11. Burkhard Scherer, "Interpreting the Diamond Way: Contemporary Convert Buddhism in Transition," *Journal of Global Buddhism* 10 (2009): 17–48, 19.
12. Because the category "convert" suggests more personal commitment than is necessarily the case for many people, we add "adherents" to point to the larger group of the interested and supportive. See also Scherer, "Interpreting the Diamond Way," 20, for a discussion of different terminological options.
13. Michiro Ama, *Immigrants to the Pure Land: The Modernization, Acculturation, and Globalization of Shin Buddhism, 1898–1941* (Honolulu: University of Hawai'i Press, 2011).
14. Richard K. Payne, "Hiding in Plain Sight: The Invisibility of the Shingon Mission to the United States," in *Buddhist Missionaries in the Era of Globalization*, ed. Linda Learman (Honolulu: University of Hawai'i Press, 2005), 101–122, 104.
15. See Duncan Ryūken Williams, *American Sutra: A Story of Faith and Freedom in the Second World War* (Cambridge, MA: Belknap Press of Harvard University Press, 2019).
16. Adjusting for inflation, this is approximately $60,000 in 2021.
17. Payne, "Hiding in Plain Sight," 108.
18. Koyasan Beikoku Betsuin, "Koyasan Buddhist Temple of Los Angeles" (Los Angeles, 2016).
19. Los Angeles Buddhist Temple Federation.
20. Elizabeth Eastman, "Incense at a Funeral: The Rise and Fall of an American Shingon Temple," in *TransBuddhism: Transmission, Translation, Transformation*, ed. Nalini Bhushan, Jay L. Garfield, and Abraham Zablocki (Amherst: University of Massachusetts Press, 2009), 69–85, 71.
21. Eastman, "Incense at a Funeral," 73.
22. Eastman, "Incense at a Funeral," 79.
23. Eastman, "Incense at a Funeral," 79.
24. Eastman, "Incense at a Funeral," 82–83.
25. Henjyoji Shingon Buddhist Temple.
26. Kosho Finch, personal communication via email, September 24, 2019.
27. For a broader perspective, see Cristina Rocha, "Buddhism in Latin America," in *The Oxford Handbook of Contemporary Buddhism*, ed. Michael Jerryson (Oxford and New York: Oxford University Press, 2017), 299–315.
28. Rafael Shoji, " 'Buddhism in Syncretic Shape': Lessons of Shingon in Brazil," *Journal of Global Buddhism* 4 (2003): 70–107, 72.

29. Shoji, "'Buddhism in Syncretic Shape'," 78.
30. Shoji, "'Buddhism in Syncretic Shape'," 92.
31. Wolfram Eberhard, *A History of China* (Berkeley and Los Angeles: University of California Press, 1950), 244–245.
32. Ester Bianchi, "The Tantric Rebirth Movement in Modern China: Esoteric Buddhism Re-vivified by the Japanese and Tibetan Traditions," *Acta Orientalia Academiae Scientiarum Hung* 57, no. 1 (2004): 31–54, 39.
33. Vesna Wallace, "Introduction," in *Buddhism in Mongolian History, Culture, and Society*, ed. Vesna Wallace (Oxford and New York: Oxford University Press, 2015), xv–xxii, xvii.
34. John Blofeld, *The Jewel in the Lotus: An Outline of Present Day Buddhism in China* (Westport, CT: Hyperion Press, 1975), 152.
35. Martino Dibeltulo, "The Revival of Tantrism: Tibetan Buddhism and Modern China" (PhD diss. University of Michigan, 2015).
36. Bianchi, "The Tantric Rebirth Movement in Modern China," 36–39.
37. Dibeltulo, "The Revival of Tantrism," 67.
38. Blofeld, *The Jewel in the Lotus*.
39. Dibultelo, "The Revival of Tantrism," 206.
40. Leo Pruden, "Translator's Introduction," in *The Essentials of the Eight Traditions*, trans. Leo Pruden, 1–6 (Berkeley, CA: Numata Center for Buddhist Translation and Research, 1994), 1.
41. Dibultelo, "The Revival of Tantrism," 207.
42. Dibultelo, "The Revival of Tantrism," 204–205.
43. Dibultelo, "The Revival of Tantrism," 207.
44. Cody Bahir, "Reformulating the Appropriated and Relinking the Chain: Challenges of Lineage and Legitimacy in Zhenyan Revival," in *The Hybridity of Buddhism: Contemporary Encounters between Tibetan and Chinese Traditions in Taiwan and the Mainland*, ed. Fabienne Jagou (Paris: École française d'Extrême-Orient, 2018), 91–108, 93. Characters have been ellided in this quote. On the formation of these categories in Japan, see Michel Mohr, "Zen Buddhism during the Tokugawa Period: The Challenge to Go beyond Sectarian Consciousness," *Japanese Journal of Religious Studies* 21, no. 4 (1994): 341–372.
45. Bahir, "Reformulating the Appropriated and Relinking the Chain," 92n10.
46. Jimmy Yu, "Revisiting the Notion of *Zong*: Contextualizing the Dharma Drum Lineage of Modern Chan Buddhism," *Chung-Hwa Buddhist Journal* 26 (2013): 113–151, 116. My thanks to Cody Bahir for pointing out this essay to me.
47. Yu, "Revisiting the Notion of *Zong*," 117.
48. Cody Bahir, "The Flag of Zhenyan Flies Again: The Taiwanese Resurrection of Esoteric Buddhism through Wuguang's Appropriation of Imperially Imported Shingon" (Diss., Leiden University, 2017).
49. Cody Bahir, "Replanting the Bodhi Tree: Buddhist Sectarianism and Zhenyan Revivalism," *Pacific World: Journal of the Institute of Buddhist Studies* third series, no. 20 (2018): 95–129, 101–102.
50. Bahir, "Replanting the Bodhi Tree," 104–106.
51. Bahir, "Replanting the Bodhi Tree," 107.
52. Bahir, "Replanting the Bodhi Tree," 128. See also Cody Bahir, "Buddhist Master Wuguang's (1918–2000) Taiwanese Web of the Colonial, Exilic and Han," *Electronic Journal of East and Central Asian Religions* 1 (Autumn 2013): 81–93.
53. While apparently similar to Western appropriation of Tibetan symbols and images for their value as cultural capital, the Chinese case is complicated by the modern history of Chinese claims of political authority over Tibet, rejection of the authority of the Dalai Lama, and characterizations of Tibetan society as feudalistic. John Powers, *The Buddha Party: How the People's Republic of China Works to Define and Control Tibetan Buddhism* (Oxford and New York: Oxford University Press, 2017), 48–49.

54. Khenpo Sodargye and Dan Smyer Yü, "Revisioning Buddhism as a Science of Mind in a Secularized China: A Tibetan Perspective," *Journal of Global Buddhism* 18 (2017): 91–111, 91.
55. Powers, *The Buddha Party*, 1.
56. Black Sect tantric Buddhism and Yun Lin Temple; and Emily Wu, "Fengshui Plus Buddhism Equals What?" (Thesis, Boston Univerity, 2003), 2.
57. True Buddha School Seattle.
58. Padmakurama.
59. Padmakurama, "True Buddha School."
60. Padmakurama, "True Buddha School."
61. "Remote Empowerment for Refuge and the Practice of Tara Who Saves from Contagious Diseases," True Buddha Foundation Dharma Affairs Notification (TBF-DA Practice Notice #0005).
62. Padmakurama, "True Buddha School."
63. Cody Bahir, "Telecommunicative Transmission: Remotely Resurrecting Chinese Esoteric Buddhism," conference presentation, American Academy of Religions, November 2018, Denver, Colorado.
64. See Richard K. Payne, "Yogi Chen and the Transformation of Tantric Ritual," conference presentation, Buddhism without Borders, Institute of Buddhist Studies, Berkeley, California, 2010. That presentation was developed into three essays: Richard K. Payne, "Integrating Christ and the Saints into Buddhist Ritual: The Christian *Homa* of Yogi Chen," *Buddhist–Christian Studies* 35 (2015): 37–48; Richard K. Payne, "Self-Representation and Cultural Expectations: Yogi Chen and Religious Practices of Life-Writing," *Entangled Religions* 3 (2016): 33–82; and Richard K. Payne, "Jesus Christ, Tantric Deity: Syntax and Semantics in Ritual Change," in *On Meaning and Mantras: Essays in Honor of Frits Staal*, ed. George Thompson and Richard K. Payne (Berkeley, CA: Institute of Buddhist Studies and BDK America, 2016), 455–476.
65. B. Khantipalo, Autobiography of Yogi Chen. The autobiography was recorded in Kalimpong by Ven. Sangharakshita Sthavira and Rev. B. Khantipalo, and although undated, it must have been sometime between 1959 and 1962, the dates of Khantipalo's years in India. Sangharakshita, "Yogi Chen and the New Buddhists of India," Dharmabytes Podcast no. 719.
66. Gray Tuttle, "Uniting Religion and Politics in a Bid for Autonomy: Lamas in Exile in China and America," in *Buddhist Missionaries in the Era of Globalization*, ed. Linda Learman (Honolulu: University of Hawai'i Press, 2005), 210–232, 212.
67. Bianchi, "The Tantric Rebirth Movement in Modern China," 36. For a discussion of the concept of humanistic Buddhism, see Stuart Chandler, "Spreading Buddha's Light: The Internationalization of Foguang Shan," in *Buddhist Missionaries in the Era of Globalization*, ed. Linda Learman (Honolulu: University of Hawai'i Press, 2005), 162–184, 182n5.
68. Khantipalo, "Autobiography of Yogi Chen."
69. Bahir, "Reformulating the Appropriated and Relinking the Chain," 95.
70. Bahir, "Reformulating the Appropriated and Relinking the Chain," 97.
71. Mark Juergensmeyer, "Thinking Globally About Religion," in *The Oxford Handbook of Global Religions*, ed. Mark Juergensmeyer (Oxford and New York: Oxford University Press, 2006), 3–12, 5.
72. Stephen C. Berkwitz, *South Asian Buddhism: A Survey* (London and New York: Routledge, 2010), 199.
73. Manuel A. Vásquez and David Garbin, "Globalization," in *The Oxford Handbook of the Study of Religion*, ed. Michael Strausberg and Steven Engler (Oxford and New York: Oxford University Press, 2016), 682–701, 691.
74. Peggy Levitt, "Redefining the Boundaries of Belonging: The Institutional Character of Transnational Religious Life," *Sociology of Religion* 65, no. 1, (2004): 1–18, 10; cited in Vásquez and Garbin, "Globalization," 691.
75. Levitt, "Redefining the Boundaries of Belonging," 6; cited in Vásquez and Garbin, "Globalization," 691.

76. Leo Ching, "Globalizing the Regional, Regionalizing the Global: Mass Culture and Asianism in the Age of Late Capital," in *Globalization*, ed. Arjun Appadurai (Durham, NC, and London: Duke University Press, 2001), 279–306, 282.
77. Foundation for the Preservation of the Mahayana Tradition.
78. Glenys Eddy, "A Strand of Contemporary Tantra: Its Discourse and Practice in the FPMT," *Journal of Global Buddhism* 8 (2007): 81–106: 81.
79. Hugh Urban, *Tantra: Sex, Secrecy, Politics, and Power in the Study of Religion* (Berkeley, Los Angeles, and London: University of California Press, 2003), 7.
80. Eddy, "A Strand of Contemporary Tantra," 81.
81. Eddy, "A Strand of Contemporary Tantra," 84.
82. Eddy, "A Strand of Contemporary Tantra," 84.
83. Eddy, "A Strand of Contemporary Tantra," 86.
84. Eddy, "A Strand of Contemporary Tantra," 88.
85. S. A. McAra, "Indigenizing or Adapting? Importing Buddhism into a Settler-Colonial Society," *Journal of Global Buddhism* 8 (2007): 132–156, 132.
86. Justin Thomas McDaniel, *Architects of Buddhist Leisure: Socially Disengaged Buddhism in Asia's Museums, Monuments, and Amusement Parks* (Honolulu: University of Hawai'i Press, 2017), 78.
87. FPMT, "Progress Continues on Land of Medicine Buddha's Mahabodhi Stupa Project in California."
88. Nicole MacArgel, "Foundation for the Preservation of the Mahayana Tradition (FPMT): A Contemporary Organization for Transmitting the Dharma" (MA thesis, Graduate Theological Union, Berkeley, CA, 2017), 19.
89. FPMT, "FPMT Project News."
90. José Cabezón and Penpa Dorjee, *Sera Monastery* (Boston: Wisdom Publications, 2019), 470.
91. Cabezón and Dorjee, *Sera Monastery*, 471.
92. Edward A. Arnold, ed., *As Long as Space Endures: Essays on the Kālacakra Tantra in Honor of H.H. the Dalai Lama* (Ithaca, NY: Snow Lion, 2009), xiii.
93. Tenzin Gyatso, *Kālacakra Tantra Rite of Initiation: For the Stage of Generation*, trans. and ed. Jeffrey Hopkins, exp. ed. (Boston: Wisdom Publications, 1999).
94. H.H. the Fourteenth Dalai Lama, *The Great Exposition of Secret Mantra*, ed. Jeffrey Hopkins, 3 vols., rev. ed. (Boulder, CO: Shambhala, 2016, 2017, 2017).
95. The American Institute of Buddhist Studies, 2012.
96. The Mind-Life Institute, founded at the Dalai Lama's initiative, serves to encourage study at the interface of science and Buddhism. While much of this work has focused on the study of meditation in the context of cognitive sciences, in 2006 the institute provided a Varela grant for a research project directly related to tantra, "White Tantric Kundalini Yoga: Physiological, Behavioral, and EEG Effects of an Intensive and Immersive Yogic Meditation Experience," conducted by Heather Jaskirat Wild. It is not clear whether the fact that there has been only one grant directly related to tantra is a matter of policy or accident.
97. Alexander Gardner, "Jamyang Khyentse Wangpo," Treasury of Lives, February 2010; idem, "Jamgon Kongtrul Lodro Taye," Treasury of Lives, September 2015; see also Alexander Gardner, *The Life of Jamgon Kongtrul the Great* (Boulder, CO: Snow Lion, 2019).
98. 84,000: Translating the Words of the Buddha.
99. Tantra Text Warning.
100. The Kumarajiva Project.
101. Khyentse Vision Project.
102. Longchenpa, *Finding Rest in the Nature of Mind*, trans. Padmakara Translation Group (Boulder, CO: Shambhala, 2017), 56–57.

103. Cf. Justin von Bujdoss, "Pain, Practice, and Pure View," *Lion's Roar: Buddhist Wisdom for Our Time*, July 27, 2017; and Rod Meade Sperry and Sam Littlefare, "Letter to Sogyal Rinpoche from Current and Ex-Rigpa Members Details Abuse Allegations," *Lion's Roar: Buddhist Wisdom for Our Time*, July 20, 2017.
104. Dzongsar Jamyang Khyentse, "Guru and Student in the Vajrayana," originally posted on Facebook, now available on Buddhist Door," August 15, 2017; and Dzongsar Jamyang Khyentse, *The Guru Drinks Bourbon?* (Boulder, CO: Shambhala, 2016).
105. Lynn P. Eldershaw, "Collective Identity and the Postcharismatic Fate of Shambhala International," *Nova Religio: The Journal of Alternative and Emergent Religions* 10, no. 4 (May 2007): 72–102, 73.
106. The English language literature on the mahāsiddhas and Mahāmudrā is quite extensive. See Roger Jackson, "Mahāmudrā in India" and "Mahāmudrā in Tibet," and David Gray, "Siddhas," in *Oxford Bibliographies Online*.
107. See also Eldershaw, "Collective Identity and the Postcharismatic Fate of Shambhala International," 75.
108. Sandra Bell, "'Crazy Wisdom,' Charisma, and the Transmission of Buddhist in the United States," *Nova Religio: The Journal of Alternative and Emergent Religions* 2, no. 1 (October 1998): 55–75, 66.
109. Eldershaw, "Collective Identity and the Postcharismatic Fate of Shambhala International," 72.
110. Eldershaw, "Collective Identity and the Postcharismatic Fate of Shambhala International," 81.
111. Shambhala, "Way of Shambhala." No further information is given regarding the "Shambhala vow."
112. Padmasambhava Centers Directory.
113. Pristine Mind.
114. Dzogchen Community, 2021.
115. See Chögyal Namkhai Norbu, *Yantra Yoga: The Tibetan Yoga of Movement* (Ithaca, NY: Snow Lion, 2008).
116. Dzogchen Community, 2021. See also Chögyal Namkhai Norbu, *Dsogchen Teachings* (Ithaca, NY, and Boulder, CO: Snow Lion, 2006), and Chögyal Namkhai Norbu, *Dzogchen: The Self-Perfected State* (Ithaca, NY: Snow Lion, 1996).
117. Himalayan Bön Foundation, "Welcome," 2021.
118. Himalayan Bön Foundation, "A Khrid Dzogchen Training Program," 2021.
119. Himalayan Bön Foundation, "Outreach Projects," 2021.
120. Namdroling Monastery, 2021.
121. Naomi Worth, "My Own Pure Body, Channels, and Elements: The Teaching and Practice of Tibetan Yoga at Namdroling," *Religions*, 12, no. 6 (2021): 404.
122. For processes of transplantation, see Martin Baumann, "The Transplantation of Buddhism to Germany: Processive Modes and Strategies of Adaptation," *Method & Theory in the Study of Religion* 6, no. 1 (1994): 35–61.
123. George Dreyfus, "The Shuk-den Affair: History and Nature of a Quarrel," *Journal of the International Association of Buddhist Studies* 21, no. 2 (1998): 227–270, 245.
124. For a full discussion, see the Association of Gelug Masters, the Geluk International Foundation, and the Association for the Preservation of Geluk Monasticism, eds., *Understanding the Case Against Shukden: The History of a Contested Tibetan Practice*, trans. Gavin Kilty (Boston: Wisdom Publications, 2019).
125. Jeannine Chandler, "Invoking the Dharma Protector: Western Involvement in the Dorje Shugden Controversy," in *Buddhism beyond Borders: New Perspectives on Buddhism in the United States*, ed. Scott A. Mitchell and Natalie E. F. Quli (Albany: State University of New York Press, 2015), 75–91, 81.
126. For a discussion of this practice from within the tradition, see Dzongsar Jamyang Khyentse, *The Guru Drinks Bourbon?*
127. John Makransky, "Competing Paradigms in Western Spread of Tibetan Buddhism," conference presentation, Tantra and Daoism: A Multidisciplinary Conference on the Globalization of Religion and Its Experience, Boston University, Boston, Massachusetts, April 19–21, 2002.

128. Makransky, personal communication, August 9, 2002.
129. Chandler, "Invoking the Dharma Protector," 82.
130. Casey Kemp, personal communication via email, October 7, 2019.
131. David Gellner, "Himalayan Conundrum? A Puzzling Absence in Ronald M. Davidson's *Indian Esoteric Buddhism*," *Journal of the International Association of Buddhist Studies* 27, no. 2 (2004): 411–417, 413.
132. Sarah LeVine and David N. Gellner, *Rebuilding Buddhism: The Theravada Movement in Twentieth-Century Nepal* (Cambridge, MA: Harvard University Press, 2005), 31.
133. LeVine and Gellner, *Rebuilding Buddhism*, 35.
134. LeVine and Gellner, *Rebuilding Buddhism*, 35.
135. LeVine and Gellner, *Rebuilding Buddhism*, 36.
136. LeVine and Gellner, *Rebuilding Buddhism*, 35.
137. LeVine and Gellner, *Rebuilding Buddhism*, 36.
138. LeVine and Gellner, *Rebuilding Buddhism*, 254.
139. Richard K. Payne and Michael Witzel, eds., *Homa Variations: The Study of Ritual Change across the* Longue Durée (Oxford and New York: Oxford University Press, 2016), ix.
140. See Lhundub Sopa, Roger Jackson, and John Newman, *The Wheel of Time: The Kalachakra in Context*, ed. Beth Simon (Madison, WI: Deer Park Books, 1985), vii.
141. Laura Harrington, "Exorcising the Mandala: Kālacakra and the Neo-Pentecostal Response," *Journal of Global Buddhism* 13 (2012): 147–171.
142. Laura Harrington, "Exorcising the Mandala: Kālacakra and the Neo-Pentecostal Response," *Journal of Global Buddhism* 13 (2012): 147–171, 148.
143. Harrington, "Exorcising the Mandala," 149.
144. Harrington, "Exorcising the Mandala," 150.
145. Harrington, "Exorcising the Mandala," 155.
146. Harrington, "Exorcising the Mandala," 160.
147. Harrington, "Exorcising the Mandala," 162.
148. Csordas, "Introduction: Modalities of Transnational Transcendence"; and Rodney Stark and William Sims Bainbridge, *A Theory of Religion* (New Brunswick, NJ: Rutgers University Press, 1996).
149. Linda Learman, "Introduction."
150. Jonathan Walters, "Rethinking Buddhist Missions," 2 vols. (PhD diss., University of Chicago, 1992), Vol. 1, 5; cited in Learman, "Introduction," 2.
151. Dibeltulo, "The Revival of Tantrism"; see also Martino Dibeltulo Concu, "Tantrism, Modernity, History: On Lü Cheng's Philological Method," in *Sino-Tibetan Buddhism across the Ages*, ed. Shen Weirong and Ester Bianchi (Leiden: Brill, 2021).
152. Bianchi, "The Tantric Rebirth Movement in Modern China."
153. Cody Bahir, "Reenchanting Buddhism via Modernizing Magic: Guru Wuguang of Taiwan's Philosophy and Science of 'Superstition'" (PhD diss., Leiden University, 2017); Bahir, "Buddhist Master Wuguang's (1918–2000) Taiwanese Web"; Bahir, "Reformulating the Appropriated and Relinking the Chain; Bahir, "Replanting the Bodhi Tree"; and Bahir, "Telecommunicative Transmission."
154. Powers, *The Buddha Party*.
155. See Richard K. Payne, "Globalization," in *The Bloomsbury Handbook of Japanese Religions*, ed. Erica Baffelli, Fabio Rambelli, and Andrea Castiglioni, ch. 12, pp. 99–106 (London: Bloomsbury, 2021).
156. Eastman, "Incense at a Funeral."
157. Payne, "Hiding in Plain Sight."
158. Shoji, "'Buddhism in Syncretic Shape'."

159. Tuttle, "Uniting Religion and Politics in a Bid for Autonomy."
160. Chandler, "Invoking the Dharma Protector"; LeVine and Gellner, *Rebuilding Buddhism*; and Harrington, "Exorcising the Mandala."

Richard K. Payne

GUARDIAN/PROTECTOR DEITIES IN TIBETAN BUDDHISM

INTRODUCTION

In the tantric hermeneutics that suffuses Tibetan Buddhism, protector deities (Skt. *dharmapāla,* Tib. *chos skyong*) are identified as the third of the so-called three roots (Tib. *rtsa gsum*). The three roots are essentially an esoteric tantric parallel to the exoteric "three jewels" of Buddhism (i.e., the buddha, the dharma, and the sangha). Further, the three roots are a convenient schematic for dividing and classifying different types of tantric deities: the gurus or spiritual teachers who are the tantric equivalent of the buddha, the meditational deities (Tib. *yi dam*), which are seen as parallel to or embodiments of the dharma, and the protectors (or *ḍākinīs,* fierce tantric goddesses who often have a protective function) are the tantric equivalent of the sangha, the spiritual community of Buddhism.

This is not to say, however, that protector deities are especially "tantric" (however that term is defined) or, for that matter, particularly Tibetan. *Dharmapālas* have been a key theological aspect of Buddhism since its inception and are a significant (and still largely understudied) part of Buddhist pantheons throughout Asia. Among the earliest Indian Buddhist texts are spells for invoking forest spirits, called *yakṣas,* to protect monks from misfortune and evil forces.[1] But with the emphasis on wrathful imagery and the taming of dangerous spiritual forces so central to tantric Buddhist theology in particular came a massive proliferation of rituals, mythic literature, and art focusing on the (usually) wrathful dharma protectors. The warlike culture of imperial and postimperial Tibet was also an especially fertile ground for the growth of religious cults centered on these (primarily) wrathful deities.[2] But what exactly, doctrinally and cosmologically speaking, are Buddhist dharma protectors? How exactly are they significant and what distinguishes them within the enormous, kaleidoscopic pantheons of Buddhism, specifically Tibetan Tantric Buddhism?

THE COSMOLOGY OF PROTECTORS

Traditionally the Buddhist worldview, generally speaking, holds that the universe is populated by innumerable beings that fall into various broad categories represented by the (usually) five or six realms of possible rebirth. Most of these beings are various species of ethereal entities that are often, somewhat misleadingly, called "spirits" or "demons" in Western scholarly literature.[3] Some have argued that the Greek word daemon is a more appropriate umbrella term for these types of entities in the study of Eurasian religions.[4] Like most preindustrial societies (and some postindustrial ones), Tibetans have traditionally viewed the world as teeming with various species of these nonhuman, often (but not always) invisible daemons. There are various general terms for these beings in Tibetan, including lhadre (*lha 'dre*, "god-demons," or "gods and demons") and *drekpa* (*'dregs pa*, "haughty ones"). Traditional Tibetan sources provide assorted taxonomies for classifying different types of daemons, but these taxonomies are far from standardized, and the daemonic species lists often vary, sometimes wildly, depending on the source. Many of the categories of daemon used in Tibetan sources were imported from India and were often mapped onto similar pre-Buddhist Tibetan daemon species.

A few of the most important species of Indo-Tibetan daemons that are often mentioned in the taxonomies are *deva* (Tib. *lha*), *yakṣa* (Tib. *gnod sbyin*), *nāga* (Tib. *klu*), *rākṣasa* (Tib. *srin po*), *graha* (Tib. *gza'*), *mātṝkās* (Tib. *ma mo*), and *māra* (Tib. *bdud*). Certain other species that are quite popular in Tibetan contexts but do not have obvious Indian parallels include beings like *tsen* (*btsan*), *damsi* (*dam sri*), and teurang (*the'u rang*).[5] While most of these species have specific distinguishing characteristics (*nāgas/klu*, for instance, are typically, though not always, associated with the water and are depicted as serpentine), in certain cases the different categories can be somewhat interchangeable. Also, hybridization is common, where certain types of daemons are described by more than one species name (i.e., "*klu-bdud*").

Many of these daemonic beings are portrayed in liturgical and narrative Buddhist literature as being "dharma protectors," which is to say they are understood to have taken refuge in the buddha and sworn to protect his teachings. In many cases they are believed to be protecting Buddhism (and specifically the human followers of Buddhism) from other daemonic beings who are non-Buddhist and who may cause various obstacles to harm Buddhists. In other cases, they may be invoked to protect against human threats. As such, these beings effectively constitute a "spiritual" sangha, a community of daemonic beings that support the human sangha.

Historically, the most popular and cosmologically most important protector deities are classified as *lokottara* (hypercosmic) deities (Tib. *'Jigs rten las 'das pa'i srung ma*), which is to say they have transcended the world and have achieved the same enlightenment as a buddha. These transcendent protector deities are believed to have at least reached the eighth bodhisattva level, the stage of "irreversibility," and so it is considered impossible for them to regress again to an unenlightened state. As such they are entirely benevolent in their intentions despite their wrathful appearance and fearsome methods. Other protectors, however, are classified as unenlightened and "worldly" or encosmic (Skt. *laukika*, Tib. *'Jigs rten pa'i srung ma*) and in a sense are no different from, or perhaps even soteriologically inferior to, a human practitioner of the dharma. In Tibetan Buddhist art, both hypercosmic and encosmic deities are typically depicted in the forms of various species of *lhadre*, but in the case of the enlightened protectors, this is simply a skillful means, a mere appearance meant to help them "tame" or forcibly convert hostile non-Buddhist daemons or humans.[6]

As a rule, *dharmapālas* that were imported from India (or at least are believed to have originally come from India) into Tibet are translocal, hypercosmic, enlightened protectors. The cosmological and soteriological status of high-level Indian enlightened protectors such as Mahākāla (Tib. Nag po Chen po) and Śrī Devī (Tib. Dpal ldan Lha mo) is such that they are often regarded as simply docetic manifestations of buddhas or bodhisattvas with a specific protective function. In contrast, local Tibetan protectors that are often associated with a specific place, such as the mountain god Yarlha Shampo (Yar lha Sham po), most of whom are believed to have been later converted to the dharma by tantric Buddhist saints such as Padmasambhava (8th century), Milarepa (1052–1135), and Rwa Lotsāwa (1016–1128?), are usually considered unenlightened or encosmic protectors. However, there are certain cases of local protectors who may start their careers, so to speak, as a worldly guardian of a particular region or monastery and, due to their popularity and increasing importance, are "promoted" to the rank of a hypercosmic enlightened deity.

One especially well-known example of a case like this is found with the deity Pehar (Pe har), who in the historical record began as the worldly protector of Tibet's first Buddhist monastery, Samye (Bsam yas), and later was promoted to be one of the main protectors of the Dalai Lamas' theocratic state, with his own retinue of manifested "ministers," one of whom is still the official state oracle of the Tibetan exile government.[7] Pehar is only one of many protector deities (usually of the encosmic variety) who are ritually summoned and channeled through special spirit mediums for a variety of divination and apotropaic purposes.[8]

Other protector deities blur the seemingly tidy theoretical line between enlightened and worldly and even the distinction between guru, yidam, and protector. Tibetan Buddhism contains a host of different teaching and tantric transmission lineages, schools, and subschools, and there are different specific protector deities, or forms of protectors, associated with each one. Opinions about which protectors are enlightened and which are worldly often come down to what informant one is asking or the textual source at which one is looking. For instance, the special protector of the Drikung Kagyu (Bri gung bka' brgyud) school, not particularly worshipped as such outside of that particular school, is a goddess named Achi Chokyi Drolma (A phyi chos kyi sgrol ma) and is believed to be a kind of ascended form of the grandmother of Jigten Gonpo ('Jig rten mgon po rin chen dpal, 1143–1217), the founder of the Drikung Kagyu. It is said that in life, she was an enlightened tantric practitioner who vowed to be reborn as a *dharmapāla* to protect future generations of Drikung disciples, but in certain liturgical contexts in the Drikung Kagyu, she can also be invoked as a meditational deity and as a guru.[9] Thus, even the distinctions between guru, meditational deity, and protector deity mentioned at the outset can be seriously blurred in practice.

PROTECTOR RITUALS

Tibetan tantric Buddhism is hyperritualized. There are dozens of different genres of rituals and liturgies for invoking, worshipping, meditating upon, or self-identifying with and making offerings to a massive (implicit) pantheon of deities.[10] Protector rituals form a key part of this tradition to the point that there is a special day set aside on the Tibetan liturgical calendar, the 29th day of every lunar month, that is specifically dedicated to making offerings to protector deities, though many Tibetans, lay and monastic, will engage in some kind of ritual worship of one or more protector deities every day.

Protector rituals can be extremely long and complex ceremonies invoking long lists of many different deities or brief rather generic liturgies invoking only one. Some are performed in monasteries or temples publicly, involving complex dances by masked and costumed dancers, while others are performed privately in the homes of lay devotees. There are supplication prayers (*gsol 'debs*), fire offering (*sbyin sreg*), smoke offering (*bsang*), and thread-cross (*mdos*) rituals, to name but a few, that invoke and propitiate protectors in various ways. The most ubiquitous protector-oriented ritual in Tibetan culture is the "golden libation" (*gser skyems*), where an offering of usually alcohol or tea is made to the *dharmapālas*, especially on the lunar calendar's "protector day." Such rituals are done on a regularly scheduled basis, but can also be performed as needed if a practitioner feels it is warranted, or at the advice of a guru.[11]

The reasons for invoking protectors can also vary quite broadly. Rituals may be done to appease them on a regular basis simply for a desired general apotropaic effect. Worldly protectors, being unenlightened, are seen as potentially quite volatile and liable to cause harm as likely as help. Thus, regular offerings are made to them as a way of pacifying their tempers and keeping them happy. Even enlightened protectors are said to have retinues of unenlightened daemons which can be angered if offerings are not made in a correct and timely way. The assistance and good will of protectors, both enlightened and worldly, are often seen as critical necessities in both day-to-day secular life and in religious training. During meditation and practice retreats, for instance, Tibetan monastics and yogis will make sure to regularly make offerings and prayers to protectors as a key and indispensable part of their tantric *sādhanā* as a way of ensuring obstacles do not hinder their spiritual practice.

Beyond general apotropaic insurance, however, lamas and tantric yogis will commonly invoke protectors in the capacity of "familiar spirits" for specific goals. Protectors are commonly invoked in liturgical texts to carry out the four types of enlightened action (*phrin las rnam bzhi*), or the four types of tantric magic, namely, pacification (*zhi*), increase (*rgyas*), overpowering (*dbang*), and destruction (*drag*). Here a practitioner will invoke and exhort the protector deity from the perspective of his or her meditational deity and, as such, the invocation of the protectors is done within the context of tantric generation stage (*skyed rim*) meditation. In other words, the *yogin* or *yoginī* does not (dare) command a protector from the perspective of an ordinary being, but only from the perspective of the enlightened being that the practitioner is used to seeing as him- or herself in habitual meditation. Certain protectors are also typically paired with certain *yi dam* deities, depending on the tantric lineage and school. For example, in the Gelukpa (Dge lugs pa) tradition, Palden Lhamo (Dpal ldan Lha mo) is typically invoked by the practitioner in the form of the extremely fierce meditation deity Vajrabhairava.

PROTECTOR MYTHOLOGY

While not as literarily developed as the Hindu mythology of India found, for example, in the *Brāhmaṇa* and *Purāṇa* collections, the mythological literature of Tibetan Buddhist protectors is quite extensive and is perhaps the most understudied feature of tantric deities in scholarship. In Tibetan Buddhism, the mythology of protectors (and deities in general) is historically most developed within the Nyingma (Rnying ma) school and by primarily Nyingma authors. Concordantly, the cult of protectors is especially advanced in the Nyingma school generally. Hosts of local Tibetan deities and special central Asian forms of "Indian" deities have been ritually, liturgically, iconographically, and mythologically developed by Nyingma authors and within Nyingma texts much more so than by their Sarma (Gsar ma) counterparts. In fact, certain protectors, or special forms of protectors, that became popular in the Sarma schools, such as Makzor Gyelmo (Dmag zor rgyal mo) in the Gelukpa school, (likely) originally come from Nyingma literature.

Mythological narratives about protectors (and meditational deities as well) are commonly found in the Mahāyoga tantras of the *Nyingma Gyubum* (*Rnying ma Rgyud 'bum*) and similar

Mahāyoga "terma" (*gter ma*) treasure texts. Nyingma tantras focused on protector deities are typically ritual instructions for how to invoke, worship, and command them, packaged with narratives (typically called *lo rgyus*, "histories") that function as a kind of "charter myth" for the ritual, explaining the origins of the deity (often in the form of a theogony identifying the protector deity's parents and the circumstances of their birth) and the context in which they became protectors of the Buddhist dharma.[12] While there are, of course, also histories of protector deities by Sarma authors, even these tend to be inspired by or taken directly from Nyingma sources. The most extensive extant premodern collection of protector deity mythology, Lelung Zhepe Dorje's 1734 *The Biographies from the Ocean of Oath-Bound Protectors* (*Dam can bstan srung rgya mtsho'i rnam thar*), draws mainly on Nyingma sources.[13]

The following presents a series of iconographic and mythological profiles of several especially important protector deities in the implicit pantheon of Tibetan Buddhism. Due to space limitations, the focus is mainly on deities and their close associates that appear in a comprehensively theogonic text called *The History of Abse* (*A bse'i byung khungs lo rgyus mdo tsam brjod pa*). Written by Lelung's son, Kunga Migyur Dorje (Kun dga' mi 'gyur rdo rje, 1721–1769), *The History of Abse* draws on several scriptural sources and likely oral traditions to lay out a family tree of Buddhist protectors in five generations. While there is a certain level of arbitrariness in the choices of this text and these protectors, all these deities have historically been particularly popular subjects in Tibetan liturgy, literature, and art and have had pride of place in the major schools of Tibetan Buddhism up to the present day, and thus serve as a good representative sample or cross section of protector deity cults in Tibetan Buddhism.

MAHĀKĀLA AND THE ŚAIVITE COMPLEX

By far the most ubiquitous dharma protector in Tibetan Buddhism, and also historically quite popular in Indian Buddhism and in Buddhism in other areas of Asia, is Mahākāla (Nag po chen po). In Tibetan Buddhism, Mahākāla is in some sense synonymous with the concept of a protector, since he is often simply called Gonpo (Mgon po, "protector").[14] However, it is perhaps more useful to think of Mahākāla as a category of deity than a singular god, since there are a bewildering number of myriad forms attributed to or classified under the name Mahākāla. In general, Mahākāla is typically depicted in liturgical descriptions and related paintings as black in color (unsurprising given that his name lierally translates as "the great black one"), with the appearance of a *yakṣa* or *rākṣasa* demon—thick-limbed, heavy body, snarling fanged mouth, and enraged, blood-shot eyes (usually three).[15] Beyond that very basic description, however, the various forms of Mahākāla can vary quite widely. Some of the more commonly worshipped forms include six-armed (Mgon po phyag drug), four-faced (Mgon po zhal bzhi pa), raven-headed (Mgon po bya rog gdong can), the Lord of the Pavilion (Gur gyi mgon po), and Black Cloak (Ber nag chen) Mahākāla. There is the Brāhmanarūpa form, which has a more typical human shape with the appearance of an Indian *brahmin*, and a six-armed form which is especially propitiated as a wealth deity and is distinctly white rather than the typical black. The black six-armed form is particularly popular in the Gelukpa school, the Lord of the Pavilion in the Sakya (Sa skya), and the Black Cloak form in the Karma Kagyu. A popular Nyingma form of Mahākāla is Gonpo Maning (Mgon po Ma ning, the "Eunich" Mahākāla), though he is somewhat secondary in popularity to a trinity of other Nyingma deities that are discussed later.

In general, Mahākāla is effectively a Buddhist transformation, or version, of the Indian god Śiva. Mahākāla is an epithet for Śiva (also the name of a disciple of that god) in Hinduism, and much of his Buddhist mythology, as developed primarily in various scriptures from the Nyingma tantric canon, is clearly inspired by or simply retellings of Hindu *Purāṇic* Śaivite myths. Śiva in tantric Buddhism, beginning primarily with what the Tibetan tradition classifies as the "Yoga Tantras," identifies the god Śiva, typically called Maheśvara (Dbang phyug chen po), as the primary cosmic villain and opponent of the Buddhist dharma. He is consistently described as the overlord of all worldly daemons and concordantly comes to symbolize negative emotions (anger in particular, with his consort Umā Devī typically representing the emotional poison of desire or craving) and soteriological obstacles in general, fulfilling much the same function as Māra does in the earlier sutric Buddhist tradition. As such, tantric Buddhist mythological literature also portrays him as the primary target for conversion to the Buddhist dharma and consequent transformation into a dharma protector.

Western scholars have often tended to interpret the literal demonization of the important Hindu god Śiva in Buddhism in sociopolitical terms. The argument generally goes that during the tantric age of Indian history, roughly spanning the second half of the first millennium, Buddhists and Śaivites were locked in a constant competition for patronage, and consequently (and quite naturally), the Buddhists portrayed their deities as being superior to the Śaivite gods. While this political interpretation is not necessarily entirely incorrect, it is misleadingly reductionist. Buddhist theology has always been "transtheistic" in orientation, and while the tantric myths of Śiva's subjugation are admittedly more violently graphic than previous portrayals of the buddha's superiority over worldly gods, Buddhist doctrine simply does not make sense except within a framework of *lokottara* (hypercosmic) deities as cosmologically and soteriologically superior to *laukika* (encosmic) ones.[16]

A number of Yoga and later Highest Yoga tantras describe the violent subjugation of Maheśvara by various wrathful Buddhist deities such as Vajrapāṇi. In the Nyingma tantras, Śiva is typically referred to as "Rudra," Śiva's original, malevolent Vedic form, and there are many retellings of the myth of his subjugation in different Nyingma tantric texts. The most extensive and well-known version of the Nyingma Rudra subjugation myth, told in the *Gathering of Intentions Sutra* (*Dgongs pa 'dus pa'i mdo*, and closely related versions like the one found in the famous hagiography of Padmasambhava, the *Padma Katang* [*Padma Bka' Thang*]), presents Rudra as effectively the anti-buddha, complete with a previous life story as a Buddhist aspirant in the distant past named Tharpa Nakpo (Thar pa nag po, "Black Liberator") who grievously misunderstood his guru's teachings. After committing a litany of crimes, including serial rape and murder, he took innumerable births in hell and other extremely low states of existence. Eventually he was reborn as a powerful hybrid demon named Rudra, who went on to overthrow the gods of the world brutally and ruthlessly, becoming a monstrous cosmic overlord who caused suffering to innumerable beings. The buddhas, as a means of saving the world, could only subdue Rudra by taking exceedingly wrathful (and sexual) forms that were a deliberate mimesis of him, thus explaining and justifying the wrathful and sexual practices employed in Buddhist tantra.[17]

The Rudra subjugation myth was told and retold many times, in various versions, in various Nyingma tantras and *terma* texts. Many versions explicitly link him with Mahākāla, explaining or suggesting that Rudra is identical with Mahākāla. In the *Padma Katang*, for instance, Rudra becomes Mahākāla after his subjugation and conversion to Buddhism. In other versions, Śiva is the father (or stepfather) of Mahākāla. In one elaborate story about Mahākāla from a *terma* text attributed to Jatson Nyingpo ('Ja' tshon snying po, 1585–1656), his origin is traced to a Buddhist monk apprenticed to a previous buddha in the distant past. An evil anti-Buddhist king who worshipped Māra attacked and attempted to kill the buddha's disciples. In response, the monks and nuns prayed that upon their death they would be reborn as vicious daemons, such as *yakṣas* and *rākṣasas*, so that they could consequently act in the capacity of dharma protectors to punish and subdue evildoers such as the oppressive king.

Their aspirations for rebirth as wrathful daemons were successful, and one *arhat* in particular (named "Peaceful Light") is reborn as the son of the wrathful form of the buddha (named Heruka, the typical title of wrathful tantric buddha forms, translated into Tibetan as *khrag thung* or "blood drinker") and Śiva's consort Umā Devī. The daemonic child was called Vajrarākṣa (aka Mahākāla), who set out and quickly conquered the three realms of existence and "liberated" (that is, killed) Māra's four ministers. Māra was understandably upset by the appearance of this apparent rival to his position as cosmic overlord and summoned an enormous army of *asuras*, the traditional demonic enemies of the gods in Indian mythology, and other daemonic creatures and they began to indiscriminately attack and kill sentient beings, going so far as to rout the gods in the Heaven of the Thirty-Three (Trāyastriṃśa). To stop this slaughter, Indra, the king of the gods, sent a group of goddesses to Mahākāla to entice him into becoming the leader of the gods in a counterattack against Māra. With a vast emanated army of servitor daemons and exceedingly wrathful displays, Mahākāla overwhelmed and obliterated Māra's armies, which the story describes in graphic detail.[18]

Once Māra and his armies are destroyed, the narrative especially emphasizes Mahākāla's role as the overlord and master of all encosmic daemons and thereafter is established as the supreme protector of the gods by Indra himself.[19] Tibetan Buddhist protector myths like this one, while on one level narratively simple and straightforward, skillfully weave together and transvalue the structures and mythemes of earlier Indian *Purāṇic, Māravijaya,* and *Avadāna* literature. Iconographically and mythologically, Mahākāla is the archetypal protector par excellence and, as effectively the Buddhist transvaluation of the Hindu god Śiva, he serves as a template for all other protectors, consistently recognized in theogonic descriptions as the progenitor and overlord of all protector deities.

THE GLORIOUS GODDESS(ES)

Śrī Devī, or Palden Lhamo, the Glorious Goddess, perhaps even more than Mahākāla, is best understood as a category of interrelated and similar forms and subforms of goddesses rather than as a singular deity. These subforms go by many names, some of the most well-known ones being Dungkyongma (Dung skyong ma), Jemo Remati (Rje mo re ma ti), Rangjung Gyalmo (Rang byung rgyal mo), Dustanma (Dus mtshan ma), and the Bonpo version of the goddess Sipe Gyalmo (Srid pa'i Rgyal mo), the "Queen of Existence," the latter name best capturing the general role of Palden Lhamo as the supreme goddess of samsara and specifically of the desire realm in which most sentient beings are born. As Lelung puts it in his unparalleled history of Tibetan Buddhist protectors, "This Queen of the Three Worlds is known by a hundred titles and a thousand names."[20] Perhaps her most well-known and popular form is Makzor Gyalmo (the "Army Repelling Queen") who is one of the main protectors of the Gelukpa school (and the Sakya before them) and the special protector of the Dalai Lamas from the time of the first incarnation of the lineage, Gendun Drup (Dge 'dun grub, 1391–1474), who had visions of the goddess from the time of his childhood. The Second Dalai Lama Gendun Gyatso (Dge 'dun rgya mtsho, 1475–1542) would go on to expand the cult of Palden Lhamo, establishing her oracle lake at Chokhor Gyatso (Chos 'khor rgya mtsho), which was later used to identify the successive Dalai Lama incarnations.[21] According to a history of the worship of Palden Lhamo by the Second Dalai Lama, her cult was introduced from the tantric holy land of Oddiyana (probably western India or northern Pakistan) into Tibet in the 11th century, and the first known representations of her are from Ladakh, also likely dating around the 11th century.[22] Much later, as one of the main official protectors of the central Tibetan government into the 20th century, Palden Lhamo was referenced in the iconography of the modern Tibetan flag in the form of blue rays of light alongside red rays, which represent another important protector, discussed later.

Makzor Gyalmo is typically depicted as having an extremely wrathful black hag-like appearance, thick-bodied (although some related forms depict her as emaciated), with dangling breasts. She has two arms, one holding a vajra-tipped club and the other holding the skull bowl of a child born from an illicit (sometimes incestuous) union, filled with blood. She chews a corpse with vicious fangs, wears a tiger skin, and rides a donkey or horse amid a halo of apocalyptic flames over a swirling sea of blood. She has various symbolically important items tied to her saddle, including a pair of dice, representing her control over karmic fate and her status as an important divination deity.[23] She also possesses a sack of diseases, symbolizing her status as mistress over both the cause and cure of illness, and her position as the leader of the *mamo*, female daemons depicted as black hags holding sacks of diseases. As noted, there are a number of other forms of Palden Lhamo, but for the most part, iconographically they follow the same basic template. Like Mahākāla, the different main forms tend to simply add more heads and arms and include different hand implements (e.g., a scorpion-hilted sword instead of the vajra club). She is often depicted with a retinue of other popular goddesses or groups of goddesses, many of which are of Tibetan rather than Indian origin, such as the five Tseringma (Tshe ring ma) sisters and the twelve Tenma (Bstan ma bcu gnyis) goddesses. She is also commonly said to have four attendant goddesses that represent the four seasons.[24]

These different forms or epiphanies are considered separate or ultimately the same deity, depending on context and the hermeneutical and theological framework employed by the author of a particular text. In general, Palden Lhamo is essentially the feminine version of Mahākāla and is sometimes simply called Mahākalī (Tib. Nag mo chen). In Tibetan protector theogonies, she is often regarded as the daughter of Śiva and Umā and the sister and consort of Mahākāla. Her iconography, nomenclature, and mythology often appear to be essentially an amalgam of elements borrowed from Hindu goddesses. Her general appearance is reminiscent of Kalī and other related fearsome tantric goddesses like Cāmuṇḍā, but she is usually regarded in Tibet as the wrathful manifestation of Saraswatī, an enlightened wisdom deity and Buddhist version of the Hindu goddess of learning and the arts. Another related form (or common epithet) of Palden Lhamo is "Remati," perhaps related to the *Purāṇic* Revati, who is the wife of Balarāma, the older brother of Krishna. The iconography of Palden Lhamo's donkey animal vehicle, however, seems to connect her more specifically to Kāḷarātri, the seventh and most fearsome form of the Navadurga, the nine main forms of the goddess Durga. Her Tibetan mythology also references the Hindu *Śākta* theological idea that Durga is the manifestation of the combined power of all the (male) gods.[25] In the Nyingma *Pure Gold of the Glorious Black Goddess* (*Dpal lha mo nag mo gser gyi sbram bu*) *Tantra*, for instance, it is said that in a previous life she was a goddess emanated from the bodies of the gods to help them defeat the *asuras*.[26] Lelung, citing the Nyingma *Blazing Flame* (*Me lce 'bar ma*) *Tantra*, gives an elaborate origin myth of the goddess spanning multiple lives.[27]

It is said that during the time of Krakucchaṃda Buddha, the first buddha of our current era, the being who would become Palden Lhamo was a goddess of light who generated the mind of bodhicitta and practiced nothing but the ten virtues. During the time of the next buddha, Kanakamuni, she was known as the goddess "Glorious Lady" and indulged in ordinary anger. During the time of Śākyamuni Buddha, there was a monk disciple to whom she made offerings and confessed her sins. Because of the karmic ripening of these actions over three lifetimes, for practicing the ten virtues she was born as the daughter of Mahādeva, the king of the gods. For indulging her anger in the second life, she became the wife of a *rākṣasa* and took on an extremely fearsome appearance. Finally, due to her offerings, confession, and prayers to the monk, she was given empowerment by all the buddhas and was established as a supreme dharma protector.

Later, the gods and the *asuras* went to war over control of a paradisical wish-fulfilling tree. Though controlled by the gods, the *asuras* wanted access to it, which the gods would not grant. Led by their various kings, including "Herankoshu" (possibly an adaptation of "Hiraṇyakaśipu," an *asura* demon famous from Indian *Purāṇic* mythology, perhaps best known for being slain by Viṣṇu's *avatar* Narasiṃha), the *asura* armies invaded the Heaven of the Thirty-Three. To prepare for battle, the gods drank from lakes of molten metal to become extremely wrathful. The craftsman of the gods, Viśvakarmā, forged for them millions of suits of armor and a vast array of weapons which they used in battle against the *asuras*, but to no avail, as every time the *asuras* shed blood, their numbers increased as more and more magically manifested warriors sprang forth. Unable to counter this endlessly replenishing army, the gods were defeated and the *asuras* were victorious.

Then Vajrapāṇi, the bodhisattva of power and often identified as the supreme wrathful tantric buddha, emanated a blazing syllable, *hūṃ*, from his heart, which dissolved into the god Viṣṇu's forehead. Then from Viṣṇu's head burst forth a blue woman whose hair was braided with *vaidurya* jewels and who possessed all the major and minor marks of a buddha, and her name was Umā Devī. Upon seeing her, all the gods desired to make her their wife, but Vajrapāṇi declared that, for the sake of benefiting the six classes of beings and so that the *asuras* could be defeated, she should be wedded to Īśvara (Śiva). At that time, Śiva was practicing intense yogic discipline in a charnel ground, and the other gods led Umā to him. Intense desire arose between them, and Śiva and Umā made love for 49 days, producing two primary offspring, the lord of death, Mahākāla, and his sister, Cāmuṇḍī.[28] Then, as the gods' champions, these two led the gods into battle against the *asuras* once more, and it is said Mahākāla repelled the *asuras* with a spear the size of Mount Meru. But the same problem as before arose, as magically emanated *asura* soldiers sprang forth whenever *asura* blood was shed. In what seems to be a clear reference to Kalī's consumption of Raktabīja's blood in the *Devī Māhātmya*, Cāmuṇḍī decapitated Herankoshu, collected all the *asuras* blood in his skull, and drank it, thus stopping the endlessly respawning reinforcements. The goddess then constructed a fortress of the gods at her navel, seemingly a symbol that she had integrated the power of all the gods within herself and then routed the evil *asuras*, allowing the gods to retake control of the wish-fulfilling tree.

Perhaps Palden Lhamo's most well-known mythological origins, however, appear to be a Tibetan adaptation of the Indian epic the *Rāmāyana*, with the goddess taking the role of a wrathful version of Sītā. As usual, there are multiple versions of the story, but the basic plot is that the demon king of Sri Lanka abducted her and forced her to rule at his side as his queen. There she took on the appearance of a *rākṣasa* demon, developed a taste for flesh and blood, learned methods of slaughter and warfare, and acquired many weapons and tools for magical subjugation (in one version, she steals the demon king's especially powerful sword). In some versions, she kills her son (who was destined to rule next and bring great harm to beings) and ties his flayed skin around herself as she escapes, riding away on a horse or donkey. She then goes to Śākyamuni Buddha and vows to become a dharma protector. While it is said that when she first swore to be a Buddhist *dharmapāla* she was a worldly, encosmic deity, eventually she achieved enlightenment, becoming a *lokottara* or hypercosmic protector.[29]

THE NYINGMA TRINITY

As mentioned, the main protectors of a particular teaching lineage, temple, or monastery in Tibetan Buddhism are historically conditional (often based on the influence and preferences of influential lamas) and often vary wildly from one to another. But while many forms of Mahākāla and the equine-riding forms of Palden Lhamo were iconographically and mythologically developed in the context of Nyingma scriptures and liturgies, these two deity types are not especially popular in the Nyingma tradition, or at least not as much as in the Sarma schools. The three deities that are typically regarded as the main Nyingma protectors are the popular trinity of Ekajaṭī, Rāhula, and Dorje Lekpa (Rdo rje legs pa). These three are also in particular considered the principal protectors of the Nyingma *terma* traditions. The first two, Ekajaṭī and Rāhula, are based on Indian deities but over time, probably beginning in the 8th or 9th centuries during the early spread of Buddhism in Tibet and the subsequent collapse of the Tibetan Empire, they developed their own distinctive central Asian iconography. Dorje Lekpa is likely to have originally been a Tibetan deity, though he does have a Sanskrit version of his name, Vajrasādhu.

Ekajaṭī (Tib. Ral gcig ma) fulfills many of the same symbolic and cosmological roles as Palden Lhamo and in some cases is identified as simply yet another form of her. Like Palden Lhamo, she is typically depicted as reminiscent of Kalī, a black, exceedingly wrathful, hag-like goddess. Just as with Palden Lhamo, she is especially connected with and considered the queen of the disease-causing female *mamo daemons*. The name Ekajaṭī means "single braid," which refers to her single braid of hair, but in her typical Nyingma form, she has one of the most bizarre appearances of any Tibetan Buddhist deity, possessing not only just a single braid of hair, but also only one eye, one fanged tooth, one breast, and, in some cases, only one leg.[30]

The fact that she has only one of these body parts is a reference to the metaphysical idea of the fundamental oneness of ultimate reality.

Rāhula is an especially fascinating case of a relatively minor deity in Indian mythology and cosmology being radically transformed and apotheosized in the Tibetan context.[31] Rāhula (known, of course, by many other names including Gza' bdud chen po, "the great planetary demon") is primarily based on Rāhu, one of the lords of the *asuras* in Indian mythology, and in Indian astrology is regarded as arguably the most malefic of the *navagraha*, the nine planets. According to his well-known Indian origin myth, he was the only *asura* who managed to get a taste of the elixir of immortality by disguising himself as a god. Exposed by the sun and moon gods, Rāhu was then decapitated by Viṣṇu, but since he had become immortal, he continued to live as a disembodied head. He swore revenge on the sun and moon and periodically temporarily swallowed them, causing solar and lunar eclipses.

The Tibetan Rāhula is effectively a combination of Rāhu and Viṣṇu (one of his names is Khyab 'jug chen po, Skt. Mahaviṣṇu) as well as possibly an amalgam of Near and Middle Eastern and Chinese astrological ideas. In his most common Tibetan iconography, he has almost as striking and strange an appearance as Ekajaṭī. He has nine main heads, three rows of three each representing different types of daemons as well as the nine planets of Indo-Tibetan astrology, topped by a raven or crow head that protrudes from his crown. His upper body is humanoid, with two or four arms, and on his belly is yet another face with an enormous mouth with which he devours the mundane universe. His lower body is that of a snake which coils in a sea of blood. Less common forms of Rāhula show or describe him with a fully humanoid body with legs, but riding on the back of a dragon. This serpentine or draconic aspect is much more prominent in Tibetan iconography than in the Indian iconography of Rāhu and perhaps relates more closely to Near or Middle Eastern conceptions of a cosmic dragon.

As a deity of the sky or atmosphere, Rāhula is also associated with bad weather, in particular hail. The za (*gza'*) or planetary spirits, of which Rāhula is the lord, are also infamous in Tibetan medicine for causing diseases related to the brain, such as stroke and epilepsy. Given these malefic associations, there is a long tradition in Nyingma and Nyingma-aligned lineages (e.g., the Drikung Kagyu) of invoking Rāhula as in effect a daemonic familiar in working black magic to kill enemies. Famously, Tibet's master yogi, Milarepa, in the early part of his life is known to have invoked a form of Rāhula to massacre a wedding party and destroy the crops of his home village out of revenge for his family's mistreatment.[32]

An elaborate mythological tradition has grown up around Rāhula as well, which integrates even while transvaluing Rāhu's Indian mythology. According to one commentarial text, in a past life, Rāhula was a Buddhist yogi named Great Planet Man (Gza' chen skyes po), who, while dwelling in meditation in a forest near a capital city, happened to meet the four wives of the local king. These women were so impressed with his dharma teachings that they begged their lord husband to invite the yogi to become their official court chaplain, and so the king did. The yogi accepted the king's offer and remained the court priest for a year while the king was away waging war. During this time, jealous ministers at court started a rumor that Planet Man was having affairs with the king's wives. When the king returned and learned of this, he sentenced the yogi to a wrongful execution. Despite the desperate pleas of his wives, the king had Planet Man burned alive on a pyre of sandalwood. Before he died, the yogi cursed the king and declared:

> I, the young monastic seer, am unstained by corrupted vows and defilements. If I am pure, without sin, after I pass from this life, may I have the terrifying form of a *yakṣa-rākṣasa*, spewing a breath of poison and disease. Those with evil thoughts, and who are hostile, greatly arrogant kings, whoever has the five poisons, women and those who are handicapped, [those] with a great desire for wealth, monks who break the rules of discipline, warlords who commit evil actions, officials who secretly take food bribes, destroyers of the laws of the land... may I be the master who takes their life force. If, clothed in compulsions and habitual faults, I touched the bodies of the queens, having been born in the vajra hell, may I never escape! Also, the four queens of the king in every time and state, may they be inseparable from me! Acting as my servants and slaves, may [they] slaughter vow corrupters![33]

So distraught by the sage's execution were the queens that they immediately committed *sati*, throwing themselves on his pyre and committing suicide. It is implied that they were later reborn as the four animal-headed retinue goddess with whom Rāhula is commonly depicted.

In his next life, the sage was born as the son of an exceedingly wrathful *rākṣasa* father who lived on the top of the cosmic mountain Sumeru and an intensely lustful *nāga* mother who lived in the ocean. In one version of Rāhula's origins in the *Nyingma Gyubum*, he is explained to essentially be the condensed essence of the universal afflictions of ignorance, wrath, and desire. Soon after he was born, Rāhula began causing terrible calamities on a cosmic scale. In a Tibetan Buddhist retelling of Rāhu's Indian myth, Rāhula attacked heaven and stole the elixir of immortality of the gods. The sun and the moon caught him, but he swallowed them and spread eighteen kinds of disease among the gods. Frightened, Indra ran for help to Vajrapāṇi, who became enraged and smashed Rāhula's head into nine pieces with his vajra scepter. Later he cut the demon's body into eight pieces but ultimately reconstituted him. Sufficiently chastised and intimidated, Rāhula offered his life force to Vajrapāṇi and vowed from then on to act as a protector of the Buddhist dharma.

The third main Nyingma protector, Dorje Lekpa, is likely of wholly central Asian origin and is identified as one of the many deities subjugated by Padmasambhava when that great tantric Buddhist master traveled through Tibet in the 8th century. His typical appearance is distinctly Tibetan as well, as he wears a long brocade robe, boots, and broad-brimmed hat. He rides on either a lion or a goat, wields a vajra in one hand, and holds a heart in the other. He is intensely wrathful and usually red in color. Like all major protectors, Dorje Lekpa has a kaleidoscopic array of alternate forms and emanations. Perhaps the most popular of these is Garwa Nagpo (Mgar ba nag po), a patron deity of blacksmiths who carries the accessories of that trade. He also has several other forms related to marginalized social groups, with names like "Black Brigand" and "Black Tribesman." Dorje Lekpa is typically identified as the lord of the *tsen*, a particularly Tibetan class of daemon that does not have a clear Indian parallel (more on them is given later), although Dorje Lekpa's retinue of 360 "brothers" is said to include many different types of daemon. He is said to consort with the *tenma* goddesses, a popular group of twelve female protectors, also of Tibetan origin, and is sometimes grouped with other more localized deities like the mountain god Nyenchen Tanglha (Gnyen chen thang lha). Despite this local Tibetan "flavor," however, and the story of his forced conversion to Buddhism by Padmasambhava (or in other myths by the wrathful Buddhist deity

Hayagrīva), he is still consistently understood to be a fully enlightened protector, at least within the Nyingma school.

Furthermore, despite his Tibetan origin, Dorje Lekpa is often given explicit connections to India in his mythology.[34] In one of his many origin stories, quoted by Lelung from an obscure Nyingma tantra, he is said to have been a brahmin sage in a very remote past life. Possessing great intelligence and religious enthusiasm at an early age, his parents gave him permission to take monastic vows when he was only twelve. He soon completely abandoned the householder life and took to practicing intense asceticism in a thatched hut in the famous "Cool Grove" charnel ground, one of India's main legendary tantric holy places, and came to be known as the Brahmin Putapa. Rumor began circulating that this brahmin was practicing evil mantras (hostile tantric black magic practices) and the local king came to believe that the sage was attempting to undermine his authority, consequently ordering his ministers to deal with the problem. The ministers questioned Putapa, and although he denied engaging in hostile magic and claimed he only practiced pure asceticism, the ministers set fire to his hut with him inside. Just as in Rāhula's origin story, the brahmin cast a curse as he was being burned alive, vowing to be reborn as a vicious daemon by the power of his merit.

Another dark *jātaka*-style origin myth has him born as the son of a powerful family named Shritala during the time of Dīpaṃkara, the buddha of this fortunate eon immediately prior to Śākyamuni. Shritala is said to have taken lay vows before Dīpaṃkara and to have produced bodhicitta, the altruistic intention for the enlightenment of all beings. However, one day he stole his neighbor's goat and went to a charnel ground where he killed and ate it. This initial crime sent him on a downward spiral of complete moral degeneracy, to the point that he turned into a serial killer of men and a rapist of women, living in a charnel ground and indistinguishable from a demon, until one day he ate poisoned deer meat and died. The original crime of stealing and eating the goat is an implied explanation as to why Dorje Lekpa is sometimes depicted riding a goat and why he is said to have a particular taste for sacrificed goat meat.

There are also many conflicting accounts of Dorje Lekpa's subsequent rebirth as a daemon. In one of these origin myths, it is said that his father was a cat-faced *rākṣasa* demon and his mother was a monkey-faced demoness who lived in a grim city of death gods (Skt. *yāma*, Tib. *gshin rje*) in India. Together they produced an extremely fearsome son with the face of a wolf. This wolf-faced demon attacked the flock of a goat-herding sage, killing and eating one of his goats. In response, the sage went before the buddha (presumably Śākyamuni) and begged him to help subdue the monster. Śākyamuni ordered Vajrapāṇi to deal with this problem, and the latter forcibly summoned Dorje Lekpa, here called the "lord of the *tsen*," and converted him into a dharma protector.

BEGTSE, TSIU MARPO, AND THE RED TSEN HORDES

In addition to Dorje Lekpa, several other popular Tibetan protectors are associated with, and said to be the leaders of, the *tsen*. As mentioned, *tsen* are a specifically Tibetan daemon with no ready Indian parallel. They are strongly associated with Tibet's physical landscape, often believed to reside in rock formations such as cliffs or large boulders. They are typically equipped with Tibetan-style armor, helmets, banners, and weapons, usually riding horses. As such, they are essentially modeled after Tibetan cavalrymen and are the demonization (and deification) of Tibet's old imperial power.[35] Always depicted with extremely fierce red faces, they recall the emic nickname for Tibet that appears in historical chronicles: "The land of the red-faced demons" (srin po gdong dmar gyi yul).[36]

In the Geluk school, the overlord of the *tsen* is the protector Beg tse chen (Great Coat of Mail), also known as Chamsing (Lcam sring), who, along with Palden Lhamo, is one of the two main protectors of the Dalai Lama and his government. Miwang Pholhane Sonam Tobgye (Mi dbang Pho lha nas bsod nams stobs rgyas, 1689–1747), a secular ruler who briefly took power from the Dalai Lamas following a civil war in the mid-18th century, was even recognized as being a worldly incarnation of Begtse.[37] Following the conversion of Mongolia to Tibetan Buddhism, with particular emphasis on the Gelukpa school, Begtse became especially popular there, to the point that some Western scholars have incorrectly argued that Begtse was originally a Mongolian deity.[38]

Begtse, like most *tsen*, is often depicted dressed in conspicuously Tibetan armor and helmet, with a very distinctive coat of mail that is his namesake, wielding a scorpion-handled sword in his right hand and the heart and lungs of an enemy clutched to his chest with his left hand. He holds a lance in the crook of his left arm. Rather than riding a horse, he tramples an enemy horse and rider underfoot. Though likely a relatively late Tibetan deity (who is concordantly recognized as only being recently enlightened), there is some evidence that, like Palden Lhamo, he was imported from India in the 11th century. There is even a special, secret form of Begtse which has a much more Indian-style appearance, naked except for a garland of severed heads, snakes, and a flayed elephant skin. He is ithyphallic and has three heads and six arms. This manifestation is said to be a secret form of Śiva.

Begtse's mythology, as with Dorje Lekpa, also connects him to India and Indian Buddhism. It is said that in a past life, Begtse was the brother of the bodhisattva who would go on to become Śākyamuni Buddha. The latter was a Buddhist and the former a non-Buddhist who debated the bodhisattva fiercely. Finally, the bodhisattva was able to force his brother to swear to become a protector of Buddhism in a future life and bestowed upon him weapons and a helmet of power that were symbols of this status. He named him Yamshu Marpo (Yam shud dmar po), a common alternate name for Begtse. In the future, soon after Buddha Śākyamuni's enlightenment, two copper eggs were born to demonic parents. These two eggs began to fly around uncontrollably of their own accord. They flew up into the sky and attacked the gods, then they flew down underwater and attacked the *nāgas*. The eggs' parents begged the king of the gods, Mahādeva, and his consort, Ekajaṭī, for help. Mahādeva split the eggs with his trident and out jumped Yamshu Marpo and his sister, who also became his consort, explaining the alternate name Lcam Sring, which literally means "brother-sister" (although, oddly, Camsing/Begtse is not typically depicted with his consort). Mahādeva then empowered them to be the supreme rulers of the *tsen*.[39]

Another important protector regarded as a lord of the *tsen* is Tsiu Marpo (Tsi'u dmar po), also known as Jagpa Melen (Jag pa me len) and Abse (A bse). Tsiu Marpo is typically considered a worldly protector and sometimes is identified as the son of Begtse. He is also famously the leader of a group of deities called the "Seven Wild *Tsen* Brothers." Tsiu Marpo has a more typical *tsen* appearance in that he is riding a horse and wearing armor and a helmet. He is often shown wielding a spear and dragging an enemy by a lasso. Like Begtse, Tsiu Marpo seems to be a relatively recent protector and his practice was mainly popularized in the 16th century by a *terma* revealer named Ngari Panchen Pema Wangyal (Mnga' ris Paṇ chen pad+ma dbang rgyal, 1487–1542). About a century later, Tsiu Marpo is said to have replaced Pehar as the main protector of Tibet's first monastery, Samye, after Pehar was moved to Nechung. Tsiu Marpo's origin story is found in Ngari Panchen's treasure discoveries.[40]

During the time of the decline of the Buddha Kaśyapa's teachings, a prince of Khotan named Chorwa ('Phyor ba) became dedicated to the dharma, took monastic ordination, and then took residence in a forest. One day, the daughter of the local king was bathing in a nearby pool where she was attacked by a venomous snake. Chorwa came to her aid and helped tend to her wound, but two of the king's ministers saw this and misreported it, claiming that Chorwa was having illicit relations with the princess. The king ordered Chorwa found and executed. The princess tried to explain the truth of the matter and plead for the monk's life, but to no avail. Desperate, she vowed to be reborn as Chorwa's future mother and committed suicide by jumping from a cliff. Warned by a friend, Chorwa was able to flee the kingdom in time, but having learned what happened, was greatly disturbed and went mad, regressing in his morality. He went to Tibet and began killing the men and raping the women until local soldiers tracked him down and stabbed him many times. Before death, he vowed to be reborn as a terrifying daemon that would kill beings, especially those who had wronged him. He was reborn as a *tsen* from an egg in a demonic land to the west. Because of his great hatred, six other *tsen* demons were born from various parts of his body, and together they went on a killing spree and brought ruin to the three realms of existence. Finally, Avalokiteśvara, the bodhisattva of compassion, angrily brought them under control in exchange for food offerings. Later the great master Padmasambhava bestowed tantric empowerments on Chorwa and officially established him as a dharma protector.

Returning to *The History of Abse*, as noted in the section "Protector Mythology," this Tibetan Buddhist theogony links most of the deities discussed here in a comprehensive family tree. The main purpose of the text is to exalt Abse, a lord of the *tsen* similar to, or an alternate form of, Tsiu Marpo. Part of the author's theological strategy in the text is to link Abse by genetic descent with the great Indian deities. The theogony, though somewhat hard to follow due to the inclusion of alternate forms the deities take at various points, essentially runs as follows: a tantric form of Avalokiteśvara and his consort Guhyajñānaḍākinī existed originally as the primordial couple. They emanate into lower forms as Śiva and Umā Devī in order to demiurgically create the physical universe. Born to them are two children, Mahākāla and Śrī Devī. Mahākāla manifests in the form of Nāgaraksha and mates with a *naginī* woman, the fruit of which is Rāhula. Rāhula in turn takes the form of a *yakṣa* and takes a *yakśī* wife. From their union is born Begtse and his sister, here named Dongmarma (Gdong dmar ma, "Red-faced Woman"). Their child is finally Abse himself, who ultimately emanates a seemingly endless horde of vicious, harmful *tsen* and other demonic forces until they are finally brought under control and converted to protectors of the dharma by Hayagrīva, the main wrathful form of Avalokiteśvara.[41]

CONCLUSION

Protector deity cults open a plethora of theological, psychological, and political avenues, among others, for study in the fields of Buddhist and Tibetan scholarship. Despite some important exceptions, however, the wealth of ritual and narrative literature dedicated to them is largely untapped, and given the historical biases endemic to Buddhist studies in the West, it is not hard to understand why. Protector deities represent a dark seething underbelly of a tradition known for its dogged pursuit of and hyperfocus on spiritual, intellectual, and even physical perfection. Growing within, emerging from, and ultimately adapting and transvaluing a literary heritage overflowing with holy hagiographies, many protector deity origin myths are dark *jātakas*, seemingly offering warnings that the saintly life can and does go horribly wrong, and what can happen as a consequence.

As seen, Rudra, Rāhula, Dorje Lekpa, Tsiu Marpo, and others began as ideal Buddhist practitioners, but their lives took hard left turns into tragedy, depravity, and sin, leading to disruption and disaster on a cosmic scale after they were reborn as obscenely powerful demonic forces. As many scriptures and commentaries make explicit, these *lhadre*, god-demons, or *drekpa*, haughty ones, are simultaneously symbols for and literal embodiments of the varying grotesqueries of samsara, existence itself, from the microcosmic psychological level of negative emotions to the macrocosmic level of painful existential realities. And yet, putting the Mahāyana rhetoric of universal enlightenment to the ultimate test, these monsters are consistently and thoroughly redeemed and apotheosized through the skillful means of tantric ritual and hermeneutics, retooled as aspects of the hypercosmic, primordial Buddha's enlightened body, speech, mind, qualities, and activity.

As the "patron saints of blissful imperfections," the *drekpa* dharma protectors are the lowest rungs on the ladder to enlightenment.[42] To take a page from the philosophy of eastern Neoplatonism, which maps quite well onto tantric Buddhism, on the contemplative or spiritual path one must first ritually "homologize [oneself] to the material gods, gatekeepers of the immaterial gods and true union with the One."[43] Thus, practitioners and scholars of Buddhism alike lose something of the vital essence, the lifeblood, of the tradition when they ignore, brush off, or merely relegate these daemonic hordes to footnotes.

DISCUSSION OF THE LITERATURE

Western scholarship on Tibetan Buddhist protector deities has for the most part been primarily descriptive, which is to say focused on the iconography of the deity as it appears in art and described in ritual texts, and synchronic in orientation. The best and most influential example of this is Nebesky-Wojkowitz's *Oracles and Demons of Tibet*, which is mainly an iconographic and nomenclatural analysis of several of the more well-known Tibetan protector deities along with a secondary discussion of popular rituals involving them, including thread-cross, divination, and weather-making rituals. While this classic contains a number of mistakes and an outdated approach to the subject, it still remains a critically important reference tool for any scholar of Tibetan protector deities. The bias toward iconography in Buddhist scholarship is evident in the well-developed art-historical scholarship on Buddhist deities in general, including protector deities, exemplified by Rob Linrothe's *Demonic Divine*. Protector deity scholarship within the past thirty years or so, including Amy Heller's excellent work, have usually tended to focus on one deity at a time or small thematically connected groups of deities, with emphasis not only on iconography but also the historical development of their cults within a specific sociopolitical context, as well as some literary analysis of the myths and rituals related to these deities. The most thoroughly researched recent example of this kind of work is Christopher Bell's study of Pehar and his ministers in *The Dalai Lama and the Nechung Oracle*.

The scholarship related to Tibetan Buddhist protector myths in general, however, is decades behind the scholarship on culturally adjacent Hindu myths, or even Indian Buddhist narrative literature. Only one Tibetan Buddhist protector-related myth, that of Rudra's subjugation, has received serious, sustained attention from multiple scholars, and there has yet to be even a translation of more than a few versions of the myth, let alone a systematic comparative analysis of the multiple versions. There has also been very little recognition or appreciation of the complex doctrinal and theological themes encoded in these stories, with some notable exceptions such as Matthew Kapstein's "Samantabhadra and Rudra: Myths of Innate Enlightenment and Radical Evil." Another extremely useful work that relates to the theological significance of protector deities is Seyfort Ruegg's analysis of the integration of *laukika* (encosmic) deity cults in Buddhism, but it too is an outlier. Meanwhile, in Indian Buddhist studies, monographs such as Robert DeCaroli's *Haunting the Buddha* provide more in-depth, historically, and doctrinally grounded as well as broadly theoretical research on spirit cults in Buddhism than anything to come out of Tibetan studies.

Similarly, regarding the topic of ritual in relation to Tibetan Buddhist protector deities, the picture is very much the same. While there has been quite an advancement in Tibetan ritual studies scholarship in the past two decades or so, most of this relates to tantric ritual in general. Studies on particularly protector or encosmic spirit deity ritual tend to be relatively few and far in between and are often simply appended to more general profiles of specific protectors in a purely descriptive manner, without much or any theoretical consideration.

Thus, there are quite a few serious lacunae in the subfield of Tibetan protector deity studies, particularly in the realm of narrative literature, and most of what such mythic literature is available to Western scholarship has not even been translated yet, let alone considered or reflected upon in any serious, systematic way.

PRIMARY SOURCES

Bstan 'dzin Rgya mtsho. *Snga 'gyur rgyud 'bum las btus pa'i gtam rgyud phyogs bsgrigs*. Khams, Tibet: Gser rta dgon pa, 2005.

Dre'u lhas grub dbang 02 kun dga' mi 'gyur rdo rje. *A bse'i byung khungs lo rgyus mdo tsam brjod pa* (https://purl.bdrc.io/resource/MW8722). Buddhist Digital Resource Center (BDRC), 1999.

Ngag dbang blo bzang, Klong rdol. "Bstan srung dam can rgya mtsho'i mtshan tho." In *Klong rdol ngag dbang blo bzang gi gsung 'bum*, vol. 2, 461–493. Lhasa, Tibet: Bod ljongs bod yig dpe rnying dpe skrun khang, 1991.

'Ol dga' rje drung 03 Bzhad pa'i rdo rje. *Dam can bstan srung rgya mtsho'i rnam thar (dbu can bris ma)* (https://purl.bdrc.io/resource/MW9366). T.S. Tashigang, 1979. Buddhist Digital Resource Center (BDRC).

FURTHER READING

Bailey, Cameron. "The Demon Seer: Rāhula and the Inverted Mythology of Indo-Tibetan Buddhism." *Journal of the International Association of Buddhist Studies* 38 (2015): 33–72.

Bailey, Cameron. "A Tibetan Protector Deity Theogony: An Eighteenth Century 'Explicit' Buddhist Pantheon and Some of Its Political Aspects." *Revue d'Etudes Tibétaines* 37, no. 3 (2016): 13–28.

Bailey, Cameron. "The Progenitor of All Dharma Protectors: Buddhist Śaivism in Lelung Zhepe Dorje's Ocean of Oath-Bound Protectors." *Journal of Bojo Jinul* 54 (2019): 179–237.

Bell, Christopher. *Tibetan Demonology*. Cambridge, UK: Cambridge University Press, 2020.

Bell, Christopher. *The Dalai Lama and the Nechung Oracle*. Oxford: Oxford University Press, 2021.

Davidson, Ronald. "Reflections on the Maheśvara Subjugation Myth: Indic Materials, Sa-skya-pa Apologetics, and the Birth of the Heruka." *Journal of the International Association of Buddhist Studies* 14, no. 2 (1991): 197–235.

DeCaroli, Robert. *Haunting the Buddha: Indian Popular Religions and the Formation of Buddhism*. New York: Oxford University Press, 2004.

Heller, Amy. "The Great Protector Deities of the Dalai Lamas." In *Lhasa in the Seventeenth Century*. Edited by Françoise Pommaret, 81–98. Leiden, The Netherlands: Brill, 2003.

Iyanaga, Nobumi. "Recits de la soumission de Mahes'vara par Trailokyavijaya, d'apres les sources chinoises et japonaises." In *Tantric and Taoist Studies in Honour of R. A. Stein*. Edited by Michel Strickmann, vol. 3, 252. Brussels: Institut Beige des Hautes fetudes Chinoises, 1985.

Kapstein, Matthew. "Samantabhadra and Rudra: Myths of Innate Enlightenment and Radical Evil." In *The Tibetan Assimilation of Buddhism: Conversion, Contestation, and Memory*, 163–177. Oxford: Oxford University Press, 2000.

Karmay, Samten G. "The Cult of Mountain Deities and Its Political Significance." In *The Arrow and the Spindle: Studies in History, Myths, Rituals and Beliefs in Tibet*, 432–450. Kathmandu, Nepal: Mandala Book Point, 1998.

Kramrisch, Stella. *The Presence of Śiva*. Princeton, NJ: Princeton University Press, 1981.

Linrothe, Rob, and Jeff Watt. *Demonic Divine: Himalayan Art and Beyond*. Chicago: Serindia, 2004.

Mayer, Robert. "The Figure of Maheśvara/Rudra in the rÑiṅ-ma-pa Tantric Tradition." *Journal of the International Association of Buddhist Studies* 21, no. 2 (1998): 271–310.

Miller, Robert. "'The Supine Demoness' (Srin mo) and the Consolidation of Empire." *Tibet Journal* 23, no. 3 (1998): 3–22.

Nebesky-Wojkowitz, René de. *Oracles and Demons of Tibet: The Cult and Iconography of the Tibetan Protective Deities*. New Delhi: Book Faith India, 1996.

Pommaret, Françoise. "On Local and Mountain Deities in Bhutan." In *Reflections of the Mountain: Essays on the History and Social Meaning of the Mountain Cult in Tibet and the Himalaya*. Edited by Anne Marie Blondeau and Ernst Steinkellner, 39–56. Vienna: Österreichische Akademie der Wissenschaften, 1996.

Ruegg, David Seyfort. *The Symbiosis of Buddhism with Brahmanism/Hinduism in South Asia and of Buddhism with "Local Cults" in Tibet and the Himalayan Region*. Vienna: Verlag der Österreichischen Akademie der Wissenschaften, 2008.

Stein, Rolf A. "La Soumission de Rudra et Autres Contes Tantriques." *Journal Asiatique* 283, no. 1 (1995): 121–160.

Sutherland, Gail Hinich. *The Disguises of the Demon: The Development of the Yakṣa in Hinduism and Buddhism*. Albany, NY: SUNY Press, 1991.

NOTES

1. See Peter Skilling, "The Rakṣā Literature of the Śrāvakayāna," *Journal of the Pali Text Society* 15 (1992): 110–180; and Ingo Strauch, "The Evolution of the Buddhist Rakṣā Genre in the Light of New Evidence from Gandhāra: The *Manasvi-nāgarāja-sūtra from the Bajaur Collection of Kharoṣṭhī Manuscripts," *Bulletin of the School of Oriental and African Studies* 77, no. 1 (2014): 63–84.
2. See Amy Heller, "Armor and Weapons in the Iconography of Tibetan Buddhist Deities," in *Warriors of the Himalayas: Rediscovering the Arms and Armor of Tibet*, ed. Donald J. LaRocca (New Haven, CT: Yale University Press, 2006), 34–41.

3. Robert DeCaroli, in his landmark study of the cults of these beings in early Indian Buddhism, *Haunting the Buddha: Indian Popular Religions and the Formation of Buddhism* (New York: Oxford University Press, 2004), uses the slightly more useful variant term of "spirit-deity" to label them.
4. See, e.g., the use of this term by David Gordon White, *Daemons Are Forever: Contacts and Exchanges in the Eurasian Pandemonium* (Chicago: University of Chicago Press, 2021). The term *daemon* is used throughout this article to refer to these beings but is occasionally switched to "demon" to indicate an overtly and especially malevolent being.
5. For a more comprehensive discussion of "spirit typologies" in Tibetan religion, see Christopher Bell, *Tibetan Demonology* (Cambridge, UK: Cambridge University Press, 2020), 10–16.
6. On the most sophisticated discussion of the cultural and theological context of the *lokottara/laukika* distinction in Indo-Tibetan Buddhism to date, see David Seyfort Ruegg, "The Symbiosis of Buddhism with Brahmanism/Hinduism in South Asia and of Buddhism with 'Local Cults' in Tibet and the Himalayan Region," in *Beiträge zur Kultur-und Geistesgeschichte Asiens*, vol. 58 (Vienna: Verlag der Österreichischen Akademie der Wissenschaften, 2008).
7. For an extensive study of Pehar and his importance within the institution of the Dalai Lama, see Christopher Bell, *The Dalai Lama and the Nechung Oracle* (Oxford: Oxford University Press, 2021). Tibetan debates about the ontological or soteriological status of certain protectors can sometimes have ugly political dimensions, as epitomized in the infamous modern Shukden (Shugs ldan) controversy, for which see Georges Dreyfus, "The Shuk-Den Affair: Origins of a Controversy," *Journal of the International Association of Buddhist Studies* 21, no. 2 (1998): 227–270; and Frédéric Richard, "Shugs ldan and the Dalai Lama: A Conflict of Political Legitimation Processes?" *Revue d'Etudes Tibétaines* 55 (2020): 440–461.
8. On the phenomenon of Tibetan oracles, see René de Nebesky-Wojkowitz, *Oracles and Demons of Tibet: The Cult and Iconography of the Tibetan Protective Deities* (New Delhi: Book Faith India, 1956, 1996), 409–454; Hanna Havnevik, "A Tibetan Female State Oracle," in *Religion and Secular Culture in Tibet*, ed. Henk Blezer (Leiden, The Netherlands: Brill, 2002), 259–287; and Hildegard Diemberger, "Female Oracles in Modern Tibet," in *Women in Tibet*, ed. Janet Gyatso and Hanna Havnevik (New York: Columbia University Press, 2005).
9. On Achi Chokyi Drolma, see Kristen Muldowney, "Outward Beauty, Hidden Wrath: An Exploration of the Drikung Kagyü Dharma Protectress Achi Chökyi Drölma," (master's thesis, Florida State University, 2011). There are other examples of great masters said to be reborn as protector deities after their deaths; see Cameron Bailey, "A Feast for Scholars: The Life and Works of Sle lung Bzhad pa'i rdo rje," (PhD diss., University of Oxford, 2017), 229–232, for the case of Dragshul Wangpo (Drag shul dbang po), who is considered a postmortem manifestation of the 5th Lelung Rinpoche, Zhepe Dorje (Sle lung bzhad pa'i rdo rje, 1697–1740); see also Daniel Berounský, "Powerful Hero (Dpa' rtsal): Protective Deity from the 19th Century Amdo and His Mediums," in *Mongolo-Tibetica Pragensia '08*, special issue: Mediums and Shamans in Central Asia, vol. 1, no. 2, ed. Daniel Berounský (Prague: Triton, 2008), 67–115, for the case of a lama from eastern Tibet who, according to legend, died in an angry mental state and was subsequently reborn as an oracular protector deity.
10. There is no standardized "closed" pantheon of deities in Tibetan Buddhism, what scholars have termed an "explicit" pantheon, but there are loosely defined "implicit" pantheons that vary, sometimes slightly, sometimes wildly, from lineage to lineage, school to school. An "explicit" pantheon is one in which an author imposes a systematic order on "a previously loose, even amorphous collection of gods." An "implicit" pantheon, by contrast, is "less a fixed system [. . .] than a repertoire or anthology that remains always-evolving" (Bruce Lincoln, *Gods and Demons, Priests and Scholars: Critical Explorations in the History of Religions* [Chicago: University of Chicago Press, 2012], 18); see also Cameron Bailey, "A Tibetan Protector Deity Theogony: An Eighteenth Century 'Explicit' Buddhist Pantheon and Some of

Its Political Aspects," *Revue d'Etudes Tibétaines* 37, no. 3 (2016): 13–28; and Bell, *The Dalai Lama and the Nechung Oracle*, 9–12, also discusses a related and useful concept of a "polytheon" when discussing the often overlapping but distinct pantheons found in each individual Tibetan monastery and temple.

11. On protector deity rituals, see de Nebesky-Wojkowitz, *Oracles and Demons of Tibet*, 343–408; for an excellent collection of studies on Tibetan ritual generally, see José Cabezón, ed., *Tibetan Ritual* (Oxford: Oxford University Press, 2010).
12. See Robert Mayer, "The Figure of Maheśvara/Rudra in the Rnying-ma-pa Tantric Tradition," *Journal of the International Association of Buddhist Studies* 21, no. 2 (1998): 271–310, who uses the term "charter myth" to describe the Rudra subjugation myth so central in Nyingma tantric mythology and ritual.
13. From here on referred to with the abbreviation "DCTS"; see T. S. Tashigang, "'Ol dga' rje drung 03 Bzhad pa'i rdo rje[purl.bdrc.io/resource/MW9366]," *Dam can bstan srung rgya mtsho'i rnam thar (dbu can bris ma)* (DCTS) (Buddhist Digital Resource Center [BDRC], 1979) and most of the stories following are drawn directly or indirectly from this text.
14. "Gonpo" can simply be a general term meaning "protector" or "lord" that does not specifically refer to Mahākāla, or to a "dharma protector" in the sense mainly discussed here. This has led to quite a bit of confusion in Western scholarly analysis of Tibetan sources on Mahākāla, especially in regard to the supposed "75 forms of Mahākāla" that are discussed in de Nebesky-Wojkowitz, *Oracles and Demons of Tibet*, 38, and then uncritically quoted by generations of later scholars. There is in fact no clear-cut group of 75 (or 72) forms of Mahākāla, as Nebesky-Wojkowitz understands it, but Mahākāla is often said to have a retinue of 70+ "*gonpo*." The term *gonpo* in this context, however, simply refers to a group of usually 70+ worldly gods that serves as Mahākāla's retinue, who are generically referred to as "lords."
15. Tantric *sādhanā* descriptions of deities often serve as the basis for artistic representations of them, or vice versa.
16. As Rob Linrothe, "Beyond Sectarianism: Towards Reinterpreting the Iconography of Esoteric Buddhist Deities Trampling Hindu Gods," *Indian Journal of Buddhist Studies* 2 (1990): 16–25, points out, while the subjugation of Śiva in tantric Buddhist iconography may have been a potent political statement in India, in Tibet (and other Asian countries to which at least certain forms of tantric Buddhism spread, like Japan), where historically there were few, if any, Śaivites, such a statement would be essentially meaningless. Thus, in Tibetan Buddhism, Śiva's subjugation by Buddhist deities has far more meaning and power as a theological statement than as a political one.
17. On Śiva-Rudra as a converted Buddhist dharma protector, see Cameron Bailey, "The Progenitor of All Dharma Protectors: Buddhist Śaivism in Lelung Zhepe Dorje's Ocean of Oath-Bound Protectors," *Journal of Bojo Jinul* 54 (2019): 179–237. The Rudra subjugation story is the one protector deity myth that has received sufficient attention and study from Western scholars; see, e.g., Ronald Davidson, "Reflections on the Maheśvara Subjugation Myth: Indic Materials, Sa-skya-pa Apologetics, and the Birth of the Heruka," *Journal of the International Association of Buddhist Studies* 14, no. 2 (1991): 197–235; Mayer, "The Figure of Maheśvara/Rudra"; and Matthew Kapstein, "Samantabhadra and Rudra: Myths of Innate Enlightenment and Radical Evil," in *The Tibetan Assimilation of Buddhism: Conversion, Contestation, and Memory* (Oxford: Oxford University Press, 2000), 163–177. On the *Gathering of Intentions Sutra*, see Jacob Dalton, *The Taming of the Demons: Violence and Liberation in Tibetan Buddhism* (New Haven, CT: Yale University, 2011); and Jacob Dalton, *The Gathering of Intentions: A History of a Tibetan Tantra* (New York: Columbia University Press, 2016).
18. *kha nas me 'bar rgya mtsho skem zhing rngams pa'i nga ros 'ur 'ur chem chem shigs shig tu sprin nag 'khrigs shing thog dang ser 'ba brug rnams bsgrags lha min bdud kyi dmag dpon brgyad ni phu bo bka' sdod lha chen brgyad kyis bsad nas mgo bcad thod pa khrag bkang gsol zhing: snying ni gtso bo la bstab*, vol. 1 (DCTS), 148.
19. *gnod sbyin khri ni nor gyi gnyer kha la bkod: ma mo 'bum ni bran dang bka' nyan la bskos: sha za bye ba'i tshogs ni bka'i bya ra mngag gzhug la bskos nas lha thams cad bde bar bkod pas: de nas lha dbang brgya byin*

gyis chos bzang lha'i mdun sar bsu ba byas: a mo li yi rdo steng du phyag dang zhe sa phul: lha thams cad kyi mgon por mnga' gsol nas dur khrod chen po dga' ba'i tshal yang phul lo, vol. 1 (DCTS): 149.

20. DCTS 1: 179.
21. Miranda Shaw, "Palden Lhamo: Supreme Guardian Goddess of the Dalai Lamas," in *As Long as Space Endures: Essays on the Kālacakra Tantra in Honor of H. H. the Dalai Lama*, ed. Edward A. Arnold (Ithaca, NY: Snow Lion, 2009), 157–159.
22. Amy Heller, "The Great Protector Deities of the Dalai Lamas," in *Lhasa in the Seventeenth Century: The Capital of the Dalai Lama*, ed. Françoise Pommaret (Leiden, The Netherlands: Brill, 2003), 85.
23. On Tibetan dice divination, see Jan-Ulrich Sobisch, *Divining with Achi and Tārā: Comparative Remarks on Tibetan Dice and Mālā Divination: Tools, Poetry, Structures, and Ritual Dimensions* (Leiden, The Netherlands: Brill, 2019), who discusses the practice in relation to the Drikung protector Achi Chokyi Drolma, mentioned earlier.
24. See de Nebesky-Wojkowitz, *Oracles and Demons of Tibet*, 22–37.
25. Found, for instance, in the famous Śākta scripture, the *Devī Mahatmya*, for which see Thomas B. Coburn, *Encountering the Goddess: A Translation of the Devi-Mahatmya and a Study of Its Interpretation* (Albany: SUNY Press, 1991).
26. *Rnying ma rgyud 'bum (Mtshams brag dgon pa'i bris ma)* (TBRC), vol. 42, no. 28 (Thimphu, Bhutan: National Library, Royal Government of Bhutan, 1982): 542.2–573.1; quoted in Bstan 'dzin Rgya mtsho, *Snga 'gyur rgyud 'bum las btus pa'i gtam rgyud phyogs bsgrigs* (Khams, Tibet: Gser rta dgon pa, 2005), 273.
27. DCTS 1: 179–184; also briefly summarized in Amy Heller, "Notes on the Symbol of the Scorpion in Tibet," in *Les Habitants du Toit du Monde, Études Recueillies en Hommage à Alexander W. Macdonald*, ed. Samten Karmay and Philippe Sagant (Nanterre, France: Société d'Ethnologie, 1997), 283–297.
28. Mahākāla here and elsewhere in Tibetan protector mythology and theogony is explicitly linked to Yāma, the god of death in the traditional Indian pantheon.
29. See Shaw, "Palden Lhamo," 156; for a more elaborate version of this story that features two Palden Lhamo-type goddesses, Dungkyongma and Remati (the latter serves as a maid to the former), and the similarities of it to Sītā's abduction by Rāvaṇa in the *Rāmāyana*, see Heller, "Notes on the Symbol of the Scorpion in Tibet," 286–288.
30. This is a form peculiar to the Drikung Kagyu.
31. This section is primarily based on Cameron Bailey, "The Demon Seer: Rāhula and the Inverted Mythology of Indo-Tibetan Buddhism," *Journal of the International Association of Buddhist Studies* 38 (2015): 33–72.
32. See Tsangnyön Heruka, *The Life of Milarepa*. trans. Andrew Quintman (New York: Penguin Books, 2010): 32; and Dan Martin, "The Early Education of Milarepa," *The Journal of the Tibet Society* 2, no. 31 (1982): 66–67.
33. Quoted from Bailey, "The Demon Seer," 57.
34. The following stories are summarized from DCTS 2: 180–194; see also de Nebesky-Wojkowitz, *Oracles and Demons of Tibet*, 154–159; and Ladrang Kalsang, *The Guardian Deities of Tibet* (Dharamsala, India: Little Lhasa, 1996), 109–112.
35. See Todd Allen Gibson, "From Btsanpo to Btsan: The Demonization of the Tibetan Sacral Kingship," (PhD diss., Indiana University, 1991).
36. This phrase is used, for instance, by Gnubs chen sangs rgyas ye shes (9th century) in *Sgom gyi gnad gsal bar phye ba bsam gtan mig sgron* (S'w Tashigangpa, 1974): 494.3.
37. Nancy Lin, "Adapting the Buddha's Biographies: A Cultural History of the 'Wish-Fulfilling Vine' in Tibet, Seventeenth to Eighteenth Centuries," (PhD diss., University of California, Berkeley, 2011).
38. See Giuseppe Tucci, *Tibetan Painted Scrolls*, vols. 3 & 2, (Bangkok: SDI, 1999): 595; and de Nebesky-Wojkowitz, *Oracles and Demons of Tibet*, 88.

39. See Kalsang, *The Guardian Deities of Tibet*, 104–105; this story is also mentioned in abbreviated form in Ven. Khenpo Shedup Tenzin, *'Gro 'dul rdo rje alias Dre'u lhas pa grub dbang Kun dga' mi 'gyur rdo rje. A bse'i byung khungs lo rgyus mdo tsam brjod pa (ABLG)* (Kathmandu, Nepal: Buddhist Digital Resource Center (BDRC), 1999).
40. The following story is summarized from the translation found in Christopher Bell, "Tsiu Marpo: The Career of a Tibetan Protector Deity," (master's thesis, Florida State University, 2006), 29–30.
41. For a more detailed discussion of this theogony, see Bailey, "A Tibetan Protector Deity Theogony."
42. To paraphrase horror film director Guillermo del Toro's quote on monsters.
43. Gregory Shaw, *Theurgy and the Soul: The Neoplatonism of Iamblichus* (Kettering, OH: Angelico Press, 2014), 176; on the parallels between Neoplatonic theurgy and Indian tantra, see Gregory Shaw, "Platonic Tantra: Theurgists of Late Antiquity," in *Oikiosophia, Quaderni Di Studi Indo-Mediterranei X-XI: From the Intelligence of the Heart to Ecosophia*, ed. Daniela Boccassini (Milan: Mimesis Edizioni, 2018), 269–284.

Cameron Bailey

H

HISTORY OF BUDDHISMS IN CHINA: THE NANBEICHO PERIOD (LATE 4TH CENTURY TO THE SUI DYNASTY)

IMPORTANCE OF THE NANBEICHAO PERIOD

The Nanbeichao period (386–581) is undoubtedly the most important period in the history of Chinese Buddhism from the perspective of its introduction, establishment, adaptation to local culture, and the formation of its own indigenous expression. It represents a time when Buddhism went from being a foreign religion initially serving small communities of mainly expatriates to a full-fledged Chinese spiritual tradition catering for the majority of the local population.

While the important and influential sectarian formations in Chinese Buddhism are usually a major characteristic of the period of unification from the Sui dynasty up to the middle of the Tang dynasty (618–906), it is important to recognize that a good proportion of the conceptual "building blocks" for these later developments germinated and took root during the Nanbeichao period. This means that on the formative level the Chinese received input from virtually all the primary forms of Indian or Indic Buddhism that prevailed on the Indian subcontinent and in Central Asia during the Gupta period (*c.* 320–550). These inputs took the form of the translation of massive numbers of canonical scriptures, transmission of imagery and iconography, norms for monastic organization, food, science, and an integrated system of belief.[1]

Indian Buddhist practices in China were rarely if ever fully replicated but in most cases underwent radical transformation in their meeting with Chinese or Sinitic culture. One major reason for this was that Indian culture per se was usually not seen as one that was superior to the local culture but rather one that complemented it, resulting in a situation where equal cultures met. After all, Chinese traditional culture and its institutions were both entrenched and deeply engrained into the local populations at the time Buddhism first arrived in the Central Kingdom during the second half of the Eastern Han (25–220 CE). This meant that Buddhism had to accommodate and adapt to prevailing norms and systems of belief, thereby from the very beginning embarking on a course that in many cases led to deep alterations and modifications of the original Indian structures and patterns of belief.

Another aspect of the inculturation of Buddhism during the Three Kingdoms and the Nanbeichao periods has to do with the nature of the population, which was composed of many diverse ethnic groups. During most of the first half millennium after Buddhism's introduction, northern and northwestern China were dominated by a succession of non-Han ethnic groups, all of which introduced their own cultural characteristics that impacted the majority Chinese populations they ruled over in varying degrees. This also meant that the manner in which Buddhism developed in China during the period under discussion differed, sometimes quite considerably, from region to region and kingdom to kingdom.

In its elucidation of the early history of Chinese Buddhism, previous scholarship has tended to stress the differences between the so-called Barbarian dynasties (i.e., non-Han Chinese political units) in the north of China in contrast to the native dynasties of the south. While such a division may be meaningful to demarcate certain local brands of Buddhism and the religion's role vis-á-vis the religious life of rulers and ruling classes in various parts of China during the period under discussion, it is not very useful as an overarching model for understanding the actual developments that early Chinese Buddhism underwent in the course of the period from its introduction and up to the Sui unification (581–618).[2] What is more important is to differentiate between, on the one hand, those communities and areas of China that were under sustained and long-term contact with the "motherlands" of Buddhism—i.e., India and the relevant cultures of Central Asia and their representatives—and therefore more exposed to Indian and Indic cultures, and on the other hand those majority communities and groups of followers whose basic value systems remained more squarely Chinese.

THE INTRODUCTION OF BUDDHISM

Much has been written about the introduction of Buddhism in China during the eastern Han, which was a period that actually produced relatively few translations of Buddhist scriptures and very little in terms of material culture.

It is not clear exactly when Buddhism was first introduced in China. According to the legend about the dream of Emperor Ming (*r.* 57–75), Buddhism was first introduced during his reign by the two Indian monks Kaśyāpamataṇga (n.d.) and Dharmarakṣa (n.d.). These two foreign monks are further credited with having introduced the scripture called *Shisier zhang jing* (Scripture in Forty-Two Sections; T. 784.17). Whether this scripture, which is not an actual Indian composition but an anthology of excerpts lifted from several early sutras, did exist in China at such an early date (i.e., during the second half of the 2nd century) is hard to ascertain. However, there exists a rather clear-cut reference to its presence in China as early as 166 CE, where it is mentioned in a memorial of the official Xiang Kai (n.d.), addressed to Emperor Huan (*r.* 146–167).[3] The legend aside, it seems more than probable that Buddhism would have reached China before 69 CE as claimed therein. By the 2nd century BCE Buddhism had already penetrated Central Asia, and several of the larger oasis-towns along the Silk Road would probably have had small communities of Buddhist monks.[4] As the Han Chinese were already carrying on a lively trade with countries like Persia, Ferghana, and the far-away Roman Empire, it seems highly unlikely that followers of Buddhism would not have been in China proper already during the late Western Han (206 BCE–08 CE).

The most commonly cited evidence for the existence of Buddhism in Han China prior to the dream of Emperor Ming is the account of the Buddhist community under the auspices of the imperial Prince Ying in Pengcheng, capital of his fief in Chu in present-day northern Kiangsu.[5]

Among the primary features in Chinese material culture showing evidence of Buddhist influence are funerary practices from the late Eastern Han. From this period the tombs yield examples of early, locally produced buddha figures, not as primary votive images but as secondary symbols of prosperity and good luck. Likewise, a number of so-called money-trees in bronze, which show formal buddha images seated beneath the tree trunk or directly on it, the leaves of which have been made of coins, indicate that the early Chinese Buddhists, locals as well as foreigners, were tradespeople for whom religion and moneymaking went hand in hand. Given that money trees with buddha images have been found over a relatively large area, it seems self-evident that Buddhist communities were a reality in China around 200 CE.[6]

EARLY FORMATIVE PERIOD AND THE TRANSLATION OF BUDDHIST SCRIPTURES

The rendering of Indian Buddhist sutras into Chinese represents one of the seminal aspects of the Buddhist success in China. From early on the Indian and foreign translators consciously adopted a number of strategies by which they might convey the original messages of the Buddhist scriptures into Chinese without doing too much damage to the original meaning.[7] At the same time they understood that their translations must make sense to their Chinese readership.[8] Because Indian and Chinese cultures were both highly developed at the time of their meeting, it was not possible for the foreign translators to present their scriptures to Chinese readers as a one-way, hegemonic dispensation as, for example, has been the case when Christianity "colonized" many native cultures during the European imperialist era. Therefore, the translations they produced were in a good many cases "custom-tailored" to Chinese culture, an approach to translation that involved considerable adaptation and borrowing of local terminologies and concepts as a means of conveyance.[9] While this overall approach successfully presented large portions of the growing Buddhist canonical literature fairly quickly in China, it did create a number of problems. Not only did these adaptive approaches result in a certain displacement of meanings of salient Buddhist doctrines, it also opened Chinese Buddhism to a considerable Daoist and Confucian adulteration of the primary Indian concepts and practices. Hence Chinese Buddhism only partly reflects the Indian Buddhist tradition and can in many ways be said to have incorporated essential parts from the local spiritual and ethical traditions, something that has persisted down to the present.[10]

The early translations were usually made as collaborative efforts between one or more foreign specialists and a team of native monk assistants, who were more or less schooled in rendering the Indian language(s) into Chinese. This pattern persisted all the way up to the 10th century, when the last significant spate of translations from Sanskrit were made. The translation of Buddhist scriptures into Chinese often came about as a result of imperial or elite patronage, although there were also many private translation projects.

INTERACTION WITH LOCAL TRADITIONS

Despite the great respect accorded Confucianism in Chinese history and culture, it was Daoism, especially in the forms that developed after the end of the Han dynasty, that had the greatest and most sustained impact on Buddhism during the first several centuries after its introduction into the Central Kingdom. While certain aspects of Confucian thought, most notably filial piety (Ch. *xiao*) and certain hierarchical structures, did indeed leave an imprint on Buddhism, Daoism—itself in its formative stages as a full-blown religion—supplied, at least initially, both the terminology and other basic conceptualizations for navigating Chinese culture, which the Buddhists adopted for their early translations and formulations for their system of belief.[11]

It has often been overlooked that Daoism and Buddhism developed side by side from the Han and all the way into the Tang, especially after the beginning of the Nanbeichao period, and that both religions consequently were in a situation of almost constant interaction and exchange during the first 500 years of Buddhist history in China. The Buddho-Daoist interactions of the Nanbeichao period left a lasting mark on both traditions, to such a degree in fact that in many cases it makes little sense to speak of one without referring to the other.[12] Salient features that reflect this development include shared concepts, including canons, netherworld,[13] transmigration, karma, medicine, use of written talismans, cosmology, and so on.[14] One of the most significant features of the Daoist borrowing from Buddhism is reflected in the manner in which the Daoist canon was formulated as well as in the way its scriptures were written, often in direct imitation of Buddhist sutras.[15]

"Neo-Daoism" is a term coined to designate certain forms of gentry-religion and philosophic musings that developed in South China during the 4th to 5th centuries, in particular in the region around Nanjing, which served as capital to a succession of southern dynasties during the Nanbeichao period. In a certain way "Neo-Daoism" is a misnomer, as it does not refer to a development of the Daoist religion per se, but rather reflects the resurgence of a classicist interest in the Lao-Zhuang tradition prevailing in South China at that time. The followers of this movement were not only inspired by the Laozi but also dabbled in Buddhist thought, often interpreted in a Daoistic manner, something that is especially evident in the writings dubbed "Xuanxue" (abstruse learning).[16] These writings attempt at coming to terms with certain concepts and notions of Buddhism, especially the *prajñāpāramitā* literature, but are conducted in a manner that would have been quite alien to practitioners of traditional Indian Buddhism.

A more representative and informed manner of appropriating and adapting Buddhism to local Daoist usage can be testified in the development that, for lack of a better term, may be referred to as "Buddho-Daoism,"[17] which first flourished in the region around Chang'an during the second half of the 5th century, possibly due to the rise of the Daoist theocracy under the charismatic master Kou Qianzhi (*d.* 448).[18] Numerous monuments, mostly in the form of sculptural steles, document the Buddho-Daoist movement, which has been seen by some scholars as a Daoist attempt at subverting Buddhism by borrowing freely from that religion while at the same time offering soteriological methods that had a greater cultural appeal to Chinese believers.[19] It is interesting to observe that the evident liberal inclusiveness of this movement would appear to have allowed to a high degree the transfer of practices and beliefs between more formal types of Buddhism and Daoism.

BUDDHIST LITERATURE AND ITS IMPACT

A major aspect of Buddhism's introduction to China was the vast canonical literature that accompanied it. Not only was the sheer amount of scriptures, treatises, and texts on ethical conduct without compare in China prior to the arrival of Buddhism, it was also the first time in Chinese history that religious literature on this scale was becoming available to a larger segment of the population beyond the educated elite. Buddhist institutions were essentially among the few places where ordinary Chinese could learn to read and write, even if it usually meant that they had to become monks or nuns. Thus, the rise of new genres of literature in Nanbeichao China can be traced directly back to the Buddhist influence, which impacted virtually all literary genres including poetry, supernatural and edifying tales, collections of monks' biographies, historical works, and canonical catalogs.

The extensive Buddhist impact on the development of the Daoist canon has already been noted, but influences and borrowings also went the other way. An important new category of indigenous Buddhist scriptures appeared in the course of the Nanbeichao period, scriptures that are essentially different from the growing number of exegetical compositions by Chinese monks, most of which relate directly to the translated Indian works. This new type of scripture, which for the lack of a better term we classify as Chinese "apocrypha," are works that masquerade as authentic Indian Buddhist scriptures. As such they are written in imitation of authentic sutras, sometimes adopting their formats and structures, but the agenda and discourses of nearly all of them reflect special geopolitical and socioreligious situations. In other words, they address concrete Sinitic concerns and therefore tend to reflect these in their choice of vocabulary and doctrinal orientation. Examples of this class of Buddhist scriptures are the *Yanshou ming jing* (Scripture on the Extension of the Span of Life; T. 2888.85) and *Qiqian fo shenfu jing* (Scripture on the Divine Talismans of the Seven Thousand Buddhas; T. 2904.85), all of which borrow from Daoism, as well as the *Anzhai jing* (Scripture on the Pacification of Habitation; T. 1394.21) and the *Fumu enchong jing* (Scripture on [Recompensing] the Kindness of Parents; T. 2887.85), which show a strong imprint from Confucianism and Chinese culture in general. Many of the scriptures of this class were also written in response to the rise of local Buddhist cults, most notably those associated with Avalokiteśvara as a universal savior, the Future Buddha Maitreya, and so on.[20]

STUDY AND PRACTICE

The Buddhist *vinaya* and its rules of conduct for monks and nuns constitutes a special chapter in the history of Chinese Buddhism during its formative period and first five centuries in China. Monastic codices and rules for correct deportment appeared quite early in the history of Chinese Buddhism, but they were mostly fragmentary and highly condensed tracts, which only transmitted the most rudimentary outlines of the Buddhist *vinayas*. When it comes to interest in and translation activity concerning the availability of more *vinaya* texts to the Buddhist communities in China, the absolute high point was the 5th century, a time when virtually all the major works representing various different *vinaya* traditions were translated into Chinese, either in part or in their totality. Even so, there were numerous minor or abbreviated renditions in vogue from the late Han onward, many of which continued to inform the growing communities of Buddhist monastics in the course of the Nanbeichao period. This multifarious, if not chaotic, situation involving different *vinaya* traditions and interpretations of the *pratimokṣa* meant that the ethical codices varied greatly from Buddhist community to community and from region to region.[21] This fact may also explain—at least partly—why many Chinese monks and nuns did not take the complete vows of the *pratimokṣa* but only those of *śrāmaṇera* and *śrāmaṇerīkas*. It is also observable that during the period in question Chinese monastics modified certain basic modes of behavior relating to livelihood, such as food, clothes, and buildings, to better match the geophysical realities of China.

Meditation is practiced both in the form of breath-counting (Pali. *anapanna*), focusing the mind on a buddha or an object, and as analytical meditation, such as contemplating the twelve links in the chain of causation or reflecting upon evanescence by watching a dead body decompose. By the middle of the Nanbeichao we begin to see a shift in meditation practices away from what can be termed basic Hinayana-type practices based on the Nikāya tradition to Hinayana-type practices based on Mahayana doctrine such as the Perfection of Wisdom or repeating the name of the buddha (Skt. *buddhānusmṛti*), and finally to Mahayana-type practices based exclusively on Mahayana ideology. Tiantai meditation as formulated in Zhiyi's *Mohe zhiguan* during the second half of the 6th century represents the third phase. Even so, these three modes do not represent a linear development but rather a scenario in which all three types continued to coexist. Not until well into the Tang did full Mahayana-type meditation finally prevail, to the gradual exclusion of the other, older forms.

The use of spells as magical incantations (Skt. *dhāraṇī*) has a long and important history in Buddhism, and they were widespread in Indian Buddhism in the first centuries after the buddha's demise. While the use of spells was initially the domain of foreign monks in China, they quickly became popular among the local population. In southern China spells were propagated by the Central Asian monk Śrīmitra (*fl.* 4th century), who is also credited with a number of translations of spell-scriptures. As early as the late 4th century spell practices were beginning to take hold among Chinese Buddhists across the board, and by the 5th century they were already an integral part of ritual practices.[22] A number of early manuscripts of private spell compilations found among the Dunhuang material and dating from the 6th century indicate that spells and their related rituals were practiced by Chinese Buddhist monastics.[23]

SCHOOLS OF THOUGHT AND BELIEF

Toward the end of the Nanbeichao multiple currents of Buddhist doctrine and practice had entered China both through the translated canonical material as well as transmitted by foreign teachers. This material was not transmitted to the Chinese followers in a gentle or organic manner following the historical developments of Buddhism in India and Central Asia but was, in a manner of speaking, dumped on the local Buddhists en bloc. This meant that what had taken several centuries to gestate and develop in India became available in China within a relatively short period of time. This fact may at least partly explain the relatively sudden appearance of a whole range of distinct or semidistinct schools of thought and practice during the 5th–6th centuries.[24]

Zhongdao is a Chinese name for Buddhism of the Middle Way or the teachings based on the Prajñāpāramitā scriptures, which became truly important through the translation efforts of Kumārajīva (334–*c.* 413) and his circle of followers. As a foreigner who fully mastered the Chinese idiom, Kumārajīva's translations sought to convey the original meaning of the Indian scriptures in a form that prioritized their readability and conceptual accessibility in the local language.[25] In particular, the *Dazhi du lun* (Treatise on the Great Liberation), a monumental treatise on the doctrine of emptiness, left its mark on Chinese Buddhist understandings of the Prajñāpāramitā literature. By the early 5th century an actual doctrinal school of Prajñāpāramitā thought was formulated by Kumārajīva's disciple Sengchao (384–*c.* 417).[26] Eventually the doctrines of this school of thought coalesced into the formal Sanlun school, one of the earliest Buddhist sectarian formations that came into being at the very end of the Nanbeichao period, named after three primary Prajñāpāramitā treatises.[27]

Yogācāra Buddhism, concerned with the function of the mind as explained by the system of six consciousnesses (later expanded to eight and nine), was mainly propagated by adherents of the *Laṅkāvatāra* and the *Yogācārabhūmi* sutras. A major exponent of this school of thought was the monk Paramārtha (498/499–569). Formally this tradition did not become a bona fide school in institutional terms until the middle of the 7th century, with the formal establishment of the Faxiang school by Xuanzang (*c.* 602–664) and his immediate disciples.

The origin of the Nirvana school, named after the *Mahāparinirvāṇa Sūtra*, has traditionally been associated with the name of Daosheng (*c.* 360–434), a preeminent scholar-monk associated with both Kumārajīva and the emerging Pure Land tradition. The teachings of this school revolve around the teachings found in the sutra, the gist of which is the explication of sudden enlightenment, buddha-nature, and the fourfold eternal qualities of the state of nirvana.[28]

A devotional school of Buddhism, the Pure Land tradition holds a special place in the history of Chinese Buddhism. It is primarily based on the teachings of the *Sukhāvatīvyūha Sūtra*, the so-called *Small Pure Land Scripture* (*Xiao Amituo jing*), and the *Guan wuliangshou fo jing* (Scripture for Contemplating Buddha Amitāyus). The teachings of this tradition revolve around the Buddha Amitābha/Amitāyus, who formulated forty-eight vows promising that whoever prayed to him at the time of death would be transported to his special paradise for rebirth. The monk Huiyuan (344–416), another of Kumārajīva's prominent followers, has traditionally been credited with establishing Pure Land Buddhism as a major tradition in China. However, the teachings of this tradition were already gaining importance before Huiyuan's rise to prominence.[29]

Schools of Meditation (Skt. *dhyāna*; Ch. *chan*, *channa*). Initially meditation practices in China were, as already stated, dominated by so-called Hinayana types of practice that were mainly concerned with the attainment of one-pointed concentration, reflections on evanescence, and contemplating the twelve links in the chain of causation. Only later were these *dhyāna* practices bound up in a doctrinal framework based on Mahayana visions of the path (Skt. *mārga*), including the repetition of a buddha or bodhisattva's name (Ch. *nianfo*) together with visualization (Ch. *guanxiang*), the idea of a buddha-nature (Ch. *foxing*), and emptiness in accordance with the teachings on the Perfection of Wisdom (Skt. *prajñāpāramitā*). The formulation of an actual school of Chan Buddhism only took place during the succeeding Sui and early Tang dynasties. Kumārajīva's disciple Huiyuan, who was originally a disciple of the exegete Dao'an (?–385), was also a major promoter of seated meditation.[30]

Huayan Buddhism, based on readings in the voluminous *Avataṁsaka Sūtra*, is one of the latecomers to the doctrinal landscape of Chinese Buddhism. Its early history is connected with the name of the monk Dushun (558–640), and it found a ready environment toward the end of the Nanbeichao with its grandiose, cosmological visions and subtle doctrines of universal interpenetration of phenomena and the absolute. The Huayan tradition is undoubtedly one of the most important and significant Buddhist schools in the history of Chinese Buddhism and also one of those that developed furthest away from its Indian origin(s).

Although there were tendencies in Chinese Buddhism toward more marked forms of sectarianism toward the end of the Nanbeichao period, the real period of Buddhist schools—understood in an institutional and historical sense—did not really take off until the Sui and Tang dynasties.

MATERIAL CULTURE

In the course of its domestication in China, Buddhism impacted Chinese culture on a number of levels—not least in the sphere of material culture.[31] At the same time Buddhism itself underwent numerous modifications dictated by a motley mixture of cultural and geopolitical issues. Buddhist temples and monasteries in China did not follow the norms for *vihāra*s in India but were built in accordance with local architectural norms, including layouts. Thus pagodas, pavilions, kiosks, and gardens were added to temple compounds, buildings, and structures that did not exist in Indian Buddhist temples. One may say that Chinese monasteries were essentially secular buildings constructed for religious purposes. This is in fact one of the really great deviations the Chinese made in regard to the Indian Buddhist tradition as far material culture goes. In the course of time Buddhist temples were also furnished with pagodas, a sort of architectural compromise between the Indian *stūpa* and the Chinese watch tower.[32] By the time of the Northern Wei (386–530) Buddhist monasteries in Chang'an and Luoyang were large-scale compounds consisting of many tens of buildings and with monastic populations and their support units, including indentured workers and slaves, numbering in the thousands.[33]

In terms of Buddhist sanctuaries and places of worship, the Nanbeichao period is known for its cave temples, which sometimes were constructed in the vicinity of freestanding temples. Hence, as far as cave temples go, this period outshines all other periods in the history of Chinese Buddhism. The earliest Buddhist cave sanctuary in China is to all intents and purposes the Mogao Caves in Dunhuang, where the first period of activity took place during the second half of the 4th century, quickly followed by other less important examples further east. The tradition of excavating cave temples is one the Chinese inherited from India and Central Asia, and as Buddhism expanded further eastward in the course of the Eastern Han and after, cave sanctuaries in increasingly great numbers began to appear: first in the Gansu Corridor, where several important sites were established during the 4th–5th centuries, and eventually in the Central Provinces.

A common characteristic of many cave sanctuaries in China is that they combine votive caves with those for living in. In this sense they follow their Indian models, which usually have living quarters for their monk populations in close proximity to caves for worship, such as one can see in Bhaja, Bedse, Karle, Ajanta, and so on, all found in the Deccan of central India.

Patronage was one of the vital aspects in regard to the establishment of cave sanctuaries in India, and in this regard, those created in Central Asia and in the Chinese territories were no different. In particular, imperial patronage was a major element in the success of a given site, such as can be documented in all the major places like the Mogao Caves,[34] Binglingsi Mt. Majji,[35] Yun'gang,[36] and Longmen.[37]

During the Nanbeichao period Buddhist iconography underwent a number of changes, reflecting the virtually constant arrival of new forms of artistic representation that entered China via the Silk Road and the Southern Sea route. From an early reliance on Gandhāran imagery over a highly formalistic and stereotypical manner of replicating the foreign sculptural language, the Northern Wei effected a change to more local, iconic representation, taking courtly dress code as the preferred mode of depicting buddha images. After the mid-6th century a new change took place whereby the Northern Wei and earlier forms of depicting Buddhist imagery were gradually replaced by a more naturalistic and corporal treatment of the human body, reflecting the norms that dominated Gupta Buddhist art during the 5th–6th centuries. This change is especially notable in the Buddhist art of the Northern Qi dynasty (550–577), which would herald in the characteristic full-bodied and three-dimensional sculptures of the Sui dynasty.

Another major area where Indian Buddhism impacted Chinese culture was food. Traditionally a meat-eating and alcohol-drinking culture, through Buddhist persuasion vegetarianism became widespread among people at all levels of society.[38] Although the Chinese continued to consume meat, fish, and poultry, because of Buddhism many days in the calendrical year were set aside for "fasting" or abstention, which meant that forms of occasional vegetarianism, sometimes lasting for extended periods of time, have persisted up to this day in Chinese cultural practice.[39] Even Daoism, which originally did not forbid meat or alcohol for its followers, would eventually adopt vegetarianism as a standard practice for its monastics, as is clearly stipulated in the manuals for the religion's monks and nuns written during the 5th–6th centuries.[40]

Merit-making or the will to do good, a practice closely connected to the conceptual system of karma, was another common Buddhist custom that became extremely popular among people of all walks of life. Practices relating to this included, in addition to the pious donations, the liberation of animals, caring for the elderly and orphans, loan institutions, and the establishment of relief depots in case of famine.

THE LIVES OF BUDDHIST MONKS AND NUNS

Among the important local Buddhist inventions were the monumental compilations consisting of biographical material relating to the lives and careers of the primary monastic proponents of the religion in China. The earliest of these is Huichao's (*fl.* first half of the 6th century)

Gaoseng chuan (Histories of Famous Monks), which set the standard for future compilations of monks' and nuns' biographies.[41] The compilation and retelling of the life stories of famous monks and nuns, most in the form of hagiographies—a genre that in many ways parallels the Buddhist apocrypha—became major vehicles for propagating Buddhism in China during its first 500-year period.

What aligned and kept the Buddhist communities together were the injunctions of the *vinayas*, the Buddhist monastic codices, which served as common guidelines for monks and nuns. These regulations laid down the norms of formal behavior for monastics as well as for laypeople. In addition, changing governments imposed various additional regulations on monks and nuns, even to the point of installing representatives inside temples and monasteries to make sure that the law was being upheld. However, Buddhist monks and nuns in China were never unified under a common religious figure but only remained responsible to their home institutions and the teachers they had chosen to study under. Even so, the secular authorities often meddled in monastic affairs, and both monks and nuns were commandeered to perform services for the ruling families and the nobility.

In contrast to India, where cremation was a universal practice for Buddhists of all walks of life, in Nanbeichao China burial, a traditional Chinese custom, was common for Buddhists as well. This practice persisted alongside cremation, which only became more common during the Tang dynasty.

As part of funerary practices, Chinese Buddhists, on a more formal level, raised memorial steles for important clerics, in which the deceased person's spiritual career was outlined in a somewhat formal and hyperbolic fashion. These stele inscriptions represent a distinct Chinese tradition also shared by Daoists and Confucians, but which is otherwise unknown to the Indian Buddhist tradition. In time the steles were erected in combination with cremation *stūpas* and cave burials.[42]

PERSECUTIONS OF BUDDHISM

Despite the fact that the development of Buddhism in China is by and large a success story, one of the concrete factors hampering the Buddhist process of inculturation in China can be highlighted by the occasional persecutions of the religion down through history. While these persecutions sometimes took the form of religious suppression, as in the case of the short-lived but violent Northern Wei suppression of Buddhism during the reign of Emperor Wu (424–451) in the middle of the 5th century aided by the local Daoists,[43] or the lengthier but equally severe one under Emperor Wu (*r.* 561–577) of the Northern Zhou (557–579),[44] most of these were de facto attempts at curbing the political and economic power of a rapidly growing Buddhist religion.[45] In most parts of Chinese history, Buddhist institutions and monastics were exempt from taxation, something that in times when Buddhist fervor ran high could result in massive losses of revenue to the state. Moreover, due to patronage from the higher echelons of Chinese society and a tendency to amass wealth and encroach on farmland, both private and state owned, in certain periods Buddhism was correctly seen as a threat to social stability and order. However, there were times when Buddhist monasteries were seen by the political power as hotbeds for antigovernment activities, something that occasioned almost certain retaliation from the state.

POPULAR BUDDHISM

To the extent that a meaningful distinction between elite Buddhism and the faith of the commoners can be upheld during the period in question, it mainly hinges on the degree of economic muscle, education, and access to resources of the former, which again translated into the sponsoring and upkeep of Buddhist communities as well as translation and building projects on a large scale. In terms of faith, norms of practice, and piety, there was hardly any difference between the spirituality of high and low, the important exception being that the members of the higher echelons of Chinese society were able to read and write, a privilege that common people—especially the peasantry—was generally denied. Public and private expression of piety and the making of donations to the Buddhist communities were practices that appealed to Chinese from all walks of life, as is borne out in numerous donor inscriptions carved in stone. Whereas wealthy donors could finance a building or carving project on their own, it was common that local Buddhist societies made up of commoners pooled their efforts for such occasions.[46]

One of the primary trends in Chinese Buddhism of the 6th century is the belief that the religion had entered the phase in its history commonly known as the "Dharma-ending age" (Ch. *mofa*), a period characterized by a general decline and corruption. Although the teachings concerned with the Dharma-ending age certainly have their origin in Indian Buddhism, in particular in the cult of Maitreya, the Future Buddha who is to appear on earth in a distant future, it would appear that this type of belief had a much greater impact on shaping Chinese Buddhism than it had on the religion in its land of origin.[47] Consequently the cult of Maitreya became very important in China during the second half of the Nanbeichao period and fostered hope of salvation in the assembly of this buddha. At the same time, it provided nourishment to messianic beliefs and related religious and political movements including a mix-up with certain local cults and Daoism. Huisi (515–577), the ancestor of Tiantai Buddhism, was a major exponent of the beliefs in the Dharma-ending age in southern China.[48]

CONCLUSION

The Nanbeichao period undoubtedly represents a most significant period in the history of Chinese Buddhism, a time during which Buddhism went from being a mainly foreign religion to one that had not only become fully integrated into the local culture but was even shaping its future course on a number of points. The success of Buddhism in China hinged on a combination of factors, which together enabled the religion to present itself as a viable alternative to local traditions, while at the same time heralding in a series of new discourses and material forms, which stimulated the development of Chinese culture on virtually all levels.

The Nanbeichao period was also a time when incoming Buddhism underwent some of its most important changes, which partly took place as the religion underwent a considerable inculturation on the one hand and was itself shaped by local realities on the other hand. The processes that went into this change were as much caused by a necessity for Buddhism to accommodate itself to Chinese culture as by internal developments facilitated by the steady influx of Buddhist scriptures and the associated belief systems they carried with them. In addition, political, socioeconomic, and geographical realities were also features playing into the transformations that eventually became Chinese Buddhism.

REVIEW OF LITERATURE

Erik Zürcher's *Buddhist Conquest of China* is the classic of early Chinese Buddhism par excellence, and the first serious Western scholarly work to address this crucial period in the formation of Chinese Buddhism. In many ways it has been the standard model for subsequent research, and as such has influenced at least two generations of scholars in the field. Even though it still stands the passage of time, its information is now rather outmoded and has been superseded by much of the later scholarship. However, if read together with the recent compilation of Zürcher's other essays (*Buddhism in China: Collected Papers of Erik Zürcher*), many of which deal with the Nanbeichao period, it is useful and important to consult.

Kenneth Ch'en's *History of Chinese Buddhism* is a classical contribution to the field meant to cover the entire history of Chinese Buddhism, and as such only partly covers the Nanbeichao period. Nevertheless, it provides a concise and inclusive survey of the developments of Chinese Buddhism during that period. Because of the concise and yet inclusive discussion provided in this work, the section on Nanbeichao Buddhism may serve as a very useful and easy-to-use introduction. That being said, Chen's treatment of Nanbeichao Buddhism is also a bit outmoded in places, as it only reflects developments in the field up to the early 1960s.

Zenryū Tsukamoto's voluminous work, *A History of Early Chinese Buddhism* (in Leon Hurwitz's translation), represents the fruits of many decades of research. It is the most comprehensive and elaborate contribution to our understanding of Nanbeichao Buddhism in a Western language to date. Even so, it does suffer from a lopsided treatment of Chinese Buddhism during the period in question and leaves out a number of important aspects. This is mainly a result of the author's own range of interests, although it otherwise provides many more details than found in Zürcher's and Ch'en's earlier works. It is also more concerned with elucidating doctrinal issues evident in the formation of early Chinese Buddhism that the earlier works do not accomplish.

Shigeo Kamata's history of Chinese Buddhism, *Chūgoku bukkyō shi*, constitutes the most recent and all-round treatment of Nanbeichao Buddhism to date, although only half of the volumes in this lengthy work deal with Buddhism in this period. It is a modern work in the manner typical of Japanese scholarship, replete in details and data but otherwise relatively weak in analysis. Even so, it provides by far the most comprehensive and all-round treatment of the topic, but done in the manner of a standard history.

PRIMARY SOURCES

Beichao fodao zaoxiangbei jingxuan (北朝佛道造像碑精選). Compiled by Zhang Yan 張燕 and Zhao Chao 趙超. Tianjing: Tianjing guji chubanshe, 1996.

Beichao fojiao shike tapian bai pin (北朝佛教石刻拓片百品). Edited by Yan Yuanjing 顏娟英. Taibei: Zhongyang yanjiu yuan lishi yuyen yanjiu, 2008.

Chu sanzang jiji (出三藏記集). T. 2145.55.

Gaoseng chuan (高僧傳). T. 2059.50.

Hongming ji (弘明集). T. 210252.

Jinglü yixiang (經律異相). T. 2121.53.

Lidai sanbao ji (歷代三寶紀). T. 2034.49.

Luoyang qielan ji (洛陽伽藍記). T. 2092.51.

Piqiuni chuan (比丘尼傳). T. 2063.51.
Quan shanggu Sandai Qin Han San Guo Liu Chao wen (全上古三代秦漢三國六朝). 4 vols. Beijing: Zhongguo shudian chuban, 1987.
Wei shu (魏書). https://zh.wikipedia.org/zh-hant/魏书
Zhongjing mulu (眾經目錄). T. 2146.55.

FURTHER READING

Benn, James A. "Buddhism, Alcohol, and Tea in Medieval China." In *Of Tripod and Palate: Food, Politics, and Religion in Traditional China*. Edited by Roel Sterckx, 213–236. New York: Palgrave Macmillan, 2005.

Bokenkamp, Stephen R. "The Silk Worm and the Bodhi Tree: The Lingbao Attempt to Replace Buddhism in China and Our Attempt to Place Lingbao Daoism." In *Religion and Chinese Society*. Vol. 1. Edited by John Lagerwey, 317–339. Hong Kong: Chinese University Press, 2004.

Bokenkamp, Stephen R. *Ancestors and Anxiety: Daoism and the Birth of Rebirth in China*. Berkeley: University of California Press, 2007.

Bumbacher, Stephan Peter. "Early Buddhism in China: Daoist Reactions." In *The Spread of Buddhism*. Edited by Ann Heirman and Stephan P. Bumbacher, 203–246. HDO sec. 8, vol. 16. Leiden, The Netherlands: Brill, 2007.

Chen, Kenneth S. "Anti-Buddhist Propaganda during the Nan-ch'ao." *Harvard Journal of Asiatic Studies* 15, nos. 1–2 (1952): 162–192.

Chen, Kenneth S. "On the Factors Responsible for the Anti-Buddhist Persecution under the Pei-ch'ao." *Harvard Journal of Asiatic Studies* 17, nos. 1–2 (1954): 261–273.

Ch'en, Kenneth S. *Buddhism in China*. Princeton, NJ: Princeton University Press, 1964.

Ch'en, Kenneth S. *The Chinese Transformation of Buddhism*. Princeton, NJ: Princeton University Press, 1973.

Dankova, Zuzana. "Kumarajiva the Translator: His Place in the History of Translating Buddhist Scriptures into Chinese." PhD diss., University of Prague, 2006.

Despeux, Catherine. "Practiques bouddhiques et taoïques du IIIe au vie siécle (221–581)." In *Religion et société en Chine ancienne et médiévale*. Edited by John Lagerwey, 643–683. Paris: Les Éditions du Cerf, 2009.

Foard, James, Michael Solomon, and Richard K. Payne, eds. *The Pure Land Tradition: History and Development*. Berkeley, CA: Berkeley Buddhist Studies Series, 1996.

Gansusheng bowuguan, and Binglingsi shiku wenwu baoguan, eds. *Binglingsi shiku* (炳靈寺石窟). Beijing: Wenwu chubanshe, 1982.

Gernet, Jacques. *Buddhism in Chinese Society: An Economic History from the Fifth to the Tenth Centuries*. Translated by Franciscus Verellen. New York: Columbia University Press, 1995.

Guang Xing. "Filial Piety in Early Buddhism." *Journal of Buddhist Ethics* 12 (2005): 82–106.

Heirmann, Ann. "*Vinaya*: From India to China." In *The Spread of Buddhism*. Edited by Ann Heirmann and Stephan Peter Bumbacher, 167–202. Handbook of Oriental Studies, sec. 8, vol. 16. Leiden, The Netherlands, and Boston: Brill, 2007.

Heirmann, Ann. "Abridged Teaching (*Lüe Jiao*): Monastic Rules between India and China." In *Buddhism across Asia: Networks of Material, Cultural and Intellectual Exchange*. Vol. 1. Edited by Tansen Sen, 193–205. Singapore: Institute of Southeast Asian Studies, 2014.

Hirai Shunei 平井俊榮. *Chūgoku hanya shisō shi kenkyū: Kichizō to Sanron gakuha* (中国般若思想史研究: 吉藏と三論学派). Tokyo: Shunjūsha, 1976.

Hureau, Sylvie. "Les rites bouddhiques." In *Religion et société en Chine ancienne et médiévale*. Edited by John Lagerwey, 493–529. Paris: Les Éditions du Cerf, 2009.

Hureau, Sylvie. "Production et dissémination de textes bouddhiques: Traductions et apocryphes." In *Religion et société en Chine ancienne et médiévale*. Edited by John Lagerwey, 429–458. Paris: Les Éditions du Cerf, 2009.

Jenner, W. J. F. J. *Memories of Loyang: Yang Hsüan-chih and the Lost Capital (493–534)*. Oxford: Oxford University Press, 1981.

Kamata Shigeo 鎌田茂雄. *Chūgoku bukkyō shi* (中国佛教史). 6 vols. Tokyo: Tōkyō daigaku shuppankai, 1982–99.

Kieschnick, John. *The Eminent Monk: Buddhist Ideals in Medieval Chinese Hagiography*. Kuroda Institute Studies in East Asian Buddhism 10. Honolulu: University of Hawai'i Press, 1997.

Kieschnick, John. *The Impact of Buddhism on Chinese Material Culture*. Princeton, NJ, and Oxford: Princeton University Press, 2003.

Kieschnick, John. "Buddhist Vegetarianism in China." In *Of Tripod and Palate: Food, Politics, and Religion in Traditional China*. Edited by Roel Sterckx, 186–212. New York: Palgrave Macmillan, 2005.

Lagerwey, John. "Religion et politique pendant la Période de Division." In *Religion et société en Chine ancienne et médiévale*. Edited by John Lagerwey. Paris: Les Éditions du Cerf, 2009, 397–428.

Lai Pengju 賴鵬舉. *Dunhuang shiku zaoxiang sixiang yanjiu: A Study of the Thoughts in the Images in Mogao Caves at Dunhuang* (敦煌石窟造像思想研究). Beijing: Wenwu chubanshe, 2009.

Lai, Whalen. "Society and the Sacred in the Secular City: Temple Legends of the Lo-yang Ch'ieh-lan-chi." In *State and Society in Early Medieval China*. Edited by Albert E. Dien, 229–268. Stanford, CA: Stanford University Press, 1990.

Liebenthal, Walter. "Shih Hui-yuan's Buddhism as Set Forth in His Writings." *Journal of the American Oriental Society* 70, no. 4 (1950): 243–259.

Liebenthal, Walter. "A Biography of Chu Tao-sheng." *Monumenta Nipponica* 11, no. 3 (1955): 64–96.

Liebenthal, Walter. "The World Conception of Chu Tao-sheng." *Monumenta Nipponica* 12 (1956–1957): 65–103, 241–268.

Longmen shiku yanjiu 龙门石窟研究, ed. *Longmen shiku yanjiu lunwen die* (龙门石窟研究论文选). Shanghai: Shanghai renmin meishu chubanshe, 1993.

Magnin, Paul. *La vie et l'oeuvre de Huisi (517–577): les origines de la secte bouddhique chinoise du Tiantai*. Paris: Ecole Française d'Extreme-Orient, 1979.

Martin, François. "Les bouddhiques laïcs leurs idéaux et leurs pratiques." In *Religion et société en Chine ancienne et médiévale*. Edited by John Lagerwey, 531–563. Paris: Les Éditions du Cerf, 2009.

Mather, Richard B. "K'ou Ch'ien-chic and the Taoist Theocracy at the Northern Wei Court, 425–451." In *Facets of Taoism*. Edited by Anna Seidel and Holmes Welsh, 103–122. New Haven, CT, and London: Yale University Press, 1979.

McRae, John R. "Buddhism, Schools of: Chinese Buddhism." In *Encyclopedia of Religion*, ed. Lindsay Jones, 2nd ed. (New York: Macmillan Reference USA, 2004), 2:1235–1241.

Nadeau, Randall L. "The Decline of the Dharma in Early Chinese Buddhism." *Asian Review* 1 (1987).

Pu Chengzhong. *Ethical Treatment of Animals in Early Chinese Buddhism: Beliefs and Practices*. Newcastle upon Tyne, UK: Cambridge Scholars Publishing, 2014.

Rhie, Marylin Martin. *Early Buddhist Art of China and Central Asia*. Vol. 2. HDO IV/12. Leiden, The Netherlands: Brill, 2002.

Silk, Jonathan A. "Marginal Notes on a Study of Buddhism, Economy and Society in China." *Journal of the International Association of Buddhist Studies* 22, no. 2 (1999): 360–398.

Sørensen, Henrik H. "The Spell of the Great, Golden Peacock Queen: The Origin, Practices and Lore of an Early Esoteric Buddhist Tradition in China." *Pacific World: Journal of the Institute for Buddhist Studies* 3, no. 8 (2006): 89–123.

Sørensen, Henrik H. "Buddho-Daoism in Medieval and Early Pre-Modern China: A Report on Recent Findings Concerning Influences and Shared Religious Practices." *The Electronic Journal of East and Central Asian Religions* 1 (2013): 109–138.

Sørensen, Henrik H. "The Meeting of Daoist and Buddhist Spatial Imagination: The Construction of the Netherworld in Medieval China." In *Locating Religions: Contact, Diversity and Translocality*. Edited by Reinhold F. Glei and Nicholas Jaspert, 234–292. Leiden, The Netherlands, and Boston: Brill, 2017.

Sørensen, Henrik H. "Spells and Magical Practices as Reflected in the Early Chinese Buddhist Sources (c. 300–600 CE) and their Implications for the Rise and Development of Esoteric Buddhism." In *Chinese and Tibetan Tantric Buddhism*. Edited by Meir Shahar and Yael Bentor, 41–71. Leiden, The Netherlands: Brill, 2017.

Swartz, Wendy, Robert Campany, Yang Lu, and Jessey Choo, eds. *Early Medieval China: A Sourcebook*. New York: Columbia University Press, 2013.

Tanaka, Kenneth K. *The Dawn of Chinese Pure Land Buddhist Doctrine: Ching-ying Hui-yuan's Commentary on the Visualization Sutra*. Albany: State University of New York Press, 1990.

Tsukamoto Zenryū. *A History of Early Chinese Buddhism*. 2 vols. Translated by L. Leon Hurwitz. Tokyo, New York, and San Francisco: Kodansha International, 1985.

Wang-Toutain, Françoise. "Entre spéculation métaphysique et devotion: La doctrine bouddhique en Chine avant le VIIe sciècle." In *Religion et société en Chine ancienne et médiévale*. Edited by John Lagerwey, 601–641. Paris: Les Éditions du Cerf, 2009.

Wong, Dorothy C. *Chinese Steles: Pre-Buddhist and Buddhist Use of a Symbolic Form*. Honolulu: University of Hawaii Press, 2004.

Zacchetti, Stefano. "Notions and Visions of the Canon in Early Chinese Buddhism." In *Spreading the Buddha's Word in East Asia: The Formation and Transformation of the Chinese Buddhist Canon*. Edited by Jiang Wu and Lucille Chia, 81–108. New York: Columbia University Press, 2016.

Zürcher, Erik. *The Buddhist Conquest of China: The Spread and Adaptation of Buddhism in Early Medieval China*. Leiden, The Netherlands: Brill, 1959.

Zürcher, Erik. "'Prince Moonlight.' Messianism and Eschatology in Early Medieval Chinese Buddhism." *T'oung Pao* 68, nos. 1–3 (1982): 1–75.

Zürcher, Erik. *Buddhism in China: Collected Papers of Erik Zürcher*. Edited by Jonathan A. Silk. Leiden, The Netherlands: Brill, 2014.

NOTES

1. Erik Zürcher, *Buddhism in China: Collected Papers of Erik Zürcher*, ed. Jonathan A. Silk (Leiden, The Netherlands: Brill, 2014), 339–351, 539–566.
2. This argument follows the idea that there was a cultured elite in the South steeped in Chinese classical philosophy versus uncouth barbarian rulers in the North. To a large degree this vision of Buddhist history in China during the period in question reflects an unholy mixture of Sinocentrism on the one hand and a Western positivist perspective on the other. As such it has more of an ideological slant privileging an imagined elite than an authentic perspective based on a proper reading of the primary sources tempered with information gathered from archaeological finds and monuments in situ. See Zenryū Tsukamoto, *A History of Early Chinese Buddhism*, vol. 1, trans. L. Hurwitz (Tokyo, New York, and San Francisco: Kodansha International, 1985), 239–450.
3. Kenneth Ch'en, *Buddhism in China* (Princeton, NJ: Princeton University Press, 1964), 34–36.
4. For a general discussion of legends concerning the introduction of Buddhism to China, see Erik Zürcher, *The Buddhist Conquest of China: The Spread and Adaptation of Buddhism in Early Medieval China* (Leiden, The Netherlands: Brill, 1959), 18–32.
5. Most probably the Kongwangshan Buddhist carvings near Lianyun in northern Jiangsu are products of Prince Ying's Buddhist community. Ch'en and others speculate that the early Buddhist *sangha* in China consisted of foreigners only, and although this might have been the case we do not really know enough about the early Chinese Buddhist sangha to substantiate such a claim. Quite possibly there were Chinese monks at large at an early time (i.e., 1st–2nd century). Ch'en, *Buddhism in China*, 33–34.
6. Tsukamoto, *Early Chinese Buddhism*, 39–112.
7. Zürcher, *Buddhism in China*, 27–62, 419–446, 513–538.

8. Stefano Zacchetti, "Notions and Visions of the Canon in Early Chinese Buddhism," in *Spreading the Buddha's Word in East Asia: The Formation and Transformation of the Chinese Buddhist Canon*, ed. Jiang Wu and Lucille Chia (New York: Columbia University Press, 2016), 81–108.
9. Zürcher, *Buddhism in China*, 27–62, 419–446, 513–538.
10. Sylvie Hureau, "Production et dissémination de textes bouddhiques: Traductions et apocryphes," in *Religion et société en Chine ancienne et médiévale*, ed. John Lagerwey (Paris: Les Éditions du Cerf, 2009), 429–458.
11. Henrik H. Sørensen, "Buddho-Daoism in Medieval and Early Pre-Modern China: A Report on Recent Findings Concerning Influences and Shared Religious Practices," *Electronic Journal of East and Central Asian Religions* 1 (2013): 99–123; and Stephan Peter Bumbacher, "Early Buddhism in China: Daoist Reactions," in *The Spread of Buddhism*, ed. Ann Heirman and Stephan P. Bumbacher, HDO sec. 8, vol. 16 (Leiden, The Netherlands: Brill, 2007), 203–246.
12. Catherine Despeux, "Practiques bouddhiques et taoïques du IIIe au vie siécle (221–581)," in *Religion et société en Chine ancienne et médiévale*, ed. John Lagerwey (Paris: Les Éditions du Cerf, 2009), 643–683.
13. Henrik H. Sørensen, "The Meeting of Daoist and Buddhist Spatial Imagination: The Construction of the Netherworld in Medieval China," in *Locating Religions: Contact, Diversity and Translocality*, ed. Reinhold F. Glei and Nicholas Jaspert (Leiden, The Netherlands, and Boston: Brill, 2017), 234–292.
14. Zürcher, *Buddhism in China*, 187–258. For aspects of the conflation between Buddhist and Daoist notions of cosmology, see Henrik H. Sørensen, "Concerning the Role and Iconography of the Astral Deity Sudṛṣti (Miaojian 妙見) in Esoteric Buddhism," in *China and beyond in the Mediaeval Period: Cultural Crossings and Inter-regional Connections*, ed. Dorothy Wong and Gustav Heldt (New Delhi and Singapore: Manohar, 2014), 403–420.
15. Zürcher, *Buddhism in China*, 105–164.
16. For a brief review of this movement, see Ch'en, *Buddhism in China*, 61–68.
17. Sørensen, "Buddho-Daoism," 109–138.
18. Ch'en, *Buddhism in China*, 147–151. See also Richard B. Mather, "K'ou Ch'ien-chic and the Taoist Theocracy at the Northern Wei Court, 425–451," in *Facets of Taoism*, ed. Anna Seidel and Holmes Welsh (New Haven, CT, and London: Yale University Press, 1979), 103–122.
19. Stephen R. Bokenkamp, "The Silk Worm and the Bodhi Tree: The Lingbao Attempt to Replace Buddhism in China and Our Attempt to Place Lingbao Daoism," in *Religion and Chinese Society*, vol. 1, ed. John Lagerwey (Hong Kong: Chinese University Press, 2004), 317–339.
20. The *Gaowang Guanyin jing* (Scripture of the High King Avalokiteśvara; T. 2898.85) is an example of a scripture edifying the cult of Avalokiteśvara. A classical collection of miracle tales is the *Guanshiyin yingyan ji [sanzhong]* (Records of Responses from Avalokitśvara [Three Kinds]), Gu xiaoshuo congkan (Beijing: Zhonghua shuju, 1994). See also Donald E. Gjertson, "The Early Buddhist Miracle Tale, a Preliminary Survey," *Journal of the American Oriental Society* 101, no. 3 (1981): 287–301.
21. Ann Heirman, "Vinaya: From India to China," in *The Spread of Buddhism*, ed. Ann Heirman and Stephan P. Bumbacher, HDO sec. 8, vol. 16 (Leiden, The Netherlands: Brill, 2007), 167–202.
22. For one example of a spell-scripture of great importance, see Henrik H. Sørensen, "The Spell of the Great, Golden Peacock Queen: The Origin, Practices and Lore of an Early Esoteric Buddhist Tradition in China," *Pacific World: Journal of the Institute for Buddhist Studies* 3, no. 8 (2006): 89–123.
23. Henrik H. Sørensen, "Spells and Magical Practices as Reflected in the Early Chinese Buddhist Sources (c. 300–600 CE) and Their Implications for the Rise and Development of Esoteric Buddhism," in *Chinese and Tibetan Tantric Buddhism*, ed. Meir Shahar and Yael Bentor (Leiden, The Netherlands: Brill, 2017), 41–71; and Sylvie Hureau, "Les rites bouddhiques," in *Religion et société en Chine ancienne et médiévale*, ed. John Lagerwey (Paris: Les Éditions du Cerf, 2009), 493–529.
24. Françoise Wang-Toutain, "Entre spéculation métaphysique et devotion: La doctrine bouddhique en Chine avant le VIIe sciècle," in *Religion et société en Chine ancienne et médiévale*, ed. John Lagerwey (Paris: Les Éditions du Cerf, 2009), 601–641.

25. Zuzana Dankova, "Kumarajiva the Translator: His Place in the History of Translating Buddhist Scriptures into Chinese" (PhD diss., University of Prague, 2006); Kamata Shigeo, *Chūgoku bukkyō shi*, vol. 2 (Tokyo: Tōkyō daigaku shuppankai, 1983), 207–310; and Ch'en, *Buddhism in China*, 81–88.
26. Kamata, *Chūgoku bukkyō shi*, 285–295.
27. Ch'en, *Buddhism in China*, 131–134. See Hirai Shunei, *Chūgoku hanya shisō shi kenkyū: Kichizō to Sanron gakuha* (Tokyo: Shunjūsha, 1976).
28. See Walter Liebenthal, "A Biography of Chu Tao-sheng," *Monumenta Nipponica* 11, no. 3 (1955): 64–96; and Walter Liebenthal, "The World Conception of Chu Tao-sheng," *Monumenta Nipponica* 12 (1956–1957): 65–103, 241–268.
29. Tsukamoto, *Early Chinese Buddhism*, 757–898; Kamata, *Chūgoku bukkyō shi*, 311–406; and Liebenthal, "Shih Hui-yüan's Buddhism as Set Forth in His Writings," *Journal of the American Oriental Society* 70, no. 4 (1950): 243–259.
30. Zürcher, *Buddhist Conquest*, 184–204. See also Tsukamoto, *Early Chinese Buddhism*, 655–756.
31. See John Kieschnick, *The Impact of Buddhism on Chinese Material Culture* (Princeton, NJ: Princeton University Press, 2003).
32. Kieschnick, *Impact of Buddhism*, 185–188.
33. For a detailed description of the situation in Luoyang at the eve of the Northern Wei, see W. J. F. Jenner, *Memories of Loyang: Yang Hsüan-chih and the Lost Capital (493–534)* (Oxford: Oxford University Press, 1981); and Whalen Lai, "Society and the Sacred in the Secular City: Temple Legends of the Lo-yang Ch'ieh-lan-chi," in *State and Society in Early Medieval China*, ed. Albert E. Dien (Stanford, CA: Stanford University Press, 1990), 229–268.
34. Lai Pengju, *Dunhuang shiku caoxiang sixiang yanjiu: A Study of the Thoughts in the Images in Mogao Caves at Dunhuang* (Beijing: Wenwu chubanshe, 2009).
35. Michael Sullivan, *The Cave Temples of Maichishan* (London: Faber & Faber, 1969).
36. James O. Caswell, *Written and Unwritten: A New History of the Buddhist Caves at Yungang* (Vancouver: University of British Columbia Press, 1988). See also, Yi Lidu, "The Third-Phase of the Yungang Cave Complex—Its Architectural Structure, Subject Matter, Composition and Style, Volume One" (PhD diss., University of Toronto, 2010).
37. Longmen shiku yanjiu, ed., *Longmen shiku yanjiu lunwen die* (Shanghai: Shanghai renmin meishu chubanshe, 1993); and Gansusheng bowuguan and Binglingsi shiku wenwu baoguan, eds., *Binglingsi shiku* (Beijing: Wenwu chubanshe, 1982).
38. John Kieschnick, "Buddhist Vegetarianism in China," in *Of Tripod and Palate: Food, Politics, and Religion in Traditional China*, ed. Roel Sterckx (New York: Palgrave Macmillan), 186–212. See also James A. Benn, "Buddhism, Alcohol, and Tea in Medieval China," in *Of Tripod and Palate: Food, Politics, and Religion in Traditional China*, ed. Roel Sterckx (New York: Palgrave Macmillan), 213–236.
39. Pu Chengzhong, *Ethical Treatment of Animals in Early Chinese Buddhism: Beliefs and Practices* (Newcastle upon Tyne, UK: Cambridge Scholars Publishing, 2014).
40. Livia Kohn, *Cosmos and Community: The Ethical Dimension of Daoism* (Cambridge, MA: Three Pines Press, 2004), 42–56.
41. Arthur F. Wright, *Studies in Chinese Buddhism* (New Haven, CT: Yale University Press, 1990), 73–111. See also, John Kieschnick, *The Eminent Monk: Buddhist Ideals in Medieval Chinese Hagiography*, Kuroda Institute Studies in East Asian Buddhism 10 (Honolulu: University of Hawai'i Press, 1997).
42. Dorothy C. Wong, *Chinese Steles: Pre-Buddhist and Buddhist Use of a Symbolic Form* (Honolulu: University of Hawaii Press, 2004), 63–174.
43. Cf. Ch'en, *Buddhism in China*, 147–151.
44. Cf. Ch'en, *Buddhism in China*, 147–151.
45. Jacques Gernet, *Buddhism in Chinese Society: An Economic History from the Fifth to the Tenth Centuries*, trans. Franciscus Verellen (New York: Columbia University Press, 1995).

46. François Martin, "Les bouddhiques laïcs leurs idéaux et leurs pratiques," in *Religion et société en Chine ancienne et médiévale*, ed. John Lagerwey (Paris: Les Éditions du Cerf, 2009), 531–563.
47. Randall L. Nadeau, "The Decline of the Dharma in Early Chinese Buddhism," *Asian Review* 1 (1987).
48. Paul Magnin, *La vie et l'oeuvre de Huisi (517–577): les origines de la secte bouddhique chinoise du Tiantai* (Paris: Ecole Française d'Extreme-Orient, 1979).

Henrik H. Sørensen

HOMA: TANTRIC FIRE RITUAL

HOMA: FIRE OFFERINGS IN A TANTRIC MODE

While there are a vast range of rituals in which fire plays a prominent role, one of the unique aspects of the homa is that it serves as an effective marker of tantric movements. It is a ritual practice that is shared by all such movements and is found across the entire extent of the tantric world. The ritual minimally involves making offerings into fire, a practice found in many religious traditions. However, what distinguishes the practice of the homa is that the offerings are made within the context of a conceptual and symbolic ritual system that is identifiably tantric in nature. This includes such elements as the use of symbolic hand gestures (mudrā), use of verbal expressions based on Sanskrit (mantra), and geometric diagrams in which the deities are either made present or represented (mandala and yantra). These and other individual elements that might be taken as markers of tantric practice[1] are found in a variety of religious traditions both within India and well beyond. However, a focus on individual religious elements as defining characteristics of tantra, or alternatively considering a list of such elements offered in the spirit of a polythetic definition, cannot indicate the systematic character of tantra—or any other religious tradition.[2]

Instead of focusing on the individual elements, an examination of tantric practice—especially one as emblematic of tantra as is the homa—provides a quite natural basis for seeing tantra as an integral, coherent system.[3] For example, in the Japanese Shingon tradition, this offering is set within a key concept of tantric ideology, that of ritual identification between the deity evoked, the hearth-altar, and the practitioner. Far from being an isolated element in a list of characteristics, this provides one point of entrée into the system of tantric thought, which ramifies into cosmology, philosophical anthropology, ritual efficacy, theories of language, and symbolic systems. As in the course of its history the homa has spread out of the Indian subcontinent to may different religious cultures, it also engages the same range of topics in those several religious cultures as well.

ORIGINS AND HISTORY: FIRE, CULT, AND THE ORIGINS OF THE HUMAN

There is a reasonable argument to be made for associating the origin of humans as social animals with fire. Fire-keeping is perhaps the oldest form of collective human behavior, an activity requiring coordination among several different members of a group.[4] Benoît Dubreuil has pointed out, for example, that cooked food requires the collection of large amounts of firewood. This in turn implies a division of labor, that is, cooperation both in cooking and in fuel gathering.[5] Fire-keeping (both maintenance and containment)[6] is thought to have preceded the ability to make fire by many millennia. Estimates for the use of fire range from 300,000 years ago at the most conservative to as much as 1.5 million years ago.[7] We note that both fire-keeping and fire-making were so important as to require the ritualization of behaviors, thus assuring that the correct actions would be carried out. It seems most likely that it is this kind of ritualized practice[8] that lies at the heart of fire cults.

BREADTH OF TRADITIONS EMPLOYING THE HOMA

Indo-European Fire Cult. The analysis of Indo-European religions suggests that there was a common set of practices related to fire.[9] These are found in both Roman and Greek ritual praxis, as well as in Indo-Iranian and Vedic cultures. There are several specific continuities between the Greco-Roman use of fire and the tantric. For example, different kinds of fires have differently shaped hearths—see the section "Vedic and Indo-Iranian" for the details of the tantric Buddhist associations of hearth-shape and ritual function. In Rome, the fires for Vesta, goddess of the domestic realm, were kept on a circular hearth. Among the three fires of Vedic practice, the domestic fire (*gārhapatiya*) is also maintained on a circular hearth. Iranian practice also employed three hearths, the domestic one being circular. And in tantric Buddhist practice, the fire for protection (*śāntika*) is built on a circular hearth as well. The association between the concept of the domestic and the function of protection is a suggestive, if not perfect, match.

In Roman, Vedic, and tantric traditions, fire is conceived as the agency by which offerings are carried from this world to the gods and are at the same time purified. In the Vedic tradition, fire is also anthropomorphized as Agni. Agni is a multiform deity found both in beneficent forms, such as the cooking fire and ritual fire, and in destructive forms, such as wildfires and the cremation fire—though the latter is also ambivalent as that which first purifies and then carries the deceased to the realm of the ancestors. Similarly in Vedic ritual Agni purifies the offerings made into a fire and transmits them to the deities. Not only is Agni a deity symbolically key to Vedic rituals employing fire, but he is also to tantic homa as well. In Japan, both the Tendai and Shingon traditions of tantric Buddhism employ the figure of Agni (J. Katen, 火天, literally "fire god"). He is most usually the first deity evoked in a sequence of offerings.[10]

Across this range of traditions, the symbolic homologies of fire with a variety of bodily functions are also similar. Thus, fire is likened to sexuality, to digestion, and to breath. Associations specifically between the fire ritual and sexuality themselves constitute a wide symbolic range. In Greek tradition, the hearth of Hestia is considered feminine, while the fire in the hearth is itself masculine. A different pairing of symbolic associations regards the widespread technology of making fire by means of a "fire drill." This involves a flat board laid on the ground that has a depression into which a vertical stick is placed and rapidly rotated. The friction creates heat that causes fine shavings or grass to catch a flame, which is then fed. In Vedic interpretations, the flat board and the vertical stick are feminine and masculine, respectively. By analogy with the symbolism of sexual intercourse, desire (*kāma*) is identified with inner heat (*tapas*), which is itself produced ritually, especially through yogic practices.

Another analogy is made between the ritual fire and digestion, and indeed one of the forms of Agni is the digestive fire. Just as a person consumes food and digests it, so the ritual fire consumes offerings and transforms them into the food of the gods.[11] Just as digestion has been homologized with fire, so has the breath. One such instance is the transformation of the twice-daily *agnihotra* ritual into an interior ritual, the *prāṇāgnihotra*. In the *prāṇāgnihotra*, which may also be understood as a kind of yogic practice, the breath takes the place of the external ritual. Having become qualified to perform the *agnihotra*, a brahman is enjoined to perform it twice each day. This continuity of twice-daily performance is then equated with the continuity of the breath.

This brief summary indicates how widely the symbolic and ritual practices that form the historical background to the tantric homa are spread across the full range of Indo-European religious tradition. However, the homa per se appears to derive more specifically from both Vedic and Indo-Iranian sources.

Vedic and Indo-Iranian. Much of the literature on the historical development of the homa leaves the impression of a simple linear sequence beginning with the Vedic practices and then—in some as yet to be identified fashion—transforming into the tantric form, that is, the homa. Vedic rites are commonly segregated into two kinds, the *śrauta* and the *gṛhya*, often rendered as solemn and household (or domestic), respectively. The two kinds differ in several ways. Whereas the solemn rites generally require three fires (or more in the case of such major rites as the *agnicayana*),[12] the household rites require only one. Solemn rites employ the services of several priests, the household rites only one—generally not the householder as such, but rather the household priest. Similarly, while the fire is referred to as the household fire, it is not the cooking fire in the kitchen, but rather a separate fire in the family shrine room.[13] The similarity between the household rites and the homa—single fire, one practitioner—and the fact that such rites would have been very widely known in medieval India suggest that these may have been the model upon which the homa was developed. As yet, however, no study connecting any specific household rite and the homa has established a clear relation.[14]

Holly Grether has noted that while "the *homa* of the tantric schools share certain features with the Brahmanical rites that evolve in the Vedic tradition, it more closely parallels the development of the ritual paradigm in the Zoroastrian tradition."[15] She suggests that there are several layers involved in creating the similarities. First are the well-established commonalities of Vedic ritual and early Zoroastrian, which she claims indicate diffusion from a common source.[16] More specificly she suggests direct Zoroastrian influences on the formation of the tantric homa. She argues that "elements of *homa* such as the structure of the rite, role of the main priest, ritual implements used, *mantric* recitation, and the mesocosmic function of the ritual space are to be counted among those that are shared with the sacrifice (*yasna*) of the Zoroastrians."[17] Grether has highlighted, in particular, one of the consistent patterns in Indo-Iranian and Indo-European fire rituals, that is, both the homa and its antecedents, as the ritual framing of fire by water—sequences of ritual acts involving the use of water. She argues that "most Asian fire rites have a symmetrical frame structure, with water sequences framing the central fire offering. This basic structure characterizes early Vedic and Avestan sacrifices, as well as medieval and contemporary fire rituals across Asia."[18] The argument that these symbolic and formal similarities indicate a formative Zoroastrian influence on the development of the tantric homa is supported by the history of Buddhism in Gandhāra.

Located in the northwest corner of the subcontinent, in what is now Pakistan, Gandhāra was close to Bactria, the home of Zoroastrianism, and was ruled as part of the Greco-Bactrian

Kingdom (*c.* 250 to 125 BCE), and then as part of the Indo-Greek Kingdom (*c.* 180 BCE to 10 CE). A Buddhist presence in the area of Gandhāra dates from the time of Aśoka (r. *c.* 268–232 BCE), who had rock edicts inscribed in the region. Trade routes that provided contact between the cultures of the Eastern Mediterranean (Hellenistic), Iran, India, and Central Asia ran through Gandhāra. In his study of Gandhāran art, Giovanni Verardi argues for Gandhāra as the locale for early adoption of the homa into Buddhist practice, first as an accomodation for Buddhist laity and then as a monastic rite.[19] It is this latter that Verardi sees as then becoming an esoteric and tantric rite within Buddhism, one performed by a *vajrācārya.*[20] During the period examined by Verardi, the local religious culture would have continued to be deeply influenced by Zoroastrian practices. Although Verardi considers only Vedic and Brahmanic influences in this early adoption of homa into Buddhist practice, Grether's analyses serve to complement those with indigenous Zoroastrian influences as well. An additional factor in the development of tantric homa in Northwest India was the Śaivite tradition.[21]

Śaiva. The Śaiva Siddhānta homa as found in texts such as the *Somaśambhupaddhati* exemplifies fire ritual practices on the subcontinent during the medieval period (*c.* 500–1200).[22] In contrast to the now-common term "Hindu," Dominic Goodall has suggested that "various soteriologies and schools of thought might be enumerated, but three streams are commonly separated out: Vedic orthodoxy and those of the heterodox Vaiṣṇavas and Śaivas."[23] He has also pointed out that despite the present identification of the Śaiva Siddhānta tradition with South India, the "pan-Indian character of the early sect has been obscured, because almost all of the extant works that bear the names of the twenty-eight principal scriptures of the Śaiva Siddhānta have been substantially altered or entirely rewritten in South India."[24]

The *Somaśambhupaddhati* is an important Śaiva Siddhānta ritual text dating from the end of the 11th century and includes instructions for performing a homa.[25] An examination of this specific homa highlights both similarities and differences between it and other tantric homa rituals. This text includes instructions for a ritual construction of the hearth-altar, such as digging up the site upon which the hearth is to be constructed, collecting the earth, leveling the ground, purification by aspersion, pounding the ground firm, sweeping the site clean, and lastly coating the site. These ritual actions are the symbolic representations of the actions required for the actual establishment of a hearth-altar and are also directly related to other building rituals found in the region.[26]

Some tantric rituals employ the symbolism of making the deities present in the ritual enclosure by inviting them; however, the Śaiva Siddhānta text employs the imagery of a symbolic birth of the deity into the ritual enclosure. This involves the full range of sexual imagery, that is, impregnation, gestation, and birth, as well as the other rituals of childhood: Two deities (identified as Brahmā and Sarasvati) are installed in the hearth-altar, and burning coals identified as Śiva's semen are then poured in while the practitioner visualizes the act of impregnation.[27] By these ritual actions, Agni is born as the ritual fire in the hearth-altar.[28]

Jain. Since the 1990s, scholars have turned their attention not only to the ritual traditions within Jainism[29] but more specifically to the tantric aspects of Jain ritual.[30] As part of a more general pattern of tantric development, Alexis Sanderson has linked the rise of Jain tantra—including homa—to royal support.[31] This suggests the desire for success in interstate conflict as described by Ronald Davidson.[32] Use of the term "tantra" regularly circulates around a fairly small set of characteristics, with scholars of different traditions creating somewhat divergent, though overlapping, usages. Citing the work of Shridhar Andhare, John E. Cort notes Andhare's observation that "tantric rituals employ both phonetic chants (mantra) and visual diagrams (*yantra, maṇḍala*) and that there is usually a close connection between the mantra and *maṇḍala* of any particular ritual."[33] At the same time, Jain thinkers have argued that it is not possible for a Jina to be made present in the icon employed in *mandala* rituals. In this way, then, Jain rituals differ from those of other tantric traditions, such as the Buddhist, in which the deities are made manifest (evoked) in the ritual enclosure. Cort characterizes Jain ritual as working "as a form of reflexive meditation, in which the worshipper actualizes in him- or herself the supreme virtues that are symbolized in the icon."[34]

Ellen Gough has studied Jain ritual most extensively and notes that the ritual is performed in both the Svetambara and Digambara traditions. She informs us that the Svetambara use homa in conjunction with ceremonies of dedication (*pratiṣṭhā*) following the reading of Sakalacandrāgni's text. It is also performed at the completion of the worship by a mendicant leader with a cloth mandala on which the *surimantra* is inscribed, as well as at the end of multiday worship ceremonies.[35]

In Gough's judgment, the Digambara tradition performs the homa more frequently than does the Svetambara. One kind of ceremony that employs the homa as part of a larger ritual program is the worship (*vidhana*) of a mandala made of colored powder. These worship services are usually concluded with a homa that is performed in three hearths: circular, square, and triangular. While the number of hearths is suggestive of continuity with the Vedic tradition, neither the shapes nor the arrangement of the three hearths of Jain ceremonials are identical with Vedic. In the latter, the circular domestic altar (*gārhapatya*) is at the west end of the rectangular ritual enclosure (*prācīnavaṃśa*), the demilune southern altar (*dakṣiṇāgni*) is about midway on the southern edge of the ritual enclosure, and the offering or oblation altar (*āhavanīya*) is at the eastern end of the ritual enclosure.[36] Thus, the three form a rather flat scalene triangle. The three fires are identified with the three realms: the domestic fire with this world, the southern fire with the intermediate realm, and the offering fire with the world of the gods.[37] In contrast, the three Jain altars are arranged in a straight line toward the altar, triangular at the end farthest from the altar, square in the middle, and circular closest to the altar.

While these three shapes match shapes used in other tantric traditions, whether this similarity is signficant or not is not clear at this time. Despite some similarities between the shapes of the altars and the continents of Indian cosmology, these similarities do not appear to be symbolically significant. Tadeusz Skorupski points out that "we have no tangible evidence to assert that they are related to each other, like the three Vedic fires are related to the three Vedic worlds."[38]

The Homa in Central Asia. The homa (Tib. sbyin sreg, སྦྱིན་སྲེག་) was brought to Tibet as part of the tantric Buddhist ritual corpus. As with other ritual systems, the homa can either stand alone as a ritual in its own right or be appended to other more complex ritual and ceremonial performances. Stephan Beyer has noted in his study of the cult of Tārā that in some cases, homa may be performed with hundreds of offerings, and that consequently the ritual is continued over weeks, during which time the fire is never allowed to die out completely.[39]

The timing of homas is linked to the phases of the moon in some traditions of practice in Tibet. In Beyer's study of the cult of Tārā, he notes that since Tārā is a peaceful deity, only homas of pacification and increase are employed—subjugation and destruction being "out of character for her."[40] Rites of pacifying are to be performed during the waning moon, while those of increase during the waxing moon, the symbolic connections being evident.

In the case of some Tibetan homa, the altar is a temporary one, in which case the construction mentioned in the section Śaiva in regard to Śaiva Siddhānta homa is literally performed, not only ritually. Richard K. Kohn describes the construction of a hearth-altar as part of the Maṇi Rimdu ritual cycle, earth being piled and pressed to form "a square about eight inches high and a foot and a half on a side."[41] As in many other tantric homa, the hearth-altar is homologized with a mandala, and in this case a Mani Rimdu mandala is drawn on the surface of the raised bed of formed earth. Not only has the homa moved from one ritual culture to others, but at the same time it has also crossed the boundaries of different material cultures. This has in some cases necessitated substitutions, local materials taking the place of ones previously employed in a different setting. Kohn notes, for example, that at "Thami, where firewood is scarce, yak dung is used instead" in place of the sticks of kindling that form the main body of the homa fire. On the other hand, unlike Japan where sesame oil is used as a substitute for clarified butter (ghee), Tibet does have a dairy culture, and so ghee is available for use in the ritual.[42]

Christopher P. Atwood has examined the fire cult in Mongolia, specifically regarding the contested question of the relation between Buddhism and shamanism.[43] Although he does not refer to any of these rites as homa, Atwood notes that fire rituals in Mongolia are "fully integrated into the Buddhist pantheon."[44] Within the more than twenty different types of fire rituals that have been published, he identifies three groups.[45] Most are household based, seeking to harmonize the family with national and cosmic orders. The second kind is a liturgy similar to many other invocations of Tibet and Mongolia. Atwood notes that neither of these is particularly tantric in nature, while the third category "are completely tantric rituals."[46] He is specifically referring here to the rituals'

> point-by-point description of how to dissolve the conventional world into emptiness and how to visualize the deity of fire out of the Sanskrit mantras, with her *uṣṇīṣa* knot of hair, white face, and other attributes typical of a Buddhist goddess.[47] The rituals then detail how to make these thus created deities deliver the various benefits and close with a confirmation of the presence of the deity in the fire and a dissolution into the mantra *oṃ ah hūṃ*.[48]

The Homa in East Asia. The homa has proven to be highly adaptable, and three examples demonstrate different dimensions of this adapability. The first is the creation of a Northern Dipper homa in China, the second is the use of the homa in the Yoshida Shintō tradition in Japan, and the third is the practice of large, outdoor homas by Shugendō practitioners, also in Japan. These three adaptations evidence two of the four kinds of borrowing described by Erik Zürcher in his "Buddhist Influence on Early Taoism." There, he sketched a fourfold typology for categorizing the ways that one religious tradition borrows elements from another. He refers to these as formal borrowing, conceptual borrowing, borrowed complexes, and pervasive influence. While formal borrowing identifies items of literary and narrative style, conceptual borrowing involves the borrowing of a single element, such as one from cosmology or doctrine, but in relative isolation. The borrowing of entire complexes is "the absorption of a coherent cluster of ideas and/or practices."[49] Pervasive influences are the most subtle and, therefore, most difficult to clearly identify. While Zürcher's focus is largely on doctrinal and symbolic religious elements, these same categories can be employed to characterize ritual practices.[50] The adaptations of the homa described here are instances of the second and third kinds of borrowings, that is, conceptual borrowing and borrowed complexes.

Although the Northern Dipper is not important in the Sanskritic forms of tantric Buddhism, it was very important in Daoist traditions—whether understood narrowly as specific Daoist religious lineages or broadly as underpinning much of popular Chinese religion. We have argued that given these differences, a Northern Dipper homa was therefore composed in China, probably so as to be able to offer a ritual that met local expectations, and in direct competition with Daoist ritual practices.[51] The Shingon tradition retains a Northern Dipper homa as part of its present-day ritual corpus. The offerings made in the course of the Shingon Northern Dipper homa include a set of eight, one for the constellation as a whole and another seven for each of the stars individually. This may be understood as an instance of what Zürcher called conceptual borrowing. In this case, the Northern Dipper has been borrowed as a symbolic unit and adapted into the performance of a tantric Buddhist ritual.

The second and third examples are instances of a borrowed complex, which differs from the other kinds of borrowing described by Zürcher in that the coherence of the homa as a ritual complex maintains the unity of the practice and its meanings. In examining such borrowing across religious and cultural boundaries, the most stable part in the process is the structure. This is so consistent that it can be considered a principle of ritual borrowing, the principle of the conservation of structure.[52]

The Yoshida tradition of Shintō (吉田神道, also known as Yuiitsu Shintō, 唯一神道), was established in the 15th century by Yoshida Kanetomo (吉田兼倶, 1434–1511). It dominated Shintō from then into the second half of the 19th century, when Buddhism and Shintō were forcefully separated by governmental mandate. Kanetomo developed a three-part ritual system, all three of which were adapted from esoteric Buddhist practice. The third of these three rituals is known as the "Yoshidashintō daigoma," or the great fire ritual of Yoshida Shintō. The basic structure of ritual actions is the same as found in the other homa discussed here—the practitioner comes to the altar, purifies the ritual space, ignites the fire, and makes various offerings into it, thus evidencing, at this basic level, the principle of the conservation of structure. The similarity extends further, however, to include the ritual accoutrements, such as the ladles used to make offerings into the fire and the wands used for purifications, as well as the use of mantra (written in Siddham script) and mudrā. Kanetomo did make certain changes to the symbolism involved, using, for example, a hexagonal hearth, and scheduling ritual activities in accord with the yin/yang dichotomy.

The Shugendō tradition of mountain asceticism originates in 7th-century Japan, drawing on indigenous beliefs regarding the mountains as dwelling places of the gods, local Shintō traditions, Daoism, and esoteric Buddhism. In the 17th century, all Shugendō temples were required to affiliate with either Tendai or Shingon. In the second half of the 19th century, it was banned as superstitious and, therefore, a hindrance to Japan's modernization, leading some to affiliate with the Shintō shrines that had themselves been separated from Buddhism. With the new constitution following World War II, freedom of religion became official policy, and several Shugendō lineages re-emerged, now acting independently of formal affiliation with either Buddhist or Shintō institutions.

Evidencing its historical affiliation with esoteric Buddhism, contemporary Shugendō maintains what is known as "saitō goma" (柴灯護摩). This ritual complex is borrowed from esoteric Buddhism, but with some significant adaptations. It is performed out of doors, unlike Buddhist homas in Japan, which are performed inside temple buildings. Large logs, from eight to twelve feet in length, are stacked in the form of a square, filled with flammable materials, and then covered over with green boughs. The greenery produces a great deal of smoke, and in some cases, after the fire has burnt down the embers are spread for fire-walking, one of the "magico-spiritual powers" that accomplished Shugendō practitioners are expected to have attained. As with the other homas discussed, the basic ritual structure follows that of esoteric Buddhist homas. Like the Yoshida Shintō homa, the Shugendō version also employs mantra and mudrā.[53]

FUNCTIONAL CATEGORIES OF THE HOMA

Although tantric schools of ritual practice differ in their specifics, there are common functional categories employed throughout. The number of such categories varies, however, including instances of three, four, and five, which are examined here.

Michel Strickmann examined two texts translated into Chinese by Bodhiruci around 709.[54] He identifies these texts as containing the earliest occurrence of the term "homa," rendered phonetically as "hu-ma" and written with the same characters used today (護摩). Strickmann glosses the names of the different functional categories in English as pacification (*śāntika*, 息災), "for assuring domestic and personal security"; augmentation (*pauṣṭika*, 增益), "for the increase of worldly goods and benefits"; and subjugation (*abhicāraka*, 降伏), "for the conquest of assailing demons or, indeed, human adversaries assimilated to demons."[55] These different functional categories of homa are part of a complex ritual system, each "requiring a hearth of different shape and dimensions, special apparatus and offerings, and a particular spacial orientation and time schedule."[56] To this list we can add color of the clothing that the practitioner is to wear as well.

In contrast to the texts examined by Strickmann, the *Sarvadurgatipariśodhanatantra* includes four functions. Tadeusz Skorupski has provided translations of the tantra's description of each of the four, together with explanations based on Vajravarman's commentary (T. 3453).[57] In his discussion of this tantra, Steven Neal Weinberger gives us the Tibetan and glosses these as "pacification of illness and so forth (*zhi ba*, *śānti*), increase of resources (*rgyas pa*, *pauṣṭika*), control of others (*dbang*, *vaśīkaraṇa*), and violent subjugation (*drag po* or *mngon spyod*, *abhicāraka*)."[58]

In the case of present day-Japan, the different functions of various rituals are usually identified as five (goshuhō, 五種法). These five are for protection/pacification (*śāntika*, *sokusai*, 息災), for prosperity (*pauṣtika*, *sōyaku/zōyaku*, 增益), for subduing adversaries (*ābhicaraka*, gōbuku/jōbuku, 降伏), for emotional affinity (*vaśikarana*, *keiai*, 敬愛), and for summoning (aṇkuśa, kōshō/kōchō, 鉤召). Whether as sets of three, four, or five, or even eight, these

Table 1. Symbolic Associations for Different Homa Categories

Category	Shape	Direction	Time	Color
Śānti	Circular	North	2 pm	White
Pauṣti	Square	East	Dawn	Yellow
Abhicāra	Triangular	South	10 am or noon	Black
Vaśikarana	Lotus	West	Night	Red
Aṇkuśa	Vajra	Any	Any	Any

categories originate in different tantric systems in India. The Indic origin is indicated, for example, by their use as general ritual categories, not only in Japan but also in Tibetan practice.[59]

Each of these functional categories is correlated with a variety of other symbolic factors, including the shape of the hearth-altar to be used, the direction that the practitioner is to be facing, the time of day at which the homa is to be performed, and the color of the practitioner's garb, as shown in table 1.

As alluded to, a more extensive list of eight functions is known from the Samvarodaya tantra. Shinichi Tsuda renders these as pacifying, increasing welfare, expelling and exorcising, hostility and killing, subduing and attracting, paralyzing and bewildering, expelling, and burning with fever.[60] The formation of a system of eight kinds may have been motivated by the sense of completeness from having one for each of the cardinal and intercardinal directions. Such correlations are found throughout tantric systems of thought, as well as in many other kinds of religious systems. The significance of such correlations as instances of metonymy is discussed in the section "Ritual Efficacy."

ORGANIZING PRINCIPLES FOR RITUAL ACTIONS: RITUAL SYNTAX

Homas are evocations; that is, they make the deities to whom offerings are to be made present within the ritual enclosure. They are found as rituals both performed independently and embedded within larger ceremonial activities. For example, Sarah Haynes found in the Tibetan rituals associated with Sarasvatī both instances in which the homa was a stand-alone ritual and instances in which it was integrated into a larger, more complex ritual performance.[61] Nawaraj Chaulagain has also noted that in Nepal, both independent performances of the homa and performances as part of ritual complexes are found.[62]

In addition, as a tantric ritual, homas also include an act of identification between the chief deity (Jpn. honzon, 本尊) and the practitioner.[63] These characteristics are reflected in the basic fivefold structure of Shingon homas, which Taisen Miyata has identified as purifying, constructing, encountering, identifying, and dissociating—ritual identification taking place in the encountering section.[64]

"Purifying" refers to the practitioner's self-purification of his or her own body, speech, and mind—the three aspects of human existence in Buddhist thought. This step also includes such actions as the symbolic putting on of armor for the practitioner's own protection.

Preparation of the ritual space is the next step, "constructing"; the practitioner symbolically constructs the space within which the ritual will be performed and the hearth-altar upon which the fire will be built and lays out and purifies the offerings to be made to the deities.[65]

The setting is now complete for the deities to be evoked within the ritual space, referred to as "encountering." The deities are invited to the ritual; a jeweled carriage is sent for them where they reside in the cosmic mandala. Once in place, the ritual space is enclosed with walls of vajras and flames to protect the ritual from demonic interference.[66]

In most of the Shingon homas, there are five sets of offerings made during this phase of the ritual. These are first to Agni (Katen, 火天), the Vedic god of fire who purifies the offerings made into the fire and carries them to the deities, as discussed in the section "Indo-European Fire Cult." The second is known as the "lord of the assembly," who varies according to the chief deity of the particular ritual. Thus, for example, the homa used for training of Shingon priests has Acalanatha Vidyārāja (Fudō Myōō, 不動明王) as the chief deity, with Prajñāpāramitā Buddha's Mother bodhisattva as the lord of the assembly. While during "encountering" the deities and the practitioner are understood to be separate from one another, in the next phase, "identifying," this separation is removed. Identification is only performed with the "chief deity" (honzon, 本尊), that is, the principal deity for whom the ritual is being performed. Identification takes place in the midst of making offerings to the chief deity. Once identification is complete, the practitioner resumes making offerings—completing those for the chief deity and then moving on to the fourth and fifth sets of offerings. These are first for a variety of deities, and then for various protectors, a set of Vedic deities, and asterisms.

Completing the last of the five sets of offerings, the final phase of the homa is "dissociating." This phase recapitulates in brief the actions that took place at the start of the ritual. Here at the end, this includes returning the deities to their original location in the cosmic mandala, transferring the benefits generated by performing the ritual, dissolving the protective boundaries of vajras, taking off the protective armor, and departing the ritual hall.

The symmetry of these actions at the end with those at the beginning is a regular feature of the Shingon homas, as well as other homas. We can represent this pattern in abstract as

$$A \rightarrow B \rightarrow C \rightarrow D \rightarrow C^* \rightarrow B^* \rightarrow A^*$$

in which the central ritual action, "*D*," is flanked symmetrically by the opening and closing sequence of actions (the closing actions marked by an asterisk). I have called the symmetry represented here, in which the actions repeated in the second half of the ritual are in reverse order, "mirror-image symmetry." "Sequential symmetry," in which the repeated actions are performed in the same order in the second as in the first half, would look like this:

$$A \rightarrow B \rightarrow C \rightarrow D \rightarrow A^* \rightarrow B^* \rightarrow C^*.$$

This simplified schema is only suggestive; in the actual homas I have studied, the actions are much more complex, and both kinds of symmetry are found.

As alluded to previously, the closing actions are usually performed in an abbreviated fashion, some actions being left out of more complex sets, or fewer numbers of repetitions of actions performed. I have called this "terminal abbreviation," and like symmetry, terminal abbreviation is also a common feature of homas. Another feature is recursion, which was identified by Frits Staal.[67] As mentioned, there are five sets of offerings made in the course of most Shingon homas—to Agni, lord of the assembly, chief deity, other deities, and what are known in some homas as the "worldly deities." Each of these forms a complete ritual unit in itself, beginning with preparations and invitation of the deity, offerings in the middle, and leave-taking and closing at the end. The five different sets of offerings are therefore recursively inserted into the frame ritual. They would look something like this:

$$A \rightarrow B \rightarrow C \rightarrow D^1 \rightarrow D^2 \rightarrow D^3 \rightarrow D^4 \rightarrow D^5 \rightarrow C^* \rightarrow B^* \rightarrow A^*$$

with D^1 through D^5 corresponding to the five sets of offerings made in the course of the homa. The consistency of these patterns, and the way in which recursion is employed for transforming one ritual into another, led Staal to describe this regularity as ritual syntax.

SYMBOLISMS OF THE HOMA

Interiorization. One of the distinctions sometimes taken for marking the shift of ritual practice away from the world of Vedic ritual practice to that of tantra is the interiorization of ritual. Yael Bentor has discussed the variety of practices this phrase has been used to identify. In her examination of Tibetan rites, she identified five kinds of interiorization. These are (1) fire offerings of breathing, inner heat, and the subtle body; (2) fire offerings of "great bliss" performed together with a tantric consort; (3) fire offerings of food (digestive fire); (4) mental fire offerings (imagination or visualization); and (5) fire offerings of enlightened wisdom, which destroys the mistaken conception of duality.[68] While some of these may be understood simply as analogies—because it burns away the mistaken conception of duality, enlightened wisdom is like the homa fire—traditional conceptions of the relation were probably stronger, that is, a kind of homologizing that faced in both directions. In other words, rather than simply an anaology, the ritual fire is enlightened wisdom and the offerings are one's own misplaced affections and mistaken conceptions (*kleśāvaraṇa* and *jñeyāvaraṇa*).

Also, the interiorization of ritual was not a psychologization of ritual, but rather a turning to the interior of the body. Focusing on the period from the 8th to 9th centuries, Jacob Dalton has pointed out that by

> the end of these two crucial centuries, a new ritual discourse of the bodily interior was in place. The tantric subject had become the site for the entire ritual performance; the body's interior provided the devotee, the altar, the oblations, and the buddha to be worshipped.[69]

The process of reinterpreting ritual as a practice interior to the body was not smooth and uniform. The *Vairocanābhisaṃbodhi tantra* (as known in Chinese translation) was probably compiled in the mid-7th century,[70] and thus predates the period to which Dalton refers. It also, however, evidences the interiorization of ritual. Together with the *Tattvasaṃgraha tantra*, the *Vairocanābhisaṃbodhi* became the central texts for the esoteric tradition, Zhenyan, in China up through the time that Kūkai studied there and brought the two lineages[71] to Japan, establishing Shingon. After that time, the *Susiddhikara tantra* also became an important text in Chinese tantric tradition and was brought to Japan by Tendai priests.

The *Vairocanābhisaṃbodhi tantra* explains the importance of the internal homa as the unity in diversity of the fire, the deity evoked, and the practitioner:

> One performs external *homa*, accomplishing *siddhi* [perfections, powers] at will.
> Next, in one's inner heart that which is of one nature but tripartite, Three places [loci, in the sense of principal agents of the ritual] united to form one, represents the internal *homa* of the *yogin*.[72]

The sutra describes this inner homa as counteracting karmic action and rebirth, and in that sense combines the fourth and fifth aspects described by Bentor. Buddhaguhya comments on the inner homa, saying that

> You should dissolve your five psycho-physical constituents [the five *skandhas*: *rūpa* (matter or form), *vedanā* (sensations or feeling), *saṃjñā* (perception or discrimination), *samskāra* (habits or conditioning), and *vijñāna* (conscious awareness)] into emptiness. Also the material objects, such as the external hearth and so forth, and likewise the perceptual awarenesses of the six senses which arise should also each be dissolved. Then preventing them from arising again, you should abide in the non-conceptualizing *samādhi*, [in which] even that *bodhicitta* which thus destroys and suspends them is counteracted by non-arising insight. That is the internal *homa*.[73]

The relation between the interior homa and the one performed physically is not universally agreed upon. Michel Strickmann, examining Yixing's commentary on the *Vairocanābhisaṃbodhi tantra* (*Da rijing shu*, T. 1796) notes that Yixing

> clarifies the scripture's implications regarding the true sense of Inner Homa. It is, first, a recognition of the identity of the divinity, the fire, and the officiant. Moreover it signifies the unity of the Three Mysteries of body, speech, and mind—in other words, mudra, mantra, and visualization of the deity... [Quoting Yixing] "Thus in general the meaning of Homa is with the fire of wisdom to burn the kindling of the kleśas until all are entirely consumed." It is thus the Inner Homa, at the center of the rite, that confers meaning and efficacy on all that precedes and follows it—the Outer Homa within which it is encapsulated. And though the meditation may be used to effectuate various sorts of Homa, Homa performed without this meditative support is meaningless, even heretical: "One would simply be burning the kindling and vainly using up the offerings. Not only would one be committing a profane act, but moreover it would be devoid of all efficacy."[74]

Another adaptation of internalized imagery is also found in the Jain tradition. Paul Dundas quotes the *Uttarādhyayana sūtra* in which Harikeśa, a Jain monk of untouchable origin, explains to Brahmans that

> Austerity is my sacrificial fire, my life is the place where the fire is kindled. Mental and physical efforts are my ladle for the oblation and my body is the dung fuel for the fire, my

actions my firewood. I offer up an oblation praised by the wise seers consisting of my restraint, effort and calm.[75]

In the *Saṁvarodaya tantra*, each aspect of the homa ritual is given meaning. For example, white mustard seeds pacify calamities—an apotropaic function of white mustard employed in rites that Strickmann has called "proto–homa."[76] Similarly, ghee brings about prosperity, sesame seeds destroy evil, corn brings wealth, and wheat removes illness. The list goes on at some length, but we note that the two ladles are identified with wisdom (*prajñā*) and skillful means (*upāya*), and that the union of the two is the practice of the non-duality of wisdom and means.[77] The bringing together of the two ladles, the smaller being placed inside the larger and in some cases rubbed back and forth, is also explained in terms of sexual symbolism.

Sex and Fire. A great deal of commentarial effort has been given to the question of whether the transgressive practices, such as yogic sex, described in the tantras are meant literally or not.[78] In a detailed study of six early tantras Tsunehiko Sugiki has discussed what he calls "psychosomatic fire oblation," which is an internalized form of practice employing the subtle body. Ideas regarding esoteric physiology form the conceptual ground for this understanding of the homa as an internalized practice. The kinds of practices studied by Sugiki do not clearly delineate between the different kinds of interiorization identified by Yael Bentor, but rather have aspects of subtle body, great bliss, and enlightened wisdom employed together. These internal practices also employ the phonic symbolism of "seed" syllable mantras (*bīja mantra*).

Sugiki has shown that there was a progression from literal to symbolic forms of sexual yogas over the course of time. In these texts, equivalences are made between the implements and actions of the homa and the elements of the sexual yogas. In two of the tantras, for example, the small ritual ladle and the hearth are identified with the yogi's penis and his female partner's vagina: "Through the union of their genital organs the practitioner controls the movements of the winds in his body and ignites the yogic subtle fire. The yogic subtle fire blazes upward, burning up concepts such as 'the five sense faculties' (i.e., rice or offered articles) and 'the five aggregates' (i.e., firewood and fuel) that the practitioner conceives." The process of interior transformations continues with the heat rising to the crown of the head, transforming the bowl of ghee there into the "awakening mind" fluid (ghee/semen): "The awakening mind flows downward in his body. He offers the awakening mind to the vagina of his female partner(s) (i.e., hearth) through his penis (i.e., the small ritual ladle)."[79]

Ritual Efficacy. Described in section Functional Categoreis of the Homa are the associations of the different types of homa performance and the factors of the hearth-altar, time of day of the performance, direction the practitioner is to face while performing the homa, and the color of the practitioner's garb. These kinds of associations are very common, not only in tantra but also throughout religions. Since the theoretical disjunction of magic, religion, and science in the 19th century, such associative thinking has been dismissed as "magical thought," and like other culturally bound categories employed in religious studies, magic has (at least until relatively recently) been treated as unproblematically universal. Consequently, some authors have used the term "magic" in their discussions of tantric practice. For example, Stephen Beyer defines magic as "the manipulation of a distant object through control of a simulacrum that is in some way associated with it, whether by name, resemblance, or attribution."[80] Beyer seems to accept that magic can be used as a universal category and applied in the context of any religious tradition, including the Tibetan tantric practices that he studied.

Several scholars have pointed out, however, that magic is a contrastive category, formulated as part of a three-way distinction among magic, science, and religion.[81] Wouter Hanegraaff has noted: "Because all traditional definitions have depended on an implicit or explicit contrast with either religion or science, the very concept of 'magic' appears to collapse together with these distinctions; any further use of it seems to imply support for scientifically untenable theories."[82] He does go on to point out, however, that the term has endured despite scholarly recognition of its contrastive nature.

While appropriate as an etic term, given the polemic role it has played historically, both inside the academy and out, it seems impossible to sublate magic as a universal category without introducing connotations from Western discourses inappropriately into discussions of traditions historically outside those discourses. The negative connotations entailed by the word deriving from the history of Christian theology, or the reactionary positive connotations from defenders of Western esotericism, make application of the category to tantric practices problematic. It has also carried negative connotations when used in psychological discourse, that is, as "magical thinking," a kind of unrealistic or even pathological belief in extraordinary means to wish fulfillment. The link frequently made between such associative thinking and ritual[83] further complicates the utility of the term "magic" by introducing cultural values dating from the Reformation (devaluation of ritual) and Enlightenment (positive valuation of reason). Laurie Patton has suggested that in place of magic, "it is more historically accurate and intellectually productive to name it metonymy, or more broadly, associational thought."[84]

Emically, most tantric traditions consider ritual to be effective because of the identity of practitioner and deity. This conception of ritual efficacy informs the practice of homa within these traditions and distinguishes such tantric rituals as the homa from other rituals, whether conducted within a tantric tradition or not, that have a dualism between practitioner and deity evident in devotional or sacrificial actions. In some tantric traditions, the identity is created as a specific ritual action, symbolically central to the ritual, while in other traditions, such identity is established in an initiation preceding ritual practice and therefore is not expressed as a distinct ritual action. In tantric Buddhist homas, such as those found in Japan, there is a threefold identification—the deity becomes manifest as the fire in the hearth-altar and is identical with the practitioner. Thus, the mouth of the hearth-altar is also the mouth of the deity and the mouth of the practitioner; the material offerings are the practitioner's own adventitious obscurations and are burned in the fire that is both the digestive fire and the fire of wisdom/gnosis. Tantric Buddhist thinkers employ the non-dualism of Madhyamaka thought, asserting that the body, speech, and mind of the practitioner is already the body, speech, and mind of the deity, as both are identically empty of any permanent essence.

REVIEW OF LITERATURE

At the end of the 19th century, Hōriou Tōki published a detailed explication of a set of ritual manuals, including the homa, as found in the Tendai and Shingon schools of Japan. The work provides images and explanations of the mūdras and ritual actions for each of the four kinds of rituals found in the training of priests in these two traditions.[85]

Further study of the homa in Western language scholarship seems to have been taken up next in the last quarter of the 20th century. Translations of a variety of tantric materials have made the homa, as performed by different ritual traditions, available for both contextual and comparative study. An exemplary instance of this is the translation of the massive *Somaśambhupaddhati* by Hélène Brunner, which includes a chapter describing homa in the context of Śaiva tradition.[86] Similarly, the *Vairocanābhisaṃbodhi tantra* contains chapters valuable for studying the early medieval Buddhist practice of homa.[87]

Interested in the historical and cultural links between the homa as found in modern Bali and its Indian predecessors, Christian Hooykaas examined the homa performances of Bauddha Brahmans.[88] His study gives a translation of one ritual manual and explicates the homa performance in Bali, both detailing the homa itself and the larger ritual and religious contexts within which it is found. A set of homa ritual instructions are found in Tadeusz Skorupski's translations of the *Sarvadurgatipariśodhana tantra* and of a commentary on the same text by Vajravarman.[89] Michel Strickmann gave a historical and descriptive overview of the homa in East Asia in two works.[90] In both, Strickmann makes the methodological point that contemporary Japanese ritual and ritual texts provide an important resource for understanding the ritual life of Tang China.

The contemporary Tendai tradition of Japan was studied by Michael Saso, who gives a detailed narrative description of a present-day Tendai homa, along with similar treatments of two other rites of Tendai esoteric practice. Saso's work is self-described as preliminary, and as such provides little context for the descriptions of these rituals.[91] Richard K. Payne studied the homa as found in the other tantric tradition of Japan, the Shingon.[92] That work focuses on the homa, giving historical and doctrinal context, as well as providing a translation and detailed narrative description of one Shingon ritual manual. The work also outlines the other three rituals of the Shingon training sequence, which are given in appendices. These latter two works are similar to Tōki's early study, being informed by the set of rituals at the core of the training of a tantric priest in Japan.

To date, cross-cultural and comparative study of the homa has played a smaller, but we believe increasing, role. One consideration is the relation between tantric forms of the homa and the broader Indo-European roots of Vedic culture.[93] More focused is Holly Grether's works on the relation between tantric homa and the Zoroastrian *yasna*.[94] In addition to the historical and cross-cultural perspectives, the extensive spread of the homa provides a means of studying ritual change both across the boundaries of religious cultures and across longer periods of time than has usually been the case in the study of ritual change. While the individual essays are relatively focused on specific traditions and times, taken together the collection of thirteen essays by Richard Payne and Michael Witzel provides materials toward such studies.[95]

PRIMARY SOURCES

This article incorporates both a survey of the homa and my own firsthand research. That research has largely focused on Shingon (真言), an esoteric (mikkyō, 密教) tradition of Buddhism found in Japan. While I have attempted to integrate as much breadth as possible in order to meet the interests of any reader, many of the specific instances or analyses will, therefore, naturally refer to Buddhist tradition, the esoteric tradition within Buddhism, and the Shingon material with which I am most familiar. However, although the details may differ between traditions and religious cultures, my own studies have found extensive similarities of performance across a wide range of cultures and settings, so as to constitute the homa per se as a significantly coherent ritual practice. There are debates within the field of Buddhist studies regarding the nature and identity of the esoteric Buddhist tradition. It is neither possible nor desireable to survey these here. I have found Ronald M. Davidson's use of the terminology of an "Esoteric movement," that is, not sect or lineage, most useful, as well as his thinking behind this terminology most convincing. See his *Indian Esoteric Buddhism: A Social History of the Tantric Movement.*[96]

FURTHER READING

Atwood, Christopher P. "Buddhism and Popular Ritual in Mongolian Religion: A Reexamination of the Fire Cult." *History of Religions* 36, no. 2 (1996): 112–139.

Bentor, Yael. "Interiorized Fire Rituals in India and in Tibet." *Journal of the American Oriental Society* 120, no. 4 (2000): 594–613.

Beyer, Stephan. *The Cult of Tārā: Magic and Ritual in Tibet.* Berkeley and Los Angeles: University of California Press, 1973.

Chaulagain, Nawaraj. "The *Navarātra Homa*: Liver, Enchantment, and Engendering the Divine *Śaktis*." In *Homa Variations: Ritual Change across the* Longue Durée. Edited by Richard K. Payne and Michael Witzel, 314–336. Oxford and New York: Oxford University Press, 2015.

Grether, Holly. "Tantric Homa Rites in the Indo-Iranian Ritual Paradigm." *Journal of Ritual Studies* 21, no. 1 (2007): 16–32.

Grether, Holly. "Burning Demons and Sprinkling Mantras: A History of Fire Sacrifice in South and Central Asia." PhD diss., University of California, Santa Barbara, 2010.

Grether, Holly. "The Ritual Interplay of Fire and Water." In *Homa Variations: Ritual Change across the* Longue Durée. Edited by Richard K. Payne and Michael Witzel, 47–66. Oxford and New York: Oxford University Press, 2015.

Payne, Richard K. *The Tantric Ritual of Japan: Feeding the Gods, The Shingon Fire Ritual.* New Delhi: International Academy of Indian Culture, 1991.

Payne, Richard K. "Tongues of Flame: Homologies in the Tantric *Homa*." In *The Roots of Tantra.* Edited by Katherine Anne Harper and Robert L. Brown, 193–210. Albany: State University of New York Press, 2002.

Payne, Richard K. "Ritual Syntax and Cognitive Theory." *Pacific World: Journal of the Institute of Buddhist Studies*, 3rd ser., 6 (2004): 195–227.

Payne, Richard K. "Ritual Studies in the *Longue Durée*: Comparing Shingon and Śaiva Siddhānta *Homas*." *Pacific World: Journal of the Institute of Buddhist Studies*, 3rd ser., 13 (Fall 2011): 223–262.

Payne, Richard K. "Fire on the Mountain: The Shugendō *Saitō Goma*." In *Homa Variations: Ritual Change across the* Longue Durée. Edited by Richard K. Payne and Michael Witzel, 337–370. Oxford and New York: Oxford University Press, 2015.

Payne, Richard K. "The Homa of the Northern Dipper." In *Tantric Traditions on the Move: Their Development through Time, and Transmission through Cultural Space.* Edited by David B. Gray and Ryan Richard Overby, 284–307. Oxford and New York: Oxford University Press, 2016.

Payne, Richard K. and Michael Witzel, eds. *Homa Variations: Ritual Change across the* Longue Durée. Oxford and New York: Oxford University Press, 2015.

Saso, Michael. *Homa Rites and Mandala Meditation in Tendai Buddhism.* New Delhi: International Academy of Indian Culture, 1991.

Skorupski, Tadeusz. "Tibetan Homa Rites." In *Agni: The Vedic Ritual of the Fire Altar*. Edited by Frits Staal, 2 vols., 2:403–417. Berkeley, CA: Asian Humanities Press, 1983.

Skorupski, Tadeusz. "Buddhist Permutations and Symbolism of Fire." In *Homa Variations: Ritual Change across the* Longue Durée. Edited by Richard K. Payne and Michael Witzel, 67–125. Oxford and New York: Oxford University Press, 2015.

Strickmann, Michel. "Homa in East Asia." In *Agni: The Vedic Ritual of the Fire Altar,* edited by Fritz Staal, 2 vols., 2:418–455. Berkeley, CA: Asian Humanities Press, 1983.

Sugiki, Tsunehiko. "Oblation, Nonconception, and Body: Systems of Psychosomatic Fire Oblation in Esoteric Buddhism in Medieval South Asia." In *Homa Variations: Ritual Change across the* Longue Durée. Edited by Richard K. Payne and Michael Witzel. Oxford and New York: Oxford University Press, 2015.

Tachikawa, Musashi, Shrikant Bahulkar, and Madhavi Kolhatkar. *Indian Fire Ritual.* Delhi: Motilal Banarsidass, 2001.

NOTES

1. For example, Teun Goudriaan gives a list of eighteen characteristics for tantra in a wide sense of "a conglomerate of ritual and yogic practices and presuppositions." See his "Introduction" to Sanjukta Gupta, Dirk van Hoens, and Teun Goudriann, *Hindu Tantrism* (Leiden, The Netherlands, and Cologne: Brill, 1979), 7. Similarly, Stephen Hodge lists twelve "features which characterize the spirit of Buddhist tantric thought" in *The Mahā-Vairocana-Abhisaṃbodhi Tantra, With Buddhaguhya's Commentary,* translated by Stephen Hodge (London and New York: RoutledgeCurzon, 2003), 4.
2. Francisca Cho and Richard King Squier, "Religion as a Complex and Dynamic System," *Journal of the American Academy of Religion* 81, no. 2 (2013): 357–398.
3. Technically, it is neither a closed system nor a fully open one, but rather what could be called a semipermeable one.
4. Don Ross, "Coordination and the Foundations of Social Intelligence," in *The Oxford Handbook of Philosophy of Social Science,* ed. Harold Kincaid (Oxford and New York: Oxford University Press, 2012), 481–506.
5. Benoît Dubreuil, *Human Evolution and the Origins of Hierarchies: The State of Nature* (Cambridge, UK: Cambridge University Press, 2010), 87.
6. Haim Ofek, *Second Nature: Economic Origins of Human Evolution* (Cambridge, UK: Cambridge University Press, 2001), 157.
7. Ibid., 3.
8. See Catherine Bell, *Ritual Theory, Ritual Practice* (Oxford and New York: Oxford University Press, 1992), 140.
9. The entirety of this section draws on Richard K. Payne, "Tongues of Flame: Homologies in the Tantric *Homa*," in *The Roots of Tantra*, ed. Katherine Anne Harper and Robert L. Brown (Albany: State University of New York Press, 2002), 193–210.
10. For the Tendai instance, see Michael Saso, *Homa Rites and Maṇḍala Meditation in Tendai Buddhism* (New Delhi: International Academy of Indian Culture, 1991), 59.
11. Carlos Lopez, "Food and Immortality in the Veda: A Gastronomic Theology?" *Electronic Journal of Vedic Studes* 3, no. 3 (1997): 11–20; p. 15, http://www.ejvs.laurasianacademy.com/issues.html.
12. See Frits Staal, ed., *Agni: The Vedic Ritual of the Fire Altar*, 2 vols. (Berkeley, CA: Asian Humanities Press, 1983).
13. For further details on this issue, see Timothy Lubin, "The Vedic *Homa* and the Standardization of Hindu *Pūjā*," in *Homa Variations: Ritual Change across the* Longue Durée, ed. Richard K. Payne and Michael Witzel (Oxford and New York: Oxford University Press, 2015), n24.

14. Richard K. Payne, "Ritual Syntax and Cognitive Theory" *Pacific World: Journal of the Institute of Buddhist Studies*, 3rd ser., 6 (2004): 195–227; p. 211. This article demonstrates a negative instance, that is, arguing that the *agnihotra* cannot be the direct forebear of the tantric homa.
15. Holly Grether, "Tantric Homa Rites in the Indo-Iranian Ritual Paradigm," *Journal of Ritual Studies* 21, no. 1 (2007): 16–32; p. 16.
16. Holly Grether, "Burning Demons and Sprinkling Mantras: A History of Fire Sacrifice in South and Central Asia," PhD diss., University of California, Santa Barbara, 2010, 55.
17. Ibid., 56–57.
18. Holly Grether, "The Ritual Interplay of Fire and Water," in *Homa Variations: Ritual Change across the* Longue Durée, ed. Richard K. Payne and Michael Witzel (Oxford and New York: Oxford University Press, 2015), 48.
19. Giovanni Verardi, Homa *and Other Fire Rituals in Gandhāra* (Naples: Istituto Universitario Orientale, 1994).
20. Ibid., 5.
21. Alexis Sanderson, "Kashmir," *Brill Encyclopedia of Hinduism*, vol. 1, 99–126.
22. Shaman Hatley, "Tantric Śaivism in Early Medieval India: Recent Research and Future Directions," *Religion Compass* 4, no. 10 (2010): 615–628, http://dx.doi.org/10.1111/j.1749-8171.2010.00240.x.
23. Dominic Goodall, ed., *Hindu Scriptures*, translated by Dominic Goodall (Berkeley and Los Angeles: University of California Press, 1996), xxxi.
24. Ibid., xxxiii.
25. *Somaśudapaddhati*, translated by Hélêne Brunner-Lachaux, 3 vols. (Pondicherry: Institut Français d'Indologie, 1963, 1968, 1977). The relevant section has been translated into English as an appendix to Richard K. Payne, "Ritual Studies in the *Longue Durée*: Comparing Shingon and Śaiva Siddhānta *Homas*," *Pacific World: Journal of the Institute of Buddhist Studies*, 3rd ser., 13 (Fall 2011): 223–262.
26. Payne, "Ritual Studies in the *Longue Durée*," 232–234. See also Richard K. Payne, "From Vedic India to Buddhist Japan: Continuities and Discontinuities in Esoteric Ritual," in *Esoteric Buddhism and the Tantras in East Asia*, ed. Charles Orzech, Henrik Sørensen, and Richard K. Payne (Leiden, The Netherlands, and Boston: Brill, 2011), 1040–1054, esp. 1048–1051.
27. Payne, "Ritual Studies in the *Longue Dureé*," 234–236.
28. See also Carl Gustav Diehl, *Instrument and Purpose: Studies in Rites and Rituals in South India* (Lund: CWK Gleerup, 1956), 124–129.
29. See, for example, Caroline Humphrey and James Laidlaw, *The Archetypal Actions of Ritual: A Theory of Ritual Illustrated by the Jain Rite of Worship* (Oxford and New York: Oxford University Press, 1994); Lawrence A. Babb, *Absent Lord: Ascetics and Kings in Jain Ritual Culture* (Berkeley and Los Angeles: University of California Press, 1996); and John E. Cort, ed., *Open Boundaries: Jain Communities and Cultures in Indian History* (Albany: State University of New York Press, 1998).
30. See, for example, Ellen Gough, "Jain *Mantraśāstra* and the *Ṛṣimaṇḍala Yantra*," *Jaina Studies: Newsletter of the Centre of Jaina Studies* 4 (March 2009): 36–38.
31. Alexis Sanderson, "The Śaiva Age: The Rise and Dominance of Śaivism during the Early Medieval Period," in *Genesis and Development of Tantrism*, ed. Shingo Einoo (Tokyo: Institute of Oriental Culture, Univesity of Tokyo, 2009), 41–350, 243.
32. Ronald M. Davidson, *Indian Esoteric Buddhism: A Social History of the Tantric Movement* (New York: Columbia University Press, 2002), 118–144.
33. John E. Cort, "Contemporary Jain Maṇḍala Rituals," in *Victorious Ones: Jain Images of Perfection*, ed. Phyllis Granoff (New York and Ahmedabad: Rubin Museum of Art), 140–157; 141.
34. Ibid., 144.
35. See also Paul Dundas, "Becoming Gautama: Mantra and History in Śvétāmbara Jainism," in *Open Boundaries: Jain Communities and Cultures in Indian History*, ed. Paul Dundas (Albany: State University of New York Press, 1998), 31–52.

36. The English glosses used here follow those of Frits Staal, ed., *Agni: The Vedic Ritual of the Fire Altar.*
37. Tadeusz Skorupski, "Buddhist Permutations and Symbolism of Fire," in *Homa Variations: Ritual Change across the* Longue Durée, ed. Richard K. Payne and Michael Witzel (Oxford and New York: Oxford University Press, 2015), 67–125, 72.
38. Ibid., 72.
39. Stephan Beyer, *The Cult of Tārā: Magic and Ritual in Tibet* (Berkeley and Los Angeles: University of California Press, 1973), 272. Full description of a homa is found on pp. 265–274.
40. Ibid., 264.
41. Richard J. Kohn, *Lord of the Dance: The Mani Rimdu Festival in Tibet and Nepal* (Albany: State University of New York Press, 2001), 241.
42. Ibid., 242.
43. See also Geoffrey Samuel, *Civilized Shamans: Buddhism in Tibetan Societies* (Washington, DC, and London: Smithsonian Institution Press, 1993).
44. Christopher P. Atwood, "Buddhism and Popular Ritual in Mongolian Religion: A Reexamination of the Fire Cult," *History of Religions* 36, no. 2 (1996): 112–139; p. 124.
45. Ibid., 124.
46. Ibid., 128.
47. Although Atwood refers to this deity as a goddess, the iconography may well be that of Agni. Unfortunately, the description provided is inadequate to make a definite identification.
48. Atwood, "Buddhism and Popular Ritual in Mongolian Religion," 128–129.
49. Erik Zürcher, "Buddhist Influence on Early Taoism: A Survey of Scriptural Evidence, " *T'oung-pao* 66 (1980), 84–147; 87.
50. For a more extended discussion of this adaptation of Zürcher's schema, see Richard K. Payne, "The Homa of the Northern Dipper," in *Tantric Traditions on the Move: Their Development through Time, and Transmission through Cultural Space,* ed. David B. Gray and Ryan Richard Overbey (Oxford and New York: Oxford University Press, 2016), 284–307.
51. Ibid., 296–297.
52. Richard K. Payne, "Conversions of Tantric Buddhist Ritual: The Yoshida Shintō *Jūhachishintō* Ritual," in *Transformations and Transfer of Tantra in Asia and Beyond,* ed. István Keul (Berlin and Boston: Walter de Gruyter, 2012), 365–398.
53. For a fuller description and more detailed analysis, see Richard K. Payne, "Fire on the Mountain: The Shugendō *Saitō Goma,*" in *Homa Variations: Ritual Change across the* Longue Durée, ed. Richard K. Payne and Michael Witzel (Oxford and New York: Oxford University Press, 2015), 337–370.
54. These are T. 951 and T. 952.
55. Michel Strickmann, "Homa in East Asia," in *Agni: The Vedic Ritual of the Fire Altar,* ed. Frits Staal, 2 vols., (Berkeley, CA: Asian Humanities Press, 1983), 2:434.
56. Ibid.
57. Tadeusz Skorupski, "Tibetan Homa Rites," in *Agni: The Vedic Ritual of the Fire Altar,* ed. Frits Staal, 2 vols. (Berkeley, CA: Asian Humanities Press, 1983), 2:403–417.
58. Steven Neal Weinberger, "The Significance of Yoga Tantra and the *Compendium of Principles (Tattvasaṃgraha Tantra)* within Tantric Buddhism in India and Tibet," PhD diss., University of Virginia, 2003, 213.
59. On the use of the category system in other kinds of rite, see Yael Bentor, *Consecration of Images and Stūpas in Indo-Tibetan Tantric Buddhism* (Leiden, The Netherlands, and New York: Brill, 1996), as for example, increase, 80, and protection, 207. On the pacifying fire offering as part of consecration rites, see 330.
60. *The Saṁvarodaya-Tantra: Selected Chapters,* trans. Shinichi Tsuda (Tokyo: Hokuseido Press, 1974), 307–308.

61. Sarah Haynes, "In Praise of Sarasvatī: An Examination of Tibetan Buddhist Ritual in Text and Life," PhD diss., University of Calgary, 2006, 4.
62. Nawaraj Chaulagain, "The *Navarātra Homa*: Liver, Enchantment, and Engendering the Divine *Śaktis*," in *Homa Variations: Ritual Change across the* Longue Durée, ed. Richard K. Payne and Michael Witzel (Oxford and New York: Oxford University Press, 2015), 314–336.
63. While most tantric traditions include ritual identification, there is an important, and importantly ambiguous, exception to be noted. In the Śaiva Siddhanta tradition, there is no specific ritual action of identification between the deity and the practitioner. This has been variously explained to me as a consequence either of the tradition being philosophically dualist or of the assertion that as fully initiated the practitioner already is the deity. These two explanations are not necessarily contradictory, of course.
64. Miyata Taisen, *A Study of the Ritual Mudrās in the Shingon Tradition* (Sacramento: Northern California Koyasan Temple, 1984).
65. In his study of the *darśapūrṇamāsa* ritual, part of the Vedic ritual corpus, Musashi Tachikawa describes this stage in terms of the creation of a "meta-world." Musashi Tachikawa, Shrikant Bahulkar, and Madhavi Kolhatkar, *Indian Fire Ritual* (Delhi: Motilal Banarsidass, 2001), 21.
66. Although the ritual symbolism differs, this indicates a concern similar to that of Vedic practice, in which the second fire is set to the south as a protection against demonic forces.
67. Staal discussed recursion in several of his publications, including "From Meanings to Trees," *Journal of Ritual Studies* 7, no. 2 (1993): 11–32.
68. Yael Bentor, "Interiorized Fire Rituals in India and in Tibet," *Journal of the American Oriental Society* 120, no. 4 (2000): 594–613.
69. Jacob Dalton, "The Development of Perfection: The Interiozation of Buddhist Ritual in the Eighth and Ninth Centuries," *Journal of India Philosophy* 32 (2004): 1–30; p. 2.
70. *The Mahā-Vairocana-Abhisaṃbodhi Tantra*, trans. Stephen Hodge, 14.
71. There is an important and continuing discussion regarding the provenance of the dual tradition, that is, the pairing of the Vajraśekhara and Vairocanābhisaṃbodhi. Shingon sectarian historiography has generally attributed the synthesis of the two into a unified dual system in which the two sets of ritual, text, and mandala are matched with one another to the founder of the Shingon tradition, Kūkai. There are, however, important suggestions that the pairing of these two specific tantric lineages was already in place at earlier dates, perhaps even being done in Indian tantric milieus. This theory is still preliminary, and depends on the interpretation of archeaological evidence, such as the finds at Famensi. These finds are, however, open to alternative interpretations.
72. *The Vairocanābhisaṃbodhi Sutra*, trans. Rolf W. Giebel (Berkeley, CA: Numata Center for Buddhist Translation and Research, 2005), 193. For alternate translations, see Michel Strickmann, "Homa in East Asia," 2:438; and *The Mahā-Vairocana-Abhisṃbodhi Tantra*, trans. Stephen Hodge, 386. See also Koichi Shinohara, *Spells, Images, and Maṇḍalas: Tracing the Evolution of Esoteric Buddhist Rituals* (New York: Columbia University Press, 2014), esp. chap. 7, "Yixing's Commentary on the *Mahāvairocana Sūtra*: Creating the Great Maṇḍala," 147–167.
73. Hodge, trans., *The Mahā-Vairocana-Abhisṃbodhi Tantra*, 390.
74. Michel Strickmann, "Homa in East Asia," 2:418–455, 443–444.
75. Paul Dundas, *The Jains*, 2nd ed. (London and New York: Routledge, 2002), 15.
76. Strickmann, "Homa in East Asia," 2:429.
77. Tsuda, 313. Strickmann, "Homa in East Asia," includes a photograph, 2:441.
78. See, for example, David Gordon White, *The Alchemical Body: Siddha Traditions in Medieval India* (Chicago and London: University of Chicago Press, 1996), and Introduction, *Tantra in Practice*, edited by David Gordon White (Princeton, NJ: Princeton University Press, 2000), especially 15–18. Also David Gray, *The Cakrasamvara Tantra (The Discourse of Śrī Heruka): A Study and Annotated Translation* (New York: American Institute of Buddhist Studies, 2007).

79. Tsunehiko Sugiki, "Oblation, Nonconception, and Body: Systems of Psychosomatic Fire Oblation in Esoteric Buddhism in Medieval South Asia," in *Homa Variations: Ritual Change across the* Longue Durée, ed. Richard K. Payne and Michael Witzel (Oxford and New York: Oxford University Press, 2015), 167–213; 175–176.
80. Beyer, *The Cult of Tārā*, 92.
81. Stanley Tambiah, *Magic, Science, and Religion, and the Scope of Rationality* (Cambridge, UK: Cambridge University Press, 1990).
82. Wouter Hanegraaff, *New Age Religion and Western Culture: Esotericism in the Mirror of Secular Thought* (Leiden, The Netherlands, and New York: Brill, 1996), 80.
83. As well as the all-too-familiar association between ritual and obsessional behaviors initiated by Sigmund Freud.
84. Laurie Patton, *Bringing the Gods to Mind: Mantra and Ritual in Early Indian Sacrifice* (Berkeley and Los Angeles: University of California Press, 2005), 16.
85. Hōriou Tōki, *Si-do-in-dzou: Gestes de l'officiant dans les cérémonies mystiques des sectes Tendaï et Singon* (Paris: Ernest Leroux, 1899).
86. Hélène Brunner, trans., *Somaśambhupaddhati*), 1:230–277.
87. Two translations and a study of the work are of value in this regard: Stephen Hodge, trans., *The* Mahā-Vairocana-Abhisaṃbodhi Tantra; Rolf W. Giebel, trans., *The Vairocanābhisaṃbodhi sutra*; and Alex Wayman, "Study of the *Vairocanābhisaṁbodhitantra*," in *The Enlightenment of Vairocana*, ed. Alex Wayman (Delhi: Motilal Banarsidass, 1992), 1–205.
88. Christian Hooykaas, "Homa in India and Bali," in *Tantric and Taoist Studies in Honour of R.A. Stein*, ed. Michel Strickmann, 3 vols. (Brussels: Institut Belge des Hautes Études Chinoises, 1983), 2:512–591.
89. Tadeusz Skorupski, *The* Sarvadurgatipariśodhana tantra*: Elimination of All Evil Destinies* (Delhi: Motilal Banarsidass, 1983); and commentary in "Tibetan Homa Rites," in *Agni*, 2:403–417.
90. Michel Strickmann, "Homa in East Asia," in *Agni*, 2:418–455; ibid., *Mantras et Mandarins: Le Bouddhisme tantrique in Chine* (Paris: Éditions Gallimard, 1996), chap. 7, "Le culte Tantrique du feu," 337–368.
91. Michael Saso, *Homa Rites and Maṇḍala Meditation in Tendai Buddhism*. On the preliminary status of the work, see p. 10.
92. Richard K. Payne, *The Tantric Ritual of Japan: Feeding the Gods, the Shingon Fire Ritual* (New Delhi: Aditya Prakashan, 1991).
93. Richard K. Payne, "Tongues of Flame," in *The Roots of Tantra*, 193–210.
94. Holly Grether, "Tantric Homa Rites in the Indo-Iranian Ritual Paradigm," 16–32, and "The Ritual Interplay of Fire and Water," in *Homa Variations*, 47–66.
95. Payne, Richard K. and Michael Witzel, eds., *Homa Variations: Ritual Change across the* Longue Durée.
96. Ronald M. Davidson, *Indian Esoteric Buddhism: A Social History of the Tantric Movement* (New York: Columbia University Press, 2002).

Richard K. Payne

HSING YUN

THE LIFE OF HSING YUN

Analysis of hagiographies of Buddhist monks demonstrates that they often emphasize uncanny and supernatural events that surround famous monks and nuns. Unlike those traditional hagiographical accounts, Hsing Yun's biographies relay his humanity.[1] Although Hsing Yun was unusually adept from a very young age, there is nothing supernatural about his story, though it is an intriguing one.

Hsing Yun was born Li Kuo-shen 李國深 in Jiangsu Province in mainland China in 1927. His biographies relay that he was a vegetarian by the age of four due to the influence of his grandmother. A few years later his father went missing while on a business trip to Nanjing, perhaps a victim of the Nanjing Massacre of 1937. Hsing Yun became a novice monk the following year at Qixia Temple 栖霞寺 outside Nanjing. He received the Dharma transmission as part of the forty-eighth generation of the Linji Chan School in 1941. Afterward, he went on to a Buddhist seminary to continue his education, which would become the guiding mission in his life. While at the seminary, Hsing Yun learned about the Chinese Buddhist reformer Tai Xu 太虛 (1890–1947), who first promoted the idea of "humanistic Buddhism" (*renjian fojiao* 人间佛家). Many of the early projects Hsing Yun took on after college placed him in the role of teacher or school administrator. Education and humanistic Buddhism continue to be central to the mission of Fo Guang Shan.

China faced constant turbulence during Hsing Yun's youth. The Second Sino-Japanese war lasted for most of the first two decades of his life, perhaps even claiming the life of his father. The Chinese Civil War restarted in 1945, even before the unconditional surrender of the Japanese forces. Hsing Yun was caught up in the war between the Communist Party and the Guomindang (GMD). While serving as an elementary school principal, he was arrested by the Communists under the assumption that he was a GMD spy. Hsing Yun and a group of other monastics followed the GMD as they retreated to Taiwan in 1949, where he was arrested again on the charge of espionage, though this time the GMD suspected he was spying for the Communists. Despite these challenging circumstances, Hsing Yun kept his focus on educating rural areas and spreading Buddhist teachings.

His passion for rural education on the island of Taiwan led him to focus his efforts in Yilan County in the north and the outskirts of Kaohsiung in the south. Hsing Yun spent his first two decades in Taiwan building a lay community promoting secular and sectarian education by building schools and temples. Hsing Yun and other monastics in Taiwan found themselves competing against Christian missionaries from the West, who often had more resources. Despite this disadvantage, Buddhism grew rapidly in Taiwan in conjunction with the economic growth it experienced in the latter half of the 20th century. As the members of his community—and the donations from the community—expanded, Hsing Yun decided to start building the main campus of Fo Guang Shan in the outskirts of Kaohsiung in 1967, and the project continued for twenty-five years.

Hsing Yun served as the head abbot of Fo Guang Shan until 1985, when he passed the leadership to Hsin Ping 心平, who remained abbot until his untimely death in 1995. (Hsing Yun stayed active with Fo Guang Shan and pursued expanding it globally. Fo Guang Shan completed its first temple in North America in 1988, when it opened Hsi Lai Temple 西来寺 ("Coming to the West"). Hsing Yun traveled extensively, opening temples around the world and meeting world leaders including Pope John Paul II, the Dalai Lama, and many heads of state. Among the most important achievements for Fo Guang Shan was the creation of Buddha's Light International Association (BLIA) in 1992. The organization offers membership for Fo Guang Shan laity, though most Fo Guang Shan monastics are members as well. In 1995, Hsing Yun claimed BLIA had reached one million members.[2] Given that BLIA does not publish an exact number of their membership, it is hard to determine the current number of members, though one article suggested around six million total "Fo Guang Shan people."[3]

Hsing Yun's health has deteriorated with his advanced age, and he suffered from multiple strokes, in 2011 and 2016.[4] Pictures indicate he is mostly wheelchair bound, and diabetes has made him nearly blind.[5] He was active spreading the dharma on most social media platforms until 2016. Hsin Bao 心保, the current head abbot of Fo Guang Shan, took over writing the new year's greeting letter to the Fo Guang Shan community in 2017, the fiftieth anniversary of Fo Guang Shan. Nevertheless, Hsing Yun has remained active despite his advanced age. He attended the 2018 BLIA World Conference meeting, which was held at Fo Guang Shan.[6] Promotions of Hsing Yun also feature his "one-stroke calligraphy," a hobby that he has developed late in life. Most controversial, however, is his continued commentary on China–Taiwan relations. In a press conference in China in 2009, Hsing Yun claimed that "there are no Taiwanese in Taiwan," in an attempt to communicate that Chinese and Taiwanese should view themselves as one family.[7] Despite scorn and objections to his statements, Hsing Yun continues to seemingly support reunification of Taiwan and China. In a December 2018 column for Taiwan's *China Times*, Hsing Yun lamented the state of political affairs in Taiwan, admitted he has always felt more Chinese despite over sixty years of living in Taiwan, and urged the people of Taiwan not to lose their traditional Chinese culture.[8] However, in a 2017 *New York Times* interview in which he was asked if Taiwan is part of China, he did not repeat his 2009 remarks, though again claiming to "belong to the same family."[9]

It is clear that Hsing Yun is no stranger to controversy. His success has brought him critique throughout his career as leader of Fo Guang Shan. The two main critiques of Hsing Yun spotlight the wealth of Fo Guang Shan and his politics. The current monetary value of the Fo Guang Shan empire is hard to estimate, but Hsing Yun reported it as high as five billion USD in the late 1990s.[10] Although that figure is likely exaggerated, the extreme wealth of Fo Guang Shan has brought critics wary of such extreme material wealth of not-for-profit religious organizations. To their credit, Fo Guang Shan monastics have not provided any reasons to doubt their integrity. Fo Guang Shan does provide monastics with a small monthly stipend, reported to be around USD 16 in 2002.[11] Hsing Yun is also critiqued due to his political record. Despite his arrest by the GMD, he later went on to join the party, even serving on the central committee. His political record indicates a preference for conservatism, but Hsing Yun has admitted at times to feeling forced to cooperate with both sides in order to promote his main agenda, compassion for all.[12] As referenced earlier, Hsing Yun has recently come under fire for his support of the Chinese Communist Party, though he insists that the spread of Buddhism remains his sole focus.[13]

HUMANISTIC BUDDHISM

Hsing Yun's teaching blends the Linji Chan school, where he received his ordination and transmission, with Pure Land Buddhism. This combination provides Fo Guang Shan with a unique style of humanistic Buddhism, which remains at the heart of their mission. Adding to that uniqueness is Hsing Yun's acceptance of "traditional modernism" as the best form of practicing Buddhism in order to keep it attractive and relevant in modern society.[14] Hsing Yun credits this style with the revival of Buddhism in Taiwan in the late 20th century. This influx of membership in Taiwan has permitted Fo Guang Shan to evolve into a global organization and spread Hsing Yun's humanistic Buddhist vision to all people. Therefore, it is worth considering the four main objectives of Fo Guang Shan's mission: culture, charity, cultivation, and education.

The cultural and educational objectives are often paired. Fo Guang Shan's cultural mission involves the propagation of the dharma in conjunction with Chinese history and culture. As a result, they have found that an effective way of promoting that culture is through education, which is why Fo Guang Shan is heavily invested in education on every level. The specific culture that Hsing Yun promotes asserts the belief that the earth can be reformed into a pure land. Unlike Japanese Pure Land sects that often emphasize the "other power" (Jp. *tariki* 他力) of Amitabha's vows that permits one to be reborn in his pure land, Hsing Yun advocates for an equal amount of "communal power."[15] The power and efforts of the community ensure that they must remain engaged with the world and actively seek to make it a better place for all humans.

Given that Fo Guang Shan promotes Buddhist and Chinese culture, one might assume that the organization has a traditional approach to propagating culture, but that is not the case. Hsing Yun has always adjusted to modern technologies in order to aid his pursuits. Hsing Yun strongly believes that Buddhism needs to adjust to modern lifestyles if it is to truly attract and help modern people. In other words, Hsing Yun seeks a "middle path" that balances the traditional approaches of Buddhism with the emerging ideas and technologies of the moment. Hsing Yun has modeled this through his progressive attitudes toward nuns occupying some of the highest positions in the organization (though no female has served as head abbot of Fo Guang Shan), as well as promoting a democratic structure and representative body for the monastic community. This choice to adapt to modern views means that Fo Guang Shan favors flexible interpretations of Buddhist texts over literalism.[16] Therefore, Hsing Yun is often quick to welcome new technologies (automobiles, air conditioning, media platforms) as long as they promote their cultural objectives.

Reflecting modern attitudes on wealth, Hsing Yun does not view wealth as inherently problematic, as long as it is accrued through ethical means. Greed, however, is another issue. To discourage greedy behaviors, Fo Guang Shan elicits donations from its members and visitors, which remain a significant source of income in addition to sales of merchandise, books, and tuition for its educational facilities.[17] Fo Guang Shan does not charge for its ritual services, though a minimum contribution is suggested.[18] While much of this income goes toward the operations budget of its many facilities and programs, a significant percentage of the annual budget is allocated for philanthropic endeavors and emergency aid. Thus, Fo Guang Shan expects and needs its members to be charitable to the organization so it, in turn, can fund charitable projects and help those in need with its ample budget.

The last mission objective, cultivation, is at the heart of everything Fo Guang Shan does. Whether they are building new temples in new communities, starting television stations and schools, or giving to needy communities, it is all to cultivate an awareness of the dharma. Each Fo Guang Shan branch offers services, retreats, and programming to help its members and monastics continually cultivate their religious practice. This promotion of self-cultivation is joined with the charitable, cultural, and educational acts in order to purify the world and bring it closer to a pure land.

REVIEW OF LITERATURE

There are several good biographical works on Hsing Yun. Perhaps the most essential is Fu Chi-Ying's biography, *Handing Down the Light: The Biography of Venerable Master Hsing Yun.*[19] Fu's biography is the only English biography published by Fo Guang Shan's own publishing house. It is the basis of many biographical sections featured on the various Fo Guang Shan–affiliated websites. The second chapter of Stuart Chandler's *Establishing a Pure Land on Earth: The Foguang Buddhist Perspective on Modernization and Globalization* is another great source that was based on Chandler's ethnographic work on Fo Guang Shan in the 1990s.[20]

The most recent study of note uses a media studies approach to review popular-media biographical depictions of Hsing Yun. Jack Meng-Tat Chia's article, "Toward a Modern Buddhist Hagiography: Telling the Life of Hsing Yun in Popular Media," analyzes a variety of popular media (comics, songs, documentaries, etc.) produced by Fo Guang Shan.[21] He finds that hagiographies of modern monks, at least in the case of Hsing Yun, are very different than traditional Buddhist hagiographies. Instead of showcasing the uncanny, otherworldly abilities of the holy monk, Hsing Yun's biographical depictions profile him as a worldly, kind, and generous monk. This depiction better suits the humanistic Buddhism that he espouses.

In another recent article, "Christianity as Model and Analogue in the Formation of the 'Humanistic' Buddhism of Tai Xu and Hsing Yun," Yu-Shuang Yao and Richard Gombrich compare Hsing Yun's version of humanistic Buddhism to his teacher, Tai Xu.[22] They demonstrate that humanistic Buddhism shares some strong similarities with both Protestant Christianity and Roman Catholicism. Lastly, Ian Johnson and Adam Wu's interview with Hsing Yun in The *New York Times* demonstrates his attempts to build Fo Guang Shan in China; the corresponding article, "Is a Buddhist Group Changing China? Or Is China Changing It?" delves into the eponymous question in consideration of the relationship between Fo Guang Shan and the Chinese Communist Party.[23]

DIGITAL MATERIALS

FoGuangPedia (https://foguangpedia.org/) is a digital archive for resources associated with Fo Guang Shan. The site grants access to the latest news and publications from Fo Guang Shan. It also hosts a relevant wiki that users can edit, learn, and share. Additionally, the site collects translated excerpts of many of Hsing Yun's works.

FURTHER READING

Chandler, Stuart. *Establishing a Pure Land on Earth: The Foguang Buddhist Perspective on Modernization and Globalization*. Honolulu: University of Hawai'i Press, 2004.

Chia, Jack Meng-Tat. "Toward a Modern Buddhist Hagiography: Telling the Life of Hsing Yun in Popular Media." *Asian Ethnology* 74, no. 1 (2015): 141–165.

Chung, Oscar. "Buddha's Light Shines Brighter." *Taiwan Today*, April 1, 2012. https://taiwantoday.tw/news.php?post=26355&unit=20,29,29,35,45.

Clart, Philip, and Charles B. Jones. *Religion in Modern Taiwan: Tradition and Innovation in a Changing Society*. Honolulu: University of Hawai'i Press, 2003.

Fu Chi-ying. *Handing Down the Light: The Biography of Venerable Master Hsing Yun*. Translated by Amy Lui-Ma. Hacienda Heights, CA: Buddha's Light, 2003.

Hsing Yun. "我是台灣中國人" [I am a Taiwan Chinese person]. *中國時報* [China times], December 12, 2018. https://www.chinatimes.com/opinion/20181211003852-262105?chdtv.

Johnson, Ian. "Is a Buddhist Group Changing China? Or Is China Changing It?" *The New York Times*, June 24, 2017, section A:1.

Johnson, Ian, and Adam Wu. "A Buddhist Leader on China's Spiritual Needs." *The New York Times*, June 24, 2017. https://www.nytimes.com/2017/06/24/world/asia/hsing-yun-buddhism-fo-guang-shan.html.

Jones, Charles B. *Buddhism in Taiwan: Religion and the State, 1660–1990*. Honolulu: University of Hawai'i Press, 1999.

Kuo, Cheng-Tian. *Religion and Democracy in Taiwan*. Albany: State University of New York Press, 2008.

Laliberté, André. *The Politics of Buddhist Organizations in Taiwan: 1989–2003*. New York: Routledge Curzon, 2004.

Madsen, Richard. *Democracy's Dharma: Religious Renaissance and Political Development in Taiwan*. Berkeley: University of California Press, 2007.

Reinke, Jens. "Sacred Secularities: Ritual and Social Engagement in a Global Buddhist China." *Religions* 9, no. 11 (2018): 338.

Yao, Yu-Shuang, and Richard Gombrich. "Christianity as Model and Analogue in the Formation of the 'Humanistic' Buddhism of Tai Xu and Hsing Yun." *Buddhist Studies Review* 34, no. 2 (2017): 205–237.

NOTES

1. Jack Meng-Tat Chia, "Toward a Modern Buddhist Hagiography: Telling the Life of Hsing Yun in Popular Media," *Asian Ethnology* 74, no. 1 (2015): 141–165, 141.
2. André Laliberté, The Politics of Buddhist Organizations in Taiwan: 1989–2003(New York: Routledge Curzon, 2004), 82.
3. Yu-Shuang Yao and Richard Gombrich, "Christianity as Model and Analogue in the Formation of the 'Humanistic' Buddhism of Tai Xu and Hsing Yun," *Buddhist Studies Review* 34, no. 2 (2017): 205–237, 215.
4. Staff Writer, "Hsing Yun Recovering after Stroke," *Taipei Times*, December 28, 2011, 2; and I-Chia Lee, "Buddhist Master Hsing Yun Stable after Acute Stroke," *Taipei Times*, November 3, 2016, 3.
5. Ian Johnson and Adam Wu, "A Buddhist Leader on China's Spiritual Needs," *The New York Times*, June 24, 2017.
6. BLIA.org, 國際佛光會 2018 世界會員代表大會開幕 四海佛光人展現 We are one 精神 [The 2018 BLIA World Conference opening ceremony displays "we are one" spirit].
7. Iok-sin Loa, "Taiwan Buddhist Master: 'No Taiwanese,'" *Taipei Times*, March 31, 2009, 1.
8. Hsing Yun, "我是台灣中國人" [I am a Taiwan Chinese person], *中國時報* [China times], December 12, 2018.
9. Johnson and Wu, "Buddhist Leader."
10. Fu Chi-ying, *Handing Down the Light: The Biography of Venerable Master Hsing Yun*, trans. Amy Lui-Ma (Hacienda Heights, CA: Buddha's Light, 2003), 212.
11. Cheng-Tian Kuo, *Religion and Democracy in Taiwan* (Albany: State University of New York Press, 2008), 24.
12. André Laliberté, "Religious Change and Democratization in Postwar Taiwan: Mainstream Buddhist Organizations and the Kuomingtang, 1947–1996," in *Religion in Modern Taiwan*, ed. Philip Clart and Charles B. Jones (Honolulu: University of Hawai'i Press, 2003), 158–185, 174.
13. Johnson and Wu, "Buddhist Leader."
14. Stuart Chandler, *Establishing a Pure Land on Earth: The Foguang Buddhist Perspective on Modernization and Globalization*, Topics in Contemporary Buddhism (Honolulu: University of Hawai'i Press, 2004), 70–71.

15. Chandler, *Pure Land*, 60.
16. Chandler, *Pure Land*, 44.
17. Laliberté, Buddhist Organizations, 81.
18. Jens Reinke, "Sacred Secularities: Ritual and Social Engagement in a Global Buddhist China," *Religions* 9, no. 11 (2018): 224.
19. Fu, *Handing Down the Light.*
20. Chandler, *Pure Land.*
21. Chia, "Toward a Modern."
22. Yao and Gombrich, "Christianity as Model."
23. Ian Johnson, "Is a Buddhist Group Changing China? Or Is China Changing It?," *The New York Times*, June 24, 2017, A:1.

Kendall Marchman

HUINENG

THE RECEIVED HAGIOGRAPHY

The hagiography of Huineng (in earliest texts 惠能, later 慧能) known to most East Asians has been that of the imperially sanctioned *Jingde chuandeng lu* (景德傳燈録 Records of the Lamplight Transmission of the Jingde Reign) of 1004 and the "Liuzu Dashi fabao tanjing luexu" (六祖大師法寶壇經略序 Brief Preface to the Dharma-Jewel Platform Sutra of the Sixth Patriarch) attributed to Fahai 法海, who was supposedly a pupil of Huineng.[1] This was first published in the Deyi version of the *Liuzu tanjing* (六祖壇經 Platform Sutra of the 6th Patriarch) of 1290 and the Zongbao edition of 1291. The preface was influenced by the *Jingde chuandeng lu* and other earlier hagiographies. The following is a composite from these accounts, primarily the *Jingde chuandeng lu*, with interpolated comments in parentheses showing what an educated Chinese reader would understand.

Huineng's father, Lu Xingtao 盧行瑫, a native of Fanyang (the surname and toponym combined indicates he was a member of the superelite Lu clan from the metropolitan area), was demoted in the Wude era (618–626) to remote Xinzhou (southwest of modern Guangzhou) as a petty official. There he married a woman of the Li clan (other sources state she was a Gelao 獦獠 or Klao, non-Chinese who lived by hunting and slash-and-burn agriculture). Huineng was born in 638 to the accompaniment of various signs and predictions of his future sainthood (only in the "Preface"). His father died when he was three (another text, the *Caoqi Dashi zhuan* 曹溪大師傳 says he lost both parents). Impoverished, mother and son made a living as woodcutters and sellers in Nanhai (Guangzhou).

When he was twenty-four ("Preface"), Huineng heard a man reading the *Jin'gang jing* (*Vajracchedikā-prajñāpāramitā-sūtra*, Diamond Sutra). Shocked, Huineng asked about it, and the man told Huineng the name of the sutra and that he had obtained it from Grand Master Hongren 弘忍 of Huangmei (district just to the north of the Yangtze River in eastern Hubei Province, on the bank opposite from modern Jiujiang City). Huineng told his mother he was going to meet Hongren and headed for Shaozhou (modern Shaoguan, northern Guangdong Province) on a then rarely used route north. In Shaozhou, he encountered the nun Wujinzang

無盡藏, who constantly read the *Niepan jing* (*Mahāparinirvāṇa-sūtra*, Nirvana Sutra), which teaches "seeing the Buddha-nature." Huineng then explained to her what he had heard and the nun asked him about some of the Chinese characters. Admitting that he was illiterate, he declared he could still interpret the meaning because "the marvelous principle of the buddhas is unrelated to letters." This led the nun and the villagers to revere Huineng. They had him reside in the repaired Baolin Monastery 寶林寺.

Soon, Huineng realized he needed to further his practice and departed to see Hongren in 670 (contradicting the "Preface," which says he left Hongren in 661). As soon as Hongren saw Huineng, he recognized Huineng's potential. (The *Jingde chuandeng lu*, following a Chinese historiographical convention, has the account of their interaction in the hagiography of the master, Hongren.) Hongren asked Huineng where he had come from. On hearing that he had come from Lingnan (Guangdong and Guangxi provinces) and that he wanted to be a buddha (作佛 *zuofo*), Hongren said that people from Lingnan (this is polite, other accounts say Gelao) have no buddha-nature and therefore cannot become a buddha. Huineng retorted that there is no north or south (*nan*, as in Lingnan) for the buddha-nature. Knowing Huineng was extraordinary, he sent him to hull rice with a pestle behind the monastery, where Huineng worked for eight months.

Hongren (601–674), aging, felt it was time to select an heir to transmit the dharma. He set his students the task of writing a *gāthā* (Buddhist verse) as a test of their ability. The senior-most monk in the assembly, Shenxiu 神秀 (606–706), erudite but unsure of himself, wrote the following verse in secret on a wall:

The body is the bodhi tree (under which the Buddha was enlightened),
The mind is like a bright mirror.
Always try to polish it,
So that no dust remains.

Hongren, seeing it, knew it was written by Shenxiu, praised it as a basis for practice and had the monks chant it, but realized it was an inadequate understanding. Hearing it, Huineng also knew it was an incomplete understanding and had a novice write Huineng's counter verse on the wall:

Bodhi is basically not a tree,
The mind also is not a mirror.
Originally there is not a single thing,
So what need is there to wipe away dust?

On seeing this verse, Hongren ordered Huineng to come to see him that night in secret. Hongren told Huineng that he possessed the appreciative eye of the Correct Dharma as transmitted from the buddha via Mahākāśyapa down to Bodhidharma, who brought it to China, and that now Huineng was the heir to this lineage. Hongren gave Huineng the robe of Bodhidharma as proof of this, but told Huineng that he should not transmit the robe and that he should go far away and teach. That night, unbeknown to the assembly, Huineng departed. Hongren only informed the assembly of this three days later, and some monks, including Huiming, chased after Huineng. Hongren died four years later.

(The account in the *Jingde chuandeng lu* hagiography of Huineng entry resumes here, as does the "Preface" hagiography, which skipped all the events until the conferral of the robe, probably because these events are mentioned in the body of the *Platform Sutra*.) In 676, Huineng arrived at Faxing Monastery 法性寺 in Nanhai (Guangzhou), where he met Dharma Master Yinzong 印宗 (627–713). Because Huineng stated that it is the mind that is moving when one sees a banner flapping in the wind, not the wind or the banner, Yinzong knew Huineng was extraordinary (not in "Preface," as the *Platform Sutra* has a long entry on this). Yinzong became Huineng's disciple and announced to the assembly that Huineng was a "living bodhisattva." Then Yinzong and other monks officiated at Huineng's ordination as a monk on a platform.

The next year, Huineng departed for Baolin Monastery in Shaozhou. At the invitation of the prefect, he preached a sermon at Dafan Monastery 大梵寺, the sermon compiled and named the *Platform Sutra*.[2] The "Preface" records miraculous events surrounding Baolin Monastery, then lists the epitaphs for Huineng written by laymen, including Liu Zongyuan 柳宗元 in 816 (which means this part of the "Preface" cannot have been written by Fahai, Huineng's disciple), but not the final deeds of Huineng, as they are found in the sutra.

The *Jingde chuandeng lu* states that in 705 Emperor Zhongzong invited Huineng to court at the instigation of Shenxiu and Huian 慧安, but Huineng declined. It records long dialogues with the imperial envoy, Xie Jian 薛簡, on doctrine and practice. After Xie Jian reported to the emperor, in 707 Zhongzong ordered Baolin Monastery redecorated and named Faquan Monastery 法泉寺. A sermon to the assembly follows.

In 712, Huineng informed the assembly that the robe of transmission would not be handed on because people now had faith, and he allowed the assembly to disband. Then he ordered his close disciples to build a (burial) stupa for him in his birthplace, Xinzhou. In 713 he left Shaozhou, predicting that someone would try to steal his head from his corpse. He passed away in Xinzhou on August 28 accompanied by miraculous signs. His corpse was taken to Caoqi 曹溪 (near Shaozhou), where it was lacquered and placed together with the robe of faith in a stupa there. The predicted robbery of his head, which failed, happened in 722, instigated by a Silla Korean monk. There follows a list of imperial requests and honors and of events at the monastery. The *Jingde chuandeng lu* then lists his disciples, including Xingsi 行思 and Huairang 懷讓.

THE FABRICATION OF THE HAGIOGRAPHY

This romance, in which a poor youth of the backwoods makes a perilous journey to find the truth, engages in a crucial struggle with a rival and returns triumphant after being pursued, was undoubtedly appealing, but it is fiction. Not only are these hagiographies late and contain unrealistic elements despite some attempts at verisimilitude, such as exact dates and places, they have also been questioned due to discoveries from 1926 of manuscripts in a cache at the Dunhuang Caves, which show that Shenhui 神會 (684–758) created the basic hagiography of Huineng. These texts have to be read critically, with an eye to their provenance, purpose, and sociopolitical context.

The earliest evidence for the existence of Huineng is found in the *Lengqie shizi ji* (楞伽師資記 Record of the Masters and Disciples of the Laṅka [School]) of ca. 713–716, written by the elite monk Jingjue 淨覺 (683–ca. 750), the brother of an empress. Jingjue simply lists

Huineng among Hongren's ten pupils, writing that "Huineng of Shaozhou and the Korean monk Chidŏk of Yangzhou were capable of being teachers of humans, but were individuals of merely one region."[3] This was the view from the metropolis, Luoyang, but it demonstrates that Huineng was accepted as being a pupil of Hongren (601–674) and that he taught in the remote southern district of Shaozhou.

Attempts have been made to identify a contemporary eyewitness account of Huineng in a poem by Song Zhiwen 宋之問 (650–730) and a poem on donating incense after Huineng's death by Zhang Yue 張說 (667–730). However, both poems are only mentioned in the 980s (Song's first in the *Wenyuan yinghua* 文苑英華 of 986, and both in the *Song gaoseng zhuan* 宋高僧傳 of 988), not by earlier champions of Huineng such as Shenhui. Because of problems of provenance, the poems of some authors attributed to other authors, questions about itineraries and dates, and questions about the title of Song's poem, "Going from Hengyang to Shaozhou, I Visited Chan Master Neng," 自衡陽至韶州謁能禪師 when the name of the master in the poem is not given, this evidence is dubious.[4] Even though Song was exiled twice to Lingnan, it is unlikely he ever went to Shaozhou, where all sources state Huineng was resident.[5] Zhang's poem also says Huineng's remains were in Nanhai (Guangzhou), not Shaozhou. It also seems to have been a late invention.

THE ROLE OF SHENHUI

In 1983, a buried tomb inscription for Shenhui (684–758) by his pupil Huikong 慧空 was discovered at Longmen near Luoyang. Dated December 31, 765, it claimed Shenhui was an heir to Huineng in a lineage from Bodhidharma.

The Dunhuang manuscripts on Shenhui's activities do not indicate dates of initial composition and their authors are mostly otherwise unknown, and the sequence of the texts is uncertain.[6] The *Nanyang Heshang dunjiao jietuo chanmen zhiliaoxing tanyu* (南陽和上頓教解脱禅門直了性壇語 Platform Discourse on Sudden Enlightenment, Release, and the Chan Gate Direct Realization of the Nature by the Reverend of Nanyang), which from the toponym Nanyang makes some think it dates 720–745, merely says about the buddha's imprimatur given to those who are qualified that "the six generations of patriarchal masters [in China] transmitted [enlightenment] from mind to mind," which implies the transmission from Bodhidharma to Huineng.[7]

What is probably the next text, the *Putidamo Nanzong ding shifei lun* (On Determining the Rights and Wrongs of the Southern Lineage of Bodhidharma), recorded by Dugu Pei 獨孤沛, states that on February 15, 732, on the date of the Lantern Festival in Buddhist monasteries, Shenhui invited people to participate in an unrestricted mass assembly (無遮大會 *wuzhe dahui*) at Dayun Monastery in Huatai (Hua County, Henan, on bank of the Yellow River).[8] This is dubious because up to around this date the unrestricted mass assemblies were always instituted by monarchs (in 519, 527, 532, 546, 558, 582, 601, 606, 618, and 710). The only exception was in 738, when Xuanyan 玄儼 (675–742), held unrestricted mass assemblies for ordination ceremonies in northern Zhejiang with lavish support from local governors.[9] As Emperor Xuanzong (r. 712–756) was intent on restricting Buddhism, he did not sponsor these assemblies.[10] No sponsor is named for this assembly at which "Shenhui rose to the lion throne and preached for the students of Buddhism of the empire."[11] Nor is Shenhui's protagonist,

Chongyuan 崇遠 of Shandong, despite it being claimed he was even known abroad, known elsewhere in the literature.[12] There probably was an assembly (but not a mass assembly), because Zongmi 宗密 (780–841), writing between 823 and 841, cryptically noted that the magistrates of Baima and Weinan counties in Huazhou, where Huatai is located, took civil action (文事 *wenshi*) against Shenhui and he "nearly died three times." Shenhui fled, disguised as a merchant.[13] This description of the ignominious defeat of Shenhui contrasts vividly with the depiction of the assembly as being extensively decorated and Shenhui's hubristic claim to be a 10th-stage bodhisattva, virtually a buddha incarnate, and of overcoming his interlocutors.[14]

In his polemic, Shenhui claimed that Huineng of Shaozhou was the heir to the robe of Bodhidharma, which he had received from Hongren, but it was not to be transmitted to anyone else.[15] Shenhui had to say this, for claiming to be Huineng's successor, the obvious question would have been why Shenhui could not show people the robe.

Shenhui states that Huineng and Shenxiu had studied together under Hongren, something modern scholars doubt.[16] Shenhui said that Shenxiu told Empress Wu that she should consult Huineng and that an associate of Puji 普寂 (651–739), a chief disciple of Shenxiu, went in December 709 to Shaozhou to steal the robe, but failed.[17] Shenhui further made the outrageous claim that Huineng's corpse was attacked three times by Zhang Xingchang 張行昌, an associate of Puji, with a sword to decapitate it, and that Wu Pingyi 武平一, the scholar who compiled Song Zhiwen's no-longer-extant collected works, erased a stele for Huineng in order to make Shenxiu the 6th patriarch.[18]

Dugu Pei writes that after the 733 account of the assembly was compiled, another text, the *Shizi xiemo zhuan* (師資血脈傳 Account of the Bloodlines of the Masters and Disciples) was written. It possibly dates to ca. 752 when inscriptions were erected for a portrait hall of the patriarchs in Luoyang, and it may be the appendix to the *Nanyang Heshang wenda zazhengyi* (南陽和尚問答雜徵義 The Dialogues of the Reverend of Nanyang Soliciting the Meaning) that was collated in Beiting, to the northwest of Dunhuang in 791, just before this outpost was lost to a Tibetan invasion.[19] Part of the text used in the collation was by Liu Cheng 劉澄, registrar of Tangshan Prefecture in Hangzhou, possibly the father of a woman who died in 789.[20] Although this *Shizi xiemo zhuan* was said in one version to have been in answer to a question by Chongyuan about the six patriarchs, possibly at the 732 assembly, there is doubt about this because Shenhui commissioned the famed poet-painter Wang Wei 王維 (701–759/761) to write a funerary inscription, the "Neng Chanshi bei" 能禅師碑 (Stele for Chan Master Neng), which contains none of the details found in the *Shizi xiemo zhuan*.[21] The inscription, possibly written around 752, is undated, vague, gives no dates for Huineng's birth or death, and contains material not used by Shenhui and his followers.[22] Although Wang Wei was probably writing under constraints, such as his and his mother's connections with Shenhui's rivals and the genre, the paucity of concrete information and plenitude of literary tropes about the south suggest that Shenhui's hagiography of Huineng was yet to be fleshed out or that Wang was skeptical of some of the claims.[23]

Wang Wei states, probably for the first time, that Huineng's surname was Lu, but he gives no toponym and says he was not born into a distinguished family and lived among the southern barbarians. Wang mentions Huineng served under Hongren and worked in the kitchen, becoming enlightened there. Hongren recognized that Huineng was enlightened, but did not announce this to the assembly, only giving Huineng the robe when Hongren was near death. Huineng returned south where he lived among the common people for sixteen years. After this, he met Yinzong, who asked Huineng about the meaning of the *Nirvana Sutra,* making Yinzong realize Huineng was a buddha incarnate (*nirmāṇakāya*) and had him ordained. Huineng's teachings became popular, and rulers, Empress Wu and Emperor Zhongzong, wanted to invite him to court. Huineng did not go to court, but he was given imperial gifts. He died to the accompaniment of miracles and his corpse was shifted to Caoqi and enshrined there.

Wang says Shenhui arrived at Shaozhou when Huineng was old and Shenhui middle-aged. Wang says Shenhui made the last offering to Huineng, just as Shenhui claimed in Dugu Pei's account. Apparently, many people did not accept Huineng's sainthood.[24]

In what is assumed to be the *Shizi xiemo zhuan* account of Huineng, Shenhui fills in more details and has a prediction made by Huineng that a person will establish the lineage (宗 *zong*) forty years after Huineng's death.[25] This likely indicates the construction of the hall of the patriarchs in 752 and that the *Shizi xiemo zhuan* was written after this date.[26] This hagiography is almost the same as the received hagiography. It includes information on his clan toponym, his father, and so on. It does not include the famous verse contest between Shenxiu and Huineng, the ordination by Yinzong, the invitations to court, or the attempted theft of the head of his "mummy."

Thus, Shenhui was the prime fabricator of the legend of Huineng, with Wang Wei possibly responsible for the reference to Yinzong. Shenhui had constructed a hagiography of Huineng to aggrandize himself, making Shenhui the true successor to a lineage of one heir per generation to the truth of Buddhism that stretched unbroken back to the buddha in a form of "Chan" exceptionalism. Yet, despite Shenhui's claims and Wang's claims that Shenhui, when middle-aged (the term Wang used, 中年 *zhongnian,* indicates forties or fifties, which for Shenhui would have been at least a decade after Huineng's death), met the elderly Huineng in Caoqi, there is evidence that he may never have done so.[27] This suggests that the hagiography is entirely a fabrication built up over several decades by Shenhui.

COMPETING CLAIMS

Shenhui's propaganda was effective because rival versions of the hagiography, with different emphases, began appearing from around the 780s. The first to appear was in the *Lidai fabao ji* (歷代法寶記 Record of the Dharma-Jewel through the Ages) of 774 or later. Its chief concern was to assert that the robe of transmission was taken from Huineng, with his assent, by Empress Wu in 696, who then gave the robe to Zhishen 智詵 (609–702), another disciple of Hongren. This built on Wang Wei's account and the *Shizi xiemo zhuan.*[28] The most important contribution it made to the received tradition was the dialogue about what moves, the banner, wind, or mind, and the ordination of Huineng by Yinzong.[29] However, the list of Hongren's disciples comes from the *Lengqie shizi ji,* but the focus here was on the transmission of the robe.

The *Lidai fabao ji* account invited various responses: that of the *Caoqi Dashi zhuan* (Biography of the Great Master of Cao Creek) of 781 and the early *Platform Sutra* estimated to have been written in the 780s. The former emphasized that the robe was kept in Baolin Monastery in Caoqi, that there was a relationship of Huineng and the monastery with the imperial court, and the importance of the relics of Huineng. It states Huineng lost both parents when he was three, heard the nun read the *Nirvana Sutra,* stayed in Baolin Monastery for three years and then went to meet Hongren. It does not mention Shenxiu or the verse contest. It elaborates on the moving banner debate and the ordination of Huineng in Guangzhou and compliance with state procedures.

On the other hand, the Dunhuang *Platform Sutra* uses Huineng's "autobiography" to frame and introduce his sermons. It ignores Huineng's relics and substitutes itself for the robe. It also introduces the verse contest between Shenxiu and Huineng. Otherwise, it largely follows the *Shizi xiemo zhuan,* but does not mention the banner debate or Yinzong. The *Platform Sutra* maintains that Huineng was illiterate to the end of his life and that it is practice that differentiates people, not whether or not they are ordained. It is unconcerned with state sanction.

Elements from these competing claims then appear in the partly extant *Baolin zhuan* (寶林傳 Accounts of Baolin Monastery) of ca. 801, which was probably influenced by the *Caoqi Dashi zhuan,* but the *Baolin zhuan* Huineng hagiography is only known from a few short quotes.

ACCEPTANCE AND RECOGNITION OF HUINENG

The hagiography of Huineng seems to have largely been consolidated and accepted by the state by the early 9th century. Li Zhou 李舟 (ca. 739–ca. 787), a member of the bureaucratic elite, late in life wrote a biography of Huineng, probably following the *Caoqi Dashi zhuan.*[30] According to Zongmi, in 770, Shenhui's tomb was granted an imperial plaque describing the true lineage (as going via Huineng), and in 796 Emperor Dezong made Shenhui the 7th patriarch, implying that Huineng was the 6th patriarch.[31] In 806, in a stele for Huijian 慧堅 (719–792), a pupil of Shenhui, Xu Dai 徐岱, wrote something that seems to confirm this.[32] Explicit state recognition of Huineng as the 6th patriarch was given when Huineng was imperially granted the posthumous name Dajian in 815. Subsequently, the eminent literati Liu Zongyuan (773–819) in 816 and Liu Yuxi 劉禹錫 (772–784) in 818/819 wrote stele inscriptions for Huineng.[33] Liu Zongyuan alluded to Huineng's time with Hongren, the verse contest, his period of hiding, residence at Caoqi, and Emperor Zhongzong's invitation. Liu Yuxi also referred to the robe of transmission, Huineng's birth in Xinzhou, his interment in a stupa, the attempted theft of Huineng's head by Zhang Jingman 張淨滿, and a request in 760 by Emperor Suzong for the robe and bowl, and then the return of these items to Caoqi in 765.[34]

By the time Zanning 贊寧 wrote the hagiography of Huineng in his *Song gaoseng zhuan* (Biographies of Eminent Monks Written in the Song) of 988, virtually all of the elements of the received tradition had been legitimized as Zanning's collection of hagiographies had the sanction of the Song dynasty court.[35] Zanning's hagiography was to remain the accepted version of Huineng's life almost until the discovery of the Dunhuang manuscripts challenged it.

MODERN POPULAR MANIFESTATIONS OF HUINENG'S HAGIOGRAPHY

Numerous modern studies and pious articles have appeared on Huineng. The hagiography has even been put to nationalist uses. Building on the tale of the theft of Huineng's skull and a reference by Ch'oe Ch'iwŏn 崔致遠 (857–?) to a portrait hall of the Six(th) Patriarch(s) at

Ssanggye Monastery 雙溪寺, and then to a plaque allegedly penned by Kim Chŏnghŭi 金正喜 (1786–1856) titled "Stupa of the 6th Patriarch's Uṣṇīṣa (Cranium Crown)" 六祖頂相塔, the monks of Ssanggye Monastery in southern Korea sometime after 1854 claimed to possess a relic of Huineng. The campaign was revived around 1913 as part of a "relics campaign" that was used to assert the independence of the monastery and the superiority of Korean Buddhism over that of the colonizing Japanese.[36] More than 1,000 people attend the memorial days at the monastery each year.[37]

Pilgrims also go to worship Huineng and his relics at Nanhua Monastery 南華寺 (Baolin Monastery?) outside of Shaoguan. The monastery sells memorial cards with pictures of "the true body of the Sixth Patriarch" and Huineng's verses on them. In 1980, Xi Zhongxun 習仲勳 (1913–2009), an elder of the Communist Party and father of Chairman Xi Jinping, helped the abbot Foyuan 佛淵 (1923–2009) repair the monastery and the "mummy" (actually a hollow lacquer cast over a skeleton) that had been broken by the Red Guards during the Cultural Revolution. Foyuan had secreted the remains of the relic, then told the Buddhist authorities in Beijing, who wrote to Xi Zhongxun, who then ordered the repairs.[38]

Again, rumor has it that Mao Zedong had the *Platform Sutra* as bedside reading just before he died because it was a Buddhist sutra of the workers, even though it preached idealism.[39] Mao called Huineng a member of the common people (老百姓 *laobaixing*).[40] The image of Huineng as an illiterate, iconoclastic woodcutter had considerable appeal. In 2000, the winner of the Nobel Prize for Literature, Gao Xingjian 高行健, published a drama based on the life of Huineng. Called *Bayue xue* 八月雪 (Snow in August), and published in Taiwan in 2000 and in Hong Kong in 2001, it portrays Huineng as a mystic who defied the political establishment.[41]

In addition, a novelistic biography was written by Lu Jinchuan 陸錦川, a Daoist *qigong* expert. This was the two-volume *Huineng Dashi zhuan*, based on all the main primary sources.[42] Another biography was published in the series Du Fo jishi bai Fo (Reading the Buddha is Worshipping the Buddha), titled *Liuzu Huineng zhuan*. It was written by Layman Mingyi 明一居士 and published in Shanghai in 2011.[43]

Huineng has been a subject in popular culture, with a film, *Liuzu Huineng zhuan* (Master Hui Neng: Sixth Patriarch of Zen Buddhism) made under the directorship of Tso Nam Lee 李作楠 in Taiwan in 1987, which even has Huineng reject the advances of a beautiful temptress.[44] A martial arts film, *Mumian jiasha* 木棉袈裟 (Silk-Cotton Robe) was made in Hong Kong in 1984 under the directorship of Xu Xiaoming 徐小明 (Tsui Siu-Ming), in which Huineng is at Shaolin Monastery, and Empress Wu and Reverend Jin (a Korean monk) appear. The fight over the robe of transmission is set in the Ming dynasty.[45] There have also been TV shows, including one of sixteen episodes with the title *Liuzu Huineng zhuan* in 2018.[46]

PROBLEMS OF THE HAGIOGRAPHY

Understanding or appreciation of the Huineng hagiography depends on the attitude to religion, history, and literature adopted. Believers suspend disbelief and ignore doubts. The appreciation of the hagiography as literature, as a creative work of fiction, may accept the justification of it as a means to an end, in Buddhist terms, a skillful means. This would have it that as "it was enthusiastically adopted by centuries of Chinese Buddhists—implies that it was more representative of the deepest religious sensibilities of the Chinese people than a journalistically accurate account could have ever been."[47] However, historians, like detectives, tend to focus forensically on timelines, agents, text criticism, power, and legitimacy to reveal events and expose disinformation, not accepting that the ends justify the means. Thus, historians focus on the fabrication of the hagiography and who profited thereby. While all approaches have their own value, the focus here is historical.

As noted previously, Shenhui created a hagiography of Huineng out of a dearth of information, expanding it over time during the course of his campaign of disinformation and propaganda. Others added to it, often from different perspectives, to form the received tradition. That alone is reason for suspicion, but there are other reasons to doubt its veracity.

First is Shenhui's claim that Huineng and Shenhui himself were members of an exclusive lineage from the buddha of one patriarch per generation. Shenhui listed an unbelievably short lineage of thirteen patriarchs, with some errors.[48] This number was expanded to twenty-eight soon after Shenhui's death. There were earlier lineages of teachers, but these apparently did not claim only one teacher per generation or to be exclusive. Shenhui was attempting to forge a Chinese "imperial lineage" of seven generations, with himself its end. The *Platform Sutra*, however, states that Huineng had ten equally qualified successors, and by the 10th century the "orthodox" lineages began from two heirs, Nanyue Huairang 南嶽懷讓 (677–744) and Qingyuan Xingsi 青原行思 (d. 740). This lineage more closely resembles the secular genealogies of the elite, with a single line of forbears from antiquity to the founding ancestor of the clan (here Southern Chan), and then the descendants and branches from that founder (Huineng).[49] Shenhui's lineage, and the Northern and Niutou 牛頭 lineages, disappeared by the 9th or 10th centuries.

Second, the claim that Bodhidharma's robe was the symbol of the patriarchal lineage was unacceptable, and the excuse had to be made that Huineng halted its transmission. No reference to it exists before Shenhui, and in 818/819 Liu Yuxi explained why the robe was no longer transmitted. It was merely a skillful means, and as a thing, it had to return to nothingness or decay.[50] The robe was obsolete once the transmission went to multiple recipients and transmission was symbolized by verses and the *Platform Sutra*.[51]

Third, based on the dating of events in the claimed lives of Huineng and Shenxiu, it is clear that they never met.[52] Shenhui and Zongmi say Huineng visited Hongren in 659, and according to Zhang Yue's epitaph for Shenxiu and the *Chuanfabao ji* 傳法寶紀 (Annals of the Transmission of the Jewel of the Dharma) of ca. 713, Shenxiu left Hongren in 657. Thus, no verse contest took place except in the imagination of the *Platform Sutra* author(s).

Fourth, the tales of attempts to erase Huineng's stele and take the head from his "mummy" (*roushen* 肉身) are examples of fake news meant to discredit rivals and elevate Huineng to be a popular saint. There is no credible, independent evidence to support such claims.

Fifth, there is no secular evidence from the 8th century that Empress Wu or Emperor Zhongzong ever invited Huineng to court, and as the author of the *Lengqie shizi ji*, Jingjue, was the brother-in-law of Zhongzong, he probably would have known of this if it was fact.

Sixth, the alleged illiteracy of Huineng does not accord with the claim that he understood the doctrines of the complex *Nirvana Sutra* that was written in a literary language when he heard it for the first time. It was not written in colloquial Chinese. Moreover, to be legally ordained as a monk, from 648 a candidate had to undertake a long period of study, and from 706 candidates had to memorize a sutra.[53] Moreover, the son of the Fanyang Lu clan of aristocrats that depended for its prestige on pedigree and office-holding, even if orphaned young, would have been expected to be literate.[54] Illiteracy was demanded by doctrinal claims that Huineng made no efforts to be enlightened, and was inherently a buddha.[55] This is an aristocracy of sainthood that simultaneously acknowledges that potentially, even a nonmonk semibarbarian like Huineng could be buddha. This claim is akin to the pre-Qin Confucian notion that all people can be sages, not by learning, but by birth. Sagehood is innate, something that Xie Lingyun 謝靈雲 (385–433) interpreted as meaning buddhahood can be attained but not learned.[56] This also meant that only a patriarch can recognize another patriarch, as Hongren did with Huineng, just as "only a buddha can know a buddha."[57]

Finally, the hagiography reflects a fantasy of the transcendence of mundane reality. For example, Huineng left Hongren suddenly at night and traveled across the Jiujiang stage 九江驛 (see *Shizi xiemo zhuan*), a major crossing over the Yangtze River. He had allegedly traveled as a young man from Xinzhou to Huangmei, a journey of about three months. Travelers in Tang China, especially when the dynasty was at the height of its power, required identity papers (公驗 *gongjian*) and a passport (過所 *guosuo*) that recorded name, age, gender, place of registration, tax status, destination, reason for travel, date of departure, route, and estimated date of arrival. The passport had to be stamped or signed at each stage or pass control (関 *guan*). It had to be requested from the village head and approved by the county authorities. Attempts to bypass the checkpoint (私度関 *shiduguan*) incurred a year's penal servitude.[58] In some cases, people disguised themselves as monks (see the case of the infamous Wei Yuansong 衛元嵩, fl. 560s–570s, whose disguise failed), and monks, like Shenhui, wore lay dress to escape capture.[59] Huineng would not have been able to travel at a moment's notice, except illegally. This makes the story of the pursuit of Huineng after he left Hongren rather implausible.

APPEAL OF HUINENG

This portrayal of a déclassé child of an aristocratic clan member rising from the position of an illiterate woodcutter to the founder of a Buddhist "school," a buddha incarnate, probably appealed to many people in Tang China who felt excluded from power by the aristocratic system and resented the establishment, although Shenhui himself was an adept social climber and came from an elite background. Even the *Platform Sutra*, with its depiction of the illiterate Huineng conferring the formless precepts, as contrasted to the formal precepts of the clergy, on a mass congregation collapsed the distinction between lay and cleric, was "directed at laypeople" because everybody had the innate potential to be a buddha.[60]

In the Tang, the *Platform Sutra* seems to have been a transmission text and a ritual text, but by the Song, the image of Huineng symbolized the ability of an illiterate creole to rise to the peak of sainthood, downplaying inheritance and lineage.[61] This accorded with the Song dynasty notion that ability could be present irrespective of birth and in which the rise from poverty was valued.[62] Such ideas began to appear in the ninth century, just as Huineng's hagiography began to gain acceptance in Chan circles.[63]

However, there is doubt as to whether the *Platform Sutra* was widely circulated in the 9th and 10th centuries. It is not quoted during the Tang (at least under the name *Tanjing*), even by masters who claimed to be heirs of Huineng, although sometime between 818 and 828, Wei Chuhou 韋處厚 (773–828) wrote in a stele for Dayi 大義 (746–818) that "[Shenhui's] followers were deluded about the truth . . . eventually formed the *Platform Sutra* to transmit the lineage," and Nanyang Huizhong (d. 774), as quoted in the *Jingde chuandeng lu,* said, "The tenets of the lineage of the south takes that *Platform Sutra* and made changes and substitutions, adding and mixing in vulgar talk/exaggerations, removing the saintly intent, confusing later followers."[64] In 967, Huixin noted that students despised the text because of its obscurity. Much of this displays a negative attitude toward the text and does not mention the "autobiographical" frame. Yet, it was taken to Japan by Ennin 圓仁 in 847 and Enchin 圓珍 in the 850s, and copies were made in Dunhuang from about the same time at the earliest. Thus, the *Platform Sutra* image of Huineng was probably available across China from the 850s but had yet to become authoritative. However, the advent of printing in the Song led to its popularity (printed 1153, 1116), and the cheaper prices of prints in the Yuan (1290, 1291) made it more accessible.

DID HUINENG WRITE A COMMENTARY ON THE *DIAMOND SUTRA*?

Given that Shenhui and the *Platform Sutra* associated Huineng closely with the *Diamond Sutra,* it was natural that commentaries on the *Diamond Sutra* were attributed to Huineng. Two of these can be found in the *Xuzangjing* (Continued Buddhist Canon, compiled in Japan between 1905 and 1912) under the heading of *Jin'gang jing jieyi* 金剛經解義 (Explanations of the Meaning of the Diamond Sutra). According to Ibuki Atsushi, these are the *Jin'gang jing zhengjie* 金剛經正解 (Correct Explanations of the Diamond Sutra) and the *Jin'gang jing koujue* 金剛經口訣 (Oral Instructions on the Diamond Sutra).[65] The *Xuzangjing* text has a preface attributed to Huineng, a *Jieyi* commentary in two fascicles by Huineng, and a "Liuzu koujue houxu" 六祖口訣後序 (Later Preface to the Oral Instructions of the Sixth Patriarch) attributed to Luo Shi 羅適 and dated 1084, plus several postfaces dated 1653 and 1667.[66]

In 854, Enchin brought a *Neng Dashi Jin'gang bore jing jue* 能大師金剛般若經訣 (Instructions on the Diamond Sutra by Great Master Neng) to Japan from southeast China, and the Tang imperial library as cataloged in the *Xin Tang shu* (New History of the Tang) of 1060 listed a *Huineng Jin'gang bore jing koujue zhengyi* 慧能金剛般若經口訣正義 (Correct Meanings of the Oral Instructions of Huineng on the Diamond Sutra) in one fascicle.[67] Moreover, Wansong Xingxiu 萬松行秀 (1166–1246) quoted a *Liuzu koujue* that corresponds to the *Jin'gang jing jieyi.*[68] However, Konggu Jinglong 空谷景隆 (1392–1443) said that the *Liuzu Dashi jieyi koujue* was a commentary by Luo Shi that borrowed Huineng's name and was doctrinally shallow, the latter a reasonable assessment.[69]

Thus, a commentary attributed to Huineng existed by 854, but whether it corresponded to the text quoted by Xingxiu ca. 1223 is open to doubt. First, although the extant *Jin'gang jing jieyi* contains ideas that are shared with the Dunhuang *Platform Sutra* and Shenhui, other ideas in it are antithetical to those of the *Platform Sutra* and Shenhui. In particular, the *Jin'gang jing jieyi* allows that even the insentient has the buddha-nature, a thesis that Shenhui was diametrically opposed to and that the *Platform Sutra* arguably rejects.[70]

Second, the extant *Jin'gang jing jieyi* has either partly copied its commentary from that of Li Wenhui 李文會 (1097–1158), the *Jin'gang jing zhu* 金剛經注 as found in the *Jin'gang jing jizhu* 金剛經集註, or Li Wenhui copied from the *Jin'gang jing jieyi.*[71] Moreover, as evidence from quotes of "Liuzu says" 六祖曰 in the *Jin'gang jing jijie* of 1232 shows, there were different texts called *Jin'gang jing jieyi* in circulation by 1232.[72] Also, Luo Shi's 1084 "preface" states that he had obtained eight copies of the *Liuzu Jin'gang jing koujue* 六祖金剛經口訣, and a (reconstructed) catalog of 1034 lists two texts, the *Jin'gang jing koujue yi* 金剛經口訣義 by Huineng and the *Liuzu Dashi Jin'gang jing dayi jue* 六祖大師金剛經大義訣 in two fascicles.[73] All of this evidence suggests that a commentary attributed to Huineng existed by the early 9th century and that the *Jin'gang jing jieyi* is the oldest of the commentaries attributed to Huineng extant.[74] However, Huineng was not the author, and as the extant *Jin'gang jing jieyi* refers to Dharma Master Lingyou 靈幽 writing out an extra sixty-two characters in his 822 copy of the *Diamond Sutra*, and that "the sixth patriarch's explanation 解 was written before this," the commentary, to the contrary, dates after 822 and probably before 854.[75]

WAS THE POPULARITY OF HUINENG DUE TO THE HAGIOGRAPHICAL IMAGE OR TO HIS THOUGHT IN THE *PLATFORM SUTRA*?

Huineng's thought was not described in pre–*Platform Sutra* texts. The earliest text unconnected to Shenhui that records Huineng's purported words is the *Xiande ji yu Shuangfeng shan ta ge tanxuanli* 先德集於雙峯山塔各談玄理 (Former Virtuosos Gathered at the Stupa on Mount Shuangfeng Each Spoke of the Profound Principle), a brief text on the back of a household registration document dated 750 (Pelliot Chinese 3559), which may have been written as late as 780 or even 800. It says, "Chan Master Neng said, 'Mental operations are equal, purely one and unmixed,'" or "Mind and actions are equal."[76]

For all Shenhui's emphasis on Huineng as his key ancestor, he barely mentioned Huineng's thought, possibly because the same "mind" is transmitted across the generations. All the patriarchs taught a direct access, an immediate seeing of the buddha-nature, which must be sudden and all at once, to be followed by gradual cultivation. It is seeing the nature that is Chan, which is not quietening or controlling the mind.[77] This buddha-nature is in all sentient beings and is undifferentiated.[78] This idea was evidently derived from the *Nirvana Sutra*, but Huineng is said to have based himself of the *Diamond Sutra*, which explains Huineng's supposed focus on *prajñāpāramitā* and nonduality as found in the *Platform Sutra*.[79] It has even been argued that the sutra referred to in the Dunhuang *Platform Sutra* title was the *Diamond Sutra* and that it was only later that the word *jing* 經 (sutra) applied to the *Platform Sutra* of which Huineng was designated the author.[80]

Moreover, the only Tang dynasty mentions of Huineng's thought that can be linked to the *Platform Sutra*, but without mentioning the sutra, are to the verse contest with Shenxiu.[81] Two of the people making these references or allusions, Chengguan 澄觀 (737–838) and Zongmi (780–841), were not only master and disciple, but also were taught and influenced by members of the Shenhui lineage, and both were involved with or knew Pei Xiu 裴休 (791–864), the third author. As none of them mentions the *Platform Sutra*, it is possible that the "verse contest" came from a hagiography of Huineng and that the "Platform Sutra" sermon was combined with the hagiographical frame sometime later in the early 10th century. They do not seem to have known anything of the sermons in the Dunhuang *Platform Sutra*.[82] Given this and the rarity of quotes from before the Song, it is more likely that the hagiography was the main reason for Huineng's popularity. For example, Pei Xiu, or his Chan master Huangbo Xiyun 黃檗希運 (d. ca. 850), knew of the story of the transmission of the robe from Hongren to the illiterate Huineng and that the senior-most monk Ming (Chen Huiming 陳慧明) pursued Huineng to the top of the Dayu range in pursuit of the dharma, which also belongs to the hagiography and not the sermon section of the *Platform Sutra*.[83] The evidence of the verse contest and meeting with Huiming suggests that there may have been two versions of the *Platform Sutra* existing in the 9th century, with Pei Xiu and Huangbo Xiyun having access to (or contributed to) the non-Dunhuang version.

The fundamental doctrine of the *Platform Sutra* is that all beings have a buddha-nature or buddhaness, a potential that can be discovered not by gradual practice, but suddenly, when one does not conceive (念 *nian*) dualistically, when *prajñā* (insight) and meditation or *samādhi* are identical. This is the direct access to enlightenment in which there is no attachment, even to the aim of enlightenment. This is seemingly effortless, yet requires effort. Following enlightenment, more practice is needed. One relies on oneself, not activating conceptualization, in a formless meditation.[84]

This had the appeal of universal access to buddhahood, unhindered by the formalities of the Buddhist Order or the need for scholarly study or even literacy, which matched similar themes in the hagiography.

REVIEW OF LITERATURE

Modern literature on Huineng and the *Platform Sutra* is vast, with bibliographies made in late 2012 listing 157 books, 68 theses, and 408 articles in East Asian and European languages, and even these are far from complete.[85] The texts considered in this section are the chief critical landmark studies.

The Japanese Zen master Dōgen (1200–1253) wrote, referring to the claims by Nanyang Huizhong, that "the words 'seeing the nature' exist in the *Platform Sutra of the Sixth Patriarch*. That book is a forgery. . . . Nor is it the words of Caoqi (Huineng)."[86] Although doubts about the *Platform Sutra* very occasionally appear, it was not until 1907 that a modern scholar, Saikainō Kōyō, declared the *Platform Sutra* a forgery, as not by Huineng, based on historical evidence that Shenhui was the first to promote the Southern Chan lineage. Then, in 1913, Matsumoto Bunzaburō published *Kongōkyō to Rokuso dankyō no kenkyū*, arguing that the *Platform Sutra* had been expanded in the Song and following periods and that material in it could not have been compiled by Fahai or written by Huineng.[87] By comparing the sutra with the "Brief Preface," *Jingde chuandeng lu*, and the inscription by Wang Wei, he found contradictions over dates in Huineng's "life," and he concluded that much of the *Platform Sutra*, including the "autobiographical" parts, could not have been by Huineng and that Shenhui had created the opposition of Northern versus Southern Chan. He did allow that part of the sutra reflected Huineng's ideas.[88] Matsumoto was a pioneer of modern Chan studies.

In 1919, Ding Fubao published *Liuzu dashi Fabao tanjing jianzhu*, a detailed philological gloss on an edition made from two Ming dynasty prints of the *Platform Sutra*. This is still valuable and has been reprinted many times (sometimes under different titles) and was the basis for the first English translation of the *Platform Sutra*, Wong Mou-lam's *Sutra Spoken by the Sixth Patriarch Wei Lang on the High Seat of the Gem of the Law*, which has been revised and republished many times.[89]

The impact of the discoveries from Dunhuang date from 1917, when Yabuki Keiki (1879–1939) published a catalog of manuscripts from Dunhuang (also publicly displayed in rotograph reproductions) that contained some "Northern" Chan texts. Then, in 1930, in his *Meisha yoin*, he published the rotographs of the Stein 5475 *Platform Sutra*, the Stein 2054 manuscript of the *Lengqie shizi ji*, and the Stein 516 *Lidai fabao ji*. An edition made from Stein 516 was published in the *Taishō shinshū daizōkyō* (Taisho Tripitaka), vol. 51 in 1928, and from Stein 5475 in vol. 48 in 1932. These immediately attracted the attention of East Asian scholars.[90]

In 1927, Hu Shi (1891–1962) met Yabuki in Tokyo and learned of the existence of the Dunhuang *Platform Sutra*. Hu, who had discovered the manuscripts related to Shenhui in Paris and London in 1926, was excited by this. He had started to write a history of Chan in 1925 and then, having edited the Zongbao version of the *Platform Sutra*, wrote a study of the *Platform Sutra* that incorporated evidence from the *Caoqi Dashi zhuan*, which he had learned of from Nukariya Kaiten's *Zengaku shisōshi* of 1925.[91] In 1930, Hu published the previously unknown Shenhui texts in *Shenhui Heshang yiji* (Shanghai: Yadong tushuguan, 1930), and his claim that Shenhui was the author of the original *Platform Sutra* was soon countered.[92]

In 1932, Matsumoto, using the copy of the Dunhuang *Platform Sutra* in *Meisha yoin*, published "*Rokuso dankyō* no shoshigakuteki kenkyū," in which he also referred to the Kōshōji version of the *Platform Sutra* discovered in 1931.[93] After comparing all the extant versions of the sutra and the various prefaces, he concluded that after the Dunhuang version of the mid-9th century, the text had been added to over time, with material added from the *Caoqi Dashi zhuan* and the *Jingde chuan deng lu*, and that it was not by Shenhui.[94] This bibliographical study pioneered the genealogical studies of the sutra.

In 1931, Hu Shi and Suzuki Daisetsu, who were in communication via Suzuki's Korean student Kim Kugyŏng, published a preface to and a study of the *Lengqie shizi ji*, and in 1931 and 1933 Kim produced a critical edition of that text.[95] In 1934, Suzuki Daisetsu (Teitarō) and Kuda Rentarō published a new edition of the *Platform Sutra* by comparing the Dunhuang and the Kōshōji versions (which had been published in 1933) and a new edition of the *Shenhui yulu* by collating Hu Shi's text and the Ishii text from Dunhuang. In a traditionally bound box set, the first title of the four volumes is *Tonkō shutsudo Jinne Zenji goroku kaisetsu oyobi mokuji*.[96] Suzuki traced the origins of the Kōshōji version back to the Huixin version, which he dated to 967, and he dated the Dunhuang version to the early 9th century. He traced some additions made in the Kōshōji version and opposed the attribution of the *Platform Sutra* to Shenhui.[97] Suzuki continued his work on the *Platform Sutra*, studying more newly discovered versions, leading him to the conclusion that the early versions were meant to symbolize a lineage transmission, the Dunhuang version being written in the third generation after Huineng. He also wrote on Huineng's hagiography. These conclusions were published in *Suzuki Daisetsu Zenshisōshi kenkyū*, vol. 2.[98]

The works of Shenhui, as found in Hu Shi's 1930 edition, were translated with annotations by Jacques Gernet as *Entretiens du maître de Dhyāna Chen-hoeui du Ho-tsö (668–760)*.[99] Two landmark studies were published in 1967, Yanagida Seizan's (1922–2006) *Shoki Zenshūshisho no kenkyū* and Philip B. Yampolsky's *The Platform Sutra of the Sixth Patriarch*. Yanagida's book primarily deals with the *Lengqie shizi ji*, the works of Shenhui, the *Platform Sutra*, the *Caoqi Dashi zhuan*, the *Lidai fabao ji*, and the *Baolin zhuan*. Although he considers much of this literature fictional, by discovering the authors and the motivations of the fiction, which has its own logic, he thinks one can uncover a historical reality. This can in part be achieved by reading beyond the immediate materials. His conclusion was that the *Platform Sutra* was not by Huineng or Shenhui, but by members of the Niutou Chan lineage, although in his 2001 "Goroku no rekishi," he suggested that the Dunhuang version was written after Nanyang Huizhong (d. 775) made a criticism of a "platform sutra" and that it was written in Dunhuang by Wuzhen of the third or fourth generation after Huineng.[100] Yampolsky, who had worked with Yanagida and Iriya Yoshitaka on Ruth Fuller Sasaki's *Linji lu* translation project, produced an edition of the Dunhuang *Platform Sutra*, an English translation, an analysis of the text, and a discussion of Huineng's hagiography. He is agnostic on the authorship of the sutra, but thinks parts of it date to between 780 and 800, and the Dunhuang version to the period between 830 and 860.[101] Yampolsky built on the Japanese scholarship and the works of Hu Shi, and his book inspired many later Western scholars of this field.

In 2005, John Jorgensen wrote *Inventing Hui-neng, the Sixth Patriarch: Hagiography and Biography in Early Chan*, which built on the work of Yanagida and Yampolsky in particular. It introduces ideas from studies of South Asian and Western Christian hagiography, compares the structures of the hagiographies of Huineng with those of Confucius, and deals with the issues of relics. It gives importance to geographical perceptions of place and to authority. Jorgensen speculates that the author of the *Platform Sutra* may have been Zhenshu 甄叔 (d. 820), a disciple of Shenhui's pupil Chengguang 乘廣 (717–798). Both seem also to have been influenced by the ideas of Mazu Daoyi 馬祖道一 (709–788) and both lived south of the Yangtze River.[102]

Readings of the Platform Sūtra, edited by Morten Schlütter and Stephen F. Teiser, contains essays on the background to ideas in the *Platform Sutra*, the hagiography of Huineng, the early Chan movement, sudden enlightenment, the issues of transmission and ordination precepts, and the relation of the sutra's ideas with Chinese philosophy more broadly.[103] In the same year, in commemoration of the 30th anniversary of the foundation of the Guangdong Fojiao xiehui (Guangdong Buddhist Association), the association published facsimiles of 15 texts of the *Platform Sutra* (including the Dunhuang Museum text and the Lushun Museum text), plus the fragments of the Tangut translation and a 1952 edition of Wong Mou-lam's English translation in *Liuzu Tanjing jicheng* (Guangdong?: Guangdong Fojiao xiehui, 2012).[104]

PRIMARY SOURCES

Manuscripts. The earliest primary sources are manuscripts retrieved from a cache in the Dunhuang Caves from 1900 onward that were not identified as "Chan" until the late 1920s. They mainly exist in multiple undated copies and fragments and may contain scribal errors. They are written mainly in a Chinese influenced by the spoken language and so would not have been considered part of the literary culture of the elite. These manuscripts are the Pelliot Chinese collection (P), the Stein Chinese collection (S), and Taishō Shinshū Daizōkyō (T).

Lengqie shizi ji by Jingjue (P4564, P3294, P3537, P3436, P3703, S2054, S4272) was discovered by Hu Shi in 1926. The best edition is provided in Yanagida Seizan, *Shoki no Zenshi I*.[105] An edition is also found in T85 no. 2837 based on S2054. A translation exists in a Tibetan manuscript from Dunhuang. An annotated French translation , *Le bouddhisme Ch'an en mal d'histoire—Génèse d'une tradition religieuse dans la Chine des T'ang*, was made by Bernard Faure in 1989.[106] An English translation from the incomplete T no. 2837 was made by J. C. Cleary as "Records of the Teachers and Students of the Lanka."[107]

The following manuscripts related to Shenhui have been found at Dunhuang:

1. *Nanyang Heshang dunjiao jietuo Chanmen zhiliaoxing tanyu* (P2045, Dunhuang xian Bowuguan 77, Beijing tushuguan Han 81). An edition and Japanese translation have been made in Tōdai goroku kenkyūban, *Jinne no goroku: Dango*.[108]
2. *Putidamo Nanzong ding shifei lun* by Dugu Pei (P3047, P3488, P2045, Dunhuang xian Bowuguan 77).
3. *Nanyang Heshang wenda zazhengyi* (also called *Shenhui yulu*) (S6557, Ishii text, P3047).

The above texts are found in Hu Shi, *Shenhui Heshang yiji*; and in Yang Wenhui, *Shenhui Heshang Chanhua lu*, along with other materials.[109] Hu's editions were translated by Jacques Gernet as *Entretiens du maître de Dhyāna Chen-hoeui du Ho-tsö (668–760)*.[110] The best editions of 1 and 2 are found in Deng Wenkuan and Rong Xinjiang, eds., *Dunbo ben Chanji lujiao*.[111]

The *Lidai fabao ji* exists in many manuscripts (P2125, P3717, P3727, S516, S1611, S1776, S5916, Ishii text, T51 no. 2075). The best edition, with a Japanese translation, is Yanagida Seizan, *Shoki no Zenshi II*.[112] There is a translation in Wendi Adamek, *The Mystique of Transmission: On an Early Chan History and Its Contexts*.[113]

The *Caoqi Dashi zhuan* exists in a single manuscript from Enryaku-ji, now kept in Nara National Museum. It is dated 803 (copy). It is reproduced in Yanagida Seizan, comp., *Rokuso dankyō shohon shūsei*.[114] A photographic reproduction, an annotated edition, and translation are found in Komazawa Daigaku Zenshūshi kenkyūkai, comp., *Enō kenkyū*.[115] It is translated in John Jorgensen, *Inventing Hui-neng*.[116]

The Dunhuang *Platform Sutra* or *(Liuzu) tanjing*, i.e., *Nanzong dunjiao zuishang moheboruobolomi jing Liuzu Huineng Dashi yu Shaozhou Dafansi shifa tanjing*, in one fascicle, survives in four manuscripts (S5475, Beijing tushuguan 8024, Lushun Bowuguan, Dunhuang xian bowuguan). These are discussed in Jorgensen, "The Platform Sutra," and, Christoph Anderl, "Always a Sūtra?"[117] Facsimiles of all manuscripts are reproduced in Guangdongsheng Fojiao xiehui, *Liuzu tanjing jicheng*, n.p., 2012, together with copies of later editions.[118] Yanagida, *Rokuso dankyō shohon shūsei*, contains S5475 and later editions. The best edition is in Deng and Rong, *Dunbo ben Chanji lujiao*.[119] English ranslations of the Dunhuang version of the *Platform Sutra* are found in Yampolsky, *Platform Sutra*, from S5475, and Red Pine, *The Platform Sutra: The Zen Teaching of Hui-neng*, from the Dunhuang Museum manuscript as collated by Yang Zengwen.[120]

Engravings. Huikong, a pupil of Shenhui, wrote a funerary inscription for his master titled"Da Tang Dongdu Heze-si mogu Diqizu Guoshi Dade yu Longmen Baoying-si Longsho fu jian shenta ming bing xu" 大唐東都荷澤寺歿故第七祖國師大德於龍門寶應寺龍首腹建身塔銘並序. This is reproduced in Yang, *Shenhui Heshang Chanhua lu*,, and an annotated edition is provided in Shiga Takayoshi, ed., *Tōdai Shakkyō Bunsen yakuchū*.[121] This text is a poor-quality grave inscription for Shenhui, suggesting it had no financial support from the state or significant donors, possibly because it was written during a civil war.

Print. The following texts are print copies of stele inscriptions for Huineng meant to be displayed for public consumption. They are written in an elaborate literary Chinese, packed with allusions, and required major sponsorship. They were mostly commissioned by Buddhist believers from elite authors.

The earliest inscription, "Neng Chanshi beiming" was by Wang Wei, a noted poet. It is found in Wang Wei's collected works, *Wang Mojie quanji*, and in the collected prose works of the Tang dynasty, *Quan Tang wen* (dated 1814).[122] Annotated editions are found in Yanagida Seizan, *Shoki Zenshūshisho no kenkyū* and Shiga, *Tōdai Shakkyō Bunsen yakuchū*.[123] A partial translation is given in Jorgensen, *Inventing Hui-neng*.[124]

Liu Zongyuan, a famous literatus, wrote a stele for Huineng in 816. This "Caoqi Diliuzu cishi Dajian Chanshi bei," 曹溪第六祖賜謚大鑒禅師碑 is in Liu Zongyuan's collected works, *Hedong Xiansheng ji* 6, and in *Quan Tang wen* 589. The best edition is in Shiga, *Tōdai Shakkyō Bunsen yakuchū*.[125] A translation is provided by McRae as an appendix in his *Platform Sutra*.[126]

In 818 or 819, Liu Yuxi wrote "Da Tang Caoqi Diliuzu Dajian Chanshi dierbei bing xu," 大唐曹溪第六祖大鑒禅師第二碑並序. This is in Liu Yuxi's collected works, *Liu Mengde wenji* 30; and in Chao Xuan (968–1020)'s compilation of select Tang prose the *Tang wen zui* 63; in *Wenyuan yinghua* 867; and in *Quan Tang wen* 610. Shiga, *Tōdai Shakkyō Bunsen yakuchū*, has made an edition, but it lacks the section on the robe that is sometimes separated out and called "Foyi ming," as in *Quan Tang wen* 608.[127] This is translated in full as an appendix by McRae in his *Platform Sutra*.[128]

Song-Court Sponsored Texts. These collections were either written on commission for the early Song court or were entered into the Tripitaka, the Buddhist canon. Zanning wrote for the literary elite in elegant Chinese, often based on stele inscriptions. The *Jingde chuandeng lu* contains colloquial Chinese, but this was edited by the literatus Yang Yi 楊億 to remove vulgar expressions and standardize the language to make it acceptable.

Zanning's *Song gaoseng zhuan*, which was presented to court in 988, contains a hagiography of Huineng.[129]

Daoyuan's *Jingde chuandeng lu* is dated 1004, but it has some inserted notes of a later date. It was entered into the Tripitaka in 1011, which gave it authority in the Chinese Buddhist world. It contains the dialogue with Hongren and the verse contest and a hagiography of Huineng proper.[130]

FURTHER READING

Adamek, Wendi. *The Mystique of Transmission: On an Early Chan History and Its Contexts*. New York: Columbia University Press, 2007.

Cleary, Thomas, trans. *The Sutra of Hui-neng Grand Master of Zen: With Hui-neng's Commentary on the Diamond Sutra*. Boston: Shambala, 1998.

Dumoulin, Heinrich. *Zen Buddhism: A History*. Vol. 1, *India and China*. Translated by James W. Heisig and Paul Knitter. New York: Macmillan, 1988.

Faure, Bernard. *The Will to Orthodoxy: A Critical Genealogy of Northern Chan Buddhism*. Translated by Phyllis Brooks. Stanford, CA: Stanford University Press, 1997.

Gernet, Jacques. *Entretiens du maître de Dhyāna Chen-hoeui du Ho-tsö (668–760)*. Paris: École Française d'Extrême-Orient, 1977.

Jorgensen, John. *Inventing Hui-neng, the Sixth Patriarch: Hagiography and Biography in Early Ch'an*. Leiden, The Netherlands: Brill, 2005.

Kim, Chigyŏn, comp. *Yukcho Tan'gyŏng ŭi segye*. Seoul, Korea: Minjoksa, 1989.
Komazawa Daigaku Zenshūshi kenkyūkai, comp. *Enō kenkyū*. Tokyo: Daishūkan shoten, 1978.
Kuiken, Cornelis Jan. "The Other Neng." PhD diss., Rijksuniversiteit Groningen, 2002.
McRae, John. *The Northern School and the Formation of Early Ch'an Buddhism*. Honolulu: University of Hawai'i Press, 1986.
McRae, John R. (trans.). *The Platform Sutra of the Sixth Patriarch*. Berkeley, CA: Numata Center for Buddhist Translation and Research, 2000.
Ogawa, Takashi. *Jinne: Tonkō bunken to shoki no Zenshūshi*. Kyoto: Rinsen shoten, 2007.
Schlütter, Morten, and Stephen S. Teiser, eds. *Readings of the Platform Sutra*. New York: Columbia University Press, 2012.
Yampolsky, Philip B., trans. *The Platform Sutra of the Sixth Patriarch: The Text of the Tun-huang Manuscript, Translated with Notes*. New York: Columbia University Press, 1967.
Yanagida, Seizan. *Shoki Zenshūshisho no kenkyū*. Kyoto: Hōzōkan, 1967.
Yang, Wenhui. *Shenhui Heshang Chanhua lu*. Beijing: Zhonghua shuju, 1996.

NOTES

1. Philip B. Yampolsky, trans., *The Platform Sutra of the Sixth Patriarch: The Text of the Tun-huang Manuscript, Translated with Notes* (New York: Columbia University Press, 1967), 79–88; and Yampolsky, *Platform Sutra*, 60–63; and John R. McRae, trans., *The Platform Sutra of the Sixth Patriarch* (Berkeley, CA: Numata Center for Buddhist Translation and Research, 2000), 117–122.
2. Based on a 19th-century gazetteer, Cornelis Jan Kuiken, "The Other Neng" (PhD diss., Rijksuniversiteit Groningen, 2002), 4.16 thinks this monastery was built in 714, after Huineng died. See Yampolsky, *Platform Sutra*, 93n14, who is skeptical about this source.
3. 韶州惠能,揚州高麗僧智,此並堪為人師,但一方人物, *Yanagida* Seizan, *Zen no Goroku 2: Shoki no Zenshi 1: Ryōgashijiki, Denhōbōki* (Tokyo: Chikuma shobō, 1971), 273.
4. Discussed in He Ge'en, "Huineng zhuan zhiyi," in *Chanzong shishi kaobian: Chanxue zhuanji*, comp. Zhang Mantao (Taipei: Dahengwenhua chubanshe, n.d, reprint of He's text of 1935), 337–358. Kuiken, "Other Neng," 3.8. See also Bernard Faure, *The Will to Orthodoxy: A Critical Genealogy of Northern Chan Buddhism*, trans. Phyllis Brooks (Stanford, CA: Stanford University Press, 1997), 34–35.
5. Kuiken, "Other Neng," 5.27, not Hengyang as Kuiken argues.
6. On arguments over the sequence, see John Jorgensen, "The Platform Sūtra and the Corpus of Shenhui: Recent Critical Text Editions and Studies," *Revue Bibliographique de Sinologie* Nouvelle série, XX (2002): 426–427.
7. 六代祖師以心傳心 Yang Zengwen, *Shenhui Heshang Chanhua lu* (Beijing: Zhonghua shuju, 1996), 7.
8. Ogawa Takashi, *Jinne: Tonkō bunken to shoki no Zenshūshi* (Kyoto: Rinsen shoten, 2007), 24–25.
9. *Song gaoseng zhuan*, T50.795c21–24, and Wan Qirong 萬齊融, "Fahua-si jietan yuan bei," 法華寺戒壇院碑, in *Quan Tangwen*, comp. Dong Gao (Taipei: Dahua shuju, 1987), vol. 2, fasc. 335, 1521a. Dates from Buddhist histories such as the *Shishi jigu lue* and *Fozu tongji*. See Yanagida Seizan, *Shoki Zenshūshisho no kenkyū* (Kyoto: Hōzōkan, 1967), 113n1.
10. Stanley Weinstein, *Buddhism under the T'ang* (Cambridge, UK: Cambridge University Press, 1987), 51–54.
11. 昇師子座、為天下學者説 Yang, *Shenhui*, 18.
12. 海外知聞 Yang, *Shenhui*, 19.
13. 縣官白馬、衛南盧鄭二令文事、三度幾死。商旅縗服、曾易服執秤負歸 *Yuanjue jing dashuchao* XZJ 14.553b22–25; Yang, *Shenhui*, 135.
14. Yang, *Shenhui*, 18, 24–25.
15. Yang, *Shenhui*, 27.

16. Yang, *Shenhui*, 29; and McRae, *Platform Sutra*, 3.
17. Yang, *Shenhui*, 32–33.
18. Yang, *Shenhui*, 31.
19. John Jorgensen, *Inventing Hui-neng, the Sixth Patriarch: Hagiography and Biography in Early Ch'an* (Leiden, The Netherlands: Brill, 2005), 66; Jorgensen, *Inventing Hui-neng*, 117–118, 552–553, 555.
20. For this woman and her father, see Zhou Shaoliang and Zhao Chao, comps., *Tangdai muzhi yibian xuji* (Shanghai: Shanghai guji chubanshe, 2001), 741–742.
21. Yang, *Shenhui*, 103.
22. Yampolsky, *Platform Sutra*, 66–69; and Jorgensen, *Inventing Hui-neng*, 139.
23. Jorgensen, *Inventing Hui-neng*, 139–140, 142, 140–144.
24. Inscription translated in Jorgensen, *Inventing Hui-neng*, 145–151.
25. Translated in Jorgensen, *Inventing Hui-neng*, 133–137.
26. Jorgensen, *Inventing Hui-neng*, 135.
27. Jorgensen, *Inventing Hui-neng*, 62–64, 149, 154–155.
28. Translated in Wendi Adamek, *Mystique of Transmission: On an Early Chan History and Its Contexts* (New York: Columbia University Press, 2007), 321–323.
29. Translated in Adamek, *Mystique*, 328–329.
30. Jorgensen, *Inventing Hui-neng*, 426–427.
31. *Yuanjue jing dashuchao* XZJ 14.554a1–3.
32. Jorgensen, *Inventing Hui-neng*, 118–120. This stele was unearthed in 1945.
33. Translated in McRae, *Platform Sutra*, 123–132.
34. Discussed Jorgensen, *Inventing Hui-neng*, 439–445.
35. T50.754c-755c. See memorial presenting the text to the throne and the imperial decree of acceptance, T50.709a-b; and, for discussion of Zanning's use of sources for his Huineng hagiography, Jorgensen, *Inventing Hui-neng*, 43, 45, 74–75, 137–139.
36. John Jorgensen, "Ssanggye-sa and Local Buddhist History: Propaganda and Relics in a Struggle for Survival, 1850s – 1930s," *Seoul Journal of Korean Studies* 21, no. 1 (June 2008): 87–127.
37. Jorgensen, "Ssanggye-sa," 92.
38. See 習近平の父が守った伝統文化の価値 (The value of the traditional culture protected by Xi Jinping's father), Dokuritsu kisha no chosen Chūgoku media o kataru 独立記者の挑戦 中国でメディアを語る (goo.ne.jp), November 4, 2017. See Foyuan's testimony, anonymous, "Liuzu Huineng zhenshen wenge canzao kaitang, Xi Zhongxun xiasiling baohu" 六祖惠能真身文革惨遭开膛 习仲勋下死令保护, December 5, 2013.
39. Sahajasz. Douban dushu 豆瓣读书, "Maozedong hen xinshang liudai Chanzong Huineng de *Liuzu tanjing*" 毛泽东很欣赏六代禅宗慧能的《六祖坛经》, January 21, 2016, and ZhangXiaoxin, comp., 张小新, "Zhenzheng de Dashi! Mao Zedong Zhizhi linzhong, chuangtou yizhi baifangzhe ta de shu" 真正的大师!毛泽东直至临终, 床头一直摆放着他的书, March 6, 2017.
40. Zhang Tiejun, "Mao Zedong tan Chanzong Dazu Huineg" 毛澤東談禅宗大祖慧能 *Zhongguo gongchandang xinwen*, cpc.people.en/GB/64162/64172/85037/6874073.html, September 15, 2019.
41. Gilbert C. F. Fong, trans., *Snow in August* (Hong Kong: Chinese University Press, 2003).
42. Lu Jinchuan, *Huineng Dashi zhuan* (Cosmos Books: Hong Kong, 1995).
43. Reissued by Shanghai Wenyi chubanshe in 2016.
44. Available on YouTube, see Douban dianying, 豆瓣典電影 and Premier Movie Legend of Dajian Huineng, 慧能大师传奇 | the Sixth Patriarch.
45. See Wuxia dianying "Mumian jiasha", 35 nianhou yanyuan xianzhuang, zhujueyizai guowai 武俠電影《木棉袈裟》, 35 年後演員現狀, 主角已在國外, May 25, 2020.
46. See Da Ai Television 大愛電視, "Gaoseng zhuan: Liuzu Huineng" 高僧傳、六祖慧能、, February 25, 2021.

47. McRae, *Platform Sutra*, 3.
48. Yampolsky, *Platform Sutra*, 30, see also pp. 8–9, table 1.
49. See Nicolas Tackett, *The Destruction of the Medieval Chinese Aristocracy* (Cambridge, MA: Harvard University Press, 2014), 63n87.
50. *Foyi ming* 佛衣銘, in McRae, *Platform Sutra*, 129–131.
51. Wendi Adamek, "Transmitting Notions of Transmission," in *Readings of the Platform Sutra*, ed. Morten Schlütter and Stephen S. Teiser (New York: Columbia University Press, 2012), 120, 122.
52. McRae, *Platform Sutra*, 3; and Faure, *Will to Orthodoxy*, 20.
53. Jorgensen, *Inventing Hui-neng*, 162–163.
54. Tackett, *Aristocracy*, 35n20, 45, 64.
55. McRae, *Platform Sutra*, 1–2; and Adamek, "Transmitting," 118.
56. John Jorgensen, "The Radiant Mind: Zhu Xi and the Chan Doctrine of *Tathāgatagarbha*," in *The Buddhist Roots of Zhu Xi's Philosophical Thought*, ed. John Makeham (New York: Oxford University Press, 2018), 50–51.
57. Jorgensen, "Radiant Mind," 93–94.
58. See Cheng Xilin 程喜霖, "Tangdai de gongjian yu guosuo" 唐代的公驗與過所, *Zhongguoshi yanjiu* 1985.1, at Xinjiang's philosophy and social sciences network, June 18, 2009; and Anonymous, "Changshi: luelun Tangchao de huzhao zhidu"「常識」略論唐朝的護照制度, 豆瓣小组, June 30, 2017.
59. *Xu gaoseng zhuan* T50.657c17–18. Zongmi, *Yuanjue jing dashuchao* XZJ 14.553b12–13.
60. Paul Groner, "Ordination and Precepts in the *Platform Sūtra*," in *Readings of the Platform Sutra*, ed. Morten Schlütter and Stephen S. Teiser (New York: Columbia University Press, 2012), 134, 138, 147, 149–150; and Yampolsky, *Platform Sutra*, 125, 141ff.
61. Christoph Anderl, "Was the *Platform Sūtra* Always a Sūtra?," in *Studies in Chinese Manuscripts: From the Warring States Period to the 20th Century*, ed. Imre Galambos (Budapest: Eötvös Lorand University, 2013), 165, 167, 169, 172.
62. Tackett, *Aristocracy*, 68.
63. Tackett, *Aristocracy*, 137.
64. 習徒迷真。。。竟成檀經傳宗Jorgensen, *Inventing Hui-neng*, 630, for background, 413–415, and analysis, 631. 是南方宗旨、把他壇經改換、添糅鄙譚削除聖意惑亂後徒 T51.438a2–3. Discussed in Jorgensen, *Inventing Hui-neng*, 603–604. The meanings of these two passages are disputed. See Yampolsky, *Platform Sutra*, 97–98.
65. Ibuki Atsushi, "Enō ni kisareru sūshu no *Kongōkyō* no chūshakusho nitsuite," in *Kongō hannya kyō no shisōteki kenkyū*, comp. Abe Jion (Tokyo: Shunjusha, 1999), 423, 430n52.
66. XZJ 38.660a–661a. XZJ 38.661b–690a. An uncritical translation of the "preface" (38.660a–661a) and the text in Daochuan's *Jin'gang jingzhu* (XZJ 38.695b-753a; this is clear from reference to Zhang Wujin of 695b on p. 88 of the translation) appears in Thomas Cleary, trans., *The Sutra of Hui-neng Grand Master of Zen: With Hui-neng's Commentary on the* Diamond Sutra (Boston: Shambala, 1998), 85–144. XZJ 38.690b–693a. XZJ 38.693a–b.
67. *Enō kenkyū*, 468; T55.1094a. Ouyang Xiu and Song Qi, *Xin Tang shu* (Shanghai: Zhonghua shuju, 1975), 5:fasc. 59, p. 1528b.
68. *Enō kenkyū*, 470–471.
69. *Enō kenkyū*, 471.
70. Takeuchi Kōdō, "Enō-sen *Kongō kyō kaigi* no shisōteki tokushitsu to seiritsu o megutte," in *Kongō hannya kyō no shisōteki kenkyū*, comp. Abe Jion (Tokyo: Shunjusha, 1999), 388–393.
71. For a biography of Li Wenhui, see anonymous, October 6, 2019. Ibuki, "Enō ni kisareru," 411–413. Li's text is also available in *Jin'gang jing zhujie*, XZJ 38, CBETA X24n0468, and extracted in text「金剛經注」-李文會(南宋) at kknews.cc/other/xe6ea28html, October 5, 2018.
72. Ibuki, "Enō ni kisareru," 418–419.

73. Ibuki, "Enō ni kisareru," 419–420.
74. Ibuki, "Enō ni kisareru," 421.
75. For Lingyou, see *Song gaoseng zhuan*, T50.869b9–10. XZJ 38.685b7–8.
76. 心行平等、純一无雜 Komazawa Daigaku Zenshūshi kenkyūkai, comp., *Enō kenkyū* (Tokyo: Daishūkan shoten, 1978), 498, 613, translated and discussed in Jeffrey L. Broughton, *The Bodhidharma Anthology: The Earliest Records of Zen* (Berkeley: University of California Press, 1999), 108–109. Based on *Baolin zhuan*, 心行平等難 "the difficulty of keeping mind and actions equal," see Tanaka Ryōshō, *Hōrinden yakuchū* (Tokyo: Uchiyama shoten, 2003), 8.
77. *Putidamo Nanzong ding shifei lun*, Yang, *Shenhui*, 30–31.
78. *Nanyang Heshang wenda zazhengyi*, Yang, *Shenhui*, 109.
79. Yang, *Shenhui*, 110.
80. Anderl, "Always a Sūtra?" 154–155, 165–166.
81. Yanagida, *Shoki Zenshūshisho no kenkyū*, 266n11. These are Chengguan, *Huayan jing suishu yanyichao*, T36.164b4–5, which refers to Datong 大通 (Shenxiu) and 164c20–24, which refers to the "sixth patriarch"; and the *Wanling lu* by Pei Xiu (some date this text to 857, the date of Pei's preface to his *Chuanxin fayao*, but the *Wanling lu* was a later recompilation [see Yanagida Seizan, "Kaisetsu," in *Denshin hōyō. Enryō roku: Zen no goroku 8*, ed. Iriya Toshitaka (Tokyo: Chikuma shobō, 1969), 175]), T48.385b11–12 本來無一物、何處有塵埃, which does not name Huineng; and Zongmi's *Zhonghua chuanxindi chanmen shizi chengxi tu*, which critically refers to the verse by Shenxiu (translated in Jeffrey Lyle Broughton, *Zongmi on Chan* [New York: Columbia University Press, 2009], 84). This line from Huineng's verse of reply in the *Wanling lu*, "originally there is not a single thing" replaces the Dunhuang *Platform Sutra*'s line in the verse, 佛性常淨清 "The Buddha-nature is always pristine." See Yampolsky, *Platform Sutra*, 132. The line, "originally there is not a single thing" may have first appeared in the *Platform Sutra* that had a preface by Huixin in 967.
82. Huangbo (or Pei Xiu) mentions a patriarchal teacher saying, "All of the Dharma spoken by the Buddha was in order to remove all thought (lit. mind). If I have no mind at all, what use is all of the Dharma?" 佛說一切法、為除一切心。我無一切心、何用一切法 which Zongmi says was spoken by Huineng (see Broughton, *Zongmi*, 174, with a slight variation). See Iriya, *Denshin hōyō*, 30, 97. But these words are not in the extant *Platform Sutra*.
83. Iriya, *Denshin hōyō*, 84; *Shizi xiemo zhuan*, Yang, *Shenhui*, 120; and Dunhuang *Platform Sutra*, Yampolsky, *Platform Sutra*, 134. Note, here the *Chuanxin fayao* also says that Huineng enlightened Huiming with the words, "Not thinking of good, not thinking of evil, at just that very moment, what is your original face before your mother and father were born?" See Yampolsky, *Platform Sutra*, 110. This appears in the earliest post-Tang versions of the *Platform Sutra*. This passage in the *Chuanxin fayao* also is the first to use the sentence later adopted as a motto of the Chan school, 直指人心、見性成佛、不在言說 "directly point at the human mind, see the nature and become buddha, which does not reside in verbal teachings." See Yanagida, *Shoki Zenshūshisho no kenkyū*, 475. This passage, by referring to the robe of transmission and the gold-embroidered robe received by Kāśyapa, shows awareness of the ideas of Shenhui as in the *Putidamo Nanzong ding shifei lun*, Yang, *Shenhui*, 29.
84. Yampolsky, *Platform Sutra*, 114–118; McRae, *Platform Sutra*, 1; and, for a more detailed interpretation, see Brook Ziporyn, "The *Platform Sūtra* and Chinese Philosophy," in *Readings of the Platform Sutra*, ed. Morten Schlütter and Stephen S. Teiser (New York: Columbia University Press, 2012), 161–187.
85. Bibliographies in Shi Mingsheng, comp., *Liuzu tanjing yanjiu jicheng* (Beijing: Jincheng chubanshe, 2012).
86. *Shōbō genzō*, T82.298b25–28.
87. Matsumoto Bunzaburō, *Kongōkyō to Rokuso dankyō no kenkyū* (Kyoto: Baiyō shoten, 1913).
88. Chen Jidong, "Riben dui Liuzu Huineng ji *Liuzu tanjing* de yanjiu zongshu," in *Liuzu tanjing yanjiu jicheng*, comp. Shi Mingsheng (Beijing: Jincheng chubanshe, 2012), 126–133; and Yanagida Seizan,

"Sōsetsu," in *Tonkō Butten to Zen: Kōza Tonkō 8*, comp. Shinohara Hisao and Tanaka Ryōshō (Tokyo: Daitō shuppansha, 1980), 28–29.

89. Wong Mou-lam, *Sutra Spoken by the Sixth Patriarch Wei Lang on the High Seat of the Gem of the Law* (Shanghai: Yu Ching Press, 1930). See Ha Lei and Ding Xiaoping, "Dalu diqu Huineng ji *Liuzu tanjing* yanjiu zongshu," in *Liuzu tanjing yanjiu jicheng*, comp. Shi Mingsheng (Beijing: Jincheng chubanshe, 2012), 27.
90. Chen Jidong, "zongshu," 145–146; and Yanagida, "Sōsetsu," 3, 19–22.
91. Ogawa Takashi, *Jinne*, 11–14; and Huang Lianzhong, "Zhongguo Taiwan diqu dui Huineng ji *Liuzu tanjing* de yanjiu zongshu," in *Liuzu tanjing yanjiu jicheng*, comp. Shi Mingsheng (Beijing: Jincheng chubanshe, 2012), 61–63.
92. Hu Shi, *Shenhui Heshang yiji* (Shanghai: Yadong tushuguan, 1930). For this and more on Hu Shi's Chan studies, see Yanagida Seizan, comp., *Ko Teki Zengaku an* (Kyoto: Chūbun shuppansha, 1975). Yanagida, *Ko Teki Zengaku an*, 31.
93. "*Rokuso dankyō* no shoshigakuteki kenkyū," *Zengaku kenkyū* (1932), 17–18.
94. Chen Jidong, "zongshu," 148–152.
95. Yanagida, *Ko Teki Zengaku an*, 35–37.
96. Suzuki Daisetsu (Teitarō) and Kuda Rentarō, *Tonkō shutsudo Jinne Zenji goroku kaisetsu oyobi mokuji* (Tokyo: Morie shoten, 1934).
97. Chen Jidong, "zongshu," 152–158.
98. Chen Jidong, "zongshu," 159–161. *Suzuki Daisetsu Zenshisōshi kenkyū*, vol. 2 (Tokyo: Iwanami shoten, 1951), 310–361.
99. Jacques Gernet, *Entretiens du maître de Dhyāna Chen-hoeui du Ho-tsö (668–760)*, vol. 31 (Hanoi: Publications de l'école française d'Extrême-Orient, 1949).
100. Yanagida Seizan, "Goroku no rekishi," *Tōhō gakuhō* 57 (2001): 211–663. Chen Jidong, "zongshu," 163–167.
101. Yampolsky, *Platform Sutra*, 45, 98.
102. Jorgensen, *Inventing Hui-neng*, 624–640.
103. Morten Schlütter and Stephen F. Teiser, eds., *Readings of the Platform Sūtra* (New York: Columbia University, 2012).
104. Guangdong Fojiao xiehui, comp., *Liuzu Tanjing jicheng* (Guangdong?: Guangdong Fojiao xiehui, 2012).
105. Yanagida Seizan, *Shoki no Zenshi I* (Zen no goroku series no. 2) (Tokyo: Chikuma shobō, 1971).
106. Bernard Faure, *Le bouddhisme Ch'an en mal d'histoire—Génèse d'une tradition religieuse dans la Chine des T'ang* (Paris: École Française d'Extrême-Orient, 1989).
107. Jonathan Christopher Cleary, "Records of the Teachers and Students of the Lanka," in *Zen Dawn: Early Zen Texts from Tun Huang*, ed., J. C. Cleary (Boston and London: Shambala, 1986), 19–78.
108. Tōdai goroku kenkyūban, *Jinne no goroku: Dango* (Kyoto: Zenbunka kenkyūsho, 2006).
109. Hu Shi, *Shenhui Heshang yiji* (Shanghai, 1930; revised Ma Junwu, *Shenhui Heshang yiji: fu Hu Shi xianshengwannian de yanjiu*, Taipei: Hu Shi jinianguan, 1968). Yang Wenhui, *Shenhui Heshang Chanhua lu* (Beijing: Zhonghua shuju, 1996).
110. Jacques Gernet, *Entretiens du maître de Dhyāna Chen-hoeui du Ho-tsö (668–760)* (Paris: École Française d'Extrême-Orient, 1977).
111. Deng Wenkuan and Rong Xinjiang, eds., *Dunbo ben Chanji lujiao* (Nanjing: Jiangsu guji chubanshe, 1998).
112. Yanagida Seizan, *Shoki no Zenshi II* (Zen no goroku series no. 3) (Tokyo: Chikumashobō, 1976).
113. Wendi Adamek, *The Mystique of Transmission: On an Early Chan History and Its Contexts* (New York: Columbia University Press, 2007).

114. Yanagida Seizan, comp., *Rokuso dankyō shohon shūsei* (Kyoto: Chūbunshuppansha, 1976), 405–424.
115. *Enō kenkyū*, plates 2, ed. and trans., 25–82.
116. John Jorgensen, *Inventing Hui-neng*, 677–705.
117. John Jorgensen, "The Platform Sutra," 400–402, and Christoph Anderl, "Always a Sūtra?"
118. Guangdongsheng Fojiao xiehui, *Liuzu tanjing jicheng* (n.p., 2012).
119. Deng and Rong, *Dunbo ben Chanji lujiao*, 215–430.
120. Yampolsky, *Platform Sutra*, 125–183. Red Pine, *The Platform Sutra: The Zen Teaching of Hui-neng* (Emeryville, CA: Shoemaker and Hoard, 2006).
121. Yang, *Shenhui Heshang Chanhua lu*, 197, and Shiga Takayoshi, ed., *Tōdai Shakkyō Bunsen yakuchū* (Kyoto: Ōtani Daigaku Shinshū sōgo kenkyūsho, 1998), 195.
122. Wang Wei, *Wang Mojie quanji* (fascicle 25: 348–358) annotated by Zhao Tiancheng, with preface 1736.
123. Yanagida Seizan, *Shoki Zenshūshisho no kenkyū*, 539–558 and Shiga, *Tōdai Shakkyō Bunsen yakuchū*, 151–174.
124. Jorgensen, *Inventing Hui-neng*, 145–151.
125. Shiga, *Tōdai Shakkyō Bunsen yakuchū*, 175–184.
126. McRae, *Platform Sutra*, 123–127.
127. Shiga, *Tōdai Shakkyō Bunsen yakuchū*, 185–193.
128. McRae, *Platform Sutra*, 127–132.
129. *Song gaoseng zhuan*, T50.754c1–755c10.
130. *Jingde chuandeng lu*, T51. 222c9–223a29, T51.235b10–237a12.

John Jorgensen

HUMANISTIC BUDDHISM (RENSHENG FOJIAO 人生佛教 / RENJIAN FOJIAO 人間佛教)

The English term *humanistic Buddhism* is a contested yet official rendition of both the Chinese *rensheng fojiao* 人生佛教 (literally "Human Life Buddhism") and *renjian fojiao* 人間佛教 (literally "Human Realm Buddhism").[1] "Humanistic Buddhism" is a discursive space where multifaceted transregional Buddhist networks engage and evolve, an overarching label that identifies several selected interpretations of Buddhist doctrines and practices, as recent Chinese scholarship has recognized with the expression *duoyuan yiti* 多元一體.

This diversity is also attested by a lack of consensus on *when* and *why* humanistic Buddhism started. Is it just the reintroduction of a practice already present in premodern China or even simply the modern remanifestation of core tenets of the buddha? Or is it a new phenomenon, fully representative of the recent history of (Chinese) Buddhism? And if it is a new and modern form of Buddhism, could it be defined as the Buddhist reaction to—outcome of—the new intellectual milieu in early-20th-century China? There is not an easy and straightforward answer to these questions.

Many practitioners are inclined to see it as just the revival of the *correct* buddhadharma; whether it is in the form of humanitarian action, social activism, or other forms of civic engagement, they do not define their practice as a new dharma path but simply as the recovery and revitalization of the early model of "correct" dharma cultivation, the buddha's core teachings (*Fotuo benhuai* 佛陀本懷). Furthermore, Buddhists' engagement in societal affairs can be easily explained doctrinally and textually. The Mahāyāna understanding of the bodhisattva path, especially the perfection of giving (*dāna*), and even the empiricism found in early texts provide doctrinal and textual justifications to various practices cataloged as humanistic Buddhism.

As we reflect on the arrival of Buddhism in China, the process of adaptation of this foreign doctrine to Chinese traditional culture, and the way Buddhism absorbed native cultural paradigms, we could also read the (Buddhist) bodhisattva practice as aligned with the Confucian ideal of social responsibility. The formation of a Buddhist community that was socially aware and potentially socially active should not surprise us. Humanistic Buddhists in early-20th-century China made explicit references to Confucian values and ideals, like the Great Unity (*datong* 大同), partly to continue a long-term engagement with Confucianism and partly to reflect and embody contemporary non-Buddhist intellectual debates. Even today, "Humanistic Buddhists" find space for Confucian texts and values in their preaching. Scholars have even argued that humanistic Buddhism relates to Confucian discourses first and foremost.[2]

Chinese canonical and historical texts report the glorification of Buddhists in their interaction with the surrounding society. For instance, even in the first official collection of biographies of nuns in China, the *Biqiuni zhuan* 比丘尼傳 [T50n2063], examples of nuns who were involved in social issues in times of difficulties can be found; the nun Lingzong 令宗 (4th century), to mention one, helped by begging for food for the needy during an epidemic outbreak.[3]

If in the premodern era we find levels of Buddhist engagement in the social, it is only in the early 20th century, with the end of the Qing and the dawn of the Republican period, that this phenomenon appears more explicitly and consistently. This is when the terms *rensheng fojiao* and *renjian fojiao* were coined, and they soon became the parent terms of a larger vocabulary that includes expressions, such as *renjianhua* 人間化 and *renjian jingtu* 人間淨土, a new taxonomy protagonist of contemporary Buddhist publications. This is when related doctrines and practices were thoroughly systematized, also in conversation with Chinese native philosophical cultures and foreign ideologies. In order to strengthen the scriptural and doctrinal authority, several theorizers of humanistic Buddhism, from Taixu 太虛 to Xingyun 星雲, have referred to a passage from the *Ekottarika-āgama*, which says that the buddha obtained enlightenment in the human realm (*renjian* 人間), a clear reference to the so-called early and original Buddhism (*yuanshi fojiao* 原始佛教).[4] At the same time, the same Chinese Buddhists gave extensive lectures on the *Vimalakīrti Nirdeśa Sūtra* (*Weimojie suo shuo jing* 維摩詰所說經 [T14n0475]), as the figure of the lay Vimalakīrti was, in the Chinese mind, the champion of lay Buddhist practice, hence a model for the individual cultivation leading to the realization of the "Pure Land on Earth."[5]

HISTORICAL OVERVIEW: ONE LABEL, FOUR PHASES, MULTIPLE PATTERNS

The monks Taixu 太虛 (1890–1947) and Cihang 慈航 (1893–1954) are usually considered the first theorizers of the so-called *rensheng fojiao* and its later redefinition as *renjian fojiao* in the first half of the 20th century. Taixu and Cihang are certainly part—and representative—of a more general milieu that urged Buddhism to become more visible and active in the public domain. The period between the end of the 19th and the mid-20th centuries was characterized by substantial changes in the political, social, and religious spheres. Those were the years when Christianity won the popular consensus in various areas of China and were the years of the May Fourth movement and the anti-religious (and mostly anti-Christian) campaigns and sentiments that animated the intellectual and official domains. It was a time of reflection over Western ideologies, systems of thoughts, and beliefs, from anarchism to socialism and Marxism, and thus the time for repositioning Chinese traditional philosophies and ideas within a new framework and a new vocabulary. The creation of humanistic Buddhism was one of the Buddhist responses to that climate, advanced by innovators who wanted to change Buddhism by adding something new to it. More "conservative" networks were the other protagonists of this "narrative of reform": they still promoted reforms but in terms of a resurgence of traditional practices against the "moral vacuum" of those years.[6] To borrow Holmes Welch's words, monks like Dixian 諦閑, Tanxu 倓虛, Yinguang 印廣, Xuyun 虛雲, and Hongyi 弘一 "were persons for whom practice was of the essence, who remained aloof from the world rather than seeking for status in it, who wanted to restore Buddhism to what it had been rather than to make it into something new. They feared that, if it were made into something as new as T'ai-hsu seemed to be proposing, it would no longer be Buddhism."[7]

At the same time, in a colonized Taiwan, contemporary movements—like the New Culture movement (*Xin wenhua yundong* 新文化運動)—influenced certain Buddhist networks and urged them to innovations that resemble the Chinese humanistic Buddhism, although that label was not adopted. This is when the socialist, communist, and Marxist ideologies formed in Japan; the Taiwanese learned about Marxism through the Japanese communists and then adopted Marxist ideas to lead a revolution against the same colonizers.

The first phase of definition, planning, and attempts of concrete implementation found impediments in the official new regulations on religion in the late 1930s and even more in the conflict and later rise to power of the communist power and the establishment of the Peoples' Republic of China (PRC). The early passing of Taixu probably also undermined much strengthening of humanistic Buddhism in China before the 1980s.

Nonetheless, it is in this apparent moment of crisis that humanistic Buddhism started a second phase of development, this time in Taiwan and through the efforts of Cihang, who moved to Taiwan in the late 1940s, and a second group of voices, the so-called Taixu's legacy, which included monastics like Dongchu 東初 (1908–1977), Yinshun 印順 (1906–2005), Xingyun 星雲 (b. 1927), and Shengyan 聖嚴 (1930–2009). Their efforts combined with local dynamics heritage from the colonial period. This is how, between the late 1940s and the 1980s, Taiwan hosted a new interpretation and the second real concretization of humanistic Buddhism, and a group of local figures (including the nun Zhengyan 證嚴, b. 1937) emerged as protagonists of this phase.

Since the late 1980s, while Taiwan continued the promotion of humanistic Buddhism, facing challenges and critique of secularization, mainland China, at the dawn of the post–Cultural Revolution, proposed a recovery of the same ideology. If in 1953 the newly established Buddhist Association of China (Zhongguo fojiao xiehui 中國佛教協會; BAC hereafter) did not emphasize humanistic Buddhism, it was the post-Mao renewed BAC (restored in 1980) that chose to elect humanistic Buddhism as one of their mottos. The resuscitation of humanistic Buddhism in the mainland, and the new meaning that it came to embrace, represent the third phase of the Chinese history of humanistic Buddhism; the lay Zhao Puchu 趙樸初 (1907–2000) was a protagonist of this phase. The spirit of reform initiated by Taixu and Yuanying 圓瑛

(1878–1953) was somehow maintained at the time of the first BAC (1953), for instance, by the monk Juzan 巨讚 (1908–1984); however, it is from the 1980s that a shift in wording and discursive narratives is perceived, with explicit reference to *the* humanistic Buddhism rooted into Taixu's thought.[8]

The beginning of the 21st century is a fourth period. In recent years, the Taiwanese model of humanistic Buddhism and the Chinese post-1980 understanding of it have met, converged, and partly merged. This newly established network of Taiwanese groups in China, and the new vision of the BAC, brought about to this later stage of development.

Throughout this long and complex history, the qualifiers *rensheng* and *renjian* have functioned as overarching conceptual categories that reflected and embedded *external* intellectual and political changes as well as the narrative of reform *internal* of Buddhist networks. Humanistic Buddhism has so been subject to many—and sometimes even contradictory—interpretations. And it has become a convenient identity label claimed also by groups who are not participating in large civic engagement; for instance, temples and communities that are mostly dedicated to the liturgical calendar attest to be practicing humanistic Buddhism, since, they argue, liturgies are *for* the people and humanistic Buddhism is, first and foremost, a Buddhism for the people (Ch: *renjian fojiao shi weiren de fojiao* 人間佛教是為人的佛教).

FIRST HALF OF THE 20TH CENTURY: FIRST THEORIES AND PRACTICES OF *RENSHENG FOJIAO* AND *RENJIAN FOJIAO*

The Beginnings in Republican China. Since the dawn of the Republican era, *rensheng fojiao* and *renjian fojiao* became signifiers of Buddhist doctrine and practice, a new view on the entanglement between monastics and laity, new prospects for a role of Buddhism and Buddhists in the public domain, and a revaluation of the samsaric world. The semantic values of *rensheng* and *renjian* came to reflect the historical and intellectual background described in the previous section. The monks Taixu and Cihang are key protagonists in the first stage of development.

Monk Taixu 太虛, 1890–1947: An Anarchist, Nationalist, and Socialist Chinese Buddhist. Taixu's conceptualization of *rensheng fojiao* developed in three decades.[9] His first thoughts are found in writings from the 1910s, at the same time of his infatuation for anarchist ideologies, where he theorized the so-called human vehicle (*rencheng* 人乘) as one of his "five vehicles" (*wucheng* 五乘).[10] According to Taixu, there is a close connection between the human vehicle and the buddha vehicle, with the former rooted in the latter, hence the argument that only in a human rebirth one can aspire to the buddhahood; these texts explain extensively the correct practice of the human vehicle and how that would ultimately lead to the final enlightenment.

In the 1920s, Taixu lectured and wrote about meaning, essence, and values of "Humanistic" as qualifier (*renshengguan* 人生觀), and he defined *rensheng fojiao* as a reform movement with the potential to "Buddhicize" (*fohua* 佛化) society as a whole.[11] These were the years of the May Fourth movement, the years when Taixu claimed that his Buddhist reforms aligned with the Guomindang (GMD) ideology and argued that his *rensheng fojiao* was instrumental to "rescue the nation" (*jiuguo* 救國, another expression of the vocabulary of that period). He built bridges between his *rensheng fojiao* and Sun Yat-sen's 孫中山 ideology and not only in the education sector.[12] For instance, to echo the "Three Principles of the People," he theorized the "Three Principles of the Buddha" (*sanfo zhuyi* 三佛主義), which is a manifesto of his *rensheng fojiao* in concrete terms: the first "Principle of the sangha" (*Foseng zhuyi* 佛僧主義) defined new plans for the administration of the monastic property, especially a new training for the sangha, and the new active role that the monastics would have played in civil society. Monastics were to be citizens of the new China first and then also spiritual guidance for the nation. The second "Principle of Buddhification" (*Fohua zhuyi* 佛化主義) laid out a plan for the Buddhadharma to actively influence, and especially reshape, societal and other non-Buddhist spheres; many aspects, from education to family life, were encouraged to go through a *fohua* process.[13] Periodicals were also established to discuss the buddhification plan, and several articles were also published on the topic.[14] The lay scholars Jiang Tesheng 蔣特生 and Tang Dayuan 唐大圓 (1885–1941), both part of the "Taixu-centred network," wrote extensively on the buddhification process. Tang Dayuan's "Xin fohua zhi biaozhun" 新佛化之標準, originally written in 1922 and published in 1924, read traditional Mahāyāna as *rensheng fojiao*; he urged the combination of being active in mundane affairs (*shijian* 世間) while guided by the otherworldly buddhdharma spirit (*chushi* 出世), with the purpose to benefit and purify (*jingyi* 淨益) society at large. The third "Principle for a Buddha land" (*Foguo zhuyi* 佛國主義) proposed further restructuring of different sectors in the public domain and advanced (humanistic) Buddhist guidelines for the process of creation of the new Chinese nation.

In the 1930s, Taixu drew a more structured definition of *rensheng fojiao* and started using the term *renjian fojiao* more consistently.[15] Quoting Taixu:

> *Renjian fojiao* is a Buddhism that does not encourage human beings to take distance from the humankind . . . ; it does not encourage the monastics to stay in the temples as hermits either. It is a Buddhism that says that Buddhist principles can ameliorate society, help humanity improve, and turn the entire world into a better place.[16]

It has been argued, even by Zhao Puchu, that Taixu proposed only a human-centered *rensheng fojiao*, which the later collective society–centered *renjian fojiao* is based on. However, a careful reading of Taixu's writings can easily reveal that the attention on societal issues was clearly evident also in Taixu's *rensheng fojiao*, which makes the difference between the two denominations quite blurry.

Finally, writings from the 1940s represent Taixu's latest manifesto of *rensheng fojiao*.[17] The book *Rensheng fojiao* 人生佛教 is usually conceived as his final declaration on humanistic Buddhism, but it is a summary of all his previous positions too.[18] These last writings also demonstrate that Taixu eventually took distance from the GMD political ideology and started embracing socialist ideologies.

Monk Cihang* 慈航*, 1893–1954: Turning Buddhism into "Societal Education" (shehui jiaoyu* 社會教育*). Before moving to Taiwan in the mid-20th century, Cihang wrote short pieces that present his understanding of humanistic Buddhism, theories, and practice.[19] He wrote editorials for the periodicals *Renjian fojiao* 人間佛教 and *Fojiao renjian* 佛教人間 that he himself founded in the 1940s and revalued the potential of human existence (*rensheng* 人生)

also in other short essays.[20] Cihang explained the interconnection between Buddhism and society and thus the need of Buddhists to engage in societal affairs.[21] His arguments resonated with Taixu's position:

> We, on the one hand practice the way of the Buddha, on the other also need to catch up with the time we are living in. . . . However, there are a number of monks and nuns who do not understand this principle, . . . and neglect the critical phase our society and nation are going through.[22]

Like Taixu and other contemporary monks, Cihang also compiled several short articles on how (the newly defined humanistic) Buddhism could "rescue the nation" (*jiuguo*), proving the existence of an overarching pattern and public discourse shared by all the exponents of this *new* Buddhism.[23] And like Taixu, Cihang also conceived the reformed monks as special "religious teachers" (defined *zongjiao shi* 宗教師 by Taixu and *jiaoshi* 教師 by Cihang) who could offer not only civic but also spiritual guidance in the making of the *new* China.

In Cihang's writings, (*renjian*) Buddhism is defined as "education" (*jiaoyu* 教育). He listed Buddhism as one of the three main religions available in China and categorized it as a form of national education (*guojia de jiaoyu* 國家的教育); it is the latter that gives Buddhism the ability to "rescue the nation," Cihang argued.[24] He explained that there are three types of education: (a) the education given within the household (*jiating jiaoyu* 家庭教育), (b) the education given at school (*xuexiao jiaoyu* 學校教育), and (c) the education given within/for society (*shehui jiaoyu* 社會教育). Since Buddhism offers guidance to society and compensates for all the deficiencies of the other two forms of education (within family and school), then Buddhism is education, with a societal function, and the potential to guarantee ethical sustainability and rescue the nation. Once in Taiwan, Cihang concretized his plans further.

Humanistic Buddhism, Marxism, and Socialism. Cihang and Taixu are only two major voices in the early decades of the 20th century, but not the only protagonists of this early humanistic Buddhism. A reading of Buddhist journals from the Republican period reveals a large number of articles and authors, and hence a complex discourse. A piece from the 1930s by the monk Fafang 法舫 well summarizes the debates on humanistic Buddhism that had developed in China until then: *renjian fojiao* is depicted as the only Buddha's teachings, the "real" Buddhism that declined and needed to be restored, a Buddhism that connects with both Theravada and Mahāyāna.[25]

In 1932, the monk Jianying 鑑瑩 published a highly articulated analysis of Marxism from the perspective of the buddhadharma (*fofa* 佛法); this article reinforced the statement that Marxism and the buddhadharma walked on parallel paths, but still claimed, in its conclusion, the superiority of the latter. Jianying traced the history of Marxism, from its first formulation in Europe to the spread in East Asia; he associated Marxism with the theory of evolution, materialism, and Hegel's dialectics and highlighted Marxism's theory of class warfare for the final goal of a classless society. Jianying explained why Marxism, which is defined as the "humanistic theory" (*renjian xueli* 人間學理) for the government of society, might have not been completely in conflict with the buddhadharma. Nevertheless, after a detailed study of Marxism from the viewpoints of Buddhist traditions, Jianying identified the excellence of Buddhism in its doctrine of egalitarianism, the teaching of compassion, and the thought of no-self and emptiness.[26]

Two years later, in 1934, Shuyi 蜀一 also drew a parallel between socialism and the emerging *rensheng* and *renjian fojiao*. Socialism and *renjian* Buddhism, Shuyi argued, may seem to be similar because they both oppose distinctions in race and social classes and both advocate forms of egalitarianism. Yet socialism appears still limited in comparison with *renjian* Buddhism since the latter preaches equality among all the living beings and compassion; it is not just concerned with social egalitarianism.[27] In the same year, the monk Jichen 寄塵 (1885–1974) explained that buddha could be seen as a socialist of this time, for his fights against the caste systems and regimes of inequality.[28]

Taiwan during the Colonial Period. The expressions *rensheng fojiao* and *renjian fojiao* labeled reforms that were theorized and enacted in the first half of 20th-century China, although most of those ideas and ideals circulated in other neighboring areas too. Because of this regional discourse, some essence of *rensheng fojiao* and *renjian fojiao* may be found outside China, under different terms, and unrelated to the specific reform movement based and centered on the figure of Taixu. Colonized Taiwan offers some good examples in that respect. Lin Delin 林德林 (1890–1951), also known as the "Taiwanese Martin Luther" (*Taiwan Mading Lude* 台灣馬丁路德) and the "new monk" (*xin seng* 新僧), proposed a set of reforms in Buddhism and society. However, we need to look at Lin Qiuwu 林秋梧 (1903–1934) to see initiatives that embedded more consistently features of humanistic Buddhism.

There have been meetings and cooperation between Chinese and Taiwanese Buddhists too, for instance, via the East Asian Buddhist Union (*dongya fojiao lianhehui* 東亞佛教聯合會), established in 1920s and the World Buddhist Movement (*shijie fojiao yundong* 世界佛教運動) that commenced in 1923. Representatives of the Chinese Association for the Buddhification of the New Youth (*Fohua xin qingnian hui* 佛化新青年會) visited Taiwan in the mid-1920s, besides obvious parallels between Lin Qiuwu's reform program and the objectives of that same association.[29]

Lin Qiuwu* 林秋梧*, 1903–1934: Taiwanese Early Version of Humanistic Buddhism. Lin Qiuwu was the lay name of the monk Zhengfeng 證峰, a monk based at Kaiyuan Temple (Kaiyuan si 開元寺) in Tainan. Lin Qiuwu was, first of all, an intellectual and social activist in the New Culture movement (*xin wenhua yundong* 新文化運動), committed to embrace Marxism and oppose the colonial power.[30] In 1927 Lin visited Kaiyuan Temple and in the same year he was ordained as a Buddhist monk; he studied in Japan, at Komazawa University, under the guidance of the Soto Zen master and intellectual Nukariya Kaiten 忽滑谷快天 (1867–1934), from 1927 to 1930. And, eventually, he returned to Taiwan and Kaiyuan Temple, where he combined his monastic practice with social activism: Lin wrote about Buddhist–Marxist theories and even reproposed Guo Moruo's 郭沫若 (1892–1978) piece, from 1923, on a fictitious encounter between Marx and Confucius. The short piece revolved around a dialectic and symbolic debate between the two philosophers on differences and similarities between their systems of thought.[31]

Lin Qiuwu set up a considerable reform plan for Buddhism, articulated in six points, which, at least in part, resembles the same arguments that Taixu and others proposed in China from the 1920s to the 1940s, for instance, the call against any theistic view in Buddhism or superstitious beliefs, to be replaced with a concrete societal-oriented practice, pretty much the *rushi* principle that was popular in China in the same years. Second, Lin Qiuwu proposed a thorough reform of the sangha: monastics had to receive higher education, be trained in Western philosophies and ideologies, and engage actively in the public domain. A final point was the urgency to improve women's education and position in society, and Lin referred to both nuns and laywomen. The bodhisattva path is seen as a foundational practice for humanistic Buddhism; if Taixu and Cihang claimed that the new monks had to be first of all citizens of the new China and "religious teachers," Lin Qiuwu continued on that line but took a step further and argued that the real bodhisattvas were the avant-garde intellectuals who are reforming society and turning it into a pure land, something that reminds us of Taixu's "bodhisattva of Progress," to borrow Ritzinger's terms.[32]

SECOND HALF OF THE 20TH CENTURY AND THE EARLY 21ST CENTURY

Postcolonial Taiwan. Around the mid-20th century, when China was moving into a new political phase, with drastic changes for the religious landscape and communities, Taiwan passed from the hands of the Japanese to a Chinese (GMD) "colonization," which also meant a decreased presence of Japanese Buddhism on the island and a new process of reinvention of Chinese Buddhism. Several sangha members, including promoters of humanistic Buddhism, fled from China to Taiwan from the late 1940s to the early 1950s. The same multifaceted "narrative of reform" that unfolded in Republican China continued then in Taiwan, where negotiations between a more conservative understanding of Buddhist practice and the so-called reform Buddhism also occurred.

Within the humanistic Buddhism network, most of the Chinese monks who moved to Taiwan belonged to two groups: the Yinshun-centered circle and the Cihang-centered circle. In the only six years that he spent in Taiwan, Cihang's threefold mission that he defined as distinctive of his humanistic Buddhism (but we could see recurrent in several other protagonists of the movement), namely, the promotion of sangha education (*jiaoyu* 教育), the advancement of knowledge of Buddhist culture (*wenjua* 文化), and an active engagement in charity (*cishan* 慈善), attracted a large number of followers and are still remembered in his community in Xizhi 汐止. Like Taixu, and unlike Yinshun, Cihang remained inclined more to Chinese Mahāyāna and less to a recovery of the Indian tradition; this is why he was critical of Yinshun and even wrote an unpublished essay, titled *Jiaru meiyou dacheng* 假如沒有大乘, to defame the latter.[33] It was Yinshun, however, who became regarded as one of the main theorizers of humanistic Buddhism in Taiwan. Probably for his relationship with Taixu, senior local monks and laity chose him, rather than the elder Cihang, to lead the renaissance of Chinese Buddhism on the island, a preference that might have contributed to the tension between the two monks.

Monk Yinshun* 印順, *1906–2005: Taixu's Legacy and Indian Buddhism in Dialogue. Whether and how the monk Yinshun can be classified as a protagonist of "humanistic Buddhism" is the main question for this section.[34] What we find in his writings and an analysis of the maturing of his understanding of Buddhism may reveal a picture that is quite distant from the more popular simplistic narrative that has projected Yinshun as simply the continuator of Taixu's humanistic Buddhism. This assessment is problematic also because it does not consider all the shades of humanistic Buddhism that are found in Taixu.

One reason behind this simplistic narrative could be the importance, felt in Taiwan, to connect the humanistic Buddhism that was developing in postcolonial Taiwan to the reform Buddhism native to Republican China. This was pivotal in building further distance between Taiwanese Buddhism and the tradition of the former Japanese colonizer. The figure of Yinshun became instrumental in this mission as he was, among all the Chinese monks who fled to Taiwan, a close student of Taixu's. Yinshun was seen as the heir of Taixu and therefore the best candidate to be the patriarch founder of postcolonial Taiwanese (humanistic) Buddhism. Yinshun was the bridge between pre-communist modern Chinese Buddhism and postcolonial Taiwan, and his disciples from Taiwan were the first generation of the Taiwanese part of the humanistic Buddhism lineage rooted in Taixu. This projection explains why, after his passing, Taiwanese newspapers depicted Yinshun as a "Humanistic Buddhism" "patriarch" and discussed a possible "lineage transmission" (*yimai chuancheng* 一脈傳承) of humanistic Buddhism. This lineage transmission had the reformer monk Taixu as initial "patriarch," Tzu Chi's founder, the nun Zhengyan, as the current major representative, and frames Yinshun as the intermediate (and bridging) position between (the Chinese) Taixu and (the Taiwanese) Zhengyan.[35]

Nonetheless, a reading of Yinshun's oeuvre reveals some considerable differences from Taixu's views and certainly a distance from the humanistic Buddhism of the later Tzu Chi. In the late 1980s, Yinshun himself wrote, "The *renjian fojiao* that I am promoting has been certainly influenced by the eminent Taixu, however it is also quite different [from Taixu's]."[36] And in reference to the many humanitarian activities that were using the label of "Humanistic Buddhism," he argued that "*renjian fojiao* is not one of the many charity activities carried out in the secular world."[37]

Similarly to Taixu and others, Yinshun drew a distinction (and progression) from *rensheng fojiao* to *renjian fojiao* and claimed that *renjian fojiao* embodied the correct teachings of the buddha, as it is in the human realm that the buddhahood could be achieved.[38] Furthermore, also in line with Taixu and others, Yinshun used a passage from the *Ekottarika-āgama* to reinforce that argument.[39] And like Taixu and others, Yinshun paid attention to the practice in this world and opposed a Buddhist practice that focused on the postmortem.

Unlike Taixu, and due to the different historical and political milieu, Yinshun did not politicize his humanistic Buddhism, and he did not engage mostly in social welfare. As Yinshun stated in several of his publications, humanistic Buddhism had to embody the core essence of the buddhadharma (*qili* 契理) and also adapt to the here and now (*qiji* 契機). Therefore, he did not criticize the concrete actions that took place at the time of Taixu; instead, he highly praised the reform movement that made Buddhists (and non-Buddhists) understand the relevance of Buddhism in one's own lifetime and society. Finally, differently from Taixu and others like the monk Cihang, Yinshun proposed a revaluation of Indian Buddhism, merged pre-Mahāyāna and early Mahāyāna teachings, and indicated that the core of (his) humanistic Buddhism was to be found in the bodhisattva practice framed in that specific doctrinal context. In so doing, Yinshun's humanistic Buddhism also participated in the revival of interest in "original Buddhism" (*yuanshi fojiao*) found in the late Qing and Republican period.[40]

Within Yinshun's writings, we read the first references to *renjian fojiao* and preliminary arguments in the 1950s, first comprehensive exposition in the 1970s, and eventually the systematization of its doctrine in the late 1980s and early 1990s.[41] The following paragraph highlights three main points that recur throughout his oeuvre and form the core of his final manifesto of humanistic Buddhism.

First, Yinshun's humanistic Buddhism implied progress from the commitment to be a bodhisattva in this world to the achievement of buddhahood. To quote his own words:

> Humanistic Buddhism [*renjian fojiao*] is the essence of the all Buddhadharma. It develops through the process 'Human being—bodhisattva—Buddha', which means, human beings developing the Bodhi-mind and cultivating the bodhisattva practice, to finally achieving the buddhahood through the bodhisattva path.[42]

Second, humanistic Buddhism practice is worded not just as bodhisattva practice but also as "Human bodhisattva Practice" (*ren pusa xing* 人菩薩行) and is rooted into the early Buddhism at the time of the buddha: "The Human bodhisattva Practice entailed by 'Humanistic Buddhism' is based on the Buddhadharma at the time of the Buddha Sakyamuni."[43] It is a Buddhist practice that embodies not just the "original" buddhadharma but also its development at the time of (Nāgārjuna's) early Mahāyāna, or, to use Yinshun's words: "It is with *renjian fojiao* and the Human bodhisattva practice (*ren pusa xing* 人菩薩行) that Buddhadharma (*fofa* 佛法) and Early Mahāyāna (*chuqi dasheng* 初期大乘) reveal themselves."[44] Yinshun elaborated this argument further in his *panjiao* 叛教, where he identified different forms of bodhisattva practice, going from the early Indian Mahāyāna (namely, early Mādhyamika) to late Indian Mahāyāna (namely, Yogācāra).[45] And finally, in terms of doctrine, what is this human bodhisattva practice? It is based, according to Yinshun, on the threefold mind (*san xin* 三心): the bodhi mind (*puti xin* 菩提心), the great compassion mind (*dabei xin* 大悲心), the realization of the empty nature (*kongxing jian* 空性見).[46]

Even if Yinshun argued that humanistic Buddhism needed to fit the here and now (*qiji*), he was critical of certain developments that had developed in Taiwan at the end of the 20th century; in the process of fitting the here and now, this Taiwanese humanistic Buddhism seemed not to be based on a proper knowledge of the teachings (*qili*). According to Yinshun, Taiwanese humanistic Buddhism was then generating a process of secularization and corruption of the dharma, the same problems that had occurred in the final stage of development of Indian Buddhism.[47] Yinshun denounced a practice that was labeled *renjian fojiao* but did not reflect the doctrinal spirit that he had explained in his works. To borrow his disciple Houguan's 厚觀 (b.1956) words, for Yinshun "*renjian fojiao* must not keep apart from the essence of *fojiao*, otherwise there would be just *renjian* and not *renjian 'fojiao'*!"[48]

The following paragraphs explain how Yinshun's peers and disciples continued along Yinshun's line of thought but also took some distance from him.

Monk Yanpei* 演培*, 1917–1996: The Transmission to Southeast Asia. The monk Yanpei, long-term peer and follower of Yinshun, merged Yinshun's human bodhisattva practice with Taixu's early plans and brought these two lines of thought to a new synthesis. Among the "Yinshun network," Yanpei was the monk who lectured and spread humanistic Buddhism in

Southeast Asia, including Vietnam. And since 1963, he made Singapore a new space for preaching and concretizing his own humanistic Buddhism.[49]

In a speech in 1958, Yanpei underlined the Buddhist value of the three principles of the people (*san min zhuyi* 三民主義), explained a parallel between the Buddhist "Pure Land on Earth" and the Confucian Great Unity (*datong* 大同), and promoted the *Vimalakīrti Nirdeśa Sūtra* as a valid manual for the practice of humanistic Buddhism. In so doing, Yanpei reproposed what Taixu had stressed earlier in the late 1920s.[50] In line with Taixu, as well as later exponents of humanistic Buddhism, Yanpei urged to establish a "Mahāyāna Buddhism in/for the Human Realm" (*renjian de dacheng fojiao* 人間的大乘佛教), with civic engagement as its core essence: "In sum, Buddhism is the Buddhism of the peoples (*dazhonghua de fojiao* 大眾化的佛教), and is the Buddhism that centers on benefitting others (*litahua de fojiao* 利他化的佛教)."[51] The Singapore Buddhist Welfare Services was established in 1981 within this framework. From the 1930s to the 1950s, Taixu, Cihang, and others founded Buddhist journals and run radio programs to circulate their dharma preaching; and Yanpei, to fit a new era, added another media platform: television broadcasting. From the 1990s onward, more social and even digital media will be adopted by humanistic Buddhists in China, Taiwan, and outside the Chinese region.

Post-1980 Taiwan: Transnational "Humanistic Buddhism." A new page in the history of humanistic Buddhism was written in post-1980 Taiwan. The lifting of the martial arts and the democratization process created more space and opportunities for religious groups and more venues for humanistic Buddhism to (re)define itself and be part of the private and public domains.

Instrumental was the expansion of Buddhist groups into transnational Buddhist enterprises, especially the cases of Foguangshan 佛光山 (established in 1967), Fagushan 法鼓山 (established in 1987), and Tzu Chi Foundation (*Ciji gongdehui* 慈濟功德會; founded in 1966) more specifically.[52] Xingyun 星雲 (b. 1927), founder of Foguangshan, and Shengyan 聖嚴 (1930–2009), founder of Fagushan, moved to Taiwan already in 1949, while Zhengyan 證嚴 (b. 1937), founder of Tzu Chi, is a native of Taiwan.[53] These groups claim to promote and represent humanistic Buddhism; each of them gave their own interpretations of what "Humanistic Buddhism" entails and how their programs were (or not) connected with its past and were positioned in/shaping its future.

Xingyun declared explicitly in several publications, including official biographies and autobiographies, that his humanistic Buddhism is indeed rooted in Taixu's ideals.[54] Zhengyan also acknowledged how Taixu inspired her to embark on the practice of humanistic Buddhism but admitted even more her indebtedness to Yinshun and Yinshun's humanistic Buddhism. Parallels with Taixu's *rensheng fojiao* and Yinshun's *renjian fojiao* are also found in Shengyan's declarations. Nonetheless, their portrayal of the history of humanistic Buddhism appears to focus on only some general aspects of Taixu's and Yinshun's positions, without a proper consideration of the contexts wherein these positions had emerged; the result is that these claimed connections seem quite fragile and easily contested; while the need to belong to a certain "lineage" or "narrative" appears as the main priority.

The vocabulary used by these groups includes key expressions that can be found in Taixu's or Yinshun's writings and in many other representatives of the early stages of humanistic

Buddhism. For instance, according to Xingyun, humanistic Buddhism has six characteristics: (a) "humanity-ness" (*renjian xing* 人間性), (b) "emphasis on the daily life" (*shenghuo xing* 生活性), (c) "altruism" (*lita xing* 利他性), (d) "positivity" (*xilexing* 喜樂性), (e) "adaptation to specific time and place" (*shidai xing* 時代性), and (f) "universalism" (*puji xing* 普濟性).[55] This manifesto of humanistic Buddhism recalls discourses from early-20th-century China: humanistic Buddhism should be seen as beneficial to society, from the micro-space of the family to the macro-sphere of the nation and beyond. Buddhism is not a passive culture anymore, characterized by an ascetic monastic community but an active agent in the public domain. Finally, humanistic Buddhism adjusts to the time and place (*qiji*), without losing buddha's core teaching as doctrinal essence (*qili*). Zhengyan's emphasis on the humanistic bodhisattva (*renjian pusa* 人間菩薩) also is reminiscent of previous protagonists.[56] The focus on charity and social welfare, missions of culture and education (for the sangha and the laity), adoption of media platforms—these features seem to repeat previous programs of humanistic Buddhism, although the contents and purposes of the new programs have changed to align to different political and societal environments.

There are also clear differences between the past and the present of humanistic Buddhism, like the new prominence given to transnationalism and the explicit attempt to respond to the new global challenges of the contemporary era. Expressions like "globalization" (*quanqiuhua* 全球化), "dialogue" (*duihua* 對話) especially with non-Buddhist institutions, "environmental protection" (*huanbao* 環保), and "climate change" (*qihou bianquan* 氣候變遷) are becoming keywords of this new phase and groups.

The Case of Taiwanese Nuns: Missions of Education and Civic Engagement. More nuns in Taiwan, besides the famous Zhengyan and those affiliated with organizations like Foguangshan and Fagushan, followed, sometimes explicitly and sometimes implicitly, principles of humanistic Buddhism, contributed to defining its most recent history, and certainly reinforced the role of the female order within humanistic Buddhism. Most of these nuns were prominent in the sectors of education and social welfare.

The nun Xiaoyun 曉雲 (1913–2004), a native of Hong Kong but in Taiwan since the late 1960s, had been an acclaimed painter before joining the sangha. As a nun, she continued her mission to spread the dharma through the arts and Tiantai philosophy and became popular for opening an institute of higher education in the late 1980s (then approved by the Taiwanese Ministry of Education in the early 1990s). In the early 1990s, she planned and eventually founded Huafan University (Huafan daxue 華梵大學), which still remains a renowned private university in the outskirts of Taipei. She is remembered as a philosopher, an artist, and an educator (*jiaoyujia* 教育家). She promoted what in English is usually translated as "Enlightened education" but could probably be renamed "Awakening Education" (*jue de jiaoyu* 覺的教育); she was an educator promoting Buddhist principles and Confucian values, with the aim to establish "whole persons" (*quanren* 全人) and thereafter benefit humanity. For these reasons, she received the epithet of an educator committed to realize a "Pure Land on Earth" (*yinzao renjian jingtu de jiaoyujia* 引造人間淨土的教育家).[57]

The nun Lianchan 蓮懺 is known in Taiwan with the title "guiding master of the blind" (*mangren daoshi* 盲人導師) for her service to visually impaired persons. She established the Chinese Buddhist Library for the Blind (Zhongguo fojiao mangren tushu zhongxin 中國盲

人圖書中心), in 1987; in 1990, she renovated the institute that was then upgraded to a Chinese Buddhist Cultural Centre for the Blind (*zhongguo fojiao mangren wenhua zhongxin* 中國佛教盲人文化中心).[58]

Certainly the most celebrated nun in Taiwan, after Zhengyan, is Zhaohui 昭慧 (b. 1957); a native of Myanmar, she has been Yinshun's student and follower, a promotor of "Humanistic Buddhism," strongly committed to social activism, and a professor at the Hsuan Chuang University (Xuanzang daxue 玄奘大學). Her activism is a concretization of several programs that humanistic Buddhism has endorsed: she has fought for human rights, women's rights, animal rights, environmental protection, and climate change. Zhaohui became a controversial figure in the Chinese sangha since she had advocated for the suppression of the eight chief rules for nuns (*ba jingfa* 八敬法); she was on the international news as she officiated a lesbian Buddhist wedding in 2012, which was also the very first lesbian wedding ever organized in Taiwan; among her initiatives, there is also the foundation of the Life Conservationist Association of China (*zhonghua minguo shengming xiehui* 中華民國生命協會, 1993).[59]

China after Mao: Humanistic Buddhism, the Buddhist Association of China, and Cross-Strait Exchanges. The practice of *renjian fojiao* (*jianxing renjian fojiao sixiang* 踐行人間佛教思想) is listed on the BAC website among the principles that the association abides by; other guidelines include patriotism (expressed with the usual formula *aiguo aijiao* 愛國愛教), the support to the leadership of the Chinese Communist Party, and the adherence to the socialism with "Chinese characteristics" (*Zhongguo tese shehui zhuyi* 中國特色社會主義).[60] There seems to be a new space for humanistic Buddhism in China after the establishment of the PRC and the later new opening to religion initiated by Deng Xiaoping 鄧小平. At the same time, scholars have noticed that the embedding of *renjian fojiao* within the BAC directives has changed throughout the last two to four decades, and certainly more studies on this matter are needed.[61]

Zhao Puchu* 趙樸初*, 1907–2000: Revalidating the Figure of Taixu. Zhao Puchu could be seen as the most important reformer in the modern history of Chinese Buddhism after Taixu. Zhao Puchu became well known for his positions in Chinese politics and for being the first chairman of the BAC (1980–2000) after the Cultural Revolution.[62] He is certainly the first Buddhist figure who contributed to the renaissance of humanistic Buddhism in China, a rediscovery of the figure of Taixu, and the revival of part of Taixu's *rensheng fojiao* and *renjian fojiao*; certainly, the framework of socialist ideals (*shehui zhuyi* 社會主義) is more stressed from the 1980s than in the 1940s.[63] Similar to what we have seen with Taiwanese organizations, the link to Taixu is generic, with no specific reference to the context(s) wherein Taixu developed his thought and not much consideration of the evolving definition of humanistic Buddhism throughout Taixu's career. Nonetheless, Zhao Puchu's role in revalidating the figure of Taixu in the eyes of the Buddhist and political spheres was the first step of a new phase in the history of humanistic Buddhism on the mainland. It also created a common denominator between Buddhism in the mainland after Mao and the new Buddhist organizations in Taiwan, an essential step in the process to restart and strengthen connections between Taiwanese and Chinese Buddhists at a time of fragile cross-strait relations.

Monk Xuecheng 學誠, b. 1966: Interfaith Dialogue, Transnationalism, and "Soft Power." The previous chairman of the BAC (2015 to 2018), the monk Xuecheng 學誠 (b. 1966), extended the concretization of humanistic Buddhism further. Following a trend present with Taixu, although on a different scale, Xuecheng joined contemporary Taiwanese Buddhists and lectured widely, abroad, on humanistic Buddhism. Like what Zhao Puchu proposed since the 1980s, Xuecheng also underlined a historical development that is rooted in Taixu's theories and programs and then included other protagonists like Fafang and Yinshun. Differently from Zhao Puchu, Xuecheng engaged in more, and regular, constructive exchanges with Taiwanese representatives of humanistic Buddhism, mainly the monk Xingyun and Foguangshan. While Xingyun writes in support of Xi Jinping's "Chinese dream" (*zhongguo meng* 中國夢) and one-China policy, and Foguangshan opens branch temples and cultural centers (called *wenjiaoguan* 文教館) in China, Xuecheng received an honorary doctoral degree from Foguangshan's Nanhua University in Taiwan (2017).[64] The merging of contemporary Chinese and Taiwanese humanistic Buddhism, a key feature of the fourth phase of its overall history, is then achieved.

Xuecheng's book *Xinyang yu duihua* 信仰與對話 added a new theme in the Buddhist engagement with the public sphere.[65] The strong involvement in interfaith dialogue and intercultural exchanges took Taixu's theories to a new level and indeed recalls initiatives of contemporary Taiwanese organizations like Foguangshan and Tzu Chi. The Chinese concept of "harmony" (*hexie* 和諧), which is a key element in Chinese civilization, is now finally taken beyond the Chinese borders and becomes a lesson from China to the contemporary globalized world. We should also question whether this interest in global outreach could be more than a religious mission and proselytism and perhaps another Chinese (political) "soft power" program.

Buddhist Nuns after Mao: Reproposing the Taiwanese Model? Nuns are also leading figures in this post-1980 humanistic Buddhism. Two examples are listed here. In Wenzhou, the Taiping nunnery, which was reopened and renovated in 2003 under the guidance of the nun Rufa 如法 (b. 1956), established the Taiping Charity Association (*Taiping cishan gongdehui* 太平慈善功德會) in 2008, on the occasion of the earthquake that hit Sichuan. Rufa manages this association with the laity, similar to what Zhengyan has been doing with Tzu Chi. Another example is in Tianjin, the Tianjin Buddhist Charity (*Tianjin foci jijinhui* 天津佛慈基金會), which was founded in 2005 by the nun Miaoxian 妙賢. Both admitted being inspired by Zhengyan and Tzu Chi.

THE IDEAL OF A "PURE LAND ON EARTH" (*RENJIAN JINGTU* 人間淨土)

The establishment of a "Pure Land on Earth" (or better, the transformation of the samsaric world into a pure land) has been a common objective in the practice of humanistic Buddhism, in China and Taiwan, from the early 20th century up to now. The background arguments say, as humanistic Buddhism preaches to concentrate on the in-life instead of the postmortem, then it also advances the target of experiencing a pure land in this same life, without the need to wait for a rebirth, and if any individual purifies the own heart/mind (*xin* 心), then the entire society would be "purified." However, how to reach this "purification" goal and what constitutes such a pure land vary according to the Buddhist figures in question and their historical and social environments.

In his writings from the late 1920s onward, Taixu described his "Pure Land on Earth" as a concrete space; for him, it was more than just a place where Buddhists practice the correct dharma.[66] Recent scholarship has underlined that Taixu's theorization of the Pure Land on Earth show clear influences from the *Vimalakīrti Nirdeśa Sūtra*, of anarchist ideologies, and his proposed cult of Maitreya.[67] Toward the end of his career, Taixu even proposed a similarity between the Pure Land on Earth and the Marxist classless society. Cihang wrote extensively about the creation of a Pure Land on Earth, restating how peace in local society and in the world is something that only humans could create, starting from their own self-cultivation; it was not a result of divine intervention; as he put it, *xin jing ze guotu jing* 心淨則國土淨.[68] Similar statements are found also later, in Shengyan's works for instance, and with constant reference to the *Vimalakīrti Nirdeśa Sūtra*.[69]

In the same decades but in Taiwan, Lin Qiuwu did not use terms like *renjian jingtu* (Pure Land on Earth), but his *xianshi jingtu* 現世淨土 (Pure Land in this Contemporary World), *citu de xifang* 此土的西方 (Western Paradise on this Earth), and *ditu de tiantang* 地土的天堂 (World Paradise) certainly echoed it. Quoting Lin Qiuwu, "Pure Land is not necessarily in the West, but it can be found everywhere, even in the South, North and East. And are the human beings, with their efforts, to establish it," a quotation that, according to Taiwanese historian Jiang Canteng 江燦騰, predates Yinshun's definition of Pure Land as explained in the essay *Jingtu xinlun* 淨土新論.[70] Similarly to Taixu and Yinshun (the latter only in his early stage of writing), Lin Qiuwu argued that the real pure land is the Marxist classless society and could be established in this same world. Also in line with Taixu, he drew an explicit parallel between a pure land on earth and the Confucian Great Unity; in his address at a Chinese–Vietnamese Buddhist Assembly (1958), Yanpei also made a parallel between Buddhist Pure Land on Earth (*renjian jingtu*) and the Confucian Great Unity (*datong shijie* 大同世界).

Yinshun's interpretation of traditional pure land practice and then his view of a possible Pure Land on Earth have been very controversial in China and Taiwan; even today, Chinese scholars claim that Yinshun did not understand pure land at all and read his call for a correct practice and transformation of this world into a pure land as a mere criticism and challenge to the more traditional Amidism.[71]

The present calls for protection of the environment and responses to climate change have added new narratives to the discourse of the Pure Land on Earth. In 2007, Shengyan created the Life Memorial Garden (*huanbao shengming yuanqu* 環保生命園區) as an alternative to memorial pagodas or traditional cemeteries and related to his "Four Kinds of Environmental Protection" (*sizhong huanbao* 四種環保).[72] Tzu Chi has also been a crucial player in this narrative, with, for instance, their recycling programs and the declaration of "Tzu Chi environmental sustainability days."[73]

REVIEW OF LITERATURE

Humanistic Buddhism (as a rendition of *renshengfojiao* 人生佛教 and *renjian fojiao* 人間佛教) embeds diverse meanings and practices and has been often used in combination with—or in replacement of—expressions like "(socially) engaged Buddhism," "Buddhist activism," or "modern Buddhism." Scholars have debated overlapping and distinctions among all these denominations, with the purpose to eventually highlight what Chinese and Taiwanese humanistic Buddhism might really mean.[74]

The publication of *Fojiao yu rensheng* 佛教與人生, within the well-known 100-volume collection edited by Zhang Mantao 張曼濤 (1933–1981) from the late 1970s, has been a milestone in the critical assessment of the subject. In line with the other volumes of the series, this anthology gathered mostly primary sources, and all from the first half of the 20th century; some explored *rensheng fojiao* and others discussed *renjian fojiao*. In the preface, Zhang Mantao argued that *rensheng fojiao* and *renjian fojiao* represented two phases of development of the same phenomenon: the former was more concerned about the individual human existence, while the latter concentrated on the societal dimension, moving from "human" as singular to "humans" in their plurality. This, indeed, became the standard way to see the dialectical relations between the two terms and what they imply.[75]

More recently, especially in the past decade, Chinese scholars have completed quite comprehensive and multivolume manuscripts on humanistic Buddhism. Some early works show attention only to selected figures and a primary interest in the background scenario and development in China and Taiwan, repeating the usual narrative that sees humanistic Buddhism as rooted in Taixu 太虛, then reshaped by Taixu's student Yinshun 印順, and finally brought to a new definition by Taiwan-based organizations (like Foguangshan 佛光山, Fagushan 法鼓山, and Tzuchi 慈濟), on one hand, and by new leaders of the BAC (like Zhao Puchu 趙樸初), on the other. Some of these works discuss the historical context wherein humanistic Buddhism arose; they question connections between the focus on human life and world (*renjianhua* 人間化) and the process of secularization (*shisuhua* 世俗化) of Buddhism and offer brief surveys on manifestations of humanistic Buddhism in Hong Kong and Macao. Others even elaborate on Yinshun as founder of his own "school" (*Yinshun men* 印順門) of humanistic Buddhism, which is explained as a network of figures and temples from Taiwan to Southeast Asia.[76] A later multivolume project, also authored by key Chinese scholars in the field, focuses only on the post-Taixu era and explores developments from 1949 to 2015. This anthology expands on themes that have not been fully articulated in previous works; for instance, with the expression "duoyuan yiti" 多元一體, it highlights the diversity of thoughts and practices found under the label *renjian fojiao*, it classifies a number of clear lineages, their patriarchs, and their descendants and draws a clear division into regions of interest, namely, mainland China, Taiwan, Hong Kong, Macao, and overseas.[77]

This anthology is part of the series "Humanistic Buddhist Thought Library" (*Renjian fojiao sixiang wenku* 人間佛教思想文庫); more volumes in the same series are being published these days, and each of them concerns key protagonists and their writings. Because they include both reflections on exponents and understandings of humanistic Buddhism and a selection of their writings, volumes in this series function as secondary literature, as well as a database of primary sources. This recent yet substantial output made in China reflects the relevance that humanistic Buddhism has had for the BAC since the 1980s, and even more explicitly from the beginning of the 21st century. And it also suggests the significance that the umbrella concept of humanistic Buddhism had in the Buddhist relations with the government. The series is, in fact, published by the China Religious Culture Publisher (Zongjiao wenhua chubanshe 宗教文化出版社), which was affiliated to the State Administration of Religious Affairs (*Guojia zongjiao shiwuju* 國家宗教事務局) and is now connected with the United Front Work Department (*Zhonggong Zhongyang tongyi zhanxian gongzuo bu* 中共

中央統一戰線工作部). The affiliation of the publisher may suggest motives not just academic behind the selection and analysis of figures and texts.

Studies of history and features of humanistic Buddhism in Taiwan are positioned within new frameworks, like the long-term debate on the formation of Taiwanese identity, the "localization" (*bentuhua* 本土化) discourse, and the postcolonial era. Some publications contributed to reinforce the narrative that sees Taiwanese practices of humanistic Buddhism as rooted in Taixu's *rensheng fojiao*, with the implicit conclusion that they are unrelated to any Japanese form of Buddhism.[78] Other scholars argued that the postcolonial humanistic Buddhism has also intersected with the new Taiwanese politics.[79]

The construction of a linear history of humanistic Buddhism as a discourse originated in China and later transmitted to Taiwan resulted in the automatic exclusion of Taiwanese monks, from the colonial period, who expressed likeminded views even without adopting explicitly the vocabulary of humanistic Buddhism that had emerged in Republican China. The monk Lin Qiuwu 林秋悟 and the lay Lin Delin 林德林, who have been discussed at length, are examples of figures not usually included in scholarly assessments of the humanistic Buddhism discourse.[80] This approach failed to consider the shared historical, religious, and intellectual milieu that animated the East Asian region in the first decades of the 20th century and did not sufficiently investigate whether the Taiwanese form of humanistic Buddhism might have also partaken Japanese (new) religious elements.[81]

We count numerous monographic studies on selected figures, for instance, the lay Zhao Puchu or the monks Juzan 巨讚, Yinshun, and Yanpei 演培 and their interpretation and practice of humanistic Buddhism.[82] Some are more scholarly than others authored by practitioners or members of these Buddhist networks. Other book-length manuscripts assessed humanistic Buddhism as the theory and force behind the missions of organizations like Tzu Chi Foundation and Foguangshan, also highlighting their transnational spirit and attempt to create global humanistic Buddhist communities.[83]

So far, the figure of Taixu has received most of the scholarly attention, in China and beyond; publications include general studies of his life and programs, historical and intellectual contextualization of his ideals and initiatives in Republican China, and investigations of his humanistic Buddhism in relation to contemporary monks within the large Chinese region.[84] More recently, Taixu's humanistic Buddhism and his ideal of a "Pure Land on Earth" have been interpreted in light—and as effect—of Taixu's early career as anarchist.[85]

The concept of Pure Land on Earth (*renjian jingtu* 人間淨土) is addressed in almost any of the publications on history and development of humanistic Buddhism and is also a topic of focused studies, which assess how this ideal challenged and entered in conflict with the Chinese mainstream understanding of pure land practice, besides the meaning that selected Buddhists conferred to it.[86]

Humanistic Buddhism scholarship, as so far has indicated, is then an ideology (*sixiang* 思想), a forceful essence (*jingshen* 精神), an identity marker. Expressions like *rensheng* and *renjian* have become qualifiers not only for a potential pure land, or science (see Taixu's conceptualization of a "Humanistic science," *rensheng guan de kexue* 人生觀的科學), but also are found next to other teachings and practices that are pivotal in Chinese Buddhism, especially Chan; scholarly assessments of "Humanistic Chan," with a focus on either Chinese or Taiwanese leaders and communities, have already been published.[87]

PRIMARY SOURCES

Leaders of humanistic Buddhism in the Republican era delivered lectures and wrote essays where they described the semantic values of *rensheng* 人生 as a qualifier and explained their views on the essence and function of *rensheng fojiao* 人生佛教, *renjian fojiao* 人間佛教, and *renjian jingtu* 人間淨土. These manuscripts can be easily retrieved from contemporary Buddhist journals, which are now available, in great part, in a few collections; see, for instance, the projects *Minguo fojiao qikan wenxian jicheng* 民國佛教期刊文獻集成 (209 volumes), *Minguo fojiao qikan wenxian jicheng bubian* 民國佛教期刊文獻集成補編 (86 volumes), and *Minguo fojiao qikan wenxian jicheng sanbian* (民國佛教期刊文獻集成三編 (35 volumes).[88] Digitally, these Republican journals can also be retrieved from the Chinese Periodical Full-Text Database 1911–1949 (*Minguo shiqi qikan quanwen shujuku* 民國時期期刊全文數據庫 1911–1949).

In addition, the compilation of multivolume collections and anthologies with the writing of these Buddhist voices serves to read their understanding of humanistic Buddhism within the framework of their ideologies and activities; I am referring to oeuvres like, just to mention a few, the *Complete Writings of Master Taixu* (*Taixu dashi quanshu* 太虛大師全書, edited by Yinshun 印順) and the *Complete Works of Master Cihang* (*Cihang fashi quanji* 慈航法師全集).[89] There are also more recent anthologies published (or still planned) by the China Religious Culture Publisher (*zongjiao wenhua chubanshe* 宗教文化出版社), part of the series "Humanistic Buddhist Thought Library" (*Renjian fojiao sixiang wenku* 人間佛教思想文庫) that was commenced in 2017.[90]

Buddhist journals, like *The South Seas Buddhist* (*Nanying fojiao/Nan'e Bukkyō* 南瀛佛教), are also a good place to start a study of Buddhist debates in colonial Taiwan and recover short essays on ideas and activities that embed the spirit of humanistic Buddhism, although they were not named explicitly as such.[91]

For primary sources on humanistic Buddhism from the second half of the 20th century onward, the volumes published by the China Religious Culture Publisher from the Humanistic Buddhist Thought Library and articles or monographs of contemporary exponents are recommended.[92]

Various initiatives of humanistic Buddhist institutions provide primary sources in alternative formats. For instance, Foguangshan 佛光山 has opened centers for the study of humanistic Buddhism to foster debates on the subject in connection with recent global challenges. For instance, the Foguangshan Institute of Humanistic Buddhism (*Foguangshan renjian fojiao yanjiuyuan* 佛光山人間佛教研究院) (http://www.fgsihb.org/), located in Gaoxiong (Taiwan), organizes yearly international Humanistic Buddhist Symposia (*Renjian fojiao luntan* 人間佛教論壇). These initiatives can not only offer secondary literature on the topic but also provide a window to the same humanistic Buddhist institutions to observe how they are reflecting on their ideologies and missions and reshaping them to fit the future. These activities have not been limited to Taiwan. Foguangshan also inaugurated the Centre for the Study of Humanistic Buddhism (*Renjian fojiao yanjiu zhongxin* 人間佛教研究中心 (https://www.cuhk.edu.hk/arts/cshb/)) at the Chinese University of Hong Kong, which holds yearly conferences as well. Worth mentioning is also the first dictionary on humanistic Buddhism recently published in Taiwan by the same Foguangshan.[93]

Journals and radio programs served to circulate material on humanistic Buddhism in the first two phases of its development; TV channels and the establishment of media enterprises by monasteries in Taiwan from the 1990s added a new channel of communication and proselytism in the third phase. With the beginning of the new century, as humanistic Buddhism is living its fourth period of expansion, social and digital media, from Facebook to WeChat, facilitate the dissemination of primary texts and material. Social media is a new platform, which can potentially increase the audience of humanistic Buddhist groups, and offers new possibilities and strategies of representation and projection of teachings. Visual and audio material from the social media accounts of humanistic Buddhist leaders and institutions are a new genre of primary sources to be analyzed in the 21st century.

FURTHER READING

Interested readers without access to Chinese sources could start with the short overviews presented in English article-length manuscripts:

Krause, Carsten. "The Changing Functions of *renjian fojiao* in Mainland China." *Journal of the Oxford Centre for Buddhist Studies* 17 (2019): 117–143.

Pacey, Scott. "A Buddhism for the Human World: Interpretations of *Renjian Fojiao* in Contemporary Taiwan." *Asian Studies Review* 29 (2005): 61–77.

Travagnin, Stefania. "Genealogy and Taxonomy of the Twentieth-century *Renjian Fojiao* 人間佛教: Mapping a *famen* 法門 from Mainland China and Taiwan to Europe." *Renjian fojiao xuebao* 人間佛教學報 9 (2017): 180–197.

Readers can then move on to sample monographs, also in English, that analyze specific actors and institutions, based in either China or Taiwan, that created and promoted humanistic Buddhism.

Laliberté, André. *The Politics of Buddhist Organizations in Taiwan, 1989–2003: Safeguard the Faith, Build a Pure Land, Help the Poor*. London: Routledge, 2004.

Madsen, Richard. *Democracy's Dharma: Religious Renaissance and Political Development in Taiwan*. Berkeley: University of California Press, 2007.

Ritzinger, Justin. *Anarchy in the Pure Land: Reinventing the Cult of Maitreya in Modern Chinese Buddhism*. Oxford: Oxford University Press, 2017.

For those who can read Chinese sources, two recent anthologies published in China should be recommended; one explores the overall history of humanistic Buddhism:

Deng Zimei 鄧子美, Chen Weihua 陳衛華, and Mao Dongyong 毛勤勇. *Dangdai renjian fojiao sichao* 當代人間佛教思潮. Lanzhou, China: Gansu Renmin Chubanshe, 2008.

And a later collection concentrates on post-1945 developments in China as well as Hong Kong, Taiwan, Macao, and Southeast Asia:

Deng Zimei 鄧子美 and Chen Weihua 陳衛華. *Dangdai renjian fojiao chuandenglu (1949–2015)* 當代人間佛教傳燈錄 (1949–2015), 2 vols. Beijing: Zongjiao wenhua chubanshe, 2017.

To better understand humanistic Buddhism as conceived and practiced in Taiwan today, readers could peruse the works of the leaders Yinshun, Xingyun, Shengyan, and Zhengyan, which have been listed in the "Primary Sources" section.

Specifically about Buddhist women as creators and creations of humanistic Buddhism and their new role and values within the humanistic Buddhism discourse, the following could serve as initial sources:

Eichman, Jennifer. "Prominent Nuns: Influential Taiwanese Voices." *CrossCurrents* 61, no. 3 (2011): 345–373.

Lee, Chengpang, and Ling Han. "Mothers and Moral Activists: Two Models of Women's Social Engagement in Contemporary Taiwanese Buddhism." *Nova Religio: The Journal of Alternative and Emergent Religions* 19, no. 3 (2016): 54–77.

Travagnin, Stefania. "Master Yinshun and Buddhist Nuns in/for the Human Realm. Shift and Continuity From Theory to Practice of *renjian fojiao* in Contemporary Taiwan." In *The Margins of Becoming. Identity*

and Culture in Taiwan. Edited by Carsten Storm and Mark Harrison, 83–100. Wiesbaden, Germany: Harrassowitz, 2007.
Zhaohui 昭慧, and Xingguang 性廣, eds. *Xin shiji de fojiao nüxing siwei* 新世紀的佛教女性思維. Taipei: Fajie chubanshe, 2001.

At the same time, books on the recent history of Chinese and Taiwanese Buddhism could be consulted to become more acquainted with the background of the movement and contextualize it socially and historically. Three valid references could be the following:

Chen Bing 陳兵 and Deng Zimei 鄧子美. *Ershi shiji Zhongguo fojiao* 二十世紀中國佛教. Beijing: Minzu chubanshe, 2000.
Birnbaum, Raoul. "Buddhist China at the Century's Turn." *The China Quarterly*, no. 174 (2003): 428–450.
Jiang Canteng 江燦騰. *Taiwan fojiao yu xiandai shehui* 台灣佛教與現代社會. Taipei: Dongda, 1992.

For the concept of Pure Land on Earth, Jiang Canteng's volume (1989), although published more than thirty years ago, is still a solid and comprehensive overview of its history, main promoters, and doctrine:

Jiang Canteng 江燦騰. *Renjian jingtu de zhuixun: Zhongguo jinshi fojiao sixiang yanjiu* 人間淨土的追尋:中國近世佛教思想研究. Taipei: Daoxiang chubanshe, 1989.

An emerging new corpus of scholarship addresses how Chinese and Taiwanese Buddhists transmitted and translated humanistic Buddhism in non-Asian countries; these sources could be consulted for an overview of the transnationalism and globalization of the movement; see, for instance, the following:

Lau, Arnold Lindros, and Jayeel Serrano Cornelio. "Tzu Chi and the Philanthropy of Filipino Volunteers." *Asian Journal of Social Science* 43, no. 4 (2015): 376–399.
Reinke, Jens. *Mapping Modern Mahayana: Chinese Buddhism and Migration in the Age of Global Modernity*. Boston and Berlin: De Gruyter, 2021.

NOTES

1. The use of the term *humanistic Buddhism* may be problematic as it is only one of the several English translations adopted to define *rensheng fojiao* and *renjian fojiao*, besides being the official English translation of *renjian fojiao* used by Foguangshan and the Buddhist Association of China. Western publications often refer to "Humanistic Buddhism" as "Buddhism of the Human Life" or "Human Life Buddhism" when intended in the sense of *rensheng fojiao* and "Buddhism for the Human Realm" or "Human Realm Buddhism" when it refers to *renjian fojiao*. This article uses "humanistic Buddhism" in reference to the general phenomenon of *rensheng fojiao* and *renjian fojiao* but uses *rensheng fojiao* and *renjian fojiao* when it needs to be more specific to either of them.
2. Yang Huinan 楊惠南, "'Renjian fojiao' de jingdian quanshi: shi 'yuan Ru ru Fo' huoshi huigu Yindu? 「人間佛教」的經典詮釋:是「援儒入佛」或是回歸印度?," *Zhonghua foxue xuebao* 中華佛學學報 13 (2000): 479–504.
3. See T50n2063, 936b29–c20.
4. Among the most used passages from the *Ekottarika-āgama*: 佛世尊皆出人間，非由天而得也 (T02no125, 694a4–5).
5. Eric Goodell, "Taixu's Pure Land on Earth and the *Vimalakirti*," *Foguang xuebao* 佛光學報 3, no. 1 (2017): 171–200.
6. For the intellectual atmosphere of the first two decades of the Republican period and reflections on the "narrative of reform" within the Buddhist sphere, see Stefania Travagnin, "Zhongguo he Taiwan fojiao jie de wusi yinyuan: yi 1910–1930 niandai wei kaocha zhongdian" 中國與臺灣佛教界的五四因緣——以1910–1930年代為考察重點, in *Wusi yundong yu zhongguo zongjiao tiaoshi yu fazhan* 五四運動與中國宗教的調適與發展, ed. Paul R. Katz (康豹) and 呂妙芬 (Taipei: Academia Sinica, 2020), 547–577.
7. Holmes Welch, *The Buddhist Revival in China* (Cambridge, MA: Harvard University Press, 1968), 71.

8. For more about Juzan, see Xinrong 信融, *Juzan fashi yanjiu* 巨贊法師研究 (Taipei: Xinwenfeng, 2006); and Li Xiangping, "Increased Production and Education—The New Modern Buddhist Thought and Practice of Monk Juzan," *Studies in Chinese Religions* 3 (2017): 83–100.
9. Taixu's works have been published posthumously in a multivolume collection edited by Yinshun, the *Taixu dashi quanshu* 太虛大師全書. Among the many studies on Taixu, see Guo Peng 郭朋, *Taixu dashi sixiang yanjiu* 太虛大師思想研究 (Xindian, Taiwan: Yuanming chubanshe, 1996); Don A. Pittman, *Towards a Modern Chinese Buddhism: Taixu's Reforms* (Honolulu: University of Hawai'i Press, 2001); Deng Zimei 鄧子美, *Taixu dashi quanzhuan* 太虛大師全傳 (Taipei: Huiming wenhua, 2002); Chen Yongge 陳永革, *Renjian chaoyin: Taixu dashi zhuan* 人間潮音:太虛大師傳 (Taipei: Sixing wenhua chuanbo, 2016); Deng Zimei 鄧子美, ed., *Taixu juan* 太虛卷, 2 vols. (Beijing: Zongjiao wenhua chubanshe, 2017); and Justin Ritzinger, *Anarchy in the Pure Land: Reinventing the Cult of Maitreya in Modern Chinese Buddhism* (Oxford: Oxford University Press, 2017).
10. Taixu 太虛, *Fojiao rencheng zhengfa lun* 佛教人乘正法論 (Shanghai: Shijie fojiao jushilin, 1928), later included in *Taixu dashi quanshu* 太虛大師全書, ed. Yinshun 印順, vol. 5 (Hong Kong: Zhengjue lianshe, 1950), 136–143; originally composed and delivered in 1916. The "five vehicles," as postulated by Taixu, are the "human vehicle" (*rencheng* 人乘), the "divine vehicle" (*tiancheng* 天乘), the "Śrāvaka vehicle" (*shengwencheng* 聲聞乘), the "Pratyekabuddha vehicle" (*yuanjuecheng* 緣覺乘), and the "Buddha vehicle" (*rulaicheng* 如來乘).
11. Taixu 太虛, "Fojiao de rensheng guan" 佛教的人生觀, *Haichaoyin* 2, no. 12 (1921): 1–5, later reprinted in *Taixu dashi quanshu* 太虛大師全書, ed. Yinshun 印順, vol. 43 (Hong Kong: Zhengjue lianshe, 1950), 918–925; this essay was originally composed and delivered in 1920. Taixu 太虛, "Duiyu zhongguo fojiao geming seng de xunc," 對於中國佛教革命僧的訓詞, in *Taixu dashi quanshu* 太虛大師全書, ed. Yinshun 印順, vol. 34 (Hong Kong: Zhengjue lianshe, 1950), 596–604; originally composed and delivered in 1928. This is one of the first articles in which he explained how *rensheng fojiao* overlaps with GMD ideology and the definition of the three principles of the buddha (*sanfo zhuyi* 三佛主義) along the three principles of the people (*sanmin zhuyi* 三民主義).
12. Taixu defined his "Humanistic Buddhist education" (*rensheng fojiao jiaoyu* 人生佛教教育) as in line with the GMD principles and in accordance with the (Confucian) ideal of the Great Unity (*datong de daode jiaoyu* 大同的道德教育). See Taixu 太虛. "Quanguo jiaoyu huiyi tiyi'an" 全國教育會議提議案, *Haichaoyin* 海潮音 9, no. 5 (1928): 4–7.
13. Paul R. Katz, "Chen Hailiang's Vision of Buddhist Family Life: A Preliminary Study," *Journal of Chinese Religions* 47, no. 1 (2019): 33–60.
14. The following periodicals were established in early 1920s: *Xin fohua xunkan* 新佛化旬刊, *Fohua xin qingnian* 佛化新青年, *Fohua cejinhui huikan* 佛化策進會會刊, *Fohua xunkan* 佛化旬刊, *Fohua pinglun* 佛化評論, and *Fohua zhoukan* 佛化週刊. Sample articles on "Buddhification" include Tang Dayuan 唐大圓, "Xinshi de fohua" 新式的佛化, *Haichaoyin* 海潮音 5, no. 3 (1924): 9–13; Tang Dayuan 唐大圓, "Xin fohua zhi biaozhun" 新佛化之標準, *Haichaoyin* 海潮音 5, no. 6 (1924): 12–17; Jiang Tesheng 蔣特生, "Geming yu fohua" 革命與佛化, *Fohua xunkan* 佛化旬刊 82 (1927): 3–4; Jiang Tesheng 蔣特生, "Geming yu fohua" 革命與佛化, *Fohua xunkan* 佛化旬刊 83 (1927): 2–4; Jiang Tesheng 蔣特生, "Lun fohua yu sanmin zhuyi" 論佛化與三民主義, *Foguang she shekan* 佛光社社刊 3 (1928): 10–12; Jiang Tesheng 蔣特生, "Lun fohua yu sanmin zhuyi" 論佛化與三民主義, *Haichaoyin* 海潮音 9, no. 5 (1928): 4–7; Ning Mogong 甯墨公, "Diguo zhuyi yu fohua" 帝國主義與佛化, *Haichaoyin* 海潮音 8, no. 6 (1927): 9–10; and Jueren 覺人, "Shenme shi fohua shijie" 甚麼是佛化世界, *Fohua shijie* 佛化世界 1 (1923): 2. For secondary sources on "buddhification," see Hou Kunhong 侯坤宏, *Taixu shidai: Duowei shijiao xiade minguo fojiao (1912–1949)* 太虛時代:多維視角下的民國佛教 (1912–1949) (Taipei: Zhengda chubanshe, 2018): 153–198.
15. Taixu 太虛. "Ji ren cheng fo de zhen xianshi lun" 即人成佛的真現實論, in *Taixu dashi quanshu* 太虛大師全書, ed. Yinshun, vol. 47 (Hong Kong: Zhengjue lianshe, 1950), 457–464, originally composed

and delivered in 1938. Taixu 太虛, "Zenme lai jianshe renjian fojiao" 怎麼來建設人間佛教, in *Taixu dashi quanshu* 太虛大師全書, ed. Yinshun, vol.47, 431–456, originally composed and delivered in 1933.

16. Taixu 太虛, "Zenme lai jianshe renjian fojiao" 怎麼來建設人間佛教, in *Taixu dashi quanshu* 太虛大師全書, ed. Yinshun, vol. 47, 431; originally composed and delivered in 1933. English translations are mine, if not stated otherwise.
17. Taixu 太虛, "Rensheng fojiao kaiti" 人生佛教開題, *Haichaoyin* 海潮音 26, no. 1 (1945): 4–5; Taixu 太虛, "Rensheng fojiao de cengci" 人生佛教的層次, *Haichaoyin* 海潮音 26, no. 2 (1945): 5–7; and Taixu 太虛, "Rensheng de fojiao" 人生的佛教, *Zhongliu* 中流 4, no. 7–8 (1946): 78.
18. Taixu 太虛, *Rensheng fojiao* 人生佛教 (Shanghai: Dafalun shuju, 1947).
19. For more about Cihang, see Kan Zhengzong 闞正宗, *Taiwan gaoseng* 台灣高僧 (Taipei: Puti Zhangqing, 1996), 47–92. See also Cihang 慈航. *Cihang fashi quanji* 慈航法師全集, 3 vols. (Xizhi, Taiwan: Cihang tang, 1981), collection edited and published in Taipei by the Master Cihang Memorial Foundation (Cihang fashi yongjiu jinianhui 慈航法師永久紀念會); and Cihang dashi jinianji bianyinchu 慈航大師紀念集編印處, ed., *Cihang dashi jinianji* 慈航大師紀念集, 2 vols. (Taipei: Mile Neiyuan, 1998).
20. See, for instance, the following articles then collected in *Cihang fashi quanji*, vol. 3, *Puti xinying—renshengpian* 菩提心影—人生篇, ed. Cihang fashi yongjiu jinianhui 慈航法師永久紀念會 (Xizhi, Taiwan: Cihang tang, 1981): Cihang 慈航, "Rensheng wenti" 人生問題, 1–8; Cihang 慈航, "Zenme cai jiao zuo yige wanquande ren" 怎麼才叫做一個完全的人, 14–17.
21. Cihang 慈航, "Fojiao yu shehui zhi guanxi" 佛教與社會之關係, in *Cihang fashi quanji*, vol. 3 *Puti xinying—renshengpian* 菩提心影—人生篇, ed. Cihang fashi yongjiu jinianhui 慈航法師永久紀念會 (Xizhi, Taiwan: Cihang tang, 1981), 42–46.
22. Cihang 慈航. "Fojiao yu shehui zhi guanxi" 佛教與社會之關係, 42.
23. See, for instance, the following articles then collected in *Cihang fashi quanji*, vol. 3, *Puti xinying—shiyipian* 菩提心影—釋疑篇, ed. Cihang fashi yongjiu jinianhui 慈航法師永久紀念會 (Xizhi, Taiwan: Cihang tang, 1981): Cihang 慈航, "Jiuguo yanjiu" 救國研究, 46–49; Cihang 慈航, "Fojiao keyi jiuguo" 佛教可以救國, 50–56; and Cihang 慈航, "Fojiao zenme keyi jiuguo" 佛教怎麼可以救國, 57–59. See also Cihang 慈航, "Jiuguo wenti" 救國問題, in *Cihang fashi quanji*, vol. 3 *Puti xinying—renshengpian* 菩提心影—人生篇, ed. Cihang fashi yongjiu jinianhui 慈航法師永久紀念會 (Xizhi, Taiwan: Cihang tang, 1981): 75–83.
24. The three religions were Buddhism, Christianity, and Islam; more local Chinese traditions, like Daoism, were not included.
25. Fafang 法舫, "Renjian fojiao shi guan" 人間佛教史觀, *Haichaoyin* 海潮音 15, no. 1 (1934): 41–56.
26. Jianying 鑑瑩, "Fofa de makesi zhuyi guan" 佛法的馬克思主義觀, *Haichaoyin* 海潮音 13, no. 9 (1932): 1–19; Jianying 鑑瑩, "Fofa de makesi zhuyi guan (er xu)" 佛法的馬克思主義觀(二續), *Zhengxin* 正信 1, no. 8 (1932): 3–5.
27. Shuyi 蜀一, "Renjian fojiao yu shehui zhuyi" 人間佛教與社會主義, *Haichaoyin* 海潮音 15, no. 1 (1934): 83–89.
28. Jichen 寄塵, "Fotuo de shehui zhuyi" 佛陀的社會主義, *Renhai deng* 人海燈 5 (1934): 1–3.
29. Jiang Canteng 江燦騰, *Riju shiqi Taiwan fojiao wenhua fazhanshi* 日劇時期台灣佛教文化發展史 (Taipei: Nantian, 2001), 275–285, 300–321; and Jiang Canteng 江燦騰, *Taiwan fojiao yu xiandai shehui* 台灣佛教與現代社會 (Taipei: Dongda, 1992), 3–35.
30. About Lin Qiuwu, see Li Xiaofeng 李筱峰, *Taiwan geming seng Lin Qiuwu* 台灣革命僧林秋梧 (Taipei: Zili wanbao shehui wenhua, 1991); and Charles B. Jones, 2000. "Buddhism and Marxism in Taiwan: Lin Qiuwu's Religious Socialism and Its Legacy in Modern Times," *Journal of Global Buddhism* 1 (2000): 82–111. Among Lin Qiuwu's articles, see Lin Qiuwu 林秋梧, "Wei Taiwan fojiao rejiao!" 爲臺灣佛教熱叫, *Nanying fojiaohui huibao* 南瀛佛教會會報 6, no. 6 (1928): 50–54; and Lin Qiuwu 林秋梧, "Jieji douzheng yu fojiao" 階級闘爭與佛教, *Nanying fojiaohui huibao* 南瀛佛教會會報 7, no. 2 (1929): 52–58.

31. Lin published this essay with the pen name Kan Ren 坎人 in the journal *Chidao bao* 赤道報 that he founded with his peer intellectuals and activists Zhuang Songlin 莊松林, Lin Zhan'ao 林占鰲, and Lu Neiding 盧內丁.
32. For Taixu's "bodhisattva of progress" see Ritzinger, *Anarchy in the Pure Land,* 171–209.
33. See Dao'an 道安, *Dao'an fashi yiji* 道安法師遺集 (Taipei: Dao'sn fashi jinianhui, 1981), 1280–1284.
34. Publications about Yinshun include Chuandao 釋傳道, *Yinshun daoshi renjian fojiao sixiang gaishuo* 印順導師人間佛教思想概說 (Tainan: Fojiao wentu jijinhui, 2014); Hou Kunhong 侯坤宏, *Yinshun fashi nianpu* 印順法師年譜 (Taipei: Guoshiguan, 2008); and Hou Kunhong, *Zhenshi yu fangbian: Yinshun sixiang yanjiu* 真實與方便: 印順思想研究 (Taipei: Fajie, 2009).
35. Jian Dongyuan 簡東源, "Taixu, Yinshun, Ciji yimo chuancheng" 太虛、印順、慈濟一脈傳承, *Zhongguo shibao* 中國時報, June 5, 2010, A5.
36. Yinshun 印順, "Qili qiji zhi renjian fojiao" 契理契機之人間佛教, in *Huayuji* 華雨集 vol. 4 (Taipei: Zhengwen, [1989] 1993), 44.
37. Yinshun 印順, *Fo zai renjian* 佛在人間 (Taipei: Zhengwen, 1971), 73.
38. See, for instance, Yinshun 印順, *Fo zai renjian* 佛在人間, 17–22.
39. *Fo shizun jie chu renjian, fei you tian er de ye* 佛世尊皆出人間, 非由天而得也 [T02no125, 694a4–5].
40. For an overview of the study of early Buddhism in the Republican period, see Stefania Travagnin Stefania and Anālayo, "The Three-Aṅga Theory in Master Yinshun's 印順 Scholarship: Assessing the State of Āgama Studies in Twentieth-Century China," in *Research on the Saṃyukta-āgama,* ed. Dhammadinnā (Taipei: Dharma Drum, 2020), 933–1007.
41. Yinshun 印順, *Fofa gai lun* 佛法概論 (Taipei: Zhengwen, 1950); Yinshun 印順, *Fo zai renjian* 佛在人間 (Taipei: Zhengwen, 1971); Yinshun 印順, "Qili qiji zhi renjian fojiao" 契理契機之人間佛教, in *Huayu ji* 華雨集, vol. 4 (Taipei: Zhengwen, 1993), 1–70, originally composed in 1989; and Yinshun 印順, "Tan fojiao zai renjian" 談人間在佛教, in *Yongguang ji* 永光集 (Taipei: Zhengwen, 2004), 188–190, originally composed in 1990.
42. Yinshun 印順, *Fo zai renjian* 佛在人間, 27.
43. Yinshun 印順, "Qili qiji zhi renjian fojiao" 契理契機之人間佛教, 50; and Yinshun 印順, "Qili qiji zhi renjian fojiao" 契理契機之人間佛教, 52.
44. Yinshun 印順, "Qili qiji zhi renjian fojiao" 契理契機之人間佛教, 61.
45. See Yinshun 印順, "Qili qiji zhi renjian fojiao" 契理契機之人間佛教.
46. Yinshun 印順, "Qili qiji zhi renjian fojiao" 契理契機之人間佛教, 57.
47. Yinshun 印順, "Qili qiji zhi renjian fojiao" 契理契機之人間佛教, 65–66.
48. Chen Meiling 陳美玲, "Zhuanfang Houguan yuanzhang" 專訪厚觀院長, *Fengcheng fayin* 鳳城發音 14 (2005): 5
49. Yang Shuya 楊淑雅, *Renjian fojiao—Yanpei fashi zai Xinjiapo de hongfa shiji* 人間佛教-演培法師在新加坡的弘法事蹟 (Singapore: Cuibolin chubanshe, 2006); Yu Lingpo 于凌波, "Xinjiapo fuhui jiangtang Shi Yanpei zhuan (1917–1996)" 新加坡福慧講堂釋演培傳 (1917–1996), in *Minguo gaoseng zhuan—xupian* 民國高僧傳—續編, ed. Yu Lingpo (Taipei: Zhaoming, 2000), 153–163; and Jack Meng-Tat Chia, "Buddhism in Singapore: A State of the Field Review," *Asian Culture* 33 (2009): 80–93. See also his autobiography: Yanpei 演培. *Yige fanyu seng de zibai* 一個凡愚僧的自白 (Taipei: Zhengwen, 1989).
50. Yinshun also spent positive comments on Confucianism as he analyzed world religions, see Yinshun 印順, *Wo zhi zongjiao guan* 我之宗教觀 (Taipei: Zhengwen, 1972), 55–64.
51. Yanpei 演培, *Fayu bian shi ji* 法雨徧施集 (Taipei: Tianhua, 1990), 370.
52. For an overview of these Taiwanese Buddhist organizations, see Richard Madsen, *Democracy Dharma: Religious Renaissance and Political Development in Taiwan* (Berkeley: University of California Press, 2007).

53. Among Xingyun's biographies, see Fu Zhiying 符芝瑛, *Chuan deng: Xingyun dashi zhuan* 傳燈:星雲大師傳 (Taipei: Tianxia, 1995). Reference books on Shengyan include his autobiography Shengyan 聖嚴, *Xuezhong zuyi: Shengyan fashi zizhuan* 雪中足跡:聖嚴法師自傳 (Taipei: Fagu wenhua, 2009). About Zhengyan, see Julia C. Huang, *Charisma and Compassion: Cheng Yen and the Buddhist Tzu Chi Movement* (Cambridge, MA: Harvard University Press, 2009). In several publications, Zhengyan is often transliterated as Cheng Yen.
54. See, for instance, Zhiying, *Chuan deng: Xingyun dashi zhuan.*
55. Xingyun 星雲, *Renjian Fojiao* 人間佛教 (Gaoxiong, Taiwan: Foguang chubanshe, 1995), 183–185.
56. Zhengyan 證嚴, *Renjian pusa* 人間菩薩 (Taipei: Ciji wenhua chubanshe, 1999).
57. Zhao Shichong 趙嗣崇, *Xiaoyun fashi zhuan* 曉雲法師傳 (Taizhong, Taiwan: Taiping Ciguangsi chuban, 2015); and Chen Xiuhui 陳秀慧, *Xiaoyun fashi jiaoyu qinghuai yu zhiye* 曉雲法師教育情懷與志業 (Taipei: Wanjuanlou tushu, 2019).
58. Lianchan 蓮懺. *Mangren daoshi fayulu* 盲人導師法語錄 (Taipei: Lianmen xuehui, 2003). See also Lin Xinju 林新居, *Fomen renwu fangtan lu* 佛門人物訪談錄 (Taipei: Puti changqing, 1993).
59. See Zhaohui 昭慧 and Xingguang 性廣, eds., *Xin shiji de fojiao nüxing siwei* 新世紀的佛教女性思維 (Taipei: Fajie chubanshe, 2001), 57–66, 207–211, 221–228. Yi Riqiu, trans. Adrian Chan-Wyles, "Taiwan held its First Lesbian Marriage in 2012," June 2015. Zhaohui 昭慧 and Hou Kunhong 侯坤宏, *Zhaohui fashi fangtanlu* 昭慧法師訪談錄 (Taipei: Fajie, 2017). Specifically on her social activism, see Stefania Travagnin, "Master Yinshun and Buddhist Nuns in/for the Human Realm. Shift and Continuity from Theory to Practice of *renjian fojiao* in Contemporary Taiwan," in *The Margins of Becoming. Identity and Culture in Taiwan*, ed. Carsten Storm and Mark Harrison (Wiesbaden, Germany: Harrassowitz, 2007), 83–100.
60. From "Introduction to the Buddhist Association of China" "Zhongguo fojiao xiehui jianjie" 中國佛教協會簡介.
61. Carsten Krause, "The Changing Functions of *renjian fojiao* in Mainland China," *Journal of the Oxford Centre for Buddhist Studies* 17 (2019): 117–143.
62. For more on Zhao Puchu and *renjian fojiao*, see Zhao Puchu 趙樸初, "Zhongguo fojiao de guoqu he xianzai" 中國佛教的過去和現在, in *Zhao Puchu wenji* 趙樸初文集, ed. *Zhao Puchu wenji* bianji weiyuanhui 趙樸初文集編輯委員會 (Beijing: Huawen chubanshe, [1987] 2007), 835–836; and Shengkai 聖凱, ed. *Zhao Puchu juan* 趙樸初卷 (Beijing: Zongjiao wenhua chubanshe, 2017). See also Ji Zhe, "Zhao Puchu and his Renjian Buddhism," *The Eastern Buddhist* 44, no. 2 (2013): 35–58; and Ji Zhe, "Comrade Zhao Puchu: bodhisattva under the Red Flag," in *Making Saints in Modern China*, ed. David Ownby, Vincent Goossaert, and Ji Zhe (Oxford and New York: Oxford University Press, 2017), 312–366.
63. The renewed attention on Taixu is also manifested in the several conferences organized to discuss his works; see, for instance, the conference organized in August 2017 (Ningbo, Zhejiang) in memory of the seventieth anniversary of the death of Taixu (*Taixu dashi yuanji qishi zhounian jinian dahui* 太虛大師圓寂七十週年紀念大會).
64. There are posters at Foguangshan, in Gaoxiong, reporting Xingyun's reflections on "Kanjian mengxiang de liliang" 看見夢想的力量. To quote from the poster: "The 'Chinese Dream' President Xi envisioned is very meaningful. Dreams drive aspirations, and aspirations lead to realizations. What I speak about 'Seeing the Power of Dreams' [*kanjian mengxiang de liliang* 看見夢想的力量], I wish to inspire this hope in each of you to realize your dreams. For the Chinese to become a stronger and better people, there must be unity. Today, the Chinese [*zhongguoren* 中國人] have achieved much, and we should look forward to a greater, higher future."
65. Xuecheng 學誠, *Xinyang yu duihua* 信仰與對話 (Beijing: Jiuzhou chubanshe, 2016).
66. See, for instance, Taixu 太虛, "Chuangzao renjian jingtu" 創造人間淨土, *Haichao yin* 海潮音 12, no. 1 (1930): 4–8.

67. Goodell, "Taixu's Pure Land on Earth and the *Vimalakirti*"; and Ritzinger, *Anarchy in the Pure Land,* 74–95.
68. Cihang 慈航, "Jianshe renjian jingtu" 建設人間淨土, in *Cihang fashi quanji,* vol. 3 *Puti xinying—renshengpian* 菩提心影—人生篇, ed. Cihang fashi yongjiu jinianhui 慈航法師永久紀念會 (Xizhi, Taiwan: Cihang tang, 1981), 27–30.
69. Shengyan 聖嚴, *Jingtu zai renjian* 淨土在人間 (Taipei: Fagu wenhua, 2003); Shengyan 聖嚴, *Shengyan fashi xinling huanbao* 聖嚴法師心靈環保 (Taipei: Fagu wenhua, 2004); and Charles B. Jones, "Master Sheng Yen's Pure Land Teachings: Synthesizing the Traditional and the Modern," *Shengyan yanjiu* 聖嚴研究 12 (2019): 217–241.
70. Jiang Canteng 江燦騰, *Taiwan fojiao bainian shi zhi yanjiu 1895–1995* 台灣佛教百年史之研究 1895–1995 (Taipei: Nantian shuju, 1996), 189.
71. Yinshun 印順, *Jingtu yu Chan* 淨土與禪 (Taipei: Zhengwen, 1971). See also Stefania Travagnin, "Master Yinshun and the Pure Land Thought. A Doctrinal Gap between Indian Buddhism and Chinese Buddhism," *Acta Orientalia Academiae Scientiarum Hungaricae* 57, no. 3 (2004): 271–328.
72. Namely, (1) environmental protection in spirit (*xinling huanbao* 心靈環保), (2) environmental protection in everyday life (*shenghuo huanbao* 生活環保), (3) environmental protection in nature (*ziran huanbao* 自然環保), and (4) environmental protection in society (*liyi huanbao* 禮儀環保). See Shengyan 聖嚴, *Sizhong huanbao* 四種環保 (Taipei: Fagu wenhua, 2015).
73. Chengpang Lee and Ling Han, "Recycling bodhisattva: The Tzu-Chi Movement's Response to Global Climate Change," *Social Compass* 62, no. 3 (September 2015): 311–325.
74. Sample publications include Hung-yok Ip, "Buddhist Activism and Chinese Modernity," *Journal of Global Buddhism* 10 (2009): 145–192; and Rongdao Lai and Jessica Main, "Introduction: Reformulating 'Socially Engaged Buddhism' as an Analytical Category," *The Eastern Buddhist* 44, no. 2 (2013): 1–34.
75. Zhang Mantao 張曼濤, ed., *Fojiao yu rensheng* 佛教與人生 (Taipei: Dacheng wenhua chubanshe, 1979).
76. Deng Zimei 鄧子美, Chen Weihua 陳衛華, and Mao Dongyong 毛勤勇, *Dangdai renjian fojiao sichao* 當代人間佛教思潮 (Lanzhou, China: Gansu Renmin Chubanshe, 2008).
77. Deng Zimei 鄧子美 and Chen Weihua 陳衛華, *Dangdai renjian fojiao chuandenglu (1949–2015)* 當代人間佛教傳燈錄 (1949–2015), 2 vols. (Beijing: Zongjiao wenhua chubanshe, 2017).
78. Yang Huinan 楊惠南, *Dangdai fojiao sixiang zhanwang* 當代佛教思想展望 (Taipei: Dongda, 1991). This book does mention Lin Qiuwu as a Taiwanese actor in the humanistic Buddhism movement.
79. See, for instance, André Laliberté, "'Buddhism for the Human Realm' and Taiwanese Democracy," in *Religious Organizations and Democracy in Contemporary Asia,* ed. Tung-ren Cheng and Deborah Brown (Armonk, NY: M. E. Sharpe, 2015), 55–82.
80. These two figures are discussed as reformers rather than exponents of *renjian fojiao.* See Li Xiaofeng, *Taiwan geming seng Lin Qiuwu;* and Jiang Canteng 江燦騰, "Riju shiqi Taiwan xin fojiao yundong de xianqu: 'Taiwan fojiao Mading Lude' Lin Delin de gean yanjiu" 日據時期台灣新佛教運動的先驅:「台灣佛教馬丁路德」林德林的個案研究, *Chung-Hwa Buddhist Journal* 15 (2002): 255–303.
81. The following title analyzes one of these humanistic Buddhist groups, Tzu Chi, also as similar to Japanese new religious movements: Yao Yu-Shuang, *Taiwan's Tzu Chi as Engaged Buddhism: Origins, Organization, Appeal and Social Impact* (Leiden, The Netherlands: Brill, 2012).
82. About Zhao Puchu, see Ji Zhe, "Zhao Puchu and his Renjian Buddhism," *The Eastern Buddhist* 44, no. 2 (2013): 35–58; and Ji Zhe, "Comrade Zhao Puchu: bodhisattva under the Red Flag," in *Making Saints in Modern China,* ed. David Ownby, Vincent Goossaert, and Ji Zhe (Oxford and New York: Oxford University Press, 2017), 312–366. About the monk Juzan, see Li Xiangping, "Increased Production and Education." About the monk Yinshun, see Chuandao 傳道, *Yinshun daoshi yu renjian fojiao* 印順導師

與人間佛教 (Tainan, Taiwan: Fojiao wenxian jijinhui, 2001); Zhaohui 昭慧, *Renjian fojiao de bozhongzhe* 人間佛教的播種者 (Taipei: Dongda tushu gongsi, 1995); Wen Jinke 溫金柯, *Jicheng yu pipan Yinshun fashi de renjian fojiao sixiang* 繼承與批判印順法師的人間佛教思想 (Taipei: Xiandai Chan, 2001); Jiang Canteng 江燦騰, *Dangdai Taiwan renjian fojiao sixiangjia* 當代台灣人間佛教思想家 (Taipei: Xinwenfeng chubanshe, 2001). About the monk Yanpei, see Jack Meng-Tat Chia, *Monks in Motion: Buddhism and Modernity across the South China Sea* (Oxford: Oxford University Press, 2020), 77–116, "Yen Pei: Humanistic Buddhism in the Chinese Diaspora."

83. For Tzu Foundation, see André Laliberté, *The Politics of Buddhist Organizations in Taiwan, 1989–2003: Safeguard the Faith, Build a Pure Land, Help the Poor* (London: Routledge, 2004); and Zhiru, "The Emergence of the Sahâ Triad in Contemporary Taiwan: Iconic Representation and Humanistic Buddhism." *Asia Major* 13 (2000): 83–105. For Foguangshan, see Stuart Chandler, *Establishing a Pure Land on Earth: The Foguang Buddhist Perspective on Modernization ad Globalization* (Honolulu: University of Hawai'i Press, 2004). For an example of a global "Humanistic Buddhism" community, see Jens Reinke, *Mapping Modern Mahayana: Chinese Buddhism and Migration in the Age of Global Modernity* (Boston and Berlin: De Gruyter, 2021).
84. Eric Stephen Goddell, "Taixu's (1890–1947) Creation of Humanistic Buddhism" (PhD diss., University of Virginia, Charlottesville, 2012); Guo Peng, *Taixu dashi sixiang yanjiu*; Chen Yongge, *Renjian chaoyin*; Hou Kunhong, *Taixu shidai*; and He Jianming 何建明, *Renjian fojiao yu xiandai Gang Ao fojiao: Taixu dashi, Zhumo fashi yu Gang Ao fojiao zhi* 人間佛教與現代港澳佛教:太虛大師, 竺摩法師與港澳佛教職, 2 vols. (Hong Kong: Xinxin chuban gongsi, 2006).
85. Ritzinger, *Anarchy in the Pure Land.*
86. It is well known that, for instance, Yinshun's book *Jingtu yu Chan* 淨土與禪 was burned in a public square in Taizhong (Taiwan); for these contrasts and challenges, see, among the others, Travagnin, "Master Yinshun and the Pure Land Thought."
87. Ji Zhe 汲喆, "Renjian fojiao, shenghuo chan yu hua xiandai gong an" 人間佛教, 生活禪與化現代公案, in *Zhiyuezhe: Jinghui zhanglao yu shenghuo chan xueshu yantaohui lunwenji* 指月者:淨慧長老與生活禪學術研討會論文集, ed. Li Silong 李四龍 (Beijing: Sanlian shudian, 2015), 165–177; Wang Jia 王佳, *Jinghui fashi yu xiandai renjian fojiao: yi shenghuo chan wei zhongxin* 淨慧法師與現代人間佛教:以生活禪為中心 (Beijing: Zongjiao wenhua chubanshe, 2020); and Xingguang 性廣, *Renjian fojiao chanfa jiqi dangdai shijian* 人間佛教禪法及其當代實踐 (Taipei: Fajie, 2001).
88. The three collections were edited by Huang Xianian 黃夏年 et al; the first was published in 2006 (Beijing: Zhongguo shudian), the second in 2008 (Beijing: Zhongguo shudian), and the third in 2013 (Beijing: Zhongguo shudian).
89. The collection of Taixu's works was first published in Hong Kong, by Zhengjue lianshe in 1950, and later reprinted in Taiwan by Shandao Temple 善導寺 in 1998. The collection has been made available in a CD-ROM by the Yinshun Cultural Foundation (Yinshun wenjiao jijinhui 印順文教基金會) since 2005. The collection of Cihang's writings was edited and published in Taipei by the Master Cihang Memorial Foundation (Cihang fashi yongjiu jinianhui 慈航法師永久紀念會) in 1981. A more recent edition was reprinted in 2014.
90. Among this series, see, for instance, Deng Zimei ed., *Taixu juan*. See the section "Review of Literature" for an assessment of this book series.
91. These publications are preserved in the database *Riju shiqi Taiwan fojiao shike* 日據時期台灣佛教史料.
92. For a comprehensive overview, I would start from the short texts and passages collected in the two volumes *Dangdai renjian fojiao chuandenglu (1949–2015)* edited by Deng Zimei and Chen Weihua. Monographs authored by the exponents of the humanistic Buddhism movement include Yinshun 印順, "Qili qiji zhi renjian fojiao" 契理契機之人間佛教, in *Huayu ji* 華雨集, vol. 4 (Taipei: Zhengwen,

1993, originally composed in 1989), 1–70; Xingyun 星雲, *Renjian fojiao fotuo benhuai* 人間佛教佛陀本懷 (Gaoxiong, Taiwan: Foguang wenhua, 2016); Shengyan 聖嚴, *Renjian jingtu: lilun yu shijian* 人間淨土:理論與實踐 (Taipei: Fagu wenhua, 2020); and the few volumes of *Still Thoughts* and *Jingsi Aphorisms* (*Jingsi yu* 靜思語), all authored by Zhengyan 證嚴 and printed in Taipei by Tzu Chi Publishing since 1999.

93. Foguangshan Renjian Fojiao Yanjiuyuan, ed., *The Glossary of Humanistic Buddhism* [*Zhongying renjian fojiao cihui xuan* 中英人間佛教詞彙選] (Gaoxiong, Taiwan: FGS Institute of Humanistic Buddhism, 2018).

Stefania Travagnin

I

IMAGING THE BUDDHA IN SOUTH ASIA

BEFORE AND AROUND THE IMAGE OF THE BUDDHA

A long period elapsed between the lifetime of the historical Buddha Śākyamuni, "the seer of the Śākyas," in the 5th–4th centuries BCE and the appearance of the first representations of him around the 1st century CE. This epoch attested to a fundamental change in relations between the devotee and his/her *iṣṭa-devatā* or his/her spiritual guide, when images of Brahmanical deities and historical figures from the past, such as the Jina, or the Buddha, emerged and became the focus of devotional rituals. Although aiming at portraying a man who lived in the 5th–4th centuries BCE, and despite being first represented in the 1st century CE, the image of the Buddha that appeared then shows a transformed body, the presentation of which is a direct continuation of the rules of composition noted in preceding centuries.

Although no anthropomorphic representation of the Buddha had appeared in the course of those centuries, his presence may have been alluded to in narrative reliefs depicting sites he had visited and that had become places of pilgrimage, or in the carving of symbolic motifs that may allude to episodes in his life. This phase in the development of Buddhist iconography has been a matter of controversy in the field of South Asian art history since the 19th century. Relevant to this topic is the fact that panels showing the veneration of sites or depicting symbolic elements are composed around a vertical line of symmetry, thus creating a strictly frontal image that prefigures the later structure of the representations of deities.

All the reliefs from the 2nd century BCE and later amply testify that not depicting the anthropomorphic form did not imply the impossibility or incapacity to represent the human body or any fantastic creature. Indeed, during the same period, striking three-dimensional sculptures of *yakṣa* and *yakṣī* were made, paving the way to the development that would emerge in the early centuries of our era.

Although a historical character, the Buddha was not represented as having a real human form, but showed as a metamorphosed body combining extraordinary features—a creation that reflects how the development and execution of this image was based on speculation on the possibility of representing a human who was of the highest spiritual nature. This echoes the description of the Buddha's body found in the literary sources: both "images," material and literary, developed their own forms, the textual sources allowing for a richer and more intricate elaboration of the image, with numerous features that cannot be visualized at the level of reality. Whoever initially designed these images was thus up against the dilemma of illustrating a human being who had shown deep spiritual insights and had introduced a particular way of life, a situation that echoed the writing of the Buddha's biography and that led monks and artists to evoke a fantastic life and a transformed body.[1]

This transformation does not reflect an obsolete practice in South Asia, where the human body is the basic form on which most images of deities are elaborated: the expression of the divine nature at the iconographic level, visual and literary, finds its way through a radical modification of this body with multiplication of members or heads, or with the substitution of animal and fantastic components for the human parts of the body. In contrast, deities of an animal nature, such as Garuḍa or the *nāga,* have their bodies transformed through inclusion of elements borrowed from the human body.

However, the earliest images of "deities," that is, of figures of a nonhistorical or unreal nature, such as those carved on the balustrade erected around stūpas or the three-dimensional *yakṣa* and *yakṣī*, have a human body. Their supramundane nature is then conveyed more strikingly with the possible presence of a vehicle carrying them or of an animal, real or fantastic, below their feet, and with their frontal position. Whereas the images shown in relief on a balustrade, or in the veranda of an excavated monument, are not cult images *sensu stricto,* being distributed at the fringe of the monument that is the center of the worship, the *yakṣa* and *yakṣī* images carved in the round were most probably standing beneath a tree where they were venerated.[2] These various images share the frontal view, which is the most generalized manner of showing the deity, asserting his/her universal and eternal presence and displaying his/her powers.[3]

FORMULATING THE IMAGE IN ART

Several studies have dealt with the appearance of the human representation of the Buddha and its relation to the "symbolic representations" that predated it, as well as various aspects displayed by the image in the course of time.[4] The regions of Mathurā and Gandhāra played a fundamental role in this artistic episode: reflecting different stylistic choices, the image was simultaneously created in both regions.[5] Mathurā was a major political and cultural center where a rich religious Brahmanical, Jain, and Buddhist imagery emerged, whereas Gandhāran ateliers laid the foundations for illustration of the past lives and biography of the Buddha. Thus, the image of the Buddha at Mathurā (figs. 1–2) introduces a composition that would be preserved throughout the centuries in India and abroad, perfectly fitting the Indian perception of the divine nature.[6] Three major parts constitute the cult image: the "deity" characterized by criteria such as the physical appearance, the attributes and gestures, and the dress; the pedestal on which the deity sits or stands; and the slab backing the representation of the deity. The pedestal and the back slab are elements that consolidate the sculpture, which did not remain uncarved but received a symbolic ornamentation.

A very specific choice of terms was selected to create this image: the Buddha and his attendants, the plain scalloped nimbus, the foliage of the peepal tree (*Ficus religiosa*), the divine beings in flight, and the throne with its ornamentation of fantastic and real animals observed from the 5th century onward. Those elements are organized within a particular pattern, the image of the Buddha being at the center of the composition and the attendants on either side, smaller and slightly drawing back; all three are seen in the central and lower part of the image, the flying figures in the upper part. A clear and symmetrical composition is thus achieved here: the Buddha depiction covers the axis of symmetry and all the elements are rigidly arranged around this depiction. Most of the stone was used to illustrate the deity and the

Figure 1. Buddha (named "Bodhisatva" in the inscription). Mathura. Mathura Museum.
Photo courtesy of Joachim K. Bautze.

Figure 2. The same, viewed from the side.
Source: Photo courtesy of Joachim K. Bautze.

attending figures, all sculpted in high relief, whereas the motifs on the back slab are carved in low relief. All the components remain secondary to the central depiction of the Buddha, with a subtle hierarchy introduced in the position of the attendants, carved slightly behind and below the Buddha.

All these elements show highly codified forms: the image of the Buddha is seen frontally; he is larger than the other figures around him and is characterized by a rigidity absent in the other characters. The image of the deity is perceived as an immovable axis out of which life arises: the topic of the throne adorned by animals serves to illustrate this creative potential since the animals symbolize the four elements—earth (elephant), fire (leogryph), water (*makara*, a fantastic being born out of the Ganges crocodile), and air (geese or *haṃsa*; or divine musicians). The attendants express, through the movements of their bodies and the fact that they may at times be depicted in profile, the same dynamic concept, that is, the life that flows out of the central image. Thus, the static central Buddha (or any other deity) has to be surrounded by attendants in motion; the two attitudes, static and dynamic, are in fact complementary and contribute to creating a composition where centrifugal and centripetal movements harmoniously merge into each other.[7]

The image of the deity in India is subject to strict rules of composition, with specific motifs distributed in a precise pattern of superimposed levels, which contributes to transforming the stela into a reflection of the universe.[8] The pedestal, being in direct contact with the earth, is the place where human devotees, lay people or monks, can be depicted and where an inscription mentioning their donation can be incised.[9] It also includes depiction of the lower part of the seat of the Buddha, showing the lions supporting it (or the god's vehicle), and would also be the space where the lotus bearing any divine image is carved. This level supports the back slab, which is divided into two or three superimposed levels: attendants are distributed around the Buddha (or deity); the throne is adorned with real and fantastic animals, and when the Buddha (or deity) is seated, the throne is partly hidden by the attending figures; and the upper part shows the nimbus flanked by flying divine figures.

This structure conveys a broad view of supramundane nature extending beyond the sole representation of the Buddha, which shows how it would also be adopted in Brahmanical and Jain iconography. The literary sources mentioned in the section "Formulating the Image of the Buddha in Literature" below reveal how the nature of the Buddha was also defined through reference to Brahmanical gods, either by negating some of their distinctive visible (iconographic) features or more often by extolling the moral qualities of the Buddha and reproving those of the Brahmanical gods, or by simply assimilating elements of their personalities, if not the gods themselves.[10] For instance, Maheśvara (known as Śiva from the Gupta period onward) could be identified as a form taken on by the Buddha.[11] The final result is that the Buddha is in fact treated as equal, if not indeed superior, to any deity. The human body of the Buddha is thus a transformed body, an imaginary body in the sense that it has parts that are excrescences and parts that are idealized and thus depart from reality. This body is also a source of extraordinary phenomena, for example, the Buddha shedding water and fire from all the pores of his body in one of the miracles he performed at Śrāvastī.[12]

From the very outset, the monks responsible for the literary descriptions, like the sculptors or painters with their artistic production, were faced with the fundamental problem of expressing in words and images the nature of Gautama transformed into that of the Buddha, a spiritual experience that remains invisible, of putting into words and displaying the message left by Śākyamuni, and of emphasizing the supremacy of the Buddha over the Hindu deities. This resulted in the creation of an "extraordinary" appearance reflecting the ambivalent human and supramundane nature of the Buddha: it shows the historical personage and can thus be understood as a reminder of the life and thought, as a symbolic presence of the founder, but it also includes the rich stratification of speculations bearing on the nature of the Buddha, a nature that differs from that of the common worshipper.

The iconographic rules fixed in the early centuries of our era have been preserved up to the present day, even though the supramundane nature of the Buddha has undergone interpretations that may at times radically differ from country to country, from period to period. This was made possible by the fact that in this early period the image that was created ideally crystallised the basic multiple perception of the Buddha, which could be inherited by all later trends throughout Asia. The Buddha is seen as a human being, a historical personage in whom the devotee can recognize him/herself; he is also a man who perceived his true nature and became a historical personage who had undergone the deepest spiritual modification and thus reached the highest state of spiritual perfection that a human being can achieve.

From the very early period also, the idea that buddhas preceded the historical Śākyamuni in early eons found its way into common belief: apart from their sizes (they were usually very tall), these buddhas are physically identical to the historical Buddha, and artistic representations of the former do not differ from representations of the latter.[13] Moreover, with the emergence of the Mahāyāna in the first centuries of our era and all subsequent developments of Buddhism, these concepts related to the Buddha evolved toward a more spiritual perception that would be ideally extolled in the system of the "three bodies" or *trikāya*. Whereas only one body is actually visible (the *nirmāṇakāya),* the other two exist at absolute and transcendent levels that remain elusive to the senses (*sambhoga-* and *dharmakāya*); however, these ethereal bodies are not abstract since they are mentioned and named in texts, where they display features that find their origin in the physical image of Śākyamuni, and since they are represented in art through images based on depictions of the latter. In this particular context, the buddhas do not succeed one another in the course of past eons but are distributed throughout the universe(s).

The image of the Buddha simultaneously shows these various possible perceptions: it is a representation of what is hidden deep in the soul of the devotee at the same time as it illustrates the accomplished Buddha. The image is located at a threshold between (historical) reality and spiritual accomplishment, before the present moment and the future one when he/she discovers his/her nature of "buddha"; but it also shows the simultaneity of these two only apparently opposed aspects of the human being, fully involved in everyday life but also driven by his/her spiritual longings. It refers the devotee to a departed time, the time of the Buddha Śākyamuni—long before his/her own, the time when the Buddha was alive as a historical personage, and also to the eternal present where the spiritual nature of the Buddha is alive. And it can also be the material foundation from which the meditation on the three bodies begins. This ahistorical approach to the image helps to explain the fascination it held in all Asian countries.

This iconic image would be set in Gandhāra at the center of intricate compositions with further smaller pictures of the Buddha and/or of bodhisattvas distributed around it, and it would be duplicated in various sizes, covering entire walls or façades in the excavated sites of Maharashtra from the 5th century onward.[14] This image loses its frozen aspect in the sculptural depiction of the Buddha biography, which became of major importance in Gandhāra and Andhra Pradesh before being painted on the walls of a site such as Ajanta, and where its lively presentation stresses the human nature of this character. At a later period and in Eastern India, this narrative would blend with the iconic image in reducing the depiction of the life to a fixed number of eight moments distributed in a strict composition: one central image of the Buddha surrounded by smaller ones, all mostly depicted in a strict frontal view.[15]

FORMULATING THE IMAGE OF THE BUDDHA IN LITERATURE

It is in the north of the subcontinent, around Mathurā and in Gandhāra, that profound reflection on the aspects to be taken by this image began in the first two centuries of our era. The cult image that resulted is itself a continuation of a model created in the previous centuries in that it shows the sage in frontal view and set in a symmetric composition. Moreover, the representation of the Buddha is distinguished from that of other figures surrounding him by the introduction of fantastic features specific to his physical appearance. The creation of this image apparently inspired the authors: poetic literature occasionally alludes to the physique of the

Buddha and may evoke lists of physical features that display at times an exaggeratedly fantastic form, thus contributing to the virtual creation of a totally imaginary figure.

Written by Mātṛceṭa in the 3rd or 4th century, the *Śatapañcāśatka*, "Hymn in a Hundred and Fifty Verses," evokes in a few eulogistic verses the physical appearance of the Buddha, emphasizing the emotion felt on beholding him rather than referring in detail to any part of the body (verses 52–57).[16] And in the lines in "Praise of the Speech," verse 72 includes the only specific reference to a part of the Buddha's body, praising the latter's mouth as being "pleasing to the eye."[17] The first verse of the possibly earlier *Devātiśayastuti/Devatāvimarṣastuti*, "Praise to the One Who Surpasses the Gods," by Śaṅkarasvāmin tells that like the gods Viṣṇu, Hiraṇyagarbha (Brahmā), and Hara (Śiva), the "venerable Buddha [Bhagavat Sugata]... [has not] been directly perceived by us," all of them being invisible.[18] But, contrary to these deities who are permanently in movement and action, "the Buddha... displays the excellence of a perpetual peaceful conduct" (verse 2); whereas they bear all sorts of attributes and weapons, he is free of any of them and redeemed from all passions (verse 8). Similarly, Udbhatasiddhasvāmin's *Viśeṣastava*, "Praise to the Prominence (of the Buddha)," offers a lengthy comparison between the deities and the Buddha, which contrasts the rich imagery of the Brahmanical pantheon—providing details of the aspects of the numerous gods, of the myths in which they are involved—with the Buddha, who is described solely in terms of his own moral and spiritual abilities.[19] This comparison emphasises the peaceful nature of the Buddha and the fact that he does not possess anything—unlike the gods who are at times heavily armed.

From the very moment of his birth the body of the Buddha displays extraordinary features, bringing those who approach him to a state of ecstasy.

> His supernatural powers, his qualities and his strength are immense and inexhaustible. The body of the Buddha is adorned with the thirty-two marks and the eighty sub-marks; he possesses inwardly the innumerable attributes and qualities of the buddhas: for that reason, one never grows weary of beholding him. Those who see the body of the Buddha forget the five objects of sensual pleasure of the world and do not remember anything. When one sees the body of the Buddha, happiness is total; one does not grow weary and one cannot change sight.[20]

As a matter of fact, the ascetic Asita, who examined the newborn at his birth, observed the presence of specific symbolic motifs on the child's body and the particular shape taken by parts of his body.[21] The presence of the thirty-two motifs and forms, named *lakṣaṇas*, indicates that the child is a "universal ruler" or *cakravartin*, that he is a "great being" or *mahāpuruṣa*.[22] This list of "features" is supplemented by another list of eighty secondary "attributes" (*anuvyañjana*).[23] Moreover, in the tradition of these two series, further ones have been constituted, enumerating motifs, real or abstract, that adorn the soles of the feet, the palms of the hands, and the body; for instance, a series of 108 motifs offering symbolic illustration of the cosmos is observed on the footprints painted or carved in Southeast Asia, hinting thus at the identification of the Buddha with the universe.[24]

These *lakṣaṇas* provoke wonderment in those who are present at the birth:[25] "The Buddha whose body is adorned (*alaṃkṛta*) with the thirty-two marks is beautiful (*abhirūpa*) and well-arranged (*avikṣipta*). If he had less than thirty-two marks, his body would be ugly; if he had more than thirty-two marks, he would be untidy. Thanks to the thirty-two marks, he is beautiful and well-arranged. Their number cannot be increased or decreased."[26] Not only Śākyamuni, but all buddhas triumph through their superiority in all aspects of life, such as physical beauty (*kāyarūpa*), power, clan, family, wisdom, and so forth, but without the marks, these superiorities would remain limited.[27] On his long way to buddhahood, a bodhisattva acquires these marks that impress upon his body.[28] These marks differentiate a Buddha's or bodhisattva's body from the "normal" human body, on which meditation should be led by the monk in order to become aware of its real nature, which is to be transitory, fragile, illusory, unreal, dirty, leading to death; in the buddha's words to his monks, "full of disgust (*nirvid*) and repugnance (*udvega*) for a body such as this, you should turn your aspirations (*adhimukti*) to the body of the Tathāgata."[29]

Whereas the concept of beauty is here defined by the presence of the *lakṣaṇas*, their presence also ensures that a bodhisattva will become a buddha, and their absence would thus coincide with the impossibility of reaching enlightenment. Consequently, their absence implies the loss of beauty, as conveyed with these words referring to a particular moment of his life: "so ruined by my austere abstinence was the wonted bright and pure complexion of my body."[30] Indeed, having left the city of Kapilavastu and his family, the future Buddha met on his way five mendicants, who

> became his constant companions during the six years he was engaged in his great striving, and they served him ... the Bodhisatta himself, who was determined to practise austerities in their most extreme form began to subsist on one grain of sesamum or rice a day. He even took to complete fasting. He dissuaded the deities from infusing divine energy through the pores of his skin. *Then his body which was once golden in colour turned black* from the great emaciation it had reached as a result of that fasting. *The thirty-two characteristics of a Great being were obliterated* ... [my italics].

As a result of trying to suppress his "breath he fell down unconscious" and some gods thought he had passed away.[31] Then

> the Bodhisatta regained his consciousness ... [and] ... realizing that the practice of such austerities was not the path to Enlightenment he went about gathering alms in villages and townships in order to revert to solid food, and he subsisted on it. *Then his thirty-two characteristics of a Great being re-appeared in their natural form, and the body regained its golden hue* [my italics].[32]

Disappointed by this behaviour, the five mendicants left him in his solitude: they were going to be the very first disciples, who would hear the first sermon of Śākyamuni at Sārnāth, once he had become a buddha.

The authors of the *Nidāna-kathā* here quoted at length were well aware of the opposition between the "healthy" monk and the ascetic going through such hard penances that these could threaten his existence. Despite the disgust provoked by this phase of the (future) buddha's life—his body losing the thirty-two marks, his golden hue waning and his skin darkening—this image was represented in Gandhāra in the early centuries of our era and, albeit more rarely, in Eastern India and Burma nearly one thousand years later.[33] This image of the ascetic monk is an image of death, and even the gods mistook his fainting at the end of the six-year penances for his death and reported him dead to his father Śuddhodana.[34] Śākyamuni recovered from this long phase of penance during which he came near to death; he regained his healthy appearance, and having defeated death, he pursued his way to Awakening, and his image, henceforth, proves that this path is synonymous with life.

A METAMORPHOSED BODY

The lists of thirty-two features and eighty attributes offer a detailed observation of the human body, underlying the qualities of its parts or modifying some of them and thus recreating an imaginary picture of a once historical character. The origins of some of them can probably be traced back to artistic representations, such as the webbed hands (the skin being preserved between the fingers in order to avoid any breaking of the stone), or conversely some may have inspired artists.

Parts of Śākyamuni's body can be briefly described in the short list:

> he has feet with level tread... he has long toes and fingers, he has broad and projecting heels, he has sharply arched feet... his hands and feet are soft and tender... his body is perfectly formed... he has a smooth skin... he has regular teeth... his canine-teeth are very white, his bust is equally rounded... his eyes are blue...

This description demonstrates the perfection of his body.[35] Most attributes mentioned in the long list refer to parts of the body, for instance, the hands, the fingernails, the fingers, the mouth, the teeth, the tongue, the eyes, the eyebrows, the ears, the nose, the forehead, the hair, and the abdomen. Similarly, this list mentions general characteristics: the body is rounded, smooth, regular, pure, tender, stainless, youthful, energetic, lofty, well-composed, and it has "broad and graceful limbs." Comparisons to the animal world may be brought in: "his legs are like the antelope's... he has the gait of a swan... he has a jaw like a lion's... his eyelashes are like a cow's," or to a tree: "his body is proportioned like the banyan-tree." The long list mentions the Buddha moving with the gait of a lion, an elephant, a swan, or a bull, or having the voice of a trumpeting elephant. Alteration of limbs or organs led to the creation of a fantastic image:

> he can touch his knees with his hands when standing erect... his hands and feet are webbed... there is no hollow between his shoulder-blades... his tongue is long and slender [and] the soles of his feet are marked with thousand-spoke wheel-signs... he has a tuft of hair (*ūrṇā*) between his eyebrows, the top of his head has a turban-shaped protuberance (*uṣṇīṣa*).

Comparisons are repeatedly made in the literature between the Buddha and the lion or the elephant.[36] For instance, the Buddha has "the gaze of the elephant" (*nāgāvalokita*), meaning that when looking behind him, he turns his whole body, moving as the animal does.[37] According to some sources, the skulls of buddhas are firmly attached to the trunk, and buddhas have fewer bones than human beings. Over "incalculable periods (*asaṃkhyeyakalpa*) of cultivating attention (*ekacittatā*)," many bones have melded together—resulting in this awkward movement.[38] In other words, body and mind so deeply intertwined as to act in unison. This feature is part of the physical and spiritual nature of the Buddha and survived throughout the centuries in Burma, where sculptors and painters remained aware of the analogy, translating it into their art, their images of the Buddha showing a deeply sunken head attached to a short, practically nonexistent, neck—which recalls the anatomy of an elephant, as described in an 18th-century Burmese biography of the Buddha.[39]

These two catalogues of marks developed in an early period and were probably already completed in the 1st century CE.[40] However, the image of the Buddha that emerges from the texts remained an ideal that, as such, would never be represented. Only some of the enumerated elements feature in the material image of the Buddha as produced in North India from the 1st century on, and we cannot rule out the possibility that before being integrated into the virtual representation they had first been actually represented. As a matter of fact, these "basic" elements find an echo in the composition of the divine image in an early period, regardless of the deity depicted: all the gods wear a headdress (here: the *uṣṇīṣa*), marks are seen on their forehead (here: the *ūrṇā*), their fingers are joined (here: "webbed hands"), the sexual organs are emphasised in male images (the member is here "concealed in a sheath" or *kosohitavatthaguhya*).[41] The left fist is set firmly on the left thigh when the Buddha sits or on the left hip when he stands, which is a generalized pattern in the iconography of male deities in this period. Both his "even feet" and his arms, so long that "standing and without bending he can touch his knees with either hand," are also rendered in the iconography of Jinas at Mathurā.[42] In a later period, artists would refer to the literary descriptions to illustrate some physical particularities: besides his body evoking the elephant as seen above, in Burma the Buddha may also have projecting heels, flat feet, and arms falling down to his knees "like the trunk of an elephant."[43]

In the course of the centuries and throughout the countries where worship was paid to the buddha, the forms displayed by the images basically resulted from a compromise between iconographic rules and the historical context, as will be briefly exemplified for those carved between the 1st and 6th centuries CE. The style and composition of the image as well as the forms of the volumes are elements that are shared by contemporary non-Buddhist images; they reflect the perception of the divine nature in what was considered to be its ideal form at a certain period.

REPRESENTING THE BUDDHA

The image created at Mathurā in the 1st–4th centuries CE (figs. 1–2) smiles and his eyes are wide open, looking straight toward the devotees—a feature inherited from earlier freestanding *yakṣa* images; his ears have elongated lobes, and his right hand is slightly turned forward and attached to the back slab by a protuberance that prevents it from breaking off. The surface of his head is plain, without any indication of hair, which is hidden by a thin garment, the end of which winds around the chignon topping the head.[44]

Displaying a powerful torso, he sits or stands in a dominant position recalling the contemporary Mathurā portraits of the Kushan rulers; he is the "great being" or *mahāpuruṣa* mentioned in the literary sources. With his left hand he firmly clenches his fist on his left thigh or hip while the right hand is raised in a gesture of command and nobility, half turned toward the devotees; both gestures underline his strong physical presence but also his moral authority while addressing the community of monks. He is ready to stand up, to act, and since this image serves as a model for the worshippers, he is in fact inviting them to act, to make the decision to take the path of renouncement: his steadfast expression and massive body, deprived of any ornamentation and covered by a clinging translucent garment, reflect the strength of the self, ready to follow the difficult path of renouncing all pleasure.

The inscriptions found on some of these sculptures name the figure as bodhisattva, which could mean that the sage is here depicted before the Awakening. However, this subtlety in nomenclature does not affect the visual formulation of this being: it remains an image of Gautama or Śākyamuni, regardless of whether he is still a bodhisattva or already a buddha.

A different perception of the buddha is to be seen in Gandhāra during the same period (1st–7th centuries) (figs. 3–5), as observed from an early stage in images found in the Swat Valley (fig. 3): the robe worn by the monk shows a similar pattern to the one noted at Mathurā, but the garment has lost its diaphanous quality and is fully pleated.[45] The hair is made visible, all the hair tied in a chignon at the top of the head; his eyes are wide open, as in Mathurā, but the Buddha has a moustache (figs. 3–4): both the hairstyle and the moustache are borrowed from contemporary representations of Śiva. The torso is powerful, but with a more realistic

Figure 3. Buddha flanked by Indra and Brahmā. Swat Valley (North Pakistan). Museum für Asiatische Kunst, Berlin.

Photo after *Buddha, The Spread of Buddhist Art in Asia*, ed. Tobu Museum of Art et al., exhibition catalogue planned by Akira Miyaji, Tokyo: NHK, 1998, p. 55.

Figure 4. Standing Buddha. Gandhāra. Museum für Asiatische Kunst, Berlin.
Source: Photo courtesy of Joachim K. Bautze.

rendering of the musculature. Besides this subtle combination of modified features encountered at Mathurā, the Buddha displays the gesture of meditation, encouraging an inward-looking attitude, and may even be entirely covered by his heavy monastic robe, his eyes no longer wide open: the image shifts from the powerful character encountered at Mathurā to the meditation ideal characterizing the image of the Buddha in Gandhāra.

The heavy, fully pleated garment that covers both shoulders conceals the shape of the Buddha's body; only a slight frontward movement of one leg can be sensed when he is seen standing (fig. 4). The feet, and even at times the hands, remain hidden by the monastic robe when the Buddha is seated. He looks down, the eyes practically closed as if looking inward, an expression that suggests the deep meditation in which the ascetic has sunk, and the smile is restrained (fig. 5). As a matter of fact, the Buddha from Gandhāra is the yogic master: he is the ideal ascetic who has withdrawn from the routine of daily life and has set himself on the road to becoming a universal spiritual leader, and yet he seems almost to be hiding himself in his heavy mantle. He reveals very little of himself: his mouth is small, his facial features are spare, his rippled hair covers the top part of his head, while the moustache is no longer shown. The headdress is no longer understood as being a chignon but rather is portrayed as a cranial protuberance (*uṣṇīṣa*) symbolizing the supreme enlightenment attained at Bodhgaya, and from *c.*

Figure 5. Seated Buddha. Gandhara. Government Museum and Art Gallery, Chandigarh.
Source: Photo courtesy of Joachim K. Bautze.

the 4th or 5th century on the hairstyle is completely curled; certain images show a hole drilled in this protuberance, and in later schools of Eastern India and Southeast Asia a flame may surmount the lump.[46]

Intensive contacts between monasteries led to transmission to various regions of specific aspects of the image that had emerged in Mathurā and Gandhāra; for instance, the tiny curls all turned in one direction and indistinctly covering the skull and the *uṣṇīṣa* became the characteristic hairstyle of the Buddha throughout Asia. This style, with the curls all flat, is also encountered in Andhra Pradesh (3rd–4th century), in an image owing various features to the Mathurā creation: the Buddha stands or sits in a frontal position, the pleated garment covering his left shoulder—rarely both shoulders; while holding the extremity of his robe with his raised left hand, with his raised right webbed hand he presents the gesture displayed at Mathurā when addressing his devotees and looks at them with eyes wide open (fig. 6).[47]

The assimilation of stylistic Gandhāran traits was not accomplished without their profound reworking from the 4th century on (the so-called Gupta period) at Mathurā (fig. 7), where the Buddha as depicted during the Kushan period gave way to an image imbued with restraint: he does not look at the viewer full in the face but casts his gaze downward; he is entirely covered by his robe, which clings to his body, revealing its smooth and rounded forms,

Figure 6. Events from the Buddha's life. Nagarjunakonda. Site Museum, Nagarjunakonda.
Source: Photo courtesy of Joachim K. Bautze.

while the drapery falls in ridges arranged in parallel lines. This Buddha tends to close himself off from the outer world, in contrast with his nature in the Kushan period; his face no longer expresses the powerful attention of the Kushan Buddha, but shows a subtle smile, having attained an inner spiritual peace. In the course of time, the face becomes elongated, the body slender and visible under the translucent garment, departing from the Gandhāran and early Mathurān ideals.

The body tends toward a perfect frontality and symmetry, no longer showing the slight movement of a leg seen earlier in Gandhāra; the Buddha stands in perfect equipoise, with the gesture of protection or "absence of fear" (*abhayamudrā*) shown by his webbed right hand. This is his most frequently encountered gesture; he becomes the protector of his community. This gesture observed in Gandhāra replaces the *vyāvṛtta* position of the hand only half turned toward the public seen at Mathurā during the Kushan period. His perfectly confident posture with the left fist placed on the left hip or knee is no longer to be seen, the hand holding the extremity of his garment in another gesture inherited from Gandhāra. Monks would take refuge in this Buddha, who would, moreover, protect their path while traveling: cast images

Figure 7. Standing Buddha, Mathura, Inscribed in the year 230 (*c*. 357 CE). State Museum Lucknow.
Source: Photo courtesy of Joachim K. Bautze.

were then produced, many of which were carried away and discovered outside India, where the Buddha shows the *abhayamudrā* and where, unlike the stone images produced around Mathurā but not unlike the Sārnāth carvings, he could present a light movement of a leg, thus showing him walking and accompanying his monks.[48]

The large nimbus behind the Mathurā Buddha's head is now covered with concentric symbolic ornamental bands carved with delicacy; rows of pearls, rows of twisted beaded garlands, rows of scrolls where birds turn into plants surround a central lotus flower with spread petals. Whereas the scalloped border or the rays radiating from the center on stone and metal images symbolize the light emerging from the Buddha, the central field of the nimbus illustrates the spiritual fertility that is born from the center, from the lotus when taking the path of the Buddha. The nervous line of this ornamentation, the extremely and exquisitely detailed carving, expresses life arising out of the inner peaceful circle while at the same time indicating that behind the diversification and chaos of life lies hidden this inner peace.

The lotus has an extremely rich symbolism and covers various aspects. Here, it marks the passage to higher spiritual levels, to heavenly worlds. From the very beginning of Indian art, for instance at Sanchi, we find a lotus carved on the lower surface of the architraves of the porticoes, referring to heaven, and this position is preserved for the lotus throughout the history of Buddhist architecture, for instance, on the ceiling above the buddha in the sanctuaries of Ajanta in the late 5th century, or under the vault of temples at Pagan from the late 11th to the 13th centuries. In Mathurā, the lotus was carved in the central field of large umbrellas that used to stand above images, as in the case of the over-life-size sculpture donated by Friar Bala in the 2nd century CE.[49] In all examples, the lotus refers to the higher level of the image, to the place where the soul leaves our world to reach higher spiritual planes.

The nimbus and the umbrella are thus of major importance in the composition of the buddha image. They integrate the cosmic waters and the fire of the sun, two elements that form an inherent part of the Buddha's nature, as we know from the early depiction of the Śrāvastī Miracles in Gandhāra; moreover, with their circular form they also contribute to locating the buddha at the center of the universe, a position from the 6th century on with the creation of *maṇḍalas*. The Buddha is thus perceived as the sun illuminating the universe from the very center where he sits or stands, and as such he deservedly received the name of Vairocana, another name for the sun. He is a powerful being who can use magic: while still at Śrāvastī he produced a great multiplicity of images of himself to fill the universe, all related to his person and all seated, standing, walking, or lying on lotuses originating from the main lotus of the image.

The personality has thus changed profoundly since the Kushan period; the Buddha is neither exclusively the ruler attentively watching the world around him, nor the yogic master hidden in his heavy garment. Now, he has put himself beyond our world, combining the moral power of the ruler, as the broad shoulders of his images at Mathurā still testify, and the spiritual strength of the ascetic in his monastic robe.

Yet profounder changes in the perception of the Buddha occurred at Sārnāth, the place where Śākyamuni preached for the very first time. Located in the vicinity of Benares on the Ganges, it became a major site in the 5th century, when pilgrims from China and Central Asia passed on their way to the sacred sites visited by the Buddha, and its ateliers exerted a significant influence in various parts of South and Southeast Asia, from Ajanta and other excavated sites in Maharashtra up to East India, Nepal, Bangladesh, and the Malay Peninsula in the second half of the 5th century and later. A clearly distinguishable stylistic idiom emerged, bringing to full blossom features that had been lying deep below the surface at Mathurā, and radically turning away from the Gandhāran naturalism.

The Buddha stands, his monastic robe covering his entire body (fig. 8). However, and in contrast to the image encountered in Gandhāra and at Mathurā, the garment is not pleated and it is translucent, revealing the form of the body, which is traced with elegant precise lines combined to a sensual and delicate rendering of all parts of the body. All the parts of the body smoothly blend into one another, reflecting the concept of the permanent flow of life, which is another major characteristic of Indian art in general.[50] As a matter of fact, the 5th- and 6th-century Sārnāth representations of the Buddha and bodhisattvas reveal a very specifically Indian aspect of the divine nature. Although it retains a faint allusion to the male genitalia inherited from the Kushan period, this image combines it with the curves of the female body. The slender body, the elegant movement, the soft swelling of all parts of the body—all these features contribute to reflecting a degree a feminization not previously seen in Buddhist art. What appears here is a trend that intersects all religious tendencies in the Gupta period, when goddesses again found their place by the side of male deities as attendant figures or as counterparts to male bodhisattvas from the 6th century on.

Figure 8. Standing Buddha. Sarnath. Indian Museum, Kolkata.
Source: Photo courtesy of Joachim K. Bautze.

The nimbus retains elements noted at Mathurā, such as the scalloped border, reminiscent of the rays of the sun, the twisted pearled garland, or the scrolls, but the lotus is absent here, leaving the central part devoid of any ornamentation. In a certain way this bareness echoes the diaphanous and plain dress, just as the row of petals in the nimbus reflected the concentric folds on the body in Mathurā. The Buddha is no longer the yogic master of Gandhāra, no longer the powerful ruler of Mathurā in the Kushan period, two aspects that had harmoniously merged in the 4th- and 5th-century image of Mathurā. Here the Buddha has become a transcendent character, full of compassion and love for all sentient beings, protecting them and displaying the *abhayamudrā* or showing his infinite generosity with the *varadamudrā*, and in some cases standing on the lotus; just as this flower emerges in all its purity out of muddy waters, the Buddha is unblemished, hovering over our world.

Whereas the Mathurā image preserved the equipoise position of the body, the Sārnāth Buddha only rarely retained this position, showing a slight movement of the hip with one knee put forward. The resulting asymmetrical position of the body indicates movement, the Buddha leaving, perhaps only for a while, his imperturbability at the center of the universe to act and move in our direction.[51]

IMAGE, OBJECT OF WONDER AND MERIT

Creating the image of the Buddha not only implied reflection on his physical appearance, but also entailed the possibility of depicting or alluding to his spiritual power. The literary sources offer ample evidence of the importance attributed to the golden radiance of his body, which was visually translated with the nimbus carved behind the head or the halo surrounding the entire body. What is seen beyond the material image is the monk and his magnificent appearance.

The physical appearance of Gautama was indeed a source of profound wonderment: in the *Mahāvastu*, when he saw the Bodhisattva, the old seer Vasiṣṭha

> wondered who this might be, glorious of form, dazzling more than the lightning's flash, all golden, gleaming like a smokeless, blazing fire. Broadchested was he, with mighty arms, and admirable hands and fingers; compact was his belly, slender his figure; his carriage that of an antelope, and his hips were prominent. He was like a pillar of gold, and his eyes flashed like a bull's. His bust was like that of a tiger, his feet and hands like the lotus. His body was bright with the marks won by the virtues of a hundred lives, as the moon is bright among the stars. There were no befitting bright ornaments on his limbs; these characteristics alone adorned the body of the great-souled one. As the true son of Meru's circle moved on stately as an elephant, the earth suddenly re-echoed to the tread of his feet. With his tender, deep and resonant voice, he was capable of ordering effectively all the three worlds. By all these secondary and principal characteristics which I have enumerated, he is marked as the supreme lord of all beings in the three worlds. With the radiance that flows from his entire body he fills all this grove of penance like the rising sun. Endowed as he is with the eighty minor characteristics and the thirty-two marks of excellence, this dazzling young is man is like Sanatkumāra. The great seer… [said] …Young man… thou art like a Gandharva, like the moon, like an offspring of a deva…[52]

Later on, Sujātā bursts into tears on seeing the one "whose face is like a full moon" and extols him in such words: "My eyes can never have enough of gazing upon thee, O valiant one. O thou that art lovely and brave, bearing the beautiful marks and wearing fine jewels, why dost thou pass on when my heart is utterly blind with unrequited love?"[53] He becomes an object of admiration to cowherds of the forest of Venuvana: his size recalls a golden mountain, shining like melting butter that burns, similar to gold in fusion, spreading a golden light in the depth of the forest. The only sighting of "the lion among the Śākyas" (Śākyasiṃha) brings rejoicing and the absolute conviction that he is omniscient; he brings contentment to anybody who gazes at him and thus finds the supreme happiness. His glow is extremely luminous, his body irradiates an aura, his physical marks are majestic, his qualities and his power are perfect.[54]

In this eulogy of the Buddha, it is evident that the golden color of the skin and the light that radiates out of the body are of major importance. The golden color of the skin is one of the *lakṣaṇas* in the thirty-two series, the texts telling that this color excels any gold color shown by the different levels of gods.[55] Similarly, the Buddha is said to display supreme beauty amid the radiance he displays; his sheen is then equal to the luminance of the "king of the gods" (*devarāja*).[56]

The emission of light is most probably the clearest evidence of the supramundane nature of the buddha, but it can also be used as a way of converting people.[57] Whereas in the initial list of thirty-two *lakṣaṇas*, the light appeared as a rather uniform aura framing the Buddha's body, this body becomes the source of rays of light that extend beyond any visible limit; a distinction is also made here in the nature of the rays, the first related to the physical body, the second being "rays of wisdom." [58] These rays can spread out from the wheels incised on the soles of his feet, for instance, or out of the *uṣṇīṣa*; beams of light shine out of the various parts of his body—the toes, ankles, legs, and so forth—and illuminate the entire universe.[59] Moreover, rays are emitted in the ten directions of space at very specific moments in the Buddha's life—birth, enlightenment, and first predication.[60] In the *sūtras* of the Great Vehicle, the buddha's light is "immeasurable,... no light in this world can outshine [him]; neither the splendor of the sun, nor the luster of precious stones, nor the splendor of Mount Sumeru, nor the light of the moon shine in this world like your blazing light."[61]

Texts such as the two *Sukhāvatīvyūha Sūtras*, probably written before the 4th century, where the central buddha is Amitābha, "the Buddha of Measureless Light," describe worlds inaccessible to us.[62] In their cosmic visions, they refer to innumerable buddhas who proclaim the Buddhist law or dharma (hence the nature of their bodies: *dharmakāya*) to myriads of bodhisattvas whose bodies share the nature of enjoyment (hence the term *sambhogakāya*). These buddhas could appear as magicians (*māyākāra*) whose supreme power would be seen in producing light. As an extrapolation of Śākyamuni's ability to emit light from various parts of his body, rays that arise out of Amitābha's body pervade the entire universe, radiating from the mouth, filling innumerable universes before returning to the "crown of their head."[63] All the bodhisattvas in the *Sukhāvatīvyūha* bear the thirty-two marks; all are surrounded by the immense radiance of their own bodies.[64] Translated at the visual level of sculpture or painting in India or elsewhere, and in particular in Central Asia, such impressive compositions show that the buddhas are physically identical to the historical Buddha.

The golden color that impregnates the body of Śākyamuni and, after him, any other buddha, and the phenomenon of emission of light out of his body, or out of the body of any bodhisattva or buddha, are two major elements of the buddha's nature that would find an echo in artistic representation. The large nimbus set above the shoulders and the aura traced around the entire body illustrate this light, which radiates from the Buddha's body. Both are encountered from the beginning of our era, and the light may be shown with arrow-like rays that spread around the image's entire face and/or body.[65]

In the testimony of Chinese pilgrims, it is evident that it was this feature that struck them in particular—the light that radiates from these images shining in full glory, and in particular from metal images that best convey the idea of the buddha as the sun (Vairocana) radiating from the center of the universe.[66] Throughout Asia and up to the present day, the golden complexion has belonged to the iconography of the buddha image; reading Xuanzang's 7th-century text, we learn that an image located at Pima in Central Asia "reflected constantly a bright light, it works many miracles... those who have any disease, according to the part affected, cover the corresponding place on the statue with gold-leaf, and forthwith they are healed."[67] Such practice is still carried on, for instance at the great Mahāmuni temple of Mandalay, which is allegedly covered by a coat of nearly 16 inches of gold leaf, applied in the last centuries day after day by worshippers.

Having gone through the highest spiritual experience, the Buddha is of a divine nature, and as such, like the bodhisattvas and buddhas inhabiting these numberless universes, he possesses magical power that he only reluctantly uses.[68] Similarly, his images are imbued with qualities not met with in images of other deities, always felt to be very powerful and to be alive, as a tale—again narrated by Xuanzang—testifies:

> To the south-west of the great stupa (of Peshawar) there is a figure of Buddha in white stone about eighteen feet high. It is a standing figure, and looks to the north. It has many spiritual powers, and diffuses a brilliant light. Sometimes there are people who see the image come out of an evening and go round the great stupa. Lately a band of robbers wished to go in and steal. The image immediately came forth and went before the robbers. Affrighted, they ran away; the image then returned to its own place, and remained fixed as before. The robbers, affected by what they had seen, began a new life, and went about through towns and villages telling what had happened.[69]

The power of actual images should not be underestimated, for it was images that constituted the major vector transmitting new religious beliefs.[70] Within this context, it should be remembered that another famous image had a major impact on the art of Central Asia and the Far East—the image of the Buddha that King Udayana of Vatsa ordered to be made in order to console him for the absence of the Buddha, who had gone on Mount Meru to teach his mother and the gods. Although it is usually said that this image was carved out of sandalwood before being copied by another ruler, King Prasenajit, who had his own copy made in gold, a text translated in the early 5th century into Chinese relates the golden image to Udayana.[71] This image was transported on an elephant to Saṅkāśya where the Buddha descended from the Heaven of the 33 Gods and walked on air to greet Śākyamuni, who bowed before the image and prophesied that it would be of major importance for Buddhism in the future, being in fact the model for all further representations of himself.[72] The "Udayana Image," as it is known, could walk, and it received special veneration from the 4th to the 7th century; thus it is possible that the numerous castings produced during this period in one way or another evoke this image, which the tradition considers to be contemporary to Śākyamuni, thereby serving as a model for all the images to come.[73]

IMAGE, OBJECT OF VENERATION

The creation of an image is not a purely intellectual and material exercise, for the image acts as an intermediary involved in the personal relationship between the devotee and the Buddha, and thus becomes the repository of feelings of devotion on the part of the human worshipper.[74] At the same time, it is understood to display the infinite compassion (*karuṇa*) of the Buddha for all sentient beings when he presents the *varadamudrā,* his universal teaching when he shows the *dharmacakrapravartanamudrā,* or his eternal protection when he displays the *abhayamudrā.*[75] The image is also the model of a perfect life following strict moral lines taught by the Buddha, who was an achieved monk and led the way to wisdom, remaining an exemplary figure for the religious community. From the 7th–8th century onward Bodhgaya, where Śākyamuni had become buddha, emerged as the most important site visited by pilgrims from all across the Asian world. This fundamental moment is illustrated with the seated Buddha brushing the earth with the fingertips of his right hand (*bhūmisparśamudrā*), an iconography that would supplant all others in importance and spread across all Asia. The buddha images were understood by the monks as being symbolic of his presence. As Yi Jing tells us,

> Sometimes a holy image is placed in the rooms where the priests reside, either in a window or in a niche especially made for it... Every monastery has its holy image, which is enshrined in a special temple. The priest must not fail to wash the image after it is constructed during his lifetime. And it is not allowable that the simple offering of food should be made only on a fast day. If these regulations are carried out, then to have the image in the same room is not wrong. While the Buddha was living, His disciples lived in the same rooms, and an image represents the real person; we can live in the same rooms without any harm. This traditional custom has long been practised in India.[76]

If we recognize here parts of rituals still practiced in 21st-century India such as the washing of the god, we also see that for the monks of the 7th century the image was a sign of the presence of the Buddha. The Buddha had been a monk, and the image was thus considered to be alive and to be a monk among monks, showing the way, teaching them, blessing his devotees, and protecting their way to salvation.

A PERFECT IMAGE

Interactions between the different schools were thus permanent. During the Gupta period, the Mathurā ateliers retained the earlier ideal of the powerful world ruler and merged it with the ideal of the perfect yogī master who had appeared in Gandhāra, covering the Buddha with a folded dress and somehow enhancing the materialism of the image. In contrast, the Sārnāth ateliers created an image that owes its pure and unadorned forms to the ideal of the perfect master, freed from any materiality that might be suggested by the dress.

The representation that emerged in the 5th century at Mathurā and Sārnāth marked the culmination of a complex evolution during which it had been imbued with various political and spiritual concepts that would differ according to sites and periods; this image would henceforth serve as a template for all the images of the Buddha created in South Asia and elsewhere.[77] The perception of the nature of the Buddha evolved in the course of time, linked to aesthetic and iconographic changes that are inherently bound to human nature. The authors of the *Rudrāyaṇāvadānam* in the *Divyādāna* tell how the Buddha himself left the door open to choices made by men; when asked by King Bimbisāra what kind of present should be offered to King Rudrāyaṇa, the Buddha advised him to have a portrait of himself painted and sent:

> "Your majesty," the Blessed One said, "these painters will just exhaust themselves. They can't apprehend the appearance of the Tathāgata. Instead, bring a piece of cloth here."
>
> The king brought a piece of cloth. The Blessed One cast his shadow on it and said [to the painters], now fill it in with various colors. And underneath the image write the [vows for] taking refuge and the precepts...[78]

The Buddha here became the artist making a drawing of himself, but he let the others fill it in as they liked, and as such, the image of the Buddha is recognizable throughout the Eastern world, although understandings of its meaning may differ.

REVIEW OF LITERATURE

Most often labeled "aniconic," the early phase in the development of Buddhist iconography has been a matter of controversy in the field of South Asian art history since the 19th century.[79] A widespread view was that specific motifs, such as the lotus, the tree, or the wheel, or topics such as scenes of devotion to a monument, were depicted as symbolizing particular moments in the Buddha's life, an opinion that was recently revised by Susan L. Huntington, suggesting that the depiction of sites rather refers to actual scenes of worship. This initiated a series of controversial papers between Susan L. Huntington and Vidya Dehejia.[80]

This period came to an end around the beginning of our era when the buddha image emerged in the visual arts in North India. Two contrasting opinions emerged, the first of which considered this phenomenon the result of Western influences, a position defended by Alfred Foucher, whose main publication on this topic was titled "L'art gréco-bouddhique du Gandhāra," tracing the origin of the particular style that developed in North Pakistan and Afghanistan to Alexander the Great.[81] However, research shows a much more nuanced picture, taking into account the probable presence of a Roman impact and the undisputable existence of relations with other South Asian regions.[82] Replying to this viewpoint on the origin of the buddha image, Ananda K. Coomaraswamy considered the image created at Mathurā as a genuine Indian creation that did not owe its existence to Western influence.[83] These two opposing positions survived most of the 20th century, with defendants on both sides, but without real discussion.[84] The question received renewed attention with two papers by Johanna van Lohuizen-De Leeuw and Herbert Härtel: both papers were read in 1979 and 1983, respectively at the biannual South Asian Archaeology Conference, and both led to an intensive phase of publications that have provided searching analyses of the facts behind the emergence of the buddha image and its development.[85] In this context, we should mention the in-depth study by Akira Miyaji on the early images found in the Swat Valley, and papers by Juhyung Rhi dealing with the stylistic evolution of the buddha image in Gandhāra, including comprehensive bibliographies on the topic.[86]

Specific aspects of the buddha image have been investigated in detailed research, such as the protuberance on his head; the snail form of it in the Mathurā sculptures defining the so-called "kapardin" Buddha, a neologism coined by Ananda K. Coomaraswamy as recently pointed out by Harry Falk, who proposed a more "realistic" identification to this element; the powerful male body in Mathurā or the "feminization" of the body in Sārnāth; and the image of the Buddha in South India and its impact in Southeast Asia.[87] In this context, attention has also focused on cast images, mainly from the 4th–7th century, which were produced in various regions of India before being carried away to Southeast Asia or the Far East.[88] Other aspects, such as the bejeweled image, the emaciated body, or the walking stance, may also allude to moments in the Buddha's biography, which constitutes an altogether separate topic in the study of the buddha image.[89]

DIGITAL MATERIALS

Digital South Asia Library (https://dsal.uchicago.edu/images/aiis/) is a database of photos taken in Indian museums and archaeological sites.

Gandharan Art Bibliography (https://www.carc.ox.ac.uk/GandharaConnections/bibliography.htm) is, in its own words, "a comprehensive bibliography of Gandharan art and closely related material"; in particular, it includes two long lists of publications concerning the buddha image in the chapter "Iconography."

Himalayan Art Resources (https://www.himalayanart.org/) includes links to museums and has a rich documentation of Buddhist images (not exclusively of the buddha), mainly from the Himalaya regions.

The John C. and Susan L. Huntington Photographic Archive of Buddhist and Asian Art (https://dsal.uchicago.edu/huntington/database.php) displays a comprehensive and easily searchable documentation of sculptures and paintings mainly preserved in South Asia.

FURTHER READING

Adam, Leonhard. *Buddhastatuen, Ursprung und Formen der Buddhagestalt.* Stuttgart: Verlag Strecker und Schröder, 1925.

Griswold, Alexander Brown. "Prolegomena to the Study of the Buddha's Dress in Chinese Sculpture: With Particular Reference to the Rietberg Museum's Collection." *Artibus Asiae* 26, no. 2 (1963): 85–131.

Krishan, Yuvraj. *The Buddha Image, Its Origin and Development.* New Delhi: Munshiram Manoharlal, 1996.

Schumann, Hans Wolfgang. *Buddhabildnisse, Ihre Symbolik und Geschichte.* Heidelberg/Leimen, Germany: Werner Kristkeitz Verlag, 2003.

van Lohuizen-De Leeuw, Johanna E. *The "Scythian" Period: An Approach to the History, Art, Epigraphy and Palaeography of North India from the 1st Century B.C. to the 3rd Century A.D.* Leiden, The Netherlands: E. J. Brill, 1949.

Verma, Shailendra Kumar. *Art and Iconography of the Buddha Images.* Delhi: Eastern Book Linkers, 1994.

EXHIBITION CATALOGUES AND ILLUSTRATED BOOKS

Budda ten: oinaru tabiji/Buddha, The Spread of Buddhist Art in Asia. Edited by Tobu Museum of Art et al. Exhibition catalogue planned by Akira Miyaji. Tokyo: NHK, 1998.

Cohn, William. *Buddha in der Kunst des Ostens.* Leipzig: Klinkhardt & Biermann, 1925.

Das Bild des Buddha, mit einem Vorwort von Professor Dr. Herbert Härtel. Berlin: Safari Verl., 1979.

Klimburg-Salter, Deborah E. *Buddha in Indien: Die frühindische Skulptur von König Aśoka bis zur Guptazeit.* Vienna: Kunsthistorisches Museum, 1995.

Pal, Pratapaditya, ed. *Light of Asia: Buddha Sakyamuni in Asian Art.* Los Angeles: Los Angeles County Museum of Art, 1984.

Menzies, Jackie, ed. *Buddha, Radiant Awakening.* Sydney: Art Gallery of New South Wales, 2001.

Rowland, Benjamin, Jr. *The Evolution of the Buddha Image.* New York: The Asia Society, 1963.

Snellgrove, David L., ed. *The Image of the Buddha.* Paris: UNESCO, 1978.

NOTES

1. This article deals with the visual representation of the buddha in literature and art and not with his biography, which is narrated in various texts and may include references to his appearance. One should consult the writings of Alfred Foucher, *Vie du Bouddha d'après les textes et les monuments de l'Inde*

(Paris: Payot, 1949); Hajima Nakamura, *Gotama Buddha, A Biography Based on the Most Reliable Texts,* 2 vols., trans. Gaynor Sekimori (Tokio: Kosei Publishing Company, 2001–2005); Ernst Waldschmidt, *Die Legende vom Leben des Buddha, In Auszügen aus den heiligen Texten, Aus dem Sanskrit, Pali und Chinesischen übersetzt und eingeführt, mit vielen zum Teil farbigen Illustrationen wiedergegeben nach tibetischen Tempelbildern aus dem Besitz des Berliner Museums für Völkerkunde* (Berlin: Volksverband d. Bücherfreunde Wegweiser-Verl. GmbH, 1929, reprint: Graz: Verl. für Sammler, 1982); and John Strong, *The Buddha, A Short Biography* (Oxford: Oneworld Publications, 2001), all of whom made use of these sources when writing their own biographies of the Buddha. The contributions of Étienne Lamotte, Alfred Foucher, and André Bareau to the biography of the Buddha are surveyed in André Couture, "Revue de la littérature française concernant l'hagiographie du Bouddhisme indien ancient," in *Monks and Magicians: Religious Biographies in Asia,* ed. Phyllis Granoff and Koichi Shinohara (Oakville, Ontario: Mosaic Press, 1988), 9–44, at 21–30. Further authors are mentioned in Claudine Bautze-Picron, "The Biography of the Buddha in Indian Art: How and When?" in *Biographie als religiöser und kultureller Text/Biography as a Religious and Cultural Text,* ed. Andreas Schüle (Münster: Lit Verlag, 2002), 197–239, at 198–199.

2. Gritli von Mitterwallner, "Yakṣas of Ancient Mathurā," in *Mathurā, The Cultural Heritage,* ed. Doris Meth Srinivasan (New Delhi: Manohar, 1989), 368–382.
3. Meyer Schapiro, "Frontal and Profile as Symbolic Forms," in Meyer Schapiro, *Words and Pictures: On the Literal and the Symbolic in the Illustration of a Text,* Approaches to Semiotics, Paperback Series 11 (The Hague: Mouton, 1973), 37–49; and Claudine Bautze-Picron, "De la scène narrative à l'icône: Simplification de l'image dans les bas-reliefs hindous d'Ellora," in *La norme et son application dans le monde indien: Journées de travail organisées par l'Université de Paris-III et le CNRS, ESA 7019, Paris, 28 & 29 janvier 1999,* ed. M.-L. Barazer-Billoret and J. Fezas (Paris: Publications de l'E.F.E.O., 2000), 203–219.
4. Johanna van Lohuizen-de Leeuw, "New Evidence With Regard to the Origin of the Buddha Image," *South Asian Archaeology 1979,* ed. Herbert Härtel (Berlin: Dietrich Reimer Verlag, 1981), 377–400 (with numerous references); and Maurizio Taddei, "Some Reflections on the Formation of the Buddha Image," in *Maurizio Taddei, On Gandhāra, Collected Articles,* ed. Giovanni Verardi and Anna Filigenzi (Naples: Università degli Studi di Napoli "L'Orientale," 2003), Vol. 2, 593–607. Further references are found in Bautze-Picron, "The Biography of the Buddha," 200, note 18. On the topic of the symbolic representations, see Karlsson, *Face to Face With the Absent Buddha: The Formation of Buddhist Aniconic Art,* Historia Religionum 15 (Uppsala: Acta Universitatis Upsaliensis, 1999); Kanoko Tanaka, *Absence of the Buddha Images in Early Buddhist Art: Towards Its Significance in Comparative Religion,* Emerging Perceptions in Buddhist Studies 8 (New Delhi: D.K. Printworld, 1998); and Robert DeCaroli, *Haunting the Buddha, Indian Popular Religions and the Formation of Buddhism* (Oxford: Oxford University Press, 2004).
5. Both regions exercised a profound influence in the production of the Buddha image in Gujarat in the 5th–6th century; see Ken Ishikawa, "More Gandhāra than Mathurā: Substantial and Persistent Gandhāran Influences Provincialized in the Buddhist Material Culture of Gujarat and Beyond, c. AD 400–550," in *The Global Connections of Gandhāran Art,* ed. Wannaporn Rienjang and Peter Stewart (Oxford: Archaeopress, 2020), 156–204.
6. Bautze-Picron, "De la scène narrative."
7. Sneh Pandit, *An Approach to the Indian Theory of Art and Aesthetics* (New Delhi: Sterling, 1977), 60–67.
8. See Claudine Bautze-Picron, "The 'Stele' in Bihar and Bengal, 8th to 12th c.: Structure and Motifs," *Berliner Indologische Studien* 2 (1986): 107–131 on the superimposed levels of the image; and Claudine Bautze-Picron, "The 'Stele' in Bihar and Bengal, 8th to 12th centuries: Symmetry and Composition," in *Indian Art and Archaeology,* ed. E. M. Raven and K. R. van Kooij, Panels of the 7th World Sanskrit Conference, Kern Institute, Leiden: August 23–29, 1987, vol. 10 (Leiden: Brill, 1992), 3–34 on the important rule of symmetry that dictates the composition of the whole carving. Although concerned with medieval images from Eastern India, the observations made in these two papers can apply to all the

production from North India up to 1200 CE. On the symbolism of the image, more particularly within the context of its composition, see Schapiro, "Frontal and Profile."

9. Claudine Bautze-Picron, "Between Men and Gods: Small Motifs in the Buddhist Art of Eastern India; An Interpretation," in *Function and Meaning in Buddhist Art: Proceedings of a Seminar Held at Leiden University, 21–24 October 1991*, ed. K. R. van Kooij and H. van der Veere (Groningen: Egbert Forsten, 1995), 59–79; and Claudine Bautze-Picron, "Incense, Flowers and Prayers in Honour of the Buddha: Ritualistic Scenes in Ajanta and Other Buddhist Sites of Maharashtra, Fifth to Eighth Century," in *Ratnasri: Gleanings From Indian Archaeology: Art History and Indology; Papers Presented in Memory of Dr. N R Banerji*, ed. Arundhati Banerji (New Delhi: Kaveri Books, 51–70).
10. Danièle Masset, "Une lecture bouddhiste des mythes hindous: la mise en question des modèles brahmaniques dans le Canon bouddhique tibétain," in *La norme et son application dans le monde indien: Journées de travail organisées par l'Université de Paris-III et le CNRS, ESA 7019, Paris, 28 & 29 janvier 1999*, ed. M.-L. Barazer-Billoret and J. Fezas (Paris: Publications de l'E.F.E.O., 2000), 155–173, at 156ff. The original Sanskrit texts analyzed by the author date back to the first three centuries CE ("Lecture bouddhiste," 155; Johannes Schneider, *Der Lobpreis der Vorzüglichkeit des Buddha, Udbhatasiddhasvāmins Viśeṣastava mit Prajñāvarmans Kommentar, Nach dem tibetischen Tanjur*, herausgegeben und übersetzt (Bonn: Indica et Tibetica, Band 23, 1993), 154–156, points out that the only secure period for dating the text that he publishes and translates is the *terminus ante quem* provided by the date of the translation into Tibetan, that is, around 800 CE); they are known through late Tibetan translations; commentaries, also known through Tibetan sources, were written around 800 CE by the Bengali scholar Prajñāvarman. As mentioned by Masset ("Lecture bouddhiste," 156), the comparison between the buddha and Brāhmanical deities is an early way of giving prominence to the buddha and his thought and is also encountered in Pāli literature. Regarding elements of the personality, for instance, the fifteenth feature of the thirty-two list has it that the buddha possesses *brahmasvara*; see Étienne Lamotte, *Le traité de la grande vertu de sagesse de Nāgārjuna (Mahāprajñāpāramitāśāstra)*, Vol. 1 (Louvain: Bibliothèque du Muséon 18, 1944; reprint: Louvain-la-Neuve: Publications de l'Institut Orientaliste de Louvain 25, 1981), 279
11. Masset, "Lecture bouddhiste," 168–170; Johannes Schneider, "Der Buddha als der wahre Śiva, Udbhaṭasiddhasvāmins Sarvajñamaheśvarastotra," *Berliner Indologische Studien* 8 (1995): 153–186.
12. In the simultaneous presence of water and fire, the presence of the elephant and lion can also be recognised; see Claudine Bautze-Picron, "Antagonistes et complémentaires, le lion et l'éléphant dans la personnalité du Buddha," in *Penser, dire et représenter l'animal dans le monde indien*, ed. Nalini Balbir and Georges-Jean Pinault, Sciences historiques et philologiques 345 (Paris: Librairie Honoré Champion, Éditeur, Bibliothèque de l'École des Hautes Études, 2008), 523–572, at 523–524.
13. For instance, the Buddha Dīpaṅkara possesses the very same thirty-two marks shown by Śākyamuni; the two lists given for each of them in the *Mahāvastu* are identical (J.J. Jones, *The Mahāvastu*, Vol. 1 (London: The Pali Text Society, reprint: 1987), 180–182; and J. J. Jones, *The Mahāvastu*, Vol. 2, (London: The Pali Text Society, 1976), 26. A description of the buddhas of the past is given in the *Buddhavaṃsa*; see I. B. Horner, *The Minor Anthologies of the Pali Canon, Part III: Chronicle of Buddhas (Buddhavaṃsa) and Basket of Conduct (Cariyāpiṭaka)* (London: The Pali Text Society, 1975). For further images, see Claudine Bautze-Picron, "Śākyamuni in Eastern India and Tibet from the 11th to the 13th centuries," *Silk Road Art and Archaeology* 4 (1995/1996): 355–408, at 361, figs. 1–3, 17–20.
14. Paul Harrison and Christian Luczanits, "New Light on (and From) the Muhammad Nari Stele," in *Special International Symposium on Pure Land Buddhism, International Symposium Series 1, 4th August 2011, Otani University* (Kyoto: Ryukoku University Research Center for Buddhist Cultures in Asia, 2012), 69–127 (with numerous further references); and Miyaji Akira, "Response to New Light on (and From) the Mohammad Nari Stele," in *Special International Symposium on Pure Land Buddhism,*

International Symposium Series 1, 4th August 2011, Otani University (Kyoto: Ryukoku University Research Center for Buddhist Cultures in Asia, 2012), 128–130.

15. R. D. Banerji, "Buddhacharita in Bengal," *The Modern Review (A Monthly Review and Miscellany)* 47 (1930): 104–110; Janice Leoshko, "Scenes of the Buddha's Life in Pala-Period Art," *Silk Road Art and Archaeology* 3 (1993/1994): 251–276; and Bautze-Picron, "Śākyamuni."
16. Venerable S. Dhammika, *Mātṛceṭa's Hymn to the Buddha: An English Rendering of the* Śatapañcāśatka (Kandy: Buddhist Publication Society, 1989), 23; and David R. Shackleton Bailey, *The Śatapañcāśatka of Mātṛceṭa, Sanskrit text, Tibetan transl. & commentary and Chinese transl, with an introd., engl. Transl. and notes, ed.* (Cambridge, UK: Cambridge University Press, 1951), 162. Mātṛceṭa should be dated "spätestens zu Beginn des 4. Jh.n.Chr." as mentioned by Schneider, *Lobpreis*, 13 note 4.
17. S. Dhammika, *Mātṛceṭa*, 26; and Bailey, *Śatapañcāśatka*, 166.
18. This text and two others were written by two brothers whom D. Masset very carefully dates "to the first centuries of our era" ("Lecture bouddhiste," 155); Schneider, *Lobpreis*, 13 suggests with caution a date earlier than Mātṛceṭa; Michael Hahn, "Śaṅkarasvāmin's *Devatāvimarṣastuti*," in *Vividharatnakarandaka, Festgabe für Adelheid Mette*, ed. Christine Chojnacki, Jens-Uwe Hartmann, and Volker M. Tschannerl (Swisttal-Odendorf: Indica et Tibetica Verlag, 2000), 313–329, at 318; and Masset, "Lecture bouddhiste," 158. One could thus surmise that in the veneration they pay to the buddha, the actual physical form does not matter to these writers.
19. Schneider, *Lobpreis*, 53–73; and Masset, "Lecture bouddhiste," 157.
20. From "Ses pouvoirs surnaturels . . . ses qualités . . . et sa force . . . sont immenses et illimités. Le corps du Buddha est orné des trente-deux marques . . . et des quatre-vingts sous-marques . . .; intérieurement il possède les innombrables attributs et qualités des Buddha: c'est pourquoi on ne se lasse pas de le voir. Ceux qui voient le corps du Buddha en oublient les cinq objets de la jouissance . . . du monde et ne se souviennent plus de rien. Si l'on voit le corps du Buddha, le bonheur est complet; on ne se lasse pas et on ne peut changer de spectacle," in the *Mahāprajñāpāramitāśāstra*, attributed to Nāgārjuna, and translated into Chinese by Kumārajīva – 4th to 5th century (Étienne Lamotte, *Le traité de la grande vertu de sagesse de Nāgārjuna (Mahāprajñāpāramitāśāstra)*, vol. 3 (Louvain-la-Neuve: Publications de l'Institut Orientaliste de Louvain, 1970), 1348–1349.
21. Lamotte, *Le traité*, Vol. 3, 1344–1348; André Bareau, "La jeunesse du Buddha dans les Sūtrapitaka et les Vinayapitaka anciens," *Bulletin de l'École Française d'Extrême-Orient* 61 (1974): 199–274, at 209–213; reprinted in André Bareau, *Recherche sur la biographie du Buddha dans les Sūtrapitaka et les Vinayapitaka anciens: Vol. 3. Articles complémentaires*, Monographies 178 (Paris: Presses de l'École Française d'Extrême-Orient, 1995), 43–118.
22. For this list of thirty-two features, see Lamotte, *Le traité*, Vol. 1, 271–281 (numerous references in the footnotes, in particular note 2 p. 271); Émile Sénart, *Essai sur la légende du Buddha, son caractère et ses origines* (2nd ed.) (Paris: Leroux, 1882), 87–160 (in particular 124–160); Stella Kramrisch, "Emblems of the Universal Being," *Journal of the Indian Society of Oriental Art* 3, no. 2 (1935): 148–165; and Stella Kramrisch, "Note on Uṣṇīṣa," *Journal of the Indian Society of Oriental Art* 4, no. 1 (1936): 79–83. Concerning the symbolism of the *lakṣaṇas* that belong to the nature of the "Great Man" or *mahāpuruṣa*, see Jones, *Mahāvastu*, Vol. 2, 26; Strong, *The Buddha*, 41–43 (with further references on 157–158). Guang Xing, *The Concept of the Buddha: Its Evolution From Early Buddhism to the Trikāya Theory* (Abingdon: Routledge Curzon, 2005), 29–31 provides a very useful juxtaposition of both lists.
23. The list is given by Xing, *The Concept*, 29–31 in relation to the thirty-two features list. I retain here the terms used by Peter Skilling, "Symbols on the Body, Feet, and Hands of a Buddha, Part II—Short Lists," *Journal of The Siam Society* 84, no. 1 (1996): 5–28, at 5–6 and note 4, in order to differentiate the two groups of signs; as noted by this writer, "the 80 attributes complement or supplement the 32 features" (see also Xing, *The Concept*, 28; these eighty "attributes" are named "sous-marques" by Lamotte, *Le traité*, Vol. 1, 273 note 1: quote on 274).

24. Skilling, "Short Lists"; and Peter Skilling, "Symbols on the Body, Feet, and Hands of a Buddha, Part I—Lists," *Journal of The Siam Society* 80, no. 2 (1992): 67–79. As Skilling's papers show, the "earliest long list" of these motifs includes around forty items (5th century) whereas the "later lists" can extend to up to 108 elements ("Lists", 67). Concerning the 108 features list in Southeast Asia, more particularly in Burma, see Claudine Bautze-Picron, "Some Observations on the Cosmological Buddhapadas at Pagan," *Journal of Bengal Art* 8 (2003): 19–68.
25. See, for instance, in the *Mahāvastu*: Jones, *Mahāvastu*, 2, 25–26 (or Jones, *The Mahāvastu*, 1, 180 on the marks on Dīpaṅkāra's body).
26. From Lamotte, *Le traité*, vol. 1, 280: English translation by Gelongma Karma Migme Chodron (*The Treatise on the Great Virtue of Wisdom of Nāgārjuna (Mahāprajñāpāramitāśāstra)*, 2001, 234); online publication.
27. Lamotte, *Le traité*, vol. 1, 280.
28. Étienne Lamotte, *Le traité de la grande vertu de sagesse de Nāgārjuna (Mahāprajñāpāramitāśāstra)*, Vol. 4 (Louvain-la-Neuve, Publications de l'Institut Orientaliste 12, 1976), 1905–1913. This explains how holy men can have some of these marks (1905–1906); the acquisition is progressive but bodhisattvas share the same set of marks as the buddhas.
29. English translation of Étienne Lamotte *L'Enseignement de Vimalakīrti (Vimalakīrtinirdeśa)* (Louvain-la-Neuve: Institut Orientaliste, Université Catholique de Louvain, 1987), 136–138) by Sara Boin (Étienne Lamotte, *The Teaching of Vimalakīrti (Vimalakīrtinirdeśa) From the French Translation With Indroduction and Notes (L'Enseignement de Vimalakīrti)* rendered into English by Sara Boin (Oxford: The Pali Text Society, 1994), 37–38); see also Lamotte, *Enseignement*, 132–138 and 226–229, with further reference to the *Majjhima Nikaya* 10 (*Satipatthāna Sutta*) on 132 note 21.
30. Jones, *Mahāvastu*, Vol. 2, 125.
31. N. A. Jayawickrama, *The Story of Gotama Buddha, The Nidāna-kathā of the Jātakatthakathā* (Oxford: The Pali Text Society, 1990), 89. A long version that can be read in the *Mahāvastu* is quoted in Deborah Klimburg-Salter and Maurizio Taddei, "The Uṣṇīṣa and the Brahmarandhra: An Aspect of Light Symbolism in Gandharan Buddha Images," in *Akshayanīvī, Essays Presented to Dr. Debala Mitra in Admiration of Her Scholarly Contributions*, ed. Gouriswar Bhattacharya, Bibliotheca Indo-Buddhica 88 (Delhi: Sri Satguru, 1991), 73–93, at 84–85: after Jones, *Mahāvastu*, Vol. 2, 120–122 (for the complete passage, see 120–126; for the darkening of the Bodhisattva's skin, see 123, 125).
32. Jayawickrama, *The Story*, 90. For the late Burmese version, see P. Bigandet, *The Life or Legend of Gaudama, the Buddha of the Burmese, with Annotations, The Ways to Naibban, and Notice on the Phongyies or Burmese Monks* (3rd ed.) (London: Trübner, 1880), Vol. 1, 73–75.
33. For the Gandhāra images, see Klimburg-Salter and Taddei, "Uṣṇīṣa"; for the Gandhāra and Burmese images, see Robert L. Brown, "The Emaciated Gandhāran Buddha Images: Asceticism, Health, and the Body," in *Living a Life in Accord With Dhamma: Papers in Honour of Professor Jean Boisselier on his Eightieth Birthday*, ed. Natasha Eilenberg, M. C. Subhadradis Diskul, and Robert L. Brown (Bangkok: Silpakorn University, 1997), 105–115. Brown suggests that these images do not illustrate the fasting of six years, but the austerities that he started again after having received the meal given to him by Sujātā, a village woman, ready to undergo them until he would reach enlightenment; for that reason, he quotes p. 107 the *Nidānakathā*: "May skin, indeed, and sinews, and bones wilt away, may flesh and blood in my body dry up, but till I attain to complete enlightenment the seat I will not leave!" (for another translation, see Jayawickrama, *The Story*, 94).
34. Jayawickrama, *The Story*, 89; see also the passage in the *Mahāvastu* (Jones, *Mahāvastu*, Vol. 2, 198).
35. Quotations after Jones, *Mahāvastu*, Vol. 2, 26; and Strong, *The Buddha*, 42, for the short list; for the long list, see Xing, *The Concept*, 29–31.
36. Bautze-Picron, "Antagonistes."
37. Étienne Lamotte, *Le traité de la grande vertu de sagesse de Nāgārjuna (Mahāprajñāpāramitāśāstra)*, Vol. 5 (Louvain-la-Neuve: Publications de l'Institut Orientaliste de Louvain 24, 1980), 2317–2318.

38. Lamotte, *Le Traité*, vol. 5, 2318, note 3.
39. Bigandet, *The Life*, Vol. 2, 35.
40. Xing, *The Concept*, 25.
41. Xing, *The Concept*, 29. On this swelling of the carving below the belt and between the two legs, which is also visible on Bodhisattva images of the Kushan period, see Vishakha N. Desai, "Reflections on the History and Historiography of Male Sexuality in Early Indian Art," in *Representing the Body: Gender Issues in Indian Art*, ed. Vidya Dehejia (New Delhi: Kali for Women/The Book Review Literary Trust, 1997), 42–55.
42. Xing, *The Concept*, 29.
43. Claudine Bautze-Picron, *The Buddhist Murals of Pagan: Timeless Vistas of the Cosmos* (Bangkok: Orchid Press, 2003), figs. 18, 19, 82; Giovanni Verardi, "The Buddha-Elephant," *Silk Road Art and Archaeology* 6 (Papers in honour of Francine Tissot, ed. Errington and Osmund Bopearachchi) (1999/2000): 69–74 (73 note 37 where the author stresses the fact that the projecting heels imply that the ankles are centered on the feet, confirming thus the axial cosmic position of the buddha). The similarity to the "trunk of an elephant" is mentioned in a passage translated by Gustav Roth, "The Physical Presence of the Buddha and Its Representation in Buddhist Literature," in *Investigating Indian Art: Proceedings of a Symposium on the Development of Early Buddhist and Hindu Iconography Held at the Museum of Indian Art Berlin in May 1986*, ed. Marianne Yaldiz and Wibke Lobo (Berlin: Museum für Indische Kunst Berlin/ Staatliche Museen Preußischer Kulturbesitz, 1987), 291–312, at 295.
44. This feature defines the so-called kapardin Buddha, a neologism coined by Ananda K. Coomaraswamy as recalled by Harry Falk, "Small-Scale Buddhism," in *Devadattīyam, Johannes Bronkhorst Felicitation Volume*, ed. François Voegeli et al. (Bern: Peter Lang, 2012), 491–517; a fundamental paper on the topic is Herbert Härtel, "The Concept of the Kapardin Buddha Type of Mathura," in *South Asian Archaeology 1983, Papers from the Seventh International Conference of the Association of South Asian Archaeologists in Western Europe Held in the Musées Royaux d'Art d'Histoire, Brussels*, ed. Janine Schotsmans and Maurizio Taddei (Naples: Istituto Universitario Orientale, Dipartimento di Studi Asiatici, Series Minor XXIII, 2, 1985), 653–678.
45. Akira Miyaji, "Aspects of the Earliest Buddha Images in Gandhāra," in *Miscellanies About the Buddha Image*, ed. Claudine Bautze-Picron (Oxford: BAR International Series 1888, South Asian Archaeology 2007, Special Sessions 1, Universita di Bologna & Istituto Italiano per l'Africa e l'Oriente, 2008), 25–42; and Juhyung Rhi, "Identifying Several Visual Types in Gandhāran Buddha Images," *Archives of Asian Art* 58 (2008): 43–85.
46. Juhyung Rhi, "Images, Relics, and Jewels: The Assimilation of Images in the Buddhist Relic Cult of Gandhāra: Or Vice Versa," *Artibus Asiae* 65, no. 2 (2005): 169–211; Hiram W. Woodward, "The Buddha's Radiance," *Journal of the Siam Society* 61, no. 1 (1973): 187–191; Klimburg-Salter and Taddei, "Uṣṇīṣa"; and Kramrisch, "Emblems" and "Note." Xuanzang reports a myth according to which the moonstone (Sanskrit: *candrakānta*) inserted in the *uṣṇīṣa* of the Buddha's image would let water flow in harmony with the waning and waxing moon; see Samuel Beal, *Si-yu-ki, Buddhist Records of the Western World, Translated from the Chinese of Hiuen Tsiang (A.D. 629)* (London: Kegan Paul, n.d.), Vol. 2, 252–253.
47. Akira Shimada, "A Seated Buddha Image From Amaravati: A Reinterpretation," *Artibus Asiae* 77, no. 2 (2017): 183–222, at 207, with further references.
48. Robert L. Brown, *Carrying Buddhism: The Role of Metal Icons in the Spread and Development of Buddhism* (Amsterdam: Royal Netherlands Academy of Arts and Sciences, J. Gonda Lecture, 2012), 2014; and Claudine Bautze-Picron, "The Buddha, Protecting the Noble Path," *Arts of Asia* 50, no. 6 (2020): 50–61.
49. On this aspect of the lotus's symbolism, see Giovanni Verardi, "Avatāraṇa: A Note on the Bodhisattva Image Dated in the Third Year of Kaniṣka in the Sārnāth Museum," *East and West* 35 (1985): 67–101.
50. Niharranjan Ray, *Idea and Image in Indian Art* (Delhi: Munshiram Manoharlal, 1973), 53–117; and Pandit, *An Approach*, 60–72.

51. Which leads to the representation of the "walking Buddha," rarely encountered in India but a well-known attitude seen in Thailand; see Robert L. Brown, "God on Earth: The Walking Buddha in the Art of South and Southeast Asia," *Artibus Asiae* 50 (1990): 73–107.
52. Jones, *Mahāvastu*, Vol. 2, 187–188.
53. Jones, *Mahāvastu*, Vol. 2, 191–192.
54. Lamotte, *Le traité*, Vol. 1, 148.
55. Lamotte, *Le traité*, Vol. 1, 276–277.
56. Lamotte, *Le traité*, Vol. 1, 277.
57. Lamotte, *Le traité*, Vol. 1, 441, 442: those who see the buddha radiating rays of light know that he is no ordinary man.
58. Lamotte, *Le traité*, Vol. 1, 442–443, 454–456, where this light, which is one of the thirty-two marks present at the birth and is seen by the world of ordinary humans, is differentiated from the immensely brilliant light that can also radiate from the body, but can only be seen by people with extraordinary merits.
59. Lamotte, *Le traité*, Vol. 1, 442–443; Kramrisch, "Emblems," 153–154; and Klimburg-Salter and Taddei, "Uṣṇīṣa," 85; the list is given in Lamotte, *Le traité*, Vol. 1, 444; the distribution of light in the universe is described on 445–447, the unmeasured universe is described on 447–449.
60. Lamotte, *Le traité*, Vol. 1, 445.
61. Luis O. Gómez, *The Land of Bliss, The Paradise of the Buddha of Measureless Light, Sanskrit and Chinese Versions of the Sukhāvatīvyūha Sutras, Introductions and English Translations* (Honolulu: University of Hawai'i Press, 1996), 66; the examples found in literature of the Great Vehicle being extremely numerous, here we shall confine ourselves to quotations from Gómez's translation of the two *Sukhāvatīvyha Sūtras*.
62. Gómez, *Land*, xii.
63. The term is used in relation to the production of the *nirmāṇakāya* created in order to preach the Buddhist law or dharma to human beings, "but this is not the true body of the Buddha"; see Étienne Lamotte, *Le traité de la grande vertu de sagesse de Nāgārjuna (Mahāprajñāpāramitāśāstra)*, Vol. 4 (Louvain-la-Neuve: Publications de l'Institut Orientaliste 12, 1976), 1907; Gómez, *Land*, 66–67: the monk Dharmakara not only praises the light and the voice of the buddha, but also makes the vow to rescue all living beings, pouring out "[his] radiance everywhere in world system." Thus, the light arises from all those who have become or will become buddhas; Gómez, *Land*, 95, 190.
64. Gómez, *Land*, 193.
65. Claudine Bautze-Picron, "The Nimbus in India up to the Gupta Period," *Silk Road Art and Archaeology* 1 (1990): 81–97.
66. Yi Jing, as translated by J. Takakusu, *A Record of the Buddhist Religion as Practised in India and the Malay Archipelago (A.D. 671–695) by I-Tsing* (Oxford: Clarendon Press, 1896), 45, mentions "under a canopy amply spread, the image of gold or bronze, brilliant and beautifully decorated..."
67. Beal, *Si-yu-ki*, Vol. 2, 322.
68. Gómez, *Land*, 183.
69. Beal, *Si-yu-ki*, Vol. 1, 103.
70. Chinese pilgrims made regular mention of the images that they had the opportunity to see and worship; see Beal, *Si-yu-ki*, Vol. 1, lxxxvi, 21–22, 44, 50–52 (Bamyan), 102–103, 202, 203–204, 235–236; Vol. 2, 119–126 (Bodhgaya), 215, 252, 322.
71. Martha L. Carter, *The Mystery of the Udayana Buddha*, Supplement no. 64, agli ANNALI 50/3 (Naples: Istituto Universitario Orientale, 1990), 6: this is the earliest mention of the legend, dated *c.* 385, and included in a Chinese translation of the *Ekottarāgama sūtra*.
72. Carter, "The Mystery", 7, in the "Sūtra of the Sea of Mystic Ecstasy," translated from Sanskrit into Chinese between 410 and 420.

73. Xuanzang mentions that the image carved at the request of King Udāyana was copied; see Beal, *Si-yu-ki*, Vol. 1, p. 235; Faxian describes the Prasenajit image and copies of it; see Beal, *Si-yu-ki*, Vol. 1, xliv–xlv; and Max Deeg, *Das Gaoseng-Faxian-Zhuan als religionsgeschichtliche Quelle, Der älteste Bericht eines chinesischen buddhistischen Pilgermönchs über seine Reise nach Indien mit Übersetzung des Textes*, Studies in Oriental Religions 52 (Wiesbaden: Harrassowitz Verlag, 2005), 537. On the Udāyana image, see Carter, *Mystery*.
74. As such, the worship of the buddha image as described by Yi Jing, Takakusu, *Record*, 45–46, 113–114, recalls the *pūjā* ("worship") practiced to the present day in India; see, for instance, Diana L. Eck, *Darshan: Seeing the Divine Image in India* (3rd ed.) (New York: Columbia University Press, 1996), 44–51.
75. Besides conveying further philosophical concepts, such as enlightenment (*bodhi*) and wisdom (*prajñā*), all concepts that were the object of constant reflection for the philosophers; see Ray, *Idea*, 7–52, for an in-depth study of the relationship between "idea and image" in their expression of the Bodhi.
76. Takakusu, *Record*, 113–114.
77. For a study of the image of the buddha in Eastern India up to the 12th century, see Janice Leoshko, "About Looking at Buddha Images in Eastern India," *Archives of Asian Art* 52 (2000/2001): 63–82 (with numerous references).
78. Andy Rotman, trans., *Divine Storie*, Divyādāna *Part 2* (Somerville: Wisdom, 2017), 214; see also Roth, "Physical Presence," 296–297.
79. A more appropriate expression might be "pre-iconism," introduced in Karel van Kooij, "Remarks on Festivals and Altars in Early Buddhist Art," in *Function and Meaning in Buddhist Art, Proceedings of a Seminar Held at Leiden University, 21–24 October 1991*, ed. K. R. van Kooij and H. van der Veere (Groningen: Egbert Forsten, 1995), 33–43, in particular 39: "Knowing that the Buddha image was to appear a few centuries later, we may call the gathering-typus a *pre-iconic* artistic formula, but not an aniconic one."
80. Susan L. Huntington, "Early Buddhist Art and the Theory of Aniconism," *Art Journal* 49 (1990): 401–408; Susan L. Huntington, "Aniconism and the Multivalence of Emblems, Another Look," *Ars Orientalis* 22 (1992): 111–156; and Vidya Dehejia, "Aniconism and the Multivalence of Emblems," *Ars Orientalis* 21 (1991): 45–66. The discussion was joined by Rob Linrothe, "Inquiries into the Origin of the Buddha Image: A Review," *East and West* 43, no. 1/4 (1993): 241–256; and Michael Rabe, "Letter to the Editor," *Art Journal* 51, no. 1 (1992): 125 and 127. The issue was discussed in detail in Karlsson, *Face to Face*.
81. Alfred Foucher, *L'art gréco-bouddhique du Gandhāra*, Vol. 1 (Paris: Imprimerie Nationale, 1905). A less biased opinion and indeed a clear description of the Buddha image in Gandhāra was provided by Wladimir Zwalf in *A Catalogue of the Gandhāra Sculpture in the British Museum: Vol. 1. Text* (London: The Trustees of the British Museum, 1996), 39–41; see also Stanley K. Abe, "Inside the Wonder House: Buddhist Art and the West," in *Curators of the Buddha: The Study of Buddhism Under Colonialism*, ed. Donald S. Lopez, Jr. (Chicago: University of Chicago Press, 1995), 63–106.
82. A detailed summary of the various opinions concerning the Gandharan art production was made in Zwalf, *Catalogue*, 67–76. For recent publications on the topic, see Martina Stoye, "On the Crossroads of Disciplines: Tonio Hölscher's Theory of Understanding Roman Art Images and Its Implication for the Study of Western Influence(s) in Gandhāran Art," in *The Global Connections of Gandhāran Art, Proceedings of the Third International Workshop of the Gandhāra Connections Project, University of Oxford, 18th–19th March, 2019*, ed. Wannaport Rienjang and Peter Stewart (Oxford: Archaeopress Archaeology, 2020), 29–49; and Monika Zin, "Buddhist Art's Late Bloomer: The Genius and Influence of Gandhāra," in *Problems of Chronology in Gandhāran Art, Proceedings of the First International Workshop of the Gandhāra Connections Project, University of Oxford, 23rd–24th March, 2017*, ed. Wannaport Rienjang and Peter Stewart (Oxford: Archaeopress Archaeology, 2018), 103–121.
83. Ananda K. Coomaraswamy, "Origin of the Buddha Image," *The Art Bulletin* 9 (1927): 287–328.

84. A summary of the publications concerning this question can be found in Miyaji, "Aspects of the Earliest Buddha Images," 25.
85. Van Lohuizen-De Leeuw, "New Evidence"; Härtel, "The Concept of the Kapardin Buddha"; Miyaji, "Aspects of the Earliest Buddha Images"; Juhyung Rhi, "From Bodhisattva to Buddha: The Beginning of Iconic Representation in Buddhist Art," *Artibus Asiae* 54, nos. 3/4 (1994): 207–225; and Juhyung Rhi, "Presenting the Buddha: Images, Conventions, and Significance in Early Indian Buddhism," in *Art of Merit: Studies in Buddhist Art and Conservation*, ed. David Park et al. (London: Archetype, 2013), 1–18.
86. Rhi, "Identifying Several Visual Types"; and Juhyung Rhi, "Positioning Gandhāran Buddhas in Chronology: Significant Coordinates and Anomalies," in *Problems of Chronology in Gandhāran Art, Proceedings of the First International Workshop of the Gandhāra Connections Project, University of Oxford, 23rd–24th March, 2017*, ed. Wannaporn Rienjang and Peter Stewart (Oxford: Archaeopress, 2018), 35–51.
87. Ananda K. Coomaraswamy, "The Buddha's cūḍā, Hair, uṣṇīṣa, and Crown," *The Journal of the Royal Asiatic Society of Great Britain and Ireland*, 4 (October 1928): 815–841; Monika Zin, "The *uṣṇīṣa* as a Physical Characteristic of the Buddha's Relatives and Successors," *Silk Road Art and Archaeology* 9 (2003): 107–129; Falk, "Small-Scale Buddhism;" Härtel, "The Concept of the Kapardin Buddha"; Desai, "Reflections"; John Powers, *A Bull of a Man: Images of Masculinity, Sex, and the Body in Indian Buddhism* (Cambridge, MA: Harvard University Press, 2009); Robert L. Brown, "The Feminization of the Sārnāth Gupta-Period Buddha Images," *Bulletin of the Asia Institute, New Series* 16 (2002): 165–179; Sara Schastok, "Bronzes in the Amarāvatī Style: Their Role in the Writing of Southeast Asian History," in *Ancient Indonesian Sculpture*, ed. Marijke J. Klokke and Pauline Lunsingh Scheurleer (Leiden: KITLV Press, Verhandelingen van het Koninkleik Instituut voor Taal-, Land- en Volkenkunde 165, 1994), 33–49; and Yuko Fukuroi, "The Flaming Protuberance on the Head of Tamil Buddha: Its Representations and Concepts," in *Miscellanies About the Buddha Image*, ed. Claudine Bautze-Picron (Oxford: BAR International Series 1888, South Asian Archaeology 2007, Special Sessions 1, Universita di Bologna & Istituto Italiano per l'Africa e l'Oriente, 2008), 43–64 (with further references to the image of the buddha in South India by the same author).
88. Brown, *Carrying Buddhism*; and Bautze-Picron, "The Buddha."
89. Claudine Bautze-Picron, *The Bejewelled Buddha from India to Burma: New Considerations*, Sixth Kumar Sarat Kumar Roy Memorial Lecture (New Delhi: Sanctum Books, 2010); Brown, "Emaciated Gandhāran Buddha Images"; Claudine Bautze-Picron, "The Emaciated Buddha in Southeast Bangladesh and Pagan (Myanmar)," in *Miscellanies About the Buddha Image*, ed. Claudine Bautze-Picron (Oxford: BAR International Series 1888, South Asian Archaeology 2007, Special Sessions 1, Universita di Bologna & Istituto Italiano per l'Africa e l'Oriente, 2008), 77–96; and Brown, "God on Earth." Bautze-Picron, "The Biography," includes numerous bibliographical references to the topic. References to more recent papers dealing with biographical events can be found at Gandharan Art Bibliography.

Claudine Bautze-Picron

THE IMAMURA FAMILIES AND THE MAKING OF AMERICAN BUDDHISM

IMAMURA EMYŌ AND THE NIKKEI BUDDHIST COMMUNITY

Imamura Emyō was the child of a Buddhist temple family, Sentokuji in Fukui Prefecture, which is affiliated with Nishi Honganji, one of the largest Shin Buddhist denominations (*Jōdo Shinshū*). Although it was the norm for sons of resident priests to study at the denomination's university (present-day Ryūkoku University in Kyoto), Emyō studied at Keiō University, which was founded by the notable Japanese enlightenment thinker Fukuzawa Yukichi (1835–1901). Nishi Honganji began propagating Shin Buddhism in Hawaii at the turn of the 20th century. Emyō came to Honolulu in 1899 to assist his uncle-in-law, Satomi Hōni, who became the first superintendent of the Honpa Honganji Mission of Hawaii (HHMH), and Japanese who had migrated to Hawaii as sugar plantation contract laborers from the beginning of the Meiji period (1868–1912). In 1900, Emyō succeeded Satomi's position and led the HHMH as bishop for next thirty years, until his sudden death in 1932.[1]

Propagating the Buddhist teaching to fellow immigrants was never easy for Emyō and the Issei Shin ministers. Although many Japanese immigrants came from Hiroshima and Yamaguchi Prefectures where Nishi Honganji had established itself, they were single and at an age when they were more interested in the physical pleasures of life. Emyō recalled:

> Even during daylight they (bachelor laborers) gambled openly and those who did not participate were being ostracized as sub-human. Into this smoke filled, imbibing, gambling scene I floated with my briefcase to speak of the dharma. "Bonze!" "Bad luck!" Such abuses to my face were common. Some behind me were urging each other to scatter salt. "Beat him up!" was common. I had expected a certain amount of this but found myself unprepared for the reality. . . I persevered and tried to talk to a few who seemed less unfriendly, but they too hesitated for fear of scorn from others. No one would listen.[2]

Emyō and his fellow ministers gradually won the hearts of the *Issei* laborers and the Caucasian planters. By 1924, the HHMH had succeeded in building more than thirty temples throughout the Hawaiian islands.

While meeting the *Issei* followers' daily religious needs, Emyō and his wife, Kiyoko, organized Buddhist groups and looked after the physical needs of the Issei workers' children. The HHMH formed the Young Men's Buddhist Association (YMBA) in Honolulu and published a Japanese Buddhist journal titled *Dōbō* in 1900, which was even read in Japan. In 1898, Kiyoko organized the Women's Buddhist Association in Honolulu, became the president of Honganji Women's Association in 1904, and formed the Young Women's Buddhist Association (YWBA) in 1917. Through these groups, she promoted the life of the Five Ls to Issei wives: Live, Learn, Labor, Love, and Leave ("leave" refers to the early phase of Japanese immigration known as the *dekasegi* period when Japanese migrants worked in sugar plantations, saved money, and returned to Japan). Emyō instructed fellow ministers to console the Issei parents who had felt alienated from their children because of the divided nationality between Issei and Nisei. For the Nisei youth, Emyō built a junior high school, a girls' school, and a Japanese language school as the HHMH's affiliated organizations. Kiyoko opened the HHMH's dormitories for Nisei who came from islands that neighbored Oahu and had no place to live in Honolulu, and taught Japanese at HHMH's Japanese school. She also hosted guests including Japanese scholars and Tagore from India.[3]

Emyō encouraged the Nisei to become good American citizens. In 1917, the HHMH published *Five Appeals to American Patriotism* for Nisei Buddhists. This pamphlet included the Declaration of Independence, George Washington's farewell address, James Monroe's Seventh

Annual Message, Abraham Lincoln's Gettysburg Address, and Woodrow Wilson's war message. In the Preface, Emyō wrote:

> Those of Shinshu faith [Shin Buddhist faith] are earnest in the belief that in Shinranism is the foundation of their spiritual life, and that the laws of the land are the foundation of civil life. Since we live in this country, we must be faithful and obedient to the laws of the country. Moreover, it is generally considered that those who firmly believe in religion and faithfully obey the national laws are the most desirable citizens. To be faithful and obedient to the Land of the Stars and Stripes, one must thoroughly understand the spirit of the country. In order to do this it will be most desirable to truly comprehend the aforesaid five appeals to American patriotism.[4]

Emyō's promotion of American patriotism did not mean that he embraced the sociopolitical conditions of the United States uncritically. He never accepted the Anglo-Saxon exclusivism by which Japanese Americans were discriminated against in Hawaii.

Emyō believed America's liberal discourse and considered the pluralistic climate of the United States fundamental to its democracy. He wrote *Democracy According to the Buddhist Viewpoint* in 1918 and *The Spirit of the United States and Freedom of Religion* (in Japanese) in 1920. In these works, Emyō connected the democratic principles of the United States and the egalitarian aspects of the Buddhist community—that Shakyamuni Buddha ignored the caste system of India and that Shinran referred to his followers as "honorable friends" instead of "disciples." Furthermore, Emyō considered both autocracy and modern democracy as a relative polity and pointed out that egotistic politicians had promoted false democracy and prevented American society from becoming truly egalitarian. He then questioned the ways in which American exclusionists linked autocracy with Japanese nationalism and modern democracy with American patriotism.[5]

Based on these ideals, Emyō and the HHMH supported the Japanese Americans' territory-wide sugar plantation strike of 1920. Previously, in 1904, Emyō had intervened in the Waipahu sugar plantation strike and persuaded fellow immigrants to return to work. In the 1920 strike, however, Emyō, other Issei Shin ministers, and leaders of other Japanese Buddhist denominations in Hawaii stood with the Japanese American laborers. Together with Shinto priests, they signed and sent a petition to the Hawaiian Sugar Planters' Association (HSPA), which stated:

> The Japanese religious leaders used to urge our workers to be loyal to the planters, but never demanded the planters to recognize the loyalty of the workers or sympathize with their circumstances. It is inevitable that the Japanese religious leaders would become liars, if we calmed down our fellow workers and forced them to be obedient. In the future, we shall be in a difficult position, and lose our credibility in propagation. The life of religious leaders is to express philanthropy and benevolence. We do not discern capitalists or laborers, but have an aptitude for saving one's mind and body. Therefore, we, religious leaders, stand between the capitalists and workers to avoid a conflict in the paradise of the Pacific.[6]

Emyō and the HHMH also supported the members of local temples who were plantation laborers directly affected by the strike.

In addition, when the territorial government suppressed the foreign language schools, Emyō and the HHMH supported autonomy of the Japanese language education system. In November 1920, the Hawaiian government passed Act 30, which cut the operating hours of Japanese language schools and gave the Department of Public Instruction (DPI) more authority to examine the curricula and textbooks of schools. Subsequently, Act 36 increased the qualification standards of Japanese language instructors, which made it difficult for them to teach at the Japanese language schools, and Act 171 prevented Nisei youth from attending Japanese language schools unless they passed the second grade of public school. The DPI required students to pay to attend foreign language schools. In December 1922, the Palama Japanese Language School and other Japanese language schools sued the territorial government and questioned the constitutionality of these laws. Two Japanese language schools affiliated with the HHMH joined the lawsuit, urging Emyō to clarify the HHMH's stance on the legal proceedings. Although Emyō was concerned that the HHMH's involvement in the litigation would generate further anti-Buddhist sentiment from Christians and that the HHMH would lose its credibility if they lost the case, he decided to support it after consulting with a former Hawaii Supreme Court judge. Emyō had his own reasons to support the Japanese language schools. He was influenced by America's leading educators such as John Dewey, who valued the importance of education that catered to students' individual needs to nurture creativity. The HHMH's Japanese language schools were necessary for the Nisei to understand their ethnic history and the Buddhist teachings.[7]

The 1920 strike and the Japanese language school litigation came about partially because of the religious rivalry within the Nikkei community. Unlike the Buddhist and Shinto followers, the Nikkei Christian leaders led by Okumura Takie (1865–1951) denounced the strike and sided with the DPI's superintendent to eliminate Buddhist influence from Nisei education.[8] Gary Okihiro stated: "the merging of religious belief with political allegiance by the Christian clergy was in accord with the Americanization movement's claim that Buddhism and other alien ideologies encouraged rebelliousness, while Christianity promoted patriotism."[9] Although the Japanese Christian leaders' accusation that Nikkei Buddhists were the subjects of imperial Japan was misleading, the HHMH's Buddhist acculturation did consist of an intertwining process of Americanizing and Japanizing persons of Japanese descent.

Contrary to the promotion of America's liberal and pluralistic discourse, Emyō and the HHMH supported imperial Japan and the mother temple of Nishi Honganji in Kyoto, which had developed a strong relationship with the Japan's imperial household. In Emyō's mind, the Issei should maintain their national identity and be loyal to imperial Japan. The Imperial Rescript on Education was read at various occasions and Japan's national holidays including the emperor's birthday were celebrated in the Japanese language schools affiliated with the HHMH. The HHMH's Buddhist Women's Association supported the Japanese Imperial Army's invasion of Northern China by donating clothing supplies. In 1928, Emyō received the honor of the Sixth Order of the Sacred Treasure from Emperor Hirohito (1901–1989), who was a cousin of Ōtani Kōshō (1911–2002), the 23rd abbot of Nishi Honganji.[10]

Emyō's position on imperial Japan was complicated. It was said that he did not have an enshrined portrait of the Japanese emperor and empress in his home, although such a practice was common among Japanese immigrants.[11] He extended his critique to the national polity of Japan, stating: "It is absurd to think that changeless tradition is good with a brain imbued with national polity, which was established when the Emperor issued the Imperial Rescript."[12] Therefore, what he said about Nisei education and imperial Japan on one occasion appeared to differ from what he said on other occasions. This inconsistency can be traced to his position as the leader of a large Buddhist organization in Hawaii, his pragmatism, and his openness to accept conflicting opinions.

What appears to be a double standard in Emyō's position toward the two modern nation-states—the United States and Japan—can be explained by the doctrine of the "two truths" that he was obliged to observe. This doctrine was, and still is, the foundation of Nishi Honganji. It defines the relationship between secular laws and religious laws, known as the buddha dharma. Although Shinran recognized the supremacy of faith in Amida Buddha, the Honganji leaders institutionalized his teaching and sought to balance secular laws and Buddhist laws.[13] Zonkaku (1290–1373), the eldest son of the third abbot of Honganji, considered this relationship to be "the same as that between the two wheels of a cart or the two wings of a bird."[14] Rennyo (1415–1499), the 8th abbot of Honganji, instructed his followers who had rebelled against local political authorities to "take the laws of the state as your outer aspect, store Other-Power faith deep in your hearts, and take [the principles of] humanity and justice as essential. Bear in mind that these are the rules of conduct that have been established within our tradition."[15] Rennyo's position became the Honganji's official stance toward state authority. During the Tokugawa period (1603–1867), the Honganji organization was divided into Higashi (east) and Nishi (west) Honganji and placed under the jurisdiction of the Magistrate of Temples and Shrines. During the Meiji period, state laws continued to overrule the laws of buddha dharma.[16]

Unlike in Japan where Honganji leaders mobilized the doctrine of two truths to transform their parishioners into dutiful imperial subjects and to keep Shin Buddhist faith personal, in Hawaii and on the US mainland two sets of secular rules collided. The application of the doctrine of two truths, therefore, required a new interpretation in Hawaii, as Shin clergy had to take into account the secular laws of the United States and the different national identities of the Issei and the Nisei. Emyō's apparently contradictory instructions to the Issei and Nisei can, therefore, be seen as an attempt to make sense of the doctrine of two truths in a new area outside of Japan. First, the buddha dharma was supposed to be kept and practiced within the climate of America's civil religion and in relation to the discourse of imperial Japan. Second, the buddha dharma and America's inclusive liberal discourse were interrelated. Third, the buddha dharma transcended political ideologies of both the United States and imperial Japan as the supreme truth and served as the standpoint from which the two ideologies were critiqued. Furthermore, Emyō's involvement in the Nikkei workers' 1920 strike and the Nikkei educators' lawsuit against the territorial government of Hawaii can be considered cases where the buddha dharma influenced secular laws and prompted Buddhist followers to oppose discriminatory statutes and oppressive sociopolitical conditions of the United States. It can therefore be seen as an effort to restore the supreme truth of the Buddha dharma over the secular laws, but overemphasizing Emyō's Buddhist leadership in the 1920 strike and the Japanese language school lawsuit is inappropriate. By that time, the Nikkei had become the major ethnic group in Hawaii and the territorial government found it difficult to ignore its socioeconomic influence.[17] In addition to the strong presence of ethnic Japanese in Hawaii, Emyō was surrounded by a group of Euro-Americans who were greatly interested in Buddhism.

ETHNIC SECTARIANISM AND UNIVERSAL BUDDHISM

Emyō established an English Department within the HHMH during the early 1920s. In 1921, Buddhist sympathizers Ernest Hunt and his wife Dorothy started to teach Buddhism to the children of Japanese descent in Hilo on the island of Hawaii. That same year, Thomas M. Kirby came to work at the HHMH. Kirby was ordained by the Buddhist Mission of North America, HHMH's counterpart on the mainland that became the Buddhist Churches of America (BCA) in 1944. He stayed for five years and then left for Japan, after which the Hunt couple, who were ordained by Emyō in 1924, took over Kirby's position. Hunt stayed at the HHMH until he was fired in 1937 by the bishop who succeeded Emyō.[18]

Emyō and Hunt worked together to develop the HHMH's English program, which was designed to introduce Buddhism to Euro-American residents in Honolulu and educate the Nisei. In 1927, they formed a biweekly forum and in the following year conducted a Buddhist initiation ceremony in which nine Caucasians took Buddhist vows. Emyō and Hunt continued to admit Euro-Americans to the HHMH who contributed to the expansion of the English department. Under the guidance of Emyō and Hunt, they organized study classes, a choir group for singing and chanting, and taught at the HHMH's Sunday School. Hunt visited hospitals and jails regularly and helped to publish *Vade Mecum* (1927), *The Symbolism of Buddhism* (1927), and *Buddhism in Hawaii and An Outline of Buddhism* (1929). Dorothy and others compiled Buddhist hymnals that were included in *Vade Mecum*.[19]

Taixu (1890–1947), the reformer of modern Chinese Buddhism, visited Hawaii in April 1929.[20] Taixu organized the International Buddhist Institute and built branches in European countries. Emyō and Hunt agreed to affiliate the HHMH's English department with the institute, thereafter calling it the Hawaiian Branch of the International Buddhist Institute. They published the *Hawaiian Buddhist Annual*, an English journal from 1930 to 1934. Its mission included promoting the teachings of Shakyamuni Buddha to the communities of native English speakers and Japanese Americans throughout the Hawaiian islands, making transsectarian Buddhist networks to improve the quality of human life, remove suffering caused by social injustice, and become mindful to international affairs.[21]

The Hawaiian branch of the International Buddhist Institute can be characterized as practicing a form of universal Buddhism. That is, it was a "nonethnic" or "transethnic" form of Buddhism sought by both Asian and Euro-American Buddhists during the 1920s and 1930s.[22] Universal Buddhism is part of what Donald S. Lopez Jr. calls "modern Buddhism," in which the buddha's teachings are viewed as compatible with modern notions of "reason, empiricism, science, universalism, individualism, tolerance, freedom and the rejection of religious orthodoxy."[23] In the late 19th century, Henry Steel Olcott aimed to form an International Buddhist League by combining Theravada and Mahayana Buddhism in Asia, as well as a United Buddhist World that would bring together Buddhists from the East and West.[24] In *Gospel of Buddha*, published in 1894, Paul Carus sought a form of nonsectarian Buddhism, ignoring the diversity of Asian Buddhist practices.[25] The efforts of Emyō and Hunt to establish a branch of the International Buddhist Institute in Honolulu can, therefore, be seen as an extension of the emerging universal Buddhist movement.

In fact, Emyō had already expressed his cosmopolitan Buddhist vision when the main temple hall of the HHMH was rebuilt in 1918. Instead of traditional Japanese temple architecture, he selected a design based on the Gandharan and Western styles. Lorraine Reiko Minatoshi Palumbo states:

> The Buddhists chose the Roman Tuscan column and dome, Indian style stupa forms, and classical arched windows for their first temple instead of following the traditional Congregationalist Church design. It is reasonable that [Imamura Emyō] was not looking to copy the church form. In order to achieve distinction from his opposition, he chose an architectural type that suggested new thought or a new presence while still having a form based on tradition. Imamura wanted to create a new image for Buddhism without forsaking the identity of Buddhism in exchange for acceptance. These architectural elements signify stability, historical significance, and cultural identity.[26]

Emyō felt the temple design should reflect the Buddhist teachings and combine a traditional style and Eastern and Western design concepts.[27]

Although Emyō and Hunt worked together to promote universal Buddhism in Hawaii, they held different Buddhist visions. Hunt and Western Buddhologists and other Euro-American Buddhist converts in general saw Theravada Buddhism, or the basic teachings of the Shakyamuni Buddha, as the common denominator of all forms of Buddhism. He suggested that Japanese Buddhist leaders should remove sectarian barriers and planned to replace Japanese forms of Buddhism in Honolulu with the ethical teachings of Shakyamuni.[28] As a leader of a Shin Buddhist denomination, however, Emyō aimed to promote both Shakyamuni's and Shinran's teachings in Hawaii. When Olcott visited Hawaii in 1901, Emyō invited him to lecture on Buddhism. In the same year, when the HHMH celebrated Shinran's birthday, Emyō extended an invitation to the usurped Queen Lili'uokalani and Mary Foster, a prominent landowner in Hawaii. It is unclear how much they understood of the Shin doctrine, but Foster later donated land to the HHMH. Emyō also explained Shin Buddhism to Lillian Shrewsbury Mesick and Ms. Barber, who taught English to Issei immigrants at the HHMH. Barber, a member of the Theosophical Society, considered Shinran somewhat similar to Martin Luther of the Reformation, because Shinran had made complex Buddhist philosophies understandable to the laity. In 1914, Emyō celebrated the publication of *The Essence of Japanese Buddhism* by Tsunoda Ryūsaku, who served as principal of the HHMH's junior high school and girls' high school. Despite its title, this book was one of the earliest attempts to present Shinran's life and teaching to the West.[29] According to George J. Tanabe, Jr., what Emyō actually did in Hawaii was "prune the political species of Japanese nationalism, graft in its place another political species from a different country [that is, American nationalism], also graft a philosophical species of universal Buddhism, and continue to nurture the rootstock bearing the double helix of family religion and Japanese ethnicity."[30] It is unclear whether Emyō's promotion of Shin Buddhism beyond the Nikkei community was connected to the ideological discourses created by Buddhist leaders of modern Japan, such as the notions of Eastern Buddhism and the eastward movement of Buddhism. Emyō seems to have tried to promote general Buddhism and Shin Buddhism at the same time.[31] Despite their differences on how Buddhism should be promoted in Hawaii, however, Emyō held Hunt in high esteem.

Emyō also made Buddhism accessible to the Nisei. He instructed the Issei ministers to "emphasize the teachings of the historical buddha and the ethical elements of Buddhism rather than its more philosophical and metaphysical aspects," and transformed the YMBA and YWBA, which were originally organizations of Issei Buddhists, into Nisei lay organizations.[32] (These two groups later merged and became the Young Buddhist Associations, or YBA, also known as *Bussei.*) Emyō and the Issei ministers helped a group of Nisei to organize the First Pan-Pacific YMBA Conference in Honolulu in 1930.

During the 1920s, Emyō initiated the Nisei ministers' program. The HHMH was not, however, an organization that was authorized to ordain and train Nisei ministerial candidates as dharma teachers. They were required to be ordained in Japan, study at Ryūkoku University, and receive training at the Nishi Honganji headquarters in Kyoto. There were three steps to becoming a full-fledged overseas minister: receiving ordination (*tokudo*), obtaining a dharma teacher's (*kyōshi*) certificate, and receiving official appointment to propagate outside Japan (*kaikyōshi*). As a rule for ordination, ministerial candidates were required to register at local temples in Japan; hence, Emyō had them registered at Sentokuji, his home temple in Fukui Prefecture. Later he asked the headquarters to recognize the registration of ministerial candidates of American citizens at the HHMH. Between 1926 and 1927, Emyō sent four Niseis to the Nishi Honganji headquarters. After completing ministerial training, they returned to Hawaii and worked at the HHMH. One of them, Shigeo Takeda, succeeded Hunt after he was fired.

Kanmo Imamura, the eldest son of Emyō Imamura, was probably the first Japanese American in Hawaii to receive ordination in Kyoto. Kanmo was born in August 1904 in Honolulu but was sent to Japan at the age of four because Emyō expected him to become his successor at Sentokuji. Unlike the four Niseis sent to Japan for ministerial training, Kanmo was ordained at the age of nine. According to the regulations of the Honganji organizations, nine years of age was, and still is, the minimum age required for ordination because that is the age at which Shinran took tonsure. Like his father, Kanmo studied at Keiō University and learned about general Buddhism and Shin Buddhism. After graduation, he taught Buddhism at the Nihon University and English at the Chiyoda Women's School. When his father died in 1932, Kanmo returned to Hawaii to help his mother. He then became the executive secretary of the YBA in Honolulu and resident priest of the Waipahu Honganji Buddhist Temple from 1935 to 1941.[33]

Although Kanmo served as a bishop of the HHMH in later life, Berkeley, California, was the center of his Buddhist activities. He started a correspondence with Jane Matsuura, a daughter of Issei and Shinobu Matsuura—a Shin Buddhist minister and his wife who were residing at the Guadalupe Buddhist Temple. Matsuura was attending the University of California at Berkeley and living in the Berkeley Buddhist Temple dormitory. Kanmo eventually attended the graduate school at UC Berkeley and in August 1941 he became resident minister of the Berkeley Buddhist Temple. Immediately after the bombing of Pearl Harbor, Kanmo married Jane. The Pacific War interrupted his study, and he and Jane were incarcerated at the Tulare Assembly Center near Fresno and later forced to move to the Gila River camp in Arizona. In the camp, Kanmo and Issei Buddhist priests of other denominations worked together to conduct Sunday service and other kinds of services including funeral and memorial services, supervised a YBA, and helped distribute *Bussei Digest*, a weekly Buddhist magazine for youth.[34]

In 1946, Kanmo resumed his ministerial residency in Berkeley and for the next twenty years he and his wife contributed to the expansion of the Berkeley Buddhist Temple and the

Buddhist Churches of America. While working at the UC Berkeley anthropology museum, Kanmo managed to run the temple (he did not receive a salary from the temple; his income came from the museum). He set the direction and led various temple projects. As a *bōmori* (the priest's wife, though this word is specific to Shin Buddhist tradition), Jane became manager of the temple office. She communicated with the members, prepared and mailed temple bulletins, and dealt with inquiries from nonmembers as the public relations representative for the temple. Because of her music background, Jane served as the temple's organist and led the choir. She also supervised the kindergarten dharma class, managed two dormitories, and kept the balance of accounting books for the temple and other related facilities.[35]

In November 1949, a group of students gathered at the home of Shinobu Matsuura (Jane's mother). This developed into Friday-night study classes that met biweekly or monthly for more than a decade. This class was later housed in the Berkeley Buddhist Temple and grew larger. In addition to Japanese American Shin Buddhists, Euro-American Buddhist converts and Buddhist sympathizers, such as Gary Snyder, Alex Wayman, Robert Jackson, and Jack Kerouac began to attend. Still later, the study group became the BCA's Buddhist Study Center, which finally developed into the Institute of Buddhist Studies (a graduate school for Buddhist ministry and research) in 1966. Kanmo contributed by serving on the executive committee and as director of both the study center and the institute.[36]

The Berkeley study group and *Berkeley Bussei*, the Shin Buddhist magazine funded and overseen by Kanmo and published by the Berkeley Buddhist Temple provided the venues for ethnic Shin Buddhists and Caucasian Buddhist converts to interact and exchange their views on the future of American Buddhism. According to Michael Masatsugu, Buddhist converts consisted of academics, teachers, students, veterans, artists, poets, and writers. Some of them were part of, or close to, the Beat movement, such as Allen Ginsberg, Jack Kerouac, Gary Snyder, and Philip Whalen.

The Beats developed their Buddhist interests as a result of orientalist scholarship and they saw Buddhism as a spiritual alternative to Christianity. They sought a spiritual entity that was outside of the existing social hierarchy and Cold War institutions that they considered to be the causes of domestic unease.[37] They were not interested in Shin Buddhism but rather in Zen Buddhism, yet they ignored the diversity of Zen practice and the Japanese culture associated with it. As Masatsugu states, "the Beat extracted Buddhism from its long history and transformed it into a timeless essence that harked back to the solitary, monastic practice of ancient sages."[38]

While the exchanges between Caucasian Buddhist converts and Japanese American Buddhists were generally amicable, their discussions often became personal.[39] The former criticized the latter for the ways in which ethnic Buddhists practiced their religion. They argued that Shin Buddhist doctrine was similar to that of Protestant Christianity, American Shin Buddhists modeled on Christian practice including Sunday service, and that they practiced Buddhism within the Japanese structure of temple Buddhism.[40] Because of the Euro-American Buddhist converts' criticism of Shin Buddhism, Japanese American Shin Buddhists emphasized Shakyamuni Buddha's teachings more than Shinran's teaching in *Berkeley Bussei*. As Kanmo observed, some Nisei Shin Buddhists even proposed to replace the statue of Amida Buddha—the main object of worship in the Berkeley Buddhist Temple—with that of Shakyamuni Buddha.[41] Ryan Anningson observed that because they were unable to read

Japanese and because Christians in the United States often led a movement to return to Jesus of Nazareth, the Nisei Shin Buddhists were more eager to adapt their religion to American religious culture.[42] The Nisei Shin Buddhists gathered in Berkeley and redefined their religion through their dialogues with the Euro-American Buddhist converts, but deviated from Shin Buddhist tradition, while the Caucasian Buddhist converts saw Zen Buddhism as the essence of Buddhism.

In this exchange, Kanmo, as a Shin Buddhist minister of the BCA, kept Amidist faith to himself, but he remained open-minded to choices of Buddhism made by those who gathered at the study center. His wife recalled: "Following the way of Nembutsu without walls or boundaries, beyond sectarian distinctions, he [Kanmo] oversaw the development of the Study Center."[43] Kanmo encouraged the youth to be Buddhist seekers. In an essay titled "Stream in the Sea," he wrote:

> Buddhism has taken many forms of expressions in different lands and times. In America, where its birth was but a generation ago, the forms have not yet been traditionalized. Among the English speaking groups, the temples observe different forms of ceremonies, use varying texts, and teach heterogeneous aspects of Buddhism.
>
> The important point that cannot be altered is to keep the minds open, absorb and eliminate, as long as the direction is toward the search. In time, roots will take place, a tradition may arise, but it will be up to the temples never to waver from the quality of freedom of inquiry.
>
> As the purity of a stream is ever present in the sea, as the boundless wisdom and compassion is ever abiding in the vast quandary of Bonno (klesa), this personal quest for the meaning of life must ever be the basis for the function of the temple and its organizations.[44]

Kanmo saw suffering as the beginning of the Buddhist quest, but did not limit its resolution to one tradition. Further, he seemed to reject various aspects of Shin Buddhist practice that the Issei followers had brought with them from Japan. Further research is needed to find out to what extent he reinterpreted Shin Buddhism and how he explained Amida Buddha to the Nisei and Caucasian Buddhists.

Emyō reconstructed Amida and the Pure Land in order to point out the universal aspects of Shin Buddhism. By introducing the notion of "3Ls," he made Amida Buddha more appealing to the Caucasian religious community. Emyō wrote: "Amida Buddha symbolizes Light, Love and Life—the so-called 3Ls. I strongly believe that the 3Ls transcend the ideal principles held by any ethnic group and objectives of any religious propagation. Perhaps, the 3Ls are the ideal principles for both Japanese and American people."[45] For him, the Pure Land was no longer a utopia to which people were believed to be born. "Be born into the Pure Land every day" and "Meditate and practice, as one desires for birth in the Pure Land."[46] Emyō explained that Shin Buddhism was not a religion of the afterlife but a religion of the here and now and encouraged the community of Shin Buddhist immigrants to be practical and flexible in their situations based on Shinran's sayings that those who were able to entrust themselves into Amida's original vow would immediately become "truly settled." He adapted both Shin Buddhist doctrine and the way of Shin Buddhist life to American society.

Emyō and Kanmo maintained the structure of temple Buddhism and sectarian identity, while universalizing their religion. Their challenges and the courses of action they took were different. Emyō was an Issei minister who lived in Hawaii before the Pacific War where the Nikkei were not an ethnic minority, and he was proud of its connections to imperial Japan. Fellow immigrants carried the Buddhist practice from Japan and continued to observe it in Hawaii. Emyō dealt with them primarily, although he was concerned with Buddhist education of their children and helped them better understand Buddhism. Kanmo was a Nisei minister who lived on the US mainland where the Japanese were a minority during the prime of his life—during the Pacific War and the post–World War II period. The imprisonment of persons of Japanese descent wounded the Nisei deeply, yet the Nisei Buddhists continued to seek their religious identities. For most Nisei, Japanese was not their mother tongue and works on Shin Buddhism in English were limited, which prevented the Nisei from understanding Shinran's teaching.

In addition to these disparities between Emyō and Kanmo, Euro-American Buddhist converts who gathered around them were also different. In the beginning of the 20th century, Euro-Americans were interested in Shakyamuni's teachings taught in the Theravada tradition, whereas the Beat Generation and those who came to the Berkeley Buddhist Study Center were interested in Zen Buddhism. The struggles experienced by Emyō and Kanmo to relate Shin Buddhism to, and distinguish it from, other Buddhists challenged Shin Buddhists during that time. Because of its emphasis on faith in Amida Buddha's original vow, Shin Buddhism was different from other forms of Buddhism that emphasized ethical practice and self-discipline. This difference became more visible when Japanese American Shin Buddhists came into contact with Euro-Americans who were interested in Theravada and Zen Buddhism. For Emyō and Kanmo, reinterpreting Shin Buddhism in the United States and the making of American Buddhism were inseparable from considerations of race and ethnicity, America's exclusive and liberal discourses, the influence of orientalist Buddhist scholarship, and the need to retain Japanese cultural practice.

REVIEW OF LITERATURE

Ama, Michihiro. *Immigrants to the Pure Land: The Modernization, Acculturation, and Globaliztion of Shin Buddhism, 1898–1941*. Honolulu: University of Hawai'i Press, 2011.

This book explores the ways in which Japanese Buddhism emerged into modernity and played a role in shaping Japan's national identity and in constructing ethnicity in trans-Pacific contexts. It focuses on the emergence of Shin Buddhism in Hawaii, on the West Coast of the continental United States, and in Canada as both an extended and essential experience of modern Japanese Buddhism. Shin Buddhists acculturated to their host societies by incorporating their organizations according to American religious conventions, by creating new sets of rituals such as Buddhist weddings and through the compilation of Buddhist hymnals modeled on Christian practice, by building cosmopolitan-looking temple halls, and by integrating democratic principles into Shin Buddhist doctrine. At the same time, Shin Buddhists of Japanese ancestry reappraised spiritual values of their own tradition and conformed to the state apparatus of modern Japan. Therefore, their religious acculturation consisted of an interactive process of Japanization and Americanization. The book includes a discussion of Emyō Imamura's Buddhist activities in Hawaii.

Moriya, Tomoe. *Yemyo Imamura: Pioneer American Buddhist.* Honolulu: Buddhist Study Center Press, 2000.

This book introduces Emyō Imamura's life and work. It discusses Fukuzawa Yukichi's influence on Emyō, Emyō's activities and the Shin Buddhist development in Japan before he moved to Hawaii, and his Buddhist vision in the United States. Emyō's *Democracy According to the Buddhist Viewpoint* is reprinted in this volume.

Pierce, Lori. "Constructing American Buddhisms: Discourse of Race and Religion in Territorial Hawaii." PhD diss., University of Hawai'i, 2000.

Pierce explores the relationship between race, which she treats as an ideology, and Buddhism sought by Euro-Americans as a form of universal religion in Hawaii. According to her, the discourse of Aloha and Buddhist universality concealed the racial and economic inequality as well as white supremacy in Hawaii. Ernest Hunt was, however, not a typical Caucasian Buddhist convert whose knowledge and practice derived from orientalist scholarship, but a unique figure who worked with Japanese Buddhist immigrants and sought a hybrid form of Buddhism. Similarly, for Emyō Imamura, seeking the place of Nikkei Buddhists in Hawaii was to challenge the Euro-Americancentric vision of America and expand the notion of Americanism.

PRIMARY SOURCES

A collection of Emyō's Japanese essays published primarily in the journal *Dōbō* is found in *Chōshōin ibunshū—The Collected Works of Emyō Imamura.*[47] The collection also includes a chronological record of his career and eulogies about his achievements given by Shin Buddhist leaders, Japanese dignitaries, and community leaders.

FURTHER READING

Hunter, Louise H. *Buddhism in Hawaii: Its Impact on a Yankee Community.* Honolulu: University of Hawai'i Press, 1971.

Imamura, Jane Michiko. *Kaikyo: Opening the Dharma, Memoirs of a Buddhist Priest's Wife in America.* Honolulu: Buddhist Study Center Press, 1998.

Masatsugu, Michael K. "'Beyond This World of Transiency and Impermanence': Japanese Americans, Dharma Bums, and the Making of American Buddhism during the Early Cold War Years." *Pacific Historical Review* 77, no. 3 (2008): 423–451.

Nishimoto, Sosuke, ed. *Higan: Compassionate Vow; Selected Writings of Shinobu Matsuura.* Berkeley, CA: Berkeley Buddhist Temple, 1986.

Moriya, Tomoe. *Amerika bukkyō no tanjō: Nijū seiki shotō ni okeru nikkei shūkyō no bunnka henyō.* Tokyo: Gendai shiryō shuppan, 2001.

Pierce, Lori. "Constructing American Buddhisms: Discourse of Race and Religion in Territorial Hawaii." PhD diss., University of Hawai'i, 2000.

Tanabe, George J., Jr. "Grafting Identity: The Hawaiian Branches of the Bodhi Tree." In *Buddhist Missionaries in the Era of Globalization.* Edited by Linda Learman, 77–100. Honolulu: University of Hawai'i Press.

NOTES

1. Michihiro Ama, *Immigrants to the Pure Land: The Modernization, Acculturation, and Globalization of Shin Buddhism, 1898–1941* (Honolulu: University of Hawai'i Press, 2011), 37, 133–134.
2. Quoted in Ama, *Immigrants to the Pure Land*, 43.
3. Emyō Imamura, *History of the Hongwanji Mission in Hawaii to the American Public: A Short History of the Hongwanji Buddhist Mission in Hawaii* (Honolulu: Publishing Bureau of Hongwanji Buddhist Mission, 1931), 12–13, 22; and Keiko Glenn, "Imamura, Kiyoko Hino," in *Notable Women of Hawaii*, ed. *Barbara Bennett Peterson* (Honolulu: University of Hawaii Press, 1984), 158–160.
4. Quoted in Ama, *Immigrants to the Pure Land*, 140.
5. Ama, 136–137.
6. Quoted and translated in Ama, 179.
7. Ama, 180–182. For a discussion of the contentions vis-à-vis the Japanese language schools in Hawaii, see Noriko Asato, *Teaching Mikadoism: The Attack on Japanese Language Schools in Hawaii, California, and Washington, 1919–1924* (Honolulu: University of Hawai'i Press, 2005).
8. For a discussion of Okumura, see, for instance, Hiromi Monobe, "Takie Okumura and the 'Americanization' of the Nisei in Hawaii" (PhD diss., University of Hawai'i at Manoa, 2004).
9. Gary Okihiro, *Cane Fires: The Anti-Japanese Movement in Hawaii, 1865–1945* (Philadelphia: Temple University Press, 1992), 133–134.
10. Ama, *Immigrants to the Pure Land*, 140–141; and Galen Amstutz, *Interpreting Amida: History and Orientalism in the Study of Pure Land Buddhism* (Albany: State University of New York Press, 1997), 80.
11. Moriya Tomoe, *Amerika bukkyō no tanjō: Nijū seiki shotō ni okeru nikkei shūkyō no bunnka henyō* (Tokyo: Gendai shiryō shuppan, 2001), 229; Louise Hunter, *Buddhism in Hawaii: Its Impact on a Yankee Community* (Honolulu: University of Hawai'i Press, 1971), 88–89.
12. Quoted and translated in Ama, *Immigrants to the Pure Land*, 141.
13. In *Kyōgyōshinshō*, Shinran criticized the imperial authority of medieval Japan and wrote: "The emperor and his ministers, acting against the dharma and violating human rectitude, became enraged and embittered. As a result, Master Genku [Hōnen, Shinan's teacher] and a number of his followers, without receiving any deliberation of their alleged crimes, were sentenced to death or were dispossessed of their monkhood, given secular names, and consigned to distant banishment. I was among the latter. Hence, I am not neither a monk nor one in worldly life. For this reason, I have taken the term 'stubble-haired' as my name" (*The Collected Works of Shinran*, vol. 1, 289). Dennis Hirota, Hisao Inagaki, Michio Tokunaga, and Ryushin Uryuzu, trans. and ed. 1997. *The Collected Works of Shinran* 2 vols. (Kyoto: Jōdo Shinshū Hongwanji-ha). Shinran rejected the name that the government gave him as a layman and called himself "stubble-haired" and kept his distance from the government.
14. Shigaraki Takamaro, *A Life of Awakening: The Heart of the Shin Buddhist Path* (Kyoto, Japan: Hozokan Publishing, 2005), 184.
15. Minor L. Rogers and Ann T. Rogers, *Rennyo: The Second Founder of Shin Buddhism* (Berkeley: Asian Humanities Press, 1991), 180.
16. Shigaraki, *A Life of Awakening*, 184–185.
17. By 1924, the Nikkei population in Hawaii had reached more than 125,000; see Yukiko Kimura, *Issei: Japanese Immigrants in Hawaii* (Honolulu: University of Hawai'i Press, 1988), 13, 22. During the 1940s, the Nikkei population in Hawaii had reached 37 percent, the majority of which was Nisei; see Tetsuden Kashima, *Judgment without Trial: Japanese American Imprisonment during World War II* (Seattle: University of Washington Press, 2004), 65.
18. Ama, *Immigrants to the Pure Land*, 70, 73; and Imamura, "History of the Hongwanji Mission in Hawaii to the American Public," 13–14.
19. Imamura, "History of the Hongwanji Mission in Hawaii to the American Public," 14–16.

20. For a discussion of Taixu, see David Pittman, *Toward a Modern Chinese Buddhism: Taixu's Reforms* (Honolulu: University of Hawai'i Press, 2001).
21. Ama, *Immigrants to the Pure Land*, 71; Imamura, "History of the Hongwanji Mission in Hawaii to the American Public," 15.
22. George J. Tanabe, Jr., "Grafting Identity: The Hawaiian Branches of the Bodhi Tree," in *Buddhist Missionaries in the Era of Globalization* (Honolulu: University of Hawai'i Press, 2005), 78.
23. Quoted in David L. McMahan, *The Making of Buddhist Modernism* (New York: Oxford University Press, 2008), 8.
24. Stephen Prothero, *The White Buddhist: The Asian Odyssey of Henry Steel Olcott* (Bloomington: Indiana University Press, 1996), 5–6.
25. Judith Snodgrass, *Presenting Japanese Buddhism to the West: Orientalism, Occidentalism, and the Columbian Exposition* (Chapel Hill: University of North Carolina Press, 2003), 239–240.
26. Lorraine Reiko Minatoshi Palumbo, "The Process of Transformation of the Buddhist Temple Architecture of the Japanese Society of Hawaii" (PhD diss., Waseda University, 1999), 125–126.
27. Palumbo, "Process of Transformation of the Buddhist Temple Architecture," 125.
28. Tanabe, "Grafting Identity," 90.
29. Ama, *Immigrants to the Pure Land*, 39, 62, 226, n. 59.
30. Tanabe, "Grafting Identity," 86–87.
31. To differentiate Japanese Buddhism from and emphasize its superiority over Buddhism in Southeast Asia and Northern China, Japanese Buddhist leaders promoted the notion of Eastern Buddhism, which in their view embraced all other forms of Buddhism and was the "full exposition of the Buddha's wisdom, and it was preserved in Japan, alone" (Snodgrass, *Presenting Japanese Buddhism to the West*, 198).
32. Eileen Tamura, *Americanization, Acculturation, and Ethnic Identity: The Nisei Generation in Hawaii* (Urbana: University of Illinois Press, 1994), 205.
33. Jane Michiko Imamura, *Kaikyo: Opening the Dharma, Memoirs of a Buddhist Priest's Wife in America* (Honolulu: Buddhist Study Center Press, 1998), 115–116.
34. Jane Michiko Imamura, *Kaikyo*, 9–11, 13–17.
35. Jane Michiko Imamura, 44–45. For Jane Imamura's Buddhist contribution, in addition to her memoirs see Jane Imamura Remembered for Her Contributions to Buddhism" and "Remembering Jane Imamura and her Contribution to Buddhism."
36. Buddhist Churches of America, *Buddhist Churches of America. Vol. 1: 75-Year History, 1899–1974* (Chicago: Nobart, Inc., 1974), 86, 239–240; *Buddhist Churches of America: A Legacy of the First 100 Years* (San Francisco: Buddhist Churches of America, 1998), 120.
37. Michael K. Masatsugu. "'Beyond This World of Transiency and Impermanence': Japanese Americans, Dharma Bums, and the Making of American Buddhism during the Early Cold War Years," *Pacific Historical Review* 77, no. 3 (2008): 437–440.
38. Masatsugu, "Beyond This World of Transiency and Impermanence," 440.
39. For instance, Gary Snyder continued to interact with Kanmo and Jane until they died (Masatsugu, 445).
40. Masatsugu, 446–448.
41. Ryan Anningson, "Theories of the Self, Race, and Essentialization in Buddhism in the United States during the 'Yellow Peril,' 1899–1957" (PhD diss., Wilfrid Laurier University, 2017), 243–244.
42. Anningson, "Theories of the Self, Race, and Essentialization," 244.
43. Jane Michiko Imamura, *Kaikyo*, 39–40.
44. Kanmo Imamura, quoted by Jane Michiko Imamura, 169.
45. Hawaii Honolulu Honganji, ed. *Chōshōin ibunshū: The Collected Works of Emyō Imamura* (Honolulu: Hawaii Honolulu Honganji, 1937), 74–75. Author's translation.

46. Quoted in Moriya, *Amerika bukkyō no tanjō*, 69.
47. Hawaii Honolulu Honganji, ed., *Chōshōin ibunshū—The Collected Works of Emyō Imamura* (Honolulu: Hawaii Honolulu Honganji, 1937.

Michihiro Ama

INTENTION IN THE PALI SUTTAS AND ABHIDHARMA

INTENTION (*SAṄKAPPA/SAṄKALPA*) AND THE PATH

Saṅkappa refers to a thought, and more specifically, a *purposeful* thought. It occurs throughout Buddhist discourse but is particularly significant as the second member of the eightfold path: right view, right intention, right speech, right action, right livelihood, right effort, right mindfulness, right concentration.[1] Structurally, right intention (*sammā-saṅkappa/samyak-saṅkalpa*) is what translates a right view (*sammā-diṭṭhi/saṃyag-dṛṣti*) of the buddha's teachings into the liberating program of ethical discipline and meditation embodied in the following six path factors. Like the factors concerning external vocal and bodily action, right intention is defined in terms of what is to be *avoided*, namely, thoughts or attitudes of sensual desire (*kāma*), ill will (*vyāpāda*), and harmfulness (*vihiṃsā*).[2] Although defined negatively, right intention is conceived as a powerful proactive force, comparable to the weaponry of a war chariot.[3] In addition to guiding ethical action, right intention is essential to meditation as the absence of these attitudes is essential for the wholesome and liberating states of *samādhi* to arise.

Although the equivalent Sanskrit term, *saṅkalpa*, can simply mean "thought," it usually connotes something more proactive and constructive. In the Upaniṣads, for example, *saṅkalpa* is thought that is "heavy with intention or determination or resolution," and in some instances, it means something like imagination, "a process of using the mind to bring together or to construct something that belongs initially to the world of thought."[4] These connotations can be traced to its verbal root, √*klp*, which includes the senses of producing, making, affecting, shaping, arranging, preparing, fashioning, intending, imagining, and creating.[5] Thus, in the context of Buddhist ethics, while *saṅkappa* manifests as thought and is the result of a process of reflection, it is a thought that is formed with a specific object or goal in view and helps bring that object/goal into being.[6] The proactive sense of the term is especially pronounced in the context of the path where a successful thought or intention to refrain from certain habitual thoughts, attitudes, and actions often implies strong determination or resolve. For this reason, some translators prefer "right resolve" to "right intention" or "right thought" as a translation of *sammā-saṅkappa*.

Although *saṅkappa* is a kind of thought and so decidedly cognitive in nature, as part of a complex psychological process issuing in action (or restraint from action), it is intimately associated with affective and conative mental factors. For example, the Dīgha Nikāya explains that different intentions (*saṅkappa*) lead to different desires (*chanda*) to act, and the Saṃyuttta Nikāya, that elements (*dhātu*) of ill will give rise to thoughts (*saññā*) of ill will, which can then lead to intentions (*saṅkappa*), desires (*chanda*), fevers (*pariḷāha*), and quests (*yesanā*) related to ill will.[7] This underscores the idea that *saṅkappa* translates thought into action, whether that is action leading to further entanglement in suffering and rebirth or to the freedom effected through refraining from desire, ill will, and harmfulness as in the case of right intention and the path. Contrary to some modern presentations of mindfulness that recommend cultivating a neutral attitude toward thoughts, the suttas often call for skillful opposition to and removal of unwholesome thoughts (*vitakka*) due to this understanding that habitual patterns of thought have a strong influence over moral sentiment and desire and often lead to action. Unlike *cetanā*, which is understood as initiating action, or even action itself, *saṅkappa* is not itself an action and must be accompanied by other, more conative mental factors, like energy (*viriya*) or effort (*padhāna*) in order to issue in action.[8]

In sum, although *saṅkappa* is a thought, it is a thought that is laden with purpose or resolve and can influence or be influenced by moral sentiments and desire in such a way that, when combined with effort, leads to action and thereby constructs experience in the direction of further suffering or liberation. *Saṅkappa* is sometimes used in the context of discussing karma or actions that bind one to the cycle of rebirth, but it is more soteriologically neutral and less intimately related to karma than *cetanā*. Moreover, as a key element of the path, right intention (*sammā-saṅkappa*) is an important focus of Buddhist practice.

OVERVIEW OF INTENTION (*CETANĀ*) IN THE NIKĀYAS

As a verbal noun derived from a causal form of the root √*cit* (to think, to intend), one might expect *cetanā* to mean "thinking."[9] However, a survey of its uses in the Pali suttas, and Indic Buddhist literature more broadly, suggests that *cetanā* is quite unlike *saṅkappa* in that it does not necessarily emerge from a process of reflection and does not always manifest as thought.[10] While it *can* emerge from a process of reflection and *can* rise to the level of articulate thought or be individuated in reference to a thought (e.g., "I will give alms to the monk"), *cetanā* is more fundamentally conative than cognitive. It is more of a purposeful *impulse* toward action than an explicit thought or thinking.[11]

One of the primary ways that *cetanā* is used in the suttas is to define basic sentience. Without *cetanā*, the body is dead, like a block of wood, or becomes food for another being.[12] This use predates Buddhism, and although they build on it, Buddhists never fully abandon this sense of the term.[13] Drawing on Pali materials, Nalini Devdas explains that *cetanā* can be understood as a "preliminary stirring of conative energy that vitalizes the organism and moves the body and mind towards an object of interest."[14] The 6th-century Buddhist scholar Sthiramati similarly says:

> Intention is the shaper of the mind (*cittābhisaṃskāra*), a mental stirring (*ceṣṭa*). Where it is present, it is like the vibration [or flowing] of a mind toward an object, like the vibrating [or flowing] of iron under the power of a lodestone.[15]

The idea that *cetanā* is essential to sentience or to having a mind (which are equivalent in the Buddhist view) is also reflected in the fact that *cetanā* is invariably included as an "omnipresent mental factor" or a factor that is present in every moment of awareness in later Buddhist psychology or Abhidharma.[16] This is anticipated in the suttas in the two core doctrines of the twelve links of dependent arising and five aggregates. The twelve links of dependent arising are the existential factors most salient to the perpetuation of suffering and rebirth; they include ignorance, karmic conditioning factors, consciousness, name and form, six sense organs, contact, feeling, thirst, clinging, existence, birth, and old age and death. The fourth link, name and material form (*nāma* and *rūpa*), refers to the psycho-physical personality. "Material form" (*rūpa*) is the body or its constituent elements, and "name" (*nāma*) is the mind, which includes feeling (*vedanā*), perception (*saññā*), intention (*cetanā*), contact (*phassa*), and attention (*manasikāra*),[17] a list that closely resembles the omnipresent mental factors of later Buddhist psychology.[18] "Name and form" is also sometimes described in terms of the "five aggregates" (*pañca-khandha*), another formula for summarizing the psycho-physical personality in connection to suffering. The aggregates include a similar list of mental factors: feeling (*vedanā*), perception (*saññā*), karmic conditioning factors (*saṅkhāra*), and consciousness (*viññāna*), and although *cetanā* is not named, it is included in the aggregate of the karmic conditioning factors, which are also identified as a second link of dependent arising. According to both Sanskrit and Pali commentarial traditions, *cetanā* is the most important karmic conditioning factor due to its dominant influence over all the other mental factors and its capacity to initiate action.[19]

In this way, while there are several different schemas for mapping the territory, the suttas preserve the idea that *cetanā* defines sentience by including it as an essential constituent of the psycho-physical personality. This connection to sentience, together with Devdas's and Sthiramati's descriptions of *cetanā*'s responsiveness to sensory objects, calls to mind something of the way a biological organism responds to stimuli. However, in the context of Buddhist soteriology, the responsiveness embodied in *cetanā* is never neutral, innocent, or benign (at least in ordinary persons).[20]

Cetanā is said to be caused by craving (*tanhā*), or to stir at the prompting of contact, perception, and feeling, and then give rise to craving.[21] It also identified, along with edible food, sensory contact, and consciousness, as one of the four "foods" or nutriments (*āhāra*) that fuel continued cyclic existence (*saṃsāra*) as the result of craving.[22] Although *cetanā* is more commonly associated with craving than with cognitive processes in the suttas, it is also said to give rise to and to initial and sustained thought (*vitarka* and *vicāra*), and, in the context of the twelve links of dependent arising, *cetanā* and the karmic conditioning factors (link two) are understood to shape consciousness (link three) dependent upon ignorance (link one).[23]

A Son's Flesh sutta offers the colorful image of a man who wants to live, does not want to die, wants to be happy, and does not want to suffer but is being dragged toward a fiery pit (samsara or the cycle of rebirth) by two strong men (wholesome and unwholesome karma), even as he has the intention (*cetanā*), longing (*patthanā*), and wish (*paṇidhi*) be far away from the pit.[24] The implication is that *cetanā* perpetuates suffering and rebirth as it initiates further action fueled by craving. However, by describing *cetanā* in terms of a longing for freedom from suffering, the sutta also raises the question as to whether *cetanā* can, like *saṅkappa*, play a role in the cultivation of the path or if it is inevitably entangled with karma.

Karma literally means "action," but in the Buddhist context, it refers to action that can be morally or soteriologically qualified as wholesome, unwholesome, or neutral, the results of which shape experience in this life or a future life and perpetuate the cycle of rebirth. The term *karma* is also applied figuratively to the results of action (similar to how the term is used in modern English).[25] The best-known and, arguably, most important suttas discussing the relationship between karma and *cetanā* are the *Penetrative sutta* in the Aṅguttara Nikāya, which describes *cetanā* as essential to bodily, vocal, and mental karma, and several suttas that recount the buddha's debates with the Jains in which *cetanā* is used to distinguish karma as *intentional* action from a mere happening or accident.[26]

Ancient and modern interpreters often have different views about what is at stake in this connection between *cetanā* and karma. Ancient Buddhist interpreters were primarily concerned with topics such as whether *cetanā* itself is action, merely necessary for action, or constitutive of action; how intentions come together with other internal, external, and historical factors to determine the quality and karmic result of action; whether or how *cetanā* can play a role in the practice of the path; and if *cetanā* is involved in the actions of liberated persons.[27] In contrast, modern interpreters have sometimes cited the connection between *cetanā* and karma as indicating that karma involves rational deliberation, choice, or free will—implications that appear fairly removed from *cetanā*'s role in the suttas as something that defines sentience or its entanglement with craving and ignorance or suffering and rebirth.[28] They have also taken it to imply an intentionalist ethics, the idea that intention (in a more cognitive sense of purpose, determination, or plan) is always the most important or the only factor for determining the moral quality and karmic result of action.[29]

Although there is no reason to expect the suttas to be entirely consistent, the view that emerges when the passages concerning *cetanā* are examined collectively is that *cetanā* is an impulse toward an object of interest or end that *may become* explicitly purposeful or subject to reflection under certain conditions but does not, in itself, signify voluntary action, rational deliberation, choice, autonomous agency, or free will under some description and does not serve as the sole or even always the primary factor determining the karmic result.[30] Indeed, the overarching concern in the suttas is the habitual processes by which *cetanā* shapes the human experience of suffering and how they can be ended.

A Note on Translation. Although there is no English word that adequately captures the various senses of *cetanā*, "intention" is a reasonable approximation. The formal phenomenological sense of intention as a subject or mind having an object in view captures something of the way in which *cetanā* is oriented toward an object, even if it does not capture *cetanā*'s sense of being an impulsion toward an object of desire or interest or its soteriological connection to craving, ignorance, suffering, and rebirth. As for the common sense of an intention as a determination, purpose, or plan for action or to bring about a certain result through action, it captures something of the sense *cetanā* has in distinguishing karma from a mere accident but suggests its cognitive dimension is primary rather than secondary, which is why some interpreters prefer "volition" as a translation.[31]

Another challenge with the translation "intention" is that while Anglophone philosophers often understand intention as a kind of mental representation, *cetanā* refers to a dynamic activity, "to the mental processes that *constitute* (rather than represent) purposeful actions."[32] Arguably, "an intending" better captures this dynamism and the grammatical sense of *cetanā* as a verbal noun, but "intention" has become a standard translation and is more natural in English, so it will be used in following sections of this article.

INTENTION (*CETANĀ*) AND KARMA

In the *Penetrative sutta* of the Aṅguttara Nikāya, the buddha declares, "I say, oh monks, Intention (*cetanā*), is karma. Intending, one acts with the body, speech, or mind."[33] Despite the fact that this statement occurs only once in the Nikāyas[34] and in a sutta that provides little guidance for interpretation,[35] it has become a kind of *mahāvākya* (an authoritative foundational statement), grounding modern explanations of karma and inspiring reconstructive projects in Buddhist meta-ethical theory. Although overemphasis on this statement divorced from the context of Buddhist soteriology has sometimes led to the conflation of Western and Buddhist ideas, the attention is not entirely unwarranted as historically Buddhists also relied on it when attempting to provide authoritative and coherent accounts of karma (see the section "Abhidharma Developments").[36]

Part of the challenge of interpreting the statement is that the *sutta* does not offer a comprehensive account of karma but rather discusses it as one of six topics, sensual desire, feeling, perception, taints, karma, and suffering, that must be understood in order to penetrate the dharma. This selection of topics reflects an emphasis on the *internal* dimensions of spiritual practice that serve to distinguish the buddha's teachings from those of his contemporaries. The statement on karma, in particular, is also consistent with the Buddha's critiques of the Brahmanical emphasis on external ritual action and the Jain emphasis on the physicality of moral action and ascetic discipline, which modern scholars have referred to as the Buddhist interiorization or ethicization of karma.[37]

Perhaps because Buddhists and Jains shared relatively similar practices and views,[38] the suttas take extra care to distinguish the Buddhist view on karma from the Jain view, and this can help clarify the meaning of the *Penetrative* statement.[39] In various suttas, the buddha criticizes the Jains for attributing present experience solely to past action, prioritizing the discipline of the body over the training of the mind, and underestimating the importance of the mind and intention in determining the moral quality and result of action.[40] In the *Upāli sutta*, for example, the buddha insists that of the three kinds of action (bodily, vocal, mental), mental action regarding an evil deed is the most morally reprehensible. This is supposed to contradict the Jain view that bodily action is most important. In the ensuing discussion, it becomes clear that the point at issue is the difference between a physical action that is performed intentionally, with *cetanā* (*sañcetanika*) and with an evil end in mind, such as the intention to crush insects to death with one's feet, and something done unintentionally, or what we might call an "accident," such as accidentally killing insects while walking.[41] This helps explain the difference that intention (*cetanā*) makes to action and perhaps also why it is presented as defining karma in the *Penetrative sutta*. Although the *Upāli sutta* leaves open the question as to whether *only* mental action, or vocal and bodily as well, are significant, *The Greater Exposition on Action sutta* clarifies that the buddha takes all three kinds of action, intentional action (*sañctanika kamma*) performed by way of body, speech, or mind, to have karmic results in the form of pleasant, painful, or neutral feeling.[42]

Following the definitional statement, "I say, oh monks, Intention (*cetanā*), is karma. Intending, one acts with the body, speech, or mind," the *Penetrative sutta* clarifies its greater significance. It explains that karma arises from (sensory and mental) contact and varies with respect to where (in any of the five realms of rebirth) and when (here and now, later in this life, or in a future life) its results can be experienced. It further explains that karma ends with the cessation of contact and that this is effected through the practice of the eightfold path.[43] The fact that these *soteriological* concerns overlap with but cannot be reduced to *moral* concerns intelligible to Western religious and ethical traditions may explain some of the confusion that has arisen with respect to the *Penetrative sutta* statement, in particular the tendencies to read the relationship between intention (*cetanā*) and karmic result via an analogy to free will and moral responsibility, or in terms of the idea that intention alone (especially in a more cognitive sense) determines the moral quality of an action.[44] It may also account for the understanding that intention (*cetanā*) entails rational deliberation, choice, or an element of deliberateness.

INTENTION (*CETANĀ*) AND DELIBERATENESS

Although intention (*cetanā*) defines something as an action as opposed to a mere accident, its presence does not necessarily entail that one is fully aware of what one is doing. The *Intention sutta* of the Aṅguttara Nikāya[45] discusses intentional (*sañcetana*) action that does and does not involve clear comprehension (*sampajāna*). The commentary is specific that this means clear comprehension regarding the moral quality (wholesome, unwholesome, or neutral) of an action and the nature of its results.[46] Like the *Penetrative sutta*, the *Intention sutta* is focused on the *internal* dimension of experience and, in particular, the pleasure and pain that can follow from intentional action. It explains that these karmic repercussions can occur regardless of whether the action is bodily, vocal, or mental and regardless of whether one acts of one's own accord or at the prompting of another.[47] In this way, the sutta highlights the intersubjective dimension of the formation of intentions, the overt or subtle ways that one's intentions and actions can be influenced by others. However, the more general point of the sutta seems to be that while painful or pleasant experiences can serve as a guide to discerning the quality, and thus wisdom, of the action that caused it, discerning these connections takes training. In other words, until or unless one develops clear comprehension (and mindfulness), the processes by which one's own intentional actions arise and bind one to the cycle of suffering and rebirth will not be transparent.[48]

In highlighting the fact that intentional actions may be performed with and without clear comprehension, the sutta may imply that an action can be devoid of an even more general level of understanding or awareness of what one is doing and yet still qualify as intentional and yield karmic results. This follows from the idea that intention (*cetanā*) is present in every moment of the mundane or ordinary mind (however unconscious or unaware) and is *also* definitional of karma, However, the point is a difficult one, because at first glance, it appears to contradict the idea that intention is what distinguishes karma from mere accident.

In commenting on the *Intention sutta*, after defining clear comprehension as not knowing the moral quality and result of action, Buddhaghosa offers examples that seem to suggest a more profound lack of knowledge or deliberateness with respect to both the performance of actions and the formation of intentions than this narrower definition seems to imply.[49] Regarding actions, he describes young children who imitate their parents in the performance of meritorious actions (or who misbehave) and animals who listen to the dharma or engage in similar meritorious actions without knowing what they are doing. The idea is that although children and animals do not act knowingly (*jānanta*), they still act intentionally and thus accrue karmic merit (or demerit).[50] The question arises as to how such *undeliberate* actions be intentional and how this can be consistent with the distinction between intentional action and accident outlined in the *Upāli sutta*.

In the case of young children imitating the meritorious actions of their parents, there may be a *purpose* connected to their movement, such as to imitate the physical gesture of the parent, even if they do not understand the meaning or karmic significance of the gesture. In other words, their actions are not accidents even if they are ignorant. From a Buddhist soteriological perspective, all spiritually immature persons are like children in that they act purposefully but with various degrees of ignorance with respect to karmic cause and effect.

However, purpose may be harder to imagine in the case of a cow who wanders close to a group of chanting monks and pricks up her ears. Even if she could have purposes with respect to things that seem salient for cows (e.g., her favorite salt lick or young calf), according to the common Buddhist view, other-than-human animals do not understand language. If the cow is merely *hearing* sounds and not listening to the dharma, how is this different from accidentally killing insects while walking (as in the *Upāli sutta*)? How could it be meritorious? Buddhaghosa does not elaborate, but various internal states, such as the cow's delight or the peace she feels in the presence of the chanting monks might suggest purpose, or more observably, the fact that she keeps coming back. Putting this together with the debate with the Jains, the critical difference between an intentional killing of insects while walking and an accidental one is that in the latter case, there is no *interest* in killing the insects; killing insects was not the goal or purpose of walking, and insects were not its object. This is quite unlike the case of the virtuous cow who delights in the chanting of the monks and regularly seeks their company. As in the case of the child who tries to imitate a parent, the cow's movement is coordinated with a purpose and oriented toward a goal (hearing) or object (sounds of the monks' chanting), even if she is not fully aware of what she is doing, much less its soteriological implications.

Elsewhere in the suttas, the same terms, *sampajāna* and *asampajāna*, are used to draw more general distinctions between deliberate and undeliberate actions: acting with prior reflection (or in haste), with (or without) premeditation in the case of lying, and acting attentively (or negligently).[51] Actions lacking these forms of deliberateness may seem "unintentional" from a cognitive perspective, but they can be understood as purposeful in the sense of involving an impulse toward a particular object of interest or end. Although it is this conative relationship to an object or end rather than a cognitive or reflective one that makes actions *intentional* and karmically potent from a Buddhist perspective, elements like prior reflection, premeditation, and attentiveness can affect the nature or intensity of an action, as well as its karmic result or assessments of culpability.[52]

Just as the formation of an intention need not involve prior reflection and so on, it also need not originate with or in oneself. Again commenting again on the *Intention sutta*, Buddhaghosa explains how people act under the influence of other people's intentions, at their explicit command, or at their prompting in subtler ways. With regard to the latter, he gives the example of how envy tends to spread among the lower gods and cautions that this kind of intersubjective emotional contagion is even more dangerous in the human realm where it can lead to violence.[53]

In sum, although the distinction between action and accident is critical to the Buddhist conception of intention and karma, the primary concern in the suttas is the fact that ignorant and largely unreflective actions, which are driven by craving and guided by purposive impulses are what perpetuates suffering and rebirth. From a Buddhist perspective, the fact that one may not be aware, much less in control of how one's intentions are formed, such as through the influence of habit or passion, pleasant or unpleasant sensory experience, other persons' emotions, or distorted views, and yet still experience the karmic repercussions of one's intentional actions makes the existential situation of cyclic existence all the more perilous and urgent.

INTENTION (*CETANĀ*) AND THE KARMIC CONDITIONING FACTORS

The term *saṅkhāra* or (karmic) "conditioning factor" is derived from the prefix *sam*, meaning "together," and the verb √*kṛ*, meaning "to do" or "to make" (the same root as *karma*). *Saṅkhāras* are "both things which put together, construct and compound other things, and the things that are put together, constructed, and compounded."[54] Various derivatives from the prefix and root, including the verb, *abhi-sam* √*kṛ* played an important role in Brahmanical thought describing the constructive dimensions of ritual action and, particularly, its effect on future existences and the prominent place of similar terminology in Buddhist thought reflects a conscious adaptation and critique of Brahmanical theory. This critique includes the ideas that intentional, morally qualified action (or karma) rather than ritual action (also called karma) perpetuates conditioned existence and rebirth and that the world (*loka*) built from karma is something to be transcended rather than maintained or sought, as in older Vedic thought.[55]

In Buddhist texts, the conditioned or conditioning factors (*saṅkhāra*) can refer to all conditioned phenomena or all five aggregates or, more specifically, the karmically potent mental factors that comprise the second link of dependent arising and one of the mental aggregates, in which case "*karmic* conditioning factors" is an appropriate translation. The term *saṅkhāra* can also refer to certain factors related to the development of meditation.[56]

As Buddhist thought develops, the aggregate of karmic conditioning factors comes to serve as a catchall for all the mental factors, other than perception (*saññā*) and feeling (*vedanā*), responsible for shaping the quality of mind or experience. However, in the Saṃyutta Nikāya, it is defined as the six classes of intention (*cetanā*), meaning intentions related to the six sensory objects (objects of the five physical senses and mental objects or ideas and thoughts), or intentions arising from contact with these objects.[57] Although the suttas often treat the karmic conditioning factors and intention as equivalent to each other and to karma, later commentators seek to clarify the individual contributions of the karmic conditioning factors and explain that although the aggregate includes other mental factors, the buddha identified it with intention because intention has a predominating influence over the other factors and is what initiates action.[58] Elsewhere in the Saṃyutta, the buddha explains that the aggregate is called "conditioning factors" (*saṅkhāra*) because these factors construct or condition (*abhisaṅkharonti*) what is conditioned (*saṅkhatam*), meaning all five aggregates.[59] In other words, through its influence on the other factors and its capacity to initiate action, intention plays a dynamic role in shaping and producing all psycho-physical experience.

Although intention is typically associated with craving, a more cognitive dimension comes to the fore in connection with the karmic conditioning factors in the context of the twelve links of dependent arising, where these factors (link two) arise dependent on ignorance (link one) and give rise to consciousness (link three). The Saṃyutta Nikāya explains that "what one intends (*ceteti*), plans (*pakappeti*), and has a tendency toward (*anuseti*) becomes a basis (*ārammaṇa*) for consciousnesses."[60] Intention (*cetanā*) is not named here but is clearly implied by the verb, "intends" (*ceteti*), which carries the sense of thinking or forming a purpose.[61] Together with the association to planning, this represents one of the few places in the suttas that speaks to the cognitive dimensions of intention (*cetanā*).[62] However, these cognitive senses are more pronounced in other Indian traditions' use of the term, as well as in the commentaries on the suttas and Abhidharma.[63]

This passage from the Saṃyutta also raises the question of precisely how intention (*cetanā*) conditions consciousness, and specifically, whether it may be directly involved in the construction of both the subjective and objective dimensions of experience. Interpreters disagree. Devdas reads "what one intends, plans, and has a tendency towards becomes a basis (*ārammaṇa*) for consciousness" as suggesting that what one intends becomes an object (*ārammaṇa*) for consciousness as well as a condition for its continuation.[64] Heim goes further, explaining that intending and planning are "the very constructing and fashioning of the objects of conscious experience."[65] However, Bhikkhu Bodhi explains that Buddhaghosa's commentary and Dhammapāla's sub-commentary, which emphasize the internal or subjective dimensions of intentional activity, exclude the common Abhidharma meaning of *ārammaṇa* as an object of the six senses. If this is right, then the sutta is not saying that the constructive activities of intention extend to the construction of the *objects* of consciousness, at least not directly. It is merely saying that the activity of intending (with respect to its objects or ends) is the *basis* (*ārammaṇa*) or condition (*paccaya*) for the perpetuation of consciousness.[66]

This seems consistent with the system of the Nikāyas in which objects are generally understood as "given" or available to consciousness through contact. In this view, contact itself is a problem and so must be ended to bring an end to karma (as explained in the *Penetrative sutta*).[67] This is why various forms of contact are restricted in the context of lay and, especially, monastic practice. However, the kinds of objects that one comes into contact with, how one relates to them on contact, and how this shapes future experience and rebirth are all the result of the constructive activity of intentions. In this way, intention has an indirect role in constructing the objects of experience. The commentary explains that due to the activities of intending, planning, and tending toward certain things, consciousness "grows abundantly" and develops a "bent" (*nati*) toward future goals and rebirth.[68]

Thus, even in the absence of explicit intending and planning, there may still be a tending (*anuseti*) or inclination toward objects of interest that serves to sustain consciousness and propel it toward rebirth. Buddhists disagree as to whether this involves subliminal, latent states of mind, or only active, conscious states but agree that "tendencies" (*anusaya*) are unwholesome and interact with intentions.[69] The dynamic suggested in the Nikāyas is that these unwholesome tendencies, which are conditioned by intention and other mental factors, as well as by the universal taints (*āsava*; sense desire, desire for continued states of existence, wrong views, and ignorance), can influence intentions toward certain objects or ends but lack the capacity to initiate action themselves.[70]

Setting aside the debate as to whether or not they include subliminal activity, Buddhists agree that the processes associated with the karmic conditioning factors involve both agency and patiency:[71] a dynamic, perhaps even creative, constructing of experience, which is invariably oriented toward an object or end connected to one of the six senses, on one hand, and conditioned by past actions and tendencies, on the other.[72] Intention is the most important and dynamic factor in respect to initiating action, but it is part of a complex psychological process wherein it is also conditioned by other mental factors and tendencies in addition to the pervasive conditions of craving and ignorance. The idea that the world is built from this activity (and that this is a *problem*) is underscored by the fact the suttas describe the six sense bases as "old karma" and "fashioned by intention" (*abhisañcetanā*), as well as by a hesitance to use the term intention (*cetanā*) in the context of the path.[73]

INTENTION (*CETANĀ*) AND THE PATH

At first glance, the cultivation of the path seems to involve a dynamic of agency and patiency similar to karmic conditioning: intentions, special applications of effort, and actions, on one hand, and the fruits of those actions, on the other. There are also some places in the suttas where the term *saṅkhāra* is used in connection with the cultivation of the path: in the cases of making an effort (*sasaṅkhāra*) with regard to attaining liberation, a prior resolve (*pubbe abhisaṅkhāra*) in regard to meditative attainment, or an effort (*padhāna-saṅkhara*) with regard to attaining a spiritual power.[74] Devdas compares these examples, in which *saṅkhāra* signifies an "application of energy to achieve a specific purpose," to the dynamics of *cetanā*, to the way in which "*cetanās* fuse cognitively processed purposes" with the "motivational capacities of the *saṅkhāras*."[75] However, because the Pali commentarial tradition generally resists mixing the linguistic registers of karma and spiritual praxis, it describes the *saṅkhāra* involved in the cultivation of the path as effort (*viriya*), one of the seven factors of awakening, rather than as intention (*cetanā*).[76]

While *saṅkappa* (purposive thought) combined its the preferred term for intention in the context of the path, there are a few places in the suttas where *cetanā* is used. The *Dog-duty Ascetic sutta*, for example, describes the karma that is "neither dark nor bright" and leads to the destruction of karma as involving the "intention to abandon" dark and bright karma and its results.[77] The commentary specifies that the intentions (*cetanā*) involved in the supramundane path, that is, the four levels of awakening from stream-entry to arhathood, are exclusively of this sort.[78] The sutta distinguishes these from bright actions that bring bright results, meaning the wholesome actions involved in the cultivation of the mundane path, such as the ten wholesome courses of action and the attainment of the meditative absorptions (*jhānas*) or *samādhi*.[79] According to the sutta, such actions involve unafflicted (*abyāpajjha*) conditioning factors (*saṅkhāra*) related to body, speech, or mind and lead to happy states.[80] In other words, they may be conducive to liberation but do not bring an end to karma.

The commentaries describe the intention for abandoning karma associated with neither dark nor bright karma as a "path intention" (*magga-cetanā*).[81] In contrast to ordinary intentions which lead to the perpetuation of the world, a path intention leads to the "rolling back" or reversal (*vivaṭṭa*) of the world.[82] *The Great Forty sutta* in the Majjhima Nikāya does not mention intention (*cetanā*) but clarifies the distinction between the mundane and supramundane practice of the eightfold path, explaining that the former (bright action with bright results) is "affected by taints, partaking of merit, ripening on the side of attachment (*upadhivepakko*)," and the latter is "noble, taintless, supramundane" practice in which the eight factors of the path truly become "path factors."[83] Although the mundane path is afflicted by attachment, the description of it here and elsewhere reveals a logic of abstaining from unwholesome attitudes and actions, which makes way for the lessening of attachment and natural development of wholesome states conducive to realization and liberation.[84]

While some suttas qualify the intentions (*cetanā*) involved in the path as intentions of abandoning karmic results, others suggest that intentions are not involved.[85] For example, the *No Intention Needed sutta* begins by asking, "[W]hat is the purpose and benefit of wholesome conduct?" (wholesome conduct being the foundation of the path).[86] The buddha replies that it is non-remorse and explains that one does not need to make an intention (*cetanāya karaṇīya*) for non-remorse to arise, that it arises naturally (*dhammatā*) from wholesome conduct and, from it, all the other factors of the path.[87] In this way, each stage of the path entails and fulfills the next. Relying on a more cognitive description of *cetanā*, the commentary explains that the fact the path unfolds according to this natural causal order (*kāraṇa-niyama*) eliminates any need for each stage to be brought about by intending (*cetetvā*), conceptualizing (*kappetvā*), or planning (*pakkappetvā*).[88]

In sum, both conceptions of the path, with and without intention (*cetanā*), can be understood in terms of a logic of abstaining and abandoning, which reverses the process of dependent arising to which intention (*cetanā*) is so integral. Returning to the poignant image from *A Son's Flesh sutta*, the man being dragged toward the fiery pit of samsara by his own karma cannot become free by intensifying his intention to be far away or by doubling down on his craving for a different experience but only by letting go of this craving altogether. This begins with a clear view of what is at stake (suffering and its ending) or mundane right view, and the intention (*saṅkappa*) to refrain from attitudes of sensual desire, ill will, and harmfulness (i.e., right intention, *sammā-saṅkappa*) and based on this, from unwholesome action (right speech, action, and livelihood). With the support of right effort and right mindfulness, this restraint creates the conditions for right *samādhi* to develop, leading to knowledge and liberation. As Heim observes, the Buddhist path, and especially, right intention (*sammā-saṅkappa*) and right effort, entail a "robust sense of agentive possibility" and "an enormous optimism in the human capacity to move towards complete freedom once we learn to relinquish our ordinary constructions of experience."[89]

The agency assumed in the practice of the path and the freedom enjoyed by the liberated person or arhat contribute to the impression that Buddhism is at least implicitly committed to some version of free will. Moreover, because intention (*cetanā*) is identified with karma and helps distinguish purposeful action from accident, it has seemed to some a likely candidate for a Buddhist concept of free will.[90] However, the suttas repeatedly indicate that intention (*cetanā*) is a site of bondage rather than of agency. There is also no clear evidence that premodern Buddhists understood intention (*cetanā*) itself to imply the freedoms to choose between alternative courses of action or otherwise control action typically associated with free will.[91] In sum, Buddhism may be compatible with free will under some description, but intention (*cetanā*) is not in any meaningful sense equivalent to will or free will.[92]

ABHIDHARMA DEVELOPMENTS

Although the Pali suttas and Sanskrit parallels (mostly preserved in Chinese) establish intention (*cetanā*) as the defining factor of sentience and of karma, it is left to later Buddhists to work out the details. This process began in the canonical Abhidharma works and commentaries and is further developed by later scholiasts.[93] Two of the most important for subsequent Buddhist tradition are Buddhaghosa (5th century) and Vasubandhu (4th–5th century).[94] They focus on topics such as whether intention is the same as karma, merely a necessary condition for it, or an essential constitutive element of it; how intention relates to other internal, external, and historical factors in respect to initiating an action, and determining its moral quality and karmic result; and how these factors work together to determine the culpability of an agent in a social context (e.g., monastic jurisprudence). While Buddhaghosa and Vasubandhu continue to regard intention (*cetanā*) as fundamentally conative, they also draw out more of its cognitive dimensions. Relying on a similar body of scripture, they not only agree on many points regarding the concept of intention (*cetanā*), its relationship to karma, and its results but also develop the concept in distinctive ways according to concerns and debates in their respective commentarial traditions.

Intention (*Cetanā*) and Karma. The *Penetrative sutta* statement (or its Sanskrit parallel), so influential in modern understandings of karma, also figures prominently in Buddhaghosa and Vasubandhu's presentations. Buddhaghosa begins his discussion of karma in *The Expositor* (*Attasālinī*) with the Pali statement "I say, oh monks, Intention (*cetanā*), is karma. Intending, one acts with the body, speech, or mind."[95] He takes this to mean that intention (*cetanā*) originates action[96] and is realized in body, speech, or mind.[97] In other words, intention is not a necessary precondition for action but an essential constituent of action that is simultaneous with it. However, intention is not the only element involved and is not itself action. The "doorways" of body, speech, and mind; the primary motivational roots (greed, hatred, and delusion, and their opposites); and, in some cases, path factors[98] also constitute action.[99]

Toward the beginning of the chapter on karma in his *Treasury of Higher Dharma and Commentary* (*Abhidharmakośa-bhāṣya*), after declaring that the variety of the world is born of action, Vasubandhu cites the Sanskrit parallel to the *Penetrative sutta* statement "There are two kinds of karma, intention and karma subsequent to intention."[100] He explains that both forms of karma are actually intention: an intention that is preparatory (*prayoga*) to action, that is, a pure intention or purposive thought (*saṅkalpa-cetanā*) and a subsequent intention that is the performance (*kriyā-cetanā*) of vocal or bodily action. Against an opponent's (Vaibhāṣika) view that that intention (*cetanā*) is mental karma but merely a necessary condition for vocal and bodily karma, Vasubandhu argues that *all three* kinds of action are intention and that the terms "bodily" and "vocal" are used merely metaphorically for the door, basis, or object of action. In this view, a bodily action is an intention that is focused or based on the body and moves the body here or there; similarly, a vocal action is an intention that is focused on the voice and causes vocal utterance.[101]

Compared to the Sarvāstivāda Vaibhāsika school, which describes bodily and vocal karma as material, Vasubandhu and Buddhaghosa agree that intention, as a *mental* factor, is the causally potent element in karma. Their explanations of how intention relates to the three doors (body, speech, mind) are also quite similar. However, Buddhaghosa draws several subtle distinctions between karma and intention, while Vasubandhu regularly collapses the two terms. For example, Buddhaghosa suggests that the six mental "courses of action" (covetousness, ill will, wrong view, and their opposites)[102] are more accurately understood as intensifications of the motivational roots than as intentions, where Vasubandhu insists that all the courses of action are intention, and underscores the point that the mental courses are nothing other than intention.[103] Heim suggests that Buddhaghosa makes the distinction as part of a larger effort to distinguish the logic of abstention and abandoning involved in the precepts and the practice of the path from the logic of accumulation involved in the concept of intention (*cetanā*).[104] In contrast, Vasubandhu builds his theory of karma around the view that intention plays similar roles in the transmission of karmic results and the transformation of the personality effected through the practice of the path.

Intention (*Cetanā*) and Karmic Results. Despite these differences, Buddhaghosa and Vasubandhu have similar assessments of the relationship between intention and karmic results. Both ascribe to what Heim calls an "action based ethics," as opposed to an intention, character, or agent-based ethics.[105] In brief, both assume a kind of objective moral naturalism in which intention is required for karmically potent action but is not the only factor and not always the most important factor determining its moral quality and result. Like other omnipresent mental factors, intention is neutral, neither wholesome nor unwholesome, but in ordinary persons, it is afflicted by pervasive conditions of ignorance and craving and can be moved by unwholesome or wholesome "roots," meaning the primary motivational factors (greed, hatred, delusion, or their opposites), and influenced by other wholesome, unwholesome, or neutral mental factors (karmic conditioning factors). These various internal conditions help determine the quality and result of an action, as do certain objective facts, chiefly, the quality of the object end toward which an intention is directed and the nature of the act itself.

This moral naturalism or action-based ethics is most evident in Buddhaghosa and Vasubandhu's discussions of the "courses of action" identified in the suttas/sūtras.[106] These include ten paradigmatic, karmically weighty unwholesome actions related to the body (killing, theft, sexual misconduct), speech (lying, divisive speech, harsh speech, idle chatter), and mind (covetousness, ill will, wrong view), and their opposites (i.e., restraint from these actions or opposing actions and attitudes). These actions have the capacity to determine a future rebirth when they are "complete" but can influence future conditions even when they are not.

With regard to a course of action of killing, Buddhaghosa explains that completeness requires that there is a living being, that one knows it is a living being, that there is the thought to kill, that there is an undertaking of the act of killing, and that the living being dies.[107] Vasubandhu agrees that in cases of serious moral transgression, like murder, knowledge of *what* one is doing is crucial and that one must also not be mistaken as to the identity of the object/person toward which an action is directed.[108] However, he also affirms the idea expressed in the *Intention sutta* and Buddhaghosa's commentary on it that lack of knowledge regarding the moral quality or result of an action does not nullify its result, nor does a mistaken motivating belief (e.g., the belief that an action is good when it is not). For example, someone who believes that matricide is virtuous and kills their mother still suffers the serious karmic repercussions of matricide.[109] However, relational or situational facts are also important: it is only matricide if one kills one's own mother.[110]

Regarding independent facts about the qualities of the object, Vasubandhu explains how, for example, killing a buddha is more serious than killing an ordinary person.[111] For his part, Buddhaghosa discusses how the size of an animal or the virtue of a person affect the gravity of the karmic result of killing them.[112] Both discuss how the qualities of objects stolen and of the nature of the victim affect the karmic result of theft, and conversely, how the quality of a gift and recipient affect the merit of giving.[113] While such objective facts are critical in regard to the karmic result of bodily actions, Buddhaghosa gives greater weight to internal factors such as motivation than to the literal meaning of words in relation to courses of action concerning speech, and both thinkers consider external and relational factors such as the quality of the person/group being addressed and whether they understand what is said.[114]

Both also discuss how the temporal, historical dimensions of courses of action affect karmic results. According to Vasubandhu, even an action that is complete will not necessarily be "accumulated," meaning that it will not necessarily determine a future birth, unless certain historical conditions also obtain. In addition to the primary action, there must also be preparatory (*prayoga*) and consequent (*pṛṣṭha*) actions.[115] In the case of external action, the primary action is the intention that moves the body or causes vocal utterance, while a preparatory action or intention is a mental action like forethought, and subsequent actions are intentions (any of the three kinds of action) consistent with the primary action.[116] In this way, it matters whether an action is done with forethought, from habit with a history of intention, or as the result of negligence; and if it is followed by consistent or remedial action, such as remorse or confession.[117] Other mental factors attendant to an action also affect its result, such as if one relishes in its performance or performs it with faith or with intense defilement or purity.[118] It also matters whether or how it has been practiced, cultivated, and developed.[119]

Buddhaghosa does not give as much attention to the temporal or historical dimensions of intention in his discussion of karma[120] but expresses a few similar ideas. He discusses, for example, how idle speech is worse when it is habitually practiced; how the three intentions, prior to the act of giving (the thought "I will give a gift"), concurrent with it, and the subsequent reflection ("I have given it") together form the basis of the act of giving; and how a similar series of intentions form the basis of the act of undertaking the precepts.[121]

Resultant and Functional Intention (*Cetanā*). Because intention (*cetanā*) is supposed to be present in every moment of mind and is the defining feature of purposeful action as well as of karma, some Buddhists, especially in the Pali Abhidhamma tradition, wrestle with the question of whether it is always karmically potent (always productive of karmic results) in ordinary persons, and whether it can be involved at all in the actions of arhats. For his part, Buddhaghosa provides a complex theory of cognitive processing (*citta-vīthi*) that helps explain how there can be intention (*cetanā*) in all minds, even when there is no intentional action or karmic result.[122] The basic idea is that in the first stage, an object is received in consciousness and consciousness begins to process it.[123] Here intention (*cetanā*) coordinates other mental factors and inclines them toward the object but is not motivated by the unwholesome or wholesome roots of action (greed, hatred, delusion, and their opposites). In the second stage, there is a series of moments (*javana*) in which the "mind cognizes the object fully and actively responds to it."[124] It is only here that intention (*cetanā*) becomes purposeful and initiates karmically potent action. In other words, not every moment of mind for an ordinary person is karmically productive; some moments are simply the result (*vipāka*) of previous action. Moreover, if an active intention in the second stage is not motivated by a wholesome or unwholesome root in ordinary persons, and so is karmically neutral, it is called "functional" (*kiriya*). This theory also accounts for the purposeful, but karmically impotent actions of arhats. Arhats have entirely "functional" (*kiriya*) minds, in which intention (*cetanā*) plays the role of coordinating the other factors and directing them to appropriate objects but is devoid of exertion (*āyūhana*) and any interest in the objects and so does not produce a karmic result.[125] The path intentions of abandoning, mentioned earlier, can be considered functional in this sense. Accordingly, there are four basic varieties of intention (*cetanā*): wholesome, unwholesome, resultant, and merely functional.[126]

Vasubandhu also recognizes a distinction between minds that result from previous actions (*vipāka*) and those that are productive of karmic results but does not elaborate on this in relation to intention (*cetanā*).[127] Moreover, because he understands intentions to play a role in *reversing* the karmic process similar to the role they play in perpetuating suffering and rebirth, he does not qualify neither the dark nor the bright intentions involved in the path as fundamentally different from karmically potent intentions, although he does follow scripture in taking path intentions to consist in abstinence from wrong action and abandoning karmic results.[128]

Conative and Cognitive Dimensions of Intention (*Cetanā*). Although they cannot be courses of action, Buddhaghosa and Vasubandhu agree that there can be undeliberate intentional actions, actions that involve intention (*cetanā*) in the form of a purposive impulse toward an object or end but lack any explicit thinking or planning. For example, as seen earlier, in his commentary on the *Intention sutta*, Buddhaghosa discusses intentions that arise from social emotional contagion and those belonging to young children and animals who do not understand what they are doing.[129] For his part, Vasubandhu mentions intentions that occur in dreams during sleep[130] and subscribes to the view that intentions are found in all three realms of existence and all five realms of rebirth (including animals) and in the form and formless realms and states of meditative absorptions.[131] Although many of these "intentional" actions (excluding meditative attainments[132]) may not be weighty enough to determine a future rebirth, they can still influence future conditions (typically described in terms of merit or demerit).[133] In other words, intentions that involve thinking or planning are an important subclass, but do not represent the broader category of intention (*cetanā*), which Buddhaghosa and Vasubandhu both define in more conative terms.

In his *Treasury*, Vasubandhu defines intention as a mental action (*manas-karma*), which is the shaper or constructing activity of mind (*citta-abhisaṃskāra*), referring to intention's role as the primary karmic conditioning factor responsible for perpetuating psycho-physical experience.[134] In his treatise on the five aggregates (*Pañcaskandha*), he adds that this constructive activity is in relation to an object or end that is endowed with good qualities, faults, or neither.[135] Commenting on Vasubandhu's *Thirty Verses*, Sthiramati elaborates, drawing out the energetic quality of this activity:

> Intention is the shaper of the mind (*cittābhisaṃskāra*), a mental stirring (*ceṣṭa*). Where it is present, it is like the vibration [or flowing] of a mind toward an object, like the vibrating [flowing] of iron under the power of a lodestone.[136]

Vasubandhu also acknowledges the primitive conative sense of intention as marking basic sentience or animacy in his *Treasury*, and in his *Monograph on Karma*, he further explains that karma is distinct from autonomic (Tibetan: *so so pa'i nus pa*) bodily processes by virtue of the fact that it is endowed with exertion (Tibetan: *rtsol ba*).[137] This is consistent with the idea in the *Treasury* that bodily karma is the intention that sets the body into motion (*prayarte*).[138]

However, because the cognitive qualities of an action are critical with respect to the gravity of its result, both Buddhaghosa and Vasubandhu follow earlier commentators in individuating intentions, especially those preliminary and subsequent to action, in terms of first-person thoughts (e.g., "I will give a gift" or the optative "I should do this").[139] Given the broader meaning and function of intention as an omnipresent mental factor, this cannot mean that intentions (*cetanās*) necessarily take the form of explicit thoughts but illustrates how intentions as purposive impulses can become manifest or known in thought and thus subject to conscious reflection. As suggested in the *Intention sutta,* this is critical to the practice of the path, which involves cultivating the capacity to reflect on one's intentional actions and their likely karmic results with mindfulness and clear comprehension (*sampajāna*).

In addition to individuating intentions in reference to thoughts, Vasubandhu describes the intention that occurs prior to the main action as a purposive thought (*saṅkalpa-cetanā*).[140] Elsewhere in the *Treasury,* he also refers to it as the thought (*āśaya*) or notion (*abhiprāya*), "I should do such and such," or "I will not do such and such," and explains that in order for an action to be accumulated (i.e., have a definitive karmic result), it must be intentional (*sañcetanātas*) in the sense of being performed with thought or awareness (*sañcintya kṛtam*), meaning not without forethought (*abuddhipūrvam*) or in haste (*sahasā*).[141] In his *Monograph on Karma,* Vasubandhu also describes two intentions (Tibetan: *'go ba* and *nges pa*) occurring before the intention that accomplishes the main action. Commentators have interpreted these as "deliberation" and the "judgment" or "determination" to act, respectively.[142] In the last chapter of the *Treasury,* he offers yet another sequence in order to explain the arising of action in the absence of an agent: "from memory, there is desire, and from desire, thought (*vitarka*), and from thought, effort (*prayatna*), and from effort, wind, and from that there is karma."[143] Here thought (*vitarka*) appears to stand in for the preparatory intention and karma for the intention that performs the main action.[144] However, this also reveals a close connection to the cognitive element of memory as well as the conative factors of desire and effort.

The prominence of these overtly cognitive glosses makes it easy to overlook the more primitive conative functions of intention (*cetanā*), which Vasubandhu also acknowledges.[145] In her book on the Theravāda interpretation of *cetenā,* Devdas discusses at length the ways that Buddhaghosa brings the more conative senses of intention from the suttas (energizing an organism and motivating it toward action), together with cognitive purposes that arise in the mind (*citta*), such that "[*c*]*etanā* gives active expression to the cognitive and emotive content of a specific state of mind (*citta*) and 'actualizes' or makes concrete the moral values that reside in the state of mind."[146]

At the heart of the theory are a series of vivid anthropomorphized similes that Buddhaghosa uses to explain the way intention relates to the other mental factors[147] belonging to the same moment of awareness or mind (*citta*).[148] Buddhaghosa begins by defining intention (*cetanā*) as "what intends (*cetayati*), which means that it puts together (*abhisandahati*) with itself its accompanying factors as objects."[149] The commentary glosses "puts together" with "bind" and "set in motion." According to Devdas, this means that intention (*cetanā*) "connects concomitant states to itself by focusing its motivating action on them and setting them in motion."[150]

After describing this basic nature or characteristic, Buddhaghosa explains that intention's function (*rasa*) is exertion (*āyūhana*). To explain how this works in a particularly wholesome (and harmonious) mind, he gives the simile of a landowner (intention) who works energetically alongside fifty-five strong men (the other karmic conditioning factors)[151] toward the common goal of reaping a harvest. He then explains intention's manifestation (*paccupaṭṭhānā*) as arranging (*saṃvidahana*) the other mental factors with similes of a chief disciple, a master carpenter, and an army general, whose strong resolve in their own task rallies their subordinates to engage in their respective tasks as part of a coordinated effort of reciting a lesson, building a house, and making war.[152] Devdas takes this to mean that by engaging in work in respect to its object, intention motivates the other mental factors to perform their own functions with respect to that object.[153] Heim elaborates that intentions are "assigned multiple responsibilities for their own and others' mental work; they can see what is needed and the urgency of it (the teacher is approaching) and are driven to stimulate themselves and others to action."[154] In other words, intentions perform a kind of executive function. Part of this involves the capacity to remember and cause the other factors to recall urgent work—thus providing a connection between present action and the past, also seen in Vasubandhu's theory of intention. Heim further reads the passage as saying that intention not only engages with work in respect to its object but "produces its object by its own work."[155] As in the passage from the Saṃyutta Nikāya discussed earlier, the philosophical issue at stake is whether intention (*cetanā*) directly or only indirectly constructs sensory objects as it shapes future experience.[156]

Overall, Buddhaghosa's similes reveal that intention not only involves a more conative, purposive impulse but coordination of other cognitive and emotional factors, such as thinking (*vitarka* and *vicāra*), mindfulness/memory (*sati*), clear comprehension, and right view, and non-greed, sympathetic joy, and abstention from bodily misconduct, toward a common object or end.[157] Presumably, this coordination, which happens in every moment of mind, is more harmonious in wholesome states devoid of unwholesome mental factors such as delusion, sluggishness, and doubt. In both the cases, it can but need not involve explicit thinking or planning.

Intention, Transmission, and Transformation. If Buddhaghosa's unique contributions to the Buddhist concept of intention (*cetanā*) are his theory of cognitive processing and these similes regarding the coordination of *simultaneous* mental factors, Vasubandhu's is his development of a theory regarding the role intention plays in the *longitudinal* phenomena of karmic ripening, habituation, memory, spiritual cultivation, and liberation.[158] In the chapter on karma in his Abhidharmakośa-bhāṣya, it becomes clear that he defines karma as the mental activity of intention (*cetanā*) not only because he takes this to be in accordance with scripture but also because intention is a more plausible mechanism for explaining these phenomena than the quasi-material and non-mental metaphysical factors proposed in the Vaibhāṣika-Sarvāstivāda theory.[159]

The debate centers on several topics related to karma and the path, such as how merit continues to increase after the initial performance of an action; how a karmic result ensues from the completion of a course of action when a proxy is involved; how a monk can be said to be practicing all eight branches of the path (including right speech, action, and livelihood) during the (silent and still) moment of meditative attainment; how he can be understood to uphold wholesome monastic discipline, even when his mind is unwholesome or neutral; and how renunciation (*virakti*) can block unwholesome action.[160] In each of these cases, the challenge is accounting for the continuing potency of action given the temporal gap between the initial act and its subsequent effects. While his opponents try to explain these examples in terms of extra-psychological factors, Vasubandhu attributes them to a transformation (*pariṇāma-viśeṣa*) in the causal series or continuum (*santati*) of the psycho-physical aggregates engendered by intention (*cetanā*) or, in the case of liberation, to a total transformation of the personality called a "reversal of the basis" (*āśraya-parāvṛtti*).

In the case of karmic fruition, once the series has been "infused" (*paribhāvita*) by an intention it can be affected by unknown external facts or unplanned consequences of the intentional act (e.g., by the virtues and subsequent meditative attainments of a monk to whom alms are offered[161]) as well as by unknown outcomes of the action (as when the successful completion of murder by proxy is unknown to the person who ordered it[162]). These facts or events trigger a specific transformation (*pariṇāma-viśeṣa*) of the series that may give rise to results in the present or at a future time.[163] Vasubandhu suggests that his theory's main advantage with respect to explaining these aspects of karmic fruition is simply that it is more elegant and more in conformity to scriptural categories than his opponent's theory.[164]

Vasubandhu's theory has greater advantages with respect to explaining the effects of immaterial actions and the psychologically transformative effects of the practice of the path. Because it links karmic result to the psychological factor of intention, it can better explain an increase in merit that results from wholesome mental cultivation, as when intentions directed toward the buddha during the day lead to joyful dreams of him (and an increase of merit) during sleep.[165] It also explains the transformative effect of taking monastic vows, how the restraint (*saṃvara*) which defines a monk endures even when he has an intention to engage in a prohibited action. The present contents of this monk's mind may be no different than an unrestrained person who has an intention to engage in the same action, but being a monk is supposed to make a difference. Instead of attributing this difference to a metaphysical condition resulting from the verbal or physical act of having taken monastic vows (like his opponent does), Vasubandhu explains that it is intention (*cetanā*) which constitutes monastic restraint. Due to the way he has cultivated the intention with which he took the vow or the way that intention has perfumed his mental stream, the monk is able to remember the vow.[166] This is what makes him subject to restraint, what causes him to feel shame and refrain from the act.[167] The same applies to other forms of restraint that constitute the mundane practice of the path.

Intention also plays a role in the supramundane path, in the transformation or reversal of the basis (*āśraya-parāvṛtti*). The idea, introduced earlier in the *Treasury*, is that liberating meditative insight transforms the personality in such a way that the potential for defilements to manifest (and compel karmically potent action) is destroyed, just like a burned seed can no longer produce rice.[168] In the karma chapter, Vasubandhu explains how the prior intention (*āśaya*) to abandon wrong action creates the basis (*āśraya*) for the abandonment of wrong action upon emerging from meditative attainment of insight (and, thus, how there can be the pure practice of the eightfold path even in the absence of manifest vocal or bodily action).[169] His commentators describe this as a *reversal* (*parāvṛtta*) of the basis.[170]

Both aspects of the theory, specific transformation (*pariṇāma-viśeṣa*) in the case of karmically potent action and reversal of the basis resulting from liberating insight, are developed further in the *Monograph on Karma*, where Vasubandhu explains that transformation and reversal concern a subliminal or unconscious level of mind called the storehouse consciousness (*ālayavijñāna*).[171] The storehouse consciousness is merely a resultant (*vipāka*) consciousness underlying the active consciousness where intentions take place.[172] Vasubandhu hints at this theory in the *Treasury* when he talks about the tendencies (*anuśaya*) as latent defilements that have the capacity to cause manifest defilement and even compares this to the capacity to remember previous experience, and also in the ninth chapter of the *Abhidharkamakośa*, but it is fully fleshed out in the *Monograph* where he elaborates how the storehouse consciousness carries the impressions (*vāsanā*) of past actions, which serve as potentials (*bīja*) for defilement and karmic results due to specific power (**śaktiviśeṣa*) of intentions (*cetanā*).[173] This theory prepares the ground for the claim in Vasubandhu's Yogācāra works, that the world created by karma (as expressed in the *Treasury*) is nothing other than mind, or "mind-only" (*citta-mātra*).[174]

CONCLUSION

In the suttas, the more cognitive term, *sankappa* (purposive thought) is the preferred term for intention in the context of the path, and the more conative *cetanā* (purposive impulse) is associated with basic sentience as well as with karma. As an omnipresent mental factor and an essential feature of karma, *cetanā* becomes central to Abhidharma theory. Its more basic conative functions (energizing the organism and impelling action) become fused with explicit cognitive purposes, especially in the context of discussing the nature and fruition of karmically weighty actions. While Buddhaghosa and Vasubandhu both highlight the ways that intention interacts with thought, memory, and emotion and plays a role in the mundane cultivation of the path, Vasubandhu is more inclined to treat the intentions involved in both the mundane and supermundane path as analogous to the intentions that bind one to cyclic existence. In contrast, Buddhaghosa speaks of several varieties of intention. Perhaps a greater difference is that while Buddhaghosa elaborates the way intention operates in a cognitive series constituting an act of perception and in relation to other simultaneous mental factors, Vasubandhu introduces the idea of a subliminal level of mind to explain the role of intention in transmitting karmic results and practicing the path.[175]

REVIEW OF LITERATURE

As of the early 21st century, there have not been any book-length studies devoted to the Buddhist concept of *saṅkappa*, but there have been three on *cetanā*. Nalini Devdas's *Cetanā and the Dynamics of Volition in Theravāda Buddhism* and Maria Heim's *Forerunner of All Things: Buddhaghosa on Mind, Agency, and Intention* both discuss *cetanā* as presented in the first four Nikāyas of the Pali Canon and the Theravāda Abhidhamma.[176] Devdas includes a discussion of pre-Buddhist uses of the term and a comprehensive survey of related terminology in the suttas and commentaries, while Heim focuses primarily on Buddhaghosa's view, including discussions of intention (often in terms other than *cetanā* or *saṅkappa*) presented in his commentaries on the Vinaya (monastic code) and narrative literature, in addition to his commentaries on the suttas and Abhidhamma, and independent treatises (namely, his *Atthasālinī* and *Visuddhimagga*). Karin Meyers's "Freedom and Self Control: Free Will in Light of South Asian

Buddhism" also discusses *cetanā* in the Nikāyas and the Theravāda Abhidhamma but focuses primarily on the concept in Vasubandhu's works, especially his *Treasury of Higher Dharma* and *Monograph on Karma*.[177] These three works agree that a concept of free will is not central to the Buddhist concept of intention (*cetanā*). However, attempts to draw analogies between *cetanā* and free will or related ideas like choice were common in earlier discussions of *cetanā*.[178]

Other works on the topic of *cetanā* include Karunaratna's "Cetanā" and Meyers, "The Dynamics of Intention, Freedom and Habituation According to Vasubandhu's *Abhidharmakośabhāṣya*", which summarizes significant portions of Vasubandhu's theory, and Maria Heim's "Aesthetics of Excess", which discusses *cetanā* in the context of moral emotions motivating actions.[179] There is also a substantial literature on karma relevant to the study of the topic.[180]

Essential primary sources include suttas from the Pali Nikāyas (see the "Further Reading" section) and parallels in the Chinese Āgamas as they become available in English translation.[181] For Abhidharma developments, Buddhaghosa's *Visuddhimagga* (*Path of Purification*) and *Attasālinī* (*Expositor*), Vasubandhu's *Abhidharmakośa-bhāṣya* (*Treasury of Higher Dharma and Commentary*) and *Monograph on Karma* (*Karmasiddhiprakaraṇa*)[182] are essential reading, although a more complete study would also include canonical Abhidharma works[183] and para-canonical works such as the *Milindapañha* (*Questions of King Milinda*),[184] as well as Yogācāra Abhidharma works.[185]

FURTHER READING

Bodhi, Bhikkhu, trans. *The Connected Discourses of the Buddha: A Translation of the Saṃyutta Nikāya*. Boston: Wisdom Publications, 2000. See especially: 12, no. 2 ("Analysis of Dependent Origination"), 534–535; 12.38 ("Volition"), 576–578; 12.63 ("A Son's Flesh"), 597–599; 12, no. 51 ("Thorough Investigation"), 586–589.

Bodhi, Bhikkhu, trans. *The Numerical Discourses of the Buddha: A Translation of the Aṅguttara Nikāya*. Boston: Wisdom Publications, 2012. See especially: 4, no. 171 ("Intention sutta"), 536–538; 4, no. 232 ("On Bright and Dark Karma sutta"), 601–605; 6, no. 63 ("Penetrative sutta"), 958–964; 10, nos. 1-2 ("No Intention Needed sutta"), 1339–1341; 10, nos. 211–217 ("Deed-Born Body sutta"), 1528–1544.

Devdas, Nalini. *Cetanā and the Dynamics of Volition in Theravāda Buddhism*. New Delhi: Motital Banarsidass, 2008.

Heim, Maria. *Forerunner of All Things: Buddhaghosa on Mind, Agency and Intention*. New York: Oxford University Press, 2013.

Karunaratana, Wijesinghe Sugathadas "Cetanā." In *Encyclopaedia of Buddhism*. Vol. IV. Edited by G. P. Malalasekera. Colombo, Sri Lanka: Department of Government Printing, 1979.

Meyers, Karin. "Freedom and Self-Control: Free Will in South Asian Buddhism." PhD diss., University of Chicago, 2010.

Ñāṇamoli, Bhikkhu, trans. *Visuddhimagga: The Path of Purification*. Colombo, Sri Lanka: Buddhist Publication Society, 2010.

Ñāṇamoli, Bhikkhu, and Bhikkhu Bodhi, trans. *The Middle Length Discourses of the Buddha: A New Translation of the Majjhima Nikāya*. Boston: Wisdom Publications, 1995. See especially: 56: Upāli Sutta: To Upāli, 477–492; 57: The Dog-duty Ascetic, 493–497; 117: The Great Forty, 934–940; 136: The Greater Exposition on Action 1058–1062.

Pruden, Leo M., trans. *Karmasidddhiprakaraṇa: The Treatise of Action by Vasubandhu*. French translation by Étienne Lamotte. Berkeley: Asian Humanities Press, 1987.

Sangpo, Gelong Lodro, trans. *Abhidharmakośa-bhāṣya of Vasubandhu: The Treasury of the Abhidharma and Its (Auto) Commentary*. 4 Vols. New Delhi: Motilal Banarsidass, 2012.

NOTES

1. This article draws primarily on discourses (suttas) in the first four collections (Nikāyas) of the Pali canon, Dīgha, Majjhima, Saṃyutta, and Aṅguttara, with some references to their commentaries and to later treatises of Buddhist psychology or Abhidharma (higher dharma), particularly those of Buddhaghosa and Vasubandhu.
2. Bhikkhu Bodhi, *The Connected Discourses of the Buddha: A Translation of the Saṃyutta Nikāya* (Boston: Wisdom Publications, 2000), 1528; and M. Leon Feer, ed., *Saṃyutta-Nikāya*, vol. V (London: Pali Text Society, 1884–1898), 9.
3. Bhikkhu Anālayo, *Excursions into the Thought World of the Pāli Discourses: From Craving to Liberation* (Onalaska, WA: Pariyatti, 2012), 55; Bodhi, *Connected*, 1526; and Leon Feer, Saṃyutta v, 6.
4. David Shulman, *More Than Real: A History of the Imagination in South India* (Cambridge, MA: Harvard University Press, 2012), 112; Shulman, *More Than Real*, 11. This meaning becomes more prominent in later usages, such as in the 9th-century *Yoga-Vāsiṣṭha*, but can be traced to the Upaniṣads. For a detailed discussion of *saṅkalpa* in the Upaniṣads, see Nalini Devdas, *Cetanā and the Dynamics of Volition in Theravāda Buddhism* (New Delhi: Motital Banarsidass, 2008), 51–54.
5. Monier Williams, *Dictionary, English and Sanskrit* (London: W.H. Allen, 1851), 308; T. W. Rhys Davids and William Stede, eds., *The Pali Text Society's Pali–English Dictionary* (Chipstead: Pali Text Society, 1921–1925), 187, 662; and Shulman, *More Than Real*, 18.
6. R. M. L. Gethin, *The Buddhist Path to Awakening* (Oxford: Oneworld, 2001), 192–194.
7. T. W. Rhys Davids and J. Estlin Carpenter, eds., *The Dīgha Nikāya*, vol. III (London: Pali Text Society, 1899–1911), 289; and Anālayo, *Excursions*, 60.
8. Devdas, *Cetanā*, 111, 425.
9. "Thinking" is how it was first rendered into English by C. A. F. Rhys Davids. See PTS Dictionary, *cinteti & ceteti*, 269. However, Monier Williams emphasizes to perceive, attend, be aware as well as to intend, 394; For detailed discussions of the history of interpretation and translation of cetanā, see Devdas, *Cetanā*, 1–32 (and chapters VII and IX); Karin Meyers, "Freedom & Self-Control: Free Will in Light of South Asian Buddhism" (PhD diss., University of Chicago, 2010), 140–174; and Maria Heim, *Forerunner of All Things: Buddhaghosa on Mind, Agency and Intention* (New York: Oxford University Press, 2013), 17–30.
10. Devdas, *Cetanā*, 425.
11. Devdas, *Cetanā*, 436–437, 489. Strictly speaking, Buddhists do not make a clear distinction between "conative" and "cognitive" dimensions of mental factors, and *cetanā* itself defies easy classification as exclusively conative (pertaining to impulse, desire, striving) or cognitive (pertaining thinking, reasoning, remembering). However, these terms are useful for clarifying what *cetanā* means in different Buddhist contexts and for correcting a tendency to overlook the more conative dimensions of the term in modern interpretation (see the section "Note on Translation").
12. V. Treckner and Robert Chalmers, eds., *The Majjhima-Nikāya*, vol. I (London: Pali Text Society, 1888–1902), 296; also see M. Leon Feer, ed., *The Saṃyutta-Nikāya*, vol. III (London: Pali Text Society, 1884–1898), 143.
13. Devdas, *Cetanā*, 179–183.
14. Devdas, *Cetanā*, 180.
15. *Cetanā cittābhisaṃskāro manasaśceṣṭā/yasyām satyām ālambanaṃ prati cetasaḥ praspanda iva bhavati, ayaskāntavaśād ayaḥprasyandavat.* Sylvain Lévi, ed., *Vijñaptimātratāsiddhi: Deux traités de Vasubandhu* (Paris, France: Librairie Honoré Champion, 1925), 21. Some manuscripts read *prasyanda* ("flowing") instead of *praspanda* ("vibration"). The Tripāṭhī and Dorje's dual Sanskrit–Tibetan version notes the confusion, but they prefer *prasyanda*. Rāmśaṅkara Tripāṭhī and Sempā Dorje, *Vijñaptimātratāsiddhi of Ācārya Vasubandbu* (Leh, Ladakh, India: Central Institute of Buddhist Studies, 1984), 47. In the Śāstrī

edition of Yaśomitra's commentary, the gloss on *cittābhisaṃskāra* is *cittapraspanda*. Swāmī Dwārikādās Śāstrī, ed., *Abhidharmakośa and Bhāṣya of Ācārya Vasubandhu with Sphuṭārthā Commentary of Ācārya Yaśomitra*, 2 vols. (Varanasi, India: Bauddha Bharati, 1998), 147.

16. On the connection of sentience and mind, see Lambert Schmithausen, *The Problem of the Sentience of Plants in Earliest Buddhism* (Tokyo: International Institute for Buddhist Studies, 1991), 2. This article uses the Sanskrit term *Abhidharma* to refer to Buddhist Abhidharma traditions (especially the Theravāda Abhidhamma as presented by Buddhaghosa and the Sautrāntika Abhidahrma as presented by Vasubandhu) when they are in general agreement on the point in question. When there are significant differences in view, individual schools, texts, or authors are named.
17. Saṃyutta ii.3–4; Majjhima i.53. Consciousness (*viññāna*), already named as the third link, is omitted. For more on name and form, see Bodhi, *Connected Discourses of the Buddha*, 47–49; and Roderick S. Bucknell, "Conditioned Arising Evolves: Variation and Change in Textual Accounts of the *Paṭicca-samuppāda* Doctrine," *Journal of the International Association of Buddhist Studies* 22, no. 2 (1999): 311–342. According to Buddhaghosa, intention, contact, and attention, which belong to the aggregate of conditioning factors, "have been selected to represent that aggregate here because they are operative even in the weakest classes of consciousness." Bodhi, *Connected*, 727, n. 6.
18. The *Dharmasaṅgaṇī* (first book in the Pali Abhidhamma) lists contact (*phassa*), feeling (*vedanā*), perception (*saññā*), intention (*cetanā*), and consciousness (*citta*). Later Theravāda Abhidhamma excludes consciousness (*citta*), and includes an additional three: unification of mind (*ekaggatā*), life faculty (*jīvindriya*), and attention (*manasikāra*). The Yogācāra Abhidharma (in the *Abhidharmasamuccaya*) includes contact (*sparśa*), feeling (*vedanā*), perception(*saṃjñā*), intention (*cetanā*), attention (*manaskāra*). The Sarvastivāda Abhidharma includes those five and adds desire (*chanda*), discernment (*prajñā*), mindfulness (*smṛti*), decision (*adhimokṣa*), and concentration (*samādhi*).
19. See the section "Intention (*Cetanā*) and the Karmic Conditioning Factors."
20. This is not the case for liberated persons. See the section "Abhidharma Developments."
21. Saṃyutta ii.11–12, ii.97–100; and Devdas, *Cetanā*, 182–183.
22. Saṃyutta ii.97; Majjima i.47–48, 261; and Dīgha iii.228.
23. Devdas, *Cetanā*, 182. Ignorance is typically defined as ignorance of the Four Noble Truths, meaning ignorance of the dynamics of the arising of suffering and its ending. Bhikkhu Ñāṇamoli and Bhikkhu Bodhi, *Middle Length Discourses: A New Translation of the Majjhima Nikāya* (Boston: Wisdom, 1995), 143; and Majjhima i.54.
24. Saṃyutta ii.97–100; the commentary explains that the pit is samsara and the two strong men, wholesome and unwholesome karma. Bodhi, *Connected*, 777, n. 166; Saṃyutta ii.99. Also see Devdas, *Cetanā*, 209–210.
25. In modern English, there is often no connection to action, with *karma* just meaning something like luck or fate. This article uses *karma* to mean action and *karmic result* for the figurative application.
26. Reverend Richard Morris and Prof. E. Hardy, eds., *The Aṅguttara Nikāya*, vol. III (London: Pali Text Society, 1885–1900), 415; and see section "Intention (*Cetanā*) and Karma."
27. See the section "Abhidharma Developments."
28. Aung in Shwe Zan Aung, trans. and Caroline Augusta Foley Rhys Davids, ed., *Compendium of Philosophy* [translation of *Abhidhammattha Sa"gaha*] (London: Pali Text Society, 1910), 43–44; Maurice Walshe, *The Long Discourses of the Buddha* (Boston: Wisdom, 1995), 33; Richard Gombrich, *Buddhist Precept and Practice: Traditional Buddhism in the Highlands of Ceylon* (New York: Kegan Paul, 1995), 170; S. K. Nanayakkara, "Free Will," in *Encyclopaedia of Buddhism*, vol. V, 280. On "choice" and *cetanā*, see Damien Keown, *The Nature of Buddhist Ethics* (New York: St. Martin's Press, 1991), 210–218; and a critique in Georges Dreyfus, "Meditation as Ethical Activity," *Journal of Buddhist Ethics* 2 (1995): 2.

29. Louis de la Vallée Poussin, *La Morale Bouddhique* (Saint Michel en l'Herm, France: Editions Dharma, 2001), 127; Alexis Sanderson, "The Sarvāstivāda and its Critics: Anāmavāda and the Theory of Karma," in *Buddhism into the Year 2000* (Bangkok, Thailand: Dhammakaya Foundation, 1994), 33–34; and Gombrich, *Buddhist Precept and Practice*, 289–293.
30. For reviews and critiques of these interpretations, see Devdas, *Cetanā*, chapter 1, 320–325; Meyers, "Freedom," 138–252; and Heim, *Forunner*, 17–26, 221–223.
31. Devdas prefers "volition" for *cetanā* and "intention" for *sankappa*, arguing that "volition" speaks to the broader and more complex set of functions encompassed by *cetanā*: "intending to achieve a goal, initiating action, and directing action toward the goal." Devdas, *Cetanā*, 224. For more on translation, see Devdas, *Cetanā*, 1–32 (also chapters VII and IX); Meyers, "Freedom," 140–174; and Heim, *Forerunner*, 17–30.
32. Heim, *Forerunner*, 28. She mentions this specifically in connection to Buddhaghosa's understanding, but it seems a fair characterization of the view in the suttas and in Vasubandhu's works as well.
33. Aṅguttara iii. 415: *Cetanāhaṃ, bhikkhave, kammaṃ vadāmi; cetayitvā kammaṃ karoti kāyena vacāya manasā*. Also see Devdas, *Cetanā*, 184ff.; and Heim, *Forerunner*, 38–39.
34. The *Penetrative sutta* statement occurs with some frequency in the Pali commentarial literature but perhaps not as much as one might expect given its ubiquity in modern accounts of karma. A search of the *Chaṭṭha Saṅgāyana* (https://www.tipitaka.org/chattha) revealed only thirteen additional citations. Five are from the commentarial literature on the suttas: (a) the *aṭṭhakathā* on the *Penetrativesutta*, (b) *Sīlakkandhavagga-abhinavaṭīkā* on the *Brahmajālasutta* of the *Dīghanikāya*, (c) the *aṭṭhakathā* on the *Gahapativaggo* of the *Majjhimanikāya*, and the *ṭīkās* on the (d) *Dhātusaṃyuttaṃ* and (e) *Sotāpattisaṃyuttaṃ* of the *Saṃyuttanikāya*. It is also cited in (f) Buddhaghosa's *Aṭṭhasālinī*, as well as in the (g) *Anuṭīkā* and (h) Ānanda's *Mūlaṭīkā* on the *Dhammasaṅganī*; in the (i) *Kathāvatthu* and its (j) *atthakathā*; and in the (k) *Pārājikakaṇda-atthakathā* of the *Vinaya*. Two additional citations are from (l) Ledi Sayadaw's *Anudīpanīpāṭha* and from (m) Aggavaṃsa's grammar, the *Saddanītippakaraṇaṃ*.
35. There are at least three possibilities for interpreting the sentence: (a) intention is a kind of karma but distinct from mental, vocal, or bodily action; (b) all three kinds of karma are intention; (c) intention is the essential ingredient for all three kinds of action.
36. Meyers, "Freedom," 4.1–4.2.
37. Gombrich, *Buddhist Precept and Practice*, 285–313; Richard Gombrich, *Theravāda Buddhism: A Social History from Ancient Banaras to Modern Colombo* (New York: Routledge, 2006 [1988]), 66–68; Steven Collins, *Selfless Persons: Imagery and Thought in Theravāda Buddhism* (Cambridge, UK: Cambridge University Press, 1982), 201; and Devdas, *Cetanā*, 29–32.
38. Such as rejecting fatalism, emphasizing the importance of individual effort (*viriya*), and relying on a restraint-based ascetic-ethical discipline. See Karin Meyers, "Free Persons, Empty Selves: Free Will in Light of the Two Truths," in *Free Will, Selfhood and Agency in Indian Philosophy*, ed. Edwin Bryant and Matthew Dasti (New York: Oxford University Press, 2014), 41–67, and the Kesakamala sutta (A.iii.286–287) for the Buddhist view on fatalism. See Devdas, *Cetanā*, 87–88 on the Jain view, which is at odds with the Buddhist presentation in the *Devadaha sutta* (Majjhima ii.214–228).
39. See Devdas, *Cetanā*, chapter 2; and Karin Meyers, "The Dynamics of Intention, Freedom and Habituation According to Vasubandhu's *Abhidharmakośabhāṣya*," in *A Mirror Is for Reflection: Understanding Buddhist Ethics*, ed. Jake H. Davis (New York: Oxford University Press, 2017) for discussions of Buddhist and Jain views on intentional action.
40. *Devadaha sutta*, Majjhima ii.214–228; *Mahāsaccaka sutta*, Majjhima iii.207–215; and *Upāli sutta*. Majjhima i.371–387.
41. Majjhima i.377.
42. Majjhima iii.209.

43. Aṅguttara iii.415; and Bhikkhu Bodhi, *The Numerical Discourses of the Buddha: A Translation of the Aṅguttara Nikāya* (Boston: Wisdom Publications, 2012), 963.
44. For example, Nanayakkara, "Free Will," 280; K. N. Jayatilleke, "Ethics in Buddhist Perspective," *The Wheel*, Publication No. 175/176 (1984 [1972]), 7–8; Harvey, " 'Freedom of the Will," 36; Lamotte, *Démonstration de L'Acte*, 152; e.g., Poussin, *La Morale*, 127; Lamotte, *Démonstration*, 152; and Gombrich, *Buddhist Precept and Practice*, 285–313.
45. Aṅguttara ii.158–159, see also *Bhūmija sutta*, Saṃyutta ii.37–41.
46. This is how the commentary attributed to Buddhaghosa defines it. See Bodhi, *Numerical*, 1708 n. 865. Also see Devdas, *Cetanā*, 160–161, 186–187 and Heim, *Forerunner*, 40–45. Heim translates *sampajāna* as "deliberate."
47. Aṅguttara ii.159.
48. Clear comprehension has a range of meanings in the suttas, but one of the most important is as a mental factor that supports mindfulness in interpreting the details of the phenomenal field, thereby enabling one to take effective soteriological action. This is seen in the well-known refrain in the *Satipaṭṭhāna sutta*, "ardent, clearly comprehending, and mindful" (*ātāpi, sampajāno, satimā*). Majjhima i.56. For a discussion of the importance of this term, see Bhikkhu Bodhi, "What Does Mindfulness Really Mean? A Canonical Perspective," *Contemporary Buddhism* 12, no. 1 (2011): 19–39.
49. Many commentaries are attributed to Buddhaghosa that may not be the work of a single author but generally represent a coherent body of thought. This article follows Heim in reading them as if they were the work of the 5th-century scholar Buddhaghosa.
50. Heim, *Forerunner*, 44–45.
51. Devdas, *Cetanā*, 185–188.
52. See the section "Abhidharma Developments."
53. Heim, *Forerunner*, 44.
54. Bodhi, *Connected*, 45.
55. Collins, *Selfless Persons*, 200–208; and Joanna Jurewicz, "Playing with Fire: The Pratītyasamutpāda from the Perspective of Vedic Thought," *Journal of the Pāli Text Society* 26 (2000): 77–103.
56. Bodhi, *Connected*, 45–46. On conditioning factors related to meditation see section "Intention (*Cetanā*) and the Path."
57. Saṃyutta iii.60. Also ii.247–248.
58. Aṅguttaraii.157–158, Saṃyutta ii.4, Majjhima i.54; Vasubandhu, *Abhidharmakośa* i.15ab, Śāstrī 39–40, Sangpo, 230. References to Vasubandhu's *Abhidharmakośa-bhāṣya* (Treasury of Higher Dharma Commentary) will be to chapter and section number of the root text and page numbers in either Sangpo's annotated English translation or Śāstrī's Sanskrit edition, which also contains Yaśomitra's sub-commentary. Gelong Lodrö Sangpo, trans., *Abhidharmakośa-bhāṣya of Vasubandhu: The Treasury of the Abhidharma and Its (Auto) Commentary, Translated into French by Louis de La Vallée Poussin*, 4 vols. (New Delhi: Motilal Banarsidass, 2012); Buddhaghosa, *The Expositor (Atthasālinī): Buddhaghosa's Commentary on the Dhammasaṅgaṇī, The First Book of the Abhidhamma Piṭaka*, trans. Maung Tin and ed. C. A. F. Rhys Davids (London: Pali Text Society, 1921), 147–148; and *Atthasālinī*, 111–112.
59. Saṃyutta iii.87. On the gloss of *saṅkhāras* as the five aggregates, see Bodhi, *Connected*, 1071, n. 112.
60. Saṃyutta ii.65.
61. Devdas, *Cetanā*, 109–110.
62. Devdas observes that it's hard to find any passages in the first four Nikāyas that link *cetanā* with the more cognitive meanings of the causal verb *ceteti*, such as "forming a purpose, reflecting on possibilities, choosing goal." She mentions that another sutta that makes this connection is the *Deed-Born Body sutta* (Aṅguttara v.293–303) where intentional action (*sañcetanākamma*) emerges from and expresses a citta. Devdas, *Cetanā*, 177–178.
63. Devdas, Cetanā, 177–178; on pre-Buddhist usage, chapters 1–2.

64. Devdas, *Cetanā*, 153–154.
65. Heim, *Forerunner*, 50 (also see 29, 47, and section "Constructing Experience," 46–52).
66. Bodhi, *Connected*, 757–758, n. 112.
67. Aṅguttara iii.415.
68. Devdas, *Cetanā*, 155.
69. Although the Theravāda tradition rejects the idea of subliminal mental factors, some suttas suggest tendencies could be interpreted in this way. Devdas, *Cetanā*, 137–176; and Heim, *Forerunner*, 119–122.
70. Devdas, *Cetanā*, 166.
71. See Heim's discussion, *Forerunner*, 48.
72. Devdas emphasizes this point about creativity, correlating the dynamic and creative aspects of *cetanā* to its role in citta processes as developed in the Theravāda Abhidhamma. *Cetanā*, 364.
73. Saṃyutta iv.132–133.
74. Devdas, *Cetanā*, 133–137. In addition, Bodhi mentions the bodily, vocal, and mental *saṅkhāra* related to the attainment of cessation, and mindfulness of breathing. Bodhi, *Connected*, 1071, n 112.
75. Devdas, *Cetanā*, 137. On the cognitive dimension of this process, see the section "Abhidharma Developments."
76. Bodhi, *Connected*, 46–47. Also see 1944, n. 259; 727–728, n. 7; the seven factors are: mindfulness (*sati*), investigation of dhammas (*dhammavicaya*), effort (*viriya*), joy (*pīti*), tranquility (*passaddhi*), concentration (*samādhi*), and equanimity (*upekkhā*). In contrast, Asan'ga defines *cetanā* as one of eight exertion conditions (*pradhāna-saṃskāra*) essential to mental cultivation (*bhāvanā*). Wapola Rahula and Sara Boin-Webb, trans., *Abhidharmasamuccaya* (Freemont, CA: Asian Humanities Press, 2001), 164.
77. Majjhima, i.387–392; *tassa pahānāya yā cetanā*. Majjhima i.391.
78. Bodhi, *Middle*, 1258, n. 608.
79. The opposite of the ten unwholesome courses is discussed later (see the section "Abhidharma Developments"); and Bodhi, *Middle*, 1258, n. 605 and 608.
80. Bodhi, *Middle*, 495–496; and Majjhima i.390.
81. Devdas, *Cetanā*, 226–227; 234, n.47; and Heim, *Forerunner*, 62.
82. Bodhi, *Numerical*, 1720, n. 946.
83. Majjhima i.71–78.
84. Heim refers to this as the "presence of absences." *Forerunner*, 76–80; 113–119.
85. On no intention in the path, also see Heim, *Forerunner*, 78–80; and Devdas, *Cetanā*, 219–224. Other suttas also discuss the fact that there is no intention (*cetanā*) in attaining nirvana but there is in attaining the formless absorptions (Majjhima iii.244) and the four *jhānas* (Majjhima i.350, iii.25). Ñāṇamoli and Bodhi, *Middle*, 1187, n. 551.
86. Aṅguttara v.2–4.
87. Aṅguttara v.3.i.e.
88. Devdas, *Cetanā*, 220. Also see Heim, *Forerunner*, 78–79.
89. Heim, *Forerunner*, 81–82.
90. For example, Aung, *Compendium of Philosophy*, 43–44; Walshe, *Long Discourses*, 33; Gombrich, *Buddhist Precept and Practice*, 170; and Nanayakkara, "Free Will," 280.
91. For critiques of the idea that *cetanā* implies free will, see Meyers, "Freedom," 138–252; Heim, *Forerunner*, 19–26; and Devdas, *Cetanā*, 31, 320–325.
92. For a variety of views on the topic, see Rick Repetti, ed., *Buddhist Perspectives on Free Will: Agentless Agency?* (New York: Routledge, 2016); "Cetanā is not a site for battles of the will; nor is it the site for discussions of free agency. It is not appropriate to inquire into the weakness of cetanā, as one might in worrying about the moral problem of the weakness of the will (akrasia); nor would traditional Buddhist systems connect cetanā to the notion of will-power."

93. Particularly notable are the Pali canonical Abhidhamma books of the *Dhammasaṅgaṇī* and *Vibhaṅga*, which Buddhaghosa relies on, and the *Mahāvibhāṣā* of the Sarvāstivāda tradition that informs Vasubandhu's discussion.
94. Buddhaghosa is authoritative for the Theravāda Abhidhamma tradition, and Vasubandhu (together with Asaṅga) is influential for East Asian and Tibetan Buddhism.
95. Buddhaghosa, *Expositor*, 117; and Edward Muller, *The Atthasālini: Buddhghosa's Commentary on the Dhammasaṅgaṇi*, rev. ed. (London: Pali Text Society, 1979), 88.
96. It is the "'origin from which action springs' (*cetanāmūlakattā kammassa*)." Heim, *Forerunner*, 40.
97. Devdas, *Cetanā*, 184.
98. Namely, the eight factors of the eightfold path and the seven factors of awakening.
99. Buddhaghosa, *Expositor*, 117–118; and Heim, *Forerunner*, 107–108.
100. *Dve karmaṇī cetanā karma cetayitvā* ca. *Abhidharmakośa* iv.1, Śāstrī, 447. See Bodhi, *Numerical*, 768, fn. 1417 for the Chinese parallel.
101. *Abhidharmakośa* iv. 3c, Śāstrī, 453–455, Sangpo, 1294–1296. This point about metaphor is clearly implied in the *Abhidharmakośa*, but explicitly in his *Monograph on Karma*. See Meyers, "Freedom," 298–299.
102. See section "Intention and Karmic Result" on the courses of action.
103. Buddhaghosa, *Expositor*, 134, 137; *Atthasālinī*, 101, 104; and *Abhidharmakośa* iv.78cd, Śāstrī 548.
104. Heim, *Forerunner*, 114–115. She specifically refers to his commentary on the *Vibhaṅga*, where he says that the precepts are only intentions in a figurative (*pariyāya*) sense, that they are more properly understood as abstentions (*virati*). In contrast, the idea that abstentions (*virakti*) are *cetanā* is critical to Vasubandhu's theory (see section "*Intention, Transmission, and Transformation*").
105. Heim, *Forerunner*, 66.
106. For example, *Greater Exposition on Action sutta*, Majjhima iii.207–215 and *Deed-Born Body sutta*, Aṅguttara v.282–303. Buddhaghosa discusses them in *Expositor*, 126–136. Vasubandhu in *Abhidharmakośa*, iv. 67a–89ab, and throughout the chapter.
107. Buddhaghosa, *Expositor*, 129ff; and *Atthasālinī*, 97.
108. *Abhidharmakośa* iv.73ab; Śāstrī, 540; and Meyers, "Freedom," 195–196.
109. Vasubandhu merely mentions this example at *Abhidharmakośa* iv. 68d, however, Yaśomotra explains that this delusion is not exculpating when commenting on another verse (iv. 54), Śāstrī, 522.
110. *Abhidharmakośa* iv.103, Śāstrī, 577.
111. *Abhidharmakośa* iv.103, also see iv.105ab Śāstri, 578–579, and Meyers, "Freedom," 190–196.
112. Buddhaghosa, *Expositor*, 129; and *Atthasālinī*, 97. The additional effort needed to kill a large animal is also a factor.
113. Buddhaghosa, *Expositor*, 129–130, 214; and *Abhidharmakośa*, iv. 114cd, 116a, 117ab, 118. See Meyers, "Freedom," 219–221.
114. See Heim's discussion, *Forerunner*, 71–72. Commenting on *Abhidharmakośa* iv.120 (Śāstrī, 589) Vasubandhu's commentator, Yaśomitra seems to accept a similar rule as Buddhaghosa, explaining that a lie spoken out of a habit in the heat of exposition is unwholesome but is not accumulated; Buddhaghosa, *Expositor*, 130–133; and *Abhidharmakośa* iv. 74cd–77bc.
115. This is presented as Bhadanta Dharmatrāta's view (*Abhidharmakośa* iv.4b), but the fact Vasubandhu accepts is evident in his analysis of the courses of action later in the chapter.
116. *Abhidharmakośa* iv. 68c. At *Abhidharmakośa* iv. 119, consequent action is counted as first among the six reasons for the relative gravity (*gurulaghutvā*) of an action. The other reasons include the field (*kṣetra*), the basis (*adhiṣṭhāna*, that is, which course of action), preparation (*prayoga*), intention (*cetanā*), and notion (*āśaya*).
117. *Abhidharmakośa* iv.120; and Meyers, "Freedom," 203.
118. *Abhidharmakośa* iv.54, Śāstrī, 522; *Abhidharmakośa* 115ab, Śāstrī, 586; and Meyers, "Freedom," 201–204.

119. *Abhidharmakośa* iv.85, Śāstrī, 561–562.
120. He treats the historical dimensions of intention (not necessarily *cetanā*) at greater length in his analyses of the monastic rule and stories. See Heim, *Forerunner*. Devdas (*Cetanā*, 207–208) discusses how Buddhaghosa and the Theravāda tradition do not accept a distinction between the performance of an act and its accumulation. However, both she (*Cetanā*, 208) and Heim (*Forerunner*, 117) may draw a greater distinction than is warranted between the two thinkers' views regarding preparatory intentions and intentions that perform the main action. More detailed comparative study is needed.
121. Buddhaghosa, *Expositor*, 133, 210–212; *Atthasālinī*, 100; and *Atthasālinī*, 157–159.
122. *Atthasālinī*, 270–272, *Visuddhimagga*, XIV, 115–122; Bhikkhu Ñāṇamoli, *The Path of Purification: Visuddhimagga* (Kandy, Sri Lanka: Buddhist Publication Society, 2010), 463–466. It is also discussed in the fourth chapter of the *Abhidhammattha-saṅgaha*. For the latter, see Bhikkhu Bodhi, *A Comprehensive Manual of Abhidhamma* (Onalaska, WA: BPS Pariyatti Editions, 1999), 149–170.
123. Devdas, *Cetanā*, 316.
124. Devdas, *Cetanā*, 315.
125. Devdas, *Cetanā*, 336–337 fn. 55, 461; and Heim, *Forerunner*, 63–65.
126. Heim, *Forerunner*, 63. The four varieties predate Buddhaghosa, but he elaborates the theory in terms of cognitive processing.
127. He discusses it at length in his *Monograph on Karma*, where he uses the category of resultant (*vipāka*) to refer to the subliminal storehouse consciousness (*ālayavijāna*). See Meyers, "Freedom," 244.
128. *Abhidharmakośa* iv.61–62.
129. See the section "Intention (*Cetanā*) and Deliberateness."
130. *Abhidharmakośa* iv.4ab, Śāstrī, 461. This is mentioned in the context of a debate about how merit increases for faithful persons whether they walk, stand, sleep, or are awake.
131. *Abhidharmakośa* iv. 83cd-84, Śāstrī, 560.
132. Meditative attainments (of form and formless absorptions) can determine a future birth.
133. Meyers, "Freedom," 201–204.
134. *Abhidharmakośa* ii.24 (also see i.15a-b). This line is also found in the *Milindapañha*, where the descriptions of *abhisaṅkharaṇa* imply a sense of preparation (Heim, *Forerunner*, 49). In the third chapter of the *Abhidharmakośa*, Vasubandhu also discusses this constructive activity in the context of the scriptural idea of *cetanā* as food for consciousness (iii.41cd, Śāstrī, 392).
135. See Meyers, "Freedom," 198, for a discussion of similar definitions in the literature and relevance to the idea of intention (*cetanā*) as defined by its object.
136. Lévi, *Vijñaptimātratāsiddhi*, 21; and Tripāṭhī and Dorje, *Vijñaptimātratāsiddhi*, 47.
137. *Abhidharmakośa* ii.45ab; Vasubandhu and Sumatiśīla *Karmasiddhiprakaraṇa by Ācārya Vasubandhu, Karmasiddhi Ṭīkā by Ācārya Sumatiśīla* (Varanasi, India: Pleasure of Elegant Sayings Printing Press, 1988), 171.
138. *Abhidharmakośa* iv.3c, Śāstrī 455. Vasubandhu also refers to this as the intention that accomplishes (*niṣṭhāpayati*) a course of action (iv.119, Śāstrī 589).
139. Buddhaghosa uses future and past (Buddhaghosa, *Expositor*, 211; *Atthasālinī*, 159), but Vasubandhu and his commentators seem to prefer the optative. See details in Meyers, "Freedom," 208.
140. *Abhidharmakośa* iv. 3c.
141. *Abhidharmakośa* iv. 119; Śāstrī, 589; *Abhidharmakośa* iv. 120. Yaśomitra explains that these actions can still be unwholesome (*akuśala*) and misconduct (*duścarita*). Śāstrī 589.
142. Poussin and Lamotte follow Vasubandhu's commentator Sumatiśīla in reading the first term as implying a preliminary thought regarding the means by which something might be done and the second as engaging in more sustained evaluation (*vicāra*). See Meyers, "Freedom," 205–207.
143. Śāstrī, 952–953.
144. Vasubandhu follows the tradition of older commentators of including gross (*vitarka*) and subtle thought (*vicāra*), which can also be pre-verbal, as arising either from intellect (*prajñā*) or from

intention (*cetanā*). According to Yaśomitra, the difference is that the former are based on reasoning (*abhyūhāvasthā*) and the latter are not. This suggests that thought (*vitarka*) cannot be considered purely cognitive. Meyers, "Freedom," 209–210.

145. Devdas, *Cetanā*, 207–208 discusses the cognitive dimensions of *cetanā* in Vasbandhu's *Abhidharmakośa*.
146. Devdas, *Cetanā*, 378; Devdas, *Cetanā*, 404. She emphasizes a difference between the capacities attributed to *cetanā* in the context of the Abhidhamma rubric of mind (*citta*) and mental (*cetasika*) and in its association with the karmic conditioning factors. Devdas, *Cetanā*, 411–412.
147. In some wholesome states of mind, this includes path factors; otherwise, these include the category of karmic conditioning factors.
148. As Heim observes, these similes do not simply illustrate the theory, but do "essential philosophical work." Heim, *Forerunner*, 105.
149. Heim, *Forerunner*, 103.
150. Devdas, *Cetanā*, 374.
151. See Table 2.1, Heim, *Forerunner*, 93–95.
152. Heim, *Forerunner*, 104–105. She reads this in the line: "So too [*cetanā*], produces its object by its own work, and makes the other associated factors produce it with their own actions." Devdas and Meyers read the line differently such that *cetanā*'s engaging with its object is what motivates the other factors to perform their own functions. Meyers, "Freedom," 152; and Devdas, *Cetanā*, 377.
153. Devdas, *Cetanā*, 216, 377.
154. Heim, *Forerunner*, 105.
155. Heim, *Forerunner*, 105; the difference between her reading and Devdas's hinges on the reading of *evaṃ esā pi attano kiccena ārammaṇe vattamānā* . . . (*Atthasālinī*, 112). Heim reads this as "produces its object by its own work," but another possible reading is "engaging in its own work in respect to its object" (which is also how Tin reads it, Buddhaghosa, *The Expositor*, 148). Heim explains that "*cetanā* is like a carpenter who makes a house by working and getting his subcontractors to do their specialized tasks." She clarifies that this is not idealism but constructivism: "Our cognition does not simply mirror or represent the world out there. Rather, our experience of the world and of our own mental life is constructed and shaped by the work of our own mental processes" (Heim, *Forerunner*, 105–106).
156. Both views can be considered constructivist, however, the less direct constructivist view may sit more easily with Buddhaghosa's theory regarding a purely receptive stage in the perceptual cognitive process (*citta-vīthi*), wherein resultant (*vipāka*) *cetanās* receive objects based on previous intentional activity.
157. For the various possible factors, see Heim, *Forerunner*, 93–95.
158. Vasubandhu is critical of the idea of simultaneous causation or conditioning. Meyers, "Freedom," 86–136.
159. The factors or dharmas at issue are the quasi-material entity of unmanifest form (*avijñapti-rūpa*), and the dharmas disassociated from the mind called "possession" (*prāpti*) and "non-possession," which are neither material nor mental. Meyers, "Freedom," 179–186, 217–241 for a discussion of the debate in relation to *cetanā*.
160. Meyers, "Freedom," 217–218.
161. *Abhidharmakośa* iv, 4ab, Śāstrī, 461.
162. Śāstrī, 459. Meyers, "Freedom," 224. Both Vasubandhu and his interlocutors agree that karma is not a private psychological affair and not entirely determined by intention.
163. *Abhidharmakośa* iv.4ab, Śāstrī 461. In the ninth chapter of the *Abhidharmakośa* (Śāstrī, 953) Vasubandhu identifies specific transformation as the culminating modification of the series that has the capacity to immediately produce a result.
164. *Abhidharmakośa* iv. 4ab, Śāstrī, 462–463. He says it is more pleasing (*paritoṣa*), but it is clear from the context that this because the Vaibhāṣika theory requires the introduction of metaphysical factors and

mechanisms not attested in scripture. Meyers, "Freedom," 225. Later in the ninth chapter of the *Treasury*, he acknowledges that such details of karma are only within the ken of buddhas (Śāstrī, 955).

165. *Abhidharmakośa* iv.4ab, Śāstri, 461.
166. This reflects two different readings of *bhāvanayā* (Śāstrī, 464). See Meyers, "Freedom," 238, Sangpo, 1307.
167. Meyers, "Freedom," 237–240.
168. *Abhidharmakośa* ii.36d, 170. The point about karmic result is only implied here but is made clear elsewhere. Meyers, "Freedom," 227–230.
169. *Abhidharmakośa* iv.4ab, Śāstri 463; and Meyers, "Freedom," 234–239.
170. Vasubandhu's commentators gloss as a radical transformation of the basis/personality (āśrayaparāvṛtti), Śāstri 463, Sthiramati tattvārtha 17b.
171. Meyers, "Freedom," 241–252.
172. In contrast to Buddhaghosa, who speaks of a variety of intention (*cetanā*) as resultant.
173. *Karmasiddhiprakaraṇa* and *Ṭīkā*, 98, 137.
174. As in the opening of the *Twenty Verses (Viṃśatika)*. Lévi, *Vijñaptimātratāsiddhi*, 3.
175. Vasubandhu rejects the idea of simultaneous causation (Meyers, "Freedom"), 115–127. Similarly, Buddhaghosa rejects the idea of a subliminal level of cognitive processing. Devdas, *Cetanā*, 165.
176. Devdas, *Cetanā and the Dynamics*; and Heim, *Forerunner of All Things*.
177. Karin Meyers, "Freedom and Self-Control: Free Will in Light of South Asian Buddhist Theories of Karma and Causation" (PhD diss., University of Chicago, 2010); Meyers, "Dynamics of Intention" includes a condensed overview of Vasubandhu's views on karma and *cetanā*.
178. For reviews of these interpretations, see Devdas, *Cetanā*, chapter 1, 320–325; Meyers, "Freedom," 138–252; and Heim, *Forerunner*, 17–26, 221–223.
179. W. S. Karunaratana, "Cetanā," in *Encyclopaedia of Buddhism*, vol. IV, ed. G. P. Malalasekera (Colombo: Department of Government Printing, 1979), 91–96; Meyers, "Dynamics of Intention"; Jake H. Davis, ed., *A Mirror Is for Reflection: Understanding Buddhist Ethics* (New York: Oxford University Press, 2017), 239–256; and Maria Heim, "The Aesthetics of Excess," *Journal of the American Academy of Religion* 71, no. 3 (2003): 531–554.
180. Of particular note are James McDermott, *Development in the Early Buddhist Concept of Kamma/Karma* (New Delhi: Munishiram Manoharlal, 1984); Ulrich Kragh, *Early Buddhist Theories of Action and Result* (Wien, Austria: Arbeitskreis für Tibetische und Buddhitische Studien, 2006); and Achim Bayer, *The Theory of Karman in the Abhidharmasamuccaya* (Tokyo: International Association for Buddhist Studies, 2010).
181. For an overview of the Āgamas, see Bhikkhu Analayo, "Chinese Āgamas," in *Oxford Bibliographies* Online (https://doi.org/10.1093/OBO/9780195393521-0250).
182. However it should be noted Lamotte's translation from the French, translated into English by Pruden (see "Further Reading") differs substantially from the Tibetan and the sub-commentary by Sumatiśīla. Étienne Lamotte, trans., *Traité de ka Démonstration de L'Acte*, French translation of *Karmasiddhiprakaraṇa*, *Melanges Chinois et Bouddhiques* 4 (Brussels, Belgium: L'Institut Belge des Hautes Études Chinoises, 1935–1936).
183. While the seven books of the Sarvāstivāda Abhidharma and Mahāvibhāṣa are not translated into English, the Pali Abhidhamma works most relevant to this topic, the *Dhammasaṅganī*, *Vibhaṅga*, and *Kathāvattu* are available in English translation from the Pali Text Society. Also notable among later works is the influential, *Abhidhammattha-saṅgaha*, available with an introduction and translation by Bodhi, *Comprehensive Manual*.
184. T. W. Rhys Davids, trans., The *Questions of King Milinda* (London: Pali Text Society, 1894).
185. Especially Asaṅga's *Abhidharmasamuccaya*, the Rahula and Boin-Webb translation, and Bayer, *Theory of Karma*.

Karin Meyers

J

JAPANESE BUDDHISMS IN DIASPORA

BUDDHISMS, DIASPORA, AND ITS BOUNDARIES

The title of this article addresses two relevant aspects of Buddhism, and religion more generally. First is the necessity to consider Buddhism a complex system hardly reducible to a single tradition, thus the plural noun Buddhisms; and second is the importance to relate such systems to the circulation of people, ideas, economies, and material goods. Here the specific context is that of diasporic movements. Diaspora, from the Greek *diaspeirein*, or to disperse, to scatter, implies not only the physical (and often traumatic) dispersion of people who left their homes for unknown places, but also a reconfiguration of their identities through the adaptation to such places and their cultures. In this process of relocation, religion has played an important role in keeping "consciousness of a homeland connection, real or imagined," and fostering a sense of belonging to that distant community.[1] This idea of an "imagined connection" between migrants and "a place of origin" as a clear characteristic of diaspora is highlighted by Steven Vertovec. "Imagined" for Vertovec does not mean unreal, but rather "the often strong sentiments and mental pictures according to which members of diasporas organize themselves and undertake their cultural practices." Diaspora is intended here as arising from migration, although not all migration implies what he calls a "diasporic consciousness."[2] On a similar line, one of the relevant constitutive elements in diaspora, according to Martin Baumann, is a "*recollecting identification with a fictitious or far away existent geographic territory*" including its culture and religion.[3] The importance of religious "adaptation-yet-continuity" has been also emphasized in relation to the history and social developments of diasporic groups.[4] Religions in diaspora have gone through a process of change and reshaping because of their circulation across "multiple spaces of practice" and in "circumstances and spaces different from the site of their creation."[5] Moreover, diaspora, as Manuel Vásquez highlights, "often involves intense ritualized and momentary fusions of past and future" and reclaims or creates "a common origin and tradition" to make an "inhospitable present" liveable.[6] Time and space, and their reshaping, are thus two important elements in the modeling of diasporic communities, and the building of sacred spaces in Buddhism (at times linked to an imagined bond with the homeland and a reconnection with some past traditions) has gone hand in hand with the building of religious communities. These interlinked aspects are in line with the use of the term diaspora in this article and the case of Japanese Buddhist groups analyzed below.

From its outset, Buddhism has been a missionary religion and Japan was one of the countries involved when this "foreign" religion reached the Japanese shores in the 6th century traveling from India through China and Korea. However, it was not until the 19th century that the propagation of Buddhism from Japan took place. While the dissemination of Buddhism (and other religious traditions) in the Japanese former colonies was forcibly imposed by the colonizers, developments in other parts of the world, notably the West, followed a different trajectory. The first phase of propagation was linked to the flow and history of Japanese migrants to Hawaii, North America, and Brazil.

JAPANESE BUDDHISMS IN HAWAII

The first Japanese immigrants reached Hawaii in 1868, at the outset of the Meiji period (1868–1912), as contract laborers for the sugarcane plantations.[7] The first Buddhist priest belonging to Jōdo Shinshū 浄土真宗 ("True Pure Land Buddhism," or Shin Buddhism in English) arrived in Hawaii in 1889. Other Buddhist denominations followed suit: Jōdoshū 浄土宗 (Pure Land Buddhism) in 1893; and, at the beginning of the 20th century, the Nichiren 日蓮 (1901), Shingon 真言 (1902), and Sōtō Zen 曹洞禅 (1904) schools.[8] Buddhist temples became an important locus of Japanese community life on the islands, as well as centers for the preservation of Japanese culture.

Jōdo Shinshū has always been counted among the largest Buddhist schools in Hawaii. The Nishi Honganji, or Honpa Hongwanji Mission of Hawaii, is the largest Buddhist denomination (the Higashi Honganji is present with five temples only). In 2000, among the 20,000 Buddhists on the islands, 8,000 individuals belonged to the Honpa Hongwanji.[9] Its membership at the end of 2016 was slightly more than 4,800 households.[10] The denomination has thirty-seven temples distributed on various islands and includes the Pacific Buddhist Academy, the Hongwanji Mission School (from preschool to eighth grade), the Buddhist Study Center, and various other organizations and programs.[11]

The first official overseas ministers, or *kaikyōshi* 開教師, were sent from Kyoto in 1897. They were in charge of serving the community of Japanese laborers, who in turn would financially provide for the ministers. At the time, the idea of missionizing to convert non-Japanese was not part of the headquarters' plans.[12] Shin Buddhism found fertile soil in Hawaii mainly because many of the Japanese laborers hailed from strongholds of this denomination in Japan, such as Hiroshima and Yamaguchi prefectures. This was complemented by the work toward adaptation and the "Americanization" of Jōdo Shinshū made by one of the major players of its propagation on the islands, Imamura Emyō (1867–1932). In view of his status within the history of the Hongwanji Mission in Hawaii and in relation to the discussion on how diaspora religious communities adapt their teachings to the hosting environment, his work deserves some space in this article.

Imamura served as bishop of the Honpa Hongwanji Mission from 1900 until his death in 1932.[13] Shin Buddhism flourished under his leadership and he was well aware that this could happen because "the seeds that had already been planted in the old country bore fruit."[14] This was, however, not the only reason. Imamura was able to find a successful way to make it possible through the adaptation of the Shin Buddhist tradition into the Christian environment of Hawaii. He did so by first creating a supportive community for the male workers and then, with the arrival of picture brides and women from Japan, for their families. At the same time, the members of the Japanese communities, who very often suffered from discrimination and worked under harsh conditions, needed to become loyal American citizens. Imamura played a crucial role in the process of the Americanization of Japanese Buddhist migrants. He instructed Jōdo Shinshū ministers to help in this effort and considered the understanding of "true Americanism" as a fundamental aspect of their missionary work.[15] At the same time, there was the need to make (Shin) Buddhism universal, without, however, eliminating its specificity. Such an idea of universality and identification with a time and space that was way beyond the ethnicity of Japan was translated in architectural terms in the structure of the Hongwanji Hawaii Betsuin in Honolulu (see figure 1).

The temple was complted in 1918 under Imamura and the project designed by two American architects. The construction, with its Indian/Western design (stupa, columns, and domes), linked Shin Buddhism to a more "neutral" common origin of Buddhism in a past India, in line with Imamura's idea of a pan-Asian and "cosmopolitan" Buddhism. This style reflected also the attempts toward internationalization made by the Honganji headquarters in Japan at that time, and later inspired the construction of the Tsukiji Honganji *betsuin* in Tokyo.[16] By detaching it from its actual time and space, the structure of the temple seemed more easily assimilable to the hosting environment, while at the same time retaining a connection to the homeland.

Another important aspect in this phase of assimilation of Shin Buddhism in Hawaii linked to Imamura's work was the transformation of rituals. In this venture, Imamura was assisted by the work of a British convert and his wife, Ernest and Dorothy Hunt. They were ordained as ministers by Imamura in 1924 and put in charge of the English department of the Hongwanji Mission. Hunt started preaching on the islands a form of Buddhism that was clearly in line with the early teachings (including the four noble truths and the eightfold path), rather than the later pure land developments and reliance on Amida Buddha. The Hunts contributed to the transformation of rituals and teachings through the writing of *gathas* (hymns) in English, textbooks, and a catechism for the numerous Sunday schools, in which, however, there was no mention of the founder of Jōdo Shinshū, Shinran 親鸞 (1173–1262).[17] The hymns, written in a Christian-like style (with buddha referred to as a "Lord"), were mostly focused on a nonsectarian

Figure 1. Honpa Hongwanji Hawaii Betsuin in Honolulu, Hawaii.
Source: Photograph by Elisabetta Porcu

Buddhism rooted in the early tradition.[18] They were revisited on three occasions—at the end of the 1930s, in 1962, and in 1990—with the inclusions of more specific references to Shin Buddhism and Japan.[19] The Christian flavor of these hymns, in particular the music and the use of the organ, can still be experienced today during Shin Buddhist services in Hawaii.[20] Moreover, the link with early Buddhism through the recitation of the three treasures (I take refuge in the buddha, the dharma, and the sangha) in both Pāli and English at the beginning of the service, continues to resonate in Shin Buddhist temples on the islands and the mainland. Interestingly, while Imamura was a reformist and aimed at the integration of the Japanese Shin Buddhist community in diaspora in Hawaii, by the end of his career he turned to nationalism and promoted the superiority of Japan through his Japanese writings.[21]

Despite its popularity outside of Japan, Zen Buddhism, both Sōtō and Rinzai denominations, is quite small in Hawaii. The Sōtō Mission has nine temples and Rinzai Zen (Rinzaishū 臨済宗) has only two temples. One of them, the Rinzai Zen Mission in Paia (Maui) was established in 1932 and has mainly served the Okinawan community. This is the only Rinzai Zen temple that was established in the United States before World War II.[22]

Different Japanese Buddhist schools in diasporic communities have adapted their teachings and practices to better suit their host cultures. Some of them have done so through substantial changes, while others have focused on some practices rather than others. It is well known that despite the popularity of zazen 坐禅, or sitting meditation, in the West, in Japan only a small number of practitioners (and priests) practice it and the major activity in temples is linked to funerary rituals. Sōtō Zen, which reached Hawaii in 1903, has followed a similar trajectory, and its temples have maintained continuity with Japan in providing memorial services and not offering *zazen* sessions.[23] The demographic of the Zen community in Hawaii is still closely linked to the ethnic Japanese origin of the members and the need to either keep or seek a connection with their ancestors, as well as try to preserve tradition in a conservative way.[24] At the same time, changes occurred in the rituals and the architecture of temples in the Zen case too. Examples include the use of pews within temples, organ music, and hymns, as well as the celebrations of Christmas and Easter.[25]

In relation to meditation, the choice of Zen temples in Hawaii to function as those in Japan is different, for example, from their counterpart in North America. Here, also due to an audience of non-Japanese practitioners, great emphasis has been placed on *zazen* meditation. This is a practice that has undoubtedly contributed to the popularity of Zen Buddhism in the West and the marginalization of other schools that did not offer it. In this regard, even a school like Shin Buddhism, which does not contemplate meditation among its practices, has introduced *zazen* and other forms of meditation to its temples in order to attract non-Japanese members and meet the needs of Japanese Americans interested in this practice.[26]

Shingon (Shingonshū 真言宗) in Hawaii is an example of what can be called grass-roots formation of diasporic religious communities. The first groups were formed as confraternities (*kō* 講) by migrant Shingon followers and not by ministers sent from Japan. These confraternities were named *Daishi-kō* from the posthumous name of the Shingon founder Kūkai 空海, or Kōbō Daishi 弘法大師 (774–835). The Shingon community did not have temples, but followers gathered at homes and halls of worship, or *Daishi-dō* 大師堂, which grew numerous on the islands. The institutionalization of such communities started in 1902 when the first Shingon priest sent from Japan, Rev. Yuijiri Hōgen, arrived on Maui and established the current Lahaina Shingon Mission.[27] Shingon is present on the islands with a dozen temples and a membership of about 1,700 families.[28]

Jōdoshū has a similar number of temples (thirteen) but less affiliated households (slightly more than a thousand as of 2013).[29] The Jōdo Mission of Hawaii *betsuin* in Honolulu, which was built in 1932, is a clear example of architectural hybridization. In this case, the designer had decided for a combination of Indian and Western styles—with a touch of Islamic architecture, especially visible in the minaret-like towers. While this pink temple is set within the space of Hawaii and its culture, the connection with an Indian past together with architectural elements linked to a more international setting seem to aim at representing a form of Buddhism without boundaries, as mentioned in the case of Shin Buddhism.[30] As in other cases, Jōdoshū in Hawaii was closely linked to the migration of Japanese laborers. Together with the aim of supporting them, there was also the preoccupation of the headquarters in Japan of losing members due to conversion to Christianity.

NORTH AMERICA

A small group of Japanese migrants settled in California in 1869, but it was not until 1890 that migration to the United States began in earnest.[31] Jōdo Shinshū was also the first school of Japanese Buddhism to be established on the mainland with the opening of its first temple in

San Francisco (1898), followed by various other temples in other cities in California such as Oakland, as well as temples in Seattle, Washington.[32] Two priests from Nishi Honganji were sent from the Kyoto headquarters in 1899 and the *San Francisco Chronicle* published an article on their arrival a few days later. The article was titled "Missionaries of the Buddhist Faith. Two Representatives of the Ancient Creed Are in San Francisco to Proselyte."[33] In the same year, the institution that represents Jōdo Shinshū (Honganji-ha) in the United States, the North America Buddhist Mission (from 1944, Buddhist Churches of America, or BCA), was established with its headquarters in San Francisco. Today the BCA has sixty temples and about 16,000 members throughout the states (these data exclude Hawaii). The BCA mission statement highlights not only the propagation of Shin Buddhism but also that of the three jewels (the buddha, dharma, and sangha), thus relating this organization to the propagation of a more general Buddhism, as in the case of the Hongwanji Hawaii Mission discussed.[34] Similar to Shin Buddhism in Hawaii, the priests sent to the mainland were meant to serve not only the spiritual, but also the sociocultural needs of the Japanese, and then of the Japanese American communities. A sort of mutual agreement sanctioned that the missionaries' work needed to be limited within the boundaries of the Japanese community that was striving toward integration in an often-hostile society. Anti-Japanese sentiments resulted in the 1924 Asian Exclusion Act that brought Japanese emigration in the United States to a halt. As a consequence of the inequality created by this law, many first-generation Japanese (*issei*) became members of the North America Buddhist Mission and Buddhist temples became shelter for them from an inhospitable society.[35] Things worsened during World War II and the internment of Japanese Americans in camps. Sixty percent of them were Buddhists and the great majority belonged to Shin Buddhism. It was under such difficult circumstances that crucial reforms toward the Americanization of Shin Buddhism on the mainland were adopted, in particular during a conference in 1944 in Salt Lake City, Utah. Here, a more "Christian" nuance was given to the name of the umbrella organization of Shin Buddhism on the mainland with the addition of the term "church" (Buddhist Churches of America), while the new constitution introduced the use of English as the main language in rituals.[36] Contemporary temples affiliated to the BCA make use both of English and Japanese in their rituals, dharma talks, and sutra chanting and try to create a balance between these two languages.[37] The ethnic character of the BCA has been one of its main features from its outset. However, overcoming the close ties to the Japanese American community and reaching people of non-Japanese ancestry have been crucial issues in its developments from the postwar period onward, and more so in the past couple of decades.

In the case of Rinzai Zen Buddhism, despite the participation of Shaku Sōen in the World's Parliament of Religions in Chicago (1893), the early ventures by D. T. Suzuki in the United States (he stayed in LaSalle, 1897–1909), and the stay of two of Shaku Sōen's disciples in North America at the beginning of the 20th century, the first Zen communities did not open in North America until the 1950s.[38] This late start was, however, not adverse to the propagation and popularity of Zen Buddhism in North America and other Western countries. These communities are focused on a Euro-American membership and there is no Japanese Rinzai Zen temple on the mainland.[39]

Sōtō Zen Buddhism, with its five temples, is a very small presence on the United States mainland. The first temple, Zenshūji, was established in Los Angeles in 1922. In 1937 it became the headquarters of North American Sōtō, as a branch of both head temples Eiheiji 永平寺 and Sōjiji 総持寺. Zen temples related to the diasporic communities have functioned in the same way as those of other Japanese Buddhist schools. They have stressed their cultural and social roles in addition to the spiritual one, which has been mostly related to funerary rites. The Sōtō Zen priest Soyu Matsuoka Rōshi established the Chicago Buddhist Temple in the mid-1950s, while the San Francisco Zen Center was founded by Shunryu Suzuki Rōshi in 1959. In the 1960s another, quite successful, form of Zen appeared in North America, which counts among its main proponents Maezumi Rōshi, who opened the Zen Center of Los Angeles where he resided until 1995.[40] While Jōdo Shinshū has remained an ethnic religion and hardly reached the non-Japanese community, Zen Buddhism, or better, a form of Zen Buddhism that was constructed for its exportation to the West, followed a different trajectory, thus becoming the form of Japanese Buddhism best known outside Japan. A pivotal role was played in this regard by D. T. Suzuki and other intellectuals like Nishitani Keiji and Nishida Kitarō, who were deeply influenced by Western ideas, and by their promotion of a kind of "pure" and decontextualized Zen, focused on "inner experience."[41] This kind of Zen Buddhism drew much attention in the American environment of the 1960s and constituted one of the deepest religious sources of inspiration for the counterculture movement, as Robert Bellah noted as early as the 1970s.[42] Zen Buddhism, in its "traditional" and new forms, developed in a great variety of countries and its presence today can be found at the global level.

The scene of ethnic Buddhist organizations in Canada is similar to that of the United States: it is varied and mostly linked to Asian diaspora. The history of the propagation of Japanese Buddhism in Canada started when Japanese migrants arrived in British Columbia and Alberta in 1889. The majority of them belonged to Jōdo Shinshū and this has remained the largest Japanese Buddhist community in the country. At the beginning of the 20th century, the Japanese requested ministers from the Honganji-ha, and this was the start of a long-term relation with the headquarters in Kyoto. During World War II and the phase of the internment or expulsion of Japanese Shin Buddhists from British Columbia, including the shutdown of their temples, three thousand of them moved to Alberta and the Shin Buddhist presence grew in that area.[43] As in the other cases outlined earlier, Jōdo Shinshū was a religion for the diasporic community. At the beginning, it was therefore not aimed at reaching the community (largely Christian) Euro-Canadian community. In the postwar period, Shin Buddhism was nationally organized as the Buddhist Churches of Canada (1955), which was renamed Jodo Shinshu Buddhist Temples of Canada (JSBTC) in 2008, which clearly hints to a more specific connotation rooted in Japan.

SOUTH AMERICA

Japanese diaspora in Latin America started at the end of the 19th century and continued in the 20th century with the arrival of migrant workers in Mexico (1897), Peru (1899), Brazil (1908), Argentina (1908), and Colombia (1929).[44] Brazil was, and still is, the country with the largest population of people of Japanese ancestry in South America. Moreover, it is the country where more than 50 percent of the Buddhist institutions (not only Japanese Buddhism) are located, and where about 47 percent of South American Buddhists reside.[45] The first Japanese migrants arrived in Brazil (Santos) on the ship *Kasato Maru* at the outset of the 20th century. However, it was not until the post-World War II period that missions of Japanese Buddhist groups—and other religious organizations—could enter the country and start their propagation. This was a consequence of the policies enforced by the Japanese government, in negotiation with Brazilian authorities, in order to avoid the problems of anti-Japanese sentiment experienced by the migrants in North America and Hawaii. Along with the subsidies given to families (and not single workers) to migrate, the Ministry of Foreign Affairs precluded Japanese priests from accompanying the immigrants due to the fear that a non-Catholic presence would be seen as an obstacle to the assimilation of the Japanese into Catholic Brazil. Despite all this, some religious organizations, such as the Honmon Butsuryū 本門佛立 school within Nichiren Buddhism, did send its priest who established a temple in the late 1930s; and in the 1920s and 1930s there were branches of Jōdo Shinshū and Shingon Buddhism in rural communities.[46]

The majority of the Japanese religious groups present in Brazil today established their churches, temples, and headquarters from the mid-1950s, after the end of World War II.[47] Japan's defeat in the war played a role in diminishing significantly the concerns of the "yellow peril"[48] and thus left space to open up the path of Japanese religions in the country. As in other countries mentioned earlier, Pure Land Buddhism represents the largest school of Japanese Buddhism in South America with its eighty-four temples, of which 90 percent are in Brazil. Honmon Butsuryū, a small school in Japan, which is practically absent from other countries where the Japanese diaspora occurred, is present in Brazil with eleven institutions, while Tendai 天台 has two temples and Shingon has five.[49] The centrality of Brazil in the propagation of Buddhism in South America is well documented.[50] One such example is the Sōtō Zen temple Busshinji in São Paulo city. This was founded in 1955 and functions as the headquarters of Sōtō Zen in South America, with an affiliated temple in Peru.[51]

Soon enough, non-Japanese Brazilians in the late 1950s and 1960s, due to the influence of counterculture movements and American Zen boom on intellectuals and upper-middle classes in urban Brazil, started seeking for a spiritual path based on Buddhist meditative practices. The aspect of Zen related to *zazen*, or sitting meditation, was well suited to accommodate the needs of these new spiritual seekers, and Busshinji leaders were able to attract them. This, however, was a cause for tensions between the new converts and the Japanese diasporic community, who wanted the temple to preserve its traditional role related to funerals and memorials for the ancestors and serve as a cultural center able to keep vivid the bond with their homeland and identity. The new converts focused on meditation as *the* practice of Buddhism and considered funeral Buddhism as unrelated to the "real" teachings.[52]

The issue of meditation is relevant to understanding the dynamics of global influences on local aspects of Japanese Buddhism. It is not surprising that, in the case of Busshinji, non-Japanese practitioners were expecting to practice *zazen* meditation. This is the main practice to attain *satori* (enlightenment) in this school, although this is not central in the everyday practice and administration of Zen Buddhist temples in Japan (and in Japanese Buddhist temples linked to the diasporic communities), which are almost exclusively focused on funerary and memorial rituals. Less obvious would be to expect the practice of meditation in a Buddhist tradition that does not contemplate this practice in its teachings. This is the case of Shin Buddhism, which again, in Brazil—as in Hawaii and North America—tried to adjust its teachings to become more accessible to non-Japanese members and potential converts. Meditation is one of the thorny fields in this tradition and has been a frequent cause of frictions between the headquarters in Japan and the temples/missions overseas; between the first generations of *nikkei* and second and third generations (increasingly more linked to the "new" home than the far distant Japan); between Japanese and non-Japanese members—usually more interested in meditation and *jiriki* (self-power) practices. Moreover, Shin Buddhism is strongly perceived both in North and South America as a form of ethnic Buddhism and of no particular appeal to non-Japanese Brazilians.[53] However, this school of Buddhism in Brasilia has managed to reach out the non-Japanese community and start the first Shin Buddhist "native Brazilian *sangha*."[54] At the beginning of this endeavor, *zazen*, a form of practice not related to Shin Buddhism, was offered to draw non-Japanese. This was then substituted for chanting meditation of relevant Shin Buddhist texts, like the *Shōshinge*, and a new form of contemplative meditation focused on one of the three main Pure Land sutras, the *Contemplation Sutra*. In this phase of transformation, a major role was played by the individual efforts of Shin Buddhist priests who were able to break the linguistic barriers through Portuguese translations of sutras and interpretations of the teachings; and promoted Japanese (and Asian) culture by offering classes of traditional arts, martial arts, yoga, and Japanese language.[55] This can be aptly seen as an example of an ongoing "adaptation-yet-continuity" pattern related to diaspora religions.[56]

Brazil has been a crucial node in the transmission of Japanese Buddhism to South America, in particular with regard to Zen Buddhism and the creation of new centers aimed at non-Japanese members and spiritual seekers. In the case of Argentina, the school that continues to be linked to ethnic communities, descendants of Japanese migrants, and serves its traditional role in funerary rites and memorial services for the ancestors is Jōdo Shinshū (Honganji-ha), which has a temple in Buenos Aires.[57] Zen Buddhism was not among the schools that played a part in the shaping of communities of Japanese migrants who were either Jōdo Shinshū members or converted to Christianity soon after their arrival in Argentina.[58] Nor did Japanese Zen priests or families contribute to the popularization of Zen, whose great majority of members are converted Buddhists. Moreover, as it happened in other Western countries attracted by a form of simplified and exotic Zen, this term has entered the vocabulary of everyday life in Argentina, and hybrid forms mixed with local culture, such as "Tango Zen" workshops, have been created.[59]

BUDDHISM-BASED NEW RELIGIOUS MOVEMENTS AND DIASPORA

Apart from traditional schools of Buddhism, Buddhism-based new religious movements, such as Sōka Gakkai 創価学会, Reiyūkai 霊友会, and Risshō Kōseikai 立正佼成会 have also established branches overseas. However, they are often small groups or for the great majority linked to a membership of non-Japanese or new local converts of Buddhism. While in several cases, new religious movements do not fall into the category of Japanese Buddhisms in diaspora as intended in this article, some others, like Sōka Gakkai and Risshō Kōseikai, can be aptly included also in view of their close (and "imagined") connection with the "place of origin."[60] In this context, the expansion of new religious movements outside Japan since the 1960s and their attempts to attract non-Japanese members are worthy of mention.

Soka Gakkai International (SGI) is the largest and probably the most successful Japanese Buddhist new religious movement worldwide, with its presence in countries as varied as Italy,

North America, South Korea, and South America. A small Sōka Gakkai group of about 500 non-Japanese members is active in Cuba and is the only Buddhist organization legally recognized in the country.[61] Soka Gakkai International has managed to have a global reach and is present even in countries like South Africa where Japanese religions, with very few exceptions, are practically absent.[62]

In South America, Sōka Gakkai was introduced to Brazil in 1960 while Risshō Kōseikai and Reiyūkai in the 1970s, initially with a focus on the Japanese-Brazilian population, mostly postwar migrants. Some of them, notably Sōka Gakkai, reached beyond the Japanese-Brazilian community and their membership is now mostly made of non-Japanese.[63] This was also due to the tensions its aggressive proselytization campaign known as *shakubuku* 折伏 (lit. to break and subdue) was creating among the Japanese-Brazilian community throughout the 1960s.[64] Risshō Kōseikai remains a small group in Brazil and from 1971 (it started with 657 households) to the 1980s it was mainly an ethnic religious group for postwar Japanese migrants. Since the 1980s it opened up to non-Japanese Brazilians, but it seems that this phase is still in a development stage. Reiyūkai propagation started in 1975 and since the 1990s it has reached out to the non-Japanese Brazilians in the community. All of these new religious movements were urged to adapt to the host cultures, overcome the language barriers, attain social recognition (usually through cultural and charitable activities), and avoid tensions with the predominant Catholic Church.[65]

Nichiren-Buddhism-based Risshō Kōseikai and Sōka Gakkai have established branches in North America and Hawaii since the late 1950s and early 1960s. Risshō Kōseikai did not grow much (it has about twenty centers and "churches" in North America, including Hawaii and Canada), and mostly remained confined to members of Japanese ancestry.[66] In the case of Hawaii, the group experienced various difficulties in adapting to the local cultures and frictions between ministers sent from Japan and local members arose, in particular because of language barriers and a strict adherence to the practice as it was observed in Japan.[67] In the case of SGI, after thirty years of Nichiren Shoshu Soka Gakkai of America (NSA), the organization comprising North America and Hawaii was renamed Soka Gakkai International-USA in 1991. The base of the NSA was a small group of Japanese women married to American men and the first district of SGI outside Japan was established in Hawaii during the visit of then Sōka Gakkai president Ikeda Daisaku (now president of SGI). Focusing on activities directed toward peace and happiness through Buddhism, Ikeda encouraged SGI Japanese members to adapt to the new society and culture by learning English and becoming US citizens. At the same time, as in other parts of the world, the group strove to include non-Japanese members and adjust its teachings to the needs of the hosting environments.[68]

REVIEW OF LITERATURE

To date, most of the literature on Japanese Buddhisms in diaspora is related to some traditional Buddhist schools in North America (the United States), Hawaii, and Brazil. There is still considerable research to be done both with regard to other countries and Buddhism-based new religious movements. This section, as the whole article, is only related to those studies specifically focused on the Japanese diaspora and not on the general propagation of Japanese Buddhism outside Japan.

Because of its peculiar history and developments in migration movements, the major bulk of research has been conducted on diaspora in Hawaii and the development of Japanese Buddhism, in particular Jōdo Shinshū, on the islands. This has created a sort of imbalance in scholarship that is reflected also in this article. Apart from earlier studies published in the 1970s, the history of the Honpa Hongwanji Mission (Honganji-ha) has been analyzed in historical perspective in studies by Moriya Tomoe, who has focused in particular on the figure of Imamura Emyō; and Ama Michihiro, who has analyzed the acculturation of the Jōdo Shinshū Honganji-ha from its arrival in the 19th century to 1941.[69] George Tanabe has explored issues of adaptation and reshaping of this tradition of Japanese Buddhism in Hawaii in various articles and book chapters.[70] On a more popular level, George and Willa Tanabe have also published a guide to Japanese Buddhist temples in Hawaii that details architectural aspects and a brief history of practically all Japanese Buddhist temples on the islands and provides an overview of different schools of Japanese Buddhism in Hawaii.[71] Ugo Dessì has written on the impact of globalization on Shin Buddhist practices in Hawaii and North America and the issue of meditation in the Honpa Hongwanji Mission of Hawaii. In the case of Zen Buddhism, Jørn Borup has focused on this school and questions of ethnicity related to two temples on Maui.[72]

Toward the end of the 1990s and the beginning of the 2000s, a variety of edited books have been published on Buddhism in North America with some chapters specifically related to Japanese Buddhism. Alfred Bloom provides an overview of Shin Buddhism in America with an emphasis on Japanese diaspora in his chapter in the edited book, *The Faces of Buddhism in America*.[73] The same volume contains articles on Zen Buddhism and Nichiren Shōshū/Sōka Gakkai in North America, which are, however, more focused on the non-Japanese converts.[74] On the same line, an exploration of both ethnic and convert Buddhism (not only Japanese) are the chapters by Richard Hughes Seager related to the United States and Bruce Matthews on Canada (one of the few articles on this country), with a clear focus on Shin Buddhism when related to "ethnic" Japanese Buddhism.[75] In the same period, ethnicity and cultural identity have been explored in the case of the Buddhist Churches of America (Shin Buddhism) and Zen temples in the United States.[76] Heading toward more recent times, Galen Amstutz has tackled the issue of ethno-chauvinism in relation to Pure Land Buddhism in America, and John Nelson has published a chapter on Buddhism in diaspora in North America, which includes a part on Japanese Buddhism.[77] Richard Payne has contributed one of the very few, if not the only, article entirely dedicated to Shingon Buddhism in North America and has explored how popular American religious culture and orientalist approaches have made this tradition almost invisible in the United States.[78]

As is clear from this article, the studies on Japanese Buddhism in Latin America are for the great majority focused on Brazil. Apart from this, research on Japanese Buddhism in the other countries is still scant. Among the first scholars who wrote about Japanese religions in Brazil, Nakamaki Hirochika should be mentioned as an important contributor. In his work *Japanese Religions at Home and Abroad: Anthropological Perspectives*, he delved into dynamics of transplantation and acculturation of Japanese religions abroad, in particular in their efforts to conform to the religious market. His analysis is mostly focused on some new religious movements, with a few mentions to Shin and Zen Buddhism.[79] Cristina Rocha's account on the hybridization of Japanese Sōtō Zen in Brazil was the first monograph on a Japanese religion written from the perspective of globalization theory.[80] Recently, she has provided an overview of Buddhism in Latin America and broadened the analysis to other areas, specifically Argentina and Cuba. In these two countries, however, Japanese Buddhism is more related to the community of non-Japanese adherents and therefore in line with studies of convert Buddhism.[81] Rafael Shoji and Frank Usarski have contributed to the field of Japanese religions, including Buddhism, in South America on a variety of occasions and provided general surveys in this regard.[82] Recently, Regina Matsue has written on Shin Buddhism in Brasilia and how local cultures have contributed to the creation of new forms of practice, as analyzed above.[83]

Given the historical conditions and the fact that the Japanese diaspora has reached Europe in a very limited way, research on Japanese Buddhisms in European countries has been mostly focused on new converts in Zen Buddhism, new religious movements (Soka Gakkai International), and non-Japanese communities.[84]

FURTHER READING

Ama, Michihiro. *Immigrants to the Pure Land: The Modernization, Acculturation, and Globalization of Shin Buddhism, 1898–1941*. Honolulu: University of Hawaii Press, 2011.

Amstutz, Galen. "Global Communication versus Ethno-Chauvinism: Framing Nikkei Pure Land Buddhism in North America." *Journal of Religion in Japan* 3, no. 2–3 (2014): 121–140. Special issue "New Research on Japanese Religions under Globalization," guest edited by Galen Amstutz and Ugo Dessì.

Borup, Jørn. "Aloha Buddha: The Secularization of Ethnic Japanese-American Buddhism." *Journal of Global Buddhism* 14 (2013): 23–43.

Carini, Eduardo Catón. "Buddhism in Argentina." In *Encyclopedia of Latin American Religions*. Edited by Henry Gooren, 1–10. Dordrecht: Springer, 2016.

Clarke, Peter B. "Japanese Religions in Latin America." In *Encyclopedia of Global Religion*, edited by Mark Juergensmeyer and Wade Clark Roof, 619–620. Los Angeles: SAGE, 2012.

Dessì, Ugo. "Meditation à la carte: Glocal Change in Hawaiian Jōdo Shinshū." In *The Global Repositioning of Japanese Religions: An Integrated Approach*, 98–130. London: Routledge, 2017.

Matsue, Regina Yoshie. 2013. "The Glocalization Process of Shin Buddhism in Brasilia." *Journal of Religion in Japan* 3, no. 2–3 (2014): 226–246. Special issue "New Research on Japanese Religions under Globalization," guest edited by Galen Amstutz and Ugo Dessì.

Matthews, Bruce. "Buddhism in Canada." In *Westward Dharma: Buddhism beyond Asia*. Edited by Charles S. Prebish and Martin Baumann, 120–138. Berkeley: University of California Press, 2002.

Mitchell, Scott A. "Locally Translocal American Shin Buddhism." *Pacific World* third series 12 (2010): 109–126. Special issue on "Buddhisms in Japan."

Payne, Richard. "Hiding in Plain Sight: The Invisibility of the Shingon Mission to the United States." In *Buddhist Missionaries in the Era of Globalization*. Edited by Linda Learman, 101–122. Honolulu: University of Hawaii Press, 2005.

Prebish, Charles S., and Kenneth K. Tanaka, eds. *The Faces of Buddhism in America*. Berkeley: University of California Press, 1998.

Reid, David. "Internationalization in Japanese Religion." In *Religion in Japanese Culture: Where Living Traditions Meet a Changing World*. Edited by Noriyoshi Tamaru and David Reid, 184–198. Tokyo: Kodansha International, 1996.

Rocha, Cristina. *Zen in Brazil: The Quest for Cosmopolitan Modernity*. Honolulu: University of Hawaii Press, 2006.

Rocha, Cristina. "Buddhism in Latin America." In *Handbook of Contemporary Buddhism*, edited by Michael Jerryson, 299–315. Oxford: Oxford University Press, 2017.

Tanabe, George J. Jr. "Grafting Identity: The Hawaiian Branches of the Bodhi Tree." In *Buddhist Missionaries in the Era of Globalization*. Edited by Linda Learman, 77–100. Honolulu: University of Hawaii Press, 2005.

Usarski, Frank. "Buddhism in South America: An Overview with Reference to the South American Context." In *2600 Years of Sambuddhatva: Global Journey of Awakening*. Edited by Oliver Abeynayake and Asanga Tilakaratne, 527–540. Colombo, Sri Lanka: Ministry of Buddhasasana and Religious Affairs, 2012.

Watanabe, Masako. "The Development of Japanese New Religions in Brazil and Their Propagation in a Foreign Culture." *Japanese Journal of Religious Studies* 35, no. 1 (2008): 115–144.

NOTES

1. Seán McLoughlin, "Religion, Religions, and Diaspora," in *A Companion to Diaspora and Transnationalism*, ed. Ato Quayson and Girish Daswani (Chichester, UK: Wiley–Blackwell, 2013), 125–138, 126.
2. Steven Vertovec, "Religion and Diaspora," in *New Approaches to the Study of Religion*, vol. 2, ed. Peter Antes, Armin W. Geertz, and Randi R. Warne (Berlin: De Gruyter, 2004), 275–303, 282. Vertovec points out the fact that transnational communities, that is, those related to an "ongoing exchanges of information, money and resources, . . . that members of diaspora may undertake with others in the homeland of elsewhere within the globalized ethnic community . . . comprise diasporas"—although the opposite is not always valid (p. 282). The debate on the term diaspora is a long-standing and ongoing one. Its use ranges from a narrow notion confined to the Jewish biblical literature to the most varied fields (e.g., Black/African diaspora). The term has acquired also contradictory meanings, as in Clifford's versions: a centered and territorial vs. an "emancipatory, and deterritorialized" vision. See Stéphane Dufoix, "Diasporas: Historical and Conceptual Analysis," in *The Encyclopedia of Global Human Migration*, ed. Immanuel Ness (Chichester, UK: Wiley–Blackwell, 2013), 1–8. With regard to the problematic related to the "dispersion of the term," see Rogers Brubaker, "The 'Diaspora' Diaspora," in *Ethnic and Racial Studies* 28, no. 1 (2005): 1–19. See also Brubaker's identification of three core elements constitutive of diaspora, "dispersion in space; . . . orientation to a 'homeland'; and . . . boundary-maintenance" (pp. 5–7).
3. Martin Baumann, "Diaspora: Genealogies of Semantics and Transcultural Comparison." *Numen* 47, no. 3, 313–317, 327 (italics in the original). According to Baumann, if such "identificational recollection or rebinding" is missing, the diasporic element is lost too.
4. Vertovec, "Religion and Diaspora," 285.
5. Paul Christopher Johnson, "Religion and Diaspora," in *Religion and Society: Advances in Research* 3 (2012): 95–114, 95.
6. Manuel A. Vásquez, "Studying Religion in Motion: A Networks Approach," *Method and Theory in the Study of Religion* 20, no. 2 (2008): 151–184, 163.
7. This section deals with Hawaii as separate from North America because of the history of Japanese Buddhism in Hawaii. Japanese Buddhism was introduced to Hawaii in the 19th century, long before the islands became a US state in 1959. This separation is still evident in the way Japanese Buddhist headquarters divide their overseas districts (a clear example is provided by the division of the Buddhist Churches of America and the Hongwanji Mission of Hawaii in the case of Shin Buddhism).
8. David Reid, "Internationalization in Japanese Religions," in *Religion in Japanese Culture: Where Living Traditions Meet a Changing World*, ed. Noriyoshi Tamaru and David Reid (Tokyo: Kodansha, 1996), 184–198, 191; cf. George J. Tanabe and Willa Jane Tanabe, *Japanese Buddhist Temples in Hawai'i* (Honolulu: University of Hawaii Press, 2013).
9. George J. Tanabe Jr., "Grafting Identity: The Hawaiian Branches of the Bodhi Tree," in *Buddhist Missionaries in the Era of Globalization*, ed. Linda Learman (Honolulu: University of Hawaii Press, 2005), 77–100, 77.

10. Data from Honpa Hongwanji (personal email communication with Rev. Kevin Kuniyuki, director of the Buddhist Study Center, Apr. 16, 2017).
11. See also "Organizations and Programs," *Honpa Hongwaji Mission of Hawaii*; and Tanabe and Tanabe, *Japanese Buddhist Temples in Hawai'i*, 11.
12. Tanabe, "Grafting Identity," 83–84.
13. Alfred Bloom, "Shin Buddhism in America: A Social Perspective," in *The Faces of Buddhism in America*, ed. Charles Prebish and Kenneth K. Tanaka (Berkeley: University of California Press), 33; and Ama Michihiro, *Immigrants to the Pure Land: The Modernization, Acculturation, and Globalization of Shin Buddhism, 1898–1941* (Honolulu: University of Hawaii Press, 2011), 36. Until 1918, when the new organizational system was inaugurated by the Kyoto Headquarters of the Honganji, Imamura was a "superintendent." His predecessor was Rev. Satomi Hōji, who was sent to Hawaii in 1898 and built the first Shin temple in Honolulu in 1899 (see Ama, *Immigrants to the Pure Land*, 36).
14. Imamura quoted in Tanabe, "Grafting Identity," 85.
15. Bloom, "Shin Buddhism in America"; Tanabe, "Grafting Identity."
16. See Ama, *Immigrants to the Pure Land*, 105; and Tanabe and Tanabe, *Japanese Buddhist Temples in Hawai'i*, 21.
17. See Tanabe, "Grafting Identity," 89–90.
18. Ama, *Immigrants to the Pure Land*, 94.
19. Tanabe, "Grafting Identity," 95–96.
20. In 2013, I spent six months in Hawaii as a visiting professor at the University of Hawaii and resided at the residence attached to the Honganji-ha's Buddhist Study Center. I had the opportunity to participate in the community life of the Honganji and this has enabled me to experience firsthand the differences and adaptations of Shin Buddhism in a diaspora setting. I am grateful to all the people who welcomed me, in particular, Bishop Eric Matsumoto and Rev. Kevin Kuniyuki, who made my stay truly valuable.
21. Galen Amstutz, "Global Communication versus Ethno-Chauvinism: Framing *Nikkei* Pure Land Buddhism in North America," Special issue on "New Research on Japanese Religions under Globalization," ed. Galen Amstutz and Ugo Dessì, *Journal of Religion in Japan* 3, no. 2–3 (2014): 121–140, 152.
22. Tanabe and Tanabe, *Japanese Buddhist Temples in Hawai'i*, 13.
23. Tanabe and Tanabe, *Japanese Buddhist Temples in Hawai'i*, 13.
24. Cf. Jørn Borup, "Aloha Buddha: The Secularization of Ethnic Japanese-American Buddhism." *Journal of Global Buddhism* 14 (2013): 23–43, 27.
25. Borup, "Aloha Buddha," 28.
26. See Ugo Dessì, *The Global Repositioning of Japanese Religions: An Integrated Approach* (London: Routledge, 2017), 98–130.
27. Tanabe and Tanabe, *Japanese Buddhist Temples in Hawai'i*, 7.
28. Data from Tanabe and Tanabe, *Japanese Buddhist Temples in Hawai'i*.
29. Data from Tanabe and Tanabe, *Japanese Buddhist Temples in Hawai'i*.
30. See Tanabe and Tanabe, *Japanese Buddhist Temples in Hawai'i*, 62–64.
31. Reid, "Internationalization in Japanese Religions," 190–191; and Bloom, "Shin Buddhism in America, 32–33.
32. Reid, "Internationalization in Japanese Religions," 191.
33. Kenneth K. Tanaka, "Issues of Ethnicity in the Buddhist Churches of America," in *American Buddhism: Methods and Findings in Recent Scholarship*, ed. Dunkan Ryūken Williams and Christopher S. Queen (Richmond, UK: Curzon, 1999), 5. See also Ama, *Immigrants to the Pure Land*, 35.
34. See the official website, Buddhist Churches of America.
35. Tanaka, "Issues of Ethnicity in the Buddhist Churches of America," 6–7.
36. Tanaka, "Issues of Ethnicity in the Buddhist Churches of America," 8.

37. Spencer, Anna, "Diversification in the Buddhist Churches of America: Demographic Trends and Their Implications for the Future Study of U.S. Buddhist Groups," *Journal of Global Buddhism* 15 (2014): 35–61, 49.
38. Charles S. Prebish, "Introduction," in *The Faces of Buddhism in America*, ed. Charles S. Prebish and Kenneth K. Tanaka (Berkeley: University of California Press, 1998), 1–10, 4; and Victor Sōgen G Hori, "Japanese Zen in America: Americanizing the Face in the Mirror," in *The Faces of Buddhism in America*, ed. Charles S. Prebish and Kenneth K. Tanaka (Berkeley: University of California Press, 1998), 50–78, 52.
39. Senryō Asai and Duncan Ryūken Williams, "Japanese American Zen Temples: Cultural Identity and Economics," in *American Buddhism: Methods and Findings in Recent Scholarship*, ed. Duncan Ryūken Williams and Christopher S. Queen (Richmond: Curzon, 1999), 20–35, 34.
40. Prebish, "Introduction," 4–5.
41. The perception of Japanese Buddhism in Europe and America has been influenced by a form of Zen Buddhism made for the West and characterized by orientalist/occidentalist traits.
42. Robert N. Bellah, "New Religious Consciousness and the Crisis in Modernity," in *The New Religious Consciousness*, ed. Charles Y. Glock and Robert N. Bellah (Berkeley: University of California Press, 1976), 333–352, 341.
43. Bruce Matthews, "Buddhism in Canada," in *Westward Dharma: Buddhism Beyond Asia*, ed. Charles S. Prebish and Martin Baumann (Berkeley: University of California Press, 2002), 120–138, 121.
44. Christina Rocha, "Buddhism in Latin America," in *Handbook of Contemporary Buddhism*, ed. Michael Jerryson (Oxford: Oxford University Press, 2017), 299–315, 300.
45. Frank Usarski, "Buddhism in South America: An Overview with Reference to the South American Context," in *2600 Years of Sambuddhatva: Global Journey of Awakening*, ed. Oliver Abeynayake and Asanga Tilakaratne (Colombo, Sri Lanka: Ministry of Buddhasasana and Religious Affairs, 2012), 527–540, 528.
46. Cristina Rocha, *Zen in Brazil: The Quest for Cosmopolitan Modernity* (Honolulu: University of Hawaii Press, 2006), 27, 32.
47. Peter B. Clarke, "Japanese Religions in Latin America," in *Encyclopedia of Global Religion*, ed. Mark Juergensmeyer and Wade Clark Roof (Los Angeles: SAGE, 2012), 619–620, 620.
48. Rocha, *Zen in Brazil*, 32.
49. Usarski, "Buddhism in South America," 528.
50. In particular, see Christina Rocha, *Zen in Brazil*; and "Buddhism in Latin America"; and Frank Usarski, "Buddhism in South America."
51. Usarski, "Buddhism in South America," 528.
52. Rocha, "Buddhism in Latin America," 305. See also *Zen in Brazil*.
53. Regina Yoshie Matsue, "The Glocalization Process of Shin Buddhism in Brasilia, in Special issue on "New Research on Japanese Religions under Globalization," ed. Galen Amstutz and Ugo Dessì. *Journal of Religion in Japan* 3/2–3 (2013): 226–246, 230.
54. Matsue, "The Glocalization Process of Shin Buddhism in Brasilia," 231.
55. Matsue, "The Glocalization Process of Shin Buddhism in Brasilia," 234–235; 241–243.
56. Cf. Vertovec, "Religion and Diaspora," 285.
57. Catón Eduardo Carini, "Buddhism in Argentina," in *Encyclopedia of Latin American Religions*, ed. Henry Gooren (Springer, 2015), 1–10; 3.
58. Federico Mallimaci quoted in Catón Eduardo Carini. "Las nuevas tierras del Buda: Globalización, medio de comunicación y descentralización en una minoría religiosa de la Argentina," *Debates do NER* 10/16 (2009): 49–70; 52.
59. Carini, "La nuevas tierras del Buda," 52; and Carini, "Buddhism in Argentina," 9.

60. See note 2.
61. Girardo Rodriguez Placencia, "Sōka Gakkai in Cuba: Building a 'Spiritual Bridge' to Local Particularism, the 'Mystic East' and the World," in Special issue on ""New Research on Japanese Religions under Globalization" ed. G. Amstutz and U. Dessì, *Journal of Religion in Japan* 3, no. 2–3 (2014): 198–225, 199.
62. Elisabetta Porcu, "Contemporary Japanese Buddhist Traditions," in *Handbook of Contemporary Buddhism* (Oxford: Oxford University Press, 2017), 122–139, 134. As regards Buddhism in South Africa, see Michel Clasquin-Johnson, "Buddhist Traditions in Africa," *Handbook of Contemporary Buddhism* (Oxford: Oxford University Press, 2017), 349–365.
63. Watanabe Masako, "The Development of Japanese New Religions in Brazil and Their Propagation in a Foreign Culture," *Japanese Journal of Religious Studies* 35, no. 1 (2008): 115–144, 116–117.
64. Watanabe, "The Development of Japanese New Religions in Brazil," 125.
65. Watanabe, "The Development of Japanese New Religions in Brazil," 124, 125, 128–133.
66. "North American Rissho Koseikai Locations," Rissho Kosei-kai International of North America.
67. Hawaii Association of International Buddhists, ed., *Unity in Diversity: Hawaii's Buddhist Communities* (Honolulu: Hawaii Association of International Buddhists, 1997), 157–158.
68. Hawaii Association of International Buddhists, ed., *Unity in Diversity: Hawaii's Buddhist Communities* (Honolulu: Hawaii Association of International Buddhists, 1997), 189–191. See also David Machacek and Kerry Mitchell, "Immigrant Buddhists in America," in *Global Citizens: The Soka Gakkai Buddhist Movement in the World,* ed. David Machacek and Bryan Wilson (Oxford University Press 2000), 259–279, 259.
69. Louise H. Hunter, *Buddhism in Hawaii: Its Impact on a Yankee Community* (Honolulu: University of Hawaii Press, 1971). On the history of the Honganji in Hawaii, see also Ruth M. Tabrah, "A Grateful Past, a Promising Future," in *A Grateful Past, a Promising Future: The First 100 Years of Honpa Hongwanji mission of Hawaii,* ed. Centennial Publication Committee (Honolulu: Honpa Hongwanji mission of Hawaii, 1989), 1–120. Moriya Tomoe, *Yemyo Imamura: Pioneer American Buddhist,* trans. Tsuneichi Tekeshita, ed. Alfred Bloom and Ruth Tabrah (Honolulu: Buddhist Studies Center, 2000). Ama Michihiro, *Immigrants to the Pure Land: The Modernization, Acculturation, and Globalization of Shin Buddhism, 1898–1941* (Honolulu: University of Hawaii Press, 2011).
70. For example, George J. Tanabe Jr., "Grafting Identity: The Hawaiian Branches of the Bodhi Tree," in *Buddhist Missionaries in the Era of Globalization,* ed. Linda Learman (Honolulu: University of Hawaii Press, 2005), 77–100; George J. Tanabe, 1998. "Glorious Gathas: Americanization and Japanization in Honganji Hymns," in *Engaged Pure Land Buddhism: The Challenges Facing Jōdo Shinshū in the Contemporary World: Essays in Honor of Professor Alfred Bloom,* ed. Kenneth K. Tanaka and Eisho Nasu (Berkeley, CA: Wisdom Ocean Publication), 221–237.
71. George J. and Willa Jane Tanabe, *Japanese Buddhist Temples in Hawai'i* (Honolulu: University of Hawaii Press, 2013).
72. Ugo Dessì, "Meditation à la carte: Glocal Change in Hawaiian Jōdo Shinshū," in *The Global Repositioning of Japanese Religions: An Integrated Approach* (London: Routledge, 2017), 98–130; and Jørn Borup, "Aloha Buddha: The Secularization of Ethnic Japanese-American Buddhism," *Journal of Global Buddhism* 14 (2013): 23–43.
73. Alfred Bloom, "Shin Buddhism in America: A Social Perspective," in *The Faces of Buddhism in America,* ed. Charles Prebish and Kenneth K. Tanaka (Berkeley: University of California Press, 1998), 31–47.
74. G. Victor Sōgen Hori, "Japanese Zen in America: Americanizing the Face in the Mirror," in *The Faces of Buddhism in America,* ed. Charles Prebish and Kenneth K. Tanaka (Berkeley: University of California Press, 1998), 50–78; and Jane Hurst, "Nichiren Shōshū and Soka Gakkai in America: The Pioneer Spirit," in *The Faces of Buddhism in America,* ed. Charles Prebish and Kenneth K. Tanaka (Berkeley: University of California Press, 1998), 80–97.
75. Richard Hughes Seager, "American Buddhism in the Making," in *Westward Dharma: Buddhism beyond Asia,* ed. Charles S. Prebish and Martin Baumann (Berkeley: University of California Press, 2002),

106–119; and Bruce Matthews, "Buddhism in Canada," in *Westward Dharma: Buddhism beyond Asia*, ed. Charles S. Prebish and Martin Baumann (Berkeley: University of California Press, 2002), 120–138.

76. Kenneth K. Tanaka, "Issues of Ethnicity in the Buddhist Churches of America," 3–19; Senryō Asai and Duncan Ryūken Williams, "Japanese American Zen Temples: Identity and Economics," 20–35. Both chapters are in *American Buddhism: Methods and Findings in Recent Scholarship*, ed. Duncan Ryūken Williams and Christopher S. Queen (Richmond, UK: Curzon, 1999).
77. Galen Amstutz, "Global Communication versus Ethno-Chauvinism: Framing *Nikkei* Pure Land Buddhism in North America," In Special issue on "New Research on Japanese Religions under Globalization," ed. Galen Amstutz and Ugo Dessì, *Journal of Religion in Japan* 3, no. 2–3 (2014): 121–140; and John Nelson "Diasporic Buddhisms and Converts Communities," in *The Handbook of Contemporary Buddhism*, ed. Michael Jerryson (Oxford: Oxford University Press, 2017), 381–397.
78. Richard Payne, "Hiding in Plain Sight: The Invisibility of the Shingon Mission to the United States," in *Buddhist Missionaries in the Era of Globalization*, ed. Linda Learman (Honolulu: University of Hawaii Press, 2005), 101–122.
79. Nakamaki Hirochika. *Japanese Religions at Home and Abroad: Anthropological Perspectives* (London: Routledge, 2003).
80. Cristina Rocha, *Zen in Brazil: The Quest for Cosmopolitan Modernity* (Honolulu: University of Hawaii Press, 2006).
81. Cristina Rocha, "Buddhism in Latin America," in *Handbook of Contemporary Buddhism*, ed. Michael Jerryson (Oxford: Oxford University Press, 2017), 299–315.
82. See, for example, Frank Usarski, "Buddhism in Brazil and Its Impact on the Larger Brazilian Society," in *Westward Dharma: Buddhism Beyond Asia*, ed. Charles S. Prebish and Martin Baumann (Berkeley: University of California Press, 2002), 163–176; "Buddhism in South America: An Overview with Reference to the South American Context," in *2600 Years of Sambuddhatva: Global Journey of Awakening*, ed. Oliver Abeynayake and Asanga Tilakaratne (Colombo, Sri Lanka: Ministry of Buddhasasana and Religious Affairs, 2012), 527–540; and "Japanese 'Immigrant Buddhism' in Brazil: Historical Overview and Current," in *Religion, Migration, and Mobility: The Brazilian Experience*, ed. Cristina Maria de Castro and Andrew Dawson (London: Routledge, 2017). Rafael Shoji, "'Buddhism in Syncretic Shape': Lessons of Shingon in Brazil," *Journal of Global Buddhism* 4 (2003): 70–107.
83. Regina Yoshie Matsue, "The Glocalization Process of Shin Buddhism in Brasilia," in Special issue on "New Research on Japanese Religions under Globalization," ed. Galen Amstutz and Ugo Dessì, *Journal of Religion in Japan* 3, no. 2–3 (2014): 226–246.
84. On Sōka Gakkai in Europe, see, for example, Bryan Wilson, "The British Movement and its Members," 349–374; and Maria Immacolata Macioti, "Buddhism in Action: Case Studies from Italy," 375–401. Both chapters are in *Global Citizens: The Soka Gakkai Buddhist Movement in the World*, ed. David Machaecek and Bryan Wilson (Oxford: Oxford University Press, 2000).

Elisabetta Porcu

JĀTAKA

THE *JĀTAKA* GENRE

Simply defined, a *jātaka* story is a tale of a past life of the Buddha. The buddha is said to have seen all his past lives during the night in which he attained awakening, as a result of entering an advanced meditative state.[1] He is understood to have told the stories at various stages during his teaching career, to illustrate the workings of karma, or the preparations he underwent for buddhahood, or the characters and propensities of the people around him. Several hundred stories were compiled in various texts, illustrated at Buddhist sites, and integrated into sermons, rituals, and festivals.

It is clear that *jātaka* was considered one of the genres of Buddhist composition from a fairly early period, since it is included in the lists of nine or twelve *aṅgas* (limbs) of the teaching, alongside such prominent genres as *sutra* (discourses), *udāna* (inspired utterances), and *gāthā* (verses).[2] Their preservation seems to have been assigned to specialized *jātaka-bhāṇakas*, or reciters, who would have memorized the stories and taught them on various occasions, though it is not clear quite what the stories consisted of in the early period, or how they were used.[3] In contrast to the *sutra* and *vinaya* texts, of which large parts are shared across the various schools into which Buddhism split in the few hundred years following the death of the Buddha, there is no evidence of a single shared *jātaka* collection, though individual stories are found across different schools. Rather, we find several different *jātaka* texts that preserve differing understandings of what the *jātaka* genre is and is for. The *jātaka* genre also often overlaps with other genres of Buddhist narrative, particularly avadånas. Indeed, tales of the Buddha's past lives are sometimes labeled *bodhisattva-avadānas* instead of (or as well as) *jātakas*.

There is much variety in *jātaka* tales and texts, but several key themes can be discerned that often thread through the genre. Firstly, the stories are used to demonstrate the superior vision and knowledge of the buddha, who not only is able to see his own past lives (an ability that is usually understood to testify to his mastery of meditation), but also has a story to suit every occasion. The identification of a story as a *jātaka* often seems to be made with the aim of demonstrating that all stories originate with the fantastic storyteller-teacher and supreme meditator that is the buddha.[4]

The second major association of the *jātaka* genre is with the long life story and multilife path of the buddha. *Jātaka* stories became understood as narrating the lifetimes of the buddha between his initial vow to buddhahood and his achievement of that state, in other words during his time as a bodhisattva (Sanskrit) or bodhisatta (Pali, a being destined) for buddhahood. In some collections *jātakas* are explicitly said to demonstrate the long path to buddhahood and the perfections or virtues required for its attainment. In the Theravada tradition these perfections usually number ten: giving (*dāna*), good conduct (*sīla*), renunciation (*nekkhamma*), wisdom (*paññā*), energy (*viriya*), forbearance (*khanti*), truth (*sacca*), determination (*adhiṭṭhāna*), lovingkindness (*mettā*), and equanimity (*upekkhā*). In other Indian and Mahāyāna texts we more often find six perfections—giving (*dāna*), good conduct (*śīla*), forbearance (*kṣanti*), energy (*vīrya*), meditation (*samādhi/dhyāna*), and wisdom (*prajñā*)—but the message is the same: *jātakas* illustrate these great virtues. Such illustrations not only inspire awe at the great achievements of the buddha, but also encourage the audience to pursue these virtues themselves, even if their emulation of the glorious bodhisattva (Buddha-to-be) will inevitably be weak.

One perfection above all others came to be strongly associated with the *jātakas* and that is generosity, or giving, known in Pāli and Sanskrit as *dāna*. Generosity is a key value in the Buddhist worldview, since it demonstrates nonattachment (to the thing given), compassion (for a recipient in need), or faith (for a recipient in the Buddhist monastic community), and in practical terms ensures the continuation of the monastic order, which could not survive without gifts of food and shelter. Several particularly famous *jātaka* stories take this virtue to extremes. Many stories tell of the Buddha-to-be making gifts of parts of his body, giving his eyes to a blind man, slicing off his flesh to ransom a dove from a hawk, or allowing a starving tigress to devour him.[5] Another famous tale—the most popular in the Theravāda world, where it is understood to narrate the last-but-one human life of the buddha—tells of the buddha's past life as Prince Vessantara (or Viśvantara in Sanskrit). Vessantara's great generosity leads to his being banished to the forest with his two children and loyal wife. In a heart-wrenching scene, he then gives his children to a Brahmin who wishes to have them for slaves. The next morning the king of the gods, Śakra, takes on a disguise as a Brahmin (as he does fairly regularly in the *jātakas*) and asks for Vessantara's wife, whom Vessantara freely gives. A great family reunion ensues, with Vessantara's wife (the buddha's wife in a past life) immediately returned to him, the children ransomed by their grandfather, and Vessantara invited home to rule; the evil Brahmin who beat the children cruelly dies from overeating. Such happy endings, however, cannot disguise the tension in the story, which takes generosity to an extreme that few audience members or readers are wholly comfortable with.

Stories of the bodhisattva's extreme generosity serve to demonstrate the lengths to which the buddha-to-be had to go in order to prepare himself for buddhahood. His path is shown to be extraordinarily hard, and we do not generally get the impression from *jātaka* texts that ordinary Buddhists should be emulating his extreme generosity. Rather, Buddhists are inspired by the buddha's great dedication to becoming a buddha and are grateful for his life-changing establishment of the Buddhist teachings and community. Other stories, particularly those in the *avadāna* genre, emphasize the enormous merit that can be gained from acts of devotion or small gifts given to Buddhist recipients, whether to the buddha himself, members of his monastic community, or images and reliquaries. The buddha, by becoming buddha, has instituted the greatest "field of merit" available and made it possible for his followers to achieve great spiritual and karmic benefits without going to the extraordinary lengths that he had to in his past lives during times when there was no Buddhism in the world.[6] Meanwhile, Buddhists are also inspired to emulate the buddha's actions in a weaker form, by giving a son to the monastery as an ordinand, for example, or by donating blood and registering as an organ donor.[7]

However, the buddha's long path, as we discover in *jātaka* stories, was not an individual path of gradually accrued virtue, but a communal path involving repeated interactions with others. Commenting on the long-standing propensities of key characters from the buddha's retinue, and highlighting their multilife relationship with him, appears to be another key theme of *jātaka* stories in some texts, including the copious *Jātakatthavaṇṇanā*. Story after story demonstrates the multilife hatred and incompetence of the buddha's cousin and nemesis Devadatta, while many other tales show the buddha's repeated friendships with senior monks such as his attendant Ānanda. The buddha's multilife relationship with his parents, wife, and son is also common in the stories, often reinforcing the strength of attachment to his family that had to be overcome in his final life. The *jātakas* therefore build up a sense of a whole Buddhist community moving toward its final formation, in which most of its members achieve liberation.

Jātaka tales, then, can demonstrate the buddha's prowess as a meditator and storyteller, as well as his extraordinary path, involving incredible acts of virtue, self-sacrifice, and generosity.

They can be awe-inspiring for their audiences, who can barely believe the lengths to which the buddha had to go in order to bring them the benefits of his teachings and institutions. The tales can also serve as exemplars, even if the audience's emulation of the buddha's activities may be weak in some cases. They also create a sense of community and of multilife encounters with the buddha, commenting on the characters and propensities of members of his retinue, and allowing audience members to imagine themselves into a relationship with him.

It is worth noting that the *jātaka* genre is a uniquely Buddhist genre. The Jains, while they shared the Buddhist love of multilife stories and told some stories about the past lives of their *Jinas*, did not have a *jātaka* genre, since they held that aspiring to become a liberated teacher would bind bad karma. For Jains, the karma that leads to *tīrthaṅkara*-hood is bound two lives before that attainment, without the person knowing.[8] Brahmanical Hindu literature, meanwhile, tended to prefer tales of mythical lineages and divine interventions, rather than karmic histories or multilife biographies.

JĀTAKA TEXTS

The biggest and best-known *jātaka* text is the *Jātakatthavaṇṇanā* or *Jātakatthakathā* (Commentary on the *Jātaka*), which is a collection of almost 550 stories in the Pāli language, preserved by the Theravāda school. The text has verses at its core, and these are believed to be canonical or *buddhavacana* (word of the buddha), and are preserved as part of the *Khuddaka Nikāya* of the Theravāda scriptures. However, these verses come to life only with their surrounding prose narrative, which is nonetheless considered commentarial, and was only fixed—after a long history—in the 5th century CE. The commentary is traditionally ascribed to Buddhaghosa, though this attribution is unlikely to be accurate.[9]

The stories of the *Jātakatthavaṇṇanā* follow a set structure. A "story of the present" explains the circumstances in which the buddha was prompted to tell a tale of one of his many past lives, which then forms the "story of the past." The verse or verses are usually in the story of the past. The story ends with the buddha revealing who in the past story was who in the present: minimally, the buddha himself is identified as one of the characters in the past, and usually other members of his family or monastic retinue also feature. The hundreds of *jātaka*s in this collection are presented in order of increasing number of verses, from 150 short stories containing a single verse each, through to 10 long stories that are more akin to epic ballads. A biographical preface, the *Nidāna-kathā* (Story of the origins), adds the stories of the buddha-to-be aspiring to buddhahood at the feet of twenty-four buddhas of the past, as well as of his final birth and early life, introducing a sense of chronology and path to the text as a whole.

The *Nidāna-kathā* links the *Jātakatthavaṇṇanā* with two other important *jātaka* texts of the Pāli tradition. The *Buddhavaṃsa* (Lineage of Buddha[s]) begins with the story of how Sumedha, who later becomes the buddha of our time, encounters a past buddha named Dīpaṅkara and makes an aspiration to buddhahood. This aspiration is repeated at the feet of the twenty-four past buddhas of this current time cycle, about whom a few formulaic details are given. The *Buddhavaṃsa* also records how the buddha-to-be reflected on the ten perfections needed for the attainment of buddhahood, and the *Cariyapiṭaka* (Basket of conduct) provides thirty-five short verse summaries of some of the lifetimes in which he worked toward those perfections, largely overlapping with stories found in the *Jātakatthavaṇṇanā*. These two texts, both included in the *Khuddaka Nikāya*, build on the idea that *jātaka*s are part of the sacred biography of the buddha and exemplify the path to buddhahood. This ideology, married with the set structure of the *Jātakatthavaṇṇanā* stories, also fed into the various nonclassical *jātaka* collections of Southeast Asia, which are collectively known as *Paññāsa Jātaka* (Fifty *Jātaka*s) texts.

Although the Theravāda seems to be the only school to have collected together its *jātaka*s into a single collection of such magnitude as the *Jātakatthavaṇṇanā*, *jātaka* stories are found in other important Indian texts. The *Mahāvastu* (Great story) includes many *jātaka*s in among its broadly biographical frame, often using tales of the past as mirrors for events in the life story of the buddha. The *Avadānaśataka* (One hundred stories) contains two chapters of ten *jātaka*s each, among its one hundred tales of karmic consequences. The *Divyāvadāna* (Divine stories) also includes *jātaka* stories, as do many later collections of *avadāna*s. *Jātaka*s are also embedded in some *sutra* and *vinaya* texts, most famously in the copious narratives of the *Mūlasarvāstivāda Vinaya* (Monastic regulations of the Mūlasarvāstivāda school).[10] Āryaśūra's *Jātakamālā* (Garland of *jātaka*s) retells thirty-four stories, most with parallels in the *Jātakatthavaṇṇanā*, in elegant Sanskrit verse and prose and sets a standard for subsequent *Jātakamālā* texts by other authors.[11] Stories were also collected together in *Jātakastava* (*Jātaka*-praise) texts, which eulogize the buddha's achievements with reference to his past lives.[12]

The understanding of what a *jātaka* is and what form it should take differs both within and between texts, demonstrating how widespread and diverse the genre is. For example, in the *Cariyapiṭaka* and *Jātakamālā* the stories are told in praise of the buddha's past virtues, but in the former the tales are first-person declarations in the voice of the buddha, while in the latter they are poetic compositions by a named author, in the third person. In neither text is there any narrative frame explaining why or to whom the stories were originally told. Both the *Jātakatthavaṇṇanā* and the *Mahāvastu* make it clear that the buddha was the original teller of his *jātaka* stories, thereby asserting his impressive status as visionary and revealer, and we also often see the audience response and hear tales of the past lives of other members of the buddha's community or family. The *Mahāvastu* tends to use *jātaka*s to mirror events in the final life of the buddha; for example, a cluster of stories about his wooing of his wife in the past explain the necessity of his courtship in his final life. Such mirrorings are common in the *Jātakatthavaṇṇanā* too, but there are also other relationships between past and present in that text, for example, karmic causes of present circumstances.

Karmic connections are foregrounded in the stories found in the *Avadānaśataka*, yet there is internal variety even in this text. While the first ten *jātaka*s included (*Avadānaśataka* 11–20) demonstrate the devotional relationship between the buddha-to-be and buddhas of the past that results in his receipt of honor in the present, the second set (*Avadānaśataka* 31–40) tell of extreme acts of virtue or generosity in times of no past buddha. Again the audience response is noted in the text: the first ten stories are said to inspire awe and veneration from the monastic community, while the second group is said to inspire emulation of the buddha's virtues. The focus on karma and merit in this text is in line with the generic conventions of *avadāna*s, which tend to tell stories of past and future lives, aspirations and achievements, and the power of the Buddhist "field of merit."

A further shift occurs when *jātaka* stories are included in Mahāyāna texts, for here the focus is on the bodhisattva path and the perfections as an ideal to be followed by more than just a single extraordinary individual. This tends to result in the use of stories to glorify the great achievements of the buddha as an exemplary bodhisattva, for example, in the list of fifty *jātaka*s in the *Rāṣṭrapālaparipṛcchā,* or the use of the stories in the *Bodhisattvapiṭaka* to elucidate the six perfections.[13] Here a celebration of the great past acts of the buddha is tied to the notion that he is an exemplar to be followed by all aspiring bodhisattvas. There is therefore a subtle tendency to downplay the individual in favor of the idea of a multiplicity of bodhisattvas, though it is notable that the *jātaka* genre remains almost exclusively associated with the "historical" buddha.

*JĀTAKA*S AND THE ARTS

Illustrations of *jātaka* stories have been popular at Buddhist sites at least since they first adorned the stone gateways and railings that surround the *stūpa* at Bharhut in Madhya Pradesh in the 1st century BCE.[14] Similar stone reliefs can be found at nearby Sanchi and at the South Indian sites of Kanaganahalli, Nagarjunakonda, and Amaravati, all dating to the first few centuries CE.[15] These early reliefs are often monoscenic, though sometimes several scenes are depicted in a single roundel or panel. The *Vessantara-jātaka* (or, in Sanskrit, *Viśvantara-jātaka*) is singled out for special treatment at Sanchi, where it is illustrated in a series of panels, testifying to its particular importance.

These early reliefs depicting *jātaka*s provide evidence for the widespread currency of the stories during the early centuries CE and suggest that they were considered appropriate for illustration at *stūpa* sites. This location for the stories suggests an early association between the *jātaka* genre and the sacred biography of the buddha, an association strengthened by the presence of scenes from the final life of the buddha at the same sites. As a part of what made the buddha who he was, the *jātaka*s form an important element in his long life story, a life story that often continues through the presence of his relics at the *stūpa* site.

Although *jātaka* stories appear at these early sites, at this stage there is no clear link to a textual collection. Some of the stories at Bharhut are labeled with Prākrit inscriptions, and many have been identified with stories now found in the *Jātakatthavaṇṇanā,* though the titles do not always match up with those used in this collection, and some stories have not been convincingly identified at all. At other sites stories have been identified through comparison with written texts, though some stories vary in their depiction, and some scenes cannot be recognized. The early visual history of *jātaka* stories therefore provides an alternative perspective to the extant textual collections.

The popularity of *jātaka* stories at Buddhist sites continued unabated through subsequent centuries and across the Buddhist world. The stories were included in *stūpa* complexes in Gandhara in the far northwest, an area of intense Buddhist activity in the early centuries of the Common Era.[16] The stories also appear in a different type of setting, namely, monastic cave complexes, such as the western Indian sites of Ajanta and Bagh. The Ajanta Caves (Maharashtra) include *jātaka* stories painted in intricate murals dating from the 5th century CE, often covering an entire wall with their complicated multiscenic narratives.[17] Murals in caves found along the Silk Route toward China, such as at Dunhuang and Kizil, also testify to the popularity of *jātaka* stories.[18] The depiction of *jātaka* stories was important as well in many later sites, for example the great monument at Borobudur in Java.[19]

In Southeast Asia we often find depictions of the final ten stories of the *Jātakatthavaṇṇanā*, which are understood as making up the final ten lives of the buddha and are associated with the ten perfections required for buddhahood. The first evidence of the ten being depicted together as a set is from 11th-century Mon temples of lower Burma (Myanmar), but the group of ten became particularly common from the 18th century onward, especially in Thailand.[20] The ten appear on the inside walls of temple *uposatha* halls, painted on cloth banners, or depicted on gold-lacquered scripture cabinets.[21] They are also commonly illustrated on manuscripts, especially those containing compilations of chanting texts.[22] The full quota of *jātaka* stories was not forgotten with this focus on the ten, however: Wat Khrua Wan (Thonburi, Thailand, first half of the 19th century) has over 500 of the *Jātakatthavaṇṇanā* stories painted in square panels in its *uposatha* hall, while the Ananda Temple in Pagan (Burma [Myanmar], 11th–12th century CE) has terracotta tiles depicting all 550 stories.

The inclusion of *jātaka* images in such a diverse range of Buddhist sites testifies not only to their enduring popularity, but also to their importance as part of the sacred biography of the buddha and their continued relevance as a teaching aid. Their appearance is not limited to the visual arts, for their literary value is also an important part of the stories' appeal. The tales have been reworked as plays, radio plays, television and film adaptations, poems, songs, opera, and dance, and they continue to be an important part of the cultural heritage of Buddhist countries, especially those from the Theravāda world. For example, in Burma the poetic genre Pyo usually draws on *jātaka* stories,[23] and much traditional Thai literature rests on the *jātakas*, especially the *Paññāsa Jātaka*,[24] while a series of Thai opera-ballets is reinterpreting the final ten *jātakas* of the *Jātakatthavaṇṇanā* for a modern audience.[25]

JĀTAKAS IN BUDDHIST LIFE

Textual and artistic evidence suggests that *jātaka* stories have played an important role in Buddhist life throughout history. Although we do not have much detailed information about the ways in which Buddhists have interacted with the stories, certain trends can be seen.

Jātaka stories often form a part of sermons and other forms of teaching, and it seems likely that this has always been their primary function. We know little of the early audiences for the stories, though they probably included both monks and nuns and laypeople, since the many stories vary in their messages. Some stories emphasize the importance of renunciation or focus on the dangers of sense pleasures, messages particularly suitable for a monastic audience. Many others laud the giving of gifts or moral activity, or emphasize the glories of the buddha that make Buddhism and its institutions so worthy of support; such messages are more suitable for lay supporters. The stories would have been conducive to a wide variety of teaching uses, from simple moral lessons to illustrations of the path to buddhahood.

It would be wrong, however, to view *jātakas* as simply a form of narrative teaching. Because of their association with the sacred biography of the buddha, and with the perfections that make buddhahood possible, *jātaka* stories also have various symbolic roles. Some of the ways in which they are used in visual form testify to this. For example, at some sites, *jātaka* stories have been illustrated in deliberately inaccessible places, covered from view or out of reach. In such cases the symbolic value of the stories is more important than their role as teachings, and they add some form of potency or sacrality to the site.[26] Another example is found in 18th-century central Thai manuscript culture, in which we often see *jātakas* decorating folded paper manuscripts, known as *samut khoi*. However, the text that they accompany is never the *jātaka* stories, but rather a selection of chanting texts that have no connection to the narratives. While it is possible that the illustrations are there as visual prompts for sermons, it is perhaps more likely that they are present as symbolic of buddhahood and the ten perfections. That the stories chosen are invariably the final ten stories of the *Jātakatthavaṇṇanā*, which are understood to relate the final ten lives of the buddha-to-be and his fulfillment of the ten perfections, further supports such an interpretation.[27] The ten stories and their association with the ten perfections also form the subject of popular chants, further indicating their special status not as moral tales, but as sacred biography and potent reminders of perfection. Symbolic and narrative value are not, of course, mutually exclusive: the use of *jātaka* stories in the ritual consecration of buddha images in Thailand suggests that they simultaneously remind the buddha(-image) who he is by recounting his life story and infuse him with the buddhahood that he achieved.[28]

A story that has particular potency is the *Vessantara-jātaka*, the final tale in the *Jātakatthavaṇṇanā* and a story understood in Theravāda Buddhist tradition as narrating the buddha's antepenultimate birth (and his penultimate human birth, his subsequent birth being in a heavenly realm).[29] This story has long held particular importance in the Buddhist world, as is attested by its widespread presence, often in a more elaborate form than other stories, in artistic representations. The story is also associated with a series of pilgrimage sites in Gandhara mentioned by the 6th- and 7th-century Chinese pilgrims Songyun and Xuanzang.[30] In Southeast Asia the Vessantara story is the subject of several traditions of ritual recitation and re-enactment, sometimes accompanied by special visual prompts including painted scrolls.[31] The villain of the story, the Brahmin Jūjuka who asks for Vessantara's children as slaves, has even become an object of veneration and protection in Thailand: since he is the recipient of the ultimate gift, his amulets or shrines bring prosperity and good luck.

In addition to all these areas of Buddhist life and practice, the stories played an important role in doctrinal formations, at least in the early period. The layers of the *Jātakatthavaṇṇanā*, for example, suggest that during this text's gradual consolidation the idea of a *jātaka* as illustrative of the bodhisattva path was developing.[32] This association, applied to an existing and varied body of stories, threw up certain challenges, since emerging ideas about the path to buddhahood had to be reconciled with, for example, stories of the bodhisattva's immoral conduct. The consistent maleness of the buddha in his past lives also resulted in various discussions of the extent to which being a man is a necessary prerequisite for the bodhisattva path.[33] In other schools, *jātaka* stories were also used to explore notions of buddhahood and the qualities required for it, as well as understandings of karma and merit and the place of the buddha in relation to other buddhas and bodhisattvas.

REVIEW OF LITERATURE

Scholarship on *jātaka* stories historically tended to focus on the Pāli collection and has been hampered by a number of assumptions about the value of that text. The *Jātakatthavaṇṇanā* was edited in the late 19th century, and a full team translation was completed in 1907. There was wide interest in this text during this early period of Buddhist scholarship, but its value was seen as being limited to two areas: Firstly, it was mined for data as an assumed witness to the social and cultural conditions of early India, despite the problems inherent in dating the collection and its various layers.[34] Secondly, the stories were studied as world folklore, with connections to other narrative collections both within India and outside it.[35] While such studies provided fascinating evidence for the ability of stories to cross geographic and cultural borders, they did not add much to scholarly understandings of the stories in their Buddhist context.

As an example of this early approach to *jātaka*s, T. W. Rhys Davids, one of the first scholars to examine the *Jātakatthavaṇṇanā*, described it both as "full of information on the daily habits and customs and beliefs of the people of India, and on every variety of the numerous questions that arise as to their economic and social conditions," and "the most reliable, the most complete, and the most ancient collection of folklore now extant in any literature in the world."[36] Despite the enthusiasm of Rhys Davids and others, this early approach established the view that the stories were neither very Buddhist nor an example of real literary culture. It was assumed that they held little Buddhist value, since they were simply folk tales, shared with other cultures and contexts, and used as entertainment or simple moral teachings, aimed at a popular audience, addressing worldly concerns.

In recent decades the scholarly approach to *jātaka*s has changed, however. With new attention being paid to the ways in which narrative sources provide insight into Buddhist thought, thanks in large part to the work of such scholars as Steven Collins and John Strong,[37] *jātaka*s have finally been acknowledged as a serious expression of ideas about the buddha, buddhahood, the bodhisattva path, and Buddhist ethics.[38] In addition, other texts containing *jātaka* stories, such as the *Paññāsa Jātaka*, *Avadānaśataka*, *Divyāvadāna*, and *Mahāvastu*, have begun to be studied seriously as Buddhist literature, and questions are starting to be asked about how *jātaka*s are integrated into these and other collections. Thematic studies of the *jātaka* genre have also begun to appear, most notably a pioneering study of gift-of-the-body *jātaka*s.[39] Fresh editorial and translation work is also under way, though much more is needed in this area, with the *Jātakatthavaṇṇanā* and several other *jātaka*-rich texts in need of new translations.

In addition to these studies of *jātaka* texts, there have been some important explorations of the stories' presence in the art and culture of the Buddhist world. While it was initially assumed that *jātaka* illustrations were always meant to provide a visual narrative representation of a story, recent scholarship has explored the role of *jātaka* depictions in instilling power or sacredness in a site, as part of the sacred biography of the buddha and as symbolic of the perfections.[40] A similar association between *jātaka*s and the potency of buddhahood has been shown to be behind some uses of the stories in the ritual consecration of images.[41] Further work on the uses of *jātaka* stories in Buddhist life, including sermons, rituals, and festivals, remains a key priority for our understanding of the genre.

PRIMARY SOURCES

Some of the main collections of *jātaka* stories are available in English translations:

Jātakatthavaṇṇanā. E. B. Cowell, ed. (several translators). *The Jātaka, or Stories of the Buddha's Former Births*. 6 vols. Cambridge, UK: Cambridge University Press, 1895–1907.

This full translation was an impressive achievement in its day and remains of great importance despite its sometimes turgid Victorian English, with the verses rendered in rhyming couplets and the rude bits translated into Latin. It has been reprinted multiple times and is also freely available online.

Naomi Appleton and Sarah Shaw, trans. *The Ten Great Birth Stories of the Buddha.* 2 vols. Chiang Mai: Silkworm, 2015.

The final ten stories of the collection, which are believed to narrate the final ten lives of the Buddha and his culmination of the ten perfections.

Sarah Shaw, trans. *The Jātakas: Birth Stories of the Bodhisatta.* Delhi: Penguin, 2006.

A selection of twenty-six stories from the *Jātakatthavaṇṇanā*, with introduction and notes.

Margaret Cone and Richard F. Gomrich, trans. *The Perfect Generosity of Prince Vessantara: A Buddhist Epic.* 2nd ed. Bristol, UK: Pali Text Society, 2011.

A very scholarly translation of this, the most popular story of the *Jātakatthavaṇṇanā*, by Cone, and a helpful introduction to the story by Gombrich.

***Buddhavaṃsa* and *Cariyāpiṭaka*.** I. B. Horner, trans. *The Minor Anthologies of the Pali Canon, Part III: Chronicle of Buddhas (Buddhavaṃsa) and Basket of Conduct (Cariyāpiṭaka).* Oxford: Pali Text Society, 1975.

A somewhat dated but still very usable translation of these two short texts from the *Khuddaka Nikāya.*

Paññāsa Jātaka. I. B. Horner and Padmanabh S. Jaini, trans. *Apocryphal Birth-Stories (Paññāsa-Jātaka).* 2 vols. Sacred Books of the Buddhists 38. London: Pali Text Society, 1985–1986.

A full translation of a Pāli collection from Burma, which is just one of several examples of the *Paññāsa Jātaka* genre.

Jātakamālā. Peter Khoroche, trans. *When the Buddha Was a Monkey: Ārya Śūra's Jātakamālā.* Chicago and London: University of Chicago Press, 1989.

A very accessible translation of a delightful short collection of Sanskrit *jātakas.*

Mahāvastu. J. J. Jones, trans. *The Mahāvastu.* 3 vols. London: Luzac, 1949–1956.

The *jātaka* stories are spread throughout this long biographical text, but easily identified from Jones's contents page.

Avadānaśataka. Naomi Appleton, trans. "The Second Decade of the *Avadānaśataka.*" *Asian Literature and Translation* 1, no. 7 (2013): 1–36; and "The Fourth Decade of the *Avadānaśataka*" *Asian Literature and Translation* 2, no. 5 (2014): 1–35.

These two chapters of ten stories each represent all the *jātaka* stories found in Avadånaśataka.

DIGITAL MATERIALS

- Kanganhalli, Gulbarga District, Karnataka (http://luczanits.net/sites/Kanganhalli.html).

A helpful overview of what is known so far about the South Indian site Kanaganahalli and a large number of photographs.

- Gandharan Archives Kurita. https://gandharan-archives.blogspot.com/

A blog compiled by Professor Isao Kurita showcasing images of Gandhāran art, including some wonderful examples of the story of Dīpaṅkara Buddha.

- The Huntington Archive (https://huntingtonarchive.org/).

A wonderful archive of photographs of Buddhist art, including, for example, over five hundred images of the Ajanta Caves.

FURTHER READING

Anālayo. *The Genesis of the Bodhisattva Ideal.* Hamburg Buddhist Studies 1. Hamburg: Hamburg University Press, 2010.

Appleton, Naomi. *Jātaka Stories in Theravāda Buddhism: Narrating the Bodhisatta Path.* Farnham, UK: Ashgate, 2010.

Brown, Robert L. "Narrative as Icon: The *Jātaka* Stories in Ancient Indian and Southeast Asian Architecture." In *Sacred Biography in the Buddhist Traditions of South and Southeast Asia.* Edited by Juliane Schober, 64–109. Honolulu: University of Hawaii Press, 1997.

Collins, Steven, ed. *Readings of the Vessantara Jātaka.* Readings in Buddhist Literature Series. New York: Columbia University Press, 2016.

Crosby, Kate. "The *Jātaka*." In *Theravāda Buddhism: Continuity, Diversity, and Identity.* By Kate Crosby, 99–111. Chichester, UK: Wiley–Blackwell, 2014.

Hinüber, Oskar von. *Entstehung und Aufbau der Jātaka-Sammlung: Studien zur Literatur des Theravāda-Buddhismus.* Stuttgart: Franz Steiner Verlag, 1998.

Ohnuma, Reiko. *Head, Eyes, Flesh, and Blood: Giving Away the Body in Indian Buddhist Literature.* New York: Columbia University Press, 2007.

Skilling, Peter, ed. *Past Lives of the Buddha: Wat Si Chum; Art, Architecture, and Inscriptions.* Bangkok: River, 2008.

Skilling, Peter. "Jātaka and Paññāsa-jātaka in South-East Asia." In *Buddhism and Buddhist Literature of South-East Asia: Selected Papers.* Edited by Claudio Cicuzza, 161–217. Bangkok: Fragile Palm Leaves Foundation, 2009.

Strong, John S. "Previous Lives of the Buddha." In *The Buddha: A Short Biography.* Edited by John S. Strong, 15–34. Oxford: Oneworld, 2001.

Walters, Jonathan S. "*Stūpa*, Story, and Empire: Constructions of the Buddha Biography in Early Post-Aśokan India." In *Sacred Biography in the Buddhist Traditions of South and Southeast Asia.* Edited by Juliane Schober, 160–192. Honolulu: University of Hawaii Press, 1997.

NOTES

1. For a discussion see Donald S. Lopez, "Memories of the Buddha," in *In the Mirror of Memory: Reflections on Mindfulness and Remembrance in Indian and Tibetan Buddhism*, ed. Janet Gyatso (Albany: State University of New York Press, 1992), 21–45.
2. The list of nine, which is found in Pāli scriptures (including *suttas*) as well as in the Mahāsāṅghika *Vinaya*, is understood to be older than the list of twelve, which tends to be less stable. The list may well have been expanded to mirror the Jain division of scriptures into twelve *aṅgas*.
3. On the *bhāṇaka* traditions see E. W. Adikaram, *Early History of Buddhism in Ceylon* (Dehiwala, Sri Lanka: Buddhist Cultural Centre, 1946), 24–32; and S. Mori, "The Origin and History of the Bhānaka Tradition,"

in *Ānanda: Papers on Buddhism and Indology*, ed. Y. Karunadasa (Colombo, Sri Lanka: Felicitation Volume Editorial Committee, 1990), 123–129. *Jātaka-bhāṇaka*s are mentioned in the *Milindapañha* and various Pāli commentaries, as well as in a Sri Lankan inscription from the first century CE.

4. On this aspect of the genre, which is dependent on the narrative framing as a dialogue between the buddha and his followers, see Naomi Appleton, "The Buddha as Storyteller: The Dialogical Setting of *Jātaka* Stories," in *Dialogue in Early South Asian Religions: Hindu, Buddhist and Jain Traditions*, ed. Brian Black and Laurie Patton (Farnham, UK: Ashgate, 2015), 99–112.
5. For a study of such stories see Reiko Ohnuma, *Head, Eyes, Flesh, and Blood: Giving Away the Body in Indian Buddhist Literature* (New York: Columbia University Press, 2007).
6. Ohnuma has argued that the presence or absence of a "field of merit," along with the concomitant variety in virtuous action needed on the part of the hero, is the basis of the distinction between the *jātaka* and *avadāna* genres: *Head, Eyes, Flesh, and Blood*, especially 40–48.
7. See Bob Simpson, "Impossible Gifts: Bodies, Buddhism and Bioethics in Contemporary Sri Lanka," *Journal of the Royal Anthropological Institute* 10, no. 4 (2004): 839–859.
8. Padmanabh S. Jaini, "Tīrthaṅkara-Prakṛti and the Bodhisattva Path," *Journal of the Pali Text Society* 9 (1981): 96–104; and Naomi Appleton, "The Multi-life Stories of Buddha and Mahāvīra: A Comparison," *Buddhist Studies Review* 29, no. 1 (2012): 5–16.
9. On the history and structure of this text see Oskar von Hinüber, *Entstehung und Aufbau der Jātaka-Sammlung* (Stuttgart: Franz Steiner Verlag, 1998).
10. Summaries (in German) of the many narratives found in the Tibetan version of this text, along with extensive notes, can be found in Jampa Losang Panglung, *Die Erzählstoffe des Mūlasarvāstivāda-Vinaya: Analysiert auf Grund der tibetischen Übersetzung*, Studia Philologica Buddhica Monograph Series 3 (Tokyo: Reiyukai Library, 1981).
11. For a study of two other *Jātakamāla* texts see Michael Hahn, *Haribhaṭṭa and Gopadatta: Two Authors in the Succession of Āryaśūra on the Rediscovery of Parts of Their Jātakamālās*, 2nd ed. Studia Philologica Buddhica Occasional Paper series (Tokyo: International Institute for Buddhist Studies, 1992).
12. One such text, mentioning fifty-one *jātaka* stories, is preserved in Khotanese, and a shorter one by Jñānayaśas is found in Sanskrit. See Mark J. Dresden, "The *Jātakastava* or 'Praise of the Buddha's Former Births': Indo-Scythian (Khotanese) Text, English Translation, Grammatical Notes, and Glossaries," *Transactions of the American Philosophical Society* 45, no. 5 (1955): 397–508; and D. R. Shackleton Bailey, trans., "The *Jātakastava* of Jñānayaśas," in *Asiatica: Festschrift Friedrich Weller zum 65*, ed. Johannes Schubert and Ulrich Schneider (Leipzig: Harrassowitz, 1954), 22–29.
13. Daniel Boucher, *Bodhisattvas of the Forest and the Formation of the Mahāyāna: A Study and Translation of the Rāṣṭrapālaparipṛcchā-sūtra*, Studies in the Buddhist Traditions (Honolulu: University of Hawaii Press, 2008); and Ulrich Pagel, *The Bodhisattvapiṭaka: Its Doctrines, Practices and Their Position in Mahāyāna Literature* (Tring, UK: Institute of Buddhist Studies, 1995).
14. On the *jātaka*s at Bharhut see Alexander Cunningham, *The Stūpa of Bharhut* (London: W. H. Allen, 1879), especially 48–82; and Benimadhab Barua, *Barhut, Book II: Jātaka Scenes* (Calcutta: Indian Research Institute, 1934).
15. On Nagarjunakonda and Amaravati see B. Subrahmanyam, *Jātakas in South Indian Art* (Delhi: Bharatiya Kala Prakashan, 2005). Kanaganahalli, also known as Kanganhalli and Kaganhalli, was only discovered in the late 1990s, and work is still under way to identify its many illustrations, but a good preliminary overview and a host of images can be found on the "Kanganhalli, Gulbarga District, Karnataka" page of Christian Luczanits's website. See also Monika Zin, "Narrative Reliefs in Kanaganahalli: Their Importance for Buddhist Studies," *Mārg* 63, no. 1 (2011): 13–21.
16. Isao Kurita, *Gandhāran Art*, 2 vols. (Tokyo: Nigensha, 2003). See also Isao Kurita's blog, *Gandharan Archives Kurita*.

17. Dieter Schlingloff, *Studies in the Ajanta Paintings: Identifications and Interpretations* (Delhi: Ajanta Publications, 1987); and *Guide to the Ajanta Paintings I: Narrative Wall Paintings* (Delhi: Munshiram Manoharlal, 1999).
18. A listing of *jātaka* murals in Dunhuang and elsewhere in China can be found in Alexander Peter Bell, *Didactic Narration: Jātaka Iconography in Dunhuang with a Catalogue of Jataka Representations in China* (Münster, Germany: Litt Verlag, 2000).
19. Luis O. Gómez and Hiram W. Woodward Jr., eds., *Barabuḍur: History and Significance of a Buddhist Monument* (Berkeley, CA: Asian Humanities Press, 1981).
20. Elizabeth Wray, Clare Rosenfield, Dorothy Bailey, and Joe D. Wray, *Ten Lives of the Buddha: Siamese Temple Painting and Jataka Tales* (New York and Tokyo: Weatherhill, 1996).
21. For some beautiful examples of the latter see Peter Skilling, ed., *Past Lives of the Buddha: Wat Si Chum; Art, Architecture and Inscriptions* (Bangkok: River Books, 2008), 72–73.
22. For a detailed study of one such manuscript, with reproductions of all of its illustrations, see Naomi Appleton, Sarah Shaw, and Toshiya Unebe, *Illuminating the Life of the Buddha: An Illustrated Chanting Book from Eighteenth-Century Siam* (Oxford: Bodleian Library, 2013).
23. John Okell, "'Translation' and 'Embellishment' in an Early Burmese *Jātaka* Poem," *Journal of the Royal Asiatic Society of Great Britain and Ireland* 3, no. 4 (1967): 133–148.
24. For example, see Justin McDaniel, "Creative Engagement: *Sujavaṇṇa Wua Luang* and Its Contribution to Buddhist Literature," *Journal of the Siam Society* 88, nos. 1–2 (2000): 156–177.
25. These are the work of Thai American composer Somtow Sucharitkul: DASJATI—The Ten Lives of the Buddha.
26. Robert L. Brown, "Narrative as Icon: The *Jātaka* Stories in Ancient Indian and Southeast Asian Architecture," in *Sacred Biography in the Buddhist Traditions of South and Southeast Asia*, ed. Juliane Schober (Honolulu: University of Hawaii Press, 1997), 64–109.
27. Appleton, Shaw, and Unebe, *Illuminating the Life of the Buddha*.
28. Donald Swearer, *Becoming the Buddha: The Ritual of Image Consecration in Thailand* (Princeton, NJ: Princeton University Press, 2004).
29. Steven Collins, ed., *Readings of the Vessantara Jātaka*, Readings in Buddhist Literature Series (New York: Columbia University Press, 2016).
30. Alfred Foucher, *Notes on the Ancient Geography of Gandhara (A Commentary on a Chapter of Hiuan Tsang)*, trans. from French by H. Hargreaves (Calcutta: Archaeological Survey of India, 1915).
31. For one such scroll, alongside an examination of the wider ritual tradition, see Leedom Lefferts and Sandra Cate, *Buddhist Storytelling in Thailand and Laos: The Vessantara Jataka Scroll and the Asian Civilisations Museum* (Singapore: Asian Civilisations Museum, 2012).
32. Naomi Appleton, *Jātaka Stories in Theravāda Buddhism* (Farnham, UK: Ashgate, 2010), especially 41–64.
33. Naomi Appleton, "In the Footsteps of the Buddha? Women and the Bodhisatta Path in Theravāda Buddhism," *Journal of Feminist Studies in Religion* 27, no. 1 (2011): 33–51.
34. The most comprehensive work of this kind was Ratilal N. Mehta, *Pre-Buddhist India: A Political, Administrative, Economic, Social and Geographical Survey of India Based Mainly on the Jātaka Stories* (Bombay: Examiner, 1939).
35. These studies are helpfully summarized and supplemented in Merlin Peris, *Greek Story Motifs in the Jatakas* (Colombo, Sri Lanka: Godage International, 2004).
36. T. W. Rhys Davids, *Buddhist India* (London: T. Fisher Unwin, 1903), 189, 208. See also his *Buddhist Birth Stories* (London: George Routledge, 1880).
37. In particular, John S. Strong, *The Legend of King Aśoka* (Princeton, NJ: Princeton University Press, 1989), and John S. Strong, *The Legend and Cult of Upagupta* (Princeton, NJ: Princeton University Press, 1992); and Steven Collins, *Nirvana and Other Buddhist Felicities* (Cambridge, UK: Cambridge University Press, 1998).

38. For discussions of how *jātakas* fit into constructions of the bodhisattva path, see Anālayo, *The Genesis of the Bodhisattva Ideal* (Hamburg: Hamburg University Press, 2010); and Appleton, *Jātaka Stories in Theravāda Buddhism*.
39. Ohnuma, *Head, Eyes, Flesh, and Blood*.
40. Most notably Brown, "Narrative as Icon."
41. Swearer, *Becoming the Buddha*.

Naomi Appleton

JEBTSUNDAMBA KHUTUGTUS OF MONGOLIA

THE FIRST KHALKA JEBTSUNDAMBA ZANABAZAR OR ȮNDÜR GEGEN, 1635–1723

The First Khalkha Jebtsundampa (1635–1723)—in Tibetan Lozang tenpé gyeltsen (Blo bzang bstan pa'i rgyal mtshan), in Mongolian Zanabazar and referred to as Ȯndür Gegen ("High Serenity")—was the son of the Khalkha Tüšiyetü Khan Ġombodorji.[1] As a child he was recognized as the reincarnation of Tāranātha (1575–1634), the great master of the Tibetan Jonangpa (Jo nang pa) school.[2] However, soon after he was treated by Gélukpa (dGe lugs pa) as the reincarnation of yet another master, Jamyang chöjé ('Jam dbyangs chos rje) (1379–1449), an important Gélukpa teacher. This recognition was confirmed by the Fifth Dalai Lama (1617–1682) and the Fourth (otherwise called also the First) Panchen Lama (1570–1662). Political plans of influential Tibetan clergy probably shaped this unusual situation of recognizing a boy as a reincarnation of two masters of competing traditions.

According to his biographies, the First Khalkha Jebtsundampa was educated by the Gélukpa teachers. At the beginning, master Nomon Khan or Chökyi gyelpo (Chos kyi rgyal po) from the [Chamdo] Jampa Ling (Chab mdo Byams pa gling) Monastery was invited to participate in his hair-cutting ceremony and to renounce his vows as a lay follower (*dge bsnyen*). The reincarnation of Khédrup sanggyé yéshé (mKhas grub sangs rgyas ye shes) called Wensa trülku (dBen sa sprul sku) acted as his preceptor of ordination. Namkha sönam drakpa (Nam mkha' bsod nams grags pa), master of the tantric college at the Drépung ('Bras spungs) Monastery, was invited to become his tutor. From the biography:

> At the age of fifteen... when he went to the pure fields of Ü (dBus) and Tsang (gTsang) [in Tibet] he was received by the vast processions of monks from all the monasteries... of Kubum (sKu 'bum), and Jakhyung gön (Bya khyung dgon) and Northern Radreng (Ra sgreng) and Rinchen drak (Rin chen brag) and Tangsak ganden chökhor (Thang sag dga' ldan chos 'khor) and Taklung (sTag lung) and the three: Sera and Drépung and Ganden (dGa' ldan), and Trashi lhünpo (bKra shis lhun po).[3]

The First Khalkha Jebtsundampa received many initiations from the Fifth Dalai Lama and the Fourth Panchen Lama. However, not all of them were recorded in his biography.

Backed by the authority of the Tibetan Buddhist teachers, supported by his father and Khalkha nobles, owing to his ancestry of Chinggis Khan as well as equipped with his own charisma, Öndür Gegeen was able to disseminate Buddhism on a considerable scale including the foundation of a new monastery Ribo gégyé ling (Ri bo dge rgyas gling).

The First Jebtsundamba was a personal spiritual guide to many disciples, including those who became the most important Buddhist teachers and reincarnations in Mongolia.[4] He was also a gifted artist who cast in bronze superb religious sculptures.[5] He authored a considerable number of Buddhist texts, some of them on the personal request of his disciples. In the catalog of the "Collected Works" of the First Jebtsundamba, Byambaa Ragchaa listed 125 works.[6] All of them are of religious character. There are many prayers devoted to specific Buddhist deities, practices, and offerings, as well as hymns and reverential prayers dedicated to teachers and prayers for their long lives, including prayers to the Fourth Panchen Lama, First Jebtsundamba's personal teachers, monk colleagues, and disciples (such as Gandan Śiretü, Zaya Pandita); prayers to fulfill teachers' wishes, wishes of lay people such as Cecen Khan; colophons to certain works, such as to the publication of the Buddhist texts, for example, *Aṣṭasahāsrika-prajñāpāramitā*, *Pañcarakṣā*, or *Lam rim chen mo* by Tsongkhapa, "Collected works" of the First (Fourth) Panchen Lama, tables of scripts invented by the First Jebtsundamnba, etc. Among reverential prayers there are also prayers for the rebirth of the very First Jebtsundamba written on request of different persons, including other lamas, monks, and laypeople. There are also supplications for the "swift return" of passed lamas, such as Khanchen Choijal (otherwise known as Lamyn Gegeen), Tāranātha, Panchen Lama, and others.

Legends About Zanabazar and His Consorts. It is not mentioned in his biography by Zaya Pandita, but it belongs to the legendary stories connected with Öndür Gegeen that this Buddhist master had a female consort. She was supposed to be a young girl, about sixteen years old. She was regarded as the emanation of the White Tārā.[7] It is said that owing to his tantric practices with her, Öndür Gegeen was able to cast beautiful female images. In the biography, however, Zaya Pandita referred to the consort perhaps once, as *gcung* (i.e, "younger sibling") with the name Chöpel (Chos 'phel). In the later Mongolian translation of the biography, probably from the 19th century, this name was rendered as Keüken Noyan ("Girl Prince"), which later would be used as the title of the consort.[8] The tradition states that after the passing of this consort, Öndür Gegeen made a sculpture resembling her.[9] He is said also to have had another consort, who was an emanation of the Green Tārā, depicted as having the appearance of a mature woman. Her image is believed to have been preserved as the bronze statue of the Green Tārā also cast by Öndür Gegeen. Another version of the story says that it was the same consort but looking mature.[10]

Political Conflict and the Oirat Attack. Due to political conflicts between Western and Eastern Mongols, the Khalkha lands were attacked by the Oirat Ġaldan Bośuġtu (1644–1697) and the First Jebtsundamba fled to Southern (Inner) Mongolia. Khalkha Mongols and the Jebtsundamba allied with the Manchu emperor Kangxi (r. 1662–1720). Khalkha lands were raided and even Buddhist monasteries were destroyed. The Ribo gégyé ling Monastery was completely demolished. The Erdeni Juu was partly destroyed and rebuilt later. Upon

Ġaldan Bośuġtu's defeat and the Jebtsundamba's return to his homeland, he was regarded as the main religious and political figure of the Khalkha Mongols. He supervised the repair of the damaged Erdeni Juu Monastery. In the following years he built many temples and led Buddhist activity in Khalkha Mongolia (liturgy, monastic robes, tune for recitation, etc.).[11]

The Manchu emperor Kangxi is said to have respected Ȯndür Gegeen. He invited him on several occasions, mainly at New Year, to visit his court (noted in the biography of the First Jebtsundamba). Even if the emperor did it only in order to control the Mongols, nevertheless it was a sign of his interest in Mongolia and its leader. When the emperor died in 1722 the First Jebtsundamba traveled to Beijing to pay his respect, and he died there on February 23, 1723. He was mummified and placed in a reliquary installed in 1728 at Amur Bayasqulangtu Monastery built by the next Manchu emperor in the modern Selenge province in Mongolia.[12]

Soyombo Script and Its Use as a Symbol. Among the creative activities of the First Jebtsundamba there is also the invention of two scripts. One, called today Zanabazar Square script, is not dated, but it was most probably created irst, while the so-called Soyombo, from the Sanskrit Swayambhu ("self-originated"), was invented later, in 1686.[13] The Zanabazar Square script was modeled on the Pakpa lama's ('Phags pa bla ma) square script, but written horizontally. The Soyombo script resembles Lantsa, or the Rañjana script used by the Tibetans. Both scripts, treated as secret and sacred, are syllabic scripts and used to serve as writing systems not only for Mongolian but also for Tibetan and Sanskrit languages, since these two also employ syllabic scripts. The newly invented scripts were much better suited to writing mantras and other ritual texts than the Mongolian script in which there was no differentiation between front and back vowels, which could have resulted in incorrect recitation of the mantras and incorrect effects of the tantric Buddhist rituals.

The significance of the Soyombo script lies in the fact that one of its signs has been accepted as the national symbol and placed on the Mongolian national flag. Therefore the connection between the First Jebtsundamba as an important figure for national identity of the Mongols has been preserved until modern times.

PRE-INCARNATIONS OF THE JEBTSUNDAMBAS IN INDIA AND TIBET

According to reverential prayers (*gsol 'debs*) of Tāranātha composed in the Tibetan language by the First Khalkha Jebtsundamba himself and included in his "Collected Works" (*gsung 'bum*), there were fifteen previous incarnations from the times of the buddha until the Jebtsudamba reincarnation was born in Khalkha Mongolia for the first time. On the basis of diverse versions of reverential prayers, different lists can be made.[14] They vary slightly in the number of incarnations listed and in the way the names of the incarnations are written. However, since the reverential prayer was written by Zanabazar himself, we can assume that it represents reliable tradition. It does not mean that it is a list of historical value, but it is definitely of religious importance. Zanabazar starts counting with Lodrö shintu namdak (Blo gros shin tu rnam dag)—contemporary to the buddha—after which come:

2. Chöpé dorjé (sPyod pa'i rdo rje, otherwise known as Nakpo chöpa, Nag po spyod pa);
3. Raten chenpo (Ra tna chen po);

4. Rongzom chözang (Rong zom chos bzang);
5. Darma wangchuk (Dar ma dbang phyug);
6. Özer pel ('Od zer dpal);
7. Drukdra gyeltsen ('Brug sgra rgyal mtshan);
8. Sanggyé réchen (Sangs rgyas ras chen);
9. Sanggha bhadra (Sang gha bha dra);
10. Jamyang chöjé ('Jam dbyangs chos rje);
11. Chöjé nyinjé (Chos rje nyin byed);
12. Jamgön lama ('Jam mgon bla ma);
13. Gajé sakyong (dGa' byed sa skyong);
14. Jétsün dorjédzin (rJe btsun rdo rje 'dzin), i.e., Tāranātha Künga nyingpo (Kun dga' snying po).

THE SECOND JEBTSUNDAMBA

The Second Jebtsundamba (1724–1758) was born as the son of Efu Chin van Dondovdorji, a son of Chakhundorji, the elder brother of the First Jebtsundamba Zanabazar; thus he was the nephew of the First Jebtsundamba.[15] It can be observed that it was customary to pass headship from uncle to nephew in the system of the Tibetan Buddhist tradition of Sakya (Sa skya). Perhaps it was employed here, as well. His recognition was confirmed in 1727 by the Fifth Panchen Lama Lozang yéshé (Blo bzang ye shes; 1663–1737). The recognition of this incarnation was confirmed also by the Manchu emperor. In 1728 he took initial Buddhist vows and the name Lozang tenpé drönmé (Blo bzang bstan pa'i sgron me). The incarnation of the master of Tongkhor (sTong 'khor) entitled Mañjuśrī (Modern Mong. Donkhor Manzshir), by the name of Ngakwang jampel tendzin (Ngag dbang 'jam dpal bstan 'dzin; 1695–1750) from Kuku nor was invited to become the tutor of the Second Jebtsundamba.[16] Due to the Jungar invasion on Khalkha in 1731, the Jebtsundamba traveled to Dolonnur.[17] In 1736 he went to Beijing, and after the meeting with the Manchu emperor, he returned to Khalkha.[18]

Thanks to funds provided by Lifan Yuan, the Jebtsundamba continued the religious work of the First Jebtsundamba by expanding the monasteries in the Boġda Gegeen's estate called Khüriye.[19] In 1739 he established the college of tantra called Déchen sangngak ling (bDe chen gsang sngags gling) and later introduced there the rites of Hayagriva; he founded the monastery of Manjushri Lama (in Modern Mongolia: Manzshir Lamyn Khiid) in 1750 and the college of philosophy (*mtshan nyid*) called Trashi chöpel (bKra shis chos phel) in 1756.[20]

His popularity and growing influence upon the Mongols and at the same time independence from the Qing dynasty met with the displeasure of the Qianlong emperor, who attempted to put an end to it and to suppress Jebtsundamba's freedom of movement inside Khalkha Mongolia, allowing him only to visit the Erdeni Juu Monastery. During the Chinggünjab's rebellion (1756–1757) the Jebtsundamba played an ambiguous role. He is said to have held secret talks with the Russians against the Manchus while in 1757 he openly led an assembly of Khalkha Mongols to reiterate loyalty to the Qing dynasty. He died in 1758 of smallpox, although there were rumors that the Manchus caused his death.[21] There are practically no works written by the Second Jebtsundamba; only two titles are recorded.[22]

THE THIRD TO SEVENTH JEBTSUNDAMBAS

In order to prevent the merging of religion and secular power by the Mongols, Manchu authorities forbade searching for the Jebtsundamba incarnations in Mongolia. Starting with the third incarnation, all subsequent rebirths of the Jebtsundambas were recognized among the Tibetans. Khalkha nobles requested the emperor to dissolve the Jebtsundamba estate in Khalkha and move his seat to Dolonnor, but the request was not fulfilled.

The Third Jebtsundamba, Yéshé tenpé nyima (Ye shes bstan pa'i nyi ma; 1758–1773), was found in the family of the prince of Lithang and recognized by the Sixth Panchen Lama Lozang penden yéshé (Blo bzang dpal ldan ye shes; 1738–1780).[23] The Third Jebtsundamba was taken first to Jehol where he paid respects to the Manchu emperor. He took his ordination from Changkya Rölpé dorjé (lCang skya rol pa'i rdo rje; 1717–1786). Nomön khen Jampel dorjé (No mon khan 'jam dpal rdo rje) became his tutor. He was brought to Khalkha in 1760. Tibetan physician Lozang norbu (Blo bzang nor bu), titled in Mongolian Darqan emči, who came with him from Tibet, founded the medical college. In 1763 the Third Jebtsundamba was enthroned. In the same year the Dambadarjalin (Tib. bsTan pa dar rgyas gling) Monastery was founded. The Jebtsundamba died in 1773.

The Fourth Jebtsundamba, Lozang tupten wangchuk jikmé gyatso pelzangpo (Blo bzang thub bstan dbang phyug 'jigs med rgya mtsho dpal bzang po; 1775–1813), was recognized in the family of the elder brother of the Dalai Lama.[24] His recognition was confirmed by the Sixth Panchen Lama Lozang penden yéshé (Blo bzang dpal ldan ye shes; 1738–1780) who also taught him the script. The Eighth Dalai Lama Jampel gyatso ('Jam dpal rgya mtsho; 1758–1804) bestowed on him his religious name and gave him teachings on sutra and tantra. In 1781 the Jebtsundamba headed to Khalkha. From Changkya rölpé dorjé yéshé tenpé drönmé (lCang skya Rol pa'i rdo rje ye shes bstan pa'i sgron me; 1717–1786) he took his novice monk's vows and was given the name Lozang gélek rapgyé (Blo bzang dge legs rab rgyas). He was enthroned in 1781. Ngakwang trinlé (Ngag dbang 'phrin las) from Drépung Monastery's Gomang (sGo mang) college became his tutor.[25] In 1803 the Fourth Jebtsundamba traveled to Tibet where he paid homage to the Eighth Dalai Lama and the Sixth Panchen Lama. He visited Sera, Drépung, and Ganden monasteries. In 1804 he received initiation into the Kālacakra-tantra and in 1805 brought these teachings from Tibet and introduced the Kālacakra-tantra and its practices in Khalkha Mongolia. Then Gachen yéshé chöpel (dGa' chen ye shes chos phel) was appointed to serve with his knowledge on Kālacakra in Mongolia. In 1806 the Kālacakra college was built, called in short in Mongolian Dechin galaw (bDe chen skal pa). The tantric college erected earlier by the Second Jebtsundamba was given a new name, Badam Yoga. In 1809 the Fourth Jebtsundamba built the facilities for a *choir* (*chos grwa*) college. Also, in 1809 he founded a college called in Modern Mongolian Gungaachoilin (Kun dga' chos gling) with a monastery curriculum (Modern Mong. *igchaa*, Tib. *yig cha*) of Panchen Sönam drakpa (bSod nams grags pa).

Due to his travels in Tibet, the Fourth Jebtsundamba was able to bring with him to Khalkha many religious objects. He also made several trips to China, including Beijing, where he died while returning from a pilgrimage to Wutaishan.[26] He composed many religious texts (517 titles).[27] All of the texts are religious writings, usually very short, often consisting of one or two pages, and sometimes just several verses. They comprise:

- prayers to Buddhist teachers, including texts on *guru-yoga* meditation (aimed at mingling of one's mind with his teacher's mind) such as referring to the First Jebtsundamba;
- reverential and longevity prayers, for example, devoted to Akya Khutugtu Lozang jamyang gyatso (Blo bzang 'jam dbyangs rgya mtsho);
- prayers to Tsongkhapa, Atiśa;
- prayers written on request of individuals, monks, and laypersons, for example, Tuśiyetu Khan tséten dorje (Tshe brtan rdo rje), Ahas gung tséwang dorje (Tshe dbang rdo rje), and others;
- supplications for the "swift return" of lamas, such as Noyon Khutugtu;
- rebirth stories, for example, of Dariganga Mergen Khutugtu;
- prayers to bodhisattvas and Buddhist deities including Vajrapāṇi, Mahākāla, Yamāntaka, Kālacakra, Tāra, Heruka, Palden Lhamo, Marici, and others;
- hymns to deities and lamas, such as Longdöl Lama;
- colophons to editions of Buddhist texts, such as longer and shorter versions of *Prajñāpāramitā* texts, *Bhadrakalpika-sūtra*, etc.;
- all kinds of offerings and consecrations, including sang (*bsangs*) offerings;
- prayers written at certain places, such as devoted to Mañjuśrī prayer written in Wutaishan, or to Vajrabhairava in the Drépung Monastery;

and other texts connected with Buddhist practice.

The Fifth Jebtsundamba was called Lozang tsültrim jikmé tenpé gyeltsen pelzangpo (Blo bzang tshul khrims 'jigs med bstan pa'i rgyal mtshan dpal bzang po; 1815–1841).[28] He was born in a family of commoners in Tibet and recognized by the Seventh Panchen Lama Tenpé nyima (bsTan pa'i nyi ma; 1782–1853). He was enthroned in 1820. A scholar with the *géshé* (*dge bshed*) degree obtained from the Losel ling (Blo gsal gling) college of the Drépung Monastery (in Mong. Loosolin gewsh), a specialist in tantra and medicine, Lozang jamyang (Blo bzang 'jam dbyangs), became his tutor. At the age of sixteen the Fifth Jebtsundamba received his novice vows. He continued the activities of the previous incarnations by expanding religious buildings in the Khüriye compound. He erected the Maidar süme (i.e., temple of Maitreya) with a huge statue of the Maitreya Buddha inside. He also sponsored copying of the so called Gold Kanjur part of the Buddhist canon, in Baruun Choir Monastery. At twenty-one years of age the Fifth Jebtsundamba went to Lhasa and visited the Seventh Panchen Lama. Back in Khalkha in 1838 he founded the Gandantegchenling Monastery (dGa' ldan theg chen gling) and renovated the temple of Khajid (Tib. Na ro mkha' spyod ma; Skt. Vajrayoginī) and established a permanent service there. He bestowed the initiation of Kālacakra to his disciples and Buddhist followers. He died in 1841 on the way to Lhasa. He authored over forty religious texts.[29] They do not differ in character from the compositions written by previously mentioned Jebtsundambas.

The Sixth Jebtsundamba Lozang tenpé gyeltsen (Blo bzang bstan pa'i rgyal mtshan; 1843–1848) was born in Tibet and recognized by the Seventh Panchen Lama.[30] At the age of six he was brought to Khalkha and enthroned but soon after died of smallpox.

The Seventh Jebtsundamba Ngakwang chökyi wangchuk trinlé gyatso (Ngag dbang chos kyi dbang phyug 'phrin las rgya mtsho; 1850–1868) was born in Tibet. His recognition was confirmed by both the Seventh Panchen Lama and the Ninth Dalai Lama (1838–1855).[31]

At the age of six he was brought to Khalkha and enthroned. According to the reports about his life, he overcame the shamanic powers of Sečen Khan Ardasida and was therefore greatly revered by him. However, he was said to have been influenced by the bad habits of the khan's sons, spending time engaged in archery, drinking, and smoking.[32] He composed religious texts, of which just a few survive.[33] He died when he was nineteen years old.

THE EIGHTH JEBTSUNDAMBA

The Eighth Jebtsundamba Ngakwang lozang chökyi nyima tendzin wangchuk (Ngag dbang blo bzang chos kyi nyi ma bstan 'dzin dbang phyug; 1869–1924) was born in Lhasa in the family of the Dalai Lama's officials.[34] Although Mongols hoped for the incarnation to be found in Mongolia, the Manchu emperor decided to recognize a child from Tibet.[35] He was brought to Khalkha in 1874 together with his parents. From early childhood he was interested in mechanical devices and illustrated magazines from Russia. He also had a private zoo and a collection of stuffed animals.[36] After the death of his mother he is said to have become rebellious.[37]

The accounts of the eighth incarnation are very contradictory as a result of the sources being conflicted parties. Russian and communist sources depict him in a very critical way and present an image of a very spoiled child, a rebellious young man, and finally a despot who demanded all his wishes to be granted. On the other hand, Buddhist sources see in him a great Buddhist master while some Mongolian sources make him a fighter for Mongolian independence, a skillful ruler who went all the way to promote Mongolian national identity even though he was ethnically Tibetan.

The Eighth Jebtsundamba was active as a Buddhist master. Owing to his religious studies he passed exams and received the title of *gachu* (*dga' bcu*) in 1908. In 1910 he ordered the printing of the Tibetan Kanjur, an edition called Urga Kanjur.[38] In 1911–1913 the enormous statue of Bodhisattva Avalokiteśvara called in modern Mongolian Migjid Janraisig was built and installed in the Gandantegchenlin Monastery. In 1912 the Jebtsundamba founded a *tsanid* college called Idgaachoizinlin (Yid dga' chos 'dzin gling) with a monastic curriculum of Chökyi gyeltsen (Chos kyi rgyal mtshan; 1469–1544) from the Sera college in Tibet.[39]

The Eighth Jebtsundamba composed 149 Buddhist works.[40] Among them there are *guru-yoga* meditations, reverential and longevity prayers to teachers, supplications for the "swift return" of passed lamas, offering prayers, texts necessary for Buddhist practices such as on making offerings, monastery regulations, etc. There are also several works advising (*bslab bya*) disciples, a hymn to Milarepa, verses to be included in the manual of the ritual *tsam* dance of Ikh Khuree (or Urga), a colophon to the Urga edition of Kanjur, etc. Not included in his "Collected Works" were, among others, *lung bstan* or prophecies.[41]

The Eighth Jebtsundamba had mistresses and consorts. The first mistress, Norow, was said to be the wife of Tserendorji Gung, one of his officials.[42] The second important woman was called Dondogdulam (or, according to some, Dondogdulham; 1874–1923).[43] She became his officially accepted consort, enthroned in 1902. She was regarded as the emanation of the White Tārā and also called Eke Dagina ("mother ḍākinī"). There were rumors that the Eighth Boġda Gegeen and his consort adopted a boy called Lamjaa.[44] After the death of Dondogdulam the Jebtsundamba had yet another consort.[45]

Even though he was ethnically Tibetan, the Boġda Gegeen was engaged in political activities against the Manchu Qing dynasty in Mongolia. Backed by Russia on December 29, 1911, even before the collapse of the Manchu rule in China, Bogda Gegeen was enthroned as Boġda Khaġan (modern Bogd Khaan). His era was called *Olan-a ergügdegsen* or "Elevated by Many," similarly to Mahāsaṃmata—according to Buddhist tradition the first legendary ruler of mankind. In 1913 an important document on Tibeto-Mongolian relations was signed by the representatives of both sides. Although focused on the financial side of the relations (such as bank warranties, loans, etc.), the document included references to independent Mongolia and independent Tibet, which were a novelty in the political situation of both countries until monitored by the Qing dynasty.[46]

Boġda Khaġan promulgated several political prophecies that served as tools during his rule.[47] The status of autonomy lasted until 1919 when the Chinese were able to regain control over Mongolia. However, in 1920 with Boġda Khaġan's approval, the army of the White Russians led by Baron Roman Fedorovich von Ungern-Sternberg (1886–1921) defeated the Chinese and in January 1921 helped to restore Boġda Khaġan's rule.[48] Soon after, in July 1921, the Red Army backed the Mongolian People's Party and overthrew Baron Sternberg's government. Boġda Khaġan was enthroned as the constitutional monarch of the People's Government, though with no actual power.[49] After his death in 1924 the search for the ninth incarnation of the Jebtsundamba was prohibited, since he might claim to be the rightful ruler, unite Mongolian Buddhists, and receive support to fight against the new communist regime.

There were several attempts by the Mongols to recognize the ninth incarnation, but all people involved were persecuted. Penalties included death in the so-called *38-yn esergüü khereg* (i.e., the case of the 38 [opponents] of [the revolution]) and the *Töw baigullaga* (i.e., the central organization).

There were also plans conceived by the Japanese to restore the ninth incarnation of the Jebtsundamba in Inner Mongolia in order to unite Mongols who were divided politically between Russia, China, and Japan with the slogans of the pan-Mongolian movement under Japanese political power.[50] However, all those attempts were unsuccessful.

THE NINTH JEBTSUNDAMBA

The Ninth Jebtsundamba was called Jampel namdröl chökyi gyeltsen ('Jam dpal rnam grol chos kyi rgyal mtshan; 1932–2012). Independent of Mongolian attempts, the search for the ninth incarnation of the Jebtsundamba was also conducted in Tibet.[51] A son of the Thirteenth Dalai Lama's guard born in 1932 was recognized in 1936 as the reincarnation of the Eighth Khalkha Jebtsundamba by Radreng rinpoché (Rwa sgreng rin po che), better known in the English language sources as Reting Rinpoche, the Fourteenth Dalai Lama's regent at that time. The boy's identity was kept secret due to the situation in Mongolia. At the age of seven the Jebtsundamba received novice vows from Reting Rinpoche, entered the Drépung Monastery's Gomang college in Tibet, and studied there for fourteen years. Since his identity was kept secret he could not enter the Khalkha division of the monastery. In the 1940s Reting Rinpoche was replaced and later arrested and the Jebtsundamba lost his mentor. At the age of twenty-one the Jebtsundamba left the monastery and started practicing *chö* (*gcod*) meditations.

At the age of twenty-five he renounced his vows, married, and started a family. When the Chinese occupation of Tibet began, the Jebtsundamba escaped into exile in India and continued to lead a layman's life in Darjeeling and Mysore with his family. Later he moved to Phendeling Tibetan Settlement at Mainpat in Madhya Pradesh. In the late 1980s he went to Tibet and was involved in the restoration of the Ganden püntsok ling (dGa' ldan Phun tshogs gling) Monastery, which had been devastated by the Chinese occupation. In 1990 he returned to India to Dharamsala and was officially recognized by the Dalai Lama as the Ninth Jebtsundamba.

Following the collapse of the Soviet Union and with the newly established religious freedom in Mongolia, in 1991 the Dalai Lama gave official recognition and acknowledgment to the Ninth Khalkha Jebtsundamba as the spiritual head of Buddhism in Mongolia through the Department of Religious Affairs, Central Tibetan Administration. In 1997 he was enthroned as the spiritual head of the Jo nang pa tradition of Tibetan Buddhism. His prime responsibility was to preserve the Jo nang pa tradition of the *Kālacakra-tantra*. In Dharamsala he established Takten House to conduct religious activities there.

The Ninth Jebtsundamba paid his first visit to Mongolia between October 29, 2009, and November 19, 2009. He visited many monasteries in Ulan Bator and the countryside and gave numerous teachings including initiations and oral transmissions of texts. His second visit began on May 19, 2010. In addition to his previous activities, the Ninth Jebtsundamba performed special *chö* rites and donated 16 million *tugrigs* (Mong. currency) for children with cancer. On August 18, 2010, the Ninth Jebtsundamba became a citizen of Mongolia. The Ninth Jebtsundamba issued a document containing nine principles of preserving nature: (1) pray to the three supreme jewels (buddha, dharma, sangha), (2) acquire knowledge of the environment and the ecology, (3) live simply, (4) be environmentally friendly, (5) facilitate a healthy envinronment for healthy living, (6) save water, which is precious as a wish-fulfilling gem and which nurtures life and the elements, (7) love and protect animals, (8) conserve and restore the forest, and (9) use underground resources and minerals properly.[52]

After falling ill he was visited by numerous followers—Mongolian incarnations as well as Tibetan incarnated lamas from India. The former Mongolian prime minister Batbold and President Elbegdorj also paid him visits. On March 1, 2012, the Ninth Jebtsundamba passed away. Work on the mummification of the Ninth Jebtsundamba was done by a specialist from the Losel ling college of the Drépung Monastery (revived in India by exile Tibetans).

THE TENTH JEBTSUNDAMBA

On November 23, 2016, the current Dalai Lama announced that the tenth reincarnation of the Jebtsundamba Khutugtu had been found in Mongolia. However, the boy would not be publicly enthroned due to his young age.[53]

YEKE SHABI—ESTATE OF THE JEBTSUNDAMBAS AND ITS ECONOMIC IMPACT

The Jebtsundampas had their estate and subjects. The subjects called *shabi* (plural *shabi nar* "disciples") with their livestock formed a property called Yeke Shabi ("Great Shabi"). The Jebtsundamba estate and shabi nar's affairs were administrated by a treasurer (Mong. *shangjodba*), later on helped by yet another administrator called *da lama*. The property of the Jebtsundamba was gradually growing and amounted to 55,000–90,000 heads of livestock and 90,000–115,000 subjects along with their herds and lands from 1800 to 1865.[54] Later the property began to decrease due to debts paid to Chinese merchants.[55] After the death of the Eighth Jebtsundamba, his property was confiscated by the state. Nevertheless, the economic power of the Jebtsundambas was an important factor in shaping the political situation of Mongolia in the 19th and 20th centuries.

RELIGIOUS AND POLITICAL IMPACT OF THE JEBTSUNDAMBAS

Starting with the First Khalkha Jebtsundamba, the growing religious authority and political role of the Jebtsundambas backed by Manchu policy made this line of reincarnations the central religious power in Khalkha Mongolia. This fact is of current relevance due to the revival of Buddhism in Mongolia since 1990. In communist times Zanabazar was blamed for the political dependence of the Mongols to the Manchus, but the political situation of the Mongols in the 17th century and the role played by the First Jebtsundamba are being reassessed. Zanabazar's impact on the dissemination of Buddhism and development of Mongolian culture, his authority (which united the Mongols), and his patriotism have been acknowledged. In the age of revival of Buddhism among the Mongols, Zanabazar is regarded as a spiritual leader who added elements of Mongolian national identity to Tibetan Buddhism.

Having great religious authority supported by steady economic income, the Jebtsundambas had the potential to gain political power. Gradually this situation changed the configuration of religious and lay powers in Mongolia and resulted in the 20th century in the hierocratic rule of the Eighth Jebtsundamba in the moment of gaining independence by the Mongols in 1911. In modern Mongolia the Ninth Jebtsundamba played an important role in the dissemination of Buddhism and in uniting different groups of Mongolian Buddhists. Although some sections of the society feared the Jebtsundamba's possible claim over the rule in the country and restoration of the constitutional monarchy, it did not happen. The role of the future Jebtsundambas is yet to be seen, but this line of reincarnations during more than 300 years of its presence in Mongolia has gained special potential.

REVIEW OF LITERATURE

The Jebtsundamba incarnations in Khalkha Mongolia have been the objects of scholarly works of many researchers. There has not, however, been equal treatment of all the incarnations: the most attention was devoted to the First and Eighth Jebtsundambas, who both lived for a considerably long time and who had a great impact not only on Buddhism practiced by the Mongols but also on political events—being, former de facto and the latter in reality, leaders of the Khalkha Mongols—affecting other Mongols as well.

Researchers had access to various primary sources: some used only Mongolian biographies and documents, others Mongolian and Tibetan sources; many wrote their works based only on translations of the sources. Therefore, in their works we can find many repetitions of not always reliable information.

Among hundreds of works devoted to different aspects of the Jebtsundambas in Mongolia, several are of special importance, particularly since they were written in European languages and subsequently often quoted. Aleksei Pozdneev, one of the greatest world Mongolists, devoted a separate book entitled *Urginskie khutukhty* ("The Khutugtus of Urga," 1880) to the subject. Also in his memoirs from expeditions to Mongolia, *Mongoliia i Mongoly* (1896; English translation *Mongolia and the Mongols*, 1971–1977), he included reports on the Jebtsundambas.[56] However, his works are based primarily on Mongolian biographies and informants, which can sometimes be misleading. For example, while describing the First Jebtsundamba, Pozdneev mentions that he returned from Tibet with an entourage of 600 people, while the Tibetan biography written by his disciple Zaya Pandita talks about only fifty religious specialists brought from Tibet to Khalkha Mongolia.[57] Pozdneev is also convinced that the First Jebtsundamba visited the monastery of his previous incarnation, i.e., the Jonangpa master Tāranātha, and brought scriptures, including a precious *Aṣṭasahāsrika-prajñāpāramitā* manuscript from there, while in his Tibetan biography written by Zaya Pandita there is no such information.[58] It is possible that it was not included due to Zaya Pandita's self-censorship resulting from his devotion to the Gélukpas. Since Pozdneev's works were often used and quoted as reliable sources of information, such inaccuracies easily spread, as in the works by Morris Rossabi and Patricia Berger and in the monograph *Mongolia: The Legacy of Chingis Khan*.[59] Both contributions regarding the Jebtsundambas contain in general accurate data, based, however, on selected secondary materials and translations of primary sources. Also, in the evaluation of the Eighth Jebtsundamba, it seems that his bad reputation maintained by the communists and popularized in their publications took priority over other works and reports.

Communist propagandists attempted to discredit the Eighth Jebtsundamba in many ways. One such publication was edited by Ts. Damdinsüren as memoirs of the Jebtsundamba's servant, also published in English translation by C. R. Bawden as *Tales of an Old Lama*.[60] Needless to say, it included only the stories portraying the Jebtsundamba in a negative light. The First Jebtsundamba depicted by the communists as a traitor was discussed by Ch. Kaplonski in his *Truth, History and Politics in Mongolia: The Memory of Heroes*.[61]

Important input into the evaluation of original sources was provided by Junko Miyawaki in her article "How Legends Developed About the First Jebtsundamba: In Reference to the Khalkha Mongol Submission to the Manchus in the Seventeenth Century."[62]

The most accurate and informative work on the Jebtsundambas in English so far are Chris Atwood's entries on the Jebtsundambas in his *Encyclopedia of Mongolia and Mongol Empire*.[63] Although he also included information on Zanabazar's visit to Tāranātha's monastery and him bringing books from there as well as critical remarks on the Eighth Jebtsundamba's conduct, he did so in a more balanced way than other authors.

Mongolian authors have published numerous works on the Jebtsundambas. Among them Sh. Bira's modern Mongolian rendering of biographies of the First Jebtsundamba originally written in classical Mongolian or Tibetan language deserves mention as a very valuable work.[64] Translation of the Tibetan biography of the First Jebtsundamba into modern Mongolian is also included in the work on Lamyn Gegeen by L. Terbish.[65] A very useful publication is a collection of short biographies of all Jebtsundambas together with the catalog of their works published by R. Byambaa.[66] Batsaikhan Ookhnoi published a monograph on the Eighth Jebtsundamba in Mongolian, translated also into English: *Bogdo Jebtsundamba Khutuktu, the Last King of Mongolia* (2009).

There are also Chinese and Japanese publications—for example, by Ishihama Yumiko (*Tibet Bukkyo sekai no rekisiteki kenkyu*, 2001 and other works) and J. Chengxiu (*Shiliu, shiqi, shiji Menggu zhengzhi gaige lun yu Zangchuan fojiao-yi Tumote, Kaerka zuoyi wei zhongxin*, 2002). They have not been discussed here due to the author's lack of knowledge of these languages.

PRIMARY SOURCES

Original sources can be divided between biographies written in Mongolian, biographies written in Tibetan, and other documents written in different languages.

Mongolian biographies of the Jebtsundambas were published in the following publications:

Bawden, Charles. *The Jebtsundamba Khutukhtus of Urga: Text, Translation and Notes*, Vol. 9. Asiatische Forschungen. Wiesbaden, Germany: Otto Harrassowitz, 1961.

Bira, Sh. *Öndör gegeeniĭn namtruud orshwoĭ*. Ulaanbaatar, Mongolia: n.p., 1995.

"History of Erdeni Ju or, Biography of the First Jetsundampa ZanabazarInformation About a Mongolian Manuscript Kept in the Kotwicz Collection at the Archive of Science in Cracow, Poland (K-III-19, j. 69a)." In *In the Heart of Mongolia: 100th Anniversary of W. Kotwicz's Expedition to Mongolia in 1912 (Studies and Selected Source Materials)*. Edited by Jerzy Tulisow, Osamu Inoue, Agata Bareja-Starzyńska, and Ewa Dziurzyńska, 385–391. Cracow, Poland: Polska Akademia Umiejętności, 2012.

Khürelbaġatur, L. *Öndör gegeen-ü namtar*. Kökeqota, China: Öbör mongγol-un aradun keblel-ün khuriy-a, 2009.

Tibetan biographies of the Jebtsundambas were published in the following publications:

Bareja-Starzyńska, Agata. *The Biography of the First Khalkha Jetsundampa Zanabazar by Zaya Pandita Luvsanprinlei: Studies, Annotated Translation, Transliteration and Facsimile*. Warsaw: Dom Wydawniczy Elipsa, Faculty of Oriental Studies, University of Warsaw, 2015.

Byambaa, Ragchaagiin, ed. *The Collected Works/gsung 'bum/of Blo bzang 'phrin las*. Ulaanbaatar, Mongolia: Mongol Bilig Series, 2004.

Byambaa, Ragchaagiin, ed. *Collected Works of Jebzundampa Khutukhts of Khalkha, I Rje btzun Dam pa Blo bzang bstan pa'i rgyal mtsan, II Rje btzun Dam pa Blo bzang bstan pa'i sgron me, III Rje btzun Dam pa Blo bzang bstan pa'i Ye shes bstan pa'i nyi ma*. Vol. 1. Ulaanbaatar, Mongolia: Mongol Bilig Series, 2004.

Byambaa, Ragchaagiin, ed. *The Collected Biographies of Jebzundampa Khutugtus of Khalkha*. Ulaanbaatar, Mongolia: Mongol Bilig Series, 2006.

Chandra, Lokesh. *Materials for a History of Tibetan Literature*. Vol. 28–30, Part 2, Śata-Piṭaka Series. New Delhi: International Academy of Indian Culture, 1963.

Chandra, Lokesh. *Dharmatāla's Annals of Tibet*. Vol. 225. Śata-Piṭaka Series. New Delhi: Sharada Rani, 1975.

Chandra, Lokesh. *Works of Jaya-pandita Blo-bzang-'phrin-las*. Vols. 1–4, Vols. 278–281. Śata-Piṭaka Series. New Delhi: International Academy of Indian Culture, 1981.

Chandra, Lokesh. *Life and Works of Jebtsundampa I*. Vol. 294, Śata-Piṭaka Series. New Delhi: International Academy of Indian Culture, 1982.

Other documents connected with the lives of the Jebtsundambas were published by Batsaikhan, Emgent Ookhnoi. *Bogdo Jebtsundamba Khutuktu, The Last King of Mongolia, Mongolia's National Revolution of 1911*. Ulaanbaatar, Mongolia: Admon, 2009.

DIGITAL MATERIALS

Buddhist Digital Resource Center (http://www.tbrc.org/) (formerly TBRC Tibetan Buddhist Resource Center).

Lulu, Jichang. Thinking Outside the Urn: China and the Reincarnation of Mongolia's Highest Lama (https://jichanglulu.wordpress.com/2017/03/21/urn/).

Nine Principles to Protect Environment by the Ninth Jebtsundamba (http://siteresources.worldbank.org/INTEAPREGTOPENVIRONMENT/Resources/TheMongolianBuddhistEightYearConservationPlanEnglishandMongolian.pdf).

Pandey, Anshuman. Proposal to Encode the Zanabazar Square Script in ISO/IEC 10646 (http://www.unicode.org/L2/L2014/14024-zanabazar-square.pdf).

FURTHER READING

Atwood, Christopher P. *Encyclopedia of Mongolia and Mongol Empire*. New York: Facts on File, 2004.

Bareja-Starzyńska, Agata. *The Biography of the First Khalkha Jetsundampa Zanabazar by Zaya Pandita Luvsanprinlei*. Studies, Annotated Translation, Transliteration and Facsimile. Warsaw: Dom Wydawniczy Elipsa, Faculty of Oriental Studies, University of Warsaw, 2015.

Bawden, Charles. *The Modern History of Mongolia*. London: Kegan Paul International, 1968.

Bawden, Charles. *Tales of an Old Lama*. Translated with notes by C. R. Bawden from a Mongolian text recorded and edited by Ts. Damdinsüren (Zhambal Boryn, *Öwgön Jambalyn yariya*). Tring, UK: Institute of Buddhist Studies, 1997.

Berger, Patricia. "After Xanadu: The Mongol Renaissance of the Sixteenth to Eighteenth Centures." In *Mongolia: The Legacy of Chinggis Khan*. Edited by Patricia Berger and Terese Tse Bartholomew, 50–75. San Francisco: Thames & Hudson, 1995.

Byambaa, Ragchaagiin. *The Bibliographical Guide of Mongolian Writers in the Tibetan Language and the Mongolian Translators*. Vol. 1. Ulaanbaatar, Mongolia: Mongol Bilig Series, 2004.

Christopher, Kaplonski. *Truth, History and Politics in Mongolia: The Memory of Heroes*. London: Routledge Curzon, 2004.

Klafkowski, Piotr, and Damchö Gyatso Choje. *Rosary of White Lotuses, Being a Clear Account of How the Precious Teaching of Buddha Appeared and Spread in the Great Hor Country*. Vol. 95. Asiatsiche Forschungen. Wiesbaden, Germany: Otto Harrassowitz, 1987

Miyawaki, Junko. "How Legends Developed About the First Jebtsundamba: In Reference to the Khalkha Mongol Submission to the Manchus in the Seventeenth Century." *Memoires of the Research Department of the Toyo Bunko*, no. 52 (1994): 45–67.

Pozdneev, Aleksei M. *Mongoli͡ia i Mongoly*. Saint Petersburg, Russia: Tipografiya Imperatorskoi Akademii Nauk, 1896.

Pozdneev, Aleksei M. *Mongolia and the Mongols*. Vol. 61. Uralic and Altaic Series. Edited by J. R. Krueger (Part 1–1971, Part 2–1977, translation of the *Mongoli͡ia i Mongoly* 1896). Bloomington: Indiana University Publications.

Pozdneev, Aleksei M. *Religion and Ritual in the Society: Lamaist Buddhism in Late 19th Century Mongolia*. Edited by J. R. Krueger. Bloomington, IN: The Mongolia Society, 1978.

Sárközi, Alice. *Political Prophecies in Mongolia in the 17–20th Centuries*. Wiesbaden, Germany: Otto Harrassowitz, 1992.

Teleki, Krisztina. *Monasteries and Temples of Bogdiin Khüree*. Ulaanbaatar, Mongolia: Institute of History, Mongolian Academy of Sciences, 2011.

Uranchimeg, Ts. "Zanabazaryn urlag ba dundad zuuny khojuu üeiin mongol." In *Mongolyn ikh khüree khiidiin buddyn shashny urlag*, 47–85. Ulaanbaatar, Mongolia: BCI Khewleliin kompani, 2016.

NOTES

1. Data on the First Jebtsundamba are based primarily on the biography composed by the Khalkha Zaya Pandita; see Agata Bareja-Starzyńska, *The Biography of the First Khalkha Jetsundampa Zanabazar by Zaya Pandita Luvsanprinlei. Studies, Annotated Translation, Transliteration and Facsimile* (Warsaw: Dom Wydawniczy Elipsa, Faculty of Oriental Studies, University of Warsaw, 2015). See also Christopher T. Atwood, *Encyclopedia of Mongolia and Mongol Empire* (New York: Facts on File, 2004), 272–273; Ragchaagiin Byambaa, *The Bibliographical Guide of Mongolian Writers in the Tibetan Language and the Mongolian Translators*, vol. 1 (Ulaanbaatar, Mongolia: Mongol Bilig Series, 2004), 5–56.
2. On the issue of the Jo nang pa and Dge lugs pa conflict and its influence on the recognition of the First Khalkha Jebtsundamba, see Cyrus Stearns, *The Buddha from Dolpo: A Study of the Life and Thought of the Tibetan Master Dolpopa Sherab Gyaltsen*, SUNY Series in Buddhist Studies (Albany: State University of New York Press, 1999); Bareja-Starzyńska, *Biography*; Gene Smith, "Introduction," in *The Autobiography of the First Panchen Lama Blo-bzang chos-kyi-rgyal-mtshan*, ed. Ngawang Gelek Demo with an English introduction by E. G. Smith, Gedan Sungrab Minyam Gyuphel Series, vol. 12 (New Delhi: SOMLAI, 1969).
3. Bareja-Starzyńska, *Biography*, 109–110, original text: 425.
4. Bareja-Starzyńska, 178–186, original text: 538–546.
5. Patricia Berger, "After Xanadu: The Mongol Renaissance of the Sixteenth to Eighteenth Centuries," in *Mongolia: The Legacy of Chinggis Khan*, ed. Patricia Berger and Terese Tse Bartholomew (San Francisco: Thames & Hudson, 1995), 50–75; Ts. Uranchimeg, "Zanabazaryn urlag ba dundad zuuny khojuu üeiin mongol," in *Mongolyn ikh khüree khiidiin buddyn shashny urlag* (Ulaanbaatar, Mongolia: BCI Khevleliin kompani, 2016), 51–86.
6. Ragchaagiin Byambaa, *The Bibliographical Guide*, nos. 00001–00125, 5–56.
7. Berger, "After Xanadu," 59; Charles Bawden, *The Modern History of Mongolia* (London: Kegan Paul International, 1968), 57.
8. Bareja-Starzyńska *Biography*, 173–174n563; original text 518–522.
9. Berger, "After Xanadu," 59.
10. Berger, 59.
11. Atwood, *Encyclopedia*, 272.
12. Atwood, 272–273; he mentioned also that there were rumors that the First Jebtsundamba was poisoned in Beijing.
13. For Soyombo, see Gyorgy Kara, *Books of the Mongolian Nomads: More Than Eight Centuries of Writing* (Bloomington: Indiana University, Research Institute for Inner Asian Studies, 2005); Shagdarsürüng Tseweeliin, *Mongolchuudyn üseg bichigiin towchoon*, Bibliotheca Mongolica: Monograph 1 (Ulaanbaatar, Mongolia: Center for Mongolian Studies, National University of Mongolia, 2001). For Zanabazar Square script, see Ragchaagiin Byambaa, *Zanabazaryn dörwöljin üseg* (Ulaanbaatar, Mongolia: Mongol Bilig, 2005); Agata Bareja-Starzyńska, "Some Undocumented Features of the Horizontal Square Script of Zanabazar," *Mongolo-Tibetica Pragensia* 6, no. 1 (2013): 65–77; Byambaa Ragchaa and Bareja-Starzyńska, "Notes on the Pre-existences."
14. György Somlai, "The Lineage of Tāranātha According to Kloṅ-rdol-bla-ma," in *Tibetan Studies. Proceedings of the 4th International Association for Tibetan Studies*, Schloss Hohenkamer—Munich 1985, ed. Helga Uebach and L. Panglung Jampa (Munich: Kommission für Zentralasiatische Studien, Bayerische Akademie der Wissenschaften, 1988), 449–451. Agata Bareja-Starzyńska and Byambaa Ragchaa. "Notes on the Pre-existences of the First Khalkha Jetsundampa Zanabazar According to His

Biography Written in the Horizontal Square Script." In "Oriental Studies. Past and Present. Proceedings of the International Conference of Oriental Studies, Warsaw, 2010," (special issue of) *Rocznik Orientalistyczny*, ed. Agata Bareja Starzyńska and Marek Mejor, 65, no. 1 (2012): 24–40.

15. Data based mainly on Byambaa, *The Bibliographical Guide*, 57. See also Atwood, *Encyclopedia*, 273.
16. The fourth head of the sTong 'khor Monastery was bestowed with the title of Manzshir by the Kangxi emperor; see TBRC P722. See also Bareja-Starzyńska, *Biography*, 180n648; and Soninbayir, "Manzshir khutagtiin tuukh," 5–10.
17. Atwood, *Encyclopedia*, 273. According to Byambaa it was in 1732; Byambaa, *The Bibliographical Guide*, 57.
18. Atwood, *Encyclopedia*, 273. According to Ch. Bawden's calculation based on the Mongolian biography, the meeting took place in 1737, when the Second Jebtsundamba was 14 years old. See Charles Bawden, *The Jebtsundamba Khutukhtus of Urga*. Text, Translation and Notes, Asiatische Forschungen, vol. 9 (Wiesbaden, Germany: Otto Harrassowitz, 1961), 71, f. 28r.
19. Atwood, *Encyclopedia*, 273.
20. All the data on the religious activities according to Byambaa, *The Bibliographical Guide*, 57. Atwood, *Encyclopedia*, 273, gives the date as 1755.
21. The version of the Manchu assassination of the Second Jebtsundamba is supported by Byambaa, *The Bibliographical Guide*, 57.
22. Byambaa, 58.
23. Byambaa, 59. See also Atwood, *Encyclopedia*, 268.
24. Data according to Byambaa, *The Bibliographical Guide*, 61–62. Byambaa (61) writes about the Eighth Dalai Lama. Atwood, *Encyclopedia*, 268 and Sarkozi write about the Seventh Dalai Lama; see Alice Sárközi, *Political Prophecies in Mongolia in the 17–20th Centuries* (Wiesbaden, Germany: Otto Harrassowitz, 1992), 84.
25. In TBRC P322 Blo bzang 'jam dbyangs rgya mtsho, the 40th krhi chen of the sKu 'bum monastery is mentioned as teacher of the Fourth Jebtsundamba.
26. Berger, "After Xanadu," 71.
27. Byambaa, *The Bibliographical Guide* lists 517 texts, nos. 00129–00645, 63–201.
28. Data according to Byambaa, *The Bibliographical Guide*, 203–204. See also Atwood, *Encyclopedia*, 268–269.
29. Certain works were included in one volume of his collected works, *gsung 'bum*, but apart from these more works have been found, and all of them are listed in Byambaa, *The Bibliographical Guide*, nos. 00646–00692, 205–223.
30. Byambaa, *The Bibliographical Guide*, 225. Atwood, *Encyclopedia*, 268, gives as the date of his birth 1842, probably relying on Ch. Bawden, who provided information that he was "installed in 1842"; Bawden, *The Jebtsundamba Khutukhtus of Urga*, 89, f. 46r. However, in the biographies the year of birth is mentioned as "rabbit year," and therefore it should be 1843.
31. Byambaa, *The Bibliographical Guide*, 227.
32. Atwood, *Encyclopedia*, 268–269.
33. Byambaa, *The Bibliographical Guide*, nos. 00693–00730, 228–234 presents a list of his writings, with a note that apart from those on the list, not many other works survived. Those listed are quite often prayers for the long life of lamas or supplications for the "swift return" of passed teachers as well as texts of recognition of certain reincarnated lamas.
34. Byambaa, *The Bibliographical Guide*, 235, and A. Pozdneev write that he was born in 1869; see Aleksei M. Pozdneev, *Mongolia and the Mongols*, in *Uralic and Altaic Series*, vol. 61, Part 1, ed. J. R. Krueger (Bloomington: Indiana University Publications, 1971), 370; Atwood, *Encyclopedia*, 268, writes about 1870.
35. Pozdneev, *Mongolia and the Mongols*, 364–365.
36. Pozdneev, *Mongolia and the Mongols*, 385; Berger, "After Xanadu," 71; Atwood, *Encyclopedia*, 269.
37. Atwood, *Encyclopedia*, 269.
38. See G. Bethlenfalvy, *A Hand-list of the Ulaanbaatar Manuscript of the Kanjur Rgyal-rtse them spangs-ma* (Budapest: Akadémiai Kiadó, 1982).

39. Byambaa, *The Bibliographical Guide*, 236.
40. Byambaa, 236. In the catalog they are listed as nos. 00731–00880, 237–296.
41. Works not included in his "Collected Works" are all listed in Byambaa, *The Bibliographical Guide* as nos. 00870–00880, 293–296.
42. Bawden, Charles, *Tales of an Old Lama*, trans. C. R. Bawden from a Mongolian text recorded, ed. Ts. Damdinsüren and Boryn Zhambal, *Ȯvgȯn Zhambalyn i͡arii͡a* (Tring, UK: Institute of Buddhist Studies, 1997), 99.
43. Bawden, 100.
44. Bawden, 100.
45. Bawden, *Tales of an Old Lama*, 100; Charles Bawden, *The Modern History of Mongolia* (London: Kegan Paul International, 1968), 166.
46. See *Lungta*, vol. 17, 2013: *The Centennial of the Tibeto-Mongol Treaty: 1913–2013*.
47. See Sárközi, *Political Prophecies in Mongolia*. They are preserved in several versions in Mongolian language.
48. Atwood, *Encyclopedia*, 271.
49. Atwood, 272.
50. Paul Hyer, "Politics and Religion in Inner Mongolia: Japan's Plans for the 9th Jebtsundamba 'Living Buddha,' *The Mongolian Journal of International Affairs*, 17 (2012): 64–74.
51. Fabian Sanders, "The Life and Lineage of the Ninth Khalkha Jetsun Dhampa Khutukhtu of Urga," *Central Asiatic Journal* 45, no. 2 (2001): 293–303.
52. Mongolian and English versions of the nine principles can be read online.
53. On the political background of the search for the Tenth Jebtsundamba see Jichang Lulu, "Jebtsundamba," blog.
54. Atwood, *Encyclopedia*, 497.
55. Atwood, 497–498.
56. Aleksei, M Pozdneev, *Mongolia and the Mongols, Uralic and Altaic Series*, vol. 61, ed. J. R. Krueger, (Bloomington: Indiana University Publications, Part 1, 1971; Part 2, 1977).
57. Aleksei, M Pozdneev, *Mongolia and the Mongols, Uralic and Altaic Series*, vol. 61, Part 1, ed. J. R. Krueger (Bloomington: Indiana University Publications, 1971), 328; Bareja-Starzyńska, *Biography*, 116–118, original text of the biography: 433–434.
58. In the Mongolian biography (edited and translated by Bawden), the monastery is not mentioned by name, only the fact that the Jebtsundamba visited places of his previous incarnation; see Bawden, *The Jebtsundamba Khutukhtus of Urga*, 10, 45. This fact is also mentioned by Miyawaki, "How Legends Developed about the First Jebtsundamba," 53.
59. Morris Rossabi, "Mongolia: From Chingis Khan to Independence," 25–49; Berger "After Xanadu," 50–75.
60. Bawden, *Tales of an Old Lama*.
61. Kaplonski Christopher, *Truth, History and Politics in Mongolia: The Memory of Heroes* (London: Routledge Curzon, 2004).
62. Junko Miyawaki, "How Legends Developed About the First Jebtsundamba: In Reference to the Khalkha Mongol Submission to the Manchus in the Seventeenth Century," *Memoires of the Research Department of the Toyo Bunko*, 52 (1994): 45–67.
63. Atwood, *Encyclopedia*.
64. Sh. Bira, *Öndör gegeeniin namtruud orshwoi* (Ulaanbaatar, Mongolia: n.p., 1995).
65. L. Terbish, *Lamyn Gegeen Luwsandanzanjantsan, tüünii zurkhain büteel tuurwil* (Ulaanbaatar, Mongolia: Mongol Ulsyn Ikh Surguul', Mongol Khel Soyolyn Deed Surguul', Ekh bichig, altai sudlalyn tenkhim [Printed and donated for free distribution by the Corporate Body of the Buddha Educational Foundation], 2004).
66. Byambaa, *The Bibliographical Guide*.

Agata Bareja-Starzyńska

K

THE KADAMPA: A FORMATIVE MOVEMENT OF TIBETAN BUDDHISM

THE BKA' GDAMS PA TRADITION OF TIBETAN BUDDHISM

The Bka' gdams pa[1] are one of the four major traditions or "schools" of Tibetan Buddhism that were formed in the context of the 11th-century revival of Buddhism on the Tibetan plateau.[2] Schools or traditions of Tibetan Buddhism can be characterized according to a whole range of criteria, including their philosophical views and doctrines, their preferences for specific tantric cycles, their meditation practices, their institutional identity through main monastic seats, and their lineage of teachers. The last of these criteria seems of particular importance, given the emphasis on lineage and transmission in tantric Buddhism in general, and in Tibetan Buddhism in particular. The Tibetan Buddhist teaching and transmission lineages trace themselves back to Indian teachers, which from a Tibetan point of view means that they represent an authentic form of Buddhism coming from the homeland of Buddha Śākyamuni.

In the case of the Bka' gdams pa, the Indian teacher from whom the lineage originates is Dīpaṃkaraśrījñāna (982–1054), a tantric master and Buddhist scholar from Bengal, who is also known by his Indian honorific title as Atiśa[ya] or Adhīśa, or in Tibetan as Jo bo ("the master"), Jo bo rje ("the supreme master"), or Lha gcig ("the sole lord"). He was invited to the western Tibetan kingdom of Gu ge and arrived there in 1042. He then accepted an invitation to central Tibet, where he stayed until he passed away in the autumn of 1054.

His Tibetan disciples became instrumental in passing on his legacy; the most important to be mentioned here are his translator and travel companion over nineteen years, Nag tsho lo tsa ba Tshul khrims rgyal ba (1011–*c.* 1064), as well as three students who are often named as the triad of "Khu, Rngog, and 'Brom." Khu ston's impact on the tradition is the least obvious; Rngog Legs pa'i shes rab (b. 10th century) and his nephew Rngog Blo ldan shes rab (1059–1109) founded an important school of logic and epistemology;[3] and 'Brom ston Rgyal ba'i 'byung gnas (1004–1064) is traditionally regarded as the founding father of the Bka' gdams pa tradition proper. At his monastery of Rwa sgreng (pronounced "Reting"), some of the most influential Bka' gdams pa masters taught or were trained, and the central Tibetan Bka' gdams pa tradition spread from there. The region of 'Phan yul (modern-day Phempo, figure 1), north of Lha sa and not far from Rwa sgreng, became one of their main home regions; another important center of Bka' gdams pa learning was the monastery of Lo on the northern side of the Skyid chu River.

From the 14th century onward, another important monastic seat started collecting and publicizing the Bka' gdams pa legacy: the monastery of Snar thang (pronounced "Nartang") in the province of Gtsang.[4] Several abbots of Snar thang were involved in compiling Bka' gdams pa works and creating mainstream collections of biographies and doctrinal works. Bka' gdams pa texts were reproduced early on when the technique of blockprinting became popular on the Tibetan plateau; the 16th-century blockprints of some Bka' gdams pa works helped to enhance their literary impact and ensured a transregional distribution.[5] By this time, however, the Bka' gdams pa had already disappeared as a distinct tradition, and the Dge lugs pa tradition regarded itself as the rightful heir to the Bka' gdams pa legacy.

It should be noted that the influence of the Bka' gdams pa masters reaches far beyond Bka' gdams pa and Dge lugs pa circles; Atiśa is a highly revered figure for other traditions, too (especially the Bka' brgyud pa, who trace themselves back to the tantric guru Nā ro pa, who was also one of Atiśa's teachers). Moreover, the doctrinal genres associated with the Bka' gdams pa, the expositions of the graded path to Buddhahood (*lam rim, bstan rim*) and the instructions on "mind training" (*blo sbyong*) became highly popular across school boundaries, and works of this type were composed by authors from different strands of Buddhism. The early Bka' gdams pas flourished at a time that was generally fairly nonsectarian (or perhaps better: presectarian), and it was common that students of Tibetan Buddhism studied with famous masters of different traditions. Thus, what is said here about the Bka' gdams pa should not be understood as applying to an exclusive school or sect, but rather to a strand with many interconnections within the emerging lineage network of Tibetan Buddhism.

EARLY BKA' GDAMS PA TEACHERS

Given the importance of teaching lineages, this survey needs to begin by introducing the most important early Bka' gdams pa teachers, those who shaped the tradition and are generally regarded as the most instrumental figures within the tradition. Their lives were recorded in writing at an early date and in a wide range of sources.

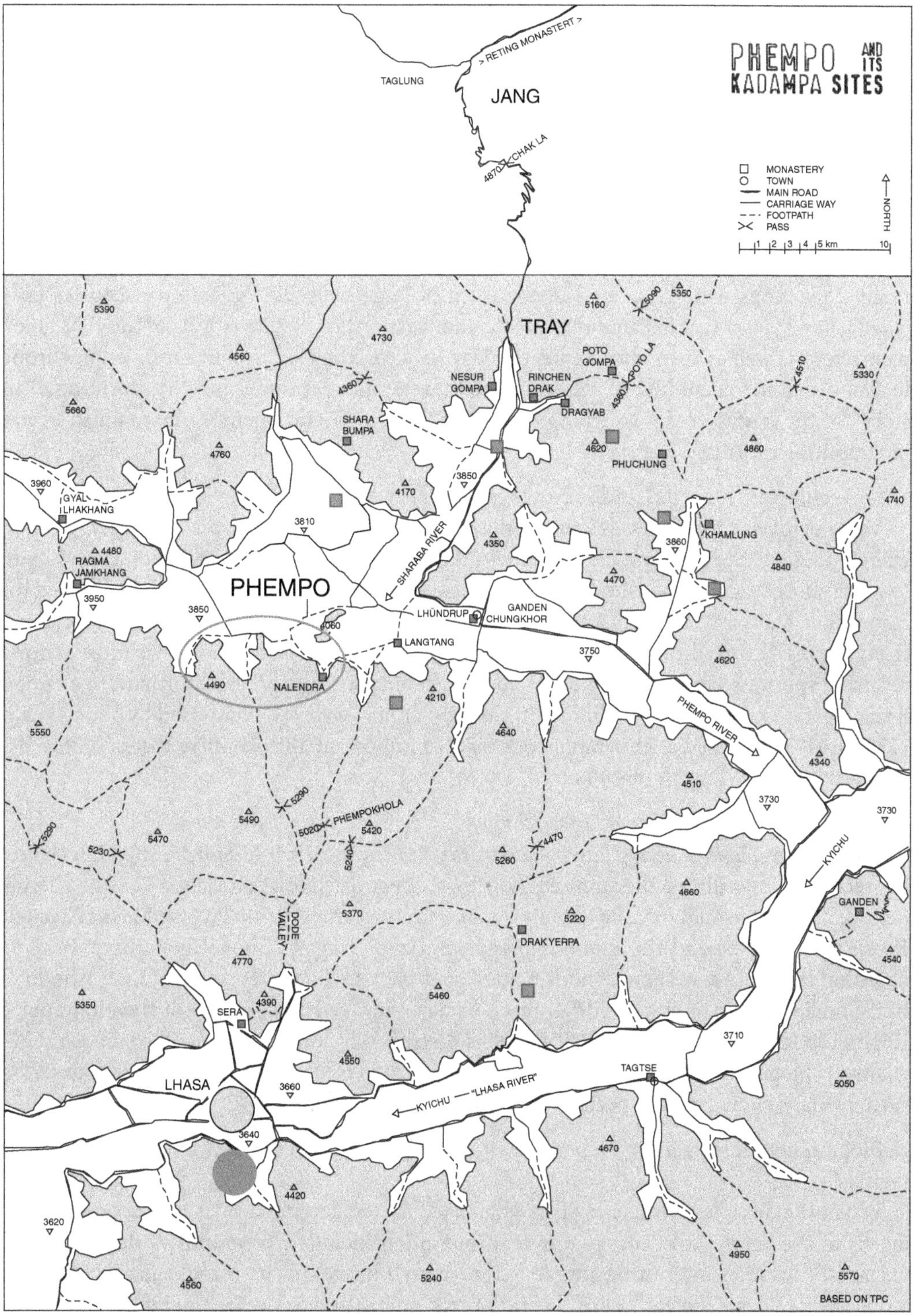

Figure 1. Map of Phempo with early Kadampa monasteries.
Source: Map courtesy of Hans-Ulrich Roesler (2004)

Biographical Sources. The earliest biographies were produced locally, in many cases by the disciples of a Buddhist teacher, who produced oral or written accounts of their teacher's life story. Most of the early accounts are relatively brief; in subsequent centuries the biographies grow in length and detail and develop a tendency toward a more hagiographical presentation. From the 13th century onward, the life stories of the Bka' gdams pa masters were also collected and assembled into collective lineage histories of the Bka' gdams tradition; this process of compiling the Bka' gdams pa legacy went hand in hand with the move to larger monastic centers, which also means a movement from local traditions to transregional mainstream traditions. From the late 15th century onward, after the emergence of the Dge lugs pa, the biography collections were circulated in the form of large-scale Bka' gdams pa histories (*Bka' gdams chos 'byung*) that became the mainstream versions of the life stories of the Bka' gdams pa masters as well as their successors, the Dge lugs pa. They are usually arranged in chronological order and according to the individual teacher–student lineages, thus forming a "life story" of the tradition as a coherent whole.[6] In terms of literary genres, the main sources of biographical information are:

a. Verse eulogies (*bstod pa*) and prayers (*gsol 'debs*)

Verse eulogies (*bstod pa*) are among the earliest biographical sources available. A famous eulogy of Atiśa, the *Bstod pa brgyad cu pa* ("Hymn in eighty verses") was composed by his long-standing student Nag tsho lo tsa ba Tshul khrims rgyal ba (b. 1011) when he learned that his teacher had passed away.[7] Another famous eulogy, the *Bstod pa sum bcu pa* ("Hymn in thirty verses"), is traditionally ascribed to 'Brom ston pa, an ascription that most scholars regard as spurious.[8] Prayers (*gsol 'debs*), too, may contain biographical information; a famous lineage prayer known under its short title as *Lam mchog sgo 'byed*, composed by Tsong kha pa (1357–1419), was used as the framework for two important 18th-century works on the Bka' gdams pa and Dge lugs pa masters.[9]

b. Individual prose biographies (*rnam thar*)

Prose biographies of Bka' gdams pa masters were composed at least from the 12th century on, recorded in writing either immediately by a direct disciple of a teacher or after a certain period of oral transmission. The latter is the case for the earliest prose biographies of Atiśa, the *Rnam thar rgyas pa* and the *Rnam thar rgyas pa yongs grags* (12th–13th century). Both are based on the same source, which ultimately goes back to an oral account by Nag tsho lo tsa ba.[10] Some early biographies of other teachers have survived as well, such as the biography of Rngog Blo ldan shes rab (1059–1109) by his disciple Gro lung pa.[11] Not all of the early Bka' gdams pa biographies are still extant, but there is reason to hope that some more may surface since plenty of new material became available in the 2000s.[12]

c. Biographical information embedded in doctrinal works, commentaries, and "collected sayings"

When the disciples of the early Bka' gdams pa masters recorded their instructions in writing from the early 12th century onward, they often included biographical details of their teachers.[13] Another interesting source for the early Bka' gdams pa masters is anthologies of "collected sayings." The earliest of these, the *Bka' gdams gsung gros thor bu* by Lce sgom Shes rab rdo rje (1124/25–1204/05), consists of short and pithy instructions of the early teachers;

a later anthology, the *Bka' gdams gces btus nor bu'i bang mdzod* (19th century), adds biographical sketches of the individual teachers to these instructional vignettes.[14]

d. Larger hagiographical compilations and lineage histories

The earliest lineage history of the Bka' gdams tradition currently known is a work by Mchims Nam mkha' grags (1210–1285), the seventh abbot of Snar thang Monastery. It is known as the *Snar thang gser phreng* ("Golden rosary of the Narthang tradition").[15] This "rosary" does not provide a full sketch of all Bka' gdams pa lineages, but traces one specific lineage, beginning in India with Atiśa's teachers including Nāropa and Ḍombhipa, followed by the life stories of Atiśa and his Tibetan disciple 'Brom ston pa, and ending with the lineage from 'Brom ston's disciple Po to ba to the abbots of Snar thang.

An anthology of a much more varied character is the *Bka' gdams glegs bam* ("The book of the Bka' gdams").[16] This work is based on a variety of biographical, legendary, and doctrinal sources and was redacted and committed to writing in 1302 in Snar thang Monastery.[17] The overall agenda of the *Bka' gdams glegs bam* is the promotion of 'Brom ston pa, who is portrayed as a manifestation of the Bodhisattva Avalokiteśvara and reincarnation of King Srong btsan sgam po (7th century), who honed and demonstrated his bodhisattva qualities over many previous lifetimes.

The late 15th century saw the emergence of comprehensive Bka' gdams pa histories (*Bka' gdams chos 'byung*) that present the main teacher–student lineages, arranging the life stories of the Bka' gdams pa masters in the form of a lineage tree. The most important ones are (in chronological order) the Bka' gdams histories by Ye shes rtse mo (1484), Bsod nams lha'i dbang po (1484), Las chen Kun dga' rgyal mtshan (1494), and Paṇ chen Bsod nams grags pa (1529).[18] They were written in a period of religio-political competition, when the Dge lugs tradition was on the rise, and Tsong kha pa's school came to be understood as the true heir to the Bka' gdams pa lineages. Another Bka' gdams pa history was composed by the famous Sa skya scholar A myes zhabs (1597–1659/60).[19] Two further important lineage histories were written in the 18th century, one by Paṇ chen bla ma Blo bzang ye shes (1663–1737) and one by Tshe mchog gling yongs 'dzin Ye shes rgyal mtshan (completed in 1787).[20]

The following survey will introduce some of the main actors of the early Bka' gdams pa tradition: the Indian teacher Atiśa Dīpaṃkaraśrījñāna and his Tibetan disciple 'Brom ston pa, as well as his three disciples known as the "three [spiritual] brothers." Among the biographical sources, preference will be given to early accounts. Because of constraints of space, other important students of Atiśa, including Nag tsho lo tsa ba Tshul khrims rgyal ba (1011–*c.* 1064), Dgon pa pa Dbang phyug rgyal mtshan (1016–1082), and Rngog Legs pa'i shes rab and his lineage, cannot receive the attention they deserve.

Atiśa Dīpaṃkaraśrījñāna, 982–1054. The following brief account of Atiśa's life is based on his earliest available biographies, the *Rnam thar rgyas pa* and the *Rnam thar rgyas pa yongs grags* (12th and 13th centuries).[21] Atiśa was born in 982 in the city of Vikramapura or Vikramapuri in Za hor (Bengal), as the middle son of the ruling family. His birth name was Candragarbha. As a young man he went to study tantra at Kālaśilā, one of the seven hills near Rājgir, and was initiated into the Hevajra Tantra; his tantric initiation name was Jñānaguhyavajra.

He studied for seven years with the yogi Avadhūtipa, and for three years he concentrated on yoga, learned tantric "vajra songs," and participated in tantric feasts (*gaṇacakra*).

When he was twenty-eight years old, he was ordained into the Vinaya of the Mahāsāṅghika school at the Mativihāra in Bodh Gayā and received the ordination name Dīpaṃkaraśrījñāna. The early biographies point out that as a tantric practitioner he could only be ordained into the Mahāsāṅghika Vinaya, an interesting remark that deserves further investigation.[22] He spent several years studying the doctrines of the "four great schools" of Indian Buddhism (Mahāsāṅghikas, Sarvāstivādins, Sammitīyas, and Sthaviravādins) as well as Abhidharma, which was taught by Dharmarakṣita at the monastery of Odantapuri. In addition to his studies of the Pāramitānaya (i.e., the Mahāyāna), he continued to study tantra with teachers such as Kusali, Jetāri, Ḍombhipa, Nāropa, and Ratnākaraśānti. His most important teacher of Mahāyāna doctrines and the "generation of the awakening mind" (*bodhicittotpāda*) became Suvarṇadvīpa Dharmakīrti (Tib. Gser gling pa Chos kyi grags pa), named after his home country Sumatra (Skt. Suvarṇadvīpa), with whom he studied Śāntideva's famous works during his visit to Sumatra. Later on, Atiśa again visited Kālaśilā, which indicates that his studies of Mahāyāna doctrines did not make him abandon his engagement with tantric practice.

Atiśa became a senior scholar (*gnas brtan chen po*) at the monastic university of Vikramaśīla, which was famous for its tantric scholarship. While Tibetan biographies highlight Atiśa's purity of conduct and accomplishment as a scholar, it is difficult to assess his role within the Indian tradition because neither his own works nor Indian commentaries on his writings have survived there. This absence may at least in part be due to the fact that the Buddhist monastic universities were destroyed not very long after his lifetime, and the survival of works from this period is slightly haphazard. In Tibet, however, Atiśa has left a rich literary legacy, consisting not only of his famous *Bodhipathapradīpa* but also numerous small-scale works as well as translations of Buddhist Sanskrit literature into Tibetan.[23]

Atiśa was invited by the kings of the western Tibetan kingdom of Gu ge, where Buddhism saw a revival under the royal patronage of King Lha bla ma Ye shes 'od ("Yeshe Ö," 947–1019/24) and his nephew and successor Byang chub 'od ("Changchub Ö," 984–1078). Two of Ye shes 'od's missions to invite scholars from India had reached Vikramaśīla, but it was only at the time of Byang chub 'od that a delegation headed by Nag tsho lo tsa ba Tshul khrims rgyal ba succeeded in bringing Atiśa to Tibet. Ratnākara, the abbot of Vikramaśīla, gave permission for this journey, but asked Nag tsho lo tsa ba to bring Atiśa back after three years. The party traveled via Nepal where Atiśa composed the *Vimalaratnalekha*, an epistle to King Neyapāla, and founded a monastery in Kathmandu.[24] In 1042 they arrived in western Tibet. At Mtho lding, the capital of the kingdom of Gu ge, Atiśa gave Buddhist instructions, had an encounter with the famous translator Rin chen bzang po ("Rinchen Sangpo," 958–1055), and met King Byang chub 'od who asked for explanations on the Śrāvakayāna, the Pāramitānaya (i.e., the Mahāyāna), and on tantra, as well as a handbook on the Guhyasamājatantra. In response to this request, Atiśa composed his famous *Bodhipathapradīpa*, which defines three categories of Buddhist practitioners and then provides step-by-step instructions for the most advanced of these, the followers of the Mahāyāna. This work laid the foundations for later Tibetan literature on the graded path to awakening (*lam rim*). While in Pu hrangs, Atiśa met 'Brom ston Rgyal ba'i 'byung gnas, and the biographies do not fail to highlight the importance of this encounter that would lead to a long-term teacher–student relationship and, ultimately, to the foundation of the Bka' gdams pa tradition.

Since the way to India was barred by civil war on the Nepalese border and 'Brom ston pa had invited him to visit the Buddhist sites of central Tibet, Atiśa did not return to Vikramaśīla, but traveled toward the province of Dbus (central Tibet). During a stay at Bsam yas, the famous first monastery of Tibet founded in the late 8th century, Atiśa collaborated in translation projects and gave tantric instructions and initiations. His student Khu ston invited him to his home region in Yar klungs, but Atiśa and 'Brom ston pa left because Khu ston did not let his own students study with Atiśa. The biographers vividly describe their clandestine flight across the Gtsang po River, with Khu ston following in hot pursuit and falling into the river. Back in Bsam yas Monastery, Atiśa was excited to discover rare Sanskrit manuscripts. A noble lady from the Mchims family began spreading slander about Atiśa, and so he and his followers left for Lhasa. Here, Atiśa is said to have discovered the *Bka' chems ka khol ma* ("pillar testament"), a famous "treasure text" (*gter ma*) related to King Srong btsan sgam po, in the Jo khang temple in 1048.[25]

Atiśa and his disciples spent the summer in the mountain hermitage of Brag Yer pa, where the dialogues recorded in the famous *Bka' gdams glegs bam* ("The book of the Bka' gdams") are said to have taken place. Then they followed an invitation to Snye thang near Lhasa, where Atiśa stayed until his death in the late autumn of 1054.[26] The *stūpa* that contained Atiśa's relics can still be visited there. After Atiśa's death, the community split up after a last joint assembly held in 1055, and it seems that the four Vinaya groups of Lhasa became involved with the Bka' gdams pa movement.[27] Atiśa's disciples left Snye thang and went their own ways, taking their share of his relics to their own new monastic residences.

'Brom ston Rgyal ba'i 'byung gnas, 1004–1064. Later authors of the Bka' gdams pa and Dge lugs pa traditions tend to highlight 'Brom ston pa's role as the most important of Atiśa's disciples and the true Tibetan founding figure of the Bka' gdams pa (*bka' gdams kyi mes po*), in spite of the fact that his role and activities are in some ways frustratingly elusive. Episodes from his life are included in the early Atiśa biography *Rnam thar rgyas pa*; the earliest full biography currently known, however, was written by Mchims Nam mkha' grags (1210–1285), the seventh abbot of Snar thang Monastery.[28] Further accounts of 'Brom ston's life can be found in the *Bka' gdams chos 'byung*-s and other religious histories such as the *Deb ther sngon po*.[29] The biographical sketch presented here is primarily based on Mchims Nam mkha' grags' *Snar thang gser phreng*.

'Brom ston was born in Phug rings in the nomad area of Byang Rtswa sgye mo in Stod lung (northwest of Lha sa) in the year 1004, according to Bka' gdams pa histories. Some biographical sources report that his childhood name was Chos 'phel.[30] The name of his father, Yag gzher sku gshen (with numerous spelling variants across the sources), points to a Bon po background, although this is not stated explicitly. His mother died early, and the young Chos 'phel who did not get on with his stepmother longed to leave home. In his fourteenth year he was sent to do trade in Snye mo, which gave him a chance to study reading and writing with a certain G.yung chos mgon.

He met the scholar Se btsun Dbang phyug gzhon nu ("Setsün Wangchuk Shönnu") from Khams (eastern Tibet) and decided to study with him. Before setting out to Khams, he took the lay vows from Zhang Sna nam Rdo rje dbang phyug ("Shang Nanam Dorje Wangchuk") and received the name Rgyal ba'i 'byung gnas. He then traveled east; in Mdo smad he studied the *Abhidharmasamuccaya* with a local household priest called Gru Nam mkha,' and then went to Khams where he studied Abhidharma and the Old Tantras with Se btsun, with whom he stayed for nineteen or twenty years. He and two of his fellow students became known collectively as "Khu, Rngog, and 'Brom" (i.e., Khu Brtson grus g.yung drung, Rngog Legs pa'i shes rab, and 'Brom Rgyal ba'i 'byung gnas). 'Brom ston also studied the "Indian language" with a scholar called Sgra tsher ma ("language thorn").

When news about Atiśa reached eastern Tibet, 'Brom ston decided to go and meet this important teacher. During his journey via central Tibet, 'Brom ston met his future patron, 'Phrang kha ber chung, and 'Brom convinced him not to go to war, but to build a temple at Phong mdo instead. He also went to visit his father and Sna nam Rdo rje dbang phyug, from whom he had taken the lay vows, and urged the Buddhist teachers of the region to invite Atiśa once the time was ripe. Farther west, in Pu hrangs, he met Atiśa, who formally accepted him as his student and gave him his own statue of the six-armed Mañjuvajra, a meditation deity of the Guhyasamāja system, which is said to be the one still housed in Rwa sgreng Monastery today.[31] 'Brom ston invited Atiśa to central Tibet and accompanied and supported him for the following twelve years, until the teacher died.

About a year after Atiśa had passed away, 'Brom ston pa and other students left Snye thang, apparently due to leadership disputes. 'Brom ston followed an invitation from a son of Phrang kha ber chung to found a monastery in the Rwa sgreng ("Reting") Valley. The investigation of the geomantic features of the valley (1056) and the consecration rituals for the monastery (1057) are described at some length, highlighting the importance of this place for the later Bka' gdams pa tradition.[32] Among the texts and doctrines taught by 'Brom ston, the biography mentions the *Prajñāpāramitā, Bodhisattvacaryāvatāra, Bodhipathapradīpa, Bhāvanākrama,* and treatises on Cittamātra and Madhyamaka philosophy. He is also said to have taught the "graded path" to awakening (*lam rim*), although he did not compose a written work on this topic himself, perhaps due to the largely oral nature of the early Bka' gdams pa movement. According to the *Snar thang gser phreng* 'Brom ston passed away on the twentieth day of the middle summer month in a dragon year, which corresponds to 1064.

The Bka' gdams pa Lineages after 'Brom ston pa. The Bka' gdams pa tradition is usually mapped out in several main lineages, although there is some slight variation in the way the teacher–disciple lineages are defined.[33] Of particular importance are three lineages originating with the "three (spiritual) brothers" (*sku mched gsum*), a term collectively used for the most important students of 'Brom ston pa at Rwa sgreng. These three lineages are the scriptural tradition (*gzhung pa*) going back to Po to ba Rin chen gsal ("Potowa Rinchensel," 1027–1105), the instructional tradition (*gdams ngag pa* or *man ngag pa*) going back to Spyan snga ba Tshul khrims 'bar ("Chengawa Tsültrimbar," 1033–1103), and the tradition of biographical and esoteric transmissions that later fed into the *Bka' gdams glegs bam* ("book of Bka' gdams"), transmitted by Phu chung ba Gzhon nu rgyal mtshan ("Puchungwa Shönnu Gyeltsen," 1031–1106).

As the designation *gzhung pa* indicates, this tradition transmitted a range of important Buddhist works, including the so-called six Bka' gdams pa core texts (*gzhung drug*): the *Jātakamālā, Udānavarga, Mahāyānasūtrālaṃkāra, Bodhisattvabhūmi, Śikṣāsamuccaya,* and

Bodhisattvacaryāvatāra. They also produced works on "mind training" (*blo sbyong*) and on the graded path to awakening (*lam rim*), including two works containing Po to ba's oral instructions on the graded path, written down by his students (see the section on "The Graded Path to Buddhahood" below). The most influential teachers among Po to ba's disciples were Glang ri thang pa Rdo rje seng ge (1054–1123), to whom the short but influential "*Blo sbyong* in Eight Verses" is attributed, and Sha ra ba Yon tan grags (1070–1141). The latter became the teacher of 'Chad kha ba Ye shes rdo rje (1101–1175), author of the famous *Blo sbyong don bdun ma* ("Mind training in seven points").[34]

The instructional lineage (*gdams ngag pa* or *man ngag pa*) goes back to Spyan snga ba, famous as an accomplished yogi and meditator, who founded the monastery of Lo (Lo dgon) in 1093 based on the Guhyasamāja mandala; this monastery became an important Bka' gdams pa seat.[35] He later stayed in Smyug rum, where his teachings continued to flourish. Among his most important students were Smyug rum pa Brtson grus 'bar (1042–1109) and Bya yul ba Gzhon nu 'od (1075–1138).

The third of the "three brothers," Phu chung ba Gzhon nu rgyal mtshan, is traditionally credited with the transmission of the biographical tradition that is codified in the *Bka' gdams glegs bam*.[36] In the *Bka' gdams chos 'byung*-s his lineage is also identified as the lineage of the blessing (*byin rlabs*), which he received from 'Brom ston pa. He is said to have focused on his own meditation practice rather than teaching larger numbers of students, and one may wonder whether his small monastery in 'Phan yul was later abandoned because he did not initiate a broader student lineage.[37]

While these three main lineages originate with 'Brom ston pa's disciples, the Bka' gdams pa tradition in the wider sense also includes lineages going back to other important students of Atiśa, such as Nag tsho lo tsa ba and his disciples, Rngog Legs pa'i shes rab and his disciples, and Dgon pa ba and his disciples.[38] In later times, after the disappearance of the Bka' gdams pa as a distinct tradition, the idea emerged that all main transmission lineages come together in Tsong kha pa Blo bzang grags pa (1357–1419), the founder of the Dge lugs pa, who is thus regarded as the heir to the entire Bka' gdams tradition.

THE GRADED PATH TO BUDDHAHOOD (*LAM RIM AND BSTAN RIM*)

The Bka' gdams pa have become famous for their systematic step-by-step approach to the Buddhist path, laid down in works on the "steps of the path" (*lam rim*) or "stages of the doctrine" (*bstan rim*). As Jackson has pointed out, the former typically operate with a subdivision into three kinds of Buddhist practitioners and the teachings related to each of them, and they normally close with a section on tantra as the most advanced (and most risky) form of practice. Works of the *bstan rim* genre tend to present the same step-by-step program, but without the division into three kinds of practitioners and they typically close with an exposition of the bodhisattva levels and buddhahood as the highest goal.[39]

Atiśa's *Bodhipathapradīpa* is the locus classicus for the definition of the three types of individuals: Buddhist beginners, the *śrāvakas*, and the Mahāyāna Buddhists, a subdivision that goes back to a stanza from Vasubandhu's *Abhidharmakośabhāṣya*.[40] Later works on the *lam rim* usually refer to Atiśa's definition of the three kinds of individuals; however, the *Bodhipathapradīpa* itself cannot be regarded as a comprehensive blueprint for the *lam rim* as a whole since it does not discuss the complete graded path, but focuses on the steps for the most advanced practitioners, those following the Mahāyāna. However, two short works preserved in the collection of the "Short Treatises of Atiśa" (*Jo bo'i chos chung*) briefly outline the path from beginning to end and thus seem to bear witness to the fact that Atiśa did indeed teach the complete *lam rim* in basically the same form as later Buddhist masters taught it. It therefore seems justified to trace these teachings back to him, even if he did not elaborate on them in detail in his written works.[41]

Numerous Bka' gdams pa masters taught or composed works on the graded path; the works that are currently available all follow a similar structure.[42] They typically begin with propaedeutic considerations for the "inferior type of individuals" who are meant to consider (a) the rare opportunity of a human rebirth with its advantages for Buddhist practice, (b) the impermanence of this state, and (c) the fact that their future fate is driven by their current actions (*karman*). These considerations are meant to lead them to the stage of the "intermediate beings" (or *śrāvakas*) who are striving for their own liberation and who are advised to consider the unsatisfactory nature of samsara and take the monastic vows. The final and longest section is for the "excellent individuals" who have developed the Mahāyāna attitude; they are encouraged to cultivate wisdom and compassion, generate *bodhicitta*, and practice the six perfections. They may also use the methods of tantra to traverse the path to awakening even faster, as long as they make sure not to contradict any of the vows they have taken.

The charm of the early Bka' gdams pa *lam rim* literature lies in its accessible and witty style, which is due to the fact that these instructions were mostly given orally in the early generations of teachers. In the case of Po to ba Rin chen gsal, his disciples committed his instructions to writing and created two highly popular works, the *Dpe chos rin chen spungs pa* ("Dharma Exemplified") and the *Be'u bum sngon po* ("Blue Compendium"). Both are fully fledged *lam rim* works, but what distinguishes them from later, more scholastic, expositions is their colloquial language and the use of similes and anecdotes to illustrate the Buddhist path, as the following example from the "Dharma Exemplified" may show:

> An abbot in Khams, who had taken the monastic vows, drank small amounts of beer. When all his students imitated him and drank beer as well, he said: "Don't drink beer, because you and I are not the same," but they didn't listen. One day he assembled the students, poured a handful of needles into each tea cup, and said: "If you want to imitate me, then take these into your mouth!" And as he poured the needles into his mouth and chewed them with a crunching noise, the others were defeated, it is said.[43]

This story is used in the text to illustrate that a good Buddhist teacher needs special abilities to restore faith and proper behavior in his students.

The humorous and down-to-earth teaching style was well suited to explain the complexities of the *lam rim* to largely untrained Tibetan audiences in the 11th and early 12th centuries and made these works highly popular. Their long-term impact has been enormous, beginning with Tsong kha pa's famous works on the graded path and continuing with numerous *lam rim* and *bstan rim* works up to the 20th and 21st centuries. Far from being limited to the Bka' gdams pa and Dge lugs pa schools, the *lam rim* and *bstan rim* genres have been adopted by other traditions, too, and expositions of the graded path to buddhahood can be found throughout the centuries and across the schools of Tibetan Buddhism.[44]

MIND TRAINING (*BLO SBYONG*)

In early Bka' gdams pa literature *blo sbyong* is frequently used as a verb ("to purify or train the mind") and qualified by the topic in which the mind should be trained. A 19th-century anthology defines *blo sbyong* in the following way: "The foundational oral instruction of the Bka' gdams pa called *blo sbyong* consists in generating the awakening mind."[45] *Blo sbyong* instructions teach various techniques that lead to this goal, such as contemplating the propaedeutic steps of the graded path, reflecting on the fact that oneself and others are equal, and mentally taking all suffering upon oneself and giving all happiness and well-being to others (*gtong len*). While *blo sbyong* as a genre is a Tibetan creation, many of its key ideas go back to Indian Mahāyāna literature; Nāgārjuna's *Ratnāvalī* is considered a source of *blo sbyong* thought, and chapter eight of Śāntideva's *Bo-dhi-sattvacaryāvatāra* is of particular importance for the idea of the equality of "self" and "other" (*parātmasamatā*).

Since *blo sbyong* instructions are defined through their topic and aims rather than their specific contents, their form is more varied than that of *lam rim* and *bstan rim* works. *Blo sbyong* texts are often fairly brief; Bka' gdams pa histories explain that they were originally given as personal oral instructions from teacher to disciple, but teachers of the 12th century began to pass them on publicly and committed them to writing. Among *blo sbyong* texts, the *Blo sbyong don bdun ma* ("Mind training in seven points") by Bya 'Chad kha ba (1101–1175) has become particularly famous, partly through the commentary by Tsong kha pa's disciple Hor ston Nam mkha' dpal (1373–1447). 'Chad kha ba himself had developed an interest in the *blo sbyong* through the "Mind training in eight lines" (*Blo sbyong tshig brgyad ma*) of Glang ri thang pa (1054–1123), and received *blo sbyong* instructions from Sha ra ba Yon tan grags (1070–1141). Later on, an extensive collection of *blo sbyong* works and related materials was compiled by two scholars of the Sa skya pa tradition, Sems dpa' chen po Gzhon nu rgyal mtshan and Mus chen Dkon mchog rgyal mtshan (1388–1469).[46] Because of its short format and straightforward instructions, the *blo sbyong* has remained highly popular, and Tibetan blockprints of *blo sbyong* texts are still reproduced in large numbers today.

Like the *lam rim*, *blo sbyong* works, too, are sometimes classified into instructions for the three types of practitioners, although this is not fundamental to the genre as such and is never expressed in the early *blo sbyong* works themselves. Even so, it is fair to say that *lam rim* and *blo sbyong* are closely related genres, and the Tibetan tradition itself tends to present them together in Buddhist compendia, doxographies, and historical works.[47] Both have had a far-reaching impact on the Buddhist traditions of Tibet, far beyond Bka' gdams pa and Dge lugs pa circles.

TANTRA AND MONASTICISM

The Bka' gdams pa have often been portrayed as a tradition that contributed to the growth of monasticism in Tibet and that valued monastic vows over tantric practice, especially the antinomian practices of the higher tantra classes.[48] It is true that the early Bka' gdams pa literature puts an emphasis on basic Buddhist ethics and Mahāyāna doctrines, rather than propagating the highly developed late tantra cycles from India. Compared to the developments in western Tibet in the 11th century, where scholars such as the famous translator Rin chen bzang po brought tantric traditions from Kashmir to Tibet and where tantric art has been preserved in the monuments of this period, the Bka' gdams pa of central Tibet appear to have been a largely rural community that was happy to establish small and unassuming monasteries, with a building style not too different from local Tibetan farmhouses, and often situated in or near their own home regions. Central Tibetan *mchod rten* (*stūpas*) of this era are mostly simple cylindrical structures with a small roof and spire, distinctly different from the vase-shaped structures of other regions and later times. The early monasteries of teachers such as Po to ba and Spyan snga ba and their disciples consist of smallish temples, usually facing south to catch the sunlight, with simple living quarters for the monks and (in some cases) nuns.[49] These establishments were not designed to look grand, but were constructed as pragmatic community environments for practicing Buddhists.

In terms of tantric transmissions, it must be remembered that Atiśa himself was steeped in the tantric traditions of Bengal, but there is no textual evidence about whether he passed these on to his Tibetan disciples to any significant degree. According to Tibetan sources, Atiśa's main meditation deities were Buddha Śākyamuni, Avalokiteśvara, Acala, and Tārā, and their meditation practice, together with the *tripiṭaka*, became known under the name of "the seven deities and teachings" (*lha chos bdun ldan*). These practices are obviously quite different from the complex rituals and antinomian practices of the late tantric period in India, or indeed of other strands of Tibetan Buddhism.

The significance of Atiśa's *Bodhipathapradīpa* lies in the fact that it condenses the highly developed Indian Buddhism of the time into a system, with a strong emphasis on the Mahāyāna; tantra is included as an advanced technique to achieve the same goal, but the work warns against practices that would lead to a breach of one's vows. The biographies of the Tibetan Bka' gdams pa teachers do not give the impression that tantric initiations and transmissions played a major role in their Buddhist training. However, physical traces of Atiśa's own tantric practice have survived. As mentioned above. Rwa sgreng houses a statue of the six-armed Mañjuvajra of the Guhyasamāja system that is said to have belonged to Atiśa himself, and Lo dgon is said to be based on the Guhyasamāja mandala. A peculiar feature of the Bka' gdams tradition is that it has created a tantric system of its own, known as the "sixteen spheres" (*thig le bcu drug*). It consists of a meditation in which the thousand-armed Avalokiteśvara is the central figure, and fifteen other figures are visualized emanating from him in a specific sequence. These figures include not only Atiśa's four main meditation deities but also Atiśa and 'Brom ston pa themselves.[50] The practice of the "sixteen spheres" seems to have played a significant role in constructing a Bka' gdams pa identity, both fulfilling the demand for a "tantra of one's own" and elevating the founding fathers of the tradition. It is being actively revived at Rwa sgreng Monastery nowadays and is documented in a voluminous modern publication.[51]

It should also be mentioned in this context that the Bka' gdams pa have their own—albeit very limited—stories of *gter ma* revelation. One of these is the "pillar testament" (*Bka' chems ka khol ma*) mentioned in the context of Atiśa's life story summarized above (Atiśa Dīpaṃkaraśrījñāna, 982–1054). The other is—to a certain degree—the "Book of the Bka' gdams" (*Bka' gdams glegs bam*): to a certain degree because this work is a compilation of very diverse materials, built around a versified explanation of Mahāyāna ethics composed by Atiśa, and including biographies, prophesies, prebirth stories, and a long section of dialogues between the early Bka' gdams pa masters. In these dialogues, the *Bka' gdams glegs bam* itself appears as a "magical book" (*'phrul pa'i glegs bam*); it manifests, but then disappears, and is finally enclosed in a *stūpa* in Stabs ka ("Tabka"). While this "magical book" seems like an inspirational, nonmaterial object, one passage mentions a concrete number of pages, which makes "the book" oscillate between a material and an immaterial object. While of course not being a *gter ma* proper, which would require a prescribed process of hiding and rediscovering the text, the *'phrul pa'i glegs bam* is certainly conceived as a book with special supernatural properties, and the process of its transmission is described with revelatory overtones.[52] Quite in tune with this, "the book" describes its contents as a secret knowledge that should not be disclosed publicly, not because of tantric esoteric practices but because—as Bka' gdams pa authors sometimes remark—the workings of *karman*, and therefore also life stories and prebirth stories, are a great mystery that can be fully gauged only by an omniscient being, i.e., a Buddha or a fully realized Buddhist master.

A FORMATIVE MOVEMENT

In conclusion, is it fair to say, as the title of this article suggests, that the Bka' gdams pa were a formative movement of Tibetan Buddhism? After all, the early Bka' gdams pa have not developed a sophisticated Sanskrit scholarship like the Sa skya pa, they have not brought forth spectacular yogi poets like the Bka' brgyud pa, they have not gained any significant political power in central Tibet, and they even disappeared as a distinct tradition altogether about four hundred years after Atiśa's arrival in Tibet. Yet, it seems justified to regard them as a formative movement in several respects, apart from creating and disseminating the instructional genres of *lam rim* and *blo sbyong* discussed in the sections on "The Graded Path to Buddhahood" and "Mind Training" above.

The central Tibetan Bka' gdams pa movement, established locally by 'Brom ston pa and disseminated by his main disciples and their students, seems to have had an enormous impact on the growing popularity of Buddhism in the region. The Tibetan biographies (*rnam thar*) of the early Bka' gdams pa masters give a vivid impression of this process. Several of these life stories begin with the remark that the family followed the indigenous Bon tradition, but the child was drawn toward Buddhism, found a Buddhist teacher and entered one of the small local monasteries, and later in life became a major figure with hundreds or even thousands of students. After the collapse of the Tibetan Empire in the 9th century, the centralized state sponsorship of Buddhism had disappeared, and there had been a rapid decline of the tradition in central Tibet. The monastic ordination lineage was reintroduced from eastern Tibet in the late 10th century, but Buddhism was far from being popular and widespread among the people on the plateau. The Bka' gdams pa began as a grass-roots movement that spread locally in the province of Dbus through the creation of relatively small-scale monasteries and hermitages, situated typically in remote places hidden at the upper end of the valleys, and thus well-suited for a secluded religious practice.

The early generations of teachers in the 11th century did not generate a large-scale written legacy, but taught their disciples orally, often on an individual basis. The oral nature of their instructions shines through in the written works that do exist: anthologies of "sayings" of the Bka' gdams pa masters and works in a highly colloquial style with dialect expressions (*yul skad*) and idiomatic language. They have a strongly local flavor, referring to specific places in central Tibet, the flora and fauna of the Tibetan plateau, local people and their customs, and well-known figures of the early Bka' gdams pa environment. Thus, they adapt the doctrines of Indian Buddhism for their audiences on the plateau, both preserving and indigenizing the Buddhist teachings.

The originally oral instructions, such as Po to ba's *Dpe chos* introduced in the section on "The Graded Path to Buddhahood" above, were written down by students in the early 12th century to preserve them for future generations. Some of these students also moved to more public places by founding monasteries in the main valleys, along the routes of travel and trade. Their biographies record rapidly growing numbers of disciples. At the same time, the teachers of the 12th century initiated public instructions on *lam rim* and *blo sbyong*, and they began composing their own written texts on this topic, beginning with works that often did not have proper titles, but were just known as "the *blo sbyong* of teacher X," or "the *lam rim* of teacher Y." This seems to indicate that the focus was on the contents of the instruction, rather than on the work as a literary composition. It is therefore sometimes hard to pin down whether a "*blo sbyong* of teacher X" was actually written down by this teacher, or by a student of the teacher, or after several steps of oral transmission. What matters to the Tibetan tradition is intellectual authorship, i.e., the individual who created the content, rather than literary authorship, i.e., the person who wrote it down. Yet, there are intriguing vignettes that reflect a growing interest in the written medium. For example, the religious history of Yar lung jo bo Shākya rin chen sde, composed in 1376, describes the origin of the *Blo sbyong don bdun ma* in the following way:

> While he was staying in 'Gres phu, ['Chad kha ba] was wondering whether he should teach these instructions publicly or not, and he intended to pass them on individually to certain suitable persons. However, he was uncertain for whom this would be beneficial or not beneficial. So he said to those present: "If you have butter, invite the meditation masters. We will hold a feast for the name-giving for these instructions of mine." At this time he had subdivided [the *blo sbyong* instructions] into seven sections and put them down in writing, and therefore it became known as *don bdun ma* ("[*Blo sbyong*] in Seven Points"). From then on, he taught [it] in public . . .[53]

According to this testimony, writing the instruction down in a structured literary form, giving a name or title to the text, and passing it on to larger numbers of students go hand in hand. The early Bka' gdams pa masters were thus among those who not only made Buddhism popular by adapting it for their Tibetan audiences but also experimented with new Tibetan writing styles, blending oral and written forms, and creating new literary genres that remained popular throughout the centuries and across the Buddhist traditions of Tibet.

REVIEW OF LITERATURE

While the figure of Atiśa Dīpaṃkaraśrījñāna attracted scholarly curiosity relatively early on, the Bka' gdams pa as a whole have—until recently—largely been neglected in academic scholarship, partly perhaps because they were overshadowed by their successors, the Dge lugs pa. Among the earlier scholarship, mention should be made of Sarat Chandra Das's sketch of Atiśa's life story published in 1893, based on two biographical sections from the *Bka' gdams glegs bam* and on Sum pa mkhan po's 18th-century work on the history of Buddhism.[54] It served as a source for Laurence A. Waddell's now outdated book on *The Buddhism of Tibet: or Lamaism*, published in 1895. Bell's *Religion of Tibet* (1931) also provides a sketch of Atiśa's life and activities. The first extensive Tibetan historical source available in English was the *Deb ther sngon po* (*The Blue Annals*) by 'Gos lo tsa ba Gzhon nu dpal (1392–1481), translated by G. N. Roerich and published in Calcutta in 1949–1953.[55] Its comprehensive nature and richness in biographical detail has made it one of the most popular sources for scholarly research on the history of Tibetan Buddhism; it served, for example, as the basis for Hadano's pioneering survey of the Bka' gdams pa tradition published in Japanese in 1954.[56]

With the growth of Tibetan studies as an academic discipline, scholarship on the Bka' gdams pa masters began to flourish in the second half of the 20th century. The first substantial monograph devoted entirely to Atiśa was published in Calcutta in 1967 by Alaka Chattopadhyaya.[57] The book is unprecedented in its detailed exploration of the subject and provides useful material, in particular in the appendices, but the academic literature as well as the Tibetan sources available to the author were limited. The first systematic collection and analysis of biographical materials related to Atiśa was undertaken by Helmut Eimer in his *Berichte über das Leben des Atiśa (Dīpaṃkaraśrījñāna)* (1977), which drew attention to the enormous number of Tibetan sources available and the broad range of literary genres that need to be considered.[58] It is a pioneering survey of sources indispensable for any scholarly work on this topic. It was followed by Eimer's synoptical edition and German paraphrase of the earliest biographical record, the *Rnam thar rgyas pa (yongs grags)*, in 1979.[59] Kaie Mochizuki has also published various studies on Atiśa and his written legacy.[60] In 2019, James Apple published a book with a detailed life story of Atiśa based on early Tibetan biographical sources and translations from a selection of works by Atiśa.[61]

It took some time until due scholarly attention was given to the Bka' gdams pa tradition as a whole. David Snellgrove's *Indo-Tibetan Buddhism* (1987) provides an insightful survey of the role of Atiśa and the early Bka' gdams pa masters.[62] However, while the 11th-century revival of Buddhism in western Tibet, with its royal patronage, high-profile scholars, and stunning art and architecture, had triggered scholarly attention already in the 1980s and 1990s, the testimonies of the Bka' gdams pa tradition in central Tibet have been studied on a broader scale beginning only at the turn of the 21st century.[63] The first detailed conspectus of the Bka' gdams pa tradition was written by Meenakshi Rai (2006).[64] The monograph provides a useful survey based on a good range of Tibetan sources, using them in a comparative way, but it does not aim to go much beyond the traditional narrative in its analysis of the material. Marie-Stella Boussemart wrote an accessible life story of 'Brom ston pa, based on Tibetan sources (1999).[65] Academic studies of individual teachers, works, and historical contexts have increased in recent years, for example through articles on lesser-known Bka' gdams pa masters, studies of the "Book of the Bka' gdams" (*Bka' gdams glegs bam*), translations and discussions of *lam rim* and *blo sbyong* works, a translation and study of Po to ba's *Dpe chos*, Vetturini's presentation and analysis of the Bka' gdams history by Bsod nams lha'i dbang po, Schuman's study of the developments at Snar thang Monastery, and Iuchi's work on various Bka' gdams pa institutions and sources.[66] Important works from the Bka' gdams tradition have been made available in translation; for example, *The Book of Kadam*; *Wisdom of the Kadam Masters*; and *Essential Mind Training: Tibetan Wisdom for Daily Life*, translated and introduced by Thupten Jinpa.[67]

PRIMARY SOURCES

Many of the Tibetan sources mentioned in this article can be accessed online at the Buddhist Digital Resource Center (https://www.tbrc.org/). A flood of Tibetan original sources has become available through two monumental series published by the Dpal brtsegs bod yig dpe rnying zhib 'jug khang: the *Bka' gdams gsung 'bum phyogs bsgrigs* (120 vols.) and the *Bod kyi lo rgyus rnam thar phyogs bsgrigs* (120 vols.). For the issues addressed here, the following primary sources are of particular relevance:

Atiśa Dīpaṃkaraśrījñāna: see the bibliography on "Bka' gdams pa Doctrines and Doctrinal Literature" below, under Eimer and Sherburne.

Bka' gdams glegs bam, vol. 1, *Jo bo rje dpal ldan a ti sha'i rnam thar bka' gdams pha chos*; vol. 2, *'Brom ston rgyal ba'i 'byung gnas kyi skyes rabs bka' gdams bu chos*. Edited by Mkha' 'gro tshe ring. Xining: Mtsho sngon mi rigs dpe skrun khang, 1994.

Bka' gdams gsung 'bum phyogs bsgrigs bzhugs so. Edited by the Dpal brtsegs bod yig dpe rnying zhib 'jug khang. 120 vols. [Chengdu]: Si khron mi rigs dpe skrun khang, 2006–2009.

Bod kyi lo rgyus rnam thar phyogs bsgrigs bzhugs so. Edited by the Dpal brtsegs bod yig dpe rnying zhib 'jug khang. 120 vols. Zi ling: Mtsho sngon mi rigs dpe skrun khang, 2010–.

Bsod nams lha'i dbang po. "Bka' gdams rin po che'i chos 'byung rnam thar nyin mor byed pa'i 'od stong." In *Two Histories of the bKa'-gdams-pa Tradition from the Library of Burmiok Athing*. 207–393. Gangtok: Gonpo Tsetsen, 1977.

Las chen Kun dga' rgyal mtshan. *Bka' gdams kyi rnam par thar pa bka' gdams chos 'byung gsal ba'i sgron me*. Lhasa: Bod ljongs mi dmangs dpe skrun khang, 2003.

Mchims Nam mkha' grags. *Snar thang gi gdan rabs gser phreng*. Lha sa: Bod ljongs bod yig dpe rnying dpe skrun khang, 2015. An *dbu can* manuscript of the same work was published in *Bod kyi lo rgyus rnam thar phyogs bsgrigs*, vol. 62 (*khu*) (Zi ling [Xining]: mTsho sngon mi rigs dpe skrun khang, 2012), folios 167a–196a.] [Also available on tbrc.org, W2CZ7888.]

Mchims Nam mkha' grags. *Rnam thar rgyas pa yongs grags*. See Eimer, *Rnam thar rgyas pa* under the Further Reading heading "The Lives of the Bka' gdams pa Masters."

Nyang Nyi ma 'od zer. *Chos 'byung me tog snying po sbrang rtsi'i bcud*. Lhasa: Bod ljongs bod yig dpe rnying dpe skrun khang, 1988. Third ed. published in 2012.

Paṇ chen Bsod nams grags pa. *Bka' gdams gsar rnying gi chos 'byung yid kyi mdzes rgyan*. In *Two Histories of the bKa'-gdams-pa Tradition from the Library of Burmiok Athing*. 1–206. Gangtok: Gonpo Tseten, 1977.

Paṇ chen Bsod nams grags pa. *Bka' gdams gsar rnying gi chos 'byung yid kyi mdzes rgyan*. Lhasa: Bod ljongs bod yig dpe rnying dpe skrun khang, 2001.

[Po to ba Rin chen gsal]. *Dpe chos dang dpe chos rin chen spungs pa*. Beijing: Mi rigs dpe skrun khang, 2001. For further editions, see Roesler, *Frühe Quellen*.

Rnam thar rgyas pa. In *Biography of Atiśa and his disciple Ḥbrom-ston: Zhö ed*. Vol. 2. Edited by Lokesh Chandra, 820–862. New Delhi: International Academy of Indian Culture, 1982. See also Eimer, *Rnam thar rgyas pa*.

DIGITAL MATERIALS

Buddhist Digital Resource Center (https://www.tbrc.org/).
The Treasury of Lives (https://www.treasuryoflives.org/).

Asian Classics Input Project (https://www.asianclassics.org/).
Himalayan Art Resources (https://www.himalayanart.org/).

FURTHER READING

HISTORY OF THE BKA' GDAMS TRADITION AND ITS INSTITUTIONS

Davidson, R. M. *Tibetan Renaissance: Tantric Buddhism in the Rebirth of Tibetan Culture.* New York: Columbia University Press, 2005. See esp. chapters 3 and 8.

Iuchi, Maho. *An Early Text on the History of Rwa sgreng Monastery: The* Rgyal ba'i dben gnas rwa sgreng gi bshad pa nyi ma'i 'od zer *of 'Brom Shes rab me lce.* Cambridge, MA: Harvard University Press, 2016.

Iuchi, Maho. "The Bka' gdams chos 'byung Genre and the Newly Published Ye shes rtse mo's Bka' gdams chos 'byung." In *The Historical Development of Tibeto-Himalayan Civilization.* Edited by Iwao Kazushi and Ikeda Takumi, 338–355. Kyoto: Rinsen Books, 2018.

Kano, Kazuo. "The Transmission of Sanskrit Manuscripts from India to Tibet: The Case of a Manuscript Collection in the Possession of Atiśa Dīpaṃkaraśrījñāna (980–1054)." In *Transfer of Buddhism across Central Asian Networks (7th to 13th Centuries).* Edited by Carmen Meinert, 82–117. Boston: Brill, 2015.

Kuijp, L. van der. "Die Dalai Lamas von Tibet und die Ursprünge der Lama-Wiedergeburten." In *Die Dalai Lamas: Tibets Reinkarnationen des Bodhisattva Avalokiteśvara.* Edited by M. Brauen, 14–31. Stuttgart: Völkerkundemuseum der Universität Zürich, 2005.

Martin, Dan, in collaboration with Yael Bentor. *Tibetan Histories: A Bibliography of Tibetan-Language Historical Works.* London: Serindia, 1997.

Miller, Amy Sims. "Jewelled Dialogues: The Role of The Book in the Formation of the Kadam Tradition within Tibet." PhD diss., University of Virginia, 2004.

Rai, Meenakshi. *Kadampa School in Tibetan Buddhism.* Delhi: Saujanya, 2006.

Roerich, George N. *The Blue Annals.* Calcutta: Asiatic Society of Bengal, 1949. See esp. Book V, *The Venerable Lord (Jo-bo-rje, Atiśa) and His Spiritual Lineage.*

Roesler, Ulrike. "On the History of Histories: The Case of the bKa' gdams pas." In *Contributions to Tibetan Buddhist Literature: Proceedings of the 11th Seminar of the International Association for Tibetan Studies, Königswinter 2006.* Edited by Orna Almogi, 393–413. Halle, Germany: International Institute for Tibetan and Buddhist Studies, 2008.

Schuman, Michael D. "Building Place and Shaping Lives: Nartang Monastery from the 12th through 15th Centuries." PhD diss., University of Virginia, 2016.

Snellgrove, David L. *Indo-Tibetan Buddhism: Indian Buddhists & their Tibetan Successors.* Boston: Shambhala, 1987. See esp. chapter V.3.

Vetturini, Gianpaolo. "The bKa' gdams pa School of Tibetan Buddhism." PhD diss., SOAS, University of London, 2007.

THE LIVES OF THE BKA' GDAMS PA MASTERS

Apple. James B. *Atiśa Dīpaṃkara: Illuminator of the Awakened Mind.* Boulder: Shambhala, 2019.

Boussemart, Marie-Stella. *Dromteunpa, l'humble yogi.* Marzens, France: Vajra Yogini, 1999.

Chattopadhyaya, Alaka. *Atīśa and Tibet: Life and Works of Dīpaṃkara Śrījñāna in Relation to the History and Religion of Tibet.* Delhi: Motilal Banarsidass, 1981.

Das, Sarat Chandra. "Indian Pandits in Tibet." *Journal of the Buddhist Text Society of India* 1, pt. 1 (1893): 1–31.

Decleer, Hubert. "Master Atiśa in Nepal: The Tham Bahīl and Five Stūpas' Foundations According to the *'Brom ston Itinerary*." *Journal of the Nepal Research Centre* 10 (1996): 27–54.

Eimer, Helmut. *Berichte über das Leben des Atiśa (Dīpaṃkaraśrījñāna): Eine Untersuchung der Quellen.* Wiesbaden, Germany: Harrassowitz, 1977.

Eimer, Helmut. Rnam thar rgyas pa: *Materialien zu einer Biographie des Atiśa Dīpaṃkaraśrījñāna.* 2 vols. Wiesbaden, Germany: Harrassowitz, 1979.

Eimer, Helmut. "Hymns and Stanzas Praising Dīpaṃkaraśrījñāna." In *Glimpses of the Sanskrit Buddhist Literature.* Edited by K. N. Mishra, 9–32. Sarnath, India: Central Institute of Higher Tibetan Studies, 1997.

Eimer, Helmut. *Testimonia for the* Bstod-pa brgyad-cu-pa: *An Early Hymn Praising Dīpaṃkaraśrījñāna (Atiśa).* Lumbini, Nepal: Lumbini International Research Institute, 2003.

Eimer, Helmut. "Sources for the Vita of 'Brom ston." In *Contributions to Tibetan Buddhist Literature.* Edited by Orna Almogi, 337–392. Halle, Germany: International Institute for Tibetan and Buddhist Studies, 2008.

Kramer, Ralf. *The Great Tibetan Translator: Life and Works of rNgog Blo ldan shes rab (1059–1109).* Munich: Indus Verlag, 2007.

Sørensen, Per K. "The Prolific Ascetic lCe-sgom Śes-rab rdo-rje alias lCe-sgom źig-po: Allusive, but Elusive." *Journal of the Nepal Research Centre* 11 (1999): 175–200.

Sørensen, Per K. "An XIth Century Ascetic of Buddhist Eclecticism: Kha-rag sgom-chuṅ." In *Tractata Tibetica et Mongolica: Festschrift für Klaus Sagaster zum 65; Geburtstag.* Edited by Karénina Kollmar-Paulenz and Christian Peter, 241–253. Wiesbaden, Germany: Harrassowitz, 2002.

BKA' GDAMS PA DOCTRINES AND DOCTRINAL LITERATURE

Ehrhard, Franz-Karl. "The Transmission of the *Thig-le bcu-drug* and the *bKa' gdams glegs bam*." In *The Many Canons of Tibetan Buddhism.* Edited by Helmut Eimer and David Germano, 29–56. Leiden, The Netherlands: Brill, 2002.

Eimer, Helmut. *Bodhipathapradīpa: Ein Lehrgedicht des Atiśa (Dīpaṃkaraśrījñāna) in der tibetischen Überlieferung.* Wiesbaden, Germany: Harrassowitz, 1978.

Jackson, David. "The bsTan Rim ("Stages of the Doctrine") and Similar Graded Path Expositions of the Bodhisattva's Path." In *Tibetan Literature: Studies in Genre.* Edited by J. I. Cabezón and R. R. Jackson, 229–243. Ithaca, NY: Snow Lion, 1996.

Jinpa, Thupten. *Mind Training: The Great Collection.* Boston: Wisdom Publications, 2006.

Jinpa, Thupten. *The Book of Kadam: The Core Texts.* Boston: Wisdom Publications, 2008.

Karmay, Samten G. "The Ordinance of Lha Bla ma Ye shes 'od." In *The Arrow and the Spindle: Studies in History, Myths, Rituals and Beliefs in Tibet.* Vol. 1. By Samten G. Karmay, 3–16. Kathmandu: Mandala Book Point, 1998.

Miyazaki, Izumi. "Atiśa (Dīpaṃkaraśrījñāna): His Philosophy, Practice and Its Sources." *Memoirs of the Research Department of the Toyo Bunko* no. 65 (2007): 61–89.

Roesler, Ulrike. *Frühe Quellen zum buddhistischen Stufenweg in Tibet. Indische und tibetische Traditionen im* dPe chos *des Po-to-ba Rin-chen-gsal.* Wiesbaden, Germany: Rei-chert Verlag, 2011.

Roesler, Ulrike, trans. "Be'u bum sngon po: The Blue Compendium: Teachings on the Graded Path by Potowa Rinchen Sal, Compiled in Verse by Dölpa Sherap Gyatso." In *Stages of the Buddha's Teachings: Three Key Texts.* Translated by U. Roesler, K. Holmes, and D. Jackson, 37–117. Boston: Wisdom Publications, 2015.

Sherburne, Richard, trans. *The Complete Works of Atiśa, Śrī Dīpaṃkara Jñāna, Jo-bo-rje: The Lamp for the Path and the Commentary, Together with the Newly Translated Twenty-Five Key Texts.* Delhi: Aditya Prakashan, 2000.

Sweet, Michael J. "Mental Purification (Blo sbyong): A Native Tibetan Genre of Religious Literature." In *Tibetan Literature: Studies in Genre.* Edited by J. I. Cabezón and R. R. Jackson, 244–260. Ithaca, NY: Snow Lion, 1996.

MATERIAL CULTURE

Henss, Michael. *The Cultural Monuments of Tibet.* Vol. 1, *The Central Regions / The Central Tibetan Province of Ü.* Munich: Prestel, 2014.

Roesler, Ulrike, and Hans-Ulrich Roesler. *Kadampa Sites of Phempo: A Guide to Some Early Buddhist Monasteries in Central Tibet.* Kathmandu: Vajra Publications, 2004.

NOTES

1. The name is explained as referring to the word of the buddha (*bka'*) as explained in the instructions (*gdams*) of Dīpaṃkaraśrījñāna, see Gianpaolo Vetturini, "The bKa' gdams pa School of Tibetan Buddhism" (PhD diss., SOAS, University of London, 2007), 165. See also Las chen Kun dga' rgyal mtshan, *Bka' gdams kyi rnam par thar pa bka' gdams chos 'byung gsal ba'i sgron me* (Lhasa: Bod ljongs mi dmangs dpe skrun khang, 2003), 3–5.
2. The Bka' gdams pa, Bka' brgyud pa, Sa skya pa, and Rnying ma pa all emerged as distinct traditions during the 11th century, even if the Rnying ma pa trace themselves back to an earlier period. On Tibetan Buddhism in this period see, for example, David L. Snellgrove, *Indo-Tibetan Buddhism: Indian Buddhists & their Tibetan Successors* (Boston: Shambhala, 1987), chapter V.3; and Ronald M. Davidson, *Tibetan Renaissance: Tantric Buddhism in the Rebirth of Tibetan Culture* (New York: Columbia University Press, 2005).
3. See Karl-Heinz Everding, "gSang phu Ne'u thog, Tibet's Earliest Monastic School (1073): Reflections on the Rise of Its Grva tshang bcu gsum and Bla khag bcu," *Zentralasiatische Studien* 38 (2009): 137–154; Pascale Hugon, "Enclaves of Learning, Religious and Intellectual Communities in Tibet: The Monastery of gSang phu Ne'u thog in the Early Centuries of the Later Diffusion of Buddhism," in *Meanings of Community across Medieval Eurasia*, ed. E. Hovden, Ch. Lutter, and W. Pohl (Leiden, The Netherlands: Brill, 2016), 289–308; and Leonard van der Kuijp, "The Monastery of Gsang-phu ne'u-thog and Its Abbatial Succession from ca. 1073 to 1250," *Berliner Indologische Studien* 3 (1987): 103–127.
4. Michael D. Schuman, "Building Place and Shaping Lives: Nartang Monastery from the 12th through 15th Centuries" (PhD diss., University of Virginia, 2016).
5. Franz-Karl Ehrhard, "The Transmission of the *Thig-le bcu-drug* and the *bKa' gdams glegs bam*," in *The Many Canons of Tibetan Buddhism*, ed. Helmut Eimer and David Germano (Leiden, The Netherlands: Brill, 2002), 29–56; and Marta Sernesi, "Bibliography and Cultural History: Remarks on the Bka' gdams glegs bam," in *The Illuminating Mirror: Tibetan Studies in Honour of Per K. Sørensen on the Occasion of his 65th Birthday*, ed. Olaf Czaja and Guntram Hazod (Wiesbaden, Germany: Dr. Ludwig Rei-chert Verlag, 2015), 411–444.
6. For more details, see Ulrike Roesler, "On the History of Histories: The Case of the bKa' gdams pas," in *Contributions to Tibetan Buddhist Literature: Proceedings of the 11th Seminar of the International Association for Tibetan Studies, Königswinter 2006*, ed. Orna Almogi (Halle, Germany: International Institute for Tibetan and Buddhist Studies, 2008), 393–413.

7. As Eimer has shown, in its transmitted form the eulogy is a composite text containing verses by Nag tsho lo tsa ba and verses composed by Atiśa's student Kṣitigarbha; see Helmut Eimer, *Testimonia for the* Bstod-pa brgyad-cu-pa*: An Early Hymn Praising Dīpaṃkaraśrījñāna (Atiśa)* (Lumbini, Nepal: Lumbini International Research Institute, 2003).
8. Helmut Eimer, "Hymns and Stanzas Praising Dīpaṃkaraśrījñāna," in *Glimpses of the Sanskrit Buddhist Literature*, ed. K. N. Mishra (Sarnath, India: Central Institute of Higher Tibetan Studies, 1997), 9–32.
9. These are Ye shes rgyal mtshan's biographies of the Bka' gdams tradition (*Byang chub lam gyi rim pa'i bla ma brgyud pa'i rnam par thar pa rgyal mtshan mdzes pa'i rgyan mchog tu phul byung nor bu'i phreng ba*) and Sum pa mkhan po's history of Buddhism (*Dpag bsam ljon bzang*). On both works, see Andrej I. Vostrikov, *Tibetan Historical Literature*, trans. Harish Chandra Gupta (Calcutta: Indian Studies: Past & Present, 1970).
10. Helmut Eimer, *Berichte über das Leben des Atiśa (Dīpaṃkaraśrījñāna): Eine Untersuchung der Quellen* (Wiesbaden, Germany: Harrassowitz, 1977), 279–292.
11. Ralf Kramer, *The Great Tibetan Translator: Life and Works of rNgog Blo ldan shes rab (1059–1109)* (Munich: Indus Verlag, 2007).
12. There are two monumental series of relevant materials: the *Bka' gdams gsung 'bum phyogs bsgrigs* (120 vols) and the *Bod kyi lo rgyus rnam thar phyogs bsgrigs* (120 vols), both published by the Dpal brtsegs bod yig dpe rnying zhib 'jug khang; see above under "Primary Sources."
13. The earliest source for the life of Po to ba Rin chen gsal, for example, is found in the 12th-century commentary on the *Be'u bum sgnon po*, a collection of Po to ba Rin chen gsal's oral instructions written by his disciple Dol pa Rin po che, and further information is given in a commentary on his *Dpe chos* written in the 14th century by 'Gro mgon Dpal ldan ye shes; see Roesler, "On the History of Histories," 399–403.
14. *Legs par bshad pa bka' gdams rin po che'i gsung gi gces btus nor bu'i bang mdzod* (Zi ling: Mtsho sngon mi rigs dpe skrun khang, 1996). The author is Tho yon Ye shes don grub bstan pa'i rgyal mtshan (1792–1855).
15. Mchims Nam mkha' grags, *Snar thang gi gdan rabs gser phreng* (Lha sa: Bod ljongs bod yig dpe rnying dpe skrun khang, 2015); see "Primary Sources" above for further editions.
16. A partial translation is available in Thupten Jinpa, *The Book of Kadam: The Core Texts* (Boston: Wisdom Publications, 2008). See also Amy Sims Miller, "Jewelled Dialogues: The Role of The Book in the Formation of the Kadam Tradition within Tibet" (PhD diss., University of Virginia, 2004).
17. On the transmission of the *Bka' gdams glegs bam*, see Ehrhard and Sernesi in note 5 above.
18. Ye shes rtse mo, *Bka' gdams rin po che'i bstan 'dzin rnams kyi byung khungs*. This work has only recently become available; see Maho Iuchi, "The Bka' gdams chos 'byung Genre and the Newly Published Ye shes rtse mo's Bka' gdams chos 'byung," in *The Historical Development of Tibeto-Himalayan Civilization*, ed. Iwao Kazushi and Ikeda Takumi (Kyoto: Rinsen Books, 2018), 338–355. Bsod nams lha'i dbang po, *Bka' gdams rin po che'i chos 'byung rnam thar nyin mor byed pa'i 'od stong*. For an analysis and translation, see Vetturini, "The bKa' gdams pa School." Las chen Kun dga' rgyal mtshan, *Bka' gdams kyi rnam par thar pa bka' gdams chos 'byung gsal ba'i sgron me*. See note 1. Paṇ chen Bsod nams grags pa, *Bka' gdams gsar rnying gi chos 'byung yid kyi mdzes rgyan*, in *Two Histories of the bKa'-gdams-pa Tradition from the Library of Burmiok Athing* (Gangtok, India: Gonpo Tseten, 1977), 1–206.
19. See Dan Martin in collaboration with Yael Bentor, *Tibetan Histories: A Bibliography of Tibetan-Language Historical Works* (London: Serindia, 1997), no. 216; and Vetturini, "The bKa' gdams pa School," 3. The title of A myes zhabs' work is *Dge ba'i bshes gnyen bka' gdams pa rnams kyi dam pa'i chos byung ba'i tshul legs par bshad pa ngo mtshar rgya mtsho*.
20. These are the *Byang chub lam gyi rim pa'i bla ma brgyud pa'i rnam thar pad ma dkar po'i phreng ba* by Paṇ chen bla ma Blo bzang ye shes (1663–1737) and the *Byang chub lam gyi rim pa'i bla ma brgyud pa'i rnam thar* by Tshe mchog gling yongs 'dzin Ye shes rgyal mtshan (on the latter see note 9).

21. Published in Helmut Eimer, *Rnam thar rgyas pa: Materialien zu einer Biographie des Atiśa Dīpaṃkaraśrījñāna*, 2 vols. (Wiesbaden, Germany: Harrassowitz, 1979). The *Rnam thar rgyas pa yongs grags* version was produced in the 13th century by Mchims Nam mkha' grags, the seventh abbot of Snar thang, and is included in his *Snar thang gser phreng* and in the *Bka' gdams glegs bam*.
22. Eimer, *Rnam thar rgyas pa*, episodes 129, 334.
23. See the appendices in Alaka Chattopadhyaya, *Atīśa and Tibet: Life and Works of Dīpaṃkara Śrījñāna in Relation to the History and Religion of Tibet* (Delhi: Motilal Banarsidass, 1967).
24. Hubert Decleer, "Master Atiśa in Nepal: The Tham Bahīl and Five Stūpas' Foundations According to the 'Brom ston Itinerary," *Journal of the Nepal Research Centre* 10 (1996): 27–54.
25. *Bka' chems ka khol ma*, ed. Smon lam rgya mtsho ([Lanzhou]: Kan su'u mi rigs dpe skrun khang, 1989). See Martin, *Tibetan Histories*, 24, no. 4. According to later biographies, the text was retrieved from a pillar, but the early biographies describe how a beggar woman indicated a place in the ground of the Jo khang Temple where Atiśa was to find the text. The protective deity guarding the treasure text allowed them to copy as much as they could within one day; see Eimer, *Rnam thar rgyas pa*, episode 337; and George N. Roerich, *The Blue Annals* (Calcutta: Asiatic Society of Bengal, 1949), 258.
26. Eimer, *Rnam thar rgyas pa*, episode 410f.
27. Roberto Vitali, "Bka' gdams pa Religious Politics in Dbus: The One Hundred Years after A ti sha's Death," in *The Illuminating Mirror: Tibetan Studies in Honour of Per K. Sørensen on the Occasion of his 65th Birthday*, ed. Olaf Czaja and Guntram Hazod (Wiesbaden, Germany: Dr. Ludwig Rei-chert Verlag, 2015), 511–525.
28. The biography is included in Mchims Nam mkha' grags, *Snar thang gser phreng* (see above under "Primary Sources"). See Helmut Eimer, "Sources for the *Vita* of 'Brom ston," in *Contributions to Tibetan Buddhist Literature*, ed. Orna Almogi (Halle, Germany: International Institute for Tibetan and Buddhist Studies, 2008), 337–392. Parallel sections are found within the early biographies of Atiśa mentioned above, the *Rnam thar rgyas pa (yongs grags)*, as well as a work by 'Brom Shes rab me lce composed around the beginning of the 14th century, see Maho Iuchi, *An Early Text on the History of Rwa sgreng Monastery: The* Rgyal ba'i dben gnas rwa sgreng gi bshad pa nyi ma'i 'od zer *of 'Brom Shes rab me lce* (Cambridge, MA: Harvard University Press, 2016), 7–12.
29. See Marie-Stella Boussemart, *Dromteunpa, l'humble yogi* (Marzens, France: Vajra Yogini, 1999); Meenakshi Rai, *Kadampa School in Tibetan Buddhism* (Delhi: Saujanya 2006), 28–38; and Roerich, *Blue Annals*, 251–265.
30. Rai, *Kadampa School*, 33.
31. Iuchi, *An Early Text*, 33; image in Michael Henss, *The Cultural Monuments of Tibet*, vol. 1, *The Central Regions/ The Central Tibetan Province of Ü* (Munich: Prestel, 2014), 285.
32. Ulrike Roesler, "A Palace for Those Who Have Eyes to See: Preliminary Remarks on the Sacred Geography of Reting (Rwa-sgreṅ)," *Acta Orientalia Vilnensia* 8, no. 1 (2007): 123–144.
33. For a brief survey, see Ulrike Roesler, *Frühe Quellen zum buddhistischen Stufenweg in Tibet: Indische und tibetische Traditionen im* dPe chos *des Po-to-ba Rin-chen-gsal* (Wiesbaden: Rei-chert Verlag, 2011), 107–115. For an alternative outline, see Rai, *Kadampa School*, 133.
34. The "*Blo sbyong* in Eight Verses" is translated in Rai, *Kadampa School*, 151–152. On the *Blo sbyong don bdun ma*, see Michael J. Sweet, "Mental Purification (Blo sbyong): A Native Tibetan Genre of Religious Literature," in *Tibetan Literature: Studies in Genre*, ed. J. I. Cabezón and R. R. Jackson (Ithaca, NY: Snow Lion, 1996), 249–250.
35. For Spyan snga ba's biography see Vetturini, "The bKa' gdams pa School," 109–114; and Roerich, *Blue Annals*, 284–285. The designation of his tradition is not entirely fixed; the term *gdams ngag pa* seems the most common, but the term *man ngag pa* is also occasionally found. See Nyang ral Nyi ma 'od zer's *Chos 'byung me tog snying* po, 434; and the *Bka' gdams gces btus nor bu'i bang mdzod*, 285. On Spyan snga ba's monastery Lo dgon see Maho Iuchi 井内真帆, "Lo ji: shyoki kadamuha ji'in no hensen" [The history of

Lo dgon pa: The vicissitudes of an early bKa' gdams pa monastery], *Ōtani daigaku kenhyū nenpō/Annual Report of Researchers of Otani University* 62 (2010): 37–77.

36. On Phu chung ba, see Vetturini, "The bKa' gdams pa School," 105–107; and Roerich, *Blue Annals*, 267–268; on his role in the transmission of the *Bka' gdams glegs bam*, see Ehrhard, "The Transmission," esp. 38–41.
37. Ulrike Roesler and Hans-Ulrich Roesler, *Kadampa Sites of Phempo: A Guide to Some Early Buddhist Monasteries in Central Tibet* (Kathmandu: Vajra Publications, 2004), 50.
38. Sketches of their lives can be found in Rai, *Kadampa School*; Roerich, *Blue Annals*; and Vetturini, "The bKa' gdams pa School."
39. David Jackson, "The bsTan rim ('Stages of the Doctrine') and Similar Graded Path Expositions of the Bodhisattva's Path," *Tibetan Literature: Studies in Genre*, ed. J. I. Cabezón and R. R. Jackson (Ithaca, NY: Snow Lion, 1996), 229–243. The distinction between *lam rim* and *bstan rim* is not very clear-cut; the colophon of Tsong kha pa's *Lam rim chen mo*, for example, names Gro lung pa's *Bstan rim chen mo* as a model for this work, which shows that the genres were perceived as similar. Similarly, Las chen Kun dga' rgyal mtshan's discussion suggests that he was not trying to draw clear borderlines (Las chen, *Bka' gdams kyi rnam par thar pa*, 5–6).
40. *Bodhipathapradīpa* stanzas 2–5. Richard Sherburne, trans., *The Complete Works of Atiśa, Śrī Dīpaṃkara Jñāna, Jo-bo-rje: The Lamp for the Path and the Commentary, Together with the Newly Translated Twenty-Five Key Texts* (Delhi: Aditya Prakashan, 2000), 4–5.
41. Sherburne, *The Complete Works*, 439–465; and Roesler, *Frühe Quellen*, 44–45. On the collection *Jo bo'i chos chung*, see also Kaie Mochizuki, "Some Remarks on the Small Texts Attributed to Dīpaṃkaraśrījñāna," *Sŭngga* (僧伽)/*Joong-ang Saṅgha University Magazine* 20 (2004): 61–74. James Apple has drawn attention to yet another virtually unknown work on the graded path attributed to Atiśa that awaits further study, see James B. Apple, *Atiśa Dīpaṃkara: Illuminator of the Awakened Mind* (Boulder, CO: Shambhala 2019), 193–232.
42. Jackson, "The bsTan rim"; and Roesler, *Frühe Quellen*, 37–44.
43. Roesler, *Frühe Quellen*, 389.
44. For a brief survey of *lam rim* works from other traditions, see David Seyfort Ruegg, introduction to *The Great Treatise on the Stages of the Path to Enlightenment*, vol. 1, by Tsong kha pa, ed. Joshua W. C. Cutler and Guy Newland (Ithaca, NY: Snow Lion, 2000), 26.
45. *Bka' gdams gces btus nor bu'i bang mdzod*, 8.
46. The collection is known as the *Blo sbyong glegs bam*. See Thupten Jinpa, *Mind Training: The Great Collection* (Boston: Wisdom Publications, 2006).
47. Roesler, *Frühe Quellen*, 13–14.
48. Chattopadhyaya, *Atīśa and Tibet*, chapter 2, emphasizes this point in defense against possible accusations against the Indian master. On the issue of antinomian practices, see also Mark Tatz, "*Maitri-pa and Atiśa*," in *Tibetan Studies: Proceedings of the 4th Seminar of the International Association for Tibetan Studies*, ed. H. Uebach and J. L. Panglung (Munich: Kommission für Zentralasiatische Studien Bayerische Akademie der Wissenschaften, 1988), 473–482.
49. Roesler and Roesler, *Kadampa Sites*, esp. 8–9 and images; examples of the cylindrical type of *stūpas* can be found in Henss, *Cultural Monuments*, vol. 1, 269, 274, 290, 291.
50. See Ehrhard, "The Transmission," 53–56.
51. *Rwa sgreng dgon pa'i nyams bzhes chos spyod kyi brjed byang chen mo*, ed. Gzigs pa sprul sku Blo bzang bzod pa and Phun tshogs rab rgyas (Lhasa: Bod ljongs mi dmangs dpe skrun khang, 2006), 82–106 and 672–717.
52. Ehrhard, "The Transmission"; and Miller, "Jewelled Dialogues."
53. Śākya rin chen sde, *Yar klungs jo bo'i chos 'byung* (Lhasa: Bod ljongs mi dmangs dpe skrun khang, 1987), 103.

54. Sarat Chandra Das, "Indian Pandits in Tibet," *Journal of the Buddhist Text Society of India* 1, pt. 1 (1893): 1–31; and *Indian Pandits in the Land of Snow*, ed. Nobin Chandra Das (Calcutta: Baptist Mission Press, 1893). See also Helmut Eimer, "The Sources for Sarat Chandra Das' Life of Atiśa (Dīpaṃkaraśrījñāna)," *Zentralasiatische Studien* 28 (1998): 7–10.
55. Roerich, *Blue Annals*.
56. Hakuyu Hadano 羽田野伯猷, "Kadamuhashi: shiryōhen (カーダム派史資料篇)" [The history of Bka' gdams pa: Materials], in *Chibetto indogaku shūsei* (チベット・インド学集成) [Collected works on Indo-Tibetan studies], vol. 1–1, by Hakuyu Hadano (Kyoto: Hōzōkan, 1954), 46–191.
57. Chattopadhyaya, *Atīśa and Tibet*.
58. In addition to his *Berichte* (1977), Helmut Eimer has published a wide range of articles on aspects of Bka' gdams pa sources, which are too numerous to be listed here.
59. Eimer, *Rnam thar rgyas pa*.
60. See, for example, Kaie Mochizuki 望月海慧, *A Study of the Mahāsūtrasamuccaya of Dīpaṃkaraśrījñāna: A Report of Grant-in-Aid for Encouragement of Young Scientists* (Minobu, Japan: Minobusan University, 2002); "Dīpaṃkaraśrījñāna's Activities at the Vikramaśīla Monastery in Relation with the Pāla Dynasty," *Tōyō Bunko* (東洋文化) 96 (2016): 63–80; and "Some Remarks on the Small Texts Attributed to Dīpaṃkaraśrījñāna," *Sŭngga* (僧伽)/*Joong-ang Saṅgha University Magazine* 20 (2004): 61–74.
61. Apple, *Atiśa Dīpaṃkara*.
62. Snellgrove, *Indo-Tibetan Buddhism*, 470–484. Insightful as this presentation is, Snellgrove seems to overstate the impact of the Bka' gdams pa on monasticism when he writes: "It would therefore seem that Atiśa and 'Brom ston pa in founding the Bka' gdams pa order were in effect the founders of the whole later Tibetan monastic tradition" (Snellgrove, *Indo-Tibetan Buddhism*, 493). A similar statement regarding 'Brom ston pa is found in *Indo-Tibetan Buddhism*, 508. However, it needs to be kept in mind that neither Atiśa nor 'Brom ston pa had taken the monks' vows according to the Mū-la-sarvā-sti-vā-da Vinaya, which is the monastic code adopted by the Tibetan Buddhists. Atiśa had been ordained according to the Mahāsāṅghika Vinaya, and 'Brom ston remained a lay Buddhist throughout his life; therefore neither of them would have been able to ordain monks in Tibet.
63. See, for example, Roberto Vitali, *The Kingdoms of Gu-ge Pu-hrang: According to the mNga'-ris rgyal-rabs by Gu-ge mkhan-chen Ngag-dbang grags-pa* (Dharamsala, India: Mtho-gliṅ gtsug lag khaṅ, 1996); Deborah E. Klimburg-Salter et al., *Tabo, a Lamp for the Kingdom: Early Indo-Tibetan Buddhist Art in the Western Himalaya* (Milan: Skira, 1997); and Davidson, *Tibetan Renaissance*, 108–116, with further references. It should be mentioned that the cultural heritage of Ladakh was explored much earlier, for example, through the pioneering work of August Hermann Francke and Giuseppe Tucci's work on the famous translator Rin chen bzang po.
64. Rai, *Kadampa School*.
65. Boussemart, *Dromteunpa*.
66. On individual teachers see, for example, Per K. Sørensen, "The Prolific Ascetic lCe-sgom Śes-rab rdo-rje alias lCe-sgom źig-po: Allusive, but Elusive," *Journal of the Nepal Research Centre* 11 (1999): 175–200; and Per K. Sørensen, "An XIth Century Ascetic of Buddhist Eclecticism: Kha-rag sgom-chuṅ," in *Tractata Tibetica et Mongolica: Festschrift für Klaus Sagaster zum 65. Geburtstag*, ed. Karénina Kollmar-Paulenz and Christian Peter (Wiesbaden, Germany: Harrassowitz, 2002), 241–253. For studies of the "Book of the Bka' gdams" (*Bka' gdams glegs bam*), see notes 5 and 16 above. On works from the Bka' gdams tradition see Jackson, "The bsTan rim"; Sweet, "Mental Purification"; Roesler, *Frühe Quellen*. On the tradition itself and its institutions see Vetturini, "The bKa' gdams pa School"; Iuchi, "Lo ji: shyoki kadamuha ji'in no hensen"; and Schuman, "Building Place and Shaping Lives."
67. Thupten Jinpa, see bibliography under "Bka' gdams pa Doctrines and Doctrinal Literature."

Ulrike Roesler

KĀLACAKRA-MAṆḌALA: SYMBOLISM AND CONSTRUCTION

INTRODUCTION

The *kālacakra-maṇḍala* is an integral part of Kālacakra tantric practice, similar to the mandalas specific to other Buddhist tantric systems of the Unexcelled Yoga Tantras (*niruttarayoga tantra*). It forms a core of the first two main phases of tantric practice: the phase of initiation (*abhiṣeka*) and the stage of generation (*utpattikrama*), which involves deity-yoga. In that respect, a kālacakra-maṇḍala can be either a physical object or a mentally visualized image. Material representations of the kālacakra-maṇḍala can be classified into two main categories. To the first category belong three-dimensional kālacakra-maṇḍalas, which traditionally have been cast in silver and gold or constructed out of other types of material. They are invariably decorated with precious substances, such as jewels, corals, pearls, and the like, and are often kept in large *stūpas*, temples, and shrines. To the second category belong two-dimensional maṇḍalas, which are of three types: those made with pulverized jewels, corals, pearls, grains, and the like; those painted on cloth (*paṭa*); and those painted on temple walls. These are architectural blueprints of a three-storied palace of nirvana, symbolizing the body, speech, and mind of the Primordial Buddha (Ādibuddha) Kālacakra. A kālacakra-maṇḍala made with powdered substances is constructed exclusively for the sake of a Kālacakra tantric initiation, whereas a cloth mandala can function as a material support both for a tantric initiation and for worship and meditation. A mural representation is never used as a material support for tantric initiations but only as a basis for meditation. In contrast to the material kālacakra-maṇḍala, one that is mentally constructed through an elaborate *sādhana* practice is not merely an objectified, mental image but also an internal, subjectivized maṇḍala located in the meditator's mind–body complex.

Whether a visual representation of the kālacakra-maṇḍala is material or purely a mental object, it is encoded with multilayered symbolic meanings. Its shape, structural organization, various constituents and colors, and deities represent specific enlightened qualities of Kālacakra's body, speech, and mind, which are the purified or sublimated aspects of our world-system (*lokadhātu*), our society, and the individual.

THE IMAGERY, STRUCTURE, AND SYMBOLIC MEANINGS OF THE KĀLACAKRA-MAṆḌALA

When interpreted as a representation of our world-system, the kālacakra-maṇḍala consists of five levels: a black wind-mandala situated in limitless space; a red fire-mandala, which is on top of the wind-mandala; a white water-mandala above it; and a yellow earth-mandala on the top. These stacked maṇḍalas differ in size; the black wind-maṇḍala is the largest in diameter, and the others are sequentially smaller in diameter. These are represented in the kālacakra-maṇḍala by the five mentioned colors, which are associated with the elements that make up the external world, the body of the individual, and the five types of gnosis. On top of the earth-mandala stands Mount Meru, and a multicolored lotus is situated in the center of its surface. Above the center of the lotus is a moon-disc, which is the same size as the center of the lotus. Above the moon-disc is a sun-disc and above that the *rāhu*-disc.

On top of these discs stands a brightly shining three-storied palace, or a vajra-pavilion, known as the mind-mandala. The mind-maṇḍala, being the top level of the palace, is placed in the very center of the colored kālacakra-maṇḍala. In its center is a radiant maṇḍala with a lotus, symbolizing Kālacakra's gnosis. On top of the lotus are the discs of the sun and moon, symbolizing wisdom and compassion, or wisdom and method. The second story of the palace is the speech-maṇḍala, symbolizing the enlightened speech. Outside that speech-mandala is the body-mandala, which is a half-size larger than the speech-maṇḍala and represents Kālacakra's body. These three mandalas, or stories, stand for the purified aspects of the individual's body, speech, and mind. Each of the maṇḍalas has four gates, situated in the four cardinal directions, thus totaling twelve gates with arches made of gold and gems. At each of the twelve gates, there are chariots. Outside the gates of the body-maṇḍala are eight cremation grounds.[1]

In the practice of a kālacakra-sādhana, these maṇḍalas are placed in the reverse order, and the wind-maṇḍala, which represents the purified forehead cakra (*lalāṭa*), is on top of the other maṇḍalas. Below it is the fire-maṇḍala, signifying the purified throat cakra; below it is the water-maṇḍala, representing the purified heart cakra; and beneath it is the earth-maṇḍala, symbolizing the purified navel cakra. From the navel cakra, Mount Meru extends down to the secret cakra, represented in the mind-maṇḍala by a lotus, while the discs of the moon, sun, and *rāhu* symbolize the three *nāḍīs* (channels) above the navel—*lalanā*, *rasanā*, and *avadhūtī*—and three *nāḍīs* below the navel, conveying the feces, urine, and seminal fluid.

The *Supreme Primordial Buddha Tantra* (*Paramādibuddhatantra*) gives us another interpretation of the symbolic meaning of the kālacakra-maṇḍala when visualized in the practice of the stage of generation for the sake of attaining the mundane accomplishments (*siddhi*). In this interpretation, the entire kālacakra-maṇḍala symbolizes the sphere of reality, or absolute space (*dharmadhātu*), identified with a purified womb into which a buddha descends. The three maṇḍalas constituting the kālacakra-maṇḍala also stand for the buddha, dharma, and sublime saṅgha. The four vajra-lines, which mark the edges of the three maṇḍalas, are said to represent the four divine abidings (*brahmavihāra*), while the quadrangular walls of the kālacakra-maṇḍala represent the four applications of mindfulness (*smṛtyupasthāna*). The twelve gates signify the twelve links of dependent origination that have been eliminated; the arches of the gates represent the twelve grounds (*bhūmi*); and the cremation grounds in the cardinal and intermediate directions represent the eightfold noble path. Here, the sixteen pillars stand for the emptiness of the five psychophysical aggregates (*skandha-śūnyatā*); the emptiness of the five elements (*dhātu-śūnyatā*), also called great emptiness (*mahāśūnyatā*); and the emptiness of ultimate reality (*paramārtha-śūnyatā*). Moreover, the upper stories represent the elements and the turrets on top of them stand for the eight types of liberation (*mokṣa*), the four purified elements (earth, water, fire, and wind) and four sense objects (form, smell, taste, and touch), and the eight qualities, such as small, large, yellow, red, and so on. The doorjambs and door wings symbolize the body, speech, and mind; the three fences of the mandalas of the mind, speech, and body represent the three vehicles; and the five colors symbolize the five faculties of faith (*śraddhendriya*) and the five powers (*bala*).[2] The pavilions of the three maṇḍalas stand for *samādhis* and *dhāraṇīs*, while the multicolored and jeweled strips of fabric represent the ten perfections. The garlands of pearls represent the eighteen unique qualities of the buddha, the decorative *bakulī* flowers represent the ten powers of a bodhisattva, and the galleries stand for the ten virtues. The sound of bells that fills the palace symbolizes liberation through emptiness, the victory banners represent the four bases of supernatural powers (*ṛdhipāda*), and the shimmering mirrors stand for the four exertions (*prahāṇa*). Moreover, the vibration of the yak-tail whisks symbolizes the seven limbs of awakening (*bodhyaṅga*), while the garlands symbolize the nine divisions of the Buddha's teachings. The corners embellished with multicolored vajras represent the four means of attracting disciples (*saṃgraha*) to the Buddhist teachings. The jewels inlaid at the junctures of the gates and turrets symbolize the jewels of the four truths of the nobles, the five great discs encompassing the palace stand for the five extrasensory perceptions (*abhijñā*), while the surrounding vajra chain symbolizes the constituents of awakening (*bodhipakṣa*). A mountain range represents bliss (*sukha*) and the light rays symbolize the gnosis-vajra, while the sun and the moon represent wisdom and compassion.[3] Although this interpretation of the symbolic meaning of the kālacakra-maṇḍala as a whole and of its constituents is given in the context of a sādhana practice, this does not preclude its reference to a physical representation of the kālacakra-maṇḍala but in fact adds to it an additional level of meaning.

Symbolism of Kālacakra's Body and Other Deities in the Kālacakra-maṇḍala. In the center of the mind-maṇḍala stands the primordial buddha Kālacakra. As expounded in the *Kālacakratantra*'s "Chapter on Sādhana" and the *Stainless Light Commentary* (*Vimalaprabhāṭīkā*), the image of primordial buddha Kālacakra represents various sublimated aspects of samsara and nirvana, the conventional and ultimate realities. In both, the iconography and the sādhana practice, Kālacakra is visualized as having a body of blue color, wearing various vajra ornaments and an apron of tiger skin. He has three necks—a blue middle neck, a red right neck, and a white left neck—and four faces, representing the four enlightened activities: the dark and fierce front face, with protruding fangs; the right, red, passionate face; the left white, peaceful face; and the yellow rear face, abiding in *samādhi*. Altogether, he has six shoulders, or three pairs of shoulders. Of the three pairs, the first is dark blue, the second is red, and the third is white. His twenty-four hands hold various weapons and ritual implements, such as a vajra, sword, cleaver, fire-arrow, vajra goad, *damaru*, hammer, spear, rod, hatchet, wheel, bell, shield, *khaṭvāṅga* with smiling faces, a skull filled with blood, bow, noose, jewel, lotus, conch, mirror, chain, and Brahmā's head. Each of his hands has five fingers, each of different colors, corresponding to the colors of the five types of gnosis and the five gross elements. His fingers glitter with seal-rings. His thumbs are yellow, the forefingers white, the middle fingers red, the ring fingers dark blue, and the smallest fingers green. Moreover, the three joints of each of his fingers are of different colors—starting from the palm of the hand, the first row of the joint is dark blue, the second row is red, and the third one is white.[4]

He is standing on discs representing the sun, moon, and *kālāgni* supported by a lotus. In terms of the symbolism of the discs regarding a person, they represent the three main nāḍīs of the subtle body—the *lalanā*, *rasanā*, and *avadhūtī*—whereas the lotus that supports them represents the heart-cakra. Kālacakra stands in the *ālīḍha* posture and tramples, with his two feet, the hearts of white Rudra and red Anaṅga (also known as Kāmadeva and referred to in the *Kālacakratantra* as Māra).[5] Anaṅga represents the four main classes of *māras*, the hindrances to the attainment of nirvana without remainder (*niravaśeṣanirvāṇa*).[6] He has one face and four arms and holds in his hands a bow, five flower-arrows, a goad, and a noose. He is being trampled by Kālacakra's red right foot. Rudra—representing the hosts of *rudras* who symbolize attachment, aversion, delusion, and pride—has one face with three eyes and four arms, which hold a trident, a *damaru*, a skull, and a *khaṭvāṅga*. He is being trampled under Kālacakra's white left foot.[7] Rati, the wife of Anaṅga, and Umā, the wife of Rudra, are stationed next to the soles of Kālacakra's two feet and have distressed facial expressions.[8]

As for the symbolic meaning of Kālacakra's body regarding time, this represents a sublimated aspect, or the transcendence of the conventional, samsaric wheel of time. His body represents a single unit of one day and one night and is said to consist of twelve *lagnas*.[9] Thus, each of his two feet represents six lagnas, making twelve altogether. Each of his three throats symbolizes four lagnas, also making twelve lagnas. Moreover, each of his four faces represents three lagnas, making twelve lagnas; lastly, each of his six shoulders represents two lagnas, symbolizing a total of twelve lagnas. His twelve arms on the right and left sides of his body represent the twelve months of a year; and each of his twenty-four hands represents a half lagna, corresponding to the classification of the twenty-four fortnights of a year. His 360 finger-joints symbolize the number of days in a year.[10]

Standing in the *alīḍha* posture, Kālacakra is in a sexual embrace with his consort Viśvamātā, who is positioned in the *pratyālīḍha* posture.[11] Her body, which is of a golden luster, is marked with *mudrās*. She wears the tiara of Vajrasattva and has four faces, twelve eyes, and eight hands. The four faces are the eastern, or front, face, which is golden yellow; the southern white face; the northern red face; and the western blue face. With her four right hands, she holds a cleaver, a goad, a damaru, and a rosary, while her four left hands hold a skull, a noose, a lotus with a hundred petals, and a jewel.

In terms of the body of the individual, Kālacakra represents semen whereas Viśvamātā represents menstrual blood.[12] In terms of ultimate reality, their union symbolizes the enlightened awareness with two mutually pervasive aspects: the transcendence of wisdom (*prajñāpāramitā*), or emptiness, represented by Viśvamātā, and compassion, or method, represented by Kālacakra.

On the eight petals—which are in the four cardinal and four intermediate directions of a lotus within the mind-maṇḍala, where Kālacakra and Viśvamātā are stationed—are eight goddesses (*śakti*). Each of the goddesses has eight arms, four faces of four different colors, and twelve eyes. Four among these goddesses—Kṛṣṇā, or Kṛṣṇadīptā, on the southeastern petal; Raktā, or Raktadīptā, on the southwestern petal; Pītā, or Pītadīptā, on the northwestern petal; and Śuklā on the northeastern petal—hold yak-tail whisks in their hands. Standing behind them are four other goddesses holding a white Dharma conch, a red Dharma gong, a black wish-fulfilling gem, and a yellow wish-fulfilling tree. With their right and left hands, these goddesses also hold emblems, including musical instruments, bowls containing various ambrosias, fruit, medicine, and sandalwood. The eight goddesses represent the eight perfections—the perfection of generosity and so on—which are said to be contained within the perfection of gnosis (*jñānapāramitā*). Thus, they all emanate from Viśvamātā, who represents wisdom, or emptiness. The stage of visualization of the eight goddesses—together with the two central deities (Kālacakra and Viśvamātā)—symbolizes the arising of Vajrasattva accompanied by his consorts (*mudrā*).[13]

On the lotuses situated in the four cardinal directions stand the four *tathāgatas*—black Amoghasiddhi, standing on the sun disc of the eastern lotus; red Ratnasaṃbhava, standing in the southern lotus; white Amitābha, situated in the northern direction; and yellow Vairocana, located in the western direction. They have six arms, three faces, and nine eyes. In the center is Akṣobhya, who is here a presiding deity among these five tathāgatas. Here, in the kālacakra-maṇḍala, the tathāgatas represent the five purified psychophysical aggregates (*skandha*) manifesting as the five types of Kālacakra's gnosis. They are accompanied by four goddesses—black Tārā, yellow Locanā, white Māmakī, and red Pāṇḍarā—who are situated in the intermediate directions and symbolize the four purified elements (*dhātu*). Tārā represents the purified wind element, Pāṇḍarā the purified fire element, Locanā the purified earth element, and Māmakī the purified water element. The color of each of the four goddesses is determined by the color of the element she represents. In the context of a kālacakra-sādhana practice, the goddesses also symbolize the four applications of mindfulness (*smṛtyupasthāna*): the mindfulness of the body (*kāya*), of feeling (*vedanā*), of mind (*citta*), and of mental phenomena (dharma).[14]

Surrounding the four tathāgatas and the four female deities in the eight directions is a set of protective, fierce male (*krodha*) and female (*krodhiṇī*) deities standing in the *ālīḍha* and *pratyalīḍdha* postures, respectively. The visualization of these three groups of deities of the mind-maṇḍala—the five tathāgatas, four goddesses, and the fierce deities—symbolizes the first stage in the development of the body-vajra, which corresponds to the fourth month of embryonic gestation in the womb, when the name-and-form aggregate (*nāmarūpa-skandha*) is formed from the elements. According to the *Stainless Light Commentary*, this sublimated phase of embryonic development is preceded by the visualization of Vajrasattva, which corresponds to the first month of embryonic gestation, when semen enters the womb. This phase also corresponds to the arising of ignorance (*avidyāṅga*), the first link in the chain of dependent origination, and symbolizes the elimination of that link.[15]

There are four bodhisattvas on the walls at the four gates of the mind-maṇḍala and an additional two bodhisattvas below the walls of the northern and southern gates. They each represent one of the six purified sense faculties (*indriya*), corresponding to the arising of the ordinary sense faculties in the embryonic development during the fifth month. The colors of the four bodhisattvas at the four gates correspond to the colors of the four tathāgatas, or the purified psychophysical aggregates, and to the colors of the elements (the four goddesses), from which arise the sense-faculties (bodhisattvas). For details, see tables 1 and 2.

Visualization of the bodhisattvas symbolizes the second phase in the development of Kālacakra's body-vajra, which corresponds to the full development of the sense faculties and sense objects in the fifth month of embryonic gestation.[16] Thus, they symbolize the purification of the fifth and sixth link—namely, the six sense objects (*āyatana*) and contact (sparśa) of the sense faculties with the sense objects—of dependent origination. In addition to these deities, there are secondary male and female deities in the mind-maṇḍala, standing in sexual union and holding different implements representing the emblems of the six buddha families.

The sixty-four yoginīs located in the speech-maṇḍala symbolize Kālacakra's speech-vajra, the purified speech of the individual. The principal yoginīs of the speech-maṇḍala represent the purified, or eliminated, factor of feeling (*vedanāṅga*), whereas the body-vajra stands for the purified factor of craving (*tṛṣṇāṅga*). On the lotuses of the body-maṇḍala, in addition to *nāgas*, pretas, and *bhūtas*, are some ninety-nine male and female deities holding various implements in their hands. They all represent the purified bodily constituents, bodily activities, desires, and counter-desires. Thus, with regard to the individual, the deities of the kālacakra-maṇḍala—which

Table 1. Bodhisattvas as Purified Aspects of the Sense Faculties and Their Origins, Colors, and Locations in the Maṇḍala

Bodhisattva	Sublimated/ purified sense faculty	Elemental origin	Color	Location
Vaigarbha/Khagarbha	Olfactory sense faculty (nose)	Wind element	Black like Tārā and Amoghasiddhi	Right of the eastern gate
Kṣitigarbha	Visual sense faculty (eye)	Fire element	Red like Pāṇḍarā and Ratnasaṃbhava	Right side of the southern gate
Sarvanīvaraṇaviṣkambhī	Bodily sense faculty	Earth element	Yellow like Locanā and Vairocana	Right side of the western gate
Lokeśvara	Gustatory faculty (tongue)	Water element	White like Māmakī and Amitābha	Right side of the northern gate
Samantabhadra	Mental faculty (mind)	Gnosis element	Blue like Kālacakra	Below the wall to the left of the northern gate below
Vajrapāṇi	Auditory sense faculty (ear)	Space element	Blue like Akṣobhya	Below the wall on the left of the southern gate

Source: Author.

Table 2. Goddesses as Purified Sense Objects and Their Corresponding Elements, Colors, and Locations in the Māṇḍala

Goddess	Purified sense object	Elemental origin	Color	Location
Sparśavajrā (touch vajrā)	Touch	Wind element	Black like Tārā	Southeastern direction
Rasavajrā (taste vajrā)	Taste	Fire element	Red like Pāṇḍarā	Southwestern direction
Gandhavajrā (smell vajrā)	Smell	Earth element	Yellow like Locanā	Northwestern direction
Rūpavajrā (form vajrā)	Form	Water element	White like Māmakī	Northwestern direction
Śabdavajrā (sound vajrā)	Sound	Gnosis element	Blue like Samantabhadra	Left of the northern gate
Dharmadhātuvajrā	Realm of phenomena/ mental object	Space element	Blue like Vajrapāṇi	Left of the southern gate

Source: Author.

corresponds to the development of the embryo's body, speech, and mind in the course of the nine months of gestation—symbolize the transformation of the person's body, speech, and mind into a single Kālacakra's four bodies: the gnosis body, represented by the lotus in the center of the mind-maṇḍala; the dharma body, represented by the mind-maṇḍala; the enjoyment body, represented by the speech-maṇḍala; and the emanation body, represented by the body-maṇḍala. The *Kālacakratantra* and the *Stainless Light Commentary* point out that all the constituents of the body, speech, and mind are taught as having the form of a maṇḍala for practical reasons—in order to stabilize the minds of inexperienced practitioners. It is further said that the deities of the mind, body, and speech mandalas of the kālacakra-maṇḍala represent the purified aspects of the three realms of samsara—the realms of desire, form, and formlessness.[17]

A RITUAL OF CONSTRUCTING A KĀLACAKRA-MAṆḌALA FOR INITIATION AND ITS PREREQUISITES

According to the *Stainless Light Commentary* (ch. 3, v. 1), the buddha taught the kālacakra-maṇḍala to enable sentient beings to gain merit and gnosis. He taught a maṇḍala in terms of mundane reality (*lokasatya*) and for the accomplishment of mundane *siddhis* and the accumulation of merit, not for the sake of attaining sublime bliss (*mahāsukha*). A vajra master (*vajrācārya*) who engages in preparing the measuring cords for a sand maṇḍala and in other activities related to the construction of a sand maṇḍala with the intention to achieve the *mahāmudrā-siddhi* through only such activity will have difficulty attaining awakening. One reason for this is that a sand maṇḍala is taught for the sake of the attainment of mundane siddhis (*laukikasiddhi*) and not for the attainment of the *mahāmudrā-siddhi* or the accumulation of gnosis. In support of this statement, Puṇḍarīka, the author of the *Stainless Light Commentary*, cites a stanza from the *Primordial Buddha Tantra* (*Ādibuddhatantra*):

> One should not apply the vajra-measuring lines nor a powder in accordance with the true nature of the mantra. For the one who does so, awakening is difficult to attain.[18]

The true meaning of the word "mantra" is here glossed as gnosis (*jñāna*), based on the interpretation that gnosis is a protection of the mind (*manas-trāṇa*). Hence, the construction of a sand maṇḍala alone, despite being a meritorious action, has limited soteriological efficacy. But this does not preclude the necessity for a vajra master to know how to build a sand maṇḍala in preparation for a Kālacakra tantric initiation. Puṇḍarīka cites Āryaśūra's *Fifty Stanzas on the Guru* (*Gurupañcaśikā*), v. 9, where Āryaśūra speaks of the qualities of a guru worthy of a disciple's veneration, among which is mentioned knowledge of how to paint a maṇḍala.[19]

In order to bestow the seven Kālacakra initiations intended for the removal of disciples' impurities and the acquisition of merit, the vajra master must set in motion the kālacakra-maṇḍala on the day of the full moon of the bright fortnight at the end of the month of Caitra.[20] This allows the disciples to meditate on the maṇḍala and recite the mantras. Prior to preparing a kālacakra-maṇḍala at the site where the initiation will be performed, the vajra master must examine the color and taste of the soil on which the maṇḍala will be constructed. This is because different colors, smells, and tastes of the soil must correspond to different maṇḍala rites, such as the rites of pacification, prosperity, killing, exorcism, attraction, dominance, paralysis,

Table 3. The Colors, Odors, and of Tastes of Soils in Relation to Mundane Rites

White soil	Black soil	Red soil	Yellow soil	Green Soil
Divine odor	Putrid odor	Lotus odor	Pungent odor	All odors
Astringent taste	Sour taste	Spicy taste	Sweet taste	All tastes
Rites of pacification and prosperity	Rites of killing and exorcism	Rites of attraction and dominance	Rites of paralyzing and confusing	All-accomplishing rite

Source: Author.

confusion, and the all-accomplishing rite (see table 3). If the soil does not correspond to the specific rite being performed, then one must dig a hole to the depth of water or a rock. This hole needs to be filled with the soil whose characteristics correspond to the desired rite and the soil mixed with liquids and bodily substances that correspond to the characteristics of the rite. The vajra master also must know how to draw the maṇḍala; otherwise, it is said, he is destined for hell.[21]

The white powder is placed in the center of the maṇḍala for the rites of pacification and prosperity, the black powder for the rites of killing and exorcism, the red powder for rites of attraction and dominance, the yellow powder for rites of paralyzing and confusing, and the green powder for the all-accomplishing rite. Since individual colors of the powders applied in the coloring of a kālacakra-maṇḍala are utilized for a corresponding rite (e.g., a white-colored powder is used for the rite of pacification and the yellow powder for the rite of paralyzing), all the aforementioned rites are said to be accomplishable through the kālacakra-maṇḍala. The purification of powder in the kālacakra-maṇḍala is accomplished through images of the maṇḍala's deities, which correspond to the lights of the five types of the gnosis of Vajrasattva.

The vajra master must, with his own hand, make a single string for measuring and delineating the lines of a maṇḍala. The length of the string should be four times the width of a maṇḍala; the string can measure up to 8 cubits in length in the case of a larger maṇḍala.[22] Using a string woven from three threads spun by a virgin girl, the vajra master is to take three such strings and intertwine them into one to the width equal to that of his thumb. The maṇḍala itself can measure from one up to 1,000 cubits. According to the *Primordial Buddha Tantra,* the mind-maṇḍala should be 12 cubits in circumference, in which case, the string should measure 24 cubits. The speech-maṇḍala should measure 16 cubits, and the body-maṇḍala should be 20 cubits. Commenting on chapter 3, verse 19, Puṇḍarīka tells us that in the case of a large kālacakra-maṇḍala measuring 1,000 cubits, the tantra does not indicate that a string measuring 2,000 cubits should be applied, simply because it would be too large.[23]

Before the vajra master draws a kālacakra-maṇḍala, his body and the bodies of his disciples, as well as the ground, must be ritually protected. Thus, having arrived at the prepared ground for a maṇḍala, the vajra master, stationed in the center and facing east, sits on a soft cushion. With a vajra, he places the syllables *oṃ, āḥ, hūṃ, ho, haṃ,* and *kṣaḥ* on his bodily cakras. The forehead cakra stands for the white disc of the moon, the throat cakra for the red disc of the sun, the heart cakra for the black disc of the *rāhu,* the navel cakra for the yellow disc of the *kālāgni,* the crown cakra (*uṣṇīṣa*) for the blue space-disc, and the secret cakra for the green disc of gnosis. After meditating on these six cakras as maṇḍalas and protecting other parts of his body, he imaginatively incinerates the hosts of *māras* and other negative entities, makes a *bali* offering to the *kṣetrapālas*, and performs a ritual protection of the country. By means of a long series of other protective rituals and meditations, he creates the wheel of protection (*rakṣācakra*) and purifies the ground, invoking and worshipping the earth goddess. After that, he prays to the buddhas of the ten directions and to the bodhisattvas and their wives for his own protection, which is needed for granting initiation into the maṇḍala. Likewise, for the sake of protection, he pegs down all the fierce deities (*krodha*) in the ten directions with pegs made from the strong wood of a *khadira* tree.[24]

The ritual purification of the ground must be performed on the fifth, the tenth, or the fifteenth day of the lunar month. For the auspicious rites, the ground must be purified on the fifth, tenth, or fifteenth lunar day of the bright fortnight, and for the inauspicious rites, it should be purified on the fifth, tenth, or fifteenth lunar day of the dark fortnight. The vajra master also must know the proper, fixed time for drawing a kālacakra-maṇḍala. A measuring string must be applied on the twelfth lunar day, an intoxicant (*madana*) offered on the thirteenth lunar day, and the colored powder of the maṇḍala applied on the fourteenth lunar day.[25]

After protecting the cakras of disciples, the vajra master must also protect the texts. He further addresses the buddhas, declaring: "I will draw a such-and-such maṇḍala of the lord for the sake of the liberation of sentient beings."[26] He must know how to interpret the bad omens that may arise during the application of the measuring string and colored powder. For example, if a measuring string breaks, this indicates impending harm to the guru and the disciples' inability to overcome obstacles. Likewise, if wind disturbs the maṇḍala powder, this forewarns of danger to the kingdom and ruin of the territory. In order to divert those dangers, the vajra master recites the Kālacakra mantra. If the bad omen reoccurs, he is advised to draw the lines, with his left leg in the squatting posture and the sole of the right foot resting on the ground.[27]

After a meditation on the chosen deity (*iṣṭadevatā*), the master places the syllables on his body, engages in the extensive recitation of mantras related to a self-empowerment, and performs a *bali* offering, the removal and binding of obstructing *māras* and demons, and 10,000 *homa* offerings. He then performs a ritual of perfuming the ritual implements, including a measuring string. While perfuming the measuring string, he recites these mantric words: "*oṃ āḥ hūṃ ṝ ḹ vajrasūtra sarvadharmair ekasvabhāva sarvadharmān ekākārasvabhāvān kuru svāhā*" ("*Oṃ āḥ hūṃ ṝ ḹ*, vajra-string that shares the same nature with all phenomena, make all phenomena have a single aspect and nature!"). Having offered the perfume, he deposits the string on the eastern side of the platform on which the kālacakra-maṇḍala will be constructed. After that, he proceeds to perfume the powder while reciting the mantra: "*oṃ aṃ iṃ ṛṃ uṃ ḷṃ suviśuddhapañcaskandhasvabhāva pañcaskandhān suviśuddhadharmān kuru kuru svāhā*" ("*Oṃ aṃ iṃ ṛṃ uṃ ḷṃ*, purified nature of the five psychophysical aggregates, make the five psychophysical aggregates into purified phenomena!"). Having offered perfume to the powder, he deposits the dishes, holding the powder on the western side of the platform.[28]

Having again subjugated the māras and offered bali, he offers the perfume, incense, and the like to the vajra string on the western side of the maṇḍala platform. Having mixed various substances intended for different rites, such as pacification, the vajra master and his disciple stretch a measuring string; the master faces east and holds the measuring string with his left hand, and the disciple faces west and holds it with his right hand. While doing so, the master recites the mantra: "*oṃ āḥ hūṃ a kāyavākcittaikabhūtāḥ sarvadharmā ekākāreṇa vajrasattvo 'haṃ vajrabhūmiṃ sūtrayāmi hūṃ āḥ phaṭ*" ("*Oṃ āḥ hūṃ a*, all phenomena being identical with the body, speech, and mind have a single aspect. I, Vajrasattva, will measure the vajra platform with a string, *hūṃ āḥ phaṭ*"). Then he utters the mantra: "*oṃ vajrasūtraikākārasvarūpeṇa jaḥ jaḥ jaḥ sarvadharmān sūtraya oṃ āḥ hūṃ ho haṃ kṣaḥ phaṭ*" ("*Oṃ* string together all phenomena *jaḥ jaḥ jaḥ* with the nature of a single aspect of the vajra string, *oṃ āḥ hūṃ ho haṃ kṣaḥ phaṭ*"). After that, both the vajra master—with his right leg in the semi-squatting posture (*ardhaparyaṅka*) and his left foot resting on the ground—and his disciple, who is in a similar posture, draw the brahma lines on the eastern and western sides of the platform.[29] Then, the vajra master, standing at the southern side of the platform with his disciple at the northern side, places the northern and southern brahma string at the four gates, above the pegs, in the eastern, western, southern, and northern areas, and lastly at the corners. After that, they incrementally place the string in the four intermediate directions. Then, starting from the eastern and western lines, they place a string in the southern and northern areas; and then from the southern and northern areas, they place it in the western and eastern areas. Having offered the perfume, incense, and so on, the vajra master ritually protects the strings and breaks them.[30]

Afterward, the vajra master stands at the eastern direction of the maṇḍala, while facing west, and his authorized disciple stands in the west, facing east. Having measured the quadrangular platform of the maṇḍala, they draw the brahma line in the center. Then the vajra master stands at the southern area of the maṇḍala, facing north, and the disciple stands at the northern area, facing south, and they place the brahma line again. They apply it to the corners in order to purify the corners. From the brahma line in the center to the southern section, there are 96 lines. There are the same number of lines from the brahma line to each of these sections: the northern, eastern, and southern sections. From the center to its border, the kālacakra-maṇḍala has 192 lines altogether. From among these lines, 48 lines delineate the mind-maṇḍala. The outline drawn by the lines of the speech-maṇḍala is twice as large as that of the mind-maṇḍala. The outline formed by the lines of the body-maṇḍala up to the gates of the great maṇḍala is twice as large as that of the speech-maṇḍala. The five walls and arches, together with the four discs of earth, water, fire, and wind and a vajra-line, delineate the body-maṇḍala up to the outer area or space.[31]

According to the *Primordial Buddha Tantra*, cited by Puṇḍarīka, the vajra master, before drawing the kālacakra-maṇḍala, must first make a smooth, quadrangular platform consisting of sixteen sections for the body-maṇḍala; then he must make the speech and mind maṇḍalas. Commenting on this instruction, Puṇḍarīka explains that each of the maṇḍalas consists of sixteen sections. Within the sixteen sections of the body-maṇḍala, a single section measures the twenty-four fingerbreadths. After the four sections within the four directions are drawn comes a drawing of eight sections on each side of the speech-maṇḍala. The sixteen sections of the speech-maṇḍala measure twelve fingerbreadths, whereas the sixteen sections for the mind-maṇḍala measure six fingerbreadths.

After drawing a brahma line, the vajra master draws the lines measuring four fingerbreadths in each of the four cardinal directions. The pericarp of the central lotus of the mind-maṇḍala is for the seat of the two principal deities. At the gates in the four cardinal directions are the lotus seats of other deities. The petals of the lotuses measure eight fingerbreadths. The lotus of the principal deities is three times larger than the seats of the remaining male and female deities. In the axial place, the lotus of Kālacakra measures twenty-four fingerbreadths; the pericarp, which forms one-third the width of the lotus, measures eight fingerbreadths. Outside the petals of the central lotus is a place for a vajra line. Placing a line between the lotuses of the deities, which measure eight fingerbreadths, the vajra master makes the platform of the fences, arches, and pillars. Then, outside the seats of the tathāgatas is a vajra line, going between them and the four goddesses. In the inner recesses are eight seats, on top of which are either vases or *kapālas*. After that, the seats of the gods and goddesses who represent the sense objects and the sense faculties are outlined. Following this, the three fences, a pavilion, ribbons, string of pearls, string of *bakulī* and *viśīrṣa* flowers, and so on are outlined.[32] After that, the walls, gates, pillars, arches, lotus seats of the deities, lines of ribbons, and so forth of the mind, speech, and body maṇḍalas are outlined according to the prescribed measurements.[33]

Preparation and Application of the Powder. After completing the drawing of the three maṇḍalas and purification of the seats of the deities, the vajra master offers the bali, together with perfumes, flowers, and the like. This is followed by the preparation of the five colored powders used for coloring the kālacakra-maṇḍala. The five colors correspond to the colors of five tathāgatas, which represent Kālacakra's five types of gnosis in the maṇḍala. The five colors also correspond to the previously mentioned colors of the five elements, in the environment and in the person's body. The powder is made by pulverizing five types of gems: the black powder is made from pulverized sapphires, the red powder from rubies, the white powder from moonstones, the yellow powder from *karketaka* gems, the blue powder from blue sapphires, and the green powder from pulverized emeralds.

In the case of a kālacakra-maṇḍala made for a universal (*sāmānya*) *cakravartin*, the yellow powder is made of pulverized gold, the white powder from pulverized pearls, the red powder from pulverized coral, the black powder from lapis lazuli, and the green powder from a mixture of the powders from the four aforementioned precious substances. For all other ordinary people, the kālacakra-maṇḍala can also be colored with powders made from common substances, such as crushed kidney beans, whole rice, and pulverized or crushed gems.

The five colors of the powders used in coloring the kālacakra-maṇḍala correspond to the colors the five tathāgatas and to the colors of the elements associated with them (see table 4).

The powder is applied in the four cardinal directions of the maṇḍala, and each of its colors corresponds to the color of one of the four faces of Kālacakra. Thus, the black powder is applied in the eastern section of the maṇḍala, corresponding to the black face of Kālacakra, which faces east and symbolizes the purification of the mind; the red color is applied in the southern section, corresponding to the red face, facing south and representing the purification of speech; the yellow powder is applied in the western section, corresponding to the yellow face, which faces

Table 4. Colors of Powders and Their Correspondences

White powder	Yellow powder	Red powder	Black powder	Blue powder
Amitābha	Vairocana	Ratnasaṃbhava	Amoghasiddhi	Akṣobhya
Water element	Earth element	Fire element	Wind element	Space element

Source: Author.

west and symbolizes the purification of gnosis; and the white powder is applied in the northern section, corresponding to Kālacakra's white face, facing north and representing the purification of the body. After that, the powder is applied in the intermediate sections of the maṇḍala, beginning with the northeastern section. This is followed by the coloring of the white terrace, red ribbons, black necklaces of pearls, garlands, semigarlands, mirrors, chowries, white *bakulī* flowers, yellow pillars, white tips, and the white and red lotuses of the deities as well as the white, red, and black lines of the walls, which represent the purified body, speech, and mind.[34]

The eight-petaled lotus in the center of the mind-maṇḍala, the seat of the presiding deity Kālacakra, is colored with green powder since green represents gnosis. Outside the lotus are sixteen pillars, four in each direction, individually marked with a decorative dagger, jewel, wheel, and lotus. Outside the central lotus, in the four intermediate directions, are a white dagger in the northeast, a red dharma gong in the southwest, a black wish-fulfilling jewel in the southeast, and a yellow wish-fulfilling tree in the northwest. The white pitchers of the goddesses who belong to the four tathāgatas of the mind-maṇḍala are in the intervals between the sixteen pillars. The white seats of the goddesses are on the top of red, or sun-colored, lotuses, and the red seats of the male deities are on top of white, or moon-colored, lotuses. The seats of the male deities are on the petals of the four cardinal directions of the eight-petaled lotus within the mind-maṇḍala, and the seats of the four goddesses are on the petals of the intermediate directions. Outside the eight petals is a row of vajras.

Within the speech-maṇḍala, the vajra master draws the lotuses for the yoginīs holding white ribbons (*paṭṭikā*) and, in the body-maṇḍala, for the *icchā* and *pratīcchā* classes of goddesses, who represent the sublimated aspects of the individual's desires and counterdesires. The eight lotuses supporting the goddesses with ribbons are in the cardinal and intermediate directions. Of these, the red lotuses are in the cardinal directions, and the white lotuses are in the intermediate directions. The five lines in the speech-maṇḍala represent the flow of the maṇḍalas of the five elements—space, wind, fire, water, and earth—in the body. Their colors correspond to the rites of pacification, paralyzing, and so on. For example, the earth element represented by the yellow line relates to killing and paralyzing due to the efficacy of the *guṇa*s of *prakṛti* and so on. The colors also correspond to the creation and dissolution of the body. For instance, the green line in the maṇḍala, which is relevant to the rites of pacification and the like, corresponds to creation, whereas the yellow line, related to the rites of killing and so forth, corresponds to dissolution.[35]

After the coloring of the speech-maṇḍala comes the coloring of the seats of the kings of *nāga*s, such as the *mārutas* ("those belonging to the wind") and others, in the outer body-maṇḍala, on the terraces (*vedikā*) beneath the arches and pillars at the boundaries of the gates. A circular, black maṇḍala of the *māruta*s is drawn at the right and left sides of the eastern gate; a triangular, red fire-maṇḍala is in the south; a quadrangular, yellow earth-maṇḍala is in the west; and a half-moon-shaped, white water-maṇḍala is in the north. Their emblems are the black, red, yellow, and white *bindu*, *swastika*, vajra, and lotus, respectively. Following this is the coloring of the black, red, yellow, white, and blue chariots at the gates and the white and red cakras of the cremation ground. Thus, throughout the kālacakra-maṇḍala, the colors of the powder must accord with a classification of the colors of the five tathāgatas.

Following completion of the coloring of the speech-maṇḍala comes the coloring of the locations of the sun and the moon in the body-maṇḍala. The rising of the moon on a *pūrṇimā* day is depicted in the northeastern direction and the setting of the sun in the southwestern direction. Above the gates, on the first upper story, in the central spot of the arch in the east, is a black dharma-wheel with a deer to its right and left. It represents the purified mind-cakra. The deities of worship (*pūjādevatā*), with their respective colors, are situated at the surrounding locations nearby. On the arch of the southern gate is a red vase of fortune (lottery vase), which represents purified speech. On its right and left sides are a conch and a lotus. On the arch of the northern gate is a kettledrum, with a white staff and a mallet on its right and left sides. On the arch of the western gate is a yellow bodhi-tree, with a male centaur (*kinnara*) on its right and a female centaur on its left.[36] In accordance with the classification of the wind and the other mentioned elements, in the central mind-maṇḍala, the applied powder of the black and other walls is elevated by the measure of a quarter of a barleycorn.[37] In the speech-maṇḍala, the elevation of the walls is doubled, and in the body-maṇḍala, it is tripled.[38]

The vajra master must be aware of what undesirable consequences follow if the lines of the maṇḍala's walls are made indistinguishable or unattractive. If the lines are unbecoming, then rites of pacification or prosperity will bring the opposite results for the vajra master's patron. If the line is too thick, it will cause illness to the vajra master's patron. If a line is bad and too thin, it indicates the loss of possessions. A broken line will cause death, and a crooked line will cause the banishment of the king and his subjects. Moreover, if an emblem is broken or if the seats of the sun and the moon are broken, the *mantrī* will not attain the *siddhi* that destroys the dangers of cyclic existence. If a coloring powder is mixed up, the patron's lineage will be broken. By saying that when there is a succession of patrons there is also a continuity of vajra masters, Puṇḍarīka reminds the vajra master that his livelihood depends on patrons of the Kālacakra initiation.[39] The vajra master is further instructed not to insert into the maṇḍala any symbol out of his desire to decorate it if that symbol is not mentioned in the tantra. If he does so, such a symbol becomes the symbol of *māras* in the vajra master's Vajrasattva family because of the excessiveness of symbols and because of doing what is contrary to the prescription given in the tantra.[40]

Purification of the Cosmic System and Body through Purification of the Kālacakra-maṇḍala. Based on the *Kālacakratantra*'s principle: "as it is in the environment, so it is in the body, and as it is in the body, so it is in the powder maṇḍala," Puṇḍarīka asserts that through a ritual purification of the kālacakra-maṇḍala, our cosmic system becomes purified. This is expressed in the *Primordial Buddha Tantra*, which reads:

> Just as it is in the environment, so it is in the body. Just as it is in the body so it is elsewhere.
>
> Being familiar with the threefold maṇḍala, the master should draw the [kālacakra-] maṇḍala.[41]

A measure of the 400,000 leagues of our cosmic system corresponds to four cubits in the person's body; and in the maṇḍala, the measure of the cosmic system can span from 1 cubit to 1,000 cubits.[42] Likewise, in the maṇḍala, the earth disc measures forty-eight fingerbreadths from the center to the boundaries of the gates in all directions. The central lotus of the presiding deities measures twenty-four fingerbreadths, and it corresponds to the enclosures of the tathāgatas in all directions of the universe that extend as far as the six continents, six oceans, and six mountains measuring 1,000 leagues. The size of the central lotus also corresponds to the measure of Meru, which extends 50,000 leagues above and below. Moreover, the earth disc, which measures 25,000 leagues in our cosmic system, extends in the maṇḍala as far as the gates of the powdered ground. According to Puṇḍarīka, the measure of the central mind-maṇḍala (*garbha-maṇḍala*) corresponds to 100,000 leagues of the cosmic system, which is occupied by six islands, oceans, continents, and Meru. In the speech-maṇḍala, a disc of the salty ocean extends from the four gates in the four directions out to the goddess Carcikā and measures forty-eight fingerbreadths in the four directions. The size of the speech-maṇḍala corresponds to the size of the water-disc of the maṇḍala of our cosmic system, which measures 200,000 leagues in all directions. The fire-disc, which measures 300,000 leagues within our cosmic system, extends in the four directions from the gates of the speech-maṇḍala up to their tips and measures forty-eight fingerbreadths. The wind-disc, which measures 400,000 leagues in our cosmic system, extends to the end of the gates of the body-maṇḍala and measures forty-eight fingerbreadths.[43] The *uṣṇīṣa* on the top of Meru, which measures 25,000 leagues in our cosmic system, is represented by a lotus in the central maṇḍala and measures twenty-four fingerbreadths. Likewise, the three parts of cosmic Meru—the face, measuring 50,000 leagues; the throat, measuring 25,000 leagues; and the face, measuring 50,000 leagues—are purified within the maṇḍala.

The abode of *nāga*s and each of the seven hells are also purified, as is the area extending from the hips to the ends of the feet in the maṇḍala. The vajra master is further instructed to purify the entire earth within the bodies of all sentient beings. Interpreting the above-cited verse from the root tantra, Puṇḍarīka explains another type of purification in the maṇḍala, pointing out that gnosis is present in the hearts of all sentient beings and that the unbeaten sound of that gnosis always has the characteristic of the *nāda*. Thus, the purified heart-cakra is represented by a central lotus in the mind-maṇḍala. The speech-maṇḍala represents the purified area of the body, extending from the throat to the navel; and the body-maṇḍala represents the purified area spanning from the space between the eyebrows to the sexual organ. The four gates of the body-maṇḍala represent the four purified apertures related to the flow of feces, urine, and semen, and to the crown cakra. The gates of the speech-maṇḍala are the four purified *nāḍīs*—*lalanā, rasaṇā, avadhūtī,* and *śaṅkhinī*—extending from the throat to the border of the navel. The gates of the mind-maṇḍala represent the purified four states of the mind—the waking, dreaming, deep sleep, and the fourth state (*tūryāvasthā*). Thus, a creation of the body, speech, and mind maṇḍalas symbolizes one's arising as the primordial buddha.[44]

In contrast to a *sādhana* on the kālacakra-maṇḍala, where the tantric adept visualizes the maṇḍala deities in their anthropomorphic forms, in many maṇḍalas painted on cloth, and here in a maṇḍala colored with powder, the presence of the deities is marked with mantric syllables. Among various mantric syllables, the syllable *oṃ* represents the body-vajra, or a maṇḍala arisen from gnosis. On the twenty-four lotuses within the kālacakra-maṇḍala are sun and moon seats, which correspond to the classification of the days of the full and new moon throughout the year. The twelve moon-seats correspond to the classification of the twelve days of the full moon within a year, and the twelve sun-seats correspond to the twelve days of the new moon. These twenty-four seats also correspond to the classification of purified wisdom (the sun) and method (the moon). On the top of the pericarp of those twenty-four lotus seats are vowels, beginning with *a*, and consonants, beginning with *ka*, and so on that include the *anusvāras* and *visargas*. On top of the bindu (*anusvāra*) is emptiness, the mother of the three worlds, Prajñāpāramitā, who has all aspects, and the form of the *nāda*, or the unbeaten sound. She is thus on the top of all mantras. Kālacakra, who is of the nature of sublime bliss, is also present there. After their presence is marked with the syllables, the syllables of the vajras of the body, speech, mind, and gnosis—which are said to have twelve aspects corresponding to the twelve purified links of dependent origination—are placed in their designated locations within the maṇḍala.

The insertion (*nyāsa*) of mantric symbols into the maṇḍala is said to be of three kinds: gross, subtle, and another different type. A gross insertion involves the form of deities transformed into symbols, such as the vajra; a subtle insertion involves the insertion of symbols such as the vajra, having transformed them into mantric seed syllables. The third type involves the insertion of the mantric seed syllables. The insertion of mantric seed syllables is followed by the insertion of emblems. The seed syllable *hūṃ* is made with blue powder on top of the discs of the sun, moon, and *rāhu*, which are located on the top of a multicolored lotus, a seat of Kālacakra. Stacked on top of each other, these three discs represent the union of the sun, moon, and *rāhu* at the time of an eclipse. With regard to a person, the lotus and the three discs represent the heart-cakra together with the *lalanā*, *rasaṇā*, and *avadhūtī*. After that, the seed syllables on the petals of Kālacakra's lotus represent generosity and the other perfections. Following this is insertion of the emblems such as the incense ladle, lamp, edibles, and conch, and a series of syllables placed in the intermediate directions and in the second row of petals. This is followed by insertion of the seed syllables of the five tathāgatas and their consorts. The insertion of the seed syllables of other male and female deities, representing the sense faculties and the sense objects, corresponds to their purification. This is followed by an insertion of the syllable of the guardians of the gates of the maṇḍala, and of the symbols and seed syllables of the remaining deities of the mind-maṇḍala. After that, the seed syllables of the deities of the speech and body maṇḍalas are inserted.[45]

After all this has been done, the vajra master, for the sake of protecting the kālacakra-maṇḍala's gates, presents to the maṇḍala his disciples who have taken the tantric vows (*vrata*) and precepts (*niyama*) and are free from the fourteen downfalls (*mūlāpati*). They stand at the four gates of the maṇḍala, fully initiated and empowered, each holding a vajra and a vajra-bell in their hands. Tantric yoginīs of the vases stand in the four intermediate directions. The vajra master then takes on the identity of the god Gaṇeśa and appoints his fifth disciple, who is skilled in all rites, as the one with power over the rites (*karma-vajrin*). In the absence of such a disciple, the vajra master, as Gaṇeśa himself, performs the homa and other rites.[46]

At the completion of a homa rite, the vajra master takes water for the purification of the mouth and offers incense to the fire. With an exhalation, he releases the fire of gnosis within his heart-cakra. He then recites the mantra: *oṃ jaḥ gaccha gaccha mahāraśmi svasthānaṃ saṃtṛpto ho punar āgamiṣyasi devasya yadāhvayāmi svāhā* ("*oṃ jaḥ*, go, go, great splendor, to your own place! Satisfied, *ho*, you will come again when I summon the deity, *svāhā*").[47] Having now become an ocean of all good qualities, he consecrates his disciple. To do that, he first recites the five-*amṛta* mantra, *oṃ āḥ hūṃ ho kṣaḥ*, seven times and places a pill consisting of the five types of flesh (*pañcapradīpa-guḍikā*) into a pearl-oyster shell or a conch shell for the purification. After that, in order to consecrate the maṇḍala, the areas outside of the maṇḍala, and ritual objects, he practices a *sādhana* with meditative concentration (*samādhi*), confesses his sins, performs the *bindu* and subtle (*sūkṣma*) yogas, and meditates on the gnosis-cakra as a pledge maṇḍala (*samaya-maṇḍala*) in the kālacakra-maṇḍala. He further makes the offerings of flowers, incense, and the like outside the maṇḍala, which he views as the body of Kālacakra.[48] Kālacakra's pervasive, black mind-vajra is in the east, in accordance with the purification of the wind element. In the north is his white body-vajra, in accordance with the purification of the water element. His red speech-vajra is in the south, in accordance with purification of the fire element; and his yellow gnosis-vajra is in the west, in accordance with purification of the earth element. A division of the maṇḍala ground also accords with Kālacakra's four faces, which correspond to the purification of the *rāhu*, the sun, the moon, and the *kālāgni*. The deities representing the four purified elements are designated in the maṇḍala with their seed syllables—*i*, *ṛ*, *u*, and *ḷ*—referred to as their origins (*yoni*) and as the nature of the four purified psychophysical aggregates: the mental formations (*saṃskāra*), feelings (*vedanā*), discernment (*saṃjñā*), and form (*rūpa*). Likewise, the syllable *a* is understood to be the origin of the space element and to have the characteristic of the aggregate of consciousness (*vijñānaskandha*).[49]

After performing various *mudrās* and reciting the given sets of mantras, the vajra master makes offerings to the deities of the kālacakra-maṇḍala and generates the bodhicitta aspiration to achieve the *mahāmudrā-siddhi* for the sake of all sentient beings. Having done so, he is now ready to bestow initiation into the kālacakra-maṇḍala to his patron and disciples. At the completion of the initiation ritual, the vajra master offers a pair of delicate, thin, and attractive garments to the yoginīs, whom he appointed earlier as the protectresses of vases, and another set of garments, crowns, and so forth to his male disciples, whom he appointed as the guardians of the maṇḍala's gates. Having dispersed the *gaṇacakra*, he performs a *pūjā* and holds a vajra and a vajra-bell. Facing Kālacakra at the eastern gate, he brings the gnostic being (*jñānasattva*) into his heart-cakra by means of a vajra-chain. Then, either with a leaf of a fig tree, his hand, or a vajra, he breaks the cakras and vajras at the outmost rim of the maṇḍala, along the path of a brahma lime. He then places a minute part of the powder on his hand and breaks the lotuses. In that way, he incrementally dismantles the maṇḍala. Having done so, he places all of the powder, together with a parasol, a chowrie, and a banner, on an elephant and carries them to a clean river that flows toward an ocean. There, he pours the powder into the river.[50]

CONCLUSION

We have seen here that the kālacakra-maṇḍala's expressiveness, with all its representational references, functions as the means of a visual and ritual communication. It mirrors the tantra's concept of the unitary reality that manifests in the diversity of our ordinary perceptions, and it expresses the tantra's method of sublimating ordinary appearances. The kālacakra-maṇḍala functions as the means by which tantric practitioners not only imagine purifying their body, speech, and mind and becoming members of the integrated Kālacakra tantric family but also reach a certain degree of purification and social integration. The given sequence of the construction of the material and mental maṇḍalas charts the path of purification, which begins with the purification and transformation of the mind and ends with the purification of the body. The fact that the tantric practitioner must observe a material kālacakra-maṇḍala used in the rite of initiation before visualizing it in the next phase of practice indicates the importance of the ocular perception of the maṇḍala for the construction of a subtler mental perception. The kālacakra-maṇḍala's efficacy in structuring the practitioner's experience and inducing the desired states of consciousness is due in part to its communication through symbolic, non-discursive signs. We have also seen here the emphasis on the efficacy of the aesthetic features of a material maṇḍala in inducing desirable results or detrimental consequences to the material well-being and life of a person when the prescribed aesthetic standards are met or ignored. This perspective on the effects of the aesthetic features of the maṇḍala on the life of a person underscores the ontological status of such features as they are embedded in the maṇḍala as a material object.

FURTHER READING

Brauen, Martin. *The Mandala: Sacred Circle in Tibetan Buddhism*. Boston: Shambhala, 1998.
Bryant, Barry. *The Wheel of Time Sand Mandala*. San Francisco: HarperSanFrancisco, 1992.
Namgal Monks. *Kalachakra*. Edited by Laura Harrington. Rome: Tibet Domani, 1996.
Wallace, Vesna A. *The Kālacakratantra. The Chapter on Sādhana, together with the Vimalaprabhā Commentary: A Study and Annotated Translation*. New York: The American Institute of Buddhist Studies and Columbia University Center for Buddhist Studies, 2010.

NOTES

1. The *Kālacakratantra*, ch. 4, vv. 8–9, and the *Vimalaprabhā*. See *Vimalaprabhā* commentary on the verse. *Vimalaprabhāṭīkā of Kalkin Śrīpuṇḍarīkā on Śrīlaghukālacakratantrarāja by Śrīmañjuśrīyaśas*, Vol. 2, ed. Vrajavallabh Dwivedi and S. S. Bahulkar, Rare Buddhist Series Texts Series, No. 12 (Sarnath, Varanasi: Central Institute of Higher Tibetan Studies, 1994), 155–156.
2. The three vehicles here are those of Śrāvakas, Pratyekabuddhas, and Bodhisattvas.
3. *Vimalaprabhāṭīkā of Kalkin Śrīpuṇḍarīkā*, 156–157.
4. *Vimalaprabhāṭīkā of Kalkin Śrīpuṇḍarīkā*, 159–160.
5. The *ālīḍha* posture is one in which the knee of the right leg is advanced and the left leg is retracted.
6. The four classes of *māras* are *skandhamāras*, or the impure psychophysical aggregates; *kleśamāras*, or mental afflictions; *mṛtyumāras*, who hinder the maintenance of life; and *devaputramāras*, who belong to the desire-realm (*kāmadhātu*) and hinder one's acts of virtue out of jealousy.
7. *Vimalaprabhāṭīkā of Kalkin Śrīpuṇḍarīkā*, 151, 157, 159.
8. *Vimalaprabhāṭīkā of Kalkin Śrīpuṇḍarīkā*, 160.
9. The moment of the sun's rising into a zodiacal sign or the sun's zodiacal signs.
10. The *Kālacakratantra*, Ch. 4, v. 2, and the *Vimalaprabhā* commentary on the verse. See the *Vimalaprabhāṭīkā of Kalkin Śrīpuṇḍarīkā*, 150–151.
11. The *pratyālīḍha* posture is a standing posture in which the left foot is advanced and the right foot is drawn back.
12. *Vimalaprabhāṭīkā of Kalkin Śrīpuṇḍarīkā*, 160–161.
13. *Vimalaprabhāṭīkā of Kalkin Śrīpuṇḍarīkā*, 161–162.
14. *Vimalaprabhāṭīkā of Kalkin Śrīpuṇḍarīkā*, 162–1633.
15. Mental formations (*saṃskārāṅga*) are said to arise in the second month of gestation, consciousness (*vijñānāṅga*) in the third month, and the form (*rūpāṅga*) in the fourth month. See *Vimalaprabhāṭīkā of Kalkin Śrīpuṇḍarīkā*, commentary on Ch. 4, v. 29, p. 166.
16. *Vimalaprabhāṭīkā of Kalkin Śrīpuṇḍarīkā*, 163–164.
17. The *Kālacakratantra*, Ch. 4, v. 48 and the *Vimalaprabhā* commentary on the verse. See *Vimalaprabhāṭīkā of Kalkin Śrīpuṇḍarīkā*, 175–176.

18. *Vimalaprabhāṭīkā of Kalkin Śrīpuṇḍarīkā*, 2: *pātanaṃ vajrasūtrāṇāṃ rajaso 'pi nipātanam| na kuryāt mantratattvena kurvato bodhi durlabhaḥ||*
19. See *Vimalaprabhāṭīkā of Kalkin Śrīpuṇḍarīkā*, Ch. 3 , p. 4: *daśatattvaparijñātā maṇḍalālekhakarmavit.*
20. Caitra is the second month of the spring. In the month of Caitra, the full moon stands in the Citra constellation.
21. The *Vimalaprabhāṭīkā of Kalkin Śrīpuṇḍarīkā*, 8–10.
22. One cubit (*hasta*) corresponds to about eighteen inches.
23. The *Kālacakratantra*, Ch. 4, vs. 8–9 and the *Vimalaprabhā*. See *Vimalaprabhā* commentary on the verse. The *Vimalaprabhāṭīkā of Kalkin Śrīpuṇḍarīkā*, 19.
24. *Acacia Catechu*; and The *Vimalaprabhāṭīkā of Kalkin Śrīpuṇḍarīkā*, 21–28.
25. Vrajavallabh, Dwivedi, and S. S. Bahulkar, Rare Buddhist Series Texts Series, No. 12 (Sarnath, Varanasi: Central Institute of Higher Tibetan Studies, 1994), 29.
26. *Kālacakratantra*, Ch. 3, v. 31, line d, *sattvānāṃ mokṣahetor amukamapi vibho maṇḍalaṃ lekhayāmi||* See *Vimalaprabhā* commentary on the verse. The *Vimalaprabhāṭīkā of Kalkin Śrīpuṇḍarīkā*, 30.
27. *Vimalaprabhā* commentary on the verse. The *Vimalaprabhāṭīkā of Kalkin Śrīpuṇḍarīkā*, 31.
28. The *Kālacakratantra*, Ch. 4, vs. 8–9, and the *Vimalaprabhā*. See *Vimalaprabhā* commentary on the verse. The *Vimalaprabhāṭīkā of Kalkin Śrīpuṇḍarīkā*, 36–37.
29. A sacred thread worn by a *brāhmaṇa* over the shoulder.
30. *Vimalaprabhā* commentary on the verse. The *Vimalaprabhāṭīkā of Kalkin Śrīpuṇḍarīkā*, 31–43.
31. *Vimalaprabhāṭīkā of Kalkin Śrīpuṇḍarīkā*, 44.
32. Mimusops Elengi.
33. *Vimalaprabhāṭīkā of Kalkin Śrīpuṇḍarīkā*, 46–49.
34. *Vimalaprabhāṭīkā of Kalkin Śrīpuṇḍarīkā*, 49–50.
35. *Vimalaprabhāṭīkā of Kalkin Śrīpuṇḍarīkā*, 51–52.
36. *Vimalaprabhāṭīkā of Kalkin Śrīpuṇḍarīkā*, 52–53.
37. A barleycorn is a unit of measure of length, nearly equal to a third of an inch or to one-sixth or one-eighth of a fingerbreadth (*aṅgulā*), based on the length of a grain of barley.
38. *Vimalaprabhāṭīkā of Kalkin Śrīpuṇḍarīkā*, 54.
39. The *Vimalaprabhāṭīkā of Kalkin Śrīpuṇḍarīkā*, 53–54.
40. *Vimalaprabhāṭīkā of Kalkin Śrīpuṇḍarīkā*, 54.
41. *yathā bāhye tathā dehe yathā dehe tathāpare| trividhaṃ maṇḍalaṃ jñātvā ācāryo maṇḍalaṃ likhet||* The verse is cited in the *Vimalaprabhāṭīkā of Kalkin Śrīpuṇḍarīkā*, 57.
42. A *hasta* ("forearm") is a unit of the measure of length, a length from the elbow till the tip of the middle finger.
43. *Vimalaprabhāṭīkā of Kalkin Śrīpuṇḍarīkā*, 55–56.
44. *Vimalaprabhāṭīkā of Kalkin Śrīpuṇḍarīkā*, 56–57.
45. For a detailed exposition of the seed syllables and symbols of the mind, speech, and body maṇḍalas, see *Vimalaprabhāṭīkā of Kalkin Śrīpuṇḍarīkā*, 58–69.
46. *Vimalaprabhāṭīkā of Kalkin Śrīpuṇḍarīkā*, 70.
47. *Vimalaprabhāṭīkā of Kalkin Śrīpuṇḍarīkā*, 77.
48. *Vimalaprabhāṭīkā of Kalkin Śrīpuṇḍarīkā*, 77–78.
49. *Vimalaprabhāṭīkā of Kalkin Śrīpuṇḍarīkā*, 79–80.
50. *Kālacakratantra*, Ch. 3, vs. 201–202, and the *Vimalaprabhā*. See *Vimalaprabhāṭīkā of Kalkin Śrīpuṇḍarīkā*, 145–146.

Vesna A. Wallace

L

LONGCHENPA

Longchen Rabjam (Klong chen rab 'byams pa, 1308–1363/1364) stands among the greatest luminaries in the history of Tibetan Buddhism, being especially revered within the Nyingma (Rnying ma) school.[1] As a paragon of both scholarly erudition and spiritual realization, in Tibet he has traditionally been accorded the rare title of Omniscient One (Kun mkhyen).[2] His achievements were many, ranging from prolific literary output to the restoration and construction of monasteries in both Tibet and Bhutan, but of particular note is the depth of his thought and writings, treasured for their accessibility to a wider, non-academic audience. His contributions can thus be approached from two angles, namely, a presentation of his life and Dharma activities set in some historical relation to the period in which he lived, and an overview of his surviving corpus.

Biographies of Longchenpa provide an important reference to understanding his significance in the long history of Tibet, as they reveal how and why he was revered there. At first glance, if one examines the various accounts of his life in relation to those of other Tibetan saints, a number of similarities are apparent.[3] Indeed, they follow the traditional structure of the hagiographical genre (*rnam thar*), first describing his birth and background, then focusing on his education and training and his ascetic practice and spiritual achievements, and then outlining his teaching and writings, the signs that appeared at the time of his death, and a list of his principal disciples.[4] There are didactic advantages to such a standardized biographical presentation, and the fundamental principles of chronology and contextualizing the key figure in terms of their tradition apply for modern readers as well; for this reason, the same structure may be followed in this presentation. Lending itself to comparison, convention also serves to reveal an extraordinary life. Here, Longchenpa truly stands out, as is exemplified by the great respect and honorific titles he was given over the centuries. He has variously been recognized as one of the three famous incarnations of Mañjuśrī (alongside Sakya Paṇḍita and Tsongkhapa), an emanation of Vimalamitra (like Kumārādza), the second Victor (Rgyal ba gnyis pa), the "second Garab Dorje (Dga' rab rdo rje)" prophesied by Śākyamuni Buddha as well as Padmasambhava, and the second Samantabhadra.[5]

In terms of his writing, Longchenpa is primarily renowned for his presentations of Dzogchen (Rdzogs chen), penned in a composition style that is both profound and direct but often poetic and aesthetically rich. However, he was also well versed in other genres. As a revealer of hidden-treasure texts (*gter ma*), he systematized and commented on a range of Seminal Essence (*Snying thig*) texts that would form a significant core of the Nyingma school's literary tradition and praxis. His philosophical explorations offer unique perspectives on Svātantrika and Prāsaṅgika Madhyamaka, particularly on the nature of the two truths, while also offering a critical overview of the analytical tradition of Buddhism. In addition, his doxographical work provides a detailed structure for the approaches of the nine vehicles—including sūtra and tantra—of the Nyingmapa, maintaining the soteriological superiority of Dzogchen, while also presenting the six paths outlined in the New Translation (Gsar ma) system.

Longchenpa's ecumenical attitude and interests were likely formed during his academic years when he received teachings from a range of masters from different schools; indeed, he maintained relationships with some of them, such as the Third Karmapa, later in life.[6] Longchenpa was also more integrative than his contemporaries involved in canonical construction, including in his own list and commentarial work certain tantras that others disdained for a lack of Indian provenance. Indeed, this perspective should not be surprising, considering his own activities in revealing hidden texts and justifying such revelations as quite valid. This very pattern would be emulated hundreds of years later even, when Jigme Lingpa ('Jigs med gling pa, 1730–1798) experienced visions of Longchenpa and made his work much more broadly known, collecting and disseminating it and continuing the Seminal Essence tradition with his Longchen Nyingtik (*Klong chen nying thig*). Due to this attention, the philosophical commentaries of Mipam (Mi pham, 1846–1912), and the successful preservation of the greatest part of Longchenpa's oeuvre across the centuries, his legacy endures today as a vital part of the Nyingma tradition.

THE EARLY LIFE OF LONGCHENPA

Longchenpa was born in the Male Earth Monkey year of 1308 in the village of Tödrong (Stod grong), located in the Yoru (g.Yo ru) region of central Tibet, and given the name Dorje Gyaltsen (Rdo rje rgyal mtshan). His father, Tensung (Bstan pa bsrungs), was a tantric yogi and scholar who belonged to the Rok Sherab Ö (Rog shes rab 'od) lineage, which traced its origins back to Gyalwa Chogyang (Rgyal ba mchog dbyangs), one of Padmasambhava's twenty-five disciples in the 8th century, and Yeshe Wangpo (Ye shes dbang po srung), one of the seven monks ordained by Śāntarakṣita (725–788). On his mother's side, Longchenpa was said to be related to Dromtönpa ('Brom ston pa, 1005–1064), the foremost disciple of the Indian master Atiśa.[7] Later in life, Longchenpa would also be recognized as the reincarnation of the *tertön* (*gter ton*) Pema Ledrel Tsal (Padma las 'brel rtsal, 1291–1315), but he did not enjoy that recognition or any institutional prestige in his childhood years.

The hagiographical tradition of Longchenpa reports miraculous portents connected to his birth. His biographies hold that his mother Sönam Gyen (Bso nams rgyan) dreamed of the sun and moon blazing in the forehead of a white snow lion, lighting up the entire world before dissolving in her womb as he was conceived. And when Longchenpa was born, the Dharma protectress Namdru Remati (Nam gru re ma ti) reportedly appeared in the guise of a black-skinned woman with bared fangs and a sword.[8] Taking the baby in her arms, she vowed to Sönam Gyen that the newborn would always enjoy her protection.[9] It is said that she already protected Longchenpa when he was but an infant, left in a field by his mother. A sudden hailstorm came up, and Sönam Gyen ran to save her son, but upon arriving where he was, she found him cradled in the arms of the black protectress.[10]

Like other well-known Buddhist scholars, Longchenpa is said to have been precocious, learning how to read and write by the age of 5. When he was 7, his father gave him empowerments in various Nyingma tantras and treasure texts, including the *Peaceful and Wrathful Aspects of the Guru* (*Gu ru zhi drag rnams kyi dbang lung*) and *Sugata Assembly of the Eight Teachings* (*Bka' brgyad bde gshegs 'dus pa*) of Nyima Özer (Nyang ral nyi ma 'od zer, 1124–1192), and instruction in astrology and Tibetan medicine. Because of his father's Rok affiliation, it is likely that the tantras comprised the Mahāyoga and Anuyoga traditions as preserved by that lineage. It is also worth noting that the commentarial tradition of the *Guhyagarbhatantra* that Longchenpa studied at an early age belonged to the tradition of Rongzom Paṇḍita (Rong zom chos kyi bzang po, 1012–1088), based on the commentary of Suryāprabhāsiṃha; later in life, he would write two important commentaries on this tantra.[11] At the age of 9, it is said that he memorized two key works in the Perfection of Wisdom cycle—namely, the "mother texts" in 8,000 lines (*Aṣṭasāhasrikāprajñāpāramitā*) and in 25,000 lines (*Pañcaviṃśatisāhasrikāprajñ āpāramitā*)—after reading them each a hundred times.[12] It was around this point that his mother died, followed by his father only two years later. Longchenpa would enter Samye monastery shortly thereafter, where he took monastic vows and begin his formal studies. From the preceptor Kunga Özer (Kun dga' 'od zer) and the abbot Samdrub Rinchen (Bsam grub rin chen), he received the refuge name Tsultrim Lodrö (Tshul khrims blo gros).

After completing the Vinaya curriculum at the age of 14, Longchenpa began teaching it to others. At 16 he began tutelage in tantra with various teachers, receiving initiations in the Nyingma tradition and the esoteric systems of other schools. From Tashi Rinchen (Bkra shis rin chen) he received the Lamdre (Lam 'bras) system of the Sakya tradition, the Kagyu school's Six Yogas (*Chos drug*) of Nāropa, and tantras featuring Vajravārāhī, Ghantapada's lineage of Cakrasaṃvara, and Mahācakra Vajrapāṇi; Wangchuk Yeshe (Dbang phyug ye shes) taught him the *Kālacakratantra*, and Zalung Rinpoche (Za lung rin po che) gave instruction in the pacification (Zhi byed) cycle of Padampa Sangye (Pha dam pa sangs rgyas, d. 1117) and cutting through (Chod).[13]

At 19, Longchenpa transitioned to continue his studies at Sangpu Neutok (Gsang phu ne'u thog), a Kadampa seminary renowned for its nonsectarian approach since its founding in

1073.[14] Here, Longchenpa immersed himself in an intensive curriculum of logic, philosophy, and debate. In addition to taking electives in ordinary topics such as grammar and poetics, he also engaged with the five treatises of Maitreya (*Byams chos sde lnga*), the *Seven Treatises on Valid Cognition* (*Tshad ma sde bdun*) of Dharmakīrti, the Prajñāpāramitā cycle, and Madhyamaka philosophy.[15] At this time, Longchenpa also received teachings from great lamas who did not necessarily belong to Sangpu Neutok's faculty. The Third Karmapa, Rangjung Dorje (Rang 'byung rdo rje, 1284–1339), tutored him in various tantras, while the historian and philosopher Dampa Sönam Gyaltsen (Dam pa bsod nams rgyal mtshan) provided education in the Sakya tradition.[16] However, despite this rich ecumenical setting, Longchenpa still had issues with academic life. Under the pen name "Power of Speech" (Ngag gi dbang po), he wrote a satirical poem—named "The Thirty Letters of the Alphabet" because it starts each new line with a different letter—that gave a cutting criticism of the rough and partisan behavior of the Khampa scholars at Sangpu Neutok.[17] Passing it to a fellow student to post on the throne in the main hall, Longchenpa departed for the mountains to engage in meditation practice.

Attended by a scholar he met on the road, Longchenpa took up residence in a cave in Chogla (Lcog la), spending eight months in total darkness.[18] During this retreat, Longchenpa had a vision of the bodhisattva Tārā that profoundly shifted his perspective of reality: appearing on horseback on the bank of a river, dressed in beautiful brocade and accompanied by music, she blessed him by placing her jeweled crown on his head. For three days, Longchenpa remained in a state of profound meditation; as he put it, "I did not wake up for a long time!"[19] This experience is said to have served as the connection for him to subsequently find the Nyingtik (*Snying thig*) teachings.

At the age of 27, Longchenpa ended his retreat to return to the Samye area. In Yartökyam (Yar stod skyam), Longchenpa found his future teacher Kumārādza (1266–1343).[20] Longchenpa was so destitute that he had nothing to offer for teachings, and he was so ashamed that he was prepared to leave, but the guru reportedly recognized his Dharma heir and personally welcomed the young man into the audience. Kumārādza had found himself in a similar situation when seeking the Vima Nyingtik (*Bi ma snying thig*) cycle from his own guru, Melong Dorje (Me long rdo rje, 1243–1303), and to receive the Seminal Essence teachings, he had needed to perform austerities and work as a painter at Kharchu (Mkhar chu) monastery near the border of Bhutan. Moreover, not only had Tārā appeared to Kumārādza in a vision to tell of this young man, he had dreamed of a "wonderful heavenly bird" that would carry his books in all directions.[21] Kumārādza prophesied that the newcomer would be foremost among his disciples.

Longchenpa thus joined an itinerant group of seventy other students who moved between uninhabited valleys, undergoing hardships and sometimes relocating even before replenishing their supplies.[22] Longchenpa is said to have subsisted for two months on only three quart-measures of flour and twenty-one mercury pills (*dngul chu*), sleeping in the same woolen sack that he wore during the day.[23] While harsh, such a severe ascetic lifestyle did not prevent Longchenpa from continuing his scholarly work. During this period, he revised and synthesized earlier compositions, and he excelled in the three disciplines of teaching, debating, and writing. In addition, he worked on translations, wrote commentaries, and penned new treatises. In their first year together, and then at Shampogangra (Sham po gangs ra), Kumārādza bestowed on Longchenpa the Vima Nyingtik, as he had done for the Third Karmapa. The *Blue*

Annals highlights Kumārādza's skill in teaching it, using "terminology peculiar to that system" rather than the traditional manner of teaching gradual stages of tantra."[24] For his part, Longchenpa regarded his guru as Vimalamitra in person. Kumārādza also shared transmissions of Dharmapāla rites as well as the major cycles of teachings of the Dzogchen tradition.[25] After spending three years with his teacher, Longchenpa set forth to go practice and share the teachings he had received.

THE LATER LIFE OF LONGCHENPA

Longchenpa moved into the role of teacher by transmitting the initiations and instructions of the Vima Nyingtik to disciples at Nyipu Shukseb (Snyi phu'i shug gseb). It was at this point that he also received the Khandro Nyingtik, a terma treasure text given by Padmasambhava to Lhacham Pemasal (Lha lcam padma gsal, 9th century) and discovered by her later incarnation (and his own previous incarnation), Pema Ledrel Tsal. This came about due to the efforts of one of his disciples, Özer Gocha ('Od zer go cha), who had recovered it after a difficult search and was able to present the terma to his teacher; this was important, as it allowed Longchenpa to properly maintain the traditional sequence of textual transmission. Around the same time, Longchenpa had a visionary encounter with the protector Shenpa Sok Drubma (Shan pa srog sgrub ma), who also gave it to him as a mind treasure (*dgongs gter*). Longchenpa still visited Kumārādza, sharing his progress and mystical experiences. He also had new ones on his travels. For example, on a trip to Lhasa, while making an offering to the famous Jowo (Jo bo) statue of Śākyamuni Buddha, a light shot from its forehead into his. This event provoked memories of Longchenpa's previous lifetimes as a scholar at Vulture Peak (Gṛdhrakūṭa) in India and at Lixian; he reported that knowledge of texts he had studied then ripened in his mindstream, enriching his understanding.[26]

The Nyingtik focus of this period continued at Chimpu (Mchims phu ri mo can) the following year when Longchenpa secluded himself with eight male and female students. Their collective practice of the Vima Nyingtik was marked by a number of ecstatic experiences, including encounters with various Dharma protectors. A particularly poignant episode involved Ekajaṭī (Ral gcig ma) possessing one yoginī in the group, who then shared a spontaneous song of realization.[27] The same protectress provided confirmation to Longchenpa that he was indeed ready to teach that cycle (while also critiquing him for seemingly minor details, such as not pronouncing the final sibilant of the word *rigs*).[28] In another vision, he again received the Khandro Nyingtik, this time from Padmasambhava. The process of opening this cycle in his mindstream continued for some time, next at Chugpodrak (Phyug po brag) with the additional assistance of Yeshe Tsogyal and Yudrönma (g.Yu sgron ma), and then at Gangri Tökar (Gangs ri thod dkar), where he finished transcribing it. The immersion of Longchenpa and his disciples in this experience entailed a continuous perception of the Dharma protectors and other wondrous sights. On one occasion, they witnessed the cosmic protector Rāhula mixing Longchenpa's ink; at other times, ḍākinīs and rainbow lights appeared in the sky.[29]

Over the next decade, most of his time was spent at Gangri Tökar. Longchenpa built his own hermitage there, Orgyen Dzong (O rgyan rdzong), on a ridge at the heart of a topographical representation of the protectress Dorje Pagmo (Rdo rje phag mo).[30] His practice deepened through realization via the direct approach (*thod rgal*) taught in the Nyingtik cycles, and this was also a rich period of composition and Dharma activity. For example, he engaged in the restoration of sacred sites, such as Lharing Drag (Lha ring brag), the ancient stūpas at Samye, and the dilapidated temple of Sha Lhakhang (Zhwa'i lha khang, built in the 9th century).[31] A particularly dramatic anecdote describes his activity at the latter, a place where he unearthed many termas: as the earth was being cleared away from the ruins, there kept emerging skulls that had been placed there as part of suppression rituals in the distant past. As darkness fell, a fierce storm arose, raining down stones and earth while Longchenpa recited mantras and put underfoot the skulls all dancing about, subjugating the disturbance. Among the frightened disciples who were there, some saw him as Guru Drakpo (Gu ru drag po), one of the terrific forms of Guru Rinpoche.[32]

Ultimately, the political upheavals taking place in central Tibet would disrupt Longchenpa's practice and work there.[33] While one account holds that Longchenpa decided to leave Tibet before the conflagration between the Pagmodrupa (Phag mo dru pa) warlord Jangchub Gyaltsen (Byang chub rgyal mtshan, 1302–1364) and the Drigung ('Bri gung) school fully erupted, there is evidence that he himself became embroiled in the civil war.[34] This happened after one of the Drigung hierarchs, Gomchen Kunga Rinchen (Sgom chen Kun dga' rin chen), learned that a sword-shaped birthmark on his back identified him as an infidel son of Māra prophesied by Padmasambhava. Seeking a way to escape this fate and the flames of hell, he found Longchenpa, who, as an emanation of Mañjuśrī, was supposedly the only person who could help him.[35] In this way, the ire of his enemy Jangchub Gyaltsen was raised. In fact, Chödrak Zangpo (Chos grags bzang po, 1300/1310–1375/1385), one of Longchenpa's disciples, does report that the warlord paid a visit to Gangri Tökar around 1350, just about the time when Longchenpa left Tibet for Bhutan.[36]

Being a place where political power was much more subordinate to religious power, Bhutan was a dear place for Longchenpa, as evidenced in the poems that he wrote there.[37] It was also a productive one. During the decade that he spent in the Himalayan kingdom, he founded eight monasteries, including Tharpa Ling (Thar pa gling) and Samten Ling (Bsam gtan gling), respectively, located near Bumthang and Paro.[38] From Bhutan, his teachings also spread to Nepal.[39] And at this point in Longchenpa's life, he began having children. While it is reported that Longchenpa had multiple sons from different mothers, here at least he fathered two children with the sister of his patron (who had been a nun when he arrived).[40] The mother needed to leave for Tibet after their secret union was discovered, after the birth of their second child, a son named Dragpa Özer (Grags pa 'od zer, 1356–1409); their earlier daughter (b. 1351) had been passed off as belonging to his consort's mother.[41] Dragpa Özer was later recognized as an emanation of Hayagrīva and a great scholar in his own right.[42]

Due to a war that was breaking out in Bhutan, Longchenpa finally returned to Tibet around 1360.[43] Through the effort of lay patrons, most notably the prince Śākya Zangpo (Si tu ShAkya bzang po), he was reconciled with Jangchub Gyaltsen, who had emerged victorious in his power struggles against the Drigung and now bore the title of T'ai Situ; Longchenpa reportedly even became the warlord's teacher.[44] One biographical tradition cites this as the period when Jangchub Gyaltsen gave the yogi his most common name, Longchen Rabjam, although it has alternatively been suggested that he received it from Kumārādza or even during his time at Samye (on the basis of the *Klong chen rab 'byams kyi rgyud* group of Dzogchen tantras).[45] At this point, Longchenpa's reputation had grown so much that he was followed constantly or forced to debate to prove his knowledge. In the latter years of his life, therefore, he mainly engaged in three types of activities: giving public teachings, continuing to restore dilapidated temples, and writing and practicing in solitude or semi-retreat conditions. Regarding the former, his teachings primarily involved the Khandro Nyingtik, although he also openly taught the "highest hidden" instructions of Dzogchen (i.e., *khregs chod* and *thod rgal*) to the masses, whether on the riverbanks in upper Uru (Dbu ru) or at various monasteries.

After a relatively short period of being back in Tibet, Longchenpa prepared his affairs and composed his last testament at the age of 56. His disciples pleaded for him to remain with them, but after discoursing on the transient nature of things, he made his way up to a cave high on the east side of the Chimpu valley.[46] There he passed away with the arising of numerous miraculous signs: even though it was winter, the snow melted, flowers came into bloom, and music spontaneously played inside and outside the cave. His relics, which included various substances in the five colors of the rainbow, were said to be as hard as diamonds; as for his reliquary, it was found in a seed-syllable HŪṂ that spontaneously appeared as a rock formation in a gully near his hermitage.[47]

THE LEGACY OF LONGCHENPA

While Longchenpa's disciples numbered in the thousands, his biographies differ in terms of whom they list. Notable in Tibet are his biographer Chödrak Zangpo (Chos grags bzang po bya bral pa bzod pa), Khyabdal Lhundrub (Khyab brdal lhun grub), Delek Gyatso (Bde legs rgya mtsho), Dragpa Senge (Grags pa seng ge), Yagde Panchen (G.yag sde paṇ chen), Sherab Gönpo (Shes rab mgon po), and Orgyen Choje (O rgyan chos rje). In Bhutan, Paljor Gyaltsen (Dpal 'byor rgyal mtshan) is remembered for continuing Longchenpa's construction of monasteries and Ösal Rangdrol ('Od gsal rang grol) for serving as his attendant.[48] Alternatively, Longchenpa's students have been categorized in various ways by Tibetan historians so that one can read of his "five heart-sons," the "four mentors who spread the teachings," and those known as "spiritually accomplished yogins."[49]

Longchenpa's son Dragpa Özer must also be mentioned in this regard, although he carried on his father's work in another capacity, fulfilling a prophecy in the Khandro Nyingtik that Pema Ledrel Tsal's next incarnation would be born in Bumthang.[50] One might remember that Longchenpa himself was supposed to be Pema Ledrel Tsal, yet the tradition does not take this to be a problem: the protectress Dorje Pagmo (Rdo rje phag mo) is said to have clarified that his life should be considered a "Pure Land" hiatus before Dragpa Özer.[51]

There are other traditions about the future incarnations of Longchenpa. For example, it is important to include Pema Lingpa (Padma gling pa, 1445–1521), based on his own claim of previously being Pema Ledrel Tsal.[52] Another alternative is found in the Geluk tradition, according to which Khedrub Je (Mkhas grub rje dge legs dpal bzang, 1385–1438) was Longchenpa reborn.[53] Generally speaking, however, the Nyingma tradition in Tibet tends to locate Longchenpa's succession of rebirths much later, beginning with Orgyen Terdak Lingpa (O rgyan gter bdag gling pa, 1646–1714) and continuing with Jigme Lingpa and Khenpo Ngagchung (Mkhan po Ngag chung, 1879–1941), also known as Ngawang Palzang (Ngag dbang dpal bzang).[54] In more modern times, the most commonly recognized current incarnations of Longchenpa have been Kyabje Thinley Norbu Rinpoche (1931–2011). Others include

H. E. Namkha Drimed Rinpoche (b. 1938 in eastern Tibet), Lingtrul Rinpoche (b. 1955 in Golok), and Gangteng Tulku (b. 1955 in Bhutan).

THE WORKS OF LONGCHENPA

In his writing, Longchenpa used and published under many names during his lifetime, and knowing them is an important aspect of understanding his oeuvre. In some cases, they are based on a historical moment in his life, but in others, they serve as pen names that help identify what kind of text he was working on. Thus, one finds his birth name, Rdo rje rgyal mtshan; his ordination name, Tshul khrims blo gros; Ngag gi dbang po, given at Samye; Klong chen rab 'byams pa, given at either Samye or Sangpu Neutok or by Kumārādza or Jangchub Gyaltsen; Bsam yas lung mang pa, given at Sangpu Neutok; Dri med 'od zer, given by Padmasambhava and Yeshe Tsogyal in a vision during his dark retreat; Rdo rje gzi brji, given by Yeshe Tsogyal in a vision; Dag gi dbang po; and the following names given in the *Grub mtha' mdzod*: Klong gsal dri med, Rdo rje sems dpa', Blo gros mchog ldan, Padma las grol, and Sna tshogs rang grol. In addition to these, he was also called by the name of his previous incarnation, Pema Ledrel Tsal, as well as Jarme Longyang (Byar med klong yangs). As noted by Stéphane Arguillère, these two monikers likely served a specific purpose, with the former reflecting that he was the bearer of a revelation rather than an author per se and the latter perhaps suggesting his role as an editor.[55]

At the same time, the "cult" of Longchenpa in Tibet is somewhat uneven. Some masters over the centuries claimed visionary experiences of him, and they strongly incorporated his work in their own; most notably, Terdak Lingpa (Gter bdag gling pa, 1646–1714) and Jigme Lingpa drew heavily from Longchenpa's writings, while Mipam significantly increased a wider knowledge of his philosophical contributions. According to Arguillère, however, the lack of any collected corpus (*gsung 'bum*) points to this great master being "fetishized, more idolized than really studied."[56] David Germano also notes the lack of fame vis-à-vis Longchenpa's writings "despite, or perhaps because of, the immensity of his accomplishment."[57] To some degree at least, this phenomenon can be explained by the disparate contents of Longchenpa's works, appealing to different types of readers, and the range of locations where they were composed. The absence of any single monastic seat after his death, a physical locus to house his writings, could have also been a factor; in a sense, this epitomizes the rather diffuse nature of the Nyingma tradition itself, not just before but also in the centuries after Longchenpa's death, especially compared to the institutionalization of the other schools.[58]

Despite all this, there were attempts to catalog Longchenpa's oeuvre even then. He himself drafted a preliminary list of his works during his exile in Bhutan, which is valuable for the texts it does not mention, suggesting that they were yet to be composed.[59] Another list, made by his disciple and biographer Chödrak Zangpo, comprises 270 titles.[60] Approximately three hundred years later, while organizing and promulgating Longchenpa's corpus for a wider audience, Jigme Lingpa compiled another list, and in the 19th century, Lagpa Sonam Chodrub (Glag bla bsod nams chos grub) put the total at 253.[61] More recently, Nyoshul Khen Rinpoche cited 307 works signed by Longchenpa, and this is the same number that Arguillère arrived at in his own detailed overview.[62] It is unlikely that the true total will ever be known, for even as new discoveries are made, tradition holds that some texts were lost forever. Dorji Wangchuk shares the story of a pack animal with Longchenpa's compositions falling into a deep ravine in Bhutan or the failure to retrieve at least a hundred of his writings from Asura Cave in Nepal.[63] What can be concluded is that Longchenpa was extremely prolific as well as wide-ranging in his literary output, which extended across his entire adult life.

Indeed, an extraordinary feature of his corpus is its breadth, something that is hard not to see as intentional. On the basis of the catalog of texts compiled in Bhutan, Gene Smith concluded that Longchenpa had the aim of providing a "unitary treatment of Buddhist thought."[64] This is supported by the thematic scheme that he himself used during his life—and the Nyingma tradition would follow—to classify his work, which divides it in terms of outer, inner, and esoteric topics. Arguillère offers a more detailed classification, including (a) profane works, hymns, poems; (b) treatises related to the Pāramitāyāna; (c) treatises related to Mantrayāna, including Māyājāla literature, diverse ritual texts, and ritual texts with a creation-stage or perfection-stage focus, respectively; (d) treatises on suchness (*de kho na nyid*), composing an introduction to Dzogchen and its various classes; and (e) teachings on Dzogchen proper, either general or on specific points.[65] The names of individual texts are included in this treatment, facilitating a helpful reference for readers seeking illumination on a specific genre or topic. Such groupings were also made in the tradition as well, resulting in the collections that, in the early 21st century, are understood as Longchenpa's major works.

The bulk of the corpus is composed of clusters of texts, which were either intentionally composed and collected as such by Longchenpa or artificially aggregated. Among the former, one finds the *Trilogy of Rest* (*Ngal gso skor gsum*), the *Trilogy of Dispelling Darkness* (*Mun sel skor gsum*), and the *Trilogy of Natural Freedom* (*Rang grol skor gsum*); arguably belonging to the latter are the *Trilogy of the Quintessence* (*Yang tig skor gsum*) and the *Seven Treasuries* (*Mdzod bdun*).[66] The first trilogy mentioned here is further divided into another set of three thematically organized trilogies: the *Trilogy of Chariots* (*Shing rta skor gsum*), the *Trilogy of Rosaries* (*Phreng ba skor gsum*), and the *Trilogy of Instruction Manuals* (*Khrid yig skor gsum*). The second offers commentary on the *Guhyagarbhatantra* but in relation to Dzogchen, while the third explores Personal Instruction Class (*man ngag gi sde*). The fourth trilogy is composed of collections of individual texts that offer commentary on the two Nyingtik cycles (*Bi ma snying thig* and *Mkha' 'gro snying thig*) that were so important to Longchenpa; the first two of the commentaries (the *Bla ma yang tig* and the *Mkha' 'gro yang tig*) speak, respectively, to these, thus forming a tetralogy known as the *Nyingtik yabshi* (*Snying thig ya bzhi*), while the final commentary (*Zab mo yang tig*) provides a commentary on both cycles.

Finally, the *Seven Treasuries* represents an artificial collection of texts in the sense that they were not organized as an integrated corpus by Longchenpa himself, and they were also composed over the span of his life. Indeed, their contents range widely from doxography to philosophical commentary, a scholarly treatment of the Nyingtik tradition, a presentation of precepts, and pith instructions on the nature of mind, along with auto-commentaries. Their respective areas of focus may further be summarized as follows: the *Wish-fulfilling Treasury* (*Yid bzhin mdzod*) provides an overview of the tantras, the *Treasury of Personal Instructions* (*Man ngag mdzod*) frames Dzogchen in terms of a philosophical system, the *Treasury of the Basic Space of Phenomena* (*Chos dbyings mdzod*) presents teachings in relation to the Expanse Class (*klong sde*) of Dzogchen, the *Treasury of Spiritual Systems* (*Grub mtha' mdzod*) offers a comprehensive overview of the various soteriological paths of Buddhism, the *Treasury of the*

Supreme Vehicle (*Theg mchog mdzod*) unpacks the key elements of the *Seventeen Dzogchen Tantras* (*Rdzogs chen rgyud bcu bdun*) and 119 related precepts, the *Treasury of Word and Meaning* (*Tshig don mdzod*) offers practical instructions in Dzogchen, and the *Treasury of the Natural State* (*Gnas lugs mdzod*) explores various Dzogchen themes.

Aside from the aforementioned major works, there also exist some whose authorship is in dispute. Among these is a treatise on logic and epistemology (*Tshad ma de kho na yid bsdus pa*), which Leonard van Kuijp convincingly argues was written a couple centuries earlier; since then, Jonathan Stotlz has shown that the author was likely a scholar from Sangpu Neutok monastery, Jepa Shönu Jangchub ('Jad pa Gzhon nu byang chub, *c.* 1150–1210).[67] Another text that has been the subject of debate is the historically focused *Chos 'byung rin po che'i gter mdzod*, which was attributed to Longchenpa by Jigme Lingpa (even though the name of the author cited in the colophon does not correspond to any of Longchenpa's known names).[68] Moreover, there exist reports of texts authored by Longchenpa that have yet to come to light, such as commentaries on *Entering the Middle Way* (*Madhyamakāvatāra*) and Fundamentals of the Middle Way (*Mūlamadhyamakakārikā*).[69]

Over the following centuries, Longchenpa came to be revered as an extraordinary treasure revealer. As early as 1400, in a biography of Padmasambhava (*Padma thang yig*) he was included under the name Drime Özer in a list of known *tertöns*.[70] Later he would come to be regarded as the progenitor of the Southern Treasure Tradition (*lho gter*), and it is worth noting that ten of Longchenpa's discovered texts are included in the *Rin chen gter mdzod*. Like other treasure revealers, he drew forth ritual objects from the earth; in Samtenling Choje in Bhutan, for example, one finds a cymbal, a *vajrakīla* dagger, and a Tārā statue that he discovered.[71] In Tibet, he discovered a range of *sādhanas* for the practice of various deities, including the twelve *tenma* goddesses (*bstan ma bcu gnyis*) and the protector Vajrasadhu (Rdo rje legs pa). And yet his rare mind treasures, drawn from a state of natural clarity, have been even more prized. Indeed, Longchenpa is purported to have exclaimed, "I am opening the door of Dharma Treasures of the inner clarity, there is no need of Dharma Treasure from the cracks of rocks."[72] While as a treasure revealer he was quite special in this regard, it is also important to remember that he was drawing on a long tradition of Dzogchen teachings, particularly those of Mind Class (*sems sde*) and Expanse Class, which could be revealed directly to the mindstream of one who had achieved great realization.[73]

Given the preceding discussion, it should come as no surprise that Longchenpa held mundane proofs of textual provenance in some disdain. This led him to push back on the conservative attitude of scholars involved in the 14th-century program of canon creation. For example, whereas Butön (Bu ston, 1290–1364) omitted the *Guhyagarbha* from his collection of tantras (following the Snar thang edition of the Bka' 'gyur), Longchenpa included it in his list of texts accepted by the Nyingma school and then proceeded to teach on it at length in the *Trilogy of Dispelling Darkness*.[74] The same holds for his approach to the *All-Creating King* (*Kun byed rgyal po*), a controversially cataphatic scripture that was similarly omitted by Butön but placed first among the Nyingma tantras; it would form the basis of Longchenpa's teaching on Mind Class in the *Trilogy of Rest* and the *Trilogy of Natural Freedom*. Regarding those who stubbornly refused to accept the authenticity of such works, Longchenpa could be extremely critical: in one instance, he blames such people as being of lesser intellect; in another, he suggests that perhaps they have been staring too long at the colophons of ordinary books.[75]

ASPECTS OF LONGCHENPA'S THOUGHT

Using his writing as a form of teaching, Longchenpa was a master at grounding and contextualizing esoteric texts to make them more accessible, as well as embedding profound teachings in seemingly simple teachings. His commentaries on the *Nyingtik Yabshi*, for example, enriched the mind treasures by means of teachings on history, philosophy, ritual, and yogic practice. His doxographical approach to Dzogchen provided crucial terminology and a valuable map for practitioners, in relation not only to other paths but also to the relative focuses of the various classes. While in relation to actual practice he taught about the openness and freedom of mind, Longchenpa clearly saw the value—and even aesthetic aspect—of a rich systemic structure. At the same time, he stressed the advantage of simplicity, the hallmark of Dzogchen, compared to overly complexifying and thinking too much.[76] His positioning of Dzogchen as superior to the other vehicles, therefore, was not so much political as soteriological.

Looking closely at Longchenpa's application of Dzogchen vis-à-vis Sūtrayāna and Mantrayāna, one finds an integrative element: like them, he argues, it has aspects of ground, path, and result (*gzhi snang, lam snang,* and *'bras snang*). And yet he also introduces how its unique hermeneutic offers an alternative to the linearity of Mahāyāna Buddhism's traditional evolutionary approach or the holographic tactic (taking the result as the path) of the resultant vehicle of tantra. Importantly, Longchenpa does not do this in the manner of his Jonangpa contemporary Dölpopa (Dol po pa, 1292–1361), equating the ground and the result; instead, he stresses that space-like mind is primally all good and that one arrives at the ground by never straying from it.[77]

Longchenpa was also rather unique in his philosophical orientation. Most notably, while he explicitly self-identified as Prāsaṅgika-Mādhyamika, he held the third promulgation of the Dharma to be definitive.[78] In not such a distant future, Tsongkhapa (1357–1419) would argue that these positions are mutually exclusive. However, unpacking Longchenpa's stance here can be a key to understanding the modus operandi that guides his writing more generally, that is, differentiating critical points on a structural basis while simultaneously highlighting and privileging what is most soteriologically effective. In this case, he follows Candrakīrti's presentation of the two truths as the most advanced line of Buddhist philosophy, and he does not tie emptiness to the third promulgation, as is done with Great Madhyamaka (Dbu ma chen po). But for Longchenpa, the philosophical vehicle only goes so far when it comes to practice. In other words, even though Prāsaṅgika-Madhyamaka works better than any other dialectical approach, it is still a provisional modality—soteriologically speaking—while the third promulgation, with its teachings on the potentiality of perfection (e.g., the *gotra*), is definitive. It could also be argued that Longchenpa's use of texts like the *Ratnagotravibhāga* has a very Dzogchen flavor (see the *Grub mtha' mdzod,* for example, where emptiness is framed as the luminosity of buddha nature); as Klaus-Dieter Mathes has noted, such a connection would have also served to tie Dzogchen to the Indian Buddhist tradition.[79]

Of course, Longchenpa had certain preferences and agendas. As shown earlier, in some cases they are explicit in his works, for he was not shy to state his mind. In others, some analysis is required to arrive at what his true aim was. As the literary style of doxography reveals positionality, with the final topic presented reflecting the stance of the author, and Longchenpa skillfully employed that genre to demonstrate his ultimate appreciation of Dzogchen.

Furthermore, Longchenpa took advantage of the rich philosophical discussion in Tibet to explore unexpected avenues. As Allison Aitken has recently pointed out, for example, his Svātantrika presentation of the two truths in his commentary to the *Yid bzhin mdzod* highlights the position of the Indian philosopher Śrīgupta, offering a fresh perspective of Madhyamaka.[80] Finally, it is important to note that as an editor of the Vima Nyingtik, by topically arranging the histories and biographies of its key figures, he not only provided a level of chronology and consistency that made Vimalamitra more widely known, but he was able to frame his guru Kumārādza as an emanation of that master, consequently elevating his own connection to the cycle. In the cases in which Longchenpa can be shown to have an agenda, however, it can almost always be explained in terms of what would serve to help people in their spiritual path. Perhaps more apparent than anything else in his writings is this dynamic, vividly expressed in a freedom to move between various modalities of presentation and content to provide appropriate teachings for a wide audience.

REVIEW OF LITERATURE

The existing literature on Longchenpa comprises a mix of academic and non-academic work, ranging from detailed research by Himalayan scholars and Western Tibetologists to elucidations and teachings on his texts by lamas, presentations by Buddhist practitioners, and translations by all those mentioned. In many cases, translations are embedded within larger treatments of Longchenpa and the Nyingma tradition, while discussions on him are also found in dedicated translations of his individual writings; in practice, the wide breadth and disparate nature of Longchenpa's corpus have led to it being treated in a variety of ways, both emic and etic. Nevertheless, a brief chronological review of scholarly investigations on the works and thoughts of Longchenpa may be provided here.

One may turn first to the translations and writings of Herbert V. Guenther, who over the course of his academic career strove to highlight the significance of Dzogchen and Longchenpa's writings on it.[81] Dudjom Rinpoche's monumental work on the history of the Nyingma school, translated and edited by Gyurme Dorje and Matthew Kapstein, freely avails itself of Longchenpa's doxographical contributions and provides an overview of his life. Tulku Thondup, Tarthang Tulku, and Nyoshul Khenpo furthered the latter aspect with their respective biographical presentations of Longchenpa for an English-speaking audience. At the turn of the millennium, Franz-Karl Erhard and Gene Smith published on the block-print history of Longchenpa's texts; subsequently, Dorji Wangchuk analyzed his writings in an attempt to provide a chronology for them, an admittedly tricky endeavor, while offering a wealth of additional information on Longchenpa's corpus and the work done on it.

In terms of dissertations, Gyurme Dorje focused on the *Phyogs bcu mun sel*, one of Longchenpa's three commentaries on the controversial *Guhyagarbhatantra*.[82] David Germano examined the Nyingtik cycles, and more specifically the *Tshig don mdzod*, in relation to the synthesis of the Dzogchen tradition with the larger context of Buddhism in Tibet. Gregory Hillis investigated the *Gnas lugs mdzod* in terms of the rhetoric of naturalness, that is, an especially Dzogchen-oriented modality of teaching. Albion M. Butters framed Longchenpa's various areas of focus (e.g., canon, philosophy, discovery of treasure texts, Dzogchen praxis) in relation to the activities of his 14th-century contemporaries, arguing for the significance of his doxographical work in the *Grub mtha' mdzod*. And Stéphane Arguillère offered an in-depth presentation and analysis (in French) of the life and works of Longchenpa, as well as a discussion of the *Chos dbying mdzod*. In all these cases, one may find partial or complete scholarly translations of the works being treated.

The last decade has seen continued work on Longchenpa. Gidi Ifergan traced the transformation in Longchenpa's thought from a rhetoric of negation, involving a critique of the soteriological value of philosophical approaches and spiritual practices, to a praxis based on natural awareness.[83] Adam Lobel examined the philosophy of practical action in the *Gnas lugs mdzod* and *Chos dbyings mdzod*, focusing specifically on spontaneity and spontaneous practice within Dzogchen, with a goal of engaging post-Heideggerian scholars on issues such as intentionality, causality, agency, ethics, and free will.[84] Also worth mentioning is Sara Lindblom's study on Longchenpa's use of Indian metaphor in the *Sgyu ma ngal gso*, arguing that it is not only didactic but also a political means to locate Dzogchen alongside Madhyamaka, in order to legitimate it and associated Nyingma tantras.[85] Most recently, Anne O. Parker's study of Longchenpa's biography by Chödrak Zangpo, which she compares to Arnold of Bonneval's co-authored Latin *vita*, or biography, of St. Bernard of Clairvaux, employs Weberian theory to illustrate a process of spiritual legitimation in medieval Tibet.[86] While more works certainly exist, as this overview cannot claim to be comprehensive, it nonetheless reveals both the substantial body of scholarship already done on Longchenpa and the opportunities that remain to explore him further.

FURTHER READING

Aitken, Allison. "The Truth about Śrīgupta's Two Truths: Longchen Rabjampa's 'Lower Svātantrikas' and the Making of a New Philosophical School." *Journal of South Asian Intellectual History* 3, no. 2 (2021): 185–225.

Arguillère, Stéphane. *Profusion de la vaste sphère: Klong-chen rab-'byams, Tibet, 1308–1364; sa vie, son œuvre, sa doctrine*. The Institute for Comparative Research in Human Culture, Orientalia Lovaniensia Analecta. Leuven, Belgium, Paris, and Dudley, MA: Peeters, 2007.

Butters, Albion M. *Illuminating the Goal: rDzogs chen and Doxography in 14th-Century Tibet*. Studia Orientalia 119. Helsinki: Finnish Oriental Society, 2018.

Cornu, Philippe. *Longchenpa, la liberté naturelle de l'esprit*. Paris: Éditions du Seuil, 1994.

Dorje, Nyoshul Khenpo Jamyang. *A Marvelous Garland of Rare Gems: Biographies of Masters of Awareness in the Dzogchen Lineage*. Translated by Richard Barron, 114. Junction City, CA: Padma Publishing, 2005.

Germano, David, and Janet Gyatso. "Longchenpa and the Possession of the Ḍākinīs." In *Tantra in Practice*. Edited by David White, 239–265. Princeton, NJ: Princeton University Press, 2000.

Guenther, Herbert V., trans. *Kindly Bent to Ease Us*, Vols. 1–3. Berkeley, CA: Dharma Publishing, 1975/1976.

Ifergan, Gigi. *The Man from Samye: Longchenpa on Praxis, Its Negation and Liberation*. New Delhi: Aditya Prakashan, 2014.

Longchenpa. *A Visionary Journey: The Story of the Wildwood Delights—The Story of the Mount Potala Delights*. Translated by Herbert Guenther. Boston: Shambhala, 1989.

Longchenpa. *Now That I Come to Die: Intimate Guidance from One of Tibet's Greatest Masters*. Translated by Tarthang Tulku. Berkeley, CA: Dharma Publishing, 2007.

Longchenpa. *Trilogy of Rest*. Books 1–3. Translated by the Padmakara Translation Group. Boulder, CO: Shambhala, 2017–2019.

Longchenpa. *You Are the Eyes of the World.* Translated by Kennard Lipman and Merrill Peterson. Ithaca, NY: Snow Lion, 2011.

Mackenzie, Jampa. *The Life of Longchenpa: The Omniscient Dharma King of the Vast Expanse.* Boston and London: Snow Lion, 2013.

Namkhai Norbu, Chogyal. *Longchenpa's Advice from the Heart.* Arcidosso, Italy: Shang Shung Institute, 2008.

Namkhai Norbu, Chogyal. *The Light of the Sun: Teachings on Longchenpa's Precious Mala of the Four Dharmas.* Arcidosso, Italy: Shang Shung Institute, 2014.

Rabjam, Longchen. *The Precious Treasury Set.* Translated by Richard Barron. Junction City, CA: Padma Publishing, 1998–2007.

Rab-jam-pa, Long-ch'en. *The Four-Themed Precious Garland: An Introduction to Dzogchen, with commentaries by Dudjom Rinpoche and Beru Khyentse Rinpoche.* Translated by Alexander Berzin, Sharpa Tulku, and Matthew Kapstein. Dharamsala, India: Library of Tibetan Works and Archives, 1978.

Thondup, Tulku. *The Practice of Dzogchen.* Edited by Harold Talbott. Ithaca, NY: Snow Lion, 1996.

Tsumagari, Shinichi. *Meaningful to Behold: A Critical Edition & Annotated Translation of Longchenpa's Biography.* Create Space, 2016.

Wangchuk, Dorji. "Cross-Referential Clues for a Relative Chronology of Klong chen pa's Works." In *Contributions to Tibetan Buddhist Literature, PIATS 2006: Tibetan Studies: Proceedings of the Eleventh Seminar of the International Association for Tibetan Studies.* Edited by Orna Almogi, 195–244. Halle, Germany: International Institute for Tibetan and Buddhist Studies, 2008.

NOTES

1. The date of Longchenpa's passing is sometimes given as 1364. On the different methods of dating his death, see Steven Goodman and Ronald M. Davidson, *Tibetan Buddhism: Reason and Revelation* (Albany: State University of New York Press, 1992), 190n6.
2. While this title has been given (in all likelihood posthumously) to great masters from other schools and is not exclusively a Nyingma tradition, only in very rare cases—such as with Longchenpa here—does it comprise their primary epithet.
3. See Tulku Thondup, *The Practice of Dzogchen*, ed. Harold Talbott (Ithaca, NY: Snow Lion, 1996), for an aggregated biography comprised of the following: Klong chen pa, *Gter 'byung rin po che'i lo rgyus*; Klong chen pa, *Zhus lan bdud rtsi gser phreng*; Klong chen pa, *Gso skor gsum gyi spyi don legs bshad rgya mtsho*; Klong chen pa, *Blo gsal ri bong gi rtogs pa brjod pa'i dris lan lha'i rnga bo che lta bu'i gtam*; 'Jigs med gling pa, *De bzhin gshegs pas legs par gsung pa'i gsung rab rgya mtsho'i snying por gyur pa rig pa 'dzin pa'i sde snod dam pa snga 'gyur rgyud 'bum rin po che'i rtogs pa brjod pa 'dzam gling tha gru khyab pa'i rgyan*; and Zhe chen rgyal tshab padma rnam rgyal, *Snga 'gyur rdo rje theg pa gtso bor gyur pa'i sgrub brgyud shing rta brgyad kyi byung ba brjod pa'i gtam mdor bsdus legs bshad padma dkar po'i rdzing bu*.
4. Outside of the biographical sources in translation cited in the notes that follow, one can also refer to the following in the original Tibetan: Glag bla chos 'grub dag chos grags bzang pos brtsam, *Klong chen pa'i rnam thar*; Bdud 'joms rin po che, *Rnying ma chos 'byung*; 'Gos lo tsA ba gzhon nu dpal, *Deb ther sngon po*; Kun bzang 'gyur med mchog grub, *Kun mkhyen chos kyi rgyal po gter chen dri med 'od zer gyi rnam par thar pa cung zad spros pa ngo mtshar skal bzang mchog gi dga' ston*; the autobiographical *Mthong snang rin po che 'od kyi drva ba*, in Longchenpa's *Snying thig ya bzhi*; Stag sgang mkhas mchog gu ru bkra shis, *Bstan pa'i snying po gsang chen snga 'gyur nges don zab mo'i chos kyi byung ba gsal bar byed pa'i legs bshad mkhas pa dga' byed ngo mtshar gtam gyi rol mtsho*.
5. Personal communication with Khenpo Palden Sherab, 2002; and Kurtis R. Schaeffer, Matthew T. Kapstein, and Gray Tuttle, eds., *Sources of Tibetan Tradition* (New York: Columbia University Press, 2013), 416.
6. For example, see Longchenpa's enduring correspondence with the Third Karmapa, preserved in his miscellaneous writings (*Gsung thor bu*).

7. Tarthang Tulku, ed., *Crystal Mirror*, Vol. V (Berkeley, CA: Dharma Publishing, 1977), 254–255.
8. This protectress appears later in Longchenpa's life as well, such as when he was recovering the Khandro Nyingtik at Chimpu. See David Germano and Janet Gyatso, "Longchenpa and the Possession of the Ḍākinīs," in *Tantra in Practice*, ed. David White (Princeton, NJ: Princeton University Press, 2000), 239–265. While Germano and Gyatso refer to her as a local deity, her name Nam gru ("Constellation") suggests a more cosmic connection with the twenty-eight *nakṣatra* deities, in particular Andromeda. Worth noting also is the generic nature of her second name, Re ma ti, used to signify four sisters among the twelve *tenma* goddesses or even as a synonym for Śrīdēvī (Dpal ldan lha mo in Tibet).
9. Tulku Thondup, *Masters of Meditation and Miracles* (Boston: Shambhala, 1996), 109.
10. Thondup, *Practice of Dzogchen*, 146. In a variant of this story, Longchenpa's mother arrived to find him missing from the spot where she had left him. Only after she started crying did the protectress appear.
11. These were the *Spyi'i khog dbub pa* and the *Rgyud kyi rnam bshad*, also known as Longchenpa's *Gsang snying 'grel ba*. See Jamgön Kongtrul Lodrö Tayé, *The Treasury of Knowledge: Book Six, Part Four: Systems of Buddhist Tantra* (Ithaca, NY: Snow Lion, 2005), 352.
12. Also included in the set of three "mother" texts (*yum gsum*) is the *Perfection of Wisdom Sutra in One Hundred Thousand Lines* (*Śatasāhasrikāprajñāpāramitā*). This metaphor is based on their description of emptiness as the "mother" of the buddhas.
13. Dudjom Rinpoche, *The Nyingma School of Tibetan Buddhism: Its Fundamentals and History, Vol. 1*, trans. and ed. Gyurme Dorje and Matthew Kapstein (Boston: Wisdom, 1991), 556; and for a more detailed review of teachings received, see Jampa Mackenzie, *The Life of Longchenpa: The Omniscient Dharma King of the Vast Expanse* (Boston and London: Snow Lion, 2013), 33–37. It is worth adding that no information exists on these individuals, save that they were instructors of Longchenpa. However, that they hailed from different traditions can be inferred by the subjects they taught.
14. Keith Dowman, *The Power-Places of Central Tibet: The Pilgrim's Guide* (New York: Routledge, 1988), 140.
15. Rinpoche, *Nyingma School of Tibetan Buddhism*, 577.
16. For a list of Longchenpa's teachers at Sangpu Neutok and their respective areas of focus, see Thondup, *Practice of Dzogchen*, 139.
17. *Rkyen la khams 'dus pa ka kha sum cu*, in *Gsung thor bu*. For a translation, see Shinichi Tsumagari, *Meaningful to Behold: A Critical Edition & Annotated Translation of Longchenpa's Biography* (Scotts Valley, CA: Create Space, 2016).
18. Mackenzie, *Life of Longchenpa*, 40.
19. Thondup, *Practice of Dzogchen*, 140.
20. The name Kumārādza is a Tibetan truncation of what in Sanskrit would be Kumārarāja ("Youthful King").
21. Tulku, *Crystal Mirror*, 256.
22. Alternatively, one reads of Kumārādza's encampment being composed of seventy shelters set up against the wind.
23. Recent research on this form of traditional Tibetan medicine for sickness related to spirits (*gdon*) reveals that the pills not only included mercury but also cannabis sativa, an assortment of other herbs, and animal musk. Christian Rätsch, *Marijuana Medicine: A World Tour of the Healing and Visionary Powers of Cannabis* (Rochester, VT: Healing Arts Press, 2001), 48.
24. George N. Roerich and Gendün Chöphel, trans., *The Blue Annals by Gö Lotsawa* (New Delhi: Motilal Banarsidass, 1988), 200.
25. Rinpoche, *Nyingma School of Tibetan Buddhism*, 580. These included the three classes of Dzogchen (Mind Class, Expanse Class, and Personal Instruction Class), the seventeen tantras, and the 119 pith instructions.
26. Thondup, *Practice of Dzogchen*, 142. Alternatively, this trip to Lhasa happened just before Longchenpa left for Bhutan, when Jangchub Gyaltsen's army tried to capture and kill him, and he was able to escape

them by disappearing. The description of the experience before the Jowo includes an entire panoply of buddhas, bodhisattvas, and deities appearing to him. See Nyoshul Khenpo Jamyang Dorje, *A Marvelous Garland of Rare Gems: Biographies of Masters of Awareness in the Dzogchen Lineage*, trans. Richard Barron (Junction City, CA: Padma Publishing, 2005), 115–116.

27. Germano and Gyatso, "Longchenpa and the Possession," 245.
28. Germano and Gyatso, "Longchenpa and the Possession," 252.
29. Rinpoche, *Nyingma School of Tibetan Buddhism*, 580; and Thondup, *Masters of Meditation and Miracles*, 112.
30. Dowman, *Power-Places of Central Tibet*, 232. To this day, some of the geographical features mentioned in his biography are still visible. Before the cave, one finds a juniper where the Dharma-protectors were believed to reside, and farther down the hill is the large slab where Rāhula ground Longchenpa's ink.
31. This activity may be linked to the biographical claims that Longchenpa was an abbot of Samye.
32. Dorje, *Marvelous Garland of Rare Gems*, 114.
33. Albion M. Butters, *Illuminating the Goal: RDzogs Chen and Doxography in 14th-century Tibet*, Studia Orientalia 119 (Helsinki: Finnish Oriental Society, 2018), 28–33; and Tsepon W. D. Shakabpa, *Tibet: A Political History* (New York: Potala, 1984), 67–82.
34. Geoffrey Samuel, *Civilized Shamans* (Washington, DC: Smithsonian Institution Press, 1993), 492.
35. Herbert Guenther, *Kindly Bent to Ease Us: From the Trilogy of Finding Comfort and Ease [Ngal gso skor gsum], Part One: Mind*, trans. *Klong chen pa*, Tibetan Translation Series (Emeryville, CA: Dharma Publishing, 1975), xv.
36. Luciano Petech, *Central Tibet and the Mongols*, Serie Orientale Roma LXV (Rome: Instituto Italiano per il Medio ed Estremo Oriente, 1990), 107.
37. Michael Aris, *Bhutan: The Early History of a Himalayan Kingdom* (Warminster, UK: Aris & Philips, 1979), 262; and Karma Ura, *Longchen's Forests of Poetry and Rivers of Composition in Bhutan* (Thimphu, Bhutan: The Centre for Bhutan Studies and GNH Research, 2016), 31–86.
38. On Longchenpa's time in Bhutan, see Dorji Penjore, "Oral Construction of Exile Life and Times of Kunkhyen Longchen Rabjam in Bumthang," *Journal of Bhutan Studies* 13 (Winter 2005): 60–73.
39. Tulku, *Crystal Mirror*, 257.
40. Roerich and Chöphel, *Blue Annals*, 202.
41. Aris, *Bhutan*, 30.
42. Penjore, "Oral Construction," 71.
43. Penjore, "Oral Construction," 62.
44. Roerich and Chöphel, *Blue Annals*, 200–202.
45. See the *Kun mkhyen chos kyi rgyal po gter chen dri med 'od zer gyi rnam par thar pa cung zad spros pa ngo mtshar skal bzang mchog gi dga' ston*, a biography of Longchenpa written in the eighteen century by Kun bzang 'gyur med mchog grub; and Matthew Kapstein, *The Tibetan Assimilation of Buddhism: Conversion, Contestation, and Memory* (New York: Oxford University Press), 245n90.
46. For a translation of the great master's last teachings to his disciples, see Chogyal Namkhai Norbu, *Longchenpa's Advice from the Heart* (Arcidosso, Italy: Shang Shung Institute, 2008).
47. Dowman, *Power-Places of Central Tibet*, 228, 232.
48. Tulku, ed. *Crystal Mirror*, XI (Berkeley, CA: Dharma Publishing, 1995), 167; and Aris, *Bhutan*, 155. For an extensive biographical description of these figures, see Dorje, *Marvelous Garland of Rare Gems*, 354–366.
49. For a list of the disciples belonging to these various categories, see https://treasuryoflives.org/biographies/view/Longchenpa/TBRC_P158.
50. See the *Zhu len bdud rtsi gser phreng* in the *Mkha' 'gro snying thig*.
51. Germano and Gyatso, "Longchenpa and the Possession," 247.
52. Aris, *Bhutan*, 27–28.

53. Jeffrey Hopkins was surprised to hear this from one of his teachers. See Jeffrey Hopkins, *Emptiness in the Mind-Only School of Buddhism* (Berkeley, CA: University of California Press, 1999), 15.
54. Khenpo Nyoshul and Surya Das, *Natural Great Perfection: rDzogs chen Teachings and Vajra Songs* (Ithaca, NY: Snow Lion, 1995), 161, 170.
55. Stéphane Arguillère, "A Biography of Klong chen rab 'byams (https://www.arguillere.org/2021/05/a-biography-of-klong-chen-rab-byams-1.html)," *Studies, Reflections and Memories on Tibetan Religions*, May 2, 2021, n3.
56. Arguillère, "A Biography of Klong chen rab 'byams."
57. David Germano, "Architecture and Absence in the Secret Tantric History of the Great Perfection (*rdzogs chen*)," *Journal of the International Association of Buddhist Studies* 17, no. 2 (1994), 203–335, 275.
58. Butters, *Illuminating the Goal*, 34–45.
59. This was done at Bumthang thar pa gling. See the *Bstan bcos kyi dkar chag rin po che'i mdzod khang* in Longchenpa's *Gsung thor bu*.
60. Chos grags bzang po, *Kun mkhyen dri med 'od zer gyi rnam thar mthong ba don ldan* (BDRC bdr:MW20468); and Thondup, *Practice of Dzogchen*, 154.
61. 'Jigs med gling pa, *Rnying rgyud dkar chag*; Glag bla bsod nams chos grub, *Dad gsum 'ju ngogs*.
62. Dorje, *Marvelous Garland of Rare Gems*, 145; and Stéphane Arguillère, *Profusion de la vaste sphère: Klong-chen rab-'byams, Tibet, 1308–1364: sa vie, son œuvre, sa doctrine*, The Institute for Comparative Research in Human Culture, Orientalia Lovaniensia Analecta (Leuven, Belgium, Paris, and Dudley, MA: Peeters, 2007), 177–194.
63. Dorji Wangchuk, "Cross-Referential Clues for a Relative Chronology of Klong chen pa's Works," in *Contributions to Tibetan Buddhist Literature, PIATS 2006: Tibetan Studies: Proceedings of the Eleventh Seminar of the International Association for Tibetan Studies*, ed. Orna Almogi (Halle, Germany: International Institute for Tibetan and Buddhist Studies, 2008), 195–244, 197n.10. Wangchuk cites Glag bla bsod nams chos grub, *Dad gsum 'ju ngogs*, for the story of Asura Cave.
64. E. Gene Smith, *Among Tibetan Texts: History and Literature of the Himalayan Plateau*, ed. Kurtis R. Schaeffer (Somerville, MA: Wisdom Publications, 2001), 34.
65. Arguillère, *Profusion de la vaste sphère*, 158–172.
66. For a critical analysis of the dating of these collections and a comparative discussion of them, see Wangchuk, "Cross-Referential Clues," 199–221 (see esp. 202, 221n87, on the later titling of the *Yang tig skor gsum* and the *Mdzod bdun*).
67. Leonard van der Kuijp, "A Treatise on Buddhist Epistemology and Logic Attributed to Klong chen Rab 'byams pa (1309–1364) and Its Place in Indo-Tibetan Intellectual History," *Journal of Indian Philosophy* 31 (2003), 381–437; and Jonathan Stoltz, "On the Authorship of the Tshad ma'i de kho na nyid bsdus pa," *Revue d'Etudes Tibétaines*, no. 56 (October 2020): 48–69.
68. Stéphane Arguillère, "What Did Longchen Rabjam Actually Write and What Is the Chronology of His Writings? (https://www.arguillere.org/2021/05/what-did-longchen-rabjam-actually-write-and-what-is-the-chronology-of-his-writings-5.html)" *Studies, Reflections and Memories on Tibetan Religions*, June 2, 2021.
69. On claims surrounding these, see Wangchuk, "Cross-Referential Clues," 230–231.
70. Giuseppe Tucci, *Tibetan Painted Scrolls* (Rome: Libreria dello Stato, 1949), 258–259n203.
71. Ura, *Longchen's Forests*, 17.
72. Thondup, *Practice of Dzogchen*, 154.
73. Dorje, *Marvelous Garland of Rare Gems*, 54.
74. For a list of the tantras that Longchenpa included in the New Translation and Ancient Translation traditions, see Albion M. Butters, "The Doxographical Genius of Kun mkhyen kLong chen rab 'byams pa" (PhD diss., Columbia University, 2006).

75. See Butters, *Illuminating the Goal*, 91–92.
76. Gregory A. Hillis, "The Rhetoric of Naturalness: A Critical Study of the gNas lugs mdzod" (PhD diss., University of Virginia, 2003), 161; and Butters, *Illuminating the Goal*, 187.
77. On the Dzogchen hermeneutic employed by Longchenpa, see Butters, *Illuminating the Goal*, 191–195.
78. This is clear in both the *Grub mtha' mdzod* and the *Tshig don mdzod*. On the latter, see David Germano, "Poetic Thought, the Intelligent Universe, and the Mystery of Self: The Tantric Synthesis of Rdzogs Chen in Fourteenth Century Tibet" (PhD diss., The University of Wisconsin-Madison, 1992), 78, 587.
79. Klaus-Dieter Mathes, *A Direct Path to the Buddha within* (Boston: Wisdom, 2008), 98, 103.
80. Allison Aitken, "The Truth about Śrīgupta's Two Truths: Longchen Rabjampa's 'Lower Svātantrikas' and the Making of a New Philosophical School," *Journal of South Asian Intellectual History* 3, no. 2 (2021): 185–225.
81. Among others, see Herbert V. Guenther, trans., *Kindly Bent to Ease Us*, Vols. 1–3 (Berkeley, CA: Dharma Publishing, 1975/1976); and Longchenpa, *A Visionary Journey: The Story of the Wildwood Delights—The Story of the Mount Potala Delights*, trans. Herbert Guenther (Boston: Shambhala, 1989).
82. Gyurme Dorje, "The *Guhyagarbhatattvaviniscayamahātantra* and its Fourteenth Century Tibetan Commentary: Phyogs bcu mun sel" (PhD diss., University of London, 1987).
83. Gidi Ifergan, *The Man from Samye: Longchenpa on Praxis, Its Negation and Liberation* (New Delhi: Aditya Prakashan, 2014).
84. Adam S. Lobel, "Allowing Spontaneity: Practice, Theory, and Ethical Cultivation in Longchenpa's Great Perfection Philosophy of Action" (PhD diss., Harvard University, 2018).
85. Sara Lindblom, "Water Moons and Other Perfectly Pure Illusions: Longchen Rabjam's Dzogchen Synthesis in *Finding Rest in Illusion*" (masters' thesis, University of Colorado at Boulder, 2020).
86. Anne O. Parker, "The Radiance of Light: Comparing the Medieval Tibetan and Medieval Latin Biographies of Longchen Rabjam and Bernard of Clairvaux" (PhD diss., Rice University, 2021).

Albion M. Butters

M

MADHYAMAKA

HISTORICAL BACKGROUND AND CONTEXT OF MADHYAMAKA

In numerous discourses, the Buddha refers to his teaching as a middle way[1] between extreme and erroneous views about the putative self (Skt. *ātman*).[2] An example of this is the frequently referenced *Kaccāyanagotta Sutta*, in which the Buddha tells Kaccāna that right view occupies a middle position between the two extreme conceptions of existence and nonexistence:

> This world, Kaccāna, for the most part depends upon a duality—upon the notion of existence and the notion of nonexistence. But for one who sees the origin of the world as it really is with correct wisdom, there is no notion of nonexistence in regard to the world. And for one who sees the cessation of the world as it really is with correct wisdom, there is no notion of existence in regard to the world... "All exists": Kaccāna, this is one extreme. 'All does not exist': this is the second extreme. Without veering towards either of these extremes, the Tathāgata teaches a Dhamma by the middle...[3]

This passage is followed by an iteration of the teaching on the twelve links of dependent origination (*pratītyasamutpāda*), which describes the process of the origination of suffering from ignorance (*avidyā*), and explains that the cessation of the first link leads to the cessation of "this whole mass of suffering."[4] Right view is the antidote to ignorance, and thus to suffering. The *Sutta* explicitly states that this middle view pertains to views about the self and to the cessation of suffering as its goal.

With the Abhidharma literature, we see the beginnings of categorization and standardization of concepts understood to be presented in the *Suttas*. Some early Buddhist traditions made this literature canonical, raising it to the status of "word of the Buddha" (*buddhavacana*), but others did not, and in some cases the latter integrated such material into the *Sutta Piṭaka*. Interpretations of the Abhidharma texts led to a proliferation of systems of exposition, and the depth and complexity of the material provided fertile ground for the further explication of Buddhist doctrine. It is against this background that Madhyamaka as a distinct doctrinal system arose. Nāgārjuna's arguments are predominantly directed against other Buddhists, presumably Ābhidharmikas. As Siderits and Katsura in their translation of the Nāgārjuna's *Root Verses of the Middle Way* (*Mūlamadhyamakakārikā*) point out, Nāgārjuna's adversaries would have shared a core set of presuppositions, which establish the parameters of what Nāgārjuna seeks to refute. These presuppositions can be summarized as follows.

What really exists, in the last analysis, and in yogic realization, is in fact a dynamic flow of fundamental, irreducible entities called dharmas. All facts about things of the conventional world, and especially the self, can be explained entirely and ultimately in terms of dharmas and their relations with one another. What one can say about composite phenomena, such as the self, is only true conventionally. Only statements grounded at the level of dharmas can be ultimately true, because only dharmas have ultimate existence. An element of the assumptions about this ultimate existence is that dharmas possess their own intrinsic natures (*svabhāva*), a unique property that is inherent to them and depends on nothing else. Nothing that lacks an intrinsic nature can be ultimate. The Buddhist goal of nirvana, the complete and final cessation of suffering, was held to be achieved through the realization of what is ultimately true about ourselves and the world. The erroneous belief that keeps us bound in saṃsāra is the mistaken assumption that the self is ultimately real, when in fact it is a conceptual fiction that we superimpose upon an impersonal stream of mental and physical phenomena.

NĀGĀRJUNA AND MAHĀYĀNA

Nāgārjuna (2nd–3rd centuries CE) is generally regarded by later Buddhist traditions and modern scholarship as the founder of the Madhyamaka "school."[5] Traditional accounts also associate Nāgārjuna with the rise of the Mahāyāna. In Tibetan traditions, Nāgārjuna (along with Asaṅga) is called one of the two "Re-openers" of the Mahāyāna and is credited with the return of the *Perfection of Wisdom* texts to the world of humans by retrieving them from the realm of the Nāgas, where they had been kept safe for centuries. He is revered as a patriarch in numerous Buddhist traditions in East Asia and Tibet, including Ch'an/Zen, Pure Land, Shingon, and the Tibetan Vajrayāna.

The emergence of the Mahāyāna is characterized by the appearance of new texts, most notably the *Perfection of Wisdom* (*Prajñāpāramitā*) sūtras, attributed to the buddha. This genre of sūtra focuses on the six, or ten, perfections of the Bodhisattva culminating in the perfection of wisdom itself called, among other things, the "mother of all the Buddhas." These texts, which depict themselves as discourses of the buddha, flatly reject the position that, while self was utterly illusory, the skandhas, the dynamic processes upon which a self was wrongly imputed, actually had an ontological status. In these sūtras we read that the five skandhas do not exist, or are empty (*śūnya*). Madhyamaka thought is traditionally understood as elucidating the meaning of such assertions in the *Perfection of Wisdom* sūtras. In Nāgārjuna's texts, arguments are made to demonstrate how and why this way of expressing the dharma is not only justified, but is in fact the actual and final intent of the Buddha's teachings.

THE TEXTUAL FOUNDATIONS OF MADHYAMAKA

In the Chinese Buddhist canon there are eight texts attributed to Nāgārjuna, and in the Tibetan canon, there are 116. Studies of Chinese Madhyamaka have tended to focus on the Sanlun school and the influence of Madhyamaka on later syncretic schools such as Tiantai, Huayan, and Chan.[6] The bulk of most modern scholarly interest in Nāgārjuna's Madhyamaka has been on just a few of the Indian texts, in some cases in their Tibetan translations. Some disagreement remains about which of them can be reliably attributed to Nāgārjuna, but there is a general consensus that the texts that the later Tibetan traditions group into the "analytic corpus" are genuine works of Nāgārjuna. In addition to the analytic corpus (*rigs tshogs*), the Tibetan categorization includes the hymnic corpus (*bstod tshogs*) and the advice corpus (gtam tshogs).[7] The analytic corpus includes the *Root Verses of the Middle Way* (*Mūlamadhyamakakārikā*), the *Sixty Stanzas on Analysis* (*Yuktiṣaṣṭikā*), the *Seventy Stanzas on Emptiness* (*Śūnyatāsaptati*), the *Dispeller of Objections* (*Vigrahavyāvatanī*), the *Treatise on Pulverization* (*Vaidalyaprakaraṇa*), and the nonextant *Proof of Conventions* (*Vyavahārasiddhi*).[8] The *Precious Garland* (*Ratnāvalī*) is sometimes substituted in the place of the latter, but it is in fact a very different sort of text from the other five, much more in accord with the advice corpus, and is often placed in that category.

The *Root Verses of the Middle Way* (MMK) was regarded by all the major commentators in India, China, and Tibet as Nāgārjuna's *magnum opus*. Modern scholarship has accepted this and has used this text as the touchstone for determining the authenticity of the other works attributed to Nāgārjuna. The *Mūlamadhyamakakārikā* consists of 447 verses in twenty-seven chapters, though some modern scholars argue that the text originally ended with chapter 25. Typical of the kārikā genre, the subject matter is presented in a terse style, leading to the composition of numerous commentaries in India, China, and Tibet to elucidate the meaning of the *Mūlamadhyamakakārikā*.

The Sixty Stanzas on Analysis (*Yuktiṣaṣṭikā*) is a text consisting of sixty-one verses that explain Mādhyamika analysis as the elimination of thinking in terms of existence and nonexistence of what is dependently originated (*pratītyasamutpāda*). The *Sixty Stanzas on Analysis* makes the striking assertion that the world is a construction of ignorance, and nirvana is precisely the realization of this fact.[9] It is extant in both Chinese and Tibetan translations. The *Seventy Stanzas on Emptiness* (*Śūnyatāsaptati*) is a text of seventy-three verses that deals with the central Madhyamaka concept of emptiness (*śūnyatā*), accompanied by a commentary said to be authored by Nāgārjuna himself. It exists only in Tibetan translation. The *Dispeller of Objections* (*Vigrahavyāvartinī*) is a seventy-verse text that answers objections to Nāgārjuna's views expressed in his other works, especially the MMK. It is available in the original Sanskrit and also in Chinese and Tibetan translations. The *Treatise on Pulverization* (*Vaidalyaprakaraṇa*) is a work that critiques the sixteen logical categories of Nyāya philosophy. It exists only in Tibetan translation. The *Precious Garland* (*Ratnāvalī*) is a 500-verse work that is said to be advice given to a king. Among the minor analytic corpus texts, the *Dispeller of Objections* is often invoked to help clarify points in the MMK, especially on the issue of Nāgārjuna's assertion that Mādhyamikas have no philosophical thesis of their own. In the major English translations and the broader attempts to establish Nāgārjuna's system, neither the Sixty Stanzas on Analysis nor the *Seventy Stanzas on Emptiness* has been much taken into account,[10] despite the fact that the 7th-century Indian commentator Candrakīrti held the *Seventy Stanzas on Emptiness*, along with the *Dispeller of Objections*, to form an appendix to the MMK.[11]

The hymns have received relatively little attention in Western scholarship despite their importance in the Tibetan traditions and many scholars' acceptance that at least some of these texts were likely written by the same author as the Mūlamadhyakakārikā.[12] In Tibet, for the proponents of the more cataphatic "other-emptiness" (*gzhan stong*) doctrine, the hymns were revered as expressing Nāgārjuna's final philosophical position and the definitive meaning of the Middle Way. For the most part, however, these texts and their message have not played a significant part in the understanding of Madhyamaka for Indian or Tibetan[13] authors or for modern scholars.

WHAT DID NĀGĀRJUNA MEAN BY "MIDDLE WAY?"

As mentioned above, the early Buddhist meaning of the idea that the buddha's teaching is a middle way was that it staked out a position between the extreme views of "all exists" and "all does not exist." These two views are often referred to as "eternalism" (*śāśvatadarśanam*) and "annihilationism" (*ucchedadarśanam*), and they specifically refer to views about the self. An eternalist view of the self holds that the self abides through time and across lives, and an annihilationist view holds that personal existence is annihilated at death, thus rendering null questions of karmic reward or retribution. The meaning of right view, in the *Kaccāyanagotta Sutta*, is defined: "Without veering towards either of these extremes, the Tathāgata teaches the Dhamma by the middle."[14] That Dhamma is the teaching of the twelve links of dependent origination.

Nāgārjuna cites the Sanskrit parallel of this *sutta* but takes its implications further. In chapter fifteen of the MMK, he says, "In 'The Instructing of Katyāyana,' both 'it exists' and 'it does not exist' are denied by the Blessed One, who clearly perceives the existent and nonexistent."[15] Here, and throughout the MMK, Nāgārjuna takes this sense of right view to apply not just to the self but to everything, including the skandhas, which are the basis for the mistaken assumption of an existent self that Ābhidarmikas held to ultimately exist. Echoing numerous statements in the *Perfection of Wisdom* sūtras, where it says that the five skandhas are as empty as the putative self, Nāgārjuna argues in the MMK and other texts of the analytic corpus that any conceivable entity can be demonstrated to be empty, that is, not existent, nonexistent, both existent and nonexistent, neither existent or nonexistent.

In chapter after chapter, Nāgārjuna subjects to analysis numerous things, from conditionality up through the buddha, the Four Noble Truths, and nirvana. In every case, the object is revealed not to exist in any ultimate sense. Though he uses a number of common patterns of argumentation, underlying them all is a method that sets up all possible ways that the object could exist, and then refutes each possibility. For example, in chapter 1 Nāgārjuna takes on the concept that things exist in the sense that they arise from causal conditions. He begins, "Not from itself, not from another, not from both, nor without a cause: never in any way is there any existing thing that has arisen."[16] The four possibilities for the arising of a thing are considered to exhaust the possibilities for a meaningful explanation of causation, and Nāgārjuna rejects each one as incoherent. To come to this conclusion, Nāgārjuna points out that dichotomous concepts like "self/other" are mutually dependent for their meaning, or existence. According to Ābhidharmikas, for a thing to be real, it must have an intrinsic nature (*svabhāva*), which makes it what it is. Nāgārjuna denies the possibility of intrinsic nature, as well as the possibility of the nature of a thing arising from something else (*parabhāva*), because "other" depends on "self." Nāgārjuna seeks to demonstrate that the Ābhidharmikas' own positions are incoherent. The conclusion here is that conditions, regarded as real things by Ābhidharmikas, are empty. "Therefore neither a product consisting of conditions nor one consisting of nonconditions exists; if the product does not exist, how can there be a condition or noncondition."[17] This discursive "emptying" of concepts that were widely accepted by scholastically inclined Buddhists of Nāgārjuna's time is the main work of the MMK, and the conclusion that Nāgārjuna reaches again and again is that when analyzed deeply, everything is revealed to lack any unique nature or essential nature of its own. Ābhidarmikas insisted that the possession of such an intrinsic nature was necessary for something to exist in an ultimate sense; thus, from their perspective Nāgārjuna seemed to be arguing that nothing really existed, and this was thought to be thoroughly incompatible with the teachings of the buddha.

It takes until chapter 24 of the MMK, "An Analysis of the Four Noble Truths," before Nāgārjuna responds to this not unreasonable concern. His response is to invoke the structure of the Two Truths, which Ābhidarmikas accept, though in a completely different way, as discussed above. Nāgārjuna's analyses have revealed that the arising and passing away of things in the phenomenal world, about which the buddha taught, is possible only because those things lack intrinsic nature—they are neither existent, nonexistent, both, or neither.

Exactly what that entails for the level of conventional truth/existence has been disputed by Nāgārjuna's Indian and Chinese commentators, as well as modern interpreters. If nothing can be said to exist (or not, or both, or neither) in any ultimate sense, numerous questions obviously arise about ethics, the path, nirvana, and more. Nāgārjuna's response to those who say that emptiness undermines all these things is to state that it is in fact the assumptions of existence/nonexistence, or existence by intrinsic nature, that would make the phenomenal world, knowledge of it, and the attainment of nirvaṇa impossible. "All is possible when emptiness is possible. Nothing is possible when emptiness is impossible... If you look upon existents as real intrinsically, in that case you regard existents as being without cause and conditions.... Effect and cause, as well as agent, instrument and act, arising and ceasing, and fruit—all these you thereby deny."[18] Later commentators, both ancient and modern, however, have struggled with the full implications of the status of the phenomenal world after it has been emptied by Mādhyamika analysis.[19]

Emptiness, however, is not some ultimate nature of the sort imagined by the Ābhidarmikas. It is just a useful way of talking, a convention, that steers a middle course between absolutism and nihilism. In probably the most famous verse of the MMK, Nāgārjuna says, "Dependent

Origination we declare to be emptiness. It [emptiness] is a dependent concept; just that is the middle path."[20] If everything is dependently originated, as the buddha taught and Nāgārjuna has argued, it follows that things cannot be accurately described as existing, not existing, both, or neither. Those concepts, and all others, are only conventional. As Mark Siderits has pithily put this, "The ultimate truth is that there is no ultimate truth."[21]

WHAT IS THE PURPOSE OF MADHYAMAKA?

A great deal of the modern scholarship on Madhyamaka approaches and engages with it as philosophy, but Buddhism has always been more than what we usually mean by this term. The Buddhist path is concerned with the eradication of existential suffering. Knowledge is for the sake of liberation from suffering and the cycle of birth and death (saṃsāra). What then does Madhyamaka have to do with this? It is worthwhile to look at what the MMK states as its purpose. It is often the case that Indian treatises such as the MMK lay out the intended purpose of the text in the opening dedicatory verse:

> I salute the Fully Enlightened One, the best of orators, who taught the doctrine of dependent origination, according to which there is neither cessation nor origination, neither annihilation nor the eternal, neither singularity nor plurality, neither the coming nor the going [of any dharma, for the purpose of nirvāṇa characterized by] the auspicious cessation of hypostatization.[22]

Nāgārjuna identifies the Buddha's fundamental teaching to be dependent origination, characterized by the negation of four pairs of concepts. The purpose of this teaching, or the fruit of its realization, is said to be cessation of "hypostatization" (*prapañca*), or the mental process of conceptualization or "thing-ification."

In chapter 18, "An Analysis of the Self," Nāgārjuna says, "Liberation is attained through the destruction of actions and defilements; actions and defilements arise because of falsifying conceptualizations; those arise from hypostatization; but hypostatization is extinguished in emptiness."[23] In the *Śūnyatāsaptati*, considered by Candrakīrti to be a supplement for understanding the MMK, Nāgārjuna says, "To imagine that things born by causes and conditions are real is called ignorance by the Teacher. From that the twelve members arise. But when one, by seeing correctly, has understood that things are empty one is not infatuated. That is the cessation of ignorance. Thereupon the twelve members stop."[24]

The final verse of an Indian treatise of this sort can also conclude or restate the purport of all that came before it. Though the two major Indian commentators, Bhāviveka[25] and Candrakīrti, take the current twenty-seven-chapter version of the MMK to be entirely composed by Nāgārjuna, some modern scholars have asserted that the final two chapters were later additions by another author. If this were so, the final verse of chapter 25, "An Analysis of Nirvāṇa," should be expected to tell us about the intent of the work. "This halting of cognizing everything, the halting of hypostatizing, is blissful. No Dharma whatsoever was ever taught by the Buddha to anyone."[26] This verse clearly echoes the dedicatory verse, though the translation here obscures this slightly in that the same phrase (*prapañcopaśamaḥ śivaḥ*) found in both verses is translated differently here. In the translation of the dedicatory verse this is rendered "the auspicious cessation of hypostatization." The second part of the dedicatory verse is the salutation to the buddha, who taught dependent origination characterized by the eight negations. In the final line of the verse at the end of chapter 25, having been through twenty-five chapters of negations, we hear that the buddha did not teach any dharma at all, to anyone. Without taking a stand on whether or not this was the final verse of the original text, this statement does indeed sum up the text's work, though concluding on a far more radical point than the one on which it started, but for which Nāgārjuna has argued thus far.

Chapter 26 is an orthodox teaching on the twelve links of dependent origination, perhaps, as the commentator Bhāviveka suggests, in response to those who would take issue with the concluding verse of the nirvana chapter. It is also worth noting that Nāgārjuna has used the doctrine of dependent origination as an argument for how things are in fact empty throughout the text up to this point, so perhaps this uncontroversial teaching of the twelve links helps us to see what he has meant by "dependent origination," and links it back to the intrinsically soteriological purpose of Madhyamaka. "Upon the cessation of ignorance there is the nonarising of volitions. But the cessation of ignorance is due to meditation on just the knowledge of this. By reason of the cessation of one factor in the twelvefold chain, another successor factor fails to arise. Thus does the entire mass of suffering completely cease."[27]

The twenty-seventh chapter is "An Analysis of Views," in which Nāgārjuna tackles the so-called indeterminate questions posed to the buddha in some sūtras. These are questions that the Buddha refused to answer, such as past and future existence of the person, the world, and so on. These questions were answered with silence, because they involved false presuppositions and thus could not be answered in a fashion that would be helpful to the questioner. Up until the final verse, most of what Nāgārjuna has said would be acceptable to his Ābhidharmika contemporaries, but the final verse says, "I salute Gautama, who, based on compassion, taught the true Dharma for the abandonment of all views."[28] In the dedicatory verse, the buddha is praised as the teacher of dependent origination, which is described in terms of four pairs of dichotomous concepts, or views, all of which are negated. Here the purpose is stated as the abandonment of *all* views, the aforementioned, and presumably any and every possible view at all about the self and the world. Chapter 24, verse 18 quoted above, suggests that even emptiness, if taken to express a view, is to be ultimately abandoned.

NĀGĀRJUNA'S MĀDHYAMIKA SUCCESSORS IN INDIA

Nāgarjuna's oeuvre gave rise to numerous commentaries on his works, and original works from authors who saw themselves standing in the Mādhyamika lineage. The earliest was Āryadeva (2nd–3rd centuries CE), who is traditionally understood to have been a direct disciple of Nāgārjuna. His major text is an original work, *The Four Hundred* (*Catuḥśataka*). This text traces the bodhisattva's path from the cultivation of virtues up through the attainment of full awakening, thus situating Madhyamaka much more explicitly in Mahāyāna thought and practice than Nāgārjuna's works. The complete text is extant only in Tibetan, and there is a full translation of Āryadeva's text into English by Karen Lang.[29]

Buddhapālita (early 6th century) wrote a commentary on Nāgārjuna's MMK which is closely related to or identical with the commentary (*Akutobhayā*) sometimes attributed to Nāgārjuna. In Buddhapālita's time, there were important new developments in Buddhist thought in the form of a highly developed epistemological system that would transform how Buddhist philosophy would be done. Buddhapālita resisted these innovations, employing only arguments that revealed the shortcomings of Nāgārjuna's opponents' positions, consistent with Nāgārjuna's own primary argumentative method.

Buddhapālita's conservatism on this point was criticized by the next major commentator, Bhāviveka (late 6th century). In his commentary on the MMK, the *Lamp of Wisdom* (*Prajñāpradīpa*), Bhāviveka took up a radically opposed position to that of Buddhapālita on the matter of what kind of argumentation was needed to establish the Mādhyamika position. This shift is perhaps a result of the further integration of the epistemological advances of Dharmakīrti (c. 650) into scholastic Mahāyāna discourse. Many thought that these new methods put Buddhists on a more solid footing in defending themselves against the critiques of non-Buddhist philosophers in India. Bhāviveka felt that the Mādhyamika position needed more than the unwanted-consequence method of argumentation (*prasaṅga*) favored by Nāgārjuna and Buddhapālita in order to give it logical establishment. Bhāviveka utilized logically elaborated syllogisms (*svatantra anumāna*) in order to argue for the conclusions of Nāgārjuna. For this reason, Bhāviveka would later be considered by the Tibetan traditions to be the founder of the Svātantrika school of interpretation. In addition to the *Lamp of Wisdom*, Bhāviveka wrote an independent verse treatise on Madhyamaka, the *Verses on the Heart of the Middle Way* (*Madhyamakahṛdayakārikā*), with a prose commentary. In this work he surveys and critiques the perspective of non-Mahāyāna Buddhists, Yogācārins, and the six philosophical systems of Hinduism. Hence, this text presents us with a snapshot of the range of philosophical positions current in India in the 6th century.

In his extensive commentary on the MMK, *Clear Words* (*Prasannapadā*), Candrakīrti (7th century) extensively critiqued Bhāviveka's introduction of the epistemological system of Dharmakīrti into the exegesis of Madhyamaka and critiqued that system itself as well as doctrines of Yogācāra. Candrakīrti, in defense of Buddhapālita, argued for exclusive reliance on *prasaṅga* arguments to establish the Mādhyamika position. This emphasis on *prasaṅga* argumentation would cause later Tibetan doxographers to see Candrakīrti to be the founder of the Prāsaṅgikā school of Madhyamaka, which came to be seen as differing from the Svātantrikas not only in terms of methodology but also in terms of holding different philosophical positions.[30] In addition to his commentary on the MMK, Candrakīrti wrote commentaries on Nāgārjuna's *Śūnyatāsaptati* and *Yuktiṣaṣṭikā* as well as one on Āryadeva's *Catuḥśataka*. His original work, *Introduction to the Middle Way* (*Madhyamakāvatāra*), was intended to be a general introduction to Madhyamaka, but with an emphasis on bodhisattva practice and realization. It is divided into ten sections on the production of the mind of awakening (*bodhicitta*), which are aligned with the ten bodhisattva stages taught in the *Sūtra on the Ten Grounds* (*Daśabhūmika Sūtra*) and the Ten Perfections. Because of this structuring, this text is far more focused on realization and soteriology than Nāgārjuna's works of the analytic corpus. Despite the professed importance of the MMK among Tibetan scholars, Candrakīrti's *Introduction to the Middle Way* has been the subject of far more commentary in Tibet.

TREATISES OF LATE INDIAN MĀDHYAMIKA THINKERS

In India, Madhyamaka was followed by Yogācāra, which, like Madhyamaka, can be seen as providing a reasoned explication of the doctrines of certain Mahāyāna sūtras, especially in the

Yogācāra case, the *Saṃdhinirmocana*. From the Yogācāra perspective, the *Perfection of Wisdom Sūtras* and Madhyamaka are understood as clearing away the pernicious illusions projected by hypostatization (*prapañca*), but the final and definitive teachings of the buddha were to be found in Yogācāra sūtras and treatises. In these texts, it is asserted that mind, once purified of hypostatization, was ultimate reality and awakening itself. Among the early commentators on Nāgārjuna's texts are several by prominent masters of the Yogācāra school. A portion of a commentary ascribed to Asaṅga (4th century) on the beginning of the MMK is found in the Chinese canon, and a commentary by Sthiramati (6th century) is also preserved there. Other commentaries by Yogācarins are also referred to in both Chinese and Tibetan sources, though they are not extant. This clearly demonstrates that Nāgārjuna's works were not seen to be necessarily in conflict with the teachings of Yogācāra.

For the most part, Madhyamaka and Yogācāra became synthesized into a complementary whole that addressed both the negation of pernicious views and the establishment of ultimate truth as consciousness. The works of Jñanagarbha, Śāntarakṣita, and Kamalaśīla set the standard for Madhyamaka orthodoxy, and it was the latter two that took Madhyamaka to Tibet as part of the first establishment of Buddhism there. In India, the Svātantika-Prāsaṅgika distinction was not the important one; it was rather one between the views of those who accepted the (conventional) existence of external objects, which included both Bhāviveka and Candrakīrti, and those who asserted a more Yogācārin understanding, in which external objects were ultimately mind-originated, though also empty in the last analysis.

This latter category included Jñanagarbha, Śāntarakṣita, and Kamalaśīla, and it was the dominant position in scholastic Buddhist India until at least the 11th century. Jñānagarbha wrote a treatise examining the Two Truths (*Satyadvayavibhaṅga*), accompanied by an autocommentary. Śāntarakṣita wrote a treatise on Madhyamaka, the *Ornament of the Middle Way* (*Madhyamakālaṃkāra*), which established the foundation of what would later be called the Yogācāra-Madhyamaka school. He also composed the *Tattvasaṃgraha*, an extensive critical study of the doctrines of the different schools of Indian philosophy at the time. A commentary on Jñānagarbha's *Satyadvayavibhaṅga* is attributed to him as well. Kamalaśīla was the disciple of Śāntarakṣita, on whose *Tattvasaṃgraha* he wrote a substantial commentary. Kamalaśīla also wrote an original work, the *Illumination of the Middle Way* (*Madhyamakāloka*), which expounds the Yogācāra-Madhymaka system in great detail, building upon and elucidating the texts of his teacher.

MADHYAMAKA IN EAST ASIA

Madhyamaka texts and teachings were brought to China by Kumārajīva (350–409), and these eventually became the foundation of an independent school, Sanlun or Three Treatise school. The three authoritative texts of Sanlun were the MMK (called the *Madhyamakaśāstra* in the Chinese canon),[31] the *Twelve Gate Treatise* (*Shih erh men lun*) attributed to Nāgārjuna, and the *One Hundred Verse Treatise* (*Pai lun*) attributed to Āryadeva. The latter two texts exist only here in Kumārajīva's translations. The text that has arguably had the greatest influence on East Asian Madhyamaka, however, was the massive *Treatise Which is a Teaching on the Great Perfection of Wisdom* (*Ta chih tu lun*), also translated by Kumārajīva. After Kumārajīva, his disciple Sengzhao was the most important figure in the establishment and development of

Chinese Madhyamaka.[32] The Mādhyamika commentaries that have figured so prominently in the Tibetan traditions' interpretation of Madhyamaka, and in modern scholarship, are not included in the Chinese canon, so the development of Mādhyamika thought took a quite different path than in Tibet. In East Asia, there has tended to be a more ontologically positivist understanding of emptiness and a general harmonization of Madhyamaka and Yogācāra, seeing them as complementary rather than opposing systems. Though Sanlun faded from importance as a distinct school of thought, Madhyamaka remained significant throughout the later development of Chinese Buddhism, influencing Tiantai, Huayan, and especially Chan.[33]

MADHYAMAKA IN TIBET

The Tibetans received Mādhyamika texts in both the first (7th–8th centuries) and second (11th–12th centuries) periods of the propagation of Buddhism there. Because scholastic monasticism was part of the institutional form that was imported, alongside Vajrayāna, Madhyamaka was important from the very beginning, and has remained so. In Tibet, monk scholars sought to establish a hierarchy of Buddhist tenet systems (*grub mtha'*) that encompassed all the Buddhist schools in an ascending order, beginning with the two Ābhidharmika, schools (Vaibhāṣika and Sautrāntika), which served as the elementary understandings of the Dharma, moving up to the Yogācāra, and culminating in the Madhyamaka. It was assumed that the understanding of the philosophical positions of each of these schools enabled one to then understand the next higher level. Ascent up through this hierarchy represented a progressively more subtle understanding of the Two Truths. The two Ābhidharma schools asserted that dharmas, understood in different ways, were ultimately real and anything that was the result of conceptual hypostatization was merely conventional. The Yogācāra was understood to assert that external objects were ultimately unreal (i.e., projected by conceptual imposition) and only consciousness was ultimately real. Madhyamaka was understood to go one step further and assert that consciousness too was empty and thus only existent conventionally.

Early in the doxographical project Tibetans followed the categorization of Madhyamaka inherited from India, in which Madhyamaka was divided into those who accepted the conventional existence of external objects (e.g., Bhāviveka and Candrakīrti), and those who declared external objects to be projections of mind and ultimately empty (Jñānagarbha, Śāntaraksita and Kamalaśīla). In the late 11th century, the Madhyamaka works of Candrakīrti were translated into Tibetan, and Tibetan doxographers began to factor them into their categorizing efforts. Shortly thereafter, the terms *Svātantrika* and *Prāsaṅgika* were coined (in Tibetan) and deployed in a new conceptualization of Madhyamaka schools. There were Tibetan scholars who accepted Candrakīrti's interpretation of Madhyamaka and those who argued forcefully against it, but in the end it was the Prāsaṅgika approach that won the day, though it remained a matter of some dispute just what the differences between this school and the Svātantrika were.

In the 14th century, it was the writings of Tsongkhapa that introduced a new distinction between Svātantrika and Prāsaṅgika, one which posited not just a methodological distinction between the two schools but also an ontological one. Prior to Tsongkhapa and continuing after him in the scholarship of the Sakya, Kagyü, and Nyingma sects, the principal difference was one of whether the Mādhyamika master used arguments that simply sought to demonstrate to the opponent the unwanted consequences of his position (*prasaṅga*), or rather utilized logically established arguments that positively proved the Mādhyamika position (*svatantra*). Tsongkhapa argued instead that there is an actual difference in how the two schools understand conventional truth. In his understanding, Svātantrikas accept the conventional reality of the manifest world. In that world there are things that are real and things that are illusory. The sophisticated epistemological system of Dharmakīrti was seen to provide tools to ascertain which are which, and to prove, in a real sense, the doctrinal position of Madhyamaka. According to Tsongkhapa, this entails a subtle realism that falls short of the definitive meaning of Nāgārjuna's texts, which is that everything is empty of intrinsic nature. Only Candrakīrti's interpretation of Madhyamaka is considered to go far enough and relegate everything in this world to the status of merely conventional.[34] Though this understanding is accepted by only one of the four major sects of Tibetan Buddhism, it has had an inestimable impact on the modern scholarship on Madhyamaka.

Despite his proclaimed exclusive adherence to Candrakīrtī's understanding of Madhyamaka, Tsongkhapa in fact relies heavily on the logico-epistemological developments of Dharmakīrti in his method of Madhyamaka argumentation and his understanding of ultimate truth. Tsongkhapa asserts that the object of Madhyamaka negation is inherent existence, but once that has been refuted, the basis of that negation, the phenomenon under analysis, can be said to exist conventionally. This move has the advantage of allowing a basis for the efficacy of logical argumentation, ethics, and religious practice. Tsongkhapa asserts that the ultimate truth, which is the emptiness of inherent existence, is itself an existent object of knowledge. This makes it possible for discursive thought to realize the ultimate truth—a claim that is unique to Tsongkhapa and the Geluk sect.

The other three major sects of Tibetan Buddhism saw Tsongkhapa's understanding of Madhyamaka as straying from the original intent of Nāgārjuna and his Indian commentators. For the Nyingma, Sakya, and Kagyu sects generally, the final purport of Madhyamaka is freedom from the extreme views of being and nonbeing. Ultimate truth is not regarded as an object of discursive knowledge, but rather the realization that things cannot be said to exist, not exist, both, or neither. Ontologically speaking, ultimate reality *qua* emptiness is reality free of hypostatization. The 19th-century Nyingma scholar Jamgön Mipham critiqued Tsongkhapa's position in his *Beacon of Certainty* and many other of his works.[35] Mipham also wrote an extensive commentary on Śāntarakṣita's *Madhyamakālaṃkāra*.[36] Though several prominent Sakya scholars wrote extensive refutations, Gorampa Sönam Sengé's *Distinguishing the Views* is probably the most powerful critique of Tsongkhapa's Madhyamaka and elucidation of the Sakya Madhyamaka.[37] Among Kagyu scholars, The Eighth and Ninth Karmapas composed commentaries on Candrakīrti's *Madhyamakāvatāra* in which Tsongkhapa's views are frequently criticized.[38]

Tibetan Buddhism is Vajrayāna Buddhism, so tantric theory has always played an important role in Tibetan doctrinal formulations. Yogācāra provides a more suitable foundation for tantric theory and practice, but Madhyamaka has nearly always been regarded as compatible with, or has served as the true doctrinal foundation of, Vajrayāna. The Nyingma and Kagyu sects have typically been more inclined to an understanding of Yogācāra and Madhyamaka as complementary teachings, and one in which both were seen through the lens of Vajrayāna thought and practice.[39] The Sakya and the Geluk sects have tended to privilege Candrakīrti's understanding as definitive (though they disagree on what that understanding is) and have kept Mādhyamika doctrine and Vajrayāna more distinct.

One formulation of Tibetan Madhyamaka explicitly based itself on tantric thinking. The "Great Madhyamaka" tradition understands Madhyamaka to include not only Nāgārjuna but also the great Yogācāra figures Asaṅga and Vasubandhu as the exemplary Mādhyamikas. Here Nāgārjuna's works from the analytic corpus serve to eliminate the hypostatizing that leads to a belief in the ultimate reality of things in the world, but his hymns express the final meaning of Madhyamaka, which is the perfected state purified of ignorance, identified with mind. Great Madhyamaka thought is characterized by its emphasis on "other-emptiness" (*gzhan stong*), which is the idea that the absolute is empty of conventional appearances but not of its own pure nature. This tradition is associated with Jonang Dolpopa Sherab Gyaltsen (1292–1361) and Tāranātha (1575–1635), as well as the Sakya scholar Shakya Chokden (1428–1507).[40] The tradition was highly influential in its time, but it was suppressed by the Fifth Dalai Lama and largely disappeared except for some regions along the Sino-Tibetan border. The 19th-century ecumenical movement (*ris med*) helped revive the knowledge of this once significant Madhyamaka vision, but it has received relatively little modern scholarly attention.

REVIEW OF LITERATURE

Most of the modern academic interest in Nāgārjuna and the Madhyamaka has been philosophical, and over time what has been of philosophical interest has evolved. As extensively discussed in his influential book *Comparative Philosophy and the Philosophy of Scholarship*,[41] Andrew Tuck has pointed out that early works tended to examine similarities between Madhyamaka and one or another European philosopher.

By the end of the 19th century, European interest in Indian religions had emerged as a positive byproduct of empire. Early orientalists, most famously Sir William Jones, discovered that India had an ancient religious and philosophical heritage equal to, or in some more enthusiastic estimates superior to, those of the West. The objects of this newfound research were primarily the "orthodox" six schools of Hindu philosophy that contemporary Indian authorities presented as the heart and pinnacle of Indian thinking. Advaita Vedānta, again in accord with Indian assumptions of the time, became particularly sought after by orientalist scholars and became popular among Western literati. Buddhism, on the other hand, was much more slowly acknowledged as a part of this grand intellectual history of India. It was the publication of Eugène Burnouf's *Introduction à l'histoire du Buddhisme indien*[42] (1844) and his annotated translation of the *Lotus Sūtra* (*Saddharmapuṇḍarīkam*) (1852) that brought Indian Buddhism into the spotlight and firmly established the idea that it was a thoroughly nihilist religion. Burnouf's sources included *Perfection of Wisdom* (*Prajñāparāmitā*) texts and Nāgārjuna's *Mūlamadhyamakakārikā* with Candrakīrti's commentary. Burnouf was not alone in his estimation of Buddhism as nihilism, and this understanding held sway in Europe throughout the 19th century.

In the early 20th century, the Belgian scholar Louis de La Vallée Poussin published what would become the definitive edition of Nāgārjuna's *Mūlamadhyamakakārikā,* along with Candrakīrti's commentary. La Vallée Poussin too saw Madhyamaka as pure nihilism, but he was a champion of Mahāyāna thought more broadly. It was the Russian scholar Fyodor Ippolitovich Stcherbatsky who first challenged this view, arguing that Madhyamaka was in fact the Buddhist parallel of Advaita Vedānta and could best be understood via Kant's dichotomous notions of noumena and phenomena. Madhyamaka could thus be read as an ancient precursor of European idealist philosophy. Stcherbatsky's understanding, fully explicated in his *Conception of Buddhist Nirvana* (1927),[43] became the new standard view about Madhyamaka, and was taken up by the Indian scholar T. R. V. Murti in his influential work *The Central Philosophy of Buddhism* (1955),[44] in which the author pushed further the linkage of Madhyamaka, Vedānta, and Kant.

Reacting to the influence of the analytic philosophy of G. E. Moore, Bertrand Russell, and the Vienna Circle, a new generation of scholars began to see Nāgārjuna as a dialectician, and the interest in his works was focused on the structure of his arguments. Only two years after Murti's book, the American Buddhist scholar Richard Robinson published the article "Some Logical Aspects of Nāgārjuna's System,"[45] in which he surveyed previous scholarship on Madhyamaka and dismissed it as philosophically unsophisticated. Unlike his predecessors, Robinson was not looking for transcendent truths, or confirmation of consistency with dominant trends in Western philosophy. He argued for taking Nāgārjuna's arguments on their own terms, in their own forms, which he elucidated with the aid of logical notation. In the end, Robinson's conclusion was that Nāgārjuna failed to successfully refute his opponents because his method of argumentation was logically or formally invalid.

The next phase of reading and explicating Madhyamaka similarly reflected the contemporaneous concerns of Western philosophy. Influenced by the works of Quine, Sellars, and especially the later Wittgenstein, several scholars began to assert that concepts such as "language game," "forms of life," and "ordinary language" provided helpful models for understanding not only what Nāgārjuna's arguments meant, but also what they were for. Such scholars[46] saw parallels between the way Wittgenstein and Nāgārjuna used language, but they also saw commonality with the primarily soteriological intent of Madhyamaka in Wittgenstein's famous statement on the purpose of philosophy, "To show the fly the way out of the fly-bottle." Further emphasizing this soteriological dimension of Madhyamaka, Frederick Streng published the first full translation of the *Mūlamadhyamakakārikā*,[47] and though he too quoted from Wittgenstein in his analysis, his primary concern was for understanding Madhyamaka and, especially, the concept of emptiness from a religious rather than a philosophical perspective.

In his seminal article "Nāgārjuna's Appeal,"[48] Richard Hayes nuances Tuck's thesis that interpretations of Madhyamaka are deeply informed by the ideological or methodological interest of the translators/interpreters by arguing that a number of Buddhist scholars have resisted this and produced translations or studies that place Nāgārjuna's works solidly in their historical and cultural contexts. Hayes highlights the work of Stanislaw Schayer, David Seyfort Ruegg, Christian Lindtner, and Kamaleswar Bhattacharya as exemplars of the ideal of detached and scientific objectivity in Madhyamaka scholarship.

In recent decades, scholars have tried to avoid the pitfalls described by Tuck and Hayes and have also argued for a deeper engagement of modern philosophy with Madhyamaka, or with Buddhist thought more broadly. These works make a plea for the inclusion of Buddhist thought, and particularly Madhyamaka, into a more globally construed notion of philosophy and engage in both exegesis and interpretation. Publications of Mark Siderits,[49] Jay Garfield,[50] Jan Westerhoff,[51] Amber Carpenter[52] and Tom Tillemans[53] are among the most significant examples of this recent phase of the study of Madhyamaka. These works typically situate Madhyamaka within its Buddhist historical context as well as interrogating the texts for their potential value to modes of modern thought.

In contemporary scholarship, the question of whether Madhyamaka thought is primarily about ultimate reality (the metaphysical interpretation) or what can be said about reality (the semantic interpretation) has become an important issue. In the past few decades the semantic interpretation has tended to predominate, but this approach is not unanimously accepted.[54]

A recent locus of controversy in interpreting Madhyamaka has centered on the question of contradiction in Madhyamaka argumentation and the ultimate purport of such arguments. Against some scholars who regard contradictions in the texts as intended to be understood metaphorically, or as expressions of skillful means (*upāya*), Jay Garfield, along with coauthors Yasuo Deguchi and Graham Priest, argues that at least some contradictions in Madhyamaka texts should be taken literally and be accepted as true (the dialetheist interpretation). This interpretation provoked a number of critical responses, resulting in an entire issue of the journal *Philosophy East and West* devoted to these critiques, along with responses by Deguchi, Garfield, and Priest.[55] Tillemans's article in this issue is an excellent example of another current interpretation that sees Madhyamaka arguments, at least in early Madhyamaka texts, as having as their purpose the complete elimination of all views about reality (the quietist interpretation). Other recent studies have been published that question Tibetan Mādhyamikas' doxographical categories, which have been accepted and employed by much of modern scholarship.[56] A renewed interest in the question of Madhyamaka's relation to the other major Mahāyāna doctrinal system, Yogācāra, has also recently come to the fore.[57]

PRIMARY SOURCES

All Buddhist traditions and modern scholarship agree that the founding author of Madhyamaka is Nāgārjuna. From among his many works, it is similarly unanimous that his *magnum opus* is *The Root Verses of the Middle Way* (*Mūlamadhyamakakārikā*). The Sanskrit text was translated into other Asian languages, most importantly Chinese and Tibetan. Modern translations from each of these languages have been made into English and other European languages. At the current stage of Madhyamaka scholarship, the definitive English translation is the one by Mark Siderits and Shōryū Katsura.[58] This translation is based on the Sanskrit original and the Tibetan translation, and utilizes all four extant Indian commentaries in its insightful yet accessible commentary. The French translation from the Sanskrit by Guy Bugault[59] is highly recommended, as is the pioneering translation from Sanskrit into Italian by Raniero Gnoli[60] and the German translation from the Chinese by Lutz Geldsetzer.[61]

Nāgārjuna's other works have often been traditionally divided into those with a methodological affinity to *The Root Verses of the Middle Way* (the analytic corpus), and his hymns and the collection of practical religious advice. Among the former, the most comprehensive and still classic collection by Lindtner[62] is an excellent starting point for those wanting to explore these works. Though the hymns evince a very different picture of Madhyamaka, and they have received relatively little attention in modern scholarship, Tibetan traditions and many modern scholars accept them as authentic works of Nāgārjuna. Lindtner's aforementioned collection includes two of the hymns, and Fernando Tola and Carmen Dragonetti's article[63] contains translations and an exhaustive discussion of these works. Among the advice texts, the *Ratnāvalī* is widely regarded as an authentic composition of Nāgārjuna and contains important similarities and complements to the *Root Verses,* though it is largely a text on ethics. The translation by Jeffrey Hopkins[64] contains a commentary by Hopkins and an edition of the Tibetan text.

The difficulty of the subject matter and the terse style of the *kārikā* form of Indian literature led to numerous commentaries on Nāgārjuna's texts, especially the *Root Verses of the Middle Way.* The Tibetan traditions and most modern scholarship typically accept that there are four Indian commentaries on the text: the *Akutobhayā* attributed to Nāgārjuna himself, the *Mūlamadhyamakavṛtti* by Buddhapālita, the *Prajñāpradīpa* of Bhāviveka, and the *Prasannapadā* of Candrakīrti. The two most important of these, and the ones that have received the greatest amount of scholarly attention, are the *Prajñāpradīpa* and the *Prasannapadā.* Their authors, Bhāviveka and Candrakīrti, came to be seen by the Tibetan traditions as embodying two distinct schools of interpretation: the Svātantrika and Prāsaṅgika, with the latter occupying the peak of the doxographical hierarchy for nearly all of the Tibetan scholastic schools. The first seven chapters of the *Prajñāpradīpa* have been translated into English in a series of articles by William Ames,[65] and a complete translation of the *Prasannapadā* into European languages has come together through the complementary efforts of a number of excellent scholars.[66]

The Mādhyamika works of Jñānagarbha, Śāntarakṣita, and Kamalaśīla have received less attention in modern scholarship. Jñānagarbha's *Distinction Between the Two Truths* has been translated by Malcolm David Eckel (*Satyadvayavibhaṅga*) and is accompanied by a useful introduction.[67] Masamichi Ichigō has published a helpful overview and full translation of Śāntarakṣita's *Ornament of the Middle Way.*[68] Though there are no complete translations of Kamalaśīla's Mādhyamika works, portions are translated and discussed by Ichigō,[69] Ryusei Keira,[70] and Sara McClintock.[71]

FURTHER READING

Bocking, Brian, trans. *Nāgārjuna in China: A Translation of the Middle Treatise.* Lewiston, NY: Edwin Mellen, 1995.

Brunnhölzl, Karl. *The Center of the Sunlit Sky: Madhyamaka in the Kagyu Tradition.* Ithaca, NY: Snow Lion, 2004.

Cabezón, José Ignacio, and Geshe Lobsang Dargyay. *Freedom from Extremes: Gorampa's "Distinguishing the Views" and the Polemics of Emptiness.* Boston: Wisdom, 2007.

Chandrakirti, and Jamgon Mipham. *Introduction to the Middle Way: Chandrakirti's Madhyamakavatara with Commentary by Jamgon Mipham.* Translated by Padmakara Translation Group. Boston and London: Shambhala, 2004.

Eckel, Malcolm David. *Jñānagarbha's Commentary on the Distinction Between the Two Truths.* SUNY Series in Buddhist Studies. Albany: State University of New York Press, 1987.

Garfield, Jay L., and Jan Westerhoff. *Madhyamaka and Yogācāra: Allies or Rivals?* Oxford and New York: Oxford University Press, 2015.

Hamilton, Sue. *Indian Philosophy: A Very Short Introduction.* Oxford and New York: Oxford University Press, 2001.

Hayes, Richard P. "Nāgārjuna's Appeal." *Journal of Indian Philosophy* 22 (1994): 299–378.

Ichigō, Masamichi. "Śāntarakṣita's Madhyamakālaṁkāra: Introduction, Edition and Translation." In *Studies in the Literature of the Great Vehicle: Three Mahāyāna Buddhist Texts.* Edited by Luis Gómez and Jonathan Silk, 141–240. Ann Arbor: Collegiate Institute for the Study of Buddhist Literature and Center for South and Southeast Asian Studies, University of Michigan, 1989.

Komarovski, Yaroslav. *Visions of Unity: The Golden Paṇḍita Shakya Chokden's New Interpretation of Yogācāra and Madhyamaka*. Albany: State University of New York Press, 2012.

Lang, Karen C. *Āryadeva's Catuḥśataka: On the Bodhisattva's Cultivation of Method and Knowledge*. Copenhagen: Akademisk Forlag, 1986.

Lindtner, Christian. *Nāgārjuniana: Studies in the Writings and Philosophy of Nāgārjuna*. New Delhi: Motilal Banarsidass, 1987.

Liu, Ming-Wood. *Madhyamaka Thought in China*. Leiden, The Netherlands: Brill, 1994.

Lopez, Donald S. *The Madman's Middle Way: Reflections of Reality of the Tibetan Monk Gendun Chöpel (Buddhism and Modernity)*. Chicago: University of Chicago Press, 2007.

MacDonald, Anne. *In Clear Words: The Prasannapadā, Chapter One, Vols. I & II*. Vienna: Verlag der Österreichischen Akademie der Wissenschaften, 2015.

McClintock, Sarah, and Georges Dreyfus. *The Svātantrika-Prāsaṅgika Distintion: What Difference Does a Difference Make?* Boston: Wisdom, 2002.

Nagao, Gadjin M. *Mādhyamika and Yogācāra: A Study of Mahāyāna Philosophies*. Translated by Leslie Kawamura. Albany: State University of New York Press, 1991.

Phuntsho, Karma. *Mipham's Dialectices and the Debates on Emptiness: To be, not to be, or neither*. London and New York: RoutledgeCurzon, 2005.

Seyfort Ruegg, David. "The Uses of the Four Positions of the *Catuḥṣkoti* and the Problem of the Description of Reality in Mahāyāna Buddhism." *Journal of Indian Philosophy* 5 (1977): 1–71.

Seyfort Ruegg, David. *The Literature of the Madhyamaka School of Philosophy in India*. A History of Indian Literature 7. Wiesbaden, Germany: Otto Harrassowitz, 1981.

Siderits, Mark, and Shōryū Katsura. *Nāgārjuna's Middle Way: The Mūlamadhyamakakārikā*. Boston: Wisdom, 2013.

Thupten Jinpa. *Self, Reason, and Reality in Tibetan Philosophy: Tsongkhapa's Quest for the Middle Way*. Ithaca, NY: Snow Lion, 2008.

Tillemans, Tom J. F. *How Do Mādhyamika's Think: and Other Essays on the Buddhist Philosophy of the Middle*. Boston: Wisdom, 2016.

Tola, Fernando, and Carmen Dragonetti. "Nāgārjuna's Catuhstava." *Journal of Indian Philosophy* 13 (1985): 1–54.

Vose, Kevin. *Resurrecting Candrakīrti: Disputes in the Tibetan Creation of Prāsaṅgika*. Boston: Wisdom, 2009.

Westerhoff, Jan. *Nāgārjuna's Madhyamaka: A Philosophical Introduction*. Oxford and London: Oxford University Press, 2009.

NOTES

1. The Sanskrit term *madhyamaka* literally means just "middle," but throughout English scholarship this has been translated as "middle way." For the sake of consistency and clarity, "middle way" will be used throughout.
2. Though many of the concepts discussed here are found in both Pali and Sanskrit sources, we will use the Sanskrit terms throughout, as Nāgārjuna composed his texts in Sanskrit, and the Indian commentaries are in Sanskrit as well.
3. *Saṃyutta Nikāya*, II.15 (5), in *The Connected Discourses of the Buddha: A New Translation of the Saṃyutta Nikāya*, trans. Bhikku Bodhi (Boston: Wisdom, 2000), 544.
4. Ibid.
5. The notion of Buddhist doctrinal schools has been a commonplace in Buddhist scholarship both traditional and modern, but this idea should be handled cautiously. The term "Madhyamaka School" really only refers to a lineage of writers (often separated by centuries) who wrote commentaries on one or another of Nāgārjuna's works, and that much later were placed into a doxographical category, primarily by the

Tibetan traditions. See, for example, Ian Charles Harris, *The Continuity of Madhyamaka and Yogācāra in Indian Mahāyāna Buddhism* (Leiden and New York: Brill, 1991); and Richard King, "Early Yogācāra and Its Relationship with the Madhyamaka School," *Philosophy East and West* 40 (1994): 659–683.

6. For a helpful overview of Madhyamaka in China, see Dan Arnold, "Madhyamaka Buddhist Philosophy: Madhyamaka in East Asia," in *Internet Encyclopedia of Philosophy*, eds. James Fieser and Bradley Dowden (2005).
7. For a discussion of this categorization, see David Seyfort Ruegg, *The Literature of the Madhyamaka School of Philosophy in India* (A History of Indian Literature 7; Wiesbaden: Otto Harrassowitz, 1981), 7–9.
8. The inclusion of the *Vyavahārasiddhi* was favored by most Tibetan scholars, but Tsongkhapa and his followers preferred the Ratnāvalī as the sixth text of this category. See Karma Phuntsho, *Mipham's Dialectics and the Debates on Emptiness: To Be, Not to Be, or Neither* (London and New York: RoutledgeCurzon, 2005), 235.
9. For a discussion of the full implications of these verses, see Eviatar Shulman, "Creative Ignorance: Nāgārjuna on the Ontological Significance of Consciousness," *Journal of the International Association of Buddhist Studies* 30, nos. 1–2 (2009): 139–173.
10. A significant exception to this is Shulman, "Creative Ignorance."
11. Christian Lindtner, *Nāgārjuniana: Studies in the Writings and Philosophy of Nāgārjuna* (New Delhi: Motilal Banarsidass, 1987), 31.
12. Āryadeva, Bhāviveka, Candrakīrti, Prajñākaramati and other Indian commentators cite one or more of these hymns and attribute them to Nāgārjuna. For an overview of this issue, see Fernando Tola and Carmen Dragonetti, "Nāgārjuna's Catuhstava," *Journal of Indian Philosophy* 13 (1985): 1–6.
13. The hymns are not found in the Chinese Buddhist canon.
14. *Saṃyutta Nikāya*, II.15 (5), in *The Connected Discourses of the Buddha: A New Translation of the Saṃyutta Nikāya*, trans. Bhikku Bodhi (Boston: Wisdom, 2000), 544.
15. Mark Siderits and Shōryū Katsura, *Nāgārjuna's Middle Way: Mūlamadhyamakakārikā* (Boston: Wisdom, 2013), 159.
16. Ibid., 18.
17. Ibid., 28.
18. Ibid., 276–277.
19. For a collection of essays on the status of conventional truth, see Cowherds, *Moonshadows: Conventional Truth in Buddhist Philosophy* (New York: Oxford University Press, 2011).
20. Siderits and Katsura, *Nāgārjuna's Middle Way*, 277.
21. Mark Siderits, *Buddhism as Philosophy: An Introduction* (Indianapolis and Cambridge: Hackett, 2007), 182.
22. Siderits and Katsura, *Nāgārjuna's Middle Way*, 13.
23. Ibid., 197.
24. Lindtner, *Nāgārjuniana*, 63–64.
25. Current scholarly consensus is that "Bhāviveka" is the proper spelling of this name, but earlier scholarship frequently used "Bhāvaviveka," or sometimes "Bhavya."
26. Siderits and Katsura, *Nāgārjuna's Middle Way*, 304.
27. Ibid., 315–316.
28. Ibid., 334.
29. Karen C. Lang, *Āryadeva's Catuḥśataka: On the Bodhisattva's Cultivation of Method and Knowledge* (Copenhagen: Akademisk Forlag, 1986).
30. For a wide-ranging examination of the differences between these two schools, see Georges B. J. Dreyfus and Sara L. McClintock, eds., *The Svātantika-Prāsaṅgika Distinction: What Difference Does a Difference Make?* (Boston: Wisdom, 2003).

31. For an English translation of the *Middle Treatise*, see Brian Bocking, trans., *Nāgārjuna in China: A Translation of the Middle Treatise* (Lewiston, NY: Edwin Mellen, 1995).
32. For a translation of an important treatise of Sengzhao, see Walter Liebenthal, *Chao Lun: The Treatises of Seng-chao: A Translation with Introduction, Notes and Appendices* (2d rev. ed.; Hong Kong: Hong Kong University Press, 1968). For an article on Sengzhao's understanding of Madhyamaka, and the ways that his thought both remains true to the Indian sources, yet reflects Chinese religious and philosophical concerns, see Shohei Ichimura, "On the Paradoxical Method of the Chinese *Mādhyamika*: Seng-chao and the *Chao-lun* Treatise," *Journal of Chinese Philosophy* 19 (1992): 51–71.
33. For an overview of the Sanlun school as well as later developments on Chinese Madhyamaka and its influence on other schools of Buddhism, see Ming-Wood Liu, *Madhyamaka Thought in China* (Leiden: Brill, 1994).
34. There are many works in English on Tsongkhapa's formulation of Madhyamaka, but for a translation of his commentary on Nāgārjuna's fundamental text, see Je Tsongkhapa, Jay L. Garfield, and Ngawang Samten, trans., *Ocean of Reasoning: A Great Commentary on Nāgārjuna's Mūlamadhyamakakārikā* (New York: Oxford University Press, 2006).
35. For a translation of this work, see John Whitney Pettit, *Mipham's Beacon of Certainty: Illuminating the View of Dzogchen, the Great Perfection* (Boston: Wisdom, 1999); for a comprehensive study of Mipham's Madhyamaka and his critiques of Tsongkhapa, see Phuntsho, *Mipham's Dialectics*.
36. Chandrakīrti and Jamgön Mipham, *Introduction to the Middle Way: Chandrakirti's Madhyamakavatara with Commentary by Jamgön Mipham*, trans. Padmakara Translation Group (Boston and London: Shambhala, 2002).
37. For a translation and study of this text, see José I. Cabezón and Geshe Lobsang Dargyay, trans., *Freedom From Extremes: Gorampa's "Distinguishing the Views" and the Polemics of Emptiness* (Boston: Wisdom, 2007).
38. For English translations see Candrakīrti and Mikyö Dorje, Ari Goldfield, Jules Levinson, Jim Scott, and Birgit Scott, trans., *The Moon of Wisdom: Chapter Six of Chandrakirti's Entering the Middle Way with Commentary by the Eighth Karmapa Mikyö Dorje's Chariot of the Dagpo Kagyü Siddhas* (Ithaca, NY: Snow Lion, 2005); and Dorje Wangchuk and Dewar Tyler, trans., *The Karmapa's Middle Way: Feast for the Fortunate* (Ithaca, NY: Snow Lion, 2008).
39. Among Nyingma scholars, Rongzom Chökyi Zangpo is an early and important figure in the establishment of the Nyingma Madhyamaka, and an example of the synthesis of Madhyamaka and Tantra. See Heidi I. Köppl, *Establishing Appearances as Divine: Rongzom Chözang on Reasoning, Madhyamaka, and Purity* (Ithaca, NY: Snow Lion, 2008).
40. For translations and studies of these two Jonang figures, see Cyrus Stearns, *The Buddha from Dolpo: A Study of the Life and Thought of the Tibetan Master Dolpopa Sherab Gyaltsen* (Ithaca, NY: Snow Lion, 2010); and Yaroslav Komarovski, *Visions of Unity: The Golden Pandita Shakya Chokden's New Interpretation of Yogācāra and Madhyamaka* (Albany, NY: State University of New York Press, 2012).
41. Andrew P. Tuck, *Comparative Philosophy and the Philosophy of Scholarship: On the Western Interpretation of Nāgārjuna* (New York: Oxford University Press, 1990).
42. Eugène Burnouf, *Introduction to the History of Indian Buddhism (Buddhism and Modernity)*, trans. Katia Buffetrille and Donald S. Lopez, Jr. (Chicago: University of Chicago Press, 2015).
43. Fyodor Shtcherbatsky, *The Conception of Buddhist Nirvana* (Delhi: Motilal Banarsidass, 1968).
44. T. R. V. Murti, *The Central Philosophy of Buddhism* (London: George Allen & Unwin, 1955).
45. Richard H. Robinson, "Some Logical Aspects of Nāgārjuna's System," *Philosophy East and West* 6, no. 4 (1957): 291–308.
46. A number of scholars, including B. K. Matilal, Ives Waldo, Nathan Katz, and Robert Thurman, utilize Wittgenstein's thought, especially in the *Philosophical Investigations*, to unpack Nāgārjuna's arguments and ultimate intent. For an extensive comparison of Nāgārjuna and Wittgenstein, see Chris Gudmunsen, *Wittgenstein and Buddhism* (London: Macmillan, 1977).

47. Frederick Streng, *Emptiness: A Study in Religious Meaning* (Nashville: Abingdon, 1967).
48. Richard P. Hayes, "Nāgārjuna's Appeal," *Journal of Indian Philosophy* 22 (1994): 299–378.
49. Siderits, *Buddhism as Philosophy*.
50. Jay L. Garfield, *Engaging Buddhism: Why It Matters to Philosophy* (Oxford and New York: Oxford University Press, 2015).
51. Jan Westerhoff, *Nāgārjuna's Madhyamaka: A Philosophical Introduction* (Oxford and New York: Oxford University Press, 2005).
52. Amber Carpenter, *Indian Buddhist Philosophy* (Ancient Philosophies; New York: Routledge, 2014).
53. Tom J. F. Tillemans, *How Do Mādhyamika's Think: and Other Essays on the Buddhist Philosophy of the Middle* (Boston: Wisdom, 2016).
54. See, for instance, Giuseppe Ferraro, "A Criticism of M. Siderits' and J. L. Garfields 'Semantic Interpretation' of Nāgārjuna's Theory of Two Truths," *Journal of Indian Philosophy* 41 (2013): 195–219. For a much broader critique of modern understanding of Madhyamaka, see Shulman, "Creative Ignorance."
55. *Philosophy East and West* 63.3 (2013) .
56. See especially Kevin Vose, *Resurrecting Candrakīrti: Disputes in the Tibetan Creation of Prāsaṇgika* (Boston: Wisdom, 2009).
57. Jay L. Garfield and Jan Westerhoff, eds., *Madhyamaka and Yogācāra: Allies or Rivals?* (Oxford and New York: Oxford University Press 2015).
58. Siderits and Katsura, *Nāgārjuna's Middle Way*.
59. Guy Bugault, ed., *Stances du milieu par excellence* (Paris: Gallimard, 2002).
60. Raniero Gnoli, ed. and trans., *Nāgārjuna Madhyamaka Kārikā: Le stanze del cammino di mezzo* (Enciclopedia di autori classici 61; Turin: P. Boringhieri, 1961).
61. Lutz Geldsetzer, ed. and trans., *Die Lehre von der Mitte: Chinesisch-Deutsch* (Philosophische Bibliotek 610; Hamburg: Felix Meiner, 2010).
62. Lindtner, *Nāgārjuniana*.
63. Tola and Dragonetti, "Nāgārjuna's Catuhstava."
64. Jeffrey Hopkins, *Nāgārjuna's Precious Garland: Buddhist Advice for Living and Liberation* (Albany, NY: Snow Lion, 2007).
65. William Ames, "Bhāvaviveka's *Prajñāpradīpa*: A Translation of Chapter One: 'Examination of Causal Conditions' (*Pratyaya*), Part One," *Journal of Indian Philosophy* 21 (1994): 209–259; "Bhāvaviveka's *Prajñāpradīpa:* A translation of Chapter Two: 'Examination of the Traversed, the Untraversed, and That Which Is Being Traversed,'" *Journal of Indian Philosophy* 23 (1995): 295–365; "Bhāvaviveka's *Prajñāpradīpa:* A Translation of Chapter Three, Four, and Five: Examining the Āyatanas, Aggregates, and Elements," *Buddhist Literature* 1 (1999): 1–119; "Bhāvaviveka's *Prajñāpradīpa:* A Translation of Chapters Six, Examination of Desire and the One Who Desires, and Seven, Examination of Origin, Duration and Cessation," *Buddhist Literature* 2 (2000): 1–91.
66. J. W. de Jong, *Cinq chapitres de la Prasannapadā* (Paris: Geuthner, 1949); Étienne Lamotte, "Le Traité de l'acte de Vasubandhu, Karmasiddhiprakaraṇa," *Mélanges Chinois et Bouddhiques* 4 (1936): 265–288; Anne MacDonald, *In Clear Words: The Prasannapadā, Chapter One. Vols. I & II* (Vienna: Verlag der Österreichischen Akadamie der Wissenschaften, 2015); Jacques May, *Candrakīrti: Prasannapadā Madhyamakavṛtti, douze chapitre traduit du sanscrit et du tibetain* (Paris: Adrien-Maisonneuve, 1959); Stanislaw Schayer, "Feuer und Brennstoff," *Rocznik Orientalistyczny* 7 (1929–1930): 26–52; Stanislaw Schayer, *Ausgewählte Kapitel aus der Prasannapadā* (Krakow: Naktadem Polskiej Akademji Umiejetnosci, 1931); and Theodore Stcherbatsky, *The Conception of Buddhist Nirvāṇa* (Delhi: Motilal Banarsidass, 1977).
67. Malcolm David Eckel, *Jñānagarbha's Commentary on the Distinction Between the Two Truths* (SUNY Series in Buddhist Studies; Albany: State University of New York Press, 1987).

68. Masamichi Ichigō, "Śāntarakṣita's Madhyamakālaṁkāra: Introduction, Edition and Translation," in *Studies in the Literature of the Great Vehicle: Three Mahāyāna Buddhist Texts,* eds. Luis Gómez and Jonathan Silk (Ann Arbor: Collegiate Institute for the Study of Buddhist Literature and Center for South and Southeast Asian Studies, University of Michigan, 1989), 141–240.
69. Masamichi Ichigō, "Śāntarakṣita and Bhāvaviveka as Opponents of the Mādhyamika in the *Madhyamakāloka,*" in *Wisdom, Compassion, and the Search for Understanding: The Buddhist Studies Legacy of Gadjin M. Nagao,* ed. Jonathan Silk (Honolulu: University of Hawai'i Press, 2000), 147–170.
70. Ryusei Keira, *Mādhyamika and Epistemology: A Study of Kamalaśīla's Method for Proving the Voidness of All Dharmas: Introduction, Annotated Translations and Tibetan Texts of Selected Sections of the Second Chapter of the* Madhyamakāloka (Vienna: Arbeitskreis für Tibetische und Buddhistische Studien, 2004).
71. Sara L. McClintock, *Omniscience and Rhetoric of Reason: Śāntarakṣita and Kamalaśīla on Rationality, Argumentation and Religious Authority* (Boston: Wisdom, 2010).

Paul B. Donnelly

MAHĀMUDRĀ IN INDIA AND TIBET

The Sanskrit term *mahāmudrā* (Tibetan: *phyag rgya chen po*), best translated as "the Great Seal," refers to a variety of Indian and Tibetan Buddhist metaphysical concepts and meditative practices concerned with the nature and attainment of ultimate reality. The term probably first occurred in Indian Buddhist tantric literature of the 7th or 8th century CE, and came to the fore in the final centuries of Buddhism's efflorescence on the subcontinent, especially in the radically "countercultural" Mahāyoga and Yoginī tantras, and in the songs, treatises, and commentaries attributed to the influential great tantric adepts (*mahāsiddhas*). Mahāmudrā was not much discussed during the early spread of Buddhist teachings in Tibet (*c.* 650–850), but it gained great prominence on the plateau during the later spread of the teaching, the so-called Tibetan Renaissance (*c.* 950–1350). In that era, it found a place of greater or lesser prominence in the ideas and practices of newly founded religious orders, especially the Marpa Kagyü (*mar pa bka' brgyud*), for which it became a central term, referring to the nature of the mind, a contemplative technique aimed at the realization of that nature, and the complete buddhahood resulting from that realization. Over the course of time, Mahāmudrā became known primarily as a style of meditation, in which the yogin or yoginī realizes the empty and luminous nature of the mind, and lives and acts from within that realization. For the past thousand years, Mahāmudrā has been a notable theme in ritual, meditative, philosophical, and literary discourse in Tibet, a touchstone for contemplatives, poets, and polemicists alike. With the spread of Tibetan Buddhism outside the plateau after 1959, Mahāmudrā has drawn the interest of scholars and practitioners in Asia and in the West, and has entered the lexicon of informed Buddhists throughout the world. This article will survey, to the extent that is possible, the historical development of usages of Mahāmudrā, from its earliest instances in India to its interpretation in the modern world, noting along the way the key teachings of the masters of the Great Seal and the controversies those teachings sometimes occasioned.

MAHĀMUDRĀ IN INDIA

The Sanskrit term *mudrā* is used widely in Indic literature. Originally, it denoted a seal of the sort used to secure and authorize important documents. It also could be a sign, a symbol, or a token. Its best-known usage is as one of a multitude of symbolic hand gestures displayed by deities, dancers, and ritual performers to "seal" or guarantee a particular identity or action. In the richly symbolic and highly ritualized world of tantric religions, mudrā refers not only to a hand gesture or bodily posture, but also to a deity or practitioner's female consort, a particularly exalted state of yogic awareness, or—in Hindu settings—a type of fermented grain consumed during ceremonies at which liquor, meat, fish, and sexual intercourse also play a role.[1] The specific term *mahāmudrā* ("great seal") is found occasionally in Hindu tantric literature—for instance in reference to a particular bodily position (*āsana*), a partner for sexual yoga practice, or the blissful gnosis of a perfected yogī—but it is in the Buddhist realm that it proved most important. Early Buddhist literature abounds in common usages of mudrā as a seal, sign, or gesture. Some Mahāyāna scholars defined Buddhism in terms of four "sealing" assertions: all contaminated entities are unsatisfactory, all conditioned phenomena are impermanent, all phenomena are empty, and nirvana is peace. Certain Mahāyāna sūtras, such as the *King of Concentrations* (*Samādhirāja*), speak of emptiness—and other key terms in Mahāyāna metaphysics—as the "seal" of all dharmas. As in Hinduism, however, in Buddhism, too, the term mahāmudrā apparently does not occur until the advent, around the 7th century, of the tantric traditions, which in a Buddhist context are usually referred to as the Mantra Vehicle, Mantrayāna, or Adamantine Vehicle, Vajrayāna.[2]

The Buddhist Tantras. The Buddhist tantras emerged from the matrix of the Great Vehicle, the Mahāyāna, with its emphasis on the spiritual ideal of the compassionate bodhisattva, its vertiginous metaphysics of emptiness and non-duality, its rich and colorful traditions of meditative practice, and its assertion that all beings eventually will attain the three "bodies" (*kāya*) of a fully awakened buddha: the Dharma Body (*dharmakāya*), Enjoyment Body (*sambhogakāya*), and Emanation Body (*nirmāṇakāya*).[3] Historians of Buddhism are far from unanimous on the relative or absolute dating of the tantras, but there is general agreement that we can trace an overall arc of development in which complex but relatively conventional systems of thought and practice, rooted in standard Mahāyāna (7th–9th centuries), are supplemented and eventually superseded by systems—some of them influenced by Hindu traditions—that employ increasingly transgressive imagery, rhetoric, and praxis (8th–11th centuries).[4] It is in the more conventional systems (most often divided by Tibetans into Action, Performance, and Yoga Tantras) that the term *mahāmudrā* first appears. For instance, the compendious Action Tantra, *The Basic Ordinance of Mañjuśrī* (*Mañjuśrīmūlakalpa*), variously refers to the Great Seal as a "five-peaked" ritual hand position signifying the attainment of all worldly and ultimate aims (e.g., chapter 2, section 26, verses15–17), a female consort through which the practitioner may gain great power (chaps. 43–47), and more abstractly, "the splendor of all mantras, pure, stainless, the destruction of evil, the attainment of all worldly aims, the achievement of all that is highest . . . the highest dharma, undeclining, the highest step" (43:22:370).[5] The yoga tantras, such as the *Compendium of the Principles of All the Tathāgatas* (*Sarvatathāgatatattvasaṃgraha*) echo the sense that Mahāmudrā is at once a hand position, a female consort, and the highest yogic attainment, but most often they define it as the clear visualization of oneself as a buddha-deity—a practice central to nearly all tantric traditions. The yoga tantras also set Mahāmudrā within a larger set of four seals—the others are the Pledge (*samaya*), Dharma, and Action (*karma*) seals—that denote various meditations and their symbolic correspondences to various worldly and transmundane categories.[6]

It is in the often transgressive Mahāyoga and Yoginī Tantras, with their strong focus on advanced meditations, practiced in the context of a subtle-body that consists of channels, winds, and "drops," that Mahāmudrā truly comes to the fore. In the most important of the Mahāyoga Tantras, *The Secret Assembly* (*Guhyasamāja*), it is explicitly described as a consort (*mudrā*) for the practice of sexual yoga as well as the realization ensuing from that practice (10:21); a contemplation-recitation that leads to attainment of the adamantine body, speech, and mind of the tathāgatas (11:1–3); and the essence of the vows of the tathāgatas—meditation on which assures buddhahood (17:45).[7] Elsewhere, the ultimate—for which Mahāmudrā clearly is one designation—is described as beyond meditation; pure in essence; space-like; free from thought or its objects; the way to awakening in which there is no awakening; beyond the aggregates, sense fields, and elements; one with the lack of self in dharmas; eternally unarisen; and in the nature of emptiness (2:3–4).[8] In the Yoginī Tantras, Mahāmudrā becomes a term of central ritual, philosophical, and soteriological importance. In the systems based on such tantras as the *Pledge Wheel* (*Cakrasaṃvara*), *Hevajra*, *Adamantine Dagger* (*Vajrakīla*), and *Wheel of Time* (*Kālacakra*), it still may be seen as one of three or four *mudrās* that "seal" tantric experiences, but it is now usually the highest in the sequence, the Great Seal that betokens a full understanding of the nature of reality. At the same time, it is often treated on its own, referring to, for instance, a goddess to be invoked; a consort in sexual yoga practice; the gnostic great bliss ensuing from that practice; the ultimate reality, emptiness, experience of which is inseparable from great bliss; and the buddhahood attained at the culmination of the tantric path (*mahāmudrāsiddhi*). To cite just one example, in the *Hevajra Tantra*, Mahāmudrā is a synonym for emptiness (part 1, chapter 10, verse 20); a consort for sexual yoga (2:8:2–5), as well as the bliss arising from that yoga (2:4:50); an empowerment that produces great bliss (2:2:31); and the "eternal state" that is the goal of tantric practice (1:8:43), the final achievement of the mind of coemergent (*sahaja*) and inseparable bliss and emptiness (2:8:5).[9]

The Mahāyoga and Yoginī tantras spawned an immense exegetical literature, including "explanatory tantras" (*vyākhyātantras*) attributed to the buddha and commentaries and treatises composed by late first-millennium authors such as the tantric Nāgārjuna, the tantric Āryadeva, and Nāropa (956–1040). Composed at a time when Mahāmudrā had gained increasing currency, these texts tended to focus on the term even more strongly than the basic tantras on which they were commenting, and to exalt it even more highly. A Hevajra-related tantra called the *Drop of Mahāmudrā* (*Mahāmudrātilaka*) gives a classic etymological definition of the term, the first of many to follow: "*mu* is awareness of voidness, *drā* is its nature of transcending duality, *mahā* is the union of the two."[10] The text goes on to describe Mahāmudrā as the "sublime mystery, indefinable, inexhaustible, and unborn . . . formless . . . unaffected by concepts . . . unstained lucidity . . . the source of all excellent qualities and spontaneous attainments."[11] Puṇḍarīka's famous *Wheel of Time* commentary, the *Stainless Light* (*Vimalaprabhā*), specifies that Mahāmudrā entails "emptiness devoid of differentiated representations and provided with all excellent aspects, [and] the accomplishment of omniscience, devoid of differentiated representations."[12] A *Guhyasamāja* explanatory tantra, the *Matrix of Gnosis* (*Jñānagarbha*), goes so far as to subsume four tantric seals under Mahāmudrā: the Action Seal (a physical consort), the Pledge Seal (tantric vows), the Gnosis Seal (a visualized consort), and the Dharma Seal (the nature of phenomena).[13]

The Great Adepts. The major exponents of the Mahāyoga and Yoginī tantras were the charismatic, wonder-working, and often quasi-legendary Buddhist tantric masters known as the great adepts (*mahāsiddhas*).[14] In prose and poetic treatises, and in songs in such poetic forms as the couplet (*dohā*), adamantine song (*vajragīti*), and performance song (*caryāgīti*), these men (and a few women) distilled essential themes from the most esoteric tantras, criticizing religious customs and social mores while celebrating the bliss and freedom found in yogic contemplation and an unconventional way of life. Though many had monastic backgrounds, they periodically or permanently repaired to cremation grounds or mountain caves, where they consorted with low-caste women, consumed forbidden substances, and generally engaged in a religious performance, or mode of conduct (*caryā*), that appeared to turn brahmanical—and Buddhist—values upside-down. In traditional accounts of their lives, their often transgressive practices inevitably culminate in the Mahāmudrā Attainment, that is, buddhahood. In their works, Mahāmudrā has many more meanings as well, and takes on great significance, whether as an explicit topic of discourse or through discussion of related terms, such as the coemergent purity of our primordial mind (*sahaja* or *nijacitta*) or the practice of "inattention" (*amanasikāra*), a type of formless, concept-free meditation. As a result, many of the adepts' writings were incorporated into anthologies of Mahāmudrā texts compiled later by Indian or Tibetan scholars. The three collections most widely recognized in Tibet are the "Seven Attainment Texts," the "Essential Trilogy," and the "Twenty-five Works on Inattention."

The Seven Attainment Texts,[15] most of which probably date from the 8th to 10th centuries, are attributed to seven different adepts who base themselves closely on one or another system of Mahāyoga or Yoginī tantra and presuppose familarity with those systems on the part of their readers. They emphasize practice over theory, but do occasionally discuss philosophical matters. It is in philosophical passages that they are likeliest to mention Mahāmudrā. In the *Attainment of Secrets* (*Guhyasiddhi*), Padmavajra refers to Mahāmudrā as that which is cultivated when one has given up practice with either a physical consort or imagined consort, and has "abandoned multiple concepts" (3:34); "the perfection of all ornaments, pacification into supreme formlessness, lucid, faultless, stainless" (4:15); and realization of the unproduced, selfless nature of mind (4:40–41).[16] In the *Attainment of Gnosis* (*Jñānasiddhi*), Indrabhūti describes it as "pervasive and without characteristics, like the sky . . . the ultimate, the unsurpassed adamantine gnosis, the all-good . . . the Dharma Body, the mirror-like gnosis" (1:44-47), and the "abandonment of all conceptuality" by which all the buddhas and adepts achieved awakening in a single life (1:56–57).[17] Other Attainment Text authors mention Mahāmudrā less often, focusing instead on synonymous concepts like the coemergent or the natural mind. Still, because the Attainment Texts deal with esoteric practices that lead to the Mahāmudrā Attainment, their inclusion in the Great Seal canon is understandable.

The Essential Trilogy comprises three poetic works attributed to the great adept Saraha, who probably lived in east India late in the first millennium CE. In legend, he is said to have learned arrow-making from a yoginī with whom he consorted; his name, literally, means "fletcher." Saraha is regarded by most Tibetan traditions as the earliest and greatest Indian exponent of Mahāmudrā, reputed to have been the guru of the great philosopher (and tantric adept) Nāgārjuna and the mountain-hermit Śavaripa, both of whom figure importantly in Tibetan Mahāmudrā lineages. The works of the Essential Trilogy—commonly designated, on the basis of their audience, as the *People, Queen,* and *King Dohā Treasuries* (*dohākoṣas*)—seldom refer to Mahāmudrā. It is explicitly mentioned only in the *Queen Dohā,* which describes it as the abiding state of natural non-duality, the sameness of samsara and nirvaṇa, a consort for sexual yoga practice, and the goal of the tantric path.[18] The *King Dohā* emphasizes the fundamental purity of mind rather than Mahāmudrā, but it does mention the four seals and implicitly equates Mahāmudrā with the unborn, empty nature of all dharmas, insisting that "all the worlds in their diversity have this very nature."[19] The *People Dohā,* the best known, most studied, and oft-quoted of the three, focuses not on Mahāmudrā, but on cognate concepts, such as the coemergent, the yoginī, great bliss, thatness, the natural mind, the stainless nature, and mind itself—all of which are equated to buddhahood, and all of which are described in terms familiar to us from discussions of Mahāmudrā elsewhere in tantric literature.[20] Saraha actually addresses Mahāmudrā in far greater detail in other texts, especially in a trilogy of adamantine songs consisting of the *Body Treasury* (*Kāyakoṣa*), *Speech Treasury* (*Vākkoṣa*), and *Mind Treasury* (*Cittakoṣa*), where it is described as "unchangeable great bliss," "experienced like ocean and space," "the sameness of all phenomena," "the nature of fruition," "unborn, nondual . . . beyond the intellect," "nothing other than oneself," "the highest union," "instantaneous full awakening," "just that," "one's own mind," and the basis of "thought-free ethics."[21] Saraha also composed texts that began to systematize ideas about Mahāmudrā, dividing it, for instance, into the triad of basis, path, and fruition, or the quartet of view, meditation, behavior, and result; these categories would be extremely influential in Tibetan discourse on the Great Seal.

The Twenty-five Works on Inattention (*amanasikāra*)[22] are attributed to Maitrīpa (986–1063), a scholar adept who studied with a number of human teachers, but received his profoundest instruction through visionary encounters with Saraha's disciple, Śavaripa. He was roughly contemporary with, and may have known, a number of other adepts who would influence understandings of Mahāmudrā in Tibet, most notably Tilopa (928–1009), a master of both the Mahāyoga and Yoginī tantras, who wrote a famous instruction-song called the *Ganges Mahāmudrā* (*phyag chen gangā mā*),[23] and his disciple, Nāropa, who wrote on Mahāmudrā, but is best known for teaching his esoteric Six Dharmas, drawn from the Mahāyoga and Yoginī tantras: inner heat, dream, illusory body, luminosity, intermediate state, and transfer of consciousness.[24] Many of Maitrīpa's own disciples—especially Vajrapāṇi (b. 1017) and the Tibetan translator Marpa Chökyi Lodrö (*mar pa chos kyi blo gros,* 1012–97) would be instrumental in the transmission of Mahāmudrā to Tibet. The Twenty-five Works on Inattention (most of which are available in Sanskrit) comprise an anthology of treatises, some in verse, some in prose, that deal with a variety of topics in Mahāyāna and Vajrayāna thought and practice. They rarely mention Mahāmudrā, and inattention itself is only occasionally discussed, while the text often regarded as most seminal, the *Ten Stanzas on Reality* (*Tattvadaśaka*), mentions neither—yet whether taken individually or as a whole, the works in the anthology still are regarded by Tibetans as foundational for understanding either concept. Maitrīpa does provide eloquent and extensive descriptions of Mahāmudrā in the *Sequence of the Four Seals* (*Caturmudrānvaya;* the text is sometimes attributed to the tantric Nāgārjuna), where it is said that it "lacks an own-being, is free from the hindrances of the knowable . . . It resembles the day-sky in the middle of autumn, stainless, and is the basis of everything perfect. It has the identity of [cyclic] existence and nirvana as its nature, consists of universal compassion, and has the unique form of great bliss";[25] and the *Teaching on Empowerment* (*Śekanirdeśa*), where the Great Seal is explicitly equated with the practice of nonabiding (*apratiṣṭhāna*) and the realization of emptiness. Maitrīpa also wrote works outside the Twenty-five Texts that deal with the Great Seal, including the *Golden Rosary of Mahāmudrā* (*Mahāmudrākaṇakamālā*), where he roots Mahāmudrā in devotion to the guru and the practice of tantra; links it to emptiness, reality, the natural mind, great bliss, inaction, and spontaneity; and explicitly states: "inattention is the path of Mahāmudrā."[26]

Esoteric and Non-dual Mahāmudrā. One of Maitrīpa's signal contributions to Mahāmudrā discourse was to imply that, as an index of ultimate reality and its realization, it was a term relevant not just to the tantras but to sūtra-based traditions, as well. He is reputed to have linked Mahāmudrā to both the *King of Concentrations Sūtra*[27] and the *Higher Continuum* (*Uttaratantra*),[28] an important Mahāyāna treatise on buddha nature often attributed to the coming buddha, Maitreya. Like many others in his era, Maitrīpa, was conversant with Mahāyāna literature from the Madhyamaka and Yogācāra philosophical schools, as well as traditions surrounding buddha nature, and sought to fuse "Perfection Vehicle" standpoints on reality with the ritual and meditative techniques developed in the Mantra Vehicle. To the degree that (a) Mahāmudrā came increasingly to connote ultimate reality, (b) many of the profoundest Mahāyāna discussions of ultimate reality are found in such pre-tantric works as the Perfection of Wisdom sūtras and the treatises of Nāgārjuna and Maitreya, and (c) association with such works remained a guarantor of legitimacy in the Indic Mahāyāna world, it is unsurprising that a handful of late Indian thinkers—including Jñānakīrti and Sahajavajra—identified a Perfection-Vehicle Mahāmudrā, though Maitrīpa himself never seems to have done so explicitly.[29]

To summarize, by the 11th century, Mahāmudrā had come to refer, in India, to a hand gesture signifying clear visualization of a deity, one of a number of "seals" (with or without hand gestures) that confirm tantric ritual procedures, a consort employed in sexual yoga practices, a meditation technique in which mind contemplates its own nature, the great bliss and luminous gnosis that result from advanced subtle-body practices, a way of living in the world freely and spontaneously, and the omniscient buddhahood that is a final outcome of the tantric path. It also had come to be synonymous with such ideas as emptiness, the middle, sameness, the coemergent, the natural mind, luminosity, the single taste, non-duality, inattention, buddha nature, non-abiding nirvana, and a buddha's Dharma Body—to name just a few. Amidst this plethora of connotations and synonyms, two major conceptions of Mahāmudrā may be discerned. Esoteric Mahāmudrā focuses on the generation of a non-conceptual, blissful gnosis of reality—the natural mind—through subtle-body practices described in the literature of the Mahāyoga and Yoginī Tantras. By contrast, non-dual Mahāmudrā focuses on attaining a direct and unmediated experience of the natural mind through a sudden transcendence of thought, image, and effort, as often described in the songs and treatises of the great adepts. Although these two approaches to Mahāmudrā are distinguishable, they are not mutually exclusive, since the Mahāyoga and Yoginī tantras contain numerous passages that suggest the unadorned views and practices of non-dual Mahāmudrā, while the great adepts who expound non-dual Mahāmudrā usually do so within a context profoundly shaped by the esoteric practices of the "higher" tantras. What's more—and crucially—nearly all approaches to Mahāmudrā are set within the affective—and often ritual—context of guru yoga, the tantrically inflected veneration of the spiritual master, whose instruction is crucial to gaining the Mahāmudrā Attainment.

MAHĀMUDRĀ IN TIBET

Although some meanings of Mahāmudrā—those of the "lower" and Mahāyoga tantras[30]—undoubtedly would have been familiar to educated Tibetans during the imperial period, or "earlier spread of the Dharma" (7th–9th centuries), it was during the "later spread of the Dharma," or Tibetan Renaissance (10th–14th centuries),[31] that it became a central topic of religious discourse in Tibet. Indeed, it can be argued that singling out Mahāmudrā as a focus of study and practice really is a Tibetan idea. Certainly, much of what we know about Indian Mahāmudrā and its practitioners we owe to Tibetan sources, and Mahāmudrā took on an importance for at least some Tibetan traditions that surpassed anything seen in India. Yet Tibetans did not simply imagine that Mahāmudrā was important in Indian Buddhism. When, after nearly two centuries of limited contact, Tibetans in the 11th century began visiting India again to collect texts and receive teachings, and Indians began traveling to Tibet carrying texts and teachings, Mahāmudrā was a far more central part of what was transmitted than it had been during the imperial period—largely due to the prominence of the Yoginī tantras and the literature they spawned, especially the works of the great adepts.

A number of Indian and Tibetan masters involved in the revival of Buddhism in Tibet focused prominently on Mahāmudrā, helping the term to stand out from the welter of concepts that were being newly transmitted across the Himalayas. In most cases, these masters—who interacted frequently with one another—came to be regarded as founders of various practice lineages that developed in Tibet, and at least some of these practice-lineages became sufficiently institutionalized that they developed into identifiable "orders" or "schools"—some of which have survived to the present day. Traditions that arose in 11th-century Tibet based primarily on the new tantric texts appearing then are generally designated as New Translation (*gsar ma*) schools. These include the Marpa Kagyü, Kadam (*bka' gdams*), Shijé (*zhi byed*), Chöd (*gcod*), Shangpa Kagyü (*shangs pa bka' brgyud*), and Sakya (*sa skya*)—as well as the one tradition that situates its origins in the imperial period: the Old Translation school, or Nyingma (*rnying ma*). All of these traditions, and others that developed later, incorporated notions of Mahāmudrā into their discourse to one degree or another.

Tibetan Renaissance Schools. Nyingma traditions find their sources of authority not in the texts and teachers of the Tibetan Renaissance but, rather, in those of Tibet's imperial period. They emphasize such commonly accepted tantras as the *Secret Assembly* and *Adamantine Dagger*, but look as well to a large collection of idiosyncratically Nyingma tantras, such as the *Secret Matrix* (*Guhyagarbha*) and *The All-Creating Sovereign* (*Kun byed rgyal po*). They honor Indian teachers like Vimalamitra, Vairocana, and—above all—Padmasambhava, a charismatic adept from northwest India who is said by Tibetans to have helped establish Buddhist practice on the plateau in the late 8th century, and to have left behind assorted teachings as Treasure-texts (*gter ma*). It is with the discovery of these Treasure-texts, during the Tibetan Renaissance, that the Nyingma begins to demarcate itself as a distinct tradition, and perhaps the most distinctive of all Nyingma systems of theory and practice is Dzogchen, (*rdzogs chen*), the Great Perfection—"an aestheticized and streamlined" style of tantric meditation, influenced by the Indian Mahāyoga Tantras, as well as Chinese Chan and native Tibetan conceptions—which came to be regarded in time as the acme of the buddha's teaching, transcending even the esoteric subtle-body practices of the Mahāyoga and Yoginī tantras.[32] Dzokchen's blend of esoteric and non-dual styles of discourse is reminiscent of that of Mahāmudrā, but because its vocabulary developed before Mahāmudrā became a major term in Indian Buddhism, there is not much discussion of Mahāmudrā in early Nyingma literature. When it is mentioned, it may—depending on the level of tantric practice under discussion—denote hand gestures, the clear visualization of oneself as a deity, or the luminous and blissful realization of emptiness effected by subtle-body practices. Nyingmapas also occasionally used Mahāmudrā in the sense of the supreme attainment at the end of the path, but in the literature of Atiyoga, their highest level of tantra, it is Dzokchen that typically is accorded this status.

The Kadam order, which lasted from the mid 11th to the late 14th century, when it was absorbed into the Geluk (*dge lugs*), is traced to the Bengali pandit Atiśa (982–1054), who lived the last twelve years of his life in Tibet. A master of the sūtra and tantra traditions, he placed special emphasis on living a morally pure life dedicated to the development of love, compassion, and the awakening mind, and articulated an all-inclusive, gradual path to awakening that became a model for the sequencing of "stages of the doctrine" (*bstan rim*) or "stages of the path" (*lam rim*) that would be adopted by every major Tibetan order. The place of Mahāmudrā in Kadam circles is uncertain. Atiśa is said to have studied the *Higher Continuum*, Saraha's songs, and other Mahāmudrā-related texts with Maitrīpa. Atiśa's foremost Tibetan disciple, Dromtönpa ('brom ston pa, 1000–1064), however, apparently urged his master not to teach Saraha's songs in Tibet, lest their antinomian rhetoric be misunderstood and taken literally—as had happened before in Tibet with tantric teachings.[33] The Kadam did, indeed, place slightly less emphasis on tantric practices, including Mahāmudrā, than other Indians and Tibetans of the 11th century, yet some historians assert that Atiśa secretly passed on instructions for meditation on the "quintessence of reality," that is,Mahāmudrā, to some of his disciples, while a Kadampa master, Parpuwa Lodrö Sengé (phar phu ba blo gros seng ge, 12th century) wrote commentaries on a number of Saraha's songs and promulgated their study, all of this suggesting that a tradition of Mahāmudrā practice persisted privately among small circles of Kadampas.[34] In any case, Kadampas were strong proponents of Mādhyamika techniques for meditating on emptiness, and when Atiśa, for example, gives instruction to the effect that "in the expanse of intrinsic reality, detached from any conception, one settles the mind without discrimination,"[35] he is describing techniques very much like those that were associated with Mahāmudrā, even if he does not use the term.

The Sakya, named after the site in Tsang (*gtsang*), west-central Tibet, where the tradition's main monastery was founded in 1073, has from its inception been connected with the locally important Khön family. Its patriarch, Khön Könchok Gyelpo (khon dkon mchog rgyal po, 1034–1102) rejected the Nyingma affiliation of his ancestors and turned to the study of the Yoginī and other later tantras. Over the course of two hundred years, the Sakya became an order that combined deep study of tantric traditions (especially the Hevajra and the Adamantine Dagger systems) with extraordinary philosophical and literary attainment, and would become for a time, under the sponsorship of the Mongol Yuan dynasty of China (1271–1368), a major political force in inner Asia. The central practice-tradition for the Sakya is Lamdré (*lam 'bras*, the Path and Fruit), an integrated system of sūtra- and tantra-based discourses and rituals rooted partly in Mahāyāna wisdom literature and centrally in the *Hevajra Tantra*. In Lamdré, the usages of "Mahāmudrā" are quite restricted: for the most part, it refers to the result of an advanced tantric path that begins with empowerment: the omniscient buddhahood known as the Mahāmudrā Attainment. It also was used occasionally to denote the view attained as the result of empowerment or a tantric practice, but in all cases the referents presuppose tantric empowerment.[36] It is worth noting, however, that despite the Sakyapas' restrictions on the use of the term Mahāmudrā, many of the meditations and other practices associated with Lamdré—under such names as the Inseparability of Samsara and Nirvāna (*'khor 'das dbyer med*) or the Three Appearances (*snang gsum*), and involving, for example, identification of the nature of mind and realizing the coemergence of an awareness of emptiness with luminosity, bliss, and non-duality—bear a striking resemblance to those approaches to ultimacy that, in other traditions, are designated as Mahāmudrā.

Mahāmudrā figured more prominently in three "minor" lineages that arose during the Tibetan Renaissance but whose practices were, within several centuries, absorbed by larger orders. The Shijé (Pacification) tradition is traced to Pa Dampa Sangyé (pha dam pa sangs rgyas, d. 1117), a peripatetic master from south India who visited Tibet five times and spent many years in China, too. His signature teaching, Shijé, derives its name from a line in the *Heart Sūtra* that associates the Perfection of Wisdom—that is, insight into emptiness—with the "pacification of all suffering." Also referred to as the Mahāmudrā of Symbols or the Stainless Drop of Mahāmudrā, Shijé involves both esoteric practices such as those of the Yoginī Tantras and direct, non-conceptual realization of the mind's true nature as taught by the great adepts, whose songs Dampa helped promulgate in Tibet. The practice of Chöd (*gcod*, "severance")—or, more fully, the "Severance Mahāmudrā whose objective is the severing of demons"—was popularized in Tibet by Dampa's great Tibetan female disciple (or grand-disciple), Machik Lapdrön (ma gcig lab sgron, 1055–1143). Like Shijé, Chöd is traced to the Perfection of Wisdom literature, in this case to passages that speak of a bodhisattva's severance of various *māras*, or demons; it also is deeply beholden to the Yoginī tantras and the teachings of the adepts. Esoteric Chöd Mahāmudrā includes teachings on both maṇḍala and subtle-body practices and on the idiosyncratic Chöd technique of offering up one's body to visualized demons in order to sever grasping at self. Non-dual Chöd Mahāmudrā is described as follows: "Primordially co-emergent, like space / It does nothing, depends on nothing. / In just the same way, the mind itself / Possesses no support, possesses no object: / Let it rest in its natural sphere, without fabrication."[37] The Shangpa Kagyü is traced to the Tibetan yogī Khyungpo Neljor (khyung po rnal 'byor, d. 1135), who studied with numerous male and female adepts in India, including Nigumā, the sister or consort of Nāropa. Along with various esoteric practices, he received a teaching called the Amulet-Box Mahāmudrā (*phyag chen ga'u ma*); because a portable amulet box usually is divided into two interlocking sections, the term came to connote the way in which, in Mahāmudrā practice, one conjoins method and wisdom, luminosity and emptiness, or bliss and emptiness. Fundamentally, the practice of the Amulet-Box Mahāmudrā involves the "natural settling" of body, speech, and mind in serenity and insight, releasing faults through gaining certainty about the true nature of mind, and recognizing that one's ordinary mind is the three bodies of a buddha.[38]

Early Marpa Kagyü. Mahāmudrā was, to a greater or lesser degree, an important concept in all the schools described above; for the Marpa Kagyü lineage, though, it was essential. The translator Marpa (1012–1097) was a wealthy farmer from south-central Tibet who traveled multiple times to India and Nepal to collect texts and teachings. There, tradition tells us, he encountered Nāropa, from whom he received such esoteric instructions as the Six Dharmas; Maitrīpa, with whom he studied a number of tantras, as well as Mahāmudrā; and many others. Thanks to Maitrīpa, Marpa says, he "realized the foundation, reality itself, as unarisen . . . took hold of the emptiness of mind . . . saw the meaning of the original nature, unelaborated, and met the mother, the three buddha bodies, in person."[39] Marpa attracted many disciples and, through his translations and teachings, was instrumental in introducing to Tibet various esoteric tantric traditions, the songs of the adepts, and other sources of discourse on Mahāmudrā. He seems to have divided Mahāmudrā into an esoteric Path of Means (*thabs lam*), centered on the Six Dharmas of Nāropa, and a more immediate non-dual Path of Liberation (*thar lam*), with each path supporting the other. Marpa's most celebrated disciple was the reformed black magician and peripatetic poet-yogin, Milarepa (mi la ras pa, 1040–1123), whose life and songs have been a source of inspiration for all Tibetans, regardless of sect.[40] For Mila, Mahāmudrā is "the natural state . . . clear, radiant, ample and relaxed, without hope or fear, . . . free from virtue or sin, without plans or expectations, neither samsara nor nirvana, . . . beyond thought, beyond concepts—unmistakable!"[41] Describing his own practice, he remarks, "to perceive the ultimate reality, I mark everything with the great seal of emptiness. This is the quintessence of non-duality."[42] At the same time, he frequently refers to Mahāmudrā as ensuing from tantric empowerment, and involving the complex, blissful experiences produced by subtle-body practices such as the Six Dharmas of Nāropa. Although both Marpa and Mila discoursed on both esoteric and non-dual Mahāmudrā, they do not seem to have taught them as separate "tracks" to buddhahood.

Milarepa's great disciple, Gampopa Sönam Rinchen (sgam po pa bsod nams rin chen, 1079–1153)—also called Dakpo Lharjé (*dvags po lha rje*), "the doctor from Dakpo," after his original profession—trained as a monk in the Kadam order after the death of his young wife. He went on to study with Mila, learning a whole range of practices from him, none more crucial than Mahāmudrā. After Mila's death, he established a retreat center at Gampo, southeast of Lhasa, where he began the process of organizing the Kagyü into a religious order, distinguished by its combination of Kadam gradualism and Mahāmudrā immediacy. It was Gampopa who brought Mahāmudrā firmly to the center of the Kagyü world-view and set the terms for most subsequent discourse about the term.[43] He emphasized a number of distinctive Mahāmudrā practices, both instantaneous and gradual. His most famous instantaneous teaching was the White Simple (*dkar po chig thub*), which focuses on the single (*chig*) spiritual "remedy"—seeing the nature of mind—that, by itself, is able (*thub*) to cure spiritual ills and effect awakening. More gradual techniques include Joinging the Coemergent (*lhan cig skyes 'byor*), which involves guru devotion, serenity, and insight; the Fivefold (*lnga ldan*) Mahāmudrā practice of awakening mind, deity yoga, guru yoga, Mahāmudrā, and dedication of merit; and the Four Yogas (*rnal 'byor bzhi*): one-pointedness, non-elaboration, single taste, and non-meditation.[44] The Four Yogas would serve as a key organizing principle for subsequent Kagyü discussions of the path of Mahāmudrā. At times, too, Gampopa equated Mahāmudrā with "ordinary mind," identifying concepts with the Dharma Body and insisting that "what is designated as 'ordinary mind' is your own cognition . . . If you recognize it, it is the gnosis of intrinsic awareness; if you fail to realize it, it is coemergent ignorance."[45]

Gampopa was perhaps most renowned for introducing—and perhaps even favoring—a Perfection (or Sūtra) Vehicle Mahāmudrā practice, which could be found in such Mahāyāna texts as the Perfection of Wisdom sūtras, with their discourse on emptiness; the *King of Concentrations Sūtra*, with its discussion of the "sameness" that is the "seal of all dharmas"; and the *Higher Continuum*, with its emphasis on the natural purity of mind, or buddha nature. This teaching did not require tantric empowerment but simply an experiential introduction to the reality of one's mind through the "pointing-out instruction" (*ngo sprod*) of the guru. Gampopa makes it clear that such a non-dual approach can be found in both Perfection and Mantra Vehicle sources, but most often he classifies Mahāmudrā as a sort of "third-way" teaching that both includes and transcends the two Mahāyāna vehicles. Nevertheless, scholars in his own and other schools who accepted two, and only two, Mahāyāna vehicles understandably viewed his insistence that Mahāmudrā could be found outside the tantras as establishing Perfection Vehicle or Sūtra Mahāmudrā, and the legitimacy of such a category would be much debated in Tibetan religious and philosophical circles.

Gampopa's major students and their many disciples were responsible for founding monasteries that became the seats of the various orders and suborders that now go under the name Dakpo Kagyü. With Gampopa as a common source, all the Dakpo Kagyü traditions placed Mahāmudrā at the center of their theoretical and practical concerns. Each, however, differed from the others in emphasis and interpretation, so that certain schools became renowned for specializing in one or another of the many approaches to Mahāmudrā offered by Gampopa and his successors. For instance, the Tselpa (*tshal pa*) Kagyü—founded by Shang Rinpoché (zhang rin po che, 1123–1193)—was famed for its promulgation of the radical White Simple Mahāmudrā teaching. The Pakdru (*phag gru*) and Drigung (*'bri gung*) Kagyü—founded, respectively, by Pakmo Drupa (phag mo gru pa, 1110–1170) and Jikten Sumgön ('jigs rten gsum mgon, 1143–1217)—were known for their teachings on the Single Intention (*dgongs gcig*) and the gradual Fivefold Mahāmudrā. The Drukpa Kagyü—founded by Lingrepa (gling ras pa, 1128–1188)—was noted for its systematization of Mahāmudrā theory and its emphasis on the practices of Joining the Coemergent and the Equal Taste (*ro snyoms*). The Karma Kagyü—founded by Düsum Khyenpa (dus gsum mkhyen pa, 1110–1193)—was renowned for its promulgation of Joining the Coemergent, its incorporation of the teachings of Saraha and other Indian adepts, its brilliant scholastic tradition, and its openness to Dzogchen. Over the course of time, each of these Marpa Kagyü schools, and others besides, produced saints and scholars alike, and contributed to the development of Mahāmudrā discourse in Tibet.

Controversy and Consolidation. The growth of Mahāmudrā as a focus of discourse in Tibetan religious circles did not proceed unquestioned. In the 13th century, Sakya Pandita Künga Gyeltsen (sa skya paṇḍita kun dga' rgyal mtshan), or Sapan (1182–1251), a brilliant historian, philosopher, literatus, and diplomat, became perhaps the first Tibetan intellectual to criticize Kagyü Mahāmudrā ideas and practices, throwing down a gauntlet that nearly every subsequent serious scholar of Mahāmudrā felt obliged to pick up. Sapan's objections to Kagyü Mahāmudrā discourse—which focus especially but not exclusively on the White Simple doctrine of Gampopa and Shang Rinpoché and the Single Intention of the Drigung—are stated most systematically in his *Clear Ascertainment of the Three Vows* (*sdom gsum rab dbye*). Sapan's criticisms there fall into two main types: historical and doctrinal. His historical argument centers on the claim that the White Simple has no real precedent in India, and is instead a Tibetan adaptation of a dicredited Chan Buddhist assertion of the possibility of immediate awakening through discarding conceptuality. According to Sapan, this position, which also influenced Dzokchen, was simply renamed "Mahāmudrā" early in the Tibetan Renaissance, so as to diguise its non-Indian origins.[46] Doctrinally, Sapan attacks three basic ideas inferable from the Kagyü texts: (a) that a single practice—even meditation on emptiness—could alone suffice for liberation (for multiple method-side practices always are required), (b) that the gnosis of Mahāmudrā could arise through solely non-conceptual meditation (because philosophical analysis is essential, too), and (c) that Mahāmudrā ever could be taught outside of the Mantra Vehicle (for its sole legitimate meaning is as the attainment resulting from prior tantric empowerment).[47] As suggested above, later Kagyü scholars were not shy about refuting Sapan's criticisms, arguing that he had ignored Indian precedents for the rhetoric of immediacy used by Tibetan Mahāmudrā commentators, overlooked evidence that Mahāmudrā was used in India in non-tantric contexts, and wrenched Tibetan non-dual Mahāmudrā discourse out of its broader context as part of a carefully constructed path system that was perfectly consonant with Mahāyāna theory and practice. In any case, Sapan's critique did virtually nothing to stifle the creativity of later Marpa Kagyü masters as they continued to develop their Mahāmudrā traditions, building on the foundation laid by Gampopa and other great Tibetan Renaissance figures, and expanding into new areas of inquiry, new ways of systematizing theory and practice, and new genres of literary expression, including histories, textual commentaries, philosophical treatises, anthologies, and polemics. Here, we can mention only the most prominent.

The first important later Marpa Kagyü contributor to Mahāmudrā discourse was the Third Karmapa, Rangjung Dorjé (rang byung rdo rje, 1284–1339).[48] Among the first recognized Tibetan reincarnates (*sprul sku*), Rangjung Dorjé lived a life typical of a charismatic lama, traveling widely, studying Buddhist literature, undergoing retreats, gaining realizations, encountering visions, writing texts in a variety of genres, engaging in diplomacy, and promoting religious and public works projects. In his writings, the Karmapa synthesized Madhyamaka, Yogācāra, buddha nature, and tantric discourse from India with various Tibetan perspectives to produce an original and influential account of Buddhist thought and practice, the hallmark of which is sharp distinction between mere cognition and true gnosis—the primordially pure awareness that all beings possess and must realize if they are to actualize their buddhahood. As heir to a number of different Kagyü lineages, Rangjung Dorjé was well versed in Mahāmudrā traditions, and composed songs, commentaries, treatises, and practice-manuals related to the Great Seal. *Instructions for the Mahāmudrā Joining the Coemergent* (*lhan cig skyes 'byor phyag chen khrid*)[49] elaborates a model for Mahāmudrā instruction—credited to Gampopa—that would be adopted by many subsequent Kagyü authors. The text begins by leading an initiated disciple through a series of preliminaries, such as developing compassion and devotion, praying to the guru visualized at the crown of one's head, absorbing the guru's blessings, and dedicating merit. Next, serenity meditation is developed, first on the basis of sense objects, then on the basis of whatever mind-states arise, and finally on a space-like awareness of clarity and non-conceptuality. Insight is induced by investigation of the nature of the serene mind—which is, whatever its object, understood to be luminous and nonconceptual, non-elaborated self-knowing, the inseparability of appearance and emptiness. Rangjung Dorjé goes on to discuss three experiences (*nyams*) that accompany Mahāmudrā meditation—bliss, luminosity, and non-conceptuality—and the ways in which they either enhance or diminish our realization. He concludes by noting that Joining the Coemergent should be practiced in concert with the Six Dharmas of Nāropa, thereby bringing together the non-dual and esoteric approaches to Mahāmudrā. His *Prayer of the Mahāmudrā of Definitive Meaning* (*nges don phyag chen smon lam*),[50] which has been discussed at length by masters of the tradition since its composition and adopted into Kagyü liturgy, provides a poetic epitome of the attitudes, realizations, and actions proper to a Mahāmudrā practitioner. The Karmapa focuses on the view and meditative practice of the Great Seal, which involve various perceptions and processes—including serenity and insight, as well as the development of both renunciation and compassion—but may be summarized as the blissful, clear, non-conceptual realization that "all phenomena are manifestations of the mind [and] the mind is without mind, empty of an essence of mind," or, even more basically, that "the nature of beings is always buddhahood."[51] This view, says Rangjung Dorjé, is held in common by practitioners of Mahāmudrā, Dzogchen, and "Great Madhyamaka."

The Third Karmapa's perspective opened the way to later attempts to synthesize Mahāmudrā and Dzokchen, and also may have influenced the development of the radical interpretation of Mahāmudrā favored by Tibetan proponents of "extrinsic emptiness" (*gzhan stong*), the view that the emptiness predicated of buddha nature and buddhahood may be quite different from the emptiness of worldly phenomena and persons. Phenomena and persons are said to be self-empty (*rang stong*) in the sense of lacking permanent, partless, independent—that is, intrinsic—existence, buddha-mind to be empty in the sense it lacks saṃsāric qualities while permitting the full manifestation of the qualities of buddhahood that are implicit in buddha nature. First articulated by the Jonang (*jo nang*) master Dölpopa Sherap Gyeltsen (dol po pa shes rab rgyal mtshan, 1292–1361), extrinsic emptiness became a popular, albeit controversial, position in Tibetan thought, adopted in one form or another by numerous Kagyü and Nyingma masters, who found it a plausible way to understand the philosophical keys to both Madhyamaka and Mahāmudrā, in particular the assertion that emptiness, when applied to supreme gnosis or buddha-mind, is an affirming negation rather than a non-affirming negation. In other words, emptiness in this context is *not* a negation pure and simple, but a negation that clears the way for the expression of the awakened qualities intrinsic to all beings.

The Kagyü Efflorescence. In the centuries after Rangjung Dorjé's passing, the fortunes of Kagyü tradition improved. Nominal Sakyapa hegemony over Tibet ended with the consolidation of power there, in the 1350s, by Jangchup Gyeltsen (byang chub rgyal mtshan) of Pakmodru (1303–1373), whose triumph ushered in an era of relative peace and prosperity, allowing religious and cultural life to develop—at least for a time—unshadowed by the prospect of war. Though shorn of political power, the Sakyapa retained their instutitonal and intellectual prestige; the Nyingma, spurred by the brilliant innovations of Longchenpa (klong chen pa, 1308–1363), found clearer articulation and greater self-confidence than they had for many years; and the "Neo-Kadam" order, eventually known as the Geluk, was founded near Lhasa by Tsongkhapa (tsong kha pa, 1357–1419). The most widespread and well-organized Marpa Kagyü sub-orders—the Karma, Drigung, and Drukpa—flourished, gaining institutional strength and continuing to develop scholarly and meditative traditions—including those surrounding Mahāmudrā—that had been established during the Tibetan Renaissance.

The last half of the 15th century produced three remarkable figures, each illustrating a distinctive aspect of Kagyü culture, who helped to further understanding of Mahāmudrā. Gö Lotsawa Shönupel (*'gos lo tsā ba gzhon nu dpal*, 1392–1481) was one of Tibet's greatest historians and a learned and subtle commentator on Indian philosophical texts. His *Blue Annals* (*deb ther sngon po*), completed in 1478, is one of the most influential of all Tibetan historical works. The longest chapter in the book, on the Marpa Kagyü, recites many narratives that prominently feature Mahāmudrā, whether as a system of philosophy, a meditation practice, or a realization required for the attainment of liberation. Gö also devotes a separate, shorter chapter to the transmission of Mahāmudrā lineages to Tibet. There, he describes Mahāmudrā as "the doctrine which seals all the meditative and religious practices, from the Pratimokṣa, which is the foundation of the Doctrine of the Buddha, to the Guhyasamāja," a salvific understanding of the nature of reality that can be grasped "only through the blessing of a holy teacher."[52] Gö also wrote a masterful commentary on the *Higher Continuum*, which he reads as a key source for a sūtra-based practice of Mahāmudrā.[53] Utterly different, on the surface, from the scholarly Gö was Tsangnyön Heruka (gtsang smyon heruka, 1452–1507), one of a number of self-professed "madmen" (*smyon pa*) who shook up the Kagyü establishment in the late 15th and early 16th centuries. He attracted both disciples and patrons, whose support enabled him to compose and publish some of the enduring masterworks of Kagyü—indeed, of Tibetan—literature. Drawing skillfully from an array of written and oral sources that had been circulating for centuries, Tsangnyön wrote *The Life of Milarepa* (*mi la rnam thar*), *The Life of Marpa the Translator* (*mar pa lo tsā ba'i rnam thar*), and *The Hundred Thousand Songs of Milarepa* (*mi la ras pa'i mgur 'bum*),[54] each of which has become a classic of Tibetan tradition, and each of which is a rich source of information on Kagyü approaches to Mahāmudrā as they developed over a number of centuries. A third key late 15th-century figure was the Seventh Karmapa, Chödrak Gyatso (chos grags rgya mtsho, 1454–1506). Identified as the Karmapa tulku at the unusually early age of nine months, he went on to live a life devoted, in varying degrees, to scholarship, meditation, diplomacy, animal protection, and public works. Two of his writings are especially relevant to Mahāmudrā. *The Ocean of Texts on Valid Cognition* (*tshad ma rigs gzhung rgya mtsho*) is the definitive Kagyü discussion of the tradition of Indian Buddhist logic, to which it gives a particular spin by tracing how the conventional processes of valid cognition may lead to a supramundane form of self-cognition (*rang rig*) that is a luminous awareness empty of duality—implicitly, Mahāmudrā. This awareness is explicitly taken to exemplify the idea of extrinsic emptiness—not in the radical sense proposed by Dölpopa, but in a "rationally structured, logically argued, moderate form"[55] that typifies Kagyü approaches to the concept. *Indian Mahāmudrā Texts* (*phyag chen rgya gzhung*) is a voluminous anthology of Tibetan translations of over two hundred Indian works explicitly or implicitly related to Mahāmudrā in all its many senses, most composed by one or another of the great adepts of late Indian Buddhist tantrism, and especially consonant with non-dual Mahāmudrā, where the Great Seal is understood primarily in terms of the natural purity of mind, buddha nature, or emptiness rather than as a function of esoteric tantric practice.[56]

The 16th century was marked by increasing conflict between the Kagyü (especially the politically powerful Karmapas) and the ascendant Geluk, but it also witnessed an unparalleled flowering of Kagyü scholasticism in general and systematic Kagyü thought about Mahāmudrā in particular, which still shapes discussions of the topic today. The Eighth Karmapa, Mikyö Dorjé (mi bskyod rdo rje, 1507–1554), was an eastern Tibetan who rose to become one of the great scholars and philosophers in Kagyü history. He was the first compiler of the great anthology of Kagyü religious poetry, *The Ocean of Kagyü Songs*, to which he contributed his own spiritual songs and reflections, prompted by dreams and visions.[57] He composed a four-session guru yoga liturgy that still is used by many Kagyüpas. He also wrote a number of smaller works on Mahāmudrā that explore the complex relation between sūtra and tantra elements in theorizing and practicing the Great Seal and that place a particular emphasis on the identity between Dharma Body and the ordinary mind.[58] Finally, Mikyö Dorjé wrote influential treatises on the key Indian sources of Tibetan religious thought and life, including a commentary on Candrakīrti's *Entry to the Middle Way* (*Madhyamakāvatāra*), which seeks to align the Madhyamaka philosophical view with Mahāmudrā as a tradition of meditation and realization, and identifies a major line of Kagyü Madhyamaka transmission that focuses on non-dual Mahāmudrā precepts taught by, among others, Saraha, Nāgārjuna, Śavaripa, and Maitrīpa in India, and Marpa, Milarepa, Gampopa, and Jikten Sumgön in Tibet.[59]

The Eighth Karmapa's younger contemporary, Dakpo Tashi Namgyel (dvags po bkra shis rnam rgyal, 1512–1587), is renowned for the clarity of his exposition of Kagyü approaches to both tantra and Mahāmudrā. His massive *Moonbeams of Mahāmudrā* (*phyag chen zla ba'i 'od zer*),[60] which remains a vital source of textual citations and meditation instructions to this day, presents a graded path of Mahāmudrā practices that begins with "common" techniques for attaining serenity and insight, then moves on to the "uncommon" techniques of Mahāmudrā: the preliminary rituals related to refuge, offering the maṇḍala, purifying defilements, and harmonizing with the guru; attainment of serenity on the basis of meditation on external objects, internal objects, and, finally, the mind itself; attainment of insight on the basis of recognizing all objects to be products of mind, and both mind and its objects to be unarisen, or empty; a deeper exploration of the nature of mind through contemplation of the coemergent identity among mind, thoughts, and appearances; maintaining unbroken realization of ultimate reality in post-meditative everyday life; overcoming errors in the practice of serenity and insight; enhancing one's realization through an even deeper recognition of the mind's empty nature and through transforming worldly suffering into the path; and attaining buddhahood through the Four Yogas: one-pointedness, non-elaboration, the single taste, and non-meditation. In the course of his exposition, Tashi Namgyel provides copious references to Indic and Tibetan sources relevant to Mahāmudrā, defends the Kagyü approach to the Great Seal against criticism from Sakyapas and others; and clearly locates Mahāmudrā within the larger frame of the Mantra Vehicle and the Perfection Vehicle, with a special emphasis on the latter. Indeed, a central concern of Tashi Namgyel is to establish the legitimacy of Gampopa's claim that Mahāmudrā is a special teaching that at once includes and transcends both Perfection and Mantra approaches to the path.

Tashi Namgyel's most brilliant disciple, and arguably the greatest of all Kagyü scholars, was the fourth Drukchen (*'brug chen*) tulku, Pema Karpo (padma dkar po, 1527–1592). Like other Kagyü masters of his era, he was preoccupied with Mahāmudrā, which he tended to regard as a practice tradition in which Sūtra and Mantra are inseparable. Consider, for instance, the mix of esoteric and non-dual imagery in the following definition: "Emptiness rich in the most excellent potentialities is termed Mahāmudrā, because it offers unchanging bliss, in which there is complete elimination [of disturbances] and complete intrinsic awareness [of what there is]."[61] His most thorough treatment of the Great Seal is the *Storehouse of Mahāmudrā* (*phyag chen gan mdzod*), which details the various textual traditions of Mahāmudrā that developed in India; refutes mistaken opinions on the topic, including those of Sapan; defines the term and relates it to basic Buddhist categories; lays out Kagyü teachings on a number of key practices, including Joining the Coemergent and the White Simple; and establishes in detail the view, meditation, and result of Joining the Coemergent, in which the mind and its appearances are understood to be inseparable from the Dharma Body. Pema Karpo also describes the practice of Joining the Coemergent in a number of popular short manuals, which still are in use today.[62]

The Ninth Karmapa, Wangchuk Dorjé (1556–1603), was the last of his line to enjoy significant temporal power. His many writings include several treatises on Mahāmudrā that remain widely read classics. The longest and most important of the three, *Ocean of Definitive Meaning* (*nges don rgya mtsho*),[63] begins with such preliminaries as an aspiration for the dharma, finding a teacher, recognizing the nature of mind in general terms, and attempting to observe mind as it is. The main practice is divided into serenity and insight meditation. In serenity meditation, one assumes the proper posture, then focuses on various external and internal objects of meditation, eventually settling on the present mind itself, and remaining focused on that, non-conceptually, in a relaxed but alert manner, neither suppressing nor chasing the thoughts that naturally arise. In insight meditation, one first examines the mind in movement and at rest, then "cuts to the root" by searching mind to see if it has an intrinsic nature. When no such nature is found, one is prepared for the four "pointing-out instructions": appearances are mind, mind is empty, emptiness is natural presence, and natural presence is self-liberated. In the concluding practices, having learned to avoid various pitfalls of meditative experience and developed various skills, one traverses the Four Yogas of Mahāmudrā, which culminate in buddhahood, or final Mahāmudrā—from which one acts creatively and compassionately in the world for the sake of others. The shorter *Mahāmudrā Eliminating the Darkness of Ignorance* (*phyag chen ma rig mun gsal*) offers a "psychological" interpretation of buddhahood, wherein the Dharma Body is simply the mind's natural emptiness, the Enjoyment Body is simply the mind's natural clarity or luminosity, and the Emanation Body is simply the appearances that arise in the mind.[64] This interpretation is particularly consonant with Mahāmudrā discourse, since it keeps its focus squarely on the mind—which, after all, whether ordinary or exalted, is, in the oft-quoted words of Saraha, "the single seed of all."[65]

Later developments. The period from 1600 until the early 19th century was marked, politically, by the rise to power of the Geluk order and a corresponding decrease in the worldly fortunes of the Kagyü. Still, the religious creativity of the Kagyü remained strong, and discourse on Mahāmudrā continued to develop. Great scholars such as Tselé Natsok Rangdrol (rtse le sna tshogs rang grol, b. 1608) and Situ Panchen Chökyi Jungné (si tu paṇ chen chos kyi byung gnas, 1700–1744) continued in the tradition of clear and systematic exposition of Mahāmudrā, writing texts that continue to guide practitioners to this day.[66] Inspired by the efforts of earlier Kagyü masters like the Third Karmapa, Karma Chakmé (1613–1678) brought together contemplative practices drawn from Kagyü Mahāmudrā and Nyingma Dzokchen into a single, synthetic system.[67] In doing so, he also anticipated the "ecumenical" spirit displayed to an even greater extent by later figures, such as Shapkar Tsokdruk Rangdrol (zhabs dkar tshogs drug rang grol, 1781–1851), who freely adopted Kagyü, Geluk, and Nyingma practices into his own unique system, and the First Jamgön Kongtrul ('jam mgon kong sprul, 1819–1899), a key figure in the coterie of eastern Tibetan scholars and thinkers known for their nonsectarian (*ris med*) approach to preserving and promulgating rare and endangered teaching traditions from all the major non-Geluk orders.[68] Jamgön Kongtrul and others of his era accentuated the synthetic tendencies already at work among the Kagyü to such a degree that, in the 20th century and beyond, Kagyü and Nyingma traditions—especially Mahāmudrā and Dzokchen—often are mastered by teachers in both orders, and sometimes are taught as complementary practices.

The last truly distinctive Great Seal tradition to develop in Tibet was that of the Geluk, which came to light with the publication, around 1600, of two texts on the "Geden Oral Transmission" (*dge ldan bka' brgyud*) of Mahāmudrā, composed by the First Panchen Lama, Losang Chökyi Gyeltsen (blo bzang chos kyi rgyal mtshan, 1570–1662)[69] This practice was authenticated by its ascription to a great founder of the Geluk, Tsongkhapa, and to a special hearing transmission (*snyan brgyud*) he initiated on the basis of instructions from the wisdom buddha, Mañjughoṣa. Geluk scholars agree, however, that the practice was not publicized until the time of the First Panchen, and it was only in the centuries after him that it became a major focus of discourse within the order. The Panchen clearly divides Mahāmudrā into two types. Mantra Mahāmudrā is the direct realization, based on advanced subtle-body yogas, of the empty luminosity (*'od gsal*) that is the sublest nature of consciousness, while Sūtra Mahāmudrā involves developing serenity and insight with regard to, respectively, the conventional and ultimate nature of the mind, as, respectively, clear and knowing, and empty of inherent existence. All of this—like most Mahāmudrā practice—is executed within the context of guru yoga. There has been some debate as to whether the Panchen intended his system to be strictly Geluk or a Geluk-Kagyü synthesis. He draws widely on Kagyü literature, and at times gives instruction in meditation techniques developed by Kagyü masters. At the same time, he sometimes chides his Kagyü contemporaries, whom he accuses of confusing the attainment of serenity with the achievement of real insight—and true insight, it is clear, comes only from an analytical and experiential understanding of the Prāsaṅgika Madhyamaka view espoused by Nāgārjuna and Candarkīrti in India and brought to perfection in Tibet by Tsongkhapa.[70] In any case, from the time of the First Panchen on, Mahāmudrā became a vital, if subsidiary, tradition of practice within the Geluk, and it remains so in the 21st century.

The world of Tibetan Buddhism changed forever with the Chinese takeover of the plateau in the 1950s. Within Tibet, especially during the period of the Cultural Revolution (c. 1966–1976), many traditions were actively suppressed, and the material culture on which religious practice depended was destroyed to a significant degree. In recent decades, there has been something of a restoration of Buddhist culture in Tibet, but under considerable restriction. Still, to the degree that some traditions continue, we can safely affirm that Mahāmudrā continues to be practiced, and even written about, on the plateau. The Tibetan exile community, some hundred thousand strong, has, since 1959, succeeded in establishing itself and preserving elements of Tibetan culture in South Asia and, more recently, in the West. Tibetan Buddhism has proven appealing to large numbers of Western students, who either study Buddhism with lamas in Asia or, increasingly, are taught by lamas who visit or reside in the

West. Scholars have observed that, of the vast range of practices developed in various Buddhist cultures, Westerners are most drawn to meditation, and of the countless meditations available, they gravitate in greatest numbers to those that appear to bring the least "cultural baggage" and, at the same time, to offer the greatest psychological benefit. Thus, great popularity has accrued to the Theravāda "mindfulness" practice of observing the flux of experience and to Zen's aesthetic and incisive penetration into the true nature of the mind and reality. Among Tibetan meditations, Mahāmudrā and Dzogchen have drawn a disproportionate amount of interest, precisely because they, too—at least in their non-dual versions—seem to involve a direct insight into how the mind is and the way things are, supposedly without recourse to metaphysics, cultural images, or social practices that Westerners might find discomfiting. Of course, in the original Indian and Tibetan context, the Great Seal was deeply embedded within a particular worldview and cultural system, and it remains to be seen whether the imprint it leaves in the West will somehow preserve the key attitudes and insights developed in Asia, or whether it will be irretrievably lost in the process of translation.

REVIEW OF LITERATURE

There is, properly speaking, no field of "Mahāmudrā studies." Some modern scholars have focused on Indian and/or Tibetan discourse about the Great Seal, but such scholarship is usually produced within the larger context of the study of Indian Buddhism, Tibetan Buddhism, or the intersection between the two. Nevertheless, the importance of Mahāmudrā in Indian and Tibetan circles, combined with the appeal of Mahāmudrā poetry, philosophy, and praxis to many contemporary Buddhists, does mean that the topic has been an increasing focus of scholarly investigation. The modern study of Mahāmudrā is skewed, to some extent, between "Dharma centers" and the academy. Many important translations of Mahāmudrā texts have been produced by organizations (and publishers) that promote the study and practice of Buddhism. At the same time, scholars affiliated with universities, colleges, and research institutes have pursued their own courses of study, producing translations, to be sure, but also tending to treat Mahāmudrā literature analytically and critically, in line with modern academic standards. These two approaches to the study of Mahāmudrā are distinctive, but far from mutually exclusive. Many texts produced by "Dharma centers" and their denizens are of very high quality, and often include the critical apparatus an academician would require. At the same time, many academic scholars are themselves also Buddhist practitioners, and their work is sometimes inflected by concerns that have arisen within their own experience of the Dharma. Suffice it to say that, over the past two centuries, important work on the Great Seal has come from both of these settings, and neither should be exalted to the detriment of the other.[71]

In the 19th and early 20th centuries, Mahāmudrā received occasional comment from pioneering scholars of Tibet, surfacing as a matter of more than passing interest only in the late 1920s, when W. Y. Evans Wentz began to publish translations, by Kazi Dawa Samdup, of a number of Tibetan Buddhist classics, including *The Life of Milarepa* and Mahāmudrā-related philosophical and meditative texts by the likes of Padampa Sangyé, Gampopa, and Pema Karpo.[72] At the same time, M. Shahidullah produced the first—and still unsurpassed—scholarly translation of the seminal songs of the great adepts Saraha and Kāṅha.[73] It was after World War II that scholarship on Mahāmudrā truly began to develop. In 1949, George Roerich, assisted by the Tibetan scholar Gendun Chöpel (1903–1951), published his translation of Gö Lotsāwa's *Blue Annals,* which is a trove of information on Mahāmudrā;[74] and in the 1950s, Herbert V. Guenther began to issue translations and analyses deeply informed by his reading of Kagyü and Nyingma sources, with Mahāmudrā often at the center of attention[75] David Snellgrove's 1959 edition, translation, and discussion of the *Hevajra Tantra* opened the door to the study of the Mahāyoga and Yoginī tantras, in which Mahāmudrā is a vital term.

In the wake of the Tibetan diaspora of 1959, Tibetans and Westerners came into contact as never before, and the long-term fruit of their exchange was the development, in Asia and in the West, of Dharma centers, usually directed by Tibetans, and an increase in the numbers of Westerners practicing Tibetan Buddhism, studying Buddhism academically, or both. To the degree that Mahāmudrā was important in many Buddhist orders, and especially attractive to Westerners because of its "simplicity," Mahāmudrā increasingly became the focus of scholarship, and, where in the 1950s and 1960s, only a handful of books on the topic were produced, by the turn of the second millennium, perhaps a dozen or more Mahāmudrā-related books were published yearly. Of particular importance to the progress of Great Seal studies were Garma C. C. Chang's translation of Milarepa's songs (1962),[76] Lobsang Lhalungpa's translation of Tashi Namgyel's great compendium of Mahāmudrā meditation (1986),[77] David Jackson's study of early Tibetan disputes over Perfection Vehicle Mahāmudrā (1994),[78] Karl Brunnhölzl's translation of Indian and Tibetan esoteric instruction texts (2007),[79] Klaus-Dieter Mathes's analysis and translation of Gö Lotāwa's Mahāmudrā-based commentary on the *Higher Continuum* (2008),[80] Peter Alan Roberts' anthology of Kagyü Mahāmudrā texts,[81] Roger Jackson and Matthew Kapstein's edited volume of essays on the Kagyü and the Great Seal (2011),[82] David Gray's inquiry into usages of *mudrā* and *mahāmudrā* in Indian Buddhist tantra (2011),[83] Lara Braitstein's study and translation of Saraha's Mahāmudrā-centered adamantine songs (2014),[84] and Ulrich Timme Kragh's massive study of the Six Dharmas of Nāropa and Mahāmudrā in the tradition of Gampopa (2015).[85]

Although for the most part, scholars of Mahāmudrā have hewed to textual analysis and doctrinal exposition, they also have engaged in lively debates, most notably one that concerns the most contested question in Tibetan Mahāmudrā circles: Was there in India—hence can there be in Tibet—a Perfection or Sūtra Vehicle Mahāmudrā? The debate was spawned by a 1982 article, in which Roger Jackson suggested that Sapan's criticism of Kagyü Mahāmudrā for its acceptance of a non-tantric Great Seal was based less on historical than polemical considerations,[86] but the main antagonists, over the next decade, were Michael Broido, who had studied with Kagyü lamas and was critical of Sapan, and David Jackson, who was expert in Sakya and defended him.[87] That phase of the debate came to an end with David Jackson's *Enlightenment by a Single Means,* but his book pointed the way to further inquiry into the possibility of an Indian form of Perfection Vehicle Mahāmudrā. That investigation has been pursued with particular vigor since the early 2000s by Klaus-Dieter Mathes, who finds in the works of Maitrīpa evidence for a Great Seal that is not exclusively tantric.[88] His conclusions, however, have been disputed by Harunaga Isaacson and Francesco Sferra, who maintain that Maitrīpa's writings do *not* provide adequate proof that he asserted a Perfection Vehicle Mahāmudrā.[89]

Research on Mahāmudrā has been facilitated in the past two decades by the publication, in Asia and the West, of the works mentioned here and many besides, but of even greater import, perhaps, has been the advent of online resources such as those of the Tibetan Buddhist Research Center and the Buddhist Canons Research Database, which give scholars access to materials with unprecedented ease and efficiency. In that sense, Mahāmudrā texts are more accessible and easier to seach than ever before. Nevertheless, "Mahāmudrā studies" is still, relatively speaking, in its infancy, and the main task for researchers remains, as it has been for a century, that of editing, translating, and interpreting the hundreds of Indian and Tibetan works on Mahāmudrā that remain unexplored, and helping us understand better the small number of works that already have seen the light of day.

PRIMARY SOURCES

Buddhist Canons Research Database. American Institute of Buddhist Studies. This service of the American Institute of Buddhist Studies (AIBS) allows Tibetan-reading scholars to search the length and breadth of the Tibetan canons of translated Buddha-word, the Kangyur (*bka' 'gyur*), and Indian treatises and commentaries, the Tengyur (*bstan 'gyur*).

Fremantle, Francesca. "A Critical Study of the Guhyasamāja Tantra." PhD Diss., School of Oriental and African Studies, London, 1971. Includes Sanskrit and Tibetan editions, along with an English translation.

Jackson, Roger R. *Tantric Treasures: Three Collections of Mystical Verse from Buddhist India*. New York: Oxford University Press, 2004. Includes Apabhraṃśa editions (supplemented by Tibetan, where necessary) of the *dohā*-treasuries of the adepts Saraha, Kāṇha, and Tilopa.

Khro ru Klu grub rgya mtsho, ed. *Nges don phyag rgya chen po'i rgya gzhung*. 11 vols. Chengdu, China: Si khron mi rigs dpe skrun khang, 2009. A book-format anthology of Mahāmudrā texts, in Tibetan. The first six volumes comprise the Seventh Karmapa's collection of Indian texts, the *Phyag chen rgya gzhung*. The final five volumes reproduce a number of Tibetan Kagyü Mahāmudrā classics, including key works by Tashi Namgyel, the Ninth Karmapa, and Jamgön Kongtrul.

Kværne, Per. *Anthology of Buddhist Tantric Songs: A Study of the Caryāgīti*. Oslo: Universitetsforlaget, 1977. Includes Apabhaṃśa and Tibetan (with English translation) of performance songs of the great adepts, supplemented by Munidatta's Sanskrit commentary.

Samdong Rinpoche and Vrajvallabh Dwivedi, eds. *Guhyādi-Aṣṭasiddhi-Saṅgraha*. Sarnath, India: Central Institute of Higher Tibetan Studies, 1987. Sanskrit and Tibetan edition of eight "Attainment Texts" composed by late-first-millennium Buddhist tantric authors.

Shastri, Haraprasad, ed. *Advayavajrasaṃgraha*. Vadodara, India: Oriental Institute, 1927. Sanskrit edition of most of the "Twenty-five Texts on Inattention" attributed to Maitrīpa.

Snellgrove, David L., ed. and trans. *The Hevajra Tantra: A Critical Study*. 2 vols. London: Oxford University Press, 1960. Includes Sanskrit and Tibetan editions, along with an English translation.

Tibetan Buddhist Resource Center. Founded by E. Gene Smith, TBRC provides scholars who can read Tibetan with access to thousands upon thousands of scanned Tibetan texts, usually for free, sometimes for a nominal fee. Nearly every important Tibetan text on Mahāmudrā may be found in the TBRC collection.

FURTHER READING

Braitstein, Lara. *The Adamantine Songs* (Vajragīti) *by Saraha: Study, Translation, and Tibetan Critical Edition.* New York: American Institute of Buddhist Studies, 2104.

Brown, Daniel P. *Pointing Out the Great Way: The Stages of Meditation in Mahāmudrā Tradition.* Boston: Wisdom Publications, 2006.

Brunnhölzl, Karl., trans. *Straight from the Heart: Buddhist Pith Instructions.* Ithaca, NY: Snow Lion Publications, 2007.

Brunnhölzl, Karl. *When the Clouds Part: The Uttaratantra and Its Meditative Tradition as a Bridge Between Sūtra and Tantra.* Boston and London: Snow Lion Publications, 2014.

Chang, Garma C. C., trans. *The Hundred Thousand Songs of Milarepa.* 2 vols. Boston: Shambhala, 1989.

Dalai Lama, H. H. the, and Alexander Berzin. *The Gelug/Kagyü Tradition of Mahāmudrā.* Ithaca, NY: Snow Lion Publications, 1997.

Fremantle, Francesca. "A Critical Study of the Guhyasamāja Tantra." PhD Diss., School of Oriental and African Studies, London, 1971.

Gray, David. "Imprints of the 'Great Seal': On the Expanding Semantic Range of the Term *mudrā* in Eighth through Eleventh Century Indian Buddhist Literature." *Journal of the International Association of Buddhist Studies* 34, nos. 1–2 (2011): 421–481.

Higgins, David. "On the Development of the Non-Mentation (*amanasikāra*) Doctrine in Indo-Tibetan Buddhism." *Journal of the International Association of Buddhist Studies* 29, no. 2 (2006): 255–304.

Jackson, David P. *Enlightenment by a Single Means: Tibetan Controversies on the "Self-Sufficient White Remedy."* Vienna: Verlag der Österreichischen Akademie der Wiseenschaften, 1994.

Jackson, Roger R. "The Indian Mahāmudrā 'Canon(s)': A Preliminary Sketch." *Indian International Journal of Buddhist Studies* 9 (2008): 151–184.

Jackson, Roger R. and Matthew T. Kapstein, eds. *Mahāmudrā and the Bka' brgyud Tradition.* Andiast, Switzerland: International Institute for Tibetan and Buddhist Studies, 2011.

Kragh, Ulrich Timme. *Tibetan Yoga and Mysticism: A Textual Study of the Yogas of Nāropa and Mahāmudrā Meditation in the Medieval Tradition of Dags po.* Studia Philologica Buddhica Monograph Series 32. Tokyo: The International Institute for Buddhist Studies, 2015.

Kvaerne, Per. "On the Concept of Sahaja in Indian Buddhist Tantric Literature." *Temenos* 11 (1975): 88–135.

Lhalungpa Lobsang P., trans. [Bkra shis rnam rgyal.] *Mahāmudrā: The Moonlight: Quintessence of Mind and Meditation.* Boston: Wisdom Publications, 2006.

Linrothe, Rob, ed. *Holy Madness: Portraits of Tantric Siddhas.* New York: Rubin Museum of Art, 2006.

Mathes, Klaus-Dieter. *A Direct Path to the Buddha Within: Gö Lotsawa's Mahāmudrā Interpretation of the Ratnagotravibhāga.* Boston: Wisdom Publications, 2008.

Mathes, Klaus-Dieter. *A Fine Blend of Mahāmudrā and Madhyamaka: Maitrīpa's Collection of Texts on Non-conceptual Realization (Amanasikāra).* Vienna: Austrian Academy of Sciences Press, 2015.

Nālandā Translation Committee, trans. *The Rain of Wisdom: The Vajra Songs of the Kagyü Gurus.* Boulder, CO: Shambhala Publications, 1980.

Rhoton, Jared Douglas, trans. *A Clear Differentiation of the Three Codes: Essential Distinctions among the Individual Liberation, Great Vehicle, and Tantric Systems.* Albany: State University of New York Press, 2002.

Roberts, Peter Alan, trans. *Mahāmudrā and Related Instructions.* Boston: Wisdom Publications, 2011.

Roerich, George N., trans. ['Gos lo tsā ba.]. *The Blue Annals.* Delhi: Motilal Banarsidass, 1976.

Schaeffer, Kurtis R. *Dreaming the Great Brahmin: Tibetan Traditions of the Buddhist Poet-Saint Saraha.* New York: Oxford University Press, 2005.

Snellgrove David L., ed. and trans. *The Hevajra Tantra: A Critical Study*. 2 vols. London: Oxford University Press, 1960.
Willis, Janice D. *Enlightened Beings: Life Stories from the Ganden Oral Tradition*. Boston: Wisdom Publications, 1995.

NOTES

1. See Roger R. Jackson, "Mahāmudrā in India," *Oxford Bibliographies* in Buddhism, 2015.
2. See David Gray, "Imprints of the 'Great Seal': On the Expanding Semantic Range of the Term *mudrā* in Eighth through Eleventh Century Indian Buddhist Literature," *Journal of the International Association of Buddhist Studies* 34, no. 1–2 (2011): 421–481.
3. Three is the most common number, but many Mahāyāna sources add a fourth, the Essence Body (*svabhāvikakāya*), and tantric authors sometimes append a fifth, the Great Bliss Body (*mahāsukhakāya*).
4. See David L. Snellgrove, *Indo Tibetan Buddhism: Indian Buddhists and Their Tibetan Successors*, 2 vols. (Boston: Shambhala Publications, 1987); and Ronald M. Davisdon, *Indian Esoteric Buddhism: A Social History of the Tantric Movement* (New York: Columbia University Press, 2002).
5. The *Basic Ordinance of Mañjuśrī* has not been fully translated into any Western language. For its usages of *mahāmudrā*, see, e.g., Glenn Wallis, *Meditating the Power of Buddhas: Ritual in the Mañjuśrīmūlakalpa* (Albany: State University of New York Press, 2002), 238–239n49; Ariane Macdonald, *Le Maṇḍala du Mañjuśrīmūlakalpa* (Paris: Adrienne-Maisonneuve, 1962), 42, 69, 99 *et passim*; and James F. Hartzell, "The Buddhist Sanskrit Tantras: 'The *Samādhi* of the Plowed Row," *The Pacific World* (Series 3) 14 (Fall 2012): 80, 139–140.
6. See Jeffrey Hopkins, *Yoga Tantra: Paths to Magical Feats* (Ithaca, NY: Snow Lion Publications, 2005).
7. Francesca Fremantle, "A Critical Study of the Guhyasamāja Tantra" (PhD Diss., School of Oriental and African Studies, London, 1971), 58, 59, 130.
8. Ibid., 34–36.
9. David L. Snellgrove, trans., *The Hevajra Tantra: A Critical Study* (London: Oxford University Press, 1960), part I, 77, 91, 105, 116, 116.
10. Lobsang P. Lhalungpa, trans., *Mahāmudrā: The Moonlight: Quintessence of Mind and Meditation* (Boston: Wisdom Publications, 2006), 93.
11. Ibid., 103, 228–229.
12. Philip Lesco, "The *Sekodeśaṭippanī:* A Brief Commentary on the Summary of the Initiation," in Edwin A. Arnold, ed., *As Long as Space Endures: Essays on the Kālacakra Tantra in Honor of H. H. the Dalai Lama* (Ithaca, NY: Snow Lion Publications 2009), 75.
13. Lhalungpa, *Mahāmudrā*, 96.
14. See Per Kvaerne, *Anthology of Buddhist Tantric Songs: A Study of the Caryāgīti* (Oslo: Universitetsforlaget, 1977); James B. Robinson, trans., Abhayadatta, *Buddha's Lions: The Lives of the Eighty-Four Siddhas* (Berkeley: Dharma Publishing, 1979); Davidson, *Indian Esoteric Buddhism*, chaps. 5–7; and Rob Linrothe, ed., *Holy Madness: Portraits of Tantric Siddhas* (New York: Rubin Museum of Art, 2006).
15. The listing of these texts is not always consistent, nor is their number; sometimes eight texts are included, as in Samdong Rinpoche and Vrajvallabh Dwivedi, eds., *Guhyādi-Aṣṭasiddhi-Saṅgraha* (Sarnath, India: Central Institute of Higher Tibetan Studies, 1987). See Roger R. Jackson, "The Indian Mahāmudrā 'Canon(s)': A Preliminary Sketch," *Indian International Journal of Buddhist Studies* 9 (2008): 160–162.
16. Samdong and Dwivedi, *Guhyādi-Aṣṭasiddhi-Saṅgraha*, 23, 29, 32.
17. Ibid., 97.

18. Roger R. Jackson, "Saraha's *Queen Dohās*," in *Yoga in Practice*, ed. David Gordon White (Princeton: Princeton University Press, 2011), 174, 178, 179, 184.
19. Thrangu Rinpoche, trans. *A Song for the King: Saraha on Mahamudra Meditation*, ed. Michele Martin (Boston: Wisdom Publications, 2006), 92, 105.
20. See Roger R. Jackson, *Tantric Treasures: Three Collections of Mystical Verse from Buddhist India* (New York: Oxford University Press, 2004), 53–115.
21. Lara Braitstein, *The Adamantine Songs* (Vajragīti) *by Saraha: Study, Translation, and Tibetan Critical Edition* (New York: American Institute of Buddhist Studies, 2104), 126, 129, 132, 133, 135, 137, 139, 140, 141, 142.
22. As with the Seven Attainment Texts, the listing of these texts is not always consistent. See, e.g., Jackson, "The Indian Mahāmudrā Canon(s)," 163–166; and Klaus-Dieter Mathes, *A Fine Blend of Mahāmudrā and Madhyamaka: Maitrīpa's Collection of Texts on Non-conceptual Realization (Amanasikāra)* (Vienna: Austrian Academy of Sciences Press, 2015).
23. See Karl Brunnhölzl, trans., *Straight from the Heart: Buddhist Pith Instructions* (Ithaca, NY: Snow Lion Publications, 2007), 93–118.
24. See Glenn R. Mullin, trans., *The Practice of the Six Yogas of Nāropa* (Ithaca, NY: Snow Lion Publications, 2006); and Ulrich Timme Kragh, "Prolegomena to the Six Doctrines of Nā ro pa: Authority and Tradition," in Roger R. Jackson and Matthew T. Kapstein, eds., *Mahāmudrā and the Bka' brgyud Tradition* (Andiast, Switzerland: International Institute for Tibetan and Buddhist Studies, 2011), 131–177.
25. Klaus-Dieter Mathes, "The 'Succession of Four Seals' (*Caturmudrānvaya*) Together with Selected Passages from Karopa's Commentary," *Tantric Studies* 1 (2008): 115.
26. Maitrīpa, *Phyag rgya chen po rdo rje'i glu gser gyi phreng ba* [*Mahāmudrāvajragītikaṇakamālā*], in Khro ru Klu grub rgya mtsho, ed., *Nges don phyag rgya chen po'i rgya gzhung* (Chengdu: Si khron mi rigs dpe skrun khang 5 (2009): 346. For a translation of this text, see Mathes, *A Fine Blend of Mahāmudrā and Madhyamaka*.
27. See Erik Pema Kunsang, trans., Thrangu Rinpoche and Khenchen Rinpoche, *King of Samadhi: Commentaries on the* Samadhi Raja Sutra *and* The Song of Lodrö Thaye (Hong Kong: Rangjung Yeshe Publications, 1994).
28. Also known as the *Distinguishing the Precious Lineage* (*Ratnagotravibhāga*); see Karl Brunnhölzl, *When the Clouds Part: The* Uttaratantra *and Its Meditative Tradition as a Bridge Between Sūtra and Tantra* (Boston and London: Snow Lion Publications, 2014).
29. On this question, see Mathes, *A Fine Blend of Mahāmudrā and Madhyamaka*; Harunaga Isaacson and Francesco Sferra, eds., *The* Sekanirdeśa *of Maitreyanātha (Advayavajra) with the* Sekanirdeśapañjikā *of Rāmapāla* (Naples: Università degli Studi di Napoli "l'Orienetale," 2014), 411–420.
30. See Roger R. Jackson, "Mahāmudrā in Tibet," *Oxford Bibliographies Online*.
31. See George N. Roerich, trans., *The Blue Annals* (Delhi: Motilal Banarsidass, 1976); Snellgrove, *Indo-Tibetan Buddhism*, vol. 2; and Ronald M. Davidson, *Tibetan Renaissance: Tantric Buddhism in the Rebirth of Tibetan Culture and the Rise of Sakya* (New York: Columbia University Press, 2004).
32. David Germano, "Architecture and Absence in the Secret Tantric History of the Great Perfection (*rdzogs chen*)," *Journal of the International Association of Buddhist Studies* 17.2 (1994): 203–335.
33. Roerich, *Blue Annals*, 843–844.
34. Kurtis R. Schaeffer, *Dreaming the Great Brahmin: Tibetan Traditions of the Buddhist Poet-Saint Saraha* (New York: Oxford University Press, 2005), 74–75.
35. Ibid., 67.
36. Cyrus Stearns, trans., *Taking the Path as Result: Core Teachings of the Sakya Lamdré Tradition* (Boston: Wisdom Publications, 2006), 42–43, 577.
37. Jérome Edou, *Machig Labdrön and the Foundations of Chöd* (Ithaca, NY: Snow Lion Publications, 1996), 165.
38. Sarah Harding, trans., *Niguma: Lady of Illusion* (Ithaca, NY: Snow Lion Publications, 2010), 32.
39. Nālandā Translation Committee, trans., *The Rain of Wisdom: The Vajra Songs of the Kagyü Gurus* (Boulder, CO: Shambhala Publications, 1980), 144–145.

40. See Andew Quintman, trans., Tsangnyön Heruka, *The Life of Milarepa* (New York: Penguin, 2010); and Garma C. C. Chang, trans., *The Hundred Thousand Songs of Milarepa*, 2 vols. (Boston: Shambhala, 1989).
41. Lama Kunga and Brian Cutillo, trans., *Miraculous Journey: Further Stories and Songs of Milarepa* (Novato, CA: Lotsawa Press, 1986), 183.
42. Lhalungpa, *Mahāmudrā*, 167.
43. See Ulrich Timme Kragh, *Tibetan Yoga and Mysticism: A Textual Study of the Yogas of Nāropa and* Mahāmudrā *Meditation in the Medieval Tradition of Dags po* (Tokyo: The International Institute for Buddhist Studies, 2015).
44. See Alexander Schiller, *Die "Vier Yoga"-Stufen der* Mahāmudrā-*Meditationstradition* (Hamburg: Department of Indian and Tibetan Studies, Universität Hamburg, 2014).
45. Lhalungpa, *Mahāmudrā*, 245.
46. Jared Douglas Rhoton, trans., *A Clear Differentiation of the Three Codes: Essential Distinctions among the Individual Liberation, Great Vehicle, and Tantric Systems* (Albany: State University of New York Press, 2002), 118–119.
47. David P. Jackson, *Enlightenment by a Single Means: Tibetan Controversies on the "Self-Sufficient White Remedy"* (Vienna: Verlag der Österreichischen Akademie der Wiseenschaften, 1994), 72.
48. See Ruth Gamble, "The View from Nowhere: The Travels of the Third Karmapa, Rang byung rdo rje in Story and Song" (PhD Diss., Australian National University, 2014).
49. Peter Alan Roberts, trans., *Mahāmudrā and Related Instructions* (Boston: Wisdom Publications, 2011), 153–168.
50. Ibid., 169–174.
51. Ibid., 170, 172.
52. Roerich, *Blue Annals*, 839–841.
53. Klaus-Dieter Mathes, *A Direct Path to the Buddha Within: Gö Lotsawa's Mahāmudrā Interpretation of the Ratnagotravibhāga* (Boston: Wisdom Publications, 2008), especially 34–45, 204–311, 367–410.
54. See, respectively, Quintman, *Life of Milarepa*; Nālandā Translation Committee, trans., *The Life of Marpa the Translator* (Boulder, CO: Prajñā Press, 1982); and Chang, *Hundred Thousand Songs*.
55. Anne Burchardi, "The Role of Rang rig in the Pramāṇa-based Gzhan stong of the Seventh Karma pa," in Jackson and Kapstein, *Mahāmudrā and the Bka' brgyud Tradition*, 340.
56. Klaus-Dieter Mathes, "The Collection of 'Indian Mahāmudrā Works' (*phyag chen rgya gzhung*) Compiled by the Seventh Karma pa Chos grags rgya mtsho," in Jackson and Kapstein, *Mahāmudrā and the Bka' brgyud Tradition*, 89–127.
57. Nālandā, *Ocean*, 310–313, 16–26
58. Jim Rheingans, "The Eighth Karmapa's Life and His Interpretation of the Great Seal" (PhD Diss., University of the West of England, 2008).
59. See David Seyfort Ruegg, "A Karma Bka' brgyud Work on the Lineages and Traditions of the Indo-Tibetan *dbu ma* (Madhyamaka)," in *The Buddhist Philosophy of the Middle: Essays on Indian and Tibetan Madhyamaka* (Boston: Wisdom Publications, 2010), 323–356.
60. See Lhalungpa, *Mahāmudrā*. A condensed version of his instruction is found in Erik Pema Kunsang, trans., Dakpo Tashi Namgyal, *Clarifying the Natural State* (Hong Kong: Rangjung Yeshe Publications, 2004).
61. Herbert V. Guenther, "Mahāmudrā—The Method of Self-Actualization," *The Tibet Journal* 1.1 (1975): 6 (translation slightly modified).
62. See W. Y. Evans-Wentz, *Tibetan Yoga and Secret Doctrines* (New York: Oxford University Press, 1958), 114–154; and Roberts, *Mahāmudrā*, 135–152.
63. See Elizabeth Callahan, trans., The Ninth Karmapa, Wangchuk Dorje, *Mahāmudrā: The Ocean of Definitive Meaning* (Seattle: Nitartha International, 2001).
64. See Alexander Berzin, trans., *The Mahāmudrā Eliminating the Darkness of Ignorance* (Dharamsala: Library of Tibetan Works and Archives, 1978), 119–120, 144–146.
65. Jackson, *Tantric Treasures*, 73.

66. See Roberts, *Mahāmudrā*, 289–332, 173–288.
67. See B. Alan Wallace, trans., *A Spacious Path to Freedom: Practical Instructions on the Union of Mahāmudrā and Atiyoga*, with commentary by Gyatrul Rinpoiche (Ithaca, NY: Snow Lion Publications, 1998).
68. See, respectively, Matthieu Ricard, trans., *The Life of Shabkar: The Autobiography of a Tibetan Yogin* (Albany: State University of New York Press, 1994); Judith Hanson, trans., *The Torch of Certainty* (Boulder, CO: Shambhala Publications, 1977); and Sarah Harding, trans., Jamgön Kongtrul, *The Treasury of Knowledge, Book Eight, Part Four: Esoteric Instructions* (Ithaca, NY: Snow Lion Publications, 2007), 208–231.
69. See His Holiness the Dalai Lama and Alexander Berzin, *The Gelug/Kagyü Tradition of Mahāmudrā* (Ithaca, NY: Snow Lion Publications, 1997).
70. See Roger R. Jackson, "The dGe ldan-bKa' brgyud Tradition of Mahāmudrā: How much dGe ldan? How Much bKa' brgyud?" in Guy Newland, ed., *Changing Minds: Contributions to the Study of Buddhism and Tibet in Honor of Jeffrey Hopkins* (Ithaca, NY: Snow Lion, 2001), 155–191.
71. For the only discussion of the "field" in English so far, see Roger R. Jackson, "The Study of Mahāmudrā in the West: A Brief Historical Overview," in Jackson and Kapstein, ed., *Mahāmudrā and the Bka' brgyud Tradition*, 3–54.
72. See e.g., *Tibet's Great Yogi Milarepa* (New York: Oxford University Press, 1928); *Tibetan Yoga and Secret Doctrines* (New York: Oxford University Press, 1935); and *The Tibetan Book of the Great Liberation* (New York: Oxford University Press, 1954).
73. M. Shahidullah, *Les chants mystiques de Kāṇha et de Saraha: Les Dohā-koṣa et les Caryā* (Paris: Adrien-Maisonneuve, 1928).
74. Roerich, *The Blue Annals*.
75. See, e.g., *Yuganaddha: The Tantric View of Life* (Varanasi: Chowkhamba, 1952); and *The Jewel Ornament of Liberation* (London: Rider, 1959).
76. Chang, *The Hundred Thousand Songs of Milarepa*.
77. Lhalungpa, *Mahāmudrā: The Moonlight*.
78. D. Jackson, *Enlightenment by a Single Means*.
79. Brunnhölzl, *Straight from the Heart*.
80. Mathes, *A Direct Path to the Buddha Within*.
81. Roberts, *Mahāmudrā and Related Instructions*. See also his *The Mind of Mahāmudrā* (Boston: Wisdom Publication, 2014), which brings together Great Seal-related texts from the 2011 anthology.
82. Jackson and Kapstein, *Mahāmudrā and the Bka' brgyud Tradition*.
83. Gray, "Imprints of the 'Great Seal.'"
84. Braitstein, *Saraha's Adamantine Songs*.
85. Kragh, *Tibetan Yoga and Mysticism*.
86. Roger Jackson, "Sa skya Paṇḍita's Account of the Bsam yas Debate: History as Polemic," *Journal of the International Association of Buddhist Studies* 5., no. 2 (1982): 89–99.
87. See, e.g., Michael M. Broido, "Sa-skya paṇḍita, the White Panacea, and the Hva-shang Doctrine," *Journal of the International Association of Buddhist Studies* 10.2 (1987): 27–68; and David P. Jackson, "Sa-skya paṇḍita the 'Polemicist': Ancient Debates and Modern Interpretations," *Journal of the International Association of Buddhist Studies* 13.2 (1990): 17–116.
88. His views are collected in Mathes, *A Fine Blend of Mahāmudrā and Madhyamaka* and in the forthcoming essay, "Sahajavajra's Integration of Tantra into Mainstream Buddhism: An Analysis of his **Tattvadaśakaṭīkā* and **Sthitisamāsa*," in *Tantric Communities in Context*.
89. Isaacson and Sferra, *The* Sekanirdeśa *of Maitreyanātha (Advayavajra)*.

Roger R. Jackson

MAÑJUŚRĪ

MAÑJUŚRĪ, THE BODHISATTVA OF DISCRIMINATING WISDOM

Mañjuśrī (T.'Jam dpal; C. Wénshū;) in Sanskrit, "Gentle Glory," also known as Mañjughoṣa ("Gentle Voice"), is one of the earliest and most important bodhisattvas in the Mahāyāna Buddhist pantheon. Mañjuśrī is the embodiment of *prajñā*, the discriminating wisdom that cuts through the ignorance that binds beings to a cycle of suffering. Like *prajñā*, Mañjuśrī is *kumārabhūta*, "ever youthful"; he is most commonly portrayed as a sixteen-year-old crown prince, wielding a flaming sword above his head with his right hand, while his left hand holds the stem of a lotus flower on which nestles a *Prajñāpāramitā* (Perfection of Prajñā) text. *"Kumārabhūta"* also speaks to Mañjuśrī's advanced spiritual status. In early Mahāyāna models of the stages to enlightenment, the *kumāra* stage was just steps away from complete buddhahood. "Mañjuśrī Kumārabhūta" thus evokes the image of a spiritual heir-apparent—a youthful, sharp, clear-eyed crown prince poised on the cusp of full spiritual power and perfection.

Euro-American scholars consider the most likely antecedent of the melodiously voiced Mañjuśrī to be a youthful celestial musician (*gandhārva*) named Pañcaśikha ("Five Crested"), who features in both Pāli and Sanskrit Buddhist works as the buddha's interlocutor. Mañjuśrī also bears a strong resemblance to the eternally youthful Brahmā Sanatkumāra, a "Lord of Speech," a youth imbued with trans-worldly wisdom in the brahmanical *Chāndogya Upaniṣad* and the Pāli Buddhist *Saṃyutta Nikāya*. In the *Janavasabha Sutta*, Brahmā Sanatkumāra manifests as none other than Pañcaśikha and extols the value of the Buddhadharma in a voice magically imbued with eight qualities.[1]

INDIAN MAHĀYĀNA

Mañjuśrī appears as both personification and spokesperson of *prajñā* in the earliest datable literary evidence of Mahāyāna works we have available in any language, namely the Chinese translations prepared from 168–189 CE by the Indo-Scythian scholar Lokakṣema and his team of translators. The bodhisattva appears in two-thirds of the extant texts. He is always portrayed as a monk, and has two key roles: he is the buddha's key interlocutor and the spiritual friend (*kalyāṇamitra*) of King Ajātaśatru, the Indian king who ruled from Magadha during the historical buddha's time. The *Druma-kinnara rājaparipcchā-sūtra* alludes to this latter role briefly. It is because of merit that King Ajātaśatru has "obtained two spiritual friends. The first one is the buddha. The second one is Mañjuśrī. Through their grace, the doubt arising from the unrighteous acts you committed was completely dispelled."[2] It is most eloquently demonstrated in the *Ajātaśatrukaukṛtya-vinodanā sūtra*, arguably the most sophisticated and engaging of the Mahāyāna sūtras translated by Lokakṣema. Many of its teachings are couched as philosophical discussions between Mañjuśrī and the Magadhan king, who struggles with the remorse he feels for murdering his father. Within this elastic frame story, Mañjuśrī imparts teachings on everything from *Prajñāpāramitā* thought to the efficacy of *dhāraṇī* (mnemonic prayers). Clad in his humble monastic robes, Mañjuśrī travels to fathomless landscapes and performs miraculous acts of transformation through the power of his meditation and *prajñā*.[3]

Most important, Mañjuśrī explicates the dharma with a fluidity and profundity that leaves the non-Mahāyāna monks speechless. The bodhisattva's insight exceeds even that of the disciples who had heard the dharma from Śākyamuni Buddha himself—the *sine qua non* of legitimacy in the Buddhist tradition. This contrast tacitly communicates a larger message: Mahāyāna thought is superior to that of the earlier, established schools. Moreover, Mañjuśrī 's perfected *prajñā* manifests as more than mere verbal or intellectual acuity: the Mañjuśrī of the *Ajātaśatrukaukṛtya-vinodanā* travels to alternate universes, emits rays of light from his pores, and manifests decillions of lotus flowers, each containing a buddha seated within.[4] Mañjuśrī in meditation is indistinguishable from the buddha himself. In fact, explains Śākyamuni Buddha, it was none other than Mañjuśrī who in a previous incarnation had inspired him and all the buddhas of the past to enter the bodhisattva path:

> It was Mañjuśrī who... caused me to conceive the Awakening Mind—my first aspiration for the sake of enlightenment... You should see that the Tathāgata Buddha's greatness, the ten powers, the fearlessnesses, the unimpeded intuition and whatever other good (qualities) are engendered by Mañjuśrī. Why is that? Because the attainment of omniscience derives from that Awakening Mind... Śāriputra, that is the way in which it should be understood. It is about that very Mañjuśrī that those who speak and teach aptly say, "He is the mother of bodhisattvas, he is the father, he is the [giver of] compassion and inspiration."[5]

The supremacy of Mañjuśrī and his *prajñā* thus functions rhetorically to assert the legitimacy of the emerging Mahāyāna movement. It is not surprising to find Mañjuśrī prominently extolled by the foundational Mahāyāna scholars of Lokakṣema's time. Nāgārjuna opens his foundational *Mūlamadhyamakakārikā* by invoking the crown prince. In his voluminous *Mahāprajñāpāramitāśastra,* Nāgārjuna describes Mañjuśrī as one of the compilers of the Mahāyāna scriptures. Nāgārjuna's disciple Aryadeva (170–270 CE) honors Mañjuśrī at the start of his *Catuhśatakaśastra,* and bows to "Mañjuśrī Jñānasattva" in his *Hastavālaprakaraṇa.* There is little question of Mañjuśrī 's rhetorical importance to the Mahāyāna textual universe well before the second century CE.[6]

Indian Buddhist writers subsequently developed the roles and rhetorical functions that Mañjuśrī served in Lokakṣema's corpus. In the *Vimalakīrtinirdeśa-sūtra,* a work of particular influence in East Asia, we find Mañjuśrī pointedly reiterating the superiority of the Mahāyāna to traditional Nikāya teachings. Mañjuśrī is the only of Śākyamuni Buddha's major monk disciples who dares to lock philosophical horns with the great lay Buddha Vimalakīrti, and so elicit his recondite and often theatrical teachings on emptiness (*śunyatā*), wisdom, and compassionate artistry (*upāya*). So incomparable is his power that he can convert even non-Buddhists to the Mahāyāna way. The Jain followers of the *Ratnakāraṇḍa-sūtra* drop to their knees before him and hail Śākyamuni Buddha. Mañjuśrī converts "incalculable numbers" of beings of the Nāga's underwater kingdom in the Lotus Sūtra (*Saddharmapuṇḍarika-sūtra),* and even brings a prostitute to the Mahāyāna path in the *Mañjuśrīvikrīḍita sūtra.* "I do not in any way possess the learning that Mañjuśrī has just defined," admits Ānanda, Śākyamuni Buddha's disciple and attendant, to the followers in the *Śuraṅgamasamādhi-sūtra.*[7]

Mañjuśrī also facilitates the teaching of new concepts and models of various Mahāyāna schools. The bodhisattva's queries in the *Saṃdhinirmocana-sūtra* engender the explication of the important "three body" (*trikāya*) model of the Yogācāra school. He inspires a lesson on Pure Land mechanics that transforms an entire assembly of disciples in the *Śuraṅgamasamādhi-sūtra*. In the *Avataṃsaka-sūtra*, the foundational text for the Huayan school of Chinese Buddhism, Mañjuśrī 's public exposition of a scripture ignites the "unhindered, unattached determination for enlightenment" in young Sudhana, and sets him on his journey to enlightenment. Appropriately, Mañjuśrī is the first of fifty-two teachers Sudhana encounters, and the first the Buddha Maitreya acknowledges at the journey's completion. "Inconceivably great is your gain," exclaims Maitreya to Sudhana, "that you have seen Mañjuśrī face to face."[8]

Maitreya's emphasis on Sudhana's "face-to-face" encounter with the crown prince was as strategic as it was poetic. In Mahāyāna circles, yogic communion with buddhas and bodhisattvas was another means by which a meditator who lived long after the death of the historical buddha could receive teachings that were deemed as legitimate as those spoken by the buddha to his own disciples. To "see Mañjuśrī face to face" was tantamount to receiving a teaching from the buddha himself.

These envisioned buddhas and bodhisattvas were sometimes said to reside in a buddha-field (*buddhakṣetra*)—a realm they created through their compassionate actions in order to ripen beings. In the *Mañjuśrībuddhakṣetra-guṇavyūha sūtra*, we learn that Mañjuśrī had vowed to create and purify his own buddha-field many eons earlier. Since then, he had "attained the ten stages of the Bodhisattva, fully acquired the ten powers of the Tathāgata and accomplished all the Buddha-dharmas." Yet why then has he not attained supreme enlightenment? "Good man," Mañjuśrī explains, "no one realizes enlightenment after he has achieved perfection in all Buddha-Dharmas. Why? Because, if one has achieved perfection in all Buddha-Dharmas, he need not realize anything more." Mañjuśrī fully understands the truth of emptiness, and so has let go of the notion of "full Buddhahood." In so saying, he makes clear that he is, through the logic of non-dualism, already fully enlightened.[9]

It is not only his buddha-field that blurs the distinction between this tenth-stage bodhisattava and a fully enlightened buddha. Mañjuśrī can share his relics in the *Mañjuśrīparinirvāna sūtra*, and great benefits accrue to those who see his image or even pronounce his name. The crown prince inspires a group of disheartened bodhisattvas in the *Śuraṅgamasamādhi-sūtra* by recounting his own long-ago attainment of nirvana. It is due to his great compassion, he explains, that he remains present to help sentient beings. "World Honored One," Mañjuśrī says to the buddha of the *Saptaśatikā-prajñāpāramitā sūtra*, "I *am* the inconceivable."[10]

Mañjuśrī 's unparalleled status in 7th-century works mirrored important changes in the landscape of Indian monasticism. After the decline of the Gupta political state, Buddhist monasteries (*vihāras*) become concentrated in the northeast regions of Bengal and Bihar, and several, including Nālandā and Vikramalaśilā, were enlarged into international hubs for scholastic training. Significantly, the curricula at these centers placed an especial emphasis on Buddhist epistemology and logic, especially the works of Dignāga (480–540) and Dharmakīrti (7th century). As the bodhisattva identified with *prajñā* and learning, Mañjuśrī gained even greater popularity and significance. Multiple stucco, bronze, and stone representations of the bodhisattva, particularly in his *kumārabhūta* form, speak to his cult status at Nālandā monastery. Typical is a 7th-century basalt sculpture of Mañjuśrī gracefully bending his torso (*ābhaṅga* posture), holding up his left hand in the gesture of gift-giving (*varada mudrā*) while his right grasps the long stalk of a lotus. His crown prince/*kumārabhūta* status is expressed by his plain, disc-like earrings, his decorated bracelet, and necklace with a spoked disc.[11]

Other contemporaneous examples emphasize his royal dimensions even more deliberately. A stucco figure of the bodhisattva sits against a large bolster, adorned not only with bracelets, arm bands, and enormous *cakra* earrings, but a necklace with a *cakra* suspended from a central amulet with tiger-claw (*vyāghranakha*) pendants, a traditional marker of protection for youths. Tellingly, his eyes are almond-shaped and open rather than lotus-shaped and downcast as is common to most of the other stucco figures—a visual allusion, perhaps, to the crown prince's association with *prajñā:* the critical, unblinking insight that sees through illusion to the truth of reality.[12]

ESOTERIC INDIAN BUDDHISM

By the 7th or 8th century, we find Mañjuśrī also appearing in esoteric Buddhist (Tantra) texts. The crown prince functionally supplants the buddha as the central teacher of the *Mañjuśrīmūlakalpa* (alt. *Mañjuśrīyamūlakalpa*), arguably one of the earliest esoteric works of Buddhist India.[13] Śākyamuni Buddha signifies the bodhisattva's importance by entrusting Mañjuśrī with a powerful six-syllable mantra: *Oṃ vakyeda nāma.* So powerful is Mañjuśrī's mantra, it releases one "from the binding fetters of existence," is "invincible against all demons," and "establish(es) the teachings of the buddhas."[14] Mañjuśrī even transforms the fiercesome Yamāntaka, the Slayer of Death into a cultivator of dharma: "Act on my behalf!... In an instant, the king of the Krodhas had gone to all regions of the world where he succeeded, thanks to his magic power, in mastering hostile beings and compelling them to enter the circle of the Assembly."[15] In this work, Yamāntaka is a wrathful attendant to the bodhisattva. Subsequently, he would become identified as a wrathful form of Mañjuśrī himself.

This attention to Mañjuśrī 's sonic forms continued. The crown prince became closely identified with the Arapacana syllabary used in Mahāyāna texts as an mnemonic device for remembering key concepts. Over time, its title served as both an alternate name for Mañjuśrī and one of his mantras: *Oṃ arapacana dhī.* The exaltation of Mañjuśrī in both sonic and physical form culminated in the late 7th- or early 8th-century *Mañjuśrīnāmasaṃgīti.* For both the monastics and laypeople of northeast India, the *Mañjuśrīnāmasaṃgīti* was the Mañjuśrī-text par excellence. It spawned twenty-two commentaries and approximately 130 related works. As its title suggests, the *Mañjuśrīnāmasaṃgīti* is comprised of multiple Mañjuśrī epithets, each of which is understood to be a syllabic manifestation of Mañjuśrī as the perfectly enlightened buddha (see Figure 1):

> The blessed one, Buddha (Mañjuśrī), the completely awakened, born from the syllable *a,* is the syllable *a,* the foremost of all phonemes, of great meaning, the supreme syllable...
>
> Of great form and great body, with great color and grand physique, with exalted name he is very noble, having a grand expansive *maṇḍala*...
>
> Without beginning or end, he is Buddha, Adibuddha without causal connection. Stainless with his unique eye of gnosis, he is embodied gnosis, the Tathāgata...
>
> Motionless, himself very clear, he hears the enlightenment of the perfect completely awakened, face-to-face with all buddhas.[16]

Figure 1. Mañjuśrī as Manjuvajra in the *Mañjuśrīnāmasaṃgīti* tradition Bengal; Pala period (c. 700–1200), 11th century.
Source: Metropolitan Museum of Art Collection.

The influence of the *Mañjuśrīnāmasaṃgīti* was fueled by its intimacy with another Indian Buddhist esoteric text, the 11th-century *Kālacakra Tantra*, one of the last tantric works to be promulgated in India before Buddhism disappeared from its homeland altogether. The *Kālacakra Tantra* cites almost seventy verses from the *Mañjuśrīnāmasaṃgīti*. Its core commentary states unequivocally that the Kālacakra is "indivisible" from the *Mañjuśrīnāmasaṃgīti*. The Kālacakra tradition and the *Mañjuśrīnāmasaṃgīti* traveled to Tibet in the 11th century. They gained particular prominence in the late 13th and early 14th century when Tibet was under Mongol rule. To this day, students in Tibet recite the *Mañjuśrīnāmasaṃgīti*, seeking to sharpen their academic performance. Mañjuśrī's continued importance underscores how thoroughly the bodhisattva has pervaded Mahāyāna Buddhism in South Asia and beyond.

BEYOND INDIA: THE CULT OF MAÑJUŚRĪ IN CHINA, CENTRAL ASIA, AND TIBET

The most prominent extra-Indian cult of Mañjuśrī was located at Wutai shan ("Five Terrace Mountain") in China's Shanxi Province. Chinese Buddhists had known of the bodhisattva from *sūtras* translated into Chinese from at least the 2nd century, including those of Lokakṣema's corpus and the *Vimalakīrtinirdeśa-sūtra*. It was Buddhabhadra's 5th-century translation of the *Avataṃsaka Sutra*, however, that fueled Mañjuśrī's rise to cult status. In this translation, the crown prince is said to actually reside in China at Mount Qingliang ("Clear and Cool Mountain"), an alternate name for the sacred mountain of Wutai shan: "Since ancient times the bodhisattva assemblies have dwelled here. Now the bodhisattva Mañjuśrī lives there with his assembly of ten thousand bodhisattvas. He is constantly present to preach the dharma."[17]

Mañjuśrī 's Chinese abode was confirmed by readings of other *sūtras*. In a 6th-century Chinese translation of the *Mañjuśrī parinirvāna sūtra*, the buddha predicts that "four hundred fifty years after my final passing, (Mañjuśrī) will go to a snowy mountain and... extensively proclaim the teachings of twelve divisions of the (Mahāyāna) scriptures."[18] He would then be brought to Gandhamadan, a Himalayan mountain known from other Sanskrit works as having five peaks. For Chinese devotees, both "Snowy Mountain" and the five peaks of Gandhamadan were clear allusions to the snowy and five-peaked Wutai shan, as well as Mañjuśrī's own association with Pañcasikh, the Five Crested figure of Pāli and early Sanskrit literature. There, Mañjuśrī would lend his assistance to local devotees:

> If sentient beings pay homage and make offerings to Mañjuśrī, then they will always be born in a land where a Buddha is present and be protected by Mañjuśrī... If a person wishes to make offerings in order to produce merit, then Mañjuśrī will transform himself into a poverty-stricken suffering wretch with no means of support and appear before the practitioner.[19]

Readers of the *Mañjuśrī-dharma-ratnagarbha-dhāranī sutra*, translated into Chinese in 710, also learned of Mañjuśrī 's Chinese home from the buddha's own prediction:

> After I have passed away, in this Jambudvīpa in the northeast quarter, there is a country called Mahā Cīna. In the center of this country there is a mountain called Five Peaks. The youth Mañjuśrī will roam about and dwell there, expounding on the dharma at the center of the mountain for the sake of sentient beings. Countless devas, nāgas, spirits, rākṣasas, kinnaras, mahoragas and other creatures human and not human encircle him, reverently making worship offerings.[20]

Buddhist pilgrims flocked to Wutai to see the crown prince; his was a buddha-field that could be reached by foot rather than through elaborate ritual visualizations or fortuitous rebirth. These devotees reported visions of miraculous cloud formations and wondrous lights, and as these accounts circulated, the scope and popularity of Mañjuśrī worship increased. A constant flow of pilgrims from India, Kashmir, Tibet, Japan, and Korea marked Wutai shan's development into an international pilgrimage site. The tantric texts of the Zhenyen school extolled Mañjuśrī 's mantra, image, and ritual invocations as the only true refuge in the times of *mofa*, the "final dharma" period. Mañjuśrī become central to followers of the Huayen, a school of thought especially popular in the Tang dynasty (618–907).

In the 8th century, Mañjuśrī worship formally entered the domain of Chinese politics. The Buddhist monk Amoghavajra (705–774) labored to establish China as a legitimate Buddhist state by promoting the worship of Mañjuśrī as the bodhisattva protector of the Tang state. He initiated the Chinese emperor as a divinely anointed Buddhist ruler, and Mañjuśrī became identified as the personal guardian of the emperor and his family, and the spiritual protector of the state in 759. An image of Mañjuśrī on his lion, said to be modeled on actual manifestations of Mañjuśrī as he appeared before the sculptor, was installed at a monastery at Wutai shan for cult worship.[21]

This time period also saw a growth of interest among Tibetans in Mañjuśrī 's earthly whereabouts. In several Tibetan writings from the 7th and 8th centuries, we find the crown prince characterized as a long-term resident of a mountain-based monastery in Khotan (*Li yul*). In the *Prophecy of Gośṛṅga* (*Ri glang ru lung bstan pa*), Mañjuśrī and the *gandharva*-king Pañcasikha accompany the buddha to a tall hill called Gośṛṅga, where the buddha espies a lake and prophesizes that it will one day become a great country. Mañjuśrī then steps forth and offers a prophecy of his own: a monastery will arise on this hill, and all beings that approach it will attain great spiritual powers.[22] In *The Prophecy of the Li Region* (*Li yul lung bstan pa*), we learn that this was not the first time Mañjuśrī had taken an interest in Khotan. Long ago, the bodhisattva had emanated as a monk named Vairocana, and taught a unique language to Khotan's Chinese and Indian inhabitants so they could communicate with each other.[23] It is Mañjuśrī as Lord of Speech who is at work here, dressed in monastic garb and serving as a bridge between Indian and Chinese cultures.

The legends of Nepal, themselves influenced by the Khotanese narratives, reinforced the Tibetan vision of Mañjuśrī as civilizing forefather. The most famous account portrays Mañjuśrī as the creator of the Kathmandu Valley. Long ago, we learn, a buddha planted a perfect light-emitting lotus flower in the center of a lake. Mañjuśrī, residing in his mountain home at Wutai shan, saw its light and realized that people were unable to reach this divine relic to worship it. The bodhisattva drew his sword and cut a gorge to drain the lake, and so created the Kathmandu Valley. As the water receded, Mañjuśrī established a *stūpa* over the lotus, which became known as the Mañjuśrī Stūpa. It was later renamed Svāyambhū, and continues to be one of the most significant Buddhist sites in Nepal.

By the 12th century, Tibetans were writing the bodhisattva Mañjuśrī back into their own early histories. In the work of a Nyang ral nyi ma 'od zer (1136–1204), it is Mañjuśrī at Wutai who facilitates the conception of King Khri srong lde btsan (742–796), the king who founded Buddhism in Tibet and oversaw the creation of Tibet's first Buddhist monastery. Through this logic, it is the bodhisattva Mañjuśrī who sparked the spread of the dharma through Tibet. The king himself became known as an emanation of Mañjuśrī.[24]

The consolidation of the Mongol empire in the 12th century further shaped Mañjuśrī worship. Seeking to bring Tibet firmly under Mongol control, Godan Khan (1206–1251), a grandson of Genghis Khan and administrator over much of China, publicly patronized Tibetan Buddhism. In 1247, he invited the illustrious Buddhist scholar Sa skya paṇḍita Kun dga' rgyal mtshan to come to his court and serve as Tibet's representative. In this capacity, Sa skya paṇḍita made several trips to Wutai shan and was later said to be a Tibetan emanation of Mañjuśrī himself. After his death, his nephew Chos rgyal 'phags pa blo gros rgyal mtshan became the personal religious teacher of the Mongol ruler Kublai Khan. He too traveled extensively to Wutai shan, and composed a range of texts that eulogized Mañjuśrī. Under the rule of Altan Khan (1507–1582), the Mongols reanimated the Tang practice of identifying its ruler with Mañjuśrī. Kublai Khan was retroactively "discovered" to have been an emanation of Mañjuśrī, as by extension, was Altan Khan, who also named one of his daughters "Mañjuśrī."[25]

Not surprisingly, the *Mañjuśrīnāmasaṃgīti* became especially popular among the Mongols of this time. Altan Khan's nephew had it translated anew into a polyglot version containing the text in Sanskrit, Tibetan, Mongolian, and Chinese. The *Mañjuśrīnāmasaṃgīti* circulated in Mongolia as a separate work, and was the opening text of the Mongolian Buddhist canon translated in 1628–1629. Today, lay donors continue to offer donations to monasteries in Ulaanbaatar for the Tibetan version of the *Mañjuśrīnāmasaṃgīti* to be recited aloud in order to remove obstacles and engender wisdom in his devotees.[26]

The Mongols were not the only rulers of China to tap Mañjuśrī's spiritual and political authority. In 1644, a nomadic people headed by the Jurchen and known as the Manchus founded the Qing dynasty (1644–1911). The Manchu rulers did not have a bloodline that linked them to Qubilai Khan and so legitimated their rule. Accordingly, they framed themselves as Qubilai's spiritual inheritors by proclaiming themselves emanations of Mañjuśri. Lest there be any doubt as to their intimacy with the crown prince, the Manchus changed their ethnonym from Jurchen to "Manju" in 1635, less than a decade before they completed their conquest of China.[27]

The height of the Mongol's religio-political associations with Mañjuśrī came when the Kangxi emperor (r. 1662–1723) referred to himself as Mañjuśrī in his preface to the officially commissioned Mongolian translation of the Tibetan Buddhist canon (1718–1720):

> Mañjuśrī, the savior of all living forms, [with the] intellect of all the Buddhas, was transformed into human form, and ascended the Fearless Lion Throne of gold, and this was none other than the sublime Emperor Kangxi-Mañjughosa who assisted and brought joy to the entire vast world.[28]

His grandson, who ruled China for the second half of the 18th century as the Qianlong emperor (r. 1735–1796), also identified himself as Mañjuśrī and was a vigorous patron of Tibetan Buddhist translation projects.

During the 18th and 19th centuries, Wutai shan continued to be an important pilgrimage site for Chinese Buddhists. For Tibeto-Mongols, however, for whom Wutai shan was considered the most sacred place to visit on earth, Mañjuśrī's mountain became a second home.

With Qing support, more than two dozen Tibeto-Mongol monasteries were established, and they attracted so many Mongol pilgrims that the site became an object of exotic interest for Chinese. By the beginning of the 19th century, Wutai was called "Tibet of China."[29] Mañjuśrī worship was thus an expression of both imperial support and Tibeto-Mongol identity.

Prominent figures from the Tibetan Buddhist tradition composed poems to the crown prince, including Thub bstan rgya tsho, the Thirteenth Dalai Lama, whose insights during his 1908 sojourn to Wutai shan were expressed in *Beautiful Clear Mirror: A Praise to Lord Mañjughoṣa's Abode*. Perhaps most famous was the work of Lcang skya rol pa'i rdo rje, a close associate of the Qianlong emperor and intermediary between the Qing court and the peoples of Inner Asia. In his *Cloud of Offerings to Please Mañjuśrī: A Song Coupled to a Place-Praise for Five-Peaked Mountain,* (1767) Lcang skya reminds all the peoples under the umbrella of Qing rule that Wutai shan was always populated by enlightening figures who, like Mañjuśrī himself, can appear in any form:

To faithful disciples who keep the holy vow,
These may appear at times just like a sage,
Or boys, or men, or women in different times,
Or Chinese monks wearing robes of brown,
As a destitute beggar wandering about,
As birds or as deer or whatever one thinks,
As medicine, flowers, plants or a forest,
As living or inanimate things they pretend.[30]

Mañjuśrī worship at Wutai shan suffered a sharp decline for much of the 20th century. Many of its monastic residents fled for safety during the Sino-Japanese War and the Japanese occupation from 1938 to 1945. Religious activities were severely curtailed during the Cultural Revolution (1966–1976). The 1980s, however, saw a new level of religious tolerance and a remarkable revival of Buddhist practice at Wutai shan fueled in part by notable pilgrimages to Mañjuśrī's home. Of especial importance was the pilgrimage by Khenpo Jikme Phuntsok Jungné, a charismatic Buddhist monk from Eastern Tibet considered by his disciples to be an emanation of Mañjuśrī. In 1980, Khenpo founded the Larung Gar Buddhist academy in Sichuan Province. In 1987, after repeated visions and instruction from Mañjuśrī, Khenpo led hundreds of his students from the Institute on a pilgrimage to Wutai shan. Thousands of pilgrims from China, Mongolia, and Tibet flocked to Wutai shan to attend his teachings, during which a magnificent image of Mañjuśrī is said to have appeared in the sky. Subsequently, Khenpo took residence in the Cave of Sudhana (Tib. Nor bzang phug), renowned for being the site where Sudhana of the *Avataṃsaka-sūtra* beheld Mañjuśrī. There, the Khenpo was said to have had multiple visions of and about the crown prince, including one that helped him discover a broken stone statue of Mañjuśrī under a tree. The image was brought back to the Khenpo's academy and housed in the Hall of Mañjuśrī. Today, it serves as an important object of Mañjuśrī worship at Larung Gar, the largest Buddhist monastic institution in the world.[31]

REVIEW OF LITERATURE

The study of Mañjuśrī is as old as the Euro-American study of Indian Buddhism, which dates back to the pioneering work of the legendary philologist Eugène Burnouf (1801–1852). In 1837, Burnouf received hundreds of Buddhist Indian Sanskrit (and some Tibetan) manuscripts from a British official of the East India Company stationed in Nepal. Virtually unknown in Europe, these manuscripts included many of the most important *sūtra* and tantras of Sanskrit Buddhism, including the *Lotus Sūtra*, the *Mañjuśrīmūlakalpa*, and a number of *Prajñāpāramitā sūtras*. The remarkable Burnouf read through this voluminous body of work and, in 1844, published the first scholarly book-length study of Buddhism in a European language. *Introduction a l'histoire du Buddhisme indian* was also an introduction to Mañjuśrī, "a bodhisattva eminent in science and in virtue, who has fulfilled all the duties imposed to his condition under innumerable buddhas prior to Śākyamuni. Indeed,

few names are so often mentioned among the Buddhists of the North as that of Mañjuśrī . . . the Chinese . . . have a most special veneration for Mañjuśrī, which is equally shared by the Tibetans and Mongols. The account by Faxian... traces the cult of which Mañjuśrī was the object back at least to the fourth century of our era. [His account] causes us to think that the existence of Mañjuśrī is connected, in ways still unknown to us, to a considerable portion of the collection of the North, the *Prajñāpāramitā*.[32]

For the remainder of the 19th century, scholarly interest, however, was less focused on Buddhism's mythical figures than on Buddhism's historical founder, Siddhartha Gautama. For this generation of scholars, the "pure" Buddhism taught by the buddha was considered rational and restrained—a sharp contrast to the ritualism, superstition, and fantasy of later, "degenerate" forms. Among the ten books of Buddhist translations printed in Max Muller's renowned "Sacred Books of the East" (1879–1910), only three were dedicated to Mahāyāna works.

In the first half of the 20th century, however, the tide began to shift. European expeditions in Central Asia recovered enormous caches of Buddhist manuscripts—most notably from the Dunhuang Cave complex in western China—that fueled new interest in Mahāyāna's "great bodhisattvas." For thinkers such as Har Dayal, such bodhisattvas were one of a "class of saints" that personified specific qualities of the buddha. Mañjuśrī, for example personified the buddha's wisdom and his melodious voice.[33]

It was Étienne Lamotte's landmark "Mañjuśrī" monograph (1960), however, that marked the beginning of serious scholarship on the history, literature, and cult worship associated with the crown prince. Over the next decades, influential French and American scholars drew upon Lamotte to explore Mañjuśrī's iconography, cult worship, and textual history. Subsequent translation studies of key Mañjuśrī texts, especially the *Mañjuśrīmūlakalpa* and the *Mañjuśrīnāmasaṃgīti*, broadened the field.[34] The cult of Mañjuśrī at Wutai shan has been widely studied.[35] Today, the study of the Buddhist revival movements at Wutai shan since the 1980s has given new impetus to the study of Mañjuśrī worship and its impact on Asian history, religion, politics, art, and cartography.[36]

PRIMARY SOURCES

In the case of Indian Buddhist works, an edition of the Sanskrit or Pali text is cited where available. The Tibetan and/or Chinese translations are given, using Tohoku (To), Derge (D), and Peking (P) for the Tibetan, and the Taisho number for the Chinese. Links to digital editions given last where available.

Ārya-ajātaśatrukaukṛttyavinodana-nāma-mahāyānasūtra: ('phags pa ma skyes dgra'i 'gyod pa bsal ba shes bya ba theg pa chen po'i mdo) To. 216; Taisho 629; D. 216.

"'phags pa ma skyes dgra'i 'gyod pa bsal ba zhes bya ba theg pa chen po'i mdo/." In bka' 'gyur (shel mkhar bris ma). Tibetan Buddhist Resource Center (TBRC) W1PD127393. 69: 660–845. [s.l.]: [s.n.], [n.d.].

Emmerick, Ronald E. "The Prophecy of the Li Region (*Li yul lung bstan pa*)" in *Tibetan Texts Concerning Khotan*. London: Oxford University Press, 1967.

KĀLACAKRATANTRA

Banerjee, Biswanath, ed. *A Critical Edition of Sri Kālacakratantrarāja (Collated with the Tibetan Version)*. Calcutta: Asiatic Society, 1985.

Paramadhibuddhoddhṛta-śrīkālacakra-nāma-tantrarāja (mchog gi dang po'i sangs rgyas las phyung ba rgyud kyi rgyal po dus kyi 'khor lo) D. 364.
Vira, Raghu, and Lokesh Candra, eds. *Kālacakratantra and Other Texts, Part 1*. New Delhi: International Academy of Indian Culture, 1966.
rgyud kyi rgyal po dpal dus kyi 'khor lo/. TBRC (http://tbrc.org) W4CZ75. 1 vols. [s.l.]: [kau lang ho], 1294.
Mañjuśrībuddhakṣetra-guṇavyūhasūtra ('jam dpal gyi sangs rgyas kyi zhing gi yon tan bkod pa) To. 59; Taisho 310.
'phags pa 'jam dpal gyi sangs rgyas kyi zhing gi yon tan bkod pa zhes bya ba. In bka' 'gyur (shel mkhar bris ma). TBRC (http://tbrc.org/) W1PD127393. 43: 679–807. [s.l.]: [s.n.], [n.d.].

MAÑJUŚRĪMŪLAKALPA

Āryamañjuśrīmūlakalpa (phags pa 'jam dpal gyi rtsa ba'i rgyu) T. 543; D. 540; Taisho 1191.
Ganapati, T., ed. *Āryamañjuśrīmūlakalpa*. Trivandrum Sanskrit Series: Part I = no. LXX, 1920; Part II = LXXVI, 1922; Part III = LXXXIV, 1925. Trivandrum: Trivandrum Sanskrit Series, 1992.
Vaidya, P. L., ed. *Mahāyānasūtrasaṃgraha, Part II*. Buddhist Sanskrit Texts, no. 18. Bihar: Mithila Institute, 1964.
chos kyi 'byung gnas. "'jam dpal rtsa rgyud." In bka' 'gyur (sde dge par phud). TBRC (http://tbrc.org) W22084. 88: 177–669. delhi: delhi karmapae chodhey gyalwae sungrab partun khang, 1976–1979.

MAÑJUŚRINĀMASAMGĪTI

Davidson, Ronald M. "The Litany of Names of Mañjuśrī." In *Tantric and Taoist Studies in Honour of Professor R. A. Stein*. Vol. 1. Edited by Michel Strickmann. Brussels: Institut Belge des Hautes Études Chinoises, 1981.
Mañjuśrījñānasattvaparamārthanāmasaṃgīti ('Jam dpal ye shes sems dpa'i don dam pa'i mtshen yang dag par brjod pa) To. 360; P. 2.
Mukherji, Durga Das, ed. *Ārya Mañjuśrināmasamgīti:* Sanskrit and Tibetan texts. Calcutta: Calcutta University Press, 1963.
Vira, Raghu, ed. *Mañjuśrī-Nāma-Sangīti in Mongolian, Tibetan, Sanskrit, and Chinese and Sekkodesa in Tibetan and Mongolian*. New Delhi: International Academy of Indian Culture, 1962.
Vira, Raghu, and Lokesh Candra, eds. *Kalacakra Tantra and Other Texts: Part I*. New Delhi: International Academy of Indian Culture, 1966.
Wayman, Alex, ed. and trans. *Chanting the Names Of Mañjuśrī: The Mañjusri-nama-samgiti, Sanskrit and Tibetan texts, Translated with Annotation and Introduction*. Boston and London: Shambhala, 1985.
bcom ldan 'das 'jam dpal ye shes sems dpa'i don dam pa'i mtshan yang dag par brjod pa. In *dpal ldan stag lung pa'i gsung rnams nor bzhi bang mdzod*. TBRC (http://tbrc.org/) W1PD166109. 18: 441–474. khun men: nor bzhi bstan rgyas tshogs pa/, 2007.

Manjusrinamasamgiti (http://gretil.sub.uni-goettingen.de/gretil/1_sanskr/4_rellit/buddh/manjnspu.htm), based on the edition by Janardan Shastri Pandey in *Bauddhastotrasamgraha*, Sarnath 1994, pp. 5-20.

SAPTAŚATIKĀ—PRAJÑĀPĀRAMITĀSŪTRA

Vaidya, P. L. *Mahayana-sutra-samgraha, Part I.* Buddhist Sanskrit Texts, no. 17. Durbhanga: Mithila Institute, 1961.

Saptaśatikāprajñāpāramitānāma mahāyāna sūtra (shes rab kyi pha rol du phyin pa bdun brgya pa zhes bya ba thek pa chen po'i mdo.) To. 24; Taisho. 232.

Mañjuśrīparivartāparaparyāyā Saptaśatikā prajñāpāramitā (http://gretil.sub.uni-goettingen.de/gretil/1_sanskr/4_rellit/buddh/bsu052_u.htm).

DIGITAL MATERIALS

Himalayan Art Resources (http://www.himalayanart.org)

The John C. and Susan L. Huntington Photographic Archive of Buddhist and Asian Art and Architecture (http://www.huntingtonarchive.osu.edu)

Tibetan Buddhist Resource Center Library (http://www.tbrc.org)

Online Index of Chinese Buddhism (http://www.buddhiststudies.net/oicb.html)

FURTHER READING

Birnbaum, Raoul. *Studies on the Mysteries of Mañjuśrī: A Group of East Asian Maṇḍalas and Their Traditional Symbolism.* Society for the Study of Chinese Religions Monograph 2. Boulder, CO: Society for the Study of Chinese Religions, 1983.

Burnouf, Eugène. *Introduction to the History of Indian Buddhism.* Edited by Katia Buffetrille and Donald S. Lopez Jr. Chicago: University of Chicago Press, 2010.

Cartelli, Mary Anne. "On a Five-Colored Cloud: The Songs of Mount Wutai." *The Journal of the American Oriental Society* 124, no. 4 (October 2004).

Chang, Garma C., ed. and trans. *A Treasury of Mahāyāna Sūtras: Selections from the Mahāratnakuta Sūtra.* University Park: Pennsylvania State University Press, 1983.

Davidson, Ronald. "The Litany of Names of Manjushri." In *Tantric and Taoist Studies in Honour of R. A. Stein.* Edited by Michel Strickmann, 1. Volume 1. Brussels: Institut Belge Des Hautes Etudes Chinoises, 1981.

Davidson, Ronald. "The Litany of the Names of Mañjuśrī." In *Religions of India in Practice.* Edited by Donald Lopez Jr., 104–125. Princeton, NJ: Princeton University Press, 1995.

Debreczeny, Karl. "Wutai Shan: Pilgrimage to Five-Peak Mountain." *Journal of the International Association of Tibetan Studies* 6 (December 2011): 1–133.

Delhey Martin. "The Textual Sources of the *Mañjuśriyamūlakalpa (Mañjuśrīmūlakalpa)*, with Special Reference to Its Early Nepalese Witness A39/4." *Journal of the Nepal Research Centre* 14 (2012): 55–75.

Harrington, Laura. " Mañjuśrī." In *Oxford Bibliographies* in Buddhism. http://www.oxfordbibliographies.com.

Harrington, Laura. "Probing Beneath the Surface: On Prajñā." In *In Vimalakirti's House: A Festschrift in Honor of Robert A. F. Thurman on the Occasion of his 70th Birthday.* Edited by Christian K. Wedemeyer, John D. Dunne, and Thomas F. Yarnall, 127–145. New York: American Institute of Buddhist Studies at Columbia University, 2015.

Harrison, Paul M. "Mañjuśrī and the Cult of the Celestial Bodhisattvas." *Chung-Hwa Buddhist Journal* 13.2 (2000): 157–193.
Hirakawa, Akira. "Mañjuśrī and the Rise of Mahāyāna Buddhism." *Journal of Asian Studies (Madras)* 1.1 (1983): 12–33.
Lalou, Marcelle. *Iconographie des étoffes peintes (pata) dans le Mañjuśrīmūlakalpa, dans Buddhica.* Vol. 6. Paris: Geuthner, 1930.
Lamotte, Étienne. "Mañjuśrī." *T'oung Pao* 48.1–3 (1960): 1–96.
Lamotte, Étienne. *L'Enseignement de Vimalakīrti.* Louvain, Belgium: Publications universitaires, 1962.
Long, Mark E. "An Eighth-Century Commentary on the Nāmasaṅgīti and the Cluster of Temples on the Prambanan Plain in Central Java." *Working Paper Series No. 20.* Nalanda-Srivijaya Centre: November 2015. https://iseas.edu.sg/articles-commentaries/nsc-working-papers.
Macdonald, Ariane. *Le maṇḍala du Mañjuśrīmūlakalpa.* Paris: Adrien-Maisonneuve, 1962.
Mallmann, Marie-Thérèse de. *Étude iconographique sur Mañjuśrī.* Paris: École Française d'Extrême-Orient, 1964.
Rhie, Marilyn, and Robert Thurman. *Wisdom and Compassion: The Sacred Art of Tibet.* New York: Harry N. Abrams, 1991.
Tribe, Anthony. "Part III: The Cult of Mañjuśrī." *Western Buddhist Review* 1 (1994).
Tribe, Anthony. "Mañjuśrī: Origins, Role and Significance. Parts I and II." *Western Buddhist Review* 2 (1997).
Tuttle, Gray. "Tibetan Buddhism at Ri bo rtse lnga/Wutai shan in Modern Times." *Journal of the International Association of Tibetan Studies* no. 2 (August 2006): 1–35.
Tuttle, Gray, and Johan Elverskog, eds. "Wutai Shan and Qing Culture." *Journal of the International Association of Tibetan Studies* 6 (December 2011): 1–428.
Wallis, Glen. *Mediating the Power of the Buddhas: Ritual in the Mañjuśrī-mūlakalpa.* Albany: State University of New York, 2002.
Wallis, Glen. "*Om Vakyeda Nāmah: Mañjuśrī's Mantra and its Uses.*" In *As Long as Space Endures: Essays in the Kālacakra Tantra in Honor of the H. H. the Dalai Lama.* Edited by Edward A. Arnold, 169–178. Ithaca, NY: Snow Lion Publications, 2009.
Williams, Paul. *Mahāyāna Buddhism: The Doctrinal Foundations.* New York: Routledge, 2009.

NOTES

1. Étienne Lamotte, "Mañjuśrī," *T'oung Pao* 48, nos. 1–3 (1960): 1–96; Marie-Thérèse de Mallmann, *Étude Iconographique sur Mañjuśrī* (Paris: École française de'Extrême-Orient, 1964); Anthony Tribe, "Mañjuśrī: Origins, Role and Significance, Parts I and II: The Cult of Mañjuśrī," *Western Buddhist Review* 2 (1997): n.p.
2. Paul Harrison, "Mañjuśrī and the Cult of the Celestial Bodhisattvas," *Chung-Hwa Buddhist Journal* 13, no. 2 (2000), 166.
3. Paul Harrison, "The Earliest Chinese Translations of Mahāyāna Buddhist Sūtras: Some Notes on the Works of Lokakṣema," *Buddhist Studies Review* 10, no. 2 (1993): 135–177; Paul Harrison, "Mañjuśrī and the Cult of the Celestial Bodhisattvas," *Chung-Hwa Buddhist Journal* 13, no. 2 (2000): 157–193.
4. In the United States, "decillion" is understood to be 10.33 By contrast, some Continental European and older British publications use the long-scale system for naming integer powers of ten, and represent decillion as 10.60 The absolute value of decillion is identical.
5. Translation mine. *'Phags pa ma skyes dgra'i 'gyod pa bsal ba shes bya ba theg pa chen po'i mdo; Ārya Ajātaśatrukaukṛtya-vinodanā-nama-mahāyāna sutra.* Derge 216, bka' 'gyur, mdo sde, Tsha 228b–229a. From Derge Kanjur and Tanjur, facsimile edition of the 18th-century redaction of the Situ Chos kyi 'byung gnas, Delhi, 1978. Numbers from Tohoku catalogue (Tokyo, 1934).

6. Christian Lindtner, ed., *Masters of Wisdom: Writings of the Buddhist Master Nāgārjuna* (Oakland: Dharma Publishing, 1986).
7. Étienne Lamotte, *L'Enseignement de Vimalakīrti* (Louvain, Belgium: Publications universitaires, 1962). English version by Sara Boin, *The Teaching of Vimalakirti* (London: PTS, 1976); Étienne Lamotte, "Mañjuśrī," *T'oung Pao* 48, nos. 1–3 (1960): 40ff; Leo Hurvitz, trans., *Scripture of the Lotus Blossom of the Fine Dharma* (New York: Columbia University Press, 1976); Étienne Lamotte, *Śuraṅgamasamādhi-sūtra: The Concentration of Heroic Progress*, trans. Sara Boin-Webb (Surrey: Curzon Press, 1998), 210.
8. Alternately entitled the *Mahāvaipulya Buddhāvataṃsaka Sūtra*. Thomas Cleary, trans., *The Flower Ornament Scripture: A Translation of the Avatamsaka Sutra*, 3 vols. (Boston: Shambala, 1984–1987).
9. Chen-chi Chang, *A Treasury of Mahāyāna Sūtras: Selections from the Mahāratnakūṭa Sūtra* (Delhi: Motilal Banarsidass, 1996), 176–177.
10. Also called the *Mahāprajñāpāramita-mañjuśrī-parivarta-sūtra*. English translation at http://lapislazulitexts.com/T08_0232.html.
11. Paul Debdanji, *The Art of Nālandā: Development of Buddhist Sculpture, A.D. 300–1200* (New Delhi: Munshiram Manoharlal Publisher, 1995), 10.
12. Fredrick M. Asher, *The Art of Eastern India, 300–800* (Minneapolis: University of Minnesota Press, 1980), 48.
13. The compilation of the MMK probably spanned the 7th to 12th centuries. Martin Delhey notes the prevalence of the unusual stem form *mañjuśrīya* in Sanskrit and Nepalese manuscripts, and argues for *Mañjuśrīyamūlakalpa* as the more likely original title. See Martin Delhey, "The Textual Sources of the *Mañjuśriyamūlakalpa (Mañjuśrīmūlakalpa)*, with Special Reference to its Early Nepalese Witness A39/4," *Journal of the Nepal Research Centre* 14 (2012): 70–71.
14. Glen Wallis, "*Om Vakyeda Nāmah:Mañjuśrī's Mantra and its Uses*," in *As Long as Space Endures: Essays in the Kālacakra Tantra in Honor of the H. H. the Dalai Lama*, ed. Edward A. Arnold (Ithaca, NY: Snow Lion Publications, 2009), 170.
15. Ariane Macdonald, *Le maṇḍala du Mañjuśrīmūlakalpa* (Paris: Adrien-Maisonneuve, 1962), 25; Rob Linrothe, *Ruthless Compassion: Wrathful Deities in Early Indo-Tibetan Esoteric Buddhist Art* (London: Serindia Publications, 1999), 26–27.
16. Ronald Davidson, "The Litany of the Names of Mañjuśrī," in *Religions of India in Practice*, ed. Ronald Davidson and Donald Lopez (Princeton, NJ: Princeton University Press, 1995), 104–125; "The Litany of Names of Mañjuśrī: Text and Translation of the *Mañjuśrīnāmasaṃgīti*," *Tantric and Taoist Studies in Honour of R.A. Stein* 1 (1981): 1–69.
17. Mary Anne Cartelli, "On a Five-Colored Cloud: The Songs of Mount Wutai," *The Journal of the American Oriental Society* (October 2004): 39.
18. Raoul Birnbaum, "The Manifestation of a Monastery: Shen-ying's Experiences on Mount Wu-t'ai in T'ang Context," *Journal of the American Oriental Society* 106, no. 1 (1986): 123.
19. This passage would be of especial importance to the Japanese Buddhist monk Eison, who encouraged the view that alms to the poor could be understood as offerings to Mañjuśrī himself. See Robert H. Sharf and Elizabeth Horton Sharf, eds., *Living Images: Japanese Buddhist Icons in Context* (Stanford, CA: Stanford University Press, 2002), 135.
20. Raoul Birnbaum, *Studies on the Mysteries of Mañjuśrī: A Group of East Asian Mandalas and Their Traditional Symbolism* (Boulder, CO: Society for the Study of Chinese Religions, 1983), 11.
21. Richard D. McBride, "Popular Esoteric Deities and the Spread of the Cults," in *Esoteric Buddhism and Tantras in East Asia*, ed. Charles D. Orzech, Henrik H. Sorenson, and Richard K. Payne (Leiden and Boston: Brill, 2010), 215–219; Karl Debreczeny, "Wutai Shan: Pilgrimage to Five-Peak Mountain," *Journal of the International Association of Tibetan Studies* 6 (December 2011): 6–7.
22. The *'phags pa glang ru lung bstan; ārya gośriṅgavyākaraṇa nāma mahāyāna sūtra*. Derge #0357, mdo sde, a: 220b6–232a7. Discussion and English translation in F. W. Thomas, *Tibetan Literary Texts and*

Documents Concerning Chinese Turkestan—Part I: Literary Texts, Oriental Translation Fund, New Series, vol. 32 (London: Royal Asiatic Society, 1935), 3–38.

23. Ronald E. Emmerick, *Tibetan Texts Concerning Khotan* (London and New York: Oxford University Press, 1967); John Brough, "Legends of Khotan and Nepal," *The Bulletin of the School of Oriental and African Studies* 12 (1948): 333–339.
24. Karl Debreczeny, "Wutai Shan: Pilgrimage to Five-Peak Mountain," *Journal of the International Association of Tibetan Studies* 6 (December 2011): 8–10.
25. Debreczeny, "Wutai Shan: Pilgrimage to Five-Peak Mountain," 16–18, 30–31; Johan Elverskog, "Wutai Shan, Qing Cosmopolitanism, and the Mongols," *Journal of the International Association of Tibetan Studies* 6 (December 2011): 248–249.
26. Isabelle Charleux, *Nomads on Pilgrimage: Mongols on Wutaishan (China), 1800–1940* (Leiden and Boston: Brill, 2015), 158–159.
27. Karl Debreczeny, "Wutai Shan: Pilgrimage to Five-Peak Mountain," *Journal of the International Association of Tibetan Studies* 6 (December 2011): 30–31.
28. Patricia Berger, "Preserving the Nation: The Political Uses of Tantric Art in China," in *Latter Days of the Law: Images of Chinese Buddhism, 850–1850*, ed. Marsha Weidner (Lawrence: Spencer Museum of Art, University of Kansas; Honolulu: University of Hawaii Press, 1994).
29. Isabelle Charleux, "Mongol Pilgrimages to Wutai Shan in the Late Qing Dynasty," *Journal of the International Association of Tibetan Studies* 6 (December 2011): 276–277.
30. Kurtis R. Schaeffer, "Tibetan Poetry on Wutai Shan," *Journal of the International Association of Tibetan Studies* 6 (December 2011): 222–224.
31. David Germano, "Re-membering the Dismembered Body of Tibet: Contemporary Tibetan Visionary Movements in the People's Republic of China," in *Buddhism in Contemporary Tibet: Religious Revival and Cultural Identity*, ed. Melvyn Goldstein and Matthew Kapstein (Berkeley: University of California Press, 1998), 53–94; Wen-Shing Lucia Chou, "The Visionary Landscape of Wutai Shan in Tibetan Buddhism from the Eighteenth to the Twentieth Century," unpublished dissertation (Berkeley: University of California at Berkeley, 2011), 120–142. See also Antonio Terrone, "Tibetan Buddhism beyond the Monastery: Revelation and Identity in rNying ma Communities of Present-day Kham," *Images of Tibet in the 19th and 20th Centuries*, Etudes thématiques 22, vol. 2 (Paris: École française d'Extrême-Orient, 2008), 747–779; Antonio Terrone, "Visions, Arcane Claims, and Treasures: Charisma and Authority in a Present-day Treasure Finder," in *Tibet, Self, and the Tibetan Diaspora: Voices of Difference*, ed. Christiaan Klieger (Proceedings of the Ninth Seminar of the IATS, Leiden, The Netherlands: Brill, 2002): 213–228.
32. Eugène Burnouf, *Introduction to the History of Indian Buddhism*, ed. Katia Buffetrille and Donald S. Lopez Jr. (Chicago: University of Chicago Press, 2010), 148.
33. Har Dayal, *The Bodhisattva Doctrine in Buddhist Sanskrit Literature* (New Delhi: Motilal Banarsidass, 1932/1970), 36.
34. Étienne Lamotte, "Mañjuśrī," *T'oung Pao* 48, no. 1–3 (1960), 1–96; Marie-Thérèse de Mallmann, *Étude Iconographique sur Mañjuśrī* (Paris: École française de'Extrême-Orient, 1964); Paul Harrison, "The Earliest Chinese Translations of Mahāyāna Buddhist Sūtras: Some Notes on the Works of Lokakṣema," *Buddhist Studies Review* 10, no. 2 (1993): 135–177; Paul M. Harrison, "Mañjuśrī and the Cult of the Celestial Bodhisattvas," *Chung-Hwa Buddhist Journal* 13, no. 2 (2000): 157–193; Raoul Birnbaum, *Studies on the Mysteries of Mañjuśrī: A Group of East Asian Mandalas and their Traditional Symbolism* (Boulder, CO: Society for the Study of Chinese Religions, 1983); Ronald M. Davidson, "The Litany of Names of Mañjuśrī: Text and Translation of the *Mañjuśrīnāmasaṃgīti*," *Tantric and Taoist Studies in Honour of R. A. Stein* 1 (1981): 1–69; Ariane Macdonald, *Le maṇḍala du Mañjuśrīmūlakalpa* (Paris: Adrien-Maisonneuve, 1962); Glen Wallis, *Mediating the Power of the Buddhas: Ritual in the Mañjuśrī-mūlakalpa* (Albany: State University of New York, 2002).

35. Cartelli, Mary Anne. "On a Five-Colored Cloud: The Songs of Mount Wutai," *Journal of the American Oriental Society* 124., no. 4 (2004): 735–757; Richard D. McBride, "Popular Esoteric Deities and the Spread of the Cults," in *Esoteric Buddhism and Tantras in East Asia*, ed. Charles D. Orzech, Henrik H. Sorenson, and Richard K. Payne (Leiden and Boston: Brill, 2010), 215–219; Gray Tuttle and Johan Elverskog, eds., "Wutai Shan and Qing Culture," *Journal of the International Association of Tibetan Studies* 6 (December 2011): 1–428.
36. David Germano, "Re-membering the Dismembered Body of Tibet: Contemporary Tibetan Visionary Movements in the People's Republic of China," in *Buddhism in Contemporary Tibet: Religious Revival and Cultural Identity*, ed. Melvyn Goldstein and Matthew Kapstein (Berkeley: University of California Press, 1998), 53–94; Wen-Shing Lucia Chou, *The Visionary Landscape of Wutai Shan in Tibetan Buddhism from the Eighteenth to the Twentieth Century*, unpublished dissertation (Berkeley: University of California Press, 2011), 120–142. See also Antonio Terrone, "Tibetan Buddhism beyond the Monastery: Revelation and Identity in rNying ma Communities of Present-day Kham," *Images of Tibet in the 19th and 20th Centuries*, Études thématiques 22, vol. 2 (Paris: École française d'Extrême-Orient, 2008), 747–779; "Visions, Arcane Claims, and Treasures: Charisma and Authority in a Present-day Treasure Finder," in *Tibet, Self, and the Tibetan Diaspora: Voices of Difference*, ed. Christiaan Klieger (Leiden, The Netherlands: Brill, 2002), 213–228.

Laura Harrington

MARITIME BUDDHISM

MARITIME HISTORY AND NETWORKS OF INTRA-ASIAN BUDDHIST TRANSMISSION

A new wave of scholarship on maritime history, Indian Ocean studies, and global history has revealed how the mainstream historical discourse has tended to focus on predominantly land-based national trajectories and has adopted a wider, maritime-focused geographical approach. The maritime-focused approach helps make sense of complex circulatory phenomena that do not fit neatly within the boundaries of nation-states, let alone geographical areas divided according to the artificial boundaries drawn by the post–World War II Area studies paradigm. Applying this perspective to Buddhist studies, one can make an argument for the important and constitutive role played by the sea and the Southern Asian littoral and insular regions in the genesis and circulation of Buddhism across the sociospatial grouping or world region of Maritime Asia. This geographically wide perspective emphasizes the maritime interactions that occurred across geographical and cultural boundaries in the region composed of a web of coastal and inland polities connected to each other through a network of cosmopolitan ports and entrepôts from the Bay of Bengal to the South and East China Seas in the course of several centuries. In so doing, it advances an alternative, and complementary, historical narrative that takes the "southern pathways," that is, the sea-based networks, into due consideration, thereby revealing the limits of a historiography that is uniquely premised on land-based, "northern pathways" of transmission of Buddhism across the Eurasian landmass.

Making a case for a multicentric circulation of Buddhism rather than a monodirectional transmission from a South Asian "homeland" to Southeast and East Asian "peripheries," recent scholarship has unveiled the multidirectional connections that exist between Buddhist

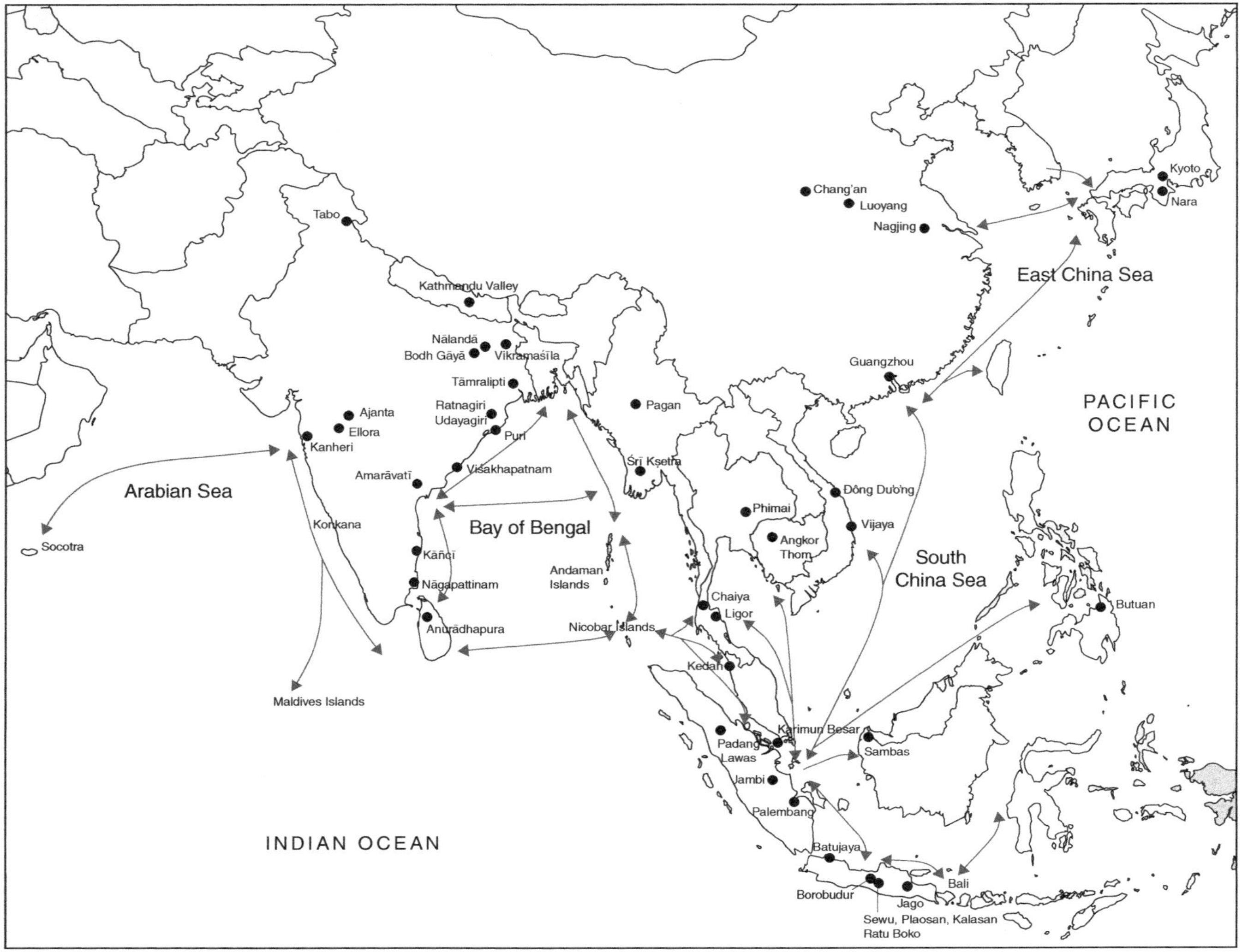

Figure 1. Buddhist sites and nodes across Maritime Asia, 500–1300 CE.
Source: Courtesy of Andrea Acri.

centers, tied to each other by overlapping networks of relations that were religious as much as economic, diplomatic, and political in nature.[1] Therefore, to understand the establishment (and disruption) of complex networks, and to better grasp such a multifaceted, transregional phenomenon as the patterns of Buddhist transmission across Maritime Asia (see Figure 1), which was shaped by sociopolitical, economic, and perhaps even environmental factors, one may try to apply, as Jason Neelis did with respect to South, Central, and East Asia, a "networks approach" or "networks model."[2] This approach individuates the nodes, conduits, and hubs that facilitated the dynamic processes of exchange, thus going beyond the metaphors of cultural "influences" that have so far characterized the scholarly discourse.

Undeniably, the overland and maritime "Silk Roads" were interlinked and complementary, forming what has been called a "great circle of Buddhism."[3] At the same time, the combined archaeological and textual evidence increasingly points to a predominant role of the maritime Silk Roads in facilitating the mobility of Buddhist agents, artifacts, texts, and ideas over long distances from the early centuries of the first millennium CE—if not earlier, as testified to by the presence of Sri Lankan and Southeast Asian toponyms in the *Mahāniddesa* and some Jātakas dating to the late third–first centuries BCE. Sea travel was the fastest, most economical, and safest way to move people and goods in the ancient world. By the 2nd century CE, the seasonal monsoon winds were fully exploited by maritime traders plying the routes connecting the ports in the Mediterranean Sea with those along the coastal and insular areas of South, Southeast, and East Asia. The sea was a connecting factor in Asian history since time immemorial.[4] Cutting across the natural boundaries and barriers of continental topography, sea-based routes formed a network of conduits that led to the formation of a medieval global Buddhist Asia. By the middle of the 7th century CE, factors such as a radical expansion of commercial maritime routes connecting South with East Asia, as well as the gradual decline of Buddhism and Buddhist exchanges in Central Asia following the Muslim conquest of Transoxiana and other sociopolitical contingencies, contributed significantly to the sea-based exchange not only of mercantile goods, but also of Buddhist beliefs and ritual practices. Unlike the Central Asian networks, the interlocking maritime networks of Buddhism survived well past the 13th century into the 19th century—for instance, the Bay of Bengal circuit linking Sri Lanka to Myanmar and Thailand, and the China Sea circuit linking China to Southeast Asia, Korea, and Japan.[5]

BUDDHISM AND MARITIME TRADE

Monks, Traders, and Kings. Traditionally, emphasis has been laid on traders and merchant guilds as the original propagators of Buddhism from its early stage and as the main agents of disseminating Maritime Buddhism across Asia.[6] Early Buddhist literature is permeated by an imaginary, highlighting the important role of seafaring in the expansion of the dharma overseas: witness the many Jātakas—such as the *Saṅkha, Suparaga,* and *Mahājānaka Jātakas,* among many others—containing references to merchants engaged in sea travel between port cities in India, Sri Lanka, and Southeast Asia.[7] Buddhist narratives of sea travel across the Bay of Bengal find a match in the available historical evidence. As suggested by the existence of monasteries near major commercial nodes and trading routes, the establishment of trade networks may have facilitated the spread of Buddhism as well as ensured its support by merchant communities. Buddhist sites in the Western Deccan, the Konkan coast, Andhra Pradesh, Odisha, and Tamil Nadu were strategically located in the vicinity of ports along the trade routes connecting the mainland to Sri Lanka and further afield to Southeast Asia. Buddhist vestiges, however scant, have been found in such remote insular locations as the Maldives Islands in the Indian Ocean and Socotra in the western Arabian Sea.[8] The widespread presence of maritime scenes of navigation and shipwreck—depicting sea travel in its political, spiritual, and economic ramifications—in sites located on/near the coast or along trading routes in South Asia, Sri Lanka, and Southeast Asia suggests that those scenes, rather than being purely symbolic and metaphysical representations of spiritual dangers, were linked to an actual imaginary.[9] This, in turn, testifies to the increasing popularity of maritime travel in Buddhist communities from the 6th century onward. The concurrent development in the same locales of "Savior Cults" focusing on the bodhisattvas Avalokiteśvara, Tārā (especially in her aspect of *aṣṭamahābhaya* or Protectress from the Eight Great Perils), and Mahāpratisarā as protectors of travelers (especially of sailors) against the perils encountered along their journeys may be due to the increasing number of merchants and monks plying the commercial routes.[10]

The vehicles of the monks' sea passages were the merchant ships that plied the maritime routes connecting the Indian Ocean to the China Sea alongside their valuable cargos. These ships also carried pilgrims, diplomats, and, indeed, religious personalities of disparate affiliations. The relationship between itinerant monks and seafaring traders may have been in many respects mutual: the monks provided (spi)ritual services to the lay community, whereas the traders ensured the sea passages of monks and their accoutrements, either directly or through donations or other forms of patronage. There is also evidence, however, of antagonistic encounters between Buddhist monks and merchants of various ethnicities and religious allegiances.[11] Furthermore, while lay householders active in trade, crafts, and warfare decidedly played a role in patronizing and spreading Buddhism through pilgrimage, travel, or migration, the success of Buddhism overseas has been too often simplistically perceived as the unique result of economic and social forces connected to a mercantile class-ideology, characterized by an inherent dynamism and opposed to a "static" Brahmanism. In fact, itinerant Buddhist monks likely circulated along the same networks that were already plied by their Brahmanical competitors, who contributed to the spread of Hindu traditions, Sanskrit language, and other Indic cultural elements to Southeast Asia since the beginning of the Common Era. It is also a fact that many of the most prominent Buddhist monks and intellectuals from the 5th century onward were themselves (ex-)Brahmins. Some biographies tended to suspiciously attribute a Brahmanical pedigree to high-ranking monks traveling to China, thereby suggesting that their descent from a merchant milieu would be undignified.[12]

The presence of Buddhist traders in a given area did not necessarily lead to the adoption of Buddhism. The biographies of itinerant monks such as Guṇavarman, Vajrabuddhi/Vajrabodhi, and Amoghavajra make it clear that royal sponsorship was essential for the religion to gain a firm foothold in the regions they visited. According to Ronald Davidson, an important factor in the rise and quick spread of esoteric (or tantric) fashions of Buddhism across Asia from the 7th century was the loss of mercantile support due to the dominance of Persian/Muslim traders on the Indian Ocean network, and the concomitant escalation in royal patronage.[13] This was made possible through the intimate relationship between ritual specialists and the political elites who, lured by the promise of invincibility, protection for the state, and superhuman powers, often employed tantric monks as "royal chaplains." In this way, they were following the pattern that already existed between Brahmanical ritualists and the courts they served. Davidson's "royal" model has been questioned by Hiram Woodward, who denies the incompatibility between mercantile and royal values, and envisages an integration of the "mercantile" and "royal" paradigms.[14] Significantly, many of the powerful dynasties that were instrumental in the sponsorship and spread of Mahāyāna and Mantranaya Buddhism ruled over domains located along the nodes of commercial and diplomatic maritime networks. Examples are the Pālas in Northeastern India, the Bhauma-Karas in Odisha, the Early Second Lambakaṇṇas in Sri Lanka, the Śailendras in Sumatra and Java, and the Tangs in China. In some cases, the maritime passages of monks were directly sponsored by kings and doubled as diplomatic missions, involving large travel parties and including dignitaries and military exponents.

Maritime Mobility. On the basis of information provided by Pliny and Faxian, the journey by merchant ship from the port city of Tāmralipti in present-day West Bengal to Sri Lanka (en route to Southeast Asia and China) would have taken only a fortnight.[15] Yijing states that his own journey from Canton to Sumatra took a month, while the remaining leg from Kedah in Peninsular Malaysia to the Nicobar Islands took ten days, and from there to Tāmralipti took fifteen days.[16] But according to other sources, because of the prevailing direction of monsoon winds, making a return voyage between China and the Indian subcontinent in one year was nearly impossible.[17]

Be that as it may, it has now become increasingly evident that the maritime mobility of Buddhist agents was quicker and easier than hitherto assumed. A case in point is the episode of the establishment of the female Buddhist order (*bhikṣunīsaṅgha*) in China. This endeavor was started by the Kashmirian monk Guṇavarman, who, however, failed to do so due to the insufficient number of senior nuns; only three of them reached China from Sri Lanka in 429 CE. After his death in 431 CE, he was succeeded by Saṅghavarman, who managed to complete this task by requesting more nuns from Sri Lanka. These eventually reached China in 438 CE on the ship of a non-Chinese merchant called Nandin (*Zhu Nanti*)—the same individual who had brought Guṇavarman to Sri Lanka and China and who is credited with translating some Sanskrit Mahāyāna scriptures into Chinese.[18] The two-way traffic between such faraway localities as Sri Lanka and China within the span of a decade suggests that Buddhist communication via the maritime routes as early as the first half of the 5th century is remarkable. It is hardly surprising, however, given the existence of 4th–6th-century Chinese records of sustained diplomatic relations and circulation of relics between the mainland and Sri Lankan and Southeast Asian localities.[19] By the 8th century, sea travel seems to have become an even easier undertaking, as suggested by the fact that the Central Asian monk Amoghavajra was even able to send back a Sanskrit text from China to his old master Ratnabuddhi in Sri Lanka after translating it.[20] In addition, several monks are known to have made it back to their places of origin. For example, the Indian Parāmiti, reached Canton by 705 and went back to his homeland by boat.[21] The Korean monk Hyecho (fl. 8th century, Amoghavajra's disciple), traveled to India twice within his lifespan—at least once, it seems, via the maritime route.[22]

Buddhist Narratives of Maritime Crossings. The Sino-Japanese and Tibetan biographies of the monks traveling from China to India and/or vice versa makes clear that travel across the maritime trading channels linking the two regions was not devoid of perils. Besides imagined entities such as marine monsters, Nāgas, and other supernatural beings, the most feared hindrances in the mind of the travelers were storms, unfavorable winds, pirates, and unskilled or unscrupulous crews.

The biographers of the Indian monk Prajña report that his sea journey to Guangzhou in China, where he arrived in 781 CE, was marred by multiple setbacks, taking in all about twenty years.[23] Another Indian monk, Maṇicintana, randomly escaped death during a storm on his way to China, while the Chinese monk Jianzhen/Ganjin (鑒真/鑑真, 688–763) allegedly attempted the dangerous crossing of the sea that separated China from Japan six times before finally making it in 754.[24]

Faxian (337/342–*c.* 422), who traveled from China to India, presents an account of his maritime journey that is striking not only for being the earliest, but also for providing rare details about his momentous voyage on a large, 200-passenger-strong merchant ship that he describes as trailing a little "emergency" boat.[25] Having encountered a storm between Sri Lanka and Sumatra, and fearing that the merchants would throw his precious Sanskrit texts overboard, he prayed to the bodhisattva Guanshyin/Avalokiteśvara. During the second leg of his journey, on a similar ship plying the route from Java to China, Faxian encountered a storm, and were it not for his patron and the monk's prayer to Guanshyin, the Brahmins, thinking that the monk was the origin of their misfortunes, would have thrown him overboard.[26]

Faxian's misfortunes are echoed in the biography of Vajrabuddhi by Lü Xiang, where it is recounted that the monk, when Vajrabuddhi was twenty days short of reaching the Chinese coast from Southeast Asia, escaped shipwreck (but lost the full version of the Sanskrit *Vajraśekhara*, thrown overboard by the captain) during a storm because he recited the *Mahāpratisarā-dhāraṇī* (*Suiqiu* 隨求), a spell manifesting the homonymous female deity.[27] A similar circumstance is associated with Vajrabuddhi's disciple Amoghavajra when he was traveling on a Southeast Asian ship (*Kunlun bo* 崑崙舶) from China to Sri Lanka in 741 CE.[28] Both Vajrabuddhi's and Amoghavajra's accounts are very similar to those expounded in the fifth narrative in the central and longest text in the Mahāpratisarā-corpus, the Sanskrit *Mahāpratisarāvidyārājñī*. In this narrative, the merchant Vimalaśaṅkha saves his ship from a storm, lightning, and meteors sent by Nāgas.[29] While the circumstances narrated in the account may reflect standard tropes in Buddhist hagiographical literature, the textual accounts speak in favor of the popularity of this *dhāraṇī* and its deity among Buddhist travellers—monks and traders alike—and match the material evidence on the propagation of the Mahāpratisarā cult across the Buddhist world.

Indeed, the *Taisho* canon informs us that in 758 Amoghavajra actually submitted a copy of this spell to Emperor Suzong (*T* 2120.829b2–21). Various textual and iconographical attestations of Mahāpratisarā are documented in Java, especially from the 8th to the 10th century, as well as in Bali, Sumatra, and Mindanao in the Philippines.[30] A gold foil recovered from the c. 10th-century Cirebon shipwreck off the Java north coast, containing a *dhāraṇī* addressed to a goddess personifying the spell, and paralleling material found in the *Ekādaśamukhadhāraṇī* and *Sādhanamālā*, confirms that passengers and/or crews actually wore this type of object as amulets intended to protect them against the dangers of voyage at sea.[31]

Imaginary and supernatural elements became predominant in the biography of the 11th-century Atiśa, who left the subcontinent for some years to study in Sumatra with the Buddhist master Dharmakīrti. He joined a group of merchants (curiously, and perhaps tellingly, originating from landlocked, mountainous Nepal) sailing to the Golden Island in search of precious stones. He encounters difficulties during his voyage across the Indian Ocean, namely, a storm supernaturally caused by the Hindu god Śiva, who tries to stop him from leaving India. To defeat Śiva and his consort, Atiśa and his disciple Kṣitigarbha manifest themselves as the wrathful tantric deities Raktayamāri and Acala, respectively; Acala launches a strike against the enemies of Buddhism: Śaivas, Muslims, and Tibetan Bon practitioners.[32] This narrative tells us a lot about the state of Buddhism in India at that time, reflecting as it does the anxieties of coeval Buddhist circles.

The Networks of Seafaring Monks in Maritime Asia. Historical evidence going back to at least the 3rd century CE provides us with a picture of the steady traffic of itinerant monks traveling both eastward and westward along the sea paths linking the swathe of territory comprised within the Indian subcontinent and Japan in search of texts, teachers, and patrons. It would seem that most of the monks who traveled both ways between India and China preferred the maritime to the overland route, or at least sought to include a maritime leg in their journey. No fewer than twenty-five monks are recorded to have arrived in China in such a way between 420 and 479 CE.[33] Seventh-century monk Yijing stated that a significant number of the Chinese and Korean monks who went to India and Southeast Asia by his time traveled by sea on merchant ships.[34] A conservative scholarly estimate records that out of the total number of 103 monks, 66 individuals were involved in the maritime transmission of Buddhism to China.[35]

While the names and life circumstances of most of those anonymous agents are bound to remain unknown, Sino-Japanese biographies allow us to reconstruct the pedigree and social circle of some prominent monks who have gone down in history as vigorous translators (e.g., of Sanskrit scriptures into Chinese), commentators, authors of original texts, initiators of lineages, and thaumaturges. According to Chinese sources,[36] the first monk to travel from India to China via the maritime route was the Sogdian Kang Senghui (康僧會), who arrived in Nanjing in 247 CE. Other South Asian monks who arrived in China in the 3rd century included Jīvaka (? Qiyu 耆域) and Kumāra (? Jiamoluo 迦摩羅). Many more monks are recorded to have arrived in Nanjing and/or Guangzhou from South and Central Asia via Sri Lanka and Southeast Asia from the 4th to the 6th century. These were Faxian (337/342–c. 422), who in traveling from China to India lost three companions along the way, and who came back by ship via Sumatra and Java. Other travelers included Dharmayaśas (? Tanmoyeshe 曇摩 耶舍) from Northwestern India, who arrived in China in 401 and was active in Guangzhou; Buddhajīva (? Fotuoshi 佛陀什, fl. 5th century) and Guṇavarman (? Qiunabamo 求那跋摩, 367–431), both from Kashmir (the latter was ordained and studied in Sri Lanka, and converted to Buddhism the royals of Java); Saṅghavarman (fl. 5th century), from Sri Lanka; Guṇabhadra (? Qiunabatuoluo 求那跋陀羅, 394–468), from Māgadha; Paramārtha (Zhendi 真諦, 499–569 CE), from Ujjain in Central India; and Bodhidharma (? Putidamo 菩提 達摩, fl. 6th century) from either South India or Central Asia; Saṅghapāla (Sengqieboluo 僧伽婆羅, 460–524) and Mandra(sena) (Mantuoluo[xian] 曼陀羅[仙], 502–519), both from Funan in mainland Southeast Asia, who reached Nanjing between the late-5th and early-6th century.

From the 7th century, a remarkably mobile, multiethnic, and cosmopolitan network of monks is associated with the propagation of the first wave of Mahāyāna Buddhist tantra (Mantranaya) via the maritime routes. Among the most prominent individuals are the Central Indian Atikūṭa (Adiquduo 阿地瞿多, fl. 650s) and Puṇyodaya (Nati 那提, fl. 650s); the Chinese Yijing (義淨, 635–713), who traveled extensively to India via Southeast Asia; the Indian Maṇicintana/Maṇicinta or Ratnacinta (Baosiwei 寶思惟, d. 721) and the South Indian Dharmaruci/Bodhiruci (Damoliuzhi 達摩流/Putiliuzhi 菩提流支, d. 727); Vajrabodhi (Jingangzhi 金剛智, 671–741) from South or Central India, and Vajrabuddhi's ordained pupil Amoghavajra (Bukong 不空, 704–774; probably a native of Samarkand); the South Indian Bodhisena (Putixianna 菩提僊那, 704–760), who traveled to China and Japan via Mainland Southeast Asia; Nāgabodhi/Nāgabuddhi (Longzhi 龍智), whose biography remains obscure but who is believed to have met Amoghavajra in Sri Lanka in the 740s, and previously Vajrabodhi; Huiguo's Javanese disciple Bianhong (辨弘, fl. late 8th century); Prajña (Boruo 般若/Bolaruo 般剌若, *c.* 744–810, from either present-day Afghanistan or South India), disciple of Amoghavajra's prominent pupil Yuanzhao (d. 800); the Chinese Jianzhen; the Japanese Kūkai (空海, 774–835); and the Korean Hyecho (慧超, fl. 8th century), disciple of Śubhakarasiṁha and then both Vajrabodhi and Amoghavajra, respectively. The networks of 7th- to 9th-century itinerant monks offer a telling picture of the extraordinary period of intra-Asian maritime connectivity that became the hallmark of the rise and spread of Esoteric Buddhist traditions in the course of just two or three generations.[37]

Sociopolitical and economic contingencies from the middle of the 9th to the end of the 10th century caused the decline and "provincialization" of Buddhism in China, as well as a reduced scale of Buddhist building activities in Southeast Asia. As a result of these dynamics, the Buddhist traffic between India and China decreased beginning in the 9th century, although smaller regional interlocking networks remained active. Sea-based transmission of Buddhism between South and Southeast Asia was sustained in the following centuries through the monks and other (possibly nonmonastic, semi-institutionalized) agents who must remain anonymous owing to the paucity of Chinese records for that period. Notable exceptions are the famous master Atiśa (aka Dīpaṅkaraśrījñāna, 980–1054), who traveled from northeastern India to the "Golden Isles" (Suvarṇadvīpa, i.e., either Sumatra or the Malay Peninsula) and stayed there for twelve years to study with Dharmakīrti from Suvarṇadvīpa, one of the five most prominent Buddhist intellectuals of his time; the (Indian?) Kīrtipaṇḍita, an adept of the Buddhist Yogatantras who was active in the Khmer domains during the reign of Jayavarman V (r. 968–*c.* 1000) in the capacity of royal guru, teaching the *Tattvasaṅgraha* and its commentary; and the *Guhasamāja* exegete Vāgīśvarakīrti, who flourished in eastern India in the early 11th century and may have been active in the Khmer domains shortly thereafter, as suggested by a verse in the Sab Bāk inscription of 1067 CE (K. 1158).[38] Almost five centuries later, the 16th-century Indian Buddhist Siddha Buddhaguptanātha is recorded by his student, the Tibetan chronicler Tāranātha, to have traveled extensively by sea from the Konkan coast to Sri Lanka, Southeast Asia (i.e., Java and Sumatra), and back to visit Buddhist vestiges and communities.[39]

In spite of the lack of biographic records, the continuation or (re)establishment of long-distance contacts across the Indian ocean from the 11th to the 13th centuries is suggested by certain notable facts: the royal-sponsored endowments sent by sea from Myanmar to Bodh Gaya, the (re)appearance of Nālandā-style imagery of Buddhist divinities in Angkor, Pagan, the Malay Peninsula, and East Java, as well as the election (arguably through initiation) of transgressive and martial forms of "Phase III" tantric Buddhism as a personal and official cult by important royal figures such as Jayavarman VII in Cambodia (r. *c.* 1181–1220), Kṛtanagara in East Java (r. 1268–92), Kublai Khan in China (r. 1260–94), and Ādityavarman in Java and Sumatra (r. ?–1375).[40] The rise of these new networks of tantric Buddhism may have been triggered by unfavorable international political developments, most notably the decline of Buddhism in northern India at the turn of the 12th and 13th centuries. Nālandā, Vikramaśīla, and Uddaṇḍapura having been razed, scholars and artisans fled to Nepal and Tibet, and possibly further afield to Southeast Asia.[41] According to Tāranātha, most of the Buddhist scholars of central north and eastern India (*madhyadeśa*) fled to mainland Southeast Asia (i.e., the kingdoms of Pegu, Campā, Kamboja, etc.) after Magadha was invaded by the Turks.[42] A northeastern Indian and/or Nepalese (Newar) influence on the Khmer architecture as well as East Javanese (and Sumatran) Buddhist art and inscriptions of that period has been noted.[43] The fact that these artisans became popular at the courts of both Kublai Khan and his sworn adversary Kṛtanagara in East Java may be indicative of maritime contacts between the two areas.[44]

From the 11th to the 16th century, the Bay of Bengal trade and diplomatic networks that connected Sri Lanka with Southeast Asia became more vigorous. This gave rise to the ascendance of the influence of Pali Buddhism on western and central mainland Southeast Asia. A new corpus of Buddhist chronicles composed between the 15th and the early 20th centuries in Thailand, Myanmar, and northern Malaysia portray the period of 1000 to 1500 as a time of intensifying contacts with Sri Lanka in the sphere of Buddhist monastic and institutional life. They show that Sri Lanka strengthened its pivotal position as a center of Theravāda monasticism and a prime repository of Buddhist relics.[45] According to the Sinhalese chronicle *Cūlavaṃsa*, King Candrabhānu (d.u.) from Southeast Asia attacked Sri Lanka in 1247 and 1262 to obtain Buddhist relics. The same interest could have been the main reason for Kublai Khan's (1215–1294) missions to Sri Lanka in 1284 and to southern India in 1272 and 1275.[46] A diaspora of Buddhist monks to Myanmar followed Sri Lanka's invasion by the Cōḻas in the 11th century, while the inverse phenomenon took place after King Vijayabāhu I (r. 1055–1110) liberated the island, whereby the exiled monks from Sri Lanka and Myanmar helped restore Buddhism in Sri Lanka.[47] Buddhist exchanges continued thereafter, from the 12th to the 16th centuries, when Sri Lankan rulers actively sent Buddhist monks, relics, and texts to Myanmar, Thailand, and Cambodia, and in their turn received monastic and diplomatic missions from Myanmar.[48] Sri Lanka maintained a leading role in the formation and transmission of "reformed" Buddhism during the colonial period until the 19th and 20th centuries. For example, the Singhalese "revivalist" monk Anagarika Dharmapāla (1864–1933) journeyed to India, Japan, China, and the United States through the maritime routes.[49]

Long-distance Buddhist interactions between India and China had significantly decreased by the 13th century and virtually ended in the mid-15th century following the Ming ban on Chinese merchants from sailing to foreign ports. The concomitant increase of Chinese diasporic communities in Southeast Asia facilitated the transmission of Buddhist ideas, including the cult of Guanyin, through maritime networks across the South China Sea.[50] In the late 19th and early 20th centuries, maritime Buddhist exchanges were restored following a Chinese diaspora to India (especially Kolkata) and Southeast Asia, most notably due to the missionary activities of the Chinese monk Taixu (太虛, 1890–1947) and his disciples.[51]

TRANS-ASIAN MARITIME NETWORKS AND THE CONSTITUTION OF SANSKRITIC BUDDHISM(S), 5TH–14TH CENTURIES

A maritime approach capitalizing on recent archaeological and epigraphic discoveries, as well as a more comprehensive reading of textual evidence from various cultural areas and historical periods, could rectify certain misconceptions. For instance, it could challenge the received idea that the southern regions of India and maritime Southeast Asia had a marginal role in the Buddhist Cosmopolis, combined with an overemphasis on the dominance of Theravāda/Pali Buddhism in Sri Lanka and mainland Southeast Asia. It could also contribute to reevaluate the importance of the western coast of India for the transmission of forms of Mahāyāna and Mantranaya Buddhism to Southeast Asia and beyond via the maritime routes. Western India, Sri Lanka, and Southeast Asia hosted important (and even predominant) Sanskritic Buddhist traditions. They also played a constitutive role in the genesis and transmission of both nascent and consolidated forms of Mahāyāna and Mantranaya Buddhism across Maritime Asia from the 5th to the 14th century. These regions constituted not only stopovers and entrepôts for traders and voyagers, but also termini in their own right. They were visited by monks and laymen alike to collect texts, relics, and icons, visit pilgrimage sites, acquire knowledge in institutionalized centers of higher learning or renowned individual masters, and receive patronage.

Western India. Buddhist architectural vestiges in the Western Deccan go back to the first century CE, and by the 6th–7th century Buddhist caves such as Ellorā, Aurangabad, and Kānherī flourish thank to the booming trade routes connecting them to the seaports of Sopara, Kalyan, and Baruch, as well as the mainland trade centre of Ujjain.[52] Those rock-cut monasteries and caves are regarded as important sites for the development of Mahāyāna and early esoteric Buddhism. Iconographic motifs that will become widespread across Maritime Asia, such as (esoteric fashions of) Tārā, Avalokiteśvara, and the Eight Great Bodhisattvas, are attested there by the late 6th–early 7th century.[53] An early and seminal Buddhist Tantra such as the *Vairocanābhisaṃbodhi* may have been composed around that time in that region.[54] The illustrated Nepalese manuscript of the *Aṣṭasāhasrikā-Prajñāpāramitā* (11th century) links a significant number of Buddhist sites to the Konkan coast.[55] Tāranātha, and earlier textual evidence, record the presence of the Singhalese monk Jayabhadra (also called Koṅkanapāda)—who was to become *vajrācārya* at Vikramaśīla—in Mahābimba in Konkan in the 9th century.[56] Mahābimba could be identified with the Bimbakāya mentioned by Tāranātha's teacher, Buddhaguptanātha, who visited Konkan in the 16th century on his way to Sri Lanka and then again when he was coming back from Java.[57] This cumulative evidence suggests the existence of enduring maritime links between Konkan, Sri Lanka, south- and northeastern India, and Southeast Asia.

Sri Lanka (and South India). From the perspective of Maritime Buddhism, Sri Lanka and South India formed a geographical and cultural dyad closely linked by sea networks. Although Buddhism in the Tamil country was a minoritarian religion living in the shadow of

Hinduism, increasing archaeological evidence suggests that it played a more important and resilient role than has hitherto been assumed. In the cosmopolitan port cities of Nagapattinam and Kāñcī, Buddhism received limited but nonetheless significant patronage, so much so that Hindu and Buddhist traditions thrived side by side, giving rise to possible cross-fertilizations.[58] Kāñcī may have acted as an incubator of early tantric fashions within the Buddhist fold, given the documented presence of proto- and mainstream tantric Śaiva traditions.[59] Circumstantial evidence and Buddhist hagiography suggest that foundational scriptures of the Yogatantra class such as the *Sarvatathāgatatattvasaṅgraha* may have been compiled in South India.[60] Prajña returned to South India from China to look for esoteric texts belonging to the Vidyādhara traditions (*chiming* 持明), and studied yogic techniques under consecration master Dharmayaśas [II]/Dharmakīrti (Damoyeshe 達摩耶舍/Facheng 法稱), while Amoghavajra received initiation into the *Vairocanābhisaṃbodhi*-system.[61]

Old Siṅhala inscriptions in Brāhmī script attest to the fact that Buddhism was firmly established in Sri Lanka by the third century BCE, probably as the result of the activities of South Indian and local traders.[62] While the island was one of the early recipients and exporters of Pali Buddhism, recent studies have underlined the numerous vestiges of Mahāyāna Buddhist Tantra existing on the island—most notably the tradition of the Abhayagiri Mahāvihāra, which might have been dominant by the 6th–7th centuries.[63] Archaeological remains and textual evidence from the later Siṅhala chronicle *Nikāyasaṅgraha* confirm the information, found in Sanskrit, Tibetan, and Chinese textual sources, that Sri Lanka (and perhaps South India, too) once hosted important lineages of Esoteric Buddhist masters and repositories of Tantras.[64]

By the 5th century, the island virtually became a compulsory stop for the monks traveling from India to China via the Andaman or Nicobar Islands and Southeast Asia. Faxian, Guṇavarman, and Guṇabhadra spent time there, and it has been hypothesized that their nonsectarian stance as documented by their activities of translation might have been acquired in the eclectic and cosmopolitan milieu of Abhayagiri.[65] Between the 7th and 8th centuries, Puṇyodaya, Vajrabuddhi, Amoghavajra, and Prajña visited Sri Lanka to obtain some rare esoteric texts in Sanskrit and receive initiation from local consecration masters, like Nāgabuddhi or Ratnabuddhi (Baojue 寶覺) and Samantabhadra (? Puxian 普賢). Maritime interactions between Sri Lanka and other centers of tantrism in the subcontinent are well documented.[66]

The fame of the eclectic Abhayagirivihāra at Anurādhapura, where a variety of Buddhist texts were studied, reached Southeast Asia. An 8th-century Siddhamātṛkā foundation inscription reports that a branch of the Sri Lankan Abhayagirivihāra, apparently intended for the use of esoteric-minded Sinhalese Buddhist monks, was established by the Śailendras on the Ratu Boko promontory in Central Java. Furthermore, the Abhayagirivihāra-related structures of Ratu Boko share with their Sri Lankan prototypes common architectural motifs, such as the peculiar double meditation platforms.[67]

The Western Indonesian Archipelago. The Western Indonesian archipelago was a strategic geographical area in the Maritime Silk Roads system. Although it has yielded significant vestiges of its glorious Hindu and Buddhist past, it is still underrepresented in contemporary scholarship. Far from being a cultural backwater that passively received Indic influences, it held an integral place in the Buddhist world as both a crossroads and a terminus of contacts since the early centuries of the Common Era. The contribution of the Austronesian-speaking region of Nusantara to the Indian Ocean trade network has been recognized in terms of providing superior shipping technology, nautical terminology, and ship crews. And yet, the creative and constitutive force of Southeast Asian agents and milieus in the transfer, transformation, and translocation of people, texts, notions, and artifacts in the Buddhist world remains to be fully appreciated. Witness the fact that a number of monks who traveled the sea routes and visited Southeast Asia—such as Guṇavarman, Paramārtha, Yijing, Vajrabodhi, Amoghavajra, and Atiśa—stirred up new developments in China as well as Tibet and the Indian subcontinent.[68] We also know about an 8th-century Javanese monk, Bianhong, who went to China to study under Huiguo and composed an Esoteric Buddhist initiation manual focusing on state protection.[69]

Sparse finds of buddha images are documented across a vast area from Sumatra and Java to Kalimantan and Sulawesi. Although their dating is uncertain, with estimates spanning from the 2nd to the 9th century, they highlight the maritime mobility of Buddhism within the archipelago.[70] It is, however, in Sumatra and Java that the majority of Buddhist vestiges concentrate. The two islands were strongholds of Mahāyāna Buddhist tantra from the 7th to the 15th century. Witness such impressive Buddhist sites as the Batang Hari river sites in Muaro Jambi and Padang Lawas in Sumatra; the Central Javanese complexes of Borobudur, Candi Sewu, Plaosan, Mendut, and Ratu Boko; and the royal temples of the Keḍiri, Siṅhasāri, and Majapahit kingdoms in East Java. Vestiges of Buddhism, such as small votive *stūpas*, are also documented on the island of Bali, where communities of tantric Buddhist ritual specialists have survived down to the present.

In his account, Faxian writes that Buddhism in Java was not worth speaking of and that Brahmanism was very strong. Just a few years thereafter, the Kashmirian monk Gunavarman, immediately before reaching China, succeeded in converting the royal family and their Javanese subjects to Buddhism. This information could be matched with the nearly contemporary archaeological remains of Batu Jaya in northwestern Java, suggesting that Buddhism was adopted at the site from the 5th century, and with 7th–early 9th century epigraphic evidence featuring Buddhist formulas traceable to a 5th-century Sarvāstivāda milieu.[71] Another report by Yijing indicates that by the middle of the 7th century the Sarvāstivāda school was prevalent in Southeast Asia and that the Chinese monk Huining 會寧 in 665 CE visited "Kaliṅga" (Java) to study and translate *Āgama* scripture with a certain Jñānabhadra for three years. Huining's pupil, Yunqi 運期, after going back to China to present a Chinese translation of the *Mahāparinirvāṇasūtra*, returned to Southeast Asia, spending more than ten years in Java and living in Śrīvijaya up to the time of Yijing.[72]

Textual and art historical remains suggest that the early esoteric developments that were emerging from the Western Deccan promptly reached Nusantara via the maritime routes. These became the basis of, and were preserved in, later religious configurations, as it may be inferred from the somewhat "archaic" character of 8th- to 9th-century Mantranaya Buddhism in Java and Sumatra. Iconographical influence stemming from the later "esoteric" phase of Ellorā and other Western Indian caves is detectable on the sculpted triptych of Mendut in Central Java, as well as in the depictions of the "courtly" 8th-century Eight Bodhisattvas known from the same temple, as well as Candi Plaosan and votive tablets from the Malay Peninsula, where they are part of a mandala arranged around a wheel-turning Śākyamuni-Vairocana.[73] Significantly, this mandalic formation is described in the "proto-tantric"

Aṣṭamaṇḍalaka, translated into Chinese by Amoghavajra (*T* 1167) and, a century earlier, by Puṇyodaya (*T* 486). Amoghavajra traveled to China via Java, and Puṇyodaya was active in mainland Southeast Asia.[74] Indeed, echoes between the iconography of the Eight Bodhisattvas in Java, Shingon Buddhism, and 8th-century Chinese translations have been discerned.[75]

The 8th- to 9th-century major architectural undertakings of the Śailendra dynasty, most notably the majestic and exquisitely crafted Buddhist monuments of Borobudur, Candi Sewu, Plaosan, and Mendut, must have ranked among the great sacred centers of the Buddhist cosmopolis, and attracted to the island a steady traffic of monks and pilgrims to the island. For instance, a 9th-century Siddhamātṛkā inscription unearthed at Candi Plaosan in the Prambanan area describes the worship of a buddha temple (*jinamandira*) by pilgrims continuously arriving from Gurjaradeśa in North India.[76] An account by Yuanzhao compiled into the *Zhenyuan xinding shijiao mulu*, as well as the Japanese master Kūkai (空海, 774–835), record that Vajrabuddhi first met Amoghavajra in Java.[77] An early 11th-century illustrated manuscript of the *Aṣṭasāhasrikā-Prajñāpāramitā* (CUL Add. 1643) dedicates one of its first vignettes to (an image of the buddha) Dīpaṅkara in Java (f. 2r), and Java figures in the early "Tantric geography" exposed by the *Manjuśriyamūlakalpa* (51.636–640).

Lastly, links between masters from the Pāla domains in Eastern India and Śailendra-sponsored Buddhism may be inferred from late 8th-century epigraphic evidence recording a certain Kumāraghoṣa, the royal preceptor from Gauḍīdvīpa who installed an image of Mañjughoṣa (Mañjuśrī) in Central Java at the request of Śailendra King Śrī Saṅgrāmadhanañjaya.[78] Furthermore, a *mahāyānika-golapaṇḍitā* (= *gauḍapaṇḍitā*, a Mahāyāna scholar from Bengal?) features in the undated short rock inscription engraved on a cliff overlooking the sea at Pasir Panjang in Karimun Besar island (Riau archipelago).[79] The fact that the latter inscription was written in Sanskrit in a nonlocal script (Nāgarī), as well as that it displays a graffiti-like character, lends credit to the hypothesis that it could have been engraved by a South Asian scholar who spent some time there en route to mainland Sumatra or Java, or to commemorate the visit of an important religious personality.[80]

Sumatra hosted renowned centers of Buddhist activity and learning. Yijing praised the high level of Buddhist scholarship he found there, where he stopped en route from Guangzhou to Nālandā and from there back to China to read Sanskrit Sūtras. It was from there that he procured the shipment of numerous Buddhist texts.[81] Yijing reports that Śākyakīrti, one of the five most distinguished Buddhist teachers of his time, traveled far and large across the "Five Indias" and finally settled in Śrīvijaya (Śrībhoja).[82] The continued existence of a high level of Buddhist scholarship and royal sponsorship of the religion is also suggested by the later figure of Shihu (施護, Dānapāla, d. 1018). In the late 10th century, this exceptionally prolific South Asian monk-translator reached China with a good knowledge of the languages of Sanfochi (Śrīvijaya) and Shepo (Java).[83]

The archaeological remains and scant epigraphic documents spread over disparate locales of the island have yielded remains of Buddhist monuments and inscriptions mostly dating back to the 10th to 13th century.[84] The *Intan* and *Cirebon* shipwrecks, discovered beneath the sea lanes linking Sumatra to Java, have yielded precious data on the 10th-century traffic of Buddhist bronze paraphernalia (e.g., *vajras*, spear-shaped sceptres, bells, statuettes, and inscribed foils), along with other commonly traded merchandise among regional entrepôts and the larger Indian Ocean and Chinese markets.[85]

A case for the possible influence of Sumatran and Javanese Buddhism on subsequent developments in India has been made with respect to the invocation of *Bhadracarī-praṇidhāna*—the text depicted in the uppermost series of reliefs on Borobudur—on the memorial *stūpa* found at the Nālandā monastery established by the Sumatran monarch Bālaputradeva for the use of pilgrims from Śrīvijaya.[86] The contribution of insular Southeast Asian masters to Vajrayāna Buddhism in Tibet, also through the handful of texts composed in Suvarṇadvīpa that were introduced into the Tibetan canon, is acknowledged by the Tibetan tradition from the 11th century. The famous master Atiśa, originary of Bengal, is said to have transmitted to Tibet the *Durbodhāloka* (a Sanskrit commentary on the *Abhisamayālaṅkāra*) composed in Southeast Asia by his teacher Dharmakīrti. Both were fervent devotees of Tārā, whose cult was widespread in insular Southeast Asia, and which may have influenced the form of cult that Atiśa reintroduced or popularized in Tibet after his stay in Suvarṇadvīpa.[87]

Contemporary transmission of Buddhist ideas from Sumatra and/or Java to the Himalayan region has been suggested on the basis of artistic and architectural similarities between the Tabo monastery in Himachal Pradesh, which Atiśa visited in 1042, and Borobudur.[88] Dharmakīrti also imparted to Atiśa the teachings of the *Kālacakratantra* and has been identified as the author of the *Netravibhaṅga*, a commentary to the *Hevajratantra*.[89] Indeed, from the 11th to the 12th century, Sumatra appears to have been a major center of the Hevajra cult. Witness the epigraphic evidence of mantra portions directly quoted from the *Hevajratantra* (which, significantly, mentions Suvarṇadvīpa), as well as the 14th-century inscription of Saruaso II, issued by Crown Prince Anaṅgavarman, son of Ādityavarman, which mentions his "daily meditation on Hevajra" (*Hevajra-nityāsmṛtiḥ*).[90] Images found at the Sumatran sites of Padang Lawas are integrated in a network that connects them to East Java, northeastern India, and mainland Southeast Asia in the 11th and 13th centuries. Overall, the sites show a kind of Buddhism that belongs to the same "Phase III" of Vajrayāna as what was present in Khmer and Cham domains between the 12th and 13th century, and in East Java and China in the 13th century.[91]

The Malay Peninsula. Given its strategic geographical location, the Malay Peninsula, which was included in the domains of Śailendra/Śrīvijayan Buddhist rulers from the 7th to the 13th century, acted as an important intersection in the traffic of merchants, monks, and pilgrims plying the maritime routes. The earliest inscription associated with Buddhism in Southeast Asia, dated to the 5th century, has been found in Kedah. Having been commissioned by "sea captain" (? *mahānāvika*) Buddhagupta from Raktamṛttikā (i.e., either Raktamṛttikā Mahāvihāra in what is now Rajbadidanga in West Bengal, or another location in the Malay Peninsula), it highlights the link between Buddhism and trade in the Peninsula prior to the establishment of monastic centers and the rise of institutional support in the Śrīvijayan period.

Also testifying to the local and translocal nature of Buddhism in the area are the many votive tablets found at multiple sites in the period from the 6th to the 12th century. Two of these tablets, recovered from sites in Kedah and tentatively dated to the 7th century, contain a passage from the Mahāyāna Sūtra *Sāgaramatiparipṛcchā*, whose Sanskrit original has survived through fragmentary quotations but has been integrally transmitted in Chinese and Tibetan translations.[92] Other specimens, such as those inscribed in northeastern Indian scripts and displaying the Eight Bodhisattvas, as well as those displaying a twelve-armed Avalokiteśvara from the Perlis caves, could have belonged to pilgrims transiting from the subcontinent (unlike the tablets recovered from difficult-to-reach caves, which rather suggest a local context of religious practice).[93] One *apramāda* gold seal bearing a short Prakrit inscription, recovered at Bang Kluay Nok in Ranong along the western coast of the central Malay Peninsula, mentions a "mariner Brahaspati" and could be compared to analogous epigraphic remains donated by mariners across the Indic world.[94] The exquisitely crafted late 8th-century bronze Avalokiteśvaras found in the Chaiya district of modern Thailand and in Bidor (Perak, Malaysia) show close similarities with the Avalokiteśvara found at Wonogiri in Central Java. This fact suggests a link between the Malay Peninsula and Java under the Śailendra, perhaps initiated by the master Vajrabuddhi himself.[95]

At its height, the Śrīvijaya kingdom extended over Sumatra, the Malay Peninsula, and Java. Besides controlling the trade routes, this polity was actively engaged in Buddhist diplomacy with India and China. In addition to the donation by Bālaputradeva at Nālandā, other gifts and diplomatic exchanges with South India and Sri Lanka are documented in inscriptions dating from the 11th to the 12th century.[96] The existence of links with the subcontinent can also be evinced from 1015 CE Nepalese Manuscript CUL Add. 1643 (f. 120r) of the *Aṣṭasāhasrikā Prajñāpāramitā*, which mentions a Lokanātha on Mount Balavatī in Kaṭahadvīpa (Kedah).[97]

The Khmer and Cam Domains. The early polities of Funan and Panpan in mainland Southeast Asia sourced relics, texts, and monks well versed in Mahāyāna teachings for China. The Indian monk Paramārtha (fl. 6th century), who became a famous and prolific translator of Mahāyāna texts in China, stayed in Funan and played an instrumental role in this traffic. Three recorded monks hailing from Funan—Nag̅asena, Saṅghapāla, and Mandrasena—visited China between the 5th and 6th centuries, carrying Sanskrit texts with them. Some of the texts translated by Paramārtha formed the core of the Yogācāra doctrine of Asaṅga and Vasubandhu in China, which in turn led to the establishment of the Dharmalakṣana school of Xuanzang in the 7th century.[98]

The maritime links of Mainland Southeast Asia extended eastward to the Indian subcontinent, if Tāranātha's claim. Tāranātha stated that, from the time of King Dharmapāla (late 8th–early 9th centuries) on, there were many students from Southeast Asian kingdoms in north and eastern India and that during the time of the four Senas, about half of the monks of Magadha were from the so-called Eastern Koki countries (including Pegu, Campā, and Kamboja in mainland Southeast Asia).[99] Although this is an apparent exaggeration, this information is not to be discounted as entirely unrealistic, for there is evidence of a steady traffic of monks across the Bay of Bengal: witness the Buddhist master Puṇyodaya, who traveled from India to China via Sri Lanka and then back to mainland Southeast Asia, and Kīrtipaṇḍita and Vāgīśvarakīrti, who were active in Khmer domains by the 10th and 11th century, respectively.

Epigraphic and archaeological evidence confirms that the Cam and Khmer realms were fully integrated in the web of intraregional Southeast Asian networks connecting the mainland and the Malay Peninsula to Java, Sumatra, and China between the 7th and 10th century. The Nham Biền stele of 908 CE relates that the courtier Rājadvāra made two trips (*siddhayātra*) to Java.[100] Possible links between Javanese and Cam Buddhism are suggested by doctrinal elements shared by the An Thái inscription and the Sanskrit-Old Javanese Esoteric Buddhist manual *Saṅ Hyaṅ Kamahāyānikan*, as well as by the importance of the "proto-tantric"

Kāraṇḍavyūhasūtra in the iconography of Đông Dương in Campa.[101] A *khakkhara* finial and several other bronze ritual objects from Dvāravatī have close parallels with Esoteric Buddhist material found in Central Java and beyond.[102]

The Philippines. Recent scholarship has reevaluated the pre-Christian, Indic heritage of what are now called the Philippine islands. In spite of the quantitatively scant evidence, qualitatively important archaeological and inscriptional finds suggest that the archipelago played a not irrelevant role in the Maritime Asian Buddhist networks. Butuan in Mindanao was visited by ships traveling the Java–China route, thanks to its important reserves of gold, as evinced by the presence of 9th-century Tang ware. Buddhist statuary, artifacts, and epigraphic documents include a clay Avalokiteśvara tablet from Luzon and an inscription from the Agusan region in Mindanao featuring a variant of a mantra contained in the *Mahāpratisarāmahāvidyārājñī*, which implies that the cult of Mahāpratisarā could have reached the Philippines from Java around the same time as Amoghavajra's missions.[103]

The gold statuette of the goddess Vajralāsyā from the Agusan region is a remarkable artifact. This icon bears stylistic and iconographical resemblances to the group of bronze statues from Nganjuk in East Java, and it probably dates to the 9th–10th centuries. Since Vajralāsyā is one of the four deities associated with providing offerings to the Buddha Vairocana and located in the southeastern corner of the Vajradhātu mandala, one may argue that a tridimensional arrangement of this mandala, or a related variant revolving around the figure of Vajrasattva, was known in the Philippines by the 10th century.[104]

REVIEW OF LITERATURE

The importance of seafaring and the maritime routes in the eastward expansion of Buddhism was highlighted long ago by influential scholars such as Édouard Chavannes, Sylvain Lévi, and George Cœdès.[105] Yet, secondary literature treating the topic of Maritime Buddhism as an integral phenomenon is scant. A small number of studies—notably those by Himanshu Ray, Tansen Sen, and Lewis Lancaster—exploring the long-distance maritime transfer of Buddhism across Asia in its religious, diplomatic, and economic ramifications has appeared in recent years on the wake of a growing interest in Maritime History/Indian Ocean Studies and Intra-Asian connections.[106] While those studies have helped popularize the idea of "Maritime Buddhism," a comprehensive, monograph-length study that synthesizes and links together the abundant and multifarious historical evidence available to us from across Asia remains to be written.

A popular way to approach Maritime Buddhism has been to focus on the lives and voyages of monks traveling by sea between the Indian subcontinent and China.[107] A recent study by Jeffrey Sundberg and Rolf Giebel has taken into account textual evidence in Chinese on the life and travels of Vajrabodhi and Amoghavajra, and matched it with historical data from South, Southeast, and East Asia.[108] The shipwreck motif as illuminated by Buddhist texts as well as art and archaeological remains has been discussed by Andrea Acri and Himanshu Ray, respectively.[109] Nautical technology and seafaring in the Indian Ocean in light of the Ajanta Buddhist cave paintings, as well as Sanskrit and Pali texts, have been surveyed by Dieter

Schlingloff.[110] Texts in East Asian languages are a particularly valuable source of information; although many have long been accessible in edited form, scholars have tended to focus on a few "classics," and the majority of them are still waiting to be translated and studied. Tibetan sources, as well as vernacular literature in, for example, Tamil, Classical Malay, and Old Javanese, would also seem to offer a promising and little-explored avenue for further research.

Although much of the existing literature bearing on Maritime Buddhism seems to be grounded on, and confined within, the boundaries of area studies, recent studies focusing on Buddhism in specific regional contexts have occasionally touched on the phenomenon of Buddhist contacts via wider trans-Asian maritime networks. See, for instance, works reevaluating Buddhism in the Tamil country or uncovering esoteric Buddhism in Sri Lanka and Southeast Asia.[111] A handful of studies have upheld a transregional and geographically wider perspective, such as Andrea Acri's edited volume *Esoteric Buddhism in Mediaeval Maritime Asia*, the articles by Max Deeg and Tansen Sen focusing on the maritime routes, and Kimiaki Tanaka's article comparing the mainland and maritime transmission of esoteric Buddhism.[112] Insightful accounts of the intricacies of Buddhism and diplomacy across South, Southeast, and East Asia have been produced by Upinder Singh, Gokul Seshadri, and Jonathan Silk.[113] Recent work by Tilman Frasch and Anne Blackburn has unraveled the networks of Pali Buddhism across Sri Lanka and Mainland Southeast Asia.[114] The study of maritime Buddhist contacts from the perspective of trade, as well as archaeology, has also been popular.[115]

Over the past decade, increasing attention has been paid to epigraphic and manuscript evidence from both mainland and insular Southeast Asia. The series of studies recently published by Arlo Griffiths on epigraphic remains and by Hudaya Kandahjaya on Old Javanese texts and inscriptions related to Borobudur are valuable to fully appreciate the important place of insular Southeast Asia in the premodern Buddhist world and in tracing the maritime connections that once linked it to other centers of Buddhism.[116] Kenneth Hall has published an article describing aspects of the Bay of Bengal–South China Sea trade networks in light of recent findings of shipwrecks in Indonesian waters. His work integrates this newly discovered evidence of Buddhist artifacts into the mainstream historical narrative.[117]

FURTHER READING

Acri, Andrea. *Esoteric Buddhism in Mediaeval Maritime Asia: Networks of Masters, Texts, Icons*. Singapore: ISEAS Publishing, 2016.

Dayalan, Duraiswamy. "Role of Archaeology in the Study of Maritime Buddhism in India." n.d.

Deeg, Max. "Maritime Routes in the Indian Ocean in Early Times According to Chinese Buddhist Texts." In *Aspects of the Maritime Silk Road: From the Persian Gulf to the East China Sea*. Edited by Ralph Kauz, 153–158. Wiesbaden, Germany: Harrassowitz Verlag, 2010.

Kandahjaya, Hudaya. *A Study on the Origin and Significance of Borobudur*. PhD diss., University of California, Berkeley, 2004.

Lancaster, Lewis. "The 'Great Circle' of Buddhism," n.d.

Pachow, Wang. "The Voyage of Buddhist Missions to South-East Asia and Far East." *University of Ceylon Review* 18, no. 3/4 (1960): 195–212 [Reprint, 1958].

Ray, Himanshu Prabha. "Narratives of Travel and Shipwreck." In *Buddhist Narrative in Asia and Beyond: In Honor of HRH Princess Maha Chakri Sirindhorn on Her Fifty-fifth Birth Anniversary*, Vol. 2. Edited by Peter Skilling and Justin McDaniel, 47–65. Bangkok: Institute of Thai Studies, Chulalongkorn University, 2012.

Ray, Himanshu Prabha. *The Winds of Change: Buddhism and the Maritime Links of Early South Asia*. New Delhi: Oxford University Press, 1994.

Sen, Tansen. "Buddhism and the Maritime Crossings." In *China and Beyond in the Mediaeval Period: Cultural Crossings and Inter-Regional Connections*. Edited by Dorothy C. Wong and G. Heldt, 39–62. Singapore/New Delhi: ISEAS Publishing/Manohar, 2014.

Sundberg, Jeffrey, and Rolf Giebel. "The Life of the Tang Court Vajrabodhi as Chronicled by Lü Xiang (呂向): South Indian and Śrī Laṅkān Antecedents to the Arrival of the Buddhist Vajrayāna in Eighth-Century Java and China," *Pacific World: Journal of the Institute of Buddhist Studies* (Third Series) 13 (2011): 129–222.

Tanaka, Kimiaki. "Comparing the Cross-Cultural Exchanges of Esoteric Buddhism through Overland and Maritime Silk Roads." In *Ancient Silk Trade Routes. Selected Works from Symposium on Cross Cultural Exchanges and Their Legacies in Asia*. Edited by Dashu Qin and Jian Yuan, 223–235. Hackensack, NJ: World Scientific, 2014.

NOTES

1. Tansen Sen, *Buddhism, Diplomacy, and Trade: The Realignment of Sino-Indian Relations, 600–1400* (Honolulu: Association for Asian Studies/University of Hawai'i Press, 2003).
2. Jason Neelis, *Early Buddhist Transmission and Trade Networks: Mobility and Exchange Within and Beyond the Northwestern Borderlands of South Asia* (Leiden, The Netherlands: Brill, 2011).
3. Lewis Lancaster, "The 'Great Circle' of Buddhism," (n.d.), and "The 'Great Circle' of Buddhism and the Connections between India and China," (n.d.). While the expression "Silk Roads" (*Die Seidenstrassen*) was coined by the German geographer Ferdinand von Richthofen in 1877, the conceptualization of "Silk roads of the sea" might go back to French scholar Édouard Chavannes. See his *Documents sur les Tou Kiue (turcs) occidentaux, Recueillis et commentés par Édouard Chavannes* (Saint Petersburg, Russia: Commissionnaires de l'Académie impérial des sciences, 1903), 233.
4. Recent surveys of the evidence of pre- and protohistorical maritime contacts between South Asia, Southeast Asia, and Southern China are Tom Hoogervorst, *Southeast Asia in the Ancient Indian Ocean World* (Oxford: Archaeopress, 2012); and Andrea Acri, Roger Blench, and Aleksandra Landmann, "Introduction: Re-connecting Histories across the Indo-Pacific," in *Spirits and Ships: Cultural Transfers in Early Monsoon Asia* (Singapore: ISEAS, 2017).
5. Sen, "Buddhism and the Maritime Crossings," in *China and Beyond in the Mediaeval Period: Cultural Crossings and Inter-Regional Connections*, eds. Dorothy C. Wong and G. Heldt (Singapore/New Delhi: ISEAS Publishing/Manohar, 2014), 55 (39–62); "Maritime Southeast Asia Between South Asia and China to the Sixteenth Century," *TRaNS: Trans-Regional and -National Studies of Southeast Asia* 2, no. 1 (2014): 33–34 (31–59).
6. Sylvain Lévi, "Les 'marchands de mer' et leur role dans le bouddhisme primitif," *Bulletin de l'Association Française des Amis de l'Orient* (October 1929): 19–39; Duraiswamy Dayalan, "Role of Trade and Tamil Traders in Promoting Buddhism," in *Sivasri: Perspectives in Indian Archaeology, Art and Culture*, ed. Duraiswamy Dayalan (New Delhi: Agam Kala Prakashan, 2013), 15–31; Lewis Lancaster, "The Great Circle of Buddhism"; Osmund Bopearachchi, "Sri Lanka and the Maritime Trade: The Impact of the Role of the Bodhisattva Avalokiteśvara as the Protector of Mariners," in *Asian Encounters: Networks of Cultural Interaction*, eds. Parul Pandya Dhar and Upinder Singh (New Delhi: Oxford University Press, 2014), 161–187; and Charles Holcombe, "Trade-Buddhism: Maritime Trade, Immigration, and the Buddhist Landfall in Early Japan," *Journal of the American Oriental Society* 119, no. 2 (1999): 280–292.
7. Sylvain Lévi, "Manimekhala, a Divinity of the Sea," *The Indian Historical Quarterly* 6, no. 4 (1931): 597–614.
8. Jost Gippert, "A Glimpse into the Buddhist Past of the Maldives; I: An Early Prakrit Inscription," *Wiener Zeitschri für die Kunde Südasiens* 48 (2004): 81–109, and "Sanskrit as a Medium of Maldivian Buddhism,"

in *Indische Kultur im Kontext: Rituale, Texte und Ideen aus Indien und der Welt; Festschri für Klaus Mylius*, ed. L. Göhler (Wiesbaden, Germany: Harrassowitz, 2005), 213–220; and Ingo Strauch, *Foreign Sailors on Socotra: The Inscriptions and Drawings from the Cave Hoq* (Bremen, Germany: Hempen Verlag, 2012).

9. Himanshu P. Ray, "Narratives of Travel and Shipwreck," in *Buddhist Narrative in Asia and Beyond: In Honor of HRH Princess Maha Chakri Sirindhorn on Her Fifty-fifth Birth Anniversary, Volume 2*, eds. Peter Skilling and Justin McDaniel (Bangkok: Institute of Thai Studies, Chulalongkorn University, 2012), 47–65.
10. Bopearachchi, "Sri Lanka and the maritime trade," 161–187; Ray, "Narratives of Travel and Shipwreck," 56–60; and John Guy, "Catalogue: Savior Cults," in *Lost Kingdoms: Hindu-Buddhist Sculpture of Early Southeast Asia*, ed. John Guy (New York: Metropolitan Museum of Art, 2014), 226–264.
11. Sen, "Buddhism and the Maritime Crossings," 42–43.
12. For example, Chinese biographies of Amoghavajra present contradictory information, describing him as either the son of a Brahman or a merchant from Central Asia: see Yi-Liang Chou, "Tantrism in China," *Harvard Journal of Asiatic Studies* 8, no. 3–4 (1945): 322 (241–332).
13. Ronald Davidson, *Indian Esoteric Buddhism: A Social History of the Tantric Movement* (New York: Columbia University Press, 2002), 82–83, 167.
14. Hiram Woodward, "Esoteric Buddhism in Southeast Asia in the Light of Recent Scholarship," *Journal of Southeast Asian Studies* 35, no. 2 (2004): 353 (329–354).
15. P. C. Chakravarti in *The History of Bengal, Volume I: Hindu Period*, ed. R. C. Majumdar (Lohanipur/Patna, India: N. V. Publications, 1971) [Reprint of first edition, Dacca: University of Dacca, 1943], 662.
16. Ray, "Providing for the Buddha: Monastic Centres in Eastern India," *Arts Asiatiques* 63 (2008): 124 (119–138).
17. Roy E. Jordaan and Brian Colless, *The Mahārāja of the Isles: The Śailendras and the Problem of Śrīvijaya* (Leiden, The Netherlands: Department of Languages and Cultures of Southeast Asia and Oceania, 2009), 112.
18. Max Deeg, "Maritime routes in the Indian Ocean in early times according to Chinese Buddhist texts," in *Aspects of the maritime Silk Road: From the Persian Gulf to the East China Sea*, ed. Ralph Kauz (Wiesbaden, Germany: Harrassowitz Verlag, 2010): 157–158 (153–158); and Jonathan Silk, "Tidings from the South Chinese court Buddhism and Overseas Relations in the Fifth Century CE," in *A Life Journey to the East*, eds. Antonino Forte and Federico Masini (Kyoto: Italian School of East Asian Studies, 2002): 31–32 (21–43).
19. Hudaya Kandahjaya, *A Study on the Origin and Significance of Borobudur* (PhD diss., University of California, Berkeley, 2004), 51–52; and Jonathan Silk, "Tidings."
20. Max Deeg, "Has Huichao Been Back to India? On a Chinese Inscription on the Back of a Pāla Bronze and the Chronology of Indian Esoteric Buddhism," in *From Turfan to Ajanta: Festschrift for Dieter Schlingloff on the Occasion of his Eightieth Birthday*, eds. Eli Franco and Monika Zin (Kathmandu, Nepal: Lumbini International Research Institute, 2010), 207–208 (197–213).
21. Wang Pachow, "The Voyage of Buddhist Missions to South-East Asia and Far East," *University of Ceylon Review* 18, no. 3/4 (1960): 211 (195–212) [Reprint, 1958].
22. Deeg, "Has Huichao Been Back to India?," 209–211.
23. Paul Copp, "Prajña," in *Esoteric Buddhism and the Tantras in East Asia*, eds. Charles D. Orzech, Henrik H. Sørensen, and Richard K. Payne (Leiden, The Netherlands: Brill, 2011), 361 (360–362); and Pachow, "The Voyage of Buddhist Missions," 210.
24. Dorothy C. Wong, "An Agent of Cultural Transmission: Jianzhen's Travels to Japan, 743–763," in *China and Beyond in the Mediaeval Period: Cultural Crossings and Inter-Regional Connections*, eds. Dorothy C. Wong and Gustav Heldt (New Delhi/New York: Manohar/Cambria Press, 2014): 63–100.
25. Haiyan Hu and Oskar von Hinüber, "Faxian's (法顯) Worship of Guanshiyin (觀世音) and the *Lotus Sūtra* of 286 (正法華經)," in *Annual Report of The International Research Institute for Advanced Buddhology at Soka University for the Academic Year 2014: Volume XVIII* (Tokyo: International Research

Institute for Advanced Buddhology Soka University, 2015), 312–313 (311–319). Strikingly enough, the detail of the large ship carrying a smaller "lifeboat" finds a parallel on an 8th-century Borobudur relief, where a similar ship (of a Malayo-Polynesian type) is depicted.

26. Hu an von Hinüber, "Faxian's (法顯) Worship," 313–314.
27. Chou, "Tantrism in China," 275, n. 19; and Jeffrey Sundberg and Rolf Giebel, "The Life of the Tang Court Vajrabodhi as Chronicled by Lü Xiang (呂向): South Indian and Śrī Laṅkān Antecedents to the Arrival of the Buddhist Vajrayāna in Eighth-Century Java and China," *Pacific World: Journal of the Institute of Buddhist Studies* (Third Series) 13 (2011): 139 (129–222).
28. Chou, "Tantrism," 290.
29. Gergely Hidas, *Mahāpratisarā-Mahāvidyārājñī. The Great Amulet, Great Queen of Spells* (New Delhi: Aditya Prakashan, 2012), 222 n. 178, 224 n. 184.
30. Gerd Mevissen, "Images of Mahāpratisarā in Bengal: Their Iconographic Links with Javanese, Central Asian and East Asian Images," *Journal of Bengal Art* 4 (2009): 99–129; Thomas Cruijsen Arlo Griffiths, and Marijke J. Klokke, "The Cult of the Buddhist *dhāraṇī* Deity Mahāpratisarā: Epigraphical and Iconographic Evidence from the Indonesian Archipelago," *Journal of the International Association of Buddhist Studies* 35 (2012): 71–157; and Roderick Orlina, "Epigraphical Evidence for the Cult of Mahāpratisarā in the Philippines," *Journal of the International Association of Buddhist Studies* 35 (2012): 91–101.
31. Arlo Griffiths, "Written Traces of the Buddhist past: *Mantras* and *Dhāraṇīs* in Indonesian Inscriptions," *Bulletin of the School of Oriental and African Studies* 77, no. 1 (2014): 157–159 (137–194).
32. Hubert Decleer, "Atiśa's Journey to Sumatra," in *Buddhism in Practice*, ed. Donald S. Lopez Jr. (Princeton, NJ: Princeton University Press, 1995): 532–540.
33. He Fangyao 何方耀, *Jin-Tang shiqi Nanhai qiufa gaoseng qunti yanjiu* 晉唐時期南 海求法高僧群體研究 [An examination of the community of eminent monks who traveled to the Southern Sea in search of the Law from the Jin to Tang periods] (Beijing: Zongjiao wenhua chubanshe, 2008), 55.
34. Pachow, "The Voyage of Buddhist Missions," 211; and Kandahjaya, *A Study*, 58.
35. Kandahjaya, *A Study*, 78. The number 103 was estimated by P. C. Bagchi, *India and China: A Thousand Years of Cultural Relations* (Calcutta: Saraswati Library, 1981), 255–277.
36. For a survey of the monks mentioned hereafter, see Pachow, "The Voyage of Buddhist Missions."
37. Andrea Acri, "Introduction: Esoteric Buddhist Networks along the Maritime Silk Routes, 7th–13th Century AD," in *Esoteric Buddhism in Mediaeval Maritime Asia*, ed. Andrea Acri (Singapore: ISEAS, 2016), 1–25.
38. Sharrock, "Kīrtipandita and the Tantras: The Revival of Buddhism in 10th century Angkor," *Udaya* 10 (2012): 203–237; and Peter-Daniel Szántó, "Vāgīśvarakīrti," in *Śaivism and the Tantric Traditions: Essays in Honour of Alexis Sanderson*, eds. Dominic Goodall et al. (Leiden, The Netherlands: Brill, forthcoming).
39. Giuseppe Tucci, "The Sea and Land Travels of a Buddhist Sādhu in the Sixteenth Century," *Indian Historical Quarterly* 7, no. 4 (1931): 683–702.
40. Upinder Singh, "Gifts from Other Lands: Southeast Asian Religious Endowments in India," in *Asian Encounters*, 48–52 (43–61); and Peter Skilling, "Geographies of Intertextuality: Buddhist Literature in Pre-modern Siam," *Aséanie* 19 (2007): 91–112.
41. Ulrich von Schroeder, *Indo-Tibetan Bronzes* (Hong Kong: Visual Dharma Publications, 1981), 311.
42. *Tāranātha's History of Buddhism in India*, translated from Tibetan by Lama Chimpa and Alaka Chattopadhyaya and ed. Debiprasad Chattopadhyaya (Calcutta: K. P. Bagchi & Company, 1980), 330.
43. For a survey and a list of the secondary literature, see Acri, "Introduction," 21–22.
44. We indeed know of a failed attempt by Kublai Khan to invade East Java: see David Bade, *Of Palm Wine, Women and War: The Mongolian Naval Expedition to Java in the 13th Century* (Singapore: ISEAS Publishing, 2013).
45. Anne M. Blackburn, "Buddhist Connections in the Indian Ocean: Changes in Monastic Mobility, 1000–1500," *Journal of the Economic and Social History of the Orient* 58, no. 5 (2015): 37–66; and

Tilman Frasch, "1456: The Making of a Buddhist Ecumene in the Bay of Bengal," in *Pelagic Passageways: The Northern Bay of Bengal World before Colonialism*, ed. Rila Mukherjee (New Delhi: Primus, 2011): 383–405.
46. Sen, "Buddhism and the Maritime Crossings," 52.
47. Sen, "Buddhism and the Maritime Crossings," 54.
48. Blackburn, "Buddhist Connections."
49. Blackburn, "The Sphere of the *Śāsana* in the Context of Colonialism," in *Buddhism Across Asia: Networks of Material, Intellectual, and Cultural Exchange, Vol. 1*, Tansen Sen, ed. (Singapore/New Delhi: ISEAS Publishing/Manohar, 2014), 371–382; and Sen, "Buddhism and the Maritime Crossings," 55; "Introduction: Buddhism in Asian History," in *Buddhism Across Asia*, xx.
50. Sen, "Introduction," xix (xi–xxx).
51. Sen, "Introduction," xx–xxi; Zhang Xing, "Buddhist Practices and Institutions of the Chinese Community in Kolkata, India," in *Buddhism Across Asia*, ed. Sen, 429–458.
52. Pia Brancaccio, "The Silk Road and the Cotton Road: Buddhist Art and Practice Between Central Asia and the Western Deccan," in *Archeologia delle Vie della Seta: Percorsi, Immagini e Cultura Materiale, Vol. 2*, ed. Bruno Genito and Lucia Caterina (Rome: Scienze e Lettere), 59–73.
53. Geri Malandra, "The Mandala at Ellora / Ellora in the Mandala," *Journal of the International Association of Buddhist Studies* 19 (1996): 181–208.
54. Alex Wayman and Ryujan Tajima, *The Enlightenment of Vairocana* (Delhi: Motilal Banarsidass, 1992): 10–11.
55. Jinah Kim, "Local Visions, Transcendental Practices: Iconographic Innovations of Indian Esoteric Buddhism," *History of Religions* 54, no. 1 (2014): 48 (34–68).
56. *Tāranātha's History of Buddhism in India*, 296, 325; and Péter-Dániel Szántó, *Selected Chapters from the Catuṣpīṭhatantra. Vol. 1. Introductory study with the annotated translation of selected chapters* (D.Phil. dissertation, Oxford University, 2012), 40.
57. Tucci, "The Sea and Land Travels of a Buddhist Sādhu in the Sixteenth Century," 690–696.
58. Sundberg and Giebel, "The Life of Vajrabodhi," 154; Peter Schalk, "Buddhism among Tamils. An Introduction," in *Buddhism among Tamils. Part 3. Extension and Conclusion*, eds. P. Schalk and Astrid Nahl (Uppsala University, Faculty of Theology, 2013), 24, 29 (21–57); and Valérie Gillet, "Pallavas and Buddhism: Interactions and Influences," in *Sivasri: Perspectives in Indian Archaeology, Art and Culture*, ed. Duraiswamy Dayalan (New Delhi: Agam Kala Prakashan, 2013), 105–135.
59. Sundberg and Giebel, "The Life of Vajrabodhi," 155.
60. Stephen Hodge, The *Mahā-Vairocana-Abhisaṃbodhi Tantra, with Buddhaguhya's commentary* (New York: RoutledgeCurzon, 2003), 11–12.
61. Copp, "Prajña," in *Esoteric Buddhism and the Tantras in East Asia*, 360–361.
62. Dayalan, "Role of Trade." Limited evidence of the spread of Buddhism via the maritime networks during the reign of the Indian King Aśoka (r. *c*. 270–232 BCE) exists in Sri Lanka, and the same idea is current in subsequent Buddhist accounts from various parts of Asia.
63. Bopearachchi, "Sri Lanka and the Maritime Trade," 164.
64. A comprehensive summary is Rangama Chandawimala, *Buddhist Heterodoxy of Abhayagiri Sect: A Study of the School of Abhayagiri in Ancient Sri Lanka* (Saarbrücken, Germany: Lambert Academic Publishing, 2013); see also Sundberg, "The Abhayagirivihāra's *Pāṃśukūlika* Monks in Second Lambakaṇṇa Śrī Laṅkā and Śailendra Java: The Flowering and Fall of a Cardinal Center of Influence in Early Esoteric Buddhism," *Pacific World*, Third Series 16 (2014): 49–185.
65. Kandahjaya, *A Study*, 46. Kandahjaya draws attention to the intriguing fact that, although Guṇavarman in Kashmir was a Sarvāstivādin monk, he did eventually expound Mahāyāna teachings in China. This would lead us to assume that he was exposed to Mahāyāna in Sri Lanka.

66. Sen, "Buddhism and the Maritime Crossings," 53; and Acri, "Introduction," 18.
67. Sundberg, "Mid-9th-Century Adversity for Sinhalese Esoteric Buddhist Exemplars in Java: Lord Kumbhayoni and the 'Rag-wearer' *Paṁsukūlika* Monks of the Abhayagirivihāra," in *Esoteric Buddhism in Mediaeval Maritime Asia*, 349–379.
68. Kandahjaya, *A Study*, 79.
69. Iain Sinclair, "Coronation and Liberation According to a Javanese Monk in China: Bianhong's Manual on the *abhiṣeka* of a *cakravartin*," in *Esoteric Buddhism in Mediaeval Maritime Asia*, 29–66.
70. Kandahjaya, *A Study*, 54.
71. Pierre-Yves Manguin and Agustijanto Indrajaya, "The Batujaya Site: New Evidence of Early Indian Influence in West Java," in *India and Southeast Asia: Reflections on Cross-cultural Exchange*, eds. Pierre-Yves Manguin, A. Mani, and Geoffrey Wade (Singapore: ISEAS Publishing, 2011), 113–136; and Johannes de Casparis, *Prasasti Indonesia II: Selected Inscriptions from the 7th to the 9th Centuries AD* (Bandung, Indonesia: Masa Baru, 75).
72. Kandahjaya, *"Saṅ Hyaṅ Kamahāyānikan*, Borobudur, and the Origins of Esoteric Buddhism in Premodern Indonesia," in *Esoteric Buddhism in Mediaeval Maritime Asia*, 85 (67–112).
73. Nicolas Revire, "From Gandhara to Candi Mendut? A Comparative Study of Bhadrāsana Buddhas and Their Related Bodhisattva Attendants in South and Southeast Asia," Paper presented at the seminar *Cultural Dialogues Between India and South-East Asia from the 7th to the 16th Centuries*, K. R. Cama Oriental Institute, Mumbai, January 17–18, 2015. Peter D. Sharrock and Emma C. Bunker, "Seeds of Vajrabodhi: Buddhist Ritual Bronzes from Java and Khorat," in *Esoteric Buddhism in Mediaeval Maritime Asia* (2016): 244 (237–252).
74. Li-Kuang Lin, "Puṇyodaya (Na-t'i), un propagateur du tantrisme en Chine et au Cambodge à l'époque de Hiuan-tsang," *Journal Asiatique* 227 (1935): 83–100.
75. Claudine Bautze-Picron, "Le Groupe des Huit Grands Bodhisattva en Inde: Genèse et Développement," in *Living a Life in Accord with Dhamma: Papers in Honor of Professor Jean Boisselier on His Eightieth Birthday*, eds. N. Eilenberg et al. (Bangkok: Silpakorn University, 1997), 28 (1–55).
76. de Casparis, *Prasasti Indonesia II*, 188–189, 202.
77. Sundberg and Giebel, "The Life," 152.
78. Himanshu Bushan Sarkar, *Corpus of the Inscriptions of Java*, 2 vols. (Calcutta: Firma K. L. Mukhopadhyay, 1971), I: 37, 45.
79. Ian Caldwell and A. Hazlewood, "The Holy Footprints of the Venerable Gautama; A New Translation of the Pasir Panjang Inscription," *Bijdragen tot de Taal-, Land- en Volkenkunde* 150 (1994): 457–480.
80. Iain Sinclair, "Gautamaśrī: A Bengali Buddhist pundit in transit through the Himalayas and the Singapore Strait." Unpublished draft paper, 2018.
81. J. Takakusu, *A Record of the Buddhist Religion as Practised in India and the Malay Archipelago, I-Tsing (A.D. 671–695)* (London: Clarendon Press, 1896), xxxvi.
82. Takakusu, *A Record*, 184.
83. Sen, *Buddhism, Diplomacy, and Trade*, 384.
84. John Miksic, "Archaeological Evidence for Esoteric Buddhism in Sumatra, 7th to 13th Century," in *Esoteric Buddhism in Mediaeval Maritime Asia*, 253–273.
85. Kenneth R. Hall, "Indonesia's Evolving International Relationships in the Ninth to Early Eleventh Centuries: Evidence from Contemporary Shipwrecks and Epigraphy," *Indonesia* 90 (2010): 15–45; Miksic, "Archaeological Evidence," 259–260; and Horst H. Liebner, *The Siren of Cirebon: A Tenth-Century Trading Vessel Lost in the Java Sea* (PhD dissertation, University of Leeds, 2014), 191–194.
86. Woodward, "Esoteric Buddhism," 353.
87. Jan Schoterman, "Traces of Indonesian Influences in Tibet," in *Esoteric Buddhism in Mediaeval Maritime Asia* 119 (113–122).

88. Natasha Kimmet, "Sharing Sacred Space: A Comparative Study of Tabo and Borobudur," in *Selected Papers from the 13th International Conference of the European Association of Southeast Asian Archaeologists, Berlin, 2010, Volume 2: Connecting Empires and States*, eds. Dominik Bonatz, Andreas Reinecke, and Mai-Lin Tjoa-Bonatz (Singapore: National University of Singapore Press, 2012), 93–101.
89. Leonard W. J. van der Kuijp, "A Treatise on Buddhist Epistemology and Logic Attributed to Klong chen Rab 'byams pa (1308–1364) and Its Place in Indo-Tibetan Intellectual History," *Journal of Indian Philosophy* 31 (2003): 420, n. 6 (381–437).
90. Griffiths, "Inscriptions of Sumatra, III: The Padang Lawas Corpus studied along with inscriptions from Sorik Merapi (North Sumatra) and Muara Takus (Riau)," in *History of Padang Lawas, North Sumatra. II: Societies of Padang Lawas (9th c.–13th c.)*, ed. Daniel Perret (Paris: Association Archipel, 2014), 211–262; and Thomas M. Hunter, "Sanskrit in a Distant Land: The Sanskritized Sections," in *A 14th Century Malay Code of Laws: The Nītisārasamuccaya by Uli Kozok* (Singapore: ISEAS Publishing, 2015), 324-327 (281–379).
91. Claudine Bautze-Picron, "Buddhist Images from Padang Lawas Region and the South Asian Connection," in *History of Padang Lawas*, 107–128.
92. D. Christian Lammerts and Arlo Griffiths, "Epigraphy: Southeast Asia," in *Brill's Encyclopedia of Buddhism Vol. I*, eds. Jonathan Silk and Vincent Eltschinger (Leiden, The Netherlands: Brill, 2015), 994 (988–1009).
93. M. Jacq-Hergoualc'h, *The Malay Peninsula: Crossroads of the Maritime Silk-Road (100 BC–1300 AD)* (Leiden, The Netherlands: Brill, 2002), 47.
94. Peter Skilling, "The Circulation of Artefacts Engraved with '*Apramāda*' and Other Mottos in Southeast Asia and India: A Preliminary Report," in *Annual Report of the International Research Institute for Advanced Buddhology at Soka University for the Academic Year 2014: Volume XVIII* (Tokyo: International Research Institute for Advanced Buddhology Soka University, 2015), 69–72 (63–77).
95. Sharrock and Bunker, "Seeds of Vajrabodhi."
96. Jacq-Hergoualch, *The Malay Peninsula*, 274–275, 346–347, 400.
97. Kim, "Local Visions, Transcendental Practices," 49, 63, 65.
98. Kandahjaya, *A Study*, 60.
99. *Tāranātha's History of Buddhism in India*, 330.
100. Philip S. E. Green, "The Many Faces of Lokeśvara: Tantric Connections in Cambodia and Campā between the Tenth and Thirteenth Centuries," *History of Religions* 54, no. 1 (2014): 80–83 (69–93).
101. Nandana Chutiwongs, "Le Bouddhisme du Champa," in *Trésors d'art du Vietnam. La sculpture du Champa Ve-XVe siècles*, eds. Pierre Baptiste and Thierry Zéphir (Paris: Réunion des Musées Nationaux and Musée des Arts Asiatiques Guimet, 2005): 80–81 (65–87). Woodward, "The Temple of Dong Duong and the Kāraṇḍavyūha Sūtra," in *From Beyond the Eastern Horizon; Essays in Honour of Professor Lokesh Chandra*, ed. Manjushree (New Delhi: Aditya Prakashan, 2011), 33–42; see also his "Review article," 348, on a 10th-century Khmer stela (K. 1154) connected with the *Kāraṇḍavyūha* bearing on one face the figure of an eight-armed Avalokiteśvara—an icon that also appears on the rear outside wall of Candi Mendut in Central Java.
102. Revire, "À propos d'une "tête" de *khakkhara* conservée au Musée national de Bangkok," *Aséanie* 24 (2009): 111–134.
103. Orlina, "Epigraphical Evidence," 91–101.
104. Florina H. Capistrano-Baker, "Butuan in Early Southeast Asia," in *Philippine Ancestral Gold*, ed. Florina H. Capistrano-Baker (Makati City, Philippines: Ayala Foundation, 2011), 253–254 (191–257).
105. Chavannes, *Documents*; Sylvain Lévi, "Manimekhala, a Divinity of the Sea," *Indian Historical Quarterly* 6, no. 4 (1931): 597 (597–614); and George Cœdès, *The Indianized States of Southeast Asia* (Honolulu: University of Hawai'i Press, 1968), 21.

106. See Ray, *The Winds of Change: Buddhism and the Maritime Links of Early South Asia* (New Delhi: Oxford University Press, 1994); Sen, "Buddhism and the Maritime Crossings" and *Buddhism, Diplomacy, and Trade*; Lancaster, "The 'Great Circle' of Buddhism;" and Deeg, "Maritime routes in the Indian Ocean."
107. Pachow, "The Voyage"; Lin, "Puṇyodaya;" S. G. M. Weerasinghe, *A History of the Cultural Relations Between Sri Lanka and China* (Colombo, Sri Lanka: Central Cultural Fund, 1995): 20–27; and Sen, "The Travel Records of Chinese Pilgrims Faxian, Xuanzang, and Yijing: Sources for Cross-Cultural Encounters between Ancient China and Ancient India," *Education about Asia* 11, no. 3 (Winter 2006): 24–33. For the maritime-related portions of Faxian's biography, see Deeg, *Das Gaoseng-Faxian-Zhuan als religionsgeschichtliche Quelle Der älteste Bericht eines chinesischen buddhistischen Pilgermönchs über seine Reise nach Indien mit Übersetzung des Textes* (Wiesbaden, Germany: Harrassowitz Verlag, 2005).
108. Sundberg and Giebel, "The Life of Vajrabodhi."
109. Ray, "Narratives of Travel and Shipwreck;" Acri, "Navigating the 'Southern Seas', Miraculously: Avoidance of Shipwreck in Buddhist Narratives of Maritime Crossings," in *Moving Spaces. Creolisation and Mobility in Africa, the Atlantic and Indian Ocean*, eds. Marina Berthet, Fernando Rosa, and Shaun Viljoen (Leiden/Boston: Brill, forthcoming).
110. Schlingloff, "Chapter 22: Ships and Seafaring," *Studies in the Ajanta Paintings: Identifications and Interpretations* (Delhi: Ajanta Publications, 1988): 195–218.
111. On South India, see Schalk, "Buddhism among Tamils"; Anne E. Monius, *Imagining a Place for Buddhism: Literary Culture and Religious Community in Tamil-Speaking South India* (Oxford: Oxford University Press, 2001); and Gokul Seshadri, "New Perspectives on Nagapattinam: The Medieval Port City in the Context of Political, Religious, and Commercial Exchanges between South India, Southeast Asia and China," in *Nagapattinam to Suvarnadwipa: Reflections on the Chola Naval Expeditions to Southeast Asia*, eds. Hermann Kulke, K. Kesavapany, and Vijay Sakhuja (Singapore: ISEAS Publishing, 2009), 102–134. On Sri Lanka, see Chandawimala, *Buddhist Heterodoxy*; Sundberg, "Appreciation of Relics, Stūpas, and Relic-Stūpas in Eighth Century Esoteric Buddhism: Taishō Tripiṭaka Texts and Archaeological Residues of Guhyā Laṅkā, Part 1," *Indian International Journal of Buddhist Studies* 18 (2017): 173–340. On Southeast Asia, see Kandahjaya, "*Saṅ Hyaṅ Kamahāyānikan*," and several other chapters in Acri, *Esoteric Buddhism in Mediaeval Maritime Asia*; McGovern, "Esoteric Buddhism in Southeast Asia," *Oxford Research Encyclopedia of Religion*; and Woodward, "Esoteric Buddhism."
112. Deeg, "Maritime routes;" Sen, "Buddhism and the Maritime Crossings;" and Tanaka, "Comparing the Cross-Cultural Exchanges."
113. Singh, "Gifts from Other Lands"; Seshadri, "New Perspectives"; and Silk, "Tidings."
114. Frasch, "1456: The Making of a Buddhist Ecumene;" "The Theravāda Buddhist Ecumene in the Fifteenth Century: Intellectual Foundations and Material Representations," in Sen, *Buddhism Across Asia*, 347–367; and Blackburn, "Buddhist Connections," "The Sphere of the Śāsana."
115. Lévi, "Les 'marchands de mer';" Dayalan, "Role of Trade;" Bopearachchi, "Sri Lanka and the Maritime Trade;" Holcombe, "Trade-Buddhism." Dayalan, "Role of Archaeology;" Ray, *The Archaeology of Seafaring in Ancient South Asia* (Cambridge, UK: Cambridge University Press, 2003); and Ray, *The Archaeology of Seafaring in Ancient South Asia* (Cambridge, UK: Cambridge University Press, 2003).
116. Griffiths, "Written Traces"; "Inscriptions of Sumatra, III"; "The 'Greatly Ferocious' Spell (*Mahāraudra-nāma-hṛdaya*): A *dhāraṇī* Inscribed on a Lead-Bronze Foil Unearthed near Borobudur," in *Epigraphic Evidence in the Pre-Modern Buddhist World: Proceedings of the Eponymous Conference Held in Vienna*, ed. K. Tropper (Vienna: Arbeitskreis für Tibetische und Buddhistische Studien, 2014), 1–36. See also Cruijsen, Griffiths, and Klokke, "The Cult"; Lammerts and Griffiths, "Epigraphy"; Griffiths, Revire, and Sanyal, "An Inscribed Bronze Sculpture of a Buddha in *bhadrāsana* at Museum Ranggawarsita in Semarang (Central Java, Indonesia)," *Artibus Asiae* 68 (2013): 3–26. Kandahjaya, *A Study*," "*Saṅ Hyaṅ*

Kamahāyānikan," "The Lord of All Virtues," *Pacific World: Journal of the Institute of Buddhist Studies* (Third Series) 11 (2009): 1–25.
117. Hall, "Indonesia's Evolving International Relationships."

Andrea Acri

MARPA LOTSAWA CHÖKYI LODRÖ

THE IMPORTANCE OF MARPA IN TIBETAN RELIGIOUS HISTORY

Marpa Chökyi Lodrö (Mar pa chos kyi blo gros, 1000?–1085?), generally called Marpa Lotsawa (Marpa "the Translator"), is the Tibetan founder of the Kagyü (*bka' brgyud*) school of Tibetan Buddhism, one of the main Tibetan Buddhist religious streams that developed in Tibet from the 11th century onward. Over the years, this religious movement has split into several subcurrents that all trace their lineages back to Marpa and his predecessors, Tilopa and Nāropa, and to Marpa's disciple Milarepa (Mi la ras pa, 1028?–1111?). After Milarepa's main disciple Gampopa (Sgam po pa, 1079–1153), the Kagyü lineage multiplied into several sub-lineages, called the "Four Primary and Eight Secondary" (*che bzhi chung brgyad*). Among these, several Kagyü sub-lineages, such as the Karma (*kar ma*), Drikung (*'bri gung*), and Drukpa (*'brug pa*) Kagyü, remain in their traditional form today. For ten centuries, the Kagyü identity has been shaped by three major figures (*mar mi dwags gsum*)—Marpa, Milarepa, and Gampopa—who each represent a distinct element of the Kagyü school and together constitute a common history and religious ancestry. In this triad, Marpa generally represents the lay family holder and independent tantric yogi, the translator who brought back precious Buddhist teachings from India and spread these key instructions in the 11th century, during the period of the "second spread" (*phyi dar*) of Buddhism in Tibet. Milarepa is the hermitic *yogin* (*rnal 'byor*), the cotton-clad one (*ras pa*) who shed all worldly life to meditate in the mountains and reached the highest accomplishment in one lifetime through a deep mastery of tantric yogic practices. Gampopa is the monastic, the one who synthesized the progressive path (*lam rim*) of the Kadampa lineage (*bka' gdams pa*) initiated by Atiśa (982–1054) with the tantric practice of the Kagyüpa—cultivation of the creation and perfection phase and mahāmudrā—thus giving rise to a more institutional Kagyü order that was embodied from the 12th century onward in a network of monasteries, sacred sites, and monastic curricula spread over the whole Tibetan plateau.

As this schematization indicates, Marpa is a cultural and religious hero in Tibet. Paintings bearing his likeness are found in most Kagyü temples around the world, and his story is often told during traditional teaching sessions. Tibetan Buddhist adepts have identified with him for centuries, and his life story has been told countless times from the 12th to the 21st century. However, multiple versions of his life exist, and the representations far exceed the truths that may be found in any of them. Although any definitive truth cannot be attained on the basis of the biographical genre only, by meticulously analyzing all the biographical sources with regard to their compositional framework and by referencing related material outside Marpa's biographical tradition as well, Marpa's life can be reconstructed to some extent. Uncertainties remain, which are inherent to the sources used—life stories written by Marpa's indirect and distant successors, who never went to the places he visited and who were themselves confronted with conflicting stories and with the functional demands of narrating a life story intended to inspire and instruct Buddhist practitioners of Marpa's transmissions. The life story narrated here, while being a synthesis of the most important early sources, does not contradict the later tradition and adopts many of the conclusions proposed by later Tibetan historians such as the Second Pawo (Dpa' bo gtsug lag phreng ba) and the Eighth Situ (Si tu paṇ chen chos kyi 'byung gnas).

Within the framework of the larger cultural landscape of Tibetan tantric Buddhism, Marpa represents the courage and perseverance of those Tibetan individuals who went to India in the 11th century in order to gain knowledge and mastery in the Highest Yoga tantras that were being practiced at that time. As declared with pious exaggeration in the *Lhorong Religious History*:

> He had in India one hundred and eight gurus. . . . There were fifty exegetical tradition holders, and thirteen who could with certainty transform appearances. In particular, there were four noble gurus–Nāro, Maitrī, Śāntibhadra . . . and Jñānagarbha. . . . Among them all, two were unrivalled: Nāro and Maitrī.[1]

Many of Marpa's masters, often collected into groups of 108, fifty, and thirteen, are not meant to be precisely identified; some of them are presented as named or unnamed tantric adepts and learned paṇḍits inhabiting the power places that Marpa visited during his sojourns in India. The four, Nāro, Maitrī, Śāntibhadra, and Jñānagarbha, are identifiable historical figures said to have been Marpa's main teachers. Among them, Nāropa and Maitrīpa occupy a special place. They are the ones who gave him the "key instructions" (*man ngag*) on cycles such as Hevajra, Cakrasaṃvara, and Guhyasamāja. These practice instructions ensured the fame and efficacy of the Kagyü lineage, and Marpa and his heirs often trace back to Nāropa's and Maitrīpa's names in their writings.

The main transmission that Marpa received from Nāropa, and to a lesser extent from Maitrīpa, was that of Hevajra, which became Marpa's chosen Buddhist deity (*yidam*). Much of Marpa's life can be read in light of the *Hevajratantra* (*Rgyud brtag pa gnyid pa*), such as the name of his wife Dakmema (the Tibetan rendering of Hevajra's consort's name, Nairātmyā), his eight consorts (the eight goddesses in Hevajra's maṇḍala), the interaction with Nāropa (his tantric conduct is described in chapter I.6 of the Tantra), and the activities of some of the people he met (for instance, the yogin who paralyzes a crow with his gaze or the woman who uses a gaze to make fruits fall, the subject of gazes being explained in chapter I.11). The most salient anecdote in Marpa's life relates an incident where he prostrated to a manifestation of Hevajra appearing in the sky rather than to his root teacher Nāropa, thus showing more deference to the meditational deity, the *yidam*, than to the guru. This is given traditionally as an explanation for the fact that Marpa's family lineage did not continue but gave rise to a teacher–disciple relation at a time when family continuity, a "bone lineage," was the norm for Tibetan lay tantric Buddhist practitioners.

Marpa was a dedicated Buddhist practitioner completely immersed in India's tantric scene, recognized by his peers and taking part with them in tantric gatherings and advanced yogic practices. The following narrative, excerpted from a biographical account by Ngamdzong

Tönpa (Ngam rdzong ston pa, 12th century), describes events said to occur during Marpa's last journey to India:

> Marpa went to the city of Lakśetra and asked where Jñānagarbha was; [he was told that] he dwelled in the forest together with a low-caste woman. That low-caste woman entered her home and came back carrying a bucket. She told him to bathe with a third of the water and drink another third. She collected the [bath] water in the drain and poured it into the water-bucket; it became white bodhicitta. The woman then crossed her legs over the bucket rim and a stream of *rakta* fell from her secret place: white and red bodhicitta merged into one. She cleansed Marpa with it, and all his mental fabrications vanished. He poured some in his mouth and then looked in the bucket: he had a dazzling vision of all the deities of the glorious Guhyasamājā maṇḍala. After that, the illustrious Jñānagarbha arrived and blessed him . . .

Marpa then left for the south, to an island in a boiling, noxious lake. While Śāntibhadra was performing a tantric feast, a woman who sat among the practitioners brought a corpse in among the assembly rows. After splitting open the skull of the corpse, she poured the *guhyamati* liquid of the glorious Śāntibhadra on the brain soaked in fresh blood. The blend of brain and urine was distributed as [the substance] of *samaya*. When it reached master Marpa, the substances were boiling. He looked inside and had a vision of the syllables of the mantra yoga of channel-wheels of the glorious Mahāmāyā.[2]

Such descriptions show the kind of advanced yogic practices, here associated with the tantras of Guhyasamāja and Mahāmāyā, that are described in the source texts and are said to have been practiced to the letter in India, although they were often euphemized or practiced only through imagination in Tibet. It is difficult to assess whether they describe what Marpa experienced in India, but it is apparent that they are what it was remembered for in Tibet: for a Tibetan who went to India, received the deepest transmissions, practiced them in an authentic fashion, and was therefore fit to import them to Tibet. Although such account are less graphic in later biographies of Marpa, they point to the fact that he often traveled off the beaten track, in the jungles and forests of India, often alone and sometimes with Indians, as a *yogin* fully immersed in the tantric practices that he received from well-known gurus such as Nāropa, as well as from unknown yogis. Unlike other translators of the period such as Drokmi Lotsāwa or Nagtso Lotsāwa who went to the well-known universities of Vikramaśīla or Nālandā, Marpa did not study in large institutions, met with his gurus in isolated hermitages, and produced very few translations, mostly of oral instructions rather than scriptures. Except for a commentary on *Guhyasamājatantra* whose attribution is controversial, all other texts attributed to his name are short works such as terse commentaries on the Hevajra tradition and instructions on creation and completion phase practices (*utpatti-* and *utpannakrama*). Notwithstanding, it is likely that he also produced other translations that did not survive (alternative versions of the *Hevajratantra* verses, for example, appear in the commentaries of his disciples).

PRIMARY SOURCES

The life of Marpa Lotsawa is mostly known, in Tibet and in the West, by the biography composed in 1505 by Tsangnyön Heruka and translated in English in 1982 as *The Life of Marpa the*

Translator by the Nālandā Translation Committee. This work is the synthesis of many biographic writings created by distant disciples of Marpa from the 12th century onward, which were themselves based on oral narratives and memories of Marpa's songs.[3] Tsangnyön's work met with great success. He was a talented writer, endowed with poetic and dramatic powers, as well as a renowned teacher and a skilled communicator who widely propagated his writings through xylographic print.[4]

Marpa's life story, however, cannot be told exclusively on the basis of Tsangnyön's work: there exist many other writings, including more than thirty biographies, either full-length or included within collections of successive life-stories of lineage masters (generally called "rosaries"). The first written evidence of Marpa's life date from the 12th century and constitute a foundational layer made up of six independent works, out of which three influenced most of the later tradition and are the main sources of Marpa's life as it is told here.[5] They are themselves based in various degrees on the songs that Marpa is said to have sung in India, Nepal and Tibet.

These three main sources are alluded to in the colophon of Tsangnyön Heruka's *Life of Marpa*.[6] He says that the first sources of Marpa's life story are: on the one hand, the oral narratives that Milarepa and Marpa Golek (Mar pa mgo legs, 11th century), two of Marpa's disciples, gave to their disciple, Ngamdzong Tönpa, and, on the other hand, those that Milarepa gave to another disciple, Rechungpa (Ras chung pa). Ngamdzong Tönpa and Rechungpa are said to have discussed their findings, and to have each told Marpa's life story. Tsangnyön Heruka says that he also added information from traditions related to Marpa's other disciples, Ngok Chödor, Tsurtön Wangngé, and Metön Tsönpo (Mes ston tshon po, 11th century).

The first main source acknowledged by Tsangnyön is the biography composed by Ngamdzong Tönpa, founder of the "Ngamdzong Aural Transmission" (*ngam rdzong snyan brgyud*).[7] It is conserved in a collection of biographies compiled by Montsepa Kunga Palden (Mon rtse pa kun dga' dpal ldan, 1407–1475).[8] Regarding the second, although Tsangnyön Heruka attributes it to Rechungpa, it is in fact a biography redacted within the Aural Transmission lineage, copied and summarized on numerous occasions, and arguably the most influential text of the corpus. The original version is found in two collections, and attributed in one of them to Martön Tsultrim Jungné (Mar ston tshul khrims 'byung gnas, late 12th century), the student of Rechungpa's disciple Kyungtsangpa (Khyung tshang pa, 1115–1176).

Tsangnyön Heruka also mentions a version of Marpa's life coming from the Ngok clan. Several early works were composed in that familial lineage, who had inherited Marpa's exegesis of the tantras and would remain central in the transmission of the Marpa Kagyü tradition until the 15th century.[9] The most important narrative does not have an author but is tentatively attributed to Ngok Dodé (Rngog mdo sde, 1078–1154), Ngok Chödor's son and Marpa's direct disciple. It bears several features of antiquity and is called "dispelling doubts" in the colophon, which is the name given by the Second Pawo to a biography that was, according to him, composed by Ngok Dodé.[10] This text was quite influential and is the source of one of the most important topoi of Marpa's biography, the long quest for his master Nāropa during his third journey to India.

Although Tsangnyön Heruka refers to biographical accounts descending from Tsurtön and Metön, no such work has been identified in the corpus, but it is possible that traces of them figure in the other three 12th-century works that did not influence the later tradition to a large extent. Among them, the first is a short biography attributed to Gampopa (1079–1153), probably redacted a generation later by Kyungtsangpa.[11] The second comes from a compilation of biographies by Lama Zhang (*bla ma zhang*, 1123–1193), influenced by Ngok Dodé as well as by Gampopa's versions. The third figures in a collection transmitted within the Dochen (Mdo chen) Kagyü tradition, a sub-branch of the Drukpa lineage.[12]

As is often the case with life accounts of characters from the beginning of the period of the second spread of Buddhism in Tibet, especially those who went to India, none of these works present a coherent representation of Marpa's life. Furthermore, no account exists from Marpa's contemporaries written in the 11th century, during Marpa's life, that could provide hard facts. The only available sources of knowledge are narratives, particularly so-called hagiographies (*rnam thar*), written within Marpa's tradition, as well as allusions and short accounts from other traditions. The following life story is therefore necessarily as tentative as all other accounts preceding it. For an inspiring account of Marpa's life in English, the reader is referred to Tsangnyön's work. That text, however, dates from the 16th century and is heavily influenced by Tsangnyön's literary creativity. It is therefore necessary to synthesize the various early narratives in order to shine a light on Marpa's life shadowy or controversial parts of it.

UNCERTAINTIES SURROUNDING THE DATES OF MARPA'S LIFE

None of Marpa's biographies agree on the subject of his dates of birth and death, and most of his life's events are undated. It therefore represents a centuries-long challenge to settle on a chronological framework—a problem with which every biographer has had to grapple since the 13th century, but which may never be conclusively solved.[13]

The dates of Marpa's birth and death can be classified along three main intervals, 1000–1081, 1012–1097, and 1024–1107. This precision arose in the 15th century when an element was added to the duodecimal animal years given in Marpa's biographies, thus reducing the fuzziness that was the norm until then. Until that point, almost all biographies state that Marpa died in a bird year, which could be 1081, 1093, or 1105, in his eighty-eighth or eightieth year. Later versions, trying to be more precise, started to diverge on the death year and proposed an ox year (1085 or 1097), or more rarely a pig year (1107). The "early tradition" starts with the mid-15th-century *Lhorong Religious History*, where the dates 997–1085 are provided. The "late version" (1024–1107) comes from an early-15th-century large piece of historical writing by Lang Lhazik Repa (Rlangs lha gzigs ras pas, 1386–1434), and the "middle way" (1012–1097) is followed mainly by Gö Lotsawa's ('Gos lo tsā ba, 1392–1481) *Blue Annals* (*Deb ther sngon po*), published in 1476, and followed by most Western writers. Later Tibetan historians generally chose the early tradition, with some variation. Thus, the second Pawo (Dpa' bo gtsug lag phreng ba, 1504–1566) indicates 1000–1085, and Katok Tsewang Norbu (Ka' thog tshe dbang nor bu, 1698–1755) advances the death by a few years, to 1081, in order to fit with the bird year claimed in early biographies. Most biographers who favored the earlier dating justified it by relying on the so-called "Ngok tradition," which reads, here in an instance from the 14th century:

> When [Ngok Dodé] reached his eighth year, the Venerable Marpa, as a Bird-year native, passed away at 89, on the 14th day of the Hare month of an Ox year and on the day of the Bird.[14]

Here, Marpa is said to have died on the fourteenth day of the second month of an unspecified Ox year. The same text also does not indicate when Dodé was born. According to the

Lhorong Religious History, it was in 1078, but in 1090 according to the *Blue Annals*. These two histories place Marpa's death in either 1085 or 1097. If Marpa was in his eighty-ninth year at that time, he may have been born in 996 or 1008, respectively.

One of the reasons it makes sense to follow the Ngok accounts for the date of Marpa's death is that they were a family lineage who largely built Marpa's fame and who relied on him for their own legitimacy. As a family whose most prominent member was Dodé, the son of Chödor, they kept good track of the fact that Dodé was seven when Marpa died, and twelve when his father died. They, like Marpa, probably did not know when Marpa was born—this was before the introduction of the Kālacakra calendar and the first duodecimal cycle in 1027. However, they may have remembered that he was old, in his eighties. This is why the *Lhorong Religious History* states that Marpa was born in 997 (choosing a lifespan of eighty-eight years rather eighty-nine), and died in 1085. That same text later allows some leeway, stating that the birth date could be pushed forward by two to five years. Thus, according to the Ngok accounts and the *Lhorong Religious History*, and most later Kagyü historians, Marpa was born at the turn of the millennium (between 997 and 1002), and died in 1085. It must be remarked, however, that early accounts coming from the Ngok tradition generally say that Marpa died in a bird year, which would then be 1081 if the early dating is chosen. Taking this into account, the second Pawo, who wrote the longest account of Marpa's life, chose the years 1000–1085. Later historians such as Katok Situ and Belo Tsewang Kunkyab ('Be lo tshe dbang kun khyab, 18th century) decided for 1000–1081, to account for the bird year. It is difficult to choose between these two versions, but it seems preferable to conclude conservatively that Marpa was born at the turn of the millennium, and died in the early to middle 1080s.

MARPA'S LIFE

Just as a definitive framing of Marpa's lifetime cannot be decided on the basis of the available biographical literature, so too for the basic discrepancies in the narration of some key events in Marpa's life. A straightforward account of Marpa's life, a standard in Tibet and in the West, is the biography redacted by Tsangnyön Heruka.[15] This version adds information not found in earlier accounts, owing to Tsangnyön's poetic license, but it is generally a synthesis of the earlier sources and the songs, with a preference for the account found in the biography written by Martön Tsultrim Jungné in the Aural Transmission. Details presented as unproblematic by Tsangnyön and some of his most detailed narratives need to be re-examined, but this account created a standard representation of Marpa as understood by Tibetan Buddhists.

"Marpa" is the translator's family name, sometimes explained as "the one from the Mar Valley." This name is not rare and several other Marpas are known, for instance, his disciple Marpa Goyak. The second Pawo says that Marpa's family originally came from Latö, further west in Tsang, and other early biographies say they came from Purang, near Mount Kailash. Marpa's ancestors settled in the southern region of Lhodrak several generations before his birth, at a place called Chukyer located not far from the northern border of today's Bhutan. There are discrepancies in the received tradition of his parents' names, but they are generally called Wangchuk Özer and Gyamo Öde (several biographies give variants after Gyamo, but none assert that she was of Chinese origin, the literal meaning of *rgya mo*; the reading *rgyal mo* is also found). They were a wealthy family with large land assets, and Marpa later also became an important landowner. The most significant among his ancestors was called "the Rich Könchok" (*phyug po dkon mchog*) and sometimes the name Könchok is also given for Marpa's father.

Marpa was born the third of five sibling and was named Chökyi Lodrö. By all accounts, he was a very turbulent child. When he was twelve, his parents sent him away to study Buddhist doctrine, and he is said to have gone to Nyugulung (Myu gu lung), the newly established hermitage of Drokmi Lotsawa in Latö, to the west of the future Sakya Monastery. Marpa is generally considered to have stayed three years at Drokmi's place, using the time to mainly learn Sanskrit and the Indian colloquial languages needed to facilitate travel to the subcontinent. This initial training is referenced in several of Marpa's songs, where Marpa laments that fees for receiving actual teachings from Drokmi were so high that he could not afford it.[16] Seeing many Tibetans heading south, he decided to do the same, and left in the direction of Nepal.

Leaving for Nepal. Marpa then passed through the religious center of Teacher Lokya (Lo skya ston pa) in Gyerphu (Dgyer/Sgyer phu), in Latö, on his way south to Nepal. He received a few instructions from the old master there and returned to his estate on later journeys, where he met Lokya's son, Lokya José Jungyal (Jo sras 'byung rgyal). The Lokyas are well known in Marpa's biography because it is at their headquarters that Marpa sang the famous song of his meeting with Saraha.[17]

At this point, or, according to other biographies, after an initial stay in Nepal, Marpa met Nyö Lotsawa Yonten Drak from Kharak (Kha rag Gnyos yon tan grags), who became an important companion on Marpa's first journey to India. The interaction between Marpa and Nyö is narrated in both translators' biographies, with general correspondences.[18] Nyö Lotsawa was a senior translator; his family narrative states that he was fifty-six and Marpa seventeen when the two met. Nyö came from a wealthy family and became famous in Tibet for his transmission of three main cycles, Guhyasamāja in the form of Mañjuvajra, the protector Trakṣad Mahākāla, and Kṛṣṇa Yamāri (Vajrabhairava).

Marpa's biographies diverge over the place and time of their meeting. The Aural Transmission says that Marpa met Nyö in a southern Tibetan inn, at Tsi Nesar (*rtsis gnas gsar*) in Nyangtö, in the Tsang region, on the road to India via Sikkim. Nyö was accompanied by several horsemen and offered his help to the poor young man, who in exchange offered his services. Together, they traveled to Nepal. There, Marpa met with two of Nāropa's disciples, the "Bold One" Chiterpa (Spyi ther pa) and Paiṇḍapa (Pen dha pa). From Citerpa, Marpa received the Catuṣpīṭha cycle, together with the protector practice of Düsolma (Dud sol ma) and the perfection phase practices of Transference (*'pho ba*) and Entering Another's Body (*grong 'jug*). Nyö did not wish to attend on this master and continued toward India instead. Other biographies, like the ones of Ngok Dodé and Ngamdzong Tönpa, state that Nyö and Marpa met after Marpa's initial stay in Nepal, either while he was back in Tibet to collect more funds, or on his way to India, and that they traveled together.

First Journey in India. After three years in Nepal—during which Marpa honed his language skills, adapted to the heat, and received tantric transmissions—he finally left for India, probably in his very early twenties, some say after a brief foray into Tibet in order to collect more funds. He and Nyö helped each other travel toward India, but parted ways upon arrival. Marpa went toward the west and Nyö toward the east. They met several times during the following years, and often it was Nyö who impelled Marpa to discover and request further teachings.

According to Ngamdzong Tönpa and many other biographies (including the *Lhorong Religious History* and the Second Pawo), when Marpa went west, he first crossed a region with "poisoned waters" that made his skin peel, layer after layer. At a place called Lakśetra, he met with Jñānagarbha, an 11th-century master of the Ārya tradition of Guhyasamāja about whom not much is known and who is distinct from the various Jñānagarbhas mentioned in the Tanjur. Marpa and Jñānagarbha are recorded to have translated a Guhyasamāja explanatory tantra found in the Kanjur.[19] From Jñānagarbha, Marpa received the Guhyasamāja transmission and the completion phase practices of the body of apparition (*sgyu lus*) and of luminosity (*'od gsal*). There, Marpa also met many yogis, several of them practicing tantric conduct (*caryā*). The biography by Ngamdzong Tönpa states:

> A large number of yogins assembled to celebrate a tantric feast, many of them, notably, were engaged in ascetic conduct. . . . At that time a yogin riding a jackal and another riding a rat also arrived. Marpa asked who they were, and was told they were Nāropa's disciples Kandhapa and Paiṇḍapa. Guru Nāropa also had 108 accomplished disciples and 28 disciples engaged in ascetic conduct. . . . As for their qualities, Kusulu the Elder once left his amulet beside him to wash his hair and a crow took it away; he used a yogic gaze that made the crow fall to the ground with the amulet. He was thus a yogin who had accomplished the four gazes: the falling gaze and so forth. Kusulu the Younger was a yogin who had mastered four out of the eight great ordinary accomplishments: he had mastered the sword, gold, magical boots and eye balm. During a ceremony, Paiṇḍapa produced a container in which beer from the town's taverns appeared and spread a sheet on which meat and food manifested. By the power of his concentration, he summoned the corpses from the charnel ground to follow him, and so forth. As for Kandhapa, he directly saw the face of his deity in the *homa*'s hearth. Such were these yogins, endowed with these and other qualities.[20]

Marpa's initial stay in India is said to have lasted five years, after which he briefly returned to Nepal in order to collect more funds. When he returned to India, he offered gold to Jñānagarbha and Paiṇḍapa, and the latter arranged a meeting with Nāropa in his hermitage of Pullahari. Marpa then met Nāropa, the famous paṇḍit and siddha who became his main guru, and one of the greatest symbols of the Kagyü lineage.

According to the Aural Transmission's biography and several others, including Tsangnyön, Marpa met Nāropa immediately when he arrived in India, led there from Nepal by Paiṇḍapa. The place where the two met is also disputed. Most claim that it was in Magadha (central India), with some saying it was in the Buddhist university of Vikramaśīla, others in Nālandā.[21] In general, Nāropa's own dwelling place is considered to be Pullahari, a hermitage in Magadha, southeast of Patna, not far from the Ganges. Many colophons and some biographies also mention an alternative hermitage in Kashmir, sometimes called Puṣpahari. Although in most early biographies Marpa generally goes toward central India to meet Nāropa, the possibility should not be excluded that the great siddha also had a hermitage in Kashmir, as he himself was said to hail from that region.[22]

When Marpa met Nāropa, he requested the transmission of Hevajra. During the initial empowerment, Nāropa manifested the nine-deity maṇḍala of Hevajra in the sky and asked Marpa whether he would like to receive the empowerment from him or from Hevajra. Amazed at that vision, Marpa chose the deity, and so Nāropa replied: "The root of blessing is the guru. As you chose the deity over the guru, the religious lineage of your family will not be of benefit!"[23]

This episode is found in most biographies (but sometimes takes place during the third journey), and it became one of the defining features of Marpa's tradition and the Kagyü lineage in general. A symbolic reminder of this episode is that the Hevajra practice manuals according to Marpa's tradition, for example, generally start with an homage to the master and *yidam* as undifferentiated. This kind of homage is a trope in writings of the Kagyü lineage. Another trope alluded to by this quote is the fact that Marpa's family lineage, that is to say especially his son Marpa Dodé, would not become his heir. It would rather be Marpa's disciples that would make his religious lineage flourish.[24]

In the Aural Transmission followed by Tsangnyön, and to a lesser extent in other biographies, Nāropa then became the center of Marpa's maṇḍala. After receiving from Nāropa the empowerment of the two tantras of Hevajra—the *Dvikalpa* (or *Hevajra Root-Tantra*) and the explanatory *Vajrapañjaratantra*—and being instructed in related practice methods (*sādhanas*) and key instructions, Marpa went away and met Nyö Lotsawa. Marpa having prevailed in a discussion about Hevajra, Nyö retorted that what he needed was in fact Guhyasamāja. Acknowledging his ignorance in that subject, Marpa returned to Nāropa, who in turn sent him to Jñānagarbha in order to learn Guhyasamāja.

The process was repeated when Nyö told Marpa about Mahāmāyā. Marpa asked Nāropa about it, and Nāropa replied that the holder of that *yoginītantra* was Śāntibhadra—also sometimes called Kukuripa, the "Dog Lover," as he was a holder of the *mahāsiddha* Kukuripa's lineage. Śāntibhadra is said to have lived in the south of India, on an "island of a noxious lake."[25] He is described as ugly and hairy, like a monkey, and he lived with a consort who is sometimes said to resemble a bitch, another justification for the name Kukuripa. From him, Marpa received the Mahāmāyā cycle, made up of the empowerment and the three yogas (of forms, mantras, and the ultimate yoga of dharma), as well as instructions and practice manuals.

At that point in Tsangnyön's version, Marpa aspired to meet Maitrīpa (986–1063). Nāropa permitted Marpa to meet with Maitrīpa, and the latter then became his second main master. While most biographies state that the two met during Marpa's first journey to India, it was especially during his second journey in the late 1040s that Marpa relied on Maitrīpa. This corresponds to the period when Nāropa was said to be engaged in tantric conduct, a time when Maitrīpa was more active as a tantric master. The place where Marpa met Maitrīpa is called the charnel ground of the Mountain Blazing like Fire, near the Ganges in eastern India. From Maitrīpa he received the Nāmasaṃgīti cycle and mahāmudrā teachings—some biographies mention the Seven Sections on Accomplishment (*grub pa sde bdun*), the Six Works on Essential Meaning (*snying po skor drug*), and the Twenty-Five Amanasikāra Works (*yid la mi byed pa'i chos nyi shu rtsa lnga*).[26]

Parting with Nyö. After twelve years in India, in some texts divided into two stays of five and seven years, respectively, Marpa returned to Tibet together with Nyö Lotsawa. By then, the two Tibetans had experienced a long friendship made up of sharing and rivalry, the amount of each varying in the sources. Even in the texts where Nyö is depicted in a cruder light, it is undeniable that he helped Marpa with gold and by guiding him in his exploration of India's tantric scene while Marpa, for his part, did not share much with Nyö, and even kept the identity of some of his masters secret. Ngamdzong describes their final interactions as follows:

> Nyö and Marpa had then reached equal fame in terms of scholarship and the rest. When they arrived at the Nepal-Tibet border, Nyö seemed outwardly to have the greatest fortune. When they reached the four parts of Latö, they were equally famous for translation and instructions. . . . When they reached the heart of Tibet (*dbus gtsang*), all the glory went to Marpa because of the instructions he held. At this reverse of fortune, Nyö became jealous. While the two were crossing Lake Nubalcha (*rnub bal cha*), in a fit of pique he threw Marpa's books into the water, so that none were left.[27]

This competitive atmosphere is also mentioned openly in Ngok Dodé's version, where it is said that Nyö threw Marpa's Guhyasamāja manuscripts into the Ganges, promising him that he could later copy his texts, but retracting this offer upon reaching Tibet. This depiction reaches its apex in Tsangnyön's version, where Nyö's treason is dramatized by Marpa's "song of shame" to Nyö, an addition by Tsangnyön. Other versions (the Aural Transmission biography, the ones written by Gampopa and Gyaltangpa) are more careful in their formulation. They state that, indeed, Marpa lost some texts, and that there were rumors that Nyö may have been responsible from it, and some give alternative versions, such as a forest fire, or that Marpa inadvertently drowned them. Yet others, such as Lama Zhang, do not mention the loss. This may be a tacit acknowledgement that, despite the end of the two translators' relationship at that stage, their distant disciples and family heirs kept good relationships and that the Nyö lineage continued to play a significant role in the Kagyü lineage (in the form of the Lhapa [*lha pa*] Kagyü sub-lineage) and in Tibet in general. Later exegetes such as Katok Situ and Belo Tsewang Künkhyab (both in the 18th century) even called those who reviled Nyö in such a way "fools," clearly alluding to Tsangnyön Heruka's one-sided dramatic narrative. According to them, in gratitude Marpa gave Nyö a statue that had belonged to Nāropa and that was then kept in the Nyö family temple.[28]

Attracting Gold and Disciples in Tibet. Whether because of Nyö or for other reasons, when Marpa came back to Tibet he lacked written traces of his transmissions. He saw clearly that his training was not complete and that he had to return to India. However, he needed to collect more gold in order to repay his guru's kindness and to request further teachings. Among early biographies, the Aural Transmission biography provides the most details on this period.

When Marpa returned home, he was not very successful. His childhood reputation remained vivid and no one from his homeland came to receive his teaching. He therefore left home again in search of gold and disciples that could provide him with funds for another costly journey south. On the way north, he met with Ngok Chödor in the vicinity of the latter's fief of Zhung (*gzhung*). Chödor finished some business and then returned to Zhung with Marpa, where the former received teachings associated with Hevajra. Marpa then went further north, where gold mines had been discovered. He stayed there for a few years, earning gold through his tantric abilities by resuscitating young infants and providing magical rites based on the Goddess Vetali. In Penyul (*'phan yul*), he met Marpa Golek who became a lifelong attendant and sponsor. Golek invited him to his residence of Tsamlung in the Dam region (*'dam gyi tsam lung*), just south of the Nyenchen Tanglha range (*gnyan chen thang lha*). There, Marpa met with success and received many more riches from Golek and other disciples.

One night, Marpa had a dream about three *ḍākinīs* singing to him instructions that revealed the meaning of a cryptic declaration uttered by Nāropa a few years prior:

The *ḍākinī* is the sky-flower.
The barren woman's [son] riding a horse is the Aural Transmission.
He wields the tortoise-hair whip of the inexpressible.
The dagger of a hare's horn is the unborn,
Which kills mental fabrications in the space of *dharmatā*.
Tilopā is the mute, beyond word, thought, and expression.
Nāropa is the blind, liberated in seeing the meaning of the meaningless.
Nāropa is the deaf on the *dharmakāya* mountain of *dharmatā*.
[Marpa] Lodrö is the cripple who runs on luminosity without coming or going.
On the sun and moon of the Bhagavan Hevajra
The dancers' many movements are of one taste.
The conches proclaim his fame in the ten directions:
They are blown for worthy human vessels of their sound.
The teaching of the wheel is the Glorious Cakrasaṃvara;
The little child of the Aural Transmission which is like a wish-fulfilling gem turns it without attachment.[29]

This inspired Marpa to return to India, and so he started his second journey south.

Second Journey to India. At this point, several things must be noted. First, Marpa is generally considered to have made three journeys to India, the number three being omnipresent in his songs. In the biographies, however, there is a wide disparity. While some rare sources (the Aural Transmission biography, for instance) mention only two journeys, most state that there were three in order to accord with the songs' declarations. The first journey, however, is generally divided into two parts of five and seven years, with a brief interruption to either Nepal or the Tibetan border to get some funds, and it is followed by the "third" journey. Yet other sources describe three distinct journeys to India, but in those cases, the second journey does not contain any noticeable detail. In Tsangnyön's version, for example, the descriptions are those found elsewhere in either the first journey (the cryptic verses, the interaction with Ākarasiddhi) or the last journey (visiting each of his former master, working on the texts).[30] Therefore, it seems preferable to conclude that there were two main journeys to India, one taking place from Marpa's early twenties until his thirties (*c.* 1020–1032), and one taking place in the mid to late 1040s.

Second, Tsangnyön describes at length that the motivation for Marpa's third journey was his disciple Milarepa's request for further teachings, and that Marpa was by then an old married man with a son, Marpa Dodé. These descriptions break with most early sources and also pose an inner contradiction as Marpa is also said in this biography to encounter the Indian master Atiśa while the latter was traveling toward central Tibet, which, according to Atiśa's bibliographic tradition, happened in 1045.[31] At that date, Milarepa was still very young and would be very unlikely to have been Marpa's disciple. Therefore, it seems warranted to discard this part of Tsangnyön's narrative and to conclude that Milarepa did not have anything to do with Marpa's last journey to Tibet.

After a few years collecting gold in Tibet and having gathered a first group of disciples, Marpa dreamt of *ḍākinīs* deciphering for him the sense of the cryptic verses imparted by Nāropa during the first travel, and he decided to set out again on a long journey to India. En route, he met with the great Indian master Atiśa who was traveling from western to central Tibet. During that meeting, Marpa received a few transmissions from Atiśa.

Atiśa had visited Nāropa before he left for Tibet in 1040, and he reportedly heard of the latter's death only a short time later. This is why Nāropa's death is generally dated to 1040. When Marpa set out for India in 1045, it was therefore clear that he would not meet Nāropa as he previously had done, and several of his masters announced to him the siddha's departure. The way they phrased this was that Nāropa had "entered tantric conduct" (*caryā*). This is a term describing a moment on a tantric practitioner's path when he passes beyond all worldly conventions.[32] Nāropa's conduct is unanimously mentioned in early biographies. For some, it only means that Nāropa does not teach any more but just sometimes conducts tantric feasts and gives his blessing. Gampopa, for instance, states that Nāropa was keeping a vow of silence and had abandoned all worldly possessions, only keeping a skull cup that he gave to Marpa. For most, however, it means that Nāropa is completely gone, and it may be an euphemistic reference to his death. In Marpa's songs and biographies, and more significantly in Ngok Dode's biography of Marpa, an event occurred at this point that is repeated in all later narratives: Marpa visited each of his gurus and prayed with them. They all predicted that he would meet Nāropa, and Marpa departed on a quest for his master in the forests and jungles of India. During that quest spanning several months, Marpa had several fleeting visions of his master who gave him short verses of instruction. Finally, Nāropa appeared in the magnificent form of the Heruka:

> After seven days, the glorious Nāropa himself arrived bearing a human skin, a skull cup, and a *khatvāṅga*. He was naked, his matted hair drawn on the top of his head, and he was adorned by the six bone ornaments. With exceedingly great joy, [Marpa] cried and shrieked, embraced [Nāropa] and pressed heart against heart, forehead against forehead. With both faces touching, [Marpa] narrated the story of his hardships and bemoaned the lord's lack of compassion. [Nāropa] answered: "It is through this complete purification of your continuum by the *maṇḍala* of body, speech, and mind that I now give you my blessing!"[33]

Then occurs the second event of Marpa's biography that came to define the Kagyü identity: seeing his master at last, Marpa took the few ounces of gold dust left in his pocket and offered them to Nāropa. The siddha then placed a few flakes upon his head, and scattered the rest, offering it to the guru and the three jewels. Awestruck, Marpa recalled the difficulties he had encountered while accumulating that gold. Recognizing his disciple's astonishment, Nāropa made the two handfuls of gold reappear and said that for him everything was gold. Then striking a brick on the floor, it became gold, and Marpa generated extraordinary confidence in his guru.

For seven months, Marpa received new instructions on Hevajra and the associated practices of the action seal (tib. *las rgya*, skt: *karmamudrā*) and inner heat (tib. *gtum mo*, skt: *caṇḍali*), on the Cakrasaṃvara Aural Transmission, on Guhyasamāja, and more. He was also encouraged to study with Maitrīpa and revise his texts with him. Finally, Nāropa instructed Marpa to return and teach in Tibet before he departed for the celestial realm accompanied by *ḍākinīs*.

Despite the agreement of Marpa's songs and biographies regarding his meeting and studying with Nāropa, discordant voices have appeared in Tibet and in the West that attempted to refute accounts of that interaction. In Western scholarship, the controversy surfaced in Ronald Davidson's *Tibetan Renaissance*, and received sustained attention due to the success of Davidson's book.[34] Yet it started in Tibet in a letter written by the Sakyapa hierarch Drakpa Gyaltsen (Grags pa rgyal mtshan, 1147–1216), and is alluded to in several late biographies of Marpa.[35] According to the Sakyapa master, Atiśa's attendant Nagtso Lotsawa (Nag 'tsho lo tsā ba, 1011–?) met Nāropa shortly before the *siddha*'s passing, and several years later he and Atiśa encountered Marpa in Nyetang. Nagtso declared that he had heard from a student of a disciple of Marpa that Marpa had said that he had not met Nāropa but that he had received his instructions from Maitrīpa. As the convoluted nature of this rumor shows, these are thirdhand statements, put in writing at least a century after the events described. Although they cannot be dismissed out of hand, they can be equally well understood within the framework of a growing competition between the Sakya and Kagyü traditions in the 12th century, and a personal rivalry between Marpa and Nagtso in the 11th century. Additionally, the controversy generally resurfaced over the years in polemical texts written by Kagyü hierarchs (the fourth Shamar [Zhwa dmar chos kyi grags, 1453–1524], an important master of the Karma Kagyü lineage and political figure of the early 16th century, or Lang Lhazik Repa, the twelfth abbot of Densatil and brother of the Phadru ruler of Tibet). Davidson's writings can also be considered in this light, since they seem to lean in the direction of the Sakya interpretation. It can therefore be concluded that this thesis does not bear as much weight as the other sources, but that ultimately all these opinions rely on writings (hagiographical, historical, or religio-political) that do not constitute facts that could prove or refute a meeting between Marpa and Nāropa in India.

Regarding Marpa's biographical writings, it can be observed that Nāropa's role was progressively emphasized over the centuries. Some early narratives assert that Marpa did not receive some specific teachings from Nāropa or that he was compelled to study with other masters as Nāropa did not teach any longer. These indications progressively disappeared from the tradition. Moreover, in some early texts, Nāropa did not have the instrumental place in Marpa's life that he had in later narratives. Therefore, Nāropa's centrality was clearly promoted over the centuries, so that he became Marpa's principal master in the Kagyü lineage.

Final Return to Tibet. After Nāropa left, Marpa made farewell visits to his Indian gurus and friends. He passed through Bodhgayā before returning to Nepal, where he also met his Newari masters, and finally made his way back to Tibet. In Bodhgayā, he is said to have for the first time "entered into another's body" (*grong 'jug*), that is to say accomplished the practice of *parapurapraveśa* that is sometimes considered part of the Six Doctrines of Nāropa (*nā ro chos drug*).[36] This practice derives from several Highest Yoga Tantras (*niruttarayogatantra*) but existed in non-Buddhist circles as well. Marpa is sometimes said to have received it during his first journey in Nepal, together with the transmission of Catuṣpīṭha, and sometimes during the third journey when Nāropa was in "tantric conduct" (or deceased), in the framework of Aural Transmission teachings. In Tibet, the practice did not spread widely and it was mainly Marpa who was famous for it, although other masters are also said to have performed it on specific occasions. According to Tsangnyön Heruka, the practice did not continue in Marpa's lineage because he intended to pass it on to his son, who suffered an accidental early death. Tsangnyön relates this to the defective choice Marpa made in prostrating to the *yidam* instead of the guru. Not all biographies agree with him, and indeed there are traces of the transmission of Entering Another's Body that did not pass through Marpa Dodé.

In the latter part of his life, from the end of the third journey onward, Marpa is said to have performed this practice several times. In Bodhgayā, he entered the body of a large dead demon and traveled in that body to a faraway rocky mountain. Later in Tibet, he is said to have entered the corpse of a yak, a sparrow, a pigeon, a lamb, a deer, and so forth. This prowess is generally described to show his mastery of the subtle energy processes (skt. *praṇā*, tib. *rlung*) that are closely related to tantric practice. In the biographies, these descriptions are used to engender faith in Marpa, although they sometimes have a comical aspect. For example, Marpa entered the body of a yak in order to carry home grass he had cut with his son. He first told his son that he would faint and re-arise in the yak, and that the son should load the grass on the yak. Then, on the way home, the son saw that the load was lopsided and so balanced it with a stone. The yak died when it reached their home, and a few hours later Marpa came back home sweating, telling his son that he had done right balancing the load, but that the extra stone had exhausted him. Such anecdotes bring a vivid and amusing quality to the narrative and help give Marpa a more human complexion.

When Marpa returned to Tibet, he again met with his disciples, married, and had children. None of the foundational biographies specify the name of his wife (or wives) and children. Details only appear in the late-12th- and 13th-century narratives and in biographies written by the Ngok family. According to these early sources, Marpa had two wives. The first and main one is sometimes called Horé (Ho re) or Jomo Zangngé (Jo mo bzang nge). She is later generally referred to as Dakmema (Tib. bdag med ma, skt. Nairātmyā), which may have been an initiatory name conferred to her by Marpa or an allusion to him being Hevajra (see "The Importance of Marpa in Tibetan Religious History" section). She had two sons. The second wife, sometimes called Chaktung (Phyag thung), had five sons, some of them also having offspring.

Among these seven children, it appears than only Dakmema's son, Marpa Dodé, was a worthy heir to his father's spiritual attainments. His story is described at length in Tsangnyön's biography of Marpa, but the narrative is greatly enlarged with details and songs that do not figure in earlier narratives. Dodé's death in particular is highly dramatized, which led to refutations in later biographies and counternarratives in Ra Lotsawa's life stories.[37] Although Tsangnyön's overall account about Marpa Dodé is unreliable, Marpa's son was clearly considered important by his contemporaries and by later biographs, and he suffered an early death. The Ngok accounts state that he died falling off a horse, and this is also the death that Tsangnyön relates. Marpa's other children, although they survived him, did not manage to retain either his teaching lineage or his residence at Drowolung in Lhodrak. According to 13th-century accounts by the treasure-revealer Guru Chöwang (Gu ru chos dbang, 1212–1270) and to the Ngok narratives, one son in particular, Jarin Korlo (Bya ri 'khor lo), kept the house but later either sold his father relics or lost them gambling. His brother did not manage to keep the residence either, and a generation later another family lived in Drowolung and maintained Marpa's estate, while the Ngok family preserved Marpa's formal teachings and his relics in Zhung.[38]

Marpa's Disciples. Despite this setback to Marpa's family lineage, his religious lineage was very successful. The biographies give various lists of disciples, but the most widespread distinguishes between four "great pillars" (*ka chen*) represented by his major students, each associated with a direction and an animal, a description that initially appeared within Milarepa's biographical tradition.[39] The four are generally listed as follows.

Ngok Chödor from Zhung is associated with the south and is the disciple who pleases Marpa with his wisdom. To him, Marpa gave the explanation of the *Hevajratantra* and so forth, as well as Merging and Transference (*bsre 'pho*), which is the name given to the Six Doctrines in the Ngok lineage. More generally, the Ngoks came to be known for their transmission of the "Seven Mandalas," six of which originate with Marpa. They were the chief representatives of Marpa's "Lineage of Explanation" (*bshad brgyud*).

Tsurtön Wangngé from Dol is associated with the east and is the disciple who pleases Marpa with his magic. To him, Marpa gave Guhyasamāja and the Pañcakrama instructions. All later Kagyü Guhyasamāja lineages (called *mar lugs*, the Mar Tradition), which were quite successful in Tibet, originate with Tsurtön. He also appears in Buddhakapāla lineages and in the transmission of the ejection (*'pho ba*) practice.

Metön from Tsangrong is associated with the west and is the disciple who pleases Marpa with his service. To him, Marpa is said to have given Mahāmāya and the practice of luminosity (*'od gsal*), as well as Hevajra and other traditions, but his lineages did not survive.

Milarepa is associated with the north and is the disciple who pleases Marpa with his devotion. To him, Marpa gave especially inner heat (*gtum mo*) and all key instructions. Milerapa is the one who continued Marpa's "practice lineage" (*sgrub brgyud*), that is to say that he is associated with the practice and realization of Marpa's key instructions coming from Nāropa and Maitrīpa. His main practice was based on Cakrasaṃvara and became known in Tibet as the Aural Tradition (Snyan brgyud). The stories relating the way Marpa received this transmission are not very detailed in his biographies, and they generally appear during Marpa's last meeting with Nāropa. Milarepa posthumously became Marpa's main disciple, and the next "pearl" in the Kagyü "Golden Rosary" lineage.

By the end of his life, Marpa had become a wealthy and powerful landowner, with a stronghold in Drowolung, Lhodrak. Milarepa's construction of a nine-story building is generally not mentioned in Marpa's biographical tradition but became a central feature of Milarepa's life story. Many narratives show that Marpa was quite famous toward the end of his life and was widely recognized as a potent holder of Nāropa's key instructions—Indian disciples even allegedly sought him out. His biographies sometimes refer to him as a "hidden yogi," that is to say one who did not spend his life in retreat but who had nevertheless obtained the resultant accomplishments.

Marpa's death, between 1081 and 1085, is generally commemorated on the full moon of the first Tibetan month, which is also the end of the period of miracles performed by Buddha Śakyamuni.

In the biographies, Marpa is associated with various tutelar figures of the past. Ngamdzong Tönpa relates a story told by the translator Ching Yonten Bar (Chings yon tan 'bar), a translator of several texts in the Kanjur and Tanjur, who was told in India that Marpa was an incarnation of Ḍombī Heruka. This 10th-century Indian siddha was known for his writings on Hevajra and part of the important groups of eight and eighty-four *mahāsiddhas*. He was considered by some of Marpa's biographers to be an emanation of the bodhisattva Samantabhadra, and the sequence Samantabhadra > Ḍombī Heruka > Marpa is followed in many biographies.[40] Another widespread association establishes a preexisting link between Marpa and Nāropa. This motif originates with Ngok Dodé's description of Marpa's quest to find Nāropa during his last journey to India. While praying with Kasoripa and Riripa, two of Nāropā's disciples, Riripa remembers one of their past lives:

In a previous life, the Brahmin Bhadrapā
Was supplicated by Dharmarāja of noble lineage
In the presence of the witnesses Kalyāṇa and Bhadra:
This fruit will come, there will be a meeting.[41]

According to him, Bhadrapā was Nāropa, Dharmarāja of noble lineage was Marpa, and Kasoripa and Riripa were Kalyāṇa and Bhadra. Later versions sometimes exchange the identity and role of Bhadrapā and Dharmarāja.

MARPA'S SONGS

Marpa was the first master of the later spread of the doctrine in Tibet to sing songs of realization (*mgur*, later called *nyams mgur*). In texts dating from the royal period, the term *mgur* refers to songs sung by the king and nobility, usually conveying success, victory, or joy.[42] This mode of expression laid a textual emphasis on personal experiences and the overcoming of obstacles. The word was not linked at that time with any Indian song tradition. During the later spread of the doctrine in Tibet, *mgur* became more religious in consequence of the exposure of Tibetans to the culture of the Indian subcontinent, where a poetic form of religious expression in the Middle Indo-Aryan dialect of Apabhraṃśa called *dohā* that expressed the realization of their author, generally in the absence of significant biographical data.[43] In the 11th century, Marpa went to the Indian subcontinent and learned its languages and culture, and is said to have received the transmission of Indian *dohās* from Maitrīpā. While this probably refers the *Dohākośa* of Saraha, it is possible that Maitrīpā also taught Marpa how to sing songs. Then, in India, Nepal, and Tibet, Marpa is said to have sung, often during tantric feasts, thus joining the Tibetan tradition of singing about episodes from one's life with the Indian tradition of songs of realization. According to Matthew Kapstein and Tulku Töndup, "drawing thematic inspiration from the Apabhraṃśa songs of the Indian Buddhist tantric masters, and imagistic and metrical resources from indigenous bardic and popular verses, Marpa created an entirely distinctive family of verse forms."[44] Marpa may have been the first in the period of the second spread of the doctrine to use this style of expression. He was followed by his disciple Milarepa, who is still regarded today as the greatest poet of Tibet, and this kind of expression became a major feature of the Kagyü lineages of Tibetan Buddhism, where the oral transmission of esoteric instructions between master and disciple is considered central.

Although Marpa and Milarepa are both famous for their songs, their styles and legacies differ. While Milarepa's earliest biographies contain sections in which songs are distinct stories depicting episodes of the poet's life, Marpa's songs never had a life of their own. This is because most do not relate specific episodes of the translator's life, but are general summaries of his journeys to India. Milarepa's style is more lyrical, describing his experience and daily yogic life in vivid and inspiring songs, while Marpa was more pragmatic, not singing on random occasions but during tantric gatherings or at the request of disciples who wanted to hear about his journeys or to receive a summary of his teachings on specific topics. As a consequence, Marpa's songs were never completely extracted from their biographical context and, although several collections of songs exist, they did not spread widely. What became famous are the "eight great songs" emphasized by Tsangnyön Heruka in his biography of Marpa and anthologized by the 8th Karmapa Mikyö Dorjé (1507–1554) in the *Ocean of Kagyü Songs* (*Bka' brgyud mgur mtsho*) without further editing.

The formal style of Marpa's songs can be divided into three main aspects: subject matter, meter, and melody pattern. As far as subject matter is concerned, half of Marpa's songs can be considered to be "biographical," while the other half are more "theoretical," that is, the songs are a presentation of his own teachings as well as of those he received from his masters. In metrical terms, Marpa's verses alternate between seven- and nine-syllable lines, a length which in the *Ocean of Kagyü Songs* is characteristic of songs from Marpa to Gampopa. This preceded the introduction into 13th-century Tibet of classical Indian poetry as codified by Daṇḍin's *Kāvyādarśa*, which is characterized by longer verses. The short prosody of Marpa's verses is also found in Tibetan folk poetry, for example in the Gesar epic.[45] Some of Marpa's songs present an indication of melody pattern, a feature found in both the Indian and Tibetan traditions, and it is likely that the melodic indications found in Marpa's songs derive from both traditions. Parallels can be found between the names of melody patterns found in the Gesar epic, names of Indian rāgas and some of Marpa's songs. Examples of melodic indications are "the voice like the drone of the tamboura," "the melody of the outstretched wings of the soaring Garuda," "the bee buzzing in the distance" and so forth.

MARPA'S WORKS

Although he is called Marpa the Translator, Marpa did not author as many translations in the Kanjur and Tanjur as some of his contemporaries like Drokmi Lotsawa or Gö Lotsawa Kukpa Lhatsé ('Gos khug pa lhas btsas, 11th century).[46] Two main compilations of his Collected Works (*gsung 'bum*) exist today in three and seven volumes, totaling less than two thousand pages. Many texts are reproductions from manuscripts rediscovered and republished in Tibet in the early 2000s.[47] A large part of these collections are biographical works presenting Marpa's life story or that of his masters (but not created by him). They also contain many tantric practice texts (empowerment and practice manuals, associated ritual texts) for the various traditions associated with Marpa, also mostly compiled by disciples. Numerous short commentaries and key instructions on mahāmudrā, tantric practice and the Six Doctrines of Nāropa are said to be redacted by Marpa or redacted by his masters and translated by him. There are also many texts associated with the Cakrasaṃvara Aural Transmission attributed to Marpa, but the authorship of these texts is often unclear.

Marpa's main writings are commentaries on the *Hevajra-* and *Vajrapañjaratantra* that gave rise to further exegesis within the Ngok lineage, and a collection of fifteen scrolls, called the *Sekarma* (*Sras mkhar ma*), revealed by the 13th-century Treasure Revealer Guru Chöwang from a wall in Marpa's residence of Drowolung and considered as the heart of Marpa's teachings.[48]

None of these texts have been the subject of much scholarly work, although several projects are being developed as of 2021. In general, the question of Marpa's literary output remains a desideratum in early Kagyü studies.

REVIEW OF LITERATURE

As the Tibetan founder of the Kagyü school, Marpa is mentioned in almost any book dealing with Tibetan Buddhism in general. Most, if not all, of these presentations rely on two main sources. First is the biography by Tsangnyön Heruka, initially partially rendered into French by Jacques Bacot in 1937 and translated fully into English in 1982 by the Nālandā Translation Committee headed by Chögyam Trungpa. Second is the *Blue Annals* (*Deb ther sngon po*), a large religious history published in 1476 by Gö Lotsawa Zhönu Pal and translated in 1949 by George Nicholas Roerich and the Tibetan scholar Gendün Chöpel. An example of an early study of Marpa based on the *Blue Annals* is an article by Turrell Wylie dealing with Marpa's tower.[49] Hubert Decleer relied on Tsangnyön's biography and on later writings by Belo Tsewang Kunkyab (18th century) and the biography of Ra Lotsawa (16th century), while examining the controversies surrounding Marpa Dodé's death.[50] Dan Martin reviewed the 1982 translation of Tsangnyön's work and made a first survey of the literature on early Kagyü biographies.[51] He also published an important work on "The Early Education of Milarepa."[52] Gene Smith published his insights into "Golden Rosaries of the Bka' brgyud Schools" in the introduction to the 1970 Tibetan edition of Montsepa's compilation. This article was reedited with his introductions to other works of Tibetan literature in *Among Tibetan Texts*.[53] Earnest study of the early Kagyü biographical sources started in 2000 with the defense of Peter Alan Roberts' dissertation on the biographies of Rechungpa, published in 2007.[54] It continued with Andrew Quintman's doctoral study of the biographies of Milarepa in 2006, published in 2014.[55] The study of Marpa's biographical traditions was the object of Cécile Ducher's MA thesis in 2011, published in 2017.[56] Marta Sernesi also contributed to the field with articles on these early sources, which she interrogated mainly from the perspective of the Aural Tradition, the development of print and the "School of Tsangnyön."[57] Cécile Ducher published articles on Marpa's songs, the Fifteen Scrolls of the *Sekarma*, and the Ngok lineage descending from Marpa.[58]

The formal teachings of Marpa, as expressed in Marpa's writings, have not been examined in detail, although there are studies related to the Marpa Kagyü teaching as it was expounded later. The English translations of Kongtrul Lodrö Thayé's (Kong sprul blo gros mtha' yas, 1813–1899) *Treasury of Knowledge* (*Shes bya mdzod*) contain presentations on Marpa's tantric transmissions.[59] Several systems of key instructions coming from Marpa figure among the *One Hundred and Eight Teaching Manuals of Jonang*.[60] Ducher describes the tantric legacy of Marpa as it was preserved by Kongtrul in his *Treasury of Kagyü Mantras* (*Bka' brgyud sngags mdzod*).[61]

DIGITAL MATERIALS

The primary sources for Marpa's life story are presented in detail in Cécile Ducher, *Building a Tradition* (https://epub.ub.uni-muenchen.de/41307/1/Ducher_2017.pdf) and are therefore not listed in detail here. Necessary references to these Tibetan sources are provided in notes to this entry, with indications of secondary sources when available.

The Treasury of Lives (https://treasuryoflives.org/biographies/view/Marpa/TBRC_P2636).

FURTHER READING

PRIMARY SOURCES—MODERN EDITIONS OF MARPA'S COLLECTED WORKS

A mgon Rin po che (Editor). "'Bri gung bka' brgyud chos mdzod chen mo las rje mar pa'i bka' 'bum." In *'Bri gung bka' brgyud chos mdzod chen mo*, Vols. 5 and 6 (out of 151). Lhasa: [s.n.], 2004.

Ser gtsug nang bstan dpe rnying 'tshol bsdu phyogs sgrig khang (Editor). *Dpal mnga' bdag sgra sgyur mar pa lo tsā ba chos kyi blo gros kyi gsung 'bum*. Gangs can khyad nor dpe tshogs, 264–266. 3 vols. Lhasa: Ser gtsug nang bstan dpe rnying 'tshol bsdu phyogs sgrig khang, 2009.

Dpal brtsegs bod yig dpe rnying zhib 'jug khang (Editor). *Lho brag mar pa lo tsā'i gsung 'bum*. 7 vols. Pe cin, Tibet: Krung go'i bod rig pa dpe skrun khang, 2011.

SECONDARY LITERATURE—BIOGRAPHIES OF MARPA IN ENGLISH

Ducher, Cécile. *Building a Tradition: The Lives of Mar Pa the Translator*. Collectanea Himalayica 5. Munich: Indus Verlag, 2017a. https://epub.ub.uni-muenchen.de/41307/1/Ducher_2017.pdf.

Gö Lotsawa Zhonnu Pal. *The Blue Annals*. Translated by George N. Roerich. Delhi: Motilal Banarsidass, 1976.

Konchog Gyaltsen (Khenpo). *The Great Kagyu Masters: The Golden Lineage Treasury*. New York: Snow Lion Publications, 1990.

Quintman Andrew. "Marpa Chokyi Lodro." In *The Treasury of Lives*. Online Publication, September 2010. https://treasuryoflives.org/biographies/view/Marpa-Chokyi-Lodro/TBRC_P2636.

Tsangnyön Heruka. *The Life of Marpa the Translator*. Translated by Nālandā Translation Committee. Boston: Shambhala, 1995.

SECONDARY LITERATURE—ON MARPA'S BIOGRAPHICAL TRADITION

Ducher, Cécile. "bKa' brgyud treasure and rNying ma revealer: The Sras mkhar ma of Mar pa Lo tsā ba." *Revue d'Études Tibétaines* 37 (2017b): 98–126. http://himalaya.socanth.cam.ac.uk/collections/journals/ret/pdf/ret_37_07.pdf.

Ducher, Cécile. "*A Lineage in Time: The Vicissitudes of the rNgog pa bka' brgyud from the 11th through 19th Centuries*." Unpublished PhD diss., EPHE/PSL, Paris, 2017.

Ducher, Cécile. "From Song to Biography and from Biography to Song: The Use of *Mgur* in Mar-pa's *rnam thar*." *Life Writing: The Selfless Ego, Part 1*, 17, no. 2 (2019): 205–219. https://doi.org/10.1080/14484528.2019.1621444.

Ducher, Cécile. "The Treasury of Kagyü Mantra: A Nineteenth-Century Collection of Marpa's Tantric Teachings." In *Reasons and Lives in Buddhist Traditions: Studies in Honor of Matthew Kapstein*, edited by Daniel Arnold, Cécile Ducher, and Pierre-Julien Hartner, 127–139. Boston: Wisdom Publications, 2019.

Ducher, Cécile. "Goldmine of Knowledge: The Collections of the gNas bcu lha khang in 'Bras spungs Monastery." *Revue d'Étude Tibétaines* 55 (2020): 121–139. http://himalaya.socanth.cam.ac.uk/collections/journals/ret/pdf/ret_55_06.pdf.

Martin, Dan. "The Early Education of Milarepa." *The Journal of the Tibet Society* 2 (1982): 52–76.
Martin, Dan. "Review of *The Life of Marpa the Translator*, translated by the Nālandā Translation Committee." *The Journal of the Tibet Society* 4 (1984): 83–92, with addendum in *The Journal of the Tibet Society* 5 (1985): 112–117.
Sernesi, Marta. "To Establish the Qualities of the Master: Considerations on Early bKa' brgyud Hagiographical Writings." In *Tīrthayātrā: Essays in Honour of Stefano Piano*, edited by Pinuccia Caracchi, Antonella Serena Comba, Alessandra Consolaro and Consolaro Pelissero, 401–424. Alessandria, Italy: Edizioni dell'Orso, 2010.
Sernesi, Marta. "A Continuous Stream of Merit: The Early Reprints of Gtsang Smyon Heruka's Hagiographical Works." In *Zentralasiatische Studien*. Vol. 40, edited by Peter Schwieger, Rudolf Kaschewsky, Petra Maurer, Dieter Schuh, Veronika Veit and Michael Weiers, 179–237. Andiast, Switzerland: International Institute for Tibetan and Buddhist Studies, 2011.

SECONDARY LITERATURE—ON THE LARGER CONTEXT OF THE SECOND SPREAD OF BUDDHISM AND THE BEGINNINGS OF THE KAGYÜ LINEAGE

Apple, James. *Atiśa Dīpaṃkara: Illuminator of the Awakened Mind*. Boulder, CO: Shambhala, 2019.
Cuevas, Bryan J. *Ra Yeshe Senge: The All Pervading Melodious Drumbeat*. New York: Penguin Books, 2015.
Davidson, Ronald M. *Tibetan Renaissance: Tantric Buddhism in the Rebirth of Tibetan Culture*. New York: Columbia University Press, 2005.
Decleer, Hubert. "The Melodious Drumsound All-Pervading, Sacred Biography of Rwa Lotsâwa: About Early Lotsâwa rnam thar and chos 'byung." In *Tibetan Studies. Vol. 1: Proceedings of the 5th International Association of Tibetan Studies Seminar*. Edited by Shōren Ihara and Zuihō Yamaguchi, 13–28. Narita, Japan: Naritasan Institute for Buddhist Studies, 1992.
Gyurme, Dorje. *One Hundred and Eight Teaching Manuals of Jonang: Essential Teachings of the Eight Practice Lineages of Tibet, Volume 18 (The Treasury of Precious Instructions)*. Ithaca, NY: Snow Lion Publications, 2021.
Harding, Sarah. *Niguma, Lady of Illusion*. Ithaca, NY: Snow Lion Publications, 2010.
Jackson, Roger R. " 'Poetry' in Tibet: Glu, mGur, sNyan ngag and Songs of Experience." In *Tibetan Literature: Studies in Genre*. Edited by José Ignacio Cabezón and Roger R. Jackson, 368–392. Ithaca, NY: Snow Lion Publications, 1996.
Jackson, Roger R. *Tantric Treasures: Three Collections of Mystical Verse from Buddhist India*. New York: Oxford University Press, 2004.
Kapstein, Matthew, and Tulku Töndup. "Tibetan Poetry." In *New Princeton Encyclopedia of Poetry and Poetics*, edited by Alex Preminger and Terry Brogan, 1290–1291. Princeton, NJ: Princeton University Press, 1993.
Khedrup Gyatso (Editor). "Kha rag gnyos kyi gdung rabs khyad par 'phags pa." In *Kha rag gnyos kyi gdung rabs and rlangs kyi po ti bse ru bsdus pa*, 1–96. Dolanji: Khedup Gyatso, 1978.
Kongtrül Lodrö Thayé. *The Treasury of Knowledge: Book Eight, Part Four: Esoteric instructions*. Translated by Sarah Harding. Ithaca, NY: Snow Lion Publications, 2007.
Kongtrül Lodrö Thayé. *The Treasury of Knowledge: Book Eight, Part Three: The Elements of Tantric Practice: A General Exposition of the Process of Meditation in the Indestructible Way of Secret Mantra*. Translated by Elio Guarisco and Ingrid McLeod. Ithaca, NY: Snow Lion Publications, 2008.
Kragh, Ulrich Timme. *Tibetan Yoga and Mysticism: A Textual Study of the Yogas of Nāropa and Mahāmudrā Meditation in the Medieval Tradition of Dags po*. Tokyo: The International Institute for Buddhist Studies, 2015.
Larsson, Stefan. *Crazy for Wisdom*. Leiden, The Netherlands: Brill, 2012.

Quintman, Andrew. "Wrinkles in Time: On the Problem of Mi la ras pa's Dates." *Acta Orientalia* 74 (2015): 3–26.

Quintman, Andrew. *The Yogin and the Madman: Reading the Biographical Corpus of Tibet's Great Saint Milarepa*. New York: Columbia University Press, 2014.

Roberts, Peter Alan. *The Biographies of Rechungpa: The Evolution of a Tibetan Hagiography*. London: Routledge, 2007.

Schott, Julian. "*Kṛṣṇacaryāpādasya Dohākośaṭīke*: As Study of its Commentaries: Edited, Translated, and Annotated, together with a Survey of his Life and Works and a Study on the *Dohā* as a Literature Genre." Unpublished PhD diss., Universität Hamburg, Hamburg, 2019.

Sernesi, Marta. "The Aural Transmission of Samvara: An Introduction to Neglected Sources for the Study of the Early Bka' brgyud." In *Mahāmudrā and the bKa'-brgyud Tradition*. Edited by Roger Jackson and Matthew Kapstein, 179–210. Andiast, Switzerland: International Institute for Tibetan and Buddhist Studies, 2011.

Sernesi, Marta. *Re-Enacting the Past: A Cultural History of the School of gTsang smyon Heruka*. Wiesbaden, Germany: Reichert Verlag, 2021.

Smith, Gene. *Among Tibetan Texts: History & Literature of the Tibetan Plateau*. Boston: Wisdom Publications, 2001.

Stearns, Cyrus. *Luminous Lives: The Story of the Early Masters of the Lam 'bras Tradition in Tibet*. Boston: Wisdom Publications, 2001.

Torricelli, Fabrizio. *Tilopā: A Buddhist Yogin of the Tenth Century*. Dharamsala, India: Library of Tibetan Works and Archives, 2018.

Wylie, Turrell. "Mar-Pa's Tower: Notes of Local Hegemons in Tibet." *History of Religions* 3, no. 2 (1964): 278–291.

Yamamoto, Carl Shigeo. *Vision and Violence: Lama Zhang and the Politics of Charisma in Twelfth-Century Tibet*. Leiden, The Netherlands: Brill, 2012.

NOTES

1. Tatsak Tsewang Gyal (Rta tshag tshe dbang rgyal, dates?), *The Lhorong Religious History, Lho rong chos 'byung* (Lhasa, China: Bod ljongs bod yig dpe rnying dpe skrung khang, 1994), 32.
2. See Cécile Ducher, *Building a Tradition: The Lives of Mar pa the Translator*. Collectanea Himalayica 5 (Munich: Indus Verlag, 2017), 246 and 263 for the Tibetan and for the English translation, respectively.
3. Cécile Ducher, "From Song to Biography and from Biography to Song: The Use of *Mgur* in Mar-pa's *rnam thar*," in *Life Writing* 17, no. 2, The Selfless Ego, Part I (2020): 205–219 describes these early biographies and Tsangnyön's sources.
4. For a study of Tsangnyön's life of Milarepa and its reception in 15th-century Tibet, see Andrew Quintman, *The Yogin and the Madman: Reading the Biographical Corpus of Tibet's Great Saint Milarepa* (New York: Columbia University Press, 2014). For a larger description of Tsangnyön's school and the place of biographies in it, see Marta Sernesi, *Re-Enacting the Past: A Cultural History of the School of gTsang smyon Heruka* (Wiesbaden, Germany: Reichert Verlag, 2021).
5. For an exhaustive presentation of all the biographies of Marpa, see Ducher, *Building a Tradition*.
6. See Tsangnyön Heruka, *The Life of Marpa the Translator*, trans. Nālandā Translation Committee (Boston: Shambhala, 1995), 204, which erroneously translates this passage by referring to one biography composed by both Rechungpa and Ngamdzong.
7. For introductory remarks on the Aural Transmission and Ngamdzong's tradition, see Marta Sernesi. "The Aural Transmission of Samvara: An Introduction to Neglected Sources for the Study of the Early Bka' brgyud," in *Mahāmudrā and the bKa'-brgyud Tradition*, ed. Roger Jackson and Matthew Kapstein (Andiast, Switzerland: International Institute for Tibetan and Buddhist Studies, 2011), 179–210.

8. The biography by Ngamdzong is edited and translated in Ducher, *Building a Tradition*, 241–273. This and all other biographies briefly described in this article are presented in detail in Ducher, *Building a Tradition*.
9. Cécile Ducher, "A Lineage in Time: The Vicissitudes of the rNgog pa bka' brgyud from the 11th through 19th centuries" (unpublished PhD diss., EPHE/PSL, Paris, 2017).
10. Translated in Ducher, *Building a Tradition*, 275–294.
11. The attribution is pseudepigraphical in Gampopa's Complete Works. The collection into which the biography is inserted ends with Gampopa's biography and states in the colophon that it was redacted by Kyungtsangpa, who was therefore in all likelihood also the one who redacted the previous life-stories (Ducher, *Building a Tradition*, 87–88).
12. For details on each of the biographies described, see Ducher, *Building a Tradition*, 45–100.
13. For an analysis of Milarepa's dates that inform the present examination, see Andrew Quintman, "Wrinkles in Time: On the Problem of Mi la ras pa's Dates," *Acta Orientalia* 74 (2015): 3–26.
14. Translation by Cécile Ducher, "A Lineage in Time," 170, quoting the *Rosary of Precious Ornaments* (*Rin po che rgyan gyi phreng ba*), 11. Additions by the author.
15. Tsangnyön, *Life of Marpa the Translator.*
16. For the centrality of Marpa's songs in the narratives of his life, see Cécile Ducher, "From Song to Biography and from Biography to Song: The Use of *Mgur* in Mar-pa's *rnam thar*," *Life Writing* 17, no. 2 (June 10, 2019): 205–219. Although several readings of the songs exist, they are generally considered reliable and are mentioned (though not quoted) from the first biographies onward. The notable exception is the Aural Transmission version, which does not use the songs and therefore omits to mention Marpa's apprenticeship with Drokmi.
17. Matthew Kapstein, "The Indian Literary Identity in Tibet," in *Literary Cultures in History: Reconstructions from South Asia*, ed. Ivan Pollock Sheldon (Berkeley: University of California Press, 2003), 747–803.
18. See "Kha rag gnyos kyi gdung rabs khyad par 'phags pa," in *Kha rag gnyos kyi gdung rabs and rlangs kyi po ti bse ru bsdus pa*, ed. Khedup Gyatso (Dolanji: Khedup Gyatso, 1978), 6–16 for Nyö Yontan Drak's biography. This text is a collective biography of the successive masters of the Nyö family lineage and was composed in 1431.
19. This tantra is called *Advayasamatāvijayamahākalparāja*. There exist two translations in Tibetan, called in short *The Longer Non-Dual Victory* (the text translated by Marpa) and the *Shorter Non-Dual Victory.* The latter was translated by Butön Rinchen Drup on the basis of an Indian manuscript to prove that the former was a Tibetan composition and not a translation. See, for instance, Gö Lotsawa Zhonnu Pal, *The Blue Annals*, trans. George N. Roerich (Delhi: Motilal Banarsidass, 1976), 417; and various articles on Butön's translation by Fan Muyou.
20. See translation in Ducher, *Building a Tradition*, 259–260 and 243–244 for the Tibetan edition.
21. More details in Ducher, *Building a Tradition*, 211–212.
22. Sarah Harding, *Niguma, Lady of Illusion* (Ithaca, NY: Snow Lion Publications, 2010), 258–259. Many later Drukpa masters accepted this location of Nāropa in Kashmir, and several monasteries and caves are now associated with Nāropa and Marpa in Kashmir and Ladakh. This trend is, however, not well represented in Marpa's biographies.
23. Ducher, *Building a Tradition*, 260. Quotation of the biography by Ngamdzong Tönpa.
24. For more detail on Marpa's family lineage and the rapid decline of his hermitage in Lhodrak, see Cécile Ducher, "bKa' brgyud treasure and rNying ma revealer: The Sras mkhar ma of Mar pa Lo tsā ba." *Revue d'Études Tibétaines* 37 (2017): 98–126.
25. *Dug mtsho gling*: this refers to the place where Śāntibhadra lives, in the south of India. See Ducher, *Building a Tradition*, 280, for an example in Marpa's biography composed by Ngog Dodé.
26. For detail on these Indian collections, see Mathes, "The Collection of 'Indian Mahāmudrā Works' Compiled by the Seventh Karma pa Chos grags rgya mtsho," in *Mahāmudrā and the bKa' brgyud*

Tradition, ed. Roger Jackson and Matthew Kapstein (Andiast, Switzerland: International Institute for Tibetan and Buddhist Studies, 2011), 89–129.

27. Ducher, *Building a Tradition*, 262–263.
28. For more details and arguments on the various versions, see Ducher, *Building a Tradition*, 227–236.
29. Ducher, *Building a Tradition*, 278. Translation of the biography by Ngok Dodé can be found in Ducher, *Building a Tradition*, 170–171. This dream-song figures in many sources.
30. Tsangnyön, *Life of Marpa the Translator*, 57–66.
31. James Apple, *Atiśa Dīpaṃkara: Illuminator of the Awakened Mind* (Boulder, CO: Shambhala, 2019), 52. Apple's source, however, seems mostly to be Marpa's biography (Tsangnyön and Pema Karpo); narratives coming from Nagtso Lotsawa also mention this encounter.
32. See Ducher, *Building a Tradition*, 213ff. This kind of tantric conduct is described in chapter I.6 of the *Hevajratantra*, for example.
33. Quotation of Ngamdzong Tönpa can be found translated in Ducher, *Building a Tradition*, 265.
34. Ronald M. Davidson, *Tibetan Renaissance: Tantric Buddhism in the Rebirth of Tibetan Culture* (New York: Columbia University Press, 2005), 142–148 and 44–49. The controversy is examined in detail in Ducher, *Building a Tradition*, 218–226.
35. The letter is found in the *Sakya Collected Works*, Vol. 7, 417–420 and trans. Davidson, *Tibetan Renaissance*, 144–146.
36. See Ducher, *Building a Tradition*, 200–209.
37. See Bryan J. Cuevas, "Rva *Lo tsā ba* and His Biographers," in *Festschrift for Per K. Sørensen on the Occasion of His 65th Birthday*, eds. Olaf Czaja and Guntram Hazod (Wiesbaden, Germany: Dr. Ludwig Reichert Verlag, 2015), 57–78; and *Ra Yeshe Senge: The All Pervading Melodious Drumbeat* (New York: Penguin Books, 2015) for descriptions of the way Marpa Dodé was killed by Ra Lotsawa. Refutations of Tsangnyön occurring later in Marpa's biographical tradition are examined in Ducher, "A Lineage in Time," 249–251.
38. Ducher, "bKa' brgyud treasure"; and "A Lineage in Time."
39. Ducher, "A Lineage in Time," 190–206.
40. See, for example, Robert N. Linrothe, *Holy Madness, Portraits of Tantric Siddhas* (New York: Rubin Museum of Art, 2006), esp. 81 and 236, and Donald S. Lopez, *Seeing the Sacred in Samsara: An Illustrated Guide to the Eighty-Four Mahāsiddhas* (Boulder, CO: Shambhala, 2019), 51.
41. Ducher, *Building a Tradition*, 198 ff.
42. Jackson, "'Poetry' in Tibet: Glu, mGur, sNyan ngag and Songs of Experience," in *Tibetan Literature: Studies in Genre*, ed. José Ignacio Cabezón and Roger R. Jackson (Ithaca, NY: Snow Lion Publications, 1996), 370.
43. See, for example, Roger R. Jackson, *Tantric Treasures: Three Collections of Mystical Verse from Buddhist India* (New York: Oxford University Press, 2004); and Julian Schott, *Kṛṣṇacaryāpādasya Dohākośaṭīke*.
44. Matthew Kapstein and Tulku Töndup, "Tibetan Poetry," in *New Princeton Encyclopedia of Poetry and Poetics*, ed. Alex Preminger and Terry Brogan (Princeton, NJ: Princeton University Press, 1993), 1290.
45. Jackson, "'Poetry' in Tibet."
46. The colophons of these canonical texts contain Marpa Chökyi Lodrö's name, sometimes together with the other names of Marpa, and sometimes with other Indian masters. Compare Dergé Kanjur: Toh 453; Dergé Tanjur: 1231, 1322, 1323, 1524, 1525, 1526, 1527, 1528, 1529t, 2454, 2330, 2332, 2333, 2338; translations in Beijing Tanjur: 4614, 4628, 4789, 4929.
47. Cécile Ducher, "Goldmine of Knowledge: The Collections of the gNas bcu lha khang in 'Bras spungs Monastery," *Revue d'Étude Tibétaines* 55 (2020): 121–139.
48. Ducher, "bKa' brgyud Treasure."

49. Turrell Wylie, "Mar-Pa's Tower: Notes of Local Hegemons in Tibet," *History of Religions* 3, no. 2 (1964): 278–291.
50. See Cuevas, *Ra Yeshe Seng*; and Hubert Decleer, "The Melodious Drumsound All-Pervading, Sacred Biography of Rwa Lotsâwa: About Early Lotsâwa rnam thar and chos 'byung," in *Tibetan Studies*. Vol. 1, *Proceedings of the 5th International Association of Tibetan Studies Seminar*, eds. Shōren Ihara and Zuihō Yamaguchi (Narita, Japan: Naritasan Institute for Buddhist Studies, 1992), 13–28.
51. Dan Martin, "The Early Education of Milarepa," *The Journal of the Tibet Society* 2 (1982): 52–76; and "Review of *The Life of Marpa the Translator*, translated by the Nālandā Translation Committee." *The Journal of the Tibet Society* 4 (1984): 83–92.
52. Martin, "Early Education of Milarepa."
53. Gene Smith, *Among Tibetan Texts: History & Literature of the Tibetan Plateau* (Boston: Wisdom Publications, 2001).
54. Peter Alan Roberts, *The Biographies of Rechungpa: The Evolution of a Tibetan Hagiography* (London: Routledge, 2007).
55. Quintman, *Yogin and the Madman.*
56. *lHo brag mar pa lo tsā'i gsung 'bum*, 7 Vols., ed. dPal brtsegs bod yig dpe rnying zhib 'jug khang (Pe cin: Krung go'i bod rig pa dpe skrun khang, 2011); (Ducher, 2017a).
57. Marta Sernesi, "To Establish the Qualities of the Master: Considerations on Early bKa' brgyud Hagiographical Writings," in *Tīrthayātrā: Essays in Honour of Stefano Piano*, ed. Pinuccia Caracchi, Antonella Serena Comba, Alessandra Consolaro and Consolaro Pelissero (Alessandria, Italy: Edizioni dell'Orso, 2010), 401–424; "A Continuous Stream of Merit: The Early Reprints of Gtsang Smyon Heruka's Hagiographical Works," in *Zentralasiatische Studien*, Vol. 40, ed. Peter Schwieger (Andiast, Switzerland: International Institute for Tibetan and Buddhist Studies, 2011), 179–237; and *Re-Enacting the Past: A Cultural History of the School of gTsang smyon Heruka* (Wiesbaden, Germany: Reichert Verlag, 2021).
58. See Ducher (2017b, 2020).
59. Particularly Kongtrül Lodrö Thayé, *The Treasury of Knowledge: Book Eight, Part Four: Esoteric instructions*, trans. Harding Sarah (Ithaca, NY: Snow Lion Publications, 2007); and *The Treasury of Knowledge: Book Eight, Part Three: The Elements of Tantric Practice: A General Exposition of the Process of Meditation in the Indestructible Way of Secret Mantra*, trans. Elio Guarisco and Ingrid McLeod (Ithaca, NY: Snow Lion Publications, 2008).
60. Gyurme Dorje, *One Hundred and Eight Teaching Manuals of Jonang* (Ithaca, NY: Snow Lion Publications, 2021).
61. Cécile Ducher, "*The Treasury of Kagyü Mantra*: A Nineteenth-Century Collection of Marpa's Tantric Teachings," in *Reasons and Lives in Buddhist Traditions: Studies in Honor of Matthew Kapstein*, ed. Dan Arnold, Cécile Ducher, and Pierre-Julien Hartner (Boston: Wisdom Publications, 2019), 127–139.

Cécile Ducher

MIPAM

MIPAM'S LIFE AND WORKS

Mipam's Life. Mipam ('Ju mi pham rgya mtsho, 1846–1912) was born to an aristocratic family in Degé (Sde dge) in eastern Tibet.[1] He became a novice monk when he was twelve, entering the monastery of Jumo Horzang Chöling ('Ju mo hor gsang chos gling), a branch of Zhechen (Zhe chen) monastery connected with the lineage of Mindröling (Smin grol gling).

There, he was a child prodigy and came to be known as "the little scholar-monk."[2] After doing a retreat for eighteen months at the Junyung hermitage ('Ju nyung ri khrod) on Mañjuśrī, it is said that he had achieved signs of accomplishment.

When Mipam was about seventeen, his homeland of Degé was taken over in the midst of a regional conflict, which eventually led to the government of the Thirteenth Dalai Lama (Thub stan rgya mtsho, 1876–1933) in central Tibet sending troops to quell the insurgence. During the fighting, Mipam went on a pilgrimage to Lhasa in central Tibet accompanied by his uncle. He was around the age of eighteen or nineteen at this time.

On the trip he stayed at a Geluk (*dge lugs*) monastery near Lhasa for about a month.[3] Here he was exposed to the Geluk tradition of scholarship, which is famous in Tibet for setting the standard of monastic education. He quickly gained fluency in dominant features of the Geluk tradition's interpretation of Buddhist thought, as well as the procedures of debate. A large part of why Mipam's work became so influential is the fact that he was able to formulate a viable alternative to the dominant Geluk interpretation of Buddhist thought, which had come to monopolize intellectual traditions of Buddhism in central Tibet since the 17th century. Through developing an articulate voice of Nyingma scholarship, his works directly challenged the Geluk hegemony on monastic education.

Mipam wrote commentaries on classic Buddhist texts based on his own Nyingma tradition. He stated clearly that he was not motivated by sectarianism, but rather by the feeling that most of the Nyingma followers were merely imitating the scholars of other traditions. He felt that the teachings of his Nyingma tradition were on the verge of becoming "like a painted butter lamp"—an artifact without much power. He said that few people even wonder about the philosophy of the Nyingma, much less ask about it. For these reasons, he composed texts in order to elucidate the Nyingma view.[4]

By emphasizing a uniquely Nyingma interpretation, Mipam's works sparked criticism from other schools, particularly from scholars in the Geluk school. On several critical points of interpretation, Mipam markedly diverged from the prevailing interpretation given within the Geluk tradition, which had come to dominate institutional scholarship in Tibet. In particular, his commentary on the Wisdom Chapter from the *Bodhicaryāvatāra* drew sharp criticism that spawned a polemical exchange with a number of prominent Geluk scholars. Mipam took up correspondence with one of his most perceptive critics from central Tibet, and they soon became friends, exchanging gifts along with polemical arguments. The rich exchange between these two exceptional scholars came to be known as "the meeting of the Sarma tiger and Nyingma lion."[5]

Mipam's writings on sutra (and Madhyamaka in particular) not only sparked controversy from the Geluk school, but also from within his own tradition. He often emphasized the importance of logic and epistemology, topics that were generally not stressed in the Nyingma tradition. Some Nyingma followers were skeptical of the role, if any, that logic and Madhyamaka analyses had in the practices of tantra, which had historically defined their tradition. Since Mipam had explicitly stated that one must understand Madhyamaka to understand the Great Perfection, those who were not inclined toward this kind of scholarship apparently were indifferent to his work, or even regarded it with suspicion.[6] Others in the Nyingma tradition, who were actively involved in scholarship on sutra topics, did not always agree with Mipam's particular exposition of Madhyamaka.

It is important to understand that before Mipam, there was no orthodox corpus of Nyingma commentaries on sutra topics. Also, monasteries had come to dominate the Tibetan landscape, and the subject matter of sutra had a central place in monastic education. As a result, for their new monastic institutions, many in the Nyingma tradition had adopted an interpretation of sutra topics from the Geluk (or Sakya) tradition, while maintaining a Nyingma tantra practice. Mipam, however, advocated a uniquely Nyingma view of sutra.

Unlike many other prominent figures of his day, Mipam did not actively promote the new "treasure" (*gter ma*) traditions, nor wrote commentaries on them.[7] Rather, he wrote numerous commentaries on a variety of diverse topics, ranging from logic, poetics, Madhyamaka (both Prāsaṅgika and Yogācāra), medicine, and astrology. He spent most of his life in meditation retreat, yet he was also a highly productive scholar and was actively involved in establishing a number of monastic colleges across eastern Tibet.

Mipam's Writings. Mipam wrote extensively, and not just on a few topics of Buddhist thought. His collected works are enormous. An early 21st-century redaction of his collected works (Kaḥtok edition) fills thirty volumes. Mipam wrote on diverse subjects such as logic, poetics, and medicine; crafts such as making ink, incense, and fireworks; and he even wrote a commentary on the *Kāma Sūtra* (*'Dod pa'i bstan bcos 'jig rten kun tu dga' ba'i gter*), the famous "sex manual" of India; in short, he was a polymath.[8] He also wrote on Tibetan translations of Indian texts, including tantras from the "new schools" (*gsar ma*), the *Guhyagarbhatantra* of his own Nyingma tradition, and buddha nature.[9]

Mipam is widely known for his contribution to the monastic curriculum, and for his work on Madhyamaka in particular, which is generally held to be the pinnacle of philosophy in Tibet. His most extensive treatment of Madhyamaka is his commentary on Śāntarakṣita's *Madhyamakālaṃkāra*. In this commentary, he showed the compatibility of Madhyamaka (and Prāsaṅgika in particular) and Yogācāra. This text not only exemplifies an important statement of his central views on Madhyamaka, but also treats several key points of Buddhist philosophy in general.

While a classic in India, the *Madhyamakālaṃkāra* had received scant attention in Tibet after Candrakīrti's *Madhyamakāvatāra* rose to prominence after it was translated into Tibetan in the 11th century. Mipam revived this important work of Yogācāra-Madhyamaka and made a strong argument—*contra* Tsongkhapa—that in the end, the view of the ultimate is the same in Yogācāra-Madhyamaka as it is in Prāsaṅgika. A Nyingma scholar, Dodrup Damchö, objected to Mipam's commentary on the *Madhyamakālaṃkāra*. His critique came from his Geluk-influenced understanding of the authentic Madhyamaka view, which treats Prāsaṅgika as incompatible with Yogācāra. Mipam responded to this criticism by supporting his position for the compatibility of the philosophies of Madhyamaka and Yogācāra in a short text entitled *Eliminating Doubts*. His portrayal of the two main Mahāyāna philosophies—Madhyamaka and Yogācāra—as compatible reflects his synthetic style and inclusive view.

Another important source for Mipam's Madhyamaka views is his commentary on the Wisdom Chapter of the *Bodhicaryāvatāra* (*Spyod 'jug sher 'grel ke ta ka*). In this text he elucidates the meaning of ultimate emptiness, nonconceptuality free from all constructs. This commentary also drew criticism, this time directly from two prominent scholars in the Geluk school. Mipam responded to each of their critiques in two provocative texts that delve deeply into several important issues of Madhyamaka.[10] These three texts unpack his view of the meaning of emptiness and Madhyamaka.

Additionally, a compilation of short instructions on the general points of scriptures, entitled *Difficult Points of Scriptures in General* (*Gzhung spyi'i dka' gnad*), is another excellent source for his views on Madhyamaka. The content in this collection notably contrasts with central features of the predominant Geluk interpretation of Madhyamaka, such as the characteristic way this tradition represents the ultimate truth as solely a negation—a lack of true existence. Another significant statement of his Madhyamaka view is the *Beacon of Certainty* (*Nges shes sgron me*), which is arranged around responses to seven incisive questions. In this short, beautiful work of philosophical poetry, Mipam illuminates the Nyingma view on Madhyamaka and the Great Perfection.

Mipam also wrote complete commentaries on three of the texts of "the five treatises of Maitreya": the *Dharmadharmatāvibhāga*, *Madhyāntavibhāga*, and *Mahāyānasūtrālaṃkāra*.[11] These three texts elaborate Yogācāra's view of the three natures and explain the ultimate truth as nonconceptual wisdom, free from duality. Significantly, Mipam presents these texts in a way that is compatible with Madhyamaka. It is notable that he wrote a massive, 760-page commentary on the *Mahāyānasūtrālaṃkāra*. While Mipam says that the *Mahāyānasūtrālaṃkāra* is a Mind-Only treatise, he emphasizes that it can also be understood as a text on the Mahāyāna in general, compatible with Madhyamaka.

Mipam lays out his view of buddha nature in a short text called *Lion's Roar: Exposition of Buddha-Nature* (*Stong thun seng ge'i nga ro*), which draws upon another of the five treatises of Maitreya, the *Uttaratantra*. Here he presents three main arguments showing why all beings have buddha nature. Also, he distinguishes his view of buddha nature, which he portrays as the unconditioned unity of emptiness and appearance, from other traditions' views of buddha-nature. Namely, he contrasts his view with: traditions that maintain buddha nature as truly real and not empty (e.g., Jonang); traditions that hold buddha nature to be simply the mind's absence of true existence (e.g., Geluk); and traditions that maintain that the cognitive quality of buddha nature—the element that is in unity with emptiness—is impermanent (e.g., Sakya). Mipam's other "Lion's Roar," his *Lion's Roar: Affirming Other-Emptiness* (*Gzhan stong khas len seng ge'i nga ro*), shows the way he establishes an "other-emptiness" (*gzhan stong*) view, a view that affirms the existence of the ultimate truth as not empty of its own essence.

Mipam affirms that all beings, without difference, are endowed with buddha nature from the beginning. While doing so, he makes an important distinction in his presentation of buddha nature between the way things appear and the way things are. In the way things appear (to sentient beings), the qualities of a buddha are a new development. In the way things are, however, he describes the qualities of the buddha as permanent, unconditioned, and a primordial endowment of all sentient beings. In claiming that the qualities of a buddha are the nature of reality, his position reflects an affirmation of "other-emptiness." Nevertheless, the fact that he also describes buddha nature as empty of its own essence distinguishes his position from one that affirms the presence of buddha nature as a non-empty, substantial reality. Indeed, the way Mipam describes buddha nature as a primordial unity of emptiness and appearance reflects his legacy of the Great Perfection, the unified ground and fruition.

As with most scholars in Tibet, most of Mipam's works do not directly address the canonical sutras, but focus on the commentarial treatises. However, he did write a few commentaries on specific sutras as well.[12] Indeed, he wrote on all three sections of the traditional Buddhist canon: Sutra, Vinaya, and Abhidharma. Mipam's works relating to the Vinaya include an interlinear commentary on the *Individual Liberation Sutra,* called *Steps to Definitive Goodness* (*Nyung ngu nges legs them skas*). Additionally, he composed an interlinear commentary on a text that discusses vows for laypeople, too.[13]

He also wrote a short text on the three vows—the vows of individual liberation, the bodhisattva vow, and the tantric commitments—entitled *Establishing the Three Vows as Essentially One* (*Sdom gsum ngo bog cig tu sgrub pa*). Harmonizing the practices of tantra with monastic vows is particularly important for followers of the Nyingma tradition after the 17th century, such as Mipam, because before then, the Nyingma tradition was primarily defined by its adherence to particular tantras and was not so strongly tied to celibate monastic institutions. With the rise of Nyingma monasteries in the 17th century, the integration of tantra and monasticism became a central concern.

Mipam also wrote on the two main classics of Abhidharma that reached Tibet: the *Abhidharmakośa* by Vasubandhu, and the *Abhidharmasamuccaya* by Asaṅga. Another important work he composed on Abhidharma is his popular *Gateway to Scholarship* (*Mkhas 'jug*), an encyclopedic textbook that draws from both Vasubandhu's and Asaṅga's presentation of Abhidharma. Moreover, he wrote commentaries on the *Pramāṇasamuccaya* and the *Pramāṇavārttika,* the two central texts by the main Buddhist scholars of logic and epistemology from India, Dignāga and Dharmakīrti. His commentary on Dharmakīrti's influential *Pramāṇavārttika* is over nine hundred pages.[14]

In addition to writing on topics of sutra, Mipam wrote several volumes on tantra as well. In particular, he wrote two important texts on Mahāyoga. For the Nyingma, the "inner-tantras" correspond to what is known as "Highest Yoga Tantra" in the new schools of translations (Sarma), so the inner-tantras represent the pinnacle of the tantras. Mipam's two texts on Mahāyoga expound upon the two main subdivisions of Mahāyoga: the *accomplishment section* and the *tantra section.* His *Discourse on the Eight Commands* (*Bka' brgyad rnam bshad*) addresses the accomplishment section of Mahāyoga, which deals primarily with the generation stage of visualizing deities, particularly the eight Mahāyoga deities. These eight deities play a significant role in Nyingma ritual and meditative practices. His *Essential Nature of Luminous Clarity* (*Spyi don 'od gsal snying po*), which is an overview of Longchenpa's commentary on *Guhyagarbhatantra,* addresses the *tantra section* of Mahāyoga. This text is a key statement of his *theory* of tantra, the view. It has a significant place in his corpus because it is the main place where he presents his outlook on the fundamental principles of tantra. Mipam also wrote an interlinear commentary on Padmasambhava's *Garland of Views,* called *Treasury of Jewels* (*Nor bu bang mdzod*), which is based on the thirteenth chapter of the *Guhyagarbhatantra.*

The *Guhyagarbhatantra* is the most important tantra in the Nyingma school. Mipam's commentary explains eleven main topics regarding this tantra—as well as the threefold ground, path, and fruition—in accord with the Great Perfection. He says that his commentary accords with the way that both Rongzom and Longchenpa explain the tantra. He termed this manner of commentary on the *Guhyagarbhatantra,* which accords with the view of the Great Perfection, the "Rong-Long" tradition (Rongzom and Longchenpa) in contrast to the "Zur" tradition that explains it as strictly a Mahāyoga text. Rongzom and Longchenpa were Mipam's primary Nyingma sources.

Drawing upon Rongzom (Rong zom chos bzang, 11th century), Mipam articulates a unique Nyingma view by extending the purview of epistemology to establish the view of tantra—that all appearances are divine—with reason through his distinctive presentation of reliable sources of knowledge (*pramāṇa*). The way he does this is through delineating four perspectives, or four reliable sources of knowledge: two that are conventional and two that are ultimate.[15] His fourfold scheme of truth adds a second tier to each of the Buddhist two truths; thus, there are two tiers of the two truths. The second tier plays a fundamental role in his comprehensive interpretation of Buddhism that integrates reliable sources of knowledge, Madhyamaka, and tantra. His incorporation of tantra within this theory of sources of knowledge is an important part of his exegesis and is a principal factor that distinguishes his Nyingma view.

His two conventional sources of knowledge are respectively based on: confined perception (*tshur mthong*) and pure vision (*dag gzigs*). Mipam describes them in his *Sword of Insight*:

> Since there are appearances that do not accord with reality,
> With regards to the conventional also there are two thoroughly conventional sources of knowledge:
> Based upon impure confined perception and
> Based upon pure vision,
> Like a person's eye and a divine eye.[16]

This division of two types of conventional knowledge is based upon two modes of understanding. The conventional knowledge based in pure vision functions to affirm a reality that is otherwise inconceivable and conflicting with ordinary perception. Conventional knowledge based in confined perception, in contrast, concerns ordinary modes of being in the world.

In parallel with the two *conventional* sources of knowledge, he also delineates two *ultimate* sources of knowledge: knowledge of the categorized ultimate (*rnam grangs pa'i don dam*) and the uncategorized ultimate (*rnam grangs ma yin pa'i don dam*), respectively. The categorized ultimate is the emptiness that can be conceived. The uncategorized ultimate, in contrast, is beyond the domain of conceptual mind. His two conventional sources of knowledge are similar to his two ultimate sources of knowledge in that the division is grounded in two distinct modes of understanding: a delimited, conceptual mode of mind; and an inconceivable mode of wisdom. In this way, he juxtaposes conceptual mind and nonconceptual wisdom.

Significantly, in the contexts of conceptual analysis, there are two distinct truths (ultimate and conventional); however, these two truths are not distinguished in nonconceptual meditative equipoise. Mipam delineates Prāsaṅgika-Madhyamaka as a discourse emphasizing the uncategorized ultimate, where there are no distinctions in accord with the perspective of wisdom in meditative equipoise. In contrast, he depicts Svātantrika-Madhyamaka as a discourse emphasizing the categorized ultimate, in the context of postmeditation where the two truths are divided and the ultimate truth can only be conceptually known. He thus makes a distinction between wisdom (*ye shes*), as the context emphasized by Prāsaṅgika, and ordinary consciousness (*rnam shes*), as the context emphasized by Svātantrika.

Mipam also depicts Prāsaṅgika as an instantaneous means to eliminate conceptual constructs, in contrast to the progressive path emphasized in Svātantrika. Other than different means of approaching the ultimate truth, however, he does not delineate a distinct view for Prāsaṅgika that is different from Svātantrika. Like the harmony he brings out between Yogācāra and Madhyamaka, he emphasizes the compatibility of Prāsaṅgika and Svātantrika by stating that the unique object of negation for the Prāsaṅgika is only the conception of the two truths as distinct. In this way, Mipam emphasizes the unity of the two truths as a characteristic of Prāsaṅgika discourse, and associates this way of coming to know reality as in accord with the way primordial purity (*ka dag*) is known in the Great Perfection. Thus, the Great Perfection plays an important role in shaping his interpretation of exoteric discourse like Madhyamaka and Yogācāra.

Another important dimension of Mipam's interpretation is his unique system of rendering the two truths in two distinct ways:

> There are two ways in which the two truths are stated within the [Buddha's] Word and śāstras: (1) from the perspective of a source of knowledge analyzing the ultimate abiding reality, emptiness is called "ultimate" and appearance is called "relative" and (2) from the perspective of a conventional source of knowledge analyzing the mode of appearance, the subjects and objects of the incontrovertible accordance between the modes of appearance and reality [i.e., authentic experience] are called "ultimate" and the opposite [i.e., inauthentic experience] are called "relative."[17]

Here he outlines a synthetic interpretation of Buddhist philosophy in two models of the two truths: for the first, whatever appears is relative truth while only emptiness, the lack of intrinsic nature, is the ultimate truth, whereas, in the second, reality experienced as it is (i.e., "authentic experience") is the ultimate truth while distorted reality (i.e., "inauthentic experience") is the relative truth. Through these two models he integrates a characteristically Madhyamaka interpretation (in the former model) with a Yogācāra interpretation (in the later model) of two truths. In Yogācāra, (nondual) wisdom is held to be the ultimate truth in contrast to (dualistic) consciousness, whereas in Madhyamaka in general, the ultimate truth is emptiness and any appearance is only ever relative truth. Mipam combines these two streams of interpretation in his unique presentation of the Nyingma view.

Mipam's main influence, Longchenpa (Klong chen rab 'byams, 1308–1363), had drawn extensively from sutras to establish the legitimacy of the contested Nyingma tantras in general and the tradition of the Great Perfection in particular. Mipam also drew from sutras in his works, but for apparently a different reason than Longchenpa. Longchenpa had primarily focused his work on the Great Perfection and used sutras to support his view of the Great Perfection as a legitimate expression of the meaning of Buddhist sutras. Mipam, in contrast, had primarily focused on commentaries of sutra topics (like Madhyamaka) and used the Great Perfection as the guiding principle of his interpretation. In other words, whereas Longchenpa directly elucidated the tradition of the Great Perfection, and used sutras to support his claims, Mipam elucidated the Great Perfection within sutra itself. A predominant feature of Mipam's commentarial style in general, across sutra and tantra, is his keen ability to interpret texts through the lens of the Great Perfection.

Mipam elaborates the distinctive view and practice of the Great Perfection in his momentous compilation known as *Trilogy of Innate Mind* (*Gnyug sems skor gsum*), a collection of his oral instructions compiled posthumously by his students.[18] These works contain his most extensive treatment of the Great Perfection, and even though it was not brought to completion, it is filled with brilliant insights that elucidate the unique features of the Great Perfection.

In addition to his extensive writing on Nyingma material, Mipam also wrote on several major texts of the Sarma tradition, or the "new schools." For instance, he wrote a commentary on the *Song of the View* by a Geluk scholar, Changkya Rolpé Dorjé.[19] The text he chose to comment on is particularly interesting because it attacks a view that negates "intrinsic existence" as something separate from phenomena, a stereotypically Geluk view. While Mipam draws upon central aspects of Geluk thought, like the author of the *Song of the View*, he also critiques what he finds as problematic within dominant strands of this tradition's interpretation.

Mipam is also credited with a commentary on Tsongkhapa's *Three Principal Aspects of the Path*, which is a pithy text summarizing the essential points of the Buddhist path in three aspects: renunciation; the altruistic intention of *bodhicitta*; and the authentic view of emptiness.[20] Additionally, he wrote a commentary on the famous *Treasury of Epistemology* of the Sakya tradition, a Tibetan classic on epistemology.[21] He also composed a short supplication to masters of the Jonang lineage.[22] Drawing upon the Bön tradition, too—a heterodox tradition that claims its roots in pre-Buddhist Tibet—he wrote an 800-page treatise on a system of divination based on knots.[23] Here, we can see that his interests were not limited to simply articulating the views of his own Nyingma tradition, but extends across Buddhist traditions.

Significantly, Mipam wrote a massive two-volume exposition on *Kālacakratantra*, as well as texts on the practices of other Sarma tantras such as *Hevajra, Guhyasamaja, Cakrasaṃvara*, and *Vajrayoginī*, among others.[24] He also composed an interlinear commentary on Saraha's *Treasury of Songs*.[25] Mipam authored several of his own songs on the view of the Great Perfection, in addition to short compositions of quintessential instructions on meditative practice.

He wrote several devotional texts as well, including an invocation to Śākyamuni Buddha entitled *Treasury of Blessings*, which is supplemented by a massive composition in 1,000 pages that expounds upon the buddha's former lives.[26] Additionally, he wrote a beautiful commentary on the famous seven-line supplication to Padmasambhava, called *White Lotus*, which draws out how the seven lines of this short supplication simultaneously resonate with several levels of meaning, including the Great Perfection.[27]

While Mipam is known for his commentaries on sutra and tantra, his writings are not limited to just these topics. For instance, he wrote a text of advice to the king of Degé.[28] Mipam had served as an advisor to the king and had received patronage from the royal family. He wrote on all of the traditional "ten arts," which include (in addition to "the inner-art" of Buddhism): linguistics, poetics, material arts, healing, logic, astrology, drama, among others. His works include a commentary on the famous fourfold medical tantra, and several short works on medicine that address pulse-reading, urinalysis, and even the concoctions of aphrodisiacs![29] He wrote a long commentary on the *Mirror of Poetry*, a classic of Indian poetics, and compiled a Sanskrit-Tibetan dictionary that includes a lexicon of words related to the Great Perfection. He also composed a divination system based on the mantra of Mañjuśrī and a short treatise on letter-writing.[30] In his *Treasure-Trove of Material Arts* (*Bzo gnas nyer mkho'i za ma tog*), he describes the crafts of painting, sculpture, jewelry, knitting, and carpentry, in addition to the process of making such things as incense, ink, herbal pills, and fireworks.

Furthermore, he compiled and edited the popular Gesar epic, which had hitherto been mainly an oral tradition. The epic portrays the exploits of King Gesar, who is acknowledged to be an incarnation of Padmasambhava, in a classic tale that unfolds in a struggle of good versus evil. He composed his own prayers and praises to Gesar, and also arranged a theatrical dance depicting Gesar and his retinue, which continues to be a popular performance at Nyingma monasteries.[31] It is remarkable for such a prominent scholar as Mipam to take such an active role in promoting folk tradition. His exemplary life and prolific works continue to be an inspiration for Buddhist scholars and practitioners inside and outside the monastery, including those living on and off the Tibetan plateau.

REVIEW OF LITERATURE

A number of scholarly works on Mipam have surfaced since the early 21st century. One example is Karma Phuntsho's published *Mipham's Dialectics and the Debates on Emptiness.* He discusses Mipam's works in light of polemical exchanges with Geluk scholars, and his work is an excellent source for Mipam's treatment of emptiness. Also, John Pettit's *Mipham's Beacon of Certainty,* which is focused around a translation of one of Mipam's texts with an annotated commentary, offers biographical information and provides a general background to central issues in Mipam's writings.

Another book-length study of Mipam by Paul Williams, *The Reflexive Nature of Awareness,* deals with the notion of "reflexive awareness" (*rang rig*) in Mipam's commentary on the ninth chapter of the *Bodhicaryāvatāra.*[32] In his book, Williams makes a case that Mipam can be understood as a proponent of "other-emptiness."[33] Matthew Kapstein, however, questions the usefulness of the indigenous labels of "self-emptiness" and "other-emptiness" in interpreting Buddhist thought and cites a danger in overly generalizing these indigenous categories.

Douglas Duckworth's *Mipam on Buddha-Nature* describes the way Mipam integrates discourses on buddha nature with those on emptiness. This book also shows the way that Mipam synthesizes the second and third "turnings of the *dharmacakra,*" Yogācāra and Prāsaṅgika interpretations, self-emptiness and other-emptiness, as well as sutra and tantra. Duckworth's *Jamgön Mipam: His Life and Teachings* further explains Mipam's works with historical and biographical background and includes several excerpts of translations from Mipam's vast corpus. There have also been several translations of Mipam's texts in recent years, which are excellent resources for appreciating the depth and breadth of his contribution to Buddhist philosophical literature.

FURTHER READING

Bötrül. *Distinguishing the Views and Philosophies: Illuminating Emptiness in a Twentieth-Century Tibetan Buddhist Classic.* Translated, annotated, and introduced by Douglas S. Duckworth. Albany: SUNY Press, 2011.

Cabezón, José, and Jamgön Mipham. *The Just King: The Tibetan Buddhist Classic on Leading an Ethical Life.* Boulder, CO: Snow Lion Publications, 2017.

Dharmachakra Translation Committee. *Ornament of the Great Vehicle Sūtras: Maitreya's Mahāyānasūtrālaṃkāra with Commentaries by Ju Mipham and Khenpo Shenga.* Ithaca, NY: Snow Lion Publications, 2014.

Dharmachakra Translation Committee. *Middle Beyond Extremes*. Ithaca, NY: Snow Lion Publications, 2006.

Dharmachakra Translation Committee and His Holiness the Fourteenth Dalai Lama. *Luminous Essence: A Guide to the Guhyagarbha Tantra*. Ithaca, NY: Snow Lion Publications, 2009.

Dilgo Khyentse. *Lion of Speech: The Life of Mipham Rinpoche*. Translated by Padmakara Translation Group. Boulder: Shambhala Publications, 2020.

Dreyfus, Georges. "Would the True Prāsaṅgika Please Stand? The Case of 'Ju Mi-pham." In *The Svātantrika-Prāsaṅgika Distinction*. Edited by Georges Dreyfus and Sara McClintock, 317–347. Boston: Wisdom Publications, 2003.

Doctor, Thomas, trans. *Speech of Delight: Mipham's Commentary on Śāntarakṣita's Ornament of the Middle Way*. Ithaca, NY: Snow Lion Publications, 2004.

Duckworth, Douglas. *Tibetan Buddhist Philosophy of Mind and Nature*. New York: Oxford University Press, 2019.

Duckworth, Douglas. "Mipam Gyatso." *Treasury of Lives*, 2013. https://treasuryoflives.org/biographies/view/Mipam-Gyatso/4228/.

Duckworth, Douglas. *Jamgön Mipam: His Life and Teachings*. Boston: Shambhala Publications, 2011.

Duckworth, Douglas. *Mipam on Buddha-Nature*. Albany: SUNY Press, 2008.

Duckworth, Douglas. "Non-Representational Language in Mipam's Re-Presentation of Other-Emptiness." *Philosophy East & West* 64, no. 4 (2014): 920–932.

Duckworth, Douglas. "Two Models of the Two Truths: Ontological and Phenomenological Approaches." *Journal of Indian Philosophy* 38, no. 5 (2010): 519–527.

Duckworth, Douglas. "Mipam's Middle Way Through Prāsaṅgika and Yogācāra." *Journal of Indian Philosophy* 38, no. 4 (2010): 431–439.

Goodman, Steven D. "Mi-pham rgya-mtsho: An Account of His Life, the Printing of His Works, and the Structure of His Treatise Entitled *mKhas-pa'i tshul la 'jug-pa'i sgo*." In *Wind Horse: Proceedings of the North American Tibetological Society*. Edited by Ronald M. Davidson, 58–78. Berkeley, CA: Asian Humanities Press, 1981.

Jamgön Mipham. *The Wisdom Chapter: Jamgön Mipham's Commentary on the Ninth Chapter of the Way of the Bodhisattva*. Translated by the Padmakara Translation Group. Boulder: Shambhala Publications, 2017.

Kapstein, Matthew. "Mipam Namgyel: The Lion's Roar Affirming Extrinsic Emptiness." In *Buddhist Philosophy: Essential Readings*. Edited by William Edelglass and Jay Garfield, 61–72. Oxford: Oxford University Press, 2009.

Kapstein, Matthew. "Mi-pham's Theory of Interpretation." In *Buddhist Hermeneutics*. Edited by Donald S. Lopez, 149–174. Honolulu: University of Hawai'i Press, 1988.

Pettit, John. *Mipham's Beacon of Certainty*. Boston: Wisdom Publications, 1999.

Phuntsho, Karma. *Mipham's Dialectics and the Debates on Emptiness*. London: RoutledgeCurzon, 2005.

Phuntsho, Karma. "Ju Mi pham rNam rgyal rGya mtsho—His Position in the Tibetan Religious Hierarchy and a Synoptic Survey of His Contributions." In *The Pandita and the Siddha: Studies in Honour of E. Gene Smith*. Edited by Ramon N. Prats. Dharamshala, India: Amnye Machen Institute, 2007.

NOTES

1. Künzang Chödrak (*sa manta bhadra dharma kirti*), *Mipam's Essential Biography and Catalogue of Works* (*Gangs ri'i khrod kyi smra ba'i seng ge gcig po 'jam dgon mi pham rgya mtsho'i rnam thar snying po bsdus pa dang gsung rab kyi dkar chag snga 'gyur bstan pa'i mdzes rgyan*), in *Mipam's Collected Works*, vol. 8, 627–628. John Pettit translates a portion of this hagiography in *Mipham's Beacon of Certainty* (Boston: Wisdom Publications, 1999), 23–39. The author of this text is unclear. Pettit attributes the author to Khenpo Künpel, Mipam's student; however, he states that there is some doubt that Khenpo Künpel is in fact the author. See Pettit, *Mipham's Beacon of Certainty*, 27, 467n.59.
2. Künzang Chödrak, *Essential Biography*, 629.

3. Künzang Chödrak, *Essential Biography*, 628–630; English trans. in Pettit, *Mipam's Beacon of Certainty*, 24.
4. Künzang Chödrak, *Essential Biography* 636–637; English trans. in Pettit, *Mipam's Beacon of Certainty*, 26–27.
5. The "Sarma tiger" refers to the Geluk scholar, Pari Rapsel (Dpa' ris blo bzang rab gsal, 1840–1910). Kuchuk, *Opening the Eye of Clear Intelligence: A History of the Transmission of the Madhyamaka View in Tibet*, 374.
6. Mipam, *Beacon of Certainty*, 19; English trans. in Pettit, 209.
7. Mipam did write a topical outline (*sa bcad*) for a treasure text of Chokgyur Lingpa, the *Concise Meaning of the* Light of Wisdom (*Lam rim ye shes snying po'i bsdus don ldeb*), in *Mipam's Collected Works*, vol. 8 (Kathmandu: Zhechen Monastery, 1987). Another short text Mipam wrote concerning the treasure tradition describes how to tell good treasure revealers from charlatans. See Mipam, *Clear Water Jewel for Examining Treasure-Revealers* (*Gter ston brtag ba chu dwangs nor bu*), in *Mipam's Collected Works*, vol. 14, 475–487. For a critical edition, translation, and analysis of this text, see Andreas Doctor, *The Tibetan Treasure Literature: Revelation, Tradition, and Accomplishment in Visionary Buddhism* (Ithaca: Snow Lion Publications, 2006). It is noteworthy that Mipam states: "I also have no hope for the fortune of a new treasure doctrine because I know that there is not the slightest thing missing (*ma chog pa rdul rtsam med*) from sutras, tantras, and commentarial treatises." Mipam, *Shedding Light on Thusness* (*Gzhan gyis brtsad pa'i lan mdor bsdus pa rigs lam rab gsal de nyid snang byed*), published in *Spyod 'jug sher 'grel ke ta ka* (Sichuan, China: Nationalities Press, 1993), 339.
8. For descriptions of the breadth of Mipam's writings, see Karma Phuntsho, *Mipham's Dialectics and the Debates on Emptiness* (London: RoutledgeCurzon, 2005), 13–19. See also Gene Smith, *Among Tibetan Texts* (Boston: Wisdom Publications, 2001), 229–233.
9. For instance, he wrote a massive two-volume commentary on the *Kālacakra*, as well as composed texts on *Hevajra, Guhyasamāja, Cakrasaṃvara*, among others.
10. He wrote *Shedding Light on Thusness* (*Gzhan gyis brtsad pa'i lan mdor bsdus pa rigs lam rab gsal de nyid snang byed*) in response to Pari Rapsel's (Dpa' ris blo bzang rab gsal, 1840–1910) critique and *Light of the Sun* (*Brgal lan nyin byed snang ba*) in response to Drakkar Tulku (Brag dkar dpal ldan bstan 'dzin snyan grags, 1866–1928).
11. Among the "five treatises of Maitreya," Mipam states that the *Uttaratantra* and *Abhisamayālaṃkāra* are Madhyamaka treatises; the *Mahāyānsūtrālaṃkāra* is a Mind-Only treatise; and that *Madhyāntavibhāga* and *Dharmadharmatāvibhāga* concern the Mahāyāna in general.
12. He wrote a commentary on the *Recollecting the Three Jewels Sutra*, called *Inexhaustible Melody of Auspiciousness* (*Bkra shis mi zad pa'i sgra dbyangs*), and also composed interlinear commentaries on the *Individual Liberation Sutra*, called *Steps to Definitive Goodness* (*Nyung ngu nges legs them skas*), and on the *Condensed Perfection of Wisdom Sutra*, called *Elegant Discourse Introducing the Unmistaken Meaning of the Intended Meaning of the Victorious Ones' Mother* (*Yon tan rin chen sdud pa'i 'grel pa rgyal ba'i yum gyi dgongs don la phyin ci ma log par 'jug pa'i legs bshad*). Additionally, he wrote a text called *Words of Maitreya* (*Ma pham zhal lung*) that correlates the *Condensed Perfection of Wisdom Sutra* with Maitreya's *Abhisamayālaṃkāra*.
13. *Mipam's Collected Works*, vol. 8, 131–134.
14. Mipam, *Treasury Illuminating Elegant Discourse* (*Legs bshad snang ba'i gter*), in *Mipam's Collected Works*, vol. 20.
15. For a discussion of the functions of Mipam's fourfold epistemology, see Matthew Kapstein, "Mi-pham's Theory of Interpretation," in *Buddhist Hermeneutics*, ed. Donald Lopez (Honolulu: University of Hawai'i Press, 1988), 159.
16. Mipam,*Sword of Insight* (*Don rnam par nges*), in *Mipam's Collected Works*, vol. 4, 800.
17. Mipam, *Words That Delight Guru Mañjughoṣa* (*'Jam byangs bla ma dgyes pa'i zhal lung*), 55–56. See also Mipam, *Light of the Sun*, in *Spyod 'jug sher 'grel ke ta ka* (Sichuan, China: Nationalities Press, 1993), 549;

Bötrül, *Stong thun gnad kyi zin thun*, in *Bötrül's Collected Works* (Sichuan, China: Nationalities Press, 2004), vol. 1, 267.

18. The first text of this trilogy, with a commentary by Khetsün Zangpo (1920–2009), has been translated by Jeffrey Hopkins, who intends to translate the whole trilogy. See Jeffrey Hopkins, *Fundamental Mind: The Nyingma View of the Great Completeness* (Ithaca: Snow Lion Publications, 2006).
19. See *Mipam's Collected Works*, vol. 4, 821–867; English translation of Mipam's text in Karl Brunnhözl, *Straight from the Heart: Buddhist Pith Instructions* (Ithaca: Snow Lion Publications, 2007), 391–428.
20. This text is mentioned in a catalogue of his works, but is not included in the Zhechen or Kaḥtok editions of his collected works.
21. Mipam, *Banner Victorious Over All: A Commentary on the Treasury of Epistemology* (*Tshad ma rigs pa'i gter mchan gyis 'grel pa phyogs las rnam par rgyal ba'i ru mtshon*), in *Mipam's Collected Works*, vol. 11, 549–752.
22. Mipam, *Supplication Supplement for the Jonang Lineage* (*Jo nang lugs kyi bshad pa'i brgyud 'debs kha skong*), in *Mipam's Collected Works*, vol. 27, 279–280.
23. Mipam, *Lamp Illuminating the Miraculous Knots* (*Srid pa 'phrul gyi ju thig gi dpyad don snang gsal sgron me*), in *Mipam's Collected Works*, vol. 16, 1–814.
24. *Mipam's Collected Works*, vol. 17 (*e*) and vol. 18 (*waṃ*).
25. Mipam, *Vajra Melodies* (*Dpal sa ra has mdzas pas do ha mdzod glu'i mchan 'grel gnyug ma'i rdo rje sgra dbyangs*), in *Mipam's Collected Works*, vol. 12, 759–795.
26. Mipam, *White Lotus: Background for the Treasury of Blessings* (*Thub chog byin rlabs gter mdzod kyi rgyab chos padma dkar po*), in *Mipam's Collected Works*, vol. 15.
27. Mipam, *White Lotus: An Explanation of the Seven-Line Supplication to Guru Padmasambhava* (*Gu ru tshig bdun gsol 'debs kyi rnam bshad padma dkar po*), in *Mipam's Collected Works*, vol. 19, 277–370; English translation in Jamgön Mipham and Padmakara Translation Group, *White Lotus* (Boston: Shambhala Publications, 2007).
28. Mipam, *Ornament of Rule* (*Rgyal po lugs kyi bstan bcos sa gzhi skyong ba'i rgyan*), in *Mipam's Collected Works*, vol. 1, 1–157; see English translation in José Cabezón, *The Just King* (Boulder: Snow Lion, 2017).
29. Karma Phuntsho, "Ju Mi pham rNam rgyal rGya mtsho—His Position in the Tibetan Religious Hierarchy and a Synoptic Survey of His Contributions," in *The Pandita and the Siddha: Studies in Honour of E. Gene Smith*, ed. Ramon N. Prats (Dharamshala, India: Amnye Machen Institute, 2007), 7.
30. Mipam, *A Divination Manual That Delights Mañjughoṣa* (*A ra pa tsa'i mo yig 'jam dpal dgyes pa'i zhal lung*), in *Mipam's Collected Works*, vol. 5, 349–398; English translation in Jay Goldberg and Doya Nardin, *Mo: Tibetan Divination System* (Ithaca: Snow Lion Publications, 1990); and Mipam, *Garland of Flowered Jewels* (*Yig bskur gyi rnam bzhag mdo tsam brjod pa me tog nor bu'i phreng ba*), in *Mipam's Collected Works*, vol. 14, 929–940.
31. See Karma Phuntsho, " 'Ju Mi pham rNam rgyal rGya mtsho," 8–9.
32. Paul Williams, *The Reflexive Nature of Awareness: A Madhyamaka Defence* (London: Curzon Press, 1998).
33. See Williams, *The Reflexive Nature of Awareness*, 199–206.

Douglas S. Duckworth

MONASTIC EDUCATION IN CONTEMPORARY ASIA

INTRODUCTION

Education is perhaps not the first thing that the wider society thinks about when they imagine contemporary Buddhists and their communities. The most famous images of contemporary

Buddhists are those of a monk or nun meditating, the images of famous monks like the Dalai Lama or Thich Naht Hanh preaching about peace or mindfulness, or, since the start of the 2010s, the images of monks in Myanmar or Sri Lanka encouraging people to "protect Buddhism," thereby inciting violence against Muslim minorities. However, beyond and behind these images lies the central and important job of education. Buddhist *sanghas* have existed for upward of two and a half millennia, even if their forms have varied across time and space, as well as their roles and relations within various societies. The preservation and propagation of the teachings of the buddha, however these are defined, remain central among the formal obligations of *sanghas*. This implies systems for transmitting these teachings, which means education. Since the start of the 20th century, and in particular since the end of the Cold War in the early 1990s, Buddhism has come to be seen as a "world religion," shaped by international images, national educational systems, and local practices. Systems of monastic education within Buddhist communities have been shaped and transformed by these same forces. In other words, contemporary monastic education should be seen as a series of systems across the Buddhist world, some of which seek to maintain traditional modes of pedagogy, others of which seek to create "modern" forms of the religion, in order to make Buddhism relevant to modern and contemporary societies.

FORMS AND DYNAMICS OF MONASTIC EDUCATION

Although monastic education can fruitfully be discussed according to a variety of factors, such as the differences between secondary and postsecondary monastic education, initially it is important to address the modes of education as well as its aims as entangled with ideas about the role of religion in society.

In general terms, monastic education in most forms has two different modes: apprentice and curricular.[1] Apprentice education, which might also be referred to as "situated learning," refers to a mode of education that is based on relationships between the student and teacher.[2] The student and teacher may have a relationship that resembles that of the apprentice and the master, and the knowledge acquired may be less important than the context within which the student is disciplined and shaped. In contrast, curricular education is the mode of education that takes place in formal school settings, and the purpose of the education is for the student to acquire specific, normally textual, knowledge. Although apprentice education situations may have a relatively consistent curriculum within a particular region or country, this is secondary to the relationship between the teacher and the student. By contrast, the material in the curriculum is a central point to curricular education. It is more likely to be a part of a bureaucratized system of learning than apprentice education, such as a public or national school system. It is also more likely to resemble what is thought of as a stereotypical school, with monks or nuns sitting at desks listening to a teacher (who may or may not be a monastic themselves). Curricular and apprentice education are ideal types, and in specific locations they might easily blend, where the relationships that are emblematic of apprentice education might be located within a school setting. Alternatively, a monk or nun might experience both modes of education, but sequentially.

The other aspect that shapes contemporary monastic education has to do with the degree of secularity. By secularity, we often understand the opposite of religion, either its absence or the nonreligious. However, since the start of the 21st century, scholarship in religious studies and anthropology has highlighted how secularity and religion are entangled with one another, and formations of the secular are really about the dynamics of determining what counts as religion and what as nonreligion in a specific local or national context. The line between the religious and nonreligious is less stable than is generally understood, in part because the categories in play are themselves unstable (certainly over time and space). This line depends on the governing system, discourses of modernity and modernization predominant in the country, and the history of both the country and religious institutions therein. Nation-states as well as global systems (of governance and information flow) determine "religiosity," and actors within respond both strategically and not, a process that Mandair and Dressler refer to as "religion-making."[3] The secularity of monastic education is very much a function of the developments of the 19th and 20th centuries. Although conditions varied, throughout much of Buddhist Asia, temples were *a*, if not *the*, locus for education (whether of apprentice or curricular mode), and monks and nuns would be likely to learn subjects that were not directly related to the teachings of the buddha, such as medicine, divination, mathematics, and so forth. Broadly speaking, prior to the 20th century, non-Buddhist knowledge played a significant role within monastic education, of both the apprentice and curricular forms. Whether this was seen as appropriate for monastics varied, but it was not seen as either "secular" or "religious" knowledge, because there was not a distinct notion of "religion." However, since the end of the 19th century, when Asian polities had to struggle with the challenge of survival in the wake of European colonialism (whether or not they were colonized), the question has become more pronounced as to whether monks, nuns, or novices should be learning non-Buddhist—that is, "secular"—information. For example, in Myanmar, when British colonizers sought to have novices learn math, most Burmese monks rejected this not because it was not Buddhist but because it reframed Buddhism from being a universal to being a "religion," that was part of an individual's choice.[4] These monks lost that particular battle, but the question of what counts as appropriate for Buddhist monastics to study remains. Indeed, although this category of the secular remains slippery from outside, internally it may be deployed by educators or institutional stakeholders as a justification for the content or purpose of monastic education. For example, some contemporary Buddhist universities specifically train monastics to be good monastics, and there are others that differ little from other comprehensive universities (public or private). This is not just a problem of the early 20th century. The question of what monastics should study remains a vital question in at least some contexts of monastic education.[5] What often shapes the contours of monastic education is the imagined role that monastics ideally play in society. When societies do not have issues with monastics practicing medicine, they will not likely have a problem with monastics learning about the body and science.

To understand this, it is important to delineate the actors and stakeholders that participate in contemporary monastic education. First, and most important, are the monastics who are also students in the various systems. The monastics include most obviously monks and nuns, but we should also consider novices (male and female) as well as female renunciants like the *mae chi* of Thailand or the *dasa sila matha* of Sri Lanka who do not or cannot take a full ordination (as in many of the Theravāda Buddhist contexts of mainland Southeast Asia and Sri Lanka). It is also necessary to consider the priests of Japan (male and female) who have served primarily pastoral and ritual specialist roles since the end of the 19th century, even if they are not for the most part celibate. The purpose of different educational systems varies significantly, and as a result, students can also vary. For example, in places like Thailand or in Tibetan Buddhist contexts, it is common for minority-aged males to ordain, either temporarily or for life. Particularly regarding the former, temporary ordination and the schools attendant upon the practice have proved to be an important alternative to public (national) education systems for at least the last seventy years.[6] A similar situation exists in Sri Lanka, where boys might decide to ordain after failing a country-wide government scholarship test. The monastery schools thus provide an important, cheaper alternative. The temporary ordination of Thailand and other Tai communities like Laos or Sipsongpannā in Southwest China, and the long- or short-term education associated with it may be a rite of passage, a place where young men were/are prepared to become full adults.[7] In Nepal, the situation is the opposite, where young women may ordain to avoid marriage and their training allows them to pursue other fields of merit.[8] In East Asia, monastic education (or priestly education in Japan) is much more likely to focus on postsecondary school students. In China, for example, Han men and women who want to ordain must have completed high school, and so monastic education is much more likely to include study in a postsecondary institute or college.[9] Similarly, a central part of the training of priests in Japan is at sectarian universities.

The other key stakeholders within contemporary monastic education are those directly attached to schools such as teachers and the patrons of schools. The status of these figures varies according to the population of the school, as well as its degree of secularity. In conditions of situated learning, the teachers are commonly monastics themselves. This is unsurprising if we consider that apprentice education is primarily about training young boys to be good monks (often in terms of the maturation process). The situation is more complicated in curricular education, in which the training is more diverse. Although there are formal monastic schools where the topics taught are primarily if not solely derived directly from the teachings of the buddha, the majority in contemporary Asia provide both Buddhist and non-Buddhist training. In these mixed-curricular contexts, it is not uncommon for monks or nuns to teach Buddhist subjects and nonmonastics to teach secular subjects. This kind of pattern used to be what one saw in the monastic high schools of Thailand, before the system shrank in the last decade. In higher Buddhist education, this pattern is even more mixed. At places like the Buddhist College of Singapore, some Buddhist topics are taught by academics with doctoral degrees; at others such as Mahachulalongkornrajavidyalaya University and Mahamakut Buddhist University, the Buddhist universities of Thailand, monks with doctoral degrees teach both Buddhist and non-Buddhist subjects.[10] The same is true of administrators of schools, although principals or deans of secondary schools or colleges that are specifically for monastics are almost always monks or nuns (an exception to this is the Japanese Buddhist universities, many of which seek to be comprehensive universities as well as training centers for priests).[11]

Generally, there are three types of patrons of monastic education: lay supporters, Buddhist sects, or institutions and states. The roles played within any specific context of monastic education is a matter of scale. Lay supporters provide important financial support for monastic education at all levels, but this is particularly the case in apprentice education taking place in villages of Southeast Asia or in Tibetan cultural contexts, or in the support of parishioners in

Japanese temple Buddhism.[12] This is because the specific temple depends upon the community around it both for financial support and labor. Buddhist sects or institutions also provide key support for schools, both in financial terms as well as through establishing curricula or standards. This is most obvious in places like Japan or in Tibetan contexts, where there are a plurality of Buddhist schools (there are a plurality of fraternities [*nikāyas*] within Theravāda communities, but the curricular differences between the Thammayut [also Dhammayutika] Nikāya and Mahā Nikāya in Thailand are not as great as those between the Shingon and the Jōdo Shinshū in Japan, for example).

The role of the state in monastic education varies significantly, with both direct and indirect roles in contemporary monastic education, an effect of the "secularity" of the education or the educational system. Across contemporary Asia, states are most likely to be involved with curricular forms of monastic education. In Theravāda polities, where monastic secondary schools are more common, governments are directly involved in approving curricula as well as funding the schools. For example, in Thailand, although the *sangha* is the body that develops the curriculum at monastic schools, the government in the guise of the National Office of Buddhism supports this work. In cases where governments are less disposed toward the free practice of religion (such as China or Laos), state entities must approve the opening of religious schools, even if they do not directly develop the curriculum.[13] The situation is somewhat more complicated regarding Buddhist colleges and universities. Governments are involved in approving the founding of universities (or their change from institutes to universities), such as in Japan during the Meiji period in particular, Sri Lanka, and Thailand.[14] Accreditation of colleges and universities may also be carried out by state entities more than private ones. In some cases, other Buddhist universities across national borders provide accreditation. In other words, contemporary Asian states are highly involved in monastic education, but it is not always a direct interaction or relationship.

There are two other distinctions in regard to contemporary monastic education: the difference between past and contemporary forms and the distinction between monastic education and Buddhist education. Although the education of monastics has been around as long as men and women have been followers of the buddha, in both apprentice and curricular forms, for the last 150 years, monastic education has been affected by two significant shifts. The first is the emergence of the idea of "Buddhism" as a world religion, and that the various parts of the Buddhist world were part of the same phenomenon. This does not mean, of course, that Buddhism did not exist prior to the mid-19th century, but the imagination of Buddhism as a singular object meant that Buddhists from around Asia began to pay attention to one another, and they began to support systems of education as either patrons (such as Japanese scholars in India) or clients (Nepali Theravada Buddhists going to Thailand to study) or both. They also paid attention to what other "Buddhists" were doing. This process, the emergence of a "Buddhist ethnoscape," intersected with both colonialism, its resistance, and the emergence of the nation-state system within Asia.[15] This last point has had a particularly profound impact on the way that educational systems for the training of monastics emerged. The training of monks and, to a lesser extent, nuns, in the 20th century became entangled with the emergence of the development of the imagination of the nation, as well as the development of educational infrastructure that sought to harness the *sanghas* to the cause of the nation. These processes have occurred unevenly throughout Asia, a reflection of the different experiences of imperialism and the conditions of the *sangha* throughout. Sometimes it was directed by the states, as was the case in Chulalongkorn's efforts to centralize the Thai Sangha by reforming the education system;[16] at other times, it emerged from the efforts of monastics themselves, as can be seen in Taixu's goal of creating a system of "modern" Buddhist institutes that could make monks and Buddhism relevant to the nation.[17] In the latter case, Buddhist institutes were an important location for monastics to debate what they believed their responsibilities were to the national community.[18] Regardless, the sense of a broader and unified Buddhist world and the entanglement of monastic education in national projects distinguishes contemporary education from its pre-1800 versions.

The second point to note is that monastic education is a subset of a wider concept we could think of as Buddhist education. This would include systems like Buddhist Sunday schools directed at lay children or schools run by monastics for lay children.[19] There are also continuing education programs, for example, in Singapore where nonmonastic Buddhists learn Pāli, and Buddhist courses and meditation centers in Asia and around the world, such as those that focus on the Goenka system.[20] These are certainly related to monastic education, and they too need to be understood in relation to the wider set of issues that emerge with the development of the idea of Buddhism and the nation-state system. Monastic education should be distinguished from Buddhist education, however, because the purpose of the former is much more specifically about training religious specialists than is the case with Buddhist education as a whole. The lines between these are not always clear, as in Southeast Asian contexts where temporary ordination is common, especially for men. In these contexts, the purpose for training young men may be more oriented toward creating good men as much as good monks. Despite the fact that the lines cannot always be sharply delineated, the set-apart status of monastics and other ritual specialists suggests that it is helpful to distinguish monastic education as a subset of Buddhist education.

THE GOALS OF DIFFERENT MODES OF MONASTIC EDUCATION

People ordain for a variety of reasons. Some of these goals hew close to the stereotyped notion of what a Buddhist motivation might be, such as a desire to cultivate wisdom or alleviate suffering. Others seem to be more oriented toward goals that are more social or material. These might include attaining access to higher levels of education, escaping a difficult living situation, fulfilling a social responsibility to become a good person (men ordaining in Thailand), or a family responsibility (children becoming priests in Japan to take over a family temple from a parent). There are also motivations that do not fit into either stereotypically Buddhist motivations or the social goals listed here, including an aesthetic attraction to being a monk.[21] Although it may be tempting to see these as radically divergent, it is better to recognize that motivations to ordain are complicated and multiple. Beyond the contingencies of the decisions of individuals, the goals of pedagogical systems are more visible, if only through a focus on both curricular decisions and the outcomes of monastic education (i.e., what happens to the monastic students after they leave a system). This comes into focus when examining in greater detail potential goals of apprentice and curricular education within Sipsongpannā, a region in Southwest China where both modes of education exist.

Sipsongpannā is a minority region of the contemporary People's Republic of China, where Theravāda Buddhism has been practiced for at least the last four centuries, perhaps longer. Like other Tai parts of mainland Southeast Asia, the Buddhists of Sipsongpannā practice temporary ordination. Many boys ordain for a period and then disrobe in order to lead a standard lay life. Prior to colonization as a part of China (a process which took much of the 20th century), almost all boys ordained at least as novices. As in Thailand, this was understood as necessary in order to be seen as full members of society; males who did not ordain were generally seen as unfit for marriage. The purpose of ordination, in other words, was to educate the boys into being men who were capable of reading and writing the local script within a Buddhist idiom. In order to ensure this, the Buddhists in the region also preferred for boys to ordain young so that they could be "tamed" and "domesticated" before puberty.[22] While the *sangha* hierarchy had close ties to the political authorities, the *sangha* was generally decentralized and like Buddhist practice in northern Thailand, individual abbots had a great deal of autonomy.[23] Just as there was no standard form of the region's script, there was no standardized set of Buddhist texts that the novices in the region were taught. What they were taught varied according to the knowledge and interests of the village abbot. However, the end goal of the education was less about producing Buddhist intellectuals and more about creating proper members of society.[24]

Since the end of the Cultural Revolution in 1976, monastic education in the region has become more complicated. Tai boys in Sipsongpannā still ordain, but they must also attend public schools.[25] One effect of this is that most novices experience situated learning in village temples and standardized, national education in the public schools at the same time. During this same period, the *sangha* of the region has also founded and run several different formal schools, explicitly to provide novices with a deeper Buddhist knowledge than most of them receive in village temples. These schools use modified versions of the curriculum used in the monastic high school system of Thailand. However, in contrast to the Thai system, which is supported by the state and partly driven by state interests, the Sipsongpannā system has developed under the auspices of the monks of the region, who are interested in developing young men who value Buddhism in combination with loyalty to their ethnic community. In looking at apprentice and curricular education together, then, it becomes clear that they have different ends. In village temples, novices are being trained to be proper human beings, with ties to the local community. At the same time, in contexts of curricular education, the novices are being trained to have a broader view of their affiliations, whether to the Chinese nation-state (in the public schools) or to the regional Buddhist culture (in the monastic high schools).

DYNAMICS OF GENDER IN CONTEMPORARY MONASTIC EDUCATION

There are at least two ways in which gender inflects systems of monastic education in contemporary Asia: the training of female monastics; and the fostering of normative notions of gender. Because the conditions in which female monastics are trained and educated are quite diverse across Asia, it is difficult to summarize training of female monastics across Asia in a short article. The conditions of the training and education of female monastics are affected by the conditions that shape the lives of women more broadly in Buddhist countries. Gendered hierarchies are common throughout Asia, and Buddhist ideologies are used to reinforce and resist those. Indeed, the lingering resistance to having girls train to be priests in 20th-century Japan has both Buddhist and Confucian roots.[26] Moreover, in places where merit-based systems have an important impact on the flow of resources to monastics, the presence or its lack of the higher ordination (*upasampadā*) impacts the amount of resources available for the training of female monastics. Novices and eight or ten precept monastics are often not seen as fertile as fields of merit as are fully ordained monastics. This is part of why female monastics have access to fewer pedagogical resources than their male counterparts in places like Nepal and other Theravāda regions, as well as in Tibetan regions, though there are exceptions to this as can be seen by the love (and support) shown to female renunciants in Sri Lanka by some villagers.[27] Female monastics have sometimes seen Buddhist institutes as important resources for fostering the status of nuns, particularly in places like Taiwan or Japan.[28] These gendered hierarchies can be affected by the existence of the higher ordination, though access to resources does not always lead to female renunciants attaining the same educational attainments as their male counterparts.[29] At the same time, understanding the conditions that female monastics find themselves in requires that we avoid simple dichotomies of freedom and unfreedom that undergird many feminist theories.[30] This can have profound implications for the goals that nuns from some Asian nation-states have in establishing educational systems.[31] Access to pedagogical resources is only one aspect in understanding the status of female renunciants.

Gender also intersects with monastic education in constructions of masculinities. Although most scholarly attention to gender and Buddhism has been focused on the status of female renunciants, and particularly the efforts to reestablish the *bhikkhunī* ordination (in Theravāda communities), scholars have also begun to consider the way that gender shapes the lives and conditions of male monastics as well. Scholars writing about Tibet and Myanmar have argued that the masculinity of monks needs to be seen in relation to wider conceptions of masculinity in their respective societies, as both complement to lay manhood, or as an ideal form of it.[32] To the degree that monastic schools train boys and men how to be proper humans, they are not only training them to be monks but how to be men as well. Casas has shown playing basketball becomes a way for novices in Sipsongpannā to display and perform their budding masculinity, which is also tied up with their likely future status as eligible laymen.[33] Moreover, Chladek has shown that whereas sites for the training of monastics such as vacation camps for novices reinforce normative forms of Thai Buddhist masculinity, they are also sites for resistance to these norms.[34]

BUDDHIST UNIVERSITIES IN CONTEMPORARY ASIA

Finally, it is worth considering Buddhist universities as a specific genre of monastic education in contemporary Asia. "Universities" are of course not new to Buddhist communities; Nalanda, the site of education and training in India for much of the first millennium, is often referred to as a university. However, although we may refer to Nalanda or some of the great monasteries of education and training in Tibet as colleges or universities, these differed significantly from the modern university which emerged in 19th-century Europe and the United States. Modern Buddhist universities in Asia generally use as their models the public or sectarian universities of Western Europe and the United States. Modern Buddhist universities, monastic or otherwise, remain a largely understudied topic.

There is significant diversity within these universities and it can be difficult to differentiate these universities from other, public universities. For example in Japan, a number of the sectarian universities that train and educate priests also train lay students (who may or may not be Buddhist). The same is true at the Thai Buddhist universities, Mahachulalongkornrajavidyalaya University and Mahamakut Buddhist University, which have been educating lay Thais as well as monks, novices, and *mae chis* for at least two decades (though these lay students are a minority of the student body). Gildow has shown how Buddhist institutes in China (which are generally post-secondary schools) need to be analyzed as relatively weak institutions nested inside other institutions of modern Chinese society.[35] At a number of universities, particularly in East Asia, there has also been a long-term secularizing process. Where one hundred years ago these Korean and Japanese universities had a clear Buddhist mission, now, many of them seem little different than other universities in the countries (except for the presence of a Buddhist studies department).[36] Similarly, regardless of whether they are populated by lay or monastic students, there are both private Buddhist universities, such as Bukkyo University in Japan, which is supported by the Jōdo Shū sect, and public ones supported by the government, such as the Buddhist and Pali University of Sri Lanka. The missions of Buddhist universities vary significantly, ranging from the goal of training all students to be modern citizens or being modern students with a Buddhist background, to being focused on training monastics to be not only well-educated in Buddhist knowledge but to be effective managers of temple properties and/or effective preachers. In addition, a number of programs have emerged within these universities or in branch campuses in Singapore or among the middle-class communities in Colombo that cater to leisure learners. In general, then, Buddhist universities that serve monastics need to be studied as part of a wider ecosystem of university education in the country in which they are situated.

An additional aspect of monastic university education in contemporary Asia is that it highlights central transnational aspects of Buddhism. Monastic universities, such as Mahachulalongkornrajavidyalaya University in Thailand, the Buddhist and Pali University of Sri Lanka, and the Buddhist College of Singapore, are at the heart of several different transnational networks. Each of these schools trains monastics from other Buddhist countries, sometimes providing links across sectarian divides, such as when Mahāyāna monks or nuns from Taiwan or China study in Sri Lanka, or monastics from both China and Southeast Asia study Mahāyāna Buddhism at the Buddhist College of Singapore. These universities can also represent transnational and transsectarian alliances and support networks, as can be seen when Mahachulalongkornrajavidyalaya University provided some essential curricular support at the founding of the Buddhist College of Singapore. At the same time, though, these monastic universities can also be locations for status building and competition. Although Thailand has its own Buddhist universities, many if not most of the highest monks in the Thai Sangha also have graduate degrees from Buddhist universities in India. The effect of these transnational interactions on national and local *sanghas* awaits further study.

REVIEW OF LITERATURE

In general, although the training of monastics has been an essential part of the lives of nuns and monks since the start of the religion, the academic study of how monastics have been educated has not been a significant part of the academic study of Buddhism until relatively recently. The scholarly turn to the training and education of monastics should be understood as taking place at the same time as a concern to understand the lived religious experience of Buddhist lives, and so has coincided with the study of the *Vinaya* and the disciplining of monastics, as in the work of Schopen, Kieffer-Pülz, and Clarke,[37] as well as a wider concern to understand the lives of Buddhists embedded in their communities. Part of what this means is understanding that the field of contemporary monastic education requires us to think a bit more broadly in terms of time. That is, the study of contemporary monastic education requires attention to scholarship focused not just on the post-Cold War period but at least on the 19th and 20th centuries as well. In very broad terms, the study of monastic education has been organized around three distinct though related problems: monastic education as a focus of modernization, monastic education as entangled with the products of nation-states, and monastic education in the development of subjectivities.

Modernization has been a central problem-space for the study of monastic education in Asia. The central question has been around the need for the *sangha* (of a given country) to reform in order to make it relevant for the changing needs of the country. A core subject has been the efforts of the Chinese monk, Taixu, to develop Buddhist institutes (*foxueyuan*) as a part of the project to develop a modern form of Buddhism. The second of Welch's three books on Chinese Buddhism in the 20th century, *The Revival of Chinese Buddhism*,[38] examines these institutes, and the projects involved with them. Taixu's legacy has been the subject of significant work since then, but the Buddhist institutes have been less so, with the exception of Lai, who sees the emergence of Buddhist institutes in China in the context of Chinese Buddhists debating the role of religion in the emerging nation-state and who they are as citizens.[39] The problem of modernization and the relevance of monastic training and exactly what monastics should study is also a problem in Southeast Asian forms of Buddhism. For example, Dhammasami and Schober show how the *sanghas* of Thailand and Burma are unable to sufficiently reform monastic education to preserve the system in the face of colonial challenges.[40] Turner centers these efforts to reform monastic education in Burma in a larger conflict between the colonial powers and Burmese (lay and monastic) over the goals of training monks, arguing that this is less about failure to reform and more about radically conflicting worldviews.[41]

As should be evident, the problem of modernization is tied up with political projects. This is seen most clearly on the scholarship on monastic education in Thailand. In the late 19th and early 20th centuries, the Thai government under Rama V (r. 168–1919) Chulālongkorn engaged in a process of centralizing control over what became the nation-state of Thailand, including asserting control over regional *sanghas* to develop a modern bureaucratic state. A core part of this was the attempt to create a standardized system of monastic education, an issue discussed in both Reynolds and Tambiah.[42] Although McDaniel has argued that the results of the Thai state's project to reform and centralize monastic education have been overstated, Choompolpaisal has shown how political discourse alters monastic education in Thailand, altering expectations of what should be learned by monks.[43] This is a point reinforced by Dhammasami who shows that the education of monks in Burma and Thailand has long been shaped by state projects.[44] The entanglements of monastic education with the state (modern or post-Cold War) is evident in other parts of Asia as well, including China, Tibet, and Sri Lanka.[45]

The third major problem in the field of contemporary monastic education is focused on the development of the subjectivity of monks and nuns. This scholarship is explicitly focused on the formation of individual lives in the context of monasteries, for example, in the pedagogical practices that inform the development of what is considered to be proper novices, whether through an emphasis on modeling and actions like sweeping and the practice of debate, meditation, or even participation in sports.[46] This scholarship is not unaware of the politics in which contemporary monasticism occurs, but as a whole it is focused on discrete monastic contexts.[47]

Finally, some of the most important scholarship on monastic education in recent decades does not specifically address the modern or contemporary as much as it looks at either continuities in monastic education or internal change. In particular, Dreyfus examines the curricula that have gone into the development of Tibetan monks.[48] Similarly, McDaniel shows how practices and curricula of monastic education persisted over centuries in Laos and Northern Thailand.[49] Moreover, Blackburn shows how change and development in monastic education in 18th-century Sri Lanka took place through internal shifts, not primarily through the effects of European colonization.[50]

NOTES

1. See Thomas Borchert, *Educating Monks: Minority Buddhism on China's Southwest Border* (Honolulu: University of Hawaii Press, 2017); and Anne Blackburn, *Buddhist Learning and Textual Practice in Eighteenth-Century Lankan Monastic Culture* (Princeton, NJ: Princeton University Press, 2001).
2. Jean Lave and Etienne Wenger, *Situated Learning. Legitimate Peripheral Participation* (Cambridge, UK: University of Cambridge Press, 1991).
3. Arvind-Pal Mandair and Markus Dressler, "Introduction: Modernity, Religion-Making, and the Postsecular," in *Secularism and Religion-Making,* ed. Markus Dressler and Arvind-Pal Mandair (New York: Oxford University Press 2011), 3–36; see also Jolyon Thomas, *Faking Liberties: Religious Freedom in American-Occupied Japan* (Chicago: University of Chicago Press, 2019).
4. Khammai Dhammasami, *Buddhism, Education and Politics in Burma and Thailand: From the Seventeenth Century to the Present* (London: Bloomsbury Press, 2017); and Alicia Turner, *Saving Buddhism: The Impermanence of Religion in Colonial Burma* (Honolulu: University of Hawaii Press, 2014), 72.
5. Douglas Gildow, "Buddhist Monastic Education: Seminaries, Academia, and the State in Contemporary China" (PhD diss., Princeton University, 2016), 10.
6. Dhitiwatana Palanee, "Buddhism and Thai Education," *South East Asian Review* 7, no. 1/2 (1982): 75–86.
7. Borchert, *Educating Monks*; Michael Ross Chaldek, "Making Monks, Making Men: The Role of Buddhist Monasticism in Shaping Northern Thai Identities" (PhD diss., University of Chicago, 2017).
8. Sarah LeVine and David Gellner, *Rebuilding Buddhism: The Theravada Movement in Twentieth-Century Nepal* (Cambridge, MA: Harvard University Press, 2005), 142–143.
9. Gildow, *Buddhist Monastic Education*; Darui Long, "Buddhist Education in Sichuan," *Educational Philosophy and Theory* 34, no. 2 (2002): 185–206.
10. See also Steven Collins and Justin McDaniel, "Buddhist 'Nuns' (*mae chi*) and the Teaching of Pali in Contemporary Thailand," *Modern Asian Studies* 44, no. 6 (2010): 1373–1408.
11. Mark Rowe and Kikuchi Hiroki., "The Current State of Sectarian Universities: A Roundtable Discussion," *Japanese Journal of Religious Studies* 31, no. 2 (2004): 429–464.
12. Stephen Covell, *Japanese Temple Buddhism: Worldliness in a Religion of Renunciation* (Honolulu: University of Hawaii Press, 2005); Jessica Starling, *Guardians of the Buddha's Home* (Honolulu: University of Hawaii Press, 2019).

13. Borchert, *Educating Monks.*
14. H. L. Seneviratne, *The Work of Kings: The New Buddhism in Sri Lanka* (Chicago: University of Chicago Press, 1999); and Dhammasami, *Buddhism, Education and Politics in Burma and Thailand.*
15. Steven Kemper, "Dharmapala's *Dharmaduta* and the Buddhist Ethnoscape," in *Buddhist Missionaries in the Era of Globalization,* ed. Linda Learman (Honolulu: University of Hawaii Press, 2005), 22–50.
16. Craig Reynolds, "The Buddhist Monkhood in Nineteenth Century Thailand" (PhD diss., Cornell University, 1972).
17. Holmes Welch, *The Buddhist Revival in China* (Cambridge, MA: Harvard University Press, 1968).
18. Lei Kuan Rongdao Lai, "Praying for the Republic: Buddhist Education, Student-Monks and Citizenship in Modern China (1991–1949)" (PhD diss., McGill University, 2013).
19. Sumi Loundon, Ilmee Hwansoo Kim, and Benny Liow, "Sunday School for Buddhists? Nurturing Spirituality in Children," in *Nurturing Child and Adolescent Spirituality: Perspectives From the World's Religious Traditions,* ed. Karen Marie Yust et al. (Lanham, MD: Rowman and Littlefield), 338–351; Monica Lindberg Falk, "Buddhism as a Vehicle for Girls' Safety and Education in Thailand," in *Little Buddhas: Children and Childhoods in Buddhist Texts and Traditions,* ed. Vanessa R. Sasson (Oxford: Oxford University Press, 2013), 266–289.
20. Thomas Borchert, "The Buddha's Precepts on Respecting Other Races and Religions? Thinking About the Relationship of Ethnicity and Theravada Buddhism," *Sojourn: Journal of Social Issues in Southeast Asia* 29, no. 3 (November 2014): 591–626, esp. 602–604; and Erik Braun, *The Birth of Insight: Meditation, Modern Buddhism and the Burmese Monk Ledi Sayadaw* (Chicago: University of Chicago Press, 2013).
21. Jeffrey Samuels, Jeffrey, *Attracting the Heart: Social Relations and the Aesthetics of Emotions in Sri Lankan Monastic Cultures* (Honolulu: University of Hawaii Press, 2010).
22. Srisawat Bunchuay, *Thai Sipsongpannā,* 3rd ed. (Bangkok: Rongphim Rapphim, 2004), 129–130.
23. Ratanaporn Sethakul, "Lanna Buddhism and Bangkok Centralization in Late Nineteenth to Early Twentieth Century," in *Theravada Buddhism in Colonial Contexts,* edited by Thomas Borchert (New York: Routledge, 2018), 81–100, esp. 85–86.
24. Borchert, *Educating Monks,* 110.
25. Shih Chih-Yu, *Negotiating Ethnicity in China: Citizenship as a Response to the State* (London: Routledge, 2002).
26. Starling, *Guardians of the Buddha's Home.*
27. LeVine and Gellner, *Rebuilding Buddhism,* 152–158; Susanne Mrozik, "'We Love our Nuns': Affective Dimensions of the Sri Lankan Bhikkhunī Revival," *Journal of Buddhist Ethics* 21 (2014): 57–95.
28. Elise Anne DeVido, 2010. *Taiwan's Buddhist Nuns* (Albany: State University of New York Press, 2010), 79; Paula Arai, *Women Living Zen: Japanese Sōtō Buddhist Nuns* (New York: Oxford University Press, 1999), 58, 109.
29. Collins and McDaniel, "Buddhist 'Nuns' (*mae chi*)."
30. Nirmala Salgado, *Buddhist Nuns and Gendered Practice: In Search of the Female Renunciant* (London: Oxford University Press, 2013).
31. See also Hiroko Kawanami, "The *Bhikkhunī* Ordination Debate: Global Aspirations, Local Concerns, With Special Emphasis on the Views of the Monastic Community in Burma," *Buddhist Studies Review* 24, no. 2 (2007): 226–244.
32. Charlene E. Makeley, *The Violence of Liberation: Gender and Tibetan Buddhist Revival in Post-Mao China* (Berkeley: University of California Press, 2007), 242; and Ward Keeler, *The Traffic in Hierarchy: Masculinity and Its Others in Buddhist Burma* (Honolulu: University of Hawaii Press, 2017), 229.
33. Roger Casas, "The Buddhist Basketball Association: Sport Practice and Cultivation of the Body Among Tai Lue Monastics," *Asia Pacific Journal of Sport and Social Science* 6, no. 1 (2017): 46–60.
34. Chladek, *Making Monks, Making Men.*

35. Gildow, "Buddhist Monastic Education."
36. Rowe and Kikuchi, "Current State of Sectarian Universities."
37. See, e.g., Gregory Schopen, *Buddhist Nuns, Monks, and Other Worldly Matters: Recent Papers on Monastic Buddhism in India* (Honolulu: University of Hawai'i Press, 2014); Petra Kieffer-Pülz, "Stretching the Vinaya Rules and Getting Away with it (11th I.B. Horner Lecture 2005)," *Journal of the Pali Text Society* XXIX (2007): 1–49; Shayne Clarke, *Family Matters in Indian Buddhist Monasticisms* (Honolulu: University of Hawai'i Press, 2013).
38. Welch, *The Buddhist Revival in China.*
39. Lai, *Praying for the Republic.*
40. Dhammasami, *Buddhism, Education and Politics in Burma and Thailand*; and Julianne Schober, "Colonial Knowledge and Buddhist Education in Burma," in *Buddhism, Power, and Political Order*, ed. Ian Harris (London: Routledge, 2007), 52–70.
41. Turner, *Saving Buddhism.*
42. Reynolds, *Buddhist Monkhood*; and Stanley Tambiah, *World Conqueror, World Renouncer: A Study of Buddhism and Polity in Thailand Against an Historical Background* (Cambridge, UK: Cambridge University Press, 1976).
43. Justin Thomas McDaniel, *Gathering Leaves and Lifting Words: Histories of Buddhist Monastic Education in Laos and Thailand.* (Seattle: University of Washington Press, 2008); and Phibul Choompolpaisal, "Political Buddhism and the Modernisation of Thai Monastic Education: From Wachirayan to Phimonlatham (1880s-1960s)," *Contemporary Buddhism* 16, no. 2 (2015): 428–450.
44. Dhammasami, *Buddhism, Education and Politics in Burma and Thailand.*
45. China: Long, "Buddhist Education in Sichuan"; Gildow, Buddhist Monastic Education; Borchert, *Educating Monks*; Tibet: Melvyn C. Goldstein, "The Revival of Monastic Life in Drepung Monastery," in *Buddhism in Contemporary Tibet*, ed. Melvyn C. Goldstein and Matthew T. Kapstein (Berkeley: University of California Press, 1998), 15–52; and Sri Lanka: Seneviratne, *The Work of Kings.*
46. Jeffrey Samuels, "Toward an Action-Oriented Pedagogy: Buddhist Texts and Monastic Education in Contemporary Sri Lanka," *Journal of the American Academy of Religion* 72, no. 4 (2004): 955–971; Michael Lempert, *Discipline and Debate: The Language of Violence in a Tibetan Buddhist Monastery* (Berkeley: University of California Press, 2012); Joanna Cook, *Meditation in Modern Buddhism: Renunciation and Change in Thai Monastic Life* (Cambridge, UK: Cambridge University Press, 2010); and Casas, "Buddhist Basketball Association."
47. Chladek, "Making Monks, Making Men."
48. Georges Dreyfus, *The Sound of Two Hands Clapping: The Education of a Tibetan Buddhist Monk* (Berkeley: University of California Press, 2003).
49. McDaniel, *Gathering Leaves and Lifting Words.*
50. Blackburn, *Buddhist Learning and Textual Practice.*

Thomas Borchert

MONGOLIAN BUDDHISM IN THE DEMOCRATIC PERIOD

MONGOLIAN BUDDHISM AND THE DEMOCRATIC REVOLUTION

Before the Mongolian Democratic Revolution of 1989–1990, the public practice of Buddhism was repressed by Mongolia's socialist government (1921–1990). From the 1940s onward there was only one functioning Buddhist temple, Gandantegchenliin Khiid, in the country.

This temple operated in Mongolia's capital city, Ulaanbaatar, performing a restricted number of activities under the watch of the Politburo. In 2010, two decades after the Mongolian Democratic Revolution, those that self-identified as Buddhist outnumbered those who professed to have no religion. Fifty-three percent of the population identified as Buddhist, while those who identified as having "no religion" accounted for 38.6 percent of the population.[1] In spite of over fifty years of active religious suppression, the government's anti-religious policies and propaganda failed to extinguish religion in Mongolia.

The presence of Buddhism in (Outer) Mongolia dates back to the 4th century CE.[2] The first major sustained interaction with Buddhism as a state religion was during the reign of Khubilai Khan (1260–1294).[3] The second was during Altan Khan's ascendancy in the 16th century. From the 16th century onward, Buddhism grew to be the main state religion in Mongolia. By the beginning of the 20th century, during Outer Mongolia's suzerainty to the Qing empire (1691–1911), Buddhist institutions held important positions of feudal power. The more established of these institutions, along with the region's aristocrats, had accumulated wealth, vast tracts of land, grazing animals, and the laborers to herd them.[4]

Following a brief period of independence headed by the Eighth Jebtsundamba (Bogd Khaan, 1869–1924) from 1911 and a series of quickly changing political affiliations and encroachments, a socialist government, backed by the Bolshevik Russians, came to power in 1921.[5] For the new socialist government, Buddhist institutions represented an alternative node of wealth, power, and influence. Toward the end of the 1930s, mirroring Stalin's purges in Russia, the tensions between the government and Buddhist institutions across the country escalated. In 1936 there were around 767 monasteries in Mongolia and around 75,000 to 100,000 lamas in the country.[6] By 1940 there were only 251 lamas left.[7] Of the population of lamas, it is estimated that around 14,000 were killed in the violence of the late 1930s.[8]

During the socialist period one temple, Gandantegchenliin Khiid, remained open. The temple's lamas, who were selected by the government, were allowed to perform truncated religious rituals and shorter versions of the extensive tantric practices that had once been carried out throughout Mongolia's religious establishments. The lamas were surveilled, and visits to the temple were restricted. Those who wanted to show their allegiance to the ruling party avoided going to the temple. Many Mongolians, afraid of the repercussions, refrained from demonstrating religious affiliations of any kind during the period. As a result of these restrictions, the temple's main visitors were the elderly, particularly old women.[9] Because of these limitations, most Mongolians who practiced religion in the socialist period did so in their homes, away from the scrutiny of the government. Inside their households, some laypeople carried out religious rituals in secret and kept sacred objects hidden.

In the mid-1980s, the Mongolian government brought in several reforms that mirrored the *glasnost* (openness, transparency) and *perestroika* (reform) restructurings that were happening in the Soviet Union. During the 1980s a group opposing the government, which was later to call itself the Mongolian Democratic Union, began to meet in secret. On International Human Rights Day, December 10, 1989, 200 people stood outside the Youth Cultural Center in Ulaanbaatar, Mongolia's capital. The protestors issued demands for the freedom of the press, greater levels of democracy, and improved human rights. Along with these demands they asked that the government acknowledge the past abuses of the socialist period, including the violence that occurred in the 1930s against Buddhism.[10] Although the government did react to the protestors' demands, their response was not accepted by the protesters and the Mongolian Democratic Union. A week later another protest was held, attracting 2,000 people.[11] The pro-democracy protests grew larger, and by January 21, in the middle of the Mongolian winter, the crowds had moved to the central square in Ulaanbaatar to the south of the parliament building, Sukhbaatar Square. There the crowd increased to an estimated 20,000 people.[12]

On March 7, 1990, ten men began a hunger strike in the central square. Hundreds of workers in Ulaanbaatar went on strike in solidarity with the hunger strikers. Protests were held in the smaller regional cities of Erdenet, Mörön, and Darkhan in solidarity with the movement. The following day, March 8, was International Women's Day, a public holiday in many socialist nations, including Mongolia. The protests swelled in size at Sukhbaatar Square, attracting crowds estimated to reach as many as 90,000 people. On March 9, fearing that the protests might turn violent in spite of the efforts of protestors committed to nonviolence, the Politburo announced that it would resign and the hunger strike ended.[13]

During the protests, cultural symbols that were repressed during the socialist era were mobilized by the protestors in order to reimagine the Mongolian nation. The protestors, rather than inventing new nationalist symbols, drew new nationalist symbols from what Caroline Humphrey calls the "deep past," an unclear historical period from which "images can be picked almost at random."[14] Along with the nationalistic image of Chinggis Khan (Genghis Khan), Buddhist symbols were used to construct alternative images of the Mongolian nation. These directly challenged the ideologies of the socialist period: first, Chinggis Khan, who had conquered the region that now encompasses Soviet Russia, and second, Buddhism, which the socialist government had sought to destroy.[15] Following the announcement that the government would resign on March 9, 1990, the pro-democracy protests continued to ensure that the government followed through with its promises. Before the first free elections in July 1990, two religious rallies were held at Ulaanbaatar's Choijin Lama Temple Museum (the former temple of the state oracle) on March 11 and April 2, 1990.[16] These protests linked the new democratic era with the freedom to practice religion, the acknowledgment of past wrongdoings, and a new nation that forged strong links to its presocialist past.

Following the Democratic Revolution of 1989–1990, Mongolians were guaranteed the freedom to publicly practice religion without persecution. Amendments were written into the new constitution to guarantee free religious practice in the country. Although successive governments have preferentially treated what most Mongolians see as the "traditional" religions of Mongolia, Buddhism and shamanism, neither is officially the state religion.[17]

The constitution does not enshrine special privileges for Buddhism or shamanism within the nation's legal system. Although neither religion is legally afforded extra entitlements, ritualized state ceremonies, including Buddhist lamas and occasionally shamans, are performed by members of the government.[18] In these ceremonies, the state utilizes Buddhism, and sometimes shamanism, to reinforce its position. In doing so, it strengthens Mongolian associations with these religions as the "traditional" religions of the Mongolian nation. Although the government assures the freedom to practice religion, all registered religious organizations are required to pay tax. Religious institutions must pay a monthly registration fee to be allowed to sponsor the visas of foreign religious specialists. Unusually, in 2016, a new temple building funded by the government was completed at the country's largest monastery compound, Gandantegchenliin Khiid.

THE REINVIGORATION OF LOCAL TEMPLES

Following the Democratic Revolution, the country saw the rapid growth of religious activities of all kinds in the early 1990s. Old men who had been lamas before the socialist period once against wore monastic robes and began to practice religion in public. As old lamas became visible in public life, many took on new students who sought a religious vocation. Others actively searched for new students, seeking out those who were good at school or those who, according to astrological predictions, might be good candidates for a religious and scholarly vocation.[19] Some old lamas and their new students were able to reinhabit old temples that had not been destroyed during the socialist purges. Others formed new collectives and established new temples within provincial centers.[20]

In the early 1990s, old lamas became the heads of the new or reinvigorated temples. They passed on their knowledge of the ritual practices to their younger students. Some transmitted rituals that they had carried out in secret during the socialist period. Others, who had not been able to maintain religious practices, taught novices what they remembered from their youth as young lamas. Old lamas tended to pass on rituals that had been easier to maintain during socialism, such as daily chanting and monthly pūjās for wrathful deities.[21] During the socialist purges of the late 1930s, high lamas were specifically targeted by the socialist government. Most either fled the country during the period or were executed. As a result, the extensive tantric rituals that these high lamas were responsible for transmitting were lost. By 1990, more than fifty years had passed wherein religion was actively suppressed. Complex tantric ritual activities involving multiple lamas, such as the Tsam (Tib. *'cham)* masked dance, were much more difficult to maintain and, as a result, were more difficult to revive. At the time of Zsuzsa Majer and Krisztina Teleki's survey in 2007, the Tsam dance had only been revived in three temples, Amarbayasgalant Khiid in Selengee Province, Züün Khüree Dashchoilin Khiid (Dashchoilin Khiid) in Ulaanbaatar, and Dashchoinkhorlin Khiid in Bulgan Province.[22] The Tsam dance is also performed annually by lamas from Gandantegchenliin Khiid in Ulaanbaatar.

In the 1990s, the efforts of old lamas to revive standing temples and build new ones were supported by the Mongolian laity. Many gave generous donations to temples when they had the means in the difficult transition period of the 1990s. Herding and urban families supported the efforts of the newly founded temples by donating food and supplies. As Mongolia is sparsely populated outside of the capital city and regional centers, it was easier for the new temples built in provincial centers and those located in the growing capital to survive after the initial period of rebuilding. Temples needed to be located near populations that could provide support for the continuation and maintenance of the temples and their sangha (*khuvrag*, the Buddhist clergy). Majer and Teleki found that, of those temples opened after the beginning of the Democratic Period, only half had survived until 2007. This was partly due to the age of the old lamas, many of whom died before they were able to establish permanent temples, and partly due to the difficulties of recruiting and maintaining younger students.[23]

In Majer and Teleki's comprehensive study, they estimated that there were 200 temples in Mongolia and that, of these, 36 were in Ulaanbaatar.[24] In addition to this figure of active local temples, there are a number of Dharma centers in the capital city. Dharma centers are Buddhist centers that focus on educating lay people. They often have a couple of resident lamas or nuns that help to run the center and teach classes. Their primary focus is to educate lay people rather than to carry out regular ritual activities. In Mongolia these centers are frequently funded by international Buddhist organizations connected to Tibetans in diaspora.

There are a number of different kinds of temples in Mongolia. Larger temples tend to be housed within enclosed compounds composed of free-standing temple buildings. Other smaller temples are often housed in a single building. Still others are housed within a *ger* (a Mongolian nomadic felt tent, also known in English as a yurt). Though ranging in size, most Mongolian temples have some common characteristics. Most temples have doors that open to the south of the temple, following the architectural design of Mongolian *gers*, which are always positioned this way. Following from the internal structure of Mongolian *gers*, they tend to have the most important shrine placed along the northern wall. Some temples have shrines covering their walls to the south, east, and/or west of the temple. Many have a high seat placed toward the north of the temple that is reserved, or inhabited by, high lamas (*Khutagt*). If a high-ranking lama is not present these seats will often be left symbolically vacant with a picture of a high lama, such as the Fourteenth Dalai Lama (Tenzin Gyatso, b. 1935) and the Ninth Jebtsundamba ('Jam dpal rnam grol chos kyi rgyal mtshan, 1933–2012), being placed upon them, marking the respect and reverence for these important teachers. Inside most temples there is a central ritual space used for carrying out the daily chanting sessions or meetings (*khural*). Most Buddhist temples contain low wooden benches facing inward toward one another, east to west. These benches are complemented by low tables on which the resident lamas or female religious specialists will place their *sūtras* (*sudar*). When lay people enter the temple from the south, they walk first to the western side of the wall and circumambulate the inside of the temple, if they choose to do so, in a clockwise direction. The majority of Mongolian temples use Tibetan as a liturgical language. This ritual language is spoken by very few Mongolians. In 2007, Teleki and Majer recorded one temple in Ulaanbaatar that read Mongolian translations of the *sūtras*.[25]

Of the institutions counted in Ulaanbaatar in 2007, Majer and Teleki recorded twenty-five temples within the Gelug lineage, eleven in the Nyingma lineage and one within the Kagyu lineage—which was running out of an office.[26] Since that time, one Sakya temple has been constructed to the east of the city center and others have opened and closed. In the post-democratic period it is common for temples to change locations or close and new ones to open. Most temples self-identify with the Gelug tradition. This was the dominant form of Buddhism in Mongolia during the Qing empire. Other lineages of Buddhism were practiced in Mongolia during the presocialist period, including the Nyingma-pa. In Ulaanbaatar, the two largest temples, Gandantegchenliin Khiid and Dashchoilin Khiid, are primarily Gelug-pa temples.

In Mongolia the categories of the Gelug-pa, Nyingma-pa, and other lineages are not clearly delineated. Often the dominant Gelug-pa is demarcated by using the term "yellow hat" (*shar malgaitan*) or "yellow religion" (*sharîn shashin*). The terms "red hat" (*ulaan malgaitan*) or "red religion" (*ulaanî shashin*) are frequently used to refer to all other Buddhist religious lineages, including the Nyingma lineage. Temples do not always exclusively practice within specific religious traditions. These classifications are unclear among laypeople and religious specialists.[27] The term for "religion" (*shashin*) in general up until recently meant Buddhism, rather than the broader concept of religion.[28] This may account partially for why the number of people identifying as "shamanist" was fairly low in the 2010 census, accounting for 2.9 percent of the population. Those practicing shamanism or Buddhism irregularly may identify as being "without religion" (*shashingui*). Buddhism can also be referred to as the "yellow religion" (*sharîn shashin*) in general, the buddha's religion (*buddîn shashin, burkhanî shashin*), or the lamas' religion (*lamîn shashin*).

Most Mongolians, whether they identify as Buddhist or not, attend Buddhist temples once a year, and most do so after the start of the Lunar New Year (*Tsagaan Sar*). When they visit temples, most people participate in the some or all of the following activities: spinning prayer wheels, circumambulating the inside and outsides of temples, touching sacred objects, making offerings at temple shrines, visiting a religious specialist to receive advice, ordering prayers, feeding the birds, performing prostrations, sitting to watch or participating in a religious service, and praying.[29] Most temples, especially the larger temples in the capital city, Betüv Khiid, Dashchoilin Khiid, and Gandantegchenliin Khiid, have places where lay people can go to pay to have prayers read in the following morning's liturgy. This is an important part of many people's visits to temples and, for some, is a source of temple critiques.[30] Some temples have set price lists for prayers, whereas at others people pay by donation. These shops are serviced either by lay people or by lamas. There are no restrictions on lamas touching money in Mongolia as there are in some other Buddhist traditions.[31]

In addition to temple rebuilding, the building of new statues has had considerable importance in the reimagining of Mongolian Buddhism in the present. Large Buddhist statues, which were important parts of the ritual landscape in the presocialist period, were destroyed during the socialist purges. One of the first major statue-building projects in the democratic era was to rebuild the large standing Avalokiteśvara (*Janraisig*) statue that was previously housed at Gandantegchenliin Khiid. The original statue was constructed between 1911 and 1913 in the newly independent Mongolian nation under the auspices of the Eighth Jebtsundamba.[32] As well as signifying the image of compassion and wisdom, the rebuilding of the standing Avalokiteśvara referenced Mongolia's previous period of independence. The country underwent significant financial hardships during the 1990s, having dismantled much of its former economy and transitioning into an new economic system. In spite of these economic difficulties, the statue of Avalokiteśvara was successfully rebuilt at the northern end of Gandantegchenliin's temple complex. Most visitors to the temple complex visit the statue to pray and spin the prayer wheels that encircle the temple's inner walls.

More recently, the building of two large statues of Maitreya (*Maidar*) have begun. Both are enlarged replicas of the artworks of Zanabazar, who, along with being the first of the Jebtsundamba lineage, is one of Mongolia's best known sculptors and artists.[33] The seated Maitreya statue, referencing the presocialist statue that was destroyed at Dashchoilin Khiid, has recently been completed. At the time of this writing the standing "Big Maitreya" project (*Ikh Maidar*) was well underway with plans to build a colossal 54-meter standing image of Maitreya to the south of Ulaanbaatar. Along with underlining the future potentials of Buddhism in the northern nation, the image of Maitreya has been linked historically to strengthening both Buddhist and state power in the region.[34]

WOMEN IN MONGOLIAN BUDDHISM

While the majority of Buddhist religious specialists in the democratic period are men, women are the main attendees of Buddhist temples and dharma centers, and they are key to religious life in Mongolia. Many Mongolians are told when to pray, when to visit temples, and on which days to avoid eating meat by their mothers and other female family members and friends. Women, as well as former male lamas, played an important role in maintaining ritual traditions within the home during the socialist period. At some dharma centers lay women lead chanting services and others teach meditation and Buddhist philosophy. Many work as translators and hold administrative positions at Buddhist temples.

In the contemporary period there are some well-known and well-respected female Buddhist religious specialists and teachers in Mongolia. Some female Buddhist religious specialists are celibate, while others, like their male counterparts, are not. Some keep their hair long, while others shave their heads and wear monastic robes. Some are clearly defined as Buddhist, while others incorporate a variety of different religious elements in their ritual practice.[35]

In 2007, Teleki and Majer recorded four female temples in Ulaanbaatar. Of these, one is a Gelug-pa nunnery that houses resident celibate nuns called the Dara Ekh Khiid or the Dolma Ling Nunnery.[36] This nunnery is funded by the Foundation for the Preservation of the Mahayana Tradition (FPMT), an international Buddhist organization. Teleki and Majer recorded two additional female Gelug-pa centers and one within the Nyingma tradition.[37] Although female Buddhists are not as visible as male lamas in Mongolia, women have been highly influential in the founding of many temples. At least ten temples have been founded, or co-founded, by women in Mongolia. Only three of these are exclusively female temples.[38] The wives of head lamas are often instrumental in organizing temple finances. However, due to the controversies surrounding the practice of non-celibate lamas, these temple wives tend not to occupy an official public role.

VOWS AND THE MONGOLIAN SANGHA

Within most Buddhist schools there are a number of different types of religious vows that monastics can take. In Mongolia, the first, which are generally taken by young novices when they enter a monastery and can also be taken by lay people, are the five *genen* or *genenmaa* vows. These make injunctions against theft, intoxicants, harmful speech, killing, and sexual misconduct. After this initial step, monastics can take a further ten precepts and become a *getsel* (for men) or a *getselmaa* (for women). In order to become fully ordained as a *gelen* (for men) or *gelenmaa* (for women), novices must take 253 precepts and 364 precepts, respectively. As Majer and Teleki note, most Mongolian male and female lamas do not observe the complete set of precepts. In their survey they found that only the *gelen* lamas observed celibacy while the *getsel* lamas tended not to, although one of the additional ten vows does prescribe it. Their survey found that around 70 to 80 percent of lamas do not follow the *getsel* vows.[39]

There is a wide range of interpretations in Mongolia about which monastic vows are necessary for lamas to wear robes and occupy positions within Mongolian Buddhist institutions. This is partly due to the high esteem of the old lamas who began to wear robes following the socialist period. As these lamas already had wives and children, most Mongolians do not see celibacy as a necessary part of being a Buddhist religious specialist. For some people, non-celibate lamas are a part of the Mongolian tradition. Others see this trend as a part of the transition period, necessary while Mongolian Buddhism reestablishes itself after socialism.[40] Before the socialist period Mongolian Buddhist institutions were relatively flexible with those who were not maintaining celibacy as part of their religious vocation. Lamas who were caught by monastic institutions, rather than being forced to disrobe, were rehabilitated through the performance of *pūjās* or the payment of a fine.[41]

The majority of lamas in Mongolia in the contemporary era are connected with the largest temples in Ulaanbaatar. This has meant that there are limited possibilities for building temple residencies where the bulk of Buddhist religious specialists live. Due to the growing size of the capital and a lack of temple resources, very few temples have residential spaces. At the time of the Democratic Revolution Ulaanbaatar's population was a little less than 600,000 people. By 2015 the city was home to over 1.3 million people. As a result of this expanding population, which has seen new apartments being built in all of the city's available spaces and the expansion of *ger* neighborhoods to the north, east, and west, many of Ulaanbaatar's existing temples have little room to expand.[42]

There are some notable exceptions to the trend of nonresidential temples. These exceptions include Betüv Khiid, which was built by Bakula Rinpoche to the southeast of Gandantegchenliin Khiid, Idgaachoinzinlin Datsan within the Gandantegchenliin Khiid (which is funded by the FPMT), the new Sakya-pa temple, the Sakya Pandita Dharma Chakra Center, and the FPMT's Dara Ekh Khiid nunnery. These temples all have the stated focus to improve monastic training and discipline. Aside from the Dara Ekh Khiid, these residences mainly house novices. They have all been influenced by transnational Buddhist networks.

Other than those religious specialists who are able to inhabit the few limited residential quarters for training lamas, the majority of Buddhist religious specialists in the capital don't live within temple complexes. Most male and female lamas live in apartments or *gers* within the city. This means that they have the same economic obligations of ordinary lay people. They pay for rent and bills, look after other family members, and buy their own food.

The lack of local lamas maintaining extensive monastic vows has been a source of criticism both from within Mongolia and from global Buddhist figures and organizations.[43] From the perspective of many global Buddhist networks and institutions, Mongolian lamas that do not follow extensive vows have lost the discipline of their lineages during the long period of socialist persecution. Many global Buddhist institutions have encouraged those Mongolian male or female lamas who have not taken vows to disrobe if they are not able to follow strict monastic rules. The Fourteenth Dalai Lama has instructed Mongolian lamas who are not following extensive monastic vows to disrobe. While many Mongolians believe married lamas to be a local variant of Buddhism and an acceptable practice, some are critical of married lamas.[44] These controversies are influenced by lamas who spend time training in monasteries in India and return to Mongolia with different expectations about monastic discipline.[45] As a result of this controversy, married lamas tend to be fairly discrete about their marital status. Their wives, even if they do perform important roles within the running of the temples, tend not to be as visible as they are in Japan.[46]

THE INFLUENCE OF TRANSNATIONAL BUDDHISM

As the government officially brought in new policies ensuring religious freedoms in the early 1990s, religious groups of all kinds entered the country. Along with Christian missionary groups, mainly from Korea and North America, transnational Buddhist organizations arrived in Mongolia hoping to help to revive Buddhism in the newly democratic nation. These organizations have helped to fund local Buddhist temples, set up independent centers, and sponsored Mongolians to study overseas. They have influenced what people expect from Buddhist temples and religion more generally. While local temples claim legitimacy from the sustained contact with old Mongolian lamas from the presocialist past, these international organizations tend to claim their lineages from unbroken textual and ritual lineages.[47]

Most of the international organizations that have influenced the resurgence of Buddhism following the socialist period are connected to Tibetans in diaspora. Tibetan Buddhism has undergone considerable changes during the 20th century. Following the Dalai Lama's expulsion from Tibet in the late 1950s, the high lamas that resettled in Europe, North America, Australasia, and India were exposed to new styles of religious instruction and new demands from Western students. Following broader patterns of "reform" within the Buddhist world, international Vajrayāna Buddhist organizations have transformed, focusing more on lay education and meditation rather than on providing ritual efficacy for lay devotees.

Following broader patterns, many transnational organizations, upon arriving in Mongolia, have carried with them an alternative perspective about "reviving" Buddhism. Their focus on lay education, meditation, and monastic discipline has sometimes clashed with local ideas about Mongolian Buddhist practice. Some of these organizations centralize monastic discipline, while others, entering the country in a time of dramatic economic upheaval, have created charitable projects. These charities tend to be eclipsed by the better funded and prolific charitable activities of Christian organizations that have arrived in Mongolia since 1990.

A number of key international figures have had a major impact on the revitalization of Buddhism in the democratic period. One of these was the Nineteenth Kushok Bakula Rinpoche (1918–2003). Born in Ladakh, he was India's ambassador to Mongolia starting in 1990. As a charismatic high lama from India, he was believed by many Mongolians to be enlightened. He built the centrally located monastic residential temple, Betüv Khiid, which focuses on providing monastic discipline and education for novices from the age of fourteen. Finished in 1999, the temple provides monthly pūjās and carries out daily prayer readings for laypeople. It sometimes provides educational activities for interested lay people.

Another important figure in the democratic period is Lama Zopa Rinpoche (b. 1945). Lama Zopa Rinpoche's global Foundation for the Preservation of the Mahayana Tradition (FPMT) has several projects in Ulaanbaatar and one dharma center in the nearby city of Darkhan. As well as the establishment of Mongolia's only celibate residential nunnery, the Dara Ekh Khiid, the FPMT built and provides funding for the educationally oriented Idgaachoinzinlin Datsan within Gandantegchenliin Khiid, which was completed in 1999. The centrally located Shredrup Ling, finished in 2000, provides regular education on Buddhist philosophy and meditation classes to lay people. The FPMT sometimes sources funding for interested students to travel overseas to study in Indian monastic institutions. The Dara Ekh Khiid provides charitable services for the local nearby community, including a hot meal program and a small health clinic.

Another Dharma center, Jampa Ling, built to the west of the Ulaanbaatar in the Third and Fourth districts, was built by an international Gelug-pa Buddhist organization. This center is headed by Panchen Ötrul Rinpoche, who visits Mongolia annually during the summer months. Jampa Ling provides weekly classes to laypeople and performs regular *pūjās*. Along with these events they have a charity, which up until recently included running a small felt factory that employed unskilled single mothers. The center is involved in translating religious texts into Mongolian and has a small printing press in the basement. Dharma centers like

Jampa Ling and Shredrup Ling provide translations to Mongolian laypeople during rituals. Laypeople participate in and sometimes lead Buddhist ritual services.

Many local temples host visiting internationally based high lamas. These figures are often Tibetans living in diaspora. Some of these high lamas visit regularly or semi-regularly, whereas others visit once or twice. High lamas may provide important tantric transmissions to Mongolian lamas and local devotees. Some provide teachings that are translated for the local community, and others fund the rebuilding of old temples. Still others fund charitable works, such as the new treatment center for children with cancer in Ulaanbaatar that was funded by the Eighth Arjia Rinpoche.

While most of the interactions with translocal Buddhist institutions tend to be with Vajrayana Buddhist organizations, there have been some interactions with Theravada monks who have visited Mongolia. There are also increasing funding opportunities coming from China for the building of temples, statues, and *stūpas*. Donations from Korea, Hong Kong, and Taiwan are becoming an important part of translocal funding networks.

From the perspective of many transnational Buddhist institutions, a lack of monastic celibacy places a limitation on the development of Buddhism in Mongolia. In an attempt to re-educate local Buddhist monastics, some of these organizations have funded young male and female novices to study overseas, though many interested students and their families pay for their own studies. Interested Mongolian students tend to study in the south of India and stay in the large Gelug-pa monasteries founded by Tibetans living in diaspora with international funding. Others train in monasteries in northern India, such as in the town of Sarnath near Varanasi. Still others study in monasteries of different lineages. In India, young monastics receive a residential monastic education and live within the regulated rules of monastic institutions.

Those who study overseas have a significant impact on Buddhist institutions when they return to Mongolia, though it should be noted that many struggle to find a place in Mongolian temples when they arrive back home. Many returning lamas have difficulties fitting into life outside of the supporting monasteries and feel the pressure from family members who see no contradiction in being a male or female lama, marrying, and starting a family. In addition to these translocal connections, some Mongolians travel to India, Nepal, and other Buddhist countries on pilgrimage. In 2017, the Dalai Lama inaugurated a new Mongolian temple in Bodh Gaya, the place where the buddha became enlightened under the Bodhi tree, in northern India.

Transnational Buddhist organizations and translocal religious connections have influenced how Mongolians see Buddhist institutions. Their emphasis on lay education and meditation has influenced local ideas about what Buddhism is and how much a person should know about religion in order to say that one is Buddhist.[48] Additionally, ideas about monastic discipline, coupled with the transfer of skills and knowledge from Tibetans in diaspora, have influenced how the local sangha interprets its own traditions, in continuity with and/or in opposition to transnational Buddhist organizations.

GEOPOLITICAL ASPECTS

Mongolian Buddhist institutions were a source of considerable power and influence during the Qing empire. The connections between Tibet and Mongolia were strong during this period. Important reincarnated lamas who lived in Mongolia were frequently born in Tibet, and many Mongolian lamas were educated within Tibetan regions. In the Democratic Period, Buddhist translocal connections once again have broad geopolitical ramifications, particularly as Mongolian Buddhist organizations reestablish ties with Tibetans in diaspora. Visits from the Fourteenth Dalai Lama to Mongolia have been a source of tension between Mongolia and its southern neighbor, China. The rebirth of one of Mongolia's most important religious reincarnation lineages, the Jebtsundamba, is being closely watched by politicians within Mongolia and China.

Mongolian Buddhist institutions, like other Buddhist institutions in the Vajrayana traditions, have tended not to be headed by a single figure. However, in the democratic period, there are three key figures, or reincarnation lineages, who have considerable authority in the present. This authority can be traced back to previous eras. These are the Abbott of Gandantegchenliin Khiid, the Khamba Lama Choijamts, the Fourteenth Dalai Lama, and the Jebtsundamba lineage.[49]

In the initial period of rebuilding after the Democratic Revolution, a meeting of Mongolian Buddhists was called and convened in 1991. As Gandantegchenliin Khiid had been the sole surviving temple during the socialist period, it was agreed upon by those present that that the abbott of the temple should be the new figure head for Mongolian Buddhism. Within two weeks of this decision, the Fourteenth Dalai Lama announced that the ninth incarnation of the lineage of the Jebtsundamba was alive and had been living in India since the middle of the 20th century.[50]

The Jebtsundamba lineage, as Agata Bareja-Starsyńska has described, is an important reincarnation lineage within Mongolian history and its importance continues into the Democratic Period.[51] The Eighth Jebtsundamba was notable as he headed Mongolia's brief period of independence from 1911 to 1921. Following the Eighth Jebtsundamba's death in 1924, the socialist government outlawed the finding of any new reincarnations in the lineage. A young boy was identified as the reincarnation of the Eighth Jebtsundamba in 1936. Although the boy was not living in Mongolia, his identity was kept secret due to concerns about his safety. In the 1950s, he had disrobed from monastic life. However, concerns about his safety caused him to flee from Tibet to India. By the time that his identity was announced in 1991, the Ninth Jebtsundamba was a householder with several children living in India.

Concerns about the potential power that the Ninth Jebtsundamba could hold, both as a former head of independent Mongolia (albeit in a previous life) and as an alternative node of power in the re-establishing Mongolian sangha, caused significant delays in the issuance of his first visa. In 1999 he was issued a visa to visit Mongolia. A couple of days after his arrival, the Chinese president, Jiang Zemin, visited Mongolia. The Chinese Communist Party viewed the Ninth Jebtsundamba and his affiliation with the Dalai Lama as being a negative force in the region.[52] After this first visit, with pressure from international and local political forces, the Ninth Jebtsundamba was not granted a visa for another ten years. The next time he visited the mood had changed. Within a year of his arrival, in 2010, he was granted Mongolian citizenship. In 2011, he was ritually enthroned as the head of Mongolian Buddhism. The ceremony was attended by the Khamba Lama Choijamts of Gandantegchenliin Khiid. In 2012, within a year of this event, the Ninth Jebtsundamba passed away.

The Fourteenth Dalai Lama's influence on the finding of the reincarnation of the Tenth Jebtsundamba has caused diplomatic friction between Mongolia and China. The Dalai Lama's visits to Mongolia have been a source of irritation for the Chinese government. Trade and diplomatic ties have frequently been severed during the Dalai Lama's visits, including the closure of road and rail transportation across the Mongolian-Chinese border. Adding to these geopolitical tensions, before passing away, the Ninth Jebtsundamba announced that he was going to be reborn in Mongolia and that it would be the Fourteenth Dalai Lama who was responsible for recognizing his rebirth.[53] During his visit to Mongolia in 2016, the Dalai Lama announced that the reincarnation had been found and, though the name of the child was not then made public, it was announced that the child had been born in Mongolia.

Although the Dalai Lama no longer heads the Tibetan government in exile, he is seen as having a negative influence on Chinese politics by the Chinese Communist Party. As the Fourteenth Dalai Lama grows older, religious figures who might be involved in the future recognition of the next incarnation in the lineage have become of increasing geopolitical importance. The Tenth Jebtsundamba, as a high ranking Gelug-pa lama born outside of China, may, if old enough, have an influence over the finding of the next Dalai Lama. Due to the present-day ties between Mongolians and Tibetans in diaspora, the potential power that the Tenth Jebtsundamba could occupy in the region is of interest to Mongolia's neighbors. Who the young incarnation is, and how they are trained, will likely be of local and geopolitical importance.

DISTINGUISHING BUDDHIST PRACTICES

Although the majority of the population of Mongolia self-identified as Buddhist in the 2010 census, it can be difficult to determine which ideas and practices are Buddhist. Not all of the public practices that were outlawed during the socialist period were Buddhist. Many of the religious practices carried out in people's homes contained a mixture of Buddhist and non-Buddhist elements. Shamanic rituals were outlawed, as were other local rituals praying to mountain and river spirits and those that made oblations to the sky. Following from the presocialist period, the delineation between shamanic, Buddhist, and other religious practices in the Democratic Period is not always clear.

Since 1990, a range of new religious forms have thrived in the country. These have often been born from a mixture of local practices, such as the reemergence of Buddhist practice, shamanism, and Islam in the western Kazakh population, and influenced by translocal organizations and individuals, such as transnational Buddhist organizations, the arrival of Christian missionary groups, and a range of other new religious activities. Most Mongolians visit a number of religious specialists when undergoing a difficult period in their lives or before making an important decision. As Mongolians tend toward religious pluralism, rather than religious exclusivity, most Mongolians do not see a problem with seeking out a number of religious specialists in times of need.[54]

Early anthropological studies of Buddhism tended to emphasize the difference between what a society following Buddhist scriptures "ought" to look like and how real Buddhist societies have deviated from these posited "norms."[55] Anthropologists, initially tending to do fieldwork in Southeast Asian Theravada countries, discovered that Buddhists often participate in practices, such as spirit and ancestor worship, that textual-based research into Buddhism would not predict. This contrast between scholarly ideas of what Buddhism "should" be and the realities of Buddhist societies has historically been thought to be particularly pronounced in societies, such as Tibet, where religious rituals seem to contain a syncretic mix of Buddhist and other religious practices.[56] In 1994, Stewart and Shaw argued that syncretism is such a universal part of religions that the term itself is rendered meaningless as an explanatory category.[57] Following this discussion, anthropological studies of Buddhist societies have been increasingly sensitive to the idea that looking at Buddhist societies in terms of how they deviate from "pure" Buddhism undermines anthropological understandings.

In Mongolia what is or is not Buddhist has been a matter of some debate. This is exacerbated by the sharing of sacred sites and a certain fuzziness in the identification and practices of religious specialists. At some ritual sites, such as sacred *ovoos* (rock cairns), it is common for state officials, Buddhist lamas, shamans, and other religious specialists to carry out libations to local deities, albeit at different times.[58] Not all ritual specialists distinguish themselves as exclusively Buddhist, shaman, or other. Some ritual specialists identify themselves as "yellow shamans" (*sharîn shashnî udgan*), that is, shamans who channel embedded local deities or guardian spirits and their followers from the Buddhist pantheon.[59]

After the end of the socialist period, as the "traditional" religions of shamanism and Buddhism began to revive, a range of new religions arrived in the capital including, but not limited to, Christianity and a variety of new religious movements. The lack of publicly sanctioned religious institutions during the socialist period and the new diversity of religious institutions in the capital have resulted in key Buddhist terms having divergent interpretations. Following the brutal religious repressions of the 1930s, many Buddhist terms were appropriated by the socialist government or simply fell out of usage. The socialist government appropriated key religious terms such as enlightenment (*gegeerel*), which was reworked to mean education.[60] The 1990s ushered in a period of religious tolerance that brought with it a new and diverse range of religious and quasi-religious groups. Some of these groups use Buddhist terms to explain non-Buddhist religious concepts. Christian groups up until recently generally used the term *burkhan* (buddha) to refer to a monotheistic God, and this has influenced how the term is understood.

REVIEW OF LITERATURE

Due to the relatively recent history of revitalized Buddhist practice in Mongolia, the literature on the subject is relatively new. The most comprehensive sociological survey of Mongolian Buddhist institutions to date is the *Documentation of Mongolian Monasteries* carried out by Kristina Teleki and Zsuzsa Majer. It is available online in both Mongolian and English.[61] Several other scholars have carried out preliminary surveys of Buddhist practice in the region, including Karénina Kollmar-Paulenz's "Buddhism in Mongolia After 1990," Agata Bareja-Starzyńska and Hanna Havnevik's "A Preliminary Study of Mongolian Buddhism in the Present Day," and Vesna Wallace's "Mediating the Power of Dharma: The Mongols' Approaches to Reviving Buddhism in Mongolia."[62]

Initial scholarly debates focusing on Mongolian Buddhism discussed two key themes. The first of these was whether or not Buddhism found in Mongolia should be called "Tibetan Buddhism," "Mongolian Buddhism," or some combination of the two. A good summary of these early debates can be found in the edited volume *The Mongolia-Tibet Interface*.[63] The second of these themes asked whether the differences between transnational Buddhist organizations and local Buddhist organizations were distinct enough that they could be considered to be, as Johan Elverskog suggested, "two Buddhisms."[64] Though these two categories can be useful for delineating different trends within religious practice, they are, at best, loose categories. Both local and translocal Buddhist organizations interact with overseas organizations and lineages and travel extensively overseas. Additionally, many local Buddhist temples provide educational classes for lay people.

Another topic arousing significant scholarly attention has been discussions of monastic vows in Mongolia. Majer and Teleki have provided an excellent sociological overview of the situation in their report on temples in Ulaanbaatar.[65] Lhavgademchig Jadamba and Bernard Schnittich's article "Negotiating Self and Other" explores how translocal and local tensions around this issue affect the rebuilding of Mongolian Buddhist identities, and my own article "Paying for Prayers" focuses on how these debates affect and are affected by donations to temples.[66] Vesna Wallace's recent article on monastic vows anchors this current debate in relation to presocialist regulations about celibacy in the region.[67]

Vesna Wallace's edited volume *Buddhism in Mongolian History, Culture, and Society* combines historical, sociological, literary, and ethnographic insights in the most comprehensive edited volume on Mongolian Buddhism to date.[68] The book includes research about Mongolian Buddhism in the democratic period looking at contemporary artworks, state rituals, and the particularities of Mongolian Buddhist practice. My own forthcoming *Enlightenment and the Gasping City* is the first full-length ethnographic book to explore Buddhism in Ulaanbaatar in detail. It discusses Buddhist ideas and practices in light of chronic air pollution and postsocialist religious uncertainties in Ulaanbaatar. Mette High's work on the relationship between Mongolian lamas and mining provides an insight into some of the practices and economic uncertainties that are affecting rural lamas.[69] Lhavgademchig Jadamba's doctoral dissertation, "Double Headed Mongolian Buddhism," provides an excellent detailed exploration of the geopolitical tensions surrounding the Jebtsundamba lineage, local politics, and international relations to date.[70]

DIGITAL MATERIALS

Lhagvademchig, Jadamba, *Double Headed Mongolian Buddhism* (http://thecessblog.com/2018/02/28/double-headed-mongolian-buddhism-by-lhagvademchig-j-shastri-visiting-researcher-university-of-shiga-prefecture)

Majer, Zsuzsa, and Krisztina Teleki, *Documentation of Mongolian Monasteries* (http://mongoliantemples.org/index.php/mn/2014-07-01-06-18-41/ub-%20temples/ubtemplesnew/10?view=newtemplemn)

FURTHER READING

Abrahms-Kavunenko, Saskia. "Religious 'Revival' After Socialism? Eclecticism and Globalisation Amongst Lay Buddhists in Ulaanbaatar." *Inner Asia* 14, no. 2 (2012): 279–297.

Abrahms-Kavunenko, Saskia. "Paying for Prayers: Perspectives on Giving in Postsocialist Ulaanbaatar." *Religion, State and Society* 43, no. 4 (2015): 327–341.

Abrahms-Kavunenko, Saskia. *Enlightenment and the Gasping City: Mongolian Buddhism at a Time of Environmental Disarray*. Ithaca, NY: Cornell University Press, 2019.

Even, Marie-Dominique. "Ritual Efficacy or Spiritual Quest? Buddhism and Modernity in Post-Communist Mongolia." In *Revisiting Rituals in a Changing Tibetan World*. Edited by Katia Buffetrille, 241–271. Leiden, The Netherlands: Brill, 2012.

Havnevik, Hanna, Byambaa Ragchaa, and Agata Bareja-Starzyńska. "Some Practices of the Buddhist Red Tradition in Contemporary Mongolia." In *The Mongolia–Tibet Interface: Opening New Research Terrains in Inner Asia*. Edited by Uradyn Bulag and Hildegard Diemberger, 223–237. Leiden, The Netherlands: Brill, 2007.

Havnevik, Hanna. "Female Temple Founders, Ritualists, and Clairvoyants in Post-Socialist Mongolian Buddhism." *Revue d'Etudes Tibétaines* 34 (2015): 35–52.

High, Mette. "Cosmologies of Freedom and Buddhist Self-Transformation in the Mongolian Gold Rush." *Journal of the Royal Anthropological Institute* 19, no. 4 (2013): 753–770.

High, Mette. "A Question of Ethics: The Creative Orthodoxy of Buddhist Monks in the Mongolian Gold Rush." *Ethnos* 83, no. 1 (2018): 80–99.

Jadamba, Lkhagvademchig, and Bernard Schittich. "Negotiating Self and Other: Transnational Cultural Flows and the Reinvention of Mongolian Buddhism." *Internationales Asienforum* 41, nos. 1–2 (2010): 83–102.

Majer, Zsuzsa. "Continuation or Disjuncture with the Past and the Tibetan Buddhist Tradition." *The Silk Road* 7 (Autumn 2009): 52–63.

Teleki, Krisztina. "Building on Ruins, Memories and Persistence: Revival and Survival of Buddhism in the Mongolian Countryside." *The Silk Road* 7 (Autumn 2009): 64–73.

Wallace, Vesna, ed. *Buddhism in Mongolia: History, Culture and Society*. Oxford: Oxford University Press, 2015.

Wallace, Vesna. "Competing Religious Conversions and Re-Conversions in Contemporary Mongolia." In *Conversion in Late Antiquity: Christianity, Islam, and Beyond*. Edited by Arietta Papaconstantinou, Neil McLynn, and Daniel Schwartz, 49–65. Farnham, U.K.: Ashgate, 2015.

NOTES

1. National Statistical Office of Mongolia 2010. *Mongolia Population Census 2010: Main Findings*.
2. Walther Heissig, *The Religions of Mongolia* (London: Routledge & Kegan Paul, 1980).
3. For more details, see Morris Rossabi, *Khubilai Khan: His Life and Times* (Berkeley: University of California Press, 1988).
4. Christopher Kaplonski, *The Lama Question: Violence, Sovereignty and Exception in Early Socialist Mongolia*. (Honolulu: University of Hawai'i Press, 2014).
5. See Agata Bareja-Starsyńska, Jebtsundamba Khutugtus of Mongolia. *Oxford Research Encyclopedia of Religion*, 2018; and Charles Bawden, *The Modern History of Mongolia* (London: Weidenfeld & Nicolson, 1968).
6. The term lama derives from the Mongolian term "lam," meaning robed Buddhist religious specialist. In the Mongolian context it is not specifically used to denote high lamas; Bawden, *Modern History of Mongolia*.
7. Bawden, *Modern History of Mongolia*.
8. These estimates vary as there was no clear count of the death toll during the period. Michael Jerryson in his book *Mongolian Buddhism: The Rise and Fall of the Sangha* (Chiang Mai, Thailand: Silkworm Books, 2007) references a plaque from the Memorial Museum for the Victims of the Political Repressions (Ulaanbaatar) that reads that around 13,680 lamas were shot during the period. Matthew King (2018)

writes in "Mongolian Buddhism in the Early 20th Century" in *Oxford Research Encyclopedia of Religion*, that conservative estimates put the number of people executed at around 30,000 people in an eighteen-month period between 1937 and 1938. This larger figure includes lamas, ethnic Buryats, aristocrats, and others believed to oppose the government.

9. Marie-Dominique Even, "Ritual Efficacy or Spiritual Quest? Buddhism and Modernity in Post-Communist Mongolia," in *Revisiting Rituals in a Changing Tibetan World*, ed. Katia Buffetrille (Leiden, The Netherlands: Brill, 2012), 252.
10. Morris Rossabi, *Modern Mongolia: From Khans to Commissars to Capitalists*. (Berkeley: University of California Press, 2005).
11. Christopher Kaplonski, *Truth, History and Politics in Mongolia: The Memories of Heroes* (London: RoutledgeCurzon, 2004), 61.
12. Kaplonski, *Truth, History and Politics in Mongolia*.
13. Rossabi, *Modern Mongolia*.
14. Caroline Humphrey, "The Moral Authority of the Past in Post-Socialist Mongolia," *Religion, State and Society* 20, no. 3 (1992): 376.
15. The symbol of Chinggis Khan in the democratic period is often linked to presocialist narratives that identified Chinggis Khan as a wheel-turning king, or Cakravartin, and an emanation of Vajrapāṇi. This Buddhicized version of Chinggis Khan often supports and links Mongolian Buddhist identities with broader nationalist narratives, thereby creating Mongolian Buddhist nationalist identities in the postsocialist period; see Vesna Wallace, "Envisioning a Mongolian Buddhist Identity Through Chinggis Khan," in *Buddhism in Mongolia: History, Culture and Society*, ed. Vesna Wallace (Oxford: Oxford University Press, 2015), 70–92; see also Caroline Humphrey, "Remembering an 'Enemy': The Bogd Khaan in Twentieth Century Mongolia," in *Memory History and Opposition Under State Socialism*, ed. Ruby Watson (Santa Fe, NM: School of American Research Press, 1994), 21–44.
16. Kaplonski, *Truth, History and Politics in Mongolia*.
17. Even, "Ritual Efficacy or Spiritual Quest?," 256.
18. Even, "Ritual Efficacy or Spiritual Quest?"; see also David Sneath, "Nationalising Civilisational Resources: Sacred Mountains and Cosmopolitical Ritual in Mongolia," *Asian Ethnicity* 15, no. 4 (2014): 458–472. For further details about the practice of shamanism in postsocialist period, see Manduahi Buyandelger, *Tragic Spirits: Shamanism, Memory, and Gender in Contemporary Mongolia* (Chicago: University of Chicago Press, 2013).
19. See Saskia Abrahms-Kavunenko, *Enlightenment and the Gasping City: Mongolian Buddhism at a Time of Environmental Disarray* (Ithaca, NY: Cornell University Press, 2019).
20. Krisztina Teleki, "Building on Ruins, Memories and Persistence: Revival and Survival of Buddhism in the Mongolian Countryside," *The Silk Road* 7 (Autumn 2009): 64–73.
21. Teleki, "Building on Ruins, Memories and Persistence," 69.
22. Teleki, "Building on Ruins, Memories and Persistence."
23. Krisztina Teleki, "Building on Ruins, Memories and Persistence," 70.
24. Zsuzsa Majer, "Continuation or Disjuncture with the Past and the Tibetan Buddhist Tradition," *The Silk Road* 7 (Autumn 2009): 52–63.
25. See Majer, "Continuation or Disjuncture with the Past." A popular *sūtra* translated into Mongolian is the Sūtra of Golden Light (Altan Gerel Sudar).
26. Majer, "Continuation or Disjuncture with the Past."
27. Hanna Havnevik, Byambaa Ragchaa, and Agata Bareja-Starzyńska, "Some Practices of the Buddhist Red Tradition in Contemporary Mongolia," in *The Mongolia–Tibet Interface: Opening New Research Terrains in Inner Asia*, ed. Uradyn Bulag and Hildegard Diemberger (Leiden, The Netherlands: Brill, 2007), 223–237.

28. Even, "Ritual Efficacy or Spiritual Quest?," 255.
29. Saskia Abrahms-Kavunenko, "Religious 'Revival' After Socialism? Eclecticism and Globalisation Amongst Lay Buddhists in Ulaanbaatar," *Inner Asia* 14, no. 2 (2012): 279–297.
30. Saskia Abrahms-Kavunenko, "Paying for Prayers: Perspectives on Giving in Postsocialist Ulaanbaatar," *Religion, State and Society* 43, no. 4 (2015): 327–341. Critiques of monastics include the perceived commodification of Buddhism, the motivations of lamas, the education of monastics, the cleanliness of temples, and whether or not lamas follow monastic vows.
31. Abrahms-Kavunenko, "Paying for Prayers."
32. Tsymzhit Vanchikova, "The Modern Religious Situation in Mongolia: Tradition and Innovation Processes," in *Religion and Ethnicity in Mongolian Societies: Historical and Contemporary Perspectives*, ed. Karénina Kollmar-Paulenz, Seline Reinhardt, and Tatiana Skrynnikova (Wiesbaden, Germany: Harrassowitz Verlag, 2014), 167–176.
33. See also Agata Bareja-Starzyńska, 2018.
34. Uranchimeg Tsultemin, "The Power and Authority of Maitreya in Mongolia Examined Through Mongolian Art," in *Buddhism in Mongolian History, Culture and Society*, ed. Vesna Wallace (Oxford: Oxford University Press, 2015).
35. Hanna Havnevik, "Female Temple Founders, Ritualists, and Clairvoyants in Post-Socialist Mongolian Buddhism," *Revue d'Etudes Tibétaines* 34 (2015): 35–52.
36. Majer, "Continuation or Disjuncture with the Past."
37. Majer, "Continuation or Disjuncture with the Past."
38. Havnevik, "Female Temple Founders."
39. Zsuzsa Majer and Krisztina Teleki, "Survey of Active Temples in Ulaanbaatar in 2005–2006, with Some Annotations in 2007."
40. Lkhagvademchig Jadamba and Bernard Schittich, "Negotiating Self and Other: Transnational Cultural Flows and the Reinvention of Mongolian Buddhism," *Internationales Asienforum* 41, nos. 1–2 (2010): 83–102.
41. Vesna Wallace, "The Interface of Mongolian Nomadic Culture, Law and Monastic Sexual Morality," *Buddhism, Law, and Society* 2 (2018): 57–75.
42. These neighborhoods are made up of one or more *gers* enclosed in wooden fenced areas with an outside toilet and often a concrete building.
43. See Abrahms-Kavunenko, "Paying for Prayers," for a more detailed exploration of this tension.
44. Abrahms-Kavunenko, "Paying for Prayers."
45. See Abrahms-Kavunenko, *Enlightenment and the Gasping City*.
46. See Steven Covell, *Japanese Temple Buddhism: Worldliness in a Religion of Renunciation* (Honolulu: University of Hawai'i Press, 2008).
47. See Covell, *Japanese Temple Buddhism*.
48. See Saskia Abrahms-Kavunenko, "The Blossoming of Ignorance: Uncertainty, Power and Syncretism amongst Mongolian Buddhists," *Ethnos* 80, no. 3 (2015): 346–363, for a look at changing expectations of religious knowledge in Ulaanbaatar.
49. See also Agata Bareja-Starzyńska, "Jebtsundamba Khutugtus of Mongolia," *Oxford Research Encyclopedia of Religion* (2018).
50. Lhavgademchig Jadamba, "Double Headed Mongolian Buddhism," *CESS Blog*, February 2018.
51. See Bareja-Starzyńska, "Jebtsundamba Khutugtus of Mongolia."
52. Jadamba, "Double Headed Mongolian Buddhism."
53. Jadamba, "Double Headed Mongolian Buddhism."
54. See Abrahms-Kavunenko, "The Blossoming of Religious Ignorance"; Abrahms-Kavunenko, "Religious 'Revival' After Socialism?"; and Manduhai Buyandelger, *Tragic Spirits*, for a more in -depth discussion of these trends.

55. David Gellner, "What Is the Anthropology of Buddhism About?," in *The Anthropology of Buddhism and Hinduism: Weberian Themes*, ed. David Gellner (New Delhi: Oxford University Press, 2002), 45–60.
56. Gellner, "What Is the Anthropology of Buddhism About?"
57. Charles Stewart and Rosalind Shaw, "Introduction: Problematizing Syncretism," in *Syncretism/Anti-Syncretism: The Politics of Religious Synthesis*, ed. Charles Stewart and Rosalind Shaw (London: Routledge, 1995), 1–26.
58. See Sneath, "Nationalising Civilisational Resources"; and Vesna Wallace, "Buddhist Sacred Mountains, Auspicious Landscapes, and their Agency," in *Buddhism in Mongolia: History, Culture and Society*, ed. Vesna Wallace (Oxford: Oxford University Press, 2015), 221–240, for a more in-depth discussion of syncretic ritual practices in Mongolia.
59. See Sneath, "Nationalising Civilisational Resources"; and Lars Højer, "The Anti-Social Contract: Enmity and Suspicion in Northern Mongolia," *Cambridge Anthropology* 24 (2004): 41–63.
60. David Sneath, "Reading the Signs by Lenin's Light: Development, Divination and Metonymic Fields in Mongolia," *Ethnos* 74, no. 1 (2009): 72–90.
61. See Zsuzsa Majer and Krisztina Teleki, "A Survey of Mongolian Monasteries Conducted in 2007."
62. Karénina Kollmar-Paulenz, "Buddhism in Mongolia After 1990," *Journal of Global Buddhism* 4 (2003): 18–34; Agata Bareja-Starzyńska and Hanna Havnevik, "A Preliminary Study of Buddhism in Present-Day Mongolia," in *Mongols from Country to City: Floating Boundaries, Pastoralism and City Life in the Mongol Lands*, ed. Ole Bruun and Li Narangoa (Copenhagen: Nordic Institute of Asian Studies, 2006), 212–236; and Vesna Wallace, "Mediating the Power of Dharma: The Mongols' Approaches to Reviving Buddhism in Mongolia," *The Silk Road Journal* 6, no. 1 (2008): 36–45.
63. Hildergard Diemberger and Uradyn Bulag, eds., *The Mongolia-Tibet Interface: Opening New Research Terrains in Inner Asia* (Leiden, The Netherlands: Brill, 2007).
64. See Abrahms-Kavunenko, "Religious 'Revival' After Socialism?"; Elverskog "Two Buddhisms in Contemporary Mongolia"; Marie-Dominque Even "Ritual Efficacy or Spiritual Quest?"; and Jadamba and Schittich, "Negotiating Self and Other."
65. Majer and Teleki, "Survey of Active Temples."
66. Abrahms-Kavuenko, "Paying for Prayers"; and Jadamba and Schittich, "Negotiating Self and Other."
67. Vesna Wallace, "The Interface of Mongolian Nomadic Culture, Law and Monastic Sexual Morality," *Buddhism, Law, and Society* 2 (2018): 57–75.
68. Vesna Wallace, ed., *Buddhism in Mongolia: History, Culture and Society* (Oxford: Oxford University Press, 2015).
69. Mette High, "A Question of Ethics: The Creative Orthodoxy of Buddhist Monks in the Mongolian Gold Rush," *Ethnos* 83, no. 1 (2018): 80–99; and Mette High, "Cosmologies of Freedom and Buddhist Self-Transformation in the Mongolian Gold Rush," *Journal of the Royal Anthropological Institute* 19, no. 4 (2013): 753–770.
70. Lkhavgademchig Jadamba, "Double Headed Mongolian Buddhism: A Historical and Anthropological Study on Identity Politics Inside the Mongolian Buddhist Institution" (PhD diss., University of Shiga Prefecture).

Saskia Abrahms-Kavunenko

MONGOLIAN BUDDHISM IN THE EARLY 20TH CENTURY

WHAT IS "MONGOLIAN BUDDHISM"?

Where is Mongolia and who were the Mongols in the early 20th century?[1] Answers to those questions are in the plural, since the form and content of Mongol communities, territories, histories, and sovereignties were subject to sustained reimagination at that time. Such imagination, in turn, was always profoundly local, even if expressed in broad abstractions such as Qing subjecthood, Russian citizenship, Tibeto-Mongolian monastic membership, or pan-Mongolism. In the first twenty or so years of the 20th century alone, Mongolian peoples were variously administered by Qing and Tsarist imperial formations, three new nation-states, and a series of breakaway autonomous units quickly (and often brutally) absorbed into Russian or Chinese political dominion.

Buddhism—a set of disciplines for self- and community formation; a technique for making place, time, community, and authority—was redefined continually as part of these broad processes. For some, a Buddhism fit for the imperial-socialist transition promised to reproduce Yuan-era political relations from the 13th-century Mongol Empire. For others, the best way forward was to simply continue imperial-era structures and narratives. These often mediated well-worn models of community conceptualization, such as of an eternal pan-Asian Buddhist kingdom in the rubric of "Our great Qing" (Mon. *manu yeke cing*), or else drew together some constellation of received concepts like *törö* (state), *ulus* (community), *qaγan* (such as a Chinggisid ruler), *cakravartin* (a Dharmic world emperor), *qutuγtu* (an incarnate lama), *shabi* (serf), *lam* (monk), *arad* (commoner), and the "Two Systems" (qoyar yosu) of "shared religio-political authority" (*šasin törü yin erke*). During the imperial-socialist transition of the early 20th century, these were set into innovative combination with Enlightenment-derived concepts of place, community, and history such as "citizen," "development," "proletariat," "democracy," "nation," and "socialism." Not only European political theory, but also nascent orientalist academic disciplines such as ethnology, folk studies, archaeology, and philology, was instrumental in these processes. For many radical progressives and reformers, a disjointed group that very much included prominent monastic leaders early on, Buddhism in a post-imperial age ought to be legible as a tradition in line with a globally circulating moderne: on the one hand, by reviving the ethical purity and orientations of the "original Buddhism" fetishized by early Euro-Russian Buddhologists in the rubric of world religions; on the other, by "rationalizing," a process that meant embracing scientific education, scientific materialism, and scientific institutions favored in many quarters by both nationalist and then socialist leaders and intelligentsia. If Buddhism could not be made legible in these ways, such reformers often ominously concluded, it ought to be erased.

As the 19th century turned into the 20th, Mongols under the Qing were organized into four ayimaγ made up of eighty-six banners (Mon. *qoshun*) in Outer Mongolia, the "great estate" (Mon. *yeke yin shabi*) of the Jebtsundamba Khutuγtus, and six leagues (Mon. chiγulγan) made from forty-nine banners in Inner Mongolia. Many other Mongolian ethnic groups lived in Tibetan regions along the Sino-Tibetan-Mongol frontiers, including in what is today Qinghai Province but also as far away as Shanxi and Zhili provinces in the People's Republic of China. Furthermore, Kalmyks and Buryats, also Mongol peoples, lived under the sovereignty of the Tsarist Empire along either side of Lake Baikal.

When the Qing and Tsarist Empires collapsed in the second decade of the 20th century, bloody contests ensued all along the Mongol frontiers of Russia and China between White Russians, Bolshevik forces, Qing loyalists, Muslim warlords, and regional factions with various affiliations. Emergent social and political desires and possibilities inspired Mongols to imagine their histories, associations, and territorial centers anew. The results were competing ethnic narratives of Mongolness (that included, in some cases, Tibetans and Manchus into their fold), competing temporalities that sought to "recover" (i.e., strategically invent) pre-Qing and Tsarist histories, and competing models of postimperial sovereignty aligned with centers as diverse as Beijing and Irkustk, Tokyo and Lhasa, Paris and Urga.

The Buddhadharma—imagined in late imperial-era frameworks by revivalists, Mongol Empire frameworks by puritans like Baron Ungern von Sternberg, in sectarian affiliation with Tibetan co-religionists, or in nativist terms by nationalist ideologues in Urga—was central to all such imagining of place, time, and sovereignty in Asia's heartland at the start of the 20th century. One particularly telling example comes from the east of Lake Baikal, in Qori Ayimaγ. There, in reaction to the revolutionary events of 1905 and 1917, a consortium of nobles and clergy elevated the monk Samdan Tsydenov to the position of "Dharmarājan of the Three Worlds and a Holder of the Religious and Civil Spheres of Authority." Though soon crushed by Soviet authorities, this anti-Bolshevik theocratic polity initiated its own Buddhist reform initiatives that elaborately fetishized the Tsarist Russian state and its deposed political leaders.[2] Over the course of the 1910s, '20s, '30s, and '40s, Mongol peoples came to be administered in various provinces and autonomous zones of first Republican China and then the People's Republic, various units of the Soviet Union, and in the socialist Mongolian People's Republic that formed in 1921.

"Buddhisms" in the plural were thus both a product of and a generative condition for each of the major sociopolitical movements that shaped the Mongol heartland of Asia in the early 20th century. For example, Buddhist ideas, institutions, networks, practices, and persons helped define and direct the transition from imperial subject to citizen, from monk or noble to proletariat and bourgeoisie, and from bannermen and slave to "Mongol." To understand this history one must first understand the transregional affiliations and imperial forms of Buddhism that were remobilized, shorn off, or dispatched in the early 20th century. Because of constraints of space, the focus in what follows will be Buddhism in the Qalq-a majority "Outer Mongolia" (aru mongγul) and its re-formation as an autonomous Mongol nation, with many referents to associated developments in "Inner Mongolia" (*öbür mongγul*) and to Mongol regions in Russian Siberia.

The "Yellow Religion." By the turn of the 20th century, the Buddhist tradition of all Mongol territories, whether under Qing or Tsarist dominion, was overwhelmingly that of the reformed Ganden tradition or, as it came to be known later, the Géluk (Tib. *dga' ldan*; *dge lugs*).[3] Known in Mongolian sources as the so-called "Yellow Hat School" (Tib. *zhwa ser chos lugs*) or, most commonly, simply as the "Yellow Religion" (Mon. sir-a yin šasin; Tib. *ser gyi chos lugs*), the Ganden tradition was founded in Central Tibet by the polymath Jé Tsongkhapa Lozang Drakpa (Tib. Rje tshong kha pa blo bzang grags pa, 1357–1419), his immediate disciples, and their powerful patrons from the Phakmodru family (Tib. phag mo gru). While all post-Yuan Tibetan traditions have histories twinned with Mongol-driven geopolitics in Inner Asia, by the early 20th century the Yellow Religion was the dominant force (and soon enough, the dominant victim).

In the early rhetoric of the school itself and in the memorialization of later followers, such as in the mammoth biographies written about Tsongkhapa by Mongol Buddhist scholars in the 18th and 19th centuries, the Géluk intervention into the already rich religious landscape of

Inner Asia was aimed at reform: to re-prioritize monastic ethics as the foundation of Mahāyāna and tantric self-cultivation, to center rigorous training in dialectics and scholasticism as the necessary intellectual foundation for meditative accomplishment, and to reinterpret the "definitive and interpretative" teachings of Nāgārjuna, Candrakīrti, Dharmakīrti, Dignāga, and other Indian paṇḍitas. This latter endeavor was pursued in Mongol lands by the 20th century through the looking glass of monastic textbooks (Tib. *yig cha*) received from the colleges of the great monastic seats of central Tibet (whose positions were regularly at odds with one another, even between colleges in a single monastery).[4]

Indeed, beginning in the 17th century, the major Géluk monasteries of central Tibet, along with a few major Tibetan Géluk institutions founded along the Sino-Tibetan-Mongol frontier in Shigatsé and Amdo, were counted as the "mother monasteries" (Tib. *ma dgon*) of hundreds of dispersed "son monasteries" (Tib. *bu dgon*) spread by the early 20th century across north China, Siberia, and all Mongol territories. Shared values and organizational structures in those three seats concerning mass ordination—a tradition it now seems solidified not as a condition for, but by means of, expansion into eastern Tibet and Mongolia—became paradigmatic in Mongol lands, much to the chagrin of many early nationalist and socialist leaders in the Mongolian People's Revolutionary Party in the revolutionary period being considered here. The many colleges of the three main Tibetan monasteries in central Tibet provided the major curricular models, ritual traditions, and philosophical interpretations of affiliates across Mongol lands until the crack of executioners' rifles silenced the raucous sounds of debate courtyards, oral recitation, and large-scale ritual in the 1930s.

Those three main seats of the Géluk school, all in the vicinity of Lhasa city in central Tibet, became major sites of Mongol education, pilgrimage, military intervention, and trade beginning in the 16th century but entering maturation during the Qing formation (1644–1912). Of those three major Géluk monastic seats, Drépung (Tib. *'Bras* spungs) may have exerted the most influence on later Mongolian Buddhist life (though individual Mongolian monastic colleges maintained collegial affiliations with all other major Tibetan Géluk monasteries). Drépung Monastery was not only the home of the incarnation lines that would become the Dalai Lamas, the most important religious figures in later Mongol imagination, but also Paṇchen Sonam Drakpa (Tib. Pan chen bsod nams grags pa, 1478–1554), a luminary whose philosophical interpretations became dominant in many Mongolian monastic manuals and philosophical textbooks. More specifically, Drépung's Gomang College (Tib. Sgo mang grwa tshang) was home to the regional houses (Tib. *khams tshan*) that most regularly housed Mongolian and Siberian pupils who had made the long journey to study in Lhasa and who, in many cases, would never return to their distant homelands.

Those Mongols who did return from their studies and those Tibetan lamas and incarnates who regularly toured through Mongol lands beginning in the 16th century often enforced a Géluk orthodoxy opposed, for example, against shamanism and "unreformed" Nyingma Buddhist influence. These Géluk orthodox figures further sought to standardize clerical Mongolian Buddhist life through emphasizing Tibetan language learning and writing to the exclusion of regional movements to adopt Mongol liturgies or native exegesis, such as the famous examples of the Third Mergen Gegegen (1717–1766).[5] So ubiquitous was this sect in Mongolia that the "Yellow Religion" become a standard by which to define spheres of ulterior religiosity, like the "Black Religion" of shamanism (Mon. qara yin šašin)[6] and unreformed

"Red" sects of Tibetan Buddhism (Mon. *ulaγan šašin*) that had been influential even in the recent past, such as those in the Qalq-a Gobi Desert inaugurated by the 19th-century luminary Danzan Ravjaa (Tib. Bstan 'dzin rab rgyas, 1803–1857).[7]

As such, while Mongolian groups maintained relations with all major Tibetan Buddhist sects, as well as with various Chinese, Uighur, Tangut, and other Central Asian Buddhist institutions and lineages, it was the Géluk school that won the day in Mongol lands. This development was inextricable from the consolidation of the Inner Asian frontiers of the Qing Empire beginning in the 17th century. In time, this consolidated into a dominant (but never hegemonic) model of religion, community identity, history, territory, and sovereignty that Johan Elverskog usefully calls the "Qing-Géluk subject."[8] The Qing-Géluk subject and its associated institutional, historical, and political forms was a hegemonic referent in most Mongol lands outside of Russian Siberia at the dawn of the 20th century.

During the 17th-century consolidation of Géluk temporal and religious authority in central Tibet under the Fifth Dalai Lama and Gushi Khan, such legends of enlightened kingship (especially centered on Avalokiteśvara, with whom the Dalai Lamas were associated, Mañjuśrī, who was identified with the Manchu emperors, and Vajrapāṇi, the enlightened source of the Jebtsundamba Qutuγtu in Qalq-a Mongolia) gained new currency and were central to the political ideology of the Géluk school's Ganden Potrang government and its affiliation with the Qing formation.[9] An entire lexicon for such religio-political authority developed in post-16th-century Inner Asian Buddhist historiography and remained important well into the 20th, such as the "Two Laws" or "Two Systems" (Tib. *chos srid lugs gnyis*; Mon. *qoyar yosu*), as well as compound nouns that collapse the two into one (Tib. bstan srid, chos srid, bstan gzhung; Mon. *törü šašin*). Some terminology subsumed these spheres of authority into one abstracted whole, such as "the unification of Dharma and politics" (ex. Tib. *chos srid zung 'brel*). Seventeenth-and 18th-century Mongolian Buddhist scholastics such as Zaya Paṇdita and the author of the *Erdeni-yin tobci* consolidated a particularly salient vision of the connections between religion and state among Mongols, Manchus, and Tibetans in the early Qing period that would hang in the background of the many varieties of sociopolitical and religious contests of the early 20th century.[10]

By the beginning of the 20th century, the Mongolian frontiers of the Qing were societies divided, administratively and conceptually, between "black" (*qar-a*) lay society and "yellow" (*sir-a*) monastic society. Each had their own regional relations to the Qing Empire and to each other, as well as uneven opportunities for political representation, economic advancement, and physical movement. These extended from incarnate lamas and hereditary nobility down to common herdsfolk, uneducated monks, vassals, and slaves.[11] As in Tibet by this time, at the top of the ecclesiastical hierarchy were incarnate lamas (Tib. *yang srid*; *sprul sku*; Mon. *qubilγan*; *qutuγtu*). The highest-ranking line of qutuγtu in Mongol lands were undoubtedly of the Jebtsundamba line, known more honorifically as the Bogda Gegegen ("Holy Enlightened One"). In the predominant Géluk hierarchy in Qing Inner Asia, the Bogda Gegegen ranked just below the Dalai Lamas and the Panchen Lamas of central Tibet. In Siberia, where Russian authorities carefully outlawed traditions of installing incarnate lamas as monastic leaders, the Bogda Gegegen and the chief Tibetan incarnates still pulled heavily on the Buryat and Kalmyk imagination.

Monastic estates in Mongolia were by the early 20th century nearly the only sedentary buildings and dominated most spheres of cultural life, including printing, education, medicine (including veterinary knowledge), astrology, and of course, Buddhist philosophical and ritual training. At this time, monastic schools generally taught using Tibetan-language sources (even if oral commentaries would have remained in local dialects) and Mongolian Buddhist authors wrote nearly exclusively in Tibetan. Outside of bureaucratic recordkeeping and diplomatic missives, monastics and educated laity even used Tibetan for writing Mongolian phonetically.

Monasteries were also dominant politically and, most egregiously for later socialist leaders, economically. According to nearly contemporaneous estimates, Buddhist monastic holdings in Outer Mongolia at the turn of the 20th century amounted to about 57 million rubles of the 257 million total national properties. In addition to donations, taxation, corvée, and so forth, Mongolian monasteries at this time bolstered their income from regular financial support from the Qing bureaucracy and from leasing land at high rates.[12] Monasteries owned some 2.5 million head of livestock in Outer Mongolia and controlled a further 1.5 million.[13] However, power in monastic infrastructure was decentered; there was no unified or inter-regional bureaucratic or administrative structure, and instead monastic estates were run by strong local corporate rule and secular affiliation. This decentered, locally embedded monastic infrastructure explains both the quick penetration of foreign ideas and progressive movements into revolutionary centers like Urga during the Qing collapse, as well as the slow, uneven, and ultimately violent overthrow of all vestiges of local monastic structure in the first three decades of the post-Qing period.

It is in this broad geopolitical and socioeconomic context that the story of Buddhism in early 20th-century Mongolia opens with a rather ominous and profoundly disruptive event: the flight of the Thirteenth Dalai Lama to Mongolia in the face of a British invasion of Lhasa in 1904. Connected to escalations in the Great Game that saw Britain preemptively responding to fears that the Russian Empire was exerting covert influence in the Tibetan frontiers of the British Raj as it had done in Afghanistan, the British Viceroy ordered the invasion of central Tibet under the leadership of Sir Francis Younghusband. Under the advice of his Buryat tutor and confidant Agvan Dorjiev, the Thirteenth Dalai Lama Tubten Gyatso retreated nearly twenty-five hundred kilometers from Lhasa to Urga. In Urga he took refuge, taught, and engaged in a distressed diplomacy for two years before moving on to Mt. Wutai and then eastern Tibet. A small body of scholarship on the Dalai Lama's time in Urga details the enormous economic strain the Tibetan contingent hoisted upon the Mongol nobility. The at best tense relationship between the Dalai Lama and the Jebtsundamba Qutuγtu has also been well documented, while the flurry of religious activity (such as mass ordination, public tantric initiation, and dialectic contests in the monastic colleges) that occurred between local Mongols and their Tibetan visitors has as yet been less comprehensively studied.[14] The Dalai Lama's flight from the British and his long sojourn in Qalq-a, China, and eastern Tibet symbolically opens three decades of profound transition in Mongol that is the subject of the remainder of this article.

THE BOGD KHAANATE PERIOD (1911–1919)

According to many Cold War-era Mongolian, Euro-American, and Soviet historians, Manchu and Tsarist neglect and aristocratic indulgence were to blame for impoverishing Mongol populations and creating optimal conditions for a "people's revolution" of one kind or another.

The people's duγuylan or "arat circle" movements that arose in protest were, prior to 1911, always regional, ultimately suppressed, and of varying character and political aspiration.[15] In Outer Mongolia, the crushing debts owed by the nobility to Chinese traders and bankers caused the exaction of increasingly high taxes from the arat commoners. The result, by the turn of the 20th century, was the concentration of wealth in the hands of just a few aristocratic estates, foreigners, and especially the monasteries that resulted in "widespread and disparate poverty."[16] There was, in Charles Bawden's estimation, the "breakdown of a traditional pattern of living under the impact of economic stagnation and the collapse of a feeling of responsibility for the public welfare on the part of the authority."[17]

As the Qing Empire began to falter in 1911 and collapse back into China, religious and aristocratic elites in the city of Urga (known then as Yeke-yin Küriye, the previously mobile "Great Encampment" of the Jebtsundamba Qutuγtu) colluded to expel the Manchu ambans and found an independent Buddhist theocracy. An ethnic Tibetan and the highest incarnate lama in Outer Mongolia, the 8th Jebtsundamba Qutuγtu (1869–1924) was duly enthroned as the Bogda Qaγan ("Holy King"), a theocratic ruler of an independent Mongolian nation-state under the reign name "Elevated by the Many" (Olana ergüg-degsen).[18] "By adding temporal authority to [the Jebtsundamba's] religious primacy," during the Bogd Khaanate, "it was possible to create a personal sovereign, replacing the Manchu Emperor, for the time being, and out of reach of the quarrels over precedence among hereditary Mongol princes."[19] In commemoration, and representative of the profound transitions in social imagination then underway, Urga was renamed Niyslel Küriye ("National Capital").

A nearly contemporaneous history of the Autonomous Period describes the centrality of Buddhist frames of reference in this early experiment in national autonomy in Asia:

> When Hsüan T'ung, the eleventh emperor of the Manchu, or Ta Ch'ing, was small, the dignitaries and aristocrats who held state power, high and low, metropolitan and provincial, civil and military, all having lost the principles and virtues of government, their despotism, cruelty, graft, greed and indiscipline exceeded all bounds, and the masses of the five races subject to the state, the Manchus, Mongols, Chinese, Tibetans and Moslems, were truly unable to bear it, and were hard put to it to find their living, so that in the southern provinces of Chinea there broke out the revolution of the revolutionary people's party known as the Ge min dan, which directly attacked the government of the Manchu Dynasty. Moreover, in Northern, Outer Mongolia, the place known as Urga was a place of extreme importance as the center and forefront and the root and the base, in fact, of all the Mongol aimaks, where the Holy Jebtsundamba Lama, worshipped and venerated by all the Mongol aimaks, had dwelt for many years, where the doctrine of the Buddha Śākyamuni flourished properly, where further all sorts of trade and industry were progressing greatly, and the people of all the tribes and sticks of Inner and Outer Mongolia mingled and settled together.[20]

All this inspired nationalist designs among progressives elsewhere in China and Tsarist Russia, especially in Siberia and Inner Mongolia, who had begun to newly conceive of a pan-Mongolian sociopolitical identity (though hardly a static, mutual, or consensual one).

So began a period of Mongolian history known as the Autonomous Period, or the "Bogd Khaanate" in the Qalq-a dialect (Bogd Khaant Mongol Ulus, 1911–1919). Although short-lived, this was a fascinating, if fraught, project to construct a "modern" and ethnically "Mongolian" Buddhist nation-state out of the mosaic of imperial-era histories and affiliations. In general, the Bogda Gegegen's administration tackled their task by combining Qing imperial administrative traditions and European parliamentary institutions (ex. ulsîn khural) with new pan-Mongolian objects of knowledge and frames of experience. Alongside influences from Russia, these also developed in dialogue with nationalist currents in post-imperial China, such as the Republican-period rhetoric of "five races under one union" (Ch. *wu zu gong he*).

However, the pacification and unification of Mongolia's new nationalist space was not only a matter of political redefinition. This transition also required sustained monastic ritual assistance and the deployment of various Buddhist discourses of authority and legitimacy. Contemporary observers such as Wladyslaw Kotwicz and Gustaf John Ramstedt recorded large-scale public cham dances, Maitreya processions, group mantra recitation, and major blessing and offering ceremonies to mark the occasion; a flourishing of public ritualism also evidenced in the very few monastic sources remaining from that period.[21] Further, using the idioms of wrathful tantric meditation and ceremony, the nationalist government employed monastic ritualists from Urga to suppress the internal and external enemies of Mongolian national autonomy (ironically employing the same techniques of ritual expulsion that had been put to use in centuries past by Tibetans to defend against Mongol invasion).[22] As just one illustrative example, "the amban Samadi Bagshi Nomu Khan Jalhantsa Qutuγtu Dambinbazar went up together with many lamas of the place to the top of a high mountain near the city of Khobdo, and recited prayers for the suppression of the enemy."[23]

Those rituals, however, were ultimately ineffective in the face of early 20th-century geopolitics. The beginning of the end of the autonomous Bogd Khaanate came during the protracted Sino-Mongol-Russian conference in Kyakhta in 1914–15. The tripartite agreement that was its outcome denied Mongolia full independence: the Mongol-Chinese border was to be demilitarized and Chinese Republican officials were to take up residence in Urga and most other major cities, such as Uliastai and Khovdo. Even so, the Mongolian government retained its power to self-govern, but soon thereafter began to lose the confidence of the newly invented Mongol citizenry because of corruption, incompetence, and disorganization. In the words of the nearly contemporaneous *Anonymous History of the Autonomous Period*:

> However, the dignitaries and aristocrats, nobles and lamas, who wielded authority in the government of Mongolia and in the various aimaks and banners, instead of uniting their minds and strength and making every effort to try and work out a policy, just struggled for advantage, trying to get for themselves more ranks, titles and salaries . . . At every move they enslaved and oppressed the ordinary people, and wasted and ruined the store of capital. In particular, such aristocratic lamas as the Erdene Shanzodba of the Great Clerical Adminstration, Ching Zorigt Chin Wang Lama Badmadorj, the Grand Lama Nyagt Bilegt Beile Lama Puntsagdorj occupied the posts of Prime Minister of the government, and chief and second minister of the Ministry of the Interior and further, they were in personal attendance upon the Holy King . . . On such pretexts as that the laymen were who were the primary princely officials were quite ignorant of the deep and intricate

doctrine of the Buddhist Faith, its limitless capabilities and its marvelous and inexhaustible competence, and so would base their actions on scraps of false and empty bookish and wordly principles derived from their personal experience, with the result that their advice and proposals would all be wrong, erroneous and misleading, they deceived the high and by-passed the low.[24]

THE PEOPLE'S REVOLUTION (1921–1937)

In 1919, the perilous semi-autonomy of Mongolia was shattered. Urga was occupied by Chinese forces and then again by White Russians in 1921 under the leadership of Baron von Ungern Sternberg, who declared that he came to defend the buddha's religion and the authority of the Bogda Gegegen against the "Reds and Atheists."[25] To great pomp and circumstance, the Bogda was brought from nearby Manzusiri Monastery where he had been held during the Chinese occupation and re-enthroned in Urga. This would be a short-lived revival, however. Mongolian socialists headed by Damdin Sükhbaatar and heavily backed (some would say led) by Soviet forces ousted the whites that same year. The Bogda Gegegen was demoted to a constitutional monarch and the Mongolian People's Republic (Bügd Nairamdakh Mongol Ard Uls) was established.

The notes of a contemporary observer named I. M. Mayskiy, while impressionistic and not entirely reliable, gives us a general sense of the social structure of Mongolian society on the eve of the socialist transition in 1921. In the four ayimaγ of Outer Mongolia (Qalq-a), there were 91 princely houses, which Mayskiy estimated to comprise 410 members (0.1 percent of the male population). According to a 1918 census, the lesser nobility comprised 5.6 percent, serfs 16.6 percent, albat 26.2 percent, and lamas 44.5 percent. (Some ten thousand lamas living in the Great Estate of the Jebtsundamba were not separately counted.)[26]

From the start, the Mongolian people's government faced this complicated ideological baggage head-on but not often with consensus. Party members understood their responsibility to free the masses from "feudal-clerical ideology," but understood the task on quite different terms from one another. Some identified as already communists, some as socialists, some as capitalist, and others still as radical-democrats bound only by necessity to the international proletariat movement. The Comintern itself had to make special accommodations to include Mongolia in its Marxist-Leninist historicization of world revolution. For example, some cadres decided that Mongolia could not be included as a member of the bourgeois countries since it was: "by nature a particular party of the poor and middle-income working arad in a primitive nomadic country, neighboring a great revolutionary state with a proletariat dictatorship."[27]

The Jebtsundamba responded to the publication of the MPP declaration in March 1921 as follows: "This is in opposition to monarchist rule. Even in great countries this (promotion of the rights of the masses) is very difficult to pursue and it is simply impossible in such an uncultured small nation as our Mongolia. It is said in historical writings that as soon as an internal threat coincides with external disorder, the fall of the state begins. If now, at such a moment, a revolutionary party sets out it would be easy not only to destroy the state but also to put an end to religion and to the nation."[28] The Jebtsundamba diplomatically summarized his attitude to the MPP as follows: "My views differ from the views of the party members not because I'm right and they are wrong, or vice versa, but because every century has its views and beliefs. Let the people of the new century realize their new mission: it's high time for the people of the old century to consider the matters of the next world."[29]

An important development in November 1921 was the "oath-taking treaty," which limited the powers of the Bogda Qaγan to a constitutional monarch. He would remain the head of state until his death in 1924. All matters religious were left to the Bogda during those three years, while all political authority passed into the hands of the people's government. There was also a rapid reform of the Shabinar Department (the Department of Religious Affairs) to reflect the separation of religious and secular spheres of administration. These reforms made it difficult for lamas to consolidate their position in the new state.[30] Even so, the educated and politically experienced lamas and aristocracy, both members of the "old society," were necessary as administrative experts for inexperienced Comintern agents and their Mongolian counterparts. Several acting or former Buddhist lamas occupied several key positions in the early iterations of the Central Committee of the revolutionary government. For example, the first Prime Minster Dogsomyn Bodoo (1885–1922) had been a lama, the next premier was Jalhanz Khutagt, one of the highest-ranking religious leaders in the country, and a prominent revolutionary leader named D. Losol was also trained as a lama prior to the revolutionary events of 1911.

Charles Bawden once wrote that, "The revolutionaries and their sympathizers were certainly not Bolsheviks; they represented a wide spectrum of origin and outlook, but the Bolshevik element ousted all others . . . there was never room in Mongolia's revolutionary development for democratic compromise."[31] Early on the poets and ideologues of revolution in Mongolia were congealed around a group Robert Rupen labeled the "Buryat Intelligentsia."[32] If high clerical Buddhism during the late-imperium was tied inextricably to the dispersed Géluk-Qing subject, and if lived religious life was always implicated in local conditions of possibility, in the twilight of the Qing and Tsarist Empire and in the dawn of socialism in Mongol lands, a new "pan-Mongolia" social imaginary emerged. In the hands of Buryat progressives and their Outer Mongolian collaborators, pan-Mongolism was tied at once to an emancipatory politics and an invented national subject, one that was anti-capitalist; reacted against the West for imposing a political, ideological, and moral dictatorship; recognized the "free creativeness" of all nationalities; recognized the special role of the general masses, and the necessity to agitate them; saw Buddhism as "refuge of national spirit."[33]

To understand the determining effect of Buryat progressive thinkers on Buddhism in early 20th-century Mongolia, one must understand the unique historical position of Buryatia between Europe and the rest of the Mongol-Tibetan world. Buryatia was incorporated into the Russian Empire in 1689. The Buryats long suffered two projects of cultural and political assimilation: russifikatsiya (forced enculturation, specifically around modes of production, as the Buryats learned agriculture); and ohristianivanie (the forced adoption of Orthodox Christianity, and the marginalization of Buddhism and indigenous traditions). The Russian state also worked to annex and nationalize Buryat Buddhism in order to weaken ties with Tibet and Mongolia. This was most successful in terms of instituting a distinct authority structure outside of the Tibet-Mongol Géluk world. There, for example, were no officially recognized incarnate lamas in Tsarist Buryatia. Power lay instead with the appointed Bandito Khambo Lam, an institution that was the invention not of a Dalai or Panchen Lama, but of the Russian state.

Very directly related to the form and content of Buddhism in early 20th-century Mongolia, the Speranski Reforms of 1822 further incorporated Buryat territories into Russian administration without coming into conflict with local tribal structures. However, the cancellation of the Speranski reforms in 1901, combined with intensified russifikatsiya and *ohristianivanie* policies and forced migration of Slavic peoples to Buryat territories, provoked a sustained critical response from leaders and intellectuals to the new pressures imposed by Russification and the augmented attacks on Buddhists and Buddhist institutions by the Orthodox Church.

Buryat Buddhism was thereby reimagined in opposition to Orthodox Christianity. Buryat intellectuals looked past pan-Buryatism (which would have tied them further into the Russian state) to pan-Mongolism, a "national" and "ethnic" imaginary distinct from the "West" (though, as in Bogdanov's statements below, many considered Western expansion inevitable, or else found the conceptual fruits of European modernity necessary in modernizing projects). These intelligentsia also argued that Buryat and Mongol customary law was not only amenable to socialist principals of communal ownership, but had historically represented some of the first instantiations of socialist principles prior to Qing and Tsarist influence.

The two most influential Buryat Intelligentsia were Ts. Jamsrano and Bogdanov. Both had very different perspectives on Buddhism, modernization, and progress politics in Inner Asia. Bogdanov was from Irkutsk and traveled widely in the west, such that he became known as a "Buryat zapadnik" (Rus. zapadnichestvo, a trend in Russian intellectual circles at this time, where "Zapadniki" marked a self-consciously "Western" view on Russia, one that importantly assumed "progress" should follow routes to democracy and nationalism).[34] He also believed that the extension and normalization of capitalist relations would circumvent any nationalist differentiation, and that the market economy would dissolve the Buryats and their "archaic Lamaism."[35] Jamsrano had been instrumental in developing non-monastic education and a secular press in Outer Mongolia even before the collapse of the Qing in 1911. By 1921 he was both a socialist and Buddhist reformer who played a decisive role in the early revolutionary history of the MPR, including writing the platform of the party and attempting to reform monastic education to include laity and scientific subjects.[36]

Despite Comintern resolutions against the "lama establishment," the period of 1924–1928 has been called the "pan-Buddhist era" and was very much colored by the ideas of the Buryat Intelligentsia like Jamsrano.[37] Buddhist reformers across Mongolia and Buryatia authored synthetic publications that, for example, combined the teachings of the buddha and Lenin. The lack of a singular god-concept in Buddhism further prompted reformers to argue that Buddhism was the true source of the theory of relativity and the source of modern thought itself.[38] Even if the official Comintern line condemned Buddhism as the "opium of the people," in the first years of the MPP many of its agents seem to have held ambiguous views about the socialist futures of the Dharma. Some urged revolutionary workers to study its tenants, while others argued that the philosophy of Marxist-Leninism thoroughly rebuked "every false point in the quasi-scientific premises of Buddhism."[39] However, such debates were not only confined to Comintern meetings or People's Congresses. They were also occurring in Buddhist monastic settings. Two examples of prominent monk-proponents of socialist reforms were the (in)famous confidante of Tsar Nikolai and the Thirteenth Dalai Lama, the Buryat Agvan Dorjiev (Mon. Agwangdorji; Tib. Ngag dbang rdo rje, 1854–1938) and Qalq-a's Darwa Paṇḍita Agwangchoijurdondubbalsang (Tib. Ngag dbang chos 'byor don grub dpal bzang po, 1870–1927).[40]

Just as elsewhere in late and postimperial and colonial Asia, where vocal but minority groups of often Western-educated Buddhist reformers invented versions of their tradition legible to a Eurocentric modernist imagination, we ought here to also note strong counter-modern and anti-reform Buddhist movements in Qalq-a and elsewhere in Mongol lands. Traces of such religious innovations are largely absent in political records and have received little scholarly attention to date. An emblematic figure in this regard is Zava Damdin Lubsangdamdin (1867–1937), a prominent Qalq-a monastic scholar, abbot, and historian. A fierce critic of the Bogda Gegegen and an interlocutor of the emergent revolutionary intelligentsia and Euro-Russian Buddhologists, Zava Damdin nevertheless proposed a subaltern historicization of the imperial-socialist transition using very different rubrics than those of the People's Party or of reformers discussed above.[41]

As the 1920s progressed, party leadership was also working to oppose the formation of an Indo-Tibetan-Mongolian religio-cultural community positioned against the socialist program. Buddhism was central to both sides of this development. Japan sought to exploit pan-Mongolism and pan-Buddhism for their own colonial and imperial ends between the 1910s and the 1930s. After 1927, the Comintern began calling pan-Mongolism a weapon of Japanese imperialism. Even in the 1930s, the Japanese were actively using pan-Buddhism and pan-Mongolism to work with Buddhist monasteries in order to expand into mainland China, Inner and Outer Mongolia, eastern Turkistan, and Tibet.

For revolutionary agitators and Soviet historians, "the one hundred thousand lamas, however, included both exploiters and the exploited,"[42] which was "comprised of incarnate lamas, clerical administrators, and church labourers."[43] To defend against foreign influence and to garner domestic loyalties, in the 1920s the USSR used the Comintern and sympathetic Mongolian lamas to gain a deeper foothold in the country. At the same time, revolutionary leaders acted to draft young cadres from among the educated classes (i.e., lamas), present lectures on the harmful role of religion, and sought to turn the general population against the widespread, imperial-era practice of sending young boys to train as monks.[44] Despite such efforts, in the first three years of the MPR (1921–1924) the number of lamas actually increased, and leading religious leaders seemed to have largely seen the USSR and its Comintern representatives as temporary allies against Chinese expansion back into Mongolia (despite ominous measures against Bodoo and the Ja Lama in 1922).

In 1921, the revolutionary government established the precursor to the Mongolian Academy of Science, the Institute of Scripts and Letters (Mongol Bichgiin Sudar Khureleen). This was a center of scholarly activity for the translation and preparation of popular literature, the collection of old books and manuscripts, the registration of monuments, and the organization of a museum. This chamber was transformed into a Learned Committee in 1930, which included departments of language and literature, history, geography, agriculture, Tibetology, and Buddhism.[45] Prominent Buddhist scholastics from Urga, such as Zawa Damdin Lubsangdamdin (1867–1937), were not only early contributors to its scholarly publications but also used the opportunity to independently twine Euro-Russian arts and sciences with received Buddhist narratives.[46]

The Bogda Gegegen died on May 20, 1924, an event that led slowly, if unevenly, to the erasure of Buddhism in Mongolia (in parallel with developments in Siberia). The Soviet government did not send its condolences in the wake of the Bogda's death, but instead prepared a plenary (held July 3, 1924) in order to resolve to establish a republic and adopt a constitution. The first constitution ominously set the goals of "fundamentally liquidating the remnants of the old despotism and transferring political rule to a genuinely arat system." At People's Congresses soon after, the electoral rights of former monastic and secular "feudalists," employers, and moneylenders were abrogated. All natural resources, very much including the expansive livestock holdings of monastic estates, were declared common property. Social equality—regardless of gender, religion, or ethnicity—was declared. All citizens (including, notably, women) over eighteen years of age who supported themselves by their own labor were given the right to vote and to be elected in the great, little, or local khurals.[47] In another symbolic transition, Niyslel Küriye ("National Capital") was renamed Ulaγanbaγatur ("Red Hero," present day Ulaanbaatar).

In light of these developments, party leaders, Comintern agents, and revolutionary intelligentsia dully engaged in the revisionisms required to fit a sparse society of nomadic pastoralists, hereditary nobility, and decentered monastic institutions into the universalist models of historical materialism. A "dictatorship of the proletariat," after all, required the invention of social classes in the Mongolian context whose newly imagined historical experience could convincingly map onto Marxist-Leninist models of historical change. "Mongolian proletariats" were found first in serfs (*shabi*) freed from monastic estates, then in women, and finally among the "lower classes" of monastics.[48]

In July 1929, Ulaγanbaγatur and Moscow signed a secret agreement that effectively incorporated the MPR into the USSR, while allowing Mongolia to keep its own state structure. As a result, Soviet policy in Mongolia shifted to the effect that fewer Comintern agents were dispatched to Mongolia in place of more technicians, educators, doctors, veterinarians, etc.[49] An important feature of this campaign was based on medicine—to supply more cheap medicine than German competitors, publish medical literature in Mongolian, and send doctors to the countryside—in order to develop a Soviet-style health care system in Mongolia. The point of this was explicitly to displace the hold of Buddhist lamas over the population in the sphere of medicine.

In the early 1930s there was a turn across the country against the utopianisms of the Buryat Intelligentsia that had colored so much of the early 1920s. For hardline factions in positions of political power at least, it was clear that the revolutionary state and the Buddhist establishment would never coexist. This came on the heels of a "Leftist Deviation" in the late 1920s that had rushed to crush Buddhist monastic influence too rashly and had ignited the people's opposition to the socialist state. Some radical elements in the MPRP had proposed to put 13,000 high-ranking monks in a concentration camp. However, Buddhist-led revolts against the party were large enough to quiet such extreme ideas, though they would resurface to terrible effect only a few years later.

THE PURGES

At the beginning of the 1930s, Outer Mongolia had some eight hundred monasteries with some 80,000 lamas, as well as over 7,700 jas monastic properties. "In view of the church's enormous influence on the population, it was not possible to resort to the confiscation of the property of the monasteries, as happened with the property of the secular feudalists and certain big church feudalists. Such a step would have been considered by believers as forced closure of the monasteries and could have caused their dissatisfaction."[50]

Instead, a program of gradual annexation and isolation of monastic assets sought to displace monastic privilege and power in Mongolia without causing widespread revolt (as did sometimes happen in some areas). For example, during the "jas campaign," the total population of monastic residents in monasteries fell from 80,000 to just 20,000 by 1932. Their livestock were transferred to collectives (negdel) and to poor arats.[51] As a result, lamas in several monastic estates led nomadic pastoralists in revolt during the summer of 1932. Such revolts would quickly occupy some 70 percent of the country, killing thousands of people, and leaving five ayimaγs in complete mutiny.[52]

As a result, even Comintern agents had to admit that the "lamas remained the cultural leaders of the Mongolian people: as teachers, the only doctors and craftsman."[53] However, the hearts and minds of the so-called exploited class of arat nomadic pastoralists were not so easily won with what was recognized as stolen monastic and aristocratic property. Furthermore, the masses bristled at state efforts to project the categories of Marxist-Leninism into Mongolia and slaughtered their livestock en masse in order to avoid high taxation and negative class association.[54]

The defeat of Left Deviationism under Comintern guidance in 1932 and the development of the "New Turn" policy briefly stopped the disrobing of monastics and the forced closure of monastic institutions. Between 1932–34, a staggering 20,000 men became monks again. Still, monastic assets were taxed in order to prevent exploitation of the arats looking after monastic-owned livestock. In the wake of the turmoil from the "jas campaign," MPRP officials worried that Japan would strengthen its influence among Outer Mongolian counterrevolutionaries within the Buddhist establishment. In fact, the number of lamas briefly increased after 1932. In the face of widespread revolts, it was hard for the state to counter illegal, prerevolutionary activity that was resurfacing among the lamas: "Leading lamas went on building temples, collecting taxes from the nomads, putting corporal punishment into practice, and getting their titles back."[55]

In the fall of 1934, following policies established at the Ninth People's Congress held that year, a plan was put into place to displace the Buddhist establishment on a discursive level. This was a cultural "struggle" waged against Buddhism and its institutions on several fronts. Party leaders resolved that the traditional Tibetan and Mongolian writing systems were to be eliminated and that a modern, reformed Mongolian written language be developed instead: "as long as the people continued reading and writing in these media, which could not express modern concepts, they would remain deaf to the cultural achievements of socialism."[56] Additionally, a change in Mongolian sympathies away from the monasteries was sought at public cham monastic dance rituals and popular naadam sporting festivals focused on archery, wrestling, and horse racing. State interventions included promoting Russian football, chess, circus performance, and more centrally mass literacy and public health campaigns promoting Russian biomedicine against traditional Tibeto-Mongolian monastic medical knowledge and practice.

Even so, the statistics obsessively collected by the socialist state painted a rather disheartening picture. After more than a decade of party support for defected lamas and the prohibitions against children and young lamas studying Buddhist philosophy, in 1934 there were some 115,000 lamas as against 200,000 yurt households. Four out of five schoolchildren in Mongolia were still receiving an education taught by lamas.[57] There was one lama, either in a monastery or living as a "Black" lama living outside the monastery, for every seven arat, while there was only one party member for every 1000 arat.[58] There were, in other words, only 8000 party members versus 115,000 active lamas twelve years into the socialist revolutionary period.

Between 1921 and 1937, the "lama question" (lam naryn asuudal in the Qalq-a dialect) became common shorthand in the Socialist Party archives for a cluster of political, economic, and social impasses. In an important study of Socialist Party responses to enduring Buddhist authority, Christopher Kaplonski sees the lama question as the very heart of "Asia's first modern revolution." He finds that it was the ambiguities, split loyalties, contingencies, and unexpected outcomes that eventually created a socialist world on the steppes of Asia's heartland. By the ominous year of 1937, state cadres estimated that there were still some 87,774 lamas out of a total population of 705,054.[59] In the 1930s, literacy circles were set up in the monasteries, but by 1937 still only five thousand out of fifty thousand poor lamas had learned to read.[60]

As a result, a special session of the MPRP Central Committee was convened in March 1937 in order to focus on anti-Buddhist campaigns. Extant sources record that antireligious agitation and propaganda was made an obligation of every party member.[61] At Stalin's behest, General Choibalsan and state judicial, police, and military forces began a systematic purge of Buddhist monastics, monasteries, and other "counter-revolutionary elements." The most conservative estimates are that some 30,000 people were executed from a population of only about 900,000 in just eighteen months spanning 1937–38.[62] Tens of thousands more were imprisoned or forcibly returned to lay life. All continuity of public Buddhist life and monasticism were ended until the democratic revolution of 1990. Soviet-era historiography would remember this obliquely as the time of the "Struggles of the Mongolian Nation for a Non-Capitalistic Route to Development."

Owen Lattimore, with some dramatic flair, observed of Mongolian Buddhism in the early revolutionary period that, "institutionally this religion, like one of its many-headed, thousand-armed deities, had a head to dominate every human thought and a hand to control every human action."[63] Even if it is true that, "in the long history of Buddhism perhaps no country or people in the world were as affected by the faith as were the Mongols of Great Mongolia," it took just years for it to be criminalized, and just months for the terror of state violence to erase its previous hegemony.[64]

Against the comforting but unsustainable anachronism that it was Russian foreigners and not Mongols who were responsible for the purges, Irina Morozova writes bluntly that: "this 'bacchanalia' was staged not by the Comintern agents, not by Russian communists, but by the Mongols themselves, who had previously been in the habit of appealing to the lamas for advice on the slightest pretext. Now they carried forward the slogan 'iron struggle.' The tsiriks (soldiers) who were now shooting the lamas, had no fear of buddha: 'their hands did not shake, but took aim with pleasure.'"[65]

CONCLUSION

Over a decades-long process a "Soviet-type command economy" was implemented in Mongolia in the wake of the purges of Buddhist institutions and their monastic populations. Solidifying only in the 1950s, this command economy "imposed a structural unity, a principle of nesting domination, on individuals and groups that were otherwise different from one another (for example, in native region, education, or religious attitudes)."[66] Connected with this consolidated system of domination was the growth of a mature and hegemonic state historiography, deeply influenced by Soviet models, which charted Mongolian national history back to the 13th century-Yuan dynasty in the historical materialist idiom of class conflict.[67] After the purges, public Buddhism in any form was essentially discontinued until the democratic movement of 1990 (an exception being the reopening of Gandetegchenlin Khiid in the capital in the second half of the 20th century as a working museum of sorts).

To explore the complicated and ultimately tragic story of Buddhism in early 20th-century Mongolia is to encounter invention; track global circulations of sociopolitical, historical, and religious representations; and peel away layers of cultural mediation and resistance. Any continuity of Buddhist tradition during the imperial-socialist transition must be looked over carefully for the ways that the idea of continuity itself was being deployed to navigate the contested landscape of sociopolitical possibility. Yet such scrutiny quickly runs past the end of pages penned by Buddhist hands outside of party cadres and preserved outside of party archives. Beyond trial proceedings and interrogation records were lamas could speak only of their "crimes." We have only a very few mostly Tibetan-language compositions by revolutionary-era monks with which to more comprehensively plumb early 20th-century Buddhism in Mongol lands. The brutal silencing of the Mongolian saṁgha in the hands of the socialist state is mirrored in a silencing in the archives, and a clear picture of Buddhist life during Asia's first experiment in state socialism remains elusive.

REVIEW OF LITERATURE

Much like the sorry fate of Buddhists in Mongolia in the early 20th century, the organization of scholarly knowledge about this period has long been defined by prevailing geopolitical winds. Early scholarly accounts of Mongolia and its Buddhism around the turn of the 20th century come from a motley crew of explorers, missionaries, and imperial agents who traveled through Mongolia during the last years of the Qing, the Bogd Khaanate, and the early years of the Mongolian People's Republic. Of note for historians of Buddhism, even if they must be used with some caution, are eyewitness accounts by explorer-scholars such as the Russians Aleksei Matveevich Pozdneev and Petr Kozlov, the Finnish Gustaf John Ramstedt, and the Polish Wladyslaw Kotwicz.[68]

As global geopolitics solidified into axes of capitalist and communist nations, a burgeoning of (often state-funded) area studies scholarship generated copious amounts of sociopolitical histories of the world's second socialist state. In those pages are troves of valuable information about Buddhism in the early 20th century. This includes systematic pictures of what traces remained of living Buddhism during the imperial-socialist transition as well as details about the bloody purges that effectively ended the public life of the dharma in Asia's heartland.[69]

In terms of more recent scholarship, a very useful critique of the very terms deployed in the study of Buddhism in Mongolia is found in Christopher Atwood's "Buddhism and Popular Ritual in Mongolia."[70] A key analysis of the sorry fate of Buddhists based on Socialist Party archives is Christopher Kaplonski's *The Lama Question*, while Larry Moses's *The Political Role of Mongolian Buddhism,* if dated, provides a close analysis of the institutional and sociopolitical structure of Mongolian Buddhism leading to the socialist period.[71] Other dedicated studies of Mongolian Buddhist chronicles, traditions, institutions, and prominent figures associated with the early 20th century are too many to mention here. Readers are encouraged to mine several broad works and notable case studies to get a sense of that broad literature. These include, but are hardly limited to, works by Walter Heissig, György Kara, Vesna Wallace, Ishihama Yumiko, Emget Ookhnoi Batsaikhan, Johan Elverskog, Uranchimeg Tsultem, Isabelle Charleux, Caroline Humphrey, and Agata Bareja-Starzyńska.[72]

In a turn away from the dominant ethno-national categories of an older area studies, fresh multi-sited pictures of Buddhist life in Mongolia are emerging influenced by frameworks connected to Global History, New Qing History, inter-Asian themes, and even environmental history. Notable monographs here are Johan Elverskog's *Our Great Qing* (2006); Caroline Humphrey and Ujeed Hürelbaatar's *A Monastery in Time: The Making of Mongolian Buddhism* (2013); a 2015 volume edited by Vesna Wallace entitled *Buddhism in Mongolian History, Culture, and Society*; and Isabelle Charleux's *Nomads on Pilgrimage: Mongols on Wutaishan, 1800–1940* (2015).[73]

Another important scholarly development has been the centering of Mongolians in the study of Buddhism and "cultural Tibet." Whereas a previous generation of historians often considered Mongolia simply a static backwater to Tibetan tradition, recent work on the Tibet-Mongol interface has clearly shown the centrality of Mongolian persons, places, institutions, and ideas in the formation of Inner Asian Buddhist tradition in the late and post-imperial period, even if the lingua franca was almost exclusively Tibetan and even if Tibetan monastic institutions in central and eastern Tibet provided the dominant (but not exclusive) models for pedagogy, ritualism, monastic organization, and literary practice. A good starting place into that literature and the growing field of inquiry it represents are the many contribution published in the 2007 Proceedings of the International Association of Tibetan Studies edited by Uradyn Bulag and Hildegard Diemberger.[74]

Finally, recent work by small teams of dedicated Mongolian and European researchers have built on Rinchen's 1979 documentation of purged monastic sites.[75] On the basis of oral history, textual analysis, and archaeological exploration, several monograph-length studies and digital resources have emerged that begin to provide clearer pictures of not only the physical presence of Buddhist monasteries prior to the purges, but also of the form and content of Buddhist life in the early 20th century. Most notable here are Krisztina Teleki and Zsuzsa Majer's ongoing work, exemplified in *Monasteries and Temples of Bogdiin Khuree, Ikh Khuree or Urga, the Old Capital City of Mongolia in the First Part of the Twentieth Century* (2006) and in an international digital research project called Documentation of Mongolian Monasteries.[76]

DIGITAL RESOURCES

Documentation of Mongolian Monasteries (http://www.mongoliantemples.org/index.php/en/)/Монголын Сүм Хийдийн Түүхэн Товчоо Төсөл

Buddhist Digital Resource Centre (https://www.tbrc.org/#!footer/about/newhome)

Treasury of Lives (https://treasuryoflives.org)

FURTHER READING

Chuluun, Sampildondov, and Uradyn E. Bulag. *The Thirteenth Dalai Lama on the Run (1904–1906): Archival Documents from Mongolia*. Leiden, The Netherlands: Brill, 2013.

'Dar pa paṇḍita. *Khyab Bdag Rdo Rje'i 'Chang 'Dar Pa Paṇḍita Nga Dbang Chos "Byor Don Grub Dpal Bzang Po"i Skyes Rabs Rnam Thar Dang Gsung Thor. Mongol Bilig: Mongolchuudin Töwd Khelt Büteeliĭg Sudlakh Tsuwral*. Ulaanbaatar, Mongolia: R. Byambaa, 2011.

Dorjiev, Agvan, Thubten Jigme Norbu, and Dan Martin. *Dorjiev Memoirs of a Tibetan Diplomat*. Tokyo: Hokke bunka kenkyū, 1991.

Humphrey, Caroline. "Remembering an Enemy: The Bogd Khaan in Twentieth Century Mongolia." In *Memory, History, and Opposition under State Socialism*. Edited by Rubie S. Watson, 21–44. Sante Fe, New Mexico: School of American Research Press; distributed by University of Washington Press, 1994.

Humphrey, Caroline, and Ujeed Hürelbaatar. *A Monastery in Time: The Making of Mongolian Buddhism*. Chicago: University of Chicago Press, 2013.

Hyer, Paul, and Sechin Jagchid. *A Mongolian Living Buddha: Biography of the Kanjurwa Khutughtu*. Albany: State University of New York Press, 1983.

Jerryson, Michael K. *Mongolian Buddhism: The Rise and Fall of the Sangha*. Chiang Mai, Thailand: Silkworm Books, 2007.

Kaplonski, Christopher. *Truth, History and Politics in Mongolia: The Memory of Heroes*. London: RoutledgeCurzon, 2004.

Kaplonski, Christopher. *The Lama Question: Violence, Sovereignty, and Exception in Early Socialist Mongolia*. Honolulu: University of Hawai'i Press, 2014.

King, Matthew. "Giving Milk to Snakes: A Socialist "Dharma Minister" and a "Stubborn" Monk on How to Reject the Dharma in Revolutionary Buryatia and Khalkha." *Journal of Religion and Violence* 4, no. 2 (2016): 205–227.

King, Matthew. "Knowing King Gésar Between Buddhist Monastery and Socialist Academy, Or the Practices of Secularism in Inner Asia." *Himalaya: The Journal of the Association for Nepal and Himalayan Studies* 36, no. 10 (2016): 44–55.

King, Matthew. "Modernities, Sense-Making, and the Inscription of Mongolian Buddhist Place." In *Buddhism in Mongolian History, Culture and Society*. Edited by Vesna Wallace, 53–69. Oxford: Oxford University Press, 2015.

Majer, Zsuzsa, and Krisctina Teleki. "Monasteries and Temples of Bogdiin Khuree, Ikh Khuree or Urga, the Old Capital City of Mongolia in the First Part of the Twentieth Century." Ulaanbaatar, Mongolia, 2006.

Mayskiy, I. M. *Mongoliya Nakanune Revolyutsii [Mongolia on the Eve of Revolution]*. Mongolia: Oriental Literature Press, 1959.

Moses, Larry William. *The Political Role of Mongol Buddhism. Indiana University Uralic Altaic Series—Asian Studies Research Institute, Indiana University*. Bloomington: Indiana University Press, 1977.

Narangoa, Li. "Japanese Imperialism and Mongolian Buddhism, 1932–1945." *Critical Asian Studies* 35, no. 4 (2003): 491–514.

Purevzhav, S. *BNMAU-D sum khiid, lam naryn asuudlyg shiidverlesen ní: 1921–1940 on*. Ulaanbaatar, Mongolia: Ulsyn khevleliin khereg erkhlekh khoroo, 1965.

Rinchen, B. *Mongol Ard Ulsin Ugsaatnĭ Sudlal Khel Shinjleliin Atlas*. Ulaanbaatar, Mongolia: Shinjleh uhaanii akademi, 1979.

Rupen, Robert A. "Cyben Zamcaranovic Zamcarano (1880-?1940)." *Harvard Journal of Asiatic Studies* 19, no. 2 (1956): 126–145.

Rupen, Robert A. *Mongols of the Twentieth Century*. Bloomington: Indiana University Publications, 1964.

Rupen, Robert A. "The Buriat Intelligentsia." *The Far Eastern Quarterly* 15, no. 3 (1956): 383–398.

Krisztina Teleki. *Monasteries and Temples of Bogdiin Khuree*. Ulaanbaatar: Institute of History, Mongolian Academy of Sciences, 2011.

Tsultem, Uranchimeg. "Cartographic Anxieties in Mongolia: The Bogd Khan's Picture-Map." *Cross-Currents: East Asian History and Cultural Review* no. 21 (2016): 66–87.

Tulisow, Jerzy, Osamu Inoue, Agata Bareja-Starzynska, and Ewa Dziurzyńska, eds. *In the Heart of Mongolia: 100th Anniversary of W. Kotwicz's Expedition to Mongolia in 1912: Studies and Selected Source Materials*. Crakow, Poland: Polish Academy of Arts and Sciences, 2012.

Wallace, Vesna A., ed. *Buddhism in Mongolian History, Culture, and Society*. New York: Oxford University Press, 2015.

Zhambal, Boryn, Charles R. Bawden, T. S. Damdinsürèn, and England Institute of Buddhist Studies. *Tales of an Old Lama*. Tring, UK: Institute of Buddhist Studies, 1997.

NOTES

1. One of the technical challenges of writing on Buddhism in early 20th-century Mongolia is that there is no scholarly consensus on either transcription or transliteration schema for vertical Uyghur script or the Cyrillic script (the latter was innovated in a language reform during the 1940s after the period this article considers). I have followed Christopher Atwood's simplified Mongolian transliteration system in this introductory article, and follow the usual Wylie transliteration system for Tibetan. Transliterations of technical terms and personal names will be given in brackets on first use, and then the simplified transcription will be used thereafter.
2. Nikolay Tsyrempilov, "Samdan Tsydenov and His Buddhist Theocratic Project," in *Biographies of Eminent Mongol Buddhists*, ed. Johan Elverskog (Halle, Germany: IITBS, International Institute for Tibetan and Buddhist Studies, 2008), 117–138.
3. Which is not to say that the so-called unreformed, older sects of Tibetan Buddhism did not maintain enduring connections with Mongolian peoples or exert influences on the form and content of Buddhism in Mongol lands. The controversial, often radically innovative and contrarian, Noyan Khutukthus of the Khalkha Gobi Desert regions is a paradigmatic case (and in particular the fifth incarnation Danzanravjaa (1803–1853) whose ecumenicalism, artistic pursuits, and charisma loom large even in the post-socialist cultural revivals happening today). See Hamid Sardar, "Danzan Ravjaa: The Fierce Drunen Lord of the Gobi," in *The Mongolia-Tibet Interface: Opening New Research Terrains in Inner Asia*, ed. Uradyn E. Bulag and Hildegard G. M. Diemberger, *Proceedings of the Tenth Seminar of the IATS, 2003* (Leiden, The Netherlands: Brill, 2007), 257–294.
4. On the concerns and organization of the early Géluk school, see Elijah S. Ary, *Authorized Lives: Biography and the Early Formation of Geluk Identity*, Studies in Indian and Tibetan Buddhism (Somerville, MA: Wisdom Publications, 2015). For studies of scholasticism and institutional histories of Géluk monastic colleges, see Georges B. J. Dreyfus, *The Sound of Two Hands Clapping the Education of a Tibetan Buddhist Monk* (Berkeley: University of California Press, 2003); Michael Lempert, *Discipline and Debate: The Language of Violence in a Tibetan Buddhist Monastery* (Berkeley: University of California Press, 2012); Martin A. Mills, *Identity, Ritual and State in Tibetan Buddhism: The Foundations of Authority in Gelukpa Monasticism* (London: RoutledgeCurzon, 2003); and José Ignacio Cabezón, *Buddhism and Language: A Study of Indo-Tibetan Scholasticism*, SUNY Series, Toward a Comparative Philosophy of Religions (Albany: State University of New York Press, 1994).
5. See Caroline Humphrey and Ujeed Hürelbaatar, *A Monastery in Time: The Making of Mongolian Buddhism*, 2013.
6. In many Mongolian cultural regions to this day there is also "yellow shamanism," a mode of shamanic practice aligned explicitly with Buddhist cosmologies and ritual technologies, or else performed with

some Buddhist affiliation or by a ritualist with training as a Buddhist lama. For examples and descriptions, see Katherine Swancutt, *Fortune and the Cursed: The Sliding Scale of Time in Mongolian Divination* (New York: Berghahn Books, 2012).

7. See, for example: Hamid Sardar, "Danzan Ravjaa: The Fierce Drunen Lord of the Gobi," in *The Mongolia-Tibet Interface: Opening New Research Terrains in Inner Asia*, ed. Uradyn E. Bulag and Hildegard G. M. Diemberger, Proceedings of the Tenth Seminar of the IATS, 2003 (Leiden: Brill, 2007), 257–94.
8. Johan Elverskog, "Mongol Time Enters a Qing World," in *Time, Temporality, and Imperial Transition: East Asia from Ming to Qing*, ed. Lynn A. Struve (Honolulu: Association for Asian Studies and University of Hawai'i Press, 2005).
9. *dGa ldan pho brang*. Originally the name of the Dalai Lama's seat at Gaden monastery in central Tibet, under the Dalai Lama V, his regent, Desi Sanggyeé Gyatso, and the Mongol forces of Gushi Khaan, the Ganden Potrang became the de facto political authority in central Tibet as part of the Qing formation. See Robert E. Buswell and Donald S. Lopez, *The Princeton Dictionary of Buddhism* (Princeton, NJ: Princeton University Press, 2013), 237. For a fascinating discussion of the legal frameworks for the Gaden Potrang government, rooted firmly in the ideology of the Two Systems, see Rebecca R. French, "Tibetan Legal Literature: The Law Codes of the DGa' Ldan Pho Brang," in *Tibetan Literature: Studies in Genre*, ed. Lhundup Sopa, Cabezón, and Roger R Jackson (Ithaca, NY: Snow Lion, 1996), 438–457.
10. Ishihama Yumiko, "The Notion of 'Buddhist Government' (chos srid) Shared by Tibet, Mongol, and Manchu in the Early 17th Century," in *The Relationship between Religion and State (chos srid zung 'brel) in Traditional Tibet: Proceedings of a Seminar Held in Lumbini, Nepal, March 2000*, ed. Christoph Cüppers (Lumbini, Nepal: Lumbini International Research Institute, 2004), 16.
11. Sechin Jagchid and Paul Hyer, *Mongolia's Culture and Society* (Boulder, CO: Westview Press, 1979), 381.
12. I. M. Mayskiy, *Mongoliya Nakanune Revolyutsii (Mongolia on the Eve of Revolution)* (Mongolia: Oriental Literature Press, 1959), 248–249. Cited in Irina Y. Morozova, *The Comintern and Revolution in Mongolia* (Cambridge, UK: White Horse Press for the Mongolia and Inner Asia Studies Unit, University of Cambridge, 2002), 91,*ff.* 6.
13. Robert A. Rupen, *Mongols of the Twentieth Century* (Bloomington: Indiana University Publications, 1964), 82.
14. Sampildondov Chuluun and Uradyn E. Bulag, *The Thirteenth Dalai Lama on the Run (1904–1906): Archival Documents from Mongolia* (Leiden, The Netherlands: Brill, 2013); and Boryn Zhambal et al., *Tales of an Old Lama* (Tring, UK: Institute of Buddhist Studies, 1997).
15. Alan J. K. Sanders, *Mongolia: Politics, Economics and Society* (London; Boulder, CO: F. Pinter; L. Rienner, 1987), 26.
16. Charles R. Bawden, *The Modern History of Mongolia* (New York: Praeger, 1968), 142.
17. Bawden, *The Modern History of Mongolia*, 147.
18. The autonomous Mongolian state was first known as "The Mongolian State Elevated by Many" (*Olnoo Örgögdcön Mongol Uls*), a name resisted by Russian authorities and indicative of the new visibility of an expansive Mongol community that included commoners.
19. Owen Lattimore, *The Mongols of Manchuria; Their Tribal Divisions, Geographical Distribution, Historical Relations with Manchus and Chinese, and Present Political Problems* (New York: H. Fertig, 1969), 122.
20. Charles Roskelly Bawden, *A Contemporary Mongolian Account of the Period of Autonomy*, 1st ed., vol. 4 (Bloomington, IN: Mongolia Society, 1970), 7.
21. Jerzy Tulisow et al., ed., *In the Heart of Mongolia: 100th Anniversary of W. Kotwicz's Expedition to Mongolia in 1912: Studies and Selected Source Materials* (crakow, Poland: Polish Academy of Arts and Sciences, 2012); Harry Halén and Suomalais-ugrilainen Seura, *Biliktu Bakshi, the Knowledgeable Teacher: G. J. Ramstedt's Career as a Scholar* (Helsinki: Finno-Ugrian Society, 1998); and G. J Ramstedt and John

Richard Krueger, *Seven Journeys Eastward, 1898–1912: Among the Cheremis, Kalmyks, Mongols, and in Turkestan, and to Afghanistan* (Bloomington, IN: Mongolia Society, 1978).

22. For example: James Gentry, "Representations of Efficacy: The Ritual Expulsion of Mongol Armies in the Consolidation and Expansion of the Tsang (Gtsang) Dynasty," in *Tibetan Ritual*, ed. José Ignacio Cabezón (Oxford: Oxford University Press, 2010), 131–164.
23. Bawden, *A Contemporary Mongolian Account of the Period of Autonomy*, 4:16.
24. Bawden, *A Contemporary Mongolian Account of the Period of Autonomy*, 4:21.
25. Veronika Veit, "Some Marginal Notes on Geser Khan in Mongol Tradition," in *Tractata Tibetica et Mongolica*, ed. Karénina Kollmar-Paulenz and Christian Peter (Wiesbaden, Germany: Otto Harrassowitz Verlag, 2002), 304.
26. Mayskiy, *Mongoliya Nakanune Revolyutsii (Mongolia on the Eve of Revolution)*, 37–42. Summarized in Sanders, *Mongolia: Politics, Economics and Society*, 33.
27. Russian State Archives of Social Political History, quoted in Morozova, *The Comintern and Revolution in Mongolia*, 76.
28. From the Russian State Archives of Social Political History, quoted in Morozova, 26.
29. From the Russian State Archives of Social Political History, quoted in Morozova, 27.
30. From the Russian State Archives of Social Political History, quoted in Morozova, 28.
31. Bawden, *The Modern History of Mongolia*, 207.
32. Robert A. Rupen, "The Buriat Intelligentsia," *The Far Eastern Quarterly* 15, no. 3 (1956): 383–398.
33. Summarized in Morozova, *The Comintern and Revolution in Mongolia*, 72.
34. Morozova, *The Comintern and Revolution in Mongolia*, 71.
35. Morozova, *The Comintern and Revolution in Mongolia*, 71.
36. Great summary of Zhamtsarano's work (including his specific roles in PC 1, his pseudonyms, etc.) in Morozova, *The Comintern and Revolution in Mongolia*, 72.
37. Larry William Moses, *The Political Role of Mongol Buddhism*, Indiana University Uralic Altaic Series—Asian Studies Research Institute, Indiana University (Bloomington: Indiana University Press, 1977), 175.
38. Unknown source, cited in Morozova, *The Comintern and Revolution in Mongolia.*
39. The Russian State Archives of Social Political History, quoted in Morozova, 32.
40. Agvan Dorjiev, Thubten Jigme Norbu, and Dan Martin, *Dorjiev Memoirs of a Tibetan Diplomat* (Tokyo: Hokke bunka kenkyū, 1991); 'Dar pa paṇḍita, *Khyab Bdag Rdo Rje'i 'Chang 'Dar Pa Paṇḍita Nga Dbang Chos "Byor Don Grub Dpal Bzang Po"i Skyes Rabs Rnam Thar Dang Gsung Thor*, Mongol Bilig: Mongolchuudin Töwd Khelt Büteeliĭg Sudlakh Tsuwral (Ulaanbaatar, Mongolia: R. Byambaa, 2011).
41. Matthew W. King, *Oceans of Milk, Oceans of Blood: A Mongolian Monk in the Ruins of the Qing Empire*, (New York: Columbia University Press, 2019); Matthew W. King, "Giving Milk to Snakes: A Socialist 'Dharma Minister' and a 'Stubborn' Monk on How to Reject the Dharma in Revolutionary Buryatia and Khalkha," *Journal of Religion and Violence* 4, no. 2 (2016): 205–27; Matthew W. King, "Knowing King Gésar Between Buddhist Monastery and Socialist Academy, Or the Practices of Secularism in Inner Asia," *Himalaya: The Journal of the Association for Nepal and Himalayan Studies* 36, no. 10 (2016): 44–55; Matthew W. King, "Modernities, Sense-Making, and the Inscription of Mongolian Buddhist Place," in *Buddhism in Mongolian History, Culture and Society*, ed. Vesna Wallace (Oxford: Oxford University Press, 2015), 53–69.
42. B. Shirendyb, *By-Passing Capitalism* (Ulaanbaatar: Mongolian People's Republic State Press, 1968), 11.
43. Sanders, *Mongolia: Politics, Economics and Society*, 32.
44. Morozova, *The Comintern and Revolution in Mongolia*, 30.
45. Sanders, *Mongolia: Politics, Economics and Society*, 134.

46. Matthew King, "Modernities, Sense-Making, and the Inscription of Mongolian Buddhist Place," in *Buddhism in Mongolian History, Culture and Society*, ed. Vesna Wallace (Oxford: Oxford University Press, 2015), 53–69.
47. William A. Brown, Urgunge Onon, and B. Shirendev, *History of the Mongolian People's Republic* (London: East Asian Research Center; Cambridge, MA: Harvard University, distributed by Harvard University Press, 1976), 6.
48. Caroline Humphrey, "Remembering an Enemy: The Bogd Khaan in Twentieth Century Mongolia," in *Memory, History, and Opposition under State Socialism*, ed. Rubie S. Watson (Sante Fe, New Mexico: School of American Research Press; distributed by University of Washington Press, 1994), 24.
49. Morozova, *The Comintern and Revolution in Mongolia*, 11–12.
50. A. P. Okladnikov et al., *Istorija Mongolskoj Narodnoj Respubliki* (Moskva, Russia: Nauka, 1983), 360.
51. Sanders, *Mongolia: Politics, Economics and Society*, 34.
52. Morozova, *The Comintern and Revolution in Mongolia*, 66.
53. The Russian State Archives of Social Political History, quoted in Morozova, 37.
54. Bawden, *The Modern History of Mongolia*, 312.
55. Morozova, *The Comintern and Revolution in Mongolia*, 38.
56. Morozova, *The Comintern and Revolution in Mongolia*, 38.
57. Sanders, *Mongolia: Politics, Economics and Society*.
58. The Russian State Archives of Social Political History. Morozova, *The Comintern and Revolution in Mongolia*, 37.
59. The Russian State Archives of Social Political History, quoted in Morozova, 38.
60. Bawden, *The Modern History of Mongolia*, 368.
61. Sanders, *Mongolia: Politics, Economics and Society*, 125.
62. Christopher Kaplonski, *Truth, History and Politics in Mongolia: The Memory of Heroes* (London: RoutledgeCurzon, 2004).
63. Owen Lattimore, *Nationalism and Revolution in Mongolia: With a Translation from the Mongol of Sh. Nachukdorji's Life of Sukebatur* (New York: Oxford University Press, 1955), 81.
64. Moses, *The Political Role of Mongol Buddhism*, 5.
65. Morozova, *The Comintern and Revolution in Mongolia*, 37.
66. Humphrey, "Remembering an Enemy: The Bogd Khaan in Twentieth Century Mongolia," 24.
67. For example, Owen Lattimore, *Nationalism and Revolution in Mongolia: With a Translation from the Mongol of Sh. Nachukdorji's Life of Sukebatur* (New York: Oxford University Press, 1955), 81.
68. Alekseĭ Matveevich Pozdneev and John Richard Krueger, *Religion and Ritual in Society: Lamaist Buddhism in Late 19th-Century Mongolia* (Bloomington, IN: Mongolia Society, 1978); Lattimore, *Nationalism and Revolution in Mongolia*; Owen Lattimore et al., "Religion and Revolution in Mongolia," *Modern Asian Studies* 1, no. 1 (1967): 81–94; Ramstedt and Krueger, *Seven Journeys Eastward, 1898–1912*; Tulisow et al., *In the Heart of Mongolia: 100th Anniversary of W. Kotwicz's Expedition to Mongolia in 1912: Studies and Selected Source Materials*; Owen Lattimore, Fujiko Isono, and Diluv Khutagt, *The Diluv Khutagt: Memoirs and Autobiography of a Mongol Buddhist Reincarnation in Religion and Revolution* (Wiesbaden, Germany: O. Harrassowitz, 1982); Paul Hyer and Sechin Jagchid, *A Mongolian Living Buddha: Biography of the Kanjurwa Khutughtu* (Albany: State University of New York Press, 1983); and Petr K. Kozlov, *Mongolija i Amdo i mertvyj gorod Chara-Choto: ėkspedicija russkogo geografičeskogo obščestva v nagornoj Azii, 1907–1909 P.K. Kozlova* (Moskva, Petrograd: Gosudarstvennoe Izdatel stvo, 1923).
69. Li Narangoa, "Japanese Imperialism and Mongolian Buddhism, 1932–1945," *Critical Asian Studies* 35, no. 4 (2003): 491–514; Alan J. K. Sanders, *The People's Republic of Mongolia: A General Reference Guide* (Oxford: Oxford University Press, 1968); Sanders, *Mongolia: Politics, Economics and Society*; Bawden, *A*

Contemporary Mongolian Account of the Period of Autonomy; Zhambal et al., *Tales of an Old Lama*; Uradyn Erden Bulag, *Nationalism and Hybridity in Mongolia* (Oxford; New York: Clarendon Press; Oxford University Press, 1998); Jagchid and Hyer, *Mongolia's Culture and Society*; Robert A. Rupen, "Cyben Zamcaranovic Zamcarano (1880–?1940)," *Harvard Journal of Asiatic Studies* 19, no. 2 (1956): 126–145; Rupen, "The Buriat Intelligentsia"; Dindub and John G. Hangin, *A Brief History of Mongolia in the Autonomous Period* (Bloomington, IN: Mongolia Society, 1977); Urgunge Onon and Derrick Pritchatt, *Asia's First Modern Revolution: Mongolia Proclaims Its Independence in 1911* (Leiden, The Netherlands: Brill, 1989); Thomas E. Ewing, *Between the Hammer and the Anvil?: Chinese and Russian Policies in Outer Mongolia, 1911–1921* (Bloomington: Research Institute for Inner Asian Studies, Indiana University, 1980); and S. Purevzhav, *BNMAU-D sum khiid, lam naryn asuudlyg shiidverlesen ní: 1921–1940 on* (Ulaanbaatar, Mongolia: Ulsyn khevleliin khereg erkhlekh khoroo, 1965).

70. Christopher P. Atwood, "Buddhism and Popular Ritual in Mongolian Religion: A Reexamination of the Fire Cult," *History of Religions* 36, no. 2 (1996): 112–139.
71. Christopher Kaplonski, *The Lama Question: Violence, Sovereignty, and Exception in Early Socialist Mongolia* (Honolulu: University of Hawai'i Press, 2014); and Moses, *The Political Role of Mongol Buddhism*.
72. Gyorgy Kara and John Richard Krueger, *Books of the Mongolian Nomads: More than Eight Centuries of Writing Mongolian* (Bloomington: Indiana University, Research Institute for Inner Asian Studies, 2005); Johan Elverskog, ed., *Biographies of Eminent Mongol Buddhists* (Halle, Germany: IITBS, International Institute for Tibetan and Buddhist Studies, 2008); Johan Elverskog, "Wutai Shan, Qing Cosmopolitanism, and the Mongols," *Journal of the International Association of Tibetan Studies*, no. 6 (2011): 243–274; Walther Heissig, *Die Familien- und Kirchengeschichtsschreibung der Mongolen* (Wiesbaden, Germany: O. Harrassowitz, 1959); Walther Heissig, *The Religions of Mongolia* (London: Routledge & Kegan Paul, 1980); Vesna Wallace, "Diverse Aspects of the Mongolian Buddhist Manuscript Culture and Realms of Its Influence," in *Buddhist Manuscript Culture: Knowledge, Ritual, and Art*, ed. Steven Berkwitz, Juliane Schober, and Claudia Brown (London: Routledge, 2008); Vesna Wallace, "Envisioning a Mongolian Buddhist Identity Through Chinggis Khan," in *Buddhism in Mongolian History, Culture, and Society* (New York: Oxford University Press, 2015); Vesna Wallace, "How Vajrapāṇi Became a Mongol," in *Buddhism in Mongolian History, Culture, and Society* (New York: Oxford University Press, 2015), 179–201; Vesna Wallace, "Legalized Violence: Punitive Measures of Buddhist Khans in Mongolia," in *Buddhist Warfare*, ed. Michael Jerryson and Mark Juergensmeyer (New York: Oxford University Press, 2010), 91–104; Vesna Wallace, "Texts as Deities: Mongols' Rituals of Worshipping Sutras and Rituals of Accomplishing Various Goals by Means of Sutras," in *Ritual in Tibetan Buddhism*, ed. José Cabezón (New York: Oxford University Press, 2009); Agata Bareja-Starzyńska, *The Biography of the First Khalkha Jetsundampa Zanabazar by Zaya Pandita Luvsanprinlei: Studies, annotated translation, transliteration and facsimile* (Warsaw, Poland: Dom Wydawniczy ELIPSA, 2015); Ishihama Yumiko, "The Notion of 'Buddhist Government' (chos srid) Shared by Tibet, Mongol, and Manchu in the Early 17th Century"; Isabelle Charleux, "Buddhist Monasteries in Southern Mongolia," in *The Buddhist Monastery: A Cross-Cultural Survey*, ed. Pierre Pichard and F Lagirarde (Paris: École française d'extrême-orient, 2003), 351–390; Matthew King, "Giving Milk to Snakes: A Socialist 'Dharma Minister' and a 'Stubborn' Monk on How to Reject the Dharma in Revolutionary Buryatia and Khalkha," *Journal of Religion and Violence* 4, no. 2 (2016): 205–227; Matthew King, "Knowing King Gésar Between Buddhist Monastery and Socialist Academy, Or the Practices of Secularism in Inner Asia," *Himalaya: The Journal of the Association for Nepal and Ḥimalayan Studies* 36, no. 10 (2016): 44–55; Michael K. Jerryson, *Mongolian Buddhism: The rise and fall of the Sangha* (Chiang Mai, Thailand: Silkworm Books, 2007); Emget Ookhnoi Batsaikhan, *Bogd Jebtsundamba Khutuktu, The Last King of Mongolia* (Ulaanbaatar, Mongolia: Admon., 2009); Uranchimeg Tsultemin, "Cartographic Anxieties in Mongolia: The Bogd Khan's Picture-Map," *Cross-Currents: East*

Asian History and Cultural Review, no. 21 (2016): 66–87; D. Ulymzhiev, "Dorzhi Banzarov-the First Buryat Scholar," *Mongolian Studies* 16 (1993): 55–57; and Alice Sárközi, *Political Prophecies in Mongolia in the 17–20th Centuries* (Wiesbaden, Germany: Otto Harrassowitz, 1992).

73. Johan Elverskog, *Our Great Qing: The Mongols, Buddhism and the State in Late Imperial China* (Honolulu: University of Hawai'i Press, 2006); Caroline Humphrey and Ujeed Hürelbaatar, *A Monastery in Time: The Making of Mongolian Buddhism*, 2013; Vesna A Wallace, ed., *Buddhism in Mongolian History, Culture, and Society* (New York: Oxford University Press, 2015); and Isabelle Charleux, *Nomads on Pilgrimage: Mongols on Wutaishan (China), 1800–1940* (Leiden, The Netherlands: Brill, 2015).
74. Uradyn E. Bulag and Hildegard Diemberger, *The Mongolia-Tibet Interface: Opening New Research Terrains in Inner Asia: PIATS 2003: Tibetan Studies: Proceedings of the Tenth Seminar of the International Association for Tibetan Studies, Oxford 2003. Managing Editor: Charles Ramble* (Leiden, The Netherlands: Brill, 2007).
75. B. Rinchen, *Mongol Ard Ulsin Ugsaatnĭ Sudlal Khel Shinjleliin Atlas* (Ulaanbaatar, Mongolia: Shinjleh uhaanii akademi, 1979).
76. Krisztina Teleki, *Monasteries and Temples of Bogdiin Khuree* (Ulaanbaatar: Institute of History, Mongolian Academy of Sciences, 2011).

Matthew W. King

MONGOLIAN BUDDHISM IN THE YUAN PERIOD

FROM THE INVESTITURE OF CHINGGIS KHAN UNTIL THE REIGN OF QUBILAI KHAN, 1206–1260

The confederation of peoples that constituted the Great Mongol Nation was an authoritarian oligarchy made up of East Asian aristocrats and elites of every stripe. They were by no means poor, isolated, or in any way benighted. The notion that they were shamanists ignorant of Buddhism is unfounded. Khitan and Tangut members of the grand confederation were Buddhist.[1] Mongols had relations with the many Buddhist nations at their borders and abroad, the Jurchen, Khitans, Uygurs, Tanguts, Chinese, Koreans, and Tibetans. By 1207 (if not even earlier) Chinggis Khan was exacting tribute from Tibet and giving audience to delegations of Tibetan monks.[2] Even so, the place of Buddhism in the budding empire's echelons of power was low. It paled in significance with the Mongols' indigenous sacerdotal tradition and its corps of *böge* "magi" priests. It paled in comparison with other foreign priestly orders such as Syriac-rite Christianity, Confucianism, and Daoism. Chinggis Khan was not Buddhist, for men of the royal family submitting to a foreign discipline, Buddhism or otherwise, was proscribed as tantamount to forfeiture of sovereignty. Mongols saw foreign religions as they saw themselves—as nations to be dealt with.[3] For a khan, conversion to a foreign religion meant bowing to another man. Mongols' sole deference, rather, was to the blue sky (*tengri*), the vault of heaven whence sovereigns create the sensible world through celestial signs that engender spatial and temporal order on earth.[4]

Mongol assimilation of Buddhism was no simple matter of preference for a personal religion but, rather, constituted one aspect of a greater geopolitical modus operandi. Bent on conquering the known world, dividing its spoils among themselves, and keeping everything in it in the family, the Mongols patronized religions as a means to the pacification of their world.

Patronage was contingent upon services rendered. In exchange for financial support, military protection, and special tax-exempt status, the Mongols charged priestly orders with praying to heaven (the sky above) and offering blessings. In practical terms, this meant that in return for patronage they expected religious orders to work to secure Mongol prosperity and support among the populace.

During the reign of Chinggis Khan, the Mongols assimilated the Buddhist traditions of the Uygurs, Tangut, Khitans, and Jurchen. The voluntary submission of the Uygur nobility in 1209 raised Buddhism's station in the empire significantly. Since 1204, Uygur Buddhist amanuenses had served in Chinggis Khan's secretarial corps. Now, Uygur Buddhists counted among the Mongol aristocracy. This foothold brought patronage to Buddhist institutions and power and privilege to its monks. Uygur Buddhist prelates carried the title *toyin*.[5] From Chinese *dao ren* 道人 by way of Old Turkic, the Mongolian word *toyin*, which today means "lama" in a general sense, during the imperial era referred specifically to a monk of noble birth. Uygur Buddhism was something of a center to the greater Buddhist world—a center both cosmopolitan and intellectual. Uygurs kept the traditions of Sogdian, Tocharian, Tibetan, and Tang Chinese Buddhist nations. They had long served as itinerant preceptors teaching Buddhism to up-and-coming Buddhist nations such as the Khitan, Tangut, Jurchen, and Korean, for whom they also acted as intermediaries. Though the Mongols would eventually favor Tibetan-rite Buddhism over Uygur Buddhism, Uygur monks became the single most potent agency in the creation of Mongolian Buddhism.

Situated at a profitable juncture on the Silk Road, the Xi Xia dynasty (1038–1227)—realm of the Minyag nation (known today as "Tangut" by the Turko-Mongolian name for it)—was a regular target of Mongol raids.[6] With the goal of world dominion before him, Chinggis Khan turned his intention from pillaging to conquest. From 1209 until 1227, the Mongols prosecuted several military campaigns culminating in full Tangut submission.[7] Several times over the course of these campaigns the Tangut threw off the Mongol yoke. Upon conclusion of the decisive 1227 campaign, the final campaign of Chinggis Khan's life, a legend (fostered by the Mongols themselves) grew that the Mongols requited Tangut recalcitrance with genocide. *The Secret History of the Mongols* states that the Mongols exterminated the Tangut, mothers and fathers, down to the offspring of their offspring.[8] This claim, however, is highly exaggerated. The Tangut nation survived the Mongol empire.[9] The Mongols disestablished the Tangut state. They executed the Tangut emperor and royal family, gave the nation over to a member of the Mongol royal family, and enrolled the feudal elite into the ranks of their own aristocracy. The Tangut elite they then scattered to the four winds, distributing them throughout their vast empire. Among this elite were eminent Tangut Buddhists. Mongol reliance on them increased apace with their appropriation of the institutions of Tangut Buddhism. Tangut Buddhism was principally a Tibetan-rite esoteric tradition but also incorporated Chinese schools popular across north China such as the *Chan* (禪) and especially the *Huayan* (華嚴) schools—both adopted through the influence of the Khitan Liao dynasty (916–1125).[10] Tangut Buddhism's distinction was the degree of secular authority Tanguts granted its institutions over the governance of a Confucian Han-style dynastic state. Qubilai Khan will look to Tangut precedents when he goes to do the same.

Campaigns against the Jurchen Jin dynasty (1115–1234) that began in 1211 and culminated with the taking of the Jurchen capital, Zhongdu (modern Beijing), in 1215 succeeded in driving the Jurchen from North China and liberating the Khitans. As Chinggis Khan established Mongol rule over the territory, he summoned leading Buddhist clerics for an audience and charged them with overseeing the continuity of Buddhist practice. They would continue to receive tax-exempt status in return for praying to heaven for the khan's longevity; that is, working under Mongol auspices.[11] The Buddhism of north China was a unique, multiethnic tradition. Cultivated by the Jin dynasty (1115–1234) and, before that, the Khitan Liao (916–1125), it kept with precedents established by the Tang dynasty (618–907)—prior to its expulsion of Buddhism (along with all foreign religions) under the Wuzong emperor (r. 840–846) in 845. The tradition comprised of Chinese schools established during the Sui-Tang era (581–907). These included the Huayan "Flower Garland" school based on the doctrine of the *Avataṃsaka Sūtra* (Ch. *Huayanjing* 華嚴經), the Chan "Meditation" school (禪宗), Pure Land (Ch. *Jingtu* 净土) Buddhism, and the Vinaya or Disciplinary school (Ch. *Lüzong* 律宗) propagated by Daoxuan (596–667).[12] Through Tibetan influence and in ecumenism with Uygur and Tangut Buddhism, north China Buddhism knew esoteric, tantric Buddhism.[13] It also assimilated aspects of the Buddhism of the South; that is, the Buddhism of the Song dynasty (960–1279). What distinguished Song, Liao, and Jin traditions was Buddhism's incorporation with Daoism and Confucianism in the tripartite *Sanjiao* (三教) "Three Teachings" religion.

With Chinggis Khan's taking of north China, two eminent Buddhist personages entered the Mongol fold, the Chan Buddhist monk Haiyun 海雲 (1202–1257) and the lay-Buddhist Khitan polymath Yelü Chucai (1189–1243). At his first meeting with Chinggis Khan in 1214, Yin Jia 印簡, known by the honorific title Haiyun Fashi 海雲法師, or simply Haiyun, was still in his teens.[14] Esteemed among members of the royal family with whom he lived for several years, he spent the remainder of his life in Mongol service. Chinggis Khan deemed him a *gaotianren* 告天人 or oracle of heaven. Under Ögedei, he received several commendations and rewards including in 1237 the honorific title "Eminent Master who Illumines Heaven and Guards the State" (*Guangtian zhenguo dashi* 光天鎮國大師). In the 1240s, Haiyun assembled a college of eminent Buddhist and Confucian sages to counsel a youthful son of Tolui, the future Qubilai Khan, on the arts of political science. They instilled in him faith in Buddhism as the vehicle most capable of engendering a pacific world.[15] When his first son was born in 1243, Qubilai afforded Haiyun the honor of naming him. In 1245, under empress regent Töregene (r. 1242–1246) Haiyun conducted a prayer service for the empire's prosperity at Wutaishan. In 1247, Emperor Güyüg (b. 1206, r. 1246–1248) granted him the title "National Preceptor" (*Ulus-un baγsi*; Ch. *guoshi* 國師) and with it, the charge to administer the Buddhist estate.[16] In 1251, Emperor Möngke (b. 1209, r. 1251–1259) confirmed Haiyun's appointment.[17] Another son of Tolui—Möngke and Qubilai's younger brother Hülegü (1218–1265)—also studied under Haiyun and would seek Haiyun's blessing before setting out on the 1251 western campaign that culminated in the founding of the Ilkhanate (1256–1335). After Qubilai founded the Yuan dynasty, he further honored Haiyun with the erection of the Haiyun Pagoda of Qingshou Temple 慶壽寺 in Daidu 大都 (modern Beijing).[18]

The Khitan nobleman Yelü Chucai (1189–1243) was versed in the Three Teachings (Ch. *Sanjiao* 三教) but favored Chan Buddhism. Adept in astronomy, literature, music, and medicine, Chinggis Khan respected his learning and, impressed as well by his physical stature and long beard, retained him in his retinue and endowed him with oracular power; that is, with authority to speak for the government. On his western campaign (1218–1225), Chinggis Khan employed Chucai as a chief secretary and charged him with a wide array of tasks, including time reckoning, auguromancy, and healing the sick. Wishing to learn the secret of longevity, Chinggis Khan ordered Chucai to summon the Daoist Master, Changchun 長春 Qiu Chuji 丘處機 (1148–1227), head of the Quanzhendao school. Chucai saw to arrangements that brought Changchun from China to Chinggis Khan's camp in the Hindukush, north of Kabul. After their meeting in 1222, the khan was so impressed with the Daoist master's teaching that he granted Quanzhen Daoists special tax-exempt status and asked them to pray to heaven and offer benedictions. In the aftermath, Changchun's discipleship took advantage of their privilege by appropriating Buddhist holdings. The conflict between Buddhists and Daoists that ensued lasted decades and led to a series of debates to determine which religion is the truer.[19]

Following Chinggis Khan's death in 1227, Mongol patronage of Buddhism expanded significantly during the reign of Ögedei (b. 1185, r. 1229–1241). Due not so much to any special intention of the Mongols, it occurred as a consequence of conquering the Buddhist nations at their periphery and appropriating their institutions. Under Ögedei, the Mongol world remained traditional and continued to rely heavily on its indigenous priesthood. John of Plano Carpini's travelogue from the 1240s shows the Mongol *törö* "state" still in the hands of *böge* priests.[20] The extent of Buddhists' power remained limited largely to Buddhist affairs. At Haiyun's request, in 1229 Ögedei gave tax-exempt status to Chan Buddhist monks. When the Mongols took the Jin capital at Kaifeng in 1233, the Mongol commander, Sübe'etei Ba'atur (1176–1248), requested permission to massacre of the city, but Yelü Chucai interceded to save the population from wanton slaughter and helped refugees resettle to the North. In this war-torn era, as an alternative to military service and corvée labor, men began pledging to Buddhist monasteries and other dispensation-granting institutions in great numbers. By 1237, Yelü Chucai recognized a need to limit the number of priests, Buddhist and Daoist both, and imposed a screening examination based on knowledge of scripture.[21] A boon to the Buddhist sangha occurred in 1235 when Ögedei, fulfilling a promise to his father to build the city, built a capital for the empire, the city of Qara-Qorum. In the city, he erected centers for religious institutions, palaces, pavilions, and temples. By the 1250s, the small city was home to twelve monasteries housing monks of the various Buddhist nations and Daoists.[22] With special deference to Buddhism, he ordered construction on a great Buddhist pavilion, pagoda, and temple complex completed by Möngke Khan in 1256.

Late in life, Ögedei instigated what became the genesis of Mongolian Buddhism when, in 1239, he assigned his second son, Köden (1206–1251), an appanage over the Tangut realm bordering Tibet and charged him with the assimilation of Tibetan Buddhism and the subjugation of Tibet.[23] In 1240, Köden sent an army under a Tangut general, Dor-ta Darqan, to invade central Tibet and secure a worthy lama-preceptor. After ransacking several monasteries, Dor-ta Darqan found his man, headmaster of the Sakya Order, Sakya Pandita Kungga gyaltsan (Sa skya pandita Kun dga' rgyal mtsan, 1182–1251).[24] In summoning the eminent sage to his court at Liangzhou (modern Wuwei), Köden was bent on patronizing Tibetan Buddhism whether Tibetans wanted him to or not. Dallying for several years, Sakya Pandita set out for the prince's camp in 1244. Traveling in the company of two nephews, Pakpa Lodrö gyeltsen ('Phags pa Blo gros rgyal mtshan, 1235–1280) and Chakna Dorje (Phyag na rdo rje, 1239–1267), he stopped frequently along the way to give teachings before arriving at court in 1246.[25]

By this time, Ögedei Khan had died, and Köden was away attending the diet (Mong. *quriltai*) that would elect his successor.[26] Köden had gone to the diet in Qara-Qorum seeking the khanship for himself. The honor went instead to Ögedei's eldest son, Güyüg (b. 1206, r. 1246–1248), whose reign was short and fraught with strife. Upon returning to his base camp in Liangzhou in 1247, Köden found Sakya Pandita and his two nephews, Phagpa and Chagna, awaiting.[27] At this time, Sakya Paṇḍita and Köden sowed the seeds of a relationship that would blossom into Mongolian Buddhism as we know it. Among the great scholars of his time, Sakya Paṇṇita (or Sapan) is now considered the founder of Mongolian Buddhism. According to Buddhist hagiography, Sakya Paṇḍita cured Köden of an illness and initiated him in the Hevajra tantra, and the two together established a certain *Yön cho* (*yon mchod*) patron-priest relationship.

These two rituals—the initiation in the Hevajra tantra and the renewal of the patron-priest relationship—thereafter became constitutional acts to the founding of a mutually established Mongol and Tibetan Buddhist state. An esoteric yogic ritual, the Hevajra tantra has a sexual aspect to it wherein yogins experience awakening in the embrace of a yoginī. On certain occasions, the two come together to consume flesh and wine, to sing and dance, and realize the consummation of bliss.[28] Mongol lords often underwent initiation with their wives. In the Yuan, the initiation would become part of an emperor's accession.[29] As for the patron-priest relationship, the term *Yön cho* is a contraction of *yöndak* (*yon bdag*) "lord of alms" or "alms-giver" (Mong. *öglige eǰen*) and *chö ne* (*mchod gnas*) "object of veneration" (Mong. *sitügen*). The compact stipulates that an alms-giver provide material support, military and financial, to a guru, who sees to the temporal needs of his patron and his patron's people. In rhetoric, the priest holds ultimate authority, for when worldly matters are at issue, patron and priest have seats of equal height but in religious matters, the monk sits higher.[30] By this rhetoric, the agreement pulls the state into an ultimately catholic Buddhist world.[31]

Buddhist histories refer to Köden's initiation as the Mongols' conversion to Buddhism. Modern scholarship too often refers to Köden as the first Mongol khan to convert. The political reality, however, was different. Köden's submission to Sakya Paṇḍita was nominal. He remained a Mongol first. In real politics, the patron-priest relationship subordinated Sakya Paṇḍita as Köden's subject and ultimately the subject of Güyüg Khan.[32] Most importantly from Köden's perspective, establishing a patron-priest relationship with Sakya Paṇḍita secured the submission of the Tibetan Buddhist world. In 1249, Köden made Sakya Paṇḍita viceroy of the Mongol empire and invested him with temporal power over Tibet. In this capacity, Sakya Paṇḍita sent a letter to Tibetan lords calling upon them to submit to the Mongols and pay tribute, which they did.[33]

The relationship between Köden and Sakya Pandita ended unceremoniously in 1251 when Möngke and the Toluids usurped power from the line of Ögedei and purged enemies of the state, descendants of Ögedei in particular. During this transitional period, Köden and Sakya Paṇḍita both died,[34] yet the relationship established between them survived. Its mantle would be taken up in the persons of Sakya Pandita's nephew, 'Phags pa lama, and Möngke's younger brother, Qubilai.

During the reign of Möngke Khan (b. 1209, r. 1251–1259), the Mongols advanced the status of Buddhism considerably. They began to favor Buddhism over other foreign religions: Christianity, Daoism, and Islam. One illustration of this advancement was the victory of

Buddhism over other religions in a series of debates. One disputation occurred in 1254 when the Franciscan friar, William of Rubruck, debated a Buddhist monk and an Islamic imam over the question of which religion is the truer.[35] The following year, Möngke held another debate, this to resolve the conflict that had ensued following Chinggis Khan's promotion of the Daoism of Changchun over the Buddhism of Yelü Chucai. Möngke summoned protagonists of both parties to court, the Daoist patriarch Li Zhichang and the abbot of the Buddhist Shaolin Monastery in Qara-Qorum, Fuyu Zhanglao. The Buddhists were declared victorious. When contention continued, Möngke scheduled another debate for the following year. However, the premature death of the Daoist interlocutor forced its postponement. Möngke then turned the matter over to Qubilai, who organized a third debate, this in 1258 in his newly built summer palace city, Kaiping (renamed Shangdu in 1264). The Buddhists won again, but dissension lingered. When the dispute devolved into bloodshed in 1280, Qubilai responded by sharply curtailing the prestige and influence of Daoism, a censure from which Daoism never recovered.[36]

The elevation of Buddhism over other foreign religions came with the promotion of Tibetan-rite Buddhism over Chinese and other Buddhist traditions, a choice that has influenced the countenance of Buddhism ever since. The change of preference occurred soon after Möngke's accession. Though upon his investiture in 1251 Möngke initially confirmed Haiyun's appointment as head of Buddhist affairs, by as early as 1252, he replaced Haiyun with Namo, a Kashmiri monk of Tibetan-rite Buddhism.[37]

Scholars speculate over the reason for the Mongols' choice of Tibetan over Chinese Buddhism. A weak, anachronistic argument has been made that the Mongols favored Tibetan Buddhism out of an affinity for Tibetan culture and Tibetan animal husbandry over Chinese culture and Chinese farming.[38] A better argument can be made for Tibetan Buddhist politics of statecraft. The Tibetan Buddhist philosophy of "all exists" (*sarvāsti*) kept with the Mongol philosophy of syncretism, the tradition of holding multiple disparate traditions in kind—rather than imposing a single, monolithic order. One can argue that the Mongols found tantric ritual preferable to others forms of practice. An argument can be made for the superiority of Tibetan scholasticism (as embodied by the likes of Sakya Paṇḍita). In this vein, one argument need not be educed. Sources show clearly that the Mongols preferred Tibetan Buddhism for its magic.[39] Derived from the Iranian tradition of the magi, Mongol religion was steeped in magic, and Mongols regarded Tibetan and Kashmiri Buddhists as the best magicians in the world.[40]

One magical adept who impressed was a certain Karma Paksi (1204–1283), the 2nd Karmapa lama of the Kagyu (Ka' brgyud) school. Karma Paksi was Qubilai's guru for a brief period in 1255. Awed by his magical prowess, Qubilai praised him so to Möngke that Möngke invited the monk for an audience in Qara-Qorum. Karma Paksi left Qubilai for Möngke and spent the remainder of his life in Möngke's court.[41] The loss of Karma Paksi reputedly irritated Qubilai and led to a rift between Sakya and Kagyu schools.[42] After Möngke's death, Qubilai would have him arrested.[43]

Buddhism advanced dramatically under Möngke but within limits. The place of Tibetan Buddhism did not supersede Uygur Buddhism, which by Möngke's reign was a well established institution. Möngke did not support Buddhism to the exclusion of other foreign religions—be they Daoism, Christianity, or Islam. Indeed, he tested the dharma against competing dogmas by subjecting Buddhists to the rigors of debate. Möngke himself was not

Buddhist. As a rule, Mongol khans did not convert to foreign religions (with the important exception of Berke [r. 1257–1266], son of Jochi, whose conversion to Islam came in the face of a threat posed by Hülegü's Ilkhanate and the Toluids). Möngke did not elevate Buddhism to the status of state religion. At its core, the empire's religion remained traditional, the influence of foreign religions circumscribed within the purview of their indigenous priesthood, the hereditary corps of *böge* priests upon whom Möngke relied heavily for counsel and sanction.

A telling account of the state of Mongol religion under Möngke is the travelogue of William of Rubruck, who, as envoy of King Louis IX of France (r. 1226–1270), lived among the Mongols for several years and was afforded audiences with Sartaq (d. 1257), son of Batu (1205–1255), that same Batu, son of Jochi (d. ?1225), and Möngke Khan himself. Having embarked under the false assumption that Mongol khans knew religion in the same way that Christian monarchs did, William of Rubruck mistakenly supposed that Sartaq was an Orthodox Christian and Möngke Khan, a Buddhist *toyin*. In the case of Möngke, William was disabused of this misapprehension straight from the horse's mouth. In an audience of May 1255, Möngke (sovereign of a realm so vast it boggles the mind) disclosed that he was not Buddhist, that Mongols venerate heaven, that as heaven has given different fingers to the hand, it has given different ways to men, and that the Mongol way is to abide by the science of soothsayers, their indigenous priesthood.[44]

FROM THE ACCESSION OF QUBILAI UNTIL THE MONGOLS' EXPULSION FROM CHINA, 1260–1368

During his reign, Qubilai Khan (b. 1215, r. 1260–1294) went one step further than Möngke had. He elevated Tibetan Buddhism to the status of state religion. This advancement might be attributed to Qubilai's profound faith in Buddhism as the world's best vehicle for achieving pacific order. While still in his twenties, Qubilai studied political science under the tutelage of the stable of eminent Buddhist and Confucianist scholars assembled for him by Haiyun. They counseled him on the possibility of using Buddhism to create a world order that might endure in peace and justice indefinitely.[45] As viceroy over north China, Qubilai put his learning into practice utilizing his brain trust to begin a series of experiments in good government. He founded a Pacification Commission and began to transform political administration, city planning, public welfare, and agriculture. At that time, Möngke's regular administration had opposed these efforts and stifled them. Upon Möngke's death in 1259, the opportunity availed itself to make his vision for the future manifest, but he would not be at liberty to do so without first securing his place as his brother's rightful heir.[46]

Qubilai Khan acceded at a time of political fragmentation, when deeds of the past had ripened to cause a rift in the royal family. The thought that Möngke and the Toluids had usurped power from the line of Ögedei muddied the question of succession. This—coupled with the fact that upon Möngke's death, the wealth, power, and territory of the Mongol empire far exceeded historical precedent—left a void of vision for the future. Facing the grim alternative of first determining the rightful khan through bloody tanistry before returning to the trying quest for absolute world dominion, Chinggisids chose instead to settle comfortably into their own individual khanates. The royal family knew that Qubilai, son of Tolui, had a vision for the future but deemed it radical. With many in the family opposed to him, in order to take the throne, Qubilai first had to defeat his youngest brother, Ariq-böke (1219–1266), in battle. Its accomplishment is said to have left him in tears.[47] Once in power, Qubilai Khan saw himself as emperor of *Dai Ön Yeke Mongγol Ulus*, that is to say, the Great Yuan Dynasty and Great Mongol Nation both. Although during his reign the royal family was less coordinated in its political objectives than at times in the past and rebellions ensued, after his conquest of Song (960–1279) in 1279, Qubilai Khan held sway like no other. In Qubilai's mind, he was the Great Khan of the Great Yuan Great Mongol Empire. The world in its entirety belonged to him and him alone. This sovereignty was entrusted to him by his family. They relied on him for their welfare.

As sovereign, Qubilai Khan refashioned the way government interacted with its people. It was said that Qubilai loved his people. Certainly, he strove to provide for them. Building from the ground up, he invested in infrastructure (road-building, shipping, tree planting, well digging), subsidized agriculture and industry, provided healthcare, and succored the poor.[48] At mid-levels of the bureaucracy, he reformed government administration and taxation policies. From the top down, he fitted these reforms under a new constitutional framework. He made Buddhism—Tibetan-rite Buddhism, and the Sakya order in particular—the state religion of a Han-style Confucian dynasty and promoted Buddhism among his kin over other religions throughout the greater empire. He made Sakya Buddhism preeminent over other foreign religions of Islam and Christianity, over Confucianism, over the Mongols' own traditional priesthood, and at times even over the Uygur Buddhist elite.

Instrumental to implementing Qubilai's vision was the service of his guru, Drogön Chögyel Pakpa Lodrö gyeltsen ('Gro mgon Chos rgyal 'Phags pa Blo gros rgyal mtshan, 1235–1280), 'Phags pa, for short. Born of the noble Khon ('Khon) family, he was but age nine when his uncle, Sapan, embarked with him and his younger brother, Chagna, for Köden's camp in 1244. In 1253, following the deaths of Sapan and Köden, Qubilai, age thirty-eight, brought the eighteen-year-old 'Phags pa to Kaiping and took him into his retinue. In 1255, 'Phags pa returned to Tibet to receive final ordination.[49] After his return to Kaiping in 1258, 'Phags pa participated in the grand debate that saw Buddhists triumph over Daoists. That same year, he officiated rites with Qubilai that would be formative of Mongolian Buddhism and influential to modern Buddhism.

'Phags pa guided Qubilai and Qubilai's consort, Chabi (< Ch. *cibei* 慈悲, for Skt. *maitrī* "loving kindness," 1227–1281), in an initiation in the Hevajra tantra, and he and Qubilai reestablished the patron-priest relationship first established between Köden and Sakya Pandita.[50] Here again, though in rhetoric 'Phags pa held ultimate authority, in reality Qubilai was lord. While this occurred when Möngke was still alive to reestablish Mongol control over Tibet, when Qubilai came to reign, Qubilai was sovereign, and 'Phags pa his subject. Their specific patron-priest relationship would become the foundation of a Borjigid-Buddhist world order that held sway in East Asia for generations. During the Yuan, the relationship transferred to each succeeding emperor and chief priest. After the expulsion of the Mongols from China, it remained the precedent for future patron-priest relationships. It was appropriated by the Ming, co-opted by the Gelukpa, and eventually transferred to the Qing. With the collapse of the Qing dynasty in 1912, Tibetans considered the relationship over. In modern times China has used Qubilai and 'Phags pa's compact to justify its claim of sovereignty over Tibet.[51]

When in 1260 Qubilai founded the Yuan Zhongtong 中統 government, 'Phags pa presided over his enthronement ceremony. In 1261, Qubilai bestowed on him the title "State Preceptor"

(*Ulus-un baγsi*; Ch. *guoshi*), granting him authority over Buddhist clergy.[52] In 1264, Qubilai sent 'Phags pa on official business back to Tibet. During his years at Sakya, 'Phags pa acted as a Mongol. He kept Mongol tradition, wore Mongol dress, and imposed Mongol ways. When he returned to court in 1268, he carried out the important task of realigning the Buddhist calendar with the Chinese. (In this realignment, the first month of the year coincided not with the first Earthly Branch or Rat term of the Chinese calendar but with the third term, the Tiger Month.[53]) On March 17, 1269 'Phags pa introduced a writing system of his own invention. Drawing from Tibetan, Uygur, and Brahmi systems, the design of his quadratic alphabet (commonly referred to as 'Phags pa script) succeeded in accurately rendering all languages in the dynasty.[54]

In 1270, 'Phags pa promulgated an annual program of Buddhist ritual to regulate the occasions of court life and court and public interaction. A sure sign of Buddhism's preeminence, in this program, a Buddhist monk presided over an emperor's enthronement. The investiture ceremony included initiations into the rites of Hevajra and Mahākāla. As an example of a public ritual in the Buddhist calendar, on the fifteenth day of the second month, Buddhist monks led a circumambulation of the imperial palace for the suppression of demons and protection of the state.[55]

In 1278, 'Phags pa composed a primer of Buddhist teaching entitled "Elucidation of the Knowable" (*Shes bya rab gsal*) on behalf of Qubilai's son, Jinggim (1243–1286), the Heir-Apparent (since 1273). Though said to have been composed at Jinggim's request, tradition dictated that the heir apparent be educated as an awakened bodhisattva with this type of guidebook for the pious layman. Known in Tibetan as *shé dzö* (*bshad mdzod*; "treasury of explanations"), this sort of formal catechism was often composed for the edification of kings and princes.[56] Unfortunately for Jinggim, he was implicated in court intrigue and, in 1285, preceded his father in death. The catechism itself, however, survived. Originally composed in Tibetan, Chinese and Mongolian translations were also made. The Tibetan version is preserved in the *Sa skya bka' 'bum* (Vol. 13) and the Chinese version in the Taisho Canon (T32, no. 1645). Two Mongolian versions, a faithful Middle Mongolian text, *Medegdekün-i belgetey-e geyigülügči* ("Prescient Elucidation of What is to be Known") and a 16th-century recension, the *Čiqula kereglegči* ("Essentials for Practice"), are extant.[57] Written in the abhidharma tradition, the text, which opens with an invocation to Sakya Pandita, is composed in five parts. Part Three, a section devoted to the animate world, gives the genesis of a Mongolian Buddhist world. In a genealogy proceeding from the deific sage-king Mahāsammata to the Solar Race of Kings to the kings of Tibet, the text goes on to say that 3,250 years after buddha's nirvana, Chinggis Khan came to rule the world.[58]

Unique to Qubilai's vision was the degree of secular power invested in Sakya monks over a Han-style Confucian dynasty. Elevating Buddhism over Confucianism required the invention of extraordinary institutions. In 1264, Qubilai created an office to govern Tibet, the "Bureau of Buddhist and Tibetan Affairs," originally named *Zongzhi yuan* 總制院 and later restructured under the name *Xuanzheng yuan* 宣政院.[59] The official business Qubilai sent 'Phags pa back to Tibet for was to implement and run it. It is worth mentioning that at the same time he also sent back 'Phags pa's brother, Chagna, investing him with secular power over Central Tibet. Pacifying Tibet proved no easy matter. When Chagna died unexpectedly in 1267, rebellion ensued. Only through swift and ruthless suppression was Tibet brought to heel.[60]

In time, Qubilai placed Sakya monks in positions of authority over the affairs of the entire empire. This meant placing them in positions over those who formerly had held them. Many felt diminished by the Sakyapa's meteoric rise to power—priests of the Mongols' sacerdotal tradition, Daoists, Syriac-rite Christians, Chan Buddhists, Uygur Buddhists, and Confucian scholars to name but a few. At court, this prerogative created tensions between Sakya prelates on one hand and members of the Uygur Buddhist aristocracy and Confucian scholars on the other. When on December 18, 1271 Qubilai proclaimed the Yuan Dynasty, his decision to subordinate the Confucian estate to Sakya Buddhism left the Confucians especially aggrieved. Court intrigue from these tensions from time to time spilled over into political violence.

An example of such intrigue was the case of Sangke (< Tib. *sengge* "lion," d. 1291). In 1287, Qubilai appointed Sangke as Chancellor of the Supreme Secretariat, a position that wielded immense power and was traditionally held by a Confucian. A Uygurized Tibetan who knew Tibetan, Chinese, Mongolian, and Uygur, Sangke had once served as 'Phags pa's interpreter. Upon 'Phags pa's death in 1280, Qubilai had sent him (along with seven thousand Mongol troops) to settle unrest in Tibet. As chancellor, Qubilai put Sangke in charge of the finances of the entire dynasty. Faced with a severe budget shortfall, Sangke introduced a new devalued currency, procured new stores of silver, expanded trade, cut expenses and raised revenues and taxes, imposed austerity measures, repealed religious exemptions, and fired incompetent officials, resorting to judicial execution of political opponents when deemed necessary. Yet, at the same time, he showed great favor to Buddhism and his friends and accumulated much wealth for himself. With the opportunity this malfeasance provided to attack him, his adversaries denounced Sangke in the presence of Qubilai, who in 1291 had him dismissed, disgraced, and executed.[61]

Precedent for investing Buddhism with secular power over a Han-style Confucian dynasty could be found in Tangut statecraft, and Qubilai availed himself of several Xixia institutions. One was the preceptorship position. By his accession, Qubilai's predecessors had already appropriated the Tangut Buddhist "preceptor" position, using the title "National Preceptor" or "Preceptor of the Nation" (*Ulus-un baγsi*; Ch. *guoshi* 國師) to designate the head of all Buddhist clergy. In 1270, Qubilai renamed the title "Imperial Preceptor" or "Preceptor of the Emperor" (*dishi* 帝師)and invested it with real power—power to speak with the authority of the emperor. This secular power he invested in its first recipient, 'Phags pa, in recognition of his many achievements (including his triumphant invention of the quadratic writing system) on the eve of the declaration of the Yuan dynasty in 1271.[62] Thereafter, the position transferred from one leading monk to another. It remained powerful throughout Yuan rule in China and even somewhat beyond.[63]

Another important Tangut influence was an imperial cult of Mahākāla. As the god of infinite time, the dharmapāla Mahākāla is annihilator of all things—even time itself. Known in Chinese as Daheitian (大黑天 "Great Black Heaven") and in Tibetan as both Nagpo Chenpo (nag po chen po "Great Black One") and Gönpo (mgon po "Protector"), the Mongols know the deity as Yeke Qara ("the Great Black One") but especially as Gombo. Personifying ferocity and intelligence, Mahākāla was the tutelary genius of the Sakya order in general and 'Phags pa in particular. Following Tangut precedent, Qubilai made Mahākāla worship a cult of imperial empowerment.[64] Mahākāla became his spiritual guide or yidam, and Qubilai himself became the embodiment of Mahākāla, the great protector of Buddhism. A ritual, which possibly involved blood offerings, invoked Mahākāla to grant victory in battle. Following Qubilai's reign, initiation in the rites of Mahākāla became part of every Yuan emperor's enthronement. Eventually, Mahākāla became the tutelary deity of the Mongols at large. From the Mongols, the cult would pass to the Manchus, who, centuries later, built a temple complex to Mahākāla in their capital city, Mukden.[65]

Keeping with Tangut precedent, Mongolian Buddhism also revitalized a cult of venerating the emperor as an emanation of Mañjuśrī through pilgrimage to Wutaishan (五臺山). Associated with the Huayan school, the mountain terrace Wutaishan (五臺山 "Five-Tower Peak") in present-day Shanxi Province had been a pilgrimage site to the earthly abode of Mañjuśrī, the bodhisattva of wisdom, since the Sui-Tang era.[66] The cult drew pilgrims from as far away as India, Kashmir, Korea, and even Japan. 'Phags pa himself is said to have made pilgrimage to the site where he composed eulogies extolling Qubilai as an emanation of Mañjuśrī. In these eulogies he bestowed upon Qubilai the epithet Sechen Khan ("Wise Emperor"), a title by which Qubilai has henceforth come to be known. During the Qing, the Mongols reaffirmed their reverence for the site.[67]

Mongolian Buddhism also assimilated the Tangut cult of venerating the emperor as a *cakravartin*, or "world-turning king." In his 1278 catechism, 'Phags pa represented Chinggis Khan as a cakravartin bodhisattva, an enlightened sage king who rules the world by turning the wheel of the dharma. Whereas in this case the title is retroactive, Qubilai and Mongol emperors henceforth actively assumed the epithet and carried its mantle. In 1267, Qubilai propagated the cult by erecting a golden wheel, symbol of the cakravartin, over the main gate to Daidu, his capital city.[68]

An alms-giver's duty is to support the Three Jewels: buddha, dharma, and saṃgha. A refuge from the world, its trials and tribulations, in ways of welfare and comity, their benefit to individuals and communities is great. But they do not come cheap. Qubilai was by no means the first sovereign to finance Buddhism, but the degree of his munificence was unprecedented. This devotion he passed on to his noble-born brethren, princes and wealthy aristocrats, and their descendants, who took it upon themselves to outdo each other in outlaying funds for establishing Buddhist institutions in their individual appanages and estates. When Tibetan Buddhism became the state religion, Mongol lords did not cease to support other traditions and religions. They continued to fund various Buddhist sects, Daoism, Christianity, and Islam. Yet, they promoted Tibetan Buddhism (and the Sakyapa in particular) with generosity estimated at roughly half of all government expenditures—literally tons of gold and silver and thousands upon thousands of bolts of silk and gold-spun cloth—all to produce nothing but the finest works of art and architecture and to support the most learned of monks.[69]

Central to the creation of a Buddhist world is the creation of a network of Buddhist centers. Yuan temples had an understated, elegant architecture that kept with Tang precedent.[70] Established along the routes, temples served the needs of local communities, facilitated diplomatic and mercantile exchange, and disseminated objects of veneration in the way of texts and icons. Mongols invested heavily to establish this network, spending vast sums on temple construction. Yesün-Temür (b. 1293, r. 1323–1328) is said to have granted 20,000 *ding* of cash and 1,000 *qing* of land for construction of the "Heavenly *Yuan* (Origin) Perpetuate the Holy (Emperor) Temple" (*Tianyuan Yansheng Si* 天元延聖寺).[71] Qubilai himself funded eight great Buddhist temples.[72]

In the west, the Mongols spent lavishly to build Buddhist infrastructure. They restored ancient Buddhist centers Islam had left to ruin and constructed visually magnificent temples and monasteries of Tibetan architecture. As microcosms of the universe, these monasteries became centers for education, the study of Sanskrit, manufacturing, agriculture, commerce, and moneylending, and were often favored over established Islamic concerns.[73] Mongols connected their newly constructed Buddhist infrastructure in the Ilkhanate with that of the greater empire. Building Buddhist edifices in strings across all major routes, they joined East and West in a network of Buddhist institutions that extended all the way from the Pacific Ocean to the Black Sea, Anatolia, and Armenia.[74]

Grander still, Qubilai funded the construction of two capital cities, Shangdu (上都) and Khanbaliq or Daidu 大都, as Buddhist world centers. In 1256, while still viceroy of North China and at the same time Möngke Khan was completing the magnificent pagoda and great temple of Qara-Qorum, Qubilai built himself a stately summer palace as a Buddhist garden paradise. Originally named Kaiping (開平), with the establishment of the Zhiyuan 至元 government in 1264, he renamed the center Shangdu (上都 "Upper Capital"). There, as was learned from Marco Polo, he housed a large enclave of Buddhist faithful and clergy, monks known by their nationalities as Tibetan or Kashmiri. These monks officiated civil order by establishing spatial and temporal order and regulating ritual practice. Marco Polo reported that they practiced necromancy, cooking and eating the flesh of those they had executed.[75] They practiced forms of magic, such as weather magic (to prevent storm clouds from passing over the palace) and legerdemain (juggling to entertain).[76] In regulating ritual practice, they appropriated rites of the indigenous *böge* priesthood. Marco Polo observed that at the beginning of fall in the Mongol calendar (August 28), Buddhist chaplains officiated the traditional Mongol mare's milk aspersion ritual, formerly conducted, as William of Rubruck mentioned, by the *böge*.[77] These *böge* soothsayers were also present at Shangdu and retained their prerogative over certain ritual practices. One of these was the cult of dead ancestors. Marco Polo noted that on the seventh day of the seventh month they faced north, uttered the names of Chinggis Khan and other deceased khans, and made libations of mare's milk in their honor.[78]

Qubilai's capital city, Khanbaliq or Daidu 大都, modern Beijing, was built over the Jurchen capital, Zhongdu, which itself was built over the Khitan capital, Yanjing. According to the city's architectural plan, Buddhist monasteries in the four cardinal directions and at the four corners of the city made Buddhism the symbolic foundation of Qubilai's world.[79] Within the Yuan capital, Qubilai established several Buddhist centers and erected a number of Buddhist temples and monuments—most of which have since been destroyed. One of these was Candan Juu ("Sandalwood Temple"), home of a large sandalwood buddha. Legend has it that the ancient Sandalwood Buddha resides only in the presence of a righteous king and possesses the magical power to walk from one to the next. Having come to rest in the realm of Qubilai, the temple burned to the ground during the Manchu Qing dynasty, around 1900, in the Boxer Rebellion.[80]

To enliven his realm with Buddhist objects of veneration, in 1273, Qubilai appointed a Nepalese artisan, Master Anige (1244–1278), head of the Directorate General for the Management of Artisans.[81] 'Phags pa had discovered Anige in a search for a worthy artist to erect a golden stupa in Amdo (Qinghai) in honor of Qubilai's enthronement.[82] When admirers judged Anige's achievement as surpassing, 'Phags pa presented him to Qubilai, who went on to commission Anige for numerous other works, including temples, stupas, and buddha sculptures in Daidu, Shangdu, and elsewhere. Anige did the metalwork decoration for both the astronomical and timekeeping instruments at the Daidu Observatory and on the royal family's imperial standards. He did portraiture and painted Qubilai and Chabi for the imperial temple. A few of Anige's works survive. The famous portraits of Qubilai and Chabi now hang in the National Palace Museum in Taipei, Taiwan.[83] His White Pagoda of Miaoying Temple still stands in Beijing.

Promulgating the dharma in a realm as vast and diverse as the Great Yuan Great Mongol Nation was no simple matter entailing translation into the languages of manifold nations. As an example of the weight of the task, in the Yuan proper, the 1345 inscription on the Juyongguan Gate of the Great Wall is a hexaglot work in Chinese, Tangut, Uygur, Tibetan, Mongolian, and Sanskrit languages. The Ilkhanate regularly patronized translation into Arabic and Persian. In this endeavor, Mongols supported not only the scholars and linguists necessary to translate and explicate texts but also the artisans and publishers requisite to print and publish them. To publish text, publishers sometimes used movable type but principally relied on xylography. Inking woodblocks was an efficient way to mass produce text but the initial carving of the blocks was time consuming and required skilled engravers. Numerous monasteries published texts but mass-production occurred at but a few centers. These were located in Daidu in the north and in the West Lake region and the cities of Suzhou and Hangzhou in the south. With the southern publishing houses still beyond his control when Qubilai first ascended, the publication of Buddhist literature increased significantly with their acquisition after the conquest of the Song dynasty (960–1279) in 1279.[84]

To undertake the concerted effort of translating, explicating, and mass-producing Buddhist literature for each nation in the empire, the Mongols assembled a college of distinguished sages from the Chinese, Tangut, Uygur, and Tibetan Buddhist nations. Incipient as a Buddhist people, Mongols themselves contributed little to this corps. Sanskritists were necessary to maintain Sanskrit as the standard medium of Buddhist expression. One Sanskritist was the Uygur Karunadas (Skt. Karuṇadāsa "servant of compassion"), a member of the Yuan academy whom Qubiliai had had study Tibetan under 'Phags pa.[85] Because Mongols were disseminating the esoteric, tantric Buddhism of Tibet, the majority of scholars were of Tibetan extraction or (as the Uygur Karunadas) at least lettered in Tibetan Buddhist tradition. The intellectual hub for this coterie was the Sakya school, which upheld the high standard in learning established by its founding Five Venerable Masters (Sakya Pandita being one). Embodying the school's tradition of scholastic excellence was the eminent textual scholar and translator, Butön Rinchendrup (Bu ston Rin chen grub, 1290–1364). Butön cataloged Buddhist texts, composed an important history of Buddhism (*Chos 'byung*, 1322), and explicated the important cosmographic treatise, the *Kālacakra tantra*.[86]

A vital contingent in this corps were Uygurs.[87] As members of the aristocracy, the Uygurs knew Mongolian and the Mongols knew Uygur (such that Mongols often deferred to Uygur when speaking at court). The Uygur and Mongolian languages bear much commonality in terms of phonology, grammar, and vocabulary, and Uygur scribes had created the Mongolian writing system by adapting their own Aramaic-derived Uygur script. For centuries, Uygur tradition had provided translation services for up-and-coming Buddhist nations such as the Khitan, Tangut, Jurchen, and Korean. Uygur sages knew Buddhist scripture, its meaning, and the depths of its complexity. They knew Sanskrit, the intermediary languages of Inner Asia through which the dharma passed, and how to render Buddhism's difficult terms and concepts, establish grammatical parallels, coin phrases, and compose verse. In short, they knew how to translate in an artful and accurate way.[88] These factors made the Uygur school of translation instrumental in transmitting the dharma into Mongolian.[89]

During the reign of Qubilai (1260–1294), translation into Mongolian was an ad hoc phenomenon. Sonom-gara (Tib. *bsod nam* "merit" + Skt. *kara* "maker") translated Sakya Pandita's aphorisms, the *Subhāṣitaratnanidhi* (Tib. *Lek shé* [Legs bshad] "elegant sayings," Mong. *Erdeni-yin sang* "treasury of jewels"), from Tibetan into Mongolian specifically for the edification of Qubilai.[90] A mandala-treatise written by 'Phags pa was translated specifically for Köden's son, Jibik-Temür.[91] Around the turn of the 14th century, however, publishing houses began to mass-produce translations of Buddhist literature.

Translation into Mongolian was spearheaded by the monk Chosgi odsir (Tib. Chos kyi 'od ser, fl. 1305–1321). Of uncertain extraction, one might deduce from biographical information and his extant works that Chosgi odsir was a Uygur born in Tibet and trained under the Sakyapa. In addition to Uygur, he was lettered in Tibetan and Mongolian. Around 1305, he translated Śāntideva didactic poem, *Bodhicaryāvatāra*, and composed a verse auto-commentary later included in the Buddhist canon in its own right.[92] In 1312, by decree of Emperor Ayurbarwada (1311–1320) one thousand copies of his translation and commentary were block-printed at the Great Temple of the White Stupa in Daidu where they were *olan-a tügügülbe* ("distributed to the many").[93] Another extant translation of his is a hymn to the Sakyapa protectress, Mahakali. Handsomely rewarded for his efforts, Chosgi odsir was eventually set up in a monastery in Daidu as head of a circle of translators. A disciple of his, Sherab Sengge (Tib. *shes rab seng ge* "lion of wisdom"), translated numerous important works into Mongolian[94] including the *Pañcarakṣā* (Mong. *Tabun sakiyan neretü sudur* "Fivefold Protection Sutra"),[95] *Suvarṇāprobhasottama-sūtra* (Mong. *Altan gereltü sudur* "Golden Light Sutra"),[96] and his master, Chosgi odsir's Tibetan translation of the *Lalitavistara-sūtra* (Mong. *Burqan baγsi-yin arban qoyar ǰokiyangγui* "The Twelve Acts of Buddha").[97]

Translation has direct benefit for teaching the literate, that is to say, the elite, but even greater indirect benefit to the entire populace. Dissemination of the dharma brings merit to those involved in the process of its creation. Hearing scripture read aloud inculcates Buddhist teaching as well as reading it for oneself does. What is more, scripture holds benefit as a talisman. At the time, the world took the very existence Buddhist scripture as a sign of peace. Especially irenic was the publication of a Buddhist canon, the reading of which constituted a potent, magical ritual for instilling comity. To this end, Yuan emperors funded the publication of canons for the peoples of the various Buddhist nations under their sway. These included a Tangut canon (*Xixia zang* 西夏藏, completed in 1302), two separate Chinese Buddhist canons, the *Puning canon* 普寧藏 (which was lost in a fire) and the *Qisha canon* 磧砂藏 (still extant), and the 1312 Tibetan canon (*bka' 'gyur*) and commentary (*bstan 'gyur*) compiled and published in manuscript form at Narthang Monastery in Tibet. The efficacy of this magic is clear in the 1340 Inscription of Arugh, Prince of Yunnan, wherein residents of Yunnan erected a stele inscription memorializing the prince's contribution of 150 pieces of silver to Kunming Monastery for an annual reading of the Buddhist canon in the name of peace.[98]

In veneration of the Three Jewels, the Mongols brought Buddhism to its widest dissemation across Asia and the Near East. A sure sign of Mongol esteem for Tibetan Buddhism was the nation's missionary work to spread the dharma throughout the world—even unto places where it was either previously unknown or long absent. When in 1251 he mounted his campaign to overthrow the Abbasid Caliphate, Hülegü (1218–1265) overran Kashmir before striking at Baghdad and came to revere West Tibetan Kashmiri monks of the Pakmo drupa (Phag mo gru pa) sect. Upon establishing the Ilkhanate (1258–1335) in 1258, he made Buddhism the religion of court. This brought Islam's adversary into the heart of the Mohammedan world.[99] With Muslims and Buddhists persistently at odds, the decision was radical and destined to fail—not for lack of trying, however.[100]

As subjects of Qubilai and the Yuan, the Ilkhanids favored the Pakmo drupa but supported monks from multiple Buddhist groups: Uygur, Tibetan, Kashmiri, and Chinese. Ilkhanids sponsored the translation of Buddhist scripture into Persian and Arabic. In these translations, translators translated "Buddha" as "Allah." The great Jewish physician, Rashid al-Din, used the teaching of a Kashmiri hermit monk to write a Buddhist catechism for Muslims.[101] In his *Compendium of Chronicles,* Rashid al-Din stated that before acceptance of Islam, the inhabitants of Mecca and Medina were Buddhists and that Chinggis Khan was a descendent of the tribes of Noah through Japheth.[102]

Mongols did least to establish Buddhism in the Ulus of Jochi, where Berke had converted to Islam already in 1257. Buddhist dominion there was limited largely to the reign Toqto'a (r. 1291–1312). Toqto'a came to power by using sympathy for Buddhism among the nobility to overthrow the standing Islamic government. Once in power, he made Uygur Buddhism the court religion before converting to Islam during the final years of his reign.[103]

In the Ulus of Chaghatay, on the other hand, Buddhism flourished. Its cities of Bukhara, Samarkand, Kashgar, Khotan, Beshbalik, Turpan, and Dunhuang had been Buddhist centers since Buddhism's inception in the region. In Khotan, where Chinese monks first heard the stories that became the *Sutra on the Wise and the Foolish* (Ch. *Xianyu jing* 賢愚經), the Buddhist establishment is said to date back to the city's founding in the 1st century BC. In 366, an itinerant monk is said to have dug the first cave grotto of Mogao near Dunhuang. In the 5th century, the great translator, Kumārajīva, was born and raised in Kucha.

In the Ulus of Chaghatay, less tension existed between Muslims and Buddhists than in other realms of the empire. Here, populations of Muslims and Buddhists had been living in proximity for centuries. Though the populace of the region was predominantly Muslim, aristocracies had often been Buddhist. The Khitans who, having fled from the Jurchen in the east to establish the Xiliao (西遼) "Western Liao" or Khara Khitai Khanate, continued to rule the region as Buddhists. Both they and the Uygur aristocracy made a policy of tolerance. In kind, Muslim subjects curbed the spirit of *jihād.*[104] When Mongols came to reign, infighting among members of the royal family notwithstanding, Chaghataids publicly perpetuated politics of peace. Rather than aggrieving one faction or another with either Sharia law or Buddhist dharma, Chaghataids promulgated the *ǰasaγ* of Chinggis Khan—this loyalty to the Chinggisid principle of sovereignty being a legacy of their patriarch, Chinggis Khan's second son, Chaghadai (d. 1242).

Buddhism flourished especially in the eastern half of the realm, where Uygurs held sway and Buddhist tradition was strong. In the early years of the empire, Buddhism thrived not so much due the designs of Chaghataid khans, but because the region was the home of Uygur Buddhism. In 1253, prior to Hülegü's founding the Ilkhanid Buddhist state, William of Rubruck's first encounter with Buddhism on his overland journey from Constantinople to the Mongol capital city, Qara-Qorum, came in the vicinity of Lake Balkhash. This was Uygur Buddhism under Chaghataid auspices. He noted the gilded opulence of its temples and remarked on the privilege of Uygur Buddhism over every other Buddhist sect.[105]

After Chaghataid khans came to recognize Qubilai and the Yuan, they too began to favor Tibetan Buddhism. The Chaghataid khan, Du'a (b. 1274, r. 1282–1307), actively supported the Drigun ('Bri gung) sect.[106] Eljigidei (r. 1327–1330) founded Buddhist temples.[107] Tarmashirin's (r. 1331–1334) very name (< Skt. *dharmaśrī*) suggests Buddhist upbringing. Though he converted his realm to Islam, he did so for political expedience without ceasing patronage of Buddhism. His successors, while continuing to espouse Islam, nonetheless continued to erect Buddhist temples and support its institutions.[108] In 1339, Yisün-temür (r. 1338–1342) issued a decree protecting a Yogācāra temple and its vineyards from banditry.[109] Tughlugh-temür (1347–1362), though a convert to Islam, nonetheless invited a Tibetan Buddhist, the Karmapa incarnate lama Rölpé dorje (Rol pa'i rdo rje, 1340–1383), to be his guru.[110] Attested by the great trove of documents found in Turpan, Chaghataids amassed a prodigious output of Buddhist literature. Compiled over a period from 1326 to 1369, much of this literature was written in Mongolian.[111] Chaghataids controlled Dunhuang and governed activity at the nearby Mogao and Yulin caves, where, until at least 1357, Mongol patrons continued to fund the creation of new grottoes.[112]

Though Qubilai's patronage of Buddhism was unprecedented, as with his predecessors', it too had its limits. Qubilai did not allow his compact with 'Phags pa to turn the Yuan into an exclusively Buddhist nation (in the way that the Holy Roman Empire was solely Roman Catholic). Not only did he support extra-Sakya Buddhist schools, he continued his patronage of other foreign religions such as Christianity, Daoism, and Islam as well. His deep faith in Buddhism notwithstanding, for Qubilai, alone at the top, surrounded by an old circle of close advisors, little changed. He wore many hats as it were, played many roles, as every sovereign must, but remained a Mongol first. Throughout his reign, he continued to uphold Mongol custom. He venerated the cult of heaven and retained the Mongols' indigenous priesthood. Though recognized as a Buddhist *cakravartin*, he personally never fully submitted to Buddhism.[113]

Even so, the reign of Qubilai Khan was a watershed moment in world history. At his passing in 1294, the Yuan dynasty, greater Mongol empire, and the world at large stood transformed by his radical vision of a Mongolian Buddhist world order.[114] In his wake, succeeding generations of Mongols had no way back to the Chinggisid principle that governed his predecessors. His reign closed the age of kings—when mighty his grandfather Chinggis Khan, and his brother Möngke reigned supreme—and heralded the dawn of the age of soteriological dominion.

With his descendants born into a Buddhist world, the Mongol conversion to Buddhism was complete. Mongols adopted Buddhist names, a common name being Sambuu (from Chinese *sanbao* 三寶 "the three jewels"). They began to give their children over to monasteries to become monks. They couched their propaganda in the moralistic idealism that Möngke Khan had eschewed. It might be presumed that they began to live their lives in accordance with Buddhist teaching as well.

A telling sign of their conversion is the rewriting of the history of their patron, Chinggis Khan. The *Yuanshi* eulogy of Chinggis Khan says that in 1266 he received a new title, Lawgiving Martial Emperor. This new title marked the re-creation of the Mongol world in Chinese dynastic tradition. Then, in 1309, he received the expanded title: Lawgiving Martial Emperor for whom the Dharma and Heaven Opened the Way to Good Fortune. This title marked the re-creation of the Mongol world as a Chinese-Buddhist-Mongolian world.

Although nominally coequal, in the relationship between dharma and heaven, just as the priest held ultimate authority over the patron in the patron-priest relationship, the dharma's propaganda, by the very nature of its abstract, rationalized faith in the unempirical, supersedes the naturalistic Mongol propaganda of heaven. This primacy is evident in a passage from the 1346 Buddhist Inscription of Qara-Qorum. The inscription states that the power of Buddhist faith creates

> the capacity of the Great Holy Man to regard the "Four Seas" [i.e., the World] as anthills, to regard the "Eight Limits (of the Earth)" as a pinch of soil, to put the whole universe in a bag, and to roll up the rivers and mountains as a mat.[115]

That is to say, through reliance on abstraction, Buddhism has the capacity to transcend world order limited to that given merely by the empirical dome of heaven.

Eventually, as the power of the emperorship became more formal than real, Mongol sovereignty yielded in obeisance to the dharma. This subordination is evident in the Vajrabhairava mandala, a large silk tapestry dated *c.* 1328–1329, now kept at the Metropolitan Museum of Art in New York City. Below the mandala's central deity, the Conqueror of Death, Yamāntaka, in the painting's lower right corner sit in prayerful supplication from right to left respectively the emperors, Tuq-Temür (r. 1328–1329, 1329–1332) and Qoshila (r. 1329), their respective wives sitting to the left.[116] Such representation would have been unthinkable to Qubilai Khan and his predecessors. Recounting the Mongols' conversion, the *Fozu lidai tongzai* (佛祖歷代通載) of 1333 says that Chinggis Khan ruled from the North over many nations with many languages as a king who turns a wheel of iron. Following his brother, Möngke, on the throne of emperor and king, Qubilai subjected many nations and territories and through his might extended the frontier. He adopted the teachings of the buddha and transformed his people in accordance with the law. Consequently, Buddhism flourished twice as much as it had before.[117]

Ironically, not long after the Mongols embraced the Buddhist world they had created, that world turned against them. The year 1351 was hard for the Mongols. For several years, the Yuan had been operating on a budget deficit that increased yearly. In 1351, the Yuan was visited by the bubonic plague. Now spread throughout Eurasia and North Africa, it caused a major contraction of the Mongol world economy. Since 1344, when massive flooding altered the course of the Yellow River, the Mongols had been funding public works projects to repair the damage. Otherwise insolvent, in 1351, the government issued an unbacked paper currency to pay wages to the thousands of workers enlisted to rebuild the Grand Canal. In the hyperinflationary spiral that ensued, those workers, facing severe economic hardship, rebelled. Donning red turbans and red clothes, rebels fought under the leadership of the White Lotus Society (Ch. *Da bai lian she* 大白蓮社), a Buddhist millennial group created to usher in apocalypse when the end was imminent. Although by 1354 the Mongols had put down the initial rebellion, by 1355 the Yuan dynasty was in shambles. That year, the "Red Turban" rebellion resumed under the leadership of a former monk, Zhu Yuanzhang (1328–1398). In 1368 Zhu drove his forces north to Daidu and on September 14, forced the reigning Yuan emperor, Toghan-Temür (b. 1320, r. 1333–1370), to flee north. That same year Zhu Yuanzhang founded the Ming dynasty (1369–1644) and came to reign as the Hongwu emperor.[118]

In the aftermath, Confucian scholars, rather unfairly it seems, blamed the Yuan collapse on emperor Toghan-Temür's personal deficiencies—in particular, a preoccupation with tantric sex. Toghan-Temür famously kept a troupe of female dancers in the imperial palace in Daidu. It offered erotic performances as entertainment to him, the emperor, whom they worshipped as a bodhisattva. The *Yuanshi* (205, p. 4583) dismissed these pursuits as debauchery. A Mongol chronicle, the *Altan tobči*, presented Toghan-Temür bemoaning his humbled estate. Stung by having his good name sullied with accusations of lewdness and perversion, he lamented the loss of the Yuan capital, saying that he lost his poor Daidu while propagating the laws of religion and becoming accustomed to it.[119]

FROM MONGOL EXPULSION FROM CHINA UNTIL ALTAN KHAN'S CONVERSION, 1368–1578

After Toghan-Temür's ignominious retreat of 1368, the Yuan contracted but did not fall. Toghan-Temür died of dysentery in 1370, but Yuan officials reestablished Qara-Qorum as a capital and inaugurated a successor, Emperor Ayushiridara (r. 1370–1378). That year, Ming forces invaded, burned Qara-Qorum, and drove the Mongols far to the north. When the Ming army retreated, however, the Mongols returned. After military operations proved unavailing, the two states stalemated. Initially, Yuan and Ming refused to recognize the other's legitimacy, but, as the gateway to Chinese industry, Ming held the upper hand. Yuan eventually weakened. It recognized the Ming emperor as the legitimate Son of Heaven and began to send officials on tribute missions. In return for tribute, Ming showed Mongols beneficence. This it expressed with the granting of titles and presenting of gifts. In 1407, the Yongle emperor agreed to horse fairs that, in exchange for horses and animal products, afforded Mongols access to Chinese grain, cloth, silk, iron kettles, and other goods. With tribute relations favorable to the Mongols, the two states settled into a fraught but stable coexistence. For another 267 years, the Mongols persevered on the Mongolian Plateau as the northern Yuan dynasty (1368–1635)—before finally giving way to the Manchu Qing dynasty (1636–1912) in 1636.

In the history of Buddhism, the era of the northern Yuan is analogous to the Hellenistic era following the fall of the Persian Empire in the 4th century BC. During the Hellenistic era, the seeds of soteriological religion sown during the Persian Empire came to fruition in the emergence of Buddhism and other soteriological religions—including Christianity and, eventually, Islam. During the northern Yuan, seeds sown by Qubilai Khan and the Mongols again came to fruition, this time in the maturation of Buddhism as an exclusive world dominion. During the northern Yuan, Mongols transformed Buddhism into its modern form. They made Géluk Buddhism the preeminent order not merely of Mongolian Buddhism but Buddhism in general and afforded it supremacy over the prerogative of the aristocracy. This transformation came not through the auspices of the Yuan itself, however, but through acts of insubordination against the state. Interestingly, in the cases of both Hellenism and the northern Yuan, the seminary that raised Buddhism was political instability among the aristocracy in the aftermath of the fall of a great empire.

With Manchu hegemony after 1636, East Asia returned to an era of relative stability. Until that time, however, the existence of the northern Yuan as an unseated, weak, and declining state sunk East Asia into a prolonged period of unrest. The question at hand was over hereditary legitimacy. Legitimacy separates a sovereign from a tyrant. Without it, one simply has no right to rule. Since 1206, political legitimacy across Eurasia came through the line of Chinggis Khan. So long as the northern Yuan retained the claim to sovereignty, the problem was how the world could realign when those who were rich and powerful were denied the legitimacy of those who had grown poor and weak. Without legitimacy, no matter how prosperous one might be, one could not form one's own state, and without one's own state one could not vie for relations with other states. Central to the issue were relations with the Ming. Mighty lords wanted special tribute relations with Ming China because that relationship brought economic advantage, but Ming policy denied them to those it deemed illegitimate.

The epitome of a nation that possessed wealth and power but lacked legitimacy were the Oirats. Having married into the royal family, the non-Chinggisid Oirats were prominent even in the time of Chinggis Khan. Under Qubilai, with the Yuan centered in China, they were charged with governing the traditional Mongolian homeland. Qubilai honored them as the only non-Chinggisids permitted the drink the fresh mare's milk of the imperial herd of white horses. He honored their chieftain with the title "Grand Master" (from Ch. *taishi* 太師), a hereditary honorific of the first degree granted to non-Chinggisids in recognition of continued service to the empire. After Yuan was expelled from China, in resuming control of the Mongolian homeland, Chinggisids sent the Oirats back to their home territory to the west. Chinggisids at this time were in precipitous decline, but Oirat power over the more slow-paced, bucolic countryside had not waned. After being displaced by their overlords, Oirat chieftains soon began attacking Chinggisids and eventually gained hegemony.

The height of Oirat power came from 1438 to 1454 under Esen Taishi (*c.* 1407–1455). As the de facto ruler of the northern steppe, Esen Taishi sought recognition from the Ming dynasty as a state sovereign in his own right. Specifically, he wanted the privilege that went with peace and intermarriage (*heqin* 和親). To win this recognition he pursued various stratagems. Since 1439, he had begun using a Yuan Chinggisid, the Emperor Togtoo-Bukha, as a puppet and sending him on tribute missions to the Ming. When this effort failed, he turned to Buddhism.[120] In 1446, Esen sent a tribute mission to the Ming emperor headed by a lama with word that the Oirats had mastered Buddhism. The delegation entreated the Ming emperor to bestow upon Esen a title, seal, robe of golden embroidery for a monk of high standing, and other Buddhist accoutrements. Replying that no precedent existed for such a request, the Ming emperor turned him down. After a subsequent failed attempt to parlay patronage of Buddhism into a dynastic title, Esen turned to yet another stratagem. On September 1, 1449, after enticing him onto the plains for battle, Esen used stealth to capture the Ming Zhengtong emperor (b.1427, r. 1435–1449, 1457–1464) at Tumu Fort (some 50 miles northwest of Beijing). For one year, he held the Ming sovereign hostage demanding marriage relations with the royal family in exchange for the emperor's release. In the heat of the moment, Ming officials coolly decided to retire the Zhengtong emperor and elevate his brother to the throne in his stead. Stymied, Esen returned the ex-emperor without condition and resumed the protocol of lobbying for privilege through Buddhism. In this vein, in 1452, Esen petitioned the Ming for Buddhist emblems of state power, icons, treasures, and ritual instruments for his Guoshi "State Preceptor." Again, Ming turned him down. Then, in 1453, being otherwise without recourse, Esen took the bold step of proclaiming himself the rightful khan of all Mongols. The first non-Chinggisid to claim sovereign legitimacy, Ming hesitantly accepted his decree, but the Chinggisids violently resisted. Among the Oirats themselves, infighting broke out over questions of position and power. Rebellion ensued. Forced to flee, Esen was killed in 1455, and soon thereafter Oirat power waned.

In response to Esen, Yuan Chinggisids rallied. In 1450, with Ming forces preoccupied with Zhengtong's kidnapping, Mongols flooded down into present day Inner Mongolia. They brought along the shrine of Chinggis Khan, his eight tents or *ordos* from the country of the Kherlen River down to the land of the Great Bend of the Yellow River—hence the name of the region, Ordos. Unable to drive them back, by 1472 the Ming attempted to keep the Mongols at bay by erecting a great wall—the Great Wall. Leading Yuan reunification was Mandukhai secen khatun (fl. 1473–1480), the widow of former emperor Manduul Khan. In 1480, she married his infant son, Batu-möngke Dayan Khan (1473–1517), and raised him to be a khan worthy of fealty.

In the early 16th century, Dayan Khan issued a new Yuan dispensation. This dispensation limited the nobility to Chinggisid loyalists and excluded Chinggisids who had gone over to the Ming (the Three Guards) as well as non-Chinggisid Oirats and Buriats. It stipulated that only descendants of Chinggis Khan—not his brothers—held supremacy. Marriage ties were not to replace ties of patrilineal descent. If commoners attempted to usurp power, all Chinggisids must retaliate. It defined Chinggis Khan's sovereignty as partible among the *tayiǰi* (< Ch. *taizi* 太子), that is, all male descendants. There was to be no *tayiǰi* without subjects and no commoner without a *tayiǰi*. It revised genealogical records and abolished previous court titles, in particular, the title *taishi* which the Oirats had sullied.

The new dispensation reorganized Yuan into six nations, known as the Six Tümen, each under a member of the royal family. Divided into two wings, east and west, the east wing was comprised of Chakhar, Khalkha, and Uriyangkhan, and the West, Ordos, Tümed, and Yüngsiyebü. The ruler of Chakhar ruled the East Wing. He was, at once, *primus inter pares*, Great Khaan of the Great Yuan. The ruler of Ordos ruled the west wing. He held the title *Jinong* "Viceroy" (Ch. *jinwang* 金王 "Golden Prince") of the Great Yuan. Primogeniture determined the succession. Symbolically, legitimacy passed through transference of Qubilai Khan's jade seal (Mong. *qasbuu tamγ-a*). Considered fraudulent by the Ming, Mongols declared this object the imperial seal of Qinshi Huangdi 秦始皇帝, used by all successive dynasties until lost by the Jurchens, but "rediscovered" by the Yuan in 1294 (the year of Qubilai's death). In making this dispensation, edicts were decreed in the traditional way with the phrase, *möngke tngri-yin küčün-dür* "by the power of eternal Heaven."[121]

After their expulsion from China, Mongols did not, as is sometimes assumed, forsake Buddhism. The northern Yuan retained the position of Imperial Preceptor. In 1374 the Sakya Imperial Preceptor, now stationed at Qara-Qorum, sent Buddhist icons to the Ming emperor.[122] Activities of the State Preceptor are attested until 1452.[123] Translation of scripture carried on. In 1431, a block print of a tetraglot, Sanskrit, Tibetan, Chinese, and Mongolian doxology to bodhisattva savioress Tārā was published in Beijing.[124] Temple-building carried on as well. Chinese sources indicate that in 1443 Chinggisid Mongols requested Ming support to construct a Buddhist temple.[125] Even following Dayan Khan's new dispensation, Mongols in the northern Yuan continued to use Tibetan-Buddhist personal names.[126] Tibetan sources show that Dayan Khan had contact with the 8th Karmapa lama, but to what extent or purpose is unknown.[127] Even so, what role (if any) Buddhism played in Dayan Khan's Yuan reformation is uncertain. What seems clear is that Dayan Khan's dispensation was a reactionary move intended not to advance Buddhism but, rather, to return Yuan to Chinggisid principles of rule. By all accounts, the period from 1453 to 1570 was as a time of Buddhist decline among Mongols of the northern Yuan. Later Buddhist chronicles remember the era as a time when "the state of this world and the buddha's religion were unstable."[128]

During Yuan's reformation, Buddhism itself was undergoing a period of transition. At the height of its dominion, institutions of Tibetan Buddhism stretched from the Pacific Ocean to the Black Sea. Even prior to Yuan expulsion from China, however, Buddhism had begun to lose its hold in the West. In the Ilkhanate, after the Buddhist reigns of Hülegü and Abaqa, growing fissures between Buddhist and Islamic partisans produced political tensions for willful agents to exploit. Soon, the Ilkhanate's Buddhist state began to destabilize. Playing on sympathy for Islam, Hülegü's son, Tegüder (r. 1282–1284), took the Ilkhan's seat by converting to Islam. He reigned as Sultan Ahmad but did not Islamicize the realm. His successor Arghun (r. 1284–1291) returned the Ilkhanate to Buddhism, but his reign ended in chaos, and religious conflict ensued. In 1295, Ghazan (r. 1295–1304) converted to Islam and Islamicized the state, ordering all Mongol elites and soldiery to convert.[129] Ghazan's brother, Kharbanda, finalized the conversion when he acceded as Sultan Öljeitü (b. 1281; r. 1304–1316). Baptized Christian, raised Buddhist, enthroned as a Sunni Muslim, and converted to Twelver Shi'ism, he proclaimed himself "The Sultan," that is, the world's preeminent Islamic ruler—greater than the Mamluk sultan of Egypt. In his early writings, Dante saw Mongols as Buddhists, but *Divina Commedia*, written around the time of Öljeitü's accession in 1304, reflects the Mongols' conversion to Islam.[130] Despite Öljeitü declaring himself the Muslim sultan of the world, Ilkhanids continued to support Buddhism to some degree until the death of the last Ilkhan, Abu Sa'id (1305–1335), in 1335. After this time, Buddhism was rapidly eclipsed in the heart of Islam.

In the realm of Jochi, the Golden Horde, Buddhism was eclipsed even earlier. There existed the same tension between Buddhism and Islam found in the Ilkhanate, but the politics played out in reverse. Though he continued supporting other religions, in 1257 Berke (r. 1257–1266), son of Jochi, had converted to Islam to garner the support of Muslims in opposition to his Buddhism-supporting brethren, Hülegü in particular. Playing on sympathy for Buddhism among the nobility, in 1291 Toqto'a (1291–1312) used conversion to Buddhism to garner power and made Uygur Buddhism the court religion. During the final years of his reign, however, he converted back to Islam. After Toqto'a's death in 1312, Özbeg Khan (r. 1313–1341) purged remaining Buddhist clerics and all who opposed the Islamization of the realm.[131]

Buddhism endured better in the Ulus of Chaghatay. In the mid-15th century, Timur the Lame (Tamerlane) made the western territory part of his Islamic Timurid state. Still, Buddhism survived in the eastern part of the ulus, what became known as Moghulistan. By the turn of the 16th, Islam had largely effaced it in the Turpan Basin. In 1516, the Buddhist caves of Dunhuang were finally closed when the khan of Turpan converted to Islam.[132]

Even in the Buddhist heartland, the highlands of Tibet, the edifice of Yuan-imposed Sakya hegemony stood on shaky ground. Tensions between Buddhist schools had existed from the inception of Mongol-mandated Sakya rule in the time of Köden and Sakya Pandita. Mongols themselves exacerbated these tensions by involving the various schools that they supported in their own family disputes by pitting them against each other. While still seated in China, certain Mongol elites had begun to disendow Sakyapa in favor of Kagyu Buddhists. When the Yuan became either unwilling or unable to enforce Sakya hegemony, tensions in Tibetan Buddhism gave way to open rifts. In 1354, with the Yuan preoccupied with the Red Turban uprising, in Tibet the Pakmodrupa (Phag mo gru pa) under Janchupgyeltsen (Byang chub rgyal mtshan, 1302–1364) overthrew the Sakyapa and established the Pakmodru dynasty (1354–1618). In throwing off the Mongol yoke, the Pakmodru reasserted Tibetan agency over Tibetan Buddhism and Tibet—this, by doing away with those who had adopted Mongol dress, customs, and language and assuming the responsibilities and prerogatives of sovereignty for themselves.[133] Despite its longevity, Pakmodru reign was far from secure. The collapse of the Yuan had created a vacuum of power across all of East Asia. The mandate of heaven was no longer clear. People were unsure of where to turn for ministration. In Tibet, the rival Karmapa posed the Pakmodru regime an ongoing threat, frequently challenged their authority, and intermittently overran the environs of Lhasa. In 1373, the Sakya hierarchy recognized Ming legitimacy and began to turn to them for patronage instead of the Yuan.[134]

One place that felt the void left by the fall of the Yuan was Amdo (A mdo). Amdo was a Tibetan hinterland, but a hinterland as well for many nations and a nexus for them. After the Ming came to power, it immediately established suzerainty over the region. Still, Chaghataids of Mohgulistan, other Chinggisids (gone over to the Ming or not), and Oirats came and went. Here a school of Buddhism was formed that would meet head on the problem of legitimacy that the Yuan collapse presented. The school was the Gelukpa (Dge lugs pa) founded by Tsongkhapa (Gtsong kha pa, 1357–1419). Born in Tsongkha "Onion Valley," Amdo, in the year of his birth, the region was still under Yuan control. It is said that, though his mother was Tibetan, the child's father, Lubum Ge (Klu 'bum dge), was a Mongol, the Yuan overseer of the region. Tsongkhapa took his initial vows under the fourth Karmapa lama, Rolpe Dorje (1340–1383) under Yuan dominion. By the time he began his religious education in 1372, Mongols in his homeland had already aligned with the Ming. At this time, he traveled to central Tibet for further education in the Kadam (Bka' gdams) tradition. Having demonstrated an aptitude for learning, the Pakmodrupa supported and promoted him. In 1409, he founded a monastery near Lhasa from which a discipleship emerged. The monastery was named Gandan (*dga' ldan* "joyful") in reference to Tuṣita Heaven (from whence bodhisattvas originate), and the discipleship was originally known as the Galuk (Dga' lugs "Joyful System"). As Tsongkhapa's teaching was less devoted to joyfulness than it was to strict discipline, his school refashioned itself the Geluk (Dge lugs "Virtuous System"). Soon, Tsongkhapa disciples founded two other major monastic centers in the vicinity of Lhasa, the Drepung ('Bras spungs) Monastery in 1416 and Sera (Se ra) in 1419.

What made the Geluk school unique was its reaffirmation of strict monastic discipline, celibacy, and abstinence from alcohol, but also its repurposing of the institution of reincarnation lineages. The Gélukpa did not invent the tradition of reincarnation or *tulku* (*sprul sku*; Mong. *bürülgü* or *qubilγan* "transformation body [of buddha]"). While the concept of reincarnation itself is ancient, Indian, and pre-Buddhist, during the Yuan, the Kagyu (Bka' brgyud) had developed it as a political institution in order to deal with the succession of abbots. The Gelukpa developed the concept into an institution that would unify Church and State in a sovereign world dominion ruled, irrespective of any one family or primogenitor, by a divinely chosen Géluk lama.

In other words, the Gelukpa used the tradition of reincarnation to create a sophisticated world order, run, as the Phagmodru ran Tibet, through the tenets of Buddhist statecraft. With the institution of reincarnate lamas in place, all that was necessary to bring a new world order into being was a patron capable of providing the government military and financial support. What inspired such remarkable ingenuity? Can it merely be coincidence that the upstart Gelukpa promulgated the institution at a time when it provided the mighty lords about the nexus of Amdo precisely what they were pining for, magic potent enough to overcome the mandate of heaven stipulating Chinggisid legitimacy through primogeniture?

Back in the northern Yuan, the unity born of Dayan Khan's reformation did not last. Economic inequality tore away at their restoration. Individual Chinggisid nobles, the *tayiǰi*, did not share wealth with one another. For income, they relied on their subjects' tribute (for whom the burden could be onerous) but also on pillaging. As a rule, they pillaged not in a united front (as their predecessors had) but rather went their own separate ways or in lesser alliances. Their individual quests for booty broke the royal family into separate fiefdoms. A 1541 Ming report, Imperial Ming Nine Border Districts Study (*Huang Ming jiu bian kao* 皇明九邊考), describes the Mongol nobility as spoiled and immoderate, their intentions bent on pillaging, exclaiming, "How declined is Mongol power!"[135]

Some princes fared better pillaging than others did. Princedoms to the west were freer to roam than the Khan of the Great Yuan, who from his seat in Chakhar in the east was hemmed in by the appanages of family members and, to the south, by the teeth of the Ming army. Western princes regularly raided the Ming's less guarded western frontier, into Amdo and Tibet, Chagataid Moghulistan, against the Yellow Uygurs of Gansu, and into the realm of the Oirats along the Ili River.

Among western princes, one became preeminent, the prince of Tümed, Altan Khan (1507–1582). Born the second son of Jinong Barsubolod, son of Dayan Khan, Altan Khan grew up raiding and pillaging with his older brother, Mergen Jinong (1506–1542). When his brother died in 1542, he became the de facto leader of the west wing of the Northern Yuan, took up the mantle of jinong, and assumed the title Altan Khan (the Mongolian equivalent of *jinong* and Chinese *jinwang* 金王 "golden prince"). He established alliances with Chaghataids and Oirats to the west. In 1558 he subdued the Yellow Uygurs of Gansu. In 1568, marriage relations with Oirats brought him a new wife, Lady Jönggen (1551–1612). For his wealth and power, Altan Khan believed himself worthy of tribute relations with the Ming. As Esen had prior, he yearly flooded the Ming emperor with tribute in hopes of establishing an alliance, but, as with Esen, the Ming rebuffed him every time. In 1550, Altan Khan began what became a twenty-year war of attrition that resulted in Ming capitulation. In 1571, the Longqing emperor (b. 1537, r. 1567–1572) opened trade relations to Altan Khan and the Three Western Tümen. Granting him the title "Prosperous Righteous Prince" (*Shunyi Wang* 順義王),the Ming emperor presented Altan Khan a great golden seal signifying his authority over lucrative Sino-Mongol border trade.

With this concession, Altan Khan's wealth and privilege exceeded that of the Great Khan of the northern Yuan. Altan Khan used his power to drive the standing Yuan emperor, Tümen Jasagtu Khan (r. 1558–1592), out of his ancestral pasturage in Chakhar east over the Khinggan Mountains into the pastures of Liaodong. Understandably put out, in a 1577 missive to the Longqing emperor, the Great Khan complained:

> The Altan Khan is the Tümen Kha'an's subject, but now that he has received a princely title and a golden seal as big as a peck, is it not as if he were made the husband and Tümen Kha'an had been reduced to the status of a wife?[136]

As this message makes clear, affluence and franchise notwithstanding, Altan Khan remained, as ever, the Great Khan's subject. He suffered Esen's fate. Unlike Chinggis, Qubilai, and his grandfather, Dayan Khan, heaven allotted Altan Khan no destiny to rule.[137] The heartless convention of primogeniture was denied him. To overcome this problem, rather than marshaling troops for battle, Altan Khan turned to religion. He converted to Geluk Buddhism.

Altan Khan's conversion was years in the making. In 1566, he sent his nephew, Khutughtai Sechen Khungtaiǐji (1540–1586) of Ordos, on a military reconnaissance into Tibet. Much as the Ögedeids had done in 1240, the purpose was to contact leading monks and establish relations.[138] Put in contact with Asing Lama (Tib. A seng bla ma ki 'Dzo dge), Altan Khan invited him to instruct him and his wife, Lady Jönggen, in Buddhist catechism.[139] In 1575, Altan Khan and Khutughtai Sechen Khungtaiji began laying the groundwork for the creation of a Buddhist nation-state in the Three Western Tümen. Then in 1576, he summoned the leading Geluk prelate, the abbot of Drepung Monastery, Sönam Gyatso (Bsod nams rgya mtsho, 1543–1588). It just so happened that Sönam Gyatso was as much in need of a patron as Altan Khan needed a priest. For generations, patrons of the rival Karmapa, the Rinpung (Rin spungs) family, had threatened the Pakmodru government with insurrection. Since the 1560s, the possibility of the Rinpungs overthrowing the Pakmodru had been imminent. Altan Khan's 1576 invitation to Sönam Gyatso arrived at the Drepung Monastery just as the Rinpung army was on the verge of taking Lhasa. Fleeing Ü (Dbus), Sönam Gyatso traveled to the Geluk stronghold on the shores of Kökenuur where he found refuge in the camp of Altan Khan at a place called Chabchiyal.[140]

On the fifteenth day of the fifth month of the Earth-Tiger year (June 19, 1578), that is to say, the occasion of the full moon of the summer solstice, the most effulgent day of the year, Sönam Gyatso met with Altan Khan and Lady Jönggen in a sacred ceremony.[141] The ceremony hearkened to past precedent. Like Qubilai and Chabi, Altan Khan and Lady Jönggen underwent a Hevajra tantric initiation, and, like Qubilai and 'Phags pa, Altan Khan and Sönam Gyatso established the patron-priest relationship. In their compact, Sönam Gyatso recognized Altan Khan as the living reincarnation of Qubilai Khan and bestowed upon him Qubilai Khan's title, *Cakravartin Sechen Khan*. He bestowed on Lady Jönggen the title *ārya Tārā*, making her the living incarnation of the bodhisattva savioress. As an emanation body of Avalokiteśvara, Sönam Gyatso recognized in himself the living reincarnation of 'Phags pa lama. For Altan Khan's part, he bestowed upon Sönam Gyatso the title *Dalai Lama Vajradhara*.[142]

The Mongolian word *dalai* literally means "ocean" but principally made a cosmological conceit signifying the horizon, specifically the "offing" of the ocean, the circumambient ocean that delimits at once the sphere of the earth and any given polity. A Eurasian commonplace, terms for "ocean" in Tibetan (*rgya mtsho*) and Sanskrit (*sāgara*) principally signified "horizon" as well. In the past, the Mongol khan had held the epithet *Dalay-yin qan* "Khan of the Circumambient Ocean," "Ruler of the Horizon," the all-encompassing ruler or ruler of all.[143] Transferred to Sönam Gyatso, the title "Dalai Lama" signifies the all-encompassing, universal guru, guru to one-and-all.

FROM THE CONVERSION OF ALTAN KHAN UNTIL THE FALL OF THE YUAN DYNASTY, 1578–1635

Scholars have deemed the era begun by Altan Khan's submission to Sönam Gyatso the Mongols' "second conversion" to Buddhism. This characterization misses the fact that the Mongols never officially abandoned Buddhism in the first place, but more importantly articulates neither the uniqueness of his action nor the magnitude of its significance. Altan Khan couched his conversion as a return to past precedent but did so as a way of forging something remarkably new. Although ostensibly an act of re-creation, Altan Khan's compact with Sönam Gyatso was fundamentally different than the one struck by Qubilai and 'Phags pa. Whereas Qubilai had checked the rhetoric of the patron-priest relationship with aristocratic propaganda that subordinated Buddhism to the mandate of heaven, Altan Khan assented to the agreement's stipulation that ultimate power lies with the priest. This assent fundamentally altered the world order, for it circumscribed the aristocracy and its heavenly mandate within the dominion of Géluk Buddhism. Under Chinggis Khan, the world had been essentially Mongol. Buddhism was but one of several religions circumscribed within the dominion of the Great Mongol Nation. Under Qubilai, Sakyapa and Tibetan Buddhism may have enjoyed certain privilege, but Buddhism's authority did not exceed that of the state. Altan Khan's assent to the terms of the patron-priest relationship created an essentially Geluk Buddhist world—a Buddhist world analogous to Christendom—in particular, the Catholic world, with the power and position of the Dalai Lama in Lhasa comparable to that of the pope in Rome.

Perhaps Altan Khan did not fully grasp the implications of his assent to Geluk supremacy. In his life, much like Qubilai, he held the cards. His wealth and power gave him leave to have his cake and eat it too, to use Geluk magic to both entertain Buddhist legitimation and retain Mongolian tradition. He was not turning sovereignty over to Buddhists so much as he was expanding his personal supremacy. Rather than overthrow the Yuan dynasty, he sought merely to carve out a sovereign state for himself, while at the same time continuing to enjoy the privileges of Chinggisid legitimacy. As Qubilai had, he accepted Buddhism but did not forsake the mandate of heaven. He still venerated Chinggis Khan as creator of the cosmos.

Magic, however, often comes with unintended consequences. Whereas in his eyes his legitimacy kept with the order that Chinggis Khan had established and Qubilai Khan sustained, in the eyes of others, not least of which the eyes of the Great Khan of the Yuan dynasty, the cosmos that made Altan Khan the reincarnation of Qubilai Khan competed with the Chinggisid mandate of heaven and threatened it. The crux of the matter was that accepting legitimation through Gélukpa magic came with a trade-off: Altan Khan could be a cakravartin and reincarnation of Qubilai Khan but at the cost of weakening the Chinggisid legacy. If Altan Khan had converted to the Gélukpa and no one else had followed suit, perhaps things would have only been better for him and nothing else would have changed. As it was, Altan Khan's conversion set off a world-altering chain reaction. Other Mongol princes followed his example. They too claimed magical legitimacy through recognition by a Tibetan lama, appropriated this the new world order, and created new princely states. Thus, Mongol conversion to the Gélukpa led to even greater decentralization and hastened the fall of the Yuan.[144]

One might take Mongol assent to Geluk supremacy as letting the genie out of the bottle, the naïve act of people unaware of their decision's political implications. In England, after all, beginning with Henry VIII's (r. 1509–1547) 1534 Act of Supremacy, the Mongols' noble-born counterparts were trying desperately to put this genie back. Likewise, it is easy to see the Mongols' conversion to the Gelukpa as an ingenious stratagem, the expedient act of people bent on gaining legitimacy when none was otherwise forthcoming. Still, there is more to consider. Whereas Dayan Khan's reformation had turned Yuan into the teeth of the winds of change, the conversion of the Mongols to Geluk Buddhism kept with the spirit of the times. Since the reign of Qubilai Khan, the rhetoric of statecraft had been moving inexorably toward the political ideology of soteriological religion, an ideology that entailed faith in abstraction, moral order, compassion, and common humanity over faith in empirical science, magic, divination, and the insistence that might makes right. Mongol conversion to Geluk Buddhism marked the dawn of the age of soteriological dominion—when religions, such as, Buddhism, Christianity, and Islam—asserted superiority to the prerogatives of the aristocracy and increasingly dominated the world.

Altan Khan died in 1582. To retain the wealth of his estate, a levirate marriage was held to wed his son, Sengge Dügüreng Khungtaiji (1521–1585), to his own stepmother, Altan Khan's Lady Jönggen, and the two continued to hold sway until Sengge Dügüreng's death in 1585. After this time, Tümed power collapsed. Such was not the fate, however, of Gelukpa Buddhism. No sooner had Altan Khan made his patron-priest compact with Sönam Gyatso than other Mongol nobles began to follow suit.

One was the Chinggisid Abatai Khan (1554–1588) of Khalkha. Abatai Khan's lot in life was determined by his birthright as the grandson of Dayan Khan's youngest son, Geresenje (1513–1548). As a youngest son, Geresenje had kept the family hearth, that is to say, an appanage over the traditional Mongolian homeland, the Mongolian Plateau including the Orkhon River watershed and the environs of Qara-Qorum, the ruined imperial capital. Abatai Khan inherited this appanage and with it, a share of his grandfather's people, the Northern Khalkha. Like Altan Khan, he ruled a vast and prosperous nation but nonetheless, for primogeniture, lacked legitimacy to promulgate his realm as a sovereign state. In 1581, Abatai invited Sönam Gyatso to travel north and initiate him. Sönam Gyatso declined the offer but sent a representative, Shiregetü Güüshi Chorjiwa (fl. 1578–1618). In 1585, Abatai Khan founded the Erdeni Zuu Monastery over the ruins of Qara-Qorum. Around that time, Abatai Khan traveled south to Kökeqota to meet Sönam Gyatso in person. Again, the Dalai Lama worked his magic. In a tantric initiation, Sönam Gyatso declared Abatai Khan to be the incarnation of the bodhisattva Vajrapani and conferred khanship upon him with the title "Great Vajra Emperor of the Dharma" (*Nom-un yeke vačir qaγan*).[145] Politically, Sönam Gyatso granted Abatai Khan sovereignty over a Buddhist nation-state and bestowed the title *Tüsiyetü Khan* upon his faithful servant.[146] After Abatai Khan's death in 1588, his body was interred at Erdeni Zuu. From the seed of his conversion grew the next major development in Mongolian Buddhism when his grandson, the Tüsiyetü (Tusheet) Khan, Gombodorji (1594–1655), established the incarnate lineage of the Jebtsundamba Khutukhtu, this in the person of Gombodorji's second son, Isidorji, remembered by the title Öndör gegen Zanabazar (1635–1723).

Géluk magic for granting legitimacy was perfectly suited to the political aspirations of the Oirats. Having suffered his incursions for decades, after the death of Altan Khan, they returned to prominence in the west from their base along the Ili River. A confederation of four nations, Khoshud, Torghud, Dörböd, and Zünghar, the Oirat chief, *primus inter pares*, was ruler of the Khoshud, who claimed descent from Chinggis Khan's brother, Qasar. Oirat conversion occurred swiftly and in earnest around the turn of the 17th century. Families of the noble-born were obliged to devote a son to the priesthood, and, in turn, the lama princes (*toyin*) who emerged from the Geluk monasteries of Tibet were obliged to proselytize the nation. Oirat political fortunes changed with the ascent of Törö Baikhu (1582–1655) in 1630. Titled Güüshi (Gu shri < Ch. *guoshi* 國師) Taishi at this time, after he succeeded in defeating Gelukpa adversaries in battle, the Fifth Dalai Lama elevated him in a tantric coronation to the title Dharmaraja (*chos rgyal*), and he became known as Güüshi Khan. In his role as the Gelukpa's strong-armed protector, Güüshi Khan settled in Amdo, where his Khoshud nation became preeminent among the region's Upper Mongols (Deedü Mongγol).[147] On the Oirat home front, a power struggle ensued between the Torghud, Dörböd, and Zünghars. In the 1630s, many Torghud and Dörböd Oirats extricated themselves from the upheaval by migrating far to the west, to the Caspian Sea and Volga River country in Caucasia. There they remained ardently devoted to Géluk Buddhism, their monks regularly journeying east. Zünghars filled the void in leadership and in 1634 formed what would prove to be the last of the great steppe empires—those bands of imperial nomadic steppe warriors that had held sway over all Eurasia since the domestication of the horse.[148]

At the turn of the 17th century, while Khalkha and the Oirats were turning to Gelukpa legitimation magic, Mongols of the Yuan East Wing, put upon by their increasingly embattled emperor, began to ally with the up-and-coming Jurchen. As a people set apart, Borjigid princes over eastern Mongol nations also sought conversion to Géluk Buddhism. A noble-born Oirat Mongol of the Khoshud, Neichi toyin (1557–1653), met their request for a missionary. A hagiography entitled "Rosary of Wish-fulfilling-jewels" (*Čindamani erikei*) describes his mission in magical terms. Neichi toyin is said to convert the eastern Mongols through charisma, the superiority of his magic, intellect, and virtue. Miraculously, he brings rain in a drought, awakens compassion for animals in a hunter, heals a gravely ill princess, effects the conversion of an indigenous priest by exorcising a demon, restores eyesight to a blind priestess, and so on. These miracles effect the khan's conversion, and he induces his people to follow.[149]

A sign of Gelukpa and Buddhist ascendancy vis-à-vis the aristocracy was the standing of the church with respect to that of the state. Soteriological orders such as Buddhism and Christianity set their religion apart from the religion of the state. As soteriological religions came to rule the world, governments promulgated dual regencies, the unification of church and state in an amalgamated catholic religion. Dual regency dominated world politics until the United States Constitution separated church and state in 1791 but even thereafter continued to hold sway until the violent wars and revolutions of the 20th century largely did away with it. In Tibetan, dual regency is referred to as "the pairing of the two (orders)" (*luk zung, lugs zung*) or simply "two orders" (*luk nyi, lugs gnyis*). This, for the Mongols, was "the custom that pairs religion and state" (*šasin törö qooslan yosu*), or simply, "the two customs" (*qoyar yosu*). As demonstrated by J. Elverskog, Altan Khan's dispensation blended Mongol and Buddhist discourses of legitimacy. The head of the religion, the Dalai Lama, turns the wheel of the dharma. The head of the state, the khan, turns the wheel of heaven. The Dalai Lama's dharma is an indissoluble silken knot; the khan's *ǰasaγ*, an invincible golden yoke.[150]

Buddhism's supremacy was manifest in several prerogatives. One was the Dalai Lama's power to grant titles. One of the first titles Sönam Gyatso granted was his own. He used his newfound authority to shore up the foundation to his new world order by sinking its cornerstone, the institution of the Dalai Lama, back to Geluk bedrock. Rather than taking it for himself, Sönam Gyatso bestowed the distinction of being the First Dalai Lama posthumously (104 years after his death) upon one of Tsongkhapa's original disciples, Gendun Drupa (Dge 'dun grub pa, 1391–1474), who in 1447 founded the Gelukpa's fourth great monastery, Tashilhunpo (Bkra shis lhun po). The title "Second Dalai Lama" he bestowed posthumously upon Gendun Gyatso (Dge 'dun rgya mtsho, 1475–1542), the reincarnation of Gendun Drupa at Tashilhunpo. Thus, through the magic of reincarnation, Sönam Gyatso became not the first Dalai Lama but the third.[151] Around 1638, assenting to the will of a nascent Geluk order among the Mongols of Khalkha, the Fifth Dalai Lama created the lineage of the Jebtsundamba Khutughtu and with it opened a gateway to the next chapter in the history of Mongolian Buddhism.[152] In 1645, the Fifth Dalai Lama created the lineage of the Panchen Lama, bestowing the title upon his teacher, Lozang chö kyi gyel tsen (Blo bzang Chos kyi rgyal mtshan, 1570–1662), this time, as the fourth reincarnation. With permission granted by a Mongol patron, this power extended even to granting the aristocratic title "khan." In granting the Dalai Lama this power, Mongols no longer depended solely on heavenly mandated destiny or the grace of a foreign emperor to hold a title. As mentioned, the Third Dalai Lama conferred khanship upon Abatai Khan; the Fifth Dalai Lama, Güüshi Khan. Some years later, the Fifth Dalai Lama granted the title *Sayin Noyan Khan* to Abatai Khan's younger brother, Tümenkin. In yet another example, around 1678, the Fifth Dalai Lama bestowed the title *Galdan Boshughtu Khan* on the Oirat ruler of Zungharia.[153] The title means "Khan by Heavenly Decree." Mongolian *γaldan*, from the Tibetan *dga' ldan* for Sanskrit *tushita*, means the "joyful" third or highest heaven. A loaded term in Gelukpa rhetoric, it refers to a realm highly abstracted in Buddhist cosmology from the empirical dome of the sky. It is both the place from whence bodhisattvas originate and namesake of the monastery whence came Tsongkhapa's discipleship.

Buddhist prerogative was upheld in jurisprudence. Upon his conversion in 1578, Altan Khan promulgated a law code that transformed his personal appanage, Tümed, into a Geluk dominion.[154] In 1582, the Great Khan of the Great Yuan, Tümen Jasaghtu Khan (r. 1558–1592), promulgated a similar code transforming Chakhar into a dominion of the Sakyapa. Another Geluk code was ratified in 1640 between the Mongols and Oirats.[155] These law codes altered the conception of what constitutes a world. Paradoxically, in monarchic dispensations (where "cosmos" means "government," "world," and "age of man"), though the king knows the world to be a world of worlds, he recognizes no other world but his own. Conversely, the soteriological dispensation knows but one world (the sphere of the earth and physical universe) and so recognizes the coexistence of different worlds, that is to say, different political states. Although states had always known the existence of—and had ways of dealing with—other states, governments veiled those ways in rhetoric of tribute. With the ascendancy of soteriological dominion, formally recognized international relations emerged. The 1640 code between Mongols and Oirats allowed for the mutual recognition of the other's state under catholic Géluk dominion. In Europe, a similar precedent was established in the 1648 Treaty of Westphalia.[156]

State-promulgated Tibetan Buddhist law codes outlawed non-Buddhist religion. Prior to the institution of the Dalai Lama, Mongols had continued to support other religions such as Christianity and Islam.[157] Now, Buddhism became the exclusive religion, and non-Buddhist religions were expelled. This move toward religious exclusion kept with a Eurasian trend. In 1502, the Spanish government ordered the Moors to convert to Christianity and in 1609 expelled Muslims who remained. It was during this era that world order settled into vast soteriological dominions, Christianity over Europe, Russia, and the Americas, Islam over Central Asia and North Africa, and Géluk Buddhism, in Inner Asia.

Geluk jurisprudence went so far as to outlaw the Mongols' own sacerdotal tradition. This tradition, it is to be noted, was not "shamanism." Shamanism is a notional religion invented in the 20th century by the anthropologist Mircea Eliade. Its notionality derives from the idea that mankind has evolved from primitive (superstitious) worship of nature to religion (soteriological religion) to science (modern science). As the name for what Eliade deemed archaic nature worship, *shamanism* refers to an abstract synthesis of ritual practices devoted to ecstatic divination magic compiled from a survey of religions of the world. No religion of any one people is defined solely by this peculiar set of practices. As has been seen, the Mongols' "magi" (*böge-nügüd*) were a hereditary priesthood venerated as intercessors between the symmetrical orders to heaven and earth and responsible for maintaining political order through marshaling science, divination propaganda, and ritual. The sacerdotal tradition included ecstatic methods of divination but much else as well—including wise counsel, time reckoning, logistics, oral history, oral literature, and medicine.

How rudely the priesthood was disbanded is debatable. Leveling its most heated vituperation, Buddhist historiography speaks of the priesthood's total annihilation in a pogrom. The biography of Altan Khan says "the ecstatic and ignorant priests and priestesses were demeaned and done away with" (*γani mungqaγ böge udaγan-i doroyitaγulun usadqaǰu*).[158] External evidence, however, suggests that this language was rhetorical. Extant liturgies reveal that certain rituals—those pertaining to the royal family, heaven, and clans—continued to be officiated by traditional priests. Many priests converted to Buddhism and joined the ranks of *baghsi* monk magicians. Others simply went on to other walks of life. Important rites and functions of the priesthood—such as time reckoning, scapulimancy, and medical and apothecary services—Buddhism appropriated. So too Buddhism assimilated and elaborated on the priesthood's network of ritual cairns (Mong. *obo, oboγ-a*) used to mark centers, landmarks, routes, and borders. Rites deemed unenlightened, such as human and animal sacrifices (especially the yearly sacrifice of horse and ox), offerings of blood and meat, hunting, the eating of meat, drinking of alcohol, and smoking, were formally condemned in Buddhism in advocacy of a moral code, the Ten Virtues.[159] In practice, however, even many of these rituals Buddhism retained. One aspect of the priestly tradition that Buddhism did eradicate was the veneration of effigies and totems. As the biography of Altan Khan puts it: "the heresies of heterodox effigies and totems were burned away" (*γadaγadu ongγod čelig-üd-ün endegüregsen-i tüimeridüged*).[160] In particular, Buddhist law stipulated that the *ongγod*, the ancestral idols at the heart of indigenous Mongolian tradition, be burned in a ritual fire. For replacement, Buddhism instituted cults of tantric deities such as the six-armed Mahākāla, Yamāntaka, Vajrasattva, and Guhyasamāja, cults that sometimes came with antinomian (blood-letting, meat-eating, alcohol-drinking, and sexual) practices of their own.[161]

Geluk ascendancy did not free patrons from the need to establish the Three Jewels. Like their ancestors, Mongols took the obligation seriously. In the Male Water Monkey Year (1572), as part of laying the groundwork for Sönam Gyatso's arrival, Altan Khan funded the construction of a citadel (Ch. *chengsi* 城寺 "city-temple"), *Kökeqota* ("Blue City"), centered on a fortified monastery dedicated to the Future Buddha, Maitreya, *Mayidari Juu*. Constructed in imitation of the lost Daidu, Altan Khan's Kökeqota was located just miles from the Yellow River in the environs of modern Baotou, several miles west of, and not to be confused with, the modern capital of Inner Mongolia, which today bears the same name (Hohhot).[162] Following their 1578 meeting, at Sönam Gyatso's request, Altan Khan built another monastery, this, to the east, in the environs of modern Hohhot, then named "Return to Civilization City" (*Guihua cheng* 歸化城). Centered on a temple housing a magnificent Shakyamuni Buddha, the monastery was originally named Juu Shakyamuni but for its large contingent of monks became known as "Great Monastery" (*Yeke Juu*). Altan Khan's son, Sengge Dügüreng, met Sönam Gyatso's request for a monastery to serve as the seat for the Dalai Lama by financing the Kumbum Monastery (*Sku 'bum byams pa gling*) at the birthplace of Tsongkhapa in Amdo, Qinghai. Completed in 1583, it would become an important hub for Inner Asian politics.[163] When Abatai Khan built Erdeni zuu in Qara-Qorum in 1585, he employed Sakyapa artisans sent from Tibet by the Third Dalai Lama. Following the model of Altan Khan's Yeke Juu Monastery, they centered the monastery on a relic of Śākyamuni Buddha, and to construct the monastery temples or *ǰuu* (pronounced *zuu* < Tib. *jo bo* "lord") they incorporated stone blocks from the razed temple of Qara-Qorum.[164]

Mongols also returned to translating the dharma into Mongolian. At Yeke Juu, Altan Khan sponsored an excellent team Tibetan scholars, translators, and printers. Having arrived in the Third Dalai Lama's entourage, these skilled artisans busied themselves compiling extant works, making new translations (from Tibetan), carving xylographs, and printing text. The obvious urgency to, and prodigiousness of, the team's output suggests a guiding principle to inculcate Buddhism to as many Mongols as quickly as possible. Leading the team was Shiregetü Güüsi Chorjiwa (fl. 1578–1618). The venerable master translated several works from Tibetan, one being the "Essentials for Practice" (*Čiqula kereglegči*), a modified version of 'Phags pa's 1278 catechism.[165] Another excellent scholar, Ayushi Güüshi (fl. 1578–1609), revised the Uygur-Mongolian script in conjunction with his translation of the *Pañcarakṣā*. Utilizing the model of the Tibetan rendition of the "fifty Indian letters," he made this reformation so that the text's many magical spells (*dharani*) would be pronounced correctly and thus retain their efficacy.[166] Altan Khan's wife, Lady Jönggen, used her considerable wealth to sponsor translation.[167] Oirats sponsored translation as well. Their eminent sage, the noble-born Khoshud prince Zaya Bandida Namkhaijamtsu (Nam mkha'i rgya mtsho, 1599–1662), created his own modification of the Uygur-Mongolian script, the "Clear Script" (*Todo bičig*). In the 1620s, the Yuan emperor Ligdan Khan (b. 1588, r. 1603/1604–1634), funded the translation of a Buddhist canon (Mong. *ghanjur*; Tib. *bka' 'gyur*) into Mongolian. With the advice of the Third Dalai Lama's chief assistant, Shiregetü Güüshi Chorjiwa, he assembled a team of thirty-five translators headed by Gungaa Odser (Tib. Kun dga' 'od zer). With texts from the early Yuan, Ming, and Altan Khan still in circulation, their work often amounted to adding new colophons to old translations. They required but a period from November 1628 to May 1629 to produce a canon of 113 volumes. Later, under the Manchu Kangxi emperor (b. 1654, r. 1662–1722), this version was modestly reworked into the modern Mongolian Buddhist canon, a block-printed edition of 108 volumes comprising 1161 works.[168]

The patronage of Mongols such as these began a renaissance of Buddhist art and culture, a renaissance that lasted from the turn of the 17th century until the mid-19th century and the coming of modernity.[169] To create this renaissance, the motivations of but a few wealthy lords started what became a tremendous transfer of wealth from the Mongols to the Buddhist establishment, especially in Tibet, and into the coffers of the Gelukpa. For their fateful meeting of 1578 alone, Altan Khan offered Sönam Gyatso a golden chalice filled with pearls and a seal poured from one hundred *lang* (ounces or taels) of pure gold.[170] In 1650, the noble-born Oirat monk, Zaya Paṇṇita, made an immense donation to the Fifth Dalai Lama that included fifty thousand taels of gold. On a 1652 peregrination to Beijing, while passing through Mongol lands, the Fifth Dalai Lama netted over ten thousand ounces of silver, seven thousand horses, and ten thousand sheep in payment for his blessed teaching.[171]

The motivations driving the Mongols' renewed patronage of Buddhism were in no small part political. Indeed, political tensions between opposing factions only increased Mongol support. At the time of the Mongol conversion to the Gelukpa, political friction in Tibet played out relative to the acting Pakmodru government. Here oppositions existed between the Gelukpa, which took the government's part, and the rival Karmapa. Antipathy between the Gelukpa and Sakyapa at this time was not prevalent. Monks of the two orders supported each other and frequently worked together. When Abatai Khan founded the Erdeni zuu Monastery, the Third Dalai Lama had the Sakya monk Lodrö nyingpo (Blo gros snying po) oversee the project and sent Sakyapa artisans from Tibet to construct the monastery temples. Thereafter, the monks in this seat of the Geluk Holy Lord, the Jebtsundamba khutukhtu, remained predominantly Sakyapa up until the 18th century. As for the Mongols, like their predecessors, they were not averse to patronizing any Buddhist school and tended to patronize multiple schools at once. Moreover, individual monks went from one camp to another. The renowned sage and translator, Shiregetü Güüsi Chorjiwa, for example, worked for the Geluk-supporting Altan Khan and Abatai Khan as well as for Ligdan Khan and the Khalkha lord, Tsoghtu taiji (1581–1637), both of whom supported the Sakyapa and Karmapa.[172]

Even so, for the Mongols, because political tension existed relative to the Yuan dynasty and the question of legitimation, when politics dictated conservatism, there was an impetus to favor the Sakyapa and Karmapa. When progressivism carried the day, Mongols favored the upstart Gelukpa—and especially the title-granting power of the Dalai Lama. Altan Khan of Tümed, Abatai Khan of Khalkha, Güüshi Khan of the Oirats, and the khans of the eastern Mongols gone over to the Jurchen all turned to the Gelukpa in challenging the Yuan's stipulation of legitimacy through primogeniture. When Altan Khan started the wheels of change in motion, the conservative Yuan renewed patronage of Buddhism but did so favoring Karmapa and Sakyapa. When the Yuan and Jurchen went to war in the 1620s, the standing Yuan emperor, Ligdan Khan, patronized the Sakyapa, while the insurgent Jurchen khan, Nurhaci (1559–1626), patronized the Gelukpa. After Ligdan Khan's death and the collapse of Chakhar in 1634, Jasaghtu Khan of Khalkha, who considered himself the rightful emperor through primogeniture, aligned with the Karmapa and Sakyapa against the Gelukpa. At the same time, Nurhaci's successor, Hongtaiji (1592–1643), having defeated Yuan forces and accepted its submission, saw himself as the rightful heir to Yuan legitimacy and likewise sponsored the Sakyapa. Eventually, in the aftermath of the fall of the Yuan, with the ascendancies of the Manchu Qing dynasty and the Fifth Dalai Lama, political tensions eased and the largely rhetorical opposition between the Gélukpa and Sakyapa dissolved as the Gelukpa became preeminent.

In the eye of the political maelstrom was the figure of the Dalai Lama. Whereas other monks were free to come and go from one lord to another, he was not. The fate of Asian politics hinged on whether the physical person embodying this particular emanation lineage lived or died. Wary of travel, when in 1582 Abatai Khan invited him to his base in Khalkha, the Third Dalai Lama declined the offer. Shortly thereafter, following the death of Altan Khan's son, Sengge Dügüreng, in 1585, Khan of the Great Yuan, Tümen Jasaghtu Khan, invited him to his court in Chakhar, but the Third Dalai Lama had sense enough to think twice. Around that time, he also received an invitation from the Ming Wanli emperor (r. 1573–1619) but again turned it down. In 1588, the Third Dalai Lama finally assented to an invitation, this from the Kharchin Mongols in eastern Mongolia. He died en route at age 45.[173]

The institution of the Dalai Lama allows the sitting Dalai Lama to decide for himself whether and where he will be reborn. It just so happened that the Third Dalai Lama decided to reappear not in Tibet but Mongolia, in the body of Altan Khan's grandson no less. Together with the princes of Tümed and other high-ranking lamas, Bandida Shiregetü Güüshi Chorjiwa affirmed the decision. The boy, Yönten Gyatso (Yon tan Rgya mtsho, 1589–1617), was examined by a commission sent from Lhasa. The commission testified to his legitimacy in a 1592 report to the abbots of the Ganden, Sera, and Drepung Monasteries. After lengthy deliberation, they confirmed him as the Fourth Dalai Lama. Enthroned and stationed in Tümed, Tibetans in Central Tibet largely ignored him for almost ten years. In 1602, his people brought him to Lhasa, and in 1603, they enthroned him in Reting and installed him at Drepung. His residency in Lhasa stirred unrest and opened rifts in the political establishment between the fragmenting Phagmodru government, the rival Rinpung and the Karmapa, Geluk officials, and the Fourth Dalai Lama's Mongol guard. In 1607, armed conflict drove him into exile. Though he eventually returned to Lhasa in 1611, the Fourth Dalai Lama's standing remained tenuous until his death in 1617 at age 28. The first and only Mongol Dalai Lama, upon his death, Geluk officials decreed that all future Dalai Lamas come from Tibet. His heart and other organs were returned to Tümed as relics.[174]

The Fourth Dalai Lama's successor met with better fortune. Remembered simply as "the Great Fifth," Ngawang Lozang Gyatso (Ngag dbang blo bzang rgya mtsho, 1617–1682) lived to see the fall of the Yuan dynasty and the rise of Géluk hegemony over the vast empires of East Asia. However, in the year of his recognition as the Dalai Lama, 1622, this glorious future was nowhere on the horizon. The Yuan emperor, Ligdan Khan, reeling from the machinations of unfaithful servants, had turned aggressive. Tibet was in chaos. The Pakmodru government, fosterer of Tsongkhapa and champion of the Gélukpa, was on the brink of collapse. Karmapa forces, funded by a new patron, Ligdan Khan, threatened Gelukpa positions across Tibet. The situation came to a head in 1632 when Ligdan Khan, driven from his base in Chakhar by the Jurchen, fled into Ordos on his way to Amdo. Facing Armageddon, the 15-year-old Dalai Lama sought protection from wherever he might find it. Having turned to both the Jurchen and

Oirats, it was the Khoshud ruler, Güüshi Taishi, who answered the call. Moving his Khoshud nation into Amdo, Güüshi Khan defeated Ligdan Khan in 1634 and then fought on for several years to eradicate Géluk adversaries both in Tibet and abroad. In 1642, upon defeating the Karmapa in Central Tibet (*Gtsang*), the Fifth Dalai Lama joined Güüshi Khan in a ceremony establishing a new patron-priest *chö yön* (*mchod yon*) relationship. The Fifth Dalai made Güüshi Khan, his strong-armed protector, an emanation of Vajrapani, and the two together remembered the relationship established between Qubilai and 'Phags pa almost four hundred years prior. With their compact, the Fifth Dalai Lama and Güüshi Khan established the Ganden phodrang (Dga' ldan pho brang) government (1642–1959). Ruled in the name of the Dalai Lama, it lasted into the 20th century, surviving numerous threats, before succumbing to a 1959 overthrow by the People's Republic of China.[175]

The brunt of the political whirlwind set loose by Altan Khan's revolutionary 1578 compact with Sönam Gyatso was borne by the penultimate Yuan emperor, Ligdan Khan (b. 1588, r. 1603/1604–1634). From the moment of his accession in 1604, the Great Khan of Great Yuan was beset on all sides with threats to his authority. In the east, the Jurchen were rising. In the west, the Oirats were a menace. To the north, Khalkha was unstable. In Tibet, the world was being remade by Gélukpa magic. The Dalai Lama, defying the mandate of heaven, bestowed transcendent legitimacy upon anyone willing to pay for it—to Altan Khan of the Tümed, Abatai Khan of Khalkha, and to the Oirats. Realizing that the time had come to reassert the Chinggisid prerogative, Ligdan Khan set out to reunify the Mongols, to extend his power over both eastern and western wings of the Six *Tümen*, and centralize the government around himself, the rightful heir to the throne of Chinggis Khan. Successful raids into China won him trading concessions from the Ming. Ligdan Khan invested the financial and political capital gained from this renewed wealth and prestige in nation building. For this, he turned to Buddhism. Keeping with tradition, he patronized the Sakyapa and Karmapa over the Gélukpa. To strike the ring of precedent, he reintroduced the imperial cult of Mahākāla at court, installing an image of the Great Black One said to have been given to 'Phags pa by Qubilai. In the name of comity, he sponsored the translation of the Buddhist canon into Mongolian. Still, whatever merit he gained through these efforts was not enough to stem the tide. In 1606, Borjigid princes over Khorchin, Kharchin, and South Khalkha granted the Jurchen ruler, Nurhaci (1559–1626), the title "khan" but retained Mongol rights. Around 1614, their princesses began to marry him. In 1616, Nurhaci founded the "Later Jin" dynasty and in 1621 conquered the ancient Jurchen homeland, Liaodong (Manchuria). By the time of Nurhaci's death in 1626, more Borjigid princes, including those over Sönid, Üjümchiin, Ongniγud, and parts of Chakhar, had aligned their appanages with the Jurchen. In 1627, Ligdan faced open rebellion and Jurchen attack. Waging a counteroffensive, the more he tried to force his brethren back into the fold, the more they turned against him. In 1632, Nurhaci's son, Hongtaiji, marshaled a large army and prosecuted an overwhelming attack. Forced to retreat, Ligdan Khan fled first to Ordos and then down into the Kökenuur region. There the forces of Güüshi Khan met him in battle. In 1634, as war waged on, he succumbed to smallpox at Shara Tala (in modern Gansu) and died. The 17th century "Yellow Chronicle" (*Sira tuγuǰi*) says of him:

> Ligdan Khan exercised the two principles of government (church and state) well but by karma suffered acts of insubordination and ruled with brutality for thirty-one years.[176]

With his death, the fall of the Yuan was imminent. In 1635, Ligdan Khan's family surrendered to Jurchen forces in Ordos. Ligdan's son, Qongghor Ejei, succeeded his father on the throne, but the chief function of the last Great Khan of the Great Yuan dynasty was merely to surrender sovereignty to Hongtaiji. In 1636, he turned over the shrine of Mahākāla, which Hongtaiji installed at the Jurchen capital of Mukden (modern Shenyang). He is also reputed to have a turned over the jade seal of heavenly ordained legitimacy.[177] With the Mongols on board, the Jurchen formed a new heavenly ordained nation-state, the "Manchu," their ruling house, the Qing 清. There were loose ends to tie up. Chinggissids over Khalkha in the north and the Ming dynasty to the south both remained unpacified. But, with the legacy of Mongolian Buddhism as the wellspring to its legitimacy and adroit use of the tools of Buddhist statecraft to master the Three Times, the Manchu Qing dynasty was well on its way to replacing the Mongol Yuan dynasty as the preeminent power in East Asia.[178]

An epilogue to the history of Yuan Buddhism is the story of a nephew of Abatai Khan, Tümenken Tsoghtu Khongtayiji (1581–1637) of Khalkha. When others deserted their emperor, Tsoght Taij remained loyal—loyal to the end. When Hongtaiji attacked Ligdan Khan in 1632, Tsoght Taij came to his emperor's defense. He left the comforts of his "White Castle" (*Čaghan bayising*), a Persian-style palace, and journeyed south to meet up with Ligdan Khan. Together, they retreated into Ordos and down into the Kökenuur region. As the situation grew desperate, Tsoght Taij sent his own son, Arslan, into the heart of Tibet to kill the Fifth Dalai Lama. Arriving in Lhasa in 1635, and perhaps realizing that the cause was lost, instead of carrying out his father's order, Arslan gave up the fight and converted to the Gélukpa, a betrayal of his father that would cost him his life.[179]

By the end of 1636, Tsoght Taij was a man without a country. His emperor, Ligdan Khan, was dead. Dead too was his own son, Arslan. The emperor's son, Qongghor Ejei, had surrendered to the Jurchen. The Yuan dynasty had fallen and the Qing dynasty been proclaimed. Still, though the tide of history had turned against him, Tsoght Taij soldiered on. In 1637, he took the field against the Fifth Dalai Lama's protector, the Khoshud Güüshi Taishi, and was slain.

Sixteen years earlier, in 1621, at the beginning of autumn, Tsoght Taij led a royal hunt of the khan's game preserve in the Khangai Mountain range. Riding a caparisoned roan, he ascended its northern mountain and upon its summit paused to gaze east. He was pining for a paternal aunt rent from him through marriage to a lord of the Ongniγuud. Himself adherent to the Sakyapa, at this time his aunt's people, the Ongniγuud, were converted to the Gelukpa. For the vast space and political distance between them, she must have felt to him a world away. It is said that with his spirit moved to tears, he made a plaintive poem of longing for her. Memorized by an attendant page, years later, in 1624, the poem was inscribed in stone by two retainers, Page Daiching and Knight Güyeng. The poem is telling not only of the disposition of the Yuan dynasty's last patriot but also the state of Mongolian Buddhism at the end of the Yuan Dynasty.[180] Its translation reads:

Although a distinction exists above and below
Between the Khan of Supernal Heaven
And the rulers and saints on earth,
In air of joyfulness and love, they are one and the same.

Although separate are the places
Of the bodhisattvas in their grottos in Akaniṣṭha Heaven
And those Awakened upon this golden Earth,
In air of care and compassion, they are one and the same.
Although there exists a difference in manner and appearance
Between the good ministers of the rulers and saints here
And the great lords of Yama, the Inquisitor,
In air of judging right from wrong, they are one and the same.
Although different are the apparent bodily forms
Of the thief who robs you from near or from afar
And the wolf prowling the edge of camp,
In air of hunger for sustenance, they are one and the same.
Although distant are the lands of the Khalkha and the Ongniγuud
Between my dear elder sister on the Onon
And sickly me who abides here on the Orkhon and the Tuul,
In air of loving and longing for each other, we are one and the same.
Should we never meet again in these bodies of ours,
From now on throughout each future birth,
As a mother loves her only child,
Let us try, in our various deeds, to help each other.

REVIEW OF LITERATURE

An integrated history of Buddhism in the Yuan dynastic era remains unrealized. Over the period from the founding of the Mongol empire under Chinggis Khan in 1206 until the rise of Qubilai Khan in 1260 hangs a pall of modern misapprehension that obscures the meaning of religion and the nature of Mongolian culture. To give the period its due will require foregoing the misconception that the Mongols were primitive shamanists and acceptance of the fact that they were a worldly oligarchy of diverse peoples that included many Buddhists. Comprehensive studies of Buddhist affairs under the five great emperors, Chinggis, Ögedei, Güyüg, Möngke, and Qubilai, have yet to be written. Scholarship on the pre-Qubilaid era has focused on isolated sources and individual figures, the itineraries of William of Rubruck and Yelü Chucai being two examples.[181] Early Mongol ties with Tibet are discussed by T. Wylie.[182] For the period from the rise of Qubilai Khan until the expulsion of the Mongols from China in 1368, scholarship flourishes. Herbert Franke has discussed Mongol reliance on the arts of Buddhist statecraft.[183] The Tibeto-Mongol interface has been studied by G. Tucci, L. Petech, and L. van der Kuijp.[184] Shen Weirong has provided the interface between Mongols, Tibetans, and Chinese.[185] Roxann Prazniak has studied Buddhist links across the Mongol empire from Yuan to Ilkhanate.[186] Translation of the dharma into Mongolian is the subject of G. Kara and P. Zieme.[187] See also the many excellent studies and translations of primary sources by F. W. Cleaves and N. Poppe's *Twelve Deeds of Buddha*.[188] Buddhist material culture has been treated by Anning Jing and N. Steinhardt.[189] For the period from 1368 until Altan Khan's conversion in 1578, Mongol sources are studied by J. Elverskog and Hidehiro Okada; the Tibetan by E. Sperling and Zahiruddin Ahmad; and the Chinese by H. Serruys.[190] For Altan Khan's pivotal conversion to the Gélukpa, see J. Elverskog's study of the *Erdeni Tunumal Sutra*. For the period following Altan Khan's conversion until the fall of the Yuan in 1635 and advent of the Qing dynasty in 1636, scholarship again is burgeoning as scholars increasingly recognize the singular importance of the Mongols in orchestrating the transition from Chinggisid to Géluk Buddhist worlds. Mongol sources are studied by A. Bareja-Starzyńska and K. Kollmar-Paulenz,[191] and the Tibetan by M. Kapstein, K. Schaeffer, and G. Tuttle.[192] For an overview of Buddhist material culture, see P. Berger and T. Bartholomew's *Mongolia: The Legacy of Chinggis Khan*.

PRIMARY SOURCES

For an overview of primary sources, let us begin with 'Phags pa lama's 1278 Buddhist catechism, the *Shes bya rab gsal* [*Elucidation of the Knowable*]. For an English translation, see C. Hoog.[193] For the Middle Mongolian version, see Uspensky and Kara.[194] For a foreign perspective on the Buddhist estate during the reign of Möngke and for the Great Khan's profession of faith, see William of Rubruck's itinerary.[195] Of Chinese sources, Yelü Chucai's *Xiyuolu* 西遊錄 [*Journey to the West*] provides insight into Buddhism's standing during the reigns of Chinggis and Ögedei. For the period from 1206 to 1368, *Yuanshi* 元史 [*History of the Yuan*] is essential.[196] See also the dynastic histories, *Songshi* 宋史 [History of the Song] and *Jinshi* 金史 [*History of the Jin*], as well as *Chuogenglu* 輟耕錄 [Record of the Ceasing of Tillage] by Tao Zongyi 陶宗儀 and *Yuanchao mingchen shilue* 元朝名臣事略 [Sketches of the Yuan Dynasty's Eminent Ministers] by Su Tianjue 蘇天爵.[197] For the period from 1368 to 1636, *Mingshi* 明史 and *Mingshilu* 明實錄 are essential.[198] Of Tibetan sources, the *Deb ther sngon po* [*Blue Annals*] by Gzhon nu dpal (1392–1481), translated by G. Roerich, is essential.[199] Another important chronicle is the 1346 *Deb ther dmar pa* [*Red Annals*] by Tshal pa Kun dga' rdo rje.[200] A source on the history of the Sakyapa is the 1629 *Sa skya gdung rabs chen mo* [*Great Sakya Lineage*] by Jam mgon A mye zhab kun dga bsod nams rgyal mtshan.[201] For the writings of 'Phags pa lama and other eminent Sakya masters, see *Sa skya bka' 'bum* [*Complete Works of the Sakya*].[202] Two important works translated by Zahiruddin Ahmad are the Fifth Dalai Lama Ngag dbang blo bzang rgya mtsho's history of Tibet and Sangs rgyas Rgya mthso's biography of the Fifth Dalai Lama.[203] For sources published under Mongol auspices, two foreign language sources are important. Although it speaks of it as "idolatry," the Persian chronicle *History of the World Conqueror* by "Ala" al-Din 'Ata Malik Juvaini (1226–1283) captures important information about the early status of Buddhism in the realm.[204] The later work, *Jāmi' al-tawārīkh* [*Compendium of Chronicles*] by Rashid al-Din (1247–1318), published in both Arabic and Persian, focuses more specifically and intentionally on Buddhism incorporating Ilkhanid and Yuan scholarship in the creation of a pro-Buddhist historiography.[205] Among Mongolian language sources, from the period 1206 until 1368, several important works are found in Tumurtogoo's compilations of Uygur script and 'Phags pa script monuments.[206] Among F. W. Cleaves' many excellent studies published in the *Harvard Journal of Asiatic Studies*, several deal with Buddhism. See his studies of Chosgi Odsir's Auto-commentary to Śāntideva's *Bodhicaryāvatāra*, the 1346 Sino-Mongolian Inscription from the Buddhist temple at Qara-Qorum, and the 1340 Inscription of Yunan Prince Arugh, which was also studied by G. Kara.[207] For Buddhist literature, see Poppe's study of the *Twelve Deeds of Buddha* and the Turfan texts published by D. Cerensodnom and Taube.[208] After the turn of the 17th century, several Mongolian Buddhist chronicles were composed. The authoritative text of Altan Khan's conversion, the *Erdeni Tunumal Sutra,* has been studied by both K. Kollmar-Paulenz and J. Elverskog.[209] Other important chronicles include the *Erdeni-yin tobchi* [*Jewel Chronicle*] of Saghang Sechen, the *Chaghan teüke* [*White History*], Lubsangdandzin's *Altan tobchi* [*Golden Chronicle*], and the *Sir-a tughujii* [Yellow Chronicle].[210] A. Bareja-Starzyńska has studied Zaya Pandita Luvsanprinlei's biography of the First Jebtsundamba Khutukhtu.[211] A Mongolian history of Mongolian Buddhism is the *Gangga-yin urusqal* [*Current of the Ganges*] by Gombojab.[212]

FURTHER READING

Ahmad, Zahiruddin. *Sino-Tibetan Relations in the Seventeenth Century.* Roma, Italy: Istituto Italiano Per Il Medio Ed Estremo Oriente, 1970.

Berger, Patricia, and Terese Tse Bartholomew. *Mongolia: The Legacy of Chinggis Khan.* San Francisco: Asian Art Museum of San Francisco, 1995.

Bosson, James E., trans. *A Treasury of Aphoristic Jewels.* Bloomington: Indiana University Press, 1969.

Cerensodnom, Dalantai, and Manfred Taube. *Die Mongolica der Berliner Turfansammlung.* Berliner Turfantexts XVI. Berlin: Akademie Verlag, 1993.

Cleaves, Francis Woodman. "The Bodistw-a Čari-a Awatar-un Tayilbur of 1312 by Čosgi Odsir." *Harvard Journal of Asiatic Studies* 17, no. 1–2 (1954): 1–129.

Dawson, Christopher, ed. *The Mission to Asia: Narratives and Letters of the Franciscan Missionaries in Mongolia and China in the Thirteenth and Fourteenth Centuries.* London: Sheed and Ward, 1955.

de Rachewiltz, Igor. "The Hsi-yu lu by Yeh-lü Ch'u-ts'ai." *Monumenta Serica* 21 (1962): 1–128.

Dunnell, Ruth. "The Hsia Origins of the Yüan Institution of Imperial Preceptor." *Asia Major* 5, no. 1 (1992): 85–111.

Elverskog, Johan. *The Jewel Translucent Sūtra.* Leiden, The Netherlands: Brill, 2003.

Franke, Herbert. *From Tribal Chieftain to Universal Emperor and God: The Legitimation of the Yüan Dynasty.* München: Verlag der Bayerischen Akademie der Wissenschaften, 1978.

Franke, Herbert. "Tibetans in Yüan China." In *China under Mongol Rule.* Edited by John D. Langlois Jr., 296–328. Princeton, NJ: Princeton University Press, 2014.

Hoog, Constance, trans. *Prince Jiṅ-gim's Textbook of Tibetan Buddhism.* Leiden, The Netherlands: E. J. Brill, 1983.

Jing, Anning. "Financial and Material Aspects of Tibetan Art under the Yuan Dynasty." *Artibus Asiae* 64, no. 2 (2004): 213–241.

Kara, György. *Books of the Mongolian Nomads: More Than Eight Centuries of Writing Mongolian.* Bloomington: Research Institute for Inner Asian Studies, 2005.

Okada, Hidehiro. "The Life of Dayan Khan." *Acta Asiatica* 11 (1966): 46–55.

Okada, Hidehiro. "The Third Dalai Lama and Altan Khan of the Tümed." In *Tibetan Studies: Proceedings of the 5th Seminar of the International Association for Tibetan Studies. Ihara Shoren and Yamaguchi Zuiho. Edited by Narita: Naritasan Shinshoji 1989,* 1992, 645–652.

Petech, Luciano. *Central Tibet and the Mongols: The Yuan-Sa-skya Period of Tibetan History.* Rome: Instituto italiano per il Medio ed Estremo Oriente, 1990.

Poppe, Nicholas. *The Twelve Deeds of Buddha: A Mongolian Version of the Lalitavistara; Mongolian Text, Notes and English Translation.* Wiesbaden, Germany: Otto Harrassowitz, 1967.

Samten, Jampa. "Overview of Mongolian Patronage to Gelugpa School of Tibetan Buddhism." *The Tibet Journal* 32, no. 3 (2007): 11–21.

Serruys, Henry. "Early Lamaism in Mongolia." *Oriens Extremus* 10, no. 2 (1963): 181–216.
Sperling, Elliot. "Hülegü and Tibet." *Acta Orientalia* 44, no. 1/2 (1990): 145–157.
Taupier, Richard. "The Rise of the Jöüngars Based on Primary Oyirod Sources." *Inner Asia* 21, no. 2 (2019): 140–161.
Tucci, Giuseppe. *Tibetan Painted Scrolls.* Rome: Libreria Dello Stato, 1949.
Tuttle, Gray, and Kurtis R. Schaeffer, eds. *The Tibetan History Reader.* Columbia University Press, 2013.

NOTES

1. Francis Woodman Cleaves, "The Historicity of the Baljuna Covenant," *Harvard Journal of Asiatic Studies* 18, no. 3–4 (1955): 357–421.
2. Rai Sarat Chandra Das, "Tibet under the Tartar Emperors of China in the 13th Century A.D.," *Journal of the Asiatic Society of Bengal* 70, no. 1 (1904): 8; Giuseppe Tucci, *Tibetan Painted Scrolls* (Rome: Libreria Dello Stato, 1949), 8; Choyiji, *Mongghol-un burqan-u shasin-u teüke* [The History of Mongolian Buddhism] (Inner Mongolia, China: Kökeqota, 1998), 83; and Klaus Sagaster, "The History of Buddhism among the Mongols," in *The Spread of Buddhism*, ed. Ann Heirman and Stephan Peter Bumbacher (Leiden, The Netherlands: Brill, 2007), 379–381.
3. Christopher Dawson, ed., *The Mission to Asia: Narratives and Letters of the Franciscan Missionaries in Mongolia and China in the Thirteenth and Fourteenth Centuries* (London: Sheed and Ward, 1955), 121.
4. Brian Baumann, "By the Power of Eternal Heaven: The Meaning of *Tenggeri* to the Government of the Pre-Buddhist Mongols," *Extrême-Orient, Extrême-Occident* 35 (2013): 234.
5. Dawson, *Mission to Asia*, 139–141.
6. Ruth W. Dunnell, "Translating History from Tangut Buddhist Texts," *Asia Major* 22, no. 1 (2009): 41.
7. H. Desmond Martin, "The Mongol Wars with Hsi Hsia (1205–27)," *Journal of the Royal Asiatic Society* 74, no. 1 (1942): 196–203.
8. Igor de Rachewiltz, trans., *The Secret History of the Mongols: A Mongolian Epic Chronicle of the Thirteenth Century* (Leiden, The Netherlands: Brill, 2006), 199–200.
9. Herbert Franke, "Tibetans in Yüan China," in *China under Mongol Rule*, ed. John D. Langlois Jr. (Princeton, NJ: Princeton University Press, 2014), 326.
10. K. J. Solonin, "Buddhist Connections between the Liao and Xixia: Preliminary Considerations," *Journal of Song-Yuan Studies* 43 (2013): 171–219.
11. Christopher P. Atwood, *Encyclopedia of Mongolia and the Mongol Empire* (New York: Facts on File, 2004), 48.
12. Hoyt Cleveland Tillman and Stephen H. West, *China under Jurchen Rule: Essays on Chin Intellectual and Cultural History* (Albany: State University of New York Press, 1995), 146.
13. Henrik Sørensen, "Esoteric Buddhism under the Liao," in *Esoteric Buddhism and the Tantras in East Asia*, ed. Charles Orzech, Henrik Sørensen, and Richard Payne (Leiden, The Netherlands: Brill, 2011), 456–464; and Tillman and West, *China under Jurchen Rule*, 146.
14. Sagaster, "History of Buddhism," 381.
15. Sechin Jagchid, *Essays in Mongolian Studies* (Provo, UT: Brigham Young University Press, 1988), 85.
16. Jagchid, *Essays in Mongolian Studies*, 105; Sagaster, "History of Buddhism," 389; and Atwood, *Encyclopedia*, 48.
17. Jagchid, *Essays in Mongolian Studies*, 105.
18. Atwood, *Encyclopedia*, 48, 117, 278.
19. Igor de Rachewiltz, "Yeh-lü Ch'u-ts'ai (1189–1243): Buddhist Idealist and Confucian Statesman," in *Confucian Personalities*, ed. Arthur F. Wright and Denis Twitchett (Stanford, CA, 1962), 189–216; Igor de Rachewiltz, "The Hsi-yu lu by Yeh-lü Ch'u-ts'ai," *Monumenta Serica* 21 (1962): 1–128; and Arthur Waley,

trans., *The Travels of an Alchemist: The Journey of the Taoist Ch'ang-Ch'un from China to the Hindukush at the Summons of Chingiz Khan*, by Li Chih-ch'ang (London: George Routledge and Sons, 1979).
20. Dawson, *Mission to Asia*, 8–14.
21. Atwood, *Encyclopedia*, 528.
22. As reported by William of Rubruck (Dawson, *Mission to Asia*, 184).
23. Luciano Petech, *Central Tibet and the Mongols: The Yuan-Sa-skya Period of Tibetan History* (Rome: Istituto italiano per il Medio ed Estremo Oriente, 1990), 7.
24. Petech, *Central Tibet*, 8; and Sagaster, "History of Buddhism," 383.
25. Sagaster, "History of Buddhism," 384.
26. Petech, *Central Tibet*, 8.
27. Atwood, *Encyclopedia*, 538–539; and Petech, *Central Tibet*, 8.
28. David L. Snellgrove, *The Hevajra Tantra: A Critical Study* (London: Oxford University Press, 1959), 11.
29. Herbert Franke, *From Tribal Chieftain to Universal Emperor and God: The Legitimation of the Yüan Dynasty* (München: Verlag der Bayerischen Akademie der Wissenschaften, 1978), 60.
30. Constance Hoog, trans., *Prince Jiṅ-gim's Textbook of Tibetan Buddhism* (Leiden, The Netherlands: E. J. Brill, 1983), 4.
31. D. Seyfort Ruegg, "Mchod yon, yon mchod and mchog gnas/yon gnas: On the Historiography and Semantics of a Tibetan Religio-Social and Religio-Political Concept," in *Tibetan History and Language: Studies Dedicated to Géza Uray on His Seventieth Birthday*, ed. E. Steinkellner (Wein, Austria: Arbeitskreis für Tibetische und Buddistische Studien, 1991), 441–453; and David Seyfort Ruegg, "The Preceptor-Donor Relation in Thirteenth-Century Tibetan Society and Polity," in *The Tibetan History Reader*, ed. Gray Tuttle et al. (New York: Columbia University Press, 2013), 211–232.
32. Petech, *Central Tibet*, 5.
33. Turrell V. Wylie, "The First Mongol Conquest of Tibet Reinterpreted," *Harvard Journal of Asiatic Studies* 37, no. 1 (1977): 103–133.
34. Sagaster, "History of Buddhism," 386.
35. Dawson, *Mongol Mission*, 91, 187–197.
36. Sagaster, "History of Buddhism," 389.
37. Atwood, *Encyclopedia*, 48; and Sagaster, "History of Buddhism," 389.
38. Jagchid, *Essays in Mongolian Studies*, 90.
39. Weirong Shen, "Magic Power, Sorcery and Evil Spirit: The Image of Tibetan Monks in Chinese Literature during the Yuan Dynasty," in *The Relationship between Religion and State (chos srid zung 'brel) in Traditional Tibet* (2004), 189.
40. Henry Yule, trans., *The Book of Ser Marco Polo the Venetian Concerning the Kingdoms and Marvels of the East*, 2 vols. (London: John Murray, 1929), 309–314.
41. Patricia Berger and Terese Tse Bartholomew, *Mongolia: The Legacy of Chinggis Khan* (San Francisco: Asian Art Museum of San Francisco, 1995), 117.
42. Petech, *Central Tibet*, 15; and Sagaster, "History of Buddhism," 388.
43. Petech, *Central Tibet*, 16.
44. Dawson, *Mongol Mission*, 194–196.
45. Jagchid, *Essays in Mongolian Studies*, 85; and Sagaster, "History of Buddhism," 382–383.
46. Atwood, *Encyclopedia*, 117–118, 458.
47. Morris Rossabi, *Khubilai Khan: His Life and Times* (Berkeley: University of California Press, 1986).
48. Herbert Franz Schurmann, trans., *Economic Structure of the Yuan Dynasty* (Cambridge, MA: Harvard University Press, 1967), 14–130.
49. Petech, *Central Tibet*, 15.
50. Petech, *Central Tibet*, 15.

51. Hoog, *Prince Jiṅ-gim's Textbook*, 4.
52. Petech, *Central Tibet*, 16.
53. Brian Baumann, *Divine Knowledge* (Leiden, The Netherlands: Brill, 2008), 60–63.
54. György Kara, *Books of the Mongolian Nomads: More Than Eight Centuries of Writing Mongolian* (Bloomington, IN: Research Institute for Inner Asian Studies, 2005), 51–54.
55. Franke, *Tribal Chieftain*, 60.
56. Hoog, *Prince Jiṅ-gim's Textbook*, 5–6.
57. György Kara, "Reading the Middle Mongol Translation of 'Phags-pa's *Shes bya rab gsal* in the St. Petersburg Manuscript and in a Print Fragment from Qaraqota," *Central Asiatic Journal* 59, no. 1–2 (2016): 43.
58. Hoog, *Prince Jiṅ-gim's Textbook*, 42.
59. Rossabi, *Khubilai Khan*, 143, 194.
60. Petech, *Central Tibet*, 21.
61. Petech, *Central Tibet*, 33–35; and Atwood, *Encyclopedia*, 488.
62. Petech, *Central Tibet*, 36–37.
63. Ruth Dunnell, "The Hsia Origins of the Yüan Institution of Imperial Preceptor," *Asia Major* 5 (1992): 86–105; Sagaster, "History of Buddhism," 389, 391–392; and Petech, *Central Tibet*, 144.
64. Elliot Sperling, "Further Remarks Apropos of the 'Ba'-rom-pa and the Tanguts," *Acta Orientalia Academiae Scientiarum Hung* 57, no. 1 (2004): 1–26.
65. Franke, *Tribal Chieftain*, 59–60; and Berger and Bartholomew, *Mongolia*, 4, 54.
66. Karl Debreczeny, "Wutai shan: Pilgrimage to Five-Peak Mountain," *Journal of the International Association of Tibetan Studies* 6 (2011): 11–13; and Solonin, "Buddhist Connections," 199.
67. Debreczeny, "Wutai shan," 1–23; and Isabella Charleux, *Nomads on Pilgrimage—Mongols on Wutaishan (China), 1800–1940* (Leiden, The Netherlands: Brill, 2015), 95.
68. David M. Robinson, *Empire's Twilight: Northeast Asia under the Mongols* (Cambridge, MA: Harvard University Press, 2009), 65–66.
69. Sagaster, "History of Buddhism," 392; Anning Jing, "Financial and Material Aspects of Tibetan Art under the Yuan Dynasty," *Artibus Asiae* 64 (2004): 213–241; and Sagaster, "History of Buddhism," 392.
70. James C. Y. Watt, *The World of Khubilai Khan: Chinese Art in the Yuan Dynasty* (New York: Metropolitan Museum of Art, 2010), 48, fig. 57.
71. George Qingzhi Zhao, *Marriage as Political Strategy and Cultural Expression: Mongolian Royal Marriages from World Empire to Yuan Dynasty*, 22, n.19; and Jing, "Financial and Material Aspects," 235, n.115.
72. Jing, "Financial and Material Aspects," 235.
73. Roxann Prazniak, "Ilkhanid Buddhism: Traces of a Passage in Eurasian History," *Comparative Studies in Society and History* 56, no. 3 (2014): 661.
74. Prazniak, "Ilkhanid Buddhism," 653.
75. Yule, *Marco Polo*, 301, n. 9.
76. Yule, *Marco Polo*, 301–302.
77. Yule, *Marco Polo*, 300–327.
78. Yule, *Marco Polo*, 308, n. 5.
79. Nancy Shatzman Steinhardt, "The Plan of Khubilai Khan's Imperial City," *Artibus Asiae* 44, no. 2–3 (1983): 151.
80. Franke, *Tribal Chieftain*, 72–76. For a precedent to the Yuan Sandalwood Buddha in the Jurchen Jin, see Tillman and West, *China under Jurchen Rule*, 161. For its destruction in 1900, see Isabella Charleux, "From North India to Buryatia: The 'Sandalwood Buddha' from the Mongols' Perspective," in *Studies on Sino-Tibetan Buddhist Art: Proceedings of the Fourth International Conference on Tibetan Archaeology and Art* (Shanghai Classics Publishing House, 2014), 1.

81. Atwood, *Encyclopedia*, 13–14.
82. Watt, *World of Khubilai Khan*, 103.
83. Anning Jing, "The Portraits of Khubilai Khan and Chabi by Anige (1245–1306), a Nepali Artist at the Yuan Court," *Artibus Asiae* 54, no. 1–2 (1994): 40–86.
84. Ying Chua, "Tantra in China," in *The Circle of Bliss: Buddhist Meditational Art*, ed. John C. Huntington and Dina Bangdel (Chicago: Serindia Publications, 2003), 47.
85. Kara, *Books*, 37–38.
86. Kara, *Books*, 37–38.
87. Peter Zieme, *Religion und Gesellschaft im uigurischen Königreich von Qočo: Kolophone und Stifter des alttürkischen buddhistischen Shrifttums aus Zentralasien* (Berlin: Springer-Verlag, 2013); and Johan Elverskog, *Uygur Buddhist Literature* (Turnhout, Belgium: Brepols, 1997).
88. Kara, *Books*, 42.
89. Kara, *Books*, 33–48.
90. Kara, *Books*, 44; see also James E. Bosson, trans., *A Treasury of Aphoristic Jewels* (Bloomington: Indiana University, 1969).
91. Kara, *Books*, 42.
92. Kara, *Books*, 274.
93. Francis Woodman Cleaves, "The Bodistw-a Čari-a Awatar-un Tayilbur of 1312 by Čosgi Odsir," *Harvard Journal of Asiatic Studies* 17 (1954): 55, 86.
94. Kara, *Books*, 46.
95. Pentti Aalto, *Qutuγ-tu Pañcarakṣā kemekü Tabun sakiyan neretü yeke kölgen sudur* (Wiesbaden, Germany: O. Harrassowitz, 1961).
96. Pentti Aalto, *Notes on the Altan Gerel (The Mongolian Version of the Suvarṇaprabhāsa-sūtra)* (Helsinki: Studia Orientalia, 1950).
97. Nicholas Poppe, *The Twelve Deeds of Buddha: A Mongolian Version of the Lalitavistara; Mongolian Text, Notes and English Translation* (Wiesbaden: Otto Harrassowitz, 1967).
98. György Kara, "L'Inscription mongole d'Aruγ, Prince de Yun-nan (1340)," *Acta Orientalia* 17, no. 2 (1964): 145–173; and Francis Woodman Cleaves, "The *Lingǰi* of Aruγ of 1340," *Harvard Journal of Asiatic Studies* 25 (1964–1965): 31–79.
99. Elliot Sperling, "Hülegü and Tibet," *Acta Orientalia* 44 (1990): 145–157.
100. Johan Elverskog, *Buddhism and Islam on the Silk Road* (Philadelphia: University of Pennsylvania Press, 2010), 139–141.
101. Karl Jahn, "Kamalashrai—Rashid al-Din's 'Life and Teaching of Buddha,' A Source for the Buddhism of the Mongol Period," *Central Asiatic Journal* 2, no. 2 (1956): 122.
102. Prazniak, "Ilkhanid Buddhism," 669.
103. Atwood, *Encyclopedia*, 50, 206–207.
104. Michal Biran, *The Empire of the Qara Khitai in Eurasian History: Between China and the Islamic World* (Cambridge, UK: Cambridge University Press, 2005), 171–201.
105. Dawson, *Mongol Mission*, 138.
106. Luciano Petech, "Tibetan Relations with Sung China and with the Mongols," in *China among Equals* (Berkeley: University of California Press, 1983), 187–189.
107. Atwood, *Encyclopedia*, 87.
108. Michel Biran, "The Chaghadaids and Islam: The Conversion of Tarmashirin Khan (1331–34)," *Journal of the American Oriental Society* 122, no. 4 (2002): 745, 746 n. 34, 748, 750.
109. Kara, *Books*, 207.
110. Atwood, *Encyclopedia*, 87.
111. Atwood, *Encyclopedia*, 87; and D. Cerensodnom and Manfred Taube, *Die Mongolica der Berliner Turfansammlung* (Berliner Turfantexts XVI, 1993).

112. Roderick Whitfield, Susan Whitfield, and Neville Agnew, *Cave Temples of Mogao at Dunhuang: Art and History on the Silk Road* (Los Angeles: Getty, 2015), 29–33.
113. Yule, *Marco Polo*, 331–458.
114. Devin DeWeese, "The Influence of the Mongols on the Religious Consciousness of Thirteenth Century Europe," *Mongolian Studies* 5 (1978–1979): 41–78.
115. Francis Woodman Cleaves, "The Sino-Mongolian Inscription of 1346," *Harvard Journal of Asiatic Studies* 15, no. 1–2 (1952): 32.
116. Berger and Bartholomew, *Mongolia*, 210.
117. Franke, *Tribal Chieftain*, 55.
118. Atwood, *Encyclopedia*, 610.
119. Charles Bawden, *The Mongol Chronicle Altan tobči: Text, Translation and Critical Notes* (Wiesbaden, Germany: Otto Harrasssowitz, 1955), 57–58.
120. Henry Serruys, "Early Lamaism in Mongolia," *Oriens Extremus* 10 (1963): 187.
121. Johan Elverskog, *The Jewel Translucent Sūtra* (Leiden, The Netherlands: Brill, 2003), 63–73.
122. Jagchid, *Essays in Mongolian Studies*, 121–122.
123. Jagchid, *Essays in Mongolian Studies*, 124.
124. Walther Heissig, "Zwei mutmaßlich mongolische Yüan-Übersetzungen und ihr Nachdruck von 1431," *Zentralasiatische Studien* 10 (1976): 7–115; and Serruys, "Early Lamaism," 187.
125. Jagchid, *Essays in Mongolian Studies*, 124.
126. Kara, *Books*, 70.
127. Rolf A. Stein, "The Evolution of Monastic Power," in *The Tibetan History Reader*, ed. Gray Tuttle and Kurtis R. Schaeffer (Columbia University Press, 2013), 205.
128. Hidehiro Okada, "The Bilig Literature in Cinggis Qaγan-u Cadig," *Mongolica* 6, no. 27 (1995): 459; and Elverskog, *Jewel Translucent*, 70.
129. Atwood, *Encyclopedia*, 50.
130. Brian Baumann, "Where the Sultan Reigns: The Redemption of a Damned Reference to the Ilkhan from Dante's *Inferno*," *Deutsches Dante-Jahrbuch* 90, no. 1 (2015): 161–178.
131. Atwood, *Encyclopedia*, 50, 206–207.
132. Whitfield, *Cave Temples of Mogao at Dunhuang*, 29–33.
133. Luciano Petech, "The Rise of the Pakmodru Dynasty," in *The Tibetan History Reader*, ed. Gray Tuttle and Kurtis R. Schaeffer (New York: Columbia University Press, 2013), 256.
134. Petech, "Rise of the Pakmodru," 260.
135. Hidehiro Okada, "The Life of Dayan Khan," *Acta Asiatica* 11 (1966): 46–55.
136. Henry Serruys, *Sino-Mongol Relations during the Ming II: The Tribute System and Diplomatic Missions*, Mélanges chinois et bouddhiques 14 (Bruxelles: Institut Belge des Hautes Études Chinoises, 1967), 104.
137. Elverskog, *Jewel Translucent*, 13–14.
138. Elverskog, *Jewel Translucent*, 152, n. 266.
139. Elverskog, *Jewel Translucent*, 129–130, n. 204.
140. Elverskog, *Jewel Translucent*, 140–141.
141. Hidehiro Okada, "The Third Dalai Lama and Altan Khan of the Tümed," in *Tibetan Studies: Proceedings of the 5th Seminar of the International Association for Tibetan Studies, Narita 1989* (1992), 645–652.
142. Jampa Samten, "Overview of Mongolian Patronage to Gelugpa School of Tibetan Buddhism," *The Tibet Journal* 32 (2007): 11–21.
143. Brian Baumann, "Whither the Ocean? The *Talu Dalai* in Sultan Öljeitü's 1305 Letter to Philip the Fair of France," *Archivum Eurasiae Medii Aevi* 19 (2012): 59–80.
144. Elverskog, *Jewel Translucent*, 15.
145. Sagaster, "History of Buddhism," 405.

146. Elverskog, *Jewel Translucent*, 15.
147. Atwood, *Encyclopedia*, 573–574.
148. Richard Taupier, "The Rise of the Jöüngars Based on Primary Oyirod Sources," *Inner Asia* 21 (2019): 140–161.
149. Walther Heissig, "A Mongolian Source to the Lamaist Suppression of Shamanism in the 17th Century," *Antrhopos* 48, no. 1–2 (1953): 1–29.
150. Elverskog, *Jewel Translucent*, 159.
151. Leonard W. J. van der Kuijp, "The Dalai Lama and the Origins of Reincarnate Lamas," in *The Tibetan History Reader*, ed. Gray Tuttle and Kurtis R. Schaeffer (New York: Columbia University Press, 2013), 335–347.
152. Junko Miyawaki, "Tibeto-Mongol Relations at the Time of First Rje btsun dam pa Qutuγtu," in *Tibetan Studies: Proceedings of the 5th Seminar of the International Association of Tibetan Studies*, ed. Ihara Shoren and Zuiho Yamaguchi (Narita: Naritasan Shinshoji, 1992), 599–604.
153. Ishihama Yumiko, "A Study of the Seals and Titles Conferred by the Dalai Lamas," in *Tibetan Studies: Proceedings of the 5th Seminar of the International Association of Tibetan Studies*, ed. Ihara Shoren and Zuiho Yamaguchi (Narita: Naritasan Shinshoji, 1992), 501–514.
154. Elverskog, *Jewel Translucent*, 158, n. 287.
155. Atwood, *Encyclopedia*, 389.
156. Munkh-Erdene, "The 1640 Great Code: An Inner Asian Parallel to the Treaty of Westphalia," *Central Asian Survey* 29, no. 3 (2010): 269–288.
157. As for Christianity, H. Okada notes that Mongols were still venerating the Virgin Mary in the 15th century. See Hidehiro Okada, "Virgin Mary in 15th Century Mongolia," *Bulletin of the Institute of China Border Area Studies* 1 (1970).
158. Elverskog, *Jewel Translucent*, 159.
159. Berger and Bartholomew, *Mongolia*, 54.
160. Elverskog, *Jewel Translucent*, 158.
161. Tucci, *Tibetan Painted Scrolls*, 46–48; Zahiruddin Ahmad, *Sino-Tibetan Relations in the Seventeenth Century* (Roma: Istituto Italiano Per Il Medio Ed Estremo Oriente, 1970), 88–92; Piotr Klafkowski, trans., *Rosary of White Lotuses* (Wiesbaden, Germany: Otto Harrassowitz, 1987), 227–228; and Heissig, "Mongolian Source," 20.
162. Elverskog, *Jewel Translucent*, 133, n. 211; and Isabelle Charleux, "Recent Research on the Maitreya Monastery in Inner Mongolia (China)," *Asia* 68, no. 1 (2014): 1–64.
163. Elverskog, *Jewel Translucent*, 133, n. 211.
164. Agata Bareja-Starzyńska, "Description of the Erdene Zuu Monastery Life (Including Čam) Based on Notes by Kotwicz," in *In the Heart of Mongolia*, ed. Jerry Tulisow et al. (Cracow, Poland: Polish Academy of Arts and Sciences, 2012), 131–189.
165. György Kara, "Zur Liste der mongolischen übersetzungen von Siregetü güüsi," in *Documenta Barbarorum: Festschrift für Walther Heissig zum 70; Geburtstag*, ed. Klaus Sagaster and Michael Weiers (Veröffentlichungen der Societas Uralo-Altaica, Wiesbaden, Germany: Otto Harrassowitz, 1983), 210–217; and Kara, *Books*, 72–73.
166. Kara, *Books*, 127–131.
167. Johan Elverskog, "Whatever Happened to Queen Jönggen?" in *Buddhism in Mongolian History, Culture, and Society*, ed. Vesna A. Wallace (Oxford: Oxford University Publishing, 2015), 3–22.
168. Kara, *Books*, 72–73.
169. Berger and Bartholomew, *Mongolia*, 3.
170. Kara, *Books*, 71.
171. Gray Tuttle, "A Tibetan Buddhist Mission to the East: The Fifth Dalai Lama's Journey to Beijing, 1652–1652," in *Proceedings of the Tenth Seminar of the IATS, 2003, Volume 3: Power, Politics, and the Reinvention of Tradition*, ed. Bryan Cuevas and Kurtis R. Schaeffer (Leiden: Brill, 2006), 65–90.

172. Kara, *Books*, 72.
173. Sagaster, "History of Buddhism," 401.
174. Elverskog, *Jewel Translucent*, 195, n. 20.
175. Petech, "Rise of the Pakmodru," 249–265.
176. Charles Bawden, *Modern History of Mongolia* (London: Kegan Paul International, 1989), 42.
177. Atwood, *Encyclopedia*, 335.
178. Nikolay Tsyrempilov, "Dge lugs pa Divided: Some Aspects of the Political Role of Tibetan Buddhism in the Expansion of the Qing Dynasty," in *Power, Politics, and the Reinvention of Tradition: Tibet in the Seventeenth and Eighteenth Centuries*, ed. Bryan J. Cuevas and Kurtis R. Schaeffer (Leiden: Brill, 2006), 47–64; Samuel M. Grupper, "Manchu Patronage and Tibetan Buddhism during the First Half of the Ch'ing Dynasty," *The Journal of the Tibet Society* 4 (1984): 47–75; and David M. Farquhar, "Empeor as Bodhisattva in the Governance of the Ch'ing Empire," *Harvard Journal of Asiatic Studies* 38, no. 1 (1978): 5–34.
179. Ahmad, *Sino-Tibetan Relations*, 116–117.
180. Brian Baumann, "The Stone Inscription of Tsogt Taij," in *Sourcs of Mongolian Buddhism*, ed. Vesna A. Wallace (Oxford: Oxford University Press, 2020), 3–5.
181. Dawson, *Mission to Asia*; and Igor de Rachewiltz, "The Hsi-yu lu by Yeh-lü Ch'u-ts'ai."
182. Wylie, "First Mongol Conquest," 103–133.
183. Franke, *Tribal Chieftain*, 1–85.
184. Tucci, *Tibetan Painted Scrolls*, 1949; Petech, *Central Tibet.*; and Leonard van der Kuijp, *The Kālacakra and the patronage of Tibetan Buddhism by the Mongol Imperial Family* (Bloomington: Indiana University, 2004).
185. Weirong Shen, "Tibetan Buddhism in Mongol-Yuan China (1206–1368)," in *Esoteric Buddhism and the Tantras in East Asia*, ed. Charles Orzech, Richard Payne, and Henrik Sørensen (Leiden: Brill, 2011), 537–549.
186. Prazniak, "Ilkhanid Buddhism," 650–680.
187. Kara, *Books of the Mongolian Nomads*, 2005.
188. Cleaves, "The Bodistw-a Čari-a Awatar-un Tayilbur of 1312 by Čosgi Odsir," 1–129.
189. Jing, "Financial and Material Aspects, 213–241"; and Nancy Steinhardt, "The Plan of Khubilai Khan's Imperial City," *Artibus Asiae* 44, no. 2–3 (1983): 137–158.
190. Elverskog, *Jewel Translucent Sutra*; Okada, "Life of Dayan Khan, 46–55"; Elliot Sperling, *Early Ming Policy toward Tibet* ([dissertation], Indiana University, 1983); Ahmad, *Sino-Tibetan Relations*; and Serruys, "Early Lamaism," 181–216.
191. Agata Bareja-Starzyńska, "The Mongolian Incarnation of Jo nang pa Tāranātha Kun dga' snying po: Öndör Gegeen Zanaabazar Blo bzang bstan pa'i rgyal mtshan (1635–1723): A Case Study of the Tibeto-Mongolian Relationship," *The Tibet Journal* 34/35 (2009–2010): 243–261; and Karenina Kollmar-Paulenz, *Erdeni tunumal neretü sudur* (Wiesbaden, Germany: Harrassowitz, 2001).
192. Gray Tuttle and Kurtis R. Schaeffer, eds., *The Tibetan History Reader* (New York: Columbia University Press, 2013).
193. Hoog, *Prince Jiṅ-gim's Textbook*.
194. Vladimir L. Uspensky, trans., *"Explanation of the Knowable" by 'Phags pa bla ma Blo gros rgyal mtshan (1235–1280)* (Tokyo: Research Institute for Languages and Cultures of Asia and Africa, 2006); and György Kara, "Reading the Middle Mongol Translation of 'Phags-pa's *Shes bya rab gsal* in the St. Petersburg Manuscript and in a Print Fragment from Qaraqota," *Central Asiatic Journal* 59, no. 1–2 (2016): 43–60.
195. Peter Jackson, *The Mission of Friar William of Rubruck* (Indianapolis, IN: Hackett Publishing, 1990).
196. Song Lian, ed., *Yuanshi* 元史 (Beijing: Zhonghua shuju, 1976).
197. Tuotuo, ed., *Songshi* 宋史 (Beijing: Zhonghua shuju, 1977); Tuotuo, ed., *Jinshi* 金史 (Beijing: Zhonghua shuju, 1975); Tao Zongyi 陶宗儀, *Chuogenglu* 輟耕錄 [Record of the Ceasing of Tillage] (Beijing: Zhonghua shuju, 1959); and Su Tianjue 蘇天爵, *Yuanchao mingchen shilue* 元朝名臣事略 [Sketches of the Yuan Dynasty's Eminent Ministers] (Beijing: Zhonghua shuju, 1962).

198. Zhang Tingyu 張廷玉, *Mingshi* 明史 (Beijing: Zhonghua shuju, 1974); and *Mingshilu* 明實錄, (Beijing: Zhonghua shuju, 1987).
199. George Roerich, *The Blue Annals* (Calcutta: The Royal Asiatic Society of Bengal, 1949).
200. Tshal pa Kun dga' rdo rje, *Deb ther dmar po* [The Red Annals] (Gangtok, Sikkim: Namgyal Institute of Tibtology, 1961). See also its Mongolian study, *Улаан дэвтэр-ийн нэгэн Төвд бичмэл эхийн орчуулга, эх бичагийн судэлгаа* (Ulaanbaatar, 2002).
201. BUDA by BDRC (https://library.bdrc.io/show/bdr:MW4CZ30702).
202. *Sa skya bka' 'bum* [The Complete Works of the Great Masters of the Sa skya Sect] (Tokyo: Toyo Bunko, 1968).
203. Zahiruddin Ahmad, trans., *The Song of the Queen of Spring or A History of Tibet*, by Ngag dbang blo bzang rgya mtsho (New Delhi: International Academy of Indian Culture, 2008); and Zahiruddin Ahmad, trans., *Life of the Fifth Dalai Lama Volume IV, Part I* by Sangs rgyas rgya mtsho (New Delhi: International Academy of Indian Culture), 1999.
204. John A. Boyle, trans., *The History of the World Conqueror* (Cambridge, MA: Harvard University Press, 1958).
205. Wheeler M. Thackston, trans., *Rashiduddin Fazlullah's Jami'u't-tawarikh: Compendium of Chronicles; A History of the Mongols* (Cambridge, MA: Harvard University Press, Department of Near Eastern Languages and Civilizations, 1999).
206. D. Tumurtogoo, *Mongolian Monuments in Uighur-Mongolian Script (XIII-XVI Centuries)* (Taipei: Academia Sinica, 2006); and D. Tumurtogoo, *Mongolian Monuments in 'Phags-pa Script* (Taipei: Academia Sinica, 2010).
207. Cleaves, "Bodistw-a Čari-a Awatar-un Tayilbur of 1312 by Čosgi Odsir," 1–129; F. W. Cleaves, "The Sino-Mongolian Inscription of 1346," *Harvard Journal of Asiatic Studies* 15 (1952): 1–123; Francis W. Cleaves, "The Lingǰi of Aruγ of 1340," *Harvard Journal of Asiatic Studies* 25 (1964–1965): 31–79; and G. Kara, "L'Inscription mongole d'Aruγ, Prince de Yun-nan (1340)," *Acta Orientalia Academiae Scientiarum Hung* 17, no. 2 (1964): 145–173.
208. Poppe, *Twelve Deeds of Buddha*; and Cerensodnom and Taube, *Die Mongolica der Berliner Turfansammlung* [Mongolica of the Turfan Collection in Berlin]
209. Kollmar-Paulenz, *Erdeni tunumal neretü sudur* [Jewel Translucent Sutra]; and Elverskog, *Jewel Translucent Sutra*.
210. Erich Haenisch, *Eine Urga-Handschrift des mongolischen Geschichtswerks von Secen Sagang* (Berlin: Akademie, 1954).; Klaus Sagaster, *Die Weisse Geschichte* (Wiesbaden, Germany: Otto Harrassowitz, 1976).; Hans-Peter Vietze and Gedeng Lubsang, *Altan tobči: Eine mongolische Chronik des XVII; Jahrhunderts von Blo bzang bstan 'jin* (Tokyo: Institute for the Study of Languages and Cultures of Asia and Africa, 1992); and Nina P. Shastina, *Shara Tudzhi: Mongol'skaia letopis' XVII v.* (Moscow and Leningrad: Akademii Nauk, 1957).
211. Agata Bareja-Starzyńska, *The Biography of the First Khalkha Jetsundampa Zanabazar by Zaya Pandita Luvsanprinlei* (Warsaw, Poland: Dom Wydawniczy ELIPSA, 2015).
212. Leonid S. Puchkovskii, ed., *Gombodzhav: Ganga-iin uruskhal* (Moscow: Akademii Nauk, 1960).

Brian Baumann

MUSLIM-BUDDHIST RELATIONS AND BUDDHISM IN MUSLIM SOURCES UNTIL THE MONGOL PERIOD

At first glance, Buddhism and Islam seem incompatible at a very fundamental level. The one God in Islam has no Buddhist equivalent. Buddhist and Islamic notions of time are diametrically opposed to each other: circular and linear. Buddhist figurative art is abhorred by many Muslims. Monasticism is one of the pillars of Buddhism, but categorically rejected in the Islamic tradition. Orientalist representations pit the violence of medieval fundamentalists against the enlightened rationalism of proto-secularists. Throughout the history of their contacts and in the present day, interactions between followers of both religions appear to reflect and confirm this antagonism. The demise of Indian Buddhism is regularly explained as the result of Muslim invasions. More lately, the Taliban infamously destroyed the Bamiyan Buddhas in front of a global audience, while Buddhist monks launch attacks against Muslims in Southeast Asia.

Recent scholarship, however, has cast doubt on the veracity of some of these accounts and on the representative nature of the conflicts and antagonistic attitudes. It has also revealed the extent to which Buddhists and Muslims enjoy a shared history of manifold encounters, often peaceful and often culturally productive, sometimes in the same social spaces. Academic traditions in the West, especially area studies, have long separated the study of Islam and the Middle East on the one hand and Buddhism and Asia on the other. As these boundaries are becoming more porous again with increasing collaborations, surveys of historical encounters between Muslims and Buddhists gain in substance. Among premodern eras, the Mongol period has received the lion's share of scholarly attention. Religious contacts are often explored against the backdrop of trade, patronage, and the transmission of knowledge in other areas such as the sciences.

A complication in any historical survey of Buddhist–Muslim relations is that chronologies do not produce linear narratives. While in some areas Muslims assumed power where Buddhists had been predominant, in other cases, such as Tibet, Islam spread into territories which only later became Buddhist. The convergence of religious, geographical, and political references thus shifted over time, but even if we should not assume too easily that a reference to Indians or Tibetans is also a reference to Buddhists, such relationships still constitute an important backdrop for religious contacts more strictly speaking. Historically, one of the greatest problems is to determine whether Muslim literary references are to Indian religions in general or to a more specific tradition such as Buddhism. Even a term so seemingly obviously referring to Buddhism such as *budd*, used in Arabic for an idol or a temple, has been applied to Buddhist as well as other Indian religious institutions.[1] Terms used by Muslims for Buddhists can be inconsistent and confusing. Another challenge is to historicize concepts of religion and the different forms in which religious identities became manifest in historical societies. Thus, what exactly in an encounter between a Muslim and a Buddhist qualifies as a Muslim–Buddhist encounter is not always obvious. Western scholarship has long disproportionately emphasized the religious identities of Muslims. As a result, the analysis of actions and objects associated with Muslims has been overdetermined by religious categories. The following survey will focus on examples where religious identities appear to be especially relevant even if these capture only a fraction of interactions between Muslims and Buddhists.

THE FIRST ENCOUNTER

The history of Islam begins with Muhammad's movement in early 7th-century western Arabia. After the death of their prophet in 632, Muslims rapidly conquered vast areas of the late antique world. By the 660s, Islamic rule had spread from modern-day Tunisia to modern-day

Afghanistan. Less than a century later, Muslim armies had brought most of the Iberian Peninsula under their control, begun a long history of expansion into the Indian subcontinent, and fought Chinese forces at the River Talas. As Muslims advanced eastwards, they entered deeper into territories in which Buddhism enjoyed a significant and continuous presence. The cities of Marw and Balkh, which had come under Muslim rule by the beginning of the 8th century, illustrate this well. Accounts of Buddhist pilgrims serve as testimonies to the presence of this religion in India and Central Asia at the eve of the Muslim conquests. The Chinese Xuanzang, who traveled from 627 to 645, is an oft-quoted source for the presence of Buddhism in the region. He "recorded an extensive Buddhist presence in several areas. By his reckoning Bamiyan in Afghanistan had 10,000 monks, the area of Sind had four hundred and sixty monasteries, and the coastal region toward Iran had one hundred and eighty monasteries with 11,000 monks."[2] The lesser-known Korean pilgrim Hyecho visited the area as a young man from 724 to 727. His account, brief and preserved in fragments, offers insights into the impact of Muslim incursions into Sind, but confirms in other cases the decline of Buddhist life before these invasions. His references to Persia and Arabia suggest that he may have traveled further west than any of the more famous Buddhist pilgrims, perhaps as the first Buddhist to encounter Muslims on their own turf, so to speak, but whether he actually visited these regions or what these geographical references meant is uncertain.[3]

The Arab-Muslim conquests unfolded as part of a larger cultural revolution in which a new empire (the caliphate) and a new religion (Islam) entered the stage of world history. Against the backdrop of these transformations, a new intellectual and literary culture flourished as well, and it increasingly manifested itself in written form and in Arabic. Because of all these circumstances, when considering Muslim encounters with Buddhists during the first two centuries or so of Islamic history, there is significantly more information available which is also based on more extensive evidence about later than earlier encounters. The further Muslims moved towards the East, the greater the likelihood to encounter Buddhists, but also the greater the likelihood that accounts of encounters were recorded and survived until today. Significant uncertainties, however, persist even in cases of documentation. The extent to which these individuals recognized each other as Muslims and Buddhists, respectively, what they may have made of such affiliations, and how they may have reported any such observations to others remains subject to speculation.

In recent representations, accounts of the earliest encounters vary considerably. The precise circumstances under which Muslims were first exposed to Buddhism or Buddhists and vice versa depend on historiographical commitments concerning the religious milieu in which Islam emerged, how far Buddhism spread to the west, and its continuous presence in these western regions. Iran is typically considered the western endpoint of Buddhism's expansion, although in recent scholarship a variety of Buddhist influences on Graeco-Roman intellectual life have been debated.[4] Depending on one's stance toward these theories, an impact of such views on Arabic-Islamic philosophy by way of Greek intermediaries might be a possibility. (For a discussion of this tradition, see the section entitled "Encounters during the Abbasid Empire.") Other examples of such mediated traces are Buddhist elements in Manichaeism, a religion known to Muslims possibly even before the first expansions into Iraq, and the legacy of Zoroastrian iconography and architecture which in Eastern Iran had been subject to Buddhist influences.[5] These examples belong to a larger category of Buddhist–Iranian entanglements in the pre-Islamic period, located especially in the Iranian-Indian border region.[6] How much Mediterranean and Middle Eastern Christians retained of any familiarity with Buddhism that circulated among early Christian authors, whether they shared any of this knowledge with Muslims or used it in any way if they converted to Islam, also remains uncertain.

Structural, social, and ideological explanations for the fate of Buddhism in its western regions often determine how scholars approach the relationship between Buddhism and Islam in general. Among the reasons Erik Seldeslachts suggested for the end of this westward spread was the absence of robust, especially state patronage for Buddhists, but also configurations of trade networks and finally the rise of Christianity in the late Roman Empire.[7] Whatever Buddhist communities existed in the Middle East, these were presumably small and only sustained by the support of merchants. (The aforementioned Hyecho even stated that Buddhism was unknown in Persia.) Likewise, in his *Buddhism and Islam on the Silk Road*, Johan Elverskog considered the control over state resources and trade networks critical for geographical shifts in Muslim–Buddhist encounters and any repercussions for mutual perceptions.

The prominence of the toponym Naw Bahār has been adduced as evidence of the widespread presence of Buddhists and their monastic institutions in Iran just before the Arab-Muslim conquests. (Naw Bahār, "new monastery," reflects the Sanskrit *nava vihāra*.) While the best known of these institutions was located in Balkh, Richard Bulliet has identified a whole set of such toponyms along trade routes in northeastern Iran and suggested that these "new monasteries" represented a distinctly Iranian branch of Buddhism.[8] In recent scholarship, literary sources are often probed with the help of archaeological evidence, a method which might be pursued in this case as well. Independent of the state of Naw Bahārs at the time of Muslim conquests, however, and the degree of destruction, it remains unclear just how "readable" these Buddhist sites were to the Muslim outsiders.

That the physical configurations of places can be ambiguous is also obvious in the case of two archaeological sites on the Persian Gulf. The cave complexes in Chehelkhāneh and Qalʿat-i Ḥaydarī have been interpreted by some scholars as Buddhist monasteries, although others have argued that these were in fact Christian structures.[9] Despite the oppression in the Sassanian Empire, which upheld Zoroastrianism as a state religion from the 3rd century onwards, both communities survived in Iran into Islamic times. That Buddhism would have spread by way of maritime trade into the Persian Gulf is consistent with larger patterns of the diffusion of Buddhism through trade.[10] (See "Maritime Buddhism.") Likewise, it seems plausible that Buddhist objects circulated west of the Indian Ocean. Discussing the journey of a Buddhist statue to the Middle East during the 9th century, Deborah Klimburg-Salter emphasized the general mobility of such objects, an observation which obtains in earlier periods as well.[11] Finbarr B. Flood has discussed the different functions of mobile objects in Hindu–Muslim contexts. An important area are Buddhist and Hindu idols sent by local Muslim rulers at the frontier to the Abbasid caliphs in Baghdad. These objects, like many others, allowed for the construction of different meanings and translation across cultural milieus. In addition to serving Muslim rulers as statements in internal competitions, "these tokens of victory also permitted a vicarious participation in the territorial expansion of the Islamic world."[12] Their symbolic and material values were intertwined. Echoing efforts to remove economically unproductive gold from Islamic sacred spaces and objects, Buddhist idols were reportedly broken up and distributed for charity. Flood's study serves as an important reminder that while Muslims may have typically encountered Buddhists while moving eastwards, Buddhist individuals and objects moved westwards as a result of the Muslim expansion.

Critical questions concern the state of these remains at the eve of the Islamic conquests and how widely Buddhist individuals, views, and objects may have spread westward beyond the area in which their presence can be documented. Only a small number of modern authors have made a case for Buddhist influences on Islam during the earliest days of Muhammad's movement in Mecca and Medina.[13] According to these views, the presence of Buddhist traders in the region of the Persian Gulf might have extended to the western shores of the Arabian Peninsula. An extensive network of trade routes and the proximity of Mecca to Red Sea ports lead to the impression that Muhammad's home region was very much connected with diverse cultural centers. Muslim religious and historical traditions about pre- and early Islamic times compiled in around the 9th century contain anecdotes about idols kept in the Kaʿba or its treasure which some modern historians have interpreted as Buddhist sculpture. Arguments about religious influence on emerging Islam often seek to undermine claims of originality. It was already the British administrator and art historian Ernest Binfield Havell (1861–1934) who took an interest in a story about a painting of the Virgin Mary with Jesus on her lap, which according to the Islamic tradition had existed in the Kaʿba where it survived into the Islamic period. According to Havell, this painting, however, may in fact have been a representation of the Buddhist deity Hāritī and her partner.[14] Havell included in his *Handbook of Indian Art* of 1920 a more general account of Buddhist influences on Islamic architecture along similar lines, suggesting that the mosque was inspired by Buddhist temples.[15] Architectural elements which had originally served as niches for idols eventually turned into mihrabs indicating the direction of prayer. In domestic contexts, such niches were later used as "cupboards or receptacles for the hookah, rose-water vessel, lamp, or other articles of domestic use."[16]

While such theories about a Buddhist presence in western Arabia at the eve of Islam remain marginal in modern scholarship, several medieval Muslim authors commented on the similarities between Arabian and Indian religious practice more generally and developed their own theories of Indian influences. In his *Book of Idols* (*Kitāb al-aṣnām*), for example, Ibn al-Kalbī (737–*c.* 820) suggested that idolatry had first emerged in India, but that when the deluge came, the waves transported these objects to Arabia.[17] Likewise, the 11th-century Persian historian Gardīzī compared Mecca and Somanātha as places for religious veneration. To his mind, these similarities were grounded in a historical connection for the temple in Somanātha "contained numerous idols of gold and silver, and the idol Manāt, which had been transported from the Kaʿba by way of Aden in the time of the Lord of the World (i.e., Muḥammad), was there."[18] Proponents of Buddhist influences on early Islam have also commented on ritual circumambulation which is prominent in both religions. Again, this similarity had already attracted attention among medieval Muslim authors such as Ibn al-Kalbī. In the early 9th century, Abū Ḥafṣ ʿUmar al-Kirmānī, author of a history of the Barmakids, a family of Buddhist converts who gained influence at the Abbasid court (see section entitled "Encounters during the Abbasid Empire"), made similar comparisons.

Theories about Buddhist references in the Qur'an, on the other hand, do not appear to proliferate in the premodern period. In modern accounts, a somewhat mysterious figure by the name of Dhū 'l-Kifl is occasionally identified with the buddha based on the supposition that Kifl is derived from Kapilavastu, the birthplace of Siddhārtha Gautama. This, however, is a marginal view. Several passages in the Qur'an reflect the presence of prized substances from India such as camphor (Arabic: *kāfūr*), ginger (Arabic: *zanjabīl*) and musk (Arabic: *misk*) in Muhammad's historical environment and thus some form of historical contact. None of these references, however, point to any significance of Indian religious ideas of practices, Buddhist or otherwise, in this milieu.

THE ARAB-MUSLIM CONQUESTS

As mentioned just above, most modern scholars date the first extensive encounters between Muslims and Buddhists to the period of the Arab-Muslim conquests in the Iranian-Indian borderlands, especially Sind. It is accordingly in the textual sources for these conquests that the earliest Muslim references to Buddhists typically appear, although a systematic and consistent distinction between Buddhists and Indians in general is usually absent. Historical and geographical works offer short descriptions of religious sites, practices, and beliefs and refer to religious communities. Two elements typically function as markers of religious practice and space: idols and monasteries or temples.

Polemical and hostile responses to Islam have long overdetermined explanations for the spread of Muhammad's movement, which has been seen as overwhelmingly violent. This is the case among Christians as much as among Buddhists and in both cases historical perceptions have left a powerful imprint on later historiography. Challenging the prevalence of narratives about the disappearance of Buddhism from India as a consequence of the Muslim conquests, Audrey Truschke has pointed out that the Muslim sources on which these accounts rely are ambiguous in the details and follow literary conventions which makes literal readings highly problematic.[19] Any understanding of Buddhist–Muslim relations during the conquest period also has to confront the asymmetry of preserved sources. Hardly any Buddhist sources have come down to us which would illustrate Buddhist attitudes to Islam during those years and Muslim sources reflect the point of view of the conquerors.

In more recent scholarship, peaceful modes of diffusion and conversion have received greater attention. Indeed, the ways by which Buddhism and Islam spread are very similar, especially in their reliance on traders, as emphasized by Silk Road historians.[20] Within the realm of political expansion, conquests were often conducted by way of peace treaty rather than military defeat. Milka Levy-Rubin has shown that conquered populations in the Middle East played an active role in the surrender treaties. Preexisting imperial structures in the late antique world were often continued under new regimes. Whether similar patterns can be identified further to the East and whether there was anything distinctly Buddhist about any role that conquered Buddhists may have played in these events is subject to further research.[21] An example which could be analyzed in such a context is the opening episode of the Muslim conquest of northwest India. In 711/712, Muslim armies under Muḥammad ibn al-Qāsim al-Thaqafī attacked the port city of Daybul in Sind, according to medieval Muslim historians, because pirates had captured a ship with Muslim passengers. The historian and geographer Yaʿqūbī (d. 897) reports that a sacred site was the main target of the attack. The local *budd*, forty cubits high, was bombarded with a mangonel and shattered.[22] Based on the record of another historian, al-Balādhurī (820–892), this *budd* has been interpreted as a Buddhist stūpa.

Derryl MacLean, however, has argued that based on archaeological evidence and the ambiguity of the word *budd*, this may have been a Śaiva temple. (How contemporaneous Muslims would have understood the difference, if at all, is unclear.) Emphasizing the difference between the local ruling authorities and Buddhists of Daybul and based on the later testimony of the *Chachnāma*, MacLean pointed out that while the former assumed no responsibility for the pirates' aggression, the Buddhists apologized to the Muslims and established a treaty with their authorities. These Buddhists were also instrumental in the eventual Muslim conquest of Daybul, presumably having recognized their own advantage in this situation.[23]

This rebalancing is not meant to deny the use of brutal force during conquests or the suffering of those who were defeated. But highlighting precisely that force was one of the conventions of history writing as well. A case is point is the 1026 attack on the Śaiva temple of Somanātha under Maḥmūd of Ghazna (971–1030), an account which is modeled after stories of the prophet Muhammad's cleansing of the Kaʿba of idols.[24] Muslim authors of conquest narratives had an interest in emphasizing the impact of these conquests, measured to some extent by the amount of violence and destruction, here especially of emblematic religious architecture and objects. To separate literary trope from reality can be a challenge, although in some cases, Arabic conquest narratives can be compared with records in other sources as well as archaeological evidence. Such studies have been conducted for the Middle East, but they can be extended into Central and South Asia. Al-Balādhurī, for example, explains that the Naw Bahār in Balkh was destroyed by the Muslim conquerors in the mid-7th century.[25] The geographer Ibn al-Faqīh, however, who also flourished in the second half of the 9th century, offered a detailed description of the Naw Bahār. The passage suggests that some of the Buddhist architecture in the city mentioned by Xuanzang almost three centuries earlier survived into the Islamic era, a theory that can be substantiated based on archaeological findings.[26] Evidence from several places in Sind confirms that Indian religious communities continued their practices well into the Islamic period.[27]

Just how much Muslim authors associated the larger Indian, Central Asian, and Buddhist world with idolatry is obvious in conquest narratives where such objects loom large as symbols of religious identity and domination. An oft-quoted account of the expansion of Arab-Muslim power into Central Asia describes a golden idol a king of Tibet sent to the Abbasid caliph al-Maʾmūn (813–833) upon his conversion to Islam. Initially sent to the capital Baghdad, like the idols in other, similar anecdotes, the object was then displayed in Mecca and later included in the treasury of the Kaʿba. Based on art historical sources, Deborah Klimburg-Salter has reconstructed the features of this object, aligning literary description and material evidence.[28] The king in question was presumably the Kabul Shāh who submitted to the Abbasids in 812–813. As Christopher Beckwith has established, this ruler was a vassal of the king of Tibet at the time in question, but contemporaneous Arabic sources often operate with large and somewhat inaccurate categories.[29]

THE THEOLOGY OF RELIGIOUS PRACTICE

Terms and concepts associated with idolatry have left a larger imprint in Islamic theology and literature about religions other than Islam. While *ṣanam* and *wathan* are regularly used in Arabic literature to denote "idol," including in Indian contexts, a term more clearly etymologically connected with Buddhism is *budd*. The word is related to the Persian *bot* which itself is rooted in "buddha," although the exact relationship between the Arabic and Persian terms has been reconstructed in different ways.[30] Unlike *ṣanam* which is used in a wide range of geographical and religious environments, *budd* and *bot* more commonly describe objects of worship in Central Asia or India. Buddhism is often conflated with other religions, as in descriptions of the attack on Daybul. Likewise, in his *Kitāb al-tanbīh wa'l-ishrāf*, the encyclopedist al-Masʿūdī (895–957) discussed beliefs surrounding the buddha in the context of the Hindu temple of Multan which attracted great interest among Muslim authors for its gold.[31] While the term *budd* thus has a more generic definition than the buddha or images of the buddha, it can be used in these specific meanings.[32] In Arabic, *budd* can also designate a temple, perhaps by extension. This twofold ambiguity—the nature of the object and its religious affiliation—accounts for the difficulty in identifying the nature of the temple in Daybul destroyed by Muslim forces in the early 8th century. Furthermore, al-Balādhurī describes Muḥammad ibn al-Qāsim as contemplating the religious status and function of the temple, concluding that it corresponded to the churches of Christians and Jews and the Zoroastrian fire-temples, illustrating the manner in which religious objects were embedded in social contexts. This observation may be a back-projection of later legal developments, specifically the regulations for the maintenance and construction of sacred sites of non-Muslims.[33]

Arabic authors such as the litterateur al-Jāḥiẓ (d. 868) or the lexicographer Ibn Durayd (837–933) assumed that *budd* was simply an Indian name for "idol." In Persian literature, the theme of *bot* as an idol became intertwined with the trope of the beautiful Turk. Conventional representations of this idealized human beauty, especially the round, moon-like face, bring to mind later Buddhist statue and betray a lasting legacy of Buddhism in Persian literature. References to *budd* can be found in other contexts as well.[34] As early as al-Masʿūdī, Muslim authors referred to a type of musk which they called *buddī*. Musk, a substance used for perfumery as well as medicine and cooking, was typically imported from Tibet, China, and India. The *buddī* type was considered weak since according to the explanation of the medieval authors, this kind of musk had been rubbed on statues and was only sold after it had been removed and replaced by fresh and more fragrant musk.

While some Muslim authors displayed a quasi-ethnographic interest in Indian religions, seeking to describe and explain noteworthy features, religions were also classified for legal reasons, as al-Balādhurī's reference to Muḥammad ibn al-Qāsim indicates. The Qur'anic regulations of rights and obligations of non-Muslims under Islamic rule reflected the religious landscape of the prophet Muhammad's western Arabian environment. With the conquests of the 7th and 8th centuries and further developments of Islamic law, however, these categories were modified to accommodate the diverse religious realities of much larger territories. The distinction between "people of the book," mostly understood to equal Jews and Christians, who were allowed to practice their religion under Muslim rule, and other religions, was hardly upheld outside of Arabia. (People who qualified for this status as tolerated religious community were referred to as *dhimmī*.) Muslim legal scholars disagreed in their interpretation and application of the distinction between protected and other religious communities and in their classification of religious communities not mentioned in the Qur'an. While some emphasized the differences among non-Muslims, others such as al-Awzāʿī (d. 774) determined that all non-Muslims who were not "people of the book" were "Majūs," a term originally denoting

Zoroastrians. Accordingly, Muslim authors sometimes identified Majūs in areas well beyond the historical homelands of Zoroastrianism. Apart from pursuing purposes of classification, they may have recognized similarities in certain rituals.

Further complications arise from historical notions of religion. Medieval Muslim writers do not display a homogeneous understanding of such a concept. While some evidence points to a narrow sense of religion as true religion, other references imply an understanding of religion as a universal category. Mālik ibn Anas (711–795), eponym of the Maliki legal school of Sunni Islam, spoke of "those among the Turks and Indians who did not have a religion (*dīn*)."[35] It is unclear whom he had in mind and whether Buddhists would have qualified as having a religion at all and separate from Hindus. What set religious communities apart from Muslims was regularly of greater interest than what defined them in positive terms. Among those classified as polytheists or idolaters, legal scholars frequently distinguished Arabs who were not granted any tolerance, from non-Arabs who were often allowed to maintain their religion and pay the *jizya*, a tax imposed on "people of the book." Critically, followers of both the Maliki and the Hanafi legal schools, which prevailed among Muslims in India, held such views. The heterogeneous responses to Indian religions in Islamic legal literature correspond to the mixed responses in practice. There is no indication that Buddhism received a different treatment than other Indian religions.

ENCOUNTERS DURING THE ABBASID EMPIRE

Buddhist–Muslim encounters during the earliest days of the Islamic empire and under the Umayyad dynasty (661–749) read like a prelude to one of the high points of these contacts. Under the Abbasids, who ruled the Islamic empire from *c.* 750, encounters intensified. The aforementioned episodes of objects sent from the eastern borderlands belong to this period. Records of Muslim–Buddhist contacts and information about Buddhism in general were now also committed to writing in Arabic. Earlier accounts may very well have existed, but they have not come down to us. The different modes of encounter determined what kind of description was presented and in which textual genres. Likewise, the general subject matter of a text framed the representation of Buddhists and Buddhism. Conquest narratives are an important case in point. The significance of trade in the Abbasid Empire is obvious in geographical literature. The caliphs in Baghdad had an interest in the world they dominated. Cartography flourished as a consequence, although as a visual parallel to geographical literature it offers very little details about the religious landscape of medieval Eurasia. While these sources offer important insights into contacts between Muslims and Buddhists, the significance of their respective religious identities is less certain.

Many of these different forms of contact came together in the imperial center Baghdad. The caliphal capital was the heart of Abbasid political and administrative organization. The armies were controlled from Baghdad, reporting and decision-making converging at the ruler's court. The new empire offered new opportunities. From across the realm, old and new elites were attracted to the capital which became a cosmopolitan metropolis of the medieval world. As the heart of political power, Baghdad also became an economic center with wealthy elites demanding high-prestige goods from distant places.

Knowledge was another of these high-prestige goods. That the elite culture of Baghdad was cosmopolitan has long been acknowledged in scholarship. The transmission of knowledge across languages, cultures, and ages has been studied especially as exemplified by the Graeco-Arabic translation movement. As mentioned above, elements of Buddhist thought might have entered the Islamic Middle East through this avenue, although there is little evidence that these elements would have been recognizable as Buddhist. Persian knowledge too was prestige knowledge and offers another possible arena for mediated Buddhist influences. In recent years, historians have paid increasing attention to India as another prestige culture and translations from Sanskrit into Arabic, often via Persian. Evidence points to a transmission of astronomical and mathematical knowledge, with greater uncertainties attaching to medicine.[36] The best known case in literature is probably the stories of the *Pañcatantra* which circulated under the title *Kalila and Dimna*.[37] The Sanskrit original had been translated into Middle Persian in the late Sassanian period, which served Ibn al-Muqaffaʿ (*c.* 721–*c.* 756) as a source for his Arabic version, itself the source of subsequent translations into a variety of languages of the medieval Mediterranean and Eurasia. Ibn al-Muqaffaʿ's version included a chapter that reflects Buddhist criticisms of Brahmans, but most of collection is not Buddhist. However, the wide circulation of this text illustrates that Buddhist ideas and texts too could have been disseminated in the Middle East. Arabic–Sanskrit contacts were not confined to the center of the empire, as bilingual coins from Sind illustrate.[38]

Another path on which knowledge about Buddhism, Buddhist views and traditions traveled to the heartlands of the Abbasid Empire was by way of Buddhists who converted to Islam and migrated westwards. If other geographical areas and religious communities can be taken as a representative pattern, conversion to Islam was presumably initially slow and then accelerated. Conversion was typically not the result of force, but rather of acculturation and appealing for the opportunities for social ascent. It is not unlikely that conversion to Islam was more attractive to some than to others. Among Christians in medieval Iberia, for example, male converts benefited a great deal more from increased opportunities for social ascent than women.[39] It seems plausible that in Central and South Asia like in other areas under Muslim rule these conversions produced religiously mixed families and that the "transition" of a family from Buddhism to Islam occurred over several generations.

The celebrities among Buddhist converts to Islam were the Barmakids, so named after the title Barmak, according to one theory derived from the Sanskrit *pramukha* ("leader"), perhaps via a Bactrian intermediary.[40] Originally keepers of the Naw Bahār in Balkh, the Barmakids had enjoyed influence in pre-Abbasid times. The circumstances of the Barmakids' conversion to Islam are controversial. One account has a Barmak become a Muslim during the caliphate of ʿUthmān (644–656). Upon his return to Balkh, he was killed and his son, also to become the Barmak, was initially raised a Buddhist and enjoyed Buddhist learning in Kashmir. He too then converted to Islam and joined the Umayyad court in Syria where his son Khālid grew up. Following Khālid ibn Barmak's involvement in the Abbasid revolution, the family rose to such power at the Abbasid court that historians speak of a decade of the Barmakids, although the extent to which the family's power was grounded in their Buddhist history is disputed.[41] Khālid himself is among those credited with the round design of the newly founded Abbasid capital Baghdad, established in 762, and the only one credited with an active role in the city's construction. Notably Christopher Beckwith has recognized in the round design a Buddhist legacy.[42] In recent historical scholarship, the family's cultural impact has received attention, in particular the role of Khālid's son Yaḥyā. Kevin van Bladel has revealed his critical role for the transmission of Sanskrit knowledge into Arabic and Johan Elverskog credits the family with being a main reason for a shift in the orientation of Islam toward the East.[43]

Just how familiar Yaḥyā ibn Khālid was with the culture of his family's ancestral homeland remains uncertain, but we are told that he sent a mission to India in order to retrieve medicinal plants and information about Indian religions. Quotations from the resulting report of Buddhist religious practices are luckily preserved in the *Fihrist*, a catalogue of books with elaborations on content compiled by the 10th-century Baghdadi bookseller al-Nadīm.[44] The passage is one of the most important premodern testimonies to Muslim perceptions of Buddhism.

Al-Nadīm declares that he read a copy of the account on Indian religions in the handwriting of the philosopher al-Kindī (*c.* 801–870), a key figure in the Graeco-Arabic translation movement and the rise of Arabic philosophy. This in itself is remarkable since it suggests an interest in India well outside the circle of people who hailed from the East or had a substantially documented interest in the East. Buddhist influences on al-Kindī's philosophical and scientific works are not a well-represented subject of research. The bookseller also tells us that he considers Yaḥyā ibn Khālid a reliable source given the Barmakids' well-known interest in India, especially its medical traditions. In fact, in al-Nadīm's catalogue, the quotations from this report stand at the beginning of the section on India and constitute a large part of it. The first quotation describes a landscape of religious sites, including objects. In Mānkīr, there are twenty thousand idols made from precious materials. The king visits the temple every year. The report singles out a golden idol on a throne under a golden dome and describes human sacrifices made in front of this idol as they are at other sites. We can then read a detailed description of the Bamiyan Buddhas. According to the report, they are called Junbukt and Zunbukt. The description will still sound familiar to modern readers: "Their forms are cared out of the sides of a great valley, cut from the rock of the mountain. The height of each one of them is eighty cubits, so that they can be seen from a great distance."[45] Worshippers are meant to approach the statues with great respect. Here too, human sacrifices take place. The author also mentions a temple with precious idols and that such objects were sent to Baghdad at the time of the Arab invasions. Al-Nadīm notices some disagreements about the location of certain temples and records his own efforts to establish the details, here adducing the authority of the contemporaneous traveler Abū Dulaf.

While so far the account speaks of Indian religions, sites, and objects in a generic sense, the next passage in the *Fihrist* offers the earliest Muslim description of Buddhist doctrine. Using again a different, but unspecified source than the report for the Barmakid, al-Nadīm explains that Indians disagree about the nature of the buddha—here, the Arabic word *al-budd* is an unambiguous reference to the buddha.

> One group assumed that the *budd* was the image of the Creator, may His greatness be exalted. Another group said that he was the image of his messenger to them. Then they disagreed at this point. One group said that the messenger was one of the angels. Another group stated that the messenger was a man among the people. Another group said that he was one of the demons (*ʿifrīt*). Another group said that the *budd* was the image of Būdāsaf the wise, who came to them from God, may his name be glorified.[46]

Like other Muslim writers about Buddhism, al-Nadīm or his source used Islamic categories in order to make discussions among Buddhists understandable to Muslim readers. The taxonomy of God, angels, messenger, and demons is common in Islamic thought. Theologians distinguished prophets, a potentially very large category, from prophets who had received a revelation and were accordingly known as "messengers." *The* messenger in the Islamic tradition is Muhammad. Al-Nadīm's representation is thus an act of cultural translation or even comparative religion.

In the next section in the *Fihrist*, religious practices of Buddhists are described. Different communities worship different representations of the buddha. Al-Nadīm also explains this in lexicographical terms:

> *Al-budd* is the generic term, while the idols (*al-aṣnām*) are like different species. The greatest *budd* looks like a man seated on a throne, with no hair on his face and with his chin and mouth sunk [close] together. He is not covered by a robe and he is as though smiling. With his hand he is stringing thirty-two [beads].

The passage illustrates the larger impact of Buddhism on Muslim literature about religion as "buddha" came to represent Indian idols. Like many others, the author does not make a clear distinction between Buddhist and other Indians. Al-Nadīm elaborates:

> A trustworthy person has said that there is an image of him in every house. These are made of all kinds of materials, according to the status of the individual. They are of gold adorned with different jewels, or of silver, brass, stone, or wood. They exalt him as he receives them, facing either from east to west, or from west to east, but for the most part they turn his back to the east, so that they face themselves towards the east. It is said that they have this image with four faces, so fashioned by engineering and accurate craftsmanship that from whatever place they approach it, they see the full face and the profile perfectly, without any part of it hidden from them. It is said that this is the form of the idol that is at Mūltān.[47]

Middle Eastern geographers of subsequent centuries were likewise fascinated by Multan. As a site of Hindu worship, however, it is beyond the scope of this survey.[48]

As in the case of the description of the statue sent by the Kabul Shāh to the Abbasid caliph al-Maʾmūn, al-Nadīm's account provides a valuable contemporaneous source for scholars of Buddhist art who may not always have access to the corresponding objects themselves. Like Klimburg-Salter, Elverskog considers the detail that the represented figure was shown as sitting on a throne critical. He concluded that the object must have shown Maitreya.[49] The four faces present a greater mystery and may point to upcoming trends in tantric Buddhist art which are not preserved in material objects. Elverskog speculates that the Arabic description captured tantric Buddhism in its emerging state, being the only premodern Muslim source to reflect tantric Buddhism at all.[50] On the other hand, the account appears to contain blatant misinformation as well. The human sacrifice might simply be a polemical trope connected with idolatry and may have brought to mind pre-Islamic Arabic practices.[51] On the other hand, the possibility of a misinterpretation remains as does that of an exaggeration.[52]

Al-Nadīm offered a precious snapshot during a period of especially rich cultural contacts, much of them represented and orchestrated by the Barmakids. The family's fall after a decade of singular influence was steep, the reasons for it remain uncertain. The fate of the Barmakids even left traces in the *Arabian Nights*, the character Jaafar of the popular Disney adaptations being a "reincarnation" of an actual historical person.[53] Elverskog sees in the fall of the Barmakids and the separation of economic zones in Eurasia the reasons for a split between Muslims and Buddhists and that Muslim knowledge of the regions and cultures east of the caliphate stagnated after the 8th century.[54] As Buddhism shifted eastwards, opportunities for Muslims to encounter actual Buddhists disappeared. According to Elverskog, the shift to maritime trade too led to a decrease of personal exchanges that involved a transmission of significant and accurate knowledge about the other.

The early Abbasid period also saw the transmission of a very important Buddhist literary tradition to the Middle East. The Arabic version of the life of the buddha known as the story of Bilawhar and Būdhāsaf (Arabic: *Bilawhar wa-Būdhāsaf*) is mostly preserved in two versions, a longer and a shorter one.[55] The original Arabic version was presumably composed in the late 8th century, which is consistent with a general Abbasid interest in Indian religion and literature. Also consistent with general patterns of cultural history is the significance of a Middle Persian intermediary which has not come down to us. Some of the structural features of the preserved versions reflect larger trends at the time, in some cases inspired by Indian and Persian precedent. Hence, it is hard to establish which elements in the preserved versions were introduced at what stage. The significance of the Persian and Arabic adaptations of the story reaches beyond the Middle East since they led to the rise of the Christian legend of Barlaam and Josaphat.

Although Buddhist versions of the life of the buddha are clearly recognizable in *Bilawhar and Būdhāsaf*, a number of differences reflect a Middle Eastern and Islamic reworking. Būdhāsaf, a name derived from *boddhisattva*, is the son of King Junaysar. Committed to idolatry, the king seeks to eradicate the rising monotheistic religion in his realm to which his son converts. These conflicts between religious communities and the oppression of the true faith may very well reflect the perspective of Shiite redactors. Several episodes in the story deal with conflicts at court and the function of courtiers who serve as go-betweens, are loyal, but also jealous and conspire. These are prominent subjects in Persian traditions which fed into Arabic literature, notably the mirror of princes genre. Structurally, characters often use parables for communication. Such embedded stories are likewise a feature of Persian influences as famously exemplified by the *Arabian Nights*. Theologically, a significant difference between the Buddhist and Islamic versions is the introduction of a teacher for Būdhāsaf, namely Bilawhar. Remarkably, the Buddha also appears in a second guise in *Bilawhar and Būdhāsaf*. Both father and son believe in *al-budd*, but they disagree about his message.

While the courtly setting of the story relates to the influx of Persian ideas into Arabic literature, the prominence of asceticism allows for the exploration of Buddhist influences on Sufism, especially during the first centuries of the tradition's history. Such theories have been presented in particular for Ibrāhīm ibn Adham (d. 777), an early ascetic born in Balkh who migrated to Syria where he became involved in military operations against Byzantium. In later legendary biographies, Ibrāhīm turned into the ruler of Balkh who resigned to become an ascetic. His story spread into North India, and Central and Southeast Asia, and it may have been in the course of these later reworkings that Buddhist elements were included.[56] The fact that similarities allowed for back-projections, however, is not grounds for dismissing the possibility that phenomenological similarities reflect actual contacts. Similarities between Yogic and Sufi traditions have also been noticed by others. Toby Mayer has presented a detailed argument for parallels between Kubrawī Sufism and Tibetan Yoga.[57] Resemblances in spiritual practices complement conceptual similarities. According to Mayer, Sufis may have developed these traits in the Mongol period and in competition with Buddhists.

CONFLICT AND KNOWLEDGE

An important insight in the recent study of cultural encounters is that violent conflict and the acquisition of knowledge about the other often go hand in hand. The relationship between power and knowledge has been widely discussed for European colonialism of the modern period, notably in Edward Said's *Orientalism*. Some scholars of premodern and non-European history have applied a similar paradigm to Eurasian encounters, including Muslim representations of India.[58] The extent to which this analytical framework, the result of a critical perspective on modern Western hegemony, should be employed for other historical contexts remains controversial. There is, however, no denying the sometimes very close relationship between those who wielded the power of the sword and those who had the power of the pen. A case in point is the most famous premodern Muslim writer on India, al-Bīrūnī (973–*c.* 1050). He had already made a name for himself in various fields of knowledge, including as the author of a work on history, *The Remaining Signs of the Past Ages*, in English translation, also known as *The Chronology of Ancient Nations*. Al-Bīrūnī, who hailed from Khwarazm in Central Asia, commented briefly on Buddhism in this book.[59] Later, he joined, perhaps not entirely voluntarily, the court of Maḥmūd of Ghazna. It was in the context of this iconic figure of Muslim aggression in India that al-Bīrūnī gained access to a much larger body of knowledge about the region, its history, culture, and science. Drawing on experts as sources, the polymath learned himself Sanskrit, a feat reflected in his Arabic translation of a key work on yoga, the *Book of Patañjali*.[60] Historians of Buddhism frequently express disappointment upon noticing just how little al-Bīrūnī had to say about Buddhism in his most famous work, *India* (Arabic: *Al-Hind*). The observation he made may account for his silence: he could not find authorities on Buddhism in India. Then again, a current count of al-Bīrūnī's works lists one hundred and eighty-four titles. He reportedly composed a treatise on the Bamiyan Buddhas which has not come down to us.[61] What has been preserved of his comments about Buddhism may thus fall short of reflecting his knowledge. On the Buddhist side, the Kālacakra Tantra reflects a greater familiarity with Muslims as a result of these confrontations.

Al-Bīrūnī's work appears to have been unknown to another important Muslim author on Indian religions. In his *Kitāb al-Milal wa'l-niḥal* (*Book of Religious Communities and Beliefs*), the Persian scholar al-Shahrastānī (1086–1158) provided the most detailed account of Buddhism written by a Muslim author before the Mongol period. The book has been variably described as a heresiography or a work of comparative religion.[62] Modern scholars have offered different impressions of al-Shahrastānī's work. Some argue that he does not seem to reflect any contemporary encounter with Buddhists. In fact, his account may even depend on information assembled for Yaḥyā al-Barmakī. Al-Shahrastānī had been born in Khorasan, where he spent most of his life, but he also went on a pilgrimage to Mecca and spent three years in Baghdad. He may have obtained his information about Buddhism in the center of the Abbasid Empire, but also closer to his own home. Bruce Lawrence identified some of the unique features of al-Shahrastānī's account, including his lists of vices and virtues and explanation of the bodhisattva. Whether some of the inaccurate details are due to his own misunderstandings or owed to a source, Buddhist or Muslim, remains an open question. Al-Shahrastānī begins with a definition of the buddha:

> The Buddha, in their opinion, means a person who is not born, who never marries nor eats food nor drinks nor grows old nor dies. The first Buddha appearing in the world was named Shakaman, which means "the noble master." Five thousand years elapsed from the time of his appearance to the time of the hijra.[63]

Both the explanation of the name and the dating are of unknown origin. Al-Shahrastānī then explains the bodhisattva, an addition to previous representations of Buddhism:

> They assert that below the rank of the Buddha is the rank of the Budisaʾiya, the latter term meaning "the one who seeks the way of truth." Indeed, one arrives at this rank only by (following certain measures for attaining moral discipline): patience and alms-giving; seeking after that which ought to be sought; abstinence and withdrawal from the world, and aloofness from its desires and pleasures; abstinence from what is forbidden; compassion for all created beings; avoidance of the ten offenses, which are: to kill any living creature; to consider it lawful (to seize) human property; to commit adultery; to lie; to utter calumnies; to use obscene language; to vilify; to slander; to say a stupid word; to deny reward (and punishment) in the afterlife; and adherence to the ten virtues, which are: to demonstrate goodness and generosity; to pardon those who offend and to overcome anger through patience; to abstain from worldly desires; to meditate on the deliverance of the soul from this transitory world to that eternal world; to exercise the intellect through knowledge and culture and much thought about the consequences of worldly things; to exert control over the direction of the soul, that it may seek after higher things; to be soft-spoken and courteous in speaking with everyone; to be kind in dealing with other men, so that their wishes become more important than one's own; to turn away totally from created beings and turn totally toward the truth; to dedicate the soul to seeking and attaining the truth.[64]

The section concludes with further comments on the nature of the Buddhas—it is worth pointing out that al-Shahrastānī used the plural here:

> This group maintains that the Buddhas came to them according to the number (of branches) of the Kil River, bringing them knowledge of the sciences and appearing to them in different kinds and as substances, the Buddhas appeared only in the families of

> kings. They claim that there is no difference among the buddhas with respect to what has been reported of them about the eternity of the world and about their assertion concerning reward already noted.[65]

Finally, al-Shahrastānī notes the particularity of the buddhas and finishes with a comparative note which reveals the lasting close connection between Buddhism and India:

> The appearance of the Buddhas has been limited to India, however, due both to the wide variety of its creatures and climates and also to the many Indians who are intent on spiritual exercises and exertion. There is no one comparable to Buddha as they have described him—if they are right in that—except al-Khidr, whom Muslims recognize.[66]

The figure adduced here is a mysterious timeless traveler who enjoyed particular popularity among mystics, but also in other Muslim circles.

Lastly, there was another guise too in which Buddhists entered Islamic theological and heresiographical literature during these first centuries of encounters. Known as Sumaniyya, their reputation was as deniers of several key principles of Islamic thought, including prophecy. The extent to which the Sumaniyya, or another group known as the "Brahmins," are a discursive figure of polemical literature is controversial in recent scholarship. One of the difficulties in determining Muslim attitudes to Buddhism is that some ideas associated with this religion are not unique to Buddhism. The belief in reincarnation is a good example, as is the tradition of caves as sacred spaces. The composition of specific religious landscapes facilitates disambiguation, but also invites circular interpretations. This challenge concerns matters of influence and whether certain Islamic schools and traditions might have absorbed Buddhist ideas and practices, but also polemical contexts.

A major difficulty also consists in determining to what extent Muslims conceived of Buddhists as a coherent group which coincided with self-identifying Buddhists. Did they, for example, identify those who worshipped the Buddhas of Bamiyan with the deniers of prophecy? As is often the case with cross-religious representations, the diversity within the described religion, here Buddhism, complicates the assessment of the description's accuracy. Describing and described tradition are both dynamic, internally as well as in their mutual relationship. Recent authors have pointed out that Muslim authors showed no awareness of the rise of tantric Buddhism, but rather for centuries perpetuated first impressions.

FURTHER READING

Akasoy, Anna, Charles Burnett, and Ronit Yoeli-Tlalim, eds. *Islam and Tibet: Interactions along the Musk Routes*. Farnham: Routledge, 2010.

Auer, Blain, and Ingo Strauch, eds. *Encountering Buddhism and Islam in Premodern Central and South Asia*. Berlin: De Gruyter, 2019.

Elverskog, Johan. "Buddhism and Islam." *Oxford Bibliographies*, May 5, 2017. https://doi.org/10.1093/OBO/9780195393521-0050.

Elverskog, Johan. *Islam and Buddhism on the Silk Road*. Philadelphia: University of Philadelphia Press, 2012.

Flood, Finbarr B. *Objects of Translation: Material Culture and Medieval "Hindu–Muslim" Encounters*. Princeton, NJ: Princeton University Press, 2009.

Gimaret, Daniel. "Bouddha et les bouddhistes dans la tradition musulmane." *Journal Asiatique* 257 (1969): 273–316.

Gimaret, Daniel, ed. *Kitāb Bilawhar wa Budasaf*. Beirut, Lebanon: Dār al-Mašriq, 1986.

Gimaret, Daniel. *Le Livre de Bilawhar et Budasf selon la version arabe ismaélienne*. Geneva, Switzerland: Droz, 1971.

Morgan, Llewelyn. *The Buddhas of Bamiyan*. Cambridge, MA: Harvard University Press, 2012.

Stern, S. M., and Sofie Walzer, eds. and trans. *Three Unknown Buddhist Stories in an Arabic Version*. Oxford: Cassirer, 1971.

Vaziri, Mostafa. *Buddhism in Iran: An Anthropological Approach to Traces and Influences*. New York: Palgrave Macmillan, 2012.

NOTES

1. For this and other terms, see Derryl N. MacLean, *Religion and Society in Arab Sind* (Leiden, the Netherlands: København, 1989), 3–4. See also Finbarr B. Flood, *Objects of Translation: Material Culture and Medieval "Hindu-Muslim" Encounters* (Princeton, NJ: Princeton University Press, 2009), 26–37 for idolatry. The difference between Buddhist and Hindu objects is mostly secondary here.
2. Johan Elverskog, *Buddhism and Islam on the Silk Road* (Philadelphia: University of Philadelphia Press, 2012), 44.
3. Donald S. Lopez Jr., *Hyecho's Journey: The World of Buddhism* (Chicago: University of Chicago Press, 2017), 19 and 25.
4. See, in particular, Christopher I. Beckwith, *Greek Buddha: Pyrrho's Encounter with Early Buddhism in Central Asia* (Princeton, NJ: Princeton University Press, 2015). For discussions of ancient Greece and Christianity, see J. Duncan M. Derrett, "Consolation and a Parable: Two Contacts between Ancient Greece and Buddhists," *Bulletin of the School of Oriental and African Studies* 65, no. 3 (2002): 518–528.
5. Erik Seldeslachts, "Greece, the Final Frontier? The Westward Spread of Buddhism," in *The Spread of Buddhism*, ed. Ann Heirman and Stephan Peter Bumbacher (Leiden, the Netherlands: Brill, 2007), 131–166, 144 for Zoroastrian architecture and 150–151 for Manichaeism.
6. Richard Foltz, "Buddhism in the Iranian World," *The Muslim World* 100, nos. 2–3 (2010): 204–214; and in general Richard Foltz, *Religions of Iran: From Prehistory to the Present* (New York: Oneworld, 2013).
7. Seldeslachts, "Greece, the Final Frontier?"
8. Richard W. Bulliet, "Naw Bahār and the Survival of Iranian Buddhism," *Journal of Persian Studies* 14 (1976): 140–145.
9. Considering both Buddhism and Christianity are Warwick Ball and David Whitehouse, "Qalʿat-i Ḥaidarī," *Iran* 14 (1976): 147–150; and Warwick Ball, "Two Aspects of Iranian Buddhism," *Bulletin of the Asia Institute of Pahlavi University* 1 (1976): 103–163; stressing the significance of maritime Buddhism, see Warwick Ball, "Some Rock-Cut Monuments in Southern Iran," *Iran* 24 (1986): 95–115; Gianroberto Scarcia, "The 'Vihar' of Qongqor-olong: Preliminary Report," *East and West* 25/1-2 (1979): 99–104; and Mostafa Vaziri, *Buddhism in Iran: An Anthropological Approach to Traces and Influences* (New York: Palgrave Macmillan, 2012), 80–88.
10. For a similar example and issues of documentation, see Ingo Strauch, "Buddhism in the West? Buddhist Indian Sailors on Socotra (Yemen) and the Role of Trade Contacts in the Spread of Buddhism," in *Buddhism and the Dynamics of Transculturality: New Approaches*, ed. Birgit Kellner (Berlin: De Gruyter, 2019), 15–52.

11. Deborah Klimburg-Salter, "Cultural Mobility, a Case Study: The Crowned Buddha of the Kabul Shāh," in *Coins, Art and Chronology II: The First Millennium C.E. in the Indo-Iranian Borderlands*, ed. Michael Alram, Deborah Klimburg-Salter, Minoru Inaba, and Matthias Pfisterer (Vienna: Österreichischen Akademie der Wissenschaften, 2010), 39–56. For the mobility of objects, see also Flood, *Objects of Translation*.
12. Flood, *Objects of Translation*, 29.
13. Markus Groß, "Buddhistische Einflüsse im frühen Islam?," in *Schlaglichter: Die beiden ersten islamischen Jahrhunderte*, ed. Markus Groß and Karl-Heinz Ohlig (Berlin: Hans Schiler, 2008), 220–274; and Markus Groß, "Frühislam und Buddhismus: Neue Indizien," in *Vom Koran zum Islam*, ed. Markus Groß and Karl-Heinz Ohlig (Berlin: Hans Schiler, 2009), 347–396. For a survey and discussion of these theories, see Anna Akasoy, "Islam and Buddhism: The Arabian Prequel?," *Entangled Religions* 8 (2019): 1–32.
14. Ernest Binfield Havell, *A Handbook of Indian Art* (London: John Murray, 1920), 106.
15. More generally, see Debashish Banerji, "The Orientalism of E. B. Havell," *Third Text* 16, no. 1 (2002): 41–56.
16. Havell, *Handbook of Indian Art*, 107.
17. Ibn al-Kalbī, *Book of Idols; Being a Translation from the Arabic of the Kitāb al-Aṣnām*, trans. Nabih Amin Faris (Princeton, NJ: Princeton University Press, 1952), 43–47.
18. Gardīzī, *The Ornament of Histories: A History of the Eastern Islamic Lands, AD 650–1041. The Original Text of Abū Saʿīd ʿAbd al-Ḥayy Gardīzī*, trans. C. Edmund Bosworth (New York: I. B. Tauris, 2011), 96. See also Richard H. Davis, *Lives of Indian Images* (Princeton, NJ: Princeton University Press, 1997), 95, for the Muslim etymology of Somanātha as derived from the pre-Islamic deity Manāt. According to this explanation, worshippers of this deity left for India when Muhammad's movement began to prevail in western Arabia.
19. Audrey Truschke, "The Power of the Islamic Sword in Narrating the Death of Indian Buddhism," *History of Religions* 57, no. 4 (2018): 406–435. For economic explanations, see Elverskog, *Buddhism and Islam*.
20. See Elverskog, *Buddhism and Islam*. For a survey, see Xinru Liu, "A Silk Road Legacy: The Spread of Buddhism and Islam," *Journal of World History* 22, no. 1 (2011): 55–81.
21. Milka Levy-Rubin, *Non-Muslims in the Early Islamic Empire: From Surrender to Coexistence* (Cambridge, UK: Cambridge University Press, 2011). For the case of the Buddhist monastery of Nalanda which came under Muslim rule in 1202 and where violent conquest narratives disguise realities of negotiation between Buddhist rulers and Muslim conquerors, see Elverskog, *Buddhism and Islam*, 2 and 49–50.
22. Matthew S. Gordon, Chase F. Robinson, Everett K. Rowson, and Michael Fishbein, eds., *The Works of Ibn Wāḍiḥ al-Yaʿqūbī: An English Translation*, 3 vols. (Leiden, the Netherlands: Brill, 2018), 998.
23. For this contrast and the complicated details of these events, see MacLean, *Religion and Society*, 1–4 and 65–66. For an analysis of the reception history of this episode and its historiographical context as well as a critical evaluation of the *Chachnāma*, see Manan Ahmed Asif, *A Book of Conquest: The Chachnama and Muslim Origins in South Asia* (Cambridge, MA: Harvard University Press, 2016). See also Finbarr Barry Flood, "Conflict and Cosmopolitanism in 'Arab' Sind," in *A Companion to Asian Art and Architecture*, ed. Rebecca M. Brown and Deborah S. Hutton (Chichester: John Wiley & Sons, 2011), 365–397.
24. Davis, *Lives of Indian Images*, 88–112. For the significance of this incident in later political history, see also Romila Thapar, *Somanatha: The Many Voices of a History* (London: Verso, 2005).
25. Arezou Azad and Hugh Kennedy, "The Coming of Islam to Balkh," in *Authority and Control in the Countryside: From Antiquity to Islam in the Mediterranean and Near East (6th–10th Century)*, ed. Alain Delattre, Marie Legendre, and Petra Sijpesteijn (Leiden, the Netherlands: Brill, 2019), 284–310, 291. For Daybul, see also Mehrdad Shokoohy and Natalie H. Shokoohy, "South Asia," in *Oxford Handbook of Islamic Archaeology*, ed. Bethany Walker, Corisande Fenwick, and Timothy Insoll (Oxford: Oxford University Press, 2020), 543–574.

26. For this example, see Azad and Kennedy, "Coming of Islam." The authors conclude that the Naw Bahār consisted of a temple complex which dominated the city, but gradually lost its functions and was eventually absorbed into post-conquest Balkh.
27. For examples, see Flood, "Conflict and Cosmopolitanism in 'Arab' Sind"; Yohanan Friedmann, "The Temple of Multān: A Note on Early Muslim Attitudes to Idolatry," *Israel Oriental Studies* 2 (1972): 176–182; Elverskog, *Buddhism and Islam,* 48; and Annette Schmiedchen, "Medieval Endowment Cultures in Western India: Buddhist and Muslim Encounters—Some Preliminary Observations," in *Encountering Buddhism and Islam in Premodern Central and South Asia,* ed. Blain Auer and Ingo Strauch (Berlin: De Gruyter, 2019), 203–2018.
28. Klimburg-Salter, "Cultural Mobility, a Case Study." For further examples of such idols, see Elverskog, *Buddhism and Islam,* 67; and Flood, *Objects of Translation,* 26–37.
29. Christopher I. Beckwith, *The Tibetan Empire in Central Asia: A History of the Struggle for Great Power among Tibetans, Turks, Arabs, and Chinese during the Early Middle Ages* (Princeton, NJ: Princeton University Press, 1987).
30. For *al-budd,* its range of usage and the more direct etymological connection with "buddha," see Daniel Gimaret, "Bouddha et les bouddhistes dans la tradition musulmane," *Journal Asiatique* 257 (1969): 273–316, 274–276.
31. Friedmann, "Temple of Multān."
32. For the literary imagery of *bot,* see Asadullah Souren Melikian-Chirvani, "Buddhism II: In Islamic Times," *Encyclopaedia Iranica,* January 1, 2000; and William L. Hanaway Jr., "Bot," *Encyclopaedia Iranica,* December 15, 1989.
33. Yohanan Friedmann, "Classification of Unbelievers in Sunnī Muslim Law and Tradition," *Jerusalem Studies in Arabic and Islam* 22 (1998): 163–195, 190; and Friedmann, "Temple of Multān," 181.
34. For the following, see Anya H. King, *Scent from the Garden of Paradise: Musk and the Medieval Islamic World* (Leiden, the Netherlands: Brill, 2017), 189.
35. Friedmann, "Classification of Unbelievers," 185.
36. Sonja Brentjes with Robert G. Morrison, "The Sciences in Islamic Societies (750–1800)," in *The New Cambridge History of Islam,* Vol. 4: *Islamic Cultures and Societies to the End of the Eighteenth Century,* ed. Robert Irwin (Cambridge, UK: Cambridge University Press, 2010), 564–639, 590–591, and 600–601. For medicine, see Oliver Kahl, *The Sanskrit, Syriac and Persian Sources in the Comprehensive Book of Rhazes* (Leiden, the Netherlands: Brill, 2015); and M. Shefer-Mossensohn and K. Abou Hershkovitz, "Early Muslim Medicine and the Indian Context: A Reinterpretation," *Medieval Encounters* 19 (2013): 274–299.
37. François de Blois, *Burzōy's Voyage to India and the Origin of the Book of Kalīlah wa Dimnah* (London: Routledge, 1990); and Nasrullah Munshi, *Kalila and Dimna,* trans. Wheeler Thackston (Indianapolis, IN: Hackett, 2019). For the Buddhist story, see Thackston's introduction, xvi.
38. Flood, "Conflict and Cosmopolitanism in 'Arab' Sind," 371.
39. Janina M. Safran, "Identity and Differentiation in Ninth-Century al-Andalus," *Speculum* 76, no. 3 (2001): 573–598.
40. Kevin van Bladel, "The Bactrian Background of the Barmakids," in *Islam and Tibet: Interactions along the Musk Routes,* ed. Anna Akasoy, Charles Burnett, and Ronit Yoeli-Tlalim (Farnham: Routledge, 2010), 43–88, 68–69 for the etymology of Barmak.
41. Bulliet, "Naw Bahār and the Survival of Iranian Buddhism."
42. Christopher I. Beckwith, "The Plan of the City of Peace: Central Asian Iranian Factors in Early 'Abbâsid Design," ' *Acta Orientalia Academiae Scientiarum Hungaricae* 38, nos. 1–2 (1984): 143–164, 146–150.
43. Elverskog, *Buddhism and Islam,* 59.
44. For this passage and further discussions of India and China, see Muḥammad ibn Isḥāq Ibn al-Nadīm, *The Fihrist of al-Nadīm: A Tenth-Century Survey of Muslim Culture,* trans. Bayard Dodge (New York: Columbia

University Press, 1970), vol. 2, 826–842. (Translations quoted here are slightly modified.) For the Arabic, see *Kitāb al-Fihrist*, ed. Ayman Fuʾād Sayyid (London: Muʾassasat al-furqān lil-turāth al-islāmī, 2014), vol. 2, 423–437. For discussions, see Elverskog, *Buddhism and Islam*, 61–80; and Llewelyn Morgan, *The Buddhas of Bamiyan* (Cambridge, MA: Harvard University Press, 2012), 105–110.
45. Al-Nadīm and Dodge, *Fihrist*, 828.
46. Al-Nadīm and Dodge, *Fihrist*, 831.
47. Al-Nadīm and Dodge, *Fihrist*, 831–832.
48. For geographical sources, see S. Razia Jafri, "Description of India (Hind and Sind) in the Works of Al-Iṣṭakhrī, Ibn Ḥauqal and Al-Maqdisī," *Bulletin of the Institute of Islamic Studies* 5 (1961): 1–36.
49. Elverskog, *Buddhism and Islam*, 76.
50. Elverskog, *Buddhism and Islam*, 79–80.
51. Elverskog, *Buddhism and Islam*, 63. See also Flood, *Objects of Translation*, 84–85, for finger sacrifice.
52. For a comparison, see Abū Zayd al-Sīrāfī, *Accounts of China and India*, ed. and trans. Tim Mackintosh-Smith, published with Ibn Faḍlān, *Mission to the Volga*, ed. and trans. James E. Montgomery (New York: New York University Press, 2014). While al-Sīrāfī refers to cannibalism in China, Ibn Faḍlān describes human sacrifice among the Vikings. In both cases, the accounts seem plausible. See 83 and note 110 for al-Sīrāfī, and 249–251 for Ibn Faḍlān.
53. Philip Kennedy, "The Fall of the Barmakids in Historiography and Fiction: Recognition and Disclosure," *Journal of Abbasid Studies* 3, no. 2 (2016): 167–238.
54. Elverskog, *Buddhism and Islam*, 82–87.
55. Donald S. Lopez and Peggy McCracken, *In Search of the Christian Buddha: How an Asian Sage Became a Medieval Sage* (New York: W. W. Norton, 2014). For some of the stemmatological discussions, see Anna Martin, "Bilawhar wa Būdīsaf (Turfan fragment)," in *Perso-Indica: An Analytical Survey of Persian Works on Indian Learned Traditions*, ed. F. Speziale and C. W. Ernst (Paris: Perso-Indica, 2018).
56. Tsugitaka Sato, "The Sufi Legend of Sultan Ibrāhīm b. Adham," *Orient* 42 (2007): 41–54.
57. Toby Mayer, "Yogic-Ṣūfī Homologies: The Case of the 'Six Principles' Yoga of Nāropa and the Kubrawiyya," *The Muslim World* 100, no. 2–3 (2010): 268–286.
58. Richard Foltz, "Muslim 'Orientalism' in Medieval Travel Accounts of India," *Studies in Religion/Sciences Religieuses* 37, no. 1 (2008): 81–95.
59. Muhammad ibn Ahmad Biruni, *The Chronology of Ancient Nations, An English Version of the Arabic Text of the Athâr-ul-bâkiya of Albîrûnî*, trans. Edward Sachau (London: Oriental Translation Fund of Great Britain & Ireland by W. H. Allen, 1879), 188–189.
60. Abū Rayḥān al-Bīrūnī, *The Yoga Sutras of Patañjali*, ed. and trans. Mario Kozah (Mineola, NY: Dover, 2020).
61. See the *Encyclopaedia Iranica* articles on Buddhism in Iran in Islamic Times (for the lost treatise about the Bamiyan Buddhas) and on al-Bīrūnī (for the number of works).
62. For a translation and detailed commentary of the section on the views of the people of India in the *Kitāb al-milal wa'l-niḥal*, see *Shahrastānī on the Indian Religions*, trans. Bruce B. Lawrence (Berlin: De Gruyter Mouton, 1976), 42–43 for the translation, 100–115 for the commentary.
63. Shahrastānī and Lawrence, *On the Indian Religions*, 42.
64. Shahrastānī and Lawrence, *On the Indian Religions*, 42–43.
65. Shahrastānī and Lawrence, *On the Indian Religions*, 43.
66. Shahrastānī and Lawrence, *On the Indian Religions*, 43.

Anna Ayse Akasoy

N

NĀGĀRJUNA

Nāgārjuna is generally acknowledged as the founder of the Madhyamaka school of Buddhist philosophy. Madhyamaka is one of the two main schools of Indian Mahāyāna thought (the other being Yogācāra). The Mahāyāna movement of Indian Buddhism began in roughly the 1st century BCE, with the appearance of a new class of sutras purporting to express the teachings of the historical buddha and other enlightened beings. These teachings go beyond what is found in earlier texts (i.e., those collected in the Pāli Nikāyas and the Chinese Āgamas) in two important respects. First, the ideal career of a Buddhist practitioner is not to become an *arhat*, one who attains nirvana and is thus released from further births, but to become a *bodhisattva*, someone who abstains from entering into final release and undergoes further rebirths in order to lead others to liberation. Second, the insight that is crucial to liberation is not merely that persons are devoid of essence but that all things are devoid of essence—that all things are empty (*śūnya*). These new sutras assert these claims but do not argue for them. Nāgārjuna set out to give rational support for the second claim, that of universal emptiness.

Very little is known about the life of Nāgārjuna. He is generally thought to have lived sometime in the 2nd or 3rd century CE and was most likely of South Indian origin. His writings show familiarity not only with contemporary Buddhist philosophical systems but also with the early work of the orthodox (Brahmanical) Nyāya school and its theory of knowledge. He is uniformly identified by later Mādhyamikas (members of the Madhyamaka school) as the founder of their tradition. But caution is called for in understanding Nāgārjuna's role as the founder of a school. It may be wrong to think of Madhyamaka and other Buddhist systems as schools in the sense of formal institutions. There is, for instance, evidence that there was considerable diversity in doctrinal views among the members of any given Buddhist monastic community, so that some of the monks or nuns of a given *vihāra* might profess identifiably Mahāyāna views while others held views more closely associated with one or another of the different Abhidharma schools. The "schools" of Indian Buddhist philosophy are perhaps best thought of as text traditions: one or a small number of foundational texts and a long line of commentaries and subcommentaries. To call Nāgārjuna the founder of Madhyamaka is just to say that he authored the texts considered authoritative for this commentarial lineage.

This brings us to another important gap in our present knowledge about Nāgārjuna. Not only do we not know with any certainty when or where he lived, but we are also not entirely sure just what he wrote. The one work that all modern scholars agree on is *Mūlamadhyamakakārikā* (MMK).[1] But given how little we actually know about Nāgārjuna's life, it has become virtually true by definition that he is the author of MMK. Of the many other works that have been traditionally attributed to him, the question that modern scholars ask is whether their style and content are consistent with what is found in MMK (as well as compatible with what is known of the historical record). One text that many scholars think passes this test is *Vigrahavyāvartanī* (VV), a sustained response to a set of objections posed by a Naiyāyika (an adherent of the orthodox Nyāya school). Receiving somewhat lower marks are *Vaidalyaprakaraṇa* (VP) and *Yuktiṣaṣṭikā* (YṢ); the former is a sustained critique of the categories of Nyāya epistemology, and the latter has much to say about the connection between the doctrine of emptiness and the goal of Buddhist practice. Also accepted by some scholars as authentic is *Ratnāvalī* (RĀ), a letter to a king that gives much advice on making worldly conduct conform to the principles revealed by the teachings of Mahāyāna.[2] All these texts are composed in verse form, a style they share with other foundational texts of the Indian schools of this era. It is commonly supposed that this style was adopted for pedagogical reasons, namely, to facilitate memorization: the pupil first memorizes the text and then recites it, at which time they receive an oral commentary from their teacher. In some cases the original author's commentary was written down and has survived. This seems to be the case with VV, and perhaps with VP as well. In the crucial case of MMK, some scholars hold that the commentary *Akutobhayā* (surviving only in Tibetan and Chinese translations) is Nāgārjuna's autocommentary, but most scholars reject this attribution. At least seven other commentaries were composed in India, only one of which (Candrakīrti's *Prasannapadā*) survives in the original Sanskrit. The terse and elliptical style of Nāgārjuna's verses makes his texts difficult to understand without a prose commentary, and yet with the possible exception of VV it is only through commentaries written much later that we are able to resolve many of the ambiguities. Fortunately, there is much agreement among the commentators about the intended meaning of many of the more difficult passages.

Since most of what is known about Nāgārjuna comes from his philosophical writings, this article focuses primarily on the philosophy to be found in MMK, VV, VP, and YṢ. The aim is to work out just what it might mean to claim that all things are empty, what reasons there might be to believe this claim, and why its acceptance might be thought to play a crucial role in attaining liberation from suffering. The first two sections briefly review the key philosophical developments in the Buddhist tradition that form the background of Nāgārjuna's doctrine of emptiness, which will help readers to better grasp just what the doctrine might mean. The next section examines several of the (many) arguments Nāgārjuna gave in support of the emptiness of all things. Doing so should help further clarify the concept and its implications. The final section addresses the pressing question of the soteriological implications of emptiness: How could this seemingly abstruse doctrine contribute to the core Buddhist project of attaining liberation from suffering?

THE ABHIDHARMA BACKGROUND

For a Mādhyamika, to assert that all things are empty (*śūnya*) is to say that nothing has intrinsic nature (*svabhāva*), that all things are devoid of essence (*nairātmya*). In ordinary usage the Sanskrit term *svabhāva* means a thing's essential nature, the property that makes the entity be the sort of thing that it is. But the concept of intrinsic nature takes on special meaning in the hands of philosophers of the Abhidharma schools as they seek to systematize the buddha's teachings concerning the path to liberation. The Buddhist path is meant to extirpate existential suffering by helping the aspirant overcome the ubiquitous but erroneous sense of an "I," the sense of being something that serves as subject of experience, agent of action, and source of value. The doctrines of nonself and impermanence have important roles to play here: what we think of as a single enduring entity turns out on analysis to be a causal series of impersonal, impermanent psychophysical elements (*skandhas*). When we look more closely, we see that the continued existence of a person just consists in one set of bodily and mental constituents existing for a while, then going out of existence, but causing a replacement set to come into existence. Nothing serves as core continuant holding them all together; they constitute a series, something we think of as one, solely due to the many causal connections among earlier and later constituents. What Abhidharma exegetes saw, however, is that this analysis leaves untouched the near-universal tendency to suppose that there must be something to serve as the owner of the series' constituents. While we may rationally acknowledge that there is nothing like a self to be found when we examine the constituents of persons, we are still inclined to view them as "me" or "mine." What explains this difficulty in extirpating the "I"-sense?

The answer that Ābhidharmikas (members of the various Abhidharma schools) arrived at is that words like "I" and "person" are merely useful ways of referring to a plurality of things when they are arranged in a certain way. Just as "six-pack" is merely a name for six cans of beer yoked together, and "chariot" is merely a convenient expression for axle, spokes, rims, and so on when assembled in the right way, so "person" is no more than a useful way of referring to a set of psychophysical elements occurring in a causal series. Our common use of these expressions can sometimes make us forget, though, that what we are talking about is not a one but a many. This may seem like a relatively minor cognitive mistake. What difference could it make whether we think of a chariot, or a tree, or a house as a single thing, and not as many things all put together is a certain way? It is replied, though, that there are reasons there cannot be such a thing as a tree understood as something that exists over and above the roots, trunk, branches, leaves, and so on. So when we think that there are such things as chariots, trees, and houses, we are superimposing on the world a concept that only reflects what is useful to us, given our interests and our cognitive limitations. This may not do much harm when it comes to concepts like *chariot* and *tree*. But things are different with expressions such as "I" and "person." According to Abhidharma, persons are no more than mental constructions and are not objective constituents of reality. It is our failure to see this that explains the difficulty we encounter when we try to uproot the "I"-sense.

Things, such as chariots, trees, houses, and persons, are not strictly speaking or objectively and mind-independently real. The obstacle to their being ultimately real is said to be that they borrow their natures from their constituents. The size, shape, and weight of the chariot are all functions of the properties of its arranged parts. Its operation of transporting a king is likewise just the functioning of the constituent parts. Regardless of what we take to be the fundamental nature of a chariot, its nature is something it has only in dependence on those parts. Its nature is extrinsic, something derived from other things. By force of reasoning, it then seems that the mark of something's being ultimately and mind-independently real is that its nature be intrinsic, and not be something it possesses only in reliance on the presence of other things. It must be the kind of thing that could exist and be the sort of thing that it is in the absence of anything else. This is the intrinsic nature test for something's being ultimately real, for being what is called a *dharma*. Abhidharma theorists devoted considerable effort to working out their classifications of the dharmas. The soteriological point of this is that once we see what the world really consists of when it is stripped of our conceptual constructions, we become better able to see through the illusion fostered by the "I"-sense.

At the same time, it was recognized that if the only concepts we could use in describing or thinking about the world were dharma- or intrinsic-nature concepts, we would never get very far in communicating our experience. Abhidharma theorists thus distinguished between two different ways in which something might be said to exist and two different ways in which a statement might be true. Things with intrinsic nature were said to be ultimately real, while such ordinary things as chariots, trees, houses, and persons were said to be only conventionally real, to be mere conceptual fictions, things that are thought to exist only due to our use of certain concepts. Likewise, statements that correctly describe how dharmas are arranged are said to be ultimately true, while statements about mere conceptual fictions can only be conventionally true. Statements that are deemed conventionally true can be useful in daily life: being told that there is a chariot available to flee the battlefield may be a lifesaver. But since chariots are, strictly speaking, mere fictions, this statement cannot be one that corresponds to how things really are. What makes it true is instead how certain dharmas happen to be arranged. So for every statement that is conventionally true and so useful for everyday purposes, there is some (usually much longer) ultimately true statement that explains its utility. This distinction between two kinds of truth and two ways for something to be said to be real was central to the enterprise of the Abhidharma schools. And while Nāgārjuna is often portrayed as radically rejecting the doctrines of Abhidharma, he actually accepts most of what has been said so far about the device of the two truths. He agrees that only things with intrinsic nature are ultimately real and that composite things that borrow their properties from their constituents are conceptual fictions. He simply adds that there can be no things with intrinsic nature. The Abhidharma position was that persons are empty of intrinsic nature and so are not ultimately real. Nāgārjuna agrees, but adds that the same holds for dharmas.[3]

ESTABLISHING EMPTINESS

One would not be alone in suspecting that this last move is tantamount to the endorsement of metaphysical nihilism, the (absurd) view that nothing whatsoever exists. The charge of nihilism was routinely made against Nāgārjuna by both Buddhist and orthodox critics. This is understandable if we see Nāgārjuna as both endorsing the Abhidharma claim that only things with intrinsic natures could be ultimately real and denying that anything has intrinsic nature. This seems tantamount to claiming that nothing really exists—a claim that is pragmatically self-refuting. (When one entertains the thought that nothing exists, at least the event of the thinking of that thought must exist.) Nāgārjuna regularly rejects the charge of nihilism (see, e.g., MMK 13.7–8, 13.15, 24.7–8; VP 73-4). But in order to see just how he thinks this accusation can be averted, we should first examine a few of the arguments he gives in support of the claim that all things are empty.

To say of something that it is empty of intrinsic nature is to say that it depends for its being the sort of thing that it is on the simultaneous existence of other things. We have already seen this idea put to use in establishing that a whole thing such as a chariot lacks intrinsic nature and so is not ultimately real: a chariot cannot have the nature of being a means of transportation unless there exist the axle, spokes, rim, and so on, the collective functioning of which constitutes the chariot's transporting something. But do the parts have their own intrinsic natures before they are assembled to make up a chariot? In MMK 10, Nāgārjuna examines the example of fuel and fire as a case of dependent existence. Among other things, he claims that fuel cannot exist as fuel apart from fire. His 7th-century CE commentator Candrakīrti applies the same reasoning to the case of a chariot, arguing that when the chariot is burned up all its parts likewise disappear (MAV 6.161).[4] The thought here is that when two things are related to one another as material cause and effect, each depends for its being what it is on the existence of the other: fuel is what it is only when there is fire, a chariot axle is what it is only when there is a chariot. Consequently, Abhidharma theorists were wrong to suppose that the ultimate constituents of ordinary objects are ultimately real bearers of intrinsic nature.

One may have doubts about the strength of this argument. The sort of dependence being demonstrated would seem to be entirely notional. We might agree that in order for a stick to be considered fuel, there must be such a thing as fire. Thinking of the stick as fuel does depend on there being fire. Still, we can imagine that this stick might never get thought of as fuel and never get burned. This does not seem to detract in any way from its being the sort of thing that it is, a stick. The property of being fuel does seem dependent on our thinking of the stick in relation to something else. But this does not seem to demonstrate the stick's emptiness all by itself. Other arguments seem called for.

Another argument concerns the relation between a dharma and its intrinsic nature or defining characteristic (*lakṣaṇa*, MMK 5). We would normally think of a dharma as an existing thing that serves as the bearer of a certain nature: fire is a thing that bears the nature of being hot, space is a thing bearing the nature of nonresistance, and so on. The present argument is meant to demonstrate the problematic nature of this relation of bearer to the nature that is borne. If the intrinsic nature is to perform its function of characterizing its bearer, that bearer must exist distinct from the nature. To be a thing that takes up its nature from its being so characterized, it must in itself lack such nature. The difficulty is that we cannot make sense of the notion of a bearer that is devoid of defining characteristic, a bare substrate that is neither hot nor cold (nor lukewarm either), neither resistant nor nonresistant (nor squishy either). While we may be tempted to suppose that this bearer is a sort of neutral gunk, we forget that to think this is to supply the bearer with its own defining characteristic, that of bare gunkiness. So the notion of bearer of defining characteristic turns out to make no sense. And in the absence of a way to make sense of this idea, the model of a dharma as something with intrinsic nature appears to lose its intelligibility.

This argument uses the common-sense model of an entity as a substance plus its properties. We think, for instance, of a pot as something that bears such properties as being hard, round, hollow, earthen, a certain color, and so on. If our understanding of dharmas uses this analysis, then since a dharma must be qualitatively simple in nature, we are led to the difficulty of the dharma itself being a bare "something I know not what." But Ābhidharmikas came to see this as a major difficulty and devised a workaround: think of the dharma not as the bearer of an intrinsic nature but as just the occurrence of the intrinsic nature that is characteristic of that sort of dharma. So if the ultimate constituents of physical objects were instances of the four elements recognized by classical Indian physics, then a fire dharma would be just the occurrence of heat at a particular place and time. We are accustomed to thinking of heat as the property of some thing, be it a fire or a stove or the water from the tea kettle. But that might reflect no more than a useful way of talking about the physical world. It might be that strictly speaking where we say there is a red hot fire there is really just the simultaneous occurrence of heat and of red color at the same place. Our notion that heat and red color must be *in* something, that they require a substance that is their bearer or substrate, might be another illusion induced by a conceptual scheme that reflects our interests and cognitive limitations. And if we employ this alternative model of dharmas as just property particulars, then Nāgārjuna's argument will fail to show that the idea of a dharma does not make sense.

An argument for emptiness that is taken by many of Nāgārjuna's interpreters, both traditional and modern, to conclusively establish the doctrine is the argument from dependent origination, that is, from the premise that every existing thing originates in dependence on a cause and ancillary supporting conditions (MMK 1, MMK 20). The literature often gives this argument pride of place because of the central role that dependent origination plays in Buddhist thought more generally. What it seeks to show is that anything that comes into existence in dependence on cause and conditions must lack intrinsic nature. It proceeds from the assumption that an account of causal production must hold either that the effect already exists in unmanifest form in its cause or that it is newly brought into existence by the cause. The first possibility is quickly dispatched, on the grounds that if the effect already existed in its cause and conditions, no effort would be needed to bring it about: the heat of fire being already present in the fuel, we could warm ourselves without having to light the firewood. If the proponent of the immanence of the effect objected that effort is needed not to produce the effect but only to make it manifest, the reply would be that this invites an infinite regress: on this model, manifestation must itself go from being unmanifest to being manifest, and a further effort will be called for to explain this, and likewise for this effort, and so on.

The second option, that cause and effect are distinct, is the consensus position of the Abhidharma schools. The basic difficulty that Nāgārjuna sees in this view is that, unlike the first option, it fails to explain why cause and conditions produce one particular sort of effect and not any other. Why should planting a barley seed in warm moist soil produce a barley sprout and not a rice sprout, a pot, or even a lawn tractor? The source of the difficulty here is that cause and effect occur successively, the cause ceasing to exist when the effect arises. We might suppose that there is some overlap in the times of their occurrence. The chariot may be said to undergo the process of coming into existence as the parts are assembled by the chariot builder, in which case the time when cause and conditions occur and the time when the effect occurs may be said to overlap. But a chariot is a mere conceptual fiction, and what we are looking for is an account of the production of something ultimately real, a dharma. Since a dharma would have to be impartite, its existence must be all-or-nothing: either it does not yet exist or else it is already produced, there is no third time when it is coming into existence. It thus remains a mystery why on this model it should only be this one specific sort of effect that comes to be when cause and conditions are assembled, and not just anything.

Thus neither account of the causal relation will work when what is at issue is the arising of ultimately real entities, things with intrinsic nature. We might take this to show that the ultimate reals arise in a purely spontaneous and utterly random way. But Nāgārjuna rejects this as inconsistent with our experience (MMK 1.1). And things do come into existence; the buddha's identification of impermanence as a fundamental feature of reality cannot be denied. We are thus left with a seemingly insoluble difficulty: dharmas must originate and yet there is no satisfactory account of how this is possible. The Madhyamaka resolution is to reject the assumption that anything is ultimately real, that there are things with intrinsic nature. Dependent origination may well be true of conventionally real things like chariots, but it could not hold for dharmas.

While this argument is widely seen as effectively establishing emptiness, there may still be a way to save dependent origination at the ultimate level. The difficulty that the argument exploits might be traceable to our tendency to think of causation in anthropomorphic terms. The cause, we think, is what produces the effect, where production is something we conceptualize in terms of human agency. It is of course manifest that no human agency is involved in the transition from seed to sprout. But perhaps this is why we tend to think of such cases of causation in the natural world as involving what we think of as a necessary connection between cause and effect. Since close examination of seed and sprout fails to disclose any such thing as a necessary connection, perhaps it is a mistake to think of causation as any more than just invariable succession of one sort of event by an event of another sort. If that is the right way to think about causation, then the fact that we cannot explain why a given sort of dharma always arises after the occurrence of a certain aggregate of events and conditions should not distress us. It might just be that this is the way that the world happens to work, and nothing more needs to be said about the matter. If causation involves no more than patterns of invariable succession, then Nāgārjuna's argument will fail to establish that things with intrinsic nature cannot be dependently originated.

We have now examined three of the arguments Nāgārjuna gives in support of the claim that nothing could bear an intrinsic nature. In each case it was suggested that the argument fails to establish emptiness. But this may not be due to logical ineptness on Nāgārjuna's part. The real problem may instead lie in our thinking of his task as one of *establishing* emptiness. A definitive proof that nothing is ultimately real (i.e., has intrinsic nature) would need to provide premises in support of its conclusion. And since the conclusion concerns what is ultimately real, those premises would have to themselves state ultimate truths about ultimate reals. But how exactly is a Mādhyamika to arrive at such premises if, as they hold, nothing can fit the description of an ultimately real entity? The best it seems we can hope for from Nāgārjuna is that he will bring out the difficulties implicit in this or that account of the ultimate nature of reality. If, as the claim of emptiness suggests, the very idea of the ultimate nature of reality is incoherent, then one cannot use ultimate truths as evidence for the claim. There simply are no such truths. All the Mādhyamika can do in that case is examine theories propounded by those who think the idea of ultimate reals makes sense and demonstrate internal inconsistencies in their views. There can be no master argument for emptiness.[5] Nāgārjuna is forced to respond to the actual views of actual opponents. And the holes we have found in those of his arguments we examined may simply reflect the fact that his actual opponents did not entertain options that are now apparent to us. On this way of understanding the dialectical situation, Nāgārjuna's strategy may be just to wear down the opponent by pointing out difficulties in each new account they give of how they think things might ultimately be.

UNDERSTANDING EMPTINESS

Having looked at several of the arguments Nāgārjuna gives in (indirect) support of the claim of emptiness, we can now begin to explore how he might address the charge that he advocates metaphysical nihilism. Nāgārjuna's short answer to this question is that if it makes no sense to say that there are ultimately real things, then it likewise cannot be said that ultimately nothing whatsoever exists (MMK 5.6). A much longer answer goes by way of the key claim that emptiness is itself empty. We begin by unpacking the short answer; doing so will eventually lead us to the longer answer, and with it perhaps a better grasp of what the claim of emptiness amounts to.

The path that the buddha taught as leading to the cessation of suffering is regularly described as a path "of the middle" (*madhyama*), and the Madhyamaka school styles itself as merely elaborating on this idea of avoiding two extremes. Various different pairs of extremes are identified as those that the buddha's teachings avoid, for instance, the pair consisting of extreme asceticism on the one hand and a life devoted to sensual pleasure on the other. But particularly prominent in early Buddhist discourses is the pair eternalism versus annihilationism. Eternalism is the view that since the self is eternal, death is not the end. Annihilationism, by contrast, claims that the person is annihilated at death, so death is the end. One might wonder how there could be a middle path between these two views—perhaps that one lives on as a zombie? But closer examination reveals that a "middle path" is not meant as a compromise view but rather a rejection of the presupposition shared by both extremes, a presupposition that generates the question at issue. In this instance of eternalism and annihilationism, the presupposition at work is, of course, that there is such a thing as an enduring "I," something about whose postmortem fate one is concerned. If the person is really just a fiction constructed on the basis of a causal series of impermanent, impersonal psychophysical elements, then the question whether I ultimately survive death or am annihilated instead simply does not arise.

Nāgārjuna's short answer to the charge of metaphysical nihilism is that his is a middle path between the extreme views of eternalism and nihilism. By "eternalism" he does not mean the view that there is an eternal self, but rather the view that ultimately real entities, whatever these may be, are eternal. He argues (at MMK 13.4–6, MMK 15.9) that this would be one consequence of entities having intrinsic natures. All change, including the change involved in ceasing to exist, would be ruled out. So the doctrine of emptiness involves the rejection of what he here calls eternalism. By "nihilism" he means metaphysical nihilism, the view that ultimately there is nothing to be found. If we apply the pattern found in early Buddhist uses of the concept of a middle path, his claim to be taking a middle path approach means that this nihilism must share a common presupposition with what he calls eternalism. And the best candidate for this role seems to be the assumption that there is such a thing as the way that things are *anyway*, that the notion of the ultimate nature of reality makes sense. The eternalist and the nihilist are both metaphysical realists: both hold that we can meaningfully ask how the world is independent of the concepts that we happen to use due to our interests and cognitive limitations. Eternalist and nihilist merely give very different answers to that question. Nāgārjuna appears to hold that if there can be no such things as entities with intrinsic nature, then the question of whether or not they exist cannot be raised. In that case, the nihilist's answer, that they do not exist, must be ruled out as unintelligible.

Nāgārjuna's short answer to the accusation of espousing nihilism thus involves the idea that emptiness is not a metaphysical thesis. His claim that all things are empty is not meant to be an account of how things ultimately are. The opponent has reasoned that if all things were indeed empty, then it would be ultimately true that all things are devoid of intrinsic nature. And since Nāgārjuna agrees with his opponent that only things with intrinsic nature could be ultimately real, this ultimate truth should entail the further ultimate truth that nothing exists. Nāgārjuna rejects this inference, though. His rejection comes by way of his claim (VV 29) that he has no thesis (*pratijñā*). By a thesis he is to be understood to mean a metaphysical thesis, a statement that is meant to characterize how things ultimately are.[6] The opponent clearly takes Nāgārjuna to be propounding emptiness in precisely this way. But that Nāgārjuna does not mean emptiness to be taken as a metaphysical thesis is part of what he is claiming when he says that emptiness is itself empty (MMK 13.7, MMK 22.11, MMK 24.18). Reflection should show that it cannot be ultimately true that anything is characterized by emptiness. In order for a statement of the form "*x* is empty" to be ultimately true, the *x* in question must be ultimately real, something with intrinsic nature. And if it is true that all things are empty, there can be no such *x*. If the emptiness claim is true at all, it must be conventionally true; that is, a statement that helps guide successful behavior.

Nāgārjuna calls those who take the teaching of emptiness as a thesis "incurable" (MMK 13.8). To take emptiness as a thesis is to miss its true status: it is said "for the sake of instruction" (MMK 22.11); that is, as an instance of Buddhist pedagogical skill. The buddha is said to have been a masterful instructor in that, when addressing a particular audience, he allegedly knew intuitively just which sort of teaching would best help that audience advance toward the goal of the cessation of suffering. Buddhist exegetes use this idea of pedagogical skill to explain why the buddha taught different things to different audiences. In particular it is said to explain why it is that when the buddha addressed lay audiences, he often emphasized the doctrine of karma and rebirth and failed to mention the doctrines of nonself and impermanence. This might seem remiss given that the doctrine of karma and rebirth is most naturally interpreted as requiring the existence of an enduring self, something belief in which is said to pose the chief obstacle to liberation. Apologists says that the buddha understood these individuals would best advance toward enlightenment if they were motivated to refrain from immoral actions, and the doctrine of karma and rebirth effectively instills such motivation. A commentator says that when Nāgārjuna claims that emptiness is taught "for the sake of instruction," the point being made about emptiness may be likened to the case of someone uttering the sound "Quiet!" in order to bring about the cessation of sound.[7] While the speaker may be thought to violate their own injunction, their utterance may nonetheless be effective. Likewise, while Nāgārjuna's teaching of emptiness may be mistaken for a metaphysical thesis, its reception may lead one to abandon the very idea of an ultimate nature of reality. Emptiness might be a "skillful means" to attain the state of metaphysical quietism, the stilling of all hypostatization (*prapañca*).

To say that emptiness is itself empty is to say that the doctrine of emptiness is not ultimately true.[8] Nāgārjuna's critics regularly raised the question of how the teaching of emptiness might achieve its professed soteriological aim if it is not itself ultimately true; that is, does not represent how things ultimately are. He responds with the example of a magical being fabricated by the buddha, and this magical being in turn producing yet another illusory being who is then used for pedagogical purposes (MMK 17.31). Today we might think of an animé such as the 1999 film *Princes et Princesses*, at the beginning of which we see three characters set out to make animés about princes and princesses. We thereby learn how an animé is created, but our instructors in this case are themselves products of this process.[9] But perhaps a better example might be a documentary in which two reporters investigate the process whereby convincing "deep fake" films are produced. We might come to suspect that the reporters in the documentary are themselves deep fakes and even go so far as to wonder whether our experience away from the screen is equally artificially generated. This would be the equivalent of first seeing emptiness as a metaphysical thesis, allowing it to generate its corrosive effects on our metaphysical realist stance, and then finally abandoning our realist understanding of emptiness. We would then have arrived at Nāgārjuna's professed goal, the quieting of all hypostatization.

THE SOTERIOLOGICAL IMPACT OF EMPTINESS

In the dedicatory verse at the outset of MMK, Nāgārjuna proclaims that the cessation of hypostatization is "auspicious," or what the Buddhist path is meant to instill. This is repeated at the end of the work, where he characterizes the Buddha's teachings as leading to the abandonment of all metaphysical views (MMK 27.30) and repeats the claim that the ceasing of hypostatization is the auspicious state or nirvana (MMK 25.24).[10] The term that is here translated as "hypostatization," *prapañca*, ordinarily means something like logorrhea or unnecessary prolixity. In the early Buddhist context, though, it comes to mean the tendency to take as real whatever we have a name and concept for. This tendency plays a crucial role in the arising of suffering as detailed in the twelve-fold chain of dependent origination. For it is through the conceptual discriminations we employ in pursuit of pleasure and avoidance of pain that we end up deploying the concepts of "I" and "mine" (DN ii.277–279), concepts that are in fact only useful designations, or mere enumerative expressions (DN i.202; SN 35.248). Suffering originates, in short, due to hypostatization or reification, taking as real what are no more than ways of talking. The buddha is thus said to "teach non-hypostatization, delighting in non-hypostatization" (AN 8.30). Nāgārjuna is therefore simply expanding the scope of the buddha's teachings to encompass not just the abandonment of views that posit an "I" but also of views that posit anything that could be taken as ultimately real. The goal, in short, is metaphysical quietism—the simple rejection of all aspiration to say how things ultimately are.

One might wonder, though, just how this expansion of scope is justified. On the original account, suffering is said to arise out of metaphysical views that posit the existence of a person (the *satkāyadṛṣṭis*). This makes perfect sense if we understand suffering as existential in nature and its cessation as something to be arrived at through extirpation of the "I"-sense (AN 3.32, 6.11). Why, though, should an Abhidharma-style scheme of metaphysics be seen as an obstacle to liberation, given that such schemes were devised precisely to demonstrate the illusory nature of the "I"-sense? We can make sense of the idea that refuting those Brahmanical systems that posit an enduring self might prove important to a Buddhist liberation project. But Nāgārjuna recognizes that this had already been done by Ābhidharmika philosophers. Why should this extra step be necessary, particularly given that it invites the accusation of nihilism?

Here is what later Mādhyamikas take to be Nāgārjuna's response:

> 46. The grasping of deeply mistaken views is the source of the arising of [the defilements of] desire and aversion. Having acknowledged existence, disputes arise from that.
> 47. That is the cause of all views, the defilements do not arise in its absence. So if one thoroughly understands this, there will be the dissolution of views and defilements.
> 48. By means of the thorough understanding of what? Due to understanding dependent origination. That which is arisen in dependence on something else is not actually arisen, so says one who best understands reality.[11] YṢ 46–48

The defilements are the three factors (desire, aversion, and delusion) that the Buddha identified as principally responsible for our remaining in samsara. Delusion is, of course, ignorance, principally ignorance of the three characteristics of reality: impermanence, nonself, and suffering. Desire and aversion are defilements precisely because they reinforce delusion by bolstering the "I"-sense. What Nāgārjuna claims here is that it is the doing of metaphysics, even metaphysics of the most seemingly innocent kind, that fuels desire and aversion. To "acknowledge existence"—to suppose that the world has an objective order of mind-independent things—is to sow the seeds of ego affirmation through attachment to one's own view and rejection of the views of others. This holds equally for ordinary people (who wouldn't call themselves metaphysicians), for non-Buddhist philosophers (whose metaphysics explicitly affirms a self), and for Buddhist metaphysicians. Following the last of these in their inquiries can, Nāgārjuna thinks, take us some way toward extirpation of the "I"-sense.[12] Still, the impulse to do metaphysics is intrinsically dangerous, so while the Buddhist path may include practice of the sort of theorizing one finds in the Abhidharma schools, this must be renounced in the end. The point of establishing emptiness is precisely to enable such renunciation.

REVIEW OF LITERATURE

It is widely agreed that Nāgārjuna's writings, while profound and suggestive, are highly elusive. Given this character, it would be hard to say anything substantive about Nāgārjuna without committing to one interpretation over other options. Modern scholarship on Nāgārjuna has brought forth an almost bewildering array of readings of the texts. This article has so far given just one such reading. That there may be other plausible ways to understand Nāgārjuna's corpus must be acknowledged. What follows is a rough catalog of the different hermeneutical approaches to be found in recent scholarly work on Nāgārjuna's thought.

It has been common, following Tuck, to classify interpretive approaches to Nāgārjuna according to a scheme divided along lines dictated by the fashions in philosophy that prevail in the world of the interpreter. Thus the readings of Stcherbatsky and Murti are said to reflect an era in which Kantianism was dominant, while the works of Robinson and Hayes reflect the rise of analytic philosophy with its emphasis on the methods of formal logic.[13] While there may be some truth to the thought behind this way of classifying hermeneutical strategies, much of the recent literature on Nāgārjuna seems to be more clearly shaped by considerations deriving from the classical Indian philosophical debate over the teaching of emptiness.

One can, for instance, draw a distinction between nihilist and nonnihilist interpretations. Some studies, such as those of Wood and Burton, claim that Nāgārjuna is correctly understood as upholding metaphysical nihilism, while others, such as Murti, de Jong, and Ruegg reject this reading in favor of one that has Nāgārjuna's dialectic aimed at indirectly indicating a sort of inexpressible ultimate.[14] The division between these two styles of interpretation clearly echoes what we find in the reception of Madhyamaka in the Indian tradition. Burton, for instance, follows a well-worn path in making the case that Nāgārjuna can only be understood as affirming metaphysical nihilism, all his protestations to the contrary notwithstanding. He thinks the arguments for emptiness are, moreover, logically flawed in just the way that Naiyāyikas maintain. Wood gives a more sympathetic nihilist reading. While he confesses himself to remain unconvinced that nothing whatsoever exists, he does think that Mādhyamikas have shown that there are serious difficulties confronting any metaphysical realist project—including one holding that the real transcends all conceptualization. Clearly opposed to nihilist readings are those such as Murti's that take Nāgārjuna to employ his negative dialectic precisely to indicate indirectly something that cannot be directly expressed, gesturing at an Absolute that is somehow beyond all categorization. While Murti does discuss some apparent affinities between Nāgārjuna and Kant, his more telling comparison is with Advaita Vedānta, a school that teaches that an ineffable Absolute is what grounds the illusory empirical world.

Both nihilist and nonnihilist interpretations attribute some form of metaphysical realism to Nāgārjuna. But the readings discussed so far take the Madhyamaka dialectic to aim at providing a characterization (whether positive or negative) of the ultimate nature of reality. A quite different sort of understanding of Nāgārjuna takes a very different lesson from his refutations of realist theses: that everything is somehow connected to everything else, namely, through relations of dependency. On this reading, the idea of the ultimate nature of reality is incoherent precisely because it misses a central feature of the world, that things originate in dependence on other things, so nothing may be said to exist in splendid ontological isolation. Nāgārjuna could be convicted of nihilism only if the lone available model of reality were the one put forward by Abhidharma, according to which the reals exist by virtue of possessing their natures intrinsically. The alternative posed by Madhyamaka may, on this reading, be likened to Indra's net, an infinitely large web at each node of which there is a jewel that somehow reflects every other. While this interpretation does not attribute to Nāgārjuna any thesis concerning the ultimate nature of reality, it may still be characterized as a metaphysical reading, insofar as it purports to characterize what it is for something to exist—namely, conventionally, through thoroughgoing interrelatedness.[15] This sort of reading has sometimes been presented as the basis for a "green" or ecologically oriented Buddhism, as for instance in Cooper and James, or as in this quotation from John Clark: "For Nāgārjuna, a being can only be understood adequately as part of a system of relations."[16]

All the interpretations discussed so far may be considered metaphysical insofar as metaphysics is the branch of philosophy concerned with what it means for something to be said to exist. A metaphysical reading is perfectly plausible in the Indian context, given that when most systems of classical Indian philosophy give their prescriptions concerning how best to live one's life they seek to ground them in the correct characterization of reality. A quite different hermeneutical strategy rejects the quest for metaphysical grounding, and so may be described as anti-realist insofar as it rejects the metaphysical realism common to nihilist, transcendental, and Indra's net readings. Here as well the inspiration may lie not in recent trends in analytic philosophy but in elements of the Indian tradition. Such readings are also described as "semantic" because they focus on the meanings of the terms we use in metaphysical inquiries. A key insight at work in these ways of understanding Nāgārjuna involves the distinction between committed versus commitmentless uses of negation—a distinction that Mādhyamika commentators made much use of in responding to their critics. So the commitmentless denial of the thesis that ultimately real things arise in one of the four logically possible ways is not tantamount to the claim that ultimately real things do not exist; it simply implies that the question of how ultimately real things arise should not be raised. More generally, the upshot of Madhyamaka dialectic is, on this reading, the prescription of metaphysical quietism, an abstention from raising and attempting to answer questions concerning how things are. Proponents of a semantic interpretation disagree over whether this strategy leads to unresolved contradictions in what Mādhyamikas do say. On the dialetheist reading espoused by Garfield, Priest, and Deguchi, such contradictions do arise, but recent developments in nonclassical logic show how the problems commonly associated with the presence of contradictions in a system can be avoided.[17] Others, such as Siderits and Westerhoff, claim that the seeming contradictions can be resolved through judicious application of semantic contextualism, the view that utterances have meaning only in a specific context of utterance.[18] What all proponents of semantic interpretive strategies share, though, is an approach to understanding Nāgārjuna that seriously considers his claim that he is not out to say how things ultimately are, but he is rather intent on helping us see that the very idea of how things ultimately are is simply devoid of meaning. This hermeneutical approach, like others to be found in the recent secondary literature, also has its antecedents in the Buddhist commentarial tradition.

PRIMARY SOURCES

AN = *Aṅguttara Nikāya*, eds. R Morris (vols. 1 and 2) and E. Hardy (vols 3–5) London: Pali Text Society, 1885-1900. Translations of individual sutras by various authors are available at the following two sites: Suttapiṭaka—navigation (suttacentral.net) and Sutta Pitaka: The Basket of Suttas (accesstoinsight.org), https://suttacentral.net/pitaka/sutta

DN = *Dīgha-nikāya*, eds. T. W. Rhys Davids and J. E. Carpenter, in 3 vols. London: Pali Text Society, 1889–1910. Translations of individual sutras by various authors are available at the following two sites: Suttapiṭaka—navigation (suttacentral.net) and Sutta Pitaka: The Basket of Suttas (accesstoinsight.org), https://suttacentral.net/pitaka/sutta

MAV = *Madhyamakāvatāra* of Candrakīrti: 2004. *Introduction to the Middle Way: Chandrakirti's Madhyamakavatara with commentary by Jamgön Mipham*, translated by the Padmakara Translation Group, Boston and London: Shambhala, 2003.

MMK = *Mūlamadhyamakakārikā*: Siderits, Mark, and Shōryū Katsura. *Nāgārjuna's Middle Way: The Mūlamadhyamakakārikā*. Boston: Wisdom, 2013.

Bugault, Guy. *Stances du millieu par excellence*. Gallimard, Paris, 2001.

Sanskrit text available at: *Majjhima Nikāya*, ed. V. Trenckner, in 3 vols. London: Pali Text Society, 1948–1960. Translations of individual sutras by various authors are available at the following two sites: Suttapiṭaka—navigation (suttacentral.net) and Sutta Pitaka: The Basket of Suttas (accesstoinsight.org), http://www.dsbcproject.org/canon-text/book/242MN =Majjhima%20Nikā

RĀ = *Ratnāvalī*: Hopkins, Jeffrey. *Buddhist Advice for Living and Liberation: Nāgārjuna's Precious Garland*. Ithaca, NY: Snow Lion, 1998. Sanskrit text available at nAgArjuna-ratnAvalI, http://gretil.sub.uni-goettingen.de/gretil/corpustei/transformations/html/sa_nAgArjuna-ratnAvalI.htm

VP = *Vaidalyaprakaraṇa*: Westerhoff, Jan. *Crushing the Categories. Vaidalyaprakaraṇa by Nāgārjuna*. Boston: Wisdom, 2018.

VV = *Vigrahavyāvartanī*: Westerhoff, Jan. *The Dispeller of Disputes: Nāgārjuna's Vigrahavyāvartanī*. Boston: Wisdom, 2018. Sanskrit text available at nAgArjuna-vigrahavy-AvartanI, http://gretil.sub.uni-goettingen.de/gretil/corpustei/transformations/html/sa_nAgArjuna-vigrahavyAvartanI.htm

YṢ = *Yuktiṣaṣṭikā*: Loizzo, Joseph. *Nāgārjuna's Reason Sixty (Yuktiṣaṣṭikā) with Chandrakīrti's Commentary*, New York: American Institute of Buddhist Studies, 2007. Scherrer-Schaub, C. A. *Yuktiṣaṣṭikāvṛtti: commentaire à la soixantaine sur le raisonnement ou du vrai enseignement de la causalité par le Maître Indien Candrakīrti*. (Mélanges Chinois et Bouddhiques, Volume XXV.) Brussels, Institut Belge des Hautes Études Chinoises, 1991. Reconstructed Sanskrit text available at nAgArjuna-yuktiSaSTikakArikA, http://gretil.sub.uni-goettingen.de/gretil/corpustei/transformations/html/sa_nAgArjuna-yuktiSaSTikakArikA.htm

FURTHER READING

Burton, David. *Emptiness Appraised: A Critical Study of Nāgārjuna's Philosophy*. Richmond, UK: Curzon, 1999.

Hayes, Richard P. "Nāgārjuna's Appeal." *Journal of Indian Philosophy* 22 (1994): 299–378.

Katsura Shōryū, and Goshima Kiyotaka. 竜樹「根本中頌」を読む (Ryūju "Konpon chūju" o yomu). Tokyo: Shunjūsha, 2016.

Lindtner, Christian. *Nāgārjuniana: Studies in the Writings and Philosophy of Nāgārjuna*. New Delhi: Motilal Banarsidass, 1987.

Murti, Tirupattur R. V. *The Central Philosophy of Buddhism*. London: Allen & Unwin, 1955.

Priest, Graham, and Jay Garfield. "Nāgārjuna and the Limits of Thought." In *Beyond the Limits of Thought*. Edited by Graham Priest and Jay Garfield, 249–270. Oxford: Clarendon Press, 2002.

Ruegg, David Seyfort. "The Uses of the Four Positions of the Catuḥṣkoti and the Problem of the Description of Reality in Mahāyāna Buddhism." *Journal of Indian Philosophy* 5 (1977): 1–71.

Siderits, Mark. *Personal Identity and Buddhist Philosophy: Empty Persons*. 2nd ed. Aldershot, UK: Ashgate, 2015.

Tuck, Andrew P. *Comparative Philosophy and the Philosophy of Scholarship: On the Western Interpretation of Nāgārjuna*. Oxford: Oxford University Press, 1990.

Westerhoff, Jan. *Nāgārjuna's Madhyamaka: A Philosophical Introduction.* Oxford: Oxford University Press, 2009.

Westerhoff, Jan. *The Golden Age of Indian Buddhist Philosophy.* Oxford: Oxford University Press, 2017.

Wood, Thomas E. *Nāgārjunian Disputations: A Philosophical Journey through an Indian Looking-Glass.* Honolulu: University of Hawai'i Press, 1994.

NOTES

1. Since there is not yet consensus on how best to translate the titles of Buddhist philosophical works, this article refers to them by their Sanskrit (or Pāli) titles and uses the widely accepted abbreviations of their titles.
2. For a far more expansive list of works deemed authentically Nāgārjuna's, see Christian Lindtner, *Nāgārjuniana: Studies in the Writings and Philosophy of Nāgārjuna* (New Delhi: Motilal Banarsidass, 1987).
3. For Nāgārjuna's extension of the domain of emptiness from persons to *dharmas* see YṢ 33–4, MMK 18.6–11.
4. Nāgārjuna argues more explicitly for the dependence of parts on whole at VP 33.
5. To say this is not to deny that Nāgārjuna uses similar styles of argumentation against different targets. For more on this see Siderits and Katsura, *Nāgārjuna's Middle Way*, 7–9.
6. This is how the term is used in the Nyāya school, and his opponent in this portion of VV is clearly a Naiyāyika. See Mark Siderits, "The Madhyamaka Critique of Epistemology I," *Journal of Indian Philosophy* 8 (1980): 307–335.
7. In Bhāviveka's commentary *Prajñāpradīpa* MMK 22.11.
8. At least the emptiness teaching is not ultimately true in the sense of corresponding to the ultimate nature of reality. The teaching may be said to be ultimately true in the quite different sense of being that the realization of which brings about liberation. It would then be *ultimately* true in the sense of being the *final* truth that must be grasped.
9. *Princes et Princesses*, directed by Michel Ocelot, (Les Armateurs, producers) 1999. Thanks to Myriam Weil for bringing this film to my attention.
10. Modern scholars disagree over whether chapters 26 and 27 are not later additions to the text. The final verse of chapter 25 more closely echoes the thought of the initial dedicatory verse, but the final verse of chapter 27 more neatly summarizes the overall dialectical situation following the preceding 26 chapters. Much of the dispute over the authenticity of chapters 26 and 27 seems driven by the fact that chapter 26 contains nothing that an orthodox Ābhidharmika could not accept. But regardless of which is the final chapter of MMK, the work does end in a verse that references the claim found at the beginning.
11. My translation of the Sanskrit original: *rāgadveṣodbhavas tīvraduṣṭadṛṣṭiparigrahaḥ|vivādās tatsamutthāś ca bhāvābhyupagame sati||sa hetuḥ sarvadṛṣṭīnāṁ kleśotpattir na taṁ vinā|tasmāt tasmin parijñāte dṛṣṭikle śaparikṣayaḥ||parijñā tasya keneti pratītyotpādadarśanāt|pratītya jātaṁ cājātam āha tattvavidāṁ varaḥ||*. For an English rendering of the Tibetan translation along with Candrakīrti's commentary, see Loizzo, "*Yuktiṣaṣṭikā*," 197–200; but it should be reiterated that attribution of YṢ to Nāgārjuna is controversial.
12. For an early Buddhist anticipation of this stance with respect to Brahmanical thinkers, see *Majjhima Nikāya* 74, in Vilhelm Trenckner, ed., *Majjhima Nikāya* (London: Pali Text Society, 1948–1960), 1:497. Translations of individual sutras by various authors are available at Suttapiṭaka and Sutta Pitaka: The Basket of Suttas and this stance toward the Abhidharma schools shows up not only in chapters 26 and 27 of MMK but also in such places as MMK 18.1–5.
13. Andrew Tuck, *Comparative Philosophy and the Philosophy of Scholarship: On the Western Interpretation of Nāgārjuna* (Oxford: Oxford University Press, 1990); Theodore Stcherbatsky, *The Conception of Buddhist Nirvana* (Delhi: Motilal Banarsidass, 1977); Tirupattur R. V. Murti, *The Central Philosophy of Buddhism* (London: Allen & Unwin, 1955); Richard Robinson, *Early Mādhyamika in India and China* (Madison: University of Wisconsin Press, 1967); and Richard Hayes, "Nāgārjuna's Appeal," *Journal of Indian Philosophy* 22 (1994): 299–378.

14. Thomas E. Wood, *Nāgārjunian Disputations: A Philosophical Journey through an Indian Looking-Glass* (Honolulu: University of Hawai'i Press, 1994); David Burton, *Emptiness Appraised: A Critical Study of Nāgārjuna's Philosophy* (Richmond, UK: Curzon Press, 1999); Jan W. de Jong, "The Problem of the Absolute in the Madhyamaka School," *Journal of Indian Philosophy* 2 (1976): 1–6; and David Seyfort Ruegg, "The Uses of the Four Positions of the Catuṣkoṭi and the Problem of the Description of Reality in Mahāyāna Buddhism," *Journal of Indian Philosophy* 5 (1977): 1–71.
15. Dan Arnold, *Buddhists, Brahmins, and Belief: Epistemology in South Asian Philosophy of Religion* (New York: Columbia University Press, 2005), 170–171.
16. David E. Cooper and Simon P. James, *Buddhism, Virtue and Environment* (Aldershot, UK: Ashgate, 2005) and John Clark, "On Being None with Nature: Nagarjuna and the Ecology of Emptiness," *Capitalism Nature Socialism* 19 (2008): 12.
17. Yasuo Deguchi, Jay Garfield, and Graham Priest, "The Way of the Dialetheist: Contradictions in Buddhism," *Philosophy East and West* 58 (2008): 395–402.
18. See, e.g., Mark Siderits, *Personal Identity and Buddhist Philosophy: Empty Persons*, 2nd ed. (Aldershot, UK: Ashgate, 2015), 187–206; and Jan Westerhoff, *Nāgārjuna's Madhyamaka: A Philosophical Introduction* (Oxford: Oxford University Press, 2009).

Mark Siderits

NAIKAN: A MEDITATION METHOD AND PSYCHOTHERAPY

THE BUDDHIST ORIGINS OF NAIKAN

A literal translation of the Japanese term *naikan* (pronounced nye-kən) is "introspection." In Buddhism, according to one dictionary, it means the practice of observing the self, or more specifically, introspection to observe the truth in the mind.[1] The term *naikan* is found in several places in Zhiyi's *Mohe Zhiguan* 摩訶止観, in which it means internal contemplation.[2] The Zen monk Hakuin 白隠 (1686–1768) used *naikan* to refer to an introspective practice for health that involved visualization, moving vital energy (*ki* 気) through the body, and contemplating four thoughts.[3] Some modern Shin Buddhist thinkers have used *naikan* to mean a method for seeking truth and interpreting Pure Land Buddhist scriptures.[4] The Shin Buddhist philosopher Kiyozawa Manshi 清沢満之 (1863–1903) created the term *naikan-shugi* 内観主義 to specifically indicate how introspection can lead people to discover the truth about themselves, which can then serve to guide how they act.[5]

The origins of Yoshimoto's Naikan method lie in a religious experience he had when he was twenty-one years old and searching to secure his faith in Amida 阿弥陀 Buddha. He grew up in a devout and wealthy Shin Buddhist household, but was anxious about whether he had an entrusting heart (*shinjin* 信心). Through a family connection, he learned about a lay Shin Buddhist group in Nara and Osaka that did a meditative practice known as *mishirabe* (self-examination). If done successfully, *mishirabe* was believed to effect a state of mind free from self-attachment and as synonymous with obtaining complete trust in Amida (*shinjin gyakutoku* 信心獲得).[6]

Those doing *mishirabe*, who were called the "sick" (*byōnin* 病人), were required to sit alone and reflect on their sins. They were not allowed to eat, drink, or sleep during *mishirabe*. It would typically last several days until the *byōnin* either quit or experienced *shukuzen kaihotsu* 宿善開発, which Yoshimoto characterized as realizing "enlightenment."[7] About every two hours, one of the so-called enlightened (*kaigonin* 開悟人) who had successfully done *mishirabe* came in to listen to "the sick" report on what they had discovered through reflecting on their lives. To help "the sick" make progress, the "enlightened" prodded them along by asking questions such as, "If you were to die now, where would you go? Would you go to heaven (*gokuraku* 極楽) or hell (*jigoku* 地獄)?" The "enlightened" would then tell "the sick" to investigate themselves and the impermanence of things.

Yoshimoto failed several times at *mishirabe* before he had a powerful experience in November 1937. Yoshimoto says in an autobiographical account how it occurred on the fourth day of his final *mishirabe*. Just before his awakening, he was suffering physical pain from lack of sleep. He thought about giving up, but the memories of how he failed the year before pushed him forward. He was doing poorly when his teacher, Komatani 駒谷, entered Yoshimoto's room to listen to his report. Yoshimoto admitted to his teacher that he was not doing well. When his teacher asked him, "Do you understand your sins?" Yoshimoto admitted that he did not feel them "deep in his heart." Komatani replied by telling Yoshimoto that his "bad karma is too strong" and that those who lack the correct karmic condition cannot be helped. As Komatani got up to leave Yoshimoto grabbed him, but Komatani pushed him away. Yoshimoto recalled what happened right after as follows: "Shuddering with guilt and fear of death, I gasped for breath in the depths of despair... After that, I fell face down unconscious. I do not know how long I was like that; it might have been minutes or hours, but when I came to I was so full of joy and all I could do was cry."[8]

Yoshimoto was never able to explain what happened but he wanted others to feel the joy he felt. He became a proponent for self-reflection that focused on people examining the wrongs they had done. Because Yoshimoto wanted to popularize this type of self-reflection, he decided in consultation with his teacher Komatani to remove the requirement to abstain from food, drink, and sleep. By the end of 1941, he began to call this modified form of *mishirabe* Naikan.

Yoshimoto understood Naikan from the perspective of Shin Buddhism as a way of seeking truth and overcoming self-attachment. But he realized shortly after modifying *mishirabe* that a person did not need to believe in Shin Buddhist doctrine for Naikan to have a positive effect. He discovered this during the war years when he offered a week of intensive Naikan to the employees of his leathercloth company. In 1943 eighteen female factory workers between the ages of fifteen and twenty volunteered to do it. Yoshimoto was pleased by the outcomes. A mother of one of the women went to see Yoshimoto to happily report how after doing Naikan her daughter had become calmer and more industrious. Yoshimoto also found that among those who did Naikan, their productivity increased, they felt less frustration and more gratitude, and that they got along better with their coworkers.[9]

Throughout his life Yoshimoto advocated for the practice of Naikan. In the 1940s and early 1950s, he framed this advocacy in religious terms, as is evident in a 1945 self-published autobiography titled *Before and After Faith: A Naikan Experience* (*Shinzen shingo: Watashi no naikan taiken* 信前信後：私の内観体験). He also set up a "Faith Consultation Office" (*Shinkō sōdansho* 信仰相談所), which in 1947 published a bulletin titled "A True Way to Save the World" (*Kyūsei shinpō* 救世真法).

He became a Shin Buddhist priest of the Kibe-ha 木辺派 and built a temple called Naikandera 内観寺, where he trained people in Naikan. After becoming a prison chaplain in 1954, he gradually started to reduce the religious language he used to describe Naikan and to argue that it was not religious. By doing so, he made it possible for Naikan to be taught at public institutions that were prohibited by law from endorsing any religious activities.

SECULARIZING NAIKAN IN PRISONS: 1954–1960

The first few months that Yoshimoto served as a prison chaplain at the Nara Youth Prison (Naikan shōnen keimusho 奈良少年刑務所) he had difficulty getting anyone to do Naikan. In hopes of attracting interest, he set up a club in the prison that met for two hours on Wednesdays, during which time they did Naikan. Their Naikan focused on examining their actions and attitudes when they were different ages. Throughout the week they also wrote Naikan diaries, which Yoshimoto read. Yoshimoto suspected at first that those who came to the club's meetings did so to avoid mandatory factory work. After a while, however, some of the youth started to open up to him about their lives and to practice Naikan seriously.

Yoshimoto also started to introduce Naikan to other juvenile detention centers and to prisons. He wrote two books about his experiences working with prisoners. Some of his writings he had translated into English and compiled as a book titled *Self-Reflection Will Guide You to the Right Way*. In that book he states that the purpose of Naikan is to "be spiritually awakened from suffering" and "to get rid of the selfishness in you, to reach the stage to be able to endure whatever difficulties you may have."[10]

To spread Naikan among correction facilities, it became necessary to present Naikan as nonreligious. Because Yoshimoto could not be at more than one prison at a time and it was hard to visit correctional facilities throughout the country, Yoshimoto wanted to train correction officers so they could teach Naikan and conduct interviews. To do this and not violate the law that prohibited public funds from being used to support religious activities, corrections officers could only guide prisoners in Naikan if it were regarded as nonreligious. So Yoshimoto started to present Naikan as a practice that was not inherently religious. In 1956, for example, he wrote that Naikan is a self-reflection method and that no law prohibits self-reflection in prisons. The following year in a booklet titled *Naikanhō no tsutaekata* 内観法の傳え方 (How to Convey the Naikan Method), Yoshimoto published a dialogue with a prison warden who argued that Naikan was not religious. The warden says it would be wrong to conclude that Naikan is religious just because Yoshimoto is a religious person and a prison chaplain. He referred to the Prime Minister Ishibashi 石橋 and said that even though Ishibashi was a Nichiren Buddhist and ordained as a Nichiren priest, that did not make all his political policies Nichiren Buddhist.[11] The warden then states that there is no constitution that prohibits self-reflection and that for Naikan, no one has to worship Amida 阿弥陀 or convert to Shinshū 真宗. So with the understanding that Naikan was not religious, Yoshimoto began to train correctional officers at his temple in Nara, so that they could lead others in Naikan without him. The training mostly involved having the officers do a week of intensive Naikan.

By 1962 there were twenty-nine prisons and ten reform schools offering Naikan.[12] Surveys of those who had done Naikan while incarcerated revealed that the recidivism rate was much lower among those who had practiced Naikan in prison. The most dramatic case was shown in

Miyazaki prison in which in 1960 the recidivism rate was only 14.4 percent for those who did Naikan, compared with 80.3 percent for those who did not.[13]

MEDICALIZATION OF NAIKAN FROM THE 1960S

Psychiatrists who worked in the prison system were the first to recognize Naikan as having psychotherapeutic benefits. In 1957 Tsushima Mamoru 津島衛, a psychiatrist at a correctional facility in Nara, praised Naikan. He said it should not simply be considered religious but seen as scientific and psychotherapeutic.[14] The following year another psychiatrist, Haraguchi Naoshi 原口直, introduced Naikan to the Jōno 城野 Medical Prison in Kitakyushu 北九州. He also told other psychiatrists about successful cases of prisoners who did Naikan.[15]

The first major publications on Naikan in relation to psychology and psychotherapy came in the 1960s. In 1962 Takeda Ryōji 武田良二, who worked in corrections, published an article on how Naikan related to psychological problems.[16] Three years later, a psychologist and professor at Shinshū 信州 University named Takeuchi Katashi 竹内硬, who did intensive Naikan with Yoshimoto, wrote an essay praising Naikan from a psychological perspective. This essay was published as the forward to Yoshimoto's autobiographical history of Naikan titled *Naikan no yonjū nen* 内観の四十年 (Forty Years of Naikan). Takeuchi also helped promote Naikan as a psychotherapeutic practice by publishing an article in 1965 in the popular Buddhist magazine *Daihōrin* 大法輪 on how Naikan restructures a person's life.[17] In that same year, Naikan as a psychotherapeutic method gained further attention among Buddhists when Satō Kōji 佐藤幸治, a psychologist and professor at Kyoto University, wrote a review of Yoshimoto's book *Forty Years of Naikan* for the major Buddhist newspaper *Chūgai Nippō* 中外日報.

Around the time of these publications, the psychologist Murase Takao 村瀬孝雄 began to study Naikan as an indigenous psychotherapy. Murase was intrigued by how Naikan developed independent of Western psychotherapeutic ideas. In an article he published in 1970, he argued that unlike Morita therapy, which was developed by a physician trained in Western medicine, Naikan had no connection with global scholarship or to the modern world of technology.[18] He pointed out how it was built not on the basis of psychological theories but rather on Yoshimoto's religious experience.

Besides theoretical writings on Naikan, we find in the 1960s Naikan emerging as a treatment in medical contexts (e.g. Figure 1). Psychiatrists began to publish findings on the results of patients who did Naikan. For example, Ishida Rokurō 石田六郎, a psychiatrist in Fukushima with a private practice, reported on the successes he was having using Naikan with patients suffering from psychosomatic and neurotic disorders. Ishida learned how to do Naikan from printed materials and audio recordings of Naikan interviews that Yoshimoto sent him.[19]

On the basis of those materials, he developed a therapy called "Naikan Analysis" (*Naikan bunseki* 内観分析), which mixed Naikan with autogenetic training, a relaxation method. His use of Naikan attracted attention when he published a report on it in 1965 in the medical journal *Nihon iji shinpō* 日本医事新報.[20]

In addition to Ishida, psychiatrists at Okayama 岡山 University Hospital came to take an interest in using Naikan with both alcoholics and patients with neurotic disorders. Suwaki Hiroshi 洲脇寛 and Yokoyama Shigeo 横山茂雄, for example, reported on their success using Naikan in 1967 to treat a seventeen-year-old male who was suffering from obsessional neurosis.[21] The

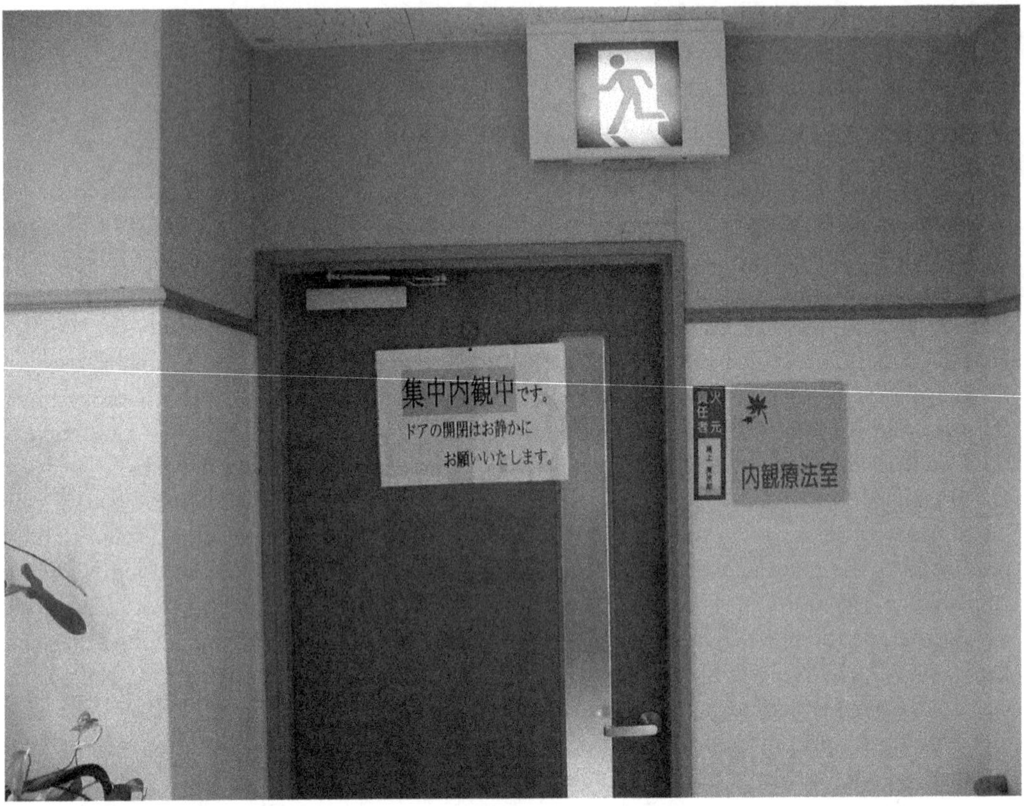

Figure 1. Naikan Therapy Room at Sanwa Chūō 三和中央 Hospital, Nagasaki 長崎.
Source: Photograph by author

positive results they were getting with Naikan led to Yoshimoto receiving an invitation to speak in 1968 with psychiatrists at Okayama University. In that same year he was also invited to Jikeikai 慈恵会 Medical University in Tokyo to give a talk, which consisted of a thirty-minute lecture followed by ninety minutes of questions on Naikan.[22] It was around the time of these talks that Yoshimoto was honing the Naikan method and formulating the three core questions of Naikan: What did I receive? What did I give back? What troubles and difficulties did I cause?

In the 1960s and early 1970s, Naikan received considerable attention in major national as well as local newspapers. Journalists told stories about Naikan's effectiveness for reforming prisoners, treating addiction, improving family relations, and helping with problems at school. Articles introducing Naikan ran headlines such as the following: "The results of Naikan Education in Hiroshima Prison—Awakening the Conscience of Inmates"; "Alcoholism Cured by Buddhist Practice"; "To Solve Family Problems, Look Objectively at Self"; "Truancy Fixed!"[23] Japan's national TV broadcasting company, NHK, introduced Naikan to the public. In 1965 and 1967 it broadcast two programs highlighting Naikan. Then between 1978 and 1982 it aired three other programs focusing on Yoshimoto and Naikan.

NAIKAN'S DEVELOPMENT BEYOND YOSHIMOTO: 1975 TO 2017

Yoshimoto was interested in promoting Naikan through publications, but he gave little effort to creating organizational structures. He did not create a strong network of Naikan practitioners that could support each other. Nor did he try to create institutions that could foster regular interaction among those who had done intensive Naikan. The creation of social organizations would be taken up by his disciples Takemoto Takahiro 竹元隆洋, a psychiatrist; and Miki Yoshihiko 三木善彦, a psychologist at a university in Osaka 大阪.

The impetus for the creation of a Naikan organization came in August 1976. Takemoto had gone to Yoshimoto's place to do Naikan for a second time. The night he arrived, Yoshimoto became ill and had to be rushed to the hospital in an ambulance. Takemoto spent the night worrying about what was going to happen to Yoshimoto and to Naikan if Yoshimoto died. He began to think about the importance of having an organization to study Naikan and to keep it going beyond Yoshimoto. He contacted Miki, and together, in consultation with Yoshimoto, they set up the Japan Naikan Association (JNA; Nihon Naikan Gakkai 日本内観学会), which had its first meeting in 1978. The association's first president was not Yoshimoto but the prominent psychologist Murase Takao.

Since its founding, the JNA has held an annual conference, at which research papers are presented on topics related to Naikan and its application for psychological disorders. In 1995 it started publishing an annual journal with research articles, case studies, reports, and book reviews.[24] Most of the articles and case studies are written by mental health care professionals and directors of Naikan centers. The JNA has also produced an annual newsletter titled "Naikan News" since 1985 that reports on Naikan events such as local conferences and workshops and on national conferences of interest to Naikan practitioners, such as those on psychiatry and psychology. It also includes responses to major Naikan presentations.

In 1998, to focus more specifically on Naikan as a medical therapy, the Japanese Naikan Medical Association was founded. It also has annual meetings and publishes a journal with research findings related to the use of Naikan as a medical treatment. It works in close cooperation with the JNA.

A nonacademic organization called the "Self Discovery Society" (Jiko hakken no kai 自己発見の会) was founded in 1990 to promote Naikan. It consisted of several regional groups that offered opportunities for those who had done intensive Naikan to interact. Up until 2011 it published a quarterly magazine titled *Yasuragi* やすら樹 (Tranquility) that had short and easy-to-read articles on Naikan. It then became dormant for several years until it was started up again by a second generation of Naikan practitioners who did not personally know Yoshimoto but who ran Naikan training centers. It has a website and started publishing a magazine in 2017 titled *Naikan Classic*.

Up until the time that Yoshimoto died in 1988, he endorsed Naikan activities promoted by his disciples and others. He did not, however, try to control them nor did he promote a certification process to set standards for how Naikan should be done. This made it easier both during and after his life for various deviations of Naikan to develop at temples and in new religions.

Two temples that included Naikan were the Gasshoen 合掌園 and Senkōbō 専光坊, both located in Mie 三重 Prefecture. Gasshoen is a Shin Kibe-ha Buddhist temple. Although it is no longer a major center for Naikan, from 1974 to 1993, when the head priest Mizuno 水野 died, the temple provided intensive Naikan for over 10,000 people. Some of the testimonials of those who had done Naikan appeared in a magazine published by the temple titled *Naikan no tomo* 内観の友 (Friends of Naikan). Twice a month the temple held meetings during which Naikan practitioners got together and shared their experiences with it. Unlike at Yoshimoto's temple, Naikan-dera, Naikan at Gasshoen was practiced as part of the religious life of the temple. During intensive Naikan retreats, for example, those doing Naikan started each day by reciting scriptures and listening to a sermon.

Similar to Gasshoen, Senkōbō has been run by a Shin Buddhist priest who has integrated religious elements with Naikan, such as the recitation of the *nenbutsu* 念仏 and Buddhist sermons. But unlike Mizuno, Senkōbō's head priest, Usami Shue 宇佐美秀慧, used Zen practices such as having the people doing Naikan come to his room in the manner of a Zen interview (*dokusan* 独参) and having those who want to do Naikan at the temple wait outside of it, sometimes for days, as is done when a Zen novice requests entry to train at a temple.

Two new religions that adopted Naikan are GLA and Hikari no Wa ひかりの輪. GLA's founder, Takahashi Shinji 高橋信次 (1927–1976), thought that Naikan was powerful for changing people and leading them to gratitude. Although Naikan is no long emphasized in GLA, in the 1980s there were two GLA-run Naikan centers in Tokyo.

In contrast to the decline of Naikan in GLA, Naikan has emerged as a core practice for Hikari no Wa, which was founded in 2007. Its founder, Jōyū 上祐, was the spokesperson for Aum in 1995 after it released sarin gas on a Tokyo subway. After denouncing Aum's leader, Asahara Shōkō 麻原彰晃, Jōyū established Hikari no Wa as a new religious organization. In 2009 it started incorporating Naikan into its religious practices. Two of its leaders did a week of intensive Naikan. For the past several years it has held one-day Naikan seminars about once every other month in different major Japanese cities during which people reflect on the three Naikan questions. After many of these seminars, Hikari no Wa puts testimonials from them on its website.

INTERNATIONALIZATION OF NAIKAN

Outside of Japan, Naikan has had the greatest influence in German-speaking regions of Europe, where thousands of people have done intensive Naikan trainings.[25] Ishii Akira 石井光, a professor fluent in German at Aoyama University, Tokyo, helped introduce the practice to Austria and Germany. In 1980 Ishii conducted the first intensive Naikan training ever held outside Japan at the Scheibbs Buddhist Center in Austria. The training's sponsor, Franz Ritter, had met Ishii in Japan in 1978 when doing Zen training at Eigenji, a temple near Kyoto. After doing intensive Naikan in 1980, Ritter started to promote and teach Naikan. In 1986 he established the first Naikan training center outside of Japan. The center moved in 1990 about fifty miles south of Vienna and was named Neue Welt Institut. The Austrian Buddhist Society recognizes it as a Buddhist institution.

A second Naikan center was opened in Austria in 1990 by Roland Dick, a one-time archeologist, and a third by Josef Hartl in 1992 called Naikan Haus Wien. Josef Hartl was a one-time drug addict and prisoner who credited Naikan with turning his life around. He was a disciple of Senkōbō's Usami. He first practiced zazen, then started practicing Naikan in 1986. He also trained to become a shiatsu provider. In 1996 he founded the Naikido Center of Vienna, which offered both Naikan and shiatsu. Among Hartl's Naikan trainees were Johanna Schuh, who opened her own training center in 2006 in Vienna called Insightvoice; and Ruedi Beiner, who offers Naikan training in Münsingen, Switzerland.

In Germany, the first Naikan training center was opened by Gerald Steinke in 1987. Steinke suffered for many years from insomnia and depression. At the recommendation of Ishii he visited Japan in 1986. After doing Naikan with Yoshimoto, Steinke's depression and insomnia disappeared. After returning to Germany, he opened a Naikan center and started offering Naikan at a prison in Göttingen. Steinke's work with prisoners led to a Naikan center being built in a prison in Peine, near Hanover, that allows up to six people at a time to do intensive Naikan.[26] Outside of prisons, intensive Naikan training is offered today in Germany at three places: Naikan Zentrum Bayerischer Wald in St. Oswald, Bavaria; Naikan Haus in Wartenberg, near Munich; and Naikan Stammhaus in Tarmstedt near Bremen.

There are also two alcohol and drug addiction treatment centers in Europe that provide Naikan as a relapse prevention method. They are die Fleckenbühler in Germany and Projekt Alp in Switzerland.

In the United States, intensive Naikan trainings have been fewer and more sporadic than in Europe. The first Naikan training in the United States, in which twelve people participated, was at a Shin Buddhist temple in San Luis Obispo in 1981. It was led by David Reynolds, an anthropologist who did intensive Naikan with Yoshimoto and later combined Naikan and Morita Therapy to formulate what he called "Constructive Living." Reynolds, who later published several popular books on Japanese psychotherapies, also helped initiated Naikan trainings in Hawaii between 2001 and 2005 that were led by the Shin Buddhist minister Sengoku Mari. The only Naikan center in North America is the ToDo Institute in Vermont run by Gregg Krech. It opened in 1992 and has offered once or so a year intensive Naikan training as well as workshops and online Naikan courses.

In Asia, Naikan can be found in China and Korea. In China, Naikan was introduced by the psychiatrist Wang Zucheng 王祖承 of the Shanghai Mental Health Center. Wang had studied in Japan for a year in the mid-1980s and started writing articles on Naikan for psychiatric journals in 1988. In 1992 he invited from Japan the director of the Yamato 大和 Naikan Institute, Maeshiro Teruaki 真栄城輝明, to give a talk at a World Health Organization meeting held in Shanghai. Maeshiro's talk was attended by over four hundred mental health specialists from around China. Soon after that meeting, Wang had a Naikan therapy room built at his hospital and started to offer Naikan therapy. Since then numerous studies have been conducted on Naikan in China as a psychiatric intervention for ailments ranging from Internet addiction to schizophrenia. In 2010 Naikan started to be covered by public health insurance and by 2014 there were fifteen medical institutions in China that used Naikan.[27]

In contrast to China, where Naikan is largely promoted by mental health professionals, in Korea its strongest advocates have been Christian leaders, particularly Catholics. The Catholic priest Heo Kuen, who accredited the intensive Naikan he did in Kagoshima in 2002 with helping him overcome his alcoholism, became the director of the Pastoral Center for Alcoholics run by the archdiocese of Seoul.[28] To help alcoholics, he began offering intensive Naikan two or three times a year. In 2006 the Korean Naikan Association had its first major meeting, which was held at a church in Seoul.

To foster cooperation among Naikan advocates in different regions of the world, two organizations were formed: the International Naikan Association (INA), which consists largely of

German-speaking Europeans; and the International Academy of Naikan Therapy (IANT), which consists mostly of mental health professionals in East Asia. The INA had its first conference in 1991 in Tokyo, but seven of its next ten conferences were in Europe. The IANT held its first conference at Tottori University in 2003. Both organizations have held conferences every two or three years since their founding.[29]

NAIKAN METHODS

Intensive Naikan involves a week of concentrated focus on Naikan's three questions. Although a few hospitals offer it as a psychotherapeutic intervention, it is typically done at Naikan training centers.[30] At some training centers it is done every week; other centers offer it once every other week, or less frequently if demand is low. At training centers, those coming to do Naikan arrive on a Sunday afternoon and leave the following Saturday or Sunday. As of 2017, a fee of about 70,000 yen is charged for the week, which covers all costs, including room and board. People arriving to do Naikan, referred to as *naikansha* 内観者, may be asked how they found out about Naikan and what they already know about it. A brief orientation is given on the first day that provides an overview of Naikan. The *naikansha* are told that they must not talk to or communicate with each other in any way during the week. Speaking is prohibited among *naikansha* in order to foster interiority and deeper self-reflection.

Each *naikansha* stays in a room with a folding screen and bedding, usually a simple futon (see figure 2). At some places the *naikansha* share a room with one or more others and at other places *naikansha* have their own private rooms. When sharing a room, the *naikansha* may be able to hear other people's interviews. Although this takes away from the privacy of interviews, it is also understood as helping *naikansha* learn how others respond to the questions and as a source of support because they are given a sense that they are not alone in the process.

Throughout the week, all *naikansha* awake at 5:00 or 6:00 a.m., depending on the center. For about the first thirty to forty-five minutes of the day, they will take care of personal hygiene; clean their room; and may do some other assigned cleaning task, such as vacuuming the hallway or washing the bathroom. The cleaning of what was just cleaned the day before and the looking for what needs to be cleaned can serve as a metaphor for repeatedly investigating and cleaning the mind with Naikan.

For the rest of the day, except when having to go to the toilet or when bathing, the *naikansha* does Naikan siting behind a folding screen (*byōbu* 屏風) in a space about three feet wide and three feet long.[31] The three questions in the interview format are often displayed inside the screen. There may also be a list of significant others to do Naikan on, such as one's mother, father, spouse, grandmother, grandfather, uncle, boss at work, etc.

To promote the continuation of self-reflection, at some centers there are Naikan-related phrases posted in the toilet area and hallways. For example, there may be quotes by the founder, Yoshimoto Ishin, such as "Before a large building is built, construction of the foundation is necessary. Naikan is building a foundation for life." Meals are brought three times a day to the screen behind which the *naikansha* eats. During mealtimes, recordings of Naikan interviews (*mensetsu* 面接) of others who have done Naikan are played for thirty to sixty minutes. These recordings allow the *naikansha* to hear ways of giving Naikan reports, but they are told not to imitate them.

Figure 2. Naikan room and screen.
Source: Photograph by author

Intensive Naikan usually starts with doing Naikan on one's mother during the first few years of elementary school. The *naikansha* reflects on what he received from his mother between the ages of six and eight, what he gave back to her at that time, and what trouble he caused her when he was between the ages of six and eight. After reflecting on these questions for ninety minutes to two hours, an "interviewer" (*mensetsusha* 面接者) who is a Naikan practitioner comes in to do an interview.

Naikan interviews follow a prescribed, ritualistic format. The interviewer enters the room, kneels before the screen, and bows. He then opens the screen, bows again, and says, "During this time what have you been examining yourself on?" If the *naikansha* is doing Naikan on his mother when he was between the ages of eight and ten years old, he replies, "During this time I have been examining myself in relation to my mother from the ages of 8 to 10. What I received from my mother was _________. What I gave back to her was _________. I caused her trouble by _________" The blanks are filled in with concrete, specific answers to the Naikan questions. For example, the *naikansha* could say "I received a chocolate birthday cake. And, when I was sick and had to take a bad tasting medicine, she mixed it in miso soup so it would be easier to take." Concrete answers that can be visualized are seen as more effective for deeper Naikan than abstract ones such as "She showed me love and supported me in my studies."

When the *naikansha* is finished reporting his answers, the *mensetsusha* says, "During the next period of time what will you examine yourself on?" The *naikansha* responds by saying, "During the next period of time I will examine myself on my mother between the ages of 11 and 13." The *mensetsusha* then says "Thank you," bows, closes the screen, bows again, then stands up and leaves the room. After about two hours, seven or eight times a day, he will return again and the ritual will be repeated.

For examining relationships, three year increments of time, as used in the example above, are common, but not mandated. Depending on how old the *naikansha* is and the number of years he interacted with his mother, the time intervals may be shorter or longer. A twenty-year-old, for example, may examine his relationship with his mother in one- or two-year intervals, while a fifty-year-old whose mother is still alive may do it in five-year intervals, particularly when he is remembering his adult years. After he finishes doing Naikan on his mother, the *naikansha* does Naikan on his father from the first years of elementary school until the present or up to his father's death. After he is done with his father, he will do Naikan on his spouse, if married, or some other important person in his life.

During midweek the *naikansha* might be invited to do Naikan on occasions when he lied or stole. He reflects on his life at different time periods and tries to remember instances of lying or stealing. He then reports on some of these during interviews. The terms "lying and stealing" are broadly defined. Lying may include not telling the whole truth, exaggerating, or giving a false impression. Stealing may include listening to or looking at something intended for others, not paying taxes, or not compensating someone for some service.

The *mensetsusha* do not counsel or console the *naikansha*. In general the guidance offered is restricted to the method. For example, if the person's answers are abstract or vague the interviewer may suggest the *naikansha* be more concrete and specific in their reporting. If the *naikansha* is having a hard time coming up with answers for the third question, the *mensetsusha* may recommend spending more time on it. Yoshimoto recommended giving 20 percent of time to the first question, 20 percent to the second, and 60 percent to the third.

To foster deeper Naikan, *mensetsusha* with extensive experience sometimes ask questions outside those in the format, such as "Why did you do that?" or "How did you think the person felt?" They may also suggest that the person do a non-Naikan activity. For example, Yanagita Kakusei 柳田鶴声, who ran a major Naikan training center called "Meisō no Mori" 瞑想の森 (literally, "meditation forest"), used to have *naikansha* make lists of resentments (*uramichō* うらみ帳) against a person they were having difficulty doing Naikan on as a way of reducing resistance to Naikan.

Although individual responses to Naikan differ, *naikansha* commonly have few and only hazy memories during the first two or three days. Consequently, their Naikan is said to be "shallow" (*asai* 浅い). On the third and fourth days, after the mind has quieted, memories arise in greater frequency and intensity. Because of this, in the latter half of the week the *naikansha* does Naikan again on his or her mother. After several days in quiet the *naikansha* often remember things that they had forgotten or have ideas about the past that never occurred to them before. During Naikan it is very common for people to cry. This is evident in Naikan testimonials. Crying is not encouraged and is discouraged if a person's crying takes too much time away from doing Naikan.

At the end of the week, the *naikansha* are asked to share their impressions or experiences doing Naikan. This may be done in an individual meeting or in a group of those who have just finished intensive Naikan. Those doing Naikan for the first time might also be given reading materials. The *mensetsusha* may recommend daily Naikan, which involves reflection on the three Naikan questions in daily life. Yoshimoto recommended doing this for two hours a day. In the first hour he suggested reflecting on an earlier period of life in relation to a particular person. Then in the second hour the *naikansha* would use the three questions to examine herself during the previous twenty-four hours. Answers to the questions might be written down in a diary, either during or right after the period of meditation. When this is done, it is called "journal Naikan" (*kiroku naikan* 記録内観).

Despite Yoshimoto's recommendation, few people do Naikan daily for two hours. Doing daily Naikan regularly, however, even for short periods of time, is encouraged. One Naikan practitioner compared it to taking a daily bath. He suggested that just like the body has to be cleaned on a regular basis, so too does the mind need to be purified and Naikan is a way of doing that.

NAIKAN CALCULATION EXERCISES

In addition to the intensive and daily Naikan methods described above, Naikan practitioners have formulated calculation exercises to encourage self-reflection. These might be done before, during, or after intensive Naikan. One such exercise poses the question, "How many meals did your mother make for you?" For this, a person can first calculate on average how many meals his mother (or his primary caretaker if it was not his mother) made for him a week when he was a particular age; then multiply that number by 52, the number of weeks in a year, to get an approximation of how many meals she made in total when he was that age. So if the person's mother made 16 meals on average for him when he was ten years old, he would multiply 16 by 52 to get 832. He would then do this for ages eleven, twelve, and all other ages during which his mother made him meals. Then he would add the totals for each age to get an approximation of how many meals his mother made throughout his life.

He can go deeper by calculating the amount of time she spent making meals for him and how much time it took her to go shopping for food. The person might point out that his mother made these meals not just for him but also for herself and others in the family as well. The truth of this is acknowledged and the Naikan guide or interviewer might say nothing in response so the person could form his own conclusions about his mother's labor. Or the guide might suggest the person simply reflect on how his life might have been if his mother had not been alive to make those meals.

Some calculation exercises might deal with money. For example, a person might calculate how much money it cost to raise her. To do this, the person would look at the cost of food, clothing, schooling, medical care, and anything else for which she needed financial support.

Money-focused calculation exercises can be used to target a particular problem such as destructive alcoholic drinking or gambling. Alcoholics, for example, might be asked at a Naikan training center or a hospital to calculate the financial costs of alcohol.[32] To do this, the alcoholic would come up with an approximation of how much he spent on alcohol each year of his drinking, then add up the totals for each year of drinking to get a grand total of how much money he spent on alcohol. Then, he might be asked to calculate how much money the consequences of his drinking costs. For example, if he was arrested for drunk driving, he would add to the total spent on alcohol how much he spent on lawyer fees and increased car insurance as a result. He would also add in the costs of any hospitalizations or rehabilitation programs and money lost from not being able to work. The alcoholic may have a vague sense that alcohol cost him a large amount of money, but Naikan advocates say that calculating and seeing a number can allow him to realize how much he gave to drinking and help him overcome any denial he may have about the seriousness of his drinking problem.

REVIEW OF LITERATURE

In 2010 the Japan Naikan Association published a list of sources on Naikan in Japanese that included over 750 items.[33] It was composed mostly of books and issues of journals. It did not include titles of individual articles in journals or the titles of essays in edited book collections; if it had, the list would have been much longer. The scholarly literature in English on Naikan is not nearly as voluminous, but as with much of the Japanese scholarship, it most commonly refers to Naikan as a therapy or treatment to achieve some social or psychological goal.

Early studies on Naikan characterized it as a moral treatment. The sociologist John Kitsuse, who first introduced Naikan to English readers, studied the use of it in prisons. He explained that Naikan led prisoners to take responsibility for their actions and provided them with a coherent interpretation of their lives.[34] He also argued that Naikan's purpose in prisons was to "produce conformance through reformation."[35] The anthropologist Takie Sugiyama Lebra, who was the first to do ethnographic fieldwork at Yoshimoto's training center, built on Kitsuse's work. She claimed that Naikan was a "moralistic type of therapy" and "the rehabilitation method that . . . best elucidates the core values of Japanese culture."[36] Legal scholars who studied Naikan in prisons have also seen it as a method for resocializing inmates.[37]

These studies set the tone for later studies of Naikan that depicted it as an indigenous psychotherapy that reveals Japanese cultural values and ideas about social relations.[38] Such studies characterize Naikan as being appropriate for the Japanese because of their particular cultural understandings of the self and human relationships. Yet some studies have argued that Naikan is not a culturally bound psychotherapy. Ozawa-de Silva, for example, has argued based on her research at Naikan centers in Austria that Naikan's mechanisms are based on social relationships (e.g., mother–child) that have relevancy in other cultures, even if their social valence is different from Japan.[39]

A number of writings on Naikan compare it to other therapies, particularly with those that originated in the West.[40] Psychoanalysis has been contrasted with Naikan.[41] While the former uses free association and a counselor who has expertise in complex theories of the mind, Naikan uses a simple structure and no academic expertise is necessary to be an interviewer. Some have argued that Naikan has similarities with Victor Frankl's meaning-focused logotherapy, in that both assume a moral self.[42]

There are research reports by psychiatrists and psychologists on how Naikan has been used to treat a wide variety of problems, including addiction (particularly alcoholism and gambling addiction), eating disorders, personality disorders, schizophrenia, psychosomatic disorders, dissociative disorder, and depression.[43] Most are based on case studies. They all tend to give a positive assessment of Naikan, but it could be argued that the numbers are not statistically significant to make any definitive conclusions.

Social scientific and psychological studies of Naikan provide a range of theories for how Naikan works to effect change. Non-Japanese scholars tend to point out how Naikan deals with anger and frustration that may be subconscious.[44] Japanese scholars tend to emphasize the role of guilt and discovered love.[45]

There are a small number of studies in English that examine Naikan's relationship with religion. Shimazono shows how Naikan is similar to New Spirituality movements.[46] Unno Taitetsu sees it as exhibiting a "utility-value of religion" that seeks practical benefits such as happiness, prosperity, peace of mind, and good health.[47] He contrasts this with religious "truth value." Kawahara Ryuzo and Ozawa-de Silva show how Naikan relates to Pure Land Buddhism in particular.[48]

PRIMARY SOURCES

Almost all primary sources on Naikan are in Japanese. Yoshimoto's autobiographical writings are the sources most important for understanding Naikan's history. Both scholars and Naikan advocates considered Yoshimoto's writings as key primary sources for understanding Naikan. His autobiographical account titled *Naikanhō* 内観法 (Naikan method) in particular is a core text for understanding Naikan.[49] Very few of Yoshimoto's writings, however, have been translated.[50] Also, of historical significance is a collection of articles on Naikan that appeared in various newspapers and magazines from 1964 to 1979.[51]

There are videos of Yoshimoto and a large number of audiocassettes of *naikansha* interviews during intensive Naikan, some of which are available through the Naikan Center in Nara.[52] There is a printed two-volume collection of testimonials in Japanese.[53] Testimonials of non-Japanese who have done intensive Naikan are available in David Reynolds's *Flowing Bridges, Quiet Waters: Japanese Psychotherapies, Morita and Naikan*; and Gregg Krech's *Question Your Life: Naikan Self-Reflection and the Transformation of Our Stories*.[54]

FURTHER READING

Blum, Mark. "Shin Buddhism in the Meiji Period." In *Cultivating Spirituality: A Modern Shin Buddhist Anthology*. Edited by Mark Blum and Robert F. Rhodes, 1–52. Albany: State University of New York Press, 2011.

Chervenkova, Velizara. *Japanese Psychotherapies: Silence and Body–Mind Interconnectedness in Morita, Naikan and Dohsa-hou*. Singapore: Springer, 2017.

Halkias, Georgios, and Richard K. Payne, eds. *Pure Lands in Asian Texts and Contexts: An Anthology*. Pure Land Buddhist Studies. Honolulu: University of Hawaii Press, 2019.

Ishida, Rokuro. "Naikan Analysis." *Psychologia* 12 (1969): 81–92.

Japanese Naikan Medical Association and Japanese Naikan Association, eds. *Naikan Therapy: Techniques and Principles for Use in Clinical Practice*. Fukuoka, Japan: Daido Gakkan, 2013.

Kawahara, Ryuzo. "Japanese Buddhist Thought and Naikan Therapy." In *Asian Culture and Psychotherapy*. Edited by Wen-Shing Tseng, Suk Choo Chang, and Masahisa Nishizono, 186–198. Honolulu: University of Hawai'i Press, 2005.

Kitsuse, John. "Moral Treatment and Reformation of Inmates in Japanese Prisons." *Psychologia* 8 (1965): 9–23.

Krech, Gregg. *Naikan: Gratitude, Grace, and the Japanese Art of Self-Reflection*. Berkeley, CA: Stone Bridge Press, 2002.

Lebra, Takie Sugiyama. "Culturally Based Moral Rehabilitation: The Naikan Method." In *Japanese Patterns of Behavior*, 201–214. Honolulu: University of Hawai'i Press, 1976.

Murase, Takeo. "Naikan Therapy." In *Culture-Bound Syndromes, Ethnopsychiatry, and Alternate Therapies*. Edited by William Lebra, 388–397. Honolulu: University of Hawai'i Press, 1976.

Murase, Takeo. "Sunao: A Central Value in Japanese Psychotherapy." In *Cultural Conceptions of Mental Health and Therapy*. Edited by Anthony J. Marsella and Geoffrey M. White, 317–329. Dordrecht, The Netherlands: D. Reidel, 1982.

Ozawa-de Silva, Chikako. *Psychotherapy and Religion in Japan: The Japanese Introspection Practice of Naikan*. London: Routledge, 2006.

Ozawa-de Silva, Chikako. "Demystifying Japanese Therapy: An Analysis of Naikan and the Ajase Complex through Buddhist Thought." *Ethos* 35 (2007): 411–446.

Ozawa-de Silva, Chikako. "Mindfulness of the Kindness of Others: The Contemplative Practice of Naikan in Cultural Context." *Transcultural Psychiatry* 52 (2015): 524–542.

Ozawa de-Silva, Chikako, and Brendan Ozawa-de Silva. "Secularizing Religious Practices: A Study of Subjectivity and Existential Transformation in Naikan Therapy." *Journal for the Scientific Study of Religion* 49 (2010): 147–161.

Reynolds, David. *The Quiet Therapies: Japanese Pathways to Personal Growth*. Honolulu: University of Hawai'i Press, 1980.

Reynolds, David. *Naikan Psychotherapy: Meditation for Self-Development*. Chicago: University of Chicago Press, 1983.

Sengoku, Mari, Hiroaki Murata, Takanobu Kawahara, Kaori Imamura, and Kazuyuki Nakagome. "Does Daily Naikan Therapy Maintain the Efficacy of Intensive Naikan Therapy against Depression?" *Psychiatry and Clinical Neurosciences* 64 (2010): 44–51.

Shimazono, Susumu. "From Salvation to Healing: Yoshimoto Naikan Therapy and Its Religious Origins." In *Religion and Psychotherapy in Modern Japan*. Edited by Christopher Harding, Iwata Fumiaki, and Yoshinaga Shin'ichi, 150–164. London: Routledge, 2015.

Suwaki, Hiroshi. "Naikan and Danshukai for the Treatment of Japanese Alcoholic Patients." *British Journal of Addiction* 74 (1979): 15–19.

NOTES

1. *Kōsetsu Bukkyōgo daijiten* 広説仏教語大辞典, ed. Nakamura Hajime 中村元 (Tokyo: Tokyo Shoseki, 2001), 1272.
2. I would like to thank Paul Swanson for pointing this out to me.
3. The last of these four thoughts Hakuin articulated is as follows: "[Contemplate] the elixir field located in the sea of vital energy—it is all the Amida Buddha of my own self. How could Amida Buddha preach the Dharma apart from that self?" (Hakuin Ekaku, *Wild Ivy*, trans. Norman Waddell [Boston: Shambhala, 2001], 118).
4. Mark Blum, "Shin Buddhism in the Meiji Period," in *Cultivating Spirituality: A Modern Shin Buddhist Anthology*, ed. Mark Blum and Robert Rhodes (Albany: State University of New York Press, 2011), 1–52; and Jeff Schroeder, "The Empirical and Esoteric: The Birth of Shin Buddhist Studies as a Modern Academic Discipline," *Japanese Religions* 39 (2014): 95–118.
5. Blum, "Shin Buddhism in the Meiji Period," 38. I would like to thank the anonymous reviewer of this article for pointing out the relevancy of Kiyozawa's *naikan-shugi*.
6. Shiozaki Ichirō 塩崎伊知朗, "Naikanhō wa dono yōni henkashita ka: Taikan-an mishirabe, zenki naikan, sanmon naikan no hikaku 内観法はどのように変化したか：諦観庵身調べ、前期内観、三問内観の比較," *Naikan Kenkyū* 内観研究 12 (2006): 63–71.

7. Jan Van Bragt translated *shukuzen kaihotsu* as "opening up of past good karma." See page 141 of "Lectures on the Tannishō" by Soga Ryōjin in *Cultvating Spirituality: A Modern Shin Buddhist Anthology*, ed. Mark Blum and Robert Rhodes (Albany: State University of New York Press, 2011). Yoshimoto refers to *shukuzen kaihotsu* as "gaining englightenment" (*satori wo uru koto* 悟りをうること) on page 25 of *Naikan he no shōtai* 内観への招待 (Osaka: Toki Shobō, 1996).
8. Yoshimoto Ishin, *Naikan no michi* 内観の道 (Koriyama, Japan: Naikan Kenshūjo, 1977), 126.
9. Yoshimoto Ishin, *Naikanhō* 内観法 (Tokyo: Shunjūsha, 2000), 130–131.
10. Yoshimoto Inobu, *Self-Reflection Will Guide You to the Right Way* (Nara, Japan: Nara Boys' Prison, 1958), 8. ("Inobu" is an alternative reading of "Ishin.")
11. Yoshimoto Ishin, *Naikanhō no tsutaekata* 内観法の傳え方 (Nara, Japan: Naikan Dōjō, 1957), 21.
12. Iwaoka Masashi 岩岡正, *Naikanhō no genryū o tazunete: Yoshimoto Ishin no iitakatta koto* 内観法の源流をたずねて：吉本伊信の言いたかったこと (Sendai, Japan: Sōei Shuppan, 2002), 103.
13. Yoshimoto Ishin, *Naikan no michi* 内観の道 (Koriyama, Japan: Naikan Kenshūjō, 1977), 63.
14. Yoshimoto Ishin, *Naikanhō no tsutaekata* (Koriyama, Japan: Naikan Dōjō, 1957), 25–27.
15. Iwaoka Masashi, *Naikanhō no genryū o tazunete: Yoshimoto Ishin no iitakatta koto* 内観法の源流をたずねて：吉本伊信の言いたかったこと (Sendai, Japan: Sōei Shuppan, 2002), 117; Okumura Nikichi 奥村二吉, Satō Kōji 佐藤幸治, and Yamamoto Haruo 山本晴雄, eds., *Naikan ryōhō* 内観療法 (Tokyo: Igaku Shoin, 1972), 1.
16. The title of this article is *Naikanhō no shiri-teki kadai* 内観法の心理的課題 (Psychological Topics for Investigation in the Naikan Method).
17. The title of the article is *Naikanhō to ningen kaizō* 内観法の人間改造 (The Naikan Method and the Creation of a Person).
18. The title of the article is *Naikanhō ni yoru jinkaku kaizen katei ni tsuite no oboekaki* 内観法による人格改善過程についての覚え書き (Notes on the Improvement Process of Personal Character through the Naikan Method).
19. Yoshimoto Ishin, *Naikan he no shōtai* 内観への招 (Osaka, Japan: Tokiwa Shobō, 1996), 83.
20. For an article in English on Naikan analysis, see Ishida Rokuro's "Naikan Analysis," *Psychologia* 12 (1969): 81–92.
21. Yoshimoto Ishin, *Naikanhō* (Tokyo: Shunjūsha, 2007), 203.
22. A transcription of this talk and the questions and answers are available in Yoshimoto, *Naikanhō*, 225–259.
23. *Naikan nijūgo nen no ayumi* 内観二十五年の歩み (Nara, Japan: Naikan Kenshūjo, 1980), 60, 155, 112, and 171.
24. In 2016 the Japan Naikan Association, according to its website, had 300 members; Retrieved from http://jpnaikan.jp/guide/kaiin.html.
25. Miki in 2008 said over 250 people a year did intensive Naikan training in Austria. See Miki Yoshihiko 三木善彦, "Ōbei ni okeru Naikan no hatten" 欧米における内観の発展 in *Naikan ryōhō* 内観療法, eds., Miki Yoshihiko 三木善彦, Maeshiro Teruaki 真栄城輝明, and Takemoto Takahiro 竹元隆洋 (Kyoto: Mineruva Shobō, 2008), 47–55, '49. Johanna Schuh estimates that between 6000 and 7000 people have done Naikan in Europe (Personal correspondence, May 2017).
26. Hatano Fumihiko 波多野二三彦, *Naikanhō wa naze kiku ka: jiko dōsatsu no kagaku* 内観法はなぜ効くか：自己洞察の科学, 5th ed. (Tokyo: Shinzansha Shuppan, 2014).
27. Zucheng Wang, "Chūgoku ni okeru Naikan ryōhō no hatten" 中国における内観療法の発展 *Naikan Igaku* 内観医学 16 (2014): 7–11.
28. *National Catholic Reporter*, December 15, 2006, 5a.
29. The author would like to thank Johanna Schuh for her guidance on the history and state of Naikan in Europe today.

30. This description is based on personal experience of doing Naikan at a Naikan training center in Tokyo; on visits to several places that do intensive Naikan in Japan; websites of different training centers; and on two published academic sources: Chikako Ozawa-de Silva, *Psychotherapy and Religion in Japan: The Japanese Introspection Practice of Naikan* (London: Routledge, 2006); and David Reynolds, *Naikan Psychotherapy: Meditation for Self-Development* (Chicago: University of Chicago Press, 1983). There is some variation among centers.
31. Miki Yoshihiko's Naikan training center is one of the few places that does not use screens or the ritualistic format. Miki said he prefers not to use them because it makes Naikan seem somewhat separate from normal daily interactions. (Interview December 1, 2014)
32. A worksheet for this is published in Yoshimoto, *Naikan no michi* 内観の道, 156.
33. See *Dai 33 kai Nihon Naikan Gakkai puroguramu, shōrokushū* 第３３回日本内観学会プログラム抄録集 (Program for the 33rd Conference of the Japan Naikan Association).
34. John Kitsuse, "A Method of Reform in Japanese Prisons," *Orient/West* 7, no. 11 (1962): 17–22.
35. See page 11 of John Kitsuse, "Moral Treatment and Reformation of Inmates in Japanese Prisons," *Psychologia* 8 (1965): 9–23.
36. See page 201 of Takie Sugiyama Lebra's *Japanese Patterns of Behavior* (Honolulu: University of Hawai'i Press, 1976).
37. Akira Ishii and Dieter Bindzus, "Prisons in Japan: Resocialization by the Means of Treatment," *Aoyama Hōgaku Ronshū* 29 (1987): 328–362.
38. See Murase Takeo, "Naikan Therapy," in *Culture-Bound Syndromes, Ethnopsychiatry, and Alternate Therapies*, ed. William Lebra (Honolulu: University of Hawai'i Press, 1976), 388–397; Murase Takeo, "Sunao: A Central Value in Japanese Psychotherapy," in *Cultural Conceptions of Mental Health and Therapy*, ed. Anthony J. Marsella and Geoffrey M. White (Dordrecht, The Netherlands: D. Reidel, 1982), 317–329.
39. Chikako Ozawa-de Silva and Brendan Ozawa-de Silva, "Secularizing Religious Practices: A Study of Subjectivity and Existential Transformation in Naikan Therapy," *Journal for the Scientific Study of Religion* 49 (2010): 147–161. Also see Chikako Ozawa-de Silva, "Mindfulness of the Kindness of Others: The Contemplative Practice of Naikan in Cultural Context," *Transcultural Psychiatry* 52, no. 4 (2015): 524–542; and Makino Rumi, "Naikan Psychotherapy in the West: A Survey of Naikan Participants," *Psychologia* 39, no. 2 (1996): 94–101.
40. Murase Takao and Frank Johnson, "Naikan, Morita, and Western Psychotherapy: A Comparison," *Archives of General Psychiatry* 31 (1974): 121–128.
41. Adeline Van Waning, "Naikan—A Buddhist Self-Reflective Approach: Psychoanalytic and Cultural Reflections," in *Freud and the Far East: Psychoanalytic Perspectives on the People and Culture of China, Japan, and Korea*, ed. Salman Akhtar (Lanham, MD: Jason Aronson, 2009), 255–273.
42. Takeuchi Katashi, "On 'Naikan' Method," *Psychologia* 8 (1965): 2–8.
43. For examples of these types of articles, see the following: Komoto Yasunobu, "The Efficacy of Group Naikan Therapy Using a Journal for Alcoholism," in *Naikan Therapy: Techniques and Principles for Use in Clinical Practice*, eds. Japanese Naikan Medical Association and Japanese Naikan Association (Fukuoka, Japan: Daido Gakkan, 2013), 151–166; Sengoku Mari, Hiroaki Murata, Takanobu Kawahara, Kaori Imamura, and Kazuyuki Nakagome, "Does Saily Naikan Therapy Maintain the Efficacy of Intensive Naikan Therapy against Depression?," *Psychiatry and Clinical Neurosciences* 64 (2010): 44–51; Komoto Yasunobu, "Brief Intervention Based on Naikan Therapy for a Severe Pathological Gambler with a Family History of Addiction: Emphasis on Guilt and Forgiveness," *Asian Journal of Gambling Issues and Public Health* 5 (2015): 1–8; Sasano Tomohisa, "A Case of a Person with Dissociative Disorder who Managed to Overcome Mourning with the Help of Naikan Therapy," *Kawasaki Journal of Medical Welfare* 7, no. 1(2001): 43–47; Sasano Tomohisa, "An Attempt at Treating a Patient with Dysthymic Disorder

and His Wife Using Naikan Therapy," *Kawasaki Journal of Medical Welfare* 8, no. 2 (2002): 81–84; Zhang Hong, Chenhu Li, and Liyu Zhao, "Single-Blind, Randomized Controlled Trial of Effectiveness of Naikan Therapy as an Adjunctive Treatment for Schizophrenia Over a One-Year Follow-up Period," *Shanghai Archives of Psychiatry* 27 (2015): 220–227.

44. See David Reynolds, *Naikan Psychotherapy: Meditation for Self-Development* (Chicago: University of Chicago Press, 1983).
45. See the studies in *Naikan Therapy: Techniques and Principles for Use in Clinical Practice.*
46. Shimazono Susumu, "From Salvation to Healing: Yoshimoto Naikan Therapy and Its Religious Origins," in *Religion and Psychotherapy in Modern Japan*, ed. Christopher Harding, Iwata Fumiaki, and Yoshinaga Shin'ichi (London: Routledge, 2015), 150–164.
47. Unno Taitetsu, "Naikan Therapy and Shin Buddhism," in *Buddhism and Psychotherapy across Cultures*, ed. Mark Unno (Boston: Wisdom, 2006), 159–168.
48. Ryuzo Kawahara, "Japanese Buddhist Thought and Naikan Therapy," in *Asian Culture and Psychotherapy*, ed. Wen-Shing Tseng, Suk Choo Chang, and Masahisa Nishizono (Honolulu: University of Hawai'i Press, 2005), 186–198; and Chikako Ozawa-de Silva, "Demystifying Japanese Therapy: An Analysis of Naikan and the Ajase Complex through Buddhist Thought," *Ethos* 35 (2007): 411–446.
49. Yoshimoto Ishin, *Naikanhō* (Tokyo: Shunjūsha, 2007).
50. Two of the few translations of Yoshimoto's writings can be found in Yoshimoto Ishin, "The Naikan Introspection Exercise," *Interpersonal Development* 5 (1974/75): 164–170; Georgios Halkias, and Richard K. Payne, eds. *Pure Lands in Asian Texts and Contexts: An Anthology*. Pure Land Buddhist Studies (Honolulu: University of Hawaii Press, 2019). The latter source gives a translation of Yoshimoto's description of his experience doing *mishirabe*.
51. This work, titled *Naikan nijū go nen no ayumi*, was published by Yoshimoto's Naikan Kenshūjo in 1980.
52. See the website http://naikan.jp/.
53. *Naikan taiken* 内観体験, vols. 1–2, ed. Yoshimoto Ishin (Nara, Japan: Naikan Kenshūjo, 1980).
54. David Reynolds, *Flowing Bridges, Quiet Waters: Japanese Psychotherapies, Morita and Naikan* (Albany: State University of New York Press, 1989); and Gregg Krech, *Question Your Life: Naikan Self-Reflection and the Transformation of Our Stories* (Monkton, VT: ToDo Institute, 2017).

Clark Chilson

NARRATIVES OF BUDDHIST RELICS AND IMAGES

HISTORIES OF POWERFUL OBJECTS

Buddhist traditions in premodern Asia display a great deal of diversity in terms of thought, practice, and cultural expression. In spite of these religious and cultural differences, Buddhist communities across Asia have tended to identify certain relics and images associated with buddhas and other fully awakened individuals as powerful objects that are worthy of veneration and protection. The power that certain relics and images are held to possess usually derives from their connection to a buddha, an individual who has attained nirvana and omniscient wisdom, while putting an end fully and finally to all the causes of suffering and rebirth in the cycle of samsara. Such connections to buddhas may either be direct or indirect, depending on the type of object in question and how it came into being. These objects are deemed powerful since they can manifest unusual abilities such as the power of locomotion and the power to generate miraculous visions, and also since it is believed that venerating these objects brings great benefits to Buddhist devotees. It is likely the case that the alleged, extraordinary natures of such powerful relics and images compelled certain individuals to narrate and recount how they were found or made, where they traveled, and the various miracles they performed as a testament to their great power.

Narratives about buddha relics and images comprise one of the important genres of Buddhist literature. The wondrous qualities associated with such powerful objects can result in narratives that appear fantastic and emotionally moving, even though they are often linked to writings that claim to be historical and therefore truthful. Such narrative texts supply devotees (and scholars) with the stories about relics and images so that they may be properly understood and venerated by Buddhist adherents in different lands. As such, these narratives work to provide the pedigrees of relics and images that have come to occupy positions of importance in the Buddhist communities in which they are found and revered. In a real sense, therefore, the narratives about relics and images are the key factors in ensuring that these sacred objects are widely recognized for the power and sacrality they are said to possess. The stories they tell lend an aura of authenticity to powerful objects that people deem worthy of special reverence.

Relics, as powerful objects, are found throughout Asian traditions of Buddhism, albeit sometimes in different forms and with varying measures of significance. In postcanonical Pāli literature, a threefold classification of relics distinguishes corporeal relics, relics of use, and commemorative relics, the latter of which often refers to images fashioned of the buddha.[1] In each case, some perceived association with the buddha or a fully awakened individual who has obtained nirvana suffices to endow a particular physical object with extraordinary power and cultural importance. Such objects often became focal points for ritualized veneration, meditative concentration, and political authority in Asian Buddhist communities. Whether it is a bone, bowl, image, or some other object, anything that was in contact with the buddha or which is a likeness of him could be suffused with power that invites veneration and could cause certain miraculous effects in the world.

Although later Buddhist traditions tend to conflate images of the buddha with his bodily remains, earlier views did not always perceive these objects to be of the same nature. In early Buddhist literature, the body of the buddha was a subject of some discussion and speculation, including descriptions of the "Thirty-Two Marks of a Great Man" that reflect his remarkable attainments in wisdom and moral perfection.[2] Despite other discourses that disparage the loathsome nature of conditioned human bodies, the buddha's body is consistently lauded for its beauty and its capacity to transform those who gaze upon it. Buddhist thought and practice consistently associate the miraculous nature of the buddha's body, which is capable of emitting colorful rays of light, streams of water and fire, and is seemingly flawless in its formal beauty, with his extraordinary attainments of awakening (*bodhi*). The emphasis on the significance of the buddha's body almost certainly enhanced the significance of his corporeal relics, but it did not elevate the importance of physical likenesses of his body early on. Indeed, there are references to venerating the relics of the buddha immediately after his death, and funerary relic shrines (*stūpas*) are among the oldest Buddhist monuments to be found in the centuries before the Common Era. The appearance of images of the buddha in stone and other materials appears to date back to around the second decade of the 1st century of the Common Era, which makes buddha images appear as a significantly later development in the material culture of the tradition.[3]

Furthermore, some of the earliest textual references to relics or "reminders" (Skt.: *caitya*) of the buddha leave out images or assign them to a lower category of importance. The *Milinda-pañhā*, for instance, identifies relics from the buddha's body and the things he used, along with the mounds (*dāgabas*) erected over the relics, and his teachings of the buddha and the sangha, as objects put forth by the Buddha for those seeking worldly blessings, good rebirths, and liberation.[4] Notably, in this listing of things toward which one should show devotion, the "relics" include only corporeal remains and objects used by the buddha. Elsewhere, in the Kalingabodhi Jātaka story, the category of commemorative reminders (*uddesika-cetiya*) of the buddha is explicitly subordinated to bodily remains and objects of use, as they do not have any direct physical connection with the buddha and are thus implicitly held to be of lower value.[5] Such distinctions made between relics and images of the buddha are important to recall, even if later Buddhist communities could at times view images as of equal standing as relics with those of the buddha's body and objects used by the buddha. This movement to see images as equivalent to relics was not universal among Buddhists, and it is worth noting that relics were sometimes inserted into buddha images to heighten their power and significance. It even appears that the practice of inserting a bodily relic or a piece of text (a kind of "dharma-relic") into an image of the buddha was a standard and expected part of image consecration rituals across Asia.[6] Suffice it to say that the identity of relics and images has existed in various degrees of tension in Buddhist traditions. While there is some overlap between these two types of powerful objects in Buddhism, there remain important distinctions that make retaining these two categories useful.

Nevertheless, despite occasional distinctions made between objects with direct or indirect connections with a fully awakened being, the three categories of relics that came to include corporeal relics, relics of use, and commemorative relics, if not quite exhaustive, helped shape the contours of Buddhist devotional practice across time and space. One could argue further that these powerful objects became the subjects of Buddhist narratives, which themselves enhanced the power with which the items were often ascribed. Written texts and oral narratives containing accounts of how relics and images appeared or were fashioned, the journeys they took leading up to their current or final place of residence, the powers they possess and the miracles they could sometimes display, and the benefits they have on the devotees that worship them all contribute to their significance as objects of devotion in Buddhism. Thus, rather than adjudicating any ontological claims made about relics and images as objects of power in themselves, we will approach the subject by examining the narratives composed about such objects and analyzing what roles these written and oral accounts perform in attributing (or, as some might say, acknowledging) the power and agency of special objects connected to the buddha and other awakened individuals. These texts will be categorized in terms of narratives of affinity that link certain objects to awakened beings, narratives of prediction that demonstrate how a relic or image was destined to find its way to a particular location, narratives of glorification that emphasize the extraordinary qualities of awakened beings and the objects associated with them, and narratives of authority that establish the significance of the ruler or monastic community that possesses a relic or image.

NARRATIVES OF AFFINITY

In order for relics and images to be seen as special and powerful objects, they need some sort of story or myth that bestows them with their extraordinary identity. These narratives can take the form of written texts, oral traditions, or some combination of the two. In East Asia, stories of relics and images are typically included as sections in other texts, but in South and Southeast Asia these narratives can also often form the basis of complete works. In Theravāda traditions found in South and Southeast Asia, discrete literary genres known in Pāli as *vaṃsas*, and in vernacular languages as *vaṁśas*, *tamnans*, and *thathanawins*, among other terms, were used to compile and circulate narratives about relics and images. These works have long been called, somewhat misleadingly, "chronicles," due to their concerns with relating past events in a chronological structure. However, whereas chronicles generally possess an open-ended structure whereby new events are recorded and added to the list of older ones by multiple authors, Buddhist *vaṃsas* and related works frequently assume the form of a "history" with a single author and a narrative framework with a discernible beginning, middle, and end.[7] An important exception to this rule is the *Mahāvaṃsa* (Great chronicle), an open-ended, Pāli text that was begun around the beginning of the 6th century CE in Sri Lanka and has been periodically extended through the centuries to the early 21st century. Many other Theravāda histories relate narratives about relics and images without being repeatedly extended by later authors.

The *vaṃsas* and related works comprise a major literary genre in Theravāda Buddhist traditions, drawing attention and importance to various relics and images as powerful objects worthy of veneration. Among the many works containing narratives of relics and images from premodern southern Asia, one could cite from Sri Lanka, the *Mahāvaṃsa*, *Mahābodhivaṃsa* (History of the great Bodhi tree), *Thūpavaṃsa* (History of the relic shrine), *Dāṭhāvaṃsa* (History of the tooth relic), and *Dhātuvaṃsa* (History of the [forehead bone] relic), with the latter works having been composed in Pāli between roughly the 10th and 13th centuries. Most of these Pāli relic *vaṃsas* were subsequently translated and expanded in the Sinhala language between the 13th and 14th centuries in Sri Lanka.[8] Related works were composed later in Myanmar, such as the 19th-century *Sāsanavaṃsa* (History of the Buddha's Dispensation) and the *Chakesadhātuvaṃsa* (History of the six hair relics) of an unknown date in Pāli, along with the late-18th-century *Vaṃsadīpanī* (Treatise on the lineage of elders) in Burmese. Thailand also has numerous works in this vein, including the 15th-century *Cāmadevīvaṃsa* (History of Queen Cāma) and the 16th-century *Jinakālamālīpakaraṇaṃ* (Sheaf of garlands of the epochs of the conqueror). Other historical narratives that mention relics and images, with or without a Pāli antecedent, appear in the vernacular languages used by Buddhists in southern Asia.[9] Some of these texts are more centrally focused on a particular relic or image, while others contain more diverse narratives that deal with a variety of subjects.

One of the distinguishing features of these Theravāda *vaṃsa* texts is their tendency to connect local events and places to the life story of Gautama Buddha and the origins of the Buddhist community of monastics and devotees in India. These texts often discuss events related to kings and the sangha while narrating accounts of how particular relics and images of the buddha came to be enshrined in local settings. In doing so, these Buddhist narratives work to extend the buddha's biography beyond his previous lives and his career as an "Awakened One." The accounts of various relics and images serve to continue his story beyond the final cessation (*parinirvāṇa*) of his life in samsara, through the instantiation of some aspects of his power and presence in relics and images that are directly connected to him. John S. Strong has described relics in this narrative work as "extensions of the Buddha's biography," wherein the story of his career is brought forward and sustained by activities and adventures concerning his relics.[10] Stories of relics become linked through narratives with different episodes of the buddha's life story. These accounts reflect aspects of the buddha's powers and virtues, while evoking or inserting incidents into his biography that are variously recalled and celebrated by Buddhists in later times and distant places. The same biographical process holds true with certain extraordinary images of the buddha. Juliane Schober has similarly noted how a buddha image can extend the life of the buddha to fit local cosmologies wherein devotees may participate in the ritual construction of the buddha's ongoing biography.[11] Buddha images that have been narratively linked with the living buddha may also, in this way, extend his story so as to incorporate Buddhist devotees into an ongoing account of how his awakening set in motion a series of events that spread his dharma and helped beings obtain higher spiritual attainments even after his passing away.

Narratives that describe relics and images as powerful objects are equally present and valued in many Mahāyāna and Vajrayāna traditions and the communities of Buddhist devotees that practice them. As a consequence, stories about the origins, effects, and enshrinement of relics and images have also been composed and transmitted in East Asian and Himalayan lands. Such narratives help to locate powerful objects connected with buddhas and *lamas* in familiar landscapes. A wide variety of pieces from physical bodies, material items associated with buddhas and other awakened individuals, iterations of speech preserved in the hearts and minds of disciples before being written down in scriptural texts, and also images and relic shrines, all said to derive from, represent, emulate, or incarnate a buddha's presence may be considered "relics."[12] The narratives associated with such relics and images in Mahāyāna and Vajrayāna forms of Buddhism may not assume as prominent a place in their respective literary traditions as the *vaṃsas* do in Theravāda, but stories about how powerful objects appeared and caused certain miraculous effects in the world are found in many Buddhist communities.

One of the apparent purposes served by Buddhist narratives about relics and images is to connect contemporary devotees with buddhas and other awakened individuals from the past. When presented in a historical framework, and recognizing the cosmological truth about the impermanence of all conditioned things, narratives that celebrate beings who attained nirvana or who fully realized "Buddha nature" must also recognize their eventual demise. The appearance of buddhas, *lamas*, and other spiritually accomplished beings is held to be a wonderful blessing, but these same beings will also disappear from the world. Numerous scholars have posited that relics and images function to make an absent buddha "present" again in the world after his *parinirvāṇa*. And yet, as Jacob Kinnard has noted, the language of "presence" in this regard is problematic for its vagueness and its theological overtones, not to mention the fact that Buddhist texts themselves rarely offer this same interpretation for relics and images.[13] In other words, it is not always clear how the historical buddha or a deceased *lama* is made "present" by their relics or image, or whether their devotees would generally hold this view of their "presence" at all. Some have posited that Buddhists affirmed the living presence of the buddha in his images as there is evidence that ancient Indian monasteries often reserved special accommodation for housing buddha images and also buried whole or broken images in *stūpas*.[14] Yet even in those cases, it is not clear whether this "actual" *presence* should be interpreted literally, figuratively, or in some other manner. Nevertheless, numerous instances of mummified Buddhist masters of China and Japan from the 7th century onward, often lacquered and transformed into icons of veneration, gesture toward the use of images that caused the deceased saints to be present in the world after their deaths.[15]

We can avoid making ontological assumptions by instead focusing on how relics and images work to extend the story of buddhas and other awakened beings into distant times and places. Narratives in written and oral forms emplace particular relics and images in ways that make some remnant of those awakened beings accessible to devotees after they have "nirvanized" out of samsara. These accounts extend their biographies in the same ways that the actual relics and images themselves extend the presence of buddhas and other awakened beings in new forms and in new places.[16] It seems impossible to think that devotees would be unable to distinguish a living buddha from the relics or an image associated with one. But those same objects are attributed with special characteristics that other inanimate objects lack entirely. It is precisely those narratives that perform the work of connecting, first, the relics and/or images with the awakened beings they represent, and second, those same awakened beings with the devotees who venerate them and their relics and images.

Narratives often establish these affinities by describing the ways that relics and images first originated and came to be established in their current locations. The *Thūpavaṃsa*, in both the Pāli and Sinhala versions, contains a series of accounts explaining how the right collarbone, a branch from the Bodhi tree, the neck bone, and a large amount (*doṇa/droṇa*) of bodily relics were obtained and eventually deposited in various shrines in Sri Lanka. Of the latter, it describes how one-eighth of the smaller relics recovered from the buddha's funeral pyre was given to the Koḷiya clan, but that a great flood destroyed the *stūpa*, and the urn of relics fell into the possession of the *nāgas* (mythical, snakelike beings), who enshrined and honored them in their watery abode.[17] Later, when King Duṭṭhagāmaṇī built a great relic shrine in Sri Lanka, the monks sent the novice Soṇuttara who was also an *arahant* (a human who has attained nirvana by the teaching of a buddha) to the *nāga* abode in order to fetch them. The novice tricked the recalcitrant *nāgas* and brought the relics back to the human world where they were deposited in the Mahāthūpa shrine in a great ceremony attended by numerous humans and deities. By recalling how these relics were obtained, the *Thūpavaṃsa* confirms that these corporeal remains may be worshipped in the Mahāthūpa in Anurādhapura, Sri Lanka, for worldly benefits and otherworldly attainments such as a heavenly rebirth.[18]

The case of the Udayana Buddha, referred to in numerous Chinese Buddhist texts, represents yet another example whereby narratives were used to establish an affinity between the buddha and a certain image. In China, the buddha image allegedly commissioned by King Udayana, who ruled during the buddha's lifetime, became the subject of several accounts describing how this special object was made and brought to China in the early centuries of the Common Era. Textual accounts of this image are numerous and vary in their details. However, some Chinese sources include details that describe how this image, carved out of sandalwood during the buddha's lifetime, was brought to China by the legendary translator monk Kumārajīva in the early 5th century, establishing affinities between the image on the one hand, and both the buddha and the monk Kumārajīva on the other. The enthusiasm of Chinese

Buddhists for this legendary sandalwood buddha image led to narratives being composed that linked certain statues to this important icon, including the Khotanese image kept in Pima and the image of Ch'angan, which benefited from the ascription of an illustrious origin as being fashioned under the direction of one of the first devotees of the buddha.[19]

Narrative texts recounting the stories behind certain relics and images often appear designed to establish affinities between the buddha and those special objects, such that the relics and images serve to extend an awareness of the buddha later in time and farther away in space. In the context of a narrative, a given relic or image may take on some of the qualities of a living buddha and can act as a kind of substitute for him. A recurring message in many of these narratives is that veneration of a relic or image carries the same benefits as worshipping a living buddha.

NARRATIVES OF PREDICTION

One of the ways that texts establish affinities between awakened beings and extraordinary objects is to cite predictions or prophesies that the former are said to have made about the latter. These narratives often link the present with the past by affirming that the retrieval and enshrinement of a particular relic was preordained by the buddha or some other awakened being. Those people who have attained the wisdom of awakening are held to have cultivated supernormal powers, including an ability to see into the future. As such, the buddha is often portrayed as predicting future events involving relics and images, or at least paving the way for their eventual locations by visiting places wherein a relic or image would later be established.[20] Other awakened beings such as *arahant*s are likewise charged with the ability to see into the past and future, and they are counted on to confirm why and how a particular relic or image was destined to travel and settle in a particular place.

The current presence of a relic in a given shrine becomes connected to its source by means of a prediction that is said to have foretold how the relic would be obtained and made available after death. In the case of the buddha relics that are held to have been enshrined in the Mahāthūpa, the relevant texts describe how the buddha himself predicted that those very relics from his cremated body would one day be established therein.

> The Order of monks said thus to him. "Friend, Soṇuttara, the Tathāgata as he lay in his death-bed addressed Sakka, the king of the deities, and told him, 'Out of my bodily relics measuring eight *doṇa*, one *doṇa* which will have been honored by the Koḷiya princes will, in the future, be established in the Great Cetiya in the Island of Tambapaṇṇi' [i.e. Sri Lanka]."[21]

By connecting the eventual transmission of those relics to the Great Relic Shrine in Sri Lanka to a prediction allegedly made by the buddha, this narrative suggests that the journey of those relics to their eventual resting place was not only preordained, but that the account itself is a continuation of the buddha's biography.

This same prediction is repeated later by a group of *arahant*s, who answer King Aśoka's question concerning why the *doṇa* of relics belonging to the Koḷiya kings was not found in the *stūpa* constructed by King Ajātasattu, and why he should not retrieve them from the *nāga* realm.

> The *arahants* replied, "Lord! When a great flood destroyed the relic shrine, the relics that were established in the shrine built by the Koḷiya kings entered into the great sea, [remaining] in the relic casket that had been placed in the relic chamber. The *nāgas* saw that relic casket, took it along to the *nāga* realm called Mañjerika, gave it to the *nāga* king Mahakeḷa, and are making offerings [to the relics]," they said. King Dharmāśoka, who heard those words, venerated the Great Sangha and announced, "Reverends! If it is the *nāga* realm, my [sphere of] command exists [there too]. I will have the relics brought." The *arahants* addressed the king, "Lord! In the future a king named Duṭagämuṇu in Laṅkādvīpa will establish those relics in the relic shrine called 'Golden Garlands.' Therefore there is no purpose in having those relics brought." They thus prevented him [from doing so].[22]

These narratives from the Pāli and Sinhala *Thūpavaṃsas* extend the relics backward and forward in chronological time. They are linked to the buddha and other notable figures in the past by the predictions made about the future destiny of the relics themselves. And they become an enduring sign of the buddha for persons to venerate far into the future.

A similar narrative effect is achieved in the account of the "Sīhaḷa-image" (Phra Sihing) found in the *Jinakālamālī*.[23] This particular image is also given an origin myth that includes an account of how it traveled from its place of origin to its eventual site in Thailand. It relates that a king in Sri Lanka requested to see what the buddha looked like 700 years after his death. A *nāga* was summoned and created an exact likeness of the buddha, which was worshipped by the Sinhala king for seven days and nights. The king had his craftsman create a dazzling image from an alloy of tin, gold, and silver, based on the one by the *nāga*, which was honored diligently by him and his descendants for generations. Some 1,100 years later, the Thai king Rama Kamhaeng came to hear of the wondrous nature of the "Sīhaḷa-image" in Sri Lanka. He dispatched an envoy to request it from the Sinhala king, who obliged him. On the way back, the ship carrying the Sīhaḷa-image was destroyed in a storm, but the image remained afloat on a single plank of wood, which miraculously carried it for three days close to shore. A local ruler had a dream about the image and went looking for it the next morning. After finding it with the help of the gods, he rescued the image, venerated it, and invited King Rama Kamhaeng to collect it. The king built a magnificent *stūpa* with an image house for the Sīhaḷa-image. Later, after the king's death, the image was captured and moved around various cities under the protection of whichever king was powerful enough to claim it. Subsequent copies of the Sīhaḷa-image were made, allowing later kings to send the image to various locations throughout their kingdoms, extending their own authority in the process.[24] The duplication or multiplication of buddha images and relics, an important narrative theme in its own right, facilitated the expansion of sacred sites in Buddhist lands and were often said to occur in conjunction with predictions.

Although there are no predictions included in the *Jinakālamālī* narrative about the Sīhaḷa-image, it is noteworthy that this account resembles other narratives that depict the miraculous origins of extraordinary objects, which then travel along a circuitous and seemingly predestined path to their resting place. The image in this case is attributed with power and associated with the buddha through physical likeness. It extends the buddha biography in a novel way, through the recollection of an ancient *nāga* who saw the living buddha and was able to recreate his image for a Sri Lankan king. The image was later given to a Thai king, and this extension of the buddha then came to reside in various Thai locations as a kind of royal palladium signifying the sovereignty of kings. Even though the image has no direct association with the living buddha, its indirect connection to him suffices to make it into an object of great power and value.

Beyond southern Asia, where narratives about relics and images comprise an important literary genre, one finds still other Buddhist traditions that contain similar types of accounts, albeit perhaps of less prominence. For example, one effort to narrate the connections between buddhas and devotees is presented in a text called *Rig pa rang shar chen po'i rgyud* (The tantra of self-arising awareness) belonging to the Tibetan Great Perfection (Dzogchen) tradition. David Germano has described how a chapter in this work indicates how the buddha prophesied and left behind certain "supports" for his body, speech, and mind after his death.[25] These supports bestowed to his devotees include bones and precious (relic) spheres, the canonical teachings found in texts, and his "inner luminosity" left in the subtle heart of all living beings.[26] Such an account contained in this Tibetan *tantra* supplies a variation on the theme of textual accounts wherein relics of the buddha serve to extend his presence in the world, connecting later devotees with awakened beings who leave traces of themselves with which the devotees can interact and possess. In many Tibetan Buddhist traditions, the accounts of relics refer not only to buddhas but also may include recently deceased *lamas* (awakened teachers) who can leave behind relics and also extend their biographies by consciously taking rebirth as a *tulku* (incarnate *lama*) who is recognized as a successor to the previous teacher and is expected to reassume that spiritual role.[27] In such cases, the written and oral biographies of renowned *lamas* and their successive rebirths serve in a similar fashion as narratives about the extensions of the lives and the presence of awakened beings.

One also finds numerous narratives from East Asia that recount how certain relics and images of the buddha were prophesied to be brought and established in lands far from where the buddha was thought to have resided centuries earlier. A scripture associated with the Chinese pilgrim Faxian describes how the living buddha patted the head of the Udayana sandalwood buddha and predicted it would be found 1,000 years after his *parinirvāṇa* in China.[28] Other Chinese texts describe it was prophesied how a robe once used by the buddha and then passed on to his disciple Mahākāśyapa was to be eventually given to the next Buddha Maitreya when he attains his awakening in the future.[29] The symbolic notion of the transmission of the master's robe to his successor carried great currency in East Asian Buddhism, and thus the appearance of narratives predicting the same type of transmission of the buddha's robe is understandable in this context. Similar narratives about the buddha's bowl, containing the predictions of its travels around Asian lands, are found in Chinese texts. Faxian recounted a story he heard in Sri Lanka in which the buddha's stone alms bowl moved from Vaiśālī to Gandhāra, before one day traveling to the land of the Western Yuezhi, and then moving in succession to Khotan, Kucha, Sri Lanka, and China, before returning to India from where it would go up to the Tuṣita Heaven and come into the possession of Maitreya ahead of his eventual buddhahood.[30] After becoming a buddha, it is predicted that Maitreya will be reunited with the alms bowl of the previous buddha and make use of it anew.

NARRATIVES OF GLORIFICATION

Buddhist narratives about relics and images do more than just connect devotees with buddhas and other awakened beings. Oftentimes such texts also reveal an interest in glorifying those same awakened beings and thus confirming why they should be venerated in the first place.

Since relics and images are often depicted as directly linked to the beings that they manifest or represent, the presence of these powerful objects speaks to their alleged attainments and foresight. In other words, the very existence of relics and images that are narratively endowed with special characteristics also confirms the power and compassion of the awakened beings who are said to have arranged for traces of themselves to persist in the world. These narratives glorify the virtues of such beings through recounting the stories of how relics and images were intentionally provided to devotees to worship in later eras. These same narratives also glorify the sources of these special relics and images through the descriptions of miracles that these objects are said to have performed.

When accounts of Buddhist relics and images reference predictions that buddhas and other awakened beings such as *lamas* make about their physical traces after their deaths, they not only extend the religious biographies of these figures but also testify to some of their extraordinary attainments. The Theravāda *vaṃsa* literature regularly cites instances where the buddha resolves that some of his relics will in the future travel across the sea and be deposited in a shrine for people to venerate and attain various felicities in their current and future lives. A clear instance of this narrative feature appears in the *Sinhala Thūpavaṃsa,* wherein the buddha is portrayed as having both the foresight and compassion to make his bodily relics available for later devotees to worship.

> Because our Buddha did not remain for much time, desiring the welfare of the world and thinking, "My Dispensation has not been spread everywhere. Taking the relics that measure even a mustard seed from me when I have passed away in *parinirvāṇa,* making relic shrines in the places where people dwell, and enshrining the relics in caskets, the many beings who make offerings will enjoy the happiness of the divine world, the *brahmā* world, and the human world," he thus made a resolution for the dispersal of the relics.[31]

By affirming that the appearance and spread of buddha relics were prophesied by the buddha himself, this account portrays people's access to relics as being akin to a gift that the buddha has given them. According to the text, the buddha's resolution (*adhiṣṭhāna*) for his relics to be spread and worshipped makes these events possible, and it suggests that he was compassionately concerned with the well-being of later devotees by enabling them to worship his relics and thereby to attain fortunate rebirths.[32]

Similar narratives about the spread of relics at the behest of the buddha are found in some *vaṃsas* from Myanmar, offering evidence for both the glorification of the buddha through his relics and the spread of this literary device across the Theravāda Buddhist world. In the 19th-century *Sāsanavaṃsa,* one finds a narrative that portrays how a young *arahant* named Gavaṃpati, born in Suvaṇṇabhūmi in lower Myanmar, invites the buddha to travel to this land by air. While preaching to an eager populace and establishing them in the three refuges and the five precepts of his dharma, the buddha is said to have given some hair relics for worship and resolved for his thirty-three teeth to be taken from his funeral pyre and brought back to Suvaṇṇabhūmi in the future.[33] This prophecy of the buddha concerning his tooth relics is related in more detail in the late-18th-century Burmese text *Vaṃsadīpanī.* Therein, Gavaṃpati is told by the buddha, "'[After my cremation] you shall carry [my] thirty-three teeth [as relics] to Suvaṇṇabhūmi and dwell there.' Thus, after the *parinirvāṇa,* . . . the *arahant* Elder Gavaṃpati, in keeping with the prophecy, took up residence in the city of Suvaṇṇabhūmi and there caused the *sāsana* to flourish."[34] This work goes on to attribute this prophesy by the buddha to an epigraph that later convinces the people of the region to embrace a party of Buddhist monks who arrive from Jambudvīpa to bring them the dharma and its fruits anew.

In addition to recalling how the buddha resolved to make his relics available to later devotees, such narratives frequently contain accounts of miracles performed by these extraordinary objects. The alleged ability of relics and images to perform miracles illustrates both the power and agency to which they are ascribed. These special relics and images are often said to imitate the actions of a living buddha by, for example, possessing the power of locomotion and the ability to generate six-colored rays of light. The 14th-century *Sinhala Bōdhivaṁśaya* (History of the Bodhi tree) contains such a narrative account when it relates where and how a sapling from the great Bodhi tree (Mahābodhi) under which the buddha sat when he attained his awakening becomes established in Sri Lanka. Following the Pāli narrative from the earlier *Mahābodhivaṃsa,* the Sinhala text describes that in the moment when the Bodhi sapling was taken off the chariot that brought it to the predestined location of its planting, it ascended about 100 feet in the air and emitted six-colored rays all across the island and the sky, and remained in the air, generating serene joy and insight in those who observed this miracle, until descending back to earth when the sun had set.[35] Other buddha relics are said to have performed similar miracles, including the buddha's tooth relic in the 12th-century *Dāṭhāvaṃsa,* his collarbone relic in the *Thūpavaṃsa,* and the frontal bone relic in the 14th-century *Sinhala Dhātuvaṃsa.*[36]

Likewise, narratives from Southeast Asian lands contain related accounts of the supernatural powers that extraordinary relics and images are said to possess. In the Pāli *Cāmadevīvaṃsa* from 15th-century Thailand, the text concludes with an account of how a casket containing some of the buddha's bodily relics emerges out of the ground at the invitation of the local king, rises up into the sky, and emits a perfumed odor and rays of the seven kinds of precious materials, before sinking back into the earth.[37] This miracle, we are told, was prophesied earlier by the buddha, confirming once again his powers of prediction and the continued powers that his relics are said to possess long after he passed away in complete nirvana. As depicted in many such narratives, miraculous displays by relics illustrate the determined resolutions that the buddha had made for them, demonstrate that they portray a will and inviolability of their own, and even reinforce the sense of their sacrality and identity with the living buddha.[38] The extraordinary power attributed to these relics and images also served as testimony to the protection that these objects extended to the buddha's dispensation after his passing away. By equating some of the miraculous actions of relics with the marvels that the buddha is said to have performed in his lifetime, these narratives make relics appear to have lives of their own. In Thai and Lao cosmology, for example, relics and statues can possess inherent power that is thought to stem from the buddha's awakening, becoming manifest in various ways such as diffusing colorful rays of light and causing prosperity, rainfall, and good fortune.[39]

Significantly, in some Burmese and Thai narratives, buddha images are also credited with manifesting miraculous powers and the qualities of an animate being. Although we do not find such narratives glorifying buddha images in texts from Sri Lanka, the presence of powerful images of the buddha is an important feature of Buddhist narratives and devotion in Southeast Asian lands. In the 15th-century Thai chronicle *Sihingkhanithan,* the narrative on the origins, travels, and duplication of the "Sīhaḷa Buddha" image (Phra Buddha Sihiṅg) is recounted. Therein, the image is described as having power and a will of its own, and the various kings who come to possess it are said to "invite" the image to occupy various locations. In one instance, the buddha image "got out of His seat and placed Himself in the air, and from Him sixfold rays were emanating in all directions."[40] The text goes on to confirm that the image itself possesses the highest fame and glory and, being devotedly worshipped akin to the living Buddha wherever it goes, the *sāsana* (dispensation) is therefore made to shine.[41] The power of this image is attributed to its alleged antiquity and close resemblance to the buddha as it is said to have been cast in Sri Lanka around the 2nd century CE. The text further asserts that while the buddha was alive, he foresaw that his images would help to liberate beings after he passes away in nirvana.[42] The Sīhaḷa Buddha image became a prized object that was transferred between kings and sometimes duplicated, since several local rulers wanted to possess this image for themselves and their kingdoms.

The movement of some of the region's most treasured buddha images from different lands and across kingdoms underlines their extraordinary qualities. Many narratives represent relics and images as objects that have agency and can travel on their own to places where they were predicted or destined to be established.[43] The Sīhaḷa Buddha's journey from its place of origin in Sri Lanka to Thai and other lands in Southeast Asia is described in terms of both the miraculous and the political. Likewise, the Emerald Buddha image (Phra Kaeo Morakot) has its own narrative account of its storied origins and travels. It is said to have been fashioned out of a precious gem obtained by the god Śakra according to the wish of the celebrated monk Nāgasena in order to make the *sāsana* shine forth.[44] This same monk is said to have made a determined resolution for seven buddha relics to enter into the image for the sake of blessing humans and gods for five thousand years.[45] The Emerald Buddha was subsequently sent from India to Sri Lanka and to four different kingdoms in Southeast Asia, in accordance with a prediction that Nāgasena made. Its travels make up a significant part of the narratives around this image, while also demonstrating its influence and popularity as an object of extraordinary power. The chronicle that narrates the history of the Emerald Buddha also verifies the power of this image by stating that those who worshipped it had their wishes granted and those who gave offerings to it were reborn in a heavenly realm.[46]

Narratives about the Mahāmuni image from Myanmar incorporate many of the same themes as found in accounts of powerful Thai Buddhist images. It is said that the Mahāmuni image was fashioned out of precious materials by the gods Sakka and Vissakamma using the living buddha as a model when he visited the kingdom of Arakan in upper Myanmar. When the image was completed, the buddha breathed upon it to impart life into it, and it is said that the image even rose to honor the buddha as his "older brother."[47] Burmese traditions about the Mahāmuni attribute various prophesies and miracles to this image, and it also has been prized and possessed by various local kings throughout history. An Arakanese text enumerates nine miracles performed by the Mahāmuni, including that its six-colored rays shone brightly in the evening when worshipped by the faithful but disappeared in the presence of heretics, that it could always expand the precincts of the shrine to accommodate more worshippers, and that birds would not fly above it.[48] Oral narratives about the image even allow that some miracles performed by the image no longer occur. It is held that the Mahāmuni used to speak, preach sermons, and advise the king, but it fell silent with the progressive decline of the buddha's *sāsana* and the increase of defilements in the world.[49]

The theme of relics and images being used to glorify certain awakened individuals and to possess their own miraculous power is also found in Buddhist traditions outside of southern Asia. Some Tibetan traditions identify not only the bones of deceased saints as extraordinary objects, but they also recognize the manifestation of *ringsel*, or "precious (relic) spheres," in the form of tiny, colorful spheres that are held to emerge from the cremated remains of a saint and that indicate the effects of that individual's spiritual endeavors and accomplishments in life.[50] These special objects are worthy of veneration as some of the physical remains of a buddha or a *lama*. The *ringsel* of accomplished spiritual teachers are specifically said to differ from those of ordinary people in their vibrancy and color.[51] Not only are the spherical *ringsel* of saints deserving of worship, but they are also attributed with power and agency that other inanimate objects do not possess. Seen as signs of spiritual mastery, *ringsel* are held to be able to multiply if they receive the appropriate reverence.[52] The agency with which such relics are attributed reflect another mode of extending the presence of a realized *lama* alongside that of intentional reincarnation as a *tulku*. As such, *ringsel* in Tibetan Buddhist traditions can act like a living *lama* by transmitting blessings to followers and replicating themselves over time.[53]

NARRATIVES OF AUTHORITY

Many of the same narratives that extend the stories of buddhas and other awakened ones, establish affinities between the buddha and devotees, and glorify the miraculous power of relics and images also serve to enhance the authority of rulers and others who make claims to such relics and images. Based on their readings of *vaṃsa* and other texts, scholars have often emphasized how relic and image veneration served to legitimate the rule of Buddhist kings. Narratives about relics and images of the buddha often highlight the power and virtue of kings who sought out, enshrined, and made offerings to these sacred objects.

It is easy to assume that the connections forged between kings and relics or images represent efforts by the authors of texts to legitimate the acts and the reigns of certain rulers. Examples of the authorizing nature of narratives on buddha relics and images frequently appear in conjunction with the transmission of Buddhism to new kingdoms in Central and East Asia. For example, the sacred Jowo Rinpoche image is held to have been brought to Tibet by the Chinese Buddhist wife of Tibet's first emperor Songtsen Gampo in the 7th century, formally marking the introduction of Buddhism and validating the righteousness of his reign. Likewise, narratives recall how in the 1st century, Emperor Ming of Han dynasty China was visited in a dream by a golden image of the buddha, foreshadowing the introduction of the religion into China and allegedly moving the emperor to send an embassy of royal officials to procure the sacred texts of this "deity." In Japan, narrative accounts of the formal introduction of Buddhism stress how a Korean king sent a buddha image and some scriptures to Japan, where members of the Soga clan that aspired to reign over the islands embraced the new religion in their successful attempt to seize power. Meanwhile, in the South Asian context, some have interpreted the account in the 6th-century *Mahāvaṃsa* of how King Duṭṭhagāmaṇī had a buddha relic placed in his royal spear as he marched into battle as a kind of mythic charter to legitimate the violence committed by the king in the name of unifying the country.[54] After the king succeeded in defeating the foreign occupiers of Sri Lanka, the *Mahāvaṃsa* went on to explain how the relic on the spear became lodged in the ground, so the king decided to build a new relic shrine over it. King Duṭṭhagāmaṇī's association with this and other relics is, in this way, frequently linked with efforts to legitimate his identity as a great Buddhist king.

Although there is a plausible argument to be made with reference to equating narratives about relics and images with strategies for legitimating Buddhist kings, it can also become an overly reductive, cynical explanation. Many of the kings who are celebrated in narratives about relics and images appear as powerful monarchs, individuals whose reputations as rulers rarely seem to have been in doubt. Instead, the political interests of these narratives seem to operate with more nuance. By bringing kings into the stories of buddha relics and images, the authors of such texts seemed to be providing models of action for current and future rulers, outlining a repertoire for the performance of righteous kingship.[55] For example, the legend of King Aśoka and his construction of 84,000 *stūpas* throughout his kingdom offered just one important model for future kings to emulate, albeit on a much smaller scale, when demonstrating their righteousness by building and repairing Buddhist monuments. From the perspectives of these narrative texts, good Buddhist kings are concerned with acquiring relics and images for the protection of their kingdoms and the well-being of their subjects, and honoring these extraordinary objects to earn merit for strengthening their rule in the present and earning fortunate rebirths in the future. This royal interest in relics and images is evident in textual accounts where kings build impressive relic shrines and make lavish offerings to relics and, similarly, where they instruct artisans to cast images or simply seize images from other lands. Although monks are often the actors who acquire relics, they usually do so on behalf of the kings to whom they entrust these sacred objects.

Numerous examples of kings who acquired and enshrined relics are found in narratives composed throughout southern Asia. In the *Sāsanavaṃsa,* King Anuruddha is depicted as having vanquished the kingdom of the Mons in lower Myanmar, taking possession of the texts of the Tipiṭaka and a collection of relics that he brought back to his own kingdom to establish the *sāsana* there.[56] This narrative account underlines the idea that righteous and powerful kings rule over lands where buddha relics are enshrined. The *Vaṃsadīpanī* also records events wherein virtuous kings are directly associated with relics. A monk named Ven. Deibbasek was said to have acquired some relics from the Mahāthūpa in Sri Lanka for the sake of spreading the *sāsana* into Burmese lands. Having then met King Thihathu there, he advised him to ensure that monks lived according to the disciplinary code and to enshrine and worship relics of the buddha so that the *sāsana* would be established for a long time.[57] The king complied and enshrined the relics in the Shwezigon Pagoda, thus signaling a new capital city for his reign. Such narratives describing how kings become the custodians of buddha relics are exceedingly common in the *vaṃsa* literature of southern Asia.

The narratives about the Bodhi tree relic also follow suit with their depictions of kings who seek to acquire and properly venerate this important relic. Narratives from Sri Lanka describe how the great southern branch of the Bodhi tree was acquired by King Aśoka and transferred over with great honor and ceremony to King Devānampiyatissa in Sri Lanka, where it was planted and enshrined in the capital city of Anurādhapura. Acting in accordance with a resolute prediction made previously by the buddha, Aśoka drew a line around the branch, which then miraculously separated itself from the rest of the Bodhi tree and settled in a golden vessel. Before sending the branch off to his royal ally in Sri Lanka, Asoka is said to have bestowed his own sovereignty over to the Bodhi tree on three occasions.[58] Subsequently, Devānampiyatissa received the Bodhi tree branch with great honor from the ship that carried it across the sea and had it conveyed like a king to his own capital city. Like Asoka, Devānampiyatissa offered his own sovereignty to the Bodhi tree and made elaborate offerings to it.[59] By offering their sovereignty to this relic, Aśoka and Devānampiyatissa demonstrated their devotion to the buddha, enhancing their authority as righteous kings in the process. This narrative, and others like it, depict Buddhist kings as intimately concerned with buddha relics: handling, enshrining, and occasionally even distributing these sacred objects for the benefit of their subjects and to authorize their own reigns.

The proliferation of relics around the Buddhist world offered numerous opportunities for kings to establish themselves as pious devotees who apparently enjoy great merit to be able to accede to the throne and to become intimately involved in worshipping important relics. Narratives help to establish the pedigrees for relics, describing where and how they came to be found in various locales across Asia. But these same accounts also help to establish the pedigrees for kings, linking the righteousness of their rules to the practices of obtaining, enshrining, and worshipping relics in their own kingdoms. Such was the case with King Kaniṣka, who ruled a vast territory in the northwest Indian subcontinent around the 1st century CE. In the 7th-century account of the travels of the Chinese pilgrim Xuanzang, he relates how the buddha's bowl relic was once stored in the king's capital in Gandhāra, and that Kaniṣka also built a large *stūpa* into which he deposited about a hectoliter of the buddha's relic bones.[60] Xuanzang narrated the legends of Kaniṣka's concern with relics, which would seem to confirm that at the very least this powerful emperor felt the need to imitate the earlier model of King Aśoka, who similarly invested great effort and resources to possess and house buddha relics in his kingdom.

Buddhist narratives, whether in the form of *vaṃsa* texts, travelogs, or other works, sometimes identify certain relics as important signifiers for the authority and sovereignty exercised by kings in Asian lands. The use of relics as royal symbols and palladia are frequently described in Buddhist literature. In medieval Japan, for instance, a number of aristocratic diaries portray imperial rites for making offerings to buddha relics that had been acquired by diplomacy and other means. From around the 7th century onward, the Japanese court incorporated buddha relics in rites to represent the emperor to the court, to maintain the safety and integrity of the realm, and to authorize an individual's accession to the throne.[61] The narrative descriptions of these rites illustrate how relics and sometimes images could be used in medieval Japan to endow an individual with imperial authority and to mark out the extent of their sovereignty through the distribution of buddha relics to various shrines throughout the realm. Imperial rites transported relics both outward from the center to bring distant shrines under the influence of the court and inward from a temple treasury to the chapel in the imperial palace.[62] The movement of these relics and their ritualized worship during these ceremonies served to offer good fortune and protection to the emperor and his realm.

Buddha images too could supply people with the means to authorize kingship and to protect the realm from harm. Important buddha images with legendary pedigrees came to be prized by numerous kings in Southeast Asia both to symbolize and sustain their rule. Drawing upon older narratives that described how great kings obtained relics, a number of Buddhist texts from Myanmar, Thailand, and Laos singled out how local kings acquired powerful buddha images that they established in their kingdoms to enhance the fortunes of the subjects and lands under their rule. During the travels of the Sīhaḷa Buddha image across various Thai and Lao polities, this extraordinary object came to be enshrined in a temple in the palace grounds of the king in Chiang Mai, acting as a royal palladium before being duplicated so that the king could send two replicas to the two major cities in his kingdom, reinforcing his sovereignty over his realm.[63] This king is further described in one text as declaring, "What a person requires, he obtains, so do I! The statue of the Buddha known under the name of Phra Sihiṅga has come to me! None of the Jambudvīpa sovereigns has more merits than I!"[64] Seeing his acquisition of the Sīhaḷa Buddha image as the culmination of his own merit and desire, the king confirms that he was in one sense destined to obtain the image. Narratives on the Sīhaḷa Buddha and the Emerald Buddha describe how these images were repeatedly seized and brought to different kingdoms around Southeast Asia. Their long and complicated journeys underline their value as royal palladia.

Various buddha relics and images have become important objects of devotion, protection, and representation for Buddhist kings across premodern and modern Asia. The tooth relic in Sri Lanka has enjoyed a special status as a relic that confirms the authority of a king and ensures the prosperity of his realm, and thus it should be worshipped and protected by all rulers in the island. By tradition, possession of the tooth relic is a requisite for a king to be recognized as righteous and deserving of his rule. In Thailand, the Emerald Buddha came to serve as the preeminent guardian of the cities where it was taken, bringing rain, prosperity, and protection from disease.[65] Since it was recaptured in the 18th century from a Lao kingdom centered in Vientiane, the Emerald Buddha has become the royal palladium of the modern Thai state. The image was enshrined in a temple in Bangkok when King Rama I moved his capital to this new city. Meanwhile, in Laos, another buddha image—the Phra Bang—remains as a palladium of the state. Held to have come from Sri Lanka via Cambodia, the Phra Bang image was ritually consecrated by Lao rulers during the New Year Festival, an act that has been repeated by high-ranking Lao politicians in the early 21st century.[66] Likewise, in Myanmar, the Mahāmuni image has also served as a royal palladium for later Burmese kings in Mandalay, offering a symbolic means to associate themselves with the reigns and observances of earlier kings.[67] Although the nature of royal palladia could change over the centuries, with certain relics and images replacing other ones, Buddhist kings consistently sought to enhance and extend their sovereignty by worshipping certain physical remains or extensions of the buddha that came to represent the authority of their rule.

THE WORK OF BUDDHIST NARRATIVES

The focus in this article on *narratives* of relics and images, rather than on the relics and images themselves, highlights how written and oral accounts of these extraordinary objects play critical roles in transmitting knowledge and devotion in Buddhist communities. From the perspectives of many if not most adherents, relics and images of buddhas and other revered individuals possess a kind of innate power derived from those fully awakened beings and can serve as substitutes for them. One could argue, however, that the extraordinary power and special status that select relics and images enjoy are in fact bestowed, at least in part, by the narratives that recall their stories and reveal why they are worthy of veneration. Such texts would have had great value for educating people about the power of these objects and the importance of the shrines that contained them. Whether these narratives appear in the forms of *vaṃsas*, diaries, or oral folklore, they serve the key purpose of attributing power and value to such objects of veneration. The variety of relics and images that Buddhists have recognized as having some sort of direct connection with the buddha has given rise to numerous narratives about these. It stands to reason, moreover, that if a relic or image were to lack a narrative about its origin, movement, and powers, it would in all probability hold a lower status among devotees, under those relics and images about which stories were told and transmitted.

One can identify four notable features of Buddhist narratives composed about relics and images. First, such narratives frequently serve to establish a sense of affinity with Buddhas and other awakened individuals by explaining how a particular relic or image is intimately connected with an extraordinary being. What makes a given relic or image more special and important than other objects is, in part, the narratives that describe how they possess a direct link to a venerable figure. Thus, relics often represent direct traces of a Buddha that have been left behind to assist devotees in gaining merit and fostering a more immediate relationship with that Buddha. Broadly speaking, such narratives may help to generate religiously valued emotions and understandings of one's relationship to a Buddha or saint, which in turn imparts a disposition to venerate that being and participate in sanctioned rituals of worship.[68] In other words, if a relic or image can generate a sense of affinity between a devotee and a Buddha, it does so by means of recounting some sort of narrative that locates the object, attributes it with power and uniqueness, and relates it to devotees living in times and places that are removed from the Buddha. While one can assert that a relic extends the biography of a buddha or other awakened saint, it requires some sort of written or oral narrative to accomplish this objective.

Second, Buddhist narratives about relics and images frequently incorporate predictions and prophesies that are meant to show how those powerful objects were in some way predestined to appear in the world and become available for people to worship and possess. When attributed to a buddha or some other awakened being, these prophecies acquire the power of a solemn resolution that helps to guide the manifestation and movement of the relic or image into the hands of a ruler or an entire community that somehow deserves to obtain it. Given the historical context in which predictions and prophecies must operate, explaining how a relic or image was obtained, displayed its powers, and traveled to its current location in the world, they can only find a place within narrative accounts. A prophecy by the Buddha about his relic or image also serves to frame the actual historical journey of these powerful objects as depicted in the sequence of narrative events. In other words, these prophecies show how the actions associated with relics and images had to take place in the manner that they did, since they were foretold by a Buddha or another awakened saint.

A third important feature of these Buddhist narratives is that they typically attribute miraculous powers to these objects and simultaneously work to glorify the Buddha or saint that serves as their referent. Accounts of relics and images are careful to distinguish these objects from the Buddha or saint to which they refer. There remains a gap, however narrow, between the relic or image and the Buddha or saint with whom they are related. Nevertheless, by virtue of their connection to an extraordinary being, relics and images are often described as manifesting many of the same powerful or supernormal characteristics. This explains why many such narratives in Buddhist traditions contain miraculous accounts of these objects. And by attributing extraordinary power to a relic or an image, that narrative also serves to reaffirm the extraordinary power of the buddha or saint to whom the revered object is connected. The intended result is increased faith and devotion on the part of the devotee who learns about the special qualities of a given relic or image. Another product of such narratives is to enhance the importance of certain shrines and temples that possess these objects, giving rise to sacred spaces and, at times, pilgrimage networks for ritualized devotion.

Fourth, since certain relics and images are said to have an affinity with a buddha or saint, and are further understood to possess similar kinds of power, such objects may thus serve to bestow authority upon those persons who may claim to keep or protect them. In many narratives about Buddhist relics and images, those individuals who have a proprietary interest in such extraordinary objects find themselves to have an enhanced stature and importance. Oftentimes, certain kings, monks, and aristocrats who are said to be responsible for a given relic or image are in turn bestowed with greater authority to act in social and political fields. In other words, their possession of a relic or connection with an image serves to enhance their power and authority. Buddha relics and images, when shown by narratives to be especially significant and powerful in their own right, effectively distribute some of the same significance and power to those who are charged with caring for and protecting them.

By performing these kinds of cultural work, Buddhist narratives about relics and images actually enhance the power and importance of those very objects. The written texts and oral accounts may have varying levels of sophistication and renown, but they are readily found in Buddhist traditions from across premodern Asia. They may often incorporate conventional themes and tropes, but they can still differ in terms of emphasis and objective. While they may not be afforded with canonical status as the words of the buddha, these narratives serve to connect devotees with Buddhas—and other awakened beings—in other ways. The accounts they convey about extraordinary objects help to make them into sources of greater sacrality and importance. Without such narrative texts, it would be difficult to imagine that buddha relics and images would enjoy the significance that they do in nearly all Buddhist traditions. Because of such narratives, Buddhist communities are able to maintain their relationships with Buddhas and saints long after they have departed this world, inspiring devotion and establishing authoritative expressions of power in both the objects themselves and the people who care for them.

REVIEW OF LITERATURE

The literature on Buddhist narratives of relics and images consists primarily of two kinds of sources. There are primary texts in editions and translations, and there is secondary scholarship that examines such narrative material. As noted, some narratives on relics and images make up the primary focus of certain texts, while in others they are part of a broader range of topics. Among primary sources with a focus on relics and images, one may locate a considerable number of narratives published in editions and translations in Pāli and other vernacular languages associated with South and Southeast Asia. The Pali Text Society has made many of the Pāli language *vaṃsa* texts available in critical editions and English translation for scholarly study. Works published in vernacular languages such as Sinhala, Burmese, and Thai are available for the most part primarily in the countries where those languages are commonly used. The extensive corpus of narratives on Buddhist relics and images from southern Asia notwithstanding, the number of studies on Pāli works besides the *Mahāvaṃsa* is quite limited. Scholarship on narratives composed in literary forms of vernacular languages are even less common.[69] Given the importance of these narratives for the spread and establishment of Buddhism across Asian lands, the relative scarcity of scholarship on these texts is a problem that would be alleviated by more attention to these works. In addition to published editions and translations of these narratives from southern Asia, there are still other manuscript texts containing material on relics and images yet to be examined.

Locating Buddhist narratives on relics and images in East and Central Asia is made more difficult by the fact that they are often included as parts of larger works that are more diffuse in subject matter. Primary accounts that relate material on relics and images exist in Chinese-, Japanese-, and Tibetan-language works, among other primary sources associated with Mahāyāna and Vajrayāna Buddhist traditions. These texts range from the accounts of East Asian pilgrim monks to the diaries of Japanese nobles, and from Tibetan *tantras* to the accounts of various *lamas* and other Buddhist saints in the Himalayan region. Since these corpuses of Buddhist texts are generally speaking vast in size, one may assume that there are many more narratives that have not yet been subjected to scholarly analysis. Perhaps the major challenge facing scholars remains locating these narratives within larger texts and collections of texts composed of diverse subjects.

Throughout Southern, East, and Central Asian Buddhist communities, there exist oral accounts of narratives associated with relics and images that are largely unexamined and understudied. Future research on local, popular traditions regarding Buddhist relics and images would be desirable to complement the written texts that contribute most to the scholarly understanding of relics and images across the Buddhist world. Such research into orally transmitted accounts would certainly require more ethnographic and vernacular language studies. These accounts may in turn offer more insights into the degrees to which written texts have shaped people's understandings of the relics and images that exist in their communities.

Secondary literature on Buddhist relics and images has increased in amount and quality in the years since Buddhist studies has begun to value material culture alongside canonical and philosophical texts. Scholarship has made great strides in examining these objects as legitimate cultural expressions of the tradition rather than as examples of so-called superstitious idolatry. By asking questions of how relics and images serve not only religious but also political and sociological interests as well, scholars in the field have begun to acknowledge, among other things, that these objects play important roles in the authorization of ruling powers, the establishment of sacred places of ritualized worship, and the economic development of religious centers.[70] In each case, scholarly attention to narratives of Buddhist relics and images helps to facilitate a better grasp of how Buddhist traditions were spread and reinforced in areas outside of those associated with the buddha's life story. Such narratives may also have functioned to displace local cultic centers and replace them with sites associated with powerful Buddhist objects.

The secondary literature on Buddhist narratives of relics and images is somewhat lesser in quantity than the studies of those objects themselves. Scholars have published numerous works on the subjects of Buddhist relics or Buddhist images as important aspects of religious practice.[71] While studies of this type add much to the scholarly understanding of Buddhist traditions, they tend to overshadow research into the narrative sources that are often used to provide details about how Buddhist relics and images were discovered, fashioned, venerated, moved, stolen, destroyed, multiplied, and subjected to other actions in different times and places. More attention should be given to the diverse ways that these narratives in Buddhist texts function as literary and cultural works that also impact the practice and perceptions of the religion. Further attention to the forms and features of the narratives on relics and images would not only increase the knowledge of such objects, but would also enhance the scholarly understanding of Buddhist literature itself.

PRIMARY SOURCES

Accounts of relics and images connected with the buddha or other Buddhist saints may be found scattered among a sizable number of texts composed in various genres. Among such works, numerous texts with narratives about Buddhist relics and images are available in English translations.

Berkwitz, Stephen, trans. *The History of the Buddha's Relic Shrine: A Translation of the* Sinhala Thūpavaṃsa. New York: Oxford University Press, 2007.

Geiger, Wilhelm, trans. *The Mahāvaṃsa, or The Great Chronicle of Ceylon*. Oxford: Pali Text Society, 2001.

Jayawickrama, N. A., trans. *The Sheaf of the Garlands of the Epochs of the Conqueror: Being a Translation of Jinakālamālīpakaraṇaṁ of Ratannapañña Thera of Thailand*. London: Luzac, 1968.

Jayawickrama, N. A., ed. and trans. *The Chronicle of the Thūpa and the Thūpavaṃsa: Being a Translation and Edition of Vācissaratthera's Thūpavaṃsa*. London: Luzac, 1971.

Law, Bimala Churn, trans. *The History of the Buddha's Religion (Sāsanavaṃsa)*. London: Luzac, 1952.

Legge, James, trans. *A Record of Buddhistic Kingdoms: Being an Account by the Chinese Monk Fâ-hien of His Travels in India and Ceylon (A.D. 399–414) in Search of the Buddhist Books of Discipline*. New York: Paragon Books, 1965.

Li Rongxi, trans. *The Great Tang Dynasty Record of the Western Regions*. Berkeley, CA: Numata Center for Buddhist Translation and Research, 1996.

Notton, Camille, trans. *The Chronicle of the Emerald Buddha*. Bangkok: Bangkok Time Press, 1932.

Notton, Camille, trans. *P'ra Buddha Sihiṅga*. Bangkok: Bangkok Time Press, 1933.

Preuss, James B. *The Thāt Phanom Chronicle: A Shrine History and Its Interpretation*. Ithaca, NY: Cornell University Press, 1976.

Swearer, Donald K., and Sommai Premchit, trans. *The Legend of Queen Cāma: Bodhiraṃsi's* Cāmadevīvaṃsa, *a Translation and Commentary*. Albany: State University of New York Press, 1998.

Thera, Vedeha. *In Praise of Mount Samanta (Samantakūṭavaṇṇanā)*. Translated by Ann Appleby Hazelwood. London: Pali Text Society, 1986.

FURTHER READING

Bentor, Yael. *Consecration of Images and Stūpas in Indo-Tibetan Tantric Buddhism*. Leiden, The Netherlands: E. J. Brill, 1996.

Berkwitz, Stephen. *Buddhist History in the Vernacular: The Power of the Past in Late Medieval Sri Lanka*. Leiden, The Netherlands: Brill, 2004.

Blackburn, Anne M. "Buddha-Relics in the Lives of Southern Asian Polities." *Numen* 57 (2010): 317–340.

Carter, Martha L. *The Mystery of the Udayana Buddha*. Naples, Italy: Instituto Universitario Orientale, 1990.

DeCaroli, Robert. *Image Problems: The Origin and Development of the Buddha's Image in Early South Asia*. Seattle: University of Washington Press, 2015.

Faure, Bernard. *The Rhetoric of Immediacy: A Cultural Critique of Chan/Zen Buddhism*. Princeton, NJ: Princeton University Press, 1991.

Faure, Bernard. "Relics and Flesh Bodies: The Creation of Ch'an Pilgrimage Sites." In *Pilgrims and Sacred Sites in China*. Edited by Susan Naquin and Chün-fang Yü, 150–189. Berkeley: University of California Press, 1992.

Germano, David, and Kevin Trainor, eds. *Embodying the Dharma: Buddhist Relic Veneration in Asia*. Albany: State University of New York Press, 2004.

Ladwig, Patrice. "Worshipping Relics and Animating Statues: Transformations of Buddhist Statecraft in Contemporary Laos." *Modern Asian Studies* 49, no. 6 (2015): 1875–1902.

Lagirarde, François. "Narratives as Ritual Histories: The Case of the Northern-Thai Buddhist Chronicles." In *Buddhist Narrative in Asia and Beyond*. Vol. 1. Edited by Peter Skilling and Justin McDaniel, 81–92. Bangkok: Chulalongkorn University, 2013.

Leider, Jacques. "Relics, Statues, and Predictions: Interpreting an Apocryphal Sermon of Lord Buddha in Arakan." *Asian Ethnology* 68, no. 2 (2009): 333–364.

Ruppert, Brian D. *Jewel in the Ashes: Buddha Relics and Power in Early Medieval Japan*. Cambridge, MA: Harvard University Asia Center, 2000.

Scheible, Kristin. *Reading the Mahāvaṃsa: The Literary Aims of a Theravāda Buddhist History*. New York: Columbia University Press, 2016.

Schober, Juliane. "In the Presence of the Buddha: Ritual Veneration of the Burmese Mahāmuni Image." In *Sacred Biography in the Buddhist Traditions of South and Southeast Asia*. Edited by Juliane Schober, 259–288. Honolulu: University of Hawai'i Press, 1997.

Sharf, Robert H. "On the Allure of Buddhist Relics." *Representations* 66 (1999): 75–99.

Sharf, Robert H. "The Buddha's Finger Bones at Famensi and the Art of Chinese Esoteric Buddhism." *Art Bulletin* 93, no. 1 (2011): 38–59.

Shinohara, Koichi. "The Story of the Buddha's Begging Bowl: Imagining a Biography of Sacred Places." In *Pilgrims, Patrons, and Place: Localizing Sanctity in Asian Religions*. Edited by Phyllis Granoff and Koichi Shinohara, 68–107. Vancouver, Canada: UBC Press, 2003.

Strong, John S. *Relics of the Buddha*. Princeton, NJ: Princeton University Press, 2004.

Swearer, Donald K. *Becoming the Buddha: The Ritual of Image Consecration in Thailand*. Princeton, NJ: Princeton University Press, 2004.

Tambiah, Stanley J. "Famous Buddha Images and the Legitimation of Kings: The Case of the Sinhala Buddha (Phra Sihing) in Thailand." *RES* 4 (1982): 5–19.

Trainor, Kevin. *Relics, Ritual, and Representation in Buddhism: Rematerializing the Sri Lankan Theravāda Tradition*. Cambridge, UK: Cambridge University Press, 1997.

Zivkovic, Tanya. *Death and Reincarnation in Tibetan Buddhism: In-between Bodies*. London: Routledge, 2014.

NOTES

1. Kevin Trainor, *Relics, Ritual, and Representation in Buddhism: Rematerializing the Sri Lankan Theravāda Tradition* (Cambridge, UK: Cambridge University Press, 1997), 89.
2. See, for instance, John Powers, *A Bull of a Man: Images of Masculinity, Sex, and the Body in Indian Buddhism* (Cambridge, MA: Harvard University Press, 2009), 21–23.
3. Sonya Rhie Quintanilla, *History of Early Stone Sculpture at Mathura, ca. 150 BCE–100 CE* (Leiden, The Netherlands: Brill, 2007), 249–250.
4. Thomas William Rhys Davids, *The Questions of King Milinda, Part II* (Delhi: Motilal Banarsidass, 1988), 229–230. This was originally published in 1894.
5. John S. Strong, *Relics of the Buddha* (Princeton, NJ: Princeton University Press, 2004), 19–20.
6. James Robson, "Relic Wary: Facets of Buddhist Relic Veneration in East Asia and Recent Scholarship," *International Journal of Buddhist Thought and Culture* 27, no. 2 (2017): 25–26.

7. Stephen C. Berkwitz, *Buddhist History in the Vernacular: The Power of the Past in Late Medieval Sri Lanka* (Leiden, The Netherlands: Brill, 2004), 25.
8. Berkwitz, *Buddhist History in the Vernacular*, 107–109.
9. In the case of northern Thai texts, see François Lagirarde, "Temps et lieux d'histoires bouddhiques: À propos de quelques 'chroniques' inédites du Lanna," *Bulletin de L'École Française d'Extrême-Orient* 94 (2007): 63–65.
10. Strong, *Relics of the Buddha*, 7.
11. Juliane Schober, "In the Presence of the Buddha: Ritual Veneration of the Burmese Mahāmuni Image," in *Sacred Biography in the Buddhist Traditions of South and Southeast Asia*, ed. Juliane Schober (Honolulu: University of Hawai'i Press, 1997), 259–288, esp. 260.
12. David Germano, "Living Relics of the Buddha(s) in Tibet," in *Embodying the Dharma: Buddhist Relic Veneration in Asia*, ed. David Germano and Kevin Trainor (Albany: State University of New York Press, 2004), 51–91, esp. 52.
13. Jacob N. Kinnard, "The Field of the Buddha's Presence," in *Embodying the Dharma*, ed. Germano and Trainor, 117–143, esp. 117–118.
14. Gregory Schopen, *Bones, Stones, and Buddhist Monks: Collected Papers on the Archaeology, Epigraphy, and Texts of Monastic Buddhism in India* (Honolulu: University of Hawai'i Press, 1997), 276–277.
15. Bernard Faure, *The Rhetoric of Immediacy: A Cultural Critique of Chan/Zen Buddhism* (Princeton, NJ: Princeton University Press, 1991), 150–160.
16. Strong, *Relics of the Buddha*, 229.
17. N. A. Jayawickrama, ed. and trans., *The Chronicle of the Thūpa and the Thūpavaṃsa: Being a Translation and Edition of Vācissaratthera's Thūpavaṃsa* (London: Luzac, 1971), 124–125. See also Stephen C. Berkwitz, trans., *The History of the Buddha's Relic Shrine: A Translation of the* Sinhala Thūpavaṃsa (New York: Oxford University Press, 2007), 231.
18. Jayawickrama, *Chronicle of the Thūpa*, 112.
19. Martha L. Carter, *The Mystery of the Udayana Buddha* (Naples, Italy: Instituto Universitario Orientale, 1990), 24–26.
20. François Lagirarde, "Narratives as Ritual Histories: The Case of the Northern-Thai Buddhist Chronicles," in *Buddhist Narrative in Asia and Beyond*, vol. 1, ed. Peter Skilling and Justin McDaniel (Bangkok: Chulalongkorn University, 2013), 88–89.
21. Jayawickrama, *Chronicle of the Thūpa*, 124. Cf. Berkwitz, *History of the Buddha's Relic Shrine*, 230–231.
22. Berkwitz, *History of the Buddha's Relic Shrine*, 231–232. Cf. Jayawickrama, *Chronicle of the Thūpa*, 125.
23. The following summary is based on the account in N. A. Jayawickrama, trans., *The Sheaf of the Garlands of the Epochs of the Conqueror: Being a Translation of Jinakālamālīpakaraṇaṁ of Ratannapañña Thera of Thailand* (London: Luzac, 1968), 120–126.
24. Stanley J. Tambiah, "Famous Buddha Images and the Legitimation of Kings: The Case of the Sinhala Buddha (Phra Sihing) in Thailand," *RES* 4 (1982): 16–17.
25. Germano, "Living Relics of the Buddha(s) in Tibet," 84.
26. Germano, "Living Relics of the Buddha(s) in Tibet," 84.
27. Tanya Zivkovic, *Death and Reincarnation in Tibetan Buddhism: In-between Bodies* (London: Routledge, 2014), 3–4.
28. Carter, *Mystery of the Udayana Buddha*, 7.
29. Strong, *Relics of the Buddha*, 218–219.
30. Koichi Shinohara, "The Story of the Buddha's Begging Bowl: Imagining a Biography and Sacred Places," in *Pilgrims, Patrons, and Place: Localizing Sanctity in Asian Religions*, ed. Phyllis Granoff and Koichi Shinohara (Vancouver, Canada: UBC Press, 2003), 87–88.
31. Berkwitz, *History of the Buddha's Relic Shrine*, 119. Cf. Jayawickrama, *Chronicle of the Thūpa*, 34.

32. Berkwitz, *Buddhist History in the Vernacular*, 251.
33. Bimala Churn Law, trans., *The History of the Buddha's Religion (Sāsanavaṃsa)* (London: Luzac, 1952), 42.
34. Patrick Arthur Pranke, *The Treatise on the Lineage of the Elders (Vaṃsadīpanī): Monastic Reform and the Writing of Buddhist History in Eighteenth-Century Burma* (PhD diss., University of Michigan, 2004), 131. (Changes in italics and spellings made by the present author for stylistic consistency.)
35. Gunapala Senadhira, ed., *Sinhala Bōdhivaṁśaya* (Colombo, Sri Lanka: Abhaya, 1965), 233–234.
36. T. W. Rhys Davids, ed., "*The Dāṭhāvaṃsa*," *Journal of the Pali Text Society* (1884): IV.51, V.26; Jayawickrama, *Chronicle of the Thūpa*, 67; and W. S. Pranandu (Fernando), ed., *Dhātuvaṁśaya* (Colombo, Sri Lanka: Saviya, 1940), 62.
37. Donald K. Swearer and Sommai Premchit, trans., *The Legend of Queen Cāma: Bodhiraṃsi's* Cāmadevīvaṃsa, *a Translation and Commentary* (Albany: State University of New York Press, 1998), 132–133.
38. Strong, *Relics of the Buddha*, 176.
39. Patrice Ladwig, "Worshipping Relics and Animating Statues: Transformations of Buddhist Statecraft in Contemporary Laos," *Modern Asian Studies* 49, no. 6 (2015): 1885–1886.
40. Camille Notton, trans., *P'ra Buddha Sihiṅga* (Bangkok: Bangkok Time, 1933), 27.
41. Notton, *P'ra Buddha Sihiṅga*, 38.
42. Notton, *P'ra Buddha Sihiṅga*, 7.
43. Ladwig, "Worshipping Relics and Animating Statues," 1897; and Lagirarde, "Narratives as Ritual Histories," 88.
44. Jayawickrama, *Sheaf of the Garlands*, 141.
45. Camille Notton, trans., *The Chronicle of the Emerald Buddha* (Bangkok: Bangkok Time, 1932), 17.
46. Notton, *Chronicle of Emerald Buddha*, 18.
47. Schober, "In the Presence of the Buddha," 268.
48. Schober, "In the Presence of the Buddha," 269.
49. Schober, "In the Presence of the Buddha," 269.
50. Germano, "Living Relics of the Buddha(s) in Tibet," 69–71.
51. Germano, "Living Relics of the Buddha(s) in Tibet," 73.
52. Zivkovic, *Death and Reincarnation in Tibetan Buddhism*, 17.
53. Zivkovic, *Death and Reincarnation in Tibetan Buddhism*, 20.
54. Alice Greenwald, "The Relic on the Spear: Historiography and the Saga of Duṭṭhagāmaṇī," in *Religion and Legitimation of Power in Sri Lanka*, ed. Bardwell L. Smith (Chambersburg, PA: Anima Books, 1978), 13–35, esp. 13–14. The original textual account may be found in Wilhelm Geiger, trans., *The Mahāvaṃsa: Or the Great Chronicle of Ceylon* (Oxford: Pali Text Society, 2001), 170. This was originally published in 1912.
55. Anne M. Blackburn, "Buddha-Relics in the Lives of Southern Asian Polities," *Numen* 57 (2010): 320.
56. Law, *History of the Buddha's Religion*, 70–71.
57. Pranke, *Treatise on the Lineage of the Elders*, 161–162.
58. Senadhira, *Sinhala Bōdhivaṁśaya*, 229.
59. Senadhira, *Sinhala Bōdhivaṁśaya*, 237. Cf. S. Arthur Strong, ed., *The Mahābodhi-Vaṁsa* (London: Pali Text Society, 1891), 170.
60. Li Rongxi, trans., *The Great Tang Dynasty Record of the Western Regions* (Berkeley, CA: Numata Center for Buddhist Translation and Research, 1996), 70–72.
61. Brian D. Ruppert, *Jewel in the Ashes: Buddha Relics and Power in Early Medieval Japan* (Cambridge, MA: Harvard University Asia Center, 2000), 263.
62. Ruppert, *Jewel in the Ashes*, 108.
63. Tambiah, "Famous Buddha Images," 11.

64. Notton, *P'ra Buddha Sihiṅga*, 45.
65. Frank E. Reynolds, "The Holy Emerald Jewel: Some Aspects of Buddhist Symbolism and Political Legitimation in Thailand and Laos," in *Religion and Legitimation of Power*, ed. Smith, 179–180.
66. Ladwig, "Worshipping Relics and Animating Statues," 1889.
67. Schober, "In the Presence of the Buddha," 280.
68. Berkwitz, *Buddhist History in the Vernacular*, 231.
69. Studies on vernacular sources on relics and images include Berkwitz, *Buddhist History in the Vernacular*, and Donald K. Swearer, *Wat Haripuñjaya: A Study of the Royal Temple of the Buddha's Relic, Lamphun, Thailand* (Missoula, MT: Scholars Press, 1976).
70. Some examples include Ruppert, *Jewel in the Ashes*; Bernard Faure, "Relics and Flesh Bodies: The Creation of Ch'an Pilgrimage Sites," in *Pilgrims and Sacred Sites in China*, ed. Susan Naquin and Chün-fang Yü (Berkeley: University of California Press, 1992), 150–189; and Yael Bentor, *Consecration of Images and Stūpas in Indo-Tibetan Tantric Buddhism* (Leiden, The Netherlands: E. J. Brill, 1996).
71. Notable examples include Strong, *Relics of the Buddha*; Trainor, *Relics, Ritual, and Representation in Buddhism*; Robert DeCaroli, *Image Problems: The Origin and Development of the Buddha's Image in Early South Asia* (Seattle: University of Washington Press, 2015); and Donald K. Swearer, *Becoming the Buddha: The Ritual of Image Consecration in Thailand* (Princeton, NJ: Princeton University Press, 2004).

Stephen C. Berkwitz

NECHUNG: A TIBETAN BUDDHIST ORACLE

Nechung (Gnas chung) is a toponym that is at once the name of a Tibetan Buddhist monastery, the shorthand for a fierce protector deity, and the title of an important state oracle, depending on the context. All three concepts are closely connected, since the human oracle is periodically possessed by the deity and his emanations, and both reside at the monastic institution for which they are labeled. Nechung Monastery is located on the outskirts of the Tibetan capital of Lhasa, downhill from Drepung ('Bras spungs)—one of the three famous Geluk (Dge lugs) monasteries, the original home of the Dalai Lama incarnations, and the site of their burgeoning government. This is significant, since the Nechung deity would come to be one of the two primary protectors of the Dalai Lamas, and the monastery's oracle would become the chief state oracle of Tibet within the religious leader's administration. The office of the Nechung Oracle achieved this high status in the 17th century as part of the Fifth Dalai Lama's (1617–1682) efforts to renovate and expand the monastery, and the human medium within this role continues to serve the Fourteenth Dalai Lama's government-in-exile. As for the Nechung deity—which can refer to an older figure named Pehar (Pe har) but more often his emanation Dorjé Drakden (Rdo rje grags ldan)—he has a mythic pedigree that can be traced back to Samyé (Bsam yas), Tibet's first Buddhist monastery. This center was established in the 8th century under the auspices of the Tibetan Buddhist emperor Trisong Deutsen (Khri srong lde'u btsan, 742–*c.* 800). As such, Nechung represents a confluence of Tibetan imperial power, the Dalai Lama's growing administration, and the most powerful of oracular offices. What follows is a concise history of Nechung's monastery, deity, and oracle, as well as their close ties to many of the important political and religious power brokers of Tibet.

A BRIEF HISTORY OF NECHUNG MONASTERY

Like many Tibetan monasteries, Nechung's origins are attributed to auspicious sights and prophetic revelation (see figure 1). According to oral tradition, the good omens and powerful topographical features of the land on which the monastery would later be founded were discussed by the great tantric master Padmasambhava and other important figures of the Tibetan Imperium in the 8th century:

> In the time of King Trisong Deutsen, the translator Vairocana once went to the place where Nechung Monastery would come to be located. There he saw various miraculous signs manifest around a birch tree, so he told master Padmasambhava about it. The master prophesied, "That birch tree is Pehar's soul tree (*bla shing*), and the pond nearby is Pehar's soul lake (*bla mtsho*).[1] In the future a monastery will appear at this place." Later, Prince Muné Tsenpo (Mu ne brtsan po; b.774)[2] established a small monastery at this site and placed four monks there. Samyé was known as the "Great Abode" (*gnas chen*) and so this area was called the "Small Abode" (*gnas chung*).[3]

During his brief kingship, Prince Muné Tsenpo was involved in several social projects that included the establishment and expansion of religious institutions.[4] However, an explicit connection to or mention of Nechung is otherwise not corroborated by Tibetan documents from the 8th to 9th century, texts from Dunhuang, or histories written shortly after the 11th century. Later written accounts of Nechung likewise fail to mention the presence of an ancient monastery at this site. Nevertheless, this oral account does provide one etiological explanation for the monastery's name of "Small Abode," contrasting it with the "Great Abode" of Samyé.

Figure 1. Nechung Monastery, Lhasa.
Source: Photo: Cecilia Haynes, 2011

Another etiology would be provided centuries later when Nechung was finally founded in the 16th century, though accounts of this event also have their inconsistencies.

René de Nebesky-Wojkowitz briefly records several different oral accounts for Nechung's founding, some of which diverge by centuries. By one popular account, Pehar had quarreled with the famed founder of the Tselpa Kagyü (Tshal pa bka' brgyud) subschool, named Lama Zhang (Bla ma zhang, 1123–1193), who responded by not allowing images of the deity to be painted among the murals in a new monastery he was establishing. In order to seek revenge, the deity took on the form of a young boy who aided the painters in their work. The painters wanted to reward the boy for his help, so he cryptically requested that they paint somewhere on the monastery walls the image of a monkey holding a lit stick of incense. The painters agreed to the strange request, and when the work on the monastery was completed, Pehar possessed the painting of the monkey and burned the monastery down with the incense stick. Understandably, Lama Zhang was outraged by this trick, so he trapped Pehar in a box through ritual means and threw him in the nearby Kyichu River (Skyid chu). Floating down the river as it flowed west along the south side of Lhasa, the trapped deity came close to Drepung Monastery, where an abbot there clairvoyantly foresaw his arrival and sent a young monk to retrieve him. As the monk was bringing the box back up the mountain to Drepung, it became supernaturally heavier, until the young monk—overpowered by its weight or his own curiosity—placed the box on a stone and opened it. Pehar immediately flew from the trap in the form of a bird and dissolved into a nearby tree, around which the Drepung abbot would build Nechung. Another account states that it was the Fifth Dalai Lama himself, not an abbot, who had Pehar retrieved and then founded the monastery.[5]

These accounts exhibit a number of discrepancies, the most glaring of which is that Drepung Monastery would not be founded until several centuries after Lama Zhang's death. It seems that a number of important figures and events were conflated around Pehar's exploits—the lineage of the Tselpa Kagyü, a Drepung abbot, and the Fifth Dalai Lama—all of which speak to a transfer of power and prestige. Guntram Hazod makes this argument specifically by claiming that Lama Zhang's presence in the oral account symbolically represents the Tselpa Kagyü community overall, and that it was a 16th-century Tselpa hierarch that disavowed Pehar. This allowed the deity to be adopted by the Gelukpa at Drepung. Pehar's transfer represents the waning of the Tselpa Kagyü's political and religious power and the waxing of the Geluk school at this time in Tibetan history.[6]

The earliest texts to discuss Nechung in detail and Pehar's role in the monastery's founding date to the turn of the 18th century. The first of these significant works is the *Nechung Record* (*Gnas chung dkar chag*), an inscription that was painted on the southern wall of Nechung's courtyard by the 1790s and composed by both the Fifth Dalai Lama and his final regent Sangyé Gyatso (1653–1705). The second work is the *Brief Hagiography of Jokpa Jangchup Penden*,[7] a text that is also attributed to Sangyé Gyatso and was likely composed a decade or so later.[8] In terms of compositional history and content, these two works are intimately linked and repeat some of the same information verbatim, but they also conflict on the details of Nechung's establishment. According to the *Nechung Record*, it was the Second Dalai Lama (1476–1542) who brought Pehar back from a monastery in Tsel (Tshal).[9] However, the *Brief Hagiography of Jokpa Jangchup Penden* claims with greater detail that the mystery abbot who foresaw Pehar's arrival was none other than the (likely) 16th-century founder and first abbot of Deyang College (Bde yangs grwa tshang) at Drepung, Jokpa Jangchup Penden (Lcog pa byang chub dpal ldan, 1404/1464–1471/1531).[10] This text provides much more information on Pehar's arrival below Drepung as well as the conversations the deity and abbot were said to have had. Once the two reached an accord, Jokpa Jangchup Penden commanded his patrons to "build a small abode (*gnas chung chung*) for my Dharma protector Pehar!"[11] This provides us with a second etiology for the monastery's name. While the text states that Nechung was founded in the Earth-Ox year, which would be 1529, there is a potential sixty-year discrepancy for Jokpa Jangchup Penden's dates. As such, it is possible that Nechung was founded earlier, in 1469, but the connection to the Second Dalai Lama in the *Nechung Record* makes the 16th-century date more likely.[12]

Interestingly, the soul tree and soul lake of the popular oral narrative are not discussed in Jokpa Jangchup Penden's hagiography, and missing from the narrative entirely is the stone on which a young monk places the box with Pehar trapped inside. Yet the soul lake has been revived, and early-20th-century photographs show the birch tree planted in the center of Nechung's courtyard. The tree was cut down during the Cultural Revolution and portions of its trunk and branches are stored in the back northwest shrine room of the monastery, where pilgrims place prayer scarves around it for blessings. Moreover, outside, and just west of Nechung's monastic compound, the stone on which the box was placed is still visible. When Pehar escaped the box as a bird, the young monk of the story is said to have cried out in contrition, "Lamakyen!" (*bla ma mkhyen*)—meaning "Lama, think of me!"—and the words miraculously appeared stamped into the stone. These words have since been painted to highlight the self-arising (*rang byung*) miracle they represent, and by 2014 a small shrine house was built around the stone. The physical evidence surrounding the monastery thus corroborates the oral account in some respects, while the earliest known textual evidence places Nechung's founding solidly in the 16th century, despite the discrepancies.

After securing temporal and religious authority in 1642 through the military aid of the Khoshut Mongolian ruler Güshi Khan (1582–1655), the Fifth Dalai Lama spent the next four decades consolidating Tibet and shoring up his nascent government.[13] Nechung was part of this political effort because the monastery too was renovated and expanded under the guidance of several ministers over the second half of the 17th century. This work and its culmination were recorded in the *Nechung Record*, which discusses the monastery's 1682 consecration. Other minor additions continued to be made over the next decade under the guidance of Sangyé Gyatso. While more additions would follow over the centuries and the monastic population would gradually increase to just over a hundred monks by the early 20th century, the monastery's appearance, size, and structure at the turn of the millennium is the result of this late-17th-century renovation. Its name was even expanded to Nechung Dorjé Drayangling (Gnas chung rdo rje sgra dbyangs gling), based on an expansive ritual text composed for Pehar by the Fifth Dalai Lama. From this time forward, Nechung would be intimately tied to the incarnation line of this religious leader.[14]

The historic site of Nechung outside Lhasa and its monastic and ritual activities were rent in two when the Fourteenth Dalai Lama went into self-imposed exile in 1959, followed by his government officials, the Nechung Oracle, and numerous other Tibetans. The Tibetan government-in-exile was established and settled in the northwestern Indian state of Himachal Pradesh, and this Central Tibetan Administration, called the Gangchen Kyishong (Gangs can skyid gshongs)—literally, "Delightful Valley of the Snowy Land"—came to be situated between the city of Dharamsala and the uphill suburb of McLeod Ganj in the Himalayan foothills. A new Nechung Monastery likewise began to develop along with the Dalai Lama's administration and other monastic institutions. This Nechung was temporarily located in an Indian house in Dharamsala before land for the new monastery was granted by the government-in-exile. Residences for the monks were built in the late 1970s and construction on the monastery proper began in May 1981. The Indian Nechung Dorjé Drayangling ('Phags yul gnas chung rdo rje sgra dbyangs gling), as it is called, was built within the compound of the Gangchen Kyishong and completed inMarch 1984. The formal consecration took place on March 31, 1985, and was presided over by the Fourteenth Dalai Lama. The Indian Nechung (see figure 2) is only a minute's walk downhill from the Library of Tibetan Works and Archives, and just past the aptly named Nechung Cafe. By the end of the 20th century both the historic Nechung and the Indian Nechung had come to house monastic communities that regularly perform ritual ceremonies. However, while the Nechung in Tibet possesses the mythic sites and objects so indicative of the historic relationship between Pehar and the Dalai Lamas, the present Nechung Oracle and Fourteenth Dalai Lama live in exile, paticipating in the vibrant centuries-old rituals and trance sessions in India. Like so many other Tibetan religious institutions, Nechung's history and activity have been split across countries.

THE MYTHIC LIVES OF THE PROTECTOR PEHAR

While Nechung is used as a shorthand in texts and in conversation to refer to the deity that possesses the Nechung Oracle, this figure is either the protector Pehar (see figure 3) or one of

Figure 2. Nechung Monastery, Gangchen Kyishong, Dharamsala.
Source: Photo: Cecilia Haynes, 2012

Figure 3. Pehar; Nechung Monastery assembly hall, Lhasa.
Source: Photo: Cecilia Haynes, 2011

his emanations, specifically his minister Dorjé Drakden. Like most divinities, there is not one comprehensive account of Pehar's biography. However, the closest is the chapter on the deity found in an extensive compilation of protector hagiographies entitled the *Ocean of Oath-Bound Guardians of the Teachings*, which was composed in 1734 by Lelung Jedrung Zhepé Dorjé (Sle lung rje drung bzhad pa'i rdo rje, 1697–1740), half a century after Nechung's renovation.[15] Prior to this work, Pehar's mythic details were scattered across various ritual texts, histories, and biographies. Although it lacks the details on Pehar's time at Samyé and eventual transfer to Nechung, Lelung's text is nonetheless fairly comprehensive in citing works on the deity's legendary origins and often quotes them verbatim. These works include important Nyingma treasure texts (*gter ma*) and biographies, such as the *Ten Point Sādhana*,[16] revealed by Nyangrel Nyima Özer (Nyang ral nyi ma 'od zer, 1124–1192), and the *Chronicle of Padmasambhava* (*Padma bka' thang*), revealed by Ogyan Lingpa (O rgyan gling pa, b. 1323).[17] Lelung also cites works either no longer extant or not accessible to nonpractitioners. One such work is the *White Crystal Rosary* (*Shel phreng dkar po*), a 12th-century treasure text likewise revealed by Nyangrel Nyima Özer and kept secret by monks at both the Tibetan and Indian Nechung Monasteries. This inaccessible text seems to be exclusively focused on Pehar's mythos; not only is it cited frequently by Lelung, the Fifth Dalai Lama was clearly familiar with the work and it was quoted extensively in an early-17th-century Sakya history of Samyé entitled the *Symphony of the Captivating Gods*.[18]

By exploring the narrative elements found within these texts, as well as in the *Nechung Record* and the *Brief Hagiography of Jokpa Jangchup Penden*, a clearer image of Pehar's life comes into focus. The deity's past lives and adventures can be divided into three major periods: (a) Pehar's lives before Tibet; (b) his establishment as Samyé's guardian; and (c) his transfer to Nechung. For the first and most diverse period, Pehar's journey begins with a past life many eons ago, when he was a devout king who chose to study under a religious master alongside his equally devout friend and minister. However, while the minister properly understood the essence of the teachings, the king did not, and his vows quickly regressed. After a brief tryst with a Brahmin's daughter, the king was admonished by his former friend for going back on his religious commitments, and in anger the king spent lifetimes seeking revenge against the minister. The king would transform into various animals, such as a snow lion, a boar, or a marmot, in order to attack his friend or disrupt his meditative practices. For each attempt, however, the great tantric deity Vajrapāṇi would subdue the vindictive king.

After lifetimes spent in Buddhist hells, the king was reborn several times into various demonic families before eventually making his way to a meditation center in Mongolia, near modern-day Qinghai Lake. Acting as the protector deity for this site, legend claims that he was eventually captured by King Trisong Deutsen's military forces and brought back to central Tibet in the 8th century. After being further subjugated by the great tantric master Padmasambhava, the spirit was named Pehar and entrusted with guarding Samyé Monastery's treasures, thus beginning the second period of the deity's mythic existence. Many of these narrative vignettes are also vividly illustrated on murals painted inside the Tsangpa Chapel (Tshangs pa lcog) of Meru Sarpa Monastery (Rme ru gsar pa) in Lhasa.[19]

While accounts are vague or conflicting, Pehar appears to hold his post at Samyé for several centuries before migrating to the region of Tsel, southeast of Lhasa, where he acted as guardian of the Kagyü hierarchs there for a time. Here the third period of Pehar's mythos intersects with the prophetic origins of Nechung, as discussed in the monastery's brief history. In the 16th century, either because he angered a Tselpa hierarch or encountered the Second Dalai Lama, or possibly both, Pehar traveled along the Kyichu River until he ended up in the foothills below Drepung. The abbot Jokpa Jangchup Penden then had servants retrieve the deity and build Pehar his "small abode" in exchange for his fealty. From then on Pehar has served the Geluk school—though not exclusively—as well as the Dalai Lamas' government from his palace of Nechung.[20]

Once at the monastery Pehar also began possessing the Nechung Oracle, giving prophecies through the generations of human mediums who held the office. While multiple deities can possess oracles in a given trance session, each is known for the particular deity who most frequently possesses them. At some point—possibly at the turn of the 18th century—Pehar ceased to be the primary deity to possess the Nechung Oracle and instead one of his emanations named Dorjé Drakden (see figure 4) took on the role. According to the major liturgical texts associated with Nechung, Dorjé Drakden is technically the minister of Kyechik Marpo (Skyes gcig dmar po), one of the four spirits believed to emanate from Pehar. With Pehar as their leader, these deities are collectively known as the five king spirits (Rgyal po sku lnga) and since Dorjé Drakden comes from one of them, he is considered a secondary emanation. While the process of how or why he came to eclipse Pehar in relation to the Nechung Oracle is unclear, whenever Nechung is used as a label for the oracle-possessing deity, it usually refers to this once-minor spirit.[21]

Figure 4. Dorjé Drakden; Meru Nyingpa Monastery assembly hall, Lhasa.
Source: Photo: Cecilia Haynes, 2011

THE STATE ORACLE OF TIBET

The Nechung Oracle has existed as a distinct office since at least the 16th century; however, the label itself does not translate a specific Tibetan term. A human medium is usually referred to as a "physical vessel" or *kuten* (*sku rten*), so the present Nechung medium, Tupten Ngödrup (Thub bstan dngos grub), is often called Nechung Kuten (Gnas chung sku rten) as an honorific title. Once in a trance, however, the person of the medium is believed to be absent altogether and replaced by the dharma protector (*chos skyong*) himself. As such, when the Nechung Oracle is quoted in texts, they are referred to generically—and sometimes vaguely—as the Nechung Dharma Protector (Gnas chung chos skyong), and only the context helps clarify that it is the deity speaking through the oracle in that instance. Regardless, this figure's rise and importance are intimately linked with the lineage of the Dalai Lamas, and he continues to be consulted for clairvoyant advice by the present incarnation and the Tibetan administration.

The earliest known reference to the Nechung Oracle is in a 1560 biography of the Second Dalai Lama, where the oracle is consulted shortly after the religious master's death in 1542.[22] This strongly implies that the Dalai Lama and the oracle had a relationship preceding this time; the Second Dalai Lama's own rites to Pehar, as well as later references to the two figures in Nechung's founding narratives, also accord with this assessment. Less than half a century later, the Nechung Oracle is mentioned again in a famous history of Altan Khan called the *Jewel Translucent Sutra*, composed in 1607. In this work, the Nechung Oracle is consulted a number of times by the Third Dalai Lama between 1575 and 1578 as he was deciding whether or not to accept the Khan's invitation to Mongolia. At Pehar's urging through the oracle, the Dalai Lama was galvanized to accept the invitation and a historic relationship was forged between the Mongolian ruler and the religious master.[23]

Beyond these two sources there is little to no mention of the Nechung Oracle in the historical record until the time of the Fifth Dalai Lama, and it is unsurprising that the deity and his medium are markedly present in this important figure's extensive writings. After achieving temporal and religious power over Tibet in 1642, the Fifth Dalai Lama and his regents spent the next forty years consolidating his power politically, economically, and ritually. Nechung was part of this expansive process since the monastery was renovated, the deity was advanced as one of the major protectors of the Dalai Lama's lineage, and the medium was promoted to state oracle. This endeavor also involved standardizing and promoting the Dalai Lama's own mythic heritage as a great incarnation and emanation of the bodhisattva Avalokiteśvara, and the Great Fifth's final regent Sangyé Gyatso was particularly adept at this.[24] This standardization included the Fifth Dalai Lama composing the biography of his third incarnation in 1646, in which there is a noticeable advancement in the relationship between the Dalai Lama and Pehar. Indeed, their friendship appears to strengthen significantly following the Second Dalai Lama's death. Before being reborn as the Third Dalai Lama, the biography claims that the religious master visited many heavenly realms while in the intermediate state. At one point, he came into the presence of Padmasambhava, where he encountered Pehar and the enlightened goddess Penden Lhamo (Dpal ldan lha mo), the other major protector of the Dalai Lamas. The following account of their interaction was spoken by Pehar through the Nechung Oracle to the Third Dalai Lama, as recorded in his biography, and was considered important enough to repeat in the *Nechung Record*:[25]

> In the center of the lotus at the heart of the 1002 Buddhas there is Padmasambhava. When we were in the Lotus Light Palace at the peak of the glorious Copper-colored Mountain, Padmasambhava instructed us to act for the improvement of the Buddha's teachings. That is to say, the Incarnate One Meaningful to Behold [the Dalai Lama],[26] through pacifying and augmenting means, performs activities that protect those who bear the Buddha's teachings; [while] I, the King Spirit Pehar, through subjugating and destructive means, accomplish activities that clear away discordant conditions and that bring about concordant conditions for him. Accordingly, both of us must also act for the improvement of the Buddha's teachings. Please consider this! In particular, Padmasambhava gave the enemies' flesh, blood, life essence, and life breath to me as food rations. For my allotted work, he entrusted me with protecting the Buddha's teachings, as well as the bearers of those teachings. Because of this, I have also never transgressed Padmasambhava's commands in the past. Again and again, I have not transgressed [his commands]. So, if there are obstacles to the activities that the One Meaningful to Behold performs in his lifetime, I will clear them away. I will accomplish all the concordant conditions! If there are harmful demons and obstructing spirits, human beings and inhuman spirits are not suitable [for dealing with them] unless they are included among the haughty ones, the eight classes of gods and spirits of the phenomenal world. I am the overlord of all eight classes, the king who is the embodiment of the haughty ones. What demons and obstructing spirits could transgress my command?

This interaction provides some insight into Pehar's character and how he views his relationship to the Dalai Lama, which is portrayed almost symbiotically; the Dalai Lama protects and promotes the Buddhist teachings through pacific means while Pehar does so through wrathful means. Shortly after this encounter, Pehar is assigned to the Dalai Lama as a special protector, and their bond is cemented from then on. The Fifth Dalai Lama extensively discusses Pehar in his ritual and biographical works, and he was even encouraged by the deity through the oracle to compose his highly detailed autobiography.[27] It is no surprise that the deity and his monastery rose so rapidly in importance at this time. As indicative of this heightened prestige, a mural of Lobzang Lekjor (Blo bzang legs 'byor) graces one side of the entryway within Nechung's assembly hall (see figure 5). This wasthe Nechung medium active when the monastery's renovations were completed at the end of the 17th century.

A more consistent lineage of Nechung Oracles would continue from this time forward, with some mediums being more effective than others. For instance, the medium Kelzang Tsültrim (Bskal bzang tshul khrims) channeled the Nechung Oracle in the mid-19th century when the deity requested that the monastery's liturgy be updated and consolidated. This resulted in the 1845 edition of Nechung's liturgical corpus that still acts as the ritual foundation for the monastery, both outside Lhasa and in exile. The next medium, Śākya Yarpel (Śākya yar 'phel), served as the Nechung Oracle the longest; he was active during the entire life of the Twelfth Dalai Lama and for much of the Thirteenth. He is also credited with having saved the Tibetan government from civil unrest, warned the Thirteenth Dalai Lama of numerous dangers, and helped strengthen the religious leader's institutional clout after a string of ineffective Dalai Lamas. For this reason, a mural of Śākya Yarpel graces the other side of Nechung Monastery's entrance within the assembly hall (see figure 6).[28] It was the medium Lobzang

Figure 5. The Nechung Oracle Lobzang Lekjor (17th century) in a trance; Nechung Monastery assembly hall, Lhasa.
Source: Photo: Cecilia Haynes, 2011

Figure 6. The Nechung Oracle Śākya Yarpel (19th century) in a trance; Nechung Monastery Assembly Hall, Lhasa.
Source: Photo: Christopher Bell, 2011

Jikmé (Blo bzang 'jigs med) who went into self-imposed exile with the Fourteenth Dalai Lama in 1959, and it is the present medium, Tupten Ngödrup, that serves him and the Tibetan government-in-exile from the Nechung Monastery established in Dharamsala. While the ineage of oracles has moved beyond Tibet, the relationship between the deity that possesses him and the Dalai Lama that consults him has remained strong.

Table 1 provides a list of the seventeen known mediums to have taken on the office of the Nechung Oracle since at least the 17th century:[29]

	Nechung Mediums	Installation	Resignation
1.	Lobzang Penden (Blo bzang dpal ldan)	Unknown	Unknown
2.	Jampa Gyatso (Byams pa rgya mtsho)	Unknown	Unknown
3.	Nangso Gönor (Nang so dgos nor)	Unknown	1647
4.	Sepo Sönam (Sras po bsod nams)	1647	1677 [?]
5a.	Unnamed medium, monastic secretary	1677 [?]	1678
5b.	Tsewang Pelwar (Tshe dbang dpal dbar)	1678	1689
6.	Kongpo Lobzang Lekjor (Kong po blo bzang legs 'byor)	1690	Unknown
7.	Tsangyang Tamdrin (Tshangs dbyangs rta mgrin)	1725	1747
8.	Ngawang Gyatso (Ngag dbang rgya mtsho)	1747	Unknown
9.	Yuloköpa (G.yu lo bkod pa)	Unknown	Unknown
10.	Kelzang Tsültrim (Bskal bzang tshul khrims)[30]	1837	1856
11.	Śākya Yarpel (Śākya yar 'phel)	1856	1900
12.	Lobzang Sönam (Blo bzang bsod nams)	1901	Unknown
13.	Gyentsen Tarchin (Rgyal mtshan mthar phyin)	1913	1915
14.	Lobzang Sönam [installed a second time]	Unknown	1936
15.	Lobzang Namgyel (Blo bzang rnam rgyal)[31]	1934/1936	1944
16.	Lobzang Jikmé (Blo bzang 'jigs med)	1945	1984
17.	Tupten Ngödrup (Thub bstan dngos grub)[32]	1987/1988	Present

NECHUNG'S MONASTIC *MAṆḌALA*

Nechung has an important connection to the Dalai Lamas, the Geluk tradition, and Tibetan Buddhist history overall. The monastery is ecumenical in nature, with a liturgical corpus containing Nyingma, Sakya, and Geluk rituals; the deity's mythic heritage is rooted in Tibet's imperial past; and the medium is the head state oracle of the Dalai Lama's government, a position the office has held since the 17th century. Nechung's institutional clout radiates throughout Tibet's historic capital of Lhasa and beyond as well. In keeping with the religious site's growing power, several monasteries and temples within Lhasa have been brought into its ritual orbit from the 17th century onward. Monasteries near Lhasa, like Tsel Yangön (Tshal yang dgon) and Gadong (Dga' gdong), as well as chapels in the city center, like Karmasha (Karma shag btsan khang), and Banakzhöl (Sbra nag zhol rgyal khang), all have emanations of Pehar as their central protector or otherwise have a connection to the deity. Meru Nyingpa Monastery (Rme ru snying pa), which lies in the center of Lhasa's old town just behind the famed Jokhang

Temple (Jo khang), likewise acts as a satellite for Nechung, whose oracle and monks would historically reside there during important holidays, especially around the Tibetan New Year. These sacred centers also share and reproduce many of Nechung's liturgical and iconographic elements, and such institutional resonances can be found in monasteries across Tibet as well as beyond the plateau. For instance, the monastery re-established in Dharamsala has its own satellites further abroad, with several Nechung centers founded across the United States.[33] This constellation of interconnected sites near and far acts as a concentric array of ritual power suggestive of a *maṇḍala*, but one securing the mundane concerns of state control and centralization rather than transcendent enlightenment. Given their close mythic and institutional connection, Nechung's rise has mirrored that of the Dalai Lamas, such that the vagaries of the oracle's influence often reflected those of the incarnate master's lineage. The monastery, deity, and oracle of Nechung are inseparably connected, and they are all closely bound to the history of the Dalai Lamas and Tibet as a whole.

DISCUSSION OF THE LITERATURE

Nechung has been the focus of few significant works of scholarship. René de Nebesky-Wojkowitz's *Oracles and Demons of Tibet* was the first work to provide consistent details on Pehar and the Nechung Oracle.[34] His chapter on Pehar draws from diverse sources to provide the deity's basic mythos and iconography, while the chapter on the Nechung Oracle discusses this figure's general attributes and offers some contemporary historical information. Both chapters are a necessary starting point for exploring the rise of Nechung's cult, though they lack a detailed examination of the deity's ritual and historical development. The first monograph to give serious attention to Nechung Monastery is Franco Ricca's *Il Tempio Oracolare di gNas-chuṅ*.[35] This work primarily concerns the architectural and iconographic qualities of the monastery, focusing on the significance of Nechung's numerous murals. The book's architectural diagrams and floor plans are especially valuable, as are the accompanying photographs and extensive lists of deities.

Anthropologist Urmila Nair focused her graduate work on examining Nechung's rituals in exile at the Nechung Monastery re-established in Dharamsala. Her master's thesis presents a sociological examination of Pehar's ontological status, while her dissertation explores Nechung's contemporary ritual performances; both works draw from her extensive ethnographic research.[36] Although Nair's portrayal of Nechung's history in Tibet is compressed and based solely on Nebesky-Wojkowitz's account, her work offers a vivid portrait of the monastery in Dharamsala and presents an extensive discussion of its ritual practices. Beyond these works, the most comprehensive study of Nechung in a Western language is Christopher Bell's *The Dalai Lama and the Nechung Oracle*.[37] This article summarizes content from Bell's book, which attempts to present a fuller picture of Pehar and Nechung Monastery's mythic origins, ritual evolution, and institutional development by drawing and expanding on pertinent primary documents and ethnographic observations.

Several modern works of Tibetan-language scholarship also serve as useful resources for understanding the cult of Pehar and the deity's place at Nechung. In the mid-1980s, a team of Tibetan scholars conducted an extensive survey of Drepung Monastery for the purposes of cultural preservation. This included transcribing the registers of the monastery's colleges, as well as documenting their histories, abbatial lineages, and sacred contents. Nechung Monastery was included in this endeavor due to its close historical ties with and physical proximity to Drepung, so the survey provides many of Nechung's historical details. This material on Drepung and Nechung was subsequently published by the Tibetan Academy of Social Sciences in 2009.[38] This is the first modern work in Tibetan to extensively discuss Nechung Monastery, its contents, and its deity.

Since the turn of the millennium, there has also been a steady accumulation of publications in Dharamsala concerning Nechung, either produced by the monastery itself or the Central Tibetan Administration. Two publications were produced in 2004 alone, one detailing Pehar's relationship with the Dalai Lamas and the other exploring the historical significance of an important Nechung festival.[39] The most extensive Tibetan monograph to focus on Nechung, which draws heavily from both of these works as well as older primary sources, is the *All-Illuminating Moon: A Dharma History of Nechung Dorjé Drayangling*,[40] composed by the late Venerable Tupten Püntsok (Thub bstan phun tshogs) and published in 2007.[41] This work provides a history of both Nechung Monastery in Tibet and the one established in Dharamsala, making it a uniquely comprehensive text; it also offers the first lengthy history of the Nechung Oracle. The final Tibetan source that merits mentioning is Mikmar Tsering's *Nechung Monastery: The Meaningful-to-Behold Record of Nechung Dorjé Drayangling, a Pleasant Grove Where Subjugation and Destruction Manifest*.[42] This is a shorter work than Tupten Püntsok's; however, it is distinct for being a bilingual book that presents the details of Nechung's history in Tibetan and Chinese. This work was published in Lhasa and reiterates much of the material collected by the Tibetan Academy of Social Sciences, where Mikmar Tsering once worked, though it also contains additional content collected by the author as well as his own valuable observations.

PRIMARY SOURCES

A myes zhabs ngag dbang kun dga' bsod nams. *Dpal bsam yas lhun gyi grub pa'i gtsug lhag khang chen po bka' srung dang bcas pa'i byon tshul legs par bshad pa chos skyong yid bzhin nor bu dges par byed pa'i yid 'phrog lha'i rol mo dgos 'dod kun 'byung*. In *Dpal sa ska pa chen po sngags 'chang thams cad mkhyen pa ngag dbang kun dga' bsod nams kyi gsung 'bum*, Amézhap Ngawang Künga Sönam, Vol. 4, 338–431. Kathmandu, Nepal: Sa skya rgyal yongs gsung rab slob gnyer khang, 2000. Originally published in 1633.

Department of Religion and Culture. *Rgyal ba'i bstan srung gnas chung sprul pa'i chos rgyal chen po'i rtogs brjod lha yi rol mo dam can dgyes pa'i sgra dbyangs*. Dharamsala, India: CTA, Gangchen Kyishong, 2004.

Mig dmar tshe ring, Gra bzhi. *Gnas chung dgon (乃琼寺): Dbang drag rol pa'i dga' tshal gnas chung rdo rje sgra dbyangs gling gi dkar chag mthong ba don ldan*. Lhasa, China: Bod ljongs mi dmangs dpe skrun khang, 2010.

Mnga' bdag nyang ral nyi ma 'od zer. *Rgyal po chen po sku lnga'i gsol mchod 'phrin las don bcu ma*. In *The Collected Works of Liturgy of the Gnas-chuṅ Rdo-rje-sgra-dbyaṅs-gliṅ Monastery: Reproduced from Blockprints from Gnas-chuṅ and Other Tibetan Establishments*, ed. Lobzang Tondan, Vol. 1, 53–75. Delhi: Lobzang Tondan, 1983.

Nechung Monastery. *Dus gsum rgyal ba thams cad kyi gno bo ma hā gu ru padma saṃ bha ba'i sku'i 'khrungs skar sprel lo sprel zla tshes bcu'i dus chen ngo sprod dang/ o rgyan las rab gling pa'i gter byon gu ru'i sku tshab mthong grol yid bzhin nor bu lha ldan du ji ltar gdan drangs tshul/*

gnas chung chos rgyal chen po'i rtogs brjod bsdus pa bcas phyogs gcig gces bsdebs. Dharamsala, India: Nechung Monastery, 2004.

Sle lung rje drung bzhad pa'i rdo rje. *Dam can bstan srung rgya mtsho'i rnam par thar pa cha shas tsam brjod pa sngon med legs bshad*, vol. 2. *Smanrtsis Shesrig Spedzod*, vol. 105. Leh, India: T. S. Tashigang, 1979. Originally published in 1734.

Thub bstan phun tshogs. *Gnas chung rdo rje sgra dbyangs gling gi chos 'byung kun gsal chu shel dbang po*. Dharamsala, India: Nechung Monastery, 2007.

Tibetan Academy of Social Sciences, ed. *Dpal ldan 'bras spungs dgon gyi dkar chag dri med dwangs gsal shel gyi me long*. Beijing: Krung go'i bod rig pa dpe skrun khang, 2009.

DIGITAL MATERIALS

Nechung Buddhist Center (http://nechungbuddhistcenter.org/). This is the website for the Nechung Buddhist Center established in San Francisco in 1999.

Nechung Dharmapala Center (http://www.nechungla.org/). This is the site for the Nechung Dharmapala Center founded in Los Angeles in 2010.

Nechung Dorje Drayang Ling (http://www.nechung.org/). This is the site for Nechung Dorje Drayang Ling, Wood Valley Temple and Retreat, the first US-based branch for Nechung, established in Pahala, Hawaii, in 1973.

Nechung Foundation (http://nechungfoundation.org/). This is the site for the New York City branch of Nechung Monastery, founded in 1994.

Tibet Album (https://tibet.prm.ox.ac.uk/). The Tibet Album, established by the Pitt Rivers Museum at the University of Oxford, houses and digitally preserves British photography in central Tibet from 1920 to 1950.

FURTHER READING

Bell, Christopher. "The Nechung Record." *Revue d'Etudes Tibétaines* 36 (2016): 143–249.

Bell, Christopher. "The Brief Hagiography of Jokpa Jangchup Penden." *Revue d'Etudes Tibétaines* 54 (2020): 147–195.

Bell, Christopher. *The Dalai Lama and the Nechung Oracle*. New York: Oxford University Press, 2021.

Nair, Urmila. *The Sociological Inflection of Ontology: A Study of the Multiple Ontological Statuses of a Tibetan Buddhist Protective Deity*. Master's thesis, University of Chicago, 2004.

Nair, Urmila. *When the Sun's Rays Are as Shadows: The Nechung Rituals and the Politics of Spectacle in Tibetan Exile*. PhD diss., University of Chicago, 2010.

Nebesky-Wojkowitz, René de. *Oracles and Demons of Tibet: The Cult and Iconography of the Tibetan Protective Deities*. New Delhi: Paljor, 1998. Originally published in 1956.

Ricca, Franco. *Il Tempio Oracolare di gNas-chuṅ: Gli Dei del Tibet più Magico e Segreto*. Alessandria, Italy: Edizioni dell'Orso, 1999.

NOTES

1. After the Cultural Revolution (1966–1976) this small pond was apparently filled in and lay housing was built on top of it. In an effort to regain some of the sacredness of the site, the housing was removed between 2007 and 2010 and a small paved-in pond was installed. The now-enclosed site of the soul lake is just northwest of the monastery proper and a minute's walk uphill.
2. This was the first of Trisong Deutsen's sons to succeed him, though his reign did not last long; see Per Sørensen, *Tibetan Buddhist Historiography: The Mirror Illuminating the Royal Genealogies, an Annotated*

Translation of the XIVth Century Tibetan Chronicle: rGyal- rabs gsal-ba'i me-long (Wiesbaden, Germany: Harrassowitz Verlag, 1994), 404–407.

3. See Mig dmar tshe ring, Gra bzhi, *Gnas chung dgon* (乃琼寺): *Dbang drag rol pa'i dga' tshal gnas chung rdo rje sgra dbyangs gling gi dkar chag mthong ba don ldan* (Lhasa, China: Bod ljongs mi dmangs dpe skrun khang, 2010), 12; see also Thub bstan phun tshogs, *Gnas chung rdo rje sgra dbyangs gling gi chos 'byung kun gsal chu shel dbang po* (Dharamsala, India: Nechung Monastery, 2007), 3, and Tibetan Academy of Social Sciences, ed., *Dpal ldan 'bras spungs dgon gyi dkar chag dri med dwangs gsal shel gyi me long* (Beijing: Krung go'i bod rig pa dpe skrun khang, 2009), 439.
4. See Sørensen, *Tibetan Buddhist Historiography*, 404–407.
5. See René de Nebesky-Wojkowitz, *Oracles and Demons of Tibet: The Cult and Iconography of the Tibetan Protective Deities* (New Delhi: Paljor, 1998), 104–106.
6. See Per Sørensen, Guntram Hazod, and Tsering Gyalbo, *Rulers on the Celestial Plain: Ecclesiastic and Secular Hegemony in Medieval Tibet: A Study of Tshal Gung-thang*, 2 vols. (Vienna: Verlag der Österreichischen Akademie der Wissenschaften, 2007), vol. 2, 627–628, see also vol. 1, 51, 216–217.
7. The full title of this work is the *Brief Hagiography of Jokpa Jangchup Pendenpa along with the Origins of the Great Dharma Protector* (*Lcog pa byang chub dpal ldan pa'i rnam thar rags bsdus chos skyong chen po'i 'byung khungs dang bcas pa*).
8. For complete translations and transcriptions of both texts, see Christopher Bell, "The Nechung Record," *Revue d'Etudes Tibétaines* 36 (2016): 143–249; Christopher Bell, "The Brief Hagiography of Jokpa Jangchup Penden," *Revue d'Etudes Tibétaines* 54 (2020): 147–195.
9. See Bell, "The Nechung Record," 168, 187–188.
10. See Bell, "The Brief Hagiography."
11. Bell, "The Brief Hagiography," 166.
12. For a discussion of Jokpa Jangchup Penden's conflicting dates, as well as the date for Nechung's founding, see Bell, "The Brief Hagiography," 148–149, 162–166; see also Sørensen, Hazod, and Gyalbo, *Rulers on the Celestial Plain*, vol. 1, 217n572.
13. For extensive and diverse explorations of this process, see Françoise Pommaret, ed., *Lhasa in the Seventeenth Century: The Capital of the Dalai Lamas*, trans. Howard Solverson (Leiden, The Netherlands: Brill, 2003).
14. For a detailed exploration of the Fifth Dalai Lama's involvement in Nechung's renovation and the religious mechanisms he and future incarnations utilized, see Christopher Bell, *The Dalai Lama and the Nechung Oracle* (New York: Oxford University Press, 2021).
15. The full title of this work is the *Unprecedented Elegant Explanation Briefly Expounding the Hagiographies and Iconographies of the Ocean of Oath-Bound Guardians of the Teachings* (*Dam can bstan srung rgya mtsho'i rnam par thar pa cha shas tsam brjod pa sngon med legs bshad*); for the chapter on Pehar, see Sle lung rje drung bzhad pa'i rdo rje, *Dam can bstan srung rgya mtsho'i rnam par thar pa cha shas tsam brjod pa sngon med legs bshad*, vol. 2. *Smanrtsis Shesrig Spedzod*, vol. 105 (Leh, India: T. S. Tashigang, 1979), 36–53.
16. The full title of this work is the *Ten-Chapter Sādhana: A Supplication Offering to the Five Great King Spirits* (*Rgyal po chen po sku lnga'i gsol mchod 'phrin las don bcu ma*); see Mnga' bdag nyang ral nyi ma 'od zer, *Rgyal po chen po sku lnga'i gsol mchod 'phrin las don bcu ma*, in *The Collected Works of Liturgy of the Gnas-chuṅ Rdo-rje-sgra-dbyaṅs-gliṅ Monastery: Reproduced from Blockprints from Gnas-chuṅ and Other Tibetan Establishments*, ed. Lobzang Tondan, Vol. 1 (Delhi: Lobzang Tondan, 1983), 53–75.
17. See O rgyan gling pa, *Padma bka' thang* (Chengdu, China: Si khron mi rigs dpe skrun khang, 1996).
18. The full title of this work is the *Symphony of the Captivating Gods That Grants All Desires and Makes the Wish-Fulfilling Dharma Protectors Rejoice: A Good Explanation for the Origins of the Great Monastery of Glorious and Spontaneously Present Samyé and Its Guardians of the Teachings* (*Dpal bsam yas lhun gyi grub pa'i gtsug lhag khang chen po bka' srung dang bcas pa'i byon tshul legs par bshad pa chos skyong yid bzhin nor bu dges par byed pa'i yid 'phrog lha'i rol mo dgos 'dod kun 'byung*), and it was composed by Amézhap Ngawang Künga Sönam (*A myes zhabs ngag dbang kun dga' bsod nams*, 1597–1659); see A myes zhabs ngag dbang kun dga' bsod nams, *Dpal*

bsam yas lhun gyi grub pa'i gtsug lhag khang chen po bka' srung dang bcas pa'i byon tshul legs par bshad pa chos skyong yid bzhin nor bu dges par byed pa'i yid 'phrog lha'i rol mo dgos 'dod kun 'byung, in *Dpal sa ska pa chen po sngags 'chang thams cad mkhyen pa ngag dbang kun dga' bsod nams kyi gsung 'bum*, Amézhap Ngawang Künga Sönam, Vol. 4 (Kathmandu, Nepal: Sa skya rgyal yongs gsung rab slob gnyer khang, 2000), 338–431.

19. See Christopher Bell, "The Mythic Murals of Meru Sarpa," *Orientations* 48, no. 1 (2017): 44–52.
20. This mythic material is summarized from A myes zhabs ngag dbang kun dga' bsod nams, *Dpal bsam*, 402–416; Sle lung rje drung bzhad pa'i rdo rje, *Dam can bstan*, 36–53; and Bell, "The Nechung Record," 165–168. See also Thub bstan phun tshogs, *Gnas chung rdo rje sgra dbyangs*, 3–5. For a detailed exploration of Pehar's mythos and an extensive analysis of it, see Bell, *The Dalai Lama and the Nechung Oracle*, 24–68.
21. For a fuller discussion of Dorjé Drakden's role and growth in popularity, see Bell, *The Dalai Lama and the Nechung Oracle*, 90–96.
22. See Sku sger yig tshang, ed., *'Phags pa 'jig rten dbang phyug gi rnam sprul rim byon gyi 'khrungs rabs deb ther nor bu'i phreng ba*, Vol. 1 (Dharamsala, India: Sku sger yig tshang, 1977), 621–622. While the day itself is not specified, the oracular consultation occurred between the eighth and eighteenth day of the third month of the Water-Tiger year (1542); for the year, see 617. The Second Dalai Lama himself passed away on the night between the seventh and eighth day of the same month and year; see 628.
23. See Johan Elverskog, *The Jewel Translucent Sutra: Altan Khan and the Mongols in the Sixteenth Century* (Leiden, The Netherlands: Brill, 2003), 143–145, 151–155.
24. See, for instance, Saṅs-rGyas rGya-mTSHo, *Life of the Fifth Dalai Lama: Volume IV, Part I*, trans. Zahiruddin Ahmad (New Delhi: International Academy of Indian Culture and Aditya Prakashan, 1999).
25. See Tā la'i bla ma 05 Ngag dbang blo bzang rgya mtsho, *Rje btsun thams cad mkhyen pa bsod nams rgya mtsho'i rnam thar dngos grub rgya mtsho'i shing rta* (Dolanji, India: Tashi Dorje, 1982), 121–122. For the *Nechung Record* excerpt, see Bell, "The Nechung Record," 190–191.
26. Tib. *Sprul sku mthong ba don ldan*. This is an epithet for the Dalai Lamas often used by the Nechung Oracle; see Urmila Nair, *When the Sun's Rays Are as Shadows: The Nechung Rituals and the Politics of Spectacle in Tibetan Exile* (PhD diss., University of Chicago, 2010), 123.
27. See Samten Karmay, trans., *The Illusive Play: The Autobiography of the Fifth Dalai Lama* (Chicago: Serindia, 2014), 18.
28. For more details on these and other Nechung mediums, see Bell, *The Dalai Lama and the Nechung Oracle*, 185–189.
29. This list is reproduced from Bell, *The Dalai Lama and the Nechung Oracle*, 184–185, which was in turn adapted and updated from Thub bstan phun tshogs, *Gnas chung*, 138.
30. Nebesky-Wojkowitz, *Oracles and Demons of Tibet*, 450–453, attempted to uncover the names of the last several Nechung mediums over the course of his research, relying on oral accounts from his Tibetan contacts. He was told of a medium during the Twelfth Dalai Lama's time named Ngag dbang, which could have been an alternative name for Kelzang Tsültrim. Nebesky-Wojkowitz seems to also conflate this figure with Śākya Yarpel in terms of timing, despite being familiar with the latter figure.
31. According to Hugh Richardson, Lobzang Namgyel was installed as the Nechung Oracle in 1934 rather than 1936; see the Tibet Album, "Nechung Oracle in Trance for the Sertreng Festival," Pitt Rivers Museum, 2006.
32. Photographs of the last three Nechung Oracles are available in Thub bstan phun tshogs, *Gnas chung*, 286–288 (these pages are unnumbered and are found in the photographs section at the end of the book). According to the Nechung Foundation, a New York branch office for the Nechung Monastery in Dharamsala chaired by Tupten Ngödrup, the latter was enthroned as the medium in 1988 rather than 1987; see Nechung Foundation, "The Nechung Oracle (Kuten-la)," 2019.
33. The first US center, named Nechung Dorje Drayang Ling, was established in Pahala, Hawaii. According to their website, their temple was founded in 1973. Other US centers for Nechung include the Nechung

Foundation in New York City, founded in 1994 by the Fourteenth Dalai Lama, the Nechung Buddhist Center in San Francisco, founded in 1999 by the present Nechung Oracle Tupten Ngödrup, and the Nechung Dharmapala Center in Los Angeles, founded in 2010, also by Tupten Ngödrup.

34. See Nebesky-Wojkowitz, *Oracles and Demons of Tibet*, 94–133 and 444–454, respectively.
35. See Franco Ricca, *Il Tempio Oracolare di gNas-chuṅ: Gli Dei del Tibet più Magico e Segreto* (Alessandria, Italy: Edizioni dell'Orso, 1999).
36. See Urmila Nair, *The Sociological Inflection of Ontology: A Study of the Multiple Ontological Statuses of a Tibetan Buddhist Protective Deity* (Master's thesis, University of Chicago, 2004); and Nair, *When the Sun's Rays Are as Shadows*, respectively.
37. See Bell, *The Dalai Lama and the Nechung Oracle.*
38. See Tibetan Academy of Social Sciences, ed., *Dpal ldan 'bras spungs*; for the material on Nechung in particular, see 439–498. I am grateful to the irreplaceable Tsering Gyalbo for generously providing me with a copy of this book.
39. See Department of Religion and Culture, *Rgyal ba'i bstan srung gnas chung sprul pa'i chos rgyal chen po'i rtogs brjod lha yi rol mo dam can dgyes pa'i sgra dbyangs* (Dharamsala, India: CTA, Gangchen Kyishong, 2004) and Nechung Monastery, *Dus gsum rgyal ba thams cad kyi gno bo ma hā gu ru padma saṃ bha ba'i sku'i 'khrungs skar sprel lo sprel zla tshes bcu'i dus chen ngo sprod dang/o rgyan las rab gling pa'i gter byon gu ru'i sku tshab mthong grol yid bzhin nor bu lha ldan du ji ltar gdan drangs tshul/gnas chung chos rgyal chen po'i rtogs brjod bsdus pa bcas phyogs gcig gces bsdebs* (Dharamsala, India: Nechung Monastery, 2004), respectively.
40. Tib. *Gnas chung rdo rje sgra dbyangs gling gi chos 'byung kun gsal chu shel dbang po.*
41. See Thub bstan phun tshogs, *Gnas chung*. I am grateful to the Venerable Yeshé Söpa (Ye shes bsod pa), head monk at Nechung Monastery, Dharamsala, for providing me with copies of this book.
42. Tib. *Gnas chung dgon* (乃琼寺): *Dbang drag rol pa'i dga' tshal gnas chung rdo rje sgra dbyangs gling gi dkar chag mthong ba don ldan*; see Mig dmar tshe ring, *Gnas chung dgon.*

Christopher Bell

NICHIREN

NICHIREN'S CAREER

Nichiren was born in 1222 in a small fishing village on the Pacific coast of eastern Japan, in Tōjō in Nagase District of Awa Province (now Chiba Prefecture), at the tip of the Bōsō peninsula. The temple Tanjōji 誕生寺 in Kominato commemorates his birthplace, but the coastline has altered over the centuries, and the exact location is not known. Nichiren described himself as "a fisherman's son," "a child of outcastes," and "a child of commoners." Scholars disagree about whether these statements point literally to Nichiren's humble birth or should be taken metaphorically as underscoring his claim that the *Lotus Sutra* saves even the lowliest of persons. Nichiren's parents evidently enjoyed some form of patronage relationship with the local estate proprietor, which would have been unusual for ordinary fishermen. Some researchers suggest that Nichiren's family may have belonged to the ranks of estate managers or lower-level samurai who served local lords as secretaries and overseers.[1]

At age twelve, Nichiren entered a nearby temple, Kiyosumidera 清澄寺 (also known as Seichōji), for study.[2] At sixteen, he was ordained by his teacher Dōzen-bō 道善房, taking the name Zeshō-bō Renchō 是聖房蓮長. While said to have been affiliated with the Tendai school, Kiyosumidera was home to several traditions. It was a major center in eastern Japan for esoteric ritual practice and also housed a substantial library. There Nichiren familiarized himself with traditional Tendai doctrine, esoteric Buddhism, and Pure Land teachings. He also prayed earnestly before the temple's chief object of worship, an image of the bodhisattva Kōkūzō 虚空蔵 (Ākāśagarbha), to become "the wisest person in Japan." This suggests that Nichiren may have practiced the *gumonjihō* 求聞持法, an esoteric rite directed to Kōkūzō to enhance one's powers of study and memory. Later he wrote that the bodhisattva appeared before him as a venerable monk and bestowed on him "a jewel of wisdom like the morning star" that enabled him to grasp the essential doctrines of each Buddhist sect.[3]

Little is known of Nichiren's life between the ages of sixteen and thirty-two. His earliest surviving essay, written at age twenty-one, finds him already engaged in a polemic that would continue throughout his life and profoundly shape his thinking. Here Nichiren argued passionately against the exclusive *nenbutsu* doctrine of Hōnen 法然 (1133–1212), revered as the founder of the Japanese Pure Land sect (Jōdoshū 浄土宗). Many people at the time, across social levels, aspired to birth after death in one of the "pure lands" of the buddhas and bodhisattvas, envisioned as both ideal postmortem realms and shortcuts on the long path to buddhahood. The most sought-after postmortem destination was the pure land of the Buddha Amida 阿弥陀 (Skt. Amitābha, Amitāyus), said to lie countless world spheres away to the west. Once born there, it was said, one would never again fall back into the samsaric realms but was assured of attaining buddhahood. People dedicated the merit of their diverse practices—sutra copying and recitation, upholding the Buddhist precepts, commissioning buddha images, and other pious acts—toward the goal of birth in Amida's Pure Land. The practice of chanting the *nenbutsu* 念仏, the name of Amida, was especially widespread, crossing both sectarian boundaries and social levels.

Hōnen had asserted that the chanted *nenbutsu* was not merely the most efficacious but the only practice by which deluded men and women of the present, degenerate Final Dharma age (*mappō* 末法) could escape samsara and achieve birth in Amida's Pure Land. This exclusive claim, rejecting all other practices, at first drew hostility from both government officials and the Buddhist clerical mainstream. But by Nichiren's time, several decades later, the exclusive *nenbutsu* was steadily gaining acceptance. In persuading converts to abandon other teachings and embrace the *nenbutsu* alone, Hōnen's followers had to counter the popularity of the *Lotus Sutra*—not only the central scripture of the influential Tendai school but a text broadly recited, copied, and worshipped for its promise of universal buddhahood. Hōnen's disciples charged, for example, that the *Lotus Sutra* was too profound for benighted persons of the Final Dharma age; those who attempted to practice it, they said, were sure to fail in their efforts and end up falling into the hells. One would do better to set aside the *Lotus Sutra* in this lifetime and instead rely upon the *nenbutsu* in order to achieve birth in Amida's Pure Land. Once born there, one could achieve the enlightenment of the *Lotus Sutra* easily.

Nichiren vehemently disagreed. Drawing on the traditional Tendai classification of the Buddhist teachings—which identifies all other teachings as partial truths and the *Lotus* alone as instantiating the buddha's full enlightenment—he argued that Hōnen's doctrine elevated provisional expedients over the buddha's ultimate teaching. Urging people to set aside the *Lotus Sutra* as beyond their capacity in the Final Dharma age was worse even than blatantly maligning the sutra, because it discouraged people from embracing the one teaching able to save them. "To be born in a country where the *Lotus Sutra* has spread, and not to believe in or practice it, is to slander the dharma," Nichiren insisted.[4]

During these early years, Nichiren made two extended trips for study, one to nearby Kamakura, seat of the Bakufu or shogunate established in 1185, and another to leading temples in western Japan in the vicinity of Kyoto and Nara. At the great Tendai center on Mt. Hiei, he is said to have stayed at the Yokawa precinct, a site of intense ascetic practice, and to have studied with the Tendai scholar-monk Shunpan 俊範, but these traditions cannot be verified. Shunpan also opposed Hōnen's teaching, and several extracts in Nichiren's possession from petitions and edicts against the exclusive *nenbutsu* could have come to him from Shunpan. During this time, Nichiren studied not only traditional Tendai, esoteric teachings, and a wide range of Buddhist scriptures and doctrines but also Confucian literature and other Chinese and Japanese classics.

By 1253, Nichiren had returned to Kiyosumidera. On the twenty-eighth day of the fourth month, 1253, he delivered his first public sermon, an event now celebrated as the founding of the Nichiren sect. While Nichiren had no intention of starting a new sect, his sermon very likely criticized the exclusive *nenbutsu* and asserted the supremacy of the *Lotus Sutra* as the sole teaching that enables buddhahood in the Final Dharma age, themes he was to develop over the next several years. Nichiren's preaching seems to have polarized the temple community into supporters and opponents. Tensions between the two factions were exacerbated by a dispute between the hereditary proprietor of the private estate where Kiyosumidera was located—the lay nun Nagoe-no-ama 名越の尼, who may have been Nichiren's patron—and the Bakufu-appointed steward, Tōjō Kagenobu 東条景信, an ardent *nenbutsu* practitioner who sought to impose this practice forcibly on the temple's clergy. Kagenobu also hunted on temple property, violating the sanctity of its precincts. Nichiren helped negotiate a successful lawsuit on Nagoe-no-ama's behalf, earning Kagenobu's enmity. Eventually he was forced to leave Kiyosumidera. From there he went to the neighboring province of Shimōsa, where he had some connection with one Toki Jōnin 富木常忍 (1216–1299), a learned warrior-bureaucrat who served in the administrative headquarters of the provincial constable. Nichiren remained in Shimōsa for a time, and Toki, along with several of his associates, became Nichiren's follower.[5]

First Remonstration. By 1257, Nichiren had moved to Kamakura. There in the surrounding hills he established a small hermitage at a place called Matsubagayatsu and began to spread his teaching. His writings from this early period develop his claims for the unique salvific power of the *Lotus Sutra*. Against the position that the *Lotus* is too profound for ordinary persons of the Final Dharma age, Nichiren countered that, precisely because it is so profound, it can liberate all people. Saichō 最澄 (766/767–822), founder of the Japanese Tendai school, had understood *mappō* to be the time when the *Lotus Sutra* would spread, an idea that Nichiren amplified. Nichiren also began to teach a form of *Lotus Sutra* practice that would be accessible to all people, namely, chanting the sutra's *daimoku* or title in the formula "*Namu Myōhō-renge-kyō*," discussed later in the section titled "The Daimoku.[6]" To a limited extent, the *daimoku* had been chanted before Nichiren.[7] It was, for example, the mantra recited in the Lotus rite or *Hokke hō* 法華法, an esoteric Tendai ritual for realizing buddhahood and gaining worldly benefits and protection. In promoting the *daimoku*, Nichiren no doubt had in mind the logic of esoteric mantra practice, in which the identity of the practitioner and the buddha is realized in the act of ritual performance. At the same time, he may have recognized, in the exclusive *nenbutsu* teaching that he so vehemently opposed, the value of a single, universally accessible practice—the chanting of a single phrase, said to be uniquely suited to the Final Dharma age—and appropriated it to the very different logic of his *Lotus*-centered teaching. For example, Nichiren rejected the Pure Land doctrine that defers attainment of buddhahood to a postmortem realm apart from this world. "Wherever a practitioner of the *Lotus Sutra* dwells should be considered the pure land," he asserted.[8]

In 1257, a major earthquake devastated Kamakura. It was the latest in a series of recent large-scale disasters, including famine, epidemics, and ominous celestial portents. For Nichiren, the country's troubles stemmed fundamentally from neglect of the *Lotus Sutra*. Of several essays he wrote on this theme, the most famous is his *Risshō ankoku ron* 立正安国論 (Establishing the true teaching and bringing peace to the land), which he submitted through an intermediary to Hōjō Tokiyori 北条時頼 (1227–1263), former regent to the shogun and the most powerful figure in the Kamakura Bakufu. Nichiren's later tradition terms this his first act of "admonishing the state" (*kokka kangyō* 国家諫暁). In this admonitory treatise Nichiren argued that because so many people had cast aside the *Lotus Sutra* and other profound Mahāyāna teachings in favor of the exclusive *nenbutsu*, the guardian deities who protect the Buddhadharma had abandoned Japan, exposing it to the predation of demons, and he urged that government officials withdraw support from teachers of Hōnen's misguided doctrine. In so arguing, Nichiren stood squarely within a common understanding of his day that saw disasters not as adventitious but as cosmic responses to moral wrongdoing or religious error.

Prompt action, he continued, was urgent. The *Risshō ankoku ron* cites sutra passages asserting that a country whose ruler fails to safeguard the true dharma will suffer such calamities as drought, famine, and epidemics, predictions eerily corresponding to the current state of affairs in Japan. Of the disasters enumerated in these sutras, only two had not materialized: internal revolt and foreign invasion. Were the situation allowed to persist, Nichiren warned, these two catastrophes would also surely occur. Conversely, if people redirected their faith to the one vehicle of the true teaching, the world would at once become a tranquil buddha land.

There is no record of the Bakufu's response. By this point, however, Hōnen's followers had won influential patrons in Kamakura, including Hōjō Shigetoki 北条重時 (1198–1261), a powerful member of the shogunate's regental family. Some disciples of Hōnen in Kamakura challenged Nichiren to debate; by his own account, he quickly defeated them. Their lay followers then complained of him to Bakufu leaders, and at one point a mob attacked his dwelling. Judging his life to be in danger, Nichiren left Kamakura, possibly taking refuge with Toki Jōnin in Shimōsa, but returned the following year. In the fifth month of 1261, he was arrested and exiled to the Izu peninsula. The reasons for this sentence are not clear. Slander and unauthorized violence were prohibited under the Bakufu's legal code, and the authorities may have felt that Nichiren's continued presence in Kamakura was a magnet for conflict. He would remain in Izu for nearly two years.

While little is known of Nichiren's circumstances in exile, his writings from this period reflect three significant developments. First, he refined his thinking about why the *Lotus Sutra* alone was appropriate for Japan at the present time. He expressed his conclusions in terms of "five principles" (*gokō* 五綱) or five interconnected perspectives from which he saw the *Lotus Sutra* as supreme: its teaching, which guarantees buddhahood for all; the time, that is, the Final Dharma age; the people's religious capacity; the country or place; and the sequence of propagation (meaning that one should not promote a dharma inferior to those that have already been established).[9] Second, in keeping with his growing emphasis on the *Lotus Sutra* as the sole vehicle of liberation in the *mappō* era, Nichiren also clarified what he meant by "slander of the dharma" (*hōbō* 謗法), the one evil that could obstruct such liberation. Nichiren took "dharma slander" not to necessarily mean verbal abuse or even malign intent but a rejection of the *Lotus Sutra* in favor of provisional teachings. The *Lotus* itself warns about frightful punishments in the Avīci hell awaiting those who slander the sutra, a fate that Nichiren now deeply feared awaited his fellow Japanese. This concern motivated his assertive proselytizing.

The *Lotus Sutra* describes the hostility that its devotees will face in a future evil age and calls on them to give their lives if need be to uphold it. These passages may reflect the experiences of the sutra's compilers, as proponents of a fledgling Mahāyāna movement, of persecution by the Buddhist mainstream. For Nichiren, they mirrored his own experience. A third theme of his Izu writings is his growing self-identification as the "votary of the *Lotus Sutra*" (*Hokekyō no gyōja* 法華経の行者), a practitioner who not only embraces the teachings of the *Lotus* but lives out its predictions by meeting great trials in propagating it.

Second Arrest and Exile. Nichiren was pardoned in the second month of 1263. For the next few years, he traveled in the eastern provinces to preach and encourage followers. In 1264, he returned briefly to his home province, Awa, to visit his ailing mother. He also renewed connections with those monks at Kiyosumidera who had been sympathetic to his message. During this visit, he and his party were ambushed at a place called Komatsubara by warriors in the service of Kagenobu, the Bakufu steward whose antagonism had forced him to leave Kiyosumidera a decade earlier. Nichiren suffered a broken arm and a sword cut across his forehead, and one of his disciples was killed defending him; two others were gravely wounded. The *Lotus Sutra*'s prophecy that its devotees will be attacked by swords had materialized.

By 1266, he had returned to Kamakura. In 1268, envoys arrived from Kublai Khan, the Mongol ruler, who had launched a campaign of conquest against China and Korea. Now he demanded that Japan acknowledge Mongol overlordship or prepare to be subjugated. For Nichiren and his followers, this turn of events signaled the fulfillment of scriptural prophecy, cited in his *Risshō ankoku ron*: a country that abandons the True Dharma will suffer attack by foreign invaders. As the Bakufu began to mobilize the country's defenses, Nichiren redoubled his efforts to communicate his message, and his following grew. He had recently begun holding lecture services on the twenty-fourth of each month, the death date of the Chinese Tiantai (J. Tendai) patriarch Zhiyi 智顗 (538–597). These gatherings served to educate his followers and solidify their resolve. At the same time, Nichiren fired off letters to government officials and leaders in the Buddhist world, repeating the admonitions stated earlier in his *Risshō ankoku ron*. Zen now joined his polemical targets as a provisional teaching unsuited to the age, as did both Shingon and Tendai esoteric teachings, evidently in response to government sponsoring of esoteric rites for protection against the Mongols. Nichiren fully understood that his attacks on other teachings were provoking antagonism. Nonetheless, convinced that the threat to Japan stemmed from widespread neglect of the *Lotus Sutra*, he felt compelled to speak out, in the sutra's words, "without begrudging bodily life."[10]

Nichiren was arrested on the twelfth day of the ninth month, 1271, probably as part of Bakufu efforts to bolster the country's defenses by subduing unruly elements at home. By Nichiren's account, Hei no Saemon-no-jō Yoritsuna 平左衛門尉頼綱, deputy chief of the board of retainers for the Hōjō shogunal regents, privately intended to have him beheaded and ordered that he be taken to the execution grounds outside Kamakura. His life was spared, it is said, when a dazzling object suddenly streaked across the night sky, terrifying his would-be executioners. While modern scholarship has questioned the historicity of the event, Nichiren himself clearly believed he had undergone a form of death and transformation on that night. He was then exiled a second time, to the bleak island of Sado in the Sea of Japan.

On Sado, Nichiren was initially assigned as living quarters a small, ruined chapel near a charnel ground; he suffered from cold, hunger, and the hostility of the locals. He also worried about his followers in Kamakura, several of whom had been had been arrested or imprisoned in the wake of his own exile. Many gave way to doubts and abandoned their faith. Nichiren himself wrestled with the question of why he and his followers should meet persecution when the *Lotus Sutra* promises its devotees "peace and security in the present life."[11] His struggle with these doubts and their eventual resolution are related in his *Kaimoku shō* 開目抄 (Opening the eyes), written during the privations of his first winter on the island, which concludes with a renewed resolve to dedicate himself to faith in the *Lotus Sutra* at all cost. "Let heaven forsake me. Let ordeals confront me. I will not begrudge bodily life.... Whatever trials we may encounter, so long as we do not cherish doubts, I and my disciples will naturally achieve buddhahood."[12] Gradually, Nichiren began to win converts among the island's inhabitants. He also maintained a steady correspondence with his followers and produced some of his most important works.

Nichiren's Sado writings show an increased identification with two figures in the *Lotus Sutra*. One is the bodhisattva Superior Conduct (Skt. Viśiṣṭacāritra, J. Jōgyō 上行), leader of a vast throng of bodhisattvas who emerge from beneath the earth and receive Śākyamuni Buddha's mandate to propagate the *Lotus* in an evil age after his nirvana. The other is the bodhisattva Never Despising (Skt. Sadāparibhūta, J. Jōfukyō 常不軽), who pays homage to everyone he meets as a future buddha, patiently bearing their scorn and abuse; by so doing, he is able to expiate his past wrongdoings and become a buddha himself. For Nichiren, the bodhisattva Superior Conduct represented his own mission to declare the truth of the *Lotus Sutra* in the present age; Nichiren's later tradition has often identified him as Superior Conduct reborn. At the same time, the bodhisattva Never Despising represented Nichiren's understanding of his present trials as a form of exculpatory suffering that would eradicate his own past sins of slander against the *Lotus Sutra* and ultimately assure his buddhahood.

Nichiren's major Sado writings include the *Kanjin honzon shō* (観心本尊抄, The contemplation of the mind and the object of worship), later designated, along with the *Risshō ankoku ron* and *Kaimoku shō*, as one of his three most important works. Dated 1273, this essay develops the doctrinal basis for chanting the *daimoku* as the form of "mind contemplation" (*kanjin* 観心) appropriate for the Final Dharma age. For Nichiren, *kanjin* was not a traditional meditation method requiring disciplined mental training. Rather, he asserted, all Śākyamuni

Buddha's "causes and effects"—the practices he undertook since the inconceivably remote past in order to realize buddhahood and the merits he gained in consequence—are fully contained within the five characters of the *daimoku* and immediately transferred to the devotee in chanting it. Thus the practitioner can realize the merits of the six perfections comprising the entirety of the bodhisattva path without needing to cultivate them as individual practices. Zhiyi had divided the *Lotus Sutra* into two parts: the first fourteen chapters, or "trace teaching" (*shakumon* 迹門), present Śākyamuni Buddha as a "manifest trace" (*suijaku* 垂迹), that is, in his transient guise as a historical figure who attained awakening in the present life, while the latter fourteen chapters or "origin teaching" (*honmon* 本門)—and especially chapter 16, "Fathoming the Lifespan of the Tathāgata"—present him in his true aspect or "original ground" (*honji* 本地) as the primordial buddha, awakened since the remotest past and constantly active in this world and others for the sake of living beings. Nichiren now began to identify the *daimoku* as the heart of the origin teaching and the dharma transmitted by this primordially enlightened Śākyamuni Buddha to the bodhisattva Superior Conduct and his followers as expressly for propagation in the Final Dharma age. The *Kanjin honzon shō* also lays the doctrinal groundwork for the calligraphic mandala, discussed in the section "The Great Mandala," that Nichiren devised as an object of worship for his followers, depicting the *Lotus* assembly where the ever-present Śākyamuni Buddha preaches.

In the second month of 1272, Hōjō Tokisuke 北条時輔, the shogunal regent's half-brother, was accused of plotting a coup, and many deemed to be collaborators were killed in Kyoto and Kamakura. Occurring just when the country needed to unite against the Mongols, this internecine struggle was alarming. It seemed to fulfill the second prediction of the *Risshō ankoku ron*, domestic rebellion, and perhaps for that reason Nichiren was transferred that spring to better quarters at the home of a local landowner. Two years later he was pardoned, possibly because he was thought to have special insight into the deepening Mongol threat. Returning to Kamakura in early spring of 1274, Nichiren was immediately summoned by Hei no Yoritsuna, the same Bakufu official responsible for his near execution and subsequent exile. Asked when the Mongols would attack, Nichiren replied—accurately, as it turned out—that they would strike within the year. Tradition says that Yoritsuna offered Nichiren official patronage if he would conduct prayer rites for the country's protection along with those being performed by other schools, but Nichiren refused. No doubt he again admonished Yoritsuna that reliance on prayer rites based on provisional teachings would invite still worse calamities; only by faith in the *Lotus Sutra* could the disaster be forestalled.

Realizing that his admonitions would not be heeded, Nichiren left Kamakura and withdrew to Mt. Minobu in Kai Province, where the local steward, Hakii (or Hakiri) Sanenaga 波木井実長, was his follower. His first dwelling there was primitive, and again he endured hunger and cold. Gradually, however, a community of followers formed around him. At this point Nichiren turned over the work of proselytizing to his chief disciples and devoted himself to writing and to training successors. The greater portion of his surviving works dates from the Minobu period and includes not only doctrinal treatises but also moving letters to his lay followers, praising their efforts, expressing gratitude for their material support, and encouraging their faith in difficult times. These letters display Nichiren's literary skills and offer insight into his perspective on the application of faith to real-world situations. From his remote retreat, Nichiren also actively supervised a network of disciples who maintained their own congregations in their respective provinces while traveling back and forth to Minobu. Through this network, Nichiren was able to receive news and communicate readily with his followers. It enabled him to guide them through critical junctures, including the two Mongol attacks of 1274 and 1281 and a local persecution of devotees in the Atsuhara area near Fuji in the late 1270s that resulted in multiple arrests and three executions.[13] However, Nichiren's health had been undermined by long years of privation. He passed away on the thirteenth day of the tenth month, 1282, after entrusting the task of propagation to his disciples.

ESSENTIALS OF NICHIREN'S TEACHING

Central to Nichiren's teaching is his claim that the *daimoku* or title of the *Lotus Sutra* embodies the whole of Buddhist truth and that chanting the *daimoku* constitutes the only efficacious practice for the present era. Buddhist scriptures say that, after the buddha's passing, his teachings will become distorted; correct practice will be lost; and liberation will become all but impossible to achieve. In East Asia, this decline process was divided into three consecutive periods: the True and Semblance Dharma ages (*shōbō* 正法, *zōbō* 像法), often said to last a thousand years each, and the Final Dharma age (*mappō*), lasting ten thousand years or more.[14] While chronologies varied, in Japan *mappō* was widely thought to have begun in 1052. Some Buddhist figures drew on notions of the Final Dharma age to urge renewed efforts in traditional disciplines of precept keeping and meditation; others, Nichiren among them, saw the *mappō* era as demanding a reformulation of Buddhist practice. Nichiren argued that provisional teachings such as *nenbutsu*, Zen, and the esoteric teachings had enabled their practitioners to achieve enlightenment during the True and Semblance Dharma ages but had lost their efficacy now in the Final Dharma age. Put differently, persons born in the *mappō* era lack the capacity to achieve enlightenment through provisional teachings. They must receive the "seed of buddhahood," the *daimoku* of the *Lotus Sutra*, the vehicle of liberation expressly intended for the people of this age. That is why *daimoku* practice entails both chanting and propagation. Nichiren spoke of the buddhahood to be achieved in *mappō* from two perspectives: as immediately accessible in the act of chanting and as culminating over a lifetime's practice. Both are inseparably connected and grounded in the same principle.

Mutual Inclusion of the Ten Realms. Tiantai/Tendai tradition holds that Śākyamuni Buddha taught for fifty years. For forty-two years he preached expedient teachings suited to the diverse capacities of his audience, and in the last eight years he preached the *Lotus Sutra* as the direct expression of his own enlightenment. Thus where earlier teachings are "provisional" (*gon* 権) and incomplete, the *Lotus Sutra* is "true" (*jitsu* 実), meaning complete and perfect. Nichiren saw the *Lotus Sutra* as complete and perfect because it enables all beings to become buddhas. While other sutras might make this claim, they did not, in his view, embody the principle that makes universal buddhahood possible. Nichiren identified this principle in Tendai terms as the "mutual inclusion of the ten Dharma-realms" (*jikkai gogu* 十界互具). Buddhist cosmology represents samsara, the realm of deluded rebirth, as a hierarchy of six paths: hell dwellers, hungry ghosts, animals, contentious *asura* demons, humans, and gods. Above these are four more realms characterized by varying degrees of awakening: the two realms of the *śrāvakas* and *pratyekabuddhas*, who cultivate detachment and cessation of desire as set forth in the so-called Hīnayāna teachings; bodhisattvas, who strive for the liberation of all; and fully awakened buddhas. In contrast to the buddha realm, which represents supreme enlightenment, the other nine realms represent delusion, or states not yet fully awakened. All ten interpenetrate, so that each realm contains all ten within itself; thus the buddha realm does not exist apart from oneself. "Some sutras say that hell lies beneath the ground," Nichiren wrote, "while others say that the Buddha dwells in the west. But close investigation shows that both exist within our five-foot body."[15]

The mutual inclusion of the ten realms expands into the larger principle of three thousand realms in a single moment of thought, or *ichinen sanzen* 一念三千. In essence, *ichinen sanzen* means that the smallest phenomenon (a single thought-moment) and the entire cosmos (three thousand realms) are mutually encompassing: the one and the many; good and evil; delusion and awakening; subject and object; self and other; and all sentient beings from hell dwellers, hungry ghosts, and animals up through bodhisattvas and buddhas, as well as their respective environments, simultaneously interpenetrate and encompass one another without losing their individual identity. First set forth by Zhiyi, this complex, architectonic principle offers a sophisticated example of how Chinese Buddhist interpreters sought to articulate the holistic interrelation of the mind and all phenomena. Nichiren described the *ichinen sanzen* principle as "the father and mother of the buddhas."[16] For him, it was what made the *Lotus Sutra* unique and qualified it as the "Wonderful Dharma" (*myōhō* 妙法).

In Nichiren's reading, the three thousand realms in a single thought-moment—or its condensed form, the mutual inclusion of the ten realms—designates both the potential for buddhahood in all beings of the nine realms as a theoretical principle (*ri no ichinen sanzen* 理の一念三千) and its actualization as the awakened state that the buddha has realized (*ji no ichinen sanzen* 事の一念三千), which encompasses and illuminates the other nine realms. Nichiren associated these two aspects respectively with the two divisions of the *Lotus Sutra*: the trace teaching or *shakumon*, which teaches that all beings can become buddhas, and the origin teaching or *honmon*, which reveals the buddha's original awakening in the remotest past and his constant presence in the world. "*Ichinen sanzen* as actuality" described for Nichiren both the primordial buddha's enlightenment and its instantiation in a concrete form of practice that makes that enlightenment accessible to all. In the *mappō* era, he taught, that concrete form comprises "three great secret Dharmas" (*sandai hihō* 三大秘法): the *daimoku*, the object of worship, and the ordination platform.

The Daimoku. *Myōhō-renge-kyō* is the title, in Japanese pronunciation, of the celebrated 406 Chinese translation of the *Lotus Sutra* by Kumārajīva (344–413), while "*Namu*" (from the Sanskrit *namas*) connotes praise, devotion, and the taking of refuge. Throughout his writings, Nichiren discusses "the *daimoku* in five or seven characters" as far more than the title of a text; *Myōhō-renge-kyō* is itself the Wonderful Dharma, "the heart of the eighty thousand sacred teachings and the eye of all buddhas."[17] Nichiren drew on a Chinese tradition of title exegesis, in which the entire meaning of a sutra was thought to be contained within its title. Zhiyi, for example, had devoted almost the whole of his commentary *Profound Meaning of the Lotus Sutra* (*Fahua xuanyi* 法華玄義) to interpreting the five characters *myō, hō, ren, ge,* and *kyō* that compose the sutra's name.[18] Just as the *Lotus Sutra* is said to be all-encompassing, so too is its title. For Nichiren, the *daimoku*, as the embodiment of *ichinen sanzen*, encompasses all phenomena, including all beings and their environments in the ten realms of existence. Nichiren's thinking about the *daimoku* also drew on widespread ideas about the efficacy of mantras, *dhāraṇīs*, and other invocations, which were believed to encapsulate enlightened states and spiritual powers and to elicit numinous responses. The *daimoku,* he taught, contains the whole of the buddha's enlightenment and makes it immediately accessible to the devotee. He expressed this idea in a famous passage from his *Kanjin honzon shō*: "Śākyamuni's causal practices and their resulting virtues are all contained within the five characters Myōhō-renge-kyō. When we embrace these five characters, he will naturally transfer to us the merit of his causes and effects."[19]

In general, the Mahāyāna sutras teach that, in order to become a buddha, one must perfect the six *pāramitās*, the practices of a bodhisattva—generosity, keeping the precepts, forbearance, assiduousness, meditation, and wisdom—over a period of three incalculable kalpas (eons). However, Nichiren, like other contemporary Tendai teachers, understood the *honmon* section of the *Lotus Sutra,* with its revelation of the buddha's constant presence in this world, as opening a perspective from which "cause," or practice (the nine realms), and "effect," or enlightenment (buddhahood), are simultaneous. He taught that all the practices that the primordial Śākyamuni Buddha carried out over countless kalpas to achieve his awakening, and all the wisdom and merit that he attained in consequence, are contained within the *daimoku* and immediately opened to the practitioner who chants it. One could say that chanting the *daimoku* aligns or "syncs" the reality of the practitioner with that of the buddha, so that the three thousand realms of the primordial buddha and those of the practitioner become identified. This is the "realization of buddhahood with this very body." Of course, religious maturity comes only with continued practice, and Nichiren urged his followers to maintain their faith throughout life. But his concept of practice did not involve aspiring to buddhahood as a remote, external goal but as grounded in an enlightenment that is always accessible via the *daimoku.*

Because he understood the *daimoku* as all-encompassing, Nichiren stressed that chanting it would confer all the goods that religious practice in his day was thought to generate: this-worldly benefits such as protection and healing and assurance for the afterlife. Beyond such specific benefits, however, he saw faith in the *Lotus Sutra* as establishing an inner freedom and stability, independent of whether one's circumstances are favorable or adverse. "Recognize suffering as suffering, enjoy pleasures for what they are, and whether in suffering or joy, keep chanting Namu Myōhō-renge-kyō," he wrote to a follower. "Then you will know the joy of the Dharma for yourself."[20]

The Great Mandala. Buddhist practitioners in medieval Japan, like those of today, often enshrined a personal object of worship (*honzon* 本尊)—a painting or statue of a buddha or bodhisattva, or perhaps a mandala—as a focus of practice. *Honzon* were regarded not as merely symbolic but as actually embodying the powers and virtues of the Buddhist holy beings that they depicted. The object of worship most widely employed within the Nichiren tradition is a calligraphic mandala that Nichiren himself devised, written entirely in Chinese characters with two Sanskrit glyphs. It is known as the *daimandara* 大曼荼羅 ("great mandala") or *gohonzon* 御本尊 ("revered object of worship"). Nichiren widely inscribed these mandalas as personal *honzon* for his followers, and more than 120 of them survive in his own hand. Since his signature appears on the *gohonzon,* receiving one was proof of a master–disciple connection with Nichiren.

On Nichiren's mandala, the *daimoku* is written vertically as a central inscription, flanked by the names of the buddhas Śākyamuni and Prabhūtaratna (Abundant Jewels), just as they sat together at the assembly of the *Lotus Sutra,* as well as the names of representative bodhisattvas, deities, and other beings, human and nonhuman, who were present on that occasion. These figures also represent the mutual inclusion of the ten realms. Illuminated by the central inscription of the *daimoku,* Nichiren explained, they reveal their enlightened aspect just as they are. Thus in doctrinal terms, the mandala embodies the nine realms encompassed by the buddha realm, or *ichinen sanzen* in actuality.

The logic underlying Nichiren's *gohonzon* resembles that of esoteric practice, in which the practitioner visualizes, often aided by use of a mandala, the union or interpenetration of oneself and the buddha (*nyūga ganyū* 入我我入), thus realizing buddhahood with this very body. For Nichiren, however, the union of the devotee and the buddha is manifested not by esoteric visualization or other meditative techniques but by faith in the *Lotus Sutra.* By chanting the *daimoku,* the devotee "enters" the mandala, the realm of the original buddha's awakening, and participates in the enlightened reality that it depicts.

In devising his *gohonzon,* Nichiren drew on earlier visual representations of the *Lotus* assembly as well as other influences, especially from esoteric Buddhism.[21] It is also noteworthy that other Buddhist teachers of his day, such as Myōe 明恵 (1173–1232) and Shinran 親鸞 (1173–1262), similarly created calligraphic *honzon* for their followers. Nichiren's mandala resembles these examples in that it did not require a professional painter or sculptor or expensive materials to produce. Thus it represents a trend toward the popularization of Buddhist iconography, previously available only to very few.[22]

The Ordination Platform. Where Nichiren himself established the *daimoku* and the object of worship, he charged his future followers with establishing an ordination platform (*kaidan* 戒壇) as the last of the "three great secret Dharmas" for the *mappō* era. Traditionally, an ordination platform is a place for receiving the Buddhist precepts and becoming a monk or nun. However, Nichiren taught that the merit of keeping the precepts is already inherent in the *daimoku,* and that embracing the *Lotus Sutra* is the only valid precept in the Final Dharma age. Thus his intentions concerning the *kaidan* are not altogether clear. He specified that it would be the "ordination platform of the origin teaching" (*honmon no kaidan* 本門の戒壇), superseding the Tendai ordination platform on Mt. Hiei, whose precepts Nichiren understood as based solely on the *shakumon* or trace teaching of the *Lotus Sutra* and no longer suited to the Final Dharma age. Only one writing in the Nichiren collection, the *Sandai hihō honjōji* (三大秘法稟承事, Transmission of the three great secret Dharmas), provides any detail, describing it as a great spiritual center for the people of the world, to be erected once the sovereign and his ministers have embraced the *Lotus Sutra.* Since ordination platforms in premodern Japan were court sponsored, Nichiren may well have envisioned the eventual acceptance of his teaching in these terms. However, a state-sponsored *kaidan* conflicts with modern notions of the separation of religion and government, and the *Sandai hihō honjōji*'s authenticity has been hotly contested, perhaps as much on ideological as on textual grounds.[23] Some among Nichiren's successors have preferred to interpret the *kaidan* metaphorically as any place where the *daimoku* is chanted, based on the *Lotus Sutra*'s teaching that wherever one upholds the sutra "is itself the place of enlightenment."[24] Whatever Nichiren's intent, his inclusion of the *kaidan* among the three great secret Dharmas reflects his awareness that practice occurs in a concrete place and must engage the larger world.

THE MISSION OF PROPAGATION

Nichiren's aim in preaching devotion to the *Lotus Sutra* was not only to guide individuals to enlightenment but to save the entire country, a task he came to see as his personal mission and responsibility. As the faith and chanting of the *daimoku* spread, he taught, the present world would become the buddha land. For that reason, he saw proselytizing as an integral part of practice.

The Choice of Shakubuku. Buddhist sutras and commentaries specify two approaches to dharma teaching: *shōju* 摂受, or leading others gradually in an open and accepting manner, without challenging their opinions, and *shakubuku* 折伏, or assertively rebuking attachment to wrong views. The choice between them, Nichiren said, should depend on the time and place. In his view, because Japan at the beginning of the Final Dharma age was a place and time where the *Lotus Sutra* was being discarded in favor of provisional teachings, the confrontational *shakubuku* method should take precedence. "When the time is right to propagate the teaching of the one vehicle, the provisional teachings become enemies," he wrote. "If they are a source of confusion, one must refute them from the standpoint of the true teaching."[25]

Convinced that only the *Lotus Sutra* leads to liberation in the *mappō* era, Nichiren understood *shakubuku* as a compassionate act, equivalent to bodhisattva practice. Whether others accepted the *Lotus* or rejected it, asserting its sole validity and urging them to take faith in it would implant the seed of buddhahood in their hearts and thereby establish for them a karmic connection to the sutra that would someday allow them to realize enlightenment, whether in this lifetime or a future one. However, Nichiren acknowledged that, even in the Final Dharma age, situations might arise that would call for a milder method, for example, in countries ignorant of the dharma.[26] This acknowledgment allowed for flexibility but also opened the way for controversy within the later Nichiren tradition, which has periodically been divided over the merits of confrontational versus accommodating approaches.

The Soteriology of Meeting Persecution. Nichiren's combative approach invited censure and attack by powerful figures in both clerical and government circles. Over the course of his tumultuous career, he found deep meaning in enduring the opposition that his efforts drew forth. First, Nichiren believed that by encountering hostility in spreading the sutra, one bears witness to its truth. The *Lotus Sutra* itself says that those who uphold it in an evil age following the Buddha's nirvana will be mocked, reviled, attacked, ousted repeatedly, and slandered to the ruling authorities by monks who are widely respected. The fact that these predictions were borne out by his own experience confirmed for Nichiren that his path was the right one. Nichiren termed this "bodily reading" (*shikidoku* 色読) of the sutra—not merely reciting it verbally or mentally embracing its teachings but living out its words. Nichiren's "bodily reading" has been described as a "circular hermeneutic" in which sutra and practitioner mirror and confirm one another: the sutra's predictions that its devotees will encounter hardships legitimated Nichiren's actions, and Nichiren's experience of persecution, in fulfilling scriptural prophecy, legitimated the *Lotus Sutra*.[27]

Nichiren further taught that enduring hardships to spread faith in the *Lotus* expiates one's offenses committed in prior lifetimes and repays one's indebtedness: to one's parents, to the ruler, to the "three jewels"—buddha, dharma, and sangha—and to all living beings. He also maintained that encountering great trials for the *Lotus Sutra*'s sake guarantees one's future buddhahood. "You must each be resolved," he told his followers. "Offering your life for the *Lotus Sutra* is like exchanging rocks for gold, or dung for rice."[28] Buddhism in general stresses the importance of breaking through egocentrism, surrendering attachments to a narrow idea of self, as a prerequisite for liberation. The sutras often express the spirit of relinquishing self-attachment through stories of heroic bodhisattvas of the past who, in their quest for supreme enlightenment, plucked out their eyes, cut off their limbs, peeled off their skin on which to transcribe Buddhist teachings, or in some fashion willingly gave up life itself for the dharma's sake. Nichiren saw such acts as beyond the capacity of ordinary people and no longer appropriate in the *mappō* era. Rather, in his view, being willing to meet harsh trials in the course of propagating the *Lotus Sutra* is equivalent to "giving one's life" and results in supreme buddhahood. Nichiren's example has proved an enduring encouragement, both to his followers and to others outside his tradition, who have risked personal welfare, even life itself, to uphold convictions that contravened prevailing orthodoxy.

Actualizing the Lotus World. The *ichinen sanzen* principle posits a radical interrelation of the living subject and his or her environment, or, in more precise Buddhist technical language, the nonduality of direct and circumstantial karmic recompense (*eshō funi* 依正不二). Because the environment mirrors the life condition of those inhabiting it, individual beings perceive and experience their surroundings differently; the world of a hell-dweller is hellish, while the world of a fully awakened person would be a buddha realm.

For Nichiren, the immanence of the buddha land in this world was not merely a truth to be realized subjectively in the faith or insight of individual practitioners; the practice of devotees would actually transform the outer world. Because all ten realms interpenetrate and encompass both living beings and their environments, manifesting buddhahood oneself in the act of chanting the *daimoku* would simultaneously draw forth buddhahood in one's surroundings. And, as the practice of the *daimoku* spread, the present world would become an ideal buddha land. Nichiren did not discuss in detail what this transformed world would look like, but in one passage he writes: "When the people all chant Namu Myōhō-renge-kyō as one, the wind will not thrash the branches nor the rain fall hard enough to erode the soil. The world will be as it was in the ages [of the ancient Chinese sage kings] Fuxi and Shennong. In this life, inauspicious disasters will be banished, and people will obtain the art of longevity," suggesting that faith in the *Lotus Sutra* could bring about harmony with nature, just rule and, in some sense, a transcending of impermanence.[29] In his teaching, actualizing the buddha land in this world becomes a concrete goal of practice and the task of *Lotus* devotees. This gives his doctrine an explicitly social dimension. Over the centuries, Nichiren's followers have sought to realize his goal, although with widely varying interpretations of what an ideal society based on the *Lotus Sutra* would look like. Nichiren's vision of manifesting the buddha land in the present world speaks powerfully to the this-worldly orientation of today's Buddhist modernism and has motivated modern and contemporary Nichiren- and *Lotus*-based movements.

Nichiren opposed the idea, common in his time, of shunning this world as wicked and impure and aspiring to birth in a pure land after death. In his later years, confronted with the need to explain what happens to *Lotus Sutra* devotees after they die, Nichiren taught that they go to "the pure land of Eagle Peak" (Ryōzen jōdō 霊山浄土), an apotheosis of Mt. Gṛdhrakūṭa (J. Ryōjusen 霊鷲山, also translated as "Vulture Peak") in Rājagṛha in India, where Śākyamuni Buddha is said to have preached the *Lotus Sutra*. Nichiren was not the first to conceive this realm as a postmortem destination. But in his understanding, the pure land of Eagle Peak is not a distinct realm apart from the present world; it exists wherever one embraces the *Lotus Sutra*. Accessible in the present, it also extends to encompass the faithful dead. This realm is precisely what Nichiren represented on his great mandala, using the *Lotus Sutra*'s mythic image of the Eagle Peak assembly where the ever-present Śākyamuni Buddha preaches to his audience. This constantly abiding "pure land" is, in other words, a timeless reality, a spatial expression of the enlightened state. Immediately accessed through faith and chanting, it is also to be manifested in the outer world through ongoing efforts in propagation.

For Nichiren, faith in the *Lotus Sutra* collapses all temporal and spatial separation between the buddha and the devotee; by upholding the sutra and chanting its *daimoku*, one can immediately enter the *Lotus* assembly and dwell in the buddha's presence. Thus the moment of chanting the *daimoku* becomes the point of intersection between linear, historical time and the timeless realm of the primordial buddha. In defining *mappō* as the historical moment when the *daimoku* of the *Lotus Sutra*, the practice of direct realization, would spread, Nichiren in effect inverted the conventional gloomy connotations of this age and redefined it as the best possible time to be alive. "Rather than be great rulers during the two thousand years of the True and Semblance Dharma ages, those concerned for their salvation should rather be common people now in the Final Dharma age," he wrote. "It is better to be a leper who chants Namu Myōhō-renge-kyō than be chief abbot of the Tendai school," the highest position in the medieval Japanese religious world.[30]

REVIEW OF LITERATURE

An immense body of scholarship on Nichiren's life and thought exists in Japanese, written from both sectarian and secular academic perspectives. To date, the Institute of Nichiren Buddhist Studies at Risshō University (Risshō Daigaku Nichiren Kyōgaku Kenkyūjo 立正大学日蓮教学研究所), which is affiliated with the denomination Nichirenshū, has played a major role in scholarly research on Nichiren.[31] The institute publishes the journal *Nichiren kyōgaku kenkyūjo kiyo* 日蓮教学研究所紀要 and has edited primary texts and produced valuable reference works, including dictionaries.[32] Scholarly journals are also published by other sects, lay organizations, and independent research institutes within the larger Nichiren Buddhist tradition. In recent years, forums have emerged to promote scholarly exchange among the various sects and lineages of Nichiren Buddhism and to include outside academics. These forums include the Hokke Komonzu Bukkyō Gakurin 法華コモンズ仏教学林 ("Lotus Commons" Buddhist Study Institute) and the journal *Hokke bukkyō kenkyū* 法華仏教研究.

Such broad collaborative efforts promise to raise Nichiren studies to a new level, as seen, for example, in the recent five-volume essay collection *Shirīzu Nichiren*.[33]

Nichiren has drawn little attention from Western researchers, especially in comparison to his near contemporaries, Dōgen 道元 (1200–1253) and Shinran, who have often been grouped with him as founders of the new Buddhist movements of Japan's Kamakura period (1185–1333). The influence of nationalistic readings of Nichiren during the Pacific War, along with his own claim for the exclusive truth of the *Lotus Sutra*, contributed for a long time to uncritical stereotyping of Nichiren in anglophone overviews of Buddhism as a militant, intolerant, or even fanatical figure. Such treatments have often conveyed more about modern normative assumptions regarding Buddhism than about Nichiren himself. In English, there are more studies of contemporary Nichirenist movements, especially Sōka Gakkai 創価学会, than there are of Nichiren.

Early examples in Western languages of serious engagement with Nichiren—although now requiring modification in light of later scholarship—include Masaharu Anesaki's *Nichiren, the Buddhist Prophet*, which, inspired by William James and the nascent field of religious psychology, depicted Nichiren as a prophet and mystic, then considered classic "types" of religious personalities.[34] Other examples are Gaston Renondeau's *La Doctrine de Nichiren*; Alicia Matsunaga and Daigan Matsunaga's *Foundation of Japanese Buddhism*; Bruno Petzold's (1873–1949) posthumously published *Buddhist Prophet Nichiren: A Lotus in the Sun*; and Laurel Rasplica Rodd's *Nichiren: Selected Writings*.[35]

Recent studies seek to understand Nichiren within larger historical and religious frameworks. Lucia Dolce's pioneering research has shed unexpected light on Nichiren's indebtedness to the thought, practice, and iconography of esoteric Buddhism.[36] Ruben Habito has placed Nichiren within the broader Buddhist use of *dhāraṇīs* and other incantations as methods of accessing spiritual power.[37] Jacqueline Stone's work examines Nichiren in his historical and intellectual contexts.[38] A landmark publication is *Revisiting Nichiren*, which also contains a bibliography of English-language work on Nichiren up until 1999.[39]

PRIMARY SOURCES

Nichiren wrote voluminously, and the four-volume *Shōwa teihon* critical edition of his writings, edited by the Institute of Nichiren Buddhist Studies at Risshō University, contains nearly five hundred writings, including doctrinal treatises and letters to his followers, as well as charts and outlines; it also contains almost four hundred fragments from additional writings.[40] Nichiren's annotated copy of the *Lotus Sutra*, in which he inscribed relevant passages of commentary, has been published separately.[41] Photographic collections of Nichiren's holographic mandalas have also been published.[42]

Two extensive collections of Nichiren's writings have appeared in English translation. Both are products of Japan-based translation committees working for the overseas propagation of Nichiren's teaching; while intended primarily for practitioners, they can, with appropriate care, be used as scholarly resources. One, supervised by Kyōtsū Hori with the assistance of other translators and editors, is the *Writings of Nichiren Shōnin*, now numbering six volumes, published by the Nichirenshū Overseas Propagation Promotion Association (NOPPA).[43] Each volume corresponds to one in the series *Nichiren Shōnin zenshū* 日蓮聖人全集, a collection of

Nichiren's writings translated into modern Japanese and annotated by leading scholars of Nichiren in Japan.[44] The English translations are based on the *Shōwa teihon* critical edition of Nichiren's work. A second collection of Nichiren's works in English is the two-volume *Writings of Nichiren Daishōnin*, published by Sōka Gakkai and available online in searchable format.[45] It is based on the single-volume Sōka Gakkai edition of Nichiren's writings.[46] Assisting in its translation was Burton Watson (1925–2017), professor emeritus of Columbia University and an accomplished translator of Chinese and Japanese literature. Two volumes of Nichiren's writings, translated by Watson and edited for a scholarly readership by his colleague, Philip Yampolsky (1920–1996), have been published by Columbia University Press.[47] (Watson also translated the *Ongi kuden* 御義口伝, a late medieval collection of oral teachings on the *Lotus Sutra* attributed to Nichiren but almost certainly the work of later disciples.)[48]

Among Nichiren's writings, more than two hundred survive, completely or partially, in his own hand; others have been handed down as copies made by early disciples or as later transcriptions and woodblock editions.[49] As is the case with many premodern Buddhist figures, some of the works transmitted as Nichiren's may be those of later disciples, and considerable scholarly disagreement surrounds the authenticity of specific texts. Disputed works include, for example, the *Sandai hihō honjōji*—mentioned in the section on "The Ordination Platform"—which mandates the establishment of a state-sponsored ordination platform. Suspicion has also been cast on writings containing accounts of seemingly miraculous events in Nichiren's life or showing strong influence of medieval Japanese Tendai "original enlightenment" (*hongaku* 本覚) discourse. Some commentators insist that interpretations of Nichiren should be based only on fully authenticatable works—an approach made possible only by the rare historical accident that so many of Nichiren's holographic writings have survived. Others opt for a more flexible stance encompassing those writings that survive only in transcription but do not contain glaring textual problems that would mark them as obvious apocrypha.[50] While future research may illuminate these issues, in the end it may prove impossible to distinguish clearly in all cases among Nichiren's own writings, those produced by immediate disciples with his approval, and later compositions attributed to him retrospectively. In this regard, Nichiren's case should be understood as representing the rule and not the exception.

DIGITAL MATERIALS

Nichiren's writings (in Japanese): The Nichirenshū Research Center for Contemporary Religion (Nichirenshū Gendai Shūkyō Kenkyūjo 日蓮宗現代宗教研究所) maintains an online database (https://genshu.nichiren.or.jp/documents/goibun/) of Nichiren's writings. These are divided into those surviving in Nichiren's holograph (*shinseki ibun* 真蹟遺文), those transmitted as later transcriptions (*shahon ibun* 写本遺文), charts (*zuroku* 図録), and fragments (*dankan* 断簡). This database follows the numbering system used in the *Shōwa Teihon Nichiren Shōnin ibun* (see note 3) and indicates its pagination. The *Chū Hokekyō*, Nichiren's annotated copy of the *Lotus Sutra*, is also available at this site.

A more sophisticated electronic database, the Nichiren Daishōnin gosho shisutemu (http://goshosystem.info/), has been made available by the research institute Kōfū Danjō 興風談所. Its use requires the installation of specialized Japanese software.

Nichiren's writings (in English): The two-volume *Writings of Nichiren Daishōnin*, published by Sōka Gakkai (1999–2006), is available online (https://www.nichirenlibrary.org/); see the section on "Primary Sources" for details. The translations are intended chiefly for Sōka Gakkai practitioners. English renderings of Buddhist terminology often differ from those used in the academic study of Buddhism, but the translations are generally clear and accurate.

A partial translation of volume 1 of the *Writings of Nichiren Shōnin*, published by the Nichirenshū Overseas Propagation Promotion Association (NOPPA), is available at GoogleBooks.

Depictions of Nichiren's life: Scenes from the life of Nichiren as depicted by the woodblock artist Utagawa Kuniyoshi 歌川国芳 (1798–1861) and others have been made available online (http://www.ris.ac.jp/library/nichiren-kichou/index.html) by the library of Risshō University.

Scholarly Studies of Nichiren in English: See "Revisiting Nichiren (https://nirc.nanzan-u.ac.jp/en/publications/jjrs/authors/)" (1999), a special issue of the *Japanese Journal of Religious Studies* co-edited by Ruben L. F. Habito and Jacqueline I. Stone. See also the university websites of Lucia Dolce (https://www.soas.ac.uk/staff/staff30872.php) and Jacqueline Stone (https://www.princeton.edu/~jstone), which include several articles on Nichiren and his tradition.

FURTHER READING

Dolce, Lucia. "Awareness of Mappō: Soteriological Interpretations of Time in Nichiren." *Transactions of the Asiatic Society of Japan*, 4th ser., 7 (1992): 81–106.

Dolce, Lucia. "Criticism and Appropriation: Nichiren's Attitude toward Esoteric Buddhism." *Japanese Journal of Religious Studies* 26, no. 3–4 (1999): 349–382.

Dolce, Lucia. "Between Duration and Eternity: Hermeneutics of the 'Ancient Buddha' of the Lotus Sutra in Chih-i and Nichiren." In *A Buddhist Kaleidoscope: Essays on the Lotus Sutra*. Edited by Gene Reeves, 223–239. Tokyo: Kōsei, 2002.

Dolce, Lucia. "Esoteric Patterns in Nichiren's Interpretation of the Lotus Sutra." PhD diss., University of Leiden, 2002.

Habito, Ruben L. F. "Bodily Reading of the Lotus Sutra." In *Readings of the Lotus Sutra*. Edited by Stephen F. Teiser and Jacqueline I. Stone, 186–208. New York: Columbia University Press, 2009.

Habito, Ruben L. F., and Jacqueline I. Stone, eds. "Revisiting Nichiren." Special issue, *Japanese Journal of Religious Studies* 26, nos. 3–4 (1999).

Lopez, Donald S. Jr., and Jacqueline I. Stone. *Two Buddhas Seated Side by Side: A Guide to the* Lotus Sutra. Princeton, NJ: Princeton University Press, 2019.

Motai Kyōkō 茂田井教亨. *Nichiren no Hokekyō kan* 日蓮の法華経観. Tokyo: Kōsei Shuppan, 1980.

Nakao Takashi 中尾尭. *Nichiren* 日蓮. Tokyo: Yoshikawa Kōbunkan, 2001.

Ōtani Gyōkō 大谷行亨. *Nichiren Shōnin no kanjin ron* 日蓮聖人の観心論. Tokyo: Sankibō Busshorin, 1999.

Satō Hiroo 佐藤弘夫. *Nichiren: Ware Nihon no hashira to naramu* 日蓮―われ日本の柱とならむ. Kyoto: Mineruba Shobō, 2003.

Stone, Jacqueline I. *Original Enlightenment and the Transformation of Medieval Japanese Buddhism*. Honolulu: University of Hawai'i Press, 1999. (See especially chap. 6, "Nichiren and the New Paradigm.")

Sueki Fumihiko 末木文美士. *Nichiren nyūmon: Gensei o utsu shisō* 日蓮入門―現世を撃つ思想. Tokyo: Chikuma Shobō, 2000.

Takagi Yutaka 高木豊. *Nichiren to sono montei* 日蓮とその門弟. Tokyo: Kōbundō, 1965.

Takagi Yutaka 高木豊. *Nichiren: Sono kōdō to shisō* 日蓮－その行動と思想. Tokyo: Hyōronsha, 1970 (Reprint 1985.)

Tamura Yoshirō 田村芳朗. *Nichiren: Junkyō no nyoraishi* 日蓮－殉教の如来使. Tokyo: Nihon Hōsō Shuppan Kyōkai, 1975.

Watanabe Hōyō 渡辺宝陽. *Nichiren bukkyōron: Sono kichō o nasu mono* 日蓮仏教論－その基調をなすもの. Tokyo: Shunjūsha, 2003.

NOTES

1. Takagi Yutaka 高木豊, *Nichiren: Sono kōdō to shisō* 日蓮－その行動と思想 (Tokyo: Hyōronsha, 1970), 13–15; and Nakao Takashi 中尾堯, *Nichiren* 日蓮 (Tokyo: Yoshikawa Kōbunkan, 2001), 18–26.
2. Ages are given according to traditional East Asian reckoning, by which people begin life at age one.
3. "Zenmui Sanzō shō" 善無畏三蔵鈔, in *Shōwa teihon Nichiren Shōnin ibun* 昭和定本日蓮聖人遺文, ed. Risshō Daigaku Nichiren Kyōgaku Kenkyūjo 立正大学日蓮教学研究所, 4 vols. (Minobu-chō, Yamanashi-ken: Sōhonzan Minobu Kuonji, 1952–1959), 1:473.
4. *Kaitai sokushin jōbutsu gi* 戒体即身成仏義, in Risshō Daigaku, *Teihon*, 1:12.
5. Takagi, *Nichiren*, 47–54; and Nakao, *Nichiren*, 54–66.
6. "*Namu Myōhō-renge-kyō*" represents proper scholarly romanization. In actual chanting, minor variations in pronunciation occur among practice groups as a matter of lineage convention. Some, for example, elide the "u" sound between "*Namu*" and "*Myōhō*."
7. Jacqueline I. Stone, "Chanting the August Title of the *Lotus Sutra*," in *Re-Visioning "Kamakura" Buddhism*, ed. Richard K. Payne (Honolulu: University of Hawai'i Press, 1998), 116–166; and Lucia Dolce, "Esoteric Patterns in Nichiren's Interpretation of the *Lotus Sutra*" (PhD diss., Leiden University, 2002), 294–315.
8. *Shugo kokka ron* 守護国家論, in Risshō Daigaku, *Teihon*, 1:129.
9. Jacqueline I. Stone, *Original Enlightenment and the Transformation of Medieval Japanese Buddhism* (Honolulu: University of Hawai'i Press, 1999), 251–255.
10. *Miaofa lianhua jing* 妙法蓮華經, *T* 262, 9:16a15, 36a5, and 43b23.
11. *T* 9:19b19–20.
12. *Kaimoku shō* 開目抄, in Risshō Daigaku, *Teihon*, 1:601, 604.
13. Jacqueline I. Stone, "The Atsuhara Affair: The *Lotus Sutra*, Persecution, and Religious Identity in the Early Nichiren Tradition," *Japanese Journal of Religious Studies* 41, no. 1 (2014): 153–189.
14. Jan Nattier, *Once upon a Future Time: Studies in a Buddhist Prophecy of Decline* (Berkeley, CA: East Asian Humanities Press, 1991), 65–118.
15. "Omonsu-dono nyōbō gohenji" 重須殿女房御返事, in Risshō Daigaku, *Teihon*, 2:1856.
16. "Shōmitsu-bō gosho" 聖密房御書, in Risshō Daigaku, *Teihon*, 1:822. See also Stone, *Original Enlightenment*, 263–266.
17. *Hokke daimoku shō* 法華題目鈔, in Risshō Daigaku, *Teihon*, 1:392.
18. Partially translated in Paul Swanson, *Foundations of T'ien-t'ai Philosophy: The Flowering of the Two Truths Theory in Chinese Buddhism* (Berkeley, CA: Asian Humanities Press, 1989), 164–256.
19. *Kanjin honzon shō* 観心本尊抄, in Risshō Daigaku, *Teihon*, 1:711; and see also Stone, *Original Enlightenment*, 267–270.
20. "Shijō Kingo-dono gohenji" 四条金吾殿御返事, in Risshō Daigaku, *Teihon*, 2:1181.
21. Lucia Dolce, "Reconsidering the Origins of Nichiren's 'Great Mandala of the Lotus Sutra,'" in *Universal and International Nature of the Lotus Sutra: Proceedings of the Seventh International Conference on the Lotus Sutra*, ed. Rissho University Executive Committee for the Seventh International Conference on the Lotus Sutra (Tokyo: Sankibō Busshorin, 2013), 187–209.

22. Takagi, *Nichiren*, 168–171.
23. Sueki Fumihiko, "Nichiren's Problematic Works," *Japanese Journal of Religious Studies* 26, nos. 3–4 (1999): 261–280, 264–273; and Jacqueline I. Stone, "'By Imperial Edict and Shogunal Decree: Politics and the Issue of the Ordination Platform in Modern Lay Nichiren Buddhism," in *Buddhism in the Modern World: Adaptations of an Ancient Tradition*, ed. Steven Heine and Charles S. Prebish (New York: Oxford, 2003), 193–219, 194–197.
24. *T* 9:52a25–26.
25. "Nyosetsu shugyō shō" 如説修行鈔, in Risshō Daigaku, *Teihon*, 1:735.
26. *Kaimoku shō*, 1:606.
27. Ruben L. F. Habito, "Bodily Reading of the *Lotus Sutra*," in *Readings of the Lotus Sutra*, ed. Stephen F. Teiser and Jacqueline I. Stone (New York: Columbia University Press, 2009), 186–208, 198–199.
28. *Shuju onfurumai gosho* 種種御振舞御書, in Risshō Daigaku, *Teihon*, 2:961–962.
29. "Nyosetsu shugyō shō," in *Teihon*, ed. Risshō Daigaku, 1:733.
30. *Senji shō* 選時抄, in *Teihon*, ed. Risshō Daigaku, 2:1009.
31. The name "Nichirenshū" is used to denote both a specific Nichiren Buddhist denomination, whose head temple is Kuonji at Mt. Minobu in Yamanashi Prefecture, and the broader Nichiren Buddhist tradition as a whole. In this case, the first meaning is indicated.
32. Nichirenshū Jiten Kankō Iinkai 日蓮宗事典刊行委員会, ed., *Nichirenshū jiten* 日蓮宗事典 (Tokyo: Nichirenshū Shūmuin, 1981); and Risshō Daigaku Nichiren Kyōgaku Kenkyūjo, ed., *Nichiren Shōnin ibun jiten* 日蓮聖人遺文辞典 (Minobu-chō, Yamanashi-ken: Sōhonzan Minobu Kuonji, 1984).
33. *Shirīzu Nichiren*, ed. Komatsu Kuniaki 小松邦彰 et al. 5 vols. (Tokyo: Shunjūsha, 2014–2015).
34. Masaharu Anesaki, *Nichiren, the Buddhist Prophet* (Cambridge, MA: Harvard University Press, 1916).
35. Gaston Renondeau, *La Doctrine de Nichiren* (Paris: Presses universitaires de France, 1953); Alicia Matsunaga and Daigan Matsunaga, *Foundation of Japanese Buddhism*, vol. 2: *The Mass Movement (Kamakura and Muromachi Periods)* (Los Angeles: Buddhist Books International, 1976), esp. chap. 3; Bruno Petzold, *Buddhist Prophet Nichiren: A Lotus in the Sun*, ed. Shotaro Iida and Wendy Simmonds (Tokyo: Hokke Jānaru, 1978); and Laurel Rasplica Rodd, *Nichiren: Selected Writings* (Honolulu: University Press of Hawaii, 1980).
36. See for example, Lucia Dolce, "Criticism and Appropriation: Nichiren's Attitude toward Esoteric Buddhism," *Japanese Journal of Religious Studies* 26, nos. 3–4 (1999): 349–382. See also other articles on Nichiren listed at Dolce's university website, https://www.soas.ac.uk/staff/staff30872.php.
37. Habito, "Bodily Reading," 186–190.
38. For example, Jacqueline I. Stone, "Nichiren and the New Paradigm," in *Original Enlightenment and the Transformation of Medieval Japanese Buddhism*, by Jacqueline I. Stone (Honolulu: University of Hawai'i Press, 1999), 239–299; and see also "Articles on the Lotus Sutra, Tendai, and Nichiren Buddhism" at Stone's university website.
39. Ruben L. F. Habito and Jacqueline I.Stone, eds., "Revisiting Nichiren," special issue, *Japanese Journal of Religious Studies* 26, nos. 3–4 (1999).
40. See *Shōwa teihon Nichiren Shōnin ibun*, note 3.
41. Yamanaka Kihachi 山中喜八, ed., *Teihon Chū Hokekyō* 定本注法華經 (Kyoto: Hōzōkan, 1980).
42. Yamanaka Kihachi 山中喜八, *Nichiren Shōnin shinseki no sekai* 日蓮聖人真蹟の世界, vol. 1 (Tokyo: Yūzankaku, 1992); and in English, see Luigi Finocchiaro and Nichiren Mandala Study Workshop, eds., *The Mandala in Nichiren Buddhism*, parts 1–2 (by the editors, 2013–2014), and http://www.lulu.com/shop/http://www.lulu.com/shop/the-nichiren-mandala-study-workshop/the-mandala-in-nichiren-buddhism-part-two-mandalas-of-the-k%C5%8Dan-period/paperback/product-23898444.html. These volumes are based chiefly on an earlier version of Yamanaka's collection, the *Nichiren Daishōnin goshinseki gohonzonshū* 日蓮大聖人御真蹟御本尊集 (Chiba: Risshō Ankoku Kai, 1975).

43. *Writings of Nichiren Shōnin*, ed. Kyōtsū Hori et al. 6 vols. (Tokyo: Nichirenshū Overseas Propagation Promotion Association, 2003–2010).
44. Watanabe Hōyō 渡辺宝陽 and Komatsu Kuniaki 小松邦彰, eds., *Nichiren Shōnin zenshū* 日蓮聖人全集, 7 vols. (Tokyo: Shunjūsha, 2011).
45. Gosho Translation Committee, ed. and trans., *Writings of Nichiren Daishōnin*. 2 vols. (Tokyo: Sōka Gakkai, 1999–2006).
46. Hori Nichikō 堀日亨 (1867–1957), ed., *Nichiren Daishōnin gosho zenshū* 日蓮大聖人御書全集 (Tokyo: Sōka Gakkai, 1952).
47. Burton Watson et al., trans., Philip B. Yampolsky, ed., *Selected Writings of Nichiren* (New York: Columbia University Press, 1990); and Burton Watson et al., trans., Philip B. Yampolsky, ed., *Letters of Nichiren* (New York: Columbia University Press, 1996).
48. Burton Watson, trans., *The Record of the Orally Transmitted Teachings* (Tokyo: Sōka Gakkai, 2004).
49. For details, see Suzuki Ichijō 鈴木一成, *Nichiren Shōnin ibun no bunkengakuteki kenkyū* 日蓮聖人遺文の文献学的研究 (Tokyo: Sankibō Busshorin, 1965), 3–10; and Yamanaka Kihachi 山中喜八, *Nichiren Shōnin shinseki no sekai* 日蓮聖人真蹟の世界, vol. 2 (Tokyo: Yūzankaku, 1993), 57–67.
50. For summaries of these arguments, see Jacqueline I. Stone, "Some Disputed Texts in the Nichiren Corpus: Textual, Hermeneutical and Historical Problems" (PhD diss., University of California, Los Angeles, 1990); and Sueki, "Nichiren's Problematic Works," 261–280. More recent work promises to shed new light on the processes by which Nichiren's works were compiled. See, for example, Emanuele D. Giglio ジッリォ・エマヌエーレ・ダヴィデ, "*Shohō jissō shō* no raireki: *Rokunai, Rokuge* no shūsei jijō to Sairen-bō den kara" 『諸法実相抄』の来歴—「録内」「録外」の集成事情と最蓮房伝から, *Indo tetsugaku bukkyōgaku kenkyū* インド哲学仏教学研究 20 (2013): 106–144.

Jacqueline Stone

P

PATRONAGE OF BUDDHIST MONASTERIES IN EASTERN INDIA, 600–1300 CE

NATURE OF PATRONAGE TO MONASTERIES

A defining feature of religion in early medieval India was the rapid expansion of Brahmanical religion.[1] Temples occupied a predominant position, and the temple acted as an institutional base for the bhakti movement. With the predominance of Brahmanical bhakti cults, Buddhism was relegated to the background in most of the regions, a significant exception being eastern India. Here Buddhism flourished, leading to the establishment of numerous monasteries of various sizes and scales. Eastern India includes the present regions of Bihar and West Bengal in India, and Bangladesh. Though the state of Odisha is taken to be a part of eastern India, the region of Orissa is not included here, as culturally and politically during early times northern and western Odisha were inclined more to central India and southern Odisha more to Andhra Pradesh. Bihar and Bengal abounded in several *mahāvihāras*, *vihāras*, and *vihārikās* (Buddhist monasteries of different scales) during the early medieval period of Indian history (*c.* 600–1300 CE). Xuanzang (600?–664 CE) was the first person who introduced scholars to many of these monasteries, which were active during his visit to the subcontinent.[2] Scholars have reference to five *mahāvihāras* from the work of Lāmā Tāranātha, though he belonged to a much later period. These *mahāvihāras* were Nalanda, Somapura, Vikramaśīla, Jagaddala, and Odantapurī.[3] In addition to these five *mahāvihāras*, the more recently published Chaprakot inscription of Gopāla IV talks about another *mahāvihāra*, at Kuṭumvavilla, which could be Chaprakot itself in the Rangpur district of northern Bangladesh.[4] Scholars have reference to Āpaṇaka *mahāvihāra* in image inscriptions from Kurkihar, Bihar, from the 9th to the beginning of the 12th centuries.[5] Gradually with archaeological excavations in various sites and inscriptional evidence one comes across numerous *vihāras* and *vihārikās* in eastern India. These monasteries were basically establishments with monks and nuns in residence. Some of them were also educational establishments where students from other regions and abroad would come. Moreover, these were places where large numbers of religious texts were being written, translated, painted, and copied. It is but natural that construction of a monastery, which was an action of faith, would also mean taking care of the sustenance of the people that inhabit the monastery and many other associated things.

But what could be the modus operandi? Naturally one way would be donation, which is a form of patronage. Royal patronage was undoubtedly an abiding feature, but there were other agencies of patronage that sustained these monasteries. Sources indicate that in the case of monasteries in eastern India, there were different kinds of patron or benefactor. These were rulers and their families, subordinate rulers or military officials, members of the monastic community, and the laity. They had to take care of three things: worship of the buddha, the multiple requirements of the monastic community, and repairs and renovation of the monastic structures. From the epigraphic evidence one learns that the founder ruler and the subordinate rulers who also constructed monasteries had some say in the functioning of the monasteries. Through the practice of *dāna* (gift giving) and in several cases *deyadhamma* (donation for the sake of acquiring merit), the laity unconditionally supported the monastic establishments, providing robes, food, and shelter for the monks and nuns as well as copies of texts, images, paintings, and the ritual objects needed for religious practices.[6] A symbiotic relation between the *saṁgha* and the lay population was the foundation of a viable Buddhist society. There was a substantial patronage from the lay community, which is evident also from the donation of images by people from various occupational groups in these monasteries. It will be worthwhile to mention here that the type of patronage in these monasteries differed from the earlier forms of patronage to early Buddhist monuments like *stūpas* and *saṁghas*. A preeminent feature of patronage to these early monuments was collective patronage; very rarely one has evidence of royal patronage: for example, from about six hundred donative records at Sanchi, only three belonged to royalty.[7] The case was different for the early medieval period. Here royal donation and donation from the elites outweighed the ordinary people, though they were not invisible. Nalanda is a classic example with evidence of donations by monarchs of all categories—including imperial, regional, and local; subordinates and other elites; and persons of the monastic order and laity—belonging to various kinds of professions or occupations. However, the pattern that emerges in Nalanda is not the same for other monasteries. When one sifts through the sources for other *mahāvihāras* like Vikramasila, Somapura, Jagaddala, and other monasteries in south Bihar and north Bengal, one perceives that the donations are mostly from rulers, subordinate rulers, monks, and perhaps elites. The laity comprising occupational or professional groups is practically absent in the records. However, the silence perhaps should not be interpreted as absence of patronage from a large social base. It could so happen that their form of patronage was through a means that did not stand the test of time. Southeastern Bengal offers a picture largely of royal patronage. One has the presence of local ruling houses who patronized Buddhist monasteries until around the 9th century CE, but after that with the emergence of the Candras as a regional power there was a shift in the pattern of patronage, in spite of the Candra ruler's claim of being a *parama saugata* (devout Buddhist).

METHODOLOGY

For an overview of the nature of patronage in the monasteries of eastern India in the early medieval period, this article intends a region-wise study, taking into consideration primarily the monasteries of south Bihar, north Bengal (West Bengal and Bangladesh), and southeastern Bengal (Bangladesh). Significantly, between the second half of the 8th century and the third quarter of the 12th century CE, the area from south Bihar to north Bengal (including Bangladesh) formed the core territory of the Pāla rulers, who were patrons of Buddhism. The evidence relating to *mahāvihāras* suggests that they were all constructed by the Pāla rulers. Eastern India saw extraordinary development of Mahāyāna Buddhism, which was nurtured in the various monasteries established by these Pāla rulers. Each of these monasteries has received scholarly attention from archaeologists, specialists of Buddhism, and historians in general, and there is substantial literature on them in a broad spectrum but not patronage per se. This article writes a narrative of patterns of patronage in each of these monasteries by sifting through the archaeological and textual sources.

MONASTERIES OF SOUTH BIHAR

Nalanda Mahāvihāra. The most celebrated monastic site not only in eastern India but in the entire South Asia was Nalanda, the oldest eastern Indian *mahāvihāra*. The site was identified by Sir Alexander Cunningham with Bargaon in Bihar following the travel accounts of the Chinese monk Xuanzang.[8] A look at the monastery's trajectory of growth would suggest that its benefactors have mostly been royal. The written records unearthed at Nalanda, like seals and inscriptions on stone and copper plates, give one an idea of the patronage. One of the earliest and most informative accounts of Nalanda was compiled by Xuanzang.[9] He noted that the revenue of one hundred villages supported the monastery. The lay community also contributed rice, butter, and milk, so that the monks need not beg for food. The structures show that it was a well-funded monastery.

From various references like clay sealings and the description of Xuanzang one learns that King Śakrāditya, identified with Kumāragupta I (*c.* 415–455 CE), was the first person to build a monastery at Nalanda—"*[ndā]-yamŚrī-Śakrāditya-Kārita . . . vihāre-chāturddisiy-ārya-(ma) hābhikṣhusaṅghasya.*"[10] His son and successor Budhagupta built a monastery to the south of it. To the east of this a monastery was built by Tathāgatagupta. To the northeast of this, King Bālāditya added a fourth monastery. To the west of this monastery, Bālāditya's son and successor Vajra built his monastery. Xuanzang writes that King Pūrṇavarman donated a copper image of Buddha in a six-story temple that was located to the southeastern side of Bālāditya's temple. The identity of Pūrṇavarman is perplexing, and Rajat Sanyal has thrown light on this.[11]

Sanyal reminds scholars of a beautifully engraved inscription by one Mādhava, son of *nagarasūttradhāra* Vāmana found at the site of Sarai mound. The inscription reads that a huge image of the buddha was donated by a king named Prathamaśiva, a ruler of Mathurā.[12] The size of the image was underscored by the statement that the image looked like the Himalayan mountains. It could be a reference to the size as well as greatness of Lord Buddha. What is striking is that the sculptor of this image was Pūrṇavarman, whose fame reached the heavens too. In a critical study of this inscription, Gouriswar Bhattacharya dates it around the end of the 6th century, thus prior to Xuanzang's presence in Nalanda. The inscription of Prathamaśiva has been wrongly ascribed to Pūrṇavarman, who was not a king but a sculptor. Sanyal has rightfully argued that the confusion was created because the visit of Prathamaśiva was prior to Xuanzang's visit and not in the 7th or 8th centuries as argued by Frederick Asher. Xuanzang relied on hearsay, and in all probability, as articulated by Sanyal, in the memory of the people of the locality the memory of Pūrṇavarman as a "local" master artist was more vibrant than the patron king Prathamaśiva, who was an outsider. Thus here one has Prathamaśiva as another patron of Nalanda. His presence in the locale is perhaps further vindicated by the reading of a monastic sealing by Sanyal in the more recently excavated Buddhist monastic site of Telhara, which was TI-LO-SHI-KA or TI-LOTSE-KA of Xuanzang's account. The sealing reads *śrīpathamaśivapuramahāvihāriy āryabhikṣusaṅghasya* ("of the council of monks of the illustrious Prathamaśivapura monastery").[13] The monastery of Telhara was named after Prathamaśiva, who in all probability was the same as King Prathamaśiva from Mathura. This monastery will be discussed in the section "Odantapuri Mahāvihāra."

Among other ruler-patrons, sealings of Harṣavardhana found in Nalanda suggest that he was a patron of Nalanda. According to Xuanzang, Harṣa endowed the revenues of about a hundred villages for the maintenance and upkeep of the inmates of Nalanda *mahāvihāra*, and two hundred households of these villages would contribute to the daily needs of the residing community of monks.[14]

The excavations at Nalanda have yielded many clay seals bearing the name of several kings. These seals provide evidence for patronage. Some of them are of kings of other kingdoms like Bhāskaravarman (king of Kāmarūpa), Dhrūvabhaṭa (referred as the king of south India), Aṅsuvarman (referred as a Nepalese king), Sarvvavarman (Maukhari ruler), and so on. Seals of officials like Paśupatisiṁha, Śrī-Sāgarasiṁha, and Devasiṁha have also been unearthed. Seals of both Dharmapāla and Devapāla are also found in Nalanda, which refer to *gandhakuṭī* built by them. Dēvapāladeva was more closely associated with this institution.[15] The Ghoshrawan Stone Inscription of Yaśōvarmadeva states that Pāla king Devapāladēva had appointed an abbot to Nalanda for the proper running of its monastic organization.[16] This is an indication of the fact that the patron had say in the administration of a monastery.[17]

Why does one find seals of almost all the royal lineages of eastern India in Nalanda? Put differently, what prompted these rulers to donate here? Sanyal has argued that by donating to this most celebrated Buddhist monastery and center of learning, the rulers were claiming a kind of legitimacy.[18] Since these rulers were already legitimate rulers of their respective kingdoms, instead of legitimacy it could be prestige and merit; patronage gave them both.

From sigillography one learns that by the 7th century CE Nalanda's fame had spread far and wide to encourage rulers beyond Magadha to donate to Nalanda. Epigraphic references also bear this out. Here particular mention may be made of a copper-plate charter from around the 8th century CE, found at the monastery of Site 1, which records a gift, presumably an endowment, from Mālāda, the son of a minister of King Yaśovarmadeva.[19] This Yaśovarman could perhaps be identified with Yaśovarman of Kanauj, who killed Jīvitagupta II, the last king of the Later Gupta dynasty of Magadha. He made multiple gifts at Nalanda, like a permanent endowment for the buddha (*akṣayanīvikā bhagavate vuddhāya*) at the temple of Bālāditya. There he offered the paraphernalia of worship such as pure water mixed with the powder of four fragrant objects, a shining lamp, clarified butter, and curd. The monks were provided with a residence and daily rice with various preparations to be redistributed at the daily *sattra*. Significantly, in the concluding imprecatory verse there is a clear indication that the lord *jina* always resided here, and so no obstacle should be created. In the opinion of Gregory Schopen, in this imprecatory verse "the sense of personal presence (*sākṣād.iha*) and permanence abiding (*sadāste*) is pronounced."[20] Thus the permanent endowment was given to the buddha himself. Sanjukta Datta suggested that this inscription throws light on aspects of the *mahāvihāra*'s built history and organization, at times corroborating information gleaned from other inscriptions—for example, the temple of Bālāditya perhaps referred to Bālāditya's *gandhakuṭī* of the seal inscription.[21] Mālāda was the owner of the monastery (*vihārasvāmī*), which gave him the right to reserve some place within it for himself.

The Pāla rulers Dharmapāla, Dēvapāla, and Mahīpāla figured as the leading patrons of Nalanda. Excavations at Nalanda give very good insight about the close association of the Pālas with this monastic establishment. Nine inscriptions belonging to the Pāla period have been found from the monastery ruins. Among them are two inscriptions from the reign of Dharmapāla, one from the reign of Gopāla II, and the rest belong to the reign of Devapāla.

Nalanda received endowments not only from the royalty but also from the lay devotees like merchants, officials, teachers, and so on. Three merchant brothers named Mudgāragomin, Śaṅkarapati, and Bṛhaspati-Siddharāja are said to have constructed one hundred *vihāras*. One hundred *vihāras* is certainly an exaggeration, but that they built some monasteries here is evident. In the 7th century CE a teacher of Nalanda named Nāgārjuna II arranged the maintenance of five hundred *mahāyāna* teachers, with the help of his treasures. Rāhulabhadra, who probably flourished as a teacher during the 7th to 8th centuries CE, established fourteen *gandhakūṭis* and fourteen schools at Nalanda.[22] Among the lay male donors are also inscriptions of Vairocana, Udayabhadra, Khacchuka, Bālāditya, and Vaidyanāthadeva, who were involved in donation at the monastery either in the form of *stūpas*, pillars, or images.[23] Among these epigraphic records, the inscription of Bālāditya stands out for its rich content, which unveils a second phase of activity at Nalanda and restoration of temple 12 by Bālāditya. The inscription states that in the eleventh regnal year of the Pāla king Mahipāla I, Bālāditya, who was a resident of Telāḍhaka, having come from Kauśāmbī, made a substantial meritorious gift following a restoration of the temple after a fire.[24]

The monks and nuns were also great patrons. One finds evidence of numerous donations by monks and nuns throughout history. At Nalanda too one has inscriptions of donor monks, of which the inscription of Vipulaśrīmitra deserves attention. The Buddhist ascetic Vipulaśrīmitra constructed the final phase of monastery number 7 in the first half of the 12th century. Along with building the *vihārikā*, Vipulaśrīmitra perhaps made an offering of the *Aṣṭasāhsarikā Prajñāpāramitā* manuscript at the temple of Khasarpaṇa Avalokiteśvara and donated four images at the *sattra* on the occasion of a festival.[25] In addition to these he made multiple donations that suggest that he was a wealthy person.

It appears that Nalanda's reputation also reached countries beyond India by the 9th century CE. A Korean inscription refers to the 13th- or 14th-century Indian monk Tinabotuo, who was trained and ordained at Nalanda before traveling to Beijing.[26] Regarding the question of international patronage, one copper-plate inscription from Nalanda is singularly important. The inscription talks about a grant of five villages by the Pāla king Devapāla in his thirty-ninth regnal year, at the request of Mahārāja Bālaputradeva, the Śailendra ruler of Suvarṇadvīpa/Yavabhūmi, in favor of a monastery built by the latter at Nalanda.[27] Mahārāja Bālaputradeva was attracted by the excellent qualities of Nālanda. The inscription can be placed in the 9th century, and the Śailendra dynasty was based in central Java. The income from the five villages was to provide for the various needs of the *bhikṣus* living there, the writing of the *dharmaratnas*, and the maintenance of the monastery. In the opinion of Upinder Singh, the grant fits in with the strong Buddhist element in the personal religious orientation and the patronage policy of the Pālas and the Śailendras.[28] The gift is described as a pious meritorious act (*dharmmādhikāra*) and *kīrtti*. Merit was naturally the main contention of both the rulers. Interestingly, for Devapāla with merit came also fame for himself and his parents, and for Bālaputra it is merit and the welfare of himself, his parents, and the world. It was perhaps the earliest endowment of a Southeast Asian ruler in South Asia.

Nalanda's paramount position as a *mahāvihāra* is further evident from the royal patronage the monastery continued to receive during the Pāla period (8th to 12th centuries CE). The temples and monasteries show several phases of renovation and construction. Of importance is monastery number 1, where different phases of construction are marked by different schools of sculptural art, starting from scroll art of the Gupta period to other varieties of the Pāla period.[29] Two damaged copper plates of Samudragupta and Dharmapāla were recovered from this monastery. Nalanda was a monastic site of unsurpassed reputation, and thus it received patronage from all quarters.

Vikramaśila Mahāvihāra. The other great monastery in Bihar was Vikramaśila. It followed the Vajrayāna tradition according to Tibetan sources, and five branches of knowledge were taught.[30] Though no monastic sealing with the name Vikramaśila has been found from the site of Antichak, the monastery is generally identified with Antichak in the Bhagalpur district of Bihar.[31] Frederick Asher argued that the monastery unearthed at Antichak is similar to the one at Paharpur known as Somapura *mahāvihāra*, on the basis of the architecture and sculptures recovered from both sites.[32] One first learns about this monastery from a manuscript of *Aṣṭasāhasrikā Prajnāpāramitā* dated in the 15th regnal year of the Pāla king Gopāla III in the second half of the 10th century CE, and subsequently in another manuscript of the same text dated in the 15th year of Gopāla IV in the late 11th century CE, both being copied at Vikramaśila. In a scribal colophon of a manuscript of Vajragarbha's *Hevajratantrapiṇḍārthtikā* it is said that the text was penned there (*śrimad Vikramaśilamahāvihāre*).[33] The biography of the Tibetan monk Dharmasvāmin (who visited Magadha around 1234 CE) records that Dharmasvāmin's uncle (1153–1216 CE) studied at Vikramaśila, but when Dharmasvāmin visited the place it was in ruins.[34] This suggests that by 1234 CE the monastery was not functioning or existing anymore. Tibetan sources speak of Vikramaśila as an important monastic university that conferred the prestigious title of Paṇḍita on Atīśa. By the late 11th century it housed around 160 *paṇḍitas* and one thousand monks.[35]

It is to be noted that the excavation revealed the remains of a colossal monastic structure set in a single culture occupation divided into three structural phases (8th to 13th centuries CE). The exterior wall appears to have been fortified, at regular intervals there are foundations of round and square towers, and the only point of access is a single gateway facing north. Significantly, many weapons of various categories (axe, shouldered celts, different kinds of daggers, knives, barbed arrowheads, etc.) have been found, which may suggest that these were for the safety of the inhabitants of the monastery.[36]

Such a huge monastery would naturally need resources to sustain it, and it is quite certain that this monastery founded by Dharmapāla himself would continue to enjoy royal patronage. Unfortunately, unlike other monasteries like Somapura or Nalanda, in case of Vikramaśila, sources are limited. No copper-plate charter is found to suggest land grants for the maintenance of the monastery. However, nonavailability should not lead one to believe that there were none. There are a few inscriptions from seals and sealings that add to knowledge. These are largely seals of individuals, whose names are given but professions or occupations are not mentioned, except in the case of two, where the donors are probably ministers (*mantrin*). There are also a few seals where the name of the person has an honorific "Śrī" as prefix. This naturally points to the elite status of the donors. These are dated mostly to the 11th and 12th centuries CE. Inscribed images were unearthed during excavations, four having the names of the donors. Of these, two are donations of a goldsmith called Mancika (Sonar Mancika), but the images could not be identified as they were broken.[37] A seated Tārā image is striking, where the inscription records that it was the *Deyadharma* of *Mahāyāna-Anuyāyinaḥ Paramopāsaka Śrī Upādhāyaya*.

Apart from the Pāla rulers, there is a royal inscription from Antichak indicating patronage in Vikramaśila by a local polity. The inscription dated to the 12th century CE is engraved in a pillar and is a *praśasti* of a local ruler, Sahura or Sahvara, who professed Buddhism, though the early rulers appear to be of Brahmanical faith.[38] Sahura established an image in the *vihāra* that was built by Rājyapāla. It appears from the inscription that he was a good fighter and a learned person. Interestingly, a few seals have been found from excavations bearing the name Sahara, which can be dated around the 12th century. It is argued that this Sahara is not same as King Sahura/Sahvara, as there is no royal epithet as a prefix to his name.[39] However, in the inscription too, though his ancestors used high-sounding epithets, he is introduced only with the honorific *Śrī*. That he was not an ordinary person is understood by the fact that at least four seals carry the name Sahara. Sahura was succeeded by his son Māsanikeśa, who caused the eulogy to be composed by Mañjuśrī, who is said to be a *paṇḍita*. The very name "Mañjuśrī" is evocative of his religious affiliation. The names of the rulers give an idea of their autochthonous origin and suggest that during the end of the Pāla rule eastern Bihar was literally under the local rulers. It is said that Sahura was a friend of the king of Gauḍa and defeated the army of the Vaṅgas. While Gauḍas meant later Pālas, Vaṅgas perhaps meant the Sena rulers. The title *Sakalabhūmipatipradipaḥ* for the first ruler Kesara along with *Rājādhirāja, Parameśvara,* and *Divyamūrtti* suggest that these rulers seem to be independent of the Pālas and offered nominal friendship. Thus, they do not fall under the category of subordinate rulers. The *praśasti* was certainly used as a tool to legitimize the authority of this local polity, which did not have a strong lineage to boast of. The choice of engraving the *praśasti* within the complex of the Vikramaśila *mahāvihāra* suggests that the ruling monarch was a patron of the monastery. The early rulers of this dynasty were adherents of Brahmanism; Hanasana is described as Lord Cakrapāṇi incarnate. Perhaps the strong presence of Buddhism and the importance of Vikramaśila *mahāvihāra* brought these local chiefs under the Buddhist network, and they were attracted to Vajrayāna Buddhism. There must have been many more donors considering the size of the monastery, but unfortunately they are invisible.

Odantapuri Mahāvihāra. Odantapuri as a *mahāvihāra* finds a place in the list of *mahāvihāras* mentioned by Tāranātha.[40] Tāranātha's statement has to be used cautiously as he belonged to the 17th century, but in the case of Odantapuri sources are so meager that this article is partly drawing from his account. Odantapuri is identified with modern Bihar Sharif in Bihar. It was founded in the 8th century CE by Gopāla, the first ruler of the Pāla dynasty, perhaps emulating Nalanda. It is also called Odantapura or Uddaṇḍapura. Unfortunately, one is limited by sources to know about the nature of patronage here. Stray references in Tāranātha's work suggest that later Pāla rulers continued to extend their patronage.[41] Moreover, during the time of Rāmapāla, a thousand monks lived in Odantapuri. Occasionally even twelve thousand monks congregated there. Odantapuri served as a model and inspiration for Tibetan Buddhists. One learns that the principal temple of Sam-Ye (Bsam-yas), built in 749 and three stories high, was modeled on Odantapuri and that several distinguished Tibetan scholars studied there.[42] It appears that the *mahāvihāra* of Odantapuri survived on the patronage it received from the Pāla rulers. However, there must have been other patrons whose history is not unearthed yet.[43]

Apart from these *mahāvihāras*, a famous *vihāra* near Nalanda was the one at Telhara, known as the *Prathamaśivapuravihāra* mentioned earlier. Xuanzang refers to it as Tilāḍhaka Monastery. It consisted of four courts, three-story pavilions, lofty terraces, and gates that opened wide leading from one to another. There were thousands of monks, all of whom studied Mahāyāna teachings.[44] Scholars and visitors from faraway lands visited this monastery. The excavations at the site (2009–2010 to 2012–2013) seem to largely confirm the account of the pilgrim.[45] The diggings have exposed walls of monasteries, inner chambers of temples, and cells belonging to different periods. The repertoire of stone sculptures of Telhara also has a long chronological span ranging from the 6th to 12th centuries CE. Clay tablets recording names of Maukhari rulers Avantivarman and Iśānavarman that were discovered from the excavations at Telhara suggest patronage by the Maukhari dynasty. A stone inscription dated in the reign of Kumārapāla, incidentally the first epigraphic record of this king, was found in Telhara.[46] As Yi Jing recounts, a Chinese scholar, known as Prajñādeva in India, visited Tilāḍhaka monastery to meet a monk renowned for his mastery of logic. While at Tilāḍhaka, Prajñādeva made a "complete translation of the *Sarvāstivādin vinaya*."[47] Hence it is apparent that at Telhara the monastery flourished primarily through royal patronage, and of course it was also supported by laity. The royalty ranged from a ruler of Mathura who gave his name to the monastery, to the Maukharīs and Pālas.

Another monastery that finds mention in an inscription from Ghosrawan was Yaśovarmapura *vihāra*. The inscription was found at the site and is of singular importance in the context of mobility of monks. It informs that a monk called Vīradeva originally hailing from Nagrahāra (near Jalalabad in western Pakistan) visited Yaśovarmanpura *vihāra* and stayed there for a long time.[48] The inscription claims that the monk was held in great esteem by the Pala ruler

Devapāla, who perhaps gave patronage to the monastery. Moreover, the name of the monastery may remind one of king Yaśovarman of Kanauj, who defeated the Later Gupta ruler Jīvitagupta II during the third or fourth decade of the 8th century CE; Yaśovarman could have been a founder benefactor of this monastery. The name of the village Ghosrawan appears to have been Ghosaligrāma in the 11th century CE, based on the colophon of a manuscript of the *Aṣṭasāhasrikā Prajñāpāramitā Sūtra* of about the same period.[49] Thus as far as the information goes, this monastery thrived on royal patronage.

PATRONAGE AT BODHGAYA

Although there is no reference to any *mahāvihāra* in Bodhgaya, in a narrative of patronage relating to Buddhism in eastern India, Bodhgaya needs to be present, albeit briefly. Faxian stated that at the place of the buddha's enlightenment, there were three monasteries; monks resided in all of them. The local people provided the monks with daily necessities in abundance, and nothing was insufficient for their needs.[50] The seat of enlightenment of Lord Buddha with its temple called Mahābodhi is the most coveted pilgrimage center for Buddhists across Asia.[51] Naturally its share of donation was much more than what the other monastic centers received. Patronage to Bodhgaya came from far and wide. Here there was a link between pilgrimage and patronage. An impressive number of sculptural remains and assemblage of votive *stūpas* are located at different positions within the Mahābodhi temple complex. Numerous donations were inscribed. The group of donor-monks was quite impressive. The donative record of Sri Lankan monk Mahānāman (588/589 CE), which talks about the temple that he built at the *bodhimaṇḍa*, is worth referring to. It shows how the pilgrim Mahānāman takes part in an important development during the 5th and 6th centuries, namely, the consolidation of the long-attested ties between Lanka and Bodhgaya.[52] Significantly, patronage from the Pāla monarchs is missing in the Mahābodhi, though their able administration perhaps facilitated the mobility of the monks and people from various parts of the subcontinent.

From around the 11th century CE, the Mahābodhi temple began to receive patronage from regions of Asia like Myanmar, Sri Lanka, Tibet, and China.[53] The reign of King Kyanzittha (1084–1112 CE) witnessed the first Burmese mission to the Bodhi tree and temple in Bodhgaya. From the Burmese inscriptions one learns that there were three such missions during the Pagan period with the purpose of repairing the Mahābodhi temple. The last mission took place from 1296 to 1298 CE, while the second cannot be dated.[54] Kyanzittha sent musical instruments to Bodhgaya during the construction of the famous temple, among which were bronze drums, together with musicians, singers, and dancers. It seems Kyanzittha got together all sorts of precious things and sent a ship with the intent to "(re)build the Holy Sri Bajras [*Vajrāsana* temple of Bodhgaya]: to buy (land?), dig a reservoir, make irrigated rice fields, make dams, cause candles and lamps to be lit which should never be quenched; and give drums, frog drums, stringed and percussion instruments."[55] An inscription datable to the 12th century mentions a Siṅghala *saṁgha* at Mahābodhi. This could bring an inflow of income derived from Sri Lankan pilgrims, as it was dominated by a monastic order of Sri Lankan affiliation.[56] There were many lay donors as well. Five 11th-century Chinese inscriptions record gifts by Chinese monks; one of these mentions that the monk had been sent to gift a stone *stūpa* at the command of the Song emperor, indicating royal patronage.[57] Inscriptional evidence of the

Pithis further suggests that around the 11th to 13th centuries CE Bodhgaya was a local center of polity.

NORTH BENGAL

Somapura Mahāvihāra. From south Bihar this article now moves on to the northern sector of the Pāla territory, which has two *mahāvihāras*, Somapura and Jagaddala, and a *vihāra* called Nandadīrghikā.

The *mahāvihāra* that finds a pride of place in various texts and inscriptions situated in present northwest Bangladesh is Somapura *mahāvihāra*, often mentioned as Paharpur, which is situated in the village of Paharpur in the Naogaon district. This is said to be one of the most sacred places of Buddhism in the eastern section of the subcontinent.

The identification of this monastery was possible through the discovery of a set of sealings, where it was inscribed *Śrī Somapure Śrī Dharmapāladeva mahā-vihāriy-āryya-bhikṣu-saṁgha sya*, meaning "to the community of monks residing at the monastery of Dharmapāladeva at Somapura."[58] The name and fame of this *mahāvihāra* spread far and wide, and it is mentioned in inscriptions from Bodhgaya and Nalanda and in Tibetan translations of certain Buddhist works.

The second inscription, known as the Indian Museum Copper Plate Inscription of Dharmapāla, Year 26, was edited by Ryosuke Furui.[59] This is a grant issued by the king to donate several land plots to Buddhists belonging to the three facilities established by a subordinate ruler and his consort. King Dharmapāla was petitioned by Mahāsāmanta Bhadraṇāga through his messenger (*dutaka*). Bhadraṇāga wished to donate these land plots to the *bhikṣu saṁghas* "residing in" (*naivāsika/nivāsin*) or belonging to a *vihāra* constructed by him in Antarāvanikā; a perfume chamber (*gandhakuṭī*) constructed by him at *Somapura-mahāvihāra*; and a *vihārikā* constructed by his consort (*rājñikā*) Saṇhāyikā at the same *mahāvihāra*. The purpose of donation was to increase the merit of the king, the petitioner himself, and his parents and make all living beings join the way to perfection. Then the special provisions for the monks for whom the donation is required are mentioned, like cloth (*cīvara*), food (*piṇḍapāta*), bedding (*śayana*), seating (*āsana*), preparation for disease (*glāna-pratyaya*), medicine (*bhaiṣajya*), and so on.

Each facility had its *saṁgha*, which had its own source of subsistence in the form of landed property or more precisely the income from it. These facts according to Furui point to the composite character of this *mahāvihāra*, and he argues that this composite character may be a clue to the difference between *mahāvihāra* and *vihāra* as categories.[60] Moreover, the reach of a monastery to the outside world, the visits of monks from other places, and the network of relationships with other monasteries perhaps also raised the status of a *vihāra* to a *mahāvihāra*.

The genealogy of Mahāsāmanta Bhadranāga deserves attention. His great grandfather Balanāga was a *sārthavāha* (caravan trader), but his father Uccaganāga was a *mahāsāmanta*, a status attained through military activity suggesting social mobility. Thus, here is the presence of a subordinate ruler of Dharmapāla who is the founder as well as patron of a monastery. From a study of the passages in a Vinaya text, Gregory Schopen has suggested that connection of a donor with a *vihāra* constructed by him makes him a *vihārasvāmin*. He continued to superintend or preside over it as a patron.[61] In addition, several stone pillar inscriptions were discovered from the site, which contain the records of the donation of pillars referring to either buddha or the three jewels. The dates assigned to them belong to the 10th and 12th centuries CE. All the donors have names ending in *garbha*, for example Ajayagarbha, Śrīgarbha, and Daśabalagarbha, except one that shows a fragmentary record of some person whose name ended in *nandin*. It is possible that these indicate continuity or the succession of monks at Somapura *mahāvihāra*.

The last epigraphic record mentioning Somapura *mahāvihāra* is the Nalanda inscription of Vipulaśrīmitra.[62] With the view to dispel entirely the eight great fears of the people, Vipulaśrīmitra built a temple of Tāriṇī (Tārā) in the illustrious Somapura, adorned with a court and tank; he further effected the renovation of the inner and outer parts of four groups of cells, which was beautifully done. It is said to be a singular feast to the eyes of the world. He further offered a charming gold ornament to the buddha with the object of keeping men on the path to enlightenment, and at Somapura he lived a monk's life. The reference in Vipulaśrīmitra's inscription to the donation of images at the *sattras* attests to the continuation of the ritual practice of maintaining feeding houses.[63] There is clear evidence of renovation taking place in the monastery around the 12th century CE. Significantly, excavations during 2007–2008, at Satyapir Bhiṭā just outside the quadrangle of Somapura Monastery have unearthed a Buddhist shrine from the 11th/12th century CE, in the courtyard of which several clay tablets depicting eight-handed Tārā and Buddhist creeds have been found.[64]

It is thus evident from the available sources that Somapura *mahāvihāra* received patronage from various categories of people over a period. During Dharmapāla's reign two levels of patronage are perceived. Being the founder of the monastery, King Dharmapāla was a natural patron, and then his *mahāsāmanta* and his wife also constructed *gandhakuṭī* and *vihārikā* in and around Somapura.

Jagaddala Mahāvihāra. Jagaddala *mahāvihāra* of Varendrī was located on the west bank of the Kotra River at the village named Jagaddala in the Naogaon district of Bangladesh.[65] It was less impressive than its illustrious counterparts. This was founded by Ramapāla, as mentioned by Sandhyākaranandī in his *Rāmacaritam*.[66] Rāmapāla established images of Avalokiteśvara and Tārā, Avalokiteśvara being the presiding deity. The well-known *siddhācāryas* Bibhūticandra, Dānaśīla, Mukṣakara Gupta, Śubhākara Gupta, and others stayed in Jagaddala *mahāvihāra* for a long time and translated a number of manuscripts into the Tibetan language.[67] The size of the *vihāra* revealed after excavation is medium. Bastions like circular cells at the four outer corners of the *vihāra* have been excavated, like those of Vikramaśila and Nandadīrghi *vihāra* in Jagjjivanpur, north Bengal. Unlike other monasteries, no inscriptions have been recovered with the name Jagaddala from the monastic site. But the fact that the name of the village is Jagaddala allows one to identify the monastery with Jagaddala *mahāvihāra* of the Tibetan sources.

A significant discovery from the site was a couple of inscribed stone pillars that helped in ascertaining the site's chronology. The pillars are inscribed in proto-Bengali characters of about the 12th/13th century CE and record the names of the writers.[68]

Jagjivanpur Vihāra. In northwest Bengal the discovery of a copper plate from the site of Jagjivanpur (Malda district) located on the banks of Punarbhaba river revealed the presence of a new *vihāra* called Nandadīrghi, which was built by Śrī Vajradeva, the *mahāsenāpati* of the Pāla king Mahendrapāla.[69] A solitary monastic sealing also bears the name of the monastery. The plan of the monastery is comparable to other monasteries of eastern India like Vikramaśila, and it also had circular bastions, probably as part of the monastery's defense mechanism. This monastic site is immensely rich in terracotta plaques, and these mostly shared the same theme as monasteries like Paharpur, Mainamati, and others.[70] The copper-plate charter of Śrī Mahendrapāla *deva* was discovered in 1987, and it revealed the identity of Pāla ruler Mahendrapāla, son of Devapāla, and dispelled the myth that the Pratihāra ruler Mahendrapāla was in possession of the Pāla territories for some time.[71]

One learns from the inscription that the monastery was built by Vajradeva, the *mahāsenāpati* of Mahendrapāla in the Nandadīrghikā *udraṅga* for the enhancement of the merit of his parents, himself, and the whole multitude of living beings. After construction the *mahāsenāpati* requested the king to grant the Nandadīrghikā *udraṅga* to this monastery for various purposes related to the functioning of the monastery. The king responded favorably to his *mahāsenāpati,* and hence this donation. Thus, here are two kinds of patron for this *vihāra*: Vajradeva, the builder patron, and King Mahendrapāla, who looked after the various aspects of sustenance of the monastery. Suresh Chandra Bhattacharyya perfectly demonstrated the relationship between services offered in the monastery and the recipients of those services from a reading of the inscription. Thus *pujana* (worship), *lekhana* (writing or copying of religious texts), and so on would be for *Bhagavato Budha-bhaṭṭāraka, Prajñāpāramitādi = sakala-dharmmanetrī-sthāna* and *Avaivarttika Bodhisatvagaṇa*. The next set of services were for monks and included *civara* (garments), *piṇḍapāta* (food and alms), *śayana* (beds), *āsana* (seats), *glāna-pratyaya* (requisites for the sick), *bhaisajya* (medicines), *pariṣkāra* (other requisites), and so on. The repair and maintenance of the *vihāra* would also be catered to from the donation.[72] It is well known that these *vihāras* were spaces where generally large-scale translations and copying of Buddhist texts occurred; surprisingly, there are no textual allusion to this monastery.

EPIGRAPHIC MENTION OF MONASTERIES

Reference can be made here to an inscription of Gopāla II from Varendra (north Bengal) that records the donation of the village Kaṅkavāsaka to a Buddhist *vihāra* constructed by *mahāsainyapati* Kokkaka, who petitioned it to Gopāla II; this is another case of construction of a *vihāra* by a general during the Pāla reign.[73] It appears from both the inscriptions that the petitioners were involved with the management of donated property.

North Bengal's continued heritage of having *mahavihāras* in the region is supported by the Chaprakot (north Bangladesh) inscription, inscribed during the reign of Pāla monarch Gopāla IV (mid-12th century), briefly referred to in the section on "Nature of Patronage to Monasteries." This inscription was engraved to commemorate the erection of a principal door or gate (*mahādvāra*) of a megamonastery (*mahāvihāra*) at Kuṭumvavilla by a senior monk (*sthavira*) named Mañjuśrījñāna. Kalyāṇavardhana built the *mahāvihāra,* and it appears that the Vardhan family, perhaps subordinate rulers of the Pāla, owned and managed it.[74]

LITTLE-KNOWN MONASTERIES

A few monasteries in West Bengal and Bihar deserve to be discussed, though their patrons are unknown. Among these, one was categorically mentioned by Xuanzang as the Raktamṛittikā *mahāvihāra,* where all the learned men of the kingdom congregated. Based on the reading of a sealing—*(L1) Śrī-Rakta[m]ṛttikā- (ma)hāvaihā (L2) rik—ārya—bhikṣu -[saṅga] s[y] a* ("[This is the seal] of the community of the noble monks of the great monastery at the illustrious Raktamṛttikā")—unearthed during excavations at Rajbaridanga in the Murshidabad district of West Bengal, it is now clear that this was the site of Raktamṛttikā *mahāvihāra* near Karṇasuvarṇa.[75] It was functioning during Xuanzang's visit, and an inscription from the 5th century CE of a *mahānāvika* Buddhagupta found from Wellesly Province in the Malay Peninsula refers to Raktamṛttikā as his abode.[76] Though no complete plan of any building complex could be obtained, the nature and character of the structural remains indicate the existence of a Buddhist monastic establishment, comprising platforms, *stūpa* basements, staircases, pavements, and so on. Thus, during the reign of Śaśāṅka this monastery was in active condition and must have been receiving patronage; but from whom is not known.[77]

In the early 21st century another monastery that caught the attention of people was at Moghalmari in West Medinipur district, West Bengal. The site represents not only the largest monastic site so far excavated in West Bengal but also bears testimony to the only example of a twin monastery in the whole of western Bengal, dating to the 6th–7th centuries CE.[78] This architecturally elaborate monastic complex had two structural phases. The sets of clay tablets and stucco images unearthed from the site merit study not only from the perspective of art but also from its wider linkages among esoteric Buddhist monastic organizations across South and Southeast Asia.[79] Sanyal has published a reading of the inscriptions on the clay tablets.[80] These inform about two monasteries, one a *mahāvihāra* and the other a *vihārikā*, named Yajñapindikamahāvihāra and Mugalayikavihārikā, respectively. The name of the patron, however, is not known. Nevertheless, this monastic complex is definitive evidence to prove the presence of a Buddhist monastery in southwestern Bengal when Xuanzang visited India.

Early-21st-century excavations at Lalpahari in Lakhisarai district of Bihar have unearthed structural remains of a Buddhist monastery with several unique structural features of early medieval eastern India. Like in some monasteries in north Bengal, here too bastions were found. Buddhist clay tablets with seated buddhas in *bhūmisparśamudrā* have also been recovered along with images of Avalokiteśvara and other deities. According to the excavator Anil Kumar, there is a *stūpa* at the center and toward the northeastern direction, a *vihāra* with open cells, and toward the west was a monastery.[81] Interestingly, wooden tablets with seated buddhas within Bodhgaya-type temples have also been found, which reinforces that it was a monastery with the regular presence of lay devotees.[82] However, information about the patrons and donors has not yet been discovered.

SOUTHEASTERN BENGAL (BANGLADESH)

Southeastern Bengal largely comprised the subregions of Samataṭa (the present Comilla-Noakhali area) and Harikela (Chittagong area). Both the subregions were under local ruling houses that generally professed Buddhism and patronized Buddhist establishments.[83] The extant remains of the monasteries, images of Buddhist deities, and copper-plate charters issued that record land donations to the monasteries by the kings of different ruling houses are indicative of the popularity of Buddhism in these subregions. This article will discuss the patronage pattern of the subregions individually.[84]

Samataṭa Area. The beginning of the 6th century witnessed the creation of Buddhist sacred structures on the initiative of the local rulers in the Kumilla-Noakhali area. Inscriptions from the region are replete with donations to *vihāra*s and *vihārikās*. The accounts of the Chinese monks form another source that supports Buddhism being a vibrant religion in the region. One learns from Yijing's account that the Buddhist monk Sheng-chi visited Samataṭa and found that more than four thousand Buddhist monks were living in the capital of Samataṭa and enjoying the patronage of King Rājabhaṭa. According to Sheng-chi, the king was a great admirer of the "three gems" and was a zealous *upāsaka*. This Rājabhaṭa is normally identified with Rājarāja, the son of Deva Khaḍga.[85]

The first example of a grant of land in favor of a community of Avaivarttika Mahāyāna monks (*mahāyānik avaivarttikabhikṣusaṅgha*) residing in a *vihāra* called Āśrama, dedicated to Avalokiteśvara, comes from Gunaighar in the Comilla area.[86] Interestingly, one finds them at Jagjivanpur in the Pundravardhana subregion around the 9th to 10th centuries. This land grant of King Vainyagupta dated 507 CE was intended to maintain the worship of the buddha and to repair the cracks in the monastery. There is reference to an already existing *rājavihāra* (*rājavihārakṣetram*) as one of the boundaries of the land to be granted. *Rājavihāra* is normally translated as "royal monastery." It may be possible to surmise that this monastery was directly under royal supervision or control, whereas the *āśramavihāra* in the same locality was a mere beneficiary.

From the 7th century CE onward, Samataṭa saw the presence of the local ruling houses, of which the Rātas, the Khaḍgas, and the Devas patronized Buddhism. This was evident from their donations to the cluster of monasteries at a site called Mainamati in Comilla and a few land grants to other monasteries.[87] Remains of monasteries loom large in the landscape of Lalmai-Mainamati. The monasteries were of great size, and perhaps they were centers of socio-religious educational and cultural activities.[88] The different monasteries in Mainamati are Salban *vihāra,* Ānanda *vihāra,* Kutilamurā, Rupbānmurā, Iṭākholāmurā, Bhoja *vihāra,* and Latikot *vihāra*. Of the land grants, the Kailan copper-plate of Śrīdhāraṇarāta refers to a sizeable grant of land for charity.[89] The copper-plate states that the *mahāsandhivigrahādhikṛta* Jayanātha distributed twenty-five *pāṭakas* of land between a Buddhist monastery, thirteen Brāhmaṇas, and himself as a beneficiary. Śrīdhāraṇarāta was a Vaiṣṇava, but his minister was a Buddhist. Royal patronage cut across the personal religion of the rulers. The Ashrafpur copper-plates of Devakhaḍga record an endowment of nine *pāṭakas* and ten *droṇas* of land in favor of four *vihāras* and *vihārikas* (*vihāravihārikachatuṣtaya*), headed by the revered preceptor Saṅghamitra.[90] Saṅghamitra also received further donations of land from prince Rājarāja for the monasteries. It appears that this was a cluster of sacred structures in the form of monasteries. Another grant from Balabhaṭṭa, of the same dynasty, recovered from the Salban *vihāra,* shows the endowment of twenty-five *pāṭakas* of land for *vihāras, stūpas,* and their repair, for the buddha, dharma, and sangha. The land was donated at the request of *mahāsandhivigrahādhikṛta* Śrī Yajñavarman, who was a devout worshipper of Buddha. This epigraph describes the "world-famous" (*bhūvanaviśmayani*) Mahābhogāśrama and eight *vihāras* adorned with a large number of white-colored *caityas*, where Buddhist philosophy and works on Buddhist religious thought were taught and discussed.[91] Here too one finds a cluster of monasteries of varying importance.

The Devas, who were devout Buddhists, followed the Khaḍgas in southeastern Bengal as the paramount power. The Deva copper-plates found in the Salban *vihāra* monastic complex and a terra cotta sealing that says *śrībhavadevamahāvihāriāryabhikṣusaṅghasya* ("of the order of the noble monks of the monastic establishment of Śrī Bhavadeva") indicate that the monastic establishment at Salban *vihāra* was known as Śrī Bhavadevamahāvihāra during the 8th century.[92] Thus, the patronage of Bhavadeva to this monastery was to such an extent that the monastery was named after him. Salban *vihāra* is the second-largest monastery of the Mainamati complex. The inscriptions recovered from various cells of the Salban *vihāra* suggest that this monastery was perhaps in use from the early 7th to 8th centuries.

Another monastery known as Ānanda *vihāra* perhaps surpassed Salban *vihāra* in size, but unfortunately it is mostly gone. It was built by Śrī Ānandadeva, the third ruler of the Deva dynasty around the end of the 7th or beginning of the 8th century CE. Among the large number of artifacts, including bronze images and terra cotta, mention must be made of a colossal bronze Avalokiteśvara. The making of such huge images needs substantial patronage, and, in this case, it appears to be royal.[93]

At Mainamati, Itakholamura occupies a central position in the southern cluster and is preeminent in height and probably the largest in ground plan. Instead of a temple in the center of the quadrangle, a rather detached and complex shrine is situated outside, on the south of the *vihāra*. Built over three phases, another important monastic structure was the Rupbanmura *vihāra*, which is the earliest. Originally of oblong shape, this monastery was made almost square with additions of cells in the next phase of its construction. A striking find among the usual is a life-size sandstone image of buddha.

Located in the center of the Mainamati cluster of monasteries, Bhoja *vihāra* had a large cruciform temple in the center of an open courtyard. This was profusely decorated with terra cotta plaques like Salban *vihāra*, and its earliest date could go back to the 8th century CE. The most spectacular find is the huge bronze Vajrasattva image.[94] The exquisitely chiseled image is decorated with various ornaments fit for a bodhisattva. It is suggested that there must have been involvement of master artisans and a religious master with a clear understanding of the iconography and its meaning.[95] This sculpture may be dated to the 9th or, at the latest, early 10th century, a period when the Candras ruled the Mainamati area.

With the Candras, one finds that the nature of patronage changed. Although their personal religion was Buddhism, not a single copper-plate charter of the Candras talks of land donation to a Buddhist monastery. They were largely directed toward the installation of Brahmanical deities or establishment of large *maṭhas*. This image, however, changes when one looks at the vast repertoire of the sculptural finds unearthed at Mainamati. The bronzes from Mainamati, which represent a great variety of iconographic types, were mainly Buddhist, though a few Brahmanical icons were also present.[96] The religious life of the region is clearly manifest in this art. A case in point is the Vajrasattva image from Bhoja *vihāra*. He was evidently the consecrated deity to whom the Bhoja *vihāra* shrine was dedicated. It is noteworthy that an independent shrine may be dedicated only to him for his worship. As no donative inscription was found on the sculpture, no reference to the donor is available. But there is no doubt that the donor was a very rich person, either a merchant or a royal dignitary. It could in all possibility be the Candra rulers, considering the supposed date of the sculpture.

Harikela Area. If one moves further south from Samataṭa into the coastal tracts of Chittagong, known as the Harikela, one finds that Buddhism prospered in this region right from the second half of the 7th century CE and received active patronage from the kings.[97] In the 7th century the Chittagong region attracted Buddhist monks from China. From Yijing's memoirs one learns that Wu-hing sailed from Siṁhala for the northeast and after a month arrived at the country of O-li-ki-lo (Harikela). Wu-hing had stayed in Harikela for one year, and then he left for Bodhgaya.[98] Another Chinese monk Tan-Kwong, who came to India by the southern sea route, arrived at A-li-ki-lo (Harikela). Having found much favor with the king of that country, he "got a temple built there." Thus, Buddhist monks were patronized by the rulers of Harikela.

An inscribed copper vase image of Devātideva talks about the grant of several *pāṭakas* of land given to the Haritaka Dharmasabhāvihāra for the enjoyment of the multitude of noble Buddhist monks for the repair and renovation work of the monastery.[99] Donation for renovations and repairs suggests continuous habitation in the monastery; the need for renovation was perhaps the demand for space. In the Chittagong copper vase grant of Attākaradeva (10th century CE) one finds that the ruling monarch is praised as a follower of Sugata, namely, the Buddha. The object of the inscription was the donation of a cell (*maṭhikā*) in honor of Munindra *bhaṭṭāraka* (the Buddha) for the attainment of perfect knowledge and for the increase of religious merit of his parents, himself, and all sentient beings.[100] The use of the term *maṭhikā* (a term used for a Brahmanical monastery) in a Buddhist context is striking. The cell was constructed in the monastery called Vela *vihāra*; some land was donated by Sahadeva with the approval of the king, for the expenses of *Tathāgatabhaṭṭāraka* and the payment of food, clothing, beds, and medicine for the monks residing in the monastery. The donation was handed over to the honorable elderly monk Dharmmadatta. This act of donation is called a *kīrtti*, and the king requests all his subjects to acknowledge this religious gift with due attention. The use of the term *kīrtti* is interesting. That such donation was regarded as *kīrtti* is also evident from its use in the Nalanda inscription of Devapāla. Donation here was perhaps not simply for gaining merit but looked upon as a mark of achievement and thus indicates the involvement of royalty in this donation to a Buddhist monastery.

The bronzes from Jhewari attest to the affluence of a Buddhist establishment near Chittagong.[101] This monastery could be Paṇḍitavihāra, referred to by Tāranātha as Piṇḍavihāra.[102] During the 10th–11th centuries Chittagong was a flourishing center of Mahāyāna-Tantrayāna Buddhism. The inscriptions on some of the metal images from Jhewari reveal the presence of donor monks. An example may be cited. A large image of the hoard identifies the donor as a *sthavira* (monastic elder). Donation of metal images naturally implies that there was a local center of production of such images, and this adds to the prominence of metal casting in southeastern Bengal. The clientele was wealthy enough to donate such images.

DONATION OF IMAGES TO MONASTERIES

These monasteries were often repositories of images, some inscribed, given as donations by lay followers and at times also by royalty.[103] In an interesting essay on the image of the donors in the Buddhist art of eastern India, Claudine Bautze-Picron indicated that images were a point of convergence of three categories of individuals—the craftsmen, lay community, and religious community—each bringing their know-how, spiritual need, or knowledge.[104] Inscribed images sometimes bear the name of the donor and their occupation or profession and in some cases also give the date of the donation, namely, the regnal year of the ruler during whose reign the donation was made, as well as family background and so on. The focus was on the occupational status and places from where they hailed rather than the *varṇa-jāti* status, which was the hallmark of the period. This suggests that the actual status of a person was more significant than the ritual status sanctioned by the normative literature. Buddhism provided a platform for commoners to indulge in donative activities from all kinds of social base. Thus, among the donors of images in eastern India are *tailika, suvarṇakāra, carmmakāra, karmmakāra,* and other groups. Merchants also formed an important category, and in south Bihar there is reference to *sādhu* (*sāhu*) as a category of merchant apart from *vaṇikas*.[105] Royal officials also donated images and inscribed their presence. Along with images, in some cases manuscripts also were donated.[106] Women constituted around 50 percent of manuscript donors in the 11th century.[107] Patronage in Nalanda, Mahābodhi, Kurkihar, Krimila, and others came from a large clientele, who were local as well as from distant lands. There were donations to smaller establishments too from the local socioeconomic group.[108] A holistic study of the records would help to assess the social composition of the donors. Pilgrims were great donors, and the Mahābodhi is a glowing example. There was a desire for recognition among the donors in addition to merit making.

CONCLUSION

These snippets of data culled after a region-wide study on patronage to Buddhist monasteries in eastern India (see Figure 1) give a broad understanding of the kinds of benefactions received by the three hierarchical units of Buddhist monastic organization, the *mahavihāra, vihāra,* and *vihārikā*. The extant archaeological remains of the monasteries confirm the presence of hierarchies among the monasteries, at least in the context of size. A close reading of the available information also reveals a certain pattern that was undoubtedly different from the collective patronage of the early historic period. Though kings, monks, merchants, and many others contributed to the making and sustaining of monasteries of all categories, in the overall assessment it was the royal patronage that reigned. The institution of land grants in the period of study made possible large-scale donations to these monasteries by the royalty and their like. The early medieval period is particularly noted for the *agrahāra* (rent-free) type of land grants by kings to Brāhmaṇas and Buddhist and Brahmanical religious institutions. This hugely changed the character of the monasteries, and they became substantial owners of land. Nalanda presents an ideal example of patronage from different quarters as well as categories of people—but this was unique to Nalanda.

The pattern of patronage that can be discerned from the study of the inscriptions of the Pāla rulers demonstrates that both the royalty and their subordinates were engaged in founding and then overseeing the upkeep of the Buddhist establishments. At Vikramaśila, apart from the Pālas, both a local ruling dynasty and lay donors were patrons of this *mahāvihāra*. Patronage was generally royal at Jagaddala *mahāvihāra*, but there were lay donors too, from the occupational group of Kāyasthas. The unearthing of monastic sites in West Bengal such as Rajbadidanga and Moghalmari demonstrate that this part of Bengal too witnessed a steady growth of monastic Buddhism in the early medieval period, though who their patrons were still remains elusive. Between the 6th and 13th centuries southeastern Bengal witnessed shifts in patronage by the royal authorities. Local rulers of Samataṭa donated to these sacred structures in the form of large monasteries and perhaps were associated with the construction of such monasteries. The patronage, being substantial, often enabled the maintenance of these monasteries. With the coming of the Candras in this area, one perceives that there was an inclination toward patronage of Brāhmaṇas and Brahmanical deities. The pattern in the Harikela region, however, was a little different. Buddhism prevailed and prospered here consistently right from the second half of the 7th century CE and received active patronage of the kings throughout.

In the case of Bihar, all the monasteries, both extant or referenced in epigraphy and texts, were located in south Bihar; if observed carefully, one notices they were located in districts like Nalanda, Lakhisarai, and Bhagalpur, which stood in a fairly linear alignment toward the east. Incidentally this very region was the power center of the Pāla monarchs, and most of the monasteries received the bulk of their patronage from the Pālas. If one leaves aside Nalanda, similarities in size, chronology, and stylistic connections between monasteries of the Pāla period may be noticed. Asher categorically delineated points of correspondence between Paharpur and Vikramaśila. The *stūpas* at both places were of the same size, along with other architectural and decorative resemblances. Again, in some cases bastion-like circular cells were constructed at the four outer corners of the monastery. The early Pāla rulers surely had a master plan for the construction of monasteries.

The earliest royal patronage at Nalanda came from the Guptas around the 5th century CE (see Table 1). Perhaps the location of Nalanda, founded in the pre-Pāla period, prompted the Pālas

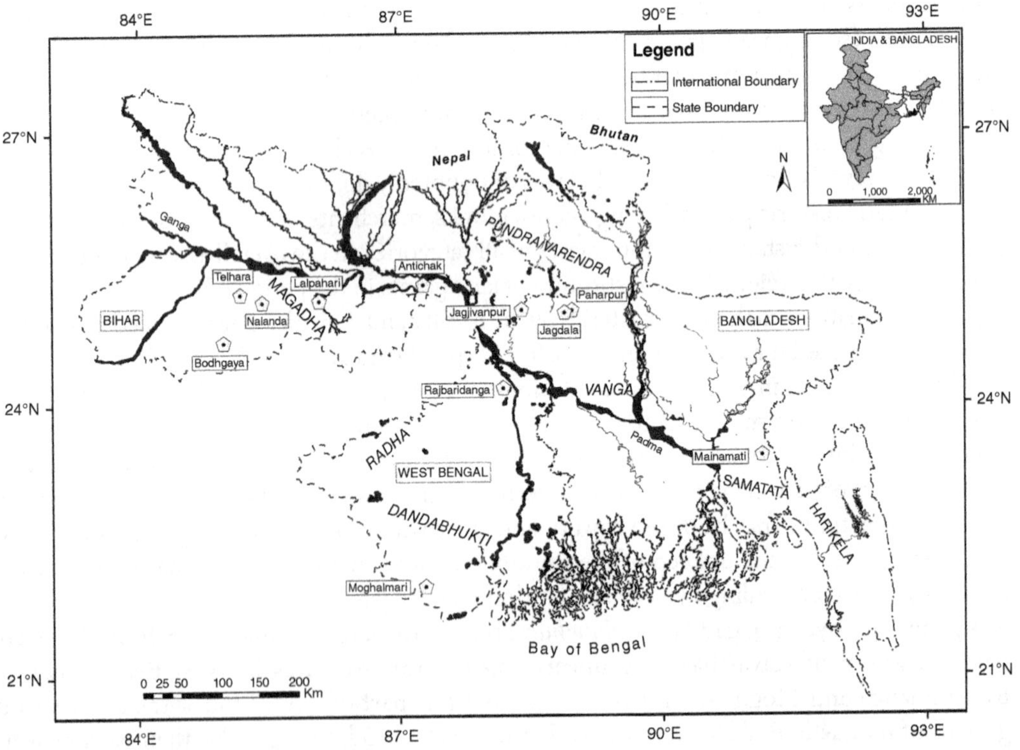

Figure 1. Buddhist sites in east India with subregions.
Source: Author

Table 1. Names and Provisional Dates of Rulers with Their Territories

Name of the Ruler	Year	Approximate Territorial Spread
Vainyagupta	Gupta] year 188 = *c*. 507–508 CE	Part of southeastern Bengal, Kumilla (Bangladesh)
Śrīdhāraṇarāta	*c*. late 7th century	Southeastern Bengal, Kumilla (Bangladesh)
Devakhaḍga	*c*. second half of 7th century	Dhaka and Kumilla (Bangladesh)
Prince Rājarāja	Late 7th century	Dhaka and Kumilla (Bangladesh)
Balabhaṭa	*c*. early 8th century	Southeastern Bengal, Kumilla (Bangladesh)
Devātideva	*c*. 715 CE	Chittagong, southeastern Bengal (Bangladesh)
Ānandadeva	*c*. mid-8th century	Southeastern Bengal, Kumilla (Bangladesh)
Bhavadeva	*c*. late 8th century	Southeastern Bengal, Kumilla (Bangladesh)
Kāntideva	*c*. early 9th century	Chittagong, southeastern Bengal (Bangladesh)
Dharmapāla	*c*. late 8th century	Bihar and Bengal (West Bengal and Bangladesh, except southeastern Bengal)
Devapāla	*c*. mid-9th century	Bihar and Bengal (West Bengal and Bangladesh, except southeastern Bengal)
Mahendrapāla	*c*. mid-9th century	Parts of Bihar and Bengal (West Bengal and Bangladesh, except southeastern Bengal)
Gopāla II	*c*. mid 10th century	North Bengal (West Bengal and Bangladesh)
Attākaradeva	*c*. early 9th century	Chittagong (southeastern Bengal, Bangladesh)
Śrīcandra	*c*. early to mid-10th century	Samatata, Vanga, and Srihatta (Bangladesh)
Gopāla III	*c*. mid-10th century	North Bengal (West Bengal and Bangladesh)

to construct monasteries in and around the region (see Table 2), which was already a stronghold of Buddhism. There are famed *stūpa* sites in north Bihar like Vaisali, Kesaria, and others, but there is not much reference to *vihāras*. Further excavations might reveal the presence of monasteries. In the case of Bengal (including Bangladesh), monasteries founded during the Pāla regime were concentrated in north Bengal, which was almost contiguous to south Bihar. We have seen that in south Bihar donors came from outside the region and from distant lands too. The geographical location of these monasteries facilitated the movement of monks and others from one monastery to another. Thus, Vipulaśrīmitra could easily travel between Nalanda and Somapura and patronize both the monasteries. Incidentally, monasteries in West Bengal in the pre-Pāla period were dispersed, with one being in Murshidabad and the other in western Medinipur; in both cases there is no telltale evidence of the nature of patronage that fostered the growth

Table 2. Coordinates of Buddhist Sites

Jagjivanpur	25°02′27.71″N	88°24′14.92″E
Rajbaridanga	24°10′48.67″N	88°11′27.28″E
Moghalmari	21°59′33.06″N	87°17′47.34″E
Paharpur	25°01′51.96″N	88°58′37.12″E
Jagdala	25°09′32.12″N	88°53′32.12″E
Mainamati	23°25′34.23″N	91°08′15.67″E
Nalanda	25°08′06.61″N	85°26′31.10″E
Antichak	25°19′26.00″N	87°17′05.00″E
Bodhgaya	24°41′45.51″N	84°59′29.38″E
Telhara	25°13′21.00″N	85°10′57.00″E
Lalpahari	25°09′03.92″N	86°06′02.03″E

of these large establishments. As for southeastern Bengal, the largest cluster of monasteries was in and around the Lalmai hills, which flourished under the royal patronage of different dynasties ruling in the subregion.[109] It is very strange that one hardly finds any donation from lay donors in southeastern Bengal. The Chittagong area, which has a substantial Buddhist population even now, cannot boast of any extant *mahāvihāra*, though monasteries are mentioned in texts and inscriptions.

Sources reveal that the momentous period of "building for the Buddha" was from the 9th to 12th centuries CE.[110] There was a spurt of building activities during that time. Religious merit accrued from these donations was surely coveted by all, irrespective of their political and social position. The period saw the rise of the local elites, subordinate rulers, and important officials. Each tried to benefit from donations made. The spurt of donations from occupational groups can be seen in the case of images donated to the monasteries. This might indicate that royalty or subordinate rulers perceived the construction of buildings as their prerogative, whereas in most cases the lay donors who engraved their names were donating images by which they gained their share of merit and recognition. They numbered much less in comparison to the early historic period. The royal donor, in a sense the patron-monarch, as the builder of monasteries perhaps looked forward to the fact that the religious merits for construction were accrued to him alone. Moreover, he could also take pride in patronage. Eventually both the benefactor and the beneficiary benefitted.

NOTES

1. For an understanding of the early medieval period, see Brajadulal Chattopadhyaya, *The Making of Early Medieval India* (Delhi: Oxford University Press, 2012).
2. Rongxi Li, trans., *The Great Tang Dynasty Records of the Western Region,* Taisho vol. 51, no. 2087 (Berkeley, CA: Numata Center for Translation and Research, 1996).

3. Lama Chimpa and Alaka Chattopadhyaya, trans., *Tāranātha's History of Buddhism in India* (Delhi: Motilal Banarsidass, 2010).
4. Ryosuke Furui, "Chaprakot Stone Inscription of the Time of Gopāla IV, Year 9," in *Centenary Commemorative Volume (1913–2013)*, ed. Alamgir Muhammad Serajuddin (Dhaka, Bangladesh: Bangladesh National Museum, 2013), 110–117.
5. Claudine Bautze-Picron, *The Forgotten Place: Stone Images from Kurkihar* (New Delhi: Archaeological Survey of India, 2015), 20.
6. For a study on *dāna*, see Anand Singh, ed., *Dāna, Reciprocity and Patronage in Buddhism* (Delhi: Primus Books, 2017). For a critical understanding of gift giving in South Asia, see Maria Heim, *Theories of the Gift in South Asia: Hindu, Buddhist, and Jain Reflections on Dana*, Religion in History, Society, and Culture Series (London: Routledge, 2015).
7. Vidya Deheija, "Collective and Popular Bases of Early Buddhist Patronage: Sacred Monuments, 100 BC to AD 250," in *The Powers of Art: Patronage in Indian Culture*, ed. Barbara Stoler Miller (Delhi: Oxford University Press, 1992), 35–45.
8. Alexander Cunningham, *The Ancient Geography of India: The Buddhist Period Including the Campaigns of Alexander and the Travels of Hwen Thsang* (London: Trubner, 1871), 469.
9. Li, *Great Tang Dynasty*, 281.
10. Hirananda Sastri, *Nalanda and Its Epigraphic Material*, Memoirs of the Archaeological Survey of India 66 (Delhi: Archaeological Survey of India, 1942), 38.
11. Rajat Sanyal, "Nalanda," in *History of Bangladesh: Early Bengal in Regional Perspectives (up to c. 1200 CE)*, vol. 1: *Archaeology, Political History, Polity*, ed. Abdul Momin Chowdhury and Ranabir Chakravarti (Dhaka, Bangladesh: Asiatic Society of Bangladesh, 2019), 297–299.
12. Dines Chandra Sircar, "Nalanda Inscription of Prathamasiva," *Epigraphia Indica* 39 (1985): 117–122.
13. Atul Kumar Verma and Rajat Sanyal, "Discovery of a Buddhist Monastery at Telhara (Bihar)," *Monthly Bulletin of the Asiatic Society* 45, no. 7 (September 2016): 10–12.
14. Li, *Great Tang Dynasty*, 250–258.
15. Sastri, *Nalanda*, 64–88.
16. Sastri, *Nalanda*, 89–91.
17. B. N. Mishra, *Nālandā: Sources and Background*, vol. 1 (Delhi: B. R. Publishing, 1988), 164–173.
18. Sanyal, "Nalanda," 305.
19. Sastri, *Nalanda*, 78–82.
20. Gregory Schopen, "The Buddha as an Owner of Property and Permanent Resident in Medieval Indian Monasteries," in *Bones, Stones and Buddhist Monks: Collected Papers on the Archaeology, Epigraphy, and Texts of Monastic Buddhism in India*, ed. Gregory Schopen (Honolulu: University of Hawai'i Press, 1997), 264.
21. Sanjukta Datta, "Prasasti, Piety and Patronage: Eastern India, c. 8th to 13th Century CE" (PhD diss., University of Delhi, 2017), 251.
22. Misra, *Nālandā*, 199–200; and also see Chitralekha Hazra Banerjee, "Nalanda from *Vihara* to *Mahavihara*: The Underlying Economic Factors," in *Urbanity and Economy: The Pre-Modern Dynamics in Eastern India*, ed. Ratnabali Chatterjee (Kolkata: Setu Prakashani, 2013), 78–95.
23. Datta, "Prasasti, Piety," 258–263.
24. Frederick M. Asher, *Nalanda* (Mumbai: Marg Publications, 2015), 50; and Sastri, *Nalanda*, 107.
25. Nani Gopal Majumdar, "Nalanda Inscription of Vipulaśrīmitra," *Epigraphia Indica* 21 (1931–1932): 97–101.
26. Tansen Sen, *Buddhism, Diplomacy, and Trade: The Realignment of Sino-Indian Relations, 600–1400* (Honolulu: Association for Asian Studies, University of Hawai'i Press, 2003), 107.
27. Nani Gopal Majumdar, "Nalanda Copper-Plate of Devapāladeva," *Monograph of the Varendra Research Society* 1 (1926): 17–31.

28. Upinder Singh, "Gifts from Other Lands, Southeast Asian Religious Endowments in India," in *Asian Encounters, Exploring Connected Histories*, ed. Upinder Singh and Parul Pandya Dhar (Delhi: Oxford University Press, 2014), 47.
29. Sanyal, "Nalanda," 301.
30. Chimpa and Chattopadhyaya, *Tāranātha's History*, 285.
31. Bindeshwari Prasad Sinha, *Archaeology in Bihar*, K. P. Jayaswal Memorial Lecture Series 5 (Patna: K. P. Jayaswal Research Institute, 1988), 104–107.
32. Frederick M. Asher, "Vikramaśila Mahāvihāra," *Bangladesh Lalitkala* 1, no. 2 (1975): 107–113.
33. Einoo Shingo, ed., *Genesis and Development of Tantrism* (Tokyo: Institute of Oriental Culture, University of Tokyo, 2009), 86–156.
34. Anant Sadashiv Altekar, ed., *Biography of Dharmasvamin, Chag lo Tsa-ba Chos-rje-dpal, a Tibetan Monk Pilgrim*, trans. George Roerich (Patna: K. P. Jayswal Research Institute, 1959), XLI–XLII.
35. Kurt Behrendt, *Tibet and India: Buddhist Traditions and Transformations* (New York: Metropolitan Museum of Art, 2014), 22–24.
36. B. S. Verma, *Antichak Excavations 2 (1971–1981)* (Delhi: Archaeological Survey of India, 2011); and Rajat Sanyal, "Antichak," in Chowdhury and Chakravarti, *History of Bangladesh*, 131–143. Here Sanyal expresses his skepticism regarding identifying Antichak with Vikramaśila *mahāvihāra*, as the two excavated monastic sealings have no connection with Vikramaśila *mahāvihāra*; rather, one of them reads *śrijayasenadeva mahāvihāra*, the other being broken.
37. Krishna Kumar Mandal, "The Matrix of Patronage, Vikramśilā Mahāvihāra," in Singh, *Dāna, Reciprocity*, 144–160.
38. Dines Chandra Sircar, *Some Epigraphical Records of the Medieval Period from Eastern India* (New Delhi: Abhinav, 1979), 23–29.
39. Mandal, "Matrix of Patronage," 151.
40. Chimpa and Chattopadhyaya, *Tāranātha's History*, 262.
41. Chimpa and Chattopadhyaya, *Tāranātha's History*, 289.
42. Giuseppe Tucci, "The Simbolism of the Temples of bSam yas," *East and West* 6, no. 4 (1956): 279–281.
43. Pratapaditya Pal, "A Forgotten Monastery of Ancient Bihar," *South Asian Studies* 4 (1988): 83.
44. Li, *Great Tang Dynasty*, 207.
45. Bijoy Kumar Choudhary, "Lesser-Known Buddhist Monasteries: Tilaḍhaka and Yaśovermapura," *Man and Environment* 41, no. 1 (2016): 17–28.
46. Sanyal, "Nalanda," 308–309.
47. Janice Leoshko, "Buddhist Images from Telhara, a Site in Eastern India," *South Asian Studies* 3 (1987): 89–97.
48. Lorenz Franz Kielhorn, "A Buddhist Stone-Inscription from Ghosrāwān," *Indian Antiquary* 17 (1888): 307–312.
49. Jinah Kim, "Unheard Voices: Women's Roles in Medieval Buddhist Artistic Production and Religious Practices in South Asia," *Journal of American Academy of Religion* 80, no. 1 (2012): 200–232, cited by Choudhary, "Lesser-Known Buddhist Monasteries," 17–18.
50. Li Rongxi, trans., *The Journey of the Eminent Monk Faxian*, Taisho vol. 51, no. 2085 (Berkeley, CA: Numata Center for Translation and Research, 1996), 197.
51. John Guy, "The Mahābodhi Temple: Pilgrim Souvenirs of Buddhist India," *Burlington Magazine* 133, no. 1059 (June 1991): 356–367.
52. Vincent Tournier, "Mahākāśyapa, His Lineage, and the Wish for Buddhahood: Reading Anew the Bodhgayā Inscriptions of Mahānāman," *Indo-Iranian Journal* 57 (2014): 12.
53. This has been discussed succinctly by Sanjukta Datta in her thesis; see Datta, "Prasasti, Piety."

54. Tilman Frasch, "A Buddhist Network in the Bay of Bengal: Relations between Bodhgaya, Burma and Sri Lanka," in *From the Mediterranean to the China Sea: Miscellaneous Notes*, ed. Claude Guillot, Denys Lombard, and Roderich Ptak (Wiesbaden, Germany: Harrassowitz Verlag, 1998), 69–92.
55. Arsenio Nicolas, "Musical Exchange between India and Southeast Asia," in *Early Interactions between South and Southeast Asia: Reflections on Cross-Cultural Exchange*, ed. Pierre-Yves Manguin, A. Mani, and Geoff Wade (Singapore: Institute of Southeast Asian Studies, 2011), 347–370.
56. Singh, "Gifts," 50.
57. Singh, "Gifts," 50.
58. For the Paharpur excavations see Kashinath Narayan Dikshit, "Excavations at Paharpur, Bengal," in *Memoirs of the Archaeological Survey of India* 55 (Delhi: Archaeological Survey of India, 1938).
59. Ryosuke Furui, "Indian Museum Copper Plate Inscription of Dharmapāla, Year 26: Tentative Reading and Study," *South Asian Studies* 27, no. 2 (2011): 145–156.
60. Furui, "Copper Plate Inscription of Dharmapāla, Year 26," 151.
61. Gregory Schopen, "The Lay Ownership of Monasteries and the Role of the Monk in Mulasarvāstivādin Monasticism," in *Buddhist Monks and Business Matters*, ed. Gregory Schopen (Honolulu: University of Hawai'i Press, 2004), 220–221, 238.
62. Majumdar, "Nalanda Inscription," 97.
63. For an understanding of the donative activities of Vipulaśrīmitra see Sanjukta Datta, "Building for the Buddha: Patrons in the Pala Kingdom," *Studies in History*, 35, no. (2) (2019): 1–16.
64. Swadhin Sen, A. K. M. S Rahman, and S. M. K. Ahsan, "Crossing the Boundaries of the Archaeology of Somapura Mahavihara: Alternative Approaches and Propositions," *Pratnatattva* 14 (2014): 49–79.
65. A. K. M. Zakariah, "JagaddalaMahavihara," *Journal of the Varendra Research Museum* 3 (1994): 29–41.
66. Radha Govinda Basak, ed., *The Ramacharitam of Sandhyakaranandin* (Calcutta: Asiatic Society, 1969), verse 3, line 7.
67. For an overview of Jagaddala see Md. Mahabub-ul Alam, "Jagaddala," in Chowdhury and Chakravarti, *History of Bangladesh*, 194–210.
68. Nazimuddin Ahmed, "Jagaddala *Mahāvihāra*," in *Banglapedia*, ed. Sirajul Islam Sajahan Miah (Dhaka, Bangladesh: Asiatic Society of Bangladesh, 2003).
69. Amal Roy, *Jagjivanpur 1996–2005: Excavation Report* (Kolkata: Directorate of Archaeology and Museums, Government of West Bengal, 2012).
70. Sheena Panja, "Jagjivanpur and Bangarh: Northern West Bengal," in Chowdhury and Chakravarti, *History of Bangladesh*, 211–218.
71. This inscription has been studied and commented upon by a number of scholars, a few of whom include Gouriswar Bhattacharya, "A New Pāla Ruler: Discovery of a Valuable Charter," *South Asian Studies* 4 (1988): 71–73; Gouriswar Bhattacharya, "The New Pāla Ruler Mahendrapāla," *Pratna Samiksha* 1 (1992): 165–170; Koluvail Vyasaraya Ramesh and Iyer S. Subramonia, "Malda District Museum Copper-Plate Charter of Mahendrapāla Deva, Year 7," *Epigraphia Indica* 42 (1992): 6–29; and the most accepted, Suresh Chandra Bhattacharya, "The Jagjivanpur Plate of Mahendrapāla Comprehensively Re-Edited," *Journal of Ancient Indian History* 23 (2005–2006): 61–125.
72. Bhattacharya, Jagjivanpur Plate, 91.
73. Ryosuke Furui, "A New Copper Plate Inscription of Gopala II," *South Asian Studies* 24 (2008): 67–75.
74. Furui, "Chaprakot Stone Inscription." For an excellent study of this inscription from the point of view of patronage, see Datta, "Building for the Buddha," 1–16.
75. Sudhir Ranjan Das, *Rajbaridanga, 1962* (Calcutta: Asiatic Society, 1968).
76. Dines Chandra Sircar, *Select Inscriptions Bearing on Indian History and Civilization*, vol. 1 (Calcutta: University of Calcutta, 1942), 497.

77. Suchandra Ghosh, "Karnasuvarna," *Banglapedia*, ed. Sirajul Islam Sajahan Miah (Dhaka: Asiatic Society of Bangladesh, 2003).
78. Asok Datta, "Excavation at Moghalmari: A Pre-Pala Buddhst Monastic Complex," *Journal of Bengal Art* 15 (2010): 275–293.
79. Rajat Sanyal and Suchandra Ghosh, "Enduring Passages, Voyaging Perceptions: New Evidence on Indian Ocean Linkages from Southwestern Bengal," in *Cross Cultural Networking in the Indian Ocean Realm, c. 100–1800 CE*, ed. Kenneth R. Hall, et al. (Delhi: Primus Books, 2019), 121–149.
80. Rajat Sanyal, "Two Monastic Sealings from Moghalmari," *Pratna Samiksha*, New Series 10 (2019): 79–93.
81. Anil Kumar, *Krimila: A Forgotten Nagar of Early Medieval Eastern India* (New Delhi: Nehru Memorial Museum and Library, 2019), 18–23.
82. Anil Kumar, personal communication (2021). The author is thankful to him for this information, which is yet to be published.
83. The concept of subregion in Bengal based on land grants was introduced by Barrie Morrison; see Barrie Morrison, *Political Centres and Cultural Regions in Early Bengal* (Tucson: University of Arizona Press, 1970). For specific understanding of southeastern Bengal, see Suchandra Ghosh, "The Trans Meghna Region: Making of a Sub-Regional Identity," *Journal of Ancient Indian History* 27 (2010–2011): 220–231.
84. An earlier publication on this may be referred to. See Suchandra Ghosh, "Nature of Royal Patronage in South-Eastern Bengal," *Journal of Bengal Art* 13–14 (2009): 109–118.
85. Latika Lahiri, *Chinese Monks in India: Biography of Eminent Monks Who Went to the Western World in Search of the Law during the Great T'ang Dynasty* (Delhi: Motilal Banarsidass, 1986), 85.
86. Sircar, *Select Inscriptions*, 340–345.
87. A. B. M. Husain, ed., *Mainamati-Devaparvata* (Dhaka, Bangladesh: Asiatic Society of Bangladesh, 1997).
88. Suchandra Ghosh, "Mainamati: An Enigmatic Centre of Buddhism in Southeastern Bangladesh," in *Nalanda, Srivijaya and Beyond: Re-Exploring Buddhist Art in Asia*, ed. Gauri Parimoo Krishnan (Singapore: Asian Civilizations Museum, 2016), 37–50.
89. Dines Chandra Sircar, "The Kailan Copper-Plate Inscription of King Sridharana Rata of Samatata," *Indian Historical Quarterly* 23 (1947): 221–241.
90. G. M. Laskar, "Ashrafpur Copper-Plate Grants of Devakhadga," *Memoirs of the Asiatic Society of Bengal* 1, no. 6 (1906): 85–89.
91. Kamala Kanta Gupta Choudhury, "Two Mainamati Copper Plate Inscriptions of the Khadga and Early Deva Times," *Bangladesh Archaeology* 1, no. 1 (1979): 141–148.
92. Dines Chandra Sircar, "Copper-Plate Inscription of King Bhavadeva of Devaparvata," *Journal of the Asiatic Society, Letters* 17, no. 2 (1951): 83–94.
93. Mokammal H. Bhuiyan, "Mainamati," in Chowdhury and Chakravarti, *History of Bangladesh*, 263–280.
94. Gouriswar Bhattacharya, "The Magnificent Bronze Image of Vajrasatva from Mainamati, Bangladesh," in *Essays on Buddhist, Hindu, Jain Iconography and Epigraphy*, ed. Enamul Haque (Dhaka, Bangladesh: International Centre for SBA, 2000), 131–132.
95. Jinah Kim, "Brahmanical-Buddhist Sculptures: Looking for 'Bengal' ness," in Chowdhury and Chakravarti, *History of Bangladesh*, 404.
96. Harunur M. Rashid, *The Early History of South-East Bengal in the Light of Archaeological Material* (Dhaka, Bangladesh: Itihas Academy, 2008).
97. Bratindranath Mukherjee, "The Original Territory of Harikela," *Bangladesh Lalitkala* 1, no. 2 (1975): 115–119.
98. I-tsing, *A Record of the Buddhist Religion as Practiced in India and the Malay Archipelago (AD671–695)*, trans. J. Junjiro Takakusu (Oxford, UK: Clarendon Press, 1896), xxxiii, xlvi, liii, 44.

99. Gouriswar Bhattacharya, "A Preliminary Report on the Inscribed Metal Vase from the National Museum of Bangladesh," in Haque, *Buddhist, Hindu, Jain Iconography*, 471–487.
100. Gouriswar Bhattacharya, "An Inscribed Metal Vase Most Probably from Chittagong, Bangladesh," *South Asian Archaeology* 1991 (1993): 323–338.
101. Asok K. Bhattacharya, *Jhewari Bronze Buddhas: A Study in History and Style* (Calcutta: Indian Museum, 1989).
102. Chimpa and Chattopadhyaya, *Tāranātha's History*, 254–255.
103. There is a continuous addition to the existing data regarding the donation of images and nature of donors after the publication of Susan Huntington's magnum opus. See Susan L. Huntington, *The "Pala-Sena" Schools of Sculptures* (Leiden, The Netherlands: E. J. Brill, 1984).
104. Claudine Bautze-Picron, *Images of Donors in the Buddhist Art of Eastern India* (2014); and also see Frederick M. Asher, "Stone and Production of Images," *East and West* 48, no. 3–4 (1998): 313–328.
105. Sayantani Pal, "Inscribed Images Donated by Merchants in Bihar and Bengal (8th–12th Century)," in *South Asian Archaeology and Art 2014*, ed. Eva Myrdal (New Delhi: Dev Publishers, 2020), 271–281.
106. Sarasi Kumar Saraswati, *Pal Yuger Citrakalā* (Calcutta: Ananda Publishers, 1978). In Bengali.
107. Jinah Kim, *Receptacle of the Sacred: Illustrated Manuscripts and the Buddhist Book Cult in South Asi* (Berkeley: University of California Press, 2013).
108. Gautam Sengupta, "Donors of Images in Eastern India c. 800–1300 AD," *Proceedings of the Indian History Congress* 43 (1982): 158–164; and also see Rajat Sanyal, "Another Inscribed Image of the Reign of Rāmapaāla from South Bihar," *Pratna Samiksha*, New Series 2 (2011): 139–144.
109. Barrie Morrison, *Lalmai: A Cultural Centre of Early Bengal* (Washington, DC: University of Washington Press, 1977).
110. This expression is borrowed from Datta, "Building for the Buddha."

Suchandra Ghosh

PERFECTIONS (SIX AND TEN) OF BODHISATTVAS IN BUDDHIST LITERATURE

THE PERFECTIONS IN BUDDHIST LITERATURE

The perfections (Sanskrit, *pāramitā*; Pāli, *pāramī*; Gāndhārī, *paramida*; Tibetan, *pha rol tu phyin pa*; Chinese, *boluomi*; Japanese, *haramitsu*) are the virtues or qualities that are fully developed by a bodhisattva (buddha-in-training) to become a buddha. A number of Buddhist traditions acknowledge that the perfections are practiced through multiple lifetimes extending over eons of time for the purpose of achieving full buddhahood for the welfare of beings.

The Sanskrit and Pāli noun *pāramitā* is derived from the adjective *parama*, meaning "high, complete, perfect." In this sense, *pāramitā* is an old noun denoting "the highest point."[1] The Theravāda tradition has consistently understood the term in this way and has commonly used another derivative, *pāramī*, as a synonym. In contrast, Mahāyāna traditions have analyzed the term as consisting of two words, *pāram itā*, meaning "gone to the beyond," signifying its purport for progress in the bodhisattva path. The Chinese and Tibetan translations of the term *pāramitā* (*du* 度 and *pha-rol-tu phyin-pa*, respectively) reflect this latter understanding of its meaning. These interpretations may differ between mainstream Buddhist (*nikāya*) and

Mahāyāna traditions, but the understandings they imply are found among most Buddhist schools. One representation regarded the term as derived from *pāram*, "other (side)," plus the past participle *ita* "gone."[2] This derivation is later preserved in the standard Tibetan translation *pha-rol-tu phyin-pa* "gone to the other shore." Other interpretations advocated that this etymology was misguided and derived *pāramitā* from the term *parama*, "excellent, supreme." The noun *pāramitā* is translated in early Chinese through "double translation" composed of *du wuji* 度無極, meaning "crossed over" (*du* 度) plus "unexcelled, limitless" (*wuji* 無極), which brings together both of the traditional etymologies.[3] A number of Buddhist works provide semantic etymologies (*nirukti*) for *pāramitā*, etymologies which explain the meaning of a term rather than its linguistic origin, based on contextual underlying factors that a text is trying to advocate. The understanding of *pāramitā* in the sense of "to reach the other shore" generally conveys the idea that a perfection enables one to go from the realm of samsara, the world of repeated rebirth and redeath, to the blissful realm of nirvana.

The conception of the perfections as a set is not found in the earliest layers of Buddhist literature.[4] Rather, the perfections as a set of practices developed sometime before the Common Era as an alternative group of spiritual practices in conjunction with revised notions of buddhahood, as well as newly considered notions of what constitutes the path leading to buddhahood. The *pāramitās* furnished an arrangement of Buddhist thought and practice that focused on the ideal of the bodhisattva and how a bodhisattva was imagined to fulfill the immeasurable qualities and virtues necessary for the attainment of buddhahood. The qualities of the *pāramitās* and their outlines for practice were extensions of earlier mainstream Buddhist arrangements of practice, such as the three trainings (*triśīkṣa*) of morality (*śīla*), concentration (*samādhi*), and insight (*prajñā*), but were modified with the underlying ethos, aspirations, and commitments for attaining incomparable buddhahood for the welfare of all beings.

The lists of perfections varied according to the genre of literature in which they appeared. What practices constituted the varied lists of perfections and how the perfections were conceived differed not only among groups but also among scholarly authors. The *pāramitās* appear in Buddhist literature as a group in varying lists, but the lists of perfections are notoriously unfixed with six and ten perfections being the most common.

The Perfections in the Jātakas. Perhaps the earliest genre of Buddhist literature in which the *pāramitās* appear are the collections of *Jātakas*, the stories of the buddha's previous lives. The *pāramitās* in these stories provide major underlying themes, such as self-sacrifice, ethical virtue, and patience, that demonstrate the magnificent qualities developed by the buddha in his previous lives by carrying out moral acts as a bodhisattva on the bodhisattva path. In the *Aviṣahya Jātaka*, for example, the bodhisattva cultivates the perfection of generosity (*dānapāramitā*) by donating alms to supplicants in spite of being reduced to poverty. The bodhisattva is a boy who refuses to steal, even after encouragement from his Brahmin teacher to do so, in the *Brāhmaṇa Jātaka*, to illustrate the cultivation of the perfection of morality (*śīlapāramitā*). In the *Kṣāntivādin Jātaka*, the bodhisattva is an ascetic who cultivates the perfection of forbearance (*kṣāntipāramitā*) by tolerating being violently disfigured by an angry king.[5] Most Buddhist groups (*nikāya*) had collections of *Jātakas* that differed in length and number. Buddhist groups and movements also understood the purport of the *Jātakas* differently, with mainstream groups like the Theravāda seeing the perfections in the *Jātakas* as qualities to be admired, while Mahāyāna movements understood the perfections in the *Jātakas* as models to emulate.

Theravāda Buddhist works, such as the *Cariyāpiṭaka,* arrange Jātaka tales on the basis of a hierarchy of perfections. The Theravāda tradition recognizes ten perfections, although only eight are listed in the *Buddhāpadāna* and seven in the *Cariyāpiṭaka*. In Theravāda traditions, the perfections provide Buddhists with a set of ideals to worship and venerate the buddha as a model of incomparable spiritual significance and superiority. The ten perfections that have become commonly accepted among Theravāda traditions serve as guides to structuring the stories of the buddha's previous lives, the Jātakas, and give evidence to the supremacy of the buddha who has fulfilled these virtues in his awakening. The ten perfections in the Theravāda tradition are (1) generosity (*dāna*), (2) morality (*sīla*), (3) renunciation (*nekhamma*), (4) insight (*pañña*), (5) energetic diligence (*viriya*), (6) patience (*khanti*), (7) truthfulness (*sacca*), (8) resolution (*adhiṭṭhāna*), (9) lovingkindness (*metta*), and (10) equanimity (*upekkhā*). A commentator on the *Cariyāpiṭaka,* Dhammapāla (post–5th century), posits two possible explanations for their sequence. The first explanation, as mentioned, is that the order of the perfections reflects the sequence in which they are undertaken. The second explanation is based on a certain order that does not follow a specific sequence of practice. Dhammapāla's commentary also expands the list of perfections into thirty perfections: ten (ordinary) perfections (*pāramī*), ten intermediate perfections (*upapāramī*), and ten supreme perfections (*paramatthapāramī*).[6]

The Perfections in Mahāyāna Sutras. A set of six perfections became common among some genres of mainstream Buddhist literature and developed into a standard list in a number of Mahāyāna sutras. However, other lists of four, five, or seven also occurred. For instance, the *Māhavibhāṣa* of the Sarvāstivādin tradition defends a list of four perfections (*dāna, śīla, vīrya,* and *prajñā*), claiming that the other perfections are subsumed under these.[7] The *Saddharmapuṇḍarīka-sūtra,* or "Lotus sutra," recognizes a tradition with six perfections but also lists five perfections in some sections of the text. Likewise, the *Rāṣṭrapālaparipṛcchā-sūtra* ("Inquiry of Rāṣṭrapāla") provides lists of five or six but also provides lists at two places in the text that include seven or eight perfections. Aberrant lists of *pāramitās* may be found in several other works as well, including the *Lalitavistara* ("The Extensive Play"), the larger *Sukhāvatīvyūha* ("The Sūtra on the Display of the [World] of Bliss"), the *Vimalakīrtinirdeśa* ("Teachings of Vimalakīrti"), and the *Mahāvastu* ("Great Story").[8] In time, a set of six perfections became standard in Mahāyāna sutras. The social and historical processes that led to the standardization of the perfections into a set of six developed, as far as currently known, off camera—that is, were never documented in written form. The six perfections are (1) generosity (*dāna*), (2) morality (*śīla*), (3) patience (*kṣānti*), (4) vigor/diligence (*vīrya*), (5) concentration (*dhyāna*), and (6) wisdom (*prajñā*). This list was expanded to complement the ten stages (*bhūmi*) traversed by a bodhisattva in the course leading to full buddhahood. The additional perfections were (7) skill-in-means (*upāya-kauśalya*), (8) resolution (*praṇidhāna*), (9) strength (*bala*), and (10) knowledge (*jñāna*).

The perfections are discussed in varying ways in Mahāyāna sutras, and it is important to recognize the heterogeneous character of the presentation of perfections in early Mahāyāna discourses. The perfections as they appear in sutras that become classified as Mahāyāna provide the themes and practices entailed in the bodhisattva ideal and constitute the practices a bodhisattva seeks to fulfill in carrying out his initial spiritual resolution (*bodhicitta*) and vows (*praṇidhāna*) to achieve buddhahood for the welfare of all beings. The discussion of *pāramitās* found in the great and diverse variety of Mahāyāna sutras generally appears in three different ways: those sutras that center on the *pāramitās*, those which partially discuss the *pāramitās*, and sutras that focus on a specific perfection. For instance, the *Ugraparipṛcchā* focuses on the perfection of generosity (*dāna*) and the *Upāliparipṛcchā* discusses morality (*śīla*).[9] A sutra that focuses on a particular perfection may incorporate other perfections into its emphasis on that particular perfection. For example, while the *Ugraparipṛcchā* focuses on the perfection of generosity (*dāna*), the sutra explains:

> If he [the householder bodhisattva] gives while relying upon the spirit of enlightenment [*bodhicitta], in that way his cultivation of the perfection of morality [*śīlapāramitā] will be fulfilled.
> If he gives while bringing to mind loving-kindness toward those beggars and not producing anger or hostility toward them, in that way his cultivation of the perfection
> of endurance [*kṣāntipāramitā] will be fulfilled.
> If he is not depressed due to a wavering mind that thinks "If I give this away, what will become of me?" in that way his perfection of exertion [*vīryapāramitā] will be fulfilled.[10]

In this way, a bodhisattva is instructed to focus on generosity while fulfilling the other perfections.

Works that partially discuss the *pāramitās* may only briefly summarize the six perfections in the context of broader thematic issues. For instance, the *Lalitavistara*, a work related to the Sarvāstivāda tradition that is classified as a Mahāyāna sutra in manuscript and in Tibetan translation, briefly summarizes the six perfections in the following manner in the broader context of discussing the life of Śākyamuni Buddha:

> The perfection of generosity (*dānapāramita*) is a gateway to the light of dharma, for it leads to the marks and signs [of a buddha], to the complete purification of the buddha realms, and to the maturing of beings who are greedy. The perfection of morality (*śīlapāramitā*) is a gateway to the light of dharma, for it enables one to pass beyond unfortunate states of existence and to mature immoral beings. The perfection of patience (*kṣāntipāramitā*) is a gateway to the light of the dharma, for it enables one to eliminate all ill will, aggression, anger, pride, infatuation, and arrogance, and to mature evil-minded beings. The perfection of diligence (*vīryapāramitā*) is a gateway to the light of dharma, for it enables one to practice all the roots of virtue and to mature beings who are lazy. The perfection of concentration (*dhyānapāramitā*) is a gateway to the light of dharma, for it enables one to arise to all states of supersensory knowledge and equipoise while maturing beings who are distracted. The perfection of wisdom (*prajñāpāramitā*) is a gateway to the light of dharma, for it enables one to eliminate the dark fog of ignorance and delusion, to abandon false views, and to mature foolish beings.[11]

Although the *Vimalakīrinirdeśa*[12] does not fully elucidate the perfections, the sutra often makes reference to them in illustrating various themes in the work. In this work, the six perfections are found in the buddha-field (*buddhakṣetra*) of the bodhisattva (I, §13), are individually explained by Vimalakīrti in order to convert various groups of people (II, §2), are qualities that constitute the seat of awakening (III, §56), and are part of the sounds of the dharma that permeates Vimalakīrti's house (VI, §13). The *Vimalakīrinirdeśa* also briefly explains that generosity is opposed to greed (*mātsarya*), that morality opposes immorality (*dauśilya*), patience opposes animosity (*vyāpāda*), energetic diligence opposes idleness (*kauśīdya*), concentration opposes distraction (*vikṣepa*), and wisdom opposes foolishness (*dauḥprajñyā*) (XI, §1).

Sutras that discuss the *pāramitās* as a set of six group them into subsets based on their overall orientation. For instance, the *Prajñāpāramitā* literature will group the six perfections into a subset of five, which is supported by the overarching perfection of wisdom (*prajñāpāramitā*). The *Aṣṭasāhasrikā* states in this regard:

> What do you think, Ānanda, does giving undedicated to omniscience get the name "*pāramitā*"? Ānanda: No, Lord. The Lord: What do you think, Ānanda, do morality, forbearance, diligence, concentration, and wisdom undedicated to omniscience get the name "*pāramitās*"? Ānanda: No, Lord. The Lord: What do you think, Ānanda, is that wisdom inconceivable which dedicates the roots of good by dedicating them to omniscience? Ānanda: Yes, inconceivable, is that wisdom, supremely inconceivable is that wisdom which dedicates the roots of good by dedicating them to omniscience. The Lord: Therefore, Ānanda, it is on account of its supremacy that wisdom gets the name "*pāramitā*," by means of which the roots of good, dedicated to omniscience, get the name "*pāramitās*." Therefore, Ānanda, it is on account of the roots of good being dedicated to omniscience that the Perfection of Wisdom (*prajñāpāramitā*) goes ahead of and is the leader, the guide, of the five perfections.[13]

The same text will also later state:

> However, Kauśika, when giving, morality, patience, diligence, and concentration are taken hold of by the perfection of wisdom, then they get the name, the appellation "perfection." For these five perfections receive an eye which leads to entrance onto the path to omniscience and to the attainment of omniscience.[14]

Other sutras outline the perfection into subsets that approach the *pāramitās* in terms of whether they constitute the equipment for merit (*puṇyasaṃbhāra*), usually including the perfections of *dāna, śīla,* and *kṣānti,* or the equipment of knowledge (*jñānasaṃbhāra*), usually including *dhyāna* and *prajñā,* with *vīrya* as a shared member between the equipment subsets.[15]

The Perfections in Indian Mahāyāna Buddhist Scholarly Works. In addition to Mahāyāna sutras, a number of Indian Mahāyāna Buddhist *śāstras* that have been preserved directly discuss the perfections. Nāgārjuna, considered to be one of the major figures in the rise of Mahāyāna traditions and famous for his articulation of the philosophy of emptiness (*śūnyatā*), composed two letters addressed to kings that advocate practicing the perfections on the bodhisattva path. Nāgārjuna's "Letter to a Friend" (*Suhṛllekha*, vs. 8) and *Ratnāvalī* (iv.80), or "Precious Garland," both mention the six perfections to be carried out by an aspiring bodhisattva. Maitreyanātha, a figure who is considered one of the founders of the Yogācāra tradition, elucidates the perfections in several works attributed to him that are preserved in Tibetan and Chinese. The *Ornament for Clear Realization* (*Abhisamayālaṃkāra*) and the *Ornament of the Mahāyāna Sūtras* (*Mahāyānasūtrālaṃkāra)* both have sections that discuss the perfections. The *Ornament for Clear Realization* (*Abhisamayālaṃkāra*), an important technical digest that outlines the bodhisattva path, discusses the perfections throughout the text, and the sixteenth chapter of the *Ornament of the Mahāyāna Sūtras* provides a summary on the six perfections.

The *Mahāprajñāpāramitāśāstra*, an enormous commentary on the "Larger Prajñāpāramitā" composed in the 4th century, attributed to Nāgārjuna and preserved in Kumārajīva's Chinese translation, the *Dazhidulun* 大智度論, contains numerous chapters that extensively outline the perfections.[16] Āryaśūra (4th century) composed his *Compendium of the Perfections* (*Pāramitāsamāsa*), a Sanskrit text in verse that outlines doctrines and practices for the six perfections. Candrakīrti, an important 7th-century Indian Buddhist Madhyamaka thinker, composed his *Madhyamakāvatāra* ("Introduction to the Middle Way"), which outlines the bodhisattva path in ten stages (*bhūmi*) based on the *Daśabhūmika sūtra* ("Discourse on the Ten Stages") and correlates the stages with ten perfections leading to buddhahood from a Madhyamaka perspective. Śāntideva, a 7th-century Indian Buddhist scholar-monk who is also considered a Madhyamaka philosopher, composed two major works that survive in Sanskrit, the *Bodhicaryāvatāra* ("Introduction to the Practice of Awakening") and *Śikṣāsamuccaya* ("Compendium of Training"), which both discuss the Mahāyāna path of perfections. The *Bodhicaryāvatāra* is one of the earliest major Madhyamaka works to take the perfections of the bodhisattva as a focus for articulating the Mahāyāna path. The work outlines how the first five perfections are guided by, and auxiliary to, the sixth perfection, the perfection of wisdom (*prajñāpāramitā*).

The diversity of Mahāyāna Buddhist sources provided various and specific accounts of the perfections, and the perfections did not become systematized into a set of six or ten until Mahāyāna movements became more developed. Even after Mahāyāna Buddhist movements became more popular in India, authors provided different accounts of the six or ten perfections, emphasizing distinctive points for their practice. Nevertheless, the characteristics of the six or ten perfections as found in Mahāyāna Buddhist literature share a number of general features. In general, the perfections were sequentially ordered in the Mahāyāna path to reflect a progressively developed cultivation of virtues leading to the goal of buddhahood. According to Candrakīrti, the bodhisattva may simultaneously practice acts of generosity, morality, patience, and so forth, but they are mastered or perfected in a sequential order beginning with generosity (*dāna*) and culminating with awareness (*jñāna*). The perfections were infused with the spiritual intent for awakening (*bodhicitta*), and the resolutions (*praṇidhāna*) to attain the goal for others, as well as the dedication or turning over (*pariṇāmana*) of the merit from one's cultivation of virtues for the benefit of all living beings in the course of reaching buddhahood.[17] The most common occurrence of the perfections among Indian Mahāyāna Buddhist sutras and *śāstra*s was in a set of six, which have the following general characteristics.

The perfection of generosity (*dānapāramitā*) is often listed first and foremost among the perfections. *Dāna* means to give an ordinary gift, to give the gift of the dharma, or to give the gift of mental peace and tranquility to another being as a symbol of self-sacrifice.[18] The perfected act of giving is a statement of great compassion, which indicated how a bodhisattva is dedicated to others and for the sake of omniscience. The perfection of giving is based on the earlier models of giving found in mainstream Buddhist literature, particularly the *Jātakas*. The story of Sadāprarudita in the *Aṣṭasāhasrikā prajñāpāramitā* ("The Perfecion of Wisdom in Eight Thousand Lines") reflects the importance of giving for the perfection of wisdom as he gives away everything for the sake of highest awakening. The multiple types of giving include *dharmadāna,* the gift of the teaching, and *āmiṣadāna,* material gifts. Mahāyāna sutras also mention *abhayadāna,* the giving of fearlessness. Bodhisattvas seek to mentally renounce the body as well as thought of ownership. Sutras often speak of the *dharmayajña* "dharma-offering" to fulfill this perfection. Mahāyāna sutras and technical digests will often describe the perfection of generosity as acts of giving that are perfected acts free of concept (*nirvikalpakapāramitā*), being triply pure (*trimaṇḍalapariśuddha*) in making no distinction between the thing given (*deya*), the donor (*dāyaka*), and the recipient (*pratigrāhaka*). The *Pañcaviṃśatisāhasrikā Prajñāpāramitā* ("The Perfecion of Wisdom in Twenty-five Thousand Lines") explicitly states this in regard to giving:

> The supramundane perfection of giving consists in the threefold complete purity. What is the threefold complete purity? In that case a *bodhisattva-mahāsattva* giving a gift does not apprehend a self, does not apprehend a recipient, and does not apprehend a gift; also he does not apprehend its [i.e., giving's] result.[19]

The passage continues by explaining that the triply pure act infuses all the perfections:

> He surrenders that gift to all beings, but does not apprehend those beings, or himself either. And, although he dedicates that gift to the supreme awakening, he does not apprehend any awakening. This is called the supra-mundane perfection of giving, and it is called "supra-mundane" because one swerves away from the world, departs from it, passes beyond it. In the same way should the difference between the worldly and the supramundane perfections of morality, patience, diligence, and concentration be understood.[20]

Śāntideva sums up *dānapāramitā* by stating that "the perfection of generosity is said to result from the mental attitude of relinquishing all that one has to people, together with the fruit of the act."[21]

The perfection of morality or ethical discipline (*śīlapāramitā*) is the attitude of abstention that refrains from harming others and, in turn, helping sentient beings by encouraging them to cultivate moral virtue. In this manner, bodhisattvas must purify their own conduct before installing others in practice. The sutras primarily discuss the perfection of morality in relation to the ten virtuous paths of actions (*daśakuśalapatha*), pure modes of conduct based on compassion and service to sentient beings.[22] The ten modes of pure conduct were often combined with the five precepts (*pañcaśīla*) as a synthetic list of eleven moral precepts (*śikṣāpada*).[23] The ten virtuous paths of actions, as listed, for example, from the *Saddharmasmṛtyupasthāna sūtra,* consists of the following abstentions: abstention from taking life (*prāṇātighātād virati*), abstention from taking what was not given (*adattādānād virati*), abstention from wrong conduct regarding the passions (*kāmamithyācārād virati*), abstention from speaking falsehood (*mṛṣāvādāt prativirati*), abstention from calumny (*paiśunyāt prativarati*), abstention from harsh speech (*pāruṣyāt prativarati*), abstention from frivolous speech (*saṃbhinnapralāpāt prativirati*), abstention from covetousness (*abhidhyāyāḥ prativirati*), abstention from malice (*vyāpādāt prativirati*), and abstention from wrong views (*mithyādṛṣṭeḥ prativirati*). Later technical digests will arrange the perfection of morality into three categories: the discipline of vows (*saṃvara–śīla*), the discipline of collecting virtuous dharmas (*kuśaladharmasaṃgrāhaka–śīla*), and the discipline of effecting the aims of sentient beings (*sattvārthakriyā–śīla*). The discipline of vows (*saṃvara-śīla*) is constituted by the ten virtuous paths of action. The discipline of collecting virtuous dharmas (*kuśaladharmasaṃgrāhaka–śīla*) seeks to increase virtuous qualities in the mind and not degenerate virtues already developed. The discipline of effecting the aims of sentient beings (*sattvārthakriyā–śīla*) focuses on the welfare of living beings and accomplishing their aims in a suitable manner without wrongdoing.[24] *Śīla* as a perfection is not concerned only with one's own morality but focuses on the moral condition of the entire world.[25]

The perfection of forbearance or patient endurance (*kṣāntipāramitā*) signifies cultivating a range of emotional and intellectual qualities to endure numerous types of hardship for the benefit of living beings. The *Pañviṃśatisāhasrikā prajñāpāramitā* mentions a twofold division of this perfection in terms of forbearance in regard to sentient beings (*sattvakṣānti*) and forbearance with regard to dharma (*dharmakṣānti*). Śāntideva notes in both his *Bodhicaryāvatāra*[26] and *Śikṣāsamuccaya*,[27] based on the *Dharmasaṅgīti Sūtra*, that *kṣānti* has three aspects: forbearance toward the endurance of suffering, forbearance in discerning the dharma; and forbearance in the endurance of injuries from others (*kṣāntis trividhā dharmsaṅgītisūtre'bhihitā duḥkhādhivāsanakṣāntiḥ dharmanidhyānakṣāntiḥ parāpakāramarṣanakṣāntiś ceti*). Forbearance is considered to be an interior mental quality that is developed within one's own mind and is not contingent upon changing other people's behavior or other external circumstances. The mental cultivation of the perfection of patient forbearance consists just in the perfect fulfillment of the mind's proficiency in ceasing one's own anger.

The fourth perfection, *vīrya* may be translated as "energy," "striving," "exertion," "vigor," "joyous perseverance," or "diligence." Śāntideva sums up *vīrya* as a perfection in his *Bodhicaryāvāra* (7.2): "What is *vīrya*? The endeavor to do what is skillful." *Vīryapāramitā* is the enthusiastic engagement in accumulating virtuous qualities and working for the welfare of all living beings. A number of Mahāyāna sutras classify *vīrya* into two types: corporeal striving and mental striving.[28] Mahāyāna scholastic texts, such as the *Bodhisattvabhūmi* ("The Stage of a Bodhisattva"), recognize three types of vīrya: armor-like exertion (*saṃnāhavīrya*), exertion which collects virtuous qualities (*kuśaladharmasaṃgrāhakavīrya*), and exertion carried out for the benefit of sentient beings (*sattvārthakriyāvīrya*).[29] *Vīrya* is devotion to courageous bodhisattva action, which aims at universal liberation, and is committed to working for the benefit of sentient beings. *Vīrya* strives for the strengthening of virtue and supports steadfastness to persevere in cultivating the other five perfections.

The fifth perfection, *dhyāna*, the perfection of meditative absorption or meditative stabilization, is a one-pointed state of mind, stabilized on virtue, that is able to fixate on an object of meditation without distraction.[30] *Dhyāna* is therefore a technical term used by Buddhists to describe higher levels of consciousness that are attained through the practice of quiescence or *śamatha* meditation.[31] Bodhisattvas cultivate and master all forms of meditations, including liberations (*vimokṣa*), concentrations (*samādhi*), and attainments (*samāpatti*).[32] The discussion on *dhyānapāramitā* in Mahāyāna sutras focuses on the ways in which meditative absorption may contribute to the actualization of the bodhisattva vow to be of benefit to sentient beings.[33] The preliminary practices leading up to *dhyānapāramitā* build upon practices found in mainstream Buddhist meditative practices, and therefore Mahāyāna discourses on *dhyānapāramitā* center upon the mastery of suspensory knowledge (*abhijñā*) and cognitive knowledge (*jñāna*). Through *dhyānapāramitā*, the bodhisattva is said to attain five supersensory powers (*abhijñā*) that assist the bodhisattva in helping other beings and installing them in the practice of the six perfections. The five supersensory powers are the divine eye (*divyacakṣus*), the divine ear (*divyaśrota*), knowledge of others' thoughts (*paracitttajñāna*), remembrance of previous births (*pūrvanivāsānusmṛti*), and supernormal power (*ṛddhi*).[34]

The sixth perfection, *prajñā*, often translated as "wisdom" or "insight," is the analytical discernment that cognizes the ontological status of things. The acquisition of *prajñā* was considered essential for establishing the other perfections of generosity, morality, patience, striving, and meditative absorption as actual "perfections." *Prajñā* as a perfection served as a guide for directing the other perfections toward buddhahood, and the other perfections worked synergistically with *prajñā* to actualize awakening. *Prajñāpāramitā* was the insight or wisdom that constituted Omniscient cognition (*sarvajñatā*) and was identified with the end itself, perfect awakening (*saṃbodhi*). *Prajñāpāramitā* was considered to be non-dual (*advaya*) awareness that was beyond all thought constructions (*vikalpa*), permeated with insight that was absolutely pure (*atyantaviśuddhi*), neither born nor extinguished (*anutpādānirodha*), and imperishable (*akṣaya*). *Prajñāpāramitā* was generally regarded as exclusively teaching the realization of emptiness (*śūnyatā*), the reality of the essencelessness of things (*dharmanairatyma*) and of people (*pudgalanairatyma*). Buddhist sources provide multiple classifications for *prajñā*, including worldly (*laukika*) and supermundane (*lokottara*), along with a number of different forms of analysis and reasonings. Within Buddhist scholastic sources, *prajñā* as a perfection developed within a sequence of understanding, beginning with the discernment or wisdom acquired from hearing (*śrutamāyi-prajñā*), leading to discernment or wisdom acquired from reflection (*cintamayā-prajñā*), that culminates in discernment or wisdom cultivated in meditation (*bhāvanāmayī-prajñā*).

In the course of the development of Mahāyāna Buddhist literature, perfections were added to the list of six to complement the ten stages or levels (*bhūmi*) traversed by a bodhisattva on the way to buddhahood. Four perfections—skillful means (*upāya-kauśalya*), resolution (*praṇidhāna*), power (*bala*), and knowledge (*jñāna*)—were added to establish a group of ten perfections (*daśapāramitā*). Skillful means (*upāya-kauśalya*) refers to the deft and proficient strategies or expedients that a bodhisattva utilizes to benefit sentient beings. *Praṇidhāna* refers to the vow or resolution that bodhisattvas make to save all living beings from samsara. *Bala* refers to the strengths or powers of bodhisattvas to guide sentient beings in their practices. *Jñāna-pāramitā* is the perfection of awareness or transcendental knowledge and is the highest wisdom of a bodhisattva correlated with the tenth stage of practice.

The perfections were incorporated into the rituals and iconography of tantric or Vajrayāna forms of Buddhism in the forms of feminine powers and forces. The *pāramitās* in Vajrayāna Buddhist literature were worshipped as deities (*pāramitādevī*) in human form with attributes of color and ornaments, and their number was increased to twelve, by adding *ratnapāramitā* ("jeweled perfection") and *vajrakarmapāramitā* to the list of ten found in Mahāyāna works.

Throughout the history of Buddhist forms of culture, the perfections have shaped the ideals and practices of those devoted to, or those seeking to emulate, buddhas and bodhisattvas. The manner in which the perfections were understood in different Buddhist cultures, such as in Tibet, Southeast Asia, or East Asia, was dependent on the Buddhist literature that was accessible or acceptable to the particular culture and the interpretative attention given to that literature.

REVIEW OF LITERATURE

Euro-North American[35] scholarship related to the understanding of *pāramitās* in Buddhist literature began, in part, with the analysis of the components of the Tibetan canonical collection known as the Kanjur (*bka' 'gyur*) in the 1830s by such scholars as H. H. Wilson and Alexander Csoma de Körös (1784–1842).[36] These scholars proposed the translation of *pāramitā* as "transcendent virtue" based on the Tibetan *pha-rol-tu phyin-pa*, literally, "reaching the other shore."

As discussed by J. W. de Jong, primary Buddhist sources in Pāli and Sanskrit only began to be studied in the 19th century.[37] Eighty-eight manuscripts were received by the Société Asiatique in 1837 from Brian Houghton Hodgson (1800–1894) in Kathmandu.[38] Eugène Burnouf (1801–1852), a prominent French scholar of Sanskrit, immediately began studying these manuscripts, particularly the *Saddharmapuṇḍarīka*. Burnouf's French translation of the *Saddharmapuṇḍarīka*, published after his death in 1852, contains an extended note on the six perfections, which examines a brief excerpt on each perfection found in the *Lalitavistara*.[39]

Robert C. Childers (1838–1876) published the first Pāli dictionary in Europe in 1875 containing an entry on *pārami* and *pāramitā*.[40] From this time onward more primary sources in Pāli and Sanskrit related to the *pāramitās* were published. This included Viggo Fausbøll's edition of *The Jātaka*,[41] E. Senart's edition of the *Mahāvastu*,[42] and Salomon Lefmann's critical edition of the *Lalitavistara*.[43] Seven volumes of Jātaka, stories of the anterior lives of the historical buddha illustrating various perfections, were translated into English and published in 1895 under the editorship of E. B. Cowell.[44] F. W. Thomas emphasized in a brief note that *pāramī* is an old noun denoting "the highest point."[45] L. De La Vallée Poussin wrote an encyclopedia entry on *bodhisattva* published in 1909 that contains sections outlining the perfections.[46] Har Dayal published in 1932 an analysis of *pāramitās* based on Buddhist Sanskrit literature that was reprinted in 2004.[47] This survey, although outdated, still remains the most thorough overview on the perfections in Indian Buddhist literature. Franklin Edgerton's dictionary on Buddhist Sanskrit published in 1953 contains entries on *pārami* and *pāramitā* that outline the use of these terms in several primary sources.[48] Edward Conze edited a survey of excerpts from Buddhist texts in 1954 (reprinted in 2012) that contains a brief section on the six perfections.[49] I. B. Horner published in 1957 a selection of ten Jātaka stories, with each one illustrating one of the ten perfections in Pāli-based traditions.[50]

In 1959, Herbert Guenther published an English translation of a 12th-century Tibetan Kagyu-pa (*bka' brgyud pa*) work by sGam-po-pa (1079–1153) that outlines the Mahāyāna path to awakening with a special section on the perfections.[51] In 1960, Conze published *The*

Prajñāpāramitā Literature, an indepth survey of the Perfection of Wisdom (*prajñāpāramitā*) literature with emphasis on Indian editions and Tibetan translations and commentaries.[52] Conze published in 1962 his *Buddhist Thought in India*, which contains a succinct discussion on the six perfections.[53] Margaret Cone and Richard Gombrich's edition of the Prince Vessantara Jātaka illustrates the perfection of generosity in a Pāli text.[54] Carol Meadows published in 1986 a Sanskrit edition, translation, and analysis of *Ārya-Śūra's Compendium of the Perfections* (*Pāramitāsamāsa*) which contains essays outlining the perfections.[55] Alex Wayman translated in 1992 a section of Tsong-kha-pa's *The Great Treatise on the Stages of the Path to Enlightenment* (*lam rim chen mo*) containing a discussion and analysis of the six perfections.[56] The perfections were outlined from a Zen Buddhist perspective by Robert Aitken[57] in 1994.

A modern and normative Gelukpa (*dge lugs pa*) perspective on the six perfections is found in Geshe Sonam Rinchen and Ruth Sonam's book published in 1998.[58] Tadeusz Skorupski published an abridged version in English of Étienne Lamotte's French translation of Nāgārjuna's *Mahāprajñāpāramitāśāstra* that focuses on the exegesis of the six perfections from a classical Indian Buddhist perspective.[59] Ven. Pandita M. Dhammagavesi's text on the ten perfections provides a normative account of the ten virtues from a modern Theravāda understanding.[60] Joshua Cutler and Guy Newland supervised the definitive team translation of Tsong-kha-pa blo bzang grags pa's *The Great Treatise on the Stages of the Path to Enlightenment* in three volumes. The second volume contains Tsong-kha-pa's exegesis on the six perfections.[61] Three separate scholarly encyclopedia entries on the perfections were published in the mid-2000s, one by D. Saddhasena on the perfections in Pāli sources,[62] an entry by Leslie Kawamura,[63] and another by Charles Hallisey.[64] Ṭhānissaro published a study guide on the ten perfections in the Theravāda tradition.[65] Volume 3 of Geshe Sopa's commentary on Tsong-kha-pa's *Lam-rim chen-mo*, published in 2008, outlines the six perfections from a contemporary Gelukpa Tibetan Buddhist orientation.[66] Dale Stuart Wright published a guide to the six perfections in 2009 that offers separate chapters on each of the six perfections, describing how each perfection is understood in traditional Buddhist sources, and then provides a critical assessment of how they may or may not contribute to dimensions of contemporary human character.[67] Naomi Appleton's work on the Jātakas contains sections that analyze the perfections in Pāli Buddhist sources.[68] Finally, Robert Buswell and Donald Lopez's *Princeton Dictionary of Buddhism* contains an entry on *pāramitā*.[69]

FURTHER READING

Appleton, Naomi. *Jātaka Stories in Theravāda Buddhism: Narrating the Bodhisatta Path*. Farnham, UK: Ashgate, 2010.

Crosby, Kate, and Andrew Skilton. *The Bodhicaryāvatāra*. Oxford: Oxford University Press, 2008.

Cutler, Joshua W. C., and Guy Newland, eds. *The Great Treatise on the Stages of the Path to Enlightenment*, translated by Lamrim Chenmo Translation Committee, 3 vols. Ithaca, NY: Snow Lion, 2002–2004.

Dayal, Har. *The Bodhisattva Doctrine in Buddhist Sanskrit Literature*. Delhi: Motilal Banarsidass, 2004.

Dhammapāla, Acariya, and Bhikkhu Bodhi. *A Treatise on the Pāramis: From the Commentary to the Cariyāpiṭaka*. Kandy, Sri Lanka: Buddhist Publication Society, 1996.

Eimer, Helmut. *Buddhistische Begriffsreihen als Skizzen des Erlösungsweges*. Vienna: Arbeitskreis für tibetische und buddhistische Studien, Universität Wien, 2006.

Furuyama Ken'ichi 古山健一. "Pāri jipparamitsu ni tsuite" パーリ十波羅蜜について [The Dasa-pāramī (or Dasa-pāramitā) in Pāli Buddhism]. *Komazawa Daigaku Daigakuin Bukkyōgaku Kenkyūkai Kiyō* 駒沢大学大学院仏教学研究会年報 30: 126–104 (81–103), 1997.

Guenther Herbert, V., ed. *The Jewel Ornament of Liberation*. The Clear Light Series. Boston: Shambhala, 1986.

Hallisey, Charles. "Pāramitās." In *Encyclopedia of Religion*. Edited by Lindsay Jones, 6993–6994. 2nd ed. Detroit: Macmillan Reference USA, 2005.

Huntington, C. W., Namgyal Wangchen, and Candrakīrti. *The Emptiness of Emptiness: An Introduction to Early Indian Mādhyamika*. Honolulu: University of Hawaii Press, 1989.

Kawamura, Leslie S. "Pāramitā [Perfection]." In *Encyclopedia of Buddhism*. Edited by Robert E. Buswell, 631–632. New York: Macmillan Reference USA, 2004.

Lamotte, Étienne. *Le Traité de la Grande Vertu de Sagesse* (*Mahāprajñāpāramitāśāstra*). 5 vols. Publications de l'Institut Orientaliste de Louvain. Louvain: Bibliothèque de l'Université, 1944–1980.

Meadows, Carol, ed. *Ārya-Śūra's Compendium of the Perfections: Text, Translation and Analysis of the Pāramitāsamāsa*. Translated by Carol Meadows. Indica et Tibetica, 8. Bonn: Indica-et-Tibetica-Verl., 1986.

Pagel, Ulrich. *The Bodhisattvapiṭaka: Its Doctrines, Practices and Their Position in Mahāyāna Literature*. Buddhica Britannica, 5. Tring, UK: Institute of Buddhist Studies, 1995.

Shyu, Ching-mei. "A Few Good Women: A Study of the Liu du ji jing (A Scripture on the Collection of the Six Perfections) from Literary, Artistic, and Gender Perspectives." PhD diss., Cornell University, 2008.

Skorupski, Tadeusz, ed. *The Six Perfections: An Abridged Version of E. Lamotte's French Translation of Nāgārjuna's Mahāprajñāpāramitāśāstra*, chapters XVI–XXX, Buddhica Britannica, 9. Tring, UK: Institute of Buddhist Studies, 2002.

Sonam Rinchen, Geshe, and Ruth Sonam. *The Six Perfections: An Oral Teaching*. Ithaca, NY: Snow Lion, 1998.

Suzuki, Hirotaka 鈴木 広隆. "Haramitsu no keifu" 波羅蜜の系譜 [Genealogy of pāramitā] *Indotetsugaku bukkyōgaku* 印度哲学仏教学 [Hokkaido Journal of Indological and Buddhist studies] 14 (1999): 55–69.

Ṭhānissaro. *The Ten Perfections: A Study Guide*. Singapore: Palelai Buddhist Temple, 2009.

Wright, Dale Stuart. *The Six Perfections: Buddhism and the Cultivation of Character*. Oxford and New York: Oxford University Press, 2009.

NOTES

1. F. W. Thomas, "Pāramitā in Pali and Sanskrit Books," *Journal of the Royal Asiatic Society of Great Britain and Ireland* (July 1904): 547–548.
2. Jan Nattier, *A Few Good Men: The Bodhisattva Path According to the Inquiry of Ugra* (*Ugraparipṛcchā*), Studies in the Buddhist Traditions (Honolulu: University of Hawai'i Press, 2003), 153n35.
3. Ibid.
4. Charles Hallisey, "Pāramitās," in *Encyclopedia of Religion*, ed. Lindsay Jones, 6993, 2nd ed. (Detroit, Macmillan Reference USA, 2005).
5. Reiko Ohnuma, *Head, Eyes, Flesh, and Blood: Giving Away the Body in Indian Buddhist Literature* (New York: Columbia University Press, 2007), 36–37.
6. Naomi Appleton, *Jātaka Stories in Theravāda Buddhism: Narrating the Bodhisatta Path* (Farnham, UK: Ashgate, 2010), 101–102; and Peter Skilling, "Vaidalya, Mahāyāna, and Bodhisatva in India: An Essay towards Historical Understanding," in *The Bodhisattva Ideal: Essays on the Emergence of Mahāyāna*, ed. Bhikkhu Nyanatusita himi, 115 (Kandy, Sri Lanka: Buddhist Publication Society 2013).
7. Daniel Boucher, *Bodhisattvas of the Forest and the Formation of the Mahāyāna: A Study and Translation of the Rāṣṭrapālaparipṛcchā-sūtra* (Honolulu: University of Hawai'i Press, 2008), 184n25.

8. Nattier, *A Few Good Men*, 153n36.
9. Ulrich Pagel, *The Bodhisattvapiṭaka: Its Doctrines, Practices and Their Position in Mahāyāna Literature*, Buddhica Britannica, 5 (Tring, UK: Institute of Buddhist Studies, 1995), 107–109.
10. Nattier, *A Few Good Men*, trans. 244, §11G(2)–(4).
11. English translation from Salomon Lefmann, *Lalita Vistara: Leben und Lehre des Çâkya-Buddha* (Halle a.S.: Buchhandlung des Waisenhauses, 1902), 34.20–35.7.
12. The following chapter and section numbers follow Lamotte's French translation and the edition of Study Group on Buddhist Sanskrit Literature. See Étienne Lamotte, *Le Traité de la Grande Vertu de Sagesse (Mahāprajñāpāramitāśāstra)*, 5 vols. Publications de l'Institut Orientaliste de Louvain (Louvain: Bibliothèque de l'Université, 1944–1980), rendered into English by Sara Boin, *The Teaching of Vimalakīrti (Vimalakīrtinirdeśa): From the French Translation with Introduction and Notes (L'enseignement de Vimalarkirti)* (Oxford: Pali Text Society, 1994); and Taishō Daigaku, *Bon-Zō-Kan taishō "Yuimakyō" "Chikōmyō shōgongyō"/ Vimalakīrtinirdeśa and Jñānālokālaṃkāra: Transliterated Sanskrit text Collated with Tibetan and Chinese Translations*, ed. Study Group on Buddhist Sanskrit Literature (Tōkyō: Taishō Daigaku Shuppankai, 2004).
13. Edward Conze, *The Perfection of Wisdom in Eight Thousand Lines & Its Verse Summary*, Wheel Series, 1 (Bolinas: Four Seasons Foundation; distributed by Book People, Berkeley, CA, 1973), 111–112.
14. Ibid., 136.
15. Carol Meadows, ed., *Ārya-Śūra's Compendium of the Perfections: Text, Translation and Analysis of the Pāramitāsamāsa*, trans. Carol Meadows, 53–64, Indica et Tibetica, 8 (Bonn: Indica-et-Tibetica-Verl., 1986).
16. Lamotte, *Le Traité de la Grande Vertu de Sagesse (Mahāprajñāpāramitāśāstra)*.
17. Meadows, *Ārya-Śūra's Compendium of the Perfections*, 54–54.
18. Ibid., 70.
19. Nalinaksha Dutt, *The Pañcaviṁśatisāhasrikā Prajñāpāramitā* (London: Luzac, 1934), 264; see also Meadows, *Ārya-Śūra's Compendium of the Perfections*, 58.
20. Edward Conze, *The Large Sutra on Perfect Wisdom: With the Divisions of the Abhisamayālaṅkāra* (Berkeley: University of California Press, 1975), 199.
21. Kate Crosby and Andrew Skilton, *The Bodhicaryāvatāra* (Oxford: Oxford University Press, 1995), 34.
22. Meadows, *Ārya-Śūra's Compendium of the Perfections*, 80.
23. Nattier, *A Few Good Men*, 107–111.
24. Mark Tatz, Asaṅga, and Tsong-kha-pa Blo-bzang-grags-pa, *Asanga's Chapter on Ethics with the Commentary of Tsong-Kha-Pa, The Basic Path to Awakening, the Complete Bodhisattva*, vol. 4., Studies in Asian Thought and Religion (Lewiston, NY: Edwin Mellen, 1986).
25. Meadows, *Ārya-Śūra's Compendium of the Perfections*, 86.
26. Crosby and Skilton, *The Bodhicaryāvatāra*, 51–61.
27. P. L Vaidya, *Śikṣasamuccaya of Śantideva* (Darbhanga: Mithila Institute of Post-Graduate Studies and Research in Sanskrit Learning, 1961), 100.
28. Meadows, *Ārya-Śūra's Compendium of the Perfections*, 93–94.
29. Pagel, *The Bodhisattvapiṭaka*, 208–209.
30. Unrai Ogiwara and Asaṅga, *Bodhisattvabhūmi: A Statement of Whole Course of the Bodhisattva (Being Fifteenth Section of Yogācārabhūmi)* (Tokyo: Sankibo Buddhist Book Store, 1971), 206–207.
31. Crosby and Skilton, *The Bodhicaryāvatāra*, 75.
32. Jens Braarvig, *Akṣayamatinirdeśasūtra* (Oslo: Solum, 1993), 183.
33. Pagel, *The Bodhisattvapiṭaka*, 217.
34. Meadows, *Ārya-Śūra's Compendium of the Perfections*, 99–100.
35. The following brief historiography focuses on major works related to the perfections published in Europe and North America. For a brief survey of related sources in modern Japanese literature, see James B. Apple, "Perfections (Six and Ten)." *Oxford Bibliographies Online in Buddhism* (2012).

36. H. H. Wilson, "Analysis of the Kah-gyur." *Journal of The Asiatic Society* 9 (September 1832): 375–392; and Alexander Csoma de Körös, "Analysis of the Sher-chin–P'hal ch'hen–Dkon-séks–Do-dé–Nyáng-dás–and Gyut; Being the 2nd, 3rd, 4th, 5th, 6th, and 7th Divisions of the Tibetan work, Entitled the Kah-gyur," *Asiastic Researches* 20, no. 2 (1839): 393–552.
37. J. W. de Jong, *A Brief History of Buddhist Studies in Europe and America* (Varanasi: Bharat-Bharati, 1976), 13.
38. Ibid., 19.
39. Eugène Burnouf, *Le lotus de la bonne loi, traduit du sanscrit, accompagné d'un commentaire et de vingt et un mémoires relatifs au bouddhisme* (Paris: Imprimerie nationale, 1852); no. VII, sur les six perfections, Vol. 2, 544–553.
40. Robert Cæsar Childers, *A Dictionary of the Pāli Language* (London: Trübner, 1875), 334–335.
41. Viggo Fausbøll, ed., *The Jātaka Together with Its Commentary Being Tales of the Anterior Births of Gotama Buddhism*, 6 vols. (London: Trübner, 1877–1896).
42. E. Senart, *Le Mahâvastu; texte sanscrit publié pour la première fois et accompagné d'introductions et d'un commentaire par É. Senart* (Paris: Imprimé par autorisation du garde des sceaux à l'Imprimerie nationale, 1882).
43. Salomon Lefmann, *Lalita Vistara: Leben und Lehre des Çâkya-Buddha* (Halle a.S.: Buchhandlung des Waisenhauses, 1902).
44. Edward B. Cowell, Robert Chalmers, W. H. D. Rouse, H. T. Francis, Robert Alexander Neil, and Charles Lang Freer, *The Jātaka; or, Stories of the Buddha's Former Births*, trans. Edward B. Cowell (Cambridge, UK: Cambridge University Press, 1895).
45. F. W. Thomas, "Pāramitā in Pali and Sanskrit Books," *Journal of the Royal Asiatic Society of Great Britain and Ireland Journal of the Royal Asiatic Society of Great Britain and Ireland* (July 1904): 547–548.
46. L. De La Vallée Poussin, "Bodhisattva," in *Encyclopædia of Religion and Ethics*, ed. James Hastings, (New York: T. & T. Clark, 1909), 2:739–753.
47. Har Dayal, *The Bodhisattva Doctrine in Buddhist Sanskrit Literature* (London: Routledge & Kegan Paul, 1932).
48. Franklin Edgerton, *Buddhist Hybrid Sanskrit Grammar and Dictionary* (New Haven, CT: Yale University Press, 1953), 341–342.
49. Edward Conze, *Buddhist Texts through the Ages: Newly Translated from the Original Pali, Sanskrit, Chinese, Tibetan, Japanese and Apabhramsa* (New York: Philosophical Library, 1954), 135–139.
50. I. B. Horner, *Ten Jātaka Stories, Each Illustrating One of the Ten Pāramitā with Pali Text* (London: Luzac, 1957).
51. Herbert V. Guenther, ed., *The Jewel Ornament of Liberation*, trans. Herbert V. Guenther (London: Rider, 1959).
52. Edward Conze, *The Prajñāpāramitā Literature* ('s-Gravenhage: Mouton, 1960). 2nd ed. revised and enlarged (New Delhi: Munshiram Manoharlal, 2000).
53. Edward Conze, *Buddhist Thought in India* (London: Allen & Unwin, 1962), 211–217.
54. Margaret Cone and Richard F. Gombrich, *The Perfect Generosity of Prince Vessantara: A Buddhist Epic* (Oxford: Clarendon, 1977).
55. Carol Meadows, *Ārya-Śūra's Compendium of the Perfections.*
56. Alex Wayman, *Ethics of Tibet: Bodhisattva Section of Tsong-Kha-Pa's Lam Rim Chen Mo*, translated from the Tibetan original (Delhi: Sri Satguru, 1992).
57. Robert Aitken, *The Practice of Perfection: The Pāramitās from a Zen Buddhist Perspective* (New York: Pantheon Books, 1994).
58. Geshe Sonam Rinchen and Ruth Sonam, *The Six Perfections: An Oral Teaching* (Ithaca, NY: Snow Lion, 1998).

59. Tadeusz Skorupski, *The Six Perfections: An Abridged Version of E. Lamotte's French Translation of Nāgārjuna's Mahāprajñāpāramitāśāstra*, chapters XVI–XXX, Buddhica Britannica (Tring, UK: Institute of Buddhist Studies, 2002), 9.
60. Ven. Pandita M. Dhammagavesi, *Ten Perfections: The Ten Virtues for Those Who Seek Enlightenment* (Schofield, N.S.W.: Lankarama Vihara, 2002).
61. Joshua W. C. Cutler and Guy Newland, eds., *The Great Treatise on the Stages of the Path to Enlightenment*, trans. Joshua W. C. Cutler et al., 3 vols. (Ithaca, NY: Snow Lion, 2002–2004).
62. D. Saddhasena, "Pāramitā," in *Encyclopaedia of Buddhism*, ed. W. G. Weeraratne, Vol. 7, fascicle 1 (Mind-Nyāyapravesa). (Kandy: Government of Sri Lanka, 2003), 312–314.
63. Leslie S. Kawamura, "Pāramitā [Perfection]," in *Encyclopedia of Buddhism*, ed. Robert E. Buswell (New York: Macmillan Reference USA, 2004), 631–632.
64. Charles Hallisey, "Pāramitās," in *Encyclopedia of Religion*, 2nd ed., ed. Lindsay Jones (Detroit: Macmillan Reference USA, 2005), 6993–6994.
65. Ṭhānissaro, *The Ten Perfections: A Study Guide* (Singapore: Palelai Buddhist Temple, 2009).
66. Geshe Lhundub Sopa, Dalai Lama, and Beth Newman, *Steps on the Path to Enlightenment, A Commentary on Tsongkhapa's Lamrim chenmo*, Vol. 3, *The Way of the Bodhisattva* (Boston: Wisdom Publications, 2008).
67. Dale Stuart Wright, *The Six Perfections: Buddhism and the Cultivation of Character* (Oxford and New York: Oxford University Press, 2009).
68. Naomi Appleton, *Jātaka Stories in Theravāda Buddhism: Narrating the Bodhisatta Path* (Farnham, UK: Ashgate, 2010).
69. Robert E. Buswell and Donald S. Lopez, *The Princeton Dictionary of Buddhism* (Princeton, NJ: Princeton University Press, 2014), 624.

James B. Apple

THE PHILOSOPHICAL WORKS AND INFLUENCE OF DIGNĀGA AND DHARMAKĪRTI

FROM ABHIDHARMA TO LOGIC AND EPISTEMOLOGY

Following some later Indian commentators, doxographical traditions that were central to the structuring of Tibetan monastic curricula represented Dignāga and Dharmakīrti as commonly exemplifying the "Sautrāntika" school of thought that originates in the Abhidharma period; both were also said, however, to embrace the idealist Yogācāra school, which represents their definitive views. Notwithstanding the possibly misleading character of such doxographical terms, this pair of characterizations succinctly captures the decisive philosophical change Dignāga and Dharmakīrti ushered in, as well as the kinds of arguments they typically made for idealism. Tibetan doxographers helpfully distinguished, in regard to the first of these doxographical terms, between two subtypes of Sautrāntikas—those who follow *scripture* (*āgama*), and those who follow *reasoning* (*yukti*)—and took Dignāga and Dharmakīrti to represent the latter; the Ābhidharmika Vasubandhu (fl. *c.* 360 CE) was in these terms chief among exemplars of *Sautrāntikas* who follow scripture. Vasubandhu's *Abhidharmakośabhāṣya*, an influential "summa" of the Abhidharma traditions of thought preserved in Sanskrit, typifies the earlier tradition of Buddhist philosophy that Dignāga and Dharmakīrti so influentially transformed. While texts such as Vasubandhu's can reasonably be understood as crystallizing early Buddhist attempts at formulating a basic ontology, the Abhidharma literature was largely driven by basically exegetical considerations. Thus, Abhidharma's project of enumerating and characterizing the "ultimately existent" (*paramārthasat*) constituents of reality—called *dharmas* in this literature—had its impetus in the challenging hermeneutical task of systematizing the many lists of categories that proliferated in the sutra literature traditionally attributed to the buddha. Much of the discussion in this literature accordingly turns on questions of scriptural interpretation and is replete with arguments to the effect that "if *X* is not the case, the buddha would not (as he did) have said such-and-such." The resultant systematization of categories aimed to provide an ultimately true description of what really exists, and the Abhidharma literature was thus understood as providing a definitive account of how Buddhist categories could be used to elaborate an exhaustively impersonal account of reality—an account, that is, consistent with the cardinal Buddhist doctrine that there are no real *selves* (*anātmavāda*). While this surely amounts to the elaboration of a complete ontology, the exegetical impetus of the project made it a basically intramural one; few who did not already take it as axiomatic that adequacy to Buddhist scriptures is a relevant constraint were apt to be persuaded by many of the arguments of this literature. This is the sense, then, in which thinkers like Vasubandhu were aptly characterized as "Sautrāntikas who follow scripture."[1]

That Dignāga and Dharmakīrti should also have been called "Sautrāntikas" makes sense given the basic commitments and orientation they share with the mainstream of the Abhidharma literature. Like thinkers in that tradition, Dignāga and Dharmakīrti, too, exhibited confidence in the possibility of specifying and characterizing what kinds of things count as ultimately existent, and in the possibility of showing how all our epistemic practices could be re-described in terms of the impersonal, momentary events that alone count as such. (This is in contrast especially to the Madhyamaka school of thought that begins with the philosopher Nāgārjuna, who argued that it cannot coherently be thought that our epistemic practices ever reach anything ultimately real. The guiding conviction of proponents of Madhyamaka was thus that the kinds of explanatory categories posited in the Abhidharma literature invariably turn out themselves to admit of the same kind of analysis that shows *selves* to be unreal.) Despite, however, the orientation they thus shared with thinkers like Vasubandhu, Dignāga and Dharmakīrti were characterized by Tibetan doxographers as "Sautrāntikas who follow *reasoning*." This aptly reflects the fundamentally different way in which they went about arguing for such views; for in contrast to the largely intramural arguments of the Abhidharma literature, the stock-in-trade of Dignāga and Dharmakīrti was epistemological arguments informed by systematic theorization of the logical form of valid inferences—arguments that could at least in principle be persuasive across party lines.

Their thoroughgoing emphasis on logical consistency led, moreover, to a radicalization of the kind of ontology characteristic of Abhidharma. Consistent with their radically nominalist bent (which itself follows from a deep suspicion of the kind of conceptual thought that necessarily involves abstractions), Dignāga and Dharmakīrti recognized that the Ābhidharmika tradition's enumeration of dharmas amounts to the enumeration of *kinds* of things—the enumeration, that is, of *types*, of which there could be innumerable tokens. (According to Vasubandhu's *Abhidharmakośabhāṣyam*, for example, there are seventy-five dharmas; that does not mean, of course, that he argued for a universe containing exactly seventy-five existents, but rather that there occur seventy-five distinct *kinds* of events.) Against this, Dignāga and Dharmakīrti held that ontological bedrock could really consist only in the unique particulars encountered in perception. In place of the Abhidharma literature's complex lists of ontologically basic kinds of things, then, Dignāga and Dharmakīrti suggest a much more austere ontology according to which only perceptible particulars finally count as "ultimately existent" (*paramārthasat*). The austere character of the resultant picture, moreover, comes fully into view only when it is appreciated that what really count as perceptible particulars must, in light of their uncompromising emphasis on the nonconceptual character of perception, be other than we typically suppose; for given Buddhists' reductionist view that temporally enduring wholes are not ultimately real, the kinds of ordinary objects conventionally understood as given to perception represent, in fact, the constructive work of conceptual thought. When this is taken into account, it seems Dignāga and Dharmakīrti must mean that only *momentary mental events* finally count as "perceptible"; it is insofar as something like this is indeed their considered view that Dignāga and Dharmakīrti were reasonably taken by the doxographical traditions as finally upholding the Yogācāra school of Buddhist idealism. Insofar, however, as they were chiefly concerned to advance maximally persuasive arguments, both thinkers characteristically exploited more intuitively plausible ideas; their route to idealism, then, goes through empiricism, in the sense that their arguments typically worked by showing what follows simply from the analysis of perception's role among our epistemic practices. Their carefully formulated arguments thus remain largely *epistemological* in key, and they seldom explicitly declare for any particular metaphysical or ontological conclusions (they did not, for example, explicitly affirm many of the doctrinal categories associated with Yogācāra)—an approach that sometimes makes it hard to discern what they finally believed, and that warrants the many modern characterizations of both thinkers as chiefly exemplifying a methodologically defined school of "Buddhist Logic" or "Buddhist Epistemology."[2]

Their epistemological predilections found expression in terms informed by sophisticated attention to the form of valid inferences. In this regard, Dignāga's brief *Hetucakraḍamaru* ("Drum of the Cycle of Reasons") formalized valid argument forms, concisely presenting what Dignāga took to be all possible relations between the terms of any formally stated inference. Abstracting from the content of any particular argument, this text can clearly be characterized as elaborating a basic table of logic. In particular, Dignāga considered all of the various ways in which the three terms of an inference—a *reason*, the *locus* in which that is instantiated, and the *conclusion* warranted thereby—could be related, thus providing a content-neutral way to characterize not only the form of valid inferences, but also the various ways in which these can be fallacious. As with Indian logic more generally, Dignāga's remains an account of *inductively* valid inferences; the role played by reference to *examples* therein is among the considerations that seemingly preclude the idea of deductive validity. (On a canonical illustration, reference to an example figures thus: "There is fire on the mountain, because there is smoke, *as we know from seeing these things together in a kitchen*.") Chief among Dharmakīrti's revisions of his predecessor's project, however, was his attempt to theorize inferences with something more like deductive certainty, though there is considerable dispute about whether that is an apt way to characterize either his aim or the result.[3]

Dignāga's sensitivity to such considerations shows up in his magnum opus, the Pramāṇasamuccaya ("Compendium of Epistemic Criteria"), which refined epistemological terms of art, attested since the early literature of the Brahmanical Nyāya school of thought, in ways conducive to characteristically Buddhist conclusions. Chiefly, while many Brahmanical schools of thought affirmed that language or the testimony of tradition ought to be reckoned among reliable epistemic criteria (as, that is, *pramāṇas*), Dignāga argued that only perception (*pratyakṣa*) and inference (*anumāna*) have this status; all other ways of knowing, he argued, are reducible to one of these. Of particular importance here was his emphasis on the essentially *nonconceptual* character of perception. While this is an intuitively plausible idea—surely the difference between *perceiving* a tree and (say) *imagining* one is that in the former case alone, one comes up against something in the world—the point becomes more radical in light of the unusually thoroughgoing reductionism characteristic of Buddhism. Given, then, the Buddhist premise that temporally enduring wholes are essentially conceptual fictions, the ordinary objects typically taken as disclosed in perception cannot finally be what counts as "perceived"; rather, it must be only momentary sense data that count as really perceptible. Indeed, Dignāga gives reason to think he finally intends the view that we are immediately, nonconceptually acquainted only with the fleeting occurrence of our own mental events. This is why his epistemology ultimately recommends the kind of idealism characteristic of Yogācāra. (Dignāga more concisely argued for idealism in his other principal work, the *Ālambanaparīkṣā*, or "Critical Investigation of Percepts.") Such a view readily makes sense as supporting fundamental Buddhist commitments; above all, this recommends the conclusion that only fleeting sensations are finally real—the thought that such sensations must be the states of a *self* (*ātma*) stands revealed as an *inferential* belief that is finally unwarranted.[4]

Dharmakīrti, who is traditionally represented as Dignāga's grand-disciple, framed his most extensive work—the Pramāṇavārttika ("Critical Commentary on Epistemic Criteria")—as a commentary on Dignāga's magnum opus. (Dharmakīrti's principal works also include the *Pramāṇaviniścaya*, or "Ascertainment of Epistemic Criteria," and the *Nyāyabindu*, "An Epitome of Philosophy.") Benefiting from intervening Brahmanical critiques of Dignāga, Dharmakīrti greatly elaborated and revised Dignāga's thought, advancing what many Indian philosophers (Buddhist and non-Buddhist alike) would take to be the definitive arguments for characteristically Buddhist positions; indeed, Dharmakīrti's influence in India effectively eclipsed Dignāga's (although only works by the latter were ever translated into Chinese). Chief among Dharmakīrti's innovations was a strong emphasis on *causal efficacy* as the criterion of the real—an emphasis expressed in an oft-quoted passage that frames the point in terms of the Buddhist idea of two levels of truth: "Whatever has the capacity for causal efficacy is ultimately existent (*paramārthasat*); everything else is conventionally existent (*saṃvṛtisat*)." These two kinds of things respectively consist, he adds, in unique particulars (*svalakṣaṇa*) and abstractions (*sāmānyalakṣaṇa*); these are the objects of (respectively) perception and inference.[5] Once again, it is an intuitively plausible idea that perception is to be distinguished by its thus being *causally* describable; surely a salient difference between *perceiving* a tree and *imagining* one is that in the former case alone one has a cognition that is actually *caused* by what it is about. Yet again, though, the point becomes more radical in light of the uncompromising reductionism of Buddhist philosophers; for given the Buddhist premise that only momentary things are ultimately real—and given, moreover, that only ultimately real things are capable of causal efficacy—we are again driven toward the conclusion that perception must finally be understood under something other than a conventional description. This dialectic typifies the generally epistemic arguments that Dharmakīrti, in particular, clearly advanced in support of idealist conclusions: starting from the intuitively plausible view that perception, uniquely among ways of knowing, can be described in causal terms, Dharmakīrti thus argued that what is caused by our perceptual encounters with the world must be mental "images" (*ākāras*); only these, he could then argue, are the direct objects of awareness, and it can only be inferentially that we suppose these to have been caused by the elements of an external world. To assent to this much is already tantamount to conceding that Dharmakīrti's idealism wins the day.[6]

Consistent with the idealism advanced by both thinkers, Dharmakīrti influentially elaborated Dignāga's thought that we are perceptually (which is to say immediately, nonconceptually) aware, finally, only of the occurrence of our own mental events. In this regard, Dharmakīrti's arguments for the perceptual character of "reflexive awareness" (*svasaṃvitti*)—the perceptual character, that is, of any cognition's awareness *of itself* as given along with whatever is represented therein—came to be taken as one of the tradition's definitive arguments for the idealist view that only cognition itself is indubitably known. Dharmakīrti argued, in particular, that anything at all that can be an object of awareness can be known *only along with the cognition to which it is present*; cognition itself must, to that extent, be understood as explanatorily basic, and it is only inferentially that one can suppose that the content of awareness represents anything external thereto. Here, too, we can see that Dharmakīrti chiefly argues *epistemologically* for a view that recommends the idealist conclusion that only mental items finally exist. Insofar, however, as his arguments remain basically epistemological, Dharmakīrti is often content to rest with the conclusion that it must be allowed that reference to an external world is just optional. The stance Dharmakīrti typically adopts is reflected in another of the later doxographical tradition's characterizations of these thinkers: "proponents of the doctrine that external objects can only be inferred" (*bāhyārthānumeyavāda*). This is eminently consistent with the basically empiricist orientation that Dharmakīrti epitomizes; classical empiricists like John Locke similarly argued, based on an intuitively plausible causal theory of perception, that we are immediately acquainted only with mental representations. (It was left to Bishop Berkeley to argue that if one holds such a view, one is effectively committed to idealism.) There are, however, moments in the works of both Dignāga and Dharmakīrti where they offer something more like metaphysical arguments to the effect that only mental events *can* exist; more on their stronger arguments below.[7]

The difference that Dharmakīrti's emphasis on causal efficacy makes shows up in his attempt to address perceived deficiencies in Dignāga's clearly inductive account of inferences.[8] This emphasis shows up, as well, in Dharmakīrti's very different (albeit complementary) elaboration of the "exclusion" (*apoha*) theory of meaning first introduced by Dignāga. Though it has been common for scholars both traditional and modern to associate Dignāga and Dharmakīrti as commonly exemplifying a unitary school of thought, it is perhaps especially with respect to the *apoha* doctrine that some important differences between them can be readily appreciated. The *apoha* doctrine is typically represented as a position in first-millennium Indian debates regarding the ontological status of universals (paradigmatically, linguistic referents), which Buddhists characteristically held to be ultimately unreal. (In contrast, many Brahmanical schools of thought—chiefly the Mīmāṃsā school, whose constitutive concern was with the interpretation of a Vedic corpus taken to represent the most significant *pramāṇa*—strongly affirmed the essential reality of linguistic referents. Indeed, the 5th-century grammarian Bhartṛhari held that linguistic items are finally the *most* real of all existents.) While it is apt to represent the *apoha* doctrine as thus advancing a kind of nominalism regarding universals, it should be understood that the scope of this elusive doctrine exceeds that; particularly as developed by Dharmakīrti, the doctrine represents a way to explain, in the absence of real universals, how all conceptual thought is constructed and why, despite its ultimate unreality, such conceptual content can nevertheless facilitate our commerce with the world. The doctrine originates with Dignāga, though, as integral to his theorization of the inferential relations that figure in the kind of reasoning theorized in his *Hetucakraḍamaru*. Let us, then, begin a more fine-grained look at some of the principal doctrines and arguments of these thinkers by starting with Dignāga's introduction of the idea that inferential relations can be exhaustively characterized in terms of "exclusions" (*apoha*).

THE *APOHA* DOCTRINE: INFERENTIAL RELATIONS AND A THEORY OF MENTAL CONTENT

According to a typical thumbnail sketch, the *apoha* theory affirms that the referents of kind-terms (*cow*, on a canonical example) are not really existent features of reality; there is no really existent property like *being a cow*, but it is possible to construct such ideas entirely through a process of exclusion. The referent of a word like *cow*, on this view, is to be understood as really arrived at just by excluding whatever is not a *non*-cow. On the face of it, this appears to be circular, since it would seem that one could conceptually exclude all *non*-cows only if one already knows what a "cow" is—and that is just what the doctrine supposedly explains. To be sure, many of the objections reasonably leveled at the doctrine by the Brahmanical interlocutors of Dignāga and Dharmakīrti involve variations on this charge, which does have something to it. That there is nevertheless a profound and interesting insight here can be brought out, however, if we begin by appreciating that Dignāga is particularly theorizing what may be called *inferential relations*.[9]

Consider, then, a canonical example of inferential relations: the relation between *being an oak* and *being a tree*. (Another canonical example, favored in many basic Tibetan debate primers, is the relation between *being blue* and *being a color*.) Dignāga's guiding thought is that every concept divides the world into two mutually exclusive classes: the class of everything that comes under that concept, and the complementary class of *everything else*. When the matter is thus understood, the question to be answered will always simply be: at what level of generality has this division been made? Dignāga's insight is that the answer to this question can be expressed (and accordingly, that relative conceptual determinacy can be explained) entirely in negative terms—which is to say, without having to specify any really existent universals. The relative determinacy of concepts like "tree" and "oak," then, can be precisely expressed without reference to timeless properties like *being a tree* or *the set of all trees*; rather, the term "tree" is contentful just insofar as it excludes from its purview everything there is that does not properly come under the concept "tree." By itself, this example seems to involve the kind of question-begging circularity already noted. Dignāga's idea, though, chiefly has to do with understanding the *relative* determinacy of concepts that invariably have their place in hierarchies of superordinate and subordinate categories. At the highest level of generality in such a hierarchy, a concept divides the world into two classes of great indeterminacy—as, for example, when we entertain the concept *being existent,* which excludes so little as to be of little practical use in most contexts. Starting at this level of generality, concepts are to be understood as having their place in branching subsets that become more narrowly circumscribed just insofar as they exclude more. Our example, then—the idea that the term "tree" excludes everything that does not come under the concept *tree*—is not really informative until we appreciate Dignāga's point that the relatively greater determinacy of a subordinate concept in the same branching hierarchy ("oak," for example) consists precisely in the fact that it excludes more than the superordinate concept "tree." The concept *oak* is narrower than the concept *tree,* then, just because *oak* excludes everything in the world that is not a tree, *plus all trees that are not oaks.* The greater determinacy of the concept "oak" is thus a function of its excluding a larger domain, the scope of which had already been narrowed by the immediately superordinate category in an ascending hierarchy of increasing generality.

While it is in the nature of *concepts* never to achieve the concreteness that characterizes spatiotemporally determinate objects—no matter how fine grained our concepts become, their approach to the world of concrete particulars is necessarily asymptotic, finally giving way to moments where one can only point at *this thing, right here*—the most determinate concepts will always be those with the greatest exclusion ranges. Among the things that recommend Dignāga's idea as an account of inferential relations is that this picture of branching hierarchies elegantly captures the asymmetry that essentially characterizes inferential relations; this makes good sense, that is, of why inferences are only warranted if, as it were, they move in the right direction in such a hierarchy. We are, then, entitled to infer that because something is an *oak* it is therefore a *tree* just because the concept *oak* excludes everything that *tree* excludes, *as well as all other trees*; we are not, however, entitled to claim that because something is a *tree* it must therefore be an *oak,* since not all trees are oaks. "This is an oak" has a more precise meaning than "this is a tree" just because everything that is incompatible with "this is a tree" is incompatible with "this is an oak," but not the other way around. This gives us a way to specify *negatively* the different scope of concepts, whose relative determinacy is expressible simply in terms of their exclusion of all the other members of a branching hierarchy of concepts; the concept *tree* excludes things like *chariots* but not things like "oak" or "maple," while "oak" excludes not only chariots (and everything else in the world that is not a tree), but additionally all trees that are not oaks.

With regard to Indian debates about the ontological status of linguistic universals, the point is that it is thus possible to account for the relative contentfulness of concepts without having to specify in what, precisely, their content "really" consists; we can account for the inferential asymmetry that defines the place of any concept (say, *tree*) in a larger scheme without having to specify either the intension ("being tall and leafy") or the extension ("the set of all woody perennial plants") of the concept. This is a desideratum, for Buddhists, since nothing one could positively specify in this way is really *real* in anything like the same way as particular trees; one can chop down a particular tree and use it for fuel, but one can do nothing of the sort with the abstract idea *being a tree.* Dignāga's *apoha* doctrine, then, is a strictly formal account of the inferentially asymmetrical relations that track the relative scope of concepts.

Still, one may reasonably object that the doctrine as so far elaborated by Dignāga cannot tell us everything we need to understand in order to make sense of why it is that despite the ultimate unreality of linguistic items, the use of language nevertheless facilitates our getting around in a world of concrete particulars; for it seems we still have no way of knowing *which* particulars are rightly brought under any specific concept. If, in terms suggested by Frege, Dignāga has thus given a good account of the relative *sense* of concepts, we are still entitled to ask for a corresponding theory of *reference*. That is just what Dharmakīrti's complementary elaboration of the *apoha* doctrine can be taken to add to the picture so far developed following Dignāga. And, given Dharmakīrti's characteristic emphasis on causal efficacy as the criterion of the real, it is as we should expect that his significantly different development of the doctrine centrally involves reference to *causal efficacy*. On Dharmakīrti's version of the doctrine, then, the idea is that the basis for our excluding whatever does not interest us at the moment is just our explanatory or practical interests—and these, he argued, can be described in terms of the *effects* we aim to bring about.[10]

If, for example, we are interested in ameliorating a fever, we may find it useful to refer to certain herbs known for their fever-reducing effects; given this, the most useful concept will be one that excludes all herbs that do not have such an effect. To be sure, this might again be thought to beg the question, since it could be objected that *capacity to produce such and such an effect* amounts to precisely the kind of abstraction that is here supposed to be explained; after all, doesn't possession of such a capacity amount to a defining characteristic of a general *type*, of which what is sought in this case would thus be a token? Dharmakīrti's thought seems to be that if usage of the concept leads us to pick some herb, it can only be *as a particular* that it produces the desired effect, since only particulars have causal efficacy. Against that, one might object that while success in producing the desired effect may indeed count as *evidence* that one had rightly used the concept in question, it leaves unaddressed the conceptually prior question of *what* was understood such that our practices could in the first place culminate in our arriving at the desired particular; while it must indeed be some particular herb that finally produces the desired effect, it seems we are still owed an account of what we understood by the concept *medicinal herb* that could lead us to any such particular in the first place. It seems, then, that variations on the circularity objection may still loom.[11]

That worry might, however, be mitigated by the fact that Dharmakīrti seems, at the end of the day, to have had in mind a rather narrower sense of the relevant "capacity to produce an effect"; in particular, he seems to have meant that what is excluded, on any occasion of concept-use, is whatever does not produce an effect that is *phenomenally* the same as what is intended. More precisely, what is excluded is whatever does not produce that effect which is a *cognition* of the expected sort; the only "sameness" that characterizes the capacity in question, then, attaches to the *judgments* that concern what is perceptually encountered in the course of using the concept, not to the supposed referents of our concepts. This means, to be sure, that there is after all something invariant across uses of a concept; however, the relevant sameness is really not a property *of the particulars in question*, but rather of the perceptual judgments produced thereby. Dharmakīrti thus means to argue not only that the construction of *kinds* is relative to our explanatory or practical interests (what we exclude, when conceiving some herb, will vary depending on whether it is fever reduction that is wanted, or the flavoring of a stew), but also that the "sameness" that constitutes the kind in question exists only (as it were) in our heads. There are, in other words, no real, mind-independent similarities that could warrant the idea that our concepts correspond to natural kinds; rather, there are only *phenomenal* similarities that guide our attention to particulars, facilitating our sorting of things in one way or another depending entirely on our interests.

Among other things, Dharmakīrti's causal application of the *apoha* idea explains why he could think that the inferential relations theorized by Dignāga can be characterized as relations of "identity" (*tādātmya*). This is as Dharmakīrti says in a concise text (the *Sambandhaparīkṣā*, or "Critical Investigation of Relations") that theorizes what he took to be the only two kinds of relations there can be: *causal* relations (which have to do with one thing's "arising from another," or *tad-utpatti*) and *identity* (*tādātmya*) relations. These kinds of relations closely track the principal kinds of reasons that can warrant judgments: those consisting, respectively, in *effects* (*kārya-hetu*), as when one infers from the presence of smoke that there must be fire; and those consisting in a conceptual "essence," or *svabhāva-hetu*, as when one knows that because something is an *oak*, it is therefore also a *tree*. The idea that the latter is an *identity* relation might seem to fly in the face of Dignāga's recognition that inferential relations are essentially characterized by asymmetry; if the relation between *being a tree* and *being an oak* is one of *identity*, how then can we make sense of the fact that inferential relations between these concepts work in one direction but not in the other? (It is true that if something is an *oak*, then it is also a *tree*, but it is not true that if something is a tree, then it is an oak; a relation of identity, however, would seem to entail the truth of the latter, as well.) In fact, Dharmakīrti accepts Dignāga's basic idea regarding inferential asymmetry; we must bear in mind, though, that Dharmakīrti's development of the *apoha* doctrine addresses a different question than had oriented Dignāga's elaboration, albeit a question complementary to Dignāga's. One can, then, retain Dignāga's thought that hierarchically branching concepts become more determinate insofar as they exclude more (and with this, the idea that inferential relations essentially involve the kind of asymmetry we have noted)—and at the same time appreciate the sense it makes for Dharmakīrti to think there is nonetheless a kind of *identity* evident in the application of concepts like *tree* and *oak*. Dharmakīrti's point is that whether we find it relevant to apply the concept *tree* or the concept *oak*, either way it will be because we are presented with the same particular object having the same causal capacities. In other words, it is as a function of our conceptual interests (and not of the particulars we encounter) that we find it relevant to attend to it at one level of generality or another; whether it is most useful to pick something out as a *tree* or as an *oak*, though, either way it is just the same object that is producing our perceptual awareness thereof.[12]

In the respective elaborations of *apoha* doctrine by Dignāga and Dharmakīrti, then, we thus find two different but complementary ways to explain the construction of conceptual content entirely in terms of "exclusions." For Dignāga, the eminently *logical* point of the doctrine is to make sense of the asymmetry that essentially characterizes inferential relations; his claim is that the relative determinacy of concepts can be characterized entirely in terms of the fact that concepts become more precise just insofar as they exclude more than the overarching concepts that subsume them. This makes good sense of why *tree* is a narrower concept than *existent*, and of why *oak* is narrower still—and it makes sense of this in such a way as to explain why inferences are valid in one direction but not the other. Dignāga's development of this idea may, however, be vulnerable to the objection that this all makes sense only if we already know *which* particulars are rightly brought under any such concept—and to the extent that is just what a theory of meaning is supposed to explain, his version of the doctrine may be thought to beg the question. Dharmakīrti's complementary development of the doctrine aims, though, to address just that problem, as Dharmakīrti instead advances the eminently *epistemic* point that our practical success in bringing particulars under concepts can be explained in terms of our excluding whatever does not produce the effects we desire on any occasion of concept-use. While Dharmakīrti's version of the doctrine, too, may be thought vulnerable to the objection that there is a vicious circularity in play—this because the idea of "sameness of effect" would seem to be tantamount to the idea of a shared defining characteristic—it is clear at least that his approach undermines realist claims (typical of Mīmāṃsā and other Brahmanical schools of thought) to the effect that the referents of words correspond to really existent natural kinds. Against such views, Dharmakīrti would have us recognize that the content of concepts is thoroughly relative to our explanatory and practical interests, and that the only "sameness" that is anywhere in view is to be found simply in our judgments.

While there is much to recommend both these versions of the *apoha* doctrine—indeed, it can be argued that some of this anticipates (among other things) some contemporary cognitive-scientific approaches to the analysis of conceptual thought[13]—the non-Buddhist interlocutors of Dignāga and Dharmakīrti were never persuaded that these influential Buddhist philosophers could answer objections to the effect that the doctrine presupposes just the sort of thing it claims to explain. The doctrine continued, however, to be refined by later Buddhist thinkers who took their bearings from Dharmakīrti, and there can be no doubt of the increasing subtlety with which *apoha* theory was elaborated; chief among later exponents of the doctrine were Śāntarakṣita (d. 788 CE), Jñānaśrīmitra (fl. late 10th century), and Ratnakīrti (fl. early 11th century).[14] Where one comes down on the ultimate tenability of the doctrine may well have to do with how promising one takes the basic epistemological commitments of Dignāga and Dharmakīrti to be; for particularly in Dharmakīrti's elaboration of it, the *apoha* doctrine turns out to relate closely to problems entailed by both thinkers' peculiarly strong emphasis on the constitutively nonconceptual character of perception. Let us turn, then, to a discussion of the characteristic epistemological contributions of Dignāga and Dharmakīrti.

EPISTEMOLOGY: NONCONCEPTUAL PERCEPTION AND ITS IDEALIST IMPLICATIONS

One way to understand particularly Dharmakīrti's deployment of the *apoha* doctrine is as addressing a problem that arises given his emphasis (shared with Dignāga) on the essentially *nonconceptual* character of perception. The problem is this: if one shares with Dignāga and Dharmakīrti the basically empiricist conviction that *perception* (*pratyakṣa*) represents a privileged kind of cognition; if (with Dharmakīrti) one emphasizes that its privileged status is owing to the fact that perceptual awareness is, uniquely, *caused* by what it is of; and if, as both thinkers urged, conceptual awareness is in contrast held to be constitutively misleading insofar as it involves ultimately unreal abstractions—if all these commitments are held, it becomes a well-nigh intractable question how (or even whether) perceptual awareness can be a constraint on (or in any other way related to) the kind of conceptual cognition that alone counts as *knowing*. It seems, that is, that one can "know" only *that* such-and-such is the case (that it is hot outside, that this tree is a maple, that everything is impermanent)—and the content of any such *that*-clause must be a complex state of affairs under some description. That just is to say, however, that it is only as *conceptualized* that anything can count as the content of an episode of knowing. The problem with taking perceptual awareness to be constitutively nonconceptual, then, is that it becomes hard to see how what is present to perception could ever figure in what is present to the kind of discursive thought that alone counts as genuinely *epistemic*.[15] In that case, though, how could perception ever count as an "epistemic criterion" (*pramāṇa*)? How could the privileged status that goes with perception's being *caused* by its object be transferred to the kind of discursive awareness that, by Dignāga and Dharmakīrti's lights, is *not* causally describable in this way? This can be understood as chief among the problems that Dharmakīrti's version of the *apoha* doctrine addresses. On this way of thinking about *apoha*, the point is that conceptual content can, after all, be described as constructed from what is given to perceptual awareness; for on Dharmakīrti's development of the doctrine, as we have seen, the conceptual process of "exclusion" explains how concepts can work even given that we cognitively encounter only the unique particulars given to perception.

Whether or not the *apoha* doctrine (or anything else) can resolve the issue, it is surely a central part of the project of Dignāga and Dharmakīrti to emphasize the nonconceptual character of perception. This is, we have noted, an intuitively plausible premise shared by most empiricists, who can be understood to take their bearings from the recognition that perception is, as Kant puts it, a faculty of "receptivity"—that perceptual awareness, in other words, is largely a function of the world's impinging upon our sensory faculties. This characterization of perception not only has, though, good empiricist bona fides, but also reflects what can be recognized as a core commitment of most Buddhist thought: the idea that conceptual thought is constitutively misleading. Indeed, there is an important sense in which conceptual thought is, for Buddhists in general, precisely the problem to be overcome by the practice of the Buddhist path. It is typical of Buddhist philosophers to urge that what a Buddha experiences is an immediate, *nonconceptual* (*nirvikalpaka*) awareness of the truths taught by the Buddhist tradition—chiefly, the truth that *selves* are not really real. This idea partly reflects, no doubt, a recognition, on the part of a basically gnostic tradition—a tradition, that is, that takes religious transformation to result from rightly *understanding* something—that there is a profound difference between merely understanding and assenting to various propositional claims, and understanding in such a way as to be thoroughly *changed* by what is known. Buddhist philosophers surely mean to emphasize, then, that the transformative gnosis they have in mind consists in something much more than simply understanding and reproducing the kinds of arguments they are in the business of making. Still, the emphasis on nonconceptual awareness goes deeper than that; the really important point, surely, is that habitual attachment to the idea of one's *self* represents the paradigm case of a specious conceptual thought. *Concepts*, that is, are essentially unreal abstractions comparable to the kinds of unitary wholes Buddhists are always concerned to refute—and the idea that our fleeting sensations must be states or parts of the "whole" that is one's *self* represents the most pernicious example of conceptual thought, the one that Buddhist philosophers always have in view.[16] The characteristically Buddhist emphasis on the desirability of taming conceptual thought goes closely together, then, with the idea that if we could but eliminate our habituated tendency to project unreal wholes, we would see that what really exists is just momentary sensations, and that there *is* no "self" over and above these.

So, the epistemology of Dignāga and Dharmakīrti advances eminently empiricist insights, but does so in large part because these are conducive to the realization of the truth most central to the Buddhist tradition. Whatever we say of their motives, though, there can be no doubt that their emphasis on the nonconceptual character of perception drives much of what is to be found in the philosophical projects of Dignāga and Dharmakīrti. Dignāga introduces this idea in the first chapter of his *Pramāṇasamuccaya,* which is dedicated to characterizing what is clearly first among *pramāṇas* for Dignāga: *pratyakṣa,* or "perception."[17] It is in verse three of the opening chapter that he characterizes perception as "devoid of conceptual construction" (*kalpanāpoḍha*). He immediately explains that "conceptual construction" here means "association with names and classes and so forth." Concerned that that characterization defines perception as lacking only overt uses of language (as though one could count as having a conceptual thought only if one explicitly utters or entertains some linguistic item), Dharmakīrti subsequently revises Dignāga on this point, emphasizing that conceptual construction denotes any thought that is so much as *suitable* for association with linguistic items—any thought whose general or abstracted character represents the kind of thing that can in principle figure as linguistic referent. This qualification is important since without it, prelinguistic and nonlinguistic beings would not exemplify conceptual thought—and it is integral to a Buddhist account that *all* beings who are not yet "awakened" (*buddha*) are habitually misled by conceptual thought.

The 8th-century commentator Dharmottara thus explains this point with respect to one of the places where Dharmakīrti advances it:

> In this regard, some thoughts have phenomenal content actually associated with expression—for example, the conception of an object which is a jar, on the part of one by whom the relevant linguistic convention is known, has as its phenomenal content an object associated with the word "jar." But some thoughts, even though not actually associated with expression, nevertheless have phenomenal content that is suitable for association with expression—for example, the conception had by a child by whom the relevant linguistic convention is not known. In this regard, if Dharmakīrti's statement said only "conception has a phenomenal content associated with expression," the conception had by someone by whom the relevant linguistic convention is unknown would not be included; but when there is reference to "suitable," the latter is also included. Even if the conception had by a new-born baby does not have phenomenal content actually associated with expression, a baby nevertheless has phenomenal content that *is* suitable for association with expression.[18]

Considering the question of how we can know, of anyone incapable of giving overt expression to their thoughts, that they nevertheless have such thoughts, Dharmottara notes that a newborn baby's purposeful behavior is intelligible only with reference to thought that is "conceptual" in the requisite sense. A newborn's seeking and settling on its mother's breast, for example, makes sense only if we understand the baby as *recognizing* something it has previously experienced as sating its hunger.[19] And recognition constitutively involves *memory,* which in turn involves reference to something not actually present—the hallmark of conceptual thought. *Perception,* in contrast, constitutively involves only actually present existents, which is why it represents a uniquely indubitable kind of awareness.

It seems, however, that even if it is allowed that the objects of perception are actually present, one might still doubt whether they really exist just as they appear; that a perceptible object (unlike a conceptual abstraction) is really present does not guarantee that it is *rightly* perceived. Indeed, this is as Dignāga and Dharmakīrti themselves would emphasize insofar as they commonly affirmed a basically *representationalist* epistemology. It follows, that is, especially from Dharmakīrti's basically causal account of perception that what we are immediately aware of is just mental representations—"aspects" or "images" (*ākāra*) comparable to the "sense data" of the classical British empiricists. This is why Dignāga and Dharmakīrti were (as noted above) represented by doxographers not as direct realists, but as "proponents of the doctrine that external objects can only be inferred"; one can at most *infer* that things "out there" in the world are as represented in any occurrent cognition. Here, then, it becomes especially important to appreciate that despite what is suggested by the English translation equivalent "perception," the word *pratyakṣa,* as Dignāga emphasized early in his account of the matter, does not refer only to *sensory* awareness; what really distinguishes perception is just that it is nonconceptual, and Dignāga argued from the beginning that it is not only sensory perception that qualifies as such. He argued that the kind of meditative awareness cultivated by skilled yogis counts as perceptual, but also (and more basically) that what he called "reflexive awareness" or "self-awareness" (*svasaṃvitti*) does, too—and in fact, there is reason to think he finally meant that only the latter kind of awareness is genuinely and nonconceptual.[20]

Dignāga's idea here is that it is in the nature of every cognition to have two basically different kinds of "aspect" (*ākāra*): one that represents what the cognition is *of* (an aspect that is, say, a tree or a cow), and one that represents the cognition's own awareness of itself as cognizing that. The latter he referred to as a cognition's "self-awareness," which effectively denotes something like the *subjectivity* of any awareness—the fact, that is, that no matter what any cognition is *of*, it is always integral to cognition that there is some felt way that that content seems *for the cognition's subject.* Dignāga's arguments for this aspect of cognition involve an appeal to the phenomenologically distinctive character of memory. Thus, he held that what distinguishes any first-order awareness from a subsequent recollection thereof is that in memory, one is aware not only of whatever it is that one had previously experienced, but also *of oneself as having experienced that*—and, he argued, the latter fact could be available to memory only if the same fact had been somehow present as part of the initial experience.[21] (One cannot be said to *remember* something not initially experienced.) This is the idea, then, that integral to any awareness is its subject's own awareness of the occurrence thereof; whenever one is aware that (say) there are cows and trees in a meadow, one is, ipso facto, also aware *that one is having an awareness of that.* And with this, we really have a plausible candidate for a uniquely indubitable sort of awareness; for while one can indeed doubt whether anything "out there" in the world really is as it seems, one cannot coherently doubt that *that is how it seems.*

Dignāga's development of this idea is, however, rather indeterminate, and there is much that is unclear about it. In Dharmakīrti's hands, however, the doctrine of *svasaṃvitti* more clearly becomes a doctrine to the effect that it is in the nature of cognitions to be self-intimating. This idea is expressed in an argument from Dharmakīrti that became one of the tradition's principal arguments for the doctrine—the so-called *sahopalambhaniyama* argument, which urges that anything at all that one can know is always characterized by the "constraint" (*niyama*) that one can be aware of it only "together with the apprehension" thereof (*saha-upalambha*).

This amounts to the familiarly idealist point that (as F. H. Bradley similarly argued in the late 19th century) "you cannot find fact unless in unity with sentience."[22] As understood by the Buddhists Dignāga and Dharmakīrti, the point cannot, of course, be that one is always aware of one's *self* as the center of awareness; rather, they clearly mean to argue just that cognition itself is explanatorily basic—as Dharmakīrti puts it in the *Pramāṇaviniścaya* (a *locus classicus* for this argument), "there is not awareness of an object simply in virtue of there *being* an object; rather, [there is awareness of an object] by virtue of there being an *awareness* thereof." *That awareness occurs*, then, is the self-evident basis of anything else we can know; hence (per *Pramāṇaviniścaya* 1.54cd), "the perception of objects does not make sense for one whose apprehension thereof is itself imperceptible."[23]

So, while any cognition's really being *of an existent object* can coherently be doubted, *there being such a cognition* cannot itself be thought to require demonstration. Of one's contemplation of the Pythagorean theorem, for example, it makes sense to ask how or whether one knows it is true ("Because I learned it in school," one might say, or, "Because I can give you the proof"); it does not, in contrast, make any sense to ask how you know simply that *that is what you are thinking of*. One is, rather, just immediately aware of whatever it is one is thinking; nothing at all could be present, Dharmakīrti argues, to someone whose own apprehension of things was not itself "perceptible" this way. It is just this self-intimating character of cognitions that Dharmakīrti means by "self-awareness" (*svasaṃvitti*), and it is easy to see how he and Dignāga could think this counts as a sort of *perceptual* awareness—for that is just to say it is an immediate, nonconceptual awareness. Recalling again the unusually thoroughgoing reductionism that is characteristic of Buddhist thought, we can see, too, how this may indeed be the *only* finally "perceptual" sort; for given the Buddhist premise that temporally enduring wholes are essentially conceptual fictions, even a seemingly perceptual awareness to the effect simply that "there is a tree" turns out already to be conceptual. What is immediately, indubitably known, in such a case, is simply *that* there is occurring an awareness to that effect. Dignāga says as much upon first introducing the idea of *svasaṃvitti*; having first characterized that as essentially *perceptual*, then, he anticipates this challenge: "If self-awareness (evident in things like our affective responses) is *perception*, then conceptual cognitions are, too." Insofar, that is, as *all* cognitions are characterized by *svasaṃvitti*, it seems that even conceptual cognitions would turn out to be, after all, "perceptual"—but that, it seems, would effectively undermine the distinction (so important for Dignāga) between perceptual and conceptual thought. Addressing this worry, Dignāga embraces the point, but explains (at *Pramāṇasamuccaya* 1.7ab) why it is not a problem: "That's true; even conceptual thought is admitted [as being perceptual] in terms of self-awareness"—but, he continues, "not with respect to its content (*artha*), because of the conceptual construction of that."[24] He thus emphasizes that in *svasaṃvitti* we are perceptually (which is just to say *nonconceptually*) aware *of* our own (conceptual) acts of judging; it is not, however, with respect to the *content* of such acts that this immediacy obtains—what is immediately apprehended is only the occurrence of judgments *as particular mental events*. Following through on the idea that we are in this sense indubitably acquainted only with the very occurrence of our mental events, Dharmakīrti and (more clearly) some of his later commentators emphasized that *svasaṃvitti* alone is a *pāramārthikapramāṇa*—only self-awareness, that is, counts as *ultimately* a *pramāṇa*, and everything else that is said by Dignāga and Dharmakīrti to count as "*pramāṇa*" is really just conventionally so.

Once again, then, intuitively plausible premises that Dignāga and Dharmakīrti share with classical empiricists—that perception represents the most basic kind of awareness, and this because perception, unlike conceptual fancies, can (Dharmakīrti emphasized) be described as caused by real objects—turn out to recommend the idealist conclusion that only the occurrence of cognition itself is indubitably known. To that extent, Dignāga and Dharmakīrti are aptly characterized as finally having meant to advance the Yogācāra school of Buddhist idealism. Nevertheless, it is typical of both thinkers to limit their arguments to an epistemological key, and generally to prescind from explicitly metaphysical or ontological conclusions; to that extent, it makes sense that traditional doxographical texts also represented them as "Sautrāntikas who follow reasoning"—a characterization that captures the modus operandi of both thinkers, who mostly restrict themselves to arguments involving the kinds of basically empiricist premises that were apt to win wide assent. Neither Dignāga nor Dharmakīrti made much reference to any specifically Yogācāra doctrines (they do not, e.g., refer to *ālayavijñāna*, or to the *trisvabhāva* doctrine), and the fuller elaboration of a complete idealist metaphysics was largely left to other thinkers in the tradition. Much as Bishop Berkeley took John Locke to have shown, then, Dignāga and Dharmakīrti mostly argued that if one accepts a basically empiricist account of perception, it turns out that one is already effectively committed to idealism.

It is, however, important to note an important exception to the generally epistemological modus operandi these thinkers shared; for Dignāga's concise *Ālambanaparīkṣā* ("Critical Investigation of Percepts") advances an argument with affinities to the essentially metaphysical argument for idealism that is most famously associated with Vasubandhu—the argument, in particular, that physical objects cannot coherently be conceived insofar as no coherent account of *atoms* can be given.[25] Dignāga's related argument concerns the intelligibility of the concept of a "percept" (*ālambana*), which returns us to Ābhidharmika categories. Thus, of the many sophisticated taxonomies of mental events and factors posited by Ābhidharmika philosophers, one of the most basic enumerates kinds of "causal conditions" (*pratyaya*) that figure in the occurrence of every moment of consciousness. Authors of the Abhidharma literature generally agreed there are four such conditions, a moment of (say) *seeing some autumn trees* must have as its causes: (1) a properly functioning ocular sense faculty (this is the *adhipati-pratyaya*, or "predominant condition"); (2) a previous moment of ocular experience (the *samanantara-pratyaya*, or "immediately preceding condition"—a category that explains how a series of fleeting moments of experience can seem, phenomenologically, to be a continuous flow; the reason we do not experience each new moment of seeing as having just popped into being is that the moments occur in continuous series); (3) a collection of other causes (the *hetupratyaya*, or "causal conditions which are causes," where *hetu* refers to another list of causes); and (4) *the autumn trees themselves*, insofar as they are among the causes of my seeing them. The latter is the *ālambana-pratyaya*, or "*percept* condition."

Dignāga's brief "Critical Investigation of Percepts" analyzes this last category, which was defined by Buddhist philosophers as satisfying two conditions; thus, the "percept" denotes that one among the *causes* of a cognition which is at the same time what the cognition is *of*. Dignāga concisely argues that no *physical* object could satisfy both these conditions, and that it therefore cannot be physical objects that are present to awareness; this is because the kinds of things we typically take cognitions to be *of* cannot, in principle, be among the causes of cognitions. The argument is simple and presupposes these premises: to be *real*, for most Buddhists as for most empiricists, just is to be capable of causally interacting with other existents; anything without this capacity does not ultimately exist. But on a Buddhist account, only *irreducible* things count as ultimately real. This means that only atomic sensible particulars (fleeting occurrences of shape and color and solidity and whatnot) could *cause* any cognition, since only these are ultimately real. The problem, though, is that it is not sensible "atoms" that are given in experience; rather, our experience typically concerns what J. L. Austin memorably referred to as "medium-sized dry goods." In terms, then, of the Buddhist category that Dignāga is analyzing, the problem is that the kinds of things that can meet the causal condition (atoms, momentary sensa) do not meet the content condition; for experience is manifestly not *of* such things. Conversely, the kinds of things that do meet the content condition (the temporally enduring wholes that show up in experience) do not, on a Buddhist view, ultimately *exist*—which is just to say they cannot cause anything. Dignāga concludes from this that nothing with a basically *atomic* structure—which is to say, no really existent external objects—can be present to awareness.

Dignāga proposes, though, that an idealist account can circumvent the problem he thus elaborates. Thus, he takes the foregoing considerations to recommend concluding that only something *intrinsic to cognition*, only something that is itself "mental," could be at once *cause* and *content* of any moment of consciousness. In order, though, to make good on his claim that something intrinsic to cognition makes sense as *causing* perceptual content, Dignāga ends up having to grant a couple of different senses of "being a cause." The first way of "being a cause" is the one that makes sense if we adopt an objective, third-personal perspective on the occurrence of mental events. From this perspective—which need not involve reference to what the subject of a cognition herself takes its content to be—what Dignāga has in mind as "intrinsic to cognition" is something temporally prior to the mental event it causes; in particular, what causes occurrent cognitions is things like mental "seeds" (*bīja*) or "latent disposition" (*vāsanā*), which denote our beginninglessly habituated capacities and tendencies to experience the world in certain ways. It makes sense to say that such things are identified from a *third*-person perspective because even though there is a sense in which these are indeed *internal* to cognition—specifically, they are carried forward "within" a mental continuum, passed down until they "ripen" within the same series—they are nevertheless *phenomenologically inaccessible*. That is, the envisioned process of long-term mental development is not transparent to the subjects thereof, and the kinds of things Dignāga has in mind—long-transmitted dispositions to act this way or that—are not themselves available to introspection. From the subject's perspective on any moment of experience, then, it is not *seen* that his or her experience represents the fruition of unconscious mental processes.

But that is of course to say that moments of experience are typically not *of* things like "habituated dispositions"; does that not, however, mean that Dignāga's appeal to these various psychological artifacts cannot, after all, satisfy the other condition on being a percept (viz., that these be what the cognition is *of*)? Dignāga can say that the artifacts of past mental events that he has in mind are not, so long as their capacities are dormant, part of experiential content; they *become* contentful only when they "ripen," at which point they show up as part of this or that experience. The Buddhist image of *seeds* is supposed to make sense of this. Just as a seed's capacity remains dormant until it is no longer a seed but a sprout, so, too, subconscious processes can continuously transmit latent dispositions until some moment when they somehow burst into consciousness. Suppose, though, that "seeds" and "habituated dispositions," even though not themselves experienced, thus meet the *content* condition insofar as they do *become* items of content upon ripening; even so, there is, Dignāga recognized, a further problem: the mental item that figures as the content of experience—a latent disposition or "seed," at just the moment that it ripens into an occurrent sense datum—has to be understood, it seems, as *part* of (as "in") that experience. But if the phenomenal content of any cognition must be understood as a *part* thereof, it becomes hard to see how it could still make sense as a *cause* of the cognition; for it does not make sense that a presently integral part of anything be at the same time a *cause* of the whole that comprises it. How could any part precede, as cause, the effect of which it is presently part?

It seems, then, that when mental content is identified from a *first-person* perspective—when we attend, that is, not to an experience's long-term psycho-genesis, but to what is most salient for the subject thereof (namely, that it seems to be an experience *of* something)—it is hard to retain the same notion of causation that figures in an account involving "seeds" and "habituated dispositions" and the like. Thus, in order to salvage his claim that something intrinsic to awareness can make sense as both *content* and *cause* thereof, Dignāga has to allow that when considered from a first-person perspective, the "percepts" that show up in experience meet the causal condition—they count, that is, as also *causes* of the cognition whose content they are—*only on a different understanding of what "being a cause" consists in.* He appeals, in particular, to an alternative understanding of "cause" according to which anything *co-occurrent* with some event—as, for example, anything's *defining characteristic* is, ipso facto, occurrent along with the thing itself—can be called one of that event's "causes."[26] So, the phenomenologically accessible content of any cognition—what the cognition seems to its subject to be *of*—can be reckoned as one of the cognition's *causes* only in the limited sense that whenever a cognition occurs, its content is present, too. Clearly, though, that is a very different sense of "cause" than when we entertain the idea that moments of experience are "caused" by a long and complex psychological past.[27]

It is not, then, an altogether straightforward matter even for an idealist to make sense at once of the *causes* and *content* of cognitions. The complexity of the issues here in play is evident in Dharmakīrti's elaboration of a line of argument clearly prefigured by Dignāga's concise "Critical Investigation of Percepts"—the line of argument, in particular, developed by Dharmakīrti around *Pramāṇavārttika* 3.208–218. In general, Dharmakīrti's commitment to causal efficacy as the criterion of the real had him rather more sanguine than Dignāga about the viability of a causal account of conventionally understood perception; for example, he entertained the thought that while Dignāga rightly argued that individual *atoms* do not cause the kind of perceptual content we typically have in mind, it is nevertheless possible for *aggregated* atoms to gain a kind of collective causal efficacy that makes it possible for them, after all, to meet both of the conditions on being a "percept" condition. Nevertheless, for Dharmakīrti, too, such a picture was just provisionally acceptable, and when he argues that this is finally unsustainable, he advances an argument much like the foregoing one from Dignāga. There is, Dharmakīrti thus argued, a fundamental contradiction between the essential *unity* of momentary cognitions and the manifold complexity that typically characterizes the content thereof—as, for example, when one is aware, in a single moment, of the variegated wings of a butterfly. Like Dignāga, then, Dharmakīrti finally argued that any attempt to reconcile momentary *cognitions* with a world of complex physical *objects* will break down. Indeed, he concludes at *Pramāṇavārttika* 3.209cd (here as elaborated by the commentator Manorathanandin) that even *idealist* alternatives are finally unsustainable so long as one remains committed to dualist conceptions of a unitary "subject" who enjoys any kinds of "objects" (whether external or internal) as content: "However things (colors, for example, whether they consist in something external or in cognition itself) are considered—whether as being unitary or as being complex—they break down, which is to say there is no way at all they can be established."[28]

Despite the elusiveness of Dharmakīrti's elaboration of the train of thought initiated by Dignāga's "Critical Investigation of Percepts," it is clear at least that both of these highly original and influential thinkers meant to advance radically revisionary accounts of the mental and of our epistemic situation; consistent with the Buddhist tradition's radical contention that we are not at all as we habitually think we are, they thus aimed to show that the analysis particularly of *perception* shows that we are really warranted only in conclusions that are fundamentally at odds with common-sense understandings of mind and world. It is clear, as well, that the foregoing line of argument differs significantly from the familiarly empiricist kinds of arguments these thinkers more typically advance; Dignāga's a priori analysis of the concept of a "percept," and Dharmakīrti's related interrogation of unitary cognitions having variegated content, represent lines of argument that are logically distinct from arguments to the effect that (e.g.,) we are immediately aware only of mental representations. Particularly as in the foregoing passage from Dharmakīrti, these basically metaphysical arguments show, as well, that the kind of disagreement concerning "external" and "internal" that is typically thought to divide realists from idealists may finally be something of a red herring. The real issue, rather, has to do with whether the *unity* taken to characterize momentary cognitions can be reconciled with the *complexity* that characterizes the content thereof (this is a distinctively Buddhist variation, surely, on the perennial philosophical problem of the relation between "the one" and "the many")—and that is, finally, just as difficult a problem for idealists as for realists. In many significant Buddhist debates subsequent to those thus initiated by Dignāga and Dharmakīrti—in, for example, the "neither-one-nor-many" argument that was the signature move of Śāntarakṣita and Kamalaśīla, and in debates among late Indian proponents of Yogācāra over whether cognition itself must finally be essentially distinct from its content, or whether instead content is integral to cognition—questions about the reality of the physical often became, accordingly, secondary to a more basic question: the question of how or whether anything at all that is properly *irreducible* can relate to the manifest complexity of ordinary experience.[29]

OTHER CONTRIBUTIONS AND INFLUENCE

There is much else to be found in the works of Dignāga and Dharmakīrti; their collective corpus is quite large, and we are still very far from having even well-established critical editions of all of their works, let alone reliable translations of these into modern languages. Recent decades have, though, seen real growth in philosophically sophisticated treatments of their work, and there are exciting developments afoot in the recovery of Sanskrit texts of their writings (many of which still remain extant only in Tibetan translation).[30] While the modern, critical study of the often elusive texts of Dignāga and Dharmakīrti thus remains, though, in a relatively fledgling state, still-flourishing Tibetan monastic curricula preserve a long tradition of engagement particularly with Dharmakīrti, whose lasting influence in India and Tibet greatly surpasses that of Dignāga.[31] (In contrast, Chinese translations of Dignāga made some of his works available in East Asia, whereas none of Dharmakīrti's works was ever translated into Chinese.) Traditionally trained Tibetan scholars well know, for example, that Dharmakīrti advanced an extensive proof, virtually unique in the tradition, of the reality of rebirth—and this in a section of his *Pramāṇavārttika* that contains, as well, an influential critique of theism, among other things.[32] And the contributions of both thinkers to the theorization of logic and dialectics clearly figures importantly in the ritualized debate practices of Tibetan scholars, which abundantly exemplify the forms of argument commonly commended by Dignāga and Dharmakīrti.[33] In the later history of Indian philosophy, too, their contributions to logic were decisively influential, and particularly the works of Dharmakīrti were much engaged by subsequent Indian thinkers, Buddhist and non-Buddhist alike. Indeed, anyone interested in classical Indian philosophies from any period subsequent to these great Buddhist thinkers will find it necessary to have some acquaintance with the thought and argument especially of Dharmakīrti, whose works posed challenges that were recognized as such by thinkers from all the various Brahmanical traditions of thought. To these other Indian philosophers, Dharmakīrti was surely most well known for the difficult but profound *apoha* theory of meaning, and for the sophisticated elaboration of a representationalist epistemology that could not go unanswered by those who argued, against him, for direct realism. And while the doctrine of *svasaṃvitti* was, in this regard, resisted especially by proponents of the Mīmāṃsā school of thought, who would have no truck with any doctrine that gave comfort to idealism, Dharmakīrti's position was taken up by other Brahmanical thinkers, albeit for ends that were antithetical to the core Buddhist doctrine of no-self (*anātmavāda*).[34] A number of great traditions of philosophical thought, then, would not be as they are but for the signal influence of Dignāga and Dharmakīrti.

REVIEW OF LITERATURE

Standard overviews of Dignāga and Dharmakīrti's thought include Richard Hayes, *Dignāga on the Interpretation of Signs*, and John Dunne, *Foundations of Dharmakīrti's Philosophy*; both volumes include significant translated excerpts from major works by the respective thinkers. Vincent Eltschinger gives an uncommonly good concise introduction to Dharmakīrti's thought, while Georges Dreyfus's *Recognizing Reality* gives a thorough, philosophically sophisticated account particularly of the Tibetan reception of Dharmakīrti. Useful overviews (by Richard Hayes and Shoryu Katsura, inter alia) of Dignāga's thought can also be found in volume 9 of Karl H. Potter, ed., *Encyclopedia of Indian Philosophies*, which is entitled *Buddhist Philosophy from 350 to 600* A.D.; a projected volume on *Buddhist Philosophy from 600 to 750* A.D. (being edited by Eli Franco) will similarly make Dharmakīrti's works available. Potter's continuously updated bibliography online to the *Encyclopedia* is a well-nigh exhaustive resource.[35]

Complete critical editions (to say nothing of modern translations) of the works of both thinkers remain desiderata; Birgit Kellner has given a thorough account of the state of progress with regard to Dharmakīrti's works, while Eli Franco's review of the inaugural volume in the series *Sanskrit Texts from the Tibetan Autonomous Region* concerns the impact of exciting new manuscript finds for the study particularly of Dignāga; the reviewed volume is a critical edition of Jinendrabuddhi's 8th-century commentary on chapter 1 of Dignāga's *Pramāṇasamuccaya.* (The availability of Jinendrabuddhi's text enabled a reconstruction, by series editor Ernst Steinkellner, of Dignāga's text itself, which is available online.) The second volume of *Sanskrit Texts from the Tibetan Autonomous Region* is a critical edition of chapters 1 and 2 of Dharmakīrti's *Pramāṇaviniścaya.* Raniero Gnoli's critical edition of chapter 1 of Dharmakīrti's *Pramāṇavārttika* is standard and is widely taken to have established the correct order of verses in that text; subsequent scholarly consensus is that the first chapter concerns *svārthānumāna* ("inference for one's own sake")—despite which, many widely available editions of the same text (e.g., Shastri's) instead give the alternative order of chapters recommended by Manorathanandin's commentary, which makes it important to note which chapter order any particular scholarly study follows.[36]

Despite the foregoing advances, Masaaki Hattori's 1968 translation of the first chapter (on *pratyakṣa*) of Dignāga's *Pramāṇasamuccaya* remains the principal point of access to Dignāga's corpus for many scholars; Ole Holten Pind has made available the same work's fifth chapter, concerning *apoha*. The 2016 collaborative volume *Dignāga's Investigation of the Percept* gives a detailed, interdisciplinary overview of Indian and Tibetan perspectives on Dignāga's concise *Ālambanaparīkṣā*. Significant translations from Dharmakīrti's much larger corpus include Tillman Vetter's German translation of the *Pramāṇaviniścaya*'s first chapter, and Tom Tillemans's annotated translation of nearly 150 verses from the fourth chapter of the *Pramāṇavārttika*; John Dunne's *Foundations of Dharmakīrti's Philosophy* also includes extensive excerpts translated from Dharmakīrti and his commentators. Important thematic studies engaging Dignāga and Dharmakīrti include Mark Siderits et al., eds., *Apoha: Buddhist Nominalism and Human Cognition*; and volume 38/3 of the *Journal of Indian Philosophy* (2010), which comprises seven articles on various aspects of *svasaṃvitti*. For annotated references to further editions, translations, and thematic studies, see Dan Arnold, "The Philosophical Works and Influence of Dignāga and Dharmakīrti," *Oxford Bibliographies Online.*[37]

FURTHER READING

Chu, Junjie. "On Dignāga's Theory of the Object of Cognition as Presented in PS(V) 1." *Journal of the International Association of Buddhist Studies* 29, no. 2 (2006): 211–253.

Dravid, Raja Ram. *The Problem of Universals in Indian Philosophy*. Delhi: Motilal Banarsidass, 1972.

Dunne, John. "Realizing the Unreal: Dharmakīrti's Theory of Yogic Perception." *Journal of Indian Philosophy* 34, no. 6 (2006): 497–519.

Eltschinger, Vincent. *Penser l'autorité des Écritures: La polémique de Dharmakīrti contre la notion brahmanique orthodoxe d'un Veda sans auter*. Vienna: Verlag der Österreichischen Akademie der Wissenschaften, 2007.

Kajiyama Yuichi. *An Introduction to Buddhist Philosophy: An Annotated Translation of the* Tarkabhāṣā *of Mokṣākaragupta*. Vienna: Arbeitskreis für tibetische und buddhistische Student Universität Vienna, 1998.

Kellner, Birgit. "Proving Idealism in Indian Buddhist Philosophy: Vasubandhu and Dharmakīrti." In *The Oxford Handbook of Indian Philosophy*. Edited by Jonardon Ganeri. New York: Oxford University Press, 2015. http://dx.doi.org/10.1093/oxfordhb/9780199314621.013.18.

MacKenzie, Matthew. "The Illumination of Consciousness: Approaches to Self-Awareness in the Indian and Western Traditions." *Philosophy East and West* 57, no. 1 (2007): 40–62.

Matilal, Bimal Krishna. *Perception: An Essay on Classical Indian Theories of Knowledge*. Oxford: Clarendon, 1966.

Matilal, Bimal Krishna. *The Character of Logic in India*. Edited by Jonardon Ganeri and Heeraman Tiwari. Albany: SUNY Press, 1998.

Mookerjee, Satkari. *The Buddhist Philosophy of Universal Flux: An Exposition of the Philosophy of Critical Realism as Expounded by Dignāga*. Delhi: Motilal Banarsidass, 1975.

Patil, Parimal G. *Against a Hindu God: Buddhist Philosophy of Religion in India*. New York: Columbia University Press, 2009.

NOTES

1. In recurrently characterizing his own position as *sautrāntika* ("following the sutras"), Vasubandhu may not have meant to refer to any "school" of thought, but only to suggest that disputes among Ābhidharmikas ought finally to be settled with reference to the sutra literature that alone was taken to express the Buddha's own teachings; later, however, the term ossified in ways that arguably make it anachronistic to read the associated school of thought back into Vasubandhu's work. On the term as a doxographical category pertaining to Vasubandhu, see Robert Kritzer, "Sautrāntika in the *Abhidharmakośabhāṣya*," *Journal of Indian Philosophy* 26, no. 2 (2003): 331–384. On the different subtypes of "Sautrāntika," see Katsumi Mimaki, "Le *Grub mtha' rnam bźag rin chen phreṅ ba* de dKon mchog 'jigs med dbaṅ po," *Zinbun: Memoirs of the Research Institute for Humanistic Studies, Kyoto University* 14 (1977): 84. On the philosophically constructive nature of Tibetan doxographical texts, see José Cabezón, "The Canonization of Philosophy and the Rhetoric of Siddhānta in Indo-Tibetan Buddhism," in *Buddha Nature: A Festschrift in Honor of Minoru Kiyota*, ed. Paul Griffiths and John Keenan (Reno, Nevada: Buddhist Books International, 1990), 7–26. On the Abhidharma literature more generally, see Steven Collins, "What Are Buddhists *Doing* When They Deny the Self?" in *Religion and Practical Reason: New Essays in the Comparative Philosophy of Religions*, ed. Frank Reynolds and David Tracy (SUNY Press, 1994), 59–86; Collett Cox, *Disputed Dharmas: Early Buddhist Theories on Existence* (Tokyo: The International Institute for Buddhist Studies, 1995); Rupert Gethin, *Foundations of Buddhism* (Oxford University Press, 1998), 202–223; Alexis Sanderson, "The Sarvāstivāda and Its Critics: Anātmavāda and the Theory of Karma," in *Buddhism into the Year 2000* (Los Angeles: Dhammakaya Foundation, 1994), 33–48; and Paul Williams, "On the Abhidharma Ontology," *Journal of Indian Philosophy* 9 (1981): 227–257.
2. For "Buddhist Logic," see Th. Stcherbatsky's dated but still useful *Buddhist Logic* (New York: Dover, 1962), the second volume of which comprises a complete translation of Dharmakīrti's *Nyāyabindu*. For "Buddhist Epistemology," see, inter alia, Mark Siderits, *Buddhism as Philosophy* (Indianapolis, IN: Hackett, 2007), 208–230. Useful overviews of these thinkers include Richard Hayes, *Dignāga on the Interpretation of Signs* (Dordrecht: Kluwer, 1988); Vincent Eltschinger, "Dharmakīrti," *Revue Internationale de Philosophie* 64, no. 3 (2010): 397–440; and John Dunne, *Foundations of Dharmakīrti's Philosophy* (Boston: Wisdom, 2004). With regard to the difficulty of determining the considered position of Dharmakīrti, the latter volume introduces the idea of a "sliding scale" of analysis, according to which Dharmakīrti's claims differ depending on whether taken from an empiricist perspective or an idealist one. For an argument that these supposedly divergent perspectives actually go more closely together than this suggests, see Dan Arnold, "Buddhist Idealism, Epistemic and Otherwise: Thoughts on the Alternating Perspectives of Dharmakīrti," *Sophia* 47, no. 1 (2008): 3–28. For a more extensive, annotated bibliography on both thinkers, see Dan Arnold, "The Philosophical Works and Influence of Dignāga and Dharmakīrti," *Oxford Bibliographies Online*, 2012.

3. On the interpretation of Indian logic in general, see Jonardon Ganeri, "Introduction: Indian Logic and the Colonization of Reason," in *Indian Logic: A Reader*, ed. Ganeri (London: Curzon, 2001), 1–25; Mark Siderits, "Deductive, Inductive, Both or Neither?" *Journal of Indian Philosophy* 31 (2003): 303–321; and Shoryu Katsura and Ernst Steinkellner, eds., *The Role of the Example* (Dṛṣṭānta) *in Classical Indian Logic* (Vienna: Arbeitskreis für Tibetische und Buddhistische Studien Universität Wien, 2004). See also Claus Oetke, *Studies on the Doctrine of Trairūpya* (Vienna: Arbeitskreis für Tibetische und Buddhistische Studien, Universität Wien, 1994); Brendan Gillon, "Dharmakīrti and the Problem of Induction," in *Studies in the Buddhist Epistemological Tradition: Proceedings of the Second International Dharmakīrti Conference*, ed. Ernst Steinkellner (Vienna: Österreichische Akademie der Wissenschaften, 1991), 53–58; and Ernst Steinkellner, "On the Interpretation of the Svabhāvahetuḥ," *Wiener Zeitschrift für die Kunde Südasiens und Archiv für Indische Philosophie* 18 (1974): 117–129. On Dignāga's *Hetucakraḍamaru*, see Huanhuan He and Leonard W. J. van der Kuijp, "Once Again on the *Hetucakraḍamaru: Rotating the Wheels," *Journal of Indian Philosophy* 44 (2016): 267–302. For Dharmakīrti's principal writings on logic, see Ernst Steinkellner, *Dharmakīrti's Early Logic: An Annotated German Translation of the Logical Parts in* Pramāṇavārttika *1 and Vṛtti* (Tokyo: International Institute for Buddhist Studies, 2013); and Ernst Steinkellner, ed., *Dharmakīrti's Hetubindu: Critically Edited by Ernst Steinkellner on the Basis of Preparatory Work by Helmut Krasser with a Transliteration of the Gilgit Fragment by Klaus Wille*, Sanskrit Texts from the Tibetan Autonomous Region 19 (Vienna: Austrian Academy of Sciences Press, 2016).
4. For a translation of Dignāga's principal work on perception, see Masaaki Hattori, *Dignāga, On Perception, Being the Pratyakṣapariccheda of Dignāga's* Pramāṇasamuccaya *from the Sanskrit Fragments and the Tibetan Versions* (Cambridge, MA: Harvard University Press, 1968). Hattori's pioneering translation is from the Tibetan translations of the *Pramāṇasamuccaya* that were all that was known to be available at the time; based on the edition of a Sanskrit commentary that has since been recovered (that of Jinendrabuddhi), Ernst Steinkellner has edited a reliable reconstruction that surely gets us closer to Dignāga's text: Ernst Steinkellner, *Dignāga's Pramāṇasamuccaya, Chapter 1: A Hypothetical Reconstruction of the Sanskrit Text with the Help of the Two Tibetan Translations on the Basis of the Hitherto Known Sanskrit Fragments and the Linguistic Materials Gained from Jinendrabuddhi's Ṭīkā* (Vienna: Österreichischen Akademie der Wissenschaften, 2005). For a critical edition of the commentary from which Dignāga's text was reconstructed, see Ernst Steinkellner, Helmut Krasser, and Horst Lasic, eds., *Jinendrabuddhi's* Viśālāmalavatī Pramāṇasamuccayaṭīkā: *Chapter 1, Part I: Critical Edition*, Sanskrit Texts from the Tibetan Autonomous Region 1 (Vienna: Österreichischen Akademie der Wissenschaften, 2005). For a translation and studies of Dignāga's *Ālambanaparīkṣā*, see Douglas Duckworth et al., eds., *Dignāga's Investigation of the Percept (Ālambana-Parīkṣā) and Its Philosophical Legacy in India and Tibet* (Oxford: Oxford University Press, 2016).
5. Quoting *Pramāṇavārttika* 3.3, which is often cited as 2.3; on the order of chapters in this work, though, scholarly consensus favors the arguments of Raniero Gnoli, made in the introduction to Raniero Gnoli, ed., *The* Pramāṇavārttikam *of Dharmakīrti: The First Chapter with the Autocommentary* (Rome: Istituto Italiano Per Il Medio ed Estremo Oriente, 1960).
6. There is presently no complete translation of either of Dharmakīrti's most extensive works, the *Pramāṇavārttika* or the *Pramāṇaviniścaya*; a critical edition of the newly available Sanskrit text of the first two chapters of the latter, however, is among the important volumes in the recently inaugurated series Sanskrit Texts from the Tibetan Autonomous Region, and collaborative work that is ongoing in Vienna stands to contribute greatly to efforts at making the whole *Pramāṇavārttika* available in translation. For the former, see Ernst Steinkellner, ed., *Dharmakīrti's* Pramāṇaviniścaya, *Chapters 1 and 2*, Sanskrit Texts from the Tibetan Autonomous Region 2 (Vienna: Austrian Academy of Sciences Press, 2007); for a German translation of (the Tibetan translation of) chapter 1 of the same text, see Tillman Vetter, *Dharmakīrti's* Pramāṇaviniścaya, *I. Kapitel: Pratyakṣam: Einleitung, Text der tibetischen*

Übersetzung, Sanskritfragmente, deutsche Übersetzung, Österreichische Akademie der Wissenschaften Philosophisch-Historische Klasse, Sitzungsberichte 250 (Vienna: Hermann Böhlaus Nachf, 1966). For a dated but still useful translation of the *Nyāyabindu,* see Stcherbatsky, *Buddhist Logic,* vol. 2; Stcherbatsky's edition of the same text has been superseded by Paṇḍita Dalsukhbhai Malvania, ed., *Paṇḍita Durveka Miśra's* Dharmottarapradīpa, 2nd ed. (Patna, India: Kashiprasad Jayaswal Research Institute, 1971); this includes the important and innovative commentary of Dharmottara, as well as the subcommentary of the Brahmin scholar Durvekamiśra. A readily available edition of the *Pramāṇavārttika* is Swami Dwarikadas Shastri, ed., *Pramāṇavārttika, Ācāryamanorathanandivṛttiyuktam* (Varanasi, India: Bauddha Bharati, 1968); for a more complete account of the state of scholarship on this extensive and difficult text, however, see Birgit Kellner, "Towards a Critical Edition of Dharmakīrti's Pramāṇavārttika," *Text Genealogy, Textual Criticism and Editorial Technique: Wiener Zeitschrift für die Kunde Südasiens* 52–53 (2009–2010): 161–211.

7. For characterizations of Dharmakīrti as typically arguing from broadly empiricist premises, see Dan Arnold, *Brains, Buddhas, and Believing: The Problem of Intentionality in Classical Buddhist and Cognitive-Scientific Philosophy of Mind* (New York: Columbia University Press, 2012), chs. 1 and 5. Dharmakīrti's strongest and most explicit argument for idealism is developed at *Pramāṇavārttika* 3.208–218, which develops a line of thought with close affinities to the argument Dignāga advanced in the *Ālambanaparīkṣā*; a helpfully concise characterization of these arguments can be found in Vincent Eltschinger, "Dharmakīrti," *Revue Internationale de Philosophie* 64, no. 3 (2010): 429–430. More on these arguments below.
8. See Richard Hayes and Brendan Gillon, "Dharmakīrti on the Role of Causation in Inference as Presented in *Pramāṇavārttika Svopajñavṛtti* 11–38," *Journal of Indian Philosophy* 36 (2008): 335–404.
9. On Dignāga's account of *apoha,* see Jonardon Ganeri, *Philosophy in Classical India: The Proper Work of Reason* (London: Routledge, 2001), 106–111; Hayes, *Dignāga on the Interpretation of Signs*; Shoryu Katsura, "The *Apoha* Theory of Dignāga," *Indogaku Bukkyogaku Kenkyu* 28, no. 1 (1979), 16–20; and, for an interpretation and translation of Dignāga's complete elaboration of the doctrine, Ole Holten Pind, *Dignāga's Philosophy of Language:* Pramāṇasamuccayavṛtti *V on* anyāpoha (Vienna: Verlag der Österreichischen Akademie der Wissenschaften, 2015), part 2. On circularity objections, see Pascale Hugon, "Breaking the Circle: Dharmakīrti's Response to the Charge of Circularity against the *Apoha* Theory and Its Tibetan Adaptation," *Journal of Indian Philosophy* 37, no. 6 (2009): 533–557.
10. On Dharmakīrti's complementary elaboration of the *apoha* doctrine, see Dunne, *Foundations of Dharmakīrti's Philosophy*; Shoryu Katsura, "Dignāga and Dharmakīrti on *Apoha*," in *Studies in the Buddhist Epistemological Tradition,* ed. Ernst Steinkellner (Vienna: Österreichische Akademie der Wissenschaften, 1991), 129–146; and Arnold, *Brains, Buddhas, and Believing,* ch. 4.
11. See Pascale Hugon, "Breaking the Circle."
12. The text in which Dharmakīrti theorizes the two kinds of relations is the *Sambandhaparīkṣā* ("Critical Investigation of Relations"), for the text of which see Erich Frauwallner, "Dharmakīrtis Sambandhaparīkṣā: Text und Übersetzung," *Wiener Zeitschrift für die Kunde Morgenlandes* 41 (1934): 261–300. On Dharmakīrti's finally causal account of the sense in which inferential relations are "identity" relations, see Dunne, *Foundations of Dharmakīrti's Philosophy,* 203–218; see, as well, Steinkellner, "On the Interpretation of the Svabhāvahetuḥ."
13. See Mark Siderits, Tom Tillemans, and Arindam Chakrabarti, eds., *Apoha: Buddhist Nominalism and Human Cognition* (New York: Columbia University Press, 2011).
14. On later elaborations of *apoha,* see especially Lawrence McCrea and Parimal Patil, *Buddhist Philosophy of Language in India: Jñānaśrīmitra on Exclusion* (New York: Columbia University Press, 2010); and Parimal Patil, *Against a Hindu God: Buddhist Philosophy of Religion in India* (New York: Columbia University Press, 2009), 195–247. A sense of the range and the many implications of the doctrine can also be gained from Siderits et al., eds., *Apoha* (note 15, above).

15. See Georges Dreyfus, "Is Perception Intentional? A Preliminary Exploration of Intentionality in Dharmakīrti," in Birgit Kellner et al., eds., *Pramāṇakīrtiḥ: Papers Dedicated to Ernst Steinkellner on the Occasion of His 70th Birthday* (Vienna: Arbeitskreis für tibetische und buddhistische Studien, Universität Wien, 2007), 95–113; Shoryu Katsura, "Dharmakīrti's Theory of Truth," *Journal of Indian Philosophy* 12.3 (1984): 215–235; and Dan Arnold, "Dharmakīrti and Dharmottara on the Intentionality of Perception: Selections from *Nyāyabindu* (*An Epitome of Philosophy*)," in *Buddhist Philosophy: Essential Readings*, ed. William Edelglass and Jay Garfield (Oxford University Press, 2009), 186–196.
16. Richard Hayes's "Principled Atheism in the Buddhist Scholastic Tradition" (*Journal of Indian Philosophy* 16 [1988]: 5–28) nicely brings out something of the ways in which many Buddhist arguments are variations on this.
17. See Masaaki Hattori, *Dignāga, On Perception.*
18. For this passage from Dharmottara's commentary on *Nyāyabindu* 1.5, see Dan Arnold, "On (Non-semantically) Remembering Conventions: Dharmakīrti and Dharmottara on *Saṃketakāla*," in *Logic and Belief in Indian Philosophy*, ed. Piotr Balcerowicz (Delhi: Motilal Banarsidass, 2009), 551; see also Stcherbatsky, *Buddhist Logic*, vol. 2, 19–20.
19. This account presupposes the reality of rebirth, which is axiomatic for these Buddhist thinkers; given that idea, a newborn is never nursing *for the first time*, and its purposeful behavior can always be explained as informed by recognition from previous lifetimes. For Dharmakīrti's proof of rebirth, see Eli Franco, *Dharmakīrti on Compassion and Rebirth* (Vienna: Arbeitskreis für tibetische und buddhistische Studien, Universität Wien, 1997).
20. For Dignāga's account of *svasaṃvitti* (or *svasaṃvedana*), see Birgit Kellner, "Self-Awareness (*svasaṃvedana*) in Dignāga's *Pramāṇasamuccaya* and *-vṛtti*—A Close Reading," *Journal of Indian Philosophy* 38, no. 3 (2010): 203–231. On the vexed question of whether *svasaṃvitti* is one of *three* kinds of perception admitted by Dignāga or one of *four*, see Eli Franco, "Did Dignāga Accept Four Types of Perception?" *Journal of Indian Philosophy* 21 (1993): 295–299.
21. See Jonardon Ganeri, "Self-Intimation, Memory and Personal Identity," *Journal of Indian Philosophy* 27 (1999): 469–483.
22. F. H. Bradley, as quoted in Ralph Barton Perry, *Present Philosophical Tendencies* (New York: Longmans, Green, 1921), 134.
23. The first quotation is from the commentary on *Pramāṇaviniścaya* 1.54cd, and the second is the half verse itself; for the text of this, see Steinkellner, *Dharmakīrti's Pramāṇaviniścaya*, pp. 40–41. For more extensive discussion of this and proximate passages, see Arnold, *Brains, Buddhas, and Believing*, 175–183. For an alternative translation, see Georges Dreyfus and Christian Lindtner, "The Yogācāra Philosophy of Dignāga and Dharmakīrti," *Studies in Central and East Asian Religions* (*Journal of the Seminar for Buddhist Studies, Copenhagen and Aarhus*) 2 (1989): 27–52. For an in-depth study of Dharmakīrti's *sahopalambhaniyama* argument, see Takashi Iwata, *Sahopalambhaniyama: Struktur und Entwicklung des Schlusses von der Tatsache, daß Erkenntnis und Gegenstand ausschließlich zusammen wahrgenommen werden, auf deren Nichtverschiedenheit* (Stuttgart: Franz Steiner Verlag, 1991). See, as well, volume 38.2 of the *Journal of Indian Philosophy* (2010), a special issue on the topic of *svasaṃvitti.*
24. Translated from Steinkellner's reconstruction (2005), 3.
25. Vasubandhu's argument to this effect is at verses 11–15 of the *Viṃśatikā*, on which see Matthew Kapstein, "Mereological Considerations in Vasubandhu's 'Proof of Idealism'," in Kapstein's *Reason's Traces: Identity and Interpretation in Indian & Tibetan Buddhist Thought* (Boston: Wisdom Publications, 2001), 181–204.
26. Dignāga can here appeal to the Ābhidharmika category of *sahabhūhetu*, which denotes the kind of "cause" (*hetu*), which simply goes "with [something's] being" (*sahabhū*); see *Abhidharmakośa* 2.50c–d, where Vasubandhu gives the relation between "characteristic" and "characterized" as an example of this.
27. On Dignāga's *Ālambanaparīkṣā*, see Douglas Duckworth et al., eds., *Dignāga's Investigation of the Percept (Ālambana-Parīkṣā) and Its Philosophical Legacy in India and Tibet* (Oxford: Oxford University Press,

2016). For a reading of that text as finally bringing into play problems regarding the relation between *third*-personal and *first*-personal perspectives on cognition, see Dan Arnold, "Philosophy of Mind's 'Hard Problem' in Light of Buddhist Idealism," in *Philosophy's Perennial Questions: Comparing Buddhist and Western Approaches*, ed. Steven Emmanuel (New York: Columbia University Press, 2021).

28. For a concise characterization of Dharmakīrti's arguments at *Pramāṇavārttika* 3.208–218, see Vincent Eltschinger, "Dharmakīrti," *Revue Internationale de Philosophie* 64, no. 3 (2010): 429–430. See, as well, Dunne, *Foundations of Dharmakīrti's Philosophy*, 98–113, and also (for translations from *Pramāṇavārttika* 3.194–224 and two commentaries thereon) 396–411.
29. On the logically distinct character of the metaphysical argument epitomized by Vasubandhu's *Viṃśatikā* (and followed by Dignāga and Dharmakīrti in the foregoing discussion), particularly vis-à-vis the epistemic arguments more typical of Dignāga and Dharmakīrti, see Dan Arnold, "Buddhist Idealism, Epistemic and Otherwise: Thoughts on the Alternating Perspectives of Dharmakīrti," *Sophia* 47, no. 1 (2008): 3–28; for a different perspective on the same issue, see Birgit Kellner, "Proving Idealism in Buddhist Philosophy: Vasubandhu and Dharmakīrti," in *The Oxford Handbook of Indian Philosophy*, ed. Jonardon Ganeri (Oxford Handbooks Online, 2015). See, as well, Isabelle Ratié, "On the Distinction between Epistemic and Metaphysical Buddhist Idealisms: A Śaiva Perspective," *Journal of Indian Philosophy* 42 (2014): 353–375. On the "neither one nor many" argument of Śāntarakṣita and Kamalaśīla, see Tom Tillemans, "The 'Neither One nor Many' Argument for *śūnyatā* and Its Tibetan Interpretations: Background Information and Source Materials," *Études de Lettres* (University of Lausanne) 3 (1982): 103–128. On late Yogācāra debates regarding the status of mental content, see Yuichi Kajiyama, "Controversy between the sākāra- and nirākāra-vādins of the yogācāra School—Some Materials," in Kajiyama's *Studies in Buddhist Philosophy (Selected Papers)* (Kyoto: Rinsen, 1989), 389–400. See, as well, Shinya Moriyama, "Ratnākaraśānti's Theory of Cognition with False Mental Images (**alīkākāravāda*) and the Neither-One-Nor-Many Argument," *Journal of Indian Philosophy* 42 (2014): 339–351; and Sara McClintock, "Kamalaśīla on the Nature of Phenomenal Content (*ākāra*) in Cognition: A Close Reading of TSP *ad* TS 3626 and Related Passages," *Journal of Indian Philosophy* 42 (2014): 327–337.
30. See Eli Franco, "A New Era in the Study of Buddhist Philosophy," *Journal of Indian Philosophy* 34, no. 3 (2006): 221–227. This is a short review article on a crucial new resource for the study of Dignāga (published as the first volume in the new series Sanskrit Texts from the Tibetan Autonomous Region): Ernst Steinkellner et al., eds., *Jinendrabuddhi's* Viśālāmalavatī Pramāṇasamuccayaṭīkā: *Chapter 1* (Vienna: Österreichischen Akademie der Wissenschaften, 2005). See, too, Birgit Kellner, "Towards a Critical Edition of Dharmakīrti's Pramāṇavārttika," *Text Genealogy, Textual Criticism and Editorial Technique: Wiener Zeitschrift für die Kunde Südasiens* 52–53 (2009–2010): 161–211.
31. See Georges Dreyfus, *Recognizing Reality: Dharmakīrti's Philosophy and Its Tibetan Interpreters* (Albany: SUNY Press, 1997).
32. See Franco, *Dharmakīrti on Compassion and Rebirth*; Richard Hayes, "Principled Atheism in the Buddhist Scholastic Tradition"; Roger Jackson, *Is Enlightenment Possible? Dharmakīrti and rGyal tshab rje on Knowledge, Rebirth, No-Self and Liberation* (Ithaca, NY: Snow Lion, 1993); and Dan Arnold, "Dharmakīrti's Dualism: Critical Reflections on a Buddhist Proof of Rebirth," *Philosophy Compass* 3, no. 5 (2008): 1079–1096.
33. See Daniel Perdue, *Debate in Tibetan Buddhism* (Ithaca, NY: Snow Lion, 1992).
34. See Alex Watson, "Bhaṭṭa Rāmakaṇṭha's Elaboration of Self-Awareness (*Svasaṃvedana*), and How It Differs from Dharmakīrti's Exposition of the Concept," *Journal of Indian Philosophy* 38 (2010): 297–321; Isabelle Ratié, "The Dreamer and the Yogin: On the Relationship between Buddhist and Śaiva Idealisms," *Bulletin of the School of Oriental and African Studies* 73, no. 3 (2010): 437–478; and Lawrence McCrea, "Abhinavagupta as Intellectual Historian of Buddhism," in *Around Abhinavagupta: Aspects of the Intellectual History of Kashmir from the Ninth to the Eleventh Century*, ed. Eli Franco and Isabelle Ratié (Berlin: LIT Verlag, 2016), 263–286.

35. Richard Hayes, *Dignāga on the Interpretation of Signs* (Dordrecht: Kluwer, 1988); John D. Dunne, *Foundations of Dharmakīrti's Philosophy* (Boston: Wisdom Publications, 2004); Vincent Eltschinger, "Dharmakīrti," *Revue Internationale de Philosophie* 64, no. 3 (2010): 397–440; Georges Dreyfus, *Recognizing Reality: Dharmakīrti's Philosophy and Its Tibetan Interpreters* (Albany: SUNY Press, 1997); Karl H. Potter, ed., *Encyclopedia of Indian Philosophies*, vol. 9: *Buddhist Philosophy from 350 to 600 A.D.* (Delhi: Motilal Banarsidass, 2003).
36. Birgit Kellner, "Towards a Critical Edition of Dharmakīrti's Pramāṇavārttika," in *Text Genealogy, Textual Criticism and Editorial Technique: Wiener Zeitschrift für die Kunde Südasiens* 52–53 (2009–2010): 161–211; Eli Franco, "A New Era in the Study of Buddhist Philosophy," *Journal of Indian Philosophy* 34, no. 3 (2006): 221–227; Ernst Steinkellner et al., eds., *Jinendrabuddhi's* Viśālāmalavatī Pramāṇasamuccayaṭīkā, Sanskrit Texts from the Tibetan Autonomous Region 1 (Vienna: Österreichischen Akademie der Wissenschaften, 2005); Ernst Steinkellner, ed., *Dharmakīrti's* Pramāṇaviniścaya, *Chapters 1 and 2*, Sanskrit Texts from the Tibetan Autonomous Region 2 (Vienna: Österreichischen Akademie der Wissenschaften, 2007); Raniero Gnoli, ed., *The* Pramāṇavārttikam *of Dharmakīrti: The First Chapter with the Autocommentary; Text and Critical Notes* (Rome: Istituto Italiano Per Il Medio ed Estremo Oriente, 1960); Swami Dwarikadas Shastri, ed., *Pramāṇavārttika, Ācāryamanorathanandivṛttiyuktam* (Varanasi, India: Bauddha Bharati, 1968).
37. Masaaki Hattori, *Dignāga, On Perception, Being the Pratyakṣapariccheda of Dignāga's* Pramāṇasamuccaya *from the Sanskrit Fragments and the Tibetan Versions* (Cambridge, MA: Harvard University Press, 1968); Ole Holten Pind, *Dignāga's Philosophy of Language:* Pramāṇasamuccayavṛtti *V on* anyāpoha, part 2 (Vienna: Verlag der Österreichischen Akademie der Wissenschaften, 2015); Douglas Duckworth et al., eds., *Dignāga's Investigation of the Percept (Ālambana-Parīkṣā) and Its Philosophical Legacy in India and Tibet* (Oxford University Press, 2016); Tillman Vetter, *Dharmakīrti's* Pramāṇaviniścaya, *I. Kapitel: Pratyakṣam: Einleitung, Text der tibetischen Übersetzung, Sanskritfragmente, deutsche Übersetzung*, Österreichische Akademie der Wissenschaften Philosophisch-Historische Klasse, Sitzungsberichte 250 (Vienna: Hermann Böhlaus Nachf, 1966); Tom J. F. Tillemans, *Dharmakīrti's* Pramāṇavārttika*: An Annotated Translation of the Fourth Chapter (parārthānumāna)*, volume 1 *(k.1–148)*, Österreichische Akademie der Wissenschaften Philosophisch-Historische Klasse, Sitzungsberichte 675 (Vienna: Verlag der Österreichischen Akademie der Wissenschaften, 2000). John Dunne, *Foundations of Dharmakīrti's Philosophy*, 331–415; Mark Siderits et al., eds., *Apoha: Buddhist Nominalism and Human Cognition* (New York: Columbia University Press, 2011). From the special issue of the *Journal of Indian Philosophy* concerning *svasaṃvitti* (38.3, 2010), see, e.g., Birgit Kellner, "Self-Awareness (*svasaṃvedana*) in Dignāga's *Pramāṇasamuccaya* and *-vṛtti*: A Close Reading," 203–231.

Dan Arnold

PILGRIMAGE IN BUDDHIST TIBET

THE SIGNIFICANCE AND FUNCTION OF PILGRIMAGE IN TIBET

Pilgrimage appears to have been an important aspect of Buddhist practice soon after the death of the buddha. The earliest evidence of Buddhist pilgrimage activity is found in two pillar inscriptions attributed to the 3rd-century BCE Mauryan emperor Aśoka. The inscription at Rummundei, in southern Nepal, identifies the site as Lumbini, the birthplace of the buddha. The inscription at Nigālī Sāgar, also in Nepal, is associated with the former Buddha

Konākamuni. The *Mahāparinibbāṇa Sūtta*, widely regarded as the *locus classicus* for the establishment of Buddhist pilgrimage, reports the buddha exhorting people to visit and pay homage to four places after his passing: the place of his birth, the site of his awakening, the site of his first teaching, and the place where he entered final nirvana.[1] One who paid such worship would guarantee worldly benefits and happiness in this world and would be born in a heavenly realm after death. He further instructs his disciple Ānanda on how the buddha should be cremated, and his remains interred in burial mounds called *stupas*, in the manner of great kings. Relic worship was categorized in two types: a portion of the buddha's cremated body or an object or place that had been in direct contact with the buddha. In either case, a stupa containing a relic was considered to be a living entity and worship of it was an encounter with the buddha himself. Later texts, such as the *Aśokāvadāna*, multiplied the number of sites associated with the buddha up to thirty-two, but from the time of the Pāla period (8th–12th centuries), a group of eight great sites (Skt. *Aṣṭamahāsthāna*) came to be widely accepted, and the Tibetans who traveled to India in the early years of the second propagation of Buddhism in Tibet in the 10th to the 11th centuries assumed the authority of this list of sites, even if they actually visited very few of them. Soon thereafter, Tibetan conceptions of India's Buddhist holy sites were transformed by Vajrayāna assumptions that relativized the importance of the eight great sites, shifting the emphasis to tantric power places (Skt. *pīṭha*) associated with Vajrayāna deities and accomplished tantric masters.[2]

Though a mainstay in the orientalist imagination of the 19th and early 20th centuries, Tibetan Buddhism and Bön only came to be well understood by scholars and the general populace in the West due to the exile of thousands of Tibetans to India and the West in the early 1960s. Beyond its borders, Tibet has come to be known for its sophisticated religious doctrines and practices. Practices such as divination, expiatory rituals, propitiation of local gods, and pilgrimage are pervasive across Tibetan Buddhist cultures, yet they have received relatively little attention in scholarly or popular circles. Particularly among nonscholars, Tibetan Buddhism is frequently seen through a Buddhist modernist lens, making it a live option for spiritually inclined people the world over. David L. McMahan has described Buddhist modernism as "the various forms of Buddhism that have been significantly shaped by an engagement with the dominant cultural and intellectual forces of modernity, such as the European Enlightenment, scientific rationalism, Romanticism and its successors, Protestantism, psychology, and modern social and political thought."[3]

Regardless of how accurately understood advanced doctrines and practices are, they are in fact a relatively small part of what Tibetan Buddhism was, and is, to Tibetans, whether within Tibet or in exile. Moreover, these sophisticated teachings and spiritual methods were, and are, only of concern or accessible to a relatively small number of religious elite. For most Tibetans, whether monks or laypeople (including the religious elite), religion's primary function is to ensure health, prosperity, longevity, and a successful afterlife rather than the classical Buddhist goal of liberation from the cycle of birth and death. As noted scholar of Tibetan Buddhism Matthew Kapstein has recently observed, "Far from seeking to transcend the world in attainments of mystical contemplation, the day-to-day concerns that motivated the religious lives of most Tibetans—laymen and clergy alike—were the problems inherent in maintaining, not transcending, the order of the world by ensuring that harvests were plentiful, cattle productive, children sound, and enemies, whether demonic or human, impotent."[4] Pilgrimage in Tibet is one such practice that is believed to accomplish these aims. Journeying to a sacred place such as a mountain, lake, cave, monastery, or the home of a holy person may well have soteriological effects for advanced tantric practitioners, impelled by visionary encounters with and blessings and empowerments from legendary power figures such as Padmasambhava, dākinīs, and high tantric deities such as Cakrasaṃvara. But for most people, pilgrimage and other ritual practices are understood to secure worldly success, purify one's evils (*sdig pa*) and pollution (*grib*), and sow the seeds for rebirth in one of the higher realms of samsara, be that one of the heavenly realms or in another fortunate human rebirth in which one can continue progress on the Buddhist path.

THE MEANING OF PILGRIMAGE IN TIBET

Throughout Western-language scholarship on this kind of practice, the term used is "pilgrimage." The study of pilgrimage has evolved from a functionalist Durkheimian understanding, to one informed by the influential theories of Victor Turner, to a less universalist perspective that highlights the diversity and contested nature of sacred places. Many sacred places in Tibet are understood differently by Buddhists and Bönpos, by local people and religious elites, or even by Buddhists and Hindus. Recent studies of Tibetan pilgrimage have tended to juxtapose particular qualities of a given site with the common characteristics of Tibetan pilgrimage while being attentive to the contested nature of these sites. While the theories of Turner and some of his followers assert that pilgrimage functions to break down, or temporarily suspend, class and other hierarchies, studies of Tibetan pilgrimage do not clearly bear this out.[5]

Like its usage in other religions, pilgrimage in Tibet refers to a journey to a place that is regarded as sacred. In the Tibetan language, the terms used for this ritual journey are *nékor* (*gnas skor*) or *néjel* (*gnas mjal*), meaning to go around or encounter or meet a *né*, or sacred place. The circumambulating can, of course, be traced to earlier Indian Buddhist practices directed toward stupas and other relics of the buddha. *Né* means simply "place" but the term carries the implicit meaning of being a place where sacred power dwells.[6] "Sacred" here does not mean something like Eliade's sui generis notion of an ultimate reality juxtaposed to the profane world. A *né* may be understood differently across time or between different groups (e.g., between Buddhists and Bönpos), but different pilgrims can disagree about the source of the power while agreeing on the fact of its presence at a *né*. The sacredness of a *né* may arise from a number of different sources, including that of autochthonous deities of place, the worldly hierophany of high tantric deities, the residual power of a great ancient Buddhist master, or even a living Buddhist master.

THE POWER OF PLACE

Central to understanding the Tibetan conception of sacred places is the idea that a *né* is possessed of, and radiates, transformative power. An ancient indigenous Tibetan concept that is connected to some pilgrimage sites is *la* (*bla*). *La*, often translated as soul or vitality, is a power that dwells in the body, but also in animals, trees, mountains, and other objects—linking individual persons, families, or even larger social units with the natural environment. At the local level, people are bound to their natal homelands by the *la* of the local mountain, but it works on a larger scale, as in the case of all adherents of Bön with Kongpo Bönri (Rkong po bon ri) in southeast Tibet. The power exists, not in just the person or the place, but rather in the transactional relationship between them. Several prominent scholars have asserted that the concept of *la* and that of deity (*lha*) were once joined in ancient Tibetan thinking.[7]

The sources of this power can be understood in a number of ways, which may overlap. Most broadly, scholars have repeatedly observed that Tibetans understand the natural world as teeming with powers, both benign and hostile, with which humans have to interact in myriad ways. From subterranean water spirits (*klu*), to local terrestrial spirits (*sa bdag, gzhi bdag*), to mountains identified with territorial deities (*yul lha*), the Tibetan landscape is alive with awesome presences with which humans must cohabit, to their benefit or peril. Territorial gods and their mountains are important recipients of pilgrimage, either being identified with a high Buddhist deity or simply continuing to exist as the territorial god alongside the new Buddhist understanding of the site. Spirits of this sort are sensitive to impurity or insult and may inflict harm upon the offender. More dangerous are numerous classes of demons, male and female, who are also quick to harm and are by nature malevolent.

Above these local spiritual presences are indigenous Tibetan deities who were subdued by the legendary tantric Buddhist master Padmasambhava or Guru Rinpoché, in the 8th century. At first inimical to the new religion, these warrior gods, mostly of a class of deity known as the "haughty ones" (*dregs pa*), were tamed by Padmasambhava and bound by oaths to protect Buddhism. These gods were integrated into the Tibetan Buddhist pantheon as dharma protectors. While serving the cause of religion, these gods are worldly protectors (*'jig rten pa'i srung ma*) (i.e., they are not awakened). Thus, they must be approached with caution and respect, constantly being reminded of their vows to protect Buddhism. Another class, the supermundane protectors (*'jig rten las 'das pa'i srung ma*), are understood to be above samsaric limitations and concerns and are often said to be manifestations of buddhas or bodhisattvas. In some cases, these higher protectors are regarded as tantric meditational deities, or *yidam* (*yi dam*), worthy of being objects of refuge, and more likely to be the source of power of a *né*.

At the top of the hierarchy of powers are the *yidam* of Vajrayāna Buddhism. These deities were brought to Tibet from India when Buddhism was propagated in Tibet in the 8th century, and again in the 11th century. Vajrayāna meditative praxis centers on the visualization of tantric deities with their retinues in their mandala palaces. The imposition of this Vajrayāna conception transformed indigenous *nés* according to Buddhist assumptions in a process that has been called the "mandalization" of Tibetan sacred sites and is part of a broader "buddhacization" of Tibetan religion. Pervasive in Vajrayāna Buddhism and tracing back to ancient Indian political models of a sovereign and his court, the mandala provides a concept for divine and kingly power from which dominion and authority flow. While these processes largely overwrote indigenous or Bön narratives of sacred sites, the process was not complete in all cases, with some major sites, such as Gang Tisé (Gangs ti se) and Amnye Machen (A myes rma chen), being understood differently by Buddhists and Bönpos.[8]

As scholar of Bön Per Kvaerne has observed, "Rituals and other religious practices, as well as meditational and metaphysical traditions are, undeniably, to a large extent similar, even identical. Concepts of history and sources of religious authority are, however, radically different and justify the claim of the Bönpos to constitute an entirely distinct religious community."[9] For Bönpos, the power of a *né* is understood to be based in the power of the founder, Tönpa Shenrap (Ston pa gshen rab), one of the deities of the Bön tantras, or a great master of the Bön lineage. Kongpo Bönri stands out as a mountain *né* that has a strong Bön identity.

Buddhist pilgrimages associated with the Nyingma (Rnying ma) sect tend to focus on the person and the power of Padmasambhava, who is regarded as a *yidam* in addition to his status as an awakened tantric master, and the founder of the Nyingma sect. Among the sects established after the second propagation of Buddhism in Tibet, the most prevalent deity and mandala that was imposed on Tibetan Buddhist sacred sites was Denchok Khorlo Dompa (Bde mchog 'khor lo sdom pa, Sanskrit: Cakrasaṃvara), hereafter referred to as Khorlo Dompa.[10] Khorlo Dompa is central to the practice of the Sakya (Sa skya), Kagyü (Bka' brgyud), and Geluk (Dge lugs) sects, and it is particularly important to the Drukpa ('Brug pa) subsect of the Kagyü, which was instrumental in establishing some of the major pilgrimage sites and routes. The *Cakrasaṃvara Tantra* is a yoginī tantra, a class of tantric teachings that emphasizes wrathful goddesses and transgressive mortuary imagery. In the mandala, the central deity couple, Khorlo Dompa and Dorjé Pakmo (Rdo rje phag mo, Skt. Vajravārāhī), ecstatically dancing in sexual union in their palace, fanged and bedecked in skulls, are surrounded by wrathful goddesses called *khandroma* (*mkha' 'gro ma*, Skt. *ḍākinī*). The presence of the *khandroma* figures prominently at numerous *nés*, protecting such sites, and if appeased, bestowing blessings and empowerments. Another important aspect of this tantra is its mapping of twenty-four pilgrimage sites (*pīṭha*), corresponding to the parts of the deity's adamantine body or that of the tantric yogi, onto the Indian subcontinent. The Sanskrit term *pīṭha* was translated into Tibetan as *né*, homologizing the indigenous concept with the new Vajrayāna one. These sites were remapped onto the Tibetan landscape, subjugating and sacralizing the Land of Snows with the power and authority of the *Cakrasaṃvara Tantra*, its practices, and its advanced practitioners, particularly Milarepa (Mi la ras pa, 1052–1135). Lapchi (La phyi), Gang Tisé, and Tsari (Tsa ri) constitute a well-known trio of holy mountains associated with Cakrasaṃvara and Milarepa.[11] One further characteristic associated with the Khorlo Dompa tradition that proved useful for the buddhacization of sacred sites is the narrative of the subjugation of Śiva (and the taking on of his attributes) by Cakrasaṃvara.[12] This account was used to justify or explain how sites that were already *nés* before the introduction of Buddhism could be transformed into or revealed to be Khorlo Dompa mandalas, or one of the twenty-four sites associated with them.

A helpful indigenous concept for understanding the power of a *né* and its transformative effect on the pilgrim is that of *jinlap* (*byin rlabs*), often translated as "blessing," though here perhaps "empowerment" is a better term. The early Tibetan kings were said to possess *jin*, meaning "splendor" or "glory," which imbued the landscape, the state, and its inhabitants. In Buddhism, the concept developed early that the charisma and power of the buddha was transformative. After his death, his mortal remains, regarded as powerful relics, were interred in stupas, which became pilgrimage sites at the major places associated with his life. The relics of other great masters came to be believed to possess a similar power, and the stupas housing them were venerated across the Buddhist world. In the Vajrayāna context, the power of Khorlo Dompa and his mandala subdue the spot as a Buddhist site and empower the environment and pilgrims who come there.

THE HISTORICAL EVOLUTION OF TIBETAN PILGRIMAGE

Though Tibetans encountered Buddhism earlier, it only began to be imported in an organized, large-scale way during the reigns of the great early Buddhist kings in the 8th century. After about one hundred years, the last Buddhist emperor, Tri Ralpachen (Khri ral pa chen, 806–838), was assassinated and replaced on the throne by his non-Buddhist brother. Members of the court unfavorable to Buddhism used this opportunity to undo the expansion of support for Buddhist monasteries and translation projects, effectively ending the period of state support of Buddhism.

There is no evidence of Tibetan pilgrimage in the period of the early kings. While it may have been the case that important imperially sponsored sites such as the Jokhang, Ramoché, and Samyé were destinations for pilgrims in the early period, early dynastic sources indicate that Buddhism was largely the concern of the court and specific clans of the aristocracy. The aforementioned sites fell into a state of disrepair after the collapse of the early dynasty and were not revived until the arrival of a contingent of monks who had been taking refuge in eastern Tibet in the late 10th century.[13] It is not until the 11th century that we have accounts of pilgrimage to India, and then the establishment and discovery of sacred sites in the Himālayan foothills and on the Tibetan plateau in the following generations.

At the beginning of the second propagation of Buddhism in Tibet, Buddhist devotees, scholars, and translators primarily sought out the sites associated with the life and major events of the buddha on the plains of India. These are the so-called eight great sites: Lumbinī, Bodh Gayā, Sārnāth, Kuśinagar, Śrāvastī, Rājgṛha, Vaiśālī, and Saṃkāśya. The accounts of the early pilgrims to India demonstrate that visiting all the major sites was ideal, but the Vajrāsana (the exact spot where the buddha attained awakening) in Bodh Gayā was by far the most visited destination. Later, the Vajrāsana became understood as the center point of a fivefold conception of holy places: Uḍḍiyāna, the source of tantric masters and lineages in the west; the mythical Shambhala in the north; Wutai Shan, the mountain home of the Bodhisattva Mañjuśrī in the east; and Potala, the mountain home of the Bodhisattva Avalokiteśvāra in the south.[14]

Other Tibetans during this period went to India in search of awakened Vajrayāna Buddhist masters (Skt. *siddha*) in order to get tantric initiation and teachings. These Tibetan tantric masters did not seem to be particularly interested in the classical Indian Buddhist sites. The 13th century saw a shift away from the sites in the Middle Gangetic region to the *pīṭhas* associated with the *Yoginītantras* and other tantric sacred places in India. The *pīṭhas* named in the Cakrasaṃvara tantric corpus were scattered across the subcontinent of India, northwest and northeast India, and parts of Tibet were increasingly understood to be home to the most important tantric sacred sites. By the 13th century, Buddhism had largely disappeared from Bodh Gayā and the other regions that Tibetans had previously visited, and the *Yoginītantras* had become more widely known and practiced, increasingly held to be the supreme teachings of the buddha. These conditions pushed Tibetan pilgrims' devotions almost entirely into the Indian Himalayan foothills and onto the Tibetan plateau.[15]

Hagiographic accounts say that the great Kagyü founders Khyungpo Neljor (Khyung po rnal 'byor, 990/1050–1127) and Marpa Chökyi Lodrö (Mar pa chos kyi blo gros, 1012–1027) visited various sites in India, including some of the eight great sites, the great Buddhist universities, charnel grounds, and *pīṭhas*. Chak Lotsāwa Chöjepal (Chag lo tsā ba chos rje dpal, 1197–1264) visited several of the eight great sites in Magadha, but also went to the charnel ground Śītavana, which was an important tantric site. Several great figures from the Kagyü sect, including Jikten Gönpo Rinchenpal ('Jig rten mgon po rin chen dpal, 1124–1217), Götsangpa Gönpo Dorjé (Rgod tshang pa mgon po rdo rje, 1189–1258), and his disciples, particularly Orgyenpa Rinchenpal (O rgyan pa rin chen dpal, 1229–1309), were instrumental in justifying and elaborating this changed conception of India's sacred places. Götsangpa is claimed to be the person who established the paradigmatic pilgrimage route around Gang Tisé, Mount Kailash. He spent time in Lahaul and Spiti and traveled to the Indian *pīṭha* of Jālandhara, where he stayed for some time. Orgyenpa followed in his teacher's footsteps, retracing most of Götsangpa's journey; but more importantly, he went to Orgyen/Uḍḍiyāna, the homeland of Padmasambhava. Orgyen was also renowned as the abode of the *khandroma*, making it one of the main points of origin of tantric teachings.[16] The routes established by these masters and their accounts of these *nés* have endured. Subsequent pilgrimage guides included these accounts, elaborated on them, and have informed the understanding of sacred sites across Tibet up to the early 21st century. Following the crackdown by the People's Republic of China (PRC) on Tibet in 1959, the practice of pilgrimage was severely curtailed. As an expression of both Buddhist and Tibetan identity, the PRC prohibited this practice for many years.

CHARACTERISTIC FEATURES OF TIBETAN PILGRIMAGE

It is common in the origin stories of the major *nés* that they were hidden, closed, or unknown before being tamed or opened by a great master. These narratives invoke the well-known stories of the taming of the indigenous gods of Tibet by Guru Rinpoché and the numerous accounts of Milarepa's victories over troublesome Tibetan spirits, deities, and the Bön master Naro Bönchung (Na ro bon chung). Both provide an explanation for why many *nés* have pre-Buddhist identities and demonstrate Buddhism's superiority to and victory over indigenous Tibetan supernatural powers. Once subdued, the *né* became accessible to pilgrims' visits and practices. The journey itself to the *né* is certainly important as part of the purificatory or transformative process, especially when that journey is full of hardships and sacrifice. However, there are many ritual activities performed along the journey and when the pilgrim arrives and "meets the *né*." The ritual practices pilgrims enact when they encounter the power place is largely consistent across different kinds of *né*, though unique features and practices are not uncommon. The sites themselves can be categorized into several types: natural sites such as mountains, lakes, and caves; human-made sites such as cities, monasteries, and temples; "hidden lands"; and holy people.

Practices at the Né. As one name for pilgrimage (*nékor*) suggests, circumambulating a *né* is a common practice. This practice can be traced back to the veneration of stupas in early Buddhism. Devotees would walk clockwise around the structure, which was believed to be enlivened by the buddha's presence via a portion of the cremated remains of his body, a piece of his body, or one his personal belongings (robes, begging bowl, etc.).[17] The eight great sacred sites were considered energized by having been a place where the buddha had dwelled and performed his awakened activities. Even early on, relics included those of other realized masters, and the stupa and its veneration spread everywhere Buddhism did. In all cases, the power of the realized being was thought to be physically present at the site. It was not just symbolic or commemorative. Those in its presence would gain both worldly and transcendent benefits.

With the introduction of Vajrayāna thought and practice, another conception of circumambulation was added. Pilgrims move around and through the mandala of the deity, basking in the power of the deities, their palace, and their entourage of *khandroma*. In the course of the circuit, pilgrims may collect empowered substances such as soil, stones, or water to take back home with them. Prostrations frequently figure into the journey to the *né* or as part of the circumambulation. The most ardent pilgrims may even do prostrations throughout the entire route, touching their bodies to the sacred ground as they move closer to the site or the completion of the circuit. Recitation of mantras or telling edifying stories about the site or great masters often figure prominently. On large-scale pilgrimages, or at particular auspicious times of the year on even local ones, lamas may give teachings or lead ritual worship. Though the focus is on the power of the high tantric deities, it is not uncommon for pilgrims to also make offerings to local deities with offerings of juniper smoke, barley flour, and the exhortation, *lha gyel lo!*, meaning "The gods are victorious!"

Benefits of Performing Pilgrimage. What one gains from the performance of pilgrimage depends on the relative spiritual status of the pilgrim. Pilgrimage is a much more common practice than the sophisticated Vajrayāna forms of meditation practiced by the religious elite, but it would be a mistake to equate pilgrimage exclusively with ordinary practitioners. Pilgrimage guides often describe these two categories of people as "ordinary people" (*so skye bo*) and "excellent" or "holy people" (*skye bo dam pa*). It is important to note here that the different experiences to be had by the more or less advanced practitioners does not necessarily correlate to a difference between monks and laypeople. Prior to 1959, a significant portion of the male population ordained, so it would be naive to assume that being a monk or nun meant that one was necessarily a serious meditator. Some monks and nuns were, of course, but being a tantric yogi has never necessitated being a celibate renunciant. Throughout the Tibetan literature on pilgrimage, it is assumed that advanced yogis have much to gain from traveling to *nés* and that their experience of them will be more profound than those of the uncultivated layperson or monk. Tibetan conceptions of the *pīṭhas* of the Khorlo Dompa corpus always allowed for an interiorized understanding, with the *pīṭhas* being present in the body of the yogi. The yogi could "visit" these sites in his or her own body, rendering the travel to the actual sites (whether understood to be in India or Tibet) unnecessary. Nonetheless, yogis have always visited physical sites. Their presence at them aided their progress in advanced meditation, and for the greatest of them, their realizations contributed to the power of the place. The power of the Khorlo Dompa maṇḍala, the presence of the *khandroma*, and the charismatic power of realized masters all contribute to the yogi's accelerated progress along the path to realization at a *né*.

For the less-advanced layperson or monk, the benefits sought from visiting a *né* tend to be more mundane. Despite the orthodox Buddhist talk of karma as exclusively determining one's good or bad fortunes, the indigenous Tibetan conceptions of evil (*sdig pa*) and pollution (*grib*) are often employed when discussing the benefits of pilgrimage. "Evil" here refers to the results of moral transgressions, while "pollution" refers to a somatic negativity that results from actions that anger various kinds of supernatural beings through transgression of social norms or contact with bodily substances. Many kinds of ritual action can mitigate or remove evil and pollution, but pilgrimage is said specifically to do so by the arduous physical effort of the pilgrim's body and by the purificatory and transformative effect of contact with the empowered landscape and its empowered substances, such as soil, rocks, plants, and water.[18]

Mountain *Nés*. Mountains are by far the most common natural features to be regarded as *nés* (*gnas ri*). The idea of a mountain as a sacred and powerful place in Tibet can be seen in the earliest Tibetan texts. The mythology of the early kings is intimately connected to mountains and their cults.[19] Across Tibet, mountains are identified with territorial deities (*yul lha*), and their veneration constitutes a significant portion of pilgrimage activity in the past and present. Mountain cults have long played important roles in the establishment and maintenance of regional and national identities in Tibet. Some mountains are regarded as both territorial deities and the dwelling of the mandala of Khorlo Dompa. Mountains that are regarded primarily as Khorlo Dompa mandalas were typically earlier thought to be territorial deities.[20] Numerous peaks across the Himalāyan ranges are regarded as sacred mountains (*gnas ri*). Many are of only regional importance, but others attract the attention of pilgrims from across the Tibetan plateau.[21] The most important *né* mountains are Gang Tisé (Gang ti se) or Mount Kailash, Tsari (Tsa ri), Lapchi (La phyi), Amnye Machen (A myes rma chen), Kawa Karpo (Kha ba dkar po), and Kongpo Bönri.[22] Probably the most important and well-known mountain pilgrimage is that of Gang Tisé, near the intersection of the borders of present-day China, India, and Nepal.

Gang Tisé is identified with Mount Meru, the central mountain and world axis according to Buddhist cosmology, which is sacred to Tibetan Buddhists, Bönpos, and Hindus.[23] To adherents of Bön, Gang Tisé is an ancient sacred site of that religion that stands at the center of the Bön kingdom of Zhangzhung. A well-known Buddhist legend has it that the great saint and yogi Milarepa subdued the Bön magician Naro Bönchung and made Gang Tisé his hermitage. The Buddhist pilgrimage route around the 6,714-meter Gang Tisé is said to have been established by the great Tibetan Kagyü master and pilgrim Götsangpa, and the Kagyü sect maintains a strong presence at the site. Drigung and Drukpa Kagyü masters established centers here—four temples were built at the four cardinal points surrounding the mountain. Gang Tisé is regarded as the physical manifestation of the maṇḍala of Khorlo Dompa, the power of which sacralizes the landscape and blesses and purifies pilgrims who traverse its circuits. Two other major mountain pilgrimage sites, Tsari and Lapchi, are conceived as Khorlo Dompa maṇḍalas as well. Though the guidebooks of each of the major pilgrimage sites laud that site's unique power, Gang Tisé holds pride of place for the claimed benefits of circumambulating the mountain. The first Drukpa Kagyü hierarch Tsangpa Gyaré Yeshé Dorjé (Gtsang pa rgya ras ye shes rdo rje, 1161–1211) is quoted as saying that one circuit would purify all the obscuration of one life, ten would purify the obscurations of a cosmic age, and one hundred circumambulations would bring buddhahood in that very lifetime.[24] Calendrical considerations are also important. A sacred mountain's great pilgrimage festival (*skor dus chen mo*) occurs once every twelve years, corresponding to the Tibetan calendrical cycle of twelve animal years. While pilgrims go to Gang Tisé and the other great *né* mountains every year, Gang Tisé's great pilgrimage festival occurs in horse years. In any given year, it is auspicious to start a pilgrimage on the fifteenth day of the fourth Tibetan month, the date on which Tibetans celebrate the birth, awakening, and *parinirvāṇa* of the buddha.

Lakes. According to the ancient Tibetan worldview, mountain sacred sites are often complemented by lakes, the two forming a gendered pair (commonly male mountain, female lake). Thirty-six kilometers south of Gang Tisé is the lake Tso Mapam (Mtsho ma pham), known in Indian languages as Manasorovar. Pilgrims who visit Gang Tisé typically include Tso Mapam as part of the journey, and nearby Rakshas Tal also attracts pilgrims. However, some lakes stand out as pilgrimage destinations of their own. In north central Tibet lies Namtso (Gnam mtsho) Lake, considered the consort of the great *né* mountain deity Nyenchen Tanglha (Gnyan chen thang lha). In south central Tibet is the divinatory Yamdrok (Yar 'brog mtsho) Lake. In eastern Tibet lies Lhamo Latso (Lha mo bla mtsho), famous for the part it plays in the selection of the Dalai Lamas. The name of the lake tells us that it is considered to be an aquatic dwelling place of the *la*, the vital principle or soul, of Palden Lhamo (Dpal ldan lha mo), the principal protector of the Dalai Lamas. The Second Dalai Lama, Gendun Gyatso (Dge 'dun rgya mtsho, 1476–1542), took Palden Lhamo as his protector and experienced visions in the lake. Since the Second Dalai Lama's time, every subsequent Dalai Lama or his regent has gone to visit the lake.[25] In the eastern Tibetan province of Amdo is Blue Lake (Mtsho sngon po). Blue Lake has a multiday circumambulation path and a number of well-documented legends surrounding it and its origins.[26]

Caves. Caves feature prominently in many sacred mountain pilgrimages. The power of caves is frequently attributed to the meditative power of advanced tantric yogis such as Guru Rinpoché, Milarepa, and other legendary tantric masters. Meditation in such caves is understood to be particularly efficacious for purification and spiritual transformation. Another type of cave is the "womb-cave," which pilgrims enter and exit through a narrow passage. Accumulated evil and pollution are purified by the transit.[27] The Bon mountain in Kongpo is somewhat unusual in that the principle sites of the maṇḍala, through which pilgrims move, are its caves. This is an excellent example of what has been called the "mandalization" of sacred sites in Tibet.[28] Caves in which "treasure texts" (*gter*) have been discovered are also considered empowered and desirable spots for meditation. Cave sites are particularly important for pilgrimages associated with Padmasambhava. The two best-known Padmasambhava caves are located beyond the contemporary borders of the Tibetan Autonomous Region. Asura Cave, located near Pharping in the Kathmandu valley, is one of the most important pilgrimages associated with Padmasambhava. It is widely held to be where he mastered the ritual system of Vajrakilāya, which is an important practice used to subdue the negative forces in Tibet.[29] In eastern Nepal lies the Halase Maratika caves where Padmasambhava attained the siddhi of long life.[30] Though not important until the 19th century, the caves (and the lake) at Rewalsar, in District Mandi in Himachal Pradesh, India, have become an important pilgrimage site for both Tibetans in Tibet and in exile.[31] A vast cave features prominently in the activities at the recently revived pilgrimage to the Drigung Powa Chenmo ('Bris gung pho ba chen mo) festival. The eight-day pilgrimage, teaching, and empowerment culminate in the teaching of *powa* *(pho ba)*, the tantric method to transfer one's consciousness to the Pure Land of Amitābha at the moment of death. The cave is said to have been empowered by the meditations of Padmasambhava's consort, Yeshé Tsogyel (Ye shes mtsho rgyal, 757–817), and its tunnels and other natural features are understood to be material correlates of the parts of the yogic body that are developed in *powa* meditation.[32]

Hidden Lands. The emphasis on "treasure texts" and their association with the Nyingma sect also bears on the concept of hidden lands (*sbas yul*). It is typically said of *nés* that they were previously unknown or inaccessible before being "opened" by a great tantric master. Hidden lands, however, are valleys said to have been hidden by Padmasambhava in case of future turmoil or to serve as sites ideal for spiritual progress for advanced practitioners.[33] The best known of these hidden lands is probably Pemakö (Padma bkod) in far southeast Tibet. This *né* was first brought to the attention of Western scholars by Jacques Bacot, and it has received attention in more recent scholarship.[34] Legends attribute the establishment of hidden lands to Padmasambhava and King Tri Songdetsen (Khri srong lde'u btsan, r. 756–796) as havens for practitioners, but texts on such sites also suggest that they were refuges for the descendants of the royal lineage.[35] The discovery of these lands peaked in the 17th and 18th centuries, which was a period in which the Nyingma sect was persecuted.[36] The notion of a secreted refuge from apocalyptic change also resonated with millennial themes in Tibetan thought, particularly those associated with the idea of Shambhala in the Kālacakra corpus.

Characteristic Features of Natural Sites. How one experiences a sacred site depends on the spiritual attainment of the person. Holy persons will actually see the deities and the *khandroma*, while ordinary beings will not be able to see them. Nonetheless, the physical landscape of a *né* manifests signs of its spiritual power for all to see. A common feature at sacred sites is the presence of various types of bodily imprints (*sku rjes*) of deities, *khandroma*, and great masters on rocks and other natural features. Full body imprints, footprints, handprints, and so on abound at sacred sites. Self-arisen images (*rang 'byung*) on the ground and on rock faces are also common. These can be images of deities, great yogis, auspicious signs, or illustrations of edifying teachings. These lithic hierophanies are not always apparent, so pilgrimage guides (*gnas bshad*) typically describe them and their locations on the route. It is common for body imprints and self-arisen images to be marked with white silk scarves (*kha btags*), anointment with butter or oil, barley flour or dough effigies, coins, and other offerings. Springs are sometimes said to pour out the "attainment water" (*bsgrub chu*) for the pilgrim and naturally occurring pools may be said to be the *khandromas*' bathing basins or the *la* lake of an autochthonous spirit or a dharma protector.

PILGRIMAGE TO HUMAN-MADE SITES AND HOLY PEOPLE

Monasteries, temples, and other human-made sites are regarded as sacred sites for the same reason as natural sites—the charismatic power of consecrated images, monks, lamas, and yogis infuse the structures that they inhabit or inhabited. Lhasa, the capital of Tibet, has long been a pilgrimage destination for Tibetans.[37] Lhasa was the capital of Tibet during the golden age of the religious kings, at which time a statue of the buddha, known as Jowo Rinpoché, was said to have been brought to Tibet by the Chinese wife of Songtsen Gampo (Srong btsan sgam po, r. 617–650), the alleged first great Buddhist king of Tibet. The statue was eventually installed in the city's central temple, the Jokhang, which is regarded as the spiritual heart of the city and called the Vajrāsana of Tibet. Pilgrims and Lhasa residents circumambulate the Jokhang and do prostrations before it. Surrounding Lhasa are the three great monasteries of the Geluk sect: Ganden, Drepung, and Sera. Southeast of Lhasa is Samyé Monastery, the first monastery in Tibet, established by the efforts of Padmasambhava and the great Indian scholar Śāntarakṣita. Pilgrimage to monasteries are done because they are inhabited by the Buddhist sangha, whose accumulated merit make veneration meritorious for pilgrims and the surrounding community. If a monastery is home to a high-ranking lama or tulku, it is understood to be empowered by his or her charismatic power, which is a result of advanced tantric practice or the spiritual eminence of a master who has returned repeatedly to this world for the sake of all sentient beings. Numerous other monasteries are also objects of pilgrimage, sometimes with local appeal and sometimes attracting pilgrims from all over Tibet and beyond.

All of the pilgrimages considered so far are to places empowered by holy persons—ultimately divine persons, but also people who attained realization of and thus identification with the high tantric deities. Most of the pilgrimages to human-made sites are also, in a sense, pilgrimages to holy people. Pilgrimage to the Potala prior to 1959 was primarily centered on the living Dalai Lama, but the enduring presence of the entire lineage can still be seen to make the palace a sacred place. Prior to 1959, large numbers of pilgrims would come to the teachings of high lamas and great teachers, most significantly the Dalai Lama, and would attend the large public Dünkhor (*dus 'khor*, Skt. Kālacakra) empowerments. As many as one hundred thousand people are said to have attended the Dünkhor empowerments in 1954 and 1956.[38] These have continued in exile.

REVIEW OF LITERATURE

The scholarly study of Tibetan pilgrimage is a relatively new field of inquiry.[39] Other than the pioneering work of Giuseppe Tucci and Robert Ekvall, most of the scholarly attention to Tibetan pilgrimage has come since the mid-1980s when China relaxed their policies toward Tibet and began to allow Tibetans to return to their pilgrimages, thus allowing Western scholars access to the sites and the pilgrims. Early scholarship tended to assume the functionalist interpretive system of Victor Turner in which pilgrimage was seen to function to temporarily suspend social status and hierarchy, bringing about an egalitarian community, "communitas," for the duration of the journey.[40] More recent scholarship on pilgrimage, while acknowledging Turner's influential model, has challenged it theoretically or tested it in the field.[41] Recent studies of Tibetan pilgrimage tend to find little evidence for Turner's thesis. Status and hierarchy often remained unchallenged, if not overtly reinforced in Tibetan pilgrimage.

The mid to late 1990s were a landmark period for scholarship on Tibetan pilgrimage. In 1994–1995 *Tibet Journal* published four special editions on sacred space. The articles were subsequently published in 1999 as *Sacred Spaces and Powerful Places in Tibetan Culture: A Collection of Essays*, edited by Toni Huber and published by the Library of Tibetan Works and Archives. In 1997, *Mandala and Landscape* was published. This volume, starting from the foundation laid down by Tucci's *Theory and Practice of Maṇḍala*, contains a wide-ranging set of articles concentrating on Tibet, but also includes articles on India, China, and Japan. Another important collection was published in 1998: *Pilgrimage in Tibet,* edited by Alex McKay. The same year saw the publication of a collection of papers presented at the 7th Seminar of the International Association for Tibetan Studies, focusing on mountain deities and their cults: *Tibetan Deities, Their Cults and Representations.* In 1999, the first book-length study of a Tibetan pilgrimage, the Tsari pilgrimage in southeast Tibet, was published: Toni Huber's *The Cult of Pure Crystal Mountain: Popular Pilgrimage and Visionary Landscape in Southeast Tibet.* At the beginning of this work, Huber attempts to diagnose the state of the field and offers suggestions for moving forward. Huber observes that three trends currently hamper progress in the study of Tibetan pilgrimage: an overemphasis on Buddhist doctrines and models, an approach that favors small-scale and localized studies, and the relative lack of a systematic approach to available data. Huber's 2008 book expands on his insights and extends the scope of his work to Tibetan pilgrimage to (and in) India. Jacob Kinnard's *Places in Motion: The Fluid Identities of Temples, Images, and Pilgrims* advances the critical engagement with Turner's theories, and though it does not specifically engage with Tibetan pilgrimage, it is a valuable contribution to the field.[42]

PRIMARY SOURCES

Great Tibetan masters began to record their pilgrimage experiences in the early years of the second propagation of Buddhism in Tibet. The great Kagyü masters Jikten Gönpo Rinchenpal ('Jig rten mgon po rin chen dpal, 1143–1217), Götsangpa Gönpo Dorjé (Rgod tshang pa mgon po rdo rje, 1189–1258), and his disciple Orgyenpa Rinchenpal (O rgyan pa rin chen dpal, 1229–1309) were among the pioneering figures to emphasize pilgrimage to sacred sites both in India and Tibet. The account of a 16th-century Tibetan master can be found in *Song of the Road: The Poetic Travel Journal of Tsarchen Losal Gyatso.*[43] Tsarchen (Tsar chen blo gsal rgya mtsho, 1503–1566) composed a prose narrative that is accompanied by verses that beautifully express the lama's experiences and realizations on the journey. Another important insider account is *The Life of Shabkar: The Autobiography of a Tibetan Yogi.*[44] Shabkar (Zhabs dkar tshogs drug rang grol) was an influential 19th-century yogi and itinerant pilgrim. His account is particularly valuable in that it highlights how Tibetan pilgrimage has both an outer, physical aspect as well as an inner, yogic one. The same can be said of *Sacred Ground: Jamgon Kongtrul on "Pilgrimage and Sacred Geography,"* which includes a translation of a pilgrimage guide by the great 19th-century Rimé scholar and encyclopedist Jamgon Kongtrul Lodrö Tayé ('Jam mgon kong sprul blo gros mtha' yas).[45] Translations of selections or complete pilgrimage guides to Tisé, Tsari, Lapchi, Amnye Machen, and the Bön mountain Kongpori can be found in the edited volumes by Huber and McKay. The monograph by Huber contains translations of large sections of the pilgrimage guide to Lapchi.[46] A number of sources have been published in Tibetan in the 20th century. The pioneer of modern pilgrimage guides was the controversial scholar and pilgrim Gendun Chöpel (Dge 'dun chos 'phel, 1903–1951), who wrote and published a book about his travels in India that is still used by Tibetans today. He also wrote guides to several sites in Tibet.[47] The *Bod kyi gnas yig bdams bsgrigs* (*A Selective Compilation of Tibetan Pilgrimage Guides*) compiles guides to both Buddhist and Bön sites across Tibet, and other collections focus on particular important sites.[48]

FURTHER READING

Blondeau, Anne-Marie. *Tibetan Deities, Their Cults and Representations: Papers Presented at a Panel of the 7th Seminar of the International Association for Tibetan Studies Graz 1999*. Vienna: Verlag Österreichischen Akademie Der Wissenschaftern, 1998.

Buffetrille, Katia. "Pilgrimage in Tibet." In *Oxford Bibliographies*. New York: Oxford University Press, 2013. http://dx.doi.org/10.1093/OBO/9780195393521-0122.

Dge 'dun chos 'phel. *Gnas yig phyogs sgrigs dad bskul lha dbang rnga sgra (The Drum Sound of Empowerment of the Gods That Arouses Faith, a Collection of Pilgrimage Guides)*. Chengdu, China: Si khrin mi rigs dpe skrun khang, 1998.

Ekvall, Robert B., and James F. Downs. *Tibetan Pilgrimage*. Tokyo: Institute for the Study of Languages and Cultures of Asia and Africa, 1987.

Gray, David. "Tantra and the Tantric Traditions of Hinduism and Buddhism." In *Oxford Research Encyclopedia of Religion*. Edited by John Barton. New York: Oxford University Press, 2016. http://dx.doi.org/10.1093/acrefore/9780199340378.013.59.

Huber, Toni. *The Cult of Pure Crystal Mountain: Popular Pilgrimage and Visionary Landscape in Southeast Tibet*. New York: Oxford University Press, 1999.

Huber, Toni. *The Holy Land Reborn: Pilgrimage and the Tibetan Reinvention of Buddhist India*. Chicago: University of Chicago Press, 2008.

Huber, Toni, ed. *Sacred Spaces and Powerful Places in Tibetan Culture*. Dharamsala: Library of Tibetan Works and Archives, 1999.

Kinnard, Jacob N. *Places in Motion: The Fluid Identities of Temples, Images, and Pilgrims*. Oxford: Oxford University Press, 2014.

Large-Blondeau, Anne-Marie. "Les pèlerinages tibétains." In *Les pèlerinages*. Edited by Jean Yoyotte, Anne-Marie Esnoul, et al., 203–245. Paris: Éditions du Seuil, 1960.

Macdonald, A. W., ed. *Maṇḍala and Landscape*. New Delhi: D. K. Printworld, 1997.

McKay, Alex, ed. *Pilgrimage in Tibet*. London: Routledge, 1998.

Ngawang Zangpo. *Sacred Ground: Jamgon Kongtrul on "Pilgrimage and Sacred Geometry."* Ithaca, NY: Snow Lion Publications, 2001.

Ricard, Matthieu, trans. *The Life of Shabkar: The Autobiography of a Tibetan Yogi*. Albany: State University of New York Press, 1994.

Stearns, Cyrus. *Song of the Road: The Poetic Travel Journal of Tsarchen Losal Gyatso*. Boston: Wisdom Publications, 2012.

NOTES

1. For an English translation from the Pali, see Maurice Walsh, *The Long Discourses of the Buddha: A Translation of the Dīgha Nikāya* (Somerville, MA: Wisdom Publications, 1987), 231–277.
2. For a thorough overview of the "shifting terrain" of the sites associated with the buddha in India, see chapter 1 of Toni Huber's *The Holy Land Reborn: Pilgrimage and the Tibetan Reinvention of Buddhist India* (Chicago: University of Chicago Press, 2008), 15–39; and for an examination of the Vajrayāna transformation of Tibetan conceptions of Indian pilgrimage sites, see Huber, *The Holy Land Reborn*, chap. 4, 85–121.
3. David L. McMahan, "Buddhist Modernism," in *Buddhism in the Modern World*, ed. David L. McMahan (New York: Routledge, 2012), 160.
4. Matthew T. Kapstein, *Tibetan Buddhism: A Very Short Introduction* (New York: Oxford University Press, 2014), 2–3.

5. Toni Huber, *The Cult of Pure Crystal Mountain: Popular Pilgrimage and Visionary Landscape in Southeast Tibet* (New York: Oxford University Press, 1999), 7–8.
6. For a discussion of this term and its implications, see Toni Huber, "Putting the Gnas Back into Gnas-skor: Rethinking Tibetan Pilgrimage Practice," in *Sacred Spaces and Powerful Places in Tibetan Culture*, ed. Toni Huber (Dharamsala: Tibetan Works and Archives, 1999), 79–80.
7. For a discussion and survey of the literature on this topic, see Geoffrey Samuel, *Civilized Shamans: Buddhism in Tibetan Societies* (Washington, DC: Smithsonian Institution Press, 1993), 186–191.
8. See Katia Buffetrille, "Reflections on Pilgrimages to Sacred Mountains, Lakes and Caves," in *Pilgrimage in Tibet*, ed. Alex McKay (Richmond: Curzon Press, 1988), 18–34. For a discussion of the contested status of Tisé between Bönpos and Buddhists, see Charles Ramble, "The Politics of Sacred Space in Bon and Tibetan Popular Tradition," in *Sacred Spaces and Powerful Places in Tibetan Culture, ed.*, Huber, 3–33.
9. Per Kvaerne, "The Bön Religion of Tibet," in *The Tibetan History Reader*, ed. Gray Tuttle and Kurtis R. Schaeffer (New York: Columbia University Press, 2013), 187.
10. The Tibetan translation of the Sanskrit includes two different readings of the name *Cakrasaṃvara*. Though it is common in Tibetan Buddhist scholarship to privilege Sanskrit, we will prefer Tibetan names and terms. For a discussion of the complexities of this name, see David B. Gray, *The Cakrasamvara Tantra (The Discourse of Śrī Heruka); Śrīherukābhidāna: A Study and Annotated Translation* (New York: The American Institute of Buddhist Studies at Columbia University, 2007), 35–37.
11. Toni Huber, "A Guide to the La-Phyi Mandala," in *Mandala and Landscape*, ed. A. W. Macdonald (New Delhi: D. K. Printworld, 2007), 234.
12. Macdonald, ed., *Mandala and Landscape*, 40–54. For the earlier subjugation of Rudra myth, see Jacob P. Dalton, *The Taming of the Demons: Violence and Liberation in Tibetan Buddhism* (New Haven, CT: Yale University Press, 2011), 159–206.
13. For a comprehensive overview of this period, see Ronald M. Davidson, *Tibetan Renaissance: Tantric Buddhism in the Rebirth of Tibetan Culture* (New York: Columbia University Press, 2005), chap. 4, 84–116.
14. Huber, *The Holy Land Reborn*, 80–83.
15. For an extensive discussion of this historical process, see Huber, *The Holy Land Reborn*, 58–121.
16. For a translation of the accounts of Orgyenpa and Taktsangrepa, see Giuseppe Tucci, *Travels of Tibetan Pilgrims in the Swat Valley* (Calcutta: Greater India Society, 1940).
17. See the collection of Gregory Schopen's pioneering articles on this topic in *Bones, Stones, and Buddhist Monks: Collected Papers on the Archeology, Epigraphy, and Texts of Monastic Buddhism in India* (Honolulu: University of Hawaii Press, 1997); and see *Embodying the Dharma: Buddhist Relic Veneration in Asia*, ed. David Germano and Kevin Trainor (Albany: State University of New York Press, 2004) for a broader discussion that includes Tibet.
18. For an extensive discussion of the effects of pilgrimage, see Huber, *The Cult of Pure Crystal Mountain*, 14–20.
19. Samten Karmay, "The Cult of Mountain Deities and Its Political Significance," in *The Arrow and the Spindle: Studies in History, Myths, Rituals and Beliefs in Tibet*, vol. 1 (Kathmandu: Mandala Book Point, 1998), 432–450.
20. Buffetrille, "Reflections to Pilgrimages to Sacred Mountains, Lakes and Caves."
21. For a sampling of articles on these kinds of sites, see Karmay, "The Cult of Mountain Deities and Its Political Significance"; Hildegard Diemberger, "The Horseman in Red: On Sacred Mountains of La stod lha (Southern Tibet)," in *Tibetan Mountain Deities, Their Cults and Representations*, ed. Anne-Marie Blondeau (Vienna: Verlag der Österreichischen Akademie der Wissenschaften, 1998), 43–55; and Elizabeth Stutchbury, "Raja Gephan—The Mountain Protector of Lahul," in Blondeau, ed., 159–168.
22. For translation of a pilgrimage guide to Tisé, see Toni Huber and Tsepak Rigzin, "A Tibetan Guide for Pilgrimage to Ti-se (Mount Kailas) and mTsho Ma-pham (Lake Masasarovar)," in *Sacred Spaces and Powerful Places in Tibetan Culture*, ed. Huber, 125–153. For a book-length study of Tsari, see Huber, *The*

Cult of Pure Crystal Mountain. For a study of Lapchi, see Huber, "A Guide to the La-phyi Maṇḍala," 233–286. For a description of the Amnye Machen pilgrimage, see Katia Buffetrille, "The Great Pilgrimage of A myes rma chen: Written Tradition, Living Realities," in Macdonald, ed., *Mandala and Landscape*, 18–34. For a description of the pilgrimage to Kawa Karpo before the Chinese occupation, see Jacques Bacot, "Pèlerinage du Dokeria (Tibet Oriental)," in *Annales du Musée Guimet* (Paris: Ernest Leroux, 1909), 1–24. For an extensive description of the great Bön pilgrimage mountain, see Charles Ramble, "The Creation of the Bon Mountain of Kongpo," in *Mandala and Landscape*, ed. Macdonald, 133–232.

23. Though consideration of Hindu veneration of the mountain falls outside the scope of this article, for a discussion of Hindu conceptions alongside Buddhist and Bön, see A. Loseries-Leick, "On the Sacredness of Mountain Kailasa in the Indian and Tibetan Sources," in *Pilgrimage in Tibet*, ed. McKay, 143–164.
24. Huber and Rigzin, "A Tibetan Guide for Pilgrimage to Ti-se (Mount Kailas) and mTsho Ma-pham (Lake Masasarovar)," 139.
25. For a brief account of the origins of this sacred lake, see Amy Heller, "The Great Protector Deities of the Dalai Lamas," in *Lhasa in the Seventeenth Century: The Capital of the Dalai Lamas*, ed. Françoise Pommaret (Leiden, The Netherlands: Brill, 2003), 82–87. For a modern account of the lake as pilgrimage site, see Keith Dowman, *The Power Places of Central Tibet: The Pilgrim's Guide* (London: Routledge & Kegan Paul, 1988), 255–263.
26. Katia Buffetrille, "The Blue Lake of A-mdo and Its Island: Legends and Pilgrimage Guide," in *Sacred Spaces and Powerful Places in Tibetan Culture*, ed. Huber, 105–124.
27. Rolf A. Stien, *Grottes-matrices et lieux saints de la déesse en Asie Orientale* (Paris: École Française d'Extrême-Orient, 1988).
28. Charles Ramble, "The Creation of the Bon Mountain of Kongpo," in *Mandala and Landscape*, ed. Macdonald, 162–172.
29. Jacob Dalton's "The Early Development of the Padmasambhava Legend in Tibet," *Journal of the American Oriental Society* 124, no. 4 (October to December, 2004): 759–772.
30. Katia Buffetrille, "The Halase Maratika Caves (Eastern Nepal): A Sacred Place Claimed by Both Hindus and Buddhists," *Pondy Papers in Social Science* (Pondicherry: Institut Français de Pondichery, 1994), 1–70.
31. Huber, *The Holy Land Reborn*, chap. 8, 232–247.
32. Matthew Kapstein, "A Pilgrimage of Rebirth Reborn: The 1992 Celebration of the Drigung Powa Chenmo," in *Buddhism in Contemporary Tibet: Religious Revival and Cultural Identity*, ed. Melvyn C. Goldstein and Matthew T. Kapstein (Berkeley: University of California Press, 1998), 95–119.
33. For an examination of the connection between "treasure finders" and hidden lands, see Franz-Karl Ehrhard, "The Role of 'Treasure Discovers' and Their Search for Himalayan Sacred Lands," in Huber, ed., *Sacred Spaces and Powerful Places in Tibetan Culture*, 227–239. For a discussion of hidden lands and political sanctuary, see Geoff Childs, "Refuge and Revitalization: Hidden Himalayan Sanctuaries (sbas yul) and the Preservation of Tibet's Imperial Lineage," *Acta Orientalia* 60 (1999): 126–158. Martin Brauen-Dolma's article, "Millenarianism in Tibetan Religion," in *Soundings in Tibetan Civilization*, ed. Barbara Nimri Aziz and Matthew Kapstein (New Delhi: Manohar, 1985), 245–256 studies the connection between hidden lands and millennial thought in Tibet.
34. Ehrhard, "The Role of 'Treasure Discoveries' and Their Writings in the Search for Himalayan Sacred Lands," 228–239.
35. Childs, "Refuge and Revitalization."
36. Franz-Karl Ehrhard, "Political and Ritual Aspects of the Search for Himalayan Sacred Lands," in *Sacred Spaces and Powerful Places in Tibetan Culture*, ed. Huber, 240–257.
37. André Alexander, *The Temples of Lhasa: Tibetan Buddhist Architecture from the 7th to the 21st Centuries*, Tibet Heritage Fund's Conservation Inventory 1 (Chicago: Serindia, 2005); and Gyurme Dorje, Tashi Tsering, Heather Stoddard, and Andre Alexander, *Jokhang: Tibet's Most Sacred Buddhist Temple* (London: Hasjörg Mayer, 2010). See also Zhang Yang's 2016 film *Paths of the Soul*.

38. "Introduction to the Kalachakra," *His Holiness, the 14th Dalai Lama of Tibet.*
39. For a comprehensive bibliography on Tibetan pilgrimage, see Katia Buffetrille, "Pilgrimage in Tibet," in *Oxford Bibliographies* (New York: Oxford University Press, 2013), http://dx.doi.org/10.1093/OBO/9780195393521-0122.
40. For a classic exposition of this theory, see Victor Turner, "Liminality and Communitas," in *The Ritual Process: Structure and Anti-Structure* (New Brunswick, NJ: Aldine Transaction, 1969), 94–130.
41. See John Eade and Michael J. Sallnow, *Contesting the Sacred: The Anthropology of Christian Pilgrimage* (London: Routledge, 1991), 4–5.
42. Jacob N. Kinnard, *Places in Motion: The Fluid Identities of Temples, Images, and Pilgrims* (Oxford: Oxford University Press, 2014), 1–26.
43. Cyrus Stearns, *Song of the Road: The Poetic Travel Journal of Tsarchen Losal Gyatso* (Boston: Wisdom Publications, 2012).
44. Matthieu Ricard, trans, *The Life of Shabkar: The Autobiography of a Tibetan Yogi* (Albany: State University of New York Press, 1994).
45. Ngawang Zangpo, *Sacred Ground: Jamgon Kongtrul on "Pilgrimage and Sacred Geometry"* (Ithaca, NY: Snow Lion Publications, 2001).
46. Huber, ed., *Sacred Spaces and Powerful Places in Tibetan Culture*; McKay, ed., *Pilgrimage in Tibet*; *Mandala and Landscape*; and Macdonald, ed., *Mandala and Landscape* (New Delhi: D. K. Printworld, 2007). For details, see note 15. For the book-length study of Tsari, see Huber, *The Cult of Pure Crystal Mountain.*
47. For the guide to sacred sites in India, see Gendun Chöpel, *Rgya gar gyi gnas chen khag la bgrod pa'i lam yig* (Calcutta: Mahabodhi Society, 1939). For a reprint edition that includes an abridged version of the India guide as well as guides to several Tibetan sites, see Gendun Chöpel, *Gnas yig phyogs sgrigs dad bskul lha dbang rnga sgra* (Chengdu, China: Si khrin mi rigs dpe skrun khang, 1998).
48. See Tshe ring dpal 'byor, *Bod kyi yig bdams bsgrigs* (Lhasa, China: Bod ljongs bod yig dpe skrun khan, 1995). For two site-specific guides see O rgyan bsod nams dang A bu dkar lo, *A myes rma chen gnas yig* (Zi ling, China: Zi ling par khang, 2002); and Rin chen rdo rje and Tshe ring chos 'phel, *Gnas chen Kha ba dkar po'i bsang mchod dang gnas yig* (Yun nan mi rigs dpe skrun khang, 1999).

Paul B. Donnelly

PILGRIMAGE IN CHINA

In Chinese, a pilgrim (*xiangke*) is one "offering incense," and going on a pilgrimage (*chaoshan jinxiang*) translates to one "offering incense to a mountain." To pilgrimage is to pay respect to a site considered numinous, to offer a donation to a deity or a bodhisattva, and/or to hope for something (e.g., a healing or merit) in return. Early historical records in Chinese show that mountains have long been considered numinous or divine, but pilgrimage need not only occur at a mountainous location. Rituals of pilgrimage are a feature of all Chinese religions and are performed at natural landscapes, significant monasteries/temples/shrines, and at sites deemed to hold spiritual magnetism. Prior to the arrival of Buddhism or Islam in China, Daoist activities identified natural environments as auspicious, mountains as homes of deities, caves as locations holding essence (*qi*), and particular buildings as useful for contemplation, reciting prayers, and offering donations to the gods. Even a mountain's crest was considered auspicious, and the building of temples at mountain locations was done in such a way as to not take away from the site's spiritual magnetism. The image of one going on pilgrimage in Chinese traditions thus often incorporates journeying to a mountain location, but the Chinese imaginary regarding pilgrimage also includes travel to cities, temples, and sites associated with a significant teacher or miraculous tale.

PILGRIMAGE IN DAOIST TRADITIONS

Although modern researchers may associate a pilgrimage site with a specific religious tradition, Chinese religious history shows that locations were fluid in terms of identity. Furthermore, they were highly contested. James Benn's work on Zhongnan shan, for example, reveals rival claims to the site. For Daoists, Zhongnan shan had strong associations with Laozi, and this was pushed by the Louguan group of Daoists. Benn's research, however, further uncovers Buddhist claims to the site. For Buddhist authors, the location was affiliated with major monks, nuns, and laypersons from Mahayana literature.[1] Claims such as these disclose multiple religious imaginaries located at a single site.

Research on Chinese pilgrimage furthermore reveals how, over time, mountainous pilgrimage sites in particular were transformed within shifting cultural imaginaries. Mountain sites originally referred to natural formations, but religious belief altered over time. Mountainous sites began to be seen as locations of deities, and state sacrificial rites occurring at mountains furthermore confirmed their auspicious nature.[2] The *Classic of the Mountains and Seas* [*Shanhaijing* 山海經] provides a record of this alteration.

Within Chinese Daoist history, textual materials reveal the importance of pilgrimaging to numinous mountains, and in the Daoist imaginary five mountains were particularly identified as holding *ling*. These were arranged directionally—north, south, east, west, and center—in accordance with the Chinese *wuxing* (five elements/phases) system from the Han period. Their worship may, however, go back as far as the Shang period. Mount Tai in the east, Mount Heng in the north, Mount Song in the center, Mount Hua in the west, and Mount Heng in the south make up the five spiritually charged mountains. In Chinese *shan* (mountain) is both singular and plural. Thus each sacred mountain is a series of mountain ranges, home to multiple temples, monasteries, and deities.

Traditions of venerating nature and practicing divination are important to Daoism, and the use of water as a metaphor for the "way"—the Dao—was included in classical Daoist philosophy from Laozi and Zhuangzi. Nature provides the ideal example for humans to emulate in their spiritual practice in order to live in accordance with the Dao. While this importance is underscored in Daoist philosophy, pilgrimage to the five mountains did not historically emerge because of philosophical texts. Instead, by the Han dynasty, the five summits (*wuyue*) developed as auspicious locations for imperial worship and sacrifice. Thus their emergence as sites of Daoist pilgrimage was very much the result of imperial patronage.

In Chinese, *yue* refers to the sacred peaks, and it is a character used frequently in the oracle bones as a range of mountains above another. Kleeman notes that we cannot be certain what mountains originally had this identification, but by the warring states era, texts including the "Canon of Yao" in the *Book of Documents* spoke of four marchmounts. By the 4th century BCE, there was a complex of numinous mountains linked to both the state as well as the well-being of the state.[3] By the Han dynasty, the marchmounts were a group of five with the central Mount Song added, and each mountain was "correlated with one of the Five Agents (*wuxing*) and, through it, with the whole system of related colors, flavors, directions, stars, season, etc."[4] After their canonization, rulers of the state have performed sacrifices to the god associated with the mountain, thus confirming them as pertinent sites of pilgrimage.

After the mountains were canonized in the 1st century BCE, Daoist adepts hoping for immortality and rulers concerned with the political legitimacy of their empires pilgrimaged to them.[5] In Chinese history, imperial patronage of the five mountains has been significant for their identification as sacred. During the late Ming, the five marchmounts received particular attention and the image of the mountain retreat as idyllic was expressed in Chinese artistic styles. During the second half of the Ming, journeying to the marchmounts became so popular among the literati that some went so far as to adopt a name associated with the goal of traveling to the mountains. For example, the intellectual Wang Yin named himself "Shanren of the Ten Marchmounts" and Guo Di called himself "Five Wanderings."[6] Individuals also published travel writings, and two gazetteers devoted to the Daoist mountains were published.

Scrolls, murals, and gardens furthermore popularized the five sacred peaks and provided individuals a means of viewing them without physically going on pilgrimage. Garden designs included artificial mountains after the likeness of the actual ones, giving individuals the sense that they had traveled to the auspicious peaks. Chinese literati enjoyed visiting gardens and parks as a leisure activity, and the Song emperor Huizong (r. 1101–1125) created the grand Genyue Park made up of unusual rocks, an artificial mountain, streams, pools, waterfalls, and grottoes. The landscape was meant to represent the forces of nature and recreate known sites of Daoist immortals.[7] Imperial patronage throughout Chinese history importantly secured the Chinese mountains as sacred realms for pilgrimage, and such support was even given in the form of replication.

Although garden creations imitating Daoist mountains conjured ideas of retreat and recreation, pilgrims have long considered them the abode of powerful immortals. And this association has instigated awe and anxiety in the traveler, not relaxation or retreat. Robson notes that since the Han period, one of the most potent feelings that travelers have felt is fear. Given that mountain homes are sites of powerful Daoist deities, a traveler might be quite terrified in regard to their safety and thus carry necessary apotropaic objects.[8] This other side of the mountain as sacred recognizes it as a supernatural site where a mortal cautiously enters the realm, recognizing that in doing so they are in danger from encountering powerful gods. The *Classic of the Mountains and Seas* provides descriptions of mountain gods as "freaks and monstrosities." "The gods surrounding Mount Min in Sichuan, for example, have horse bodies and dragon heads, while those of Great Palace Mountain have human faces on each of their three heads."[9] While the Chinese imaginary of mountains includes the viewpoint that they are auspicious sites for securing political power, they are realms of miracles and locations of transcendent treasures including materials for elixirs, as well as being the abodes of powerful deities. This power should be feared, for if a person enters a mountain range without possessing magical arts, the individual may become the victim of a disease, a tree may topple on them, a cliff may collapse, or tigers, wolves, or poisonous insects may attack them.[10] However, magical preparations would help to assure one's safe travel, as would traveling on days deemed auspicious.

Within the five marchmounts, Mount Tai in Shandong Province was a premier location for pilgrimage, and it was considered sacred not only for Daoism, but for Confucianism and Buddhism as well. Pilgrims have included individuals from all strata of society—emperors seeking to legitimize their rule, literati to gain cultural prestige, and ordinary individuals (women and peasants) to pray to their ancestors. Regarding emperors, the earliest historic records are of Qin Shihuangdi ascending the site in 219 (emperors as far back as the Yellow Emperor may have traveled there but we do not have a historic record of this).[11] Subsequently, more than seventy-two emperors pilgrimaged to the site to perform sacrifices, and importantly, many went to perform the *feng* and *shan* sacrifices—imperial rituals of offering to Heaven observed by emperors perhaps since the time of Qin Shihuangdi.[12] This ceremony represented the responsibility of the emperor to maintain harmony between Heaven and Earth, and by traversing to Mount Tai to perform the ritual, an emperor symbolically legitimized his rule. It was an important rite within Confucian ideology that provided authority to the emperor. During the Qing, both emperors Kangxi and Qianlong notably refused to perform it. Both pilgrimaged to the mountain, but they rejected the ritual for the purpose of promoting statecraft agendas—legitimizing themselves as rulers of a multiethnic state and not solely a Han one. Pilgrimage on the part of emperors thus carried with it political symbolism as well as religious significance.

In addition to using the site as a stage for political gain, pilgrimage to Mount Tai was done with the purpose of extending one's cultural capital. For Chinese literati, Confucius was the site's most important pilgrim (he was believed to have stood at the site's top), and by following in his footsteps, the individual elevated his cultural prestige. While on pilgrimage, literati contributed to the site's distinct landscape by engraving poems and calligraphy on the mountain, and the poets Du Fu and Li furthermore elevated the site's popularity by writing about the mountain and describing its mystical qualities.[13]

Ordinary (nonelite) individuals also legitimized the location as a site worthy of patronage. Given its location in the east, Mount Tai was associated with life, and while visiting the mountain, pilgrims prayed to the goddess of the mountain who was reported to grant miraculous pregnancies to couples struggling to produce an heir.[14] Males prayed to her to fulfill family obligations, and women prayed for sons for their personal welfare. During late imperial China, over one-third of Mount Tai's pilgrims were nonelite women, and pilgrimage was a chance for women to additionally create female social networks and pass on pilgrim rituals.[15] Interestingly, while the mountain was associated with birth, it was also importantly associated with death. During the late Ming, some pilgrims journeyed to the site to sacrifice their life with the hope that by doing so, they could help their ailing parents. Close to Mount Tai's peak is the "cliff for abandoning life"—a site where these filial suicides took place. Pilgrims believed that the mountain gods would look favorably upon the individual who sacrificed their life by jumping off the cliff, and because of the sacrifice, the person's parents would be restored to health. Essentially, by shortening a child's life, the parent's life might be extended. In 1523, the act was so popular that He Qiming (the governor of Shandong) ordered the building of a wall to prevent people from jumping off.[16]

Overall, the study of Mount Tai exemplifies the diversity of Daoist sacred sites in China in regard to identity and pilgrims. The site was significant for multiple religious traditions; going on pilgrimage carried with it religious, political, and cultural symbolism, and through the ritualistic act, meaningful social connections were made. Importantly, mountains considered sacred in the Daoist imaginary have not been limited to the five marchmounts, nor has the inclusion within the company of five ensured a site's popularity in terms of pilgrimage. In fact, one of the more popular Daoist mountains for pilgrimage was Mount Wudang, which was associated with the powerful deity Zhenwu. The earliest records of this deity come from the Western Han, and worship of the god continues today. From her study of scriptures, liturgical manuals, hagiographic accounts, government documents, epigraphy, iconography, gazetteers, anecdotes, and popular literature from the Song, Yuan, and Ming, scholar Shin-Yi Chao has found that Zhenwu emerged as the major Daoist god of exorcism, a minor god of internal alchemy, a source of political legitimization, and a deity for popular worship.[17] For these reasons, he became the central deity associated with Mount Wudang. Imperial worship, plus cultic and clerical activity, all located Zhenwu at Wudang. In 1412, the Yongle Emperor of the Ming contributed financial support for the building of seven large monastic complexes, plus small temples, all dedicated to the cult of Zhenwu, and he did so because he believed Zhenwu assisted his succession to the throne. The result of this construction was that pilgrims flooded the mountain and "Zhenwu became the object of one of the few truly 'national' cults, involving all levels of society."[18]

Within Daoist traditions, the mountain has been an important object of veneration. Spirits are believed to populate mountain spaces, and a mountain's physical materials provide benefit for those practicing alchemy, hoping for healing, or wishing for pregnancy. Mountain reclusion has historically been a significant practice for Daoists, but this began prior to the development of mountain monasteries. As uncovered by Bin Wei, Liu Xiang's 劉相 *Biographies of Exemplary Transcendents* [*Liexian zhuan* 列仙傳] includes records of Daoists ingesting essences in hopes of reaching immortality, and they did so at mountains. As Wei notes, "the character *xian* for immortality can be written in two ways: 仙 and 遷. The *Explication of Terms* [*Shiming* 釋名] says the following: '仙 is equivalent to 遷, as in 'to move into the mountains' 遷入山中." Another variant of the character 仚 is recorded in the *Explication of Written Characters* [*Shuowen jiezi* 說文解字]...'仚 is a person atop a mountain.'"[19] These sources dating to the Eastern Han (27–220) evidence a religious imaginary in which mountains are connected to goals of reaching immortality.

Furthermore, as developed in the Six Dynasties, the five marchmounts were sometimes viewed as the five fingers of the cosmic Laozi. They were "interconnected by an array of caves believed to be the gateways to the Taoist heavenly underworld."[20] They are essential to the Daoist imaginary, and pilgrimage by emperors, literati, and nonelite pilgrims confirmed their landscapes as sacred geography. Overall, as Dott identifies, four factors contributed to a site's spiritual magnetism: miraculous cures, apparitions of supernatural beings, sacred geography, and difficulty of access. Given the mountain's place within Chinese cosmology, when Buddhism entered China, sacred sites were a necessity to domesticate and localize the tradition. Thus pilgrimage occurred at sites already holding spiritual magnetism, and Buddhist mountains emerged at Daoist locations already deemed auspicious.

PILGRIMAGE IN CHINESE BUDDHIST TRADITIONS

As mentioned earlier, imperial support of Daoist sites helped establish mountains as centers of religious activity. This occurred in regard to Buddhist sacred sites as well. Additionally, remarkable geography, plus a site's religious features, contributed to its establishment of sacredness. Added to this was the role the ruling elite played in financially supporting monastery and temple building. Their patronage shaped sacred mountains and pilgrimage activities, and relationships between state authority and pilgrimage contributed to China's relationships with foreign nations, India and Japan included. Chinese pilgrims journeyed to India and brought back Buddhist texts, and Japanese pilgrims such as Ennin pilgrimaged to China and returned to Japan with sutras, religious implements, and teachings.

The establishment of Buddhism in China was intimately linked to the activities of pilgrims. During the 1st century CE, Buddhist teachings began spreading from India to China through cross-cultural exchanges and trade networks, and importantly, traveling Buddhist monks and pilgrims helped circulate Buddhist texts and relics. The travels of Chinese pilgrims were significant for transmitting Buddhist doctrines from India into China, as well as scriptures and sacred objects to be used in rituals and ceremonies. Faxian 法顯 (337?–422?), Xuanzang 玄奘 (602–664), and Yijing 義淨 (635–713) were among the hundreds of Chinese monks who traveled to India, and their detailed travel accounts provide a historical record of monastic institutions, rituals, and Buddhist doctrines. Faxian's travel account *A Record of the Buddhist Kingdoms* concerns his trek from Chang'an (present-day Xi'an) to India and explains the purpose of his pilgrimage to India as one to acquire texts of *vinaya* (monastic rules). While at the time of his journey texts such as the Lotus Sutra had been translated into Chinese, few *vinaya* texts were available for the growing Buddhist monastic community.[21]

Faxian's travel account reveals the importance of relics for creating a network of Buddhist pilgrims. Because of a demand for Buddhist relics in China (including physical remains of Sakyamuni Buddha), a travel network was established in which doctrines and ritual items circulated. This also nurtured a pilgrimage network of Buddhist monks and merchants, as Buddhist monasteries would provide accommodation for traders who then gave donations to the monastic communities.[22] When Xuanzang began his religious pilgrimage to India in 627, Buddhism was well established in China, and many texts had been translated into Chinese. His purpose in traveling to India was to visit sacred Buddhist sites—a desire shared by many Chinese pilgrims. Furthermore, he wanted to learn Buddhist teachings from Indian teachers, and his travel records (*The Records of the Western Regions*) provide accounts of his dialogues with Indians. His accounts, as well as Faxian's, have been far more popular than those of Yijing, who pilgrimaged from China to India between 671 and 695. But for historians, Yijing's *Memoirs of Eminent Monks* offers biographies of the numerous Buddhist monks who used either overland routes or the maritime route to pilgrimage from China into India.

The hope of these eminent pilgrims was to return to China with Buddhist texts, relics, and other ritual items so that Chinese practitioners could perform pilgrimages at domestic sacred sites. This would allow individuals to encounter the sacred in China without having to venture to India. In fact, the housing of Buddhist relics and texts indeed established sites of Buddhist pilgrimage. One example is the Famen Temple outside Xian in rural Shaanxi Province. During the Tang dynasty, imperial ceremonial rituals were performed there, and importantly, the temple functioned as a reliquary for one of the buddha's finger bones. In 1981 the pagoda collapsed, and when an archeological research team began restoring the pagoda, underground chambers were found. Inside these chambers they discovered Tang artifacts, including relic bones of the buddha. While this discovery was celebrated, it was not unexpected, given that Famen was known to be the home of one of the buddha's finger bones, which had been a gift from the Indian emperor Ashoka. During the Tang dynasty, the artifact drew large numbers of worshipers.[23]

In the study of pilgrimage in Chinese Buddhism, scholars can divide the inquiry into categories of investigation including pilgrimage to bodhisattvas, pilgrimage to monasteries and temples, pilgrimage and the state, and pilgrimage and art.

Pilgrimage to Bodhisattvas. Regarding bodhisattvas (enlightened beings), Buddhist pilgrimage reveals mountains to be locales where enlightened beings are manifested. Mountains are considered to be the abodes (*bodhimanda*) of bodhisattvas—physical locations of their pure lands. In India, sites of Buddhist pilgrimage were linked to stories of the buddha's life, but in China, sacred sites are linked to bodhisattvas. However, when Buddhism entered China, it did not carry with it sacred geography based on Chinese landscapes. Thus, when the religious tradition began to be rooted in China, numinous mountains were included into the domestication and localization of enlightened beings, and the abodes of bodhisattvas were mapped onto already established Daoist sites. Buddhist scriptures were an important source for legitimizing a site as the authentic pure land of a bodhisattva, but miracle tales occurring at a mountain further confirmed this identity and encouraged acts of pilgrimage.

Eventually four great and famous Buddhist mountains (*sida fojiao mingshan* 四大佛教名山) emerged as centers of Chinese Buddhist pilgrimage, complete with famous monasteries. Each mountain is associated with a resident bodhisattva, and pilgrims offered incense as a means of making contact with the enlightened being. Through this offering, the individual hoped to gain worldly, and otherworldly, benefits. As will be shown, four sites were linked to miraculous healings, pregnancies, and apparitions of bodhisattvas. These inspired pilgrims, as did the hope of earning merit to transfer to a loved one to relieve them of illness.

However, the compilation of four Buddhist mountains evolved over time, and other mountain monasteries were created by Buddhist monks. As recorded by Liu Yuxi 劉禹錫 (772–842), Mount Songshan was the center for Chan Buddhism during his time, with Mount Wutai being known for mysterious inspiration and Hengshan for practicing Buddhist precepts.[24] By the Kangxi period of the Qing, Mounts Wutai, Emei, Putuo, and Jiuhua had been canonized and built up as pilgrimage sites, and as was the case with Daoist mountains, imperial support, local gentry, literati, and "ordinary" pilgrims (nonelite) were all important to the establishment of the four sacred mountains. Essential to this were miracle tales locating a particular bodhisattva at each mountain home. Mount Wutai was most likely first established as the residence of Mañjuśrī Bodhisattva, followed by Mount Emei—the home of the Samantabhadra Bodhisattva, then Mount Putuo—the residence of the Avalokiteśvara Bodhisattva, and finally Mount Jiuhua—the location of the Kṣitigarbha Bodhisattva.

Mount Wutai—the "Five-Terrace mountain"—is a group of five mountains identified as the abode of Mañjuśrī Bodhisattva, and atop each of the peaks is a unique form of the bodhisattva.[25] As early as the 5th century, a legend circulated that Mañjuśrī was to be found at the site,[26] but it was in the 7th century that Chinese gazetteers began disseminating stories of apparitions of Mañjuśrī occurring at the site. Tales of such visions helped establish a cult of Mañjuśrī at Mount Wutai, and visual records of the bodhisattva's manifestations were mapped onto the mountain. The earliest Chinese texts placing Mañjuśrī on the Five-Terrace mountain come from the late 7th- to early 8th-century translations of the *Avatamsaka Sūtra*, the *Huayan jing*, and the *Mañjuśrī Precious Treasury of the Law dhāraṇī Sūtra*. Chinese supporters of a Mañjuśrī cult located at Mount Wutai used these texts as predictors of the bodhisattva's presence at the mountain.[27] In the first gazetteer about the mountain by Huixiang from the 7th century, frequent allusions to a passage from the *Avatamsaka Sūtra* were used to elevate the site's significance.[28] Pilgrimage sightings of the bodhisattva confirmed that the site was indeed the dwelling of Mañjuśrī, and such apparitions helped to sustain the mountain as sacred and worthy of devotional activity.[29] Patronage from significant individuals such as the tantric master Amoghavajra (705–774) also helped establish the site as sacred, poetry and artistic traditions located at Mount Wutai popularized the location in the imaginary, and finally miracle tales created a concrete connection between pilgrims and the bodhisattva at the mountain.

Regarding Mount Emei, predating its identification with Samantabhadra Bodhisattva, the site was a known abode of immortals. Over time, it gained popularity as a site where Samantabhadra manifested, and significantly during the Tang, the monk Chengguan pilgrimaged to Wutai and then Emei, and when annotating the *Huayan jing* "he praised Manjusri and Samantabhadra as two of the three saints of Huayan, which led to Mount E'mei being known as the 'Silver Realm' during the Five Dynasties period."[30] It was during the Tang dynasty that the transformation into a Buddhist mountain occurred, specifically in the mid-9th century after the persecution of Buddhism. Hargett explains that the monk Huitong contributed to the reconstruction of monasteries, suggesting that there was a modest-sized Buddhist community in place by the late Tang.[31] The mountain's origin tale that places Samantabhadra Bodhisattva at Mount Emei includes Master Pu, who had a sighting of the bodhisattva during the 1st century. This narrative was perhaps intended to spread the notion that Emei had been connected to Buddhist traditions for a long time. This tale aimed to establish a historical relationship between Buddhism and the mountain. But to reorient the landscape and domesticate Samantabhadra, scriptural authentication such as that from the *Surangama Sūtra* and the *Huajan jing* were necessary.

Mount Putuo is known as the home of the Avalokiteśvara Bodhisattva, and here, scriptures such as the *Avatamsaka Sūtra* were used to support the site as the place where the bodhisattva manifests. Tales of miracles occurring there further legitimized it as a sacred site, and the feminization of Avalokiteśvara in China was inseparable from the bodhisattva's domestication and localization. Furthermore, as is evident from the Putuo gazetteers during the Ming and Qing periods, pilgrimage inscribed meanings of sacredness onto Mount Putuo that helped transform it into the home of the bodhisattva. The stories of supernatural events were an essential component of the religious *imaginaire* and were at the center of texts regarding the sacred site.[32] Miracle tales included accounts of pilgrims making contact with Avalokiteśvara, and each of the Putuo gazetteers includes a section titled "efficacious wonders" that describes the miracles performed by the bodhisattva. During the late Tang period, a miracle tale circulated in which an Indian monk trekking to Putuo prayed to Avalokiteśvara and received a vision at the spot now known as the Cave of Tidal Sounds.[33] According to a 1361 gazetteer, in 848, when the foreign monk went to the cave, he burned his ten fingers to show his piety. "When the fingers were burned off, he saw the Great Being, who preached dharma to him and gave him a seven-hued precious stone. This was the first of many miracles of P'u-t'o."[34] Finally, the site's establishment benefitted from an origin tale regarding the Japanese monk Hui'e (Egaku). According to the legend, he tried to take a Guanyin image home from China but found his boat stuck near Mount Putuo. When he prayed to Avalokiteśvara, the bodhisattva guided him to a location on the island where he built a shrine. Reports of such visions led to royal patronage of the island, and they provided motivation for future pilgrims to travel to Putuo with the hope of receiving a vision of the bodhisattva.[35]

At Jiuhua, the Silla prince Jin Dizang (705–803) is said to have taken up residence at the site for cultivation practice; however, the site did not become famous because of him. Instead, it was a group of literati from the Song and Yuan periods called the Jiuhua Poetry Society (*jiuhua shishe*) that established Jiuhua as the home of Kṣitigarbha Bodhisattva.[36] By the Ming dynasty, the Three Great Sacred Peaks had appeared (Wutai, Emei, and Putuo), and the four great sacred peaks appellation that included Jiuhua may have appeared by the Wanli period but did not attain general consensus until the Kangxi period.[37]

Pilgrimage and the State. The canonization of the four great sacred peaks was the result of a long, dynamic process of Sinicization of Buddhism. Legends inspired travel to the sites, Buddhist scriptures confirmed the location as an enlightened being's home, and importantly, ongoing journeys by elite and nonelite pilgrims popularized and legitimized sites as sacred. Pilgrimages popularized locations and legitimized their association with a particular bodhisattva, and sources regarding the veneration of bodhisattvas at their mountain homes came from mountain guides, stone inscriptions, travelogs, and local gazetteers. Sources providing information regarding nonimperial patronage come from travelers' accounts, in particular gazetteers compiled by members of the local elite and produced with sponsorship from local officials. Ming and Qing gazetteers offer a unique genre of Chinese Buddhism and incorporate information regarding cultures, geography, history, tourism, and local officials. They provide accounts of pilgrims, pilgrim activities, sociopolitical contexts, and impressions of the sacred sites.

Considering imperial patronage, imperially supported temples plus poems and steles composed by emperors provide documentation of their support. Such patronage assisted in the expansion of temples and monasteries at mountain sites, which further supported pilgrimage. It is important to note that for a mountain site to be deemed "sacred" in China, it needed to be characterized as such. Over time, each of China's four sacred Buddhist mountains became centers of pilgrimage as a result of intentional processes led by political and religious leaders. At Mount Wutai, for example, Mañjuśrī has been seen as a protector bodhisattva of China since the 8th century and thus was the focus of imperial attention.[38] As detailed in "Pilgrimage in Daoist Traditions," imperial worship of mountains was an important component of Chinese politics, as mountains were the location from which to communicate with Heaven. This statecraft model was applied to worship of Mañjuśrī at Mount Wutai on the part of the state and survived throughout the Mongol, Chinese, and Manchu courts.

As Hargett details regarding Mount Emei, no single individual was responsible for redefining the mountain as a "Buddhist site"; it was a collective effort on the part of local Buddhists, lay supporters, and government officials. The Song emperors Taizu and Taizong in particular were central to this process, and while they may have had a personal interest in Buddhism, Song imperial support of Emei, as well as Wutai and Putuo, was political.[39] But the creation of a Buddhist sacred mountain was not without its challenges. One of the issues in transforming landscapes into Buddhist spaces connected to a particular bodhisattva was legitimacy. In the process of legitimizing a site as the home of a resident enlightened being, texts were evoked to confer the site's status as the mountain home of the associated bodhisattva, and temples and monasteries were built to create a local Buddhist community. But to sustain both the community and the site's identity as sacred, pilgrims were necessary.

Pilgrimage and Art. Related to the imaginary of a sacred site in China is the representation of the location and resident deities in art. As locations where the sacred manifests, mountains inspired pilgrims to create art (painting, poetry, eulogies, and songs) expressing patronage. These transmitted iconic views of a location, and paintings furthermore served as travel guides. Maps, such as those of Mount Wutai, demarcate a site's significance, and both visual and literary art reveal pilgrimage sites as locations of multiple levels of meaning and sites of Chinese and international communities.[40]

While on pilgrimage, devout Buddhists performed ritualistic acts such as three steps one bow—every three steps, the individual bowed. Furthermore, influenced by miracle tales and bodhisattva sightings, pilgrimage cults established centers for worshipping the resident bodhisattva, and such pilgrims contributed to the iconographic images, songs, and texts glorifying the bodhisattva. Such activities supported a site as one of spiritual significance, and financially, pilgrims provided patronage to local monastics through donations. They furthermore contributed to a mountain's local economy by staying at inns, dining at restaurants, buying souvenirs at shops, and so forth. But in addition to establishing a site as spatially significant in a spiritual sense, pilgrims also contributed to imaginaries regarding Buddhist locations that popularized a mountain's beauty.

"Elite" pilgrims (literati) wrote about a location's beautiful views in mountain gazetteers, and literary works by poets applauded a site's unique and remarkable environment. At Emei, for example, the works of Li Bo 李白 and Fan Chengda 范成大 popularized the site's exceptional landscape. "Of special importance here," Hargett writes, "is the dramatic nature of the mountain's topography and its remote location on the western border of China; the mountain's grotto system; the strange and unusual flora and fauna that populate Emei's landscape; and Buddha's Glory."[41] Important to the success of a mountain in terms of being popular was that the site was known (whether in a real sense or in the imaginary) as having a unique landscape. Bingenheimer's translations of Mount Putuo gazetteers confirm this. In his analysis of maps from the Hou-Tu Gazetteer 1590 [1598] (Putuoluojia shan zhi 補陀洛伽山志) and the Zhou Gazetteer 1607 [1641] (Chongxiu Putuoshan zhi 重修普陀山志) we see that visual representations of the meanings imprinted onto Mount Putuo show that the mountain's maps emphasized the site's impressionistic "'views' for the armchair traveler."[42] With later gazetteers, maps of Mount Putuo were not based on topography but on literature, and legends and poetry were weaved into the imaginary regarding how Mount Putuo was experienced. Elite pilgrims (the writers of gazetteers) were significant for a site's transformation into a Buddhist location, and their impressions of a location textualized a site as a series of shifting views. It is evident that literati played a critical role in developing a site's sacredness, and in regard to Putuo, views of the site included a Confucian–Buddhist synthesis.

Pilgrimage to Monasteries and Temples. Included in the Sinicization of Buddhism were the activities of Chan monks who reimagined locations as sacred and established Chan cultic sites. In the making of sacred sites beyond the four mountains discussed previously, monks as pilgrims established travel networks to sites associated with eminent monks, one of which was the range of Song Shan—the site of Shaolin Monastery, where the Chan patriarch

Bodhidharma was believed to have sat in meditation for nine years. In Chan ideology, pilgrimage does not, in theory, require any spatial journey. Instead, the transformative process can occur in the mind. However, in actual practice "the wanderings of the 'clouds and water' (*yunshui*), as Ch'an monks were called, soon became as structured as any pilgrimage, and both notions overlapped."[43] Like the construction of the four great Buddhist mountain sites, Chan cultic centers also developed around veneration of relics and stupas, but over time the goal of meeting a Chan master—a patriarch of the tradition—became a primary goal of disciples.[44] At times the hope of "meeting" a master meant coming into contact with a deceased patriarch, as in the case of Bodhidharma's residence at Mount Song. During the Tang, the school of martial arts was created there, and the site's lineage back to Bodhidharma was emphasized. This connection was a means of distinguishing it from other locations. As Northern Chan rose in status, monks from around China ventured to the mountain, and as famous monks continued traveling to the site, more monks were further inspired to travel there. Such journeys of monks as pilgrims helped establish Buddhist communities and sacred sites, while also creating pilgrimage networks linking Chan cultic centers.

An important aspect of Buddhist pilgrimage in Chinese traditions is the act of pilgrimaging to a temple to provide donations to monastic communities. Because of their ascetic lifestyle, monks and nuns are favored recipients of donations. They are "fields of merit," and by giving to the monastic community, an individual receives merit.[45]

> Any donation to the Buddhist sangha [community of monks and nuns] is like planting a seed in the "great field of merit"—it will grow and provide the donor with more than they originally donated... The accumulation of merit was one Buddhist option that could address their daily problems—illness, financial difficulties, and poor harvest—or their larger concerns about death and the afterlife.[46]

Within Buddhist traditions, undertaking a pilgrimage is a means of earning merit for the actor, and if one donates to a monastic community, the individual can transfer the merit earned to a deceased family member.[47] And if one transfers the merit earned, one increases the original merit that was generated.[48] Buddhist pilgrimage circuits in China therefore included cherished temples; these transactions of exchange were a foundation of Chinese Buddhist monastic economies, and donations to the sangha included providing land and monetary support.

The individuals who traveled to a pilgrimage site, the ways in which pilgrims imagined the location and inscribed meaning onto it, and the ongoing meanings associated with the site were important factors in its development. The building of Buddhist pilgrimage locations incorporated Chinese views on space and place, including the view of mountains as intermediaries between Heaven and Earth and as places where divine beings dwell. Importantly, each pilgrimage location was uniquely established and modified based on social and political influences, but the four great and famous Buddhist mountains were modeled on Mount Wutai's development into a Buddhist site. For a bodhisattva from a foreign land to be domesticated into the Chinese landscape, the enlightened being had to be localized. This was done by positioning legends and miraculous events at physical locations, but also by connecting a site to sutras. These activities, along with pilgrims, literati, and emperors providing patronage, legitimized a site as sacred. Over time, each of the four famous mountains was restructured by diverse actors in both the physical and the imaginary, and each was influenced by religious, cultural, and political events. Evident in the history of Buddhist pilgrimage sites in China is place-making as an ongoing activity, as well as sacredness as an identity whose meaning shifts over time.

PILGRIMAGE IN CONFUCIANISM

Of particular importance in pilgrimage related to Confucianism is the city of Qufu, Shangdong. As the home of Confucius, Qufu is a sacred place that attracted intellectuals to venture there. Whereas sacred mountains were pilgrimage sites for elite and nonelite travelers, Qufu was a site that attracted educated elites in particular. The Temple of Confucius (Kong Temple 孔廟) in Qufu was especially important to pilgrims, but as James Flath reveals, traveling to Qufu was very different from pilgrimaging to sacred mountains. Confucius did not become a popular cultic figure in imperial times, and even though there were monuments to Confucius on mountains such as Mount Tai, nonelite pilgrims did not have the compulsion to continue on from Mount Tai to Qufu to pay their respects at Kong Temple.[49] Qufu did not therefore, Flath argues, develop as a popular tour destination, complete with the reputation and infrastructure of popular mountain sites. Travel conditions furthermore hindered the site's development into the 20th century, as reaching Qufu is quite challenging.

Although in imperial settings Qufu did not receive the socially diverse range of travelers that nearby Mount Tai did, the community of educated elites that pilgrimaged to Qufu viewed it as a memorable destination. Shrines to Confucius were centers for veneration, and writer Bi Ziyan (1569–1638) compared Qufu's environment to that of the five sacred peaks.[50] Included in the pantheon of figures enshrined at Qufu are his immediate family members, male and female, plus chief disciples and intellectual successors (represented by statues or tablets). This grouping has been compared to canonized saints in Catholicism.[51] Qufu was of specifical significance not only for a cult of Confucius but also for official patronage. Imperial court representatives held seasonal rituals there, and dating back to the Tang, shrines venerating Confucius were ordered to be established. Following dynasties continued this, and the late imperial state sponsored renovations to the main shrine complex in Qufu.[52]

The memorial shrine to Confucius in his hometown of Qufu is not the only site of pilgrimage for individuals hoping to venerate the ancient teacher. As Julia Murray has uncovered in her work, from the 7th century onward temples for official worship were located throughout China. One of these is a shrine just outside Shanghai. In the 17th century, patrons believed it marked the location where Confucius's cap and robe were buried one thousand years following his death. Although the relics were unseen, devotees built a ritual complex at the site called Kongzhai. Here, pilgrims (predominantly scholarly elites) offered sacrifices to the ancient sage. The shrine was destroyed during the Cultural Revolution, and unlike some other sites honoring Confucius, it has not been rebuilt.[53]

PILGRIMAGE IN CHINESE ISLAM AND TIBETAN BUDDHISM

In northwest China, in the Xinjiang Uyghur Autonomous Region, holy sites (*mazar*) for the veneration of saints are scattered across the landscape. These shrines are composed of one or several tombs, a mosque, and a building for mystics.[54] Starting in the 10th century, Central

Asian and Persian merchants and missionaries began arriving in western China, bringing Islam with them. This was composed of Sunni traditions, plus Sufism. "Throughout the history of Islam in the region, believers have venerated the heroes of this religious heritage, that is to say convert kings, great proselytizers, holy fighters, learned men, pious zealots, mystical figures, and so on."[55] Considered to be saints and "friends of Allah," these individuals are seen as intermediaries between Muslim practitioners and Allah, and they have abilities beyond the ordinary human that include the ability to cure individuals. Holy sites are shrines where Sufi saints or their ancestors are buried, and they are locations for pilgrimage.

In western China, Muslim pilgrimages thus consist of journeys to a holy tomb, and such pilgrimages are different than the obligatory pilgrimage to Mecca. In Xinjiang, people visit the tombs of saints throughout the year, during religious festivals (e.g., the birthday of the Prophet Muhammad), or during religious periods in the year such as Ramadan (the month of fasting), and the sites are marked by tall branches with prayer flags placed there by believers who seek blessings from the saint interred there.[56] Both men and women participate in the veneration of saints, and while many of the large complexes have been turned into museums, small shrines in remote areas exist and pilgrimage continues.

At the shrine, practitioners recite prayers of request to Allah, circumambulate the shrine, and at times perform an animal sacrifice. The most popular rite is for pilgrims to bring a ritual object to the burial site of a Sufi shrine as a ritual offering. In a practice that is unique to Xinjiang, women create dolls from scraps of cloth and leave them on the shrine as a request for pregnancy. "These figurines are also used by shamans to cure children and to assist or to chastise people in love affairs."[57] Overall, Sufi shrines in Xinjiang are known as locations of spiritual magnetism—sites where one can communicate with spiritual powers for the curing of disease or for assistance with fertility. Some shrines are even associated with particular requests, such as the curing of a skin disease.

While on pilgrimage, practitioners historically incorporated Sufi performances including dancing and singing into the event, as well as trade fairs and festivals. Today, many of these festivals have been banned, but annual events such as the pilgrimage to the holy site of Imam Asim continue. "From Wednesday through Friday throughout the month of May the shrine is surrounded by bazaar booths and food stalls, and a wide range of activities like camel riding, wrestling, tightrope walking, magic shows, storytelling, and musical performances are available."[58]

By comparing Sufi traditions in western China to those especially of Tibetan Buddhist pilgrimage, what we find is a parallel regarding pilgrimage to sacred sites associated with known masters. Prior to Buddhism's arrival in Tibet in the 7th century, Bon traditions revered lakes, rivers, and mountains as sacred dwellings of gods and goddesses. After the arrival of Buddhism, many such sites were taken over and Bon deities were subdued as protectors of Buddhism. Over time, sites associated with esteemed masters, especially reincarnate lamas, became locations of pilgrimage, and while traveling, practitioners recite mantras and perform full prostration (dropping fully to the ground) after every three steps. In Tibetan traditions, monasteries, temples, stupas, mountains such as Kailash, and caves (especially Drak Yerpa, where Padmasambhava spent time meditation) receive pilgrims. The act of pilgrimaging to a holy site and performing ritual circuits creates merit for the practitioner, and a pilgrim is "one who circles a sacred place/person." Pilgrimage in Tibetan Buddhism is more than simply the act of traveling to a site of sacredness, and a pilgrim is identified by the ritual circumambulation performed at the end of the journey.[59]

Pilgrimage is a journey to go around or to encounter a sacred place, referred to as *né*.[60] "In the Tibetan language, the terms used for this ritual journey are nékor (*gnas skor*) or néjel (*gnas mjal*), meaning to go around (*skor*) or encounter/meet (*mjal*) a né or sacred place (*gnas*)."[61] *Né* carries the notion that the site is a place where sacred power resides, coming from deities, powers of an ancient Buddhist master, tantric deities, or a living Buddhist teacher. In the Tibetan imaginary of the natural world, both threatening and benign powers are believed to be present in the form of water spirits, terrestrial spirits, gods, and mountains. Given that the natural world is viewed as alive with powerful presences, human interaction with nature is very important and determines whether humans will benefit or suffer. Pilgrimage is thus a ritual journey to encounter né, as its transformative power can affect the pilgrim through "empowerment" or "blessing" (*jinlap* [*byin rlabs*]).

As Paul Donnelly explains, guidebooks often describe pilgrims as "ordinary people" or "excellent"/"holy people." Pilgrimage literature accepts the idea that advanced yogis will benefit greatly from traveling to a né, and their encounter will be more profound than that of an "ordinary" (noncultivated) pilgrim.[62] For laypersons or less advanced monks, pilgrimage is aimed at removing karmic transgressions or "pollution," referring to angering a supernatural being. While many ritual actions are aimed at removing such indiscretions, pilgrimage is seen as a particularly powerful form of ritual action. A pilgrim's arduous physical work, plus their encounter with an empowered landscape, creates a beneficial, transformative ritual.[63]

Another important aspect of pilgrimage in Tibetan Buddhism is the travels of pilgrims from Tibet to India. During the time of Buddhism's second transmission into Tibet, sites associated with the historical buddha were of particular importance to Tibetan pilgrimages. These included Lumbinī, Bodh Gayā, Sārnāt, Kuśinagar, Śrāvastī, Rājgṛha, Vaiśālī, and Saṃkāśya. "The accounts of the early pilgrims to India demonstrate that visiting all the major sites was ideal, but the Vajrāsana (the exact spot where the Buddha attained awakening) in Bodh Gayā was by far the most visited destination."[64] As pilgrimage routes developed further, in the west, Uḍḍiyāna was viewed as the source of tantric masters and lineages; in the north, the mythical Shambhala was sought; in the east, Wutai Shan was viewed as the mountain home of the Bodhisattva Mañjuśrī; and in the south, Potala was understood as the mountain home of the Bodhisattva Avalokiteśvāra.[65] The earliest account of Tibetans going on pilgrimage to India is from Chak Lotsāwa Chöjepal (*chag lo tsā ba chos rje dpal*, 1197–1264).

PILGRIMAGE IN MODERN CHINA

During the Cultural Revolution (1969–1979) religious activity was banned by the state, but since then rituals of pilgrimage have been revived and sacred sites have been restored. China's state-driven economic growth following market reforms in the 1980s encouraged individuals to travel around the nation and visit locations connected to Chinese history, culture, and heritage. On the local level, government officials contributed to the rebuilding of religious sites for the purpose of economic development based on tourism. Since the 1990s, local governments have supported and initiated the building or rebuilding of Buddhist and Daoist sites, but the atheist Chinese Communist Party maintains it does not support such efforts for religious participation.[66] Instead, they want to extract the economic benefits from religious tourism. Regarding Buddhist sites, examples include the local Shanghai government rebuilding the Jing'an Temple in 1997, local authorities creating scenic spots related to Buddhism around the Lingyin Temple in Hangzhou in 1999, authorities in Wuxi, Jiangsu Province erecting a 289-foot-tall "Lingshan Buddha" in the "Lingshan Scenic Culture Park" in 1997, and the opening of the Nanshan Buddhist Culture Park in Hainan with a 354-foot-tall statue of Guanyin in 2005.[67] State-owned nonreligious development companies essentially invest in "scenic parks" surrounding a religious site and contribute to temple reconstruction and the building of commercial outlets (i.e., hotels, restaurants, shops). Moreover, local governments also invest in infrastructural improvements such as roads, cable cars, train routes, and tour buses to easily assist individuals in their travels to and from a religious site. Each of the four famous Buddhist mountains has a tourism development company that manages the mountain's tourist center, transportation, entrance fees, publications, and promotions. In the case of the Mount Emei Tourism Company, 33 percent of its shares were sold on the Shenzhen Stock Exchange in 1997.

Religious sites receive government support because they have cultural assets that can be marketed for tourism. Additionally, religious relics inspire local governments to sponsor the rebuilding of temples to create transnational networks. Local governments in Zhejiang and Guangdong Provinces, for example, have brought together intellectuals and local historians to reawaken legends and compile stories of the Daoist deity Huang Daxian as part of their agenda to revive sites dedicated to the deity.[68] By gathering these tales, they collectively hope to reawaken religious memories, and given that memories are symbolic capital for soliciting overseas investment, local governments hope that through promoting cultural heritage, transnational networks will also be established.

Along with the revival of temples, the creation of scenic areas, and the reawakening of tales, legends, and miracle stories, local governments have furthermore supported the creation of festivals that celebrate local religious deities (in both Buddhist and Daoist traditions), with the intention of attracting visitors from the mainland and abroad. Interestingly, ethnographic studies have found that although the government has not given patronage to religious sites with the intention of reviving religious rituals or religious beliefs, the result has been a revival of pilgrimage. And the sites of religious tourism that survive are the ones that are deemed by visitors to be the most desirable in terms of spirituality. Case studies indicate that while a site's historical connections to a religious deity are significant, it must draw religious practitioners. A sacred site is maintained over time by its pilgrims. Considering that pilgrimage sites in China have historically grown through the steady support of pilgrims, it is not surprising that recent ethnography finds the most successful sites (in terms of visitor numbers) to be those considered to hold spiritual magnetism.

Recent scholarship tends to separate pilgrimage from tourism, with pilgrimage referring to explicit religious activities and tourism meaning nonreligious (secular) ones. Pilgrims and tourists have also been differentiated by their understandings of place. When traveling to a location, it is argued that the tourist views the place as peripheral while the pilgrim sees it as central.[69] The tourist travels away from home while the pilgrim heads *toward* a home of sorts. While such models of pilgrimage posit the pilgrim's journey as a sacred one, and the tourist's travel as a secular one, there is a great deal of overlap between pilgrims and tourists, especially in regard to notions of the sacred and the secular. Naquin and Yü suggest that understanding pilgrimage cross-culturally requires redefinition—pilgrimage is *any* journey to a sacred place to perform some religious act. Since traditional times in China, sightseeing, as well as other forms of entertainment, has been a common activity during travel, which is clear in the writings of mountain gazetteers.

Across China, religious culture is being reborn in a variety of ways, and revived pilgrimages are a significant contribution to this renewal. While local governments have invested in religious sites for economic and political reasons (similar to imperial settings), it is through the act of pilgrimage that sites are revived and legitimized as sacred. Rituals of pilgrimage indicate that individuals are searching for meaning beyond that which they can find in their nonreligious (secular) settings. As one pilgrim of Miaofengshan told writer Ian Johnson, "we're in a new era of uncontrollable desire and greed. The ancients found answers in these mountains. Maybe there is something for us to learn too."[70] As in imperial times, pilgrims in modern China travel to mountains to pay respect to deities, to revere particular gods/goddesses/bodhisattvas that are in residence at a site, to gain wisdom, for healing of diseases, and for fertility.

New forms of pilgrimage have also begun at temples and monasteries in attempts to modernize traditions. This is especially seen in the case of Buddhist temples. Longquan Monastery outside Beijing is leading the way in using technology to encourage both virtual and physical pilgrimage. Online, through the social networking application *weixin* (WeChat), blogs, and websites, individuals are able to receive guidance from respected Buddhist masters without going on a pilgrimage. However, Longquan's community also works to encourage physical pilgrimage and has created new models of visiting a temple. In 2015, the two-foot-tall robot monk Xian'er was "born" to spread Buddhist teachings. He is able to respond to questions, chant sutras, and sing songs. While he was being showcased at Longquan, on average, one thousand visitors arrived at the temple each day, hoping to capture a photo with him.[71] He was an attraction for the modern era, and while he is not always in residence at the temple, he is easily accessible through his WeChat account, online animations, and his cartoon series.

In addition to using technology to entice travelers and encourage individuals to become practitioners of Buddhism, monastic communities have also created temple stay programs, meditation retreats, small group sutra studies, and dharma camps. These are aimed at encouraging young Chinese to travel to temples, engage in Buddhist doctrine, and begin implementing Buddhist teachings into their daily life. Buddhist monks at Longquan are concerned with the ways in which young people are isolated today, as well as with Chinese society's attachments to fame and wealth.[72] One of their methods for altering this is to create short-term travel opportunities (rather than long-term pilgrimages) that include young people staying in residence at a temple or monastery. The method for reaching young people has been through entertainment online, with the intention of encouraging youths to participate in dharma assemblies, camps, or meditation retreats in which they experience monastic life, learn Buddhist teachings, and become inspired to improve their lives.[73] At the conclusion of such gatherings, a resident master transmits the precepts. If we consider pilgrimage to be any journey to a sacred site to perform a religious act, these are new forms of pilgrimage, and included in their itinerary is room for missionization.

REVIEW OF LITERATURE

Textual translations and analysis of literature dominate scholarship on Chinese pilgrimage, especially in regard to imperial settings. This includes translations of gazetteers, miracle tales, and court documents. Works have also identified the importance of steles and commissioned paintings and gardens representing pilgrimage sites. Regarding Buddhist sites, given its link to transnational communities, Mount Wutai has especially been examined. More work could importantly be done on Mount Jiuhua. For Daoist pilgrimage, the religious imaginary of mountains has especially been studied, plus the key elements in the transformation of mountain sites into pilgrimage locations. Ethnographic studies of sacred sites are providing rich investigations of pilgrimage in modern China, but more work is needed to examine ongoing constructions of sacredness.

FURTHER READING

Bokenkamp, Stephen R. *Ancestors and Anxiety: Daoism and the Birth of Rebirth in China*. Berkeley: University of California Press, 2009.

Chan, Selina Ching, and Graeme Lang. "Temples as Enterprises." In *Religion in Contemporary China: Revitalization and Innovation*. Edited by Adam Yuet Chau, 133–153. New York: Routledge, 2011.

Fu, Li-tsui Flora. *Framing Famous Mountains: Grand Tour and Mingshan Paintings in Sixteenth-Century China*. Hong Kong: Chinese University Press, 2009.

Johnson, Ian. *The Souls of China: The Return of Religion after Mao*. New York: Vintage Books, 2017.

Lopez, Donald S. R. *Religions of China in Practice*. Princeton, NJ: Princeton University Press, 1996.

Naquin, Susan, and Chün-fang Yü, eds. *Pilgrims and Sacred Sites in China*. Berkeley: University of California Press, 1992.

NOTES

1. James Benn, "One Mountain, Two Traditions: Buddhist and Taoist Claims on Zhongnan shan in Medieval Times," in *Images, Relics and Legends: The Formation and Transformation of Buddhist Sacred Sites*, ed. James Benn, Jinhua Chen, and James Robson (Oakville, Ontario: Mosaic Press, 2012), 69–90.
2. See Tian Tian 田天, *Qinhan guojia jisi shigao* 秦漢國家祭祀史稿 [History of Qin and Han state sacrifices] (Beijing: Sanlian shudian, 2015), 297–327; and Sima Qian 司馬遷, *Shiji* 史記 [Records of the Grand Historian] (Beijing: Zhonghua Book Company, 1982), 1371.
3. Terry Kleeman, "Mountain Deities in China: The Domestication of the Mountain God and the Subjugation of the Margins," *Journal of the American Oriental Society* 111, no. 2 (1994): 226–238, at 227–228.
4. Kleeman, "Mountain Deities in China," 228.
5. Flora Li-tsui Fu, *Framing Famous Mountains: Grand Tour and Mingshan Paintings in Sixteenth-Century China* (Hong Kong: Chinese University Press, 2009), 152.
6. Fu, *Framing Famous Mountains*, 152.
7. See Stephen Little and Shawn Eichman, *Taoism and the Arts of China* (Chicago: Art Institute of Chicago, 2000); and James Hargett, "Huizong's Magic Marchmount: The Genyue Pleasure Park of Kaifeng," *Monumenta Serica* 38 (1988): 1–48.
8. James Robson, *Power of Place: The Religious Landscape of the Southern Sacred Peak (Nanyue* 南嶽*) in Medieval China* (Cambridge, MA: Harvard University Asia Center, 2009).
9. Kleeman, "Mountain Deities in China," 230.
10. Kleeman, "Mountain Deities in China," 230–231.
11. Brian R. Dott, *Identity Reflections: Pilgrimages to Mount Tai in Late Imperial China* (Cambridge, MA: Harvard University Asia Center, 2004), 53.
12. Stephen Bokenkamp, "Record of the Feng and Shan Sacrifices," in *Religions of China in Practice*, ed. Donald Lopez (Princeton, NJ: Princeton University Press, 1996), 251–261.

13. Dott, *Identity Reflections*, 230.
14. Dott, *Identity Reflections*, 119.
15. Dott, *Identity Reflections*, 111.
16. Dott, *Identity Reflections*, 69.
17. Shin-Yi Chao, *Daoist Ritual, State Religion, and Popular Practices: Zhenwu Worship from Song to Ming (960–1644)* (New York: Routledge Studies in Daoism, 2011).
18. John Lagerway, "The Pilgrimage to Wudang shan," in *Pilgrims and Sacred Sites in China*, ed. Susan Naquin and Chün-fang Yü (Berkeley: University of California Press, 1992), 293–332.
19. Bin Wei, "A View of History from the Mountains: Daoist Hermitage in the Six Dynasties," *Journal of Chinese Humanities* 4, no. 2 (2019): 125–149.
20. Bernard Faure, "Relics and Flesh Bodies: The Creation of Ch'an Pilgrimage Sites," in *Pilgrims and Sacred Sites in China*, ed. Susan Naquin and Chün-fang Yü (Berkeley: University of California Press, 1992), 150–189.
21. Tansen Sen, "The Travel Records of Chinese Pilgrims Faxian, Xuanzang, and Yijing," *Education About Asia* 11, no. 3 (2006): 24–33.
22. Xinru Liu, *Ancient India and Ancient China: Trade and Religious Exchanges, AD 1–600* (Delhi: Oxford University Press, 1988); and Tansen Sen, *Buddhism, Diplomacy, and Trade: The Realignment of Sino-Indian Relations, 600–1400* (Honolulu: University of Hawai'i Press, 2003).
23. Tansen Sen, "Relic Worship at the Famen Temple and the Buddhist World of the Tang Dynasty," in *Secrets of the Fallen Pagoda: Treasures from Famen Temple and the Tang Court*, ed. Alan Chong (Singapore: Asian Civilisations Museum, 2014), 27–49.
24. See Sheng Kai, "On the Veneration of the Four Sacred Buddhist Mountains in China," *The Eastern Buddhist* 44, no. 2 (2013): 121–143.
25. Karl Debreczeny, "Wutai shan: Pilgrimage to Five-Peak Mountain," *Journal of the International Association of Tibetan Studies* 6 (2011): 1–133, at 3.
26. Sheng, "On the Veneration," 123.
27. Raoul Birnbaum, "Thoughts on T'ang Buddhist Mountain Traditions and Their Contexts," *T'ang Studies* 2 (1984): 5–23; Raoul Birnbaum, "The Manifestations of a Monastery: Shen-ying's Experiences on Mount Wu-t'ai in T'ang Context," *Journal of the American Oriental Society* 106, no. 1 (1986): 110–137; Raoul Birnbaum, "Light in the Wutai Mountains," in *The Presence of Light: Divine Radiance and Religious Experience*, ed. Matthew T. Kapstein (Chicago: University of Chicago Press, 2004), 195–226; Mary Anne Cartelli, "The Poetry of Mount Wutai: Chinese Buddhist Verse From Dunhuang" (PhD diss., Columbia University, 2002); and Susan Andrews, "Tales of Conjured Temples in Qing Period Mountain Gazetteers," *Journal of the International Association of Tibetan Studies* 6 (2011): 134–162.
28. Susan Andrews, "Representing Mount Wutai's Past: A Study of Chinese and Japanese Miracle Tales about the Five Terrace Mountain" (PhD diss., Columbia University, 2013), 6.
29. Robert Gimello, "Chang Shang-ying on Wu-t'ai Shan," in *Pilgrims and Sacred Sites in China*, ed. Susan Naquin and Chünfang Yü (Berkeley: University of California Press, 1992), 89–149; Robert Gimello, "Wu-t'ai Shan during the Early Chin Dynasty: The Testimony of Chu Pien," *Chung-Hwa Buddhist Journal* 7 (1994): 501–612; and Daniel B. Stevenson, "Tales of the Lotus Sutra," in *Buddhism in Practice*, ed. Donald S. Lopez (Princeton, NJ: Princeton University Press, 1996), 427–451.
30. Sheng, "On the Veneration," 124.
31. James M. Hargett, *Stairway to Heaven: A Journey to the Summit of Mount Emei* (Albany: State University of New York Press, 2006), 140.
32. Marcus Bingenheimer, *Island of Guanyin: Mount Putuo and Its Gazetteers* (New York: Oxford University Press, 2016), 77.
33. Chün-fang Yü, *Kuan-yin: The Chinese Transformation of Avalokiteśvara* (New York: Columbia University Press, 2001), 383.

34. Yü, *Kuan-yin*, 384.
35. Yü, *Kuan-yin*, 384.
36. Sheng, "On the Veneration," 124.
37. Sheng, "On the Veneration," 128.
38. Debreczeny, "Wutai shan," 6.
39. Hargett, *Stairway to Heaven*, 138.
40. Wen-shing Chou, "Maps of Wutai Shan: Individuating the Sacred Landscape Through Color," *Journal of the International Association of Tibetan Studies* 6 (2011): 372–388; and Natasha Heller, "Visualizing Pilgrimage and Mapping Experience: Mount Wutai on the Silk Road," in *The Journey of Maps and Images on the Silk Road*, ed. Philippe Forêt and Andreas Kaplong (Boston: Brill, 2008), 29–50.
41. Hargett, *Stairway to Heaven*, 139.
42. Bingenheimer, *Island of Guanyin*, 65.
43. Faure, "Relics and Flesh Bodies," 151.
44. Faure, "Relics and Flesh Bodies," 151.
45. Oliver Freiberger, "Profiling the Sangha: Institutional and Non-institutional Tendencies in Early Buddhist Teachings," *Marburg Journal of Religion* 5, no. 1 (2000): 1–6.
46. Michael Walsh, "The Economics of Salvation: Toward a Theory of Exchange in Chinese Buddhism," *Journal of the American Academy of Religion* 75, no. 2 (2007): 353–382, at 361.
47. Gunapala Piyasena Malalasekera, "Transference of Merit in Ceylonese Buddhism," *Philosophy East and West* 17, nos. 1–4 (1967): 85–90; Stanley J. Tambiah, *Buddhism and the Spirit Cults in North-East Thailand* (Cambridge, UK: Cambridge University Press, 1970); Richard F. Gombrich, "Merit Transference in Sinhalese Buddhism: A Case Study of the Interaction Between Doctrine and Practice," *History of Religions* 11, no. 2 (1971): 203–219; John Clifford Holt, "Assisting the Dead by Venerating the Living: Merit Transfer in the Early Buddhist Tradition," *Numen* 28, no. 1 (1981): 1–28; Heinz Bechert, "Buddha-field and the Transfer of Merit in a Theravada Source," *Indo-Iranian Journal* 35, nos. 2–3 (1992): 95–108; and Gregory Schopen, *Bones, Stones, and Buddhist Monks: Collected Papers on the Archaeology, Epigraphy, and Texts of Monastic Buddhism in India* (Honolulu: University of Hawai'i Press, 1997).
48. Walsh, "The Economics of Salvation," 361.
49. James A. Flath, *Traces of the Sage: Monument, Materiality, and the First Temple of Confucius* (Honolulu: University of Hawai'i Press, 2016), 165.
50. Bi Ziyan, *Shiyinyuan cang gao* *石隱園藏稿* [Stored manuscripts from the Garden Where Stones Are Hidden], 1781. SKQS edition.
51. Jesse Sloane, "Confucian Pilgrimage in Late Imperial and Republican China," *Sungkyun Journal of East Asian Studies* 17, no. 2 (2017): 163–190.
52. Sloane, "Confucian Pilgrimage," 165.
53. Julia Murray, "A Heavenly Aura: Confucian Modes of Relic Veneration," *Journal of the British Academy* 2 (2014): 59–99.
54. Alexandre Papas, "Pilgrimages to Muslim Shrines in West China," in *The Living Shrines of Uyghur China*, ed. Lisa Ross (New York: Monacelli Press, 2013), 11–17.
55. Papas, "Pilgrimages," 12.
56. Sanjyot Mehendale, "*Mazar* in Context," *Cross Currents: East Asian History and Culture Review* 3 (2012): 1–10, at 8.
57. Papas, "Pilgrimages," 14.
58. Papas, "Pilgrimages," 14.
59. Katia Buffetrille, "Pilgrimage in Tibet," *Oxford Bibliographies Online* (2017).
60. See Toni Huber, "Putting the Gnas Back into Gnas-skor: Rethinking Tibetan Pilgrimage Practice," in *Sacred Spaces and Powerful Places in Tibetan Culture*, ed. Toni Huber (Dharamshala, India: Tibetan Works and Archives, 1999), 79–80.

61. Paul B. Donnelly, "Where the Heroes and Sky-Goers Gather: A Study of the Saurata Pilgrimage," *Religions* 8, no. 157 (2017): 1–23.
62. Donnelly, "Where the Heroes and Sky-Goers Gather," 4.
63. For more on the general benefits of pilgrimage, see Toni Huber, *The Cult of Pure Crystal Mountain: Popular Pilgrimage and Visionary Landscape in Southeast Tibet* (New York: Oxford University Press, 1999).
64. Paul B. Donnelly, "Pilgrimage in Buddhist Tibet," *Oxford Research Encyclopedias*, 2018.
65. Toni Huber, *The Holy Land Reborn: Pilgrimage and the Tibetan Reinvention of Buddhist India* (Chicago: University of Chicago Press, 2008), 80–83.
66. Ji Zhe, "Buddhism in the Reform Era: A Secularized Revival?" in *Religion in Contemporary China: Revitalization and Innovation*, ed. Adam Yuet Chau (New York: Routledge, 2011): 32–50, at 40.
67. Ji, "Buddhism in the Reform Era," 40–41.
68. Selia Ching Chan and Grame Lang, *Building Temples in China: Memories, Tourism and Identities* (New York: Routledge, 2015), 45.
69. Justine Digance, "Pilgrimage at Contested Sites," *Annals of Tourism Research* 30 (2003): 143–159.
70. Ian Johnson, *The Souls of China: The Return of Religion after Mao* (New York: Pantheon Books, 2017), 381.
71. Yun Ke, "Finding Robot Monk Xian'er: Understanding Buddhism in Longquan Animation," *Journal of Visual and Media Anthropology* 2, no. 1 (2016): 7–24, at 13.
72. Courtney Bruntz, "Taking Tourism into Their Own Hands: Monastic Communities and Temple Transformations in China," in *Buddhist Tourism in Asia*, ed. Courtney Bruntz and Brooke Schedneck (Honolulu: University of Hawai'i Press, 2020), 144–160.
73. Shi Huikong, *Stories of Venerable Master Xuecheng* (Beijing: China Fortune Press, 2016), 100.

Courtney Bruntz

PRACTICES OF PROTECTION IN THE PALI WORLD

OVERVIEW

Principles of Protection. People may think of Buddhism primarily as a system of teachings and practices aimed at personal transformation, focused on self-mastery and transcendence. The goal is liberation from samsara, the unending cycle of suffering, death, and rebirth. The buddha's power stems precisely from his achievement of this goal. What has this to do with practices of protection? The buddha's attainments, arrived at through his realization of the *dhamma*, the truth, and his many lifetimes of meritorious action, limit the extent to which he is vulnerable to the vicissitudes of the mundane world. These vicissitudes stem from the inherent nature of all things summarized in Buddhist doctrine as impermanence, suffering (or, literally, insecurity), and the absence of an enduring, unchanging self. From the earliest times, people sought refuge from this, to share in the buddha's invulnerability by harnessing the power of the buddha, the *dhamma* (truth or Buddhist teaching), the sangha (monastic community), and other powerful entities. This was done through various means, leading to an array of protective practices in Theravada cultures.

Some early Buddhist texts teach that one should pay attention to seen sources of danger over which one has some control, especially the people we deal with on a daily basis. Treating them well, according to the values of the time, averts problems before they arise. Similarly, the purpose of many of the rules governing monastics enshrined in the *Vinaya* is to maintain harmony within the sangha and its host society, sensitive to both practical and psychological realities. These sources therefore look to our own ethical conduct and the need to pay attention to the expectations of others as a practical source of protection. The *Sīgālovāda Sutta* makes these points by explicitly reinterpreting existing devotional practices to the six directions to avert dangers from them, appearing to reject more ritualistic types of protective practice.[1] Nonetheless, more ritualistic practices such as the recitation of potent texts are also taught in the canon, including in the *Āṭānāṭiya Sutta*, which follows the *Sīgālovāda Sutta*. Moreover, one's vulnerability to obstacles that may apparently come out of nowhere means that tackling unseen sources of power is a pervasive feature of Theravada cultures. The desirability of anticipating unseen causes of danger underlies the importance of astrology, which, in turn, informs life decisions, as well as day-to-day conduct, such as when to make offerings at temples, and other types of evasive action to avoid the harmful effect of planetary conjunctions. People therefore seek protection by harnessing the power of various types of persons (human and nonhuman, both seen and unseen), texts, practices, and substances.

Sometimes such practices are obviously apotropaic, undertaken primarily with defense in mind, to mitigate against some anticipated danger or trouble. Sometimes they are practiced to invoke the power of the triple gem, specific spirits, or certain mantras to bring luck and achieve success. Some protective effects are seen primarily as side effects, the benefits accrued from practices that are primarily designed to be transformative, such as meditation or personal restraint through keeping precepts, or other meritorious action, *puṇya kamma*, such as worship or making offerings. Maintaining a mental state of lovingkindness, *mettā*, is believed to induce a beneficent response in others, including wild animals, and also to cause anyone with malevolent designs to feel as if their entire body is on fire, an agony only relieved by desisting from their intended course of action.[2] Protective practices may also be compensatory, seeking to invoke the power of meritorious action or the protective potency of external sources to delay or avoid the karmic consequences of one's bad deeds.

The paradox between the inevitability of death and suffering, according to the fruition and exhaustion of karmic consequences, and recourse to external sources of protection, is recognized within Theravada sources. For example, there is a protective set of verses called the *Unhissa-vijaya-gāthā*, "verses on the victory of the crown of the [buddha's] head," popular throughout mainland Southeast Asia because of their reputation for bestowing longevity, among other benefits. The story that narrates the origin of the verses tells of a deity who realizes his days in heaven are numbered and rebirth in hell is imminent. He desperately seeks a solution. While the chief of the gods explains that there is no way of avoiding the inevitable ripening of karmic consequences, the buddha then teaches that the verses can do just that, and the deity is able to postpone his death by reciting them.[3]

Sources of Protection. The belief in the benefits of contact with powerful persons, sounds, sights, and substances underlies many commonplace Theravada practices such as worship and offerings, water blessings, the recitation of protective texts, and the wearing of protective symbols, undertaken individually or as part of a community. Certain Buddhist texts, many of which are extracted from the Pali canon, are regarded as particularly efficacious.

The term *paritta*, literally "protection," refers to a class of such texts commonly recited for their protective properties. *Abhidhamma* texts, containing what for Theravada is the ultimate expression of the truth, are also used in this manner, especially in Myanmar. Many post-canonical and dense acrostic verses are also important. The recitation of protective texts, sometimes performed within a temporary enclosure constructed for the purpose, is a feature of almost all Theravada rituals, varying in length from a verse briefly uttered to entire cycles of texts recited in continuous rotation over a seven-day period. Some incorporate such recitation into their daily practice. The recitation benefits all within its hearing, whether human or non-human, and is believed to be both prophylactic, warding off dangers and overcoming problems, and benedictive, bringing good things and assuring success in an undertaking.[4] However, in this article, the term *protection* is used, which translates as *paritta*, because this is understood as a single concept throughout the Theravada world.

Physical substances, such as images, amulets, water, string, and sand, are also empowered during such formal recitation ceremonies. These substances then transfer the benefits to the people and places with whom they come into contact. Throughout Tai, Khmer, and Lao communities, monks sprinkle the water onto their congregations or onto items to be blessed using a small bundle of twigs dipped into a bowl of sacred water, while also chanting a further blessing. In Sri Lanka and Myanmar, it is string, tied around the wrist, rather than water, that is the primary conduit for extending *paritta*'s protective force. In Laos and neighboring regions, string is used by both Buddhists and non-Buddhists, because it is also associated with local spirit practices.

Paritta chanting is used in the consecration of buddha images throughout the Theravada world as one of a sequence of steps to empower the image, who, in turn, has the job of protecting the Buddhist teaching (*sāsana*) to ensure its five-thousand-year duration after the death (*parinibbāna*) of the buddha.[5] Tending to images then provides double protection: that of the buddha represented by the image and that of the protective rites used to empower it. Some images and places may be associated with additional protective powers because of their particularly auspicious history, association with particular kings, or precious constituents. The temple of the Mahāmuni image of Mandalay, associated with the buddha, the Indian emperor Ashoka, and local kings, is one of the most sacred sites in Myanmar.[6] The famous Emerald Buddha of Thailand, associated with the monk Nāgasena of the quasi-canonical *Milindapañha* text, is further connected with the 11th-century Burmese king Anawrahta and a series of other royal patrons.[7] Meanwhile in Sri Lanka, the Temple of the Tooth, housing a tooth relic of the buddha in Kandy, has long been associated with protecting the sovereignty of rulers of the island and the Sinhalese people.[8] It is not only the buddha or his representatives that are sought out for protection. All Theravada societies are host to a rich pantheon of supernatural beings. These may be external, such as the earth goddess, serpent god, and many tutelary deities (*anak tā*) important in Cambodia rituals, or the internal spirits (*praling* in Cambodia, *khwan* in several Tai-Lao dialects) associated with parts of the body, that need to be retained and appeased through recalling rituals to ensure or restore health.[9] People in lower Myanmar often make offerings to their local guardian spirits (*nats*) with the help of mediums, seeking help with anything from unexplained arrest to the success of one's crops, to the need to bring more customers to one's business.[10]

Another widespread physical source of protection is the amulet, made from a diverse range of potent materials, such as ground-up manuscripts of Buddhist texts; cremation ash; herbs and flowers in Cambodia, Laos, and Thailand; or something regionally specific, like the gold produced through alchemy by Buddhist wizards (*weikza*) in Myanmar. Amulets may be plain or consist of a simple Pali verse, but they usually represent a figure, ranging from different animals to a highly regarded figure, such an enlightened monk, or gods and figures from within or beyond the Theravada pantheon.[11] In mainland Southeast Asia, women's skirts and menstruation blood are regarded as powerful and dangerous for men. Yet in the case of mother and son, this relationship turns into a protective one, and an amulet made from the skirt the mother wore in childbirth protects him.[12] Perhaps unexpected within a Buddhist context are some of the more notorious types of amulets, such as those made from an aborted fetus in Cambodia and Thailand or humans sacrificed when laying the foundations of buildings in Cambodia and Burma. An untimely death causes the departed spirit to linger, and that spirit is then regarded as providing protection to the wearer or residents, respectively. This understanding of premature death reflects the Buddhist understanding that consciousness at death is the precursor to the rebirth consciousness and therefore influences the next rebirth. This means that a particularly early, sudden, or unpleasant death may cause a negative rebirth, including as a spirit at the place of death. Usually, Buddhists will try to help the departed move on to a better rebirth through the transference of merit, but in some protective practices, the trapped spirit is employed as a guardian of the holder of the object or of the place of death.[13]

Visual means used to harness the power of the buddha, dhamma, or sangha or other sources of power include potent diagrams, often referred to by the Indic term *yantra*, or a derivation thereof. The person who produces these diagrams will usually empower themselves and the substances used to employ them, as well as use special arrangements not necessarily visible in the final form to concentrate the protective power into the yantra. These yantras may be simple arrangements of letters, for example, the syllables of a particular goddess, or the words of the common homage to the buddha *na mo bu ddhā ya*, or longer, usually Pali, phrases such as the qualities of the buddha or the twenty-four conditions (*paccaya*) underlying all causality expounded in the *Paṭṭhāna*, the seventh and final text of the *Abhidhamma Piṭaka*. These are arranged into potentially complex patterns, the form sometimes reflecting the purpose. For example, in Cambodia, yantras in the form of complex, multilayered nets were used to block projectiles or hold back an enemy.[14] These diagrams may be augmented by auspicious symbols. Images of heroic figures or animals, such as tigers or serpents (*nāga*), as well as a whole host of figures can also be used in yantras. Yantras may be drawn onto cloth and then worn or placed in an area needful of protection, onto metal and then inserted under the skin, onto the skin as tattoos, or onto paper, which may be then pulverized and consumed.

PROTECTIVE TEXTS

The phrase "protective texts" refers to a wide range of texts, including mantras and syllables, which are used for prophylactic and benedictive purposes. Protective texts in Theravada cultures include a range of canonical and noncanonical *sutta* (teachings attributed to the buddha), *gāthā* "verses," *paritta* "protection" texts, and sections from the *Abhidhamma Piṭaka*, as well as abbreviations of texts. The terms *sutta*, *gāthā*, and *paritta* are not mutually exclusive, and the same text may come under more than one of these names. The term *paritta* is perhaps most commonly used to refer to texts when they are memorized and recited for protection, even if those texts also appear with other titles.

Diverse Repertoires of* Paritta *Texts. One of the earliest Buddhist texts explicitly taught for protection is the *Āṭānāṭiya Sutta* of the Pali canon. In it, the four deities who rule the four cardinal points visit the buddha and offer to teach him a set of protective verses. The verses identify deities and other supernatural beings of the different directions. Because these deities revere the buddha and his teachings, if anyone recites the *sutta,* they will protect that person from any hostile supernatural beings who have yet to follow the *dhamma.* This is in marked contrast with the reinterpretation of such a cosmology in ethical terms found in the *Sigālovāda Sutta,* which immediately precedes the *Āṭānāṭiya Sutta* in the canon.[15]

This text is among the earliest known lists of *paritta* texts, which are found in the *Milindapañha,* the commentaries (*aṭṭhakathā*), and the *Visuddhimagga* of Buddhaghosa and give nine titles in total.[16] The nine are (a) *Ratana,* (b) *Metta,* (c) *Khandha,* (d) *Mora,* (e) the *Dhajagga,* (f) the *Āṭānāṭiya,* (g) *Aṅgulimālā,* (h) *Isigili,* and (i) *Bojjhaṅga.*[17] A suffix, either *sutta* or *paritta,* is attached to each title such as the *Ratana Sutta* or the *Āṭānāṭiya-paritta.*

Different regions developed their own preferred repertoires of *paritta* at different periods. In Sri Lanka, there is the widely recited *paritta* text called the *Catubhāṇavāra,* "Four Recitations," found in a shorter recension of twenty-two texts and a longer recension of twenty-nine.[18] There are manuscripts of different versions of the Sri Lankan *Catubhāṇavāra* in Myanmar and in Thailand, but it is not recited there. In modern Myanmar, the most popular *paritta* collection consists of eleven texts and is known as the *Mahāparitta,* the "Great Protection." All but three of the eleven texts of this collection are named in the *Milindapañha* and commentarial lists. Another collection of *paritta* texts called the *Sīrimaṅgala-paritta* was compiled by the Sīrimaṅgala Paritta Association led by U Nu, the first prime minister of Myanmar, during the rains retreat of 1950. This *paritta* collection contains the eleven texts from the *Mahāparitta* and another twenty texts, to make thirty-one in total.[19] Thirty-one texts were chosen to bring protection to all the beings present in the thirty-one realms of the traditional Theravada cosmology.[20] The additional twenty texts include the *Dhammacakkappavattana Sutta,* the first sermon of the buddha; the list and summary sections of the twenty-four conditions (*paccayuddesa* and *paccayaniddesa*) found in the *Paṭṭhāna,* the seventh book of the *Abhidhamma Piṭaka*; and the *Mahāsatipaṭṭhāna Sutta,* famous for providing the textual basis of Burmese insight practice (*vipassanā*). Later *paritta* collections containing most of the thirty-one texts compiled by various monastic and lay authors of modern Myanmar seem to have been informed by the *Sīrimaṅgala paritta.* The two sections of the *Paṭṭhāna* and the *Dhammacakkappavattana Sutta* have become key components of the Burmese *paritta* tradition.

Among religious reforms initiated by King Mongkut (r. 1851–1868) of Thailand was the Ariyaka script adapted in the 1840s from Mon and Greek, intended as a universal written medium for Pali.[21] The first book printed in the Ariyaka script was Mongkut's edition of a chanting booking of eight protective texts, indicating how the harnessing of texts for protection could be at the heart of modernizing reform, in contrast to the rejection of protective practices as later developments by Western observers whose views otherwise often coincided with those of reformists. *The Royal Chanting Book* in Thai script compiled by Saṅgharāja Sā

Phussadeva under the sponsorship of King Chulalongkorn (r. 1868–1910), who continued Mongkut's reforms, has come to be regarded as the most important printed collection of *paritta* texts in Thailand. First published in 1880, making it to be one of the first Pali books to be printed, it has been reprinted regularly ever since. At the same time, when the Thai establishment published the first edition of the Pali canon in the same decade, they excluded many local and regional texts of Thailand that provide the richest evidence for protective practices. *The Royal Chanting Book* consists of various *paritta*s and *sutta*s, as well as condensed versions of the three sections of the Pali canon, the *Vinaya Piṭaka, Sutta Piṭaka* and *Abhidhamma Piṭaka,* under the titles *Phra Vinaya, Phra Sūtra,* and *Phra Paramartha,* respectively.[22]

Use of the Abhidhamma Piṭaka. The abridged version of the seven books of the *Abhidhamma Piṭaka* included in Sā's *The Royal Chanting Book* is also used for funerary chanting in Thailand, ensuring the safe and auspicious transition of the deceased to their next life. Meanwhile, in Myanmar, the whole *Abhidhamma Piṭaka,* particularly the five volumes of the *Paṭṭhāna,* is ritually chanted for protection by monastics and laypeople, either in groups or individually. The *Paṭṭhāna,* which explicates causality in terms of the innumerable ways in which mentality and materiality are interrelated, is seen as a representation of the buddha's omniscience and as a great defense against the decline of his teaching (*sāsana*). It is the most popular protective text in Myanmar. Buddhists in Myanmar believe that the *Paṭṭhāna* also guards against threats and dangers of any kind, pleasing helpful gods (*deva*) and warding off evil spirits, whom it scorches. To counteract the burning nature of the *Paṭṭhāna,* some people believe it should be recited along with the *Karaṇīyamettā Sutta,* the *paritta* text on loving-kindness, bringing a cooling effect to the reciter and others, including the maleficent spirits.[23]

While there is a distinctive emphasis on Abhidhamma in Myanmar, the protective power of *Abhidhamma* is also important in Cambodia, Thailand, and Laos, including as the set of seven sacred syllables drawn from the books of the *Abhidhamma Piṭaka,* namely, *saṅ* (for *Dhammasaṅgaṇi*), *vi* (for *Vibhaṅga*), *dhā* (for *Dhātukathā*), *pu* (for *Puggalapaññatti*), *ka* (for *Kathāvatthu*), *ya* (for *Yamaka*), and *pa* (for *Paṭṭhāna*).[24]

Protective Verses and Their Popularity. Other texts that may be chanted for protection include the *itipisogāthā,* a set of verses that recount the qualities of the "three gems," the buddha, dhamma, and sangha. The rearrangement of the syllables of these verses underlies mantra arrangements and yantra designs, including those used for tattoos in Cambodia and for candle yantra in Myanmar.[25]

A wide range of chants suitable for various auspicious occasions continue to be published throughout Southeast Asia. We often find a mixture of auspicious Pali words and vernacular glosses and explanations in such texts.[26] Some are commercially sold, others copied or memorized individually, and still others printed in batches for free distribution to mark various occasions. Burmese chanting pamphlets begin with a few Pali verses inviting the deities residing in all quarters of the world to come and listen to the words of the buddha and conclude by sharing the merit with them before sending them home. Noncanonical verses used for protection include the *Unhissavijayagāthā,* the *Mahādibbamanta,* and the *Jinapañjara-gāthā,* "Verses on the Victor's Armor."[27] A shorter text found within the *Mahādibbamanta* is the "Protective Chant of the Blessings of the Buddhas in All Directions," *Sabbadisabuddhamaṅgala Paritta,* which associates the buddha and his disciples with different points of the compass. Popular in Cambodia, it is sometimes found inscribed on the stones that mark the outer periphery of the sacred ordination enclosure of Cambodian temples.[28] The *Jinapañjara* is the most popular protective text in Thailand. It locates different buddhas, the triple gem, enlightened disciples of the buddha (arhats), and canonical *paritta* texts on different parts of the reciter's body, cloaking the whole body with powerful beings and texts. It is studied by monastic students at Buddhist universities and used as a ritual chant in Buddhist ceremonies by monastics and laypeople. Like the twenty-four conditions of the *Paṭṭhāna* in Myanmar, it is so pervasive that it is printed as color posters, cards, and yantra editions and in textbooks.[29]

A short text entitled *Sambuddhe-gāthā*, "Verses on the Buddhas," is a very popular protective text in Thailand and in Myanmar.[30] The Thai version of the text with three verses praises the 512,028, 1,024,055, and 2,048,109 Buddhas of the past, present, and future respectively, and their dhamma and sangha, invoking their protective power. The standard version of the text in Myanmar consists of only the first verse of the Thai version with one extra line, paying additional homage to innumerable "conquerors," that is, buddhas, each with their dhamma and sangha. The efficacy derives from the infinity of the triple gems invoked. In addition to these *gāthās*, shorter *gāthās*, as well as condensed acrostic verses imbued with the powers inherent in the Pali alphabet, composed by various monastic and lay literati, are widely used in Theravada societies as protective texts to bring about specific benefits and to safeguard against certain threats.

THE BROADER CONTEXT

Multifaceted Protection. Engaging in protective practices is usually multifaceted, not restricted to one type of mechanism. Seeking out tattoos and yantras has long been the practice of warriors in Southeast Asia, as part of their armor for protection during battle, a practice found to this day. In the modern day, protective practices may be the more acceptable face of protest, an act that may be at once religious, requiring respect, and provocative, drawing attention to a problem. During the Saffron Revolution of 2007, monks took to demonstration on the streets, seeking to avert the economic difficulties caused by the Burmese *junta*'s hike in fuel prices. At the same time, they recited *paritta*, seeking to allay fear and danger and convert the minds of all who listened to a state of lovingkindness.

The use of yantras and mantras has long been just one aspect of medicine within Theravada cultures. A modern adaptation of this was seen during the first major wave of the COVID-19 pandemic to hit Myanmar in March 2020. Buddhist monks had a comprehensive approach to containment. They were active in providing quarantine facilities at temples and meditation centers for returning migrant workers and quick to take up and encourage the use of masks, visors, distancing, and handwashing. They also introduced lockdown measures promptly to prevent crowds gathering at monasteries. These are all protective practices based on the emerging epidemiological understanding of causality. At the same time, they engaged in more traditional protective practices such as the chanting of *paritta*, especially the *Ratana Sutta*, even taking to the air in a helicopter to sprinkle sanctified water down onto the country from above. In the second wave, on the basis of an astrological calculation, a widely shared social media post from a monk encouraged people to chant the *Karaṇīyametta Sutta* nine times on

September 15, 2020 between 6:00 a.m. and 9:00 a.m. and sprinkle the *paritta* water at home in order to create a sacred barrier, a common practice in Myanmar. Such use of astrology in Buddhism is sometimes contested by reform-minded and modernist commentators, yet it is pervasive. Here the response to COVID-19 exemplifies the ways that protective practices may be multilayered, drawing on epidemiology, astrology, numerology, and *paritta,* as well as the status of the sangha. The sangha's status has in recent decades been extended to a further form of protection—environmental, with the symbolic wrapping of trees in saffron cloth to "ordain" them in areas of Cambodia and Thailand. This act sanctifies the trees against felling in response to the devastating deforestation that has blighted both countries.[31]

Power Dynamics. Ethnographic studies have examined the complex power relationships of Theravada Buddhist societies and the Buddhist cosmology that informs them.[32] Tannenbaum, working on power relationships between various beings in the context of Shan Buddhism, suggests that power is a basic, unquestioned part of the universe, and that power implies protection.[33] If one has access to a source of power, one is protected and this principle applies across the boundary between the seen and unseen or supernatural. People therefore turn to powerful people as well as to national, regional, and local deities for assistance.

Power can be shared and bestowed on one's followers. If one has access to power by dint of one's own religious conduct or restraint, or a meritorious act, or one's own store of perfection (*pāramī*), or through invoking powerful beings, objects or chants, then one can share that with others. Power is not constant or equally distributed throughout the universe: some beings have great power, others have little.[34] Power can be lost, either because the merit that contributed to it is used up or because one breaks the conditions of the power, for example, by breaking the precepts imposed with tattoos or the vow that sealed the pact with the source of power.

For Theravada Buddhists, the greatest power is held by the buddhas, that is, previous buddhas, the present buddha of this world (Gotama Buddha), and the next buddha of this world (Ariya Metteyya). These may be as a set of the five most recent buddhas, or of twenty-eight, or of innumerable numbers of past, present, and future buddhas. Although Gotama and other buddhas are no longer present, their power continues, often concentrated within the physical representations of them, such as relics and images, or in narrations of their great attainments or conceptualized as the ten qualities that they perfected, which are mobile and transferrable. The power of these representations may be enhanced. For example, images may contain protective texts, symbols, and even representations of organs, such as hearts and lungs within the structure of the image.[35]

Beings in the lowest hells have the least power. Gods, humans, and spirits generally rank somewhere in the middle and essentially are the same in terms of their experiences in that they can all feel pain and pleasure and are all subject to death. Gods, who reside in heavens, are regarded as more powerful than humans and mainly benevolent. One may interact with the gods not only through offerings, priests, and mediums but also through meditative states and through the recitation of *parittas* and of *Abhidhamma*. Gods from all realms and directions, including the highest formless (*arūpaloka*) realms of the Buddhist cosmology, will come to listen to *Abhidhamma* and contribute their protection.

Within the human realm, access to power often reflects social stratification, and thus the rich and the ruling class assume the apex of society because of their accumulated merit and perfection.[36] Nonetheless, there is some space within Theravada societies for the securing of power by those who are ordinarily powerless, such as spirit mediums and astrologers. Those in Bangkok, for example, are often from poor working-class and migrant backgrounds yet have transformed themselves to sources of power and protection.[37] Such roles may also give a place in society to those whose identities are otherwise marginalized, such as members of minority groups, as well as nonbinaries and nonheterosexuals, whose identity is criminalized in countries with a British colonial history.

The term *spirits* is often used to translate several different Pali and vernacular words, as a broad term to refer to some of the denizens of heavens and also of this realm, residing alongside humans. Humans are in general more powerful than spirits, although spirits may have specific areas of power, requiring negotiation. The power relationships between humans and spirits are rather complex because of the impact of one's karma and its effects on the relative power positions. For example, spirits may help humans if one keeps precepts or does wholesome deeds, an idea that can be traced to the Pali sources.[38] In contrast, spirits may harm or hinder humans if one's morality is in question. Spirits can harm humans when the bad karmic effects of the previous unwholesome karma have arisen.[39] On the other hand, some spirits and local deities demand the contested breaking of Buddhist precepts or doctrinal ideals, enjoying alcohol, blood sacrifice, or abandoned possession.[40]

A hierarchy of power also pertains to language and to physical objects. Pali, the sacred language in which the teachings of the buddha are recorded, and the Pali terms that relate to the three "gems," that is, the buddha, dhamma, and sangha, have the greatest power, from single significant syllables to full Buddhists texts, in written, oral, or visual form. Statements of truth may also offer protection, an ancient pan-global belief that informs customs of ancient India and is reflected in early Buddhist narratives.[41] As might be expected, buddha images and relics top the hierarchy of physical objects, although dangerous and lewd language and objects may also be sources of protection. Protective practices therefore relate to how one harnesses the potency of such powerful and usually beneficent beings, words, and objects; persuades those who may grant the favor of their power; or thwarts the power of those that might be disruptive.

The Economy of Protective Practices. An economy surrounds protective practices. This is broader than the offerings or fees made to those who perform them.[42] Sites associated with potent protection become the focus of pilgrimage, generating bus tours, tourism, stalls for offerings, as well as accommodation, hospitality, and vendors of various kinds. Popular sites may be associated with the buddha or his relics, such as Wat Unnalom in Cambodia containing a hair from the circle of hair between the buddha's eyes, the Temple of the Tooth in Sri Lanka, or the hair-enshrining Shwedagon Pagoda in Myanmar, or with important gods, such as the temple to the god Kataragama in Sri Lanka. New sacred sites develop, for example, when a revered monk or nun regarded as enlightened dies and their relics are enshrined. Recent examples are the shrine of the nondecayed body of the late Sunlun Sayadaw U Kavi (1878–1952) of Myanmar and that of Mae Chee Kaew (1901–1991) of Thailand.[43] Amulets associated with prestigious monks, one of many types of amulets used throughout Southeast Asia, may be issued to raise funds for specific occasions in Thailand or for the annual monastic fairs.

The contribution of protective practices to local economies may be extensive as Justin McDaniel points out in relation to such fairs: "Food vendors, carnival ride operators, astrologers, the renters of sound equipment (mics, speakers, stages, cables, etc.), local shop keepers, souvenir makers, florists, motel owners, charter bus companies, and the like" all profit from this activity.[44] The trade in amulets takes place throughout Thailand, including at dedicated markets, magazines, and online sales. In some cases, high prices—hundreds of thousands of US dollars—are placed on certain amulets, because of the miraculous powers attributed to them, and this has triggered violent robberies.[45]

Historical Evidence. Protective practices are a feature found in all forms of Asian Buddhism. While the broad principles, such as the harnessing of the triple gem, sacred texts, potent diagrams, and the power of the virtuous, are shared, the specifics within Theravada are usually particular to the tradition, and even to a specific region. Even where Theravada, with its emphasis on Pali textual authorities and a more limited pantheon, appears to share a protective practice with Mahāyāna, the route of transmission and basis of similarity often remains conjecture.[46] Even the *Unhissavijayagāthā*, which has a recognizably shared name and narrative to the popular Mahāyāna protective texts the *Uṣṇīṣavijayadhāraṇī*, is, in fact, different in both content and range of applications.[47]

Literary and archaeological evidence indicates that many of the protective practices observed in contemporary Theravada can be traced back to ancient times, the Pali canon, or even older Indic precursors, while others have spread under the influence of particular cultures. The popular *Unhissavijayagāthā* may have transferred from Chinese culture.[48] The symbolic syllables, such as *na mo bu dhā ya*, and the condensation of the seven books of the *Abhidhamma* in summary, well known throughout Thailand and beyond, are found inscribed in distinctive patterns with auspicious marks in 15th- to 16th-century stone slabs and gold leaves from Sukhodaya. They may have spread to Thai culture more broadly with the mass movements of people from there to repopulate Ayutthaya toward the end of the 16th century.[49] The special format of the *Abhidhamma* texts inscribed on the stone slabs is indicative of how *Abhidhamma*, known as the analytical and scholarly vein of Theravada that seeks to explain how causality and transformation takes place, has also long been embedded within other cultures of causality: word and alphabet alchemy and magic diagrams. Looking more closely at the cultural context within which these practices developed may help us understand the worldview which underlies them. For example, the formation and use of yantra in Cambodia relate to the transformative process of traditional Pali grammar, the chemical processes for purifying mercury and gold, as well as to complex rearrangement of scared Pali phrases, imbued with layers of esoteric meaning, distinctive to the region.

PROTECTING THE BUDDHA'S *SĀSANA*

In thinking of protective practices, we tend to think in terms of protection for individual people or groups. However, the availability of Buddhist teaching, the *dhamma*, is not inevitable and itself requires protection. Once the buddha is no longer present in the world to safeguard his teachings and provide new ones, the institutions such as the sangha and texts he has set up (collectively termed the *sāsana*, "mission" or "dispensation") begin to decline. As they decline, personal transformation becomes harder to attain. Human society and the environment also degrade. In response to the feared decline of the *sāsana*, a whole range of other practices that we might term protective have been followed. These include *saṅgīti*, "councils" to revise the Pali canon in order to ensure the continued availability of the *saddhamma*, true or "unadulterated" teachings; reviews of monks' conduct in relation to the *vinaya* rules to ensure correct monastic practice; and revivals of meditation and learning of Abhidhamma to ensure correct personal practice and access to transformative insight.[50] While other more political or economic motives may sometimes be discerned in the background, these activities cover three aspects of the *sāsana* essential for its survival: "study," *pariyatti*; "practice," *paṭipatti*; and "realization," *paṭivedha*. Such revival movements have taken place at points of crisis, such as at 1,000 years or at 2,500 years after the death of the buddha, the midway point in the predicted 5,000-year duration of the *sāsana*.[51] The latter also coincided with the European colonial period, with the attendant warfare, cruelty, looting and destruction of sacred sites, and disruption seen as particularly threatening to the survival of Buddhism. The colonial and early independence period therefore saw attempts throughout the Pali world to ensure the texts, practices, and understanding of Buddhism were authentic. These inspired reforms, quests to revive Buddhism as the buddha had taught it, as well as critiques of practices, are regarded as later accretions. These broader protective practices have shaped Theravada history, texts, and practice. They underlie Theravada's apparent conservatism as practitioners sought to reinvoke the pristine teaching from the time of the buddha to ensure its ongoing presence. They inspired the revival of meditation in the late 19th to mid-20th century, which, in turn, informed the modern spread of Buddhist-based meditation practices globally. They also inspired the modernization of monastic curricula in some part of the Theravada world such as Thailand, but the anti-secularist approach to monastic education in Burma (later Myanmar), with an emphasis on the study of *Abhidhamma* literature. This principle of protecting the *sāsana* has informed, or been used to justify, activities to control religious beliefs, practices, and expression, such as through the ecclesiastical court system (*vinicchaya*) in Myanmar.[52] Militaries and governments may also take this principle of protection as the basis for other systems of control, from the conversion of ethnic minorities and other non-Buddhists to staging a coup d'état.

CRITICISM OF PROTECTIVE PRACTICES

Protective practices that have been culturally accepted may fall out of use, come under scrutiny, and even be rejected. Some have been critiqued by scholars and reformists. Sometimes this critique is on doctrinal grounds. This might be a perceived lack of compliance with the self-reliance implied by the law of karma, belief in a pantheon that has fallen out of fashion or has become associated with a different group in the essentialization of what it means to be Buddhist, or reflects a mechanism that is no longer understood and no longer deemed Buddhist. Sometimes it is attributed to a rise in commercialism, especially in Thailand.[53]

Some critique relates to practical consequences. Burmese critics in the colonial period, including monks, worried that an excess of generosity toward the sangha or the payment for protective rites might further impoverish people already suffering from the economies of extraction to which they were subject. Reformers in Bangladesh and elsewhere during this period also criticized animal sacrifice as un-Buddhist, based on its repeated rejection in the canon, although animal sacrifice tends to continue alongside other forms of protection in many Buddhist societies. In the modern period, criticism of offerings and animal release practices might result from the environmental damage or harm to animal welfare that these practices newly entail because of commercialization, commodification, and the use of plastic. Another issue is whether the reliance on the magical intervention of protective practices, from virtuous behavior to chanting, absolves practitioners from the challenge of tackling abuses of power. This critique can be directed as much to canonical stories, such as the long-suffering wives whose virtue is praised in the *Vimānavatthu*, as to the modern-day engagement with political or domestic oppression. At the opposite end of the spectrum, we see members of powerful elites seeking to shore up popular support or compensate for abuse of power by public displays of large donations to prestigious pagodas, monasteries, or monks. The extent to which this is a cynical exercise or entails the compartmentalization of different Buddhist values is unclear.[54]

REVIEW OF LITERATURE

Protective practices are highly visible in ethnographic studies but mostly invisible in textual studies until recently. The assumption that texts and doctrines are the primary means of defining Theravada Buddhism may be a vestige of the colonial gaze particularly from a Protestant Christian or secularist perspective. Perhaps because unencumbered by Protestantism, some of the earliest studies to recognize the vernacular literature of mainland Southeast Asia came from scholars within the French colonial administration, such as Adhémard Leclère (1853–1917) and Louis Finot (1864–1935), founding director of the École française d'Extrême-Orient (EFEO). EFEO scholars such as François Bizot and Louis Gabaude have continued to document the practicalities of Cambodian, Lao, and Thai Theravada, revealing a rich culture of somatic practice across salvific and protective functions of religion.[55] Because of the overlap between protection and healing, medical anthropology is also an important resource.[56] Studies informed by an Indological emphasis on classical texts or by Weberian sociology have sought to explain the place of protective practices in a religion regarded as structured toward personal transformation. Peter Harvey has offered an important response by showing that protective practices are found in the canon and work through mechanisms such as the power of truth and the triple gem.[57] Eviatar Shulman's recent work takes this further, examining closely the metaphysical mechanisms implicit in key *paritta* texts to indicate the efficacy of *paritta*, relating the unique ontological position of the buddha in the Buddhist cosmos. Everything including benign and malevolent beings orient toward the buddha whose realization and substantiation of the truth thereby gives them direct access to the protective power that he thus embodies.

Themes that emerged in grappling with these contrasted aims of Buddhist practice are religious syncretism, the continuation of brahminical religion through Buddhism, the broadening scope of Buddhism to accommodate the needs of nonelite practitioners, the incorporation into Buddhism of underlying religion, or Buddhism as a nominal veneer over indigenous practice. Questions include whether such practices go against the doctrines of no-self, the buddha's absence, and individual karmic responsibility. Pioneering anthropological studies addressing these questions include Melford Spiro's books on Burmese Buddhism, Richard Gombrich's work on Sri Lanka, and Stanley Tambiah's books on Thai Buddhism.[58] Spiro's

Burmese Supernaturalism focuses on how the *nat* cult is in conflict with Buddhist doctrines and ethos. His *Buddhism and Society* provides a useful threefold analysis of Theravada practice according to purpose, nibbanic, kammatic, and apotropaic, with protective practices in this final category. Gombrich offers an analysis according to the state of mind of practitioners, between cognitive, based on the rational understanding of the buddha's message of self-reliance, and affective, based on the psychological need for support to deal with life. Tambiah documents a variety of Tai-Lao rites through which humans interact with spirits at the cosmological to bodily level, identifying adaptations from early Buddhism.

Bridging the big tradition and little tradition divide, Donald Swearer's work draws on history, literature, and fieldwork to document the complex processes underlying protective power, including the empowerments that bring buddha images to life.[59] B. J. Terwiel, in his pioneering *Monks and Magic*, consciously eschews "big tradition" approaches to provide a close consideration of the lived reality of Thai Buddhists, documenting many everyday protective practices including tattooing.[60] In his documentation of the history, texts, arts, and changing practices of Tai ethnic groups, Terwiel often focuses on why practices are pursued from his informants' standpoint, not on doctrine. He is comfortable with the term *magic*, often avoided for its historically pejorative use to dismiss efficacy. Tannenbaum places efficacy at the heart of her study of Shan communities, analyzing Buddhist and non-Buddhist practical religion according to hierarchies of power and protection.[61] Meanwhile, Nancy Eberhardt's work on Shan Buddhist practices is innovative in foregrounding laypeople and women rather than monastics.[62] Important close documentation of Sri Lankan *paritta* practices, informed by a strong textual foundation, has been provided by Hamalawa Saddhatissa, Lily de Silva, and G. A. Perera.[63]

Studies that build on this attention to regional practice challenge preconceptions about Theravada. Anne Blackburn shows how *paritta* texts were historically, and remain, a key part of educated monasticism, informing commentarial compositions and identity. She thus challenges earlier ethnographic accounts of *paritta* recitation as an accommodation of the needs of laypeople and demonstrates how monks engage with *paritta* texts beyond the ritual arena.[64] Kate Crosby has also challenged the perceived dichotomy of pragmatic and nibbanic religion. She has shown that both approaches are employed by the same actors and share mechanisms for bringing about change paralleled in sciences such as medicine, chemistry, and grammar.[65] Pyi Phyo Kyaw has reappraised the place of Abhidhamma in Burmese Buddhism, showing that, far from being a scholastic exercise, Abhidhamma is used as the basis of spiritual and protective transformation. Her work also expands the category of protective texts beyond the focus on *paritta*.[66]

Adding epigraphy to texts and fieldwork, Peter Skilling's extensive contribution to the subject demonstrates how protective practices have long enriched Buddhist traditions. He documents techniques of abbreviation that condense long canonical texts into short phrases and syllables. With the Sambuddhe verses, he challenges the assumption that only one buddha is relevant for Theravadins, tracing the evolution of the concept of multiple buddhas.[67] Justin McDaniel redirects us to consider the function of protective practices within society, including the materiality and economy of amulets, through narrative and close observation of contemporary culture. He also draws attention to Thai writings on the subject.[68] Bringing multiple scholars together is now proving productive in revealing the diversity and dynamics of protective texts and practices, such as Cicuzza's edited volume on protective texts of Southeast Asia, and Bénédicte Brac de la Perrière's on the long-neglected subject of Burmese *weikza*.[69]

An important shift in perspective has been the attention paid to ways in which anxieties about the survival of Buddhism have shaped the history and forms of Theravada practice, including works by Erik Braun and Alicia Turner on Burmese responses to colonialism.[70]

FURTHER READING

Bizot, François, and Oskar von Hinüber. *La guirlande de Joyaux. Textes bouddhiques du Cambodge* II. Paris: École Française d'Extrême-Orient, 1994.

Brac de la Perrière, Bénédicte, Guillaume Rozenberg, and Alicia Turner, eds. *Champions of Buddhism: Weikza Cults in Contemporary Burma*. Singapore: NUS Press, 2014.

Cicuzza, Claudio, ed. *Katā me rakkhā, katā me parittā: Protecting the Protective Texts and Manuscripts: Proceedings of the Second International Pali Studies Week*. Materials for the Study of the Tripiṭaka, Volume 14. Bangkok and Lumbini, Nepal: Fragile Palm Leaves and Lumbini International Research Institute, 2018.

De Silva, Lily. "The Paritta Ceremony of Sri Lanka: Its Antiquity and Symbolism." In *Buddhist Thought and Ritual*. Edited by David Kalupahana, 139–150. New York: Paragon House, 1991.

Eberhardt, Nancy. *Imagining the Course of Life. Self-Transformation in a Shan Buddhist Community*. Honolulu: University of Hawai'i Press, 2006.

Harris, Ian. *Cambodian Buddhism. History and Practice*. Honolulu: University of Hawai'i Press, 2005.

Harvey, Peter. "The Dynamics of Paritta Chanting in Southern Buddhism." In *Love Divine: Studies in Bhakti and Devotional Mysticism*. Edited by Karel Werner, 53–84. Surrey, UK: Curzon Press, 1993.

McDaniel, Justin Thomas. *The Lovelorn Ghost and the Magical Monk: Practicing Buddhism in Modern Thailand*. New York: Columbia University Press, 2011.

McDaniel, Justin Thomas. "The Material Turn: An Introduction to Thai Sources for the Study of Buddhist Amulets." In *Material Culture and Asian Religions: Text, Image, Object*. Edited by Benjamin Fleming and Richard Mann, 135–148. New York: Routledge, 2014.

Merrison, Lindsay. "Friends in Higher Places." 88mm documentary, DVD. DER Documentary, 2001. https://store.der.org/friends-in-high-places-p832.aspx.

Patton, Thomas. "In Pursuit of the Sorceror's Power: Sacred Diagrams as Technologies of Potency." In *Champions of Buddhism: Weikza Cults in Contemporary Burma*. Edited by Bénédicte Brac de la Perrière, Guillaume Rozenberg, and Alicia Turner, 150–153. Singapore: NUS Press, 2014.

Perera, G. Ariyapala. *Buddhist Paritta Chanting Ritual: A Comparative Study of the Buddhist Benedictory Ritual*. Dehiwala, Sri Lanka: Buddhist Cultural Centre, 2000.

Saddhatissa, Hammalawa. "The Significance of Paritta and Its Application in the Theravāda Tradition." In *Buddhist Thought and Ritual*. Edited by David J. Kalupahana, 125–138. New York: Paragon House, 1991.

Shulman, Eviatar. "The Protective Buddha: On the Cosmological Logic of Paritta," *Numen* 66 (2019): 207–242.

Skilling, Peter. "The *Rakṣā* Literature of the *Śrāvakayāna*." *Journal of Pali Text Society* 16 (1992): 109–182.

Spiro, Melford. *Burmese Supernaturalism: A Study in the Explanation and Reduction of Suffering*. Englewood Cliffs, NJ: Prentice Hall, 1967.

Swearer, Donald. "A Summary of the Seven Books of the *Abhidhamma*." In *Buddhism in Practice*. Edited by Donald S. Lopez Jr., 336–342. Princeton, NJ: Princeton University Press, 1995.

Swearer, Donald K. *Becoming the Buddha: The Ritual of Image Consecration in Thailand*. Princeton, NJ, and Oxford: Princeton University Press, 2004.

Tannenbaum, Nicola. *Who Can Compete against the World? Power-Protection and Buddhism in Shan Worldview*. Ann Arbor, MI: Association for Asian Studies, 1995.

Terwiel, Barend Jan. *Monks and Magic: An Analysis of Religious Ceremonies in Central Thailand*, 4th rev. ed. Copenhagen: NIAS Press, 2012.

Turner, Alicia. *Saving Buddhism: Moral Community and the Impermanence of Colonial Religion*. Honolulu: University of Hawai'i Press, 2014.

Walker, Trent. *Until Nirvana's Time: Buddhist Songs from Cambodia*. Boulder, CO: Shambhala Publications, 2022.

NOTES

1. Sigalovada Sutta: The Discourse to Sigala (*Dīgha Nikāya* 31), translated from the Pali by Narada Thera. *Access to Insight* (*BCBS Edition*) (November 30, 2013). For discussion see Sarah Shaw, *The Art of Listening: A Guide to the Early Teachings of Buddhism* (Boulder, CO: Shambhala, 2021), 207–221.
2. Tsunehiko Sugiki, "Warriors Who Do Not Kill in War: A Buddhist Interpretation of the Warrior's Role in Relation to the Precept against Killing," *Religions* 10, no. 11 (2020): 530.
3. Gregory Kourilsky, "The Uṇhissa-Vijaya-Sutta in Laos and Thailand: A Philological Approach," in *Katā me rakkhā, katā me parittā: Protecting the Protective Texts and Manuscripts, Proceedings of the Second International Pali Studies Week*, Materials for the Study of the Tripiṭaka Volume 14, ed. Claudio Cicuzza (Bangkok and Lumbini, Nepal: Fragile Palm Leaves and Lumbini International Research Institute, 2018), 12–13. Kourilsky analyses the differences between these verses and the protective *dhāraṇī* of the same name that circulates in Mahāyāna cultures and is associated with longevity.
4. Lily de Silva, "The Paritta Ceremony of Sri Lanka: Its Antiquity and Symbolism," in *Buddhist Thought and Ritual*, ed. David J. Kalupahana (Delhi: Motilal Banarsidass, 1991), 147.
5. Donald K. Swearer, "Consecrating the Buddha," in *Buddhism in Practice*, ed. Donald S. Lopez (Princeton, NJ: Princeton University Press, 1995), 57.
6. Pyi Phyo Kyaw and Kate Crosby, "The Buddha and His Brothers: Expressions of Power, Place and Community by the Network of Mahāmuni Images of Arakan, Bangladesh and Burma," in *Art of Merit: Studies in Buddhist Art and Its Conservation*, ed. David Park, Kuenga Wangmo, and Sharon Cather (London: Archetype Publications, 2013), 263–274.
7. Angela S. Chiu, *The Buddha in Lanna. Art, Image, Power and Place in Northern Thailand* (Honolulu: University of Hawai'i Press, 2017), 33–34. See table 2.1 in Chiu, *The Buddha in Lanna*, for a table of royal networks associated with different famous statues of Southeast Asia.
8. John S. Strong, "'The Devil Was in That Little Bone': The Portuguese Capture and Destruction of the Buddha's Tooth Relic," in *Relics and Remains: Past & Present*, Vol. 206, Supplement 5, ed. Alexandra Walsham (Oxford: Oxford University Press, 2010), 184–198.
9. Ian Harris, *Cambodian Buddhism. History and Practice* (Honolulu: University of Hawai'i Press, 2005), 52–61; and Trent Walker, *Until Nirvana's Time: Buddhist Songs from Cambodia* (Boulder, CO: Shambhala Publications, 2022), 262–263.
10. Lindsay Merrison, "Friends in Higher Places," 88mm documentary (DER Documentary, 2001), DVD.
11. Barend Jan Terwiel, *Monks and Magic: An Analysis of Religious Ceremonies in Central Thailand*, 4th rev. ed. (Copenhagen: NIAS Press, 2012), 69–72; and Justin Thomas McDaniel, "The Material Turn: An Introduction to Thai Sources for the Study of Buddhist Amulets," in *Material Culture and Asian Religions: Text, Image, Object*, ed. Benjamin Fleming and Richard Mann (New York, Routledge, 2014), 138–139.
12. Terwiel, *Monks and Magic*, 71.
13. U. Kan Hla, "Traditional Town Planning in Burma," *Journal of the Society of Architectural Historians* 37, no. 2 (1978): 92–104; Harris, *Cambodian Buddhism*, 61; and Justin Thomas McDaniel, "A Buddha in the Palm of your Hand. Amulets in Thai Buddhism," in *Enlightened Ways: The Many Streams of Buddhist Art in Thailand*, ed. Heidi Tan and Alan Chong (Singapore: Asian Civilisations Museum, 2012), 51.
14. François Bizot and Oskar von Hinüber, *La guirlande de Joyaux*, Textes bouddhiques du Cambodge II (Paris: École française d'Extrême-Orient, 1994), 54.

15. "Atanatiya Sutta: Discourse on Atanatiya" (DN 32), translated from the Pali by Piyadassi Thera, *Access to Insight (BCBS Edition)*, November 30, 2013. For discussion, see Shaw, *The Art of Listening*, 222–237.
16. Peter Skilling, "The *Raksā* Literature of the *Śrāvakayāna*," *Journal of Pali Text Society* 16 (1992): 109–182, 118.
17. For lists of the titles of *paritta* texts in a range of Pali sources, see Skilling "The *Raksā* Literature," 174–179.
18. For the full list of the two *Catubhāṇavāra* recensions, see Lily de Silva, *Paritta: A Historical and Religious Study of the Buddhist Ceremony for Peace and Prosperity in Sri Lanka* (Colombo: National Museums of Sri Lanka, 1981), 5–6.
19. For the full list of the thirty-one titles of the *Sīrimaṅgala-paritta*, see Skilling "The *Raksā* Literature," 179.
20. Sīrimaṅgala Paritta Association, *Thirimingala Payate Taw (Sīrimaṅgala-paritta)* (Yangon, Myanmar: Ministry of Religious Affairs, 1990), *cha*.
21. Justin Thomas McDaniel, *The Lovelorn Ghost and the Magical Monk: Practicing Buddhism in Modern Thailand* (New York: Columbia University Press, 2011), 145.
22. Peter Skilling, "Chanting and Inscribing: The 'Condensed Tripiṭaka' in Thai Ritual," in *Guiding Lights' for the "Perfect Nature": Studies on the Nature and the Development of Abhidharma Buddhism. A Commemorative Volume in Honor of Prof. Dr. Kenyo Mitomo for his 70th Birthday*, ed. The Planning Committee (Japan: Sankibo Busshorin, 2016), 8.
23. Pyi Phyo Kyaw, "*Paṭṭhāna* in Burmese Buddhism" (PhD thesis, King's College London, 2014), 130–132.
24. Donald K. Swearer, "A Summary of the Seven Books of the Abhidhamma," in *Buddhism in Practice*, ed. Donald S. Lopez Jr. (Princeton, NJ: Princeton University Press, 1995), 336–342, 337; and Justin Thomas McDaniel, "Philosophical Embryology: Buddhist Texts and the ritual Construction of a Fetus," in *Imagining the Fetus: The Unborn in Myth, Religion, and Culture*, ed. Jane Marie Law and Vanessa R. Sasson (Oxford and New York: Oxford University Press, 2009), 91–106.
25. Bizot and von Hinüber, *La guirlande de Joyaux*, 46–84; Thomas Patton, "In Pursuit of the Sorceror's Power: Sacred Diagrams as Technologies of Potency," in *Champions of Buddhism: Weikza Cults in Contemporary Burma*, ed. Bénédicte Brac de la Perrière, Guillaume Rozenberg, and Alicia Turner (Singapore: NUS Press, 2014), 150–153.
26. McDaniel, *The Lovelorn Ghost*, 146; and Kourilsky, "The Uṇhissa-vijaya-sutta in Laos and Thailand."
27. Cicuzza, ed., *Katā me rakkhā, katā me parittā*; and Padmanabh S. Jaini, "*Mahādibbamanta:* A *Paritta* Manuscript from Cambodia," *BSOAS* 28, no. 1 (1965): 61–80.
28. Walker, *Until Nirvana's Time*, 358–359, and, for a poem based on it, 215–216.
29. McDaniel, *The Lovelorn Ghost*, 77–85.
30. Peter Skilling, "The *Sambuddhe* Verses and Later Theravādin Buddhology," *Journal of Pali Text Society* 22 (1996): 151–183, 178.
31. Sue Darlington, "The Ordination of a Tree: The Buddhist Ecology Movement in Thailand," *Ethnology* 37, no. 1 (Winter, 1998): 1–15.
32. Terwiel, *Monks and Magic*; and Nicola Tannenbaum, *Who Can Compete against the World? Power-Protection and Buddhism in Shan Worldview* (Ann Arbor, MI: Association for Asian Studies), 1995.
33. Tannenbaum, *Who Can Compete*, 80.
34. Tannenbaum, *Who Can Compete*, 79–80.
35. Donald K. Swearer, *Becoming the Buddha: The Ritual of Image Consecration in Thailand* (Princeton, NJ, and Oxford: Princeton University Press, 2004), 53 and 262; and Woramat Malasart, "The *Dhammakāya* Text Genre and Its Significance for Tai-Khmer Buddhism and Modern Marginalisation," *Journal of the Siam Society* 109, pt. 2 (2021): 79–94, 86–87.
36. Edoardo Siani, "Alternative Divinity: Migrant Spirit Mediumship in the City of Gods," in *Diaspora: Exit, Exile, Exodus of Southeast Asia*, ed. Loredana Pazzini-Paracciani (Chiang Mai, Thailand: MAIIAM Contemporary Art Museum, 2018), 48–49.

37. Siani, "Alternative Divinity"; and Edoardo Siani, "Stranger Diviners and Their Stranger Clients: Popular Cosmology-Making and Its Kingly Power in Buddhist Thailand," *South East Asia Research* 26, no. 4 (2018): 416–431.
38. Peter Harvey, "The Dynamics of Paritta Chanting in Southern Buddhism," in *Love Divine: Studies in Bhakti and Devotional Mysticism*, ed. Karel Werner (Surrey, UK: Curzon Press, 1995), 66–71.
39. Kyaw, "*Paṭṭhāna* in Burmese Buddhism," 131–132.
40. David P. Chandler, "Royally Sponsored Human Sacrifices in Nineteenth Century Cambodia: The Cult of *Nāk Tā* Me Sā (Mahāsuramardini) at Ba Phnom," *Journal of the Siam Society* 62, no. 2 (1972): 207–222; and Nancy Eberhardt, *Imagining the Course of Life. Self-Transformation in a Shan Buddhist Community* (Honolulu: University of Hawai'i Press, 2006), 110–121.
41. Harvey, "The Dynamics of Paritta Chanting," 68–75.
42. Barend Jan Terwiel, "Tattooing in Thailand's History," *Journal of the Royal Asiatic Society of Great Britain & Ireland* 111, no. 2 (April 1979): 159.
43. Patrick Pranke, "On Saints and Wizards: Ideals of Human Perfection and Power in Contemporary Burmese Buddhism," in *Champions of Buddhism: Weikza Cults in Contemporary Burma*, ed. Bénédicte Brac de la Perrière, Guillaume Rozenberg, and Alicia Turner (Singapore: NUS Press, 2014), 30; and Martin Seeger, "'Against the Stream': The Thai Female Buddhist Saint Mae Chi Kaew Sianglam (1901–1991)," *South East Asia Research* 18, no. 3 (2010): 555–595.
44. Justin Thomas McDaniel, "Liberation Materiality: Thai Buddhist Amulets and the Benefits of Selling Sacred Stuff," *Material Religion* 11, no. 3 (2015): 401–402.
45. McDaniel, "The Material Turn," 135.
46. Kate Crosby, *Esoteric Theravada: The Story of the Forgotten Meditation Tradition of Southeast Asia* (Boulder, CO: Shambhala, 2020), 33–36.
47. Kourilsky, "The Uṇhissa-vijaya-sutta in Laos and Thailand," 14–20 and 34–41.
48. Kourilsky, "The Uṇhissa-vijaya-sutta in Laos and Thailand," 42.
49. Peter Skilling, "Calligraphic Magic: *Abhidhamma* Inscriptions from Sukhodaya," *Buddhist Studies Review* 35, no. 1–2 (2018): 161.
50. Erik C. Braun, *The Birth of Insight: Meditation, Modern Buddhism, and the Burmese Monk Ledi Sayadaw* (Chicago and London: University of Chicago Press, 2013); and Alicia Turner, *Saving Buddhism: Moral Community and the Impermanence of Colonial Religion* (Honolulu: University of Hawai'i Press, 2014).
51. Tilman Frasch, "Buddhist Councils in a Time of Transition: Globalism, Modernity and the Preservation of Textual Traditions," *Contemporary Buddhism: An Interdisciplinary Journal* 14, no. 1 (2013): 38–51, 40.
52. Janaka Ashin and Kate Crosby, "Heresy and Monastic Malpractice in the Buddhist Court Cases (Vinicchaya) of Modern Burma (Myanmar)," *Contemporary Buddhism: An Interdisciplinary Journal* 18, no. 1 (2017): 199–261.
53. McDaniel, "The Material Turn," 135.
54. Lambert Schmithausen, "Aspects of the Buddhist Attitude to War," in *Violence Denied: Violence, Non-violence and the Rationalization of Violence in South Asian Cultural History*, ed. Jan E. M. Houben and Karl R. van Kooij (Leiden, The Netherlands: Brill, 1999): 45–67, 53; and Pyi Phyo Kyaw, "In the Midst of Imperfections: How Buddhists in Burma Resolve Moral Dilemmas Encountered in Their Business Activities," *Journal of Buddhist Ethics* 24 (2017): 287–339.
55. Among François Bizot's works, see, for example, *Le don de soi-même*. Recherches sur le bouddhisme khmer III, Publications de l'École française d'Extrême-Orient 130 (Paris: École française d'Extrême-Orient, 1981); Bizot, "Notes sur les *yantra* bouddhiques d'Indochine," in *Tantric and Taoist Studies in Honour of R. A. Stein*, Mélanges Chinois et Bouddhiques 20, ed. M. Strickmann (Bruxelles: Institut Belge des Hautes Etudes Chinoises, 1981), 155–191; Bizot, *Le chemin de Lankā*. Textes bouddhiques du Cambodge I (Paris: École française d'Extrême-Orient 1992); and Bizot, *Le Bouddhisme des Thaïs*

(Bangkok: Éditions des Cahiers de France 1993). For Louis Gabaude, see, for example, *Les Cetiya de sable au Laos et au Thaïlande* (Paris: École française d'Extrême-Orient, 1979).

56. See, for example, Jan Ovesen and Ing-Britt Trankell, *Cambodians and Their Doctors. A Medical Anthropology of Colonial and Post-colonial Cambodia* (Copenhagen: NIAS Press, 2010). Medical anthropological works vary from detailed studies of specific issues to more broad cultural appraisals such as the best-selling Anne Fadiman's. *The Spirit Catches You and You Fall Down: A Hmong Child, Her American Doctors and the Collision of Two Cultures* (New York: Farrar, Straus and Giroux, 1997). While the latter is about Hmong spirit practices rather than Buddhism, it gives a sense of spirit beliefs shared by neighboring Southeast Asian ethnic groups.
57. Peter Harvey, "The Dynamics of Paritta Chanting in Southern Buddhism," 53–84.
58. Melford Spiro, *Burmese Supernaturalism: A Study in the Explanation and Reduction of Suffering* (Englewood Cliffs, NJ: Prentice Hall, 1967); and Spiro, *Buddhism and Society: A Great Tradition and Its Burmese Vicissitudes* (London: George Allen and Unwin, 1971; 2nd ed., Berkeley: University of California Press, 1981); and Richard Francis Gombrich, *Precept and Practice: Traditional Buddhism in the Rural Highlands of Ceylon* (Oxford: Clarendon Press, 1971); Stanley Jeyaraja Tambiah, *Buddhism and the Spirit Cults in North-east Thailand* (Cambridge, UK: Cambridge University Press, 1970); Stanley Jeyaraja Tambiah, *World Conqueror and World Renouncer: A Study of Buddhism and Polity in Thailand against a Historical Background*, Cambridge Studies in Social and Cultural Anthropology (New York: Cambridge University Press, 1976); Stanley Jeyaraja Tambiah, *The Buddhist Saints of the Forest and the Cult of Amulets* (New York: Cambridge University Press, 1984).
59. Swearer, *Becoming the Buddha.*
60. Terwiel, *Monks and Magic.* Terwiel, "Tattooing in Thailand's History," 156–166.
61. Tannenbaum, *Who Can Compete.*
62. Eberhardt, *Imagining the Course of Life.*
63. Hammalawa Saddhatissa, "The Significance of Paritta and Its Application in the Theravāda Tradition," in *Buddhist Thought and Ritual*, ed. David J Kalupahana (New York: Paragon House, 1991), 125–138; de Silva, "The Paritta Ceremony of Sri Lanka," 139–150; and G. Ariyapala Perera, *Buddhist Paritta Chanting Ritual: A Comparative Study of the Buddhist Benedictory Ritual* (Dehiwala, Sri Lanka: Buddhist Cultural Centre, 2000).
64. Anne M. Blackburn, "Magic in the Monastery: Textual Practice and Monastic Identity in Sri Lanka," *History of Religions* 38, no. 4 (May 1999): 354–372.
65. Kate Crosby and Jotika Khur-Yearn, "Poetic *Dhamma* and the *Zare:* Traditional Styles of Teaching Theravada amongst the Shan of Northern Thailand," *Contemporary Buddhism* 11, no. 1 (2010): 1–26; and Crosby, *Esoteric Theravada.*
66. Kyaw, "*Paṭṭhāna* in Burmese Buddhism," chap. 2.
67. Peter Skilling, "The Rakṣā Literature of the Śrāvakayāna," *Journal of Pali Text Society* 16 (1992): 109–182; Skilling, "The *Sambuddhe* Verses," 151–183; Skilling, "Chanting and Inscribing: The 'Condensed Tripiṭaka' in Thai Ritual," in *Guiding Lights' for the "Perfect Nature": Studies on the Nature and the Development of Abhidharma Buddhism. A Commemorative Volume in Honor of Prof. Dr. Kenyo Mitomo for his 70th Birthday*, ed. The Planning Committee (Japan: Sankibo Busshorin, 2016), 928–962; and Skilling, "Calligraphic Magic," 161–187.
68. McDaniel, *The Lovelorn Ghost*; McDaniel, "A Buddha in the Palm of your Hand"; and McDaniel, "The Material Turn"; McDaniel, "Liberation Materiality."
69. Cicuzza, *Katā me rakkhā, katā me parittā*; and Brac de la Perrière, Rozenberg, and Turner, *Champions of Buddhism.*
70. Braun, *The Birth of Insight*; and Turner, *Saving Buddhism.*

Kate Crosby and Pyi Phyo Kyaw

PRAJÑĀPĀRAMITĀ AND KHMER ESOTERIC BUDDHISM IN THE 10TH TO 13TH CENTURIES

INTRODUCTION

There are no in-depth studies to date that focus on the tantric forms of Prajñāpāramitā across maritime Asia in spite of her unique and extensive iconography there. The brief study of Hedwige Multzer o'Naghten only discusses Prajñāpāramitā icons within the confines of Khmer Mahāyāna Buddhist iconography.[1] Further brief studies by Emma Bunker highlight several esoteric Buddhist female bronzes and address the question of scholars' limited understanding of Prajñāpāramitā in the Khmer domain.[2] Nepalese, Tibetan, and Khotanese studies of the goddess have long noted her tantric associations and esoteric forms, given the availability of large bodies of surviving textual materials. Since there are no surviving Buddhist texts or any other type of manuscript from Cambodia's pre-Angkorian or Angkorian periods, little is known about how the various iconographic forms of the goddess were worshiped.

Studies of Hiram Woodward, Wibke Lobo, Peter Sharrock, Julia Estève, Brice Vincent, and Phillip Green have focused on Khmer esoteric Buddhism.[3] During the reign of Jayavarman VII (1182–*c.* 1218), new Buddhist religious elements with some tantric undertones developed, including certain iconographic forms of Prajñāpāramitā and other esoteric female images.

Edward Conze's extensive study, which remains the basis for work on Prajñāpāramitā literature, observed that the clearly significant Khmer Prajñāpāramitā cult fell outside the mainstream, but he did not offer a clear explanation.[4] This article argues that the Khmer Prajñāpāramitā developed from a relatively minor figure beside Avalokiteśvara in pre-Angkorian Cambodia to an increasingly important if still dependent role within an emerging tantric context beginning in the 10th century. By the 12th and 13th centuries, Prajñāpāramitā came to occupy a crucial place in the increasingly overt esoteric Buddhism in the reign of Jayavarman VII. Her multiheaded, multiarmed images produced during his reign call for reconsidering her as an independent and purely Mahāyāna Buddhist deity in the royal pantheon.

THE WAT PÔ VEAL *CAITYA* PILLAR

The evolution of the Khmer Prajñāpāramitā may be traced in a Buddhist *caitya* pillar (see figure 1) or a small tower depicting three female deities currently held at the Wat Pô Veal Museum in Battambang.[5] A *caitya* pillar depicting Prajñāpāramitā is not unusual in Khmer art as several such pillars depict the goddess along with a *nāga*-enthroned buddha, Avalokiteśvara, and Vajrapāṇi from the 10th century.[6] The goddess is well attested in art historical and epigraphic sources of Cambodia since the 8th century.

What is unusual about the Wat Pô Veal *caitya* is the depiction of three multiheaded and multiarmed tantric-looking female deities, including one in dance posture. This striking stone affirms an important place for female deities in 11th- to 13th-century Khmer Buddhist art. The eight-headed, twenty-two-armed dancing figure recalls the numerous eight-headed, sixteen-armed Hevajra bronze statues from this period.

Side A presents a standing single-headed goddess with four arms. The lower right hand holds a lotus and the left one holds a flask or a bottle. The upper right hand carries a rosary. The

Figure 1. Khmer Buddhist *caitya* pillar depicting three esoteric female Buddhist deities. Cambodia, 11th to 13th century, found in Thmà Puok in Banteay Meanchey Province. Sandstone (approx. h: 115–120 cm), Wat Pô Veal Museum, Battambang. EFEO archive no. EFEO_00595.

upper left arm is broken but perhaps held a book as in the other four-armed Khmer Prajñāpāramitā of the period (see figure 2). Side B depicts an eight-headed, twenty-two-armed dancing female figure holding no attributes. Side C bears an image of a three-headed and fourteen-armed female figure seated on a pedestal in *vajrāsana*, and side D of the *caitya* does not carry any image. Since side D is bare, it is logical to assume that side B was the front face of the *caitya*. No known Khmer Prajñāpāramitā image has three heads and fourteen arms or eight heads, but she is known with eleven heads and twenty-two arms in Khmer art. She was never depicted in dancing posture, making the *caitya* unique in Khmer art if the dancing figure is indeed Prajñāpāramitā. The eight-headed deity in the dancing posture in Khmer art is Hevajra, but he displays sixteen arms. The *caitya* appears to embody a conventional Khmer Prajñāpāramitā with four arms presented on side A and her esoteric aspects on sides B and C.

The museum label assigns the three-faced *caitya* from the village of Svay Chék, Thmà Puok district, to the 11th century. The École française d'Extrême-Orient (EFEO) archive label for the *caitya* reads "Stèle bouddhique comportant une image d'Hevajra (fin 12–début 13- Buddhist Stele with an image of Hevajra)."[7] Bruno Bruguier agrees with this Hevajra identification.[8] The

Figure 2. Four-armed Khmer Prajñāpāramitā, Cambodia, 10th-century Banteay Srei style. Sandstone (h: 42 cm), Angkor National Museum, Siem Reap. C.A. no. 023, no. 21.5371.

"Hevajra" label is misleading as the figure in question is clearly of a female deity. The *caitya* is somewhat provincial in style, hard to date, but is stylistically close to the 11th to 13th century when esoteric Buddhism was gaining prominence. In this tantric context, this article considers the Wat Pô Veal *caitya* side C may present the only known Khmer portrayal of Hevajra's consort, Nairātmyā, an aspect of Prajñāpāramitā that is addressed in the section "Prajñāparamitā on *Caitya* Pillars: Her Apparent Esoteric Manifestation."

PRAJÑĀPĀRAMITĀ: DEVELOPMENT OF LITERATURE AND DOCTRINE

The Sanskrit term *prajñā* is variously translated as "wisdom, gnosis, insight or intuitive knowledge," while *pāramitā* means perfection or complete attainment. Prajñāpāramitā literally means "Perfection of Supreme Wisdom." Originally, the word "prajñāpāramitā" referred to the large body of "Perfection of Wisdom" texts, the core of the Mahāyāna Buddhist schools, and at the same time formed a path leading toward enlightenment. However, at some point in time, this important reference to texts was understood as the personification of all the texts in the form of a female deity.

In an outstanding work of scholarship on this major deity in 1960, Edward Conze distinguished four phases in the historical development of Prajñāpāramitā thought, stretching over more than one thousand years. The first phase, which lasted from 100 BCE to 100 CE, saw the elaboration of the basic root text entitled *Aṣṭasāhasrikā Prajñāpāramitā Sūtra* (or Perfection of Wisdom in 8,000 verses).[9] Over the next two hundred years, the Perfection of Wisdom literature achieved great popularity. So much devotion was lavished upon it that the basic text expanded into large versions in ten thousand, eighteen thousand, twenty-five thousand, and one hundred thousand verses, collectively known as the Large Perfection of Wisdom literature.

The next two centuries of the development of Prajñāpāramitā, lasting until about 500 CE, saw the Prajñāpāramitā literature spread throughout India and into China but in the form of shorter texts since the large versions were unwieldy for travel. In this phase, the texts became increasingly concise and the basic concepts of Perfection Wisdom were distilled into shorter sutras and *dhāraṇīs*, the most popular forms being the *Vajracchedikā*, or the *Diamond Sutra*, and *Prajñāpāramitāhṛdaya*, or *Heart Sutra*. Sometimes the teachings were distilled down to just a single letter as seen in *Prajñāpāramitā-sarvatathāgatamātā-ekākṣrā* (or The Perfection of Wisdom in a single letter).[10] The final phase of Prajñāpāramitā development, from 600 to 1200 CE, coincided with the emergence of tantric forms of Buddhism that emphasized the ritual deployment of Prajñāpāramitā texts. A new literature developed to meet current needs such as the *Prajñāpāramitānayaśatapañcaśatikā*, also known as the *Prajñāpāramitānayasūtra* or *Adhrdyaśatikā Prajñāpāramitā* (*AP*-150 line Perfection of Insight), which included key new terms like *vajra* (thunderbolt), *gūhya* (secret), and *siddhī* (super normal accomplishment).[11] The text was so important that *mudrās*, mantras, and mandala rites were added to it by esoteric Buddhists to develop it into the voluminous scripture known as *Paramādyatantra*.[12] Prajñāpāramitā was invoked through the medium of *bīja*-mantras (seed syllables), mantras and *dhāraṇīs* that had magical virtues and could be recited for the protection of a realm, or from the calamities, or simply to earn merit. Texts for constructing mandalas, such as *Prajñāpāramitāma ṇḍalavidhi*, also became common in this period.[13] Thus a feminine force that arose in the Mahāyāna tradition soon became the prototype of all female figures in tantric Buddhism.[14]

Around the early 12th century, the *Aṣṭasāhasrikā Prajñāpāramitā Sūtra* manuscripts began to include not just the "Phase II" but also the "Phase III" esoteric Buddhist deities such as Cakrasaṃvara, Trailokyavijaya, and Hevajra.[15] It became the most favored text for manuscript illustration when tantric Buddhism was in full bloom.[16] The later Tibetan accounts of 11th- and 12th-century Indian Buddhism accord equally high esteem to the *Prajñāpāramitā* as to the major tantras, *Guhyasāmaja* and *Kālacakra*.[17]

In tantric Buddhism, *prajñā* (wisdom) was explicitly identified with nirvana and *upāya* (means) with samsara.[18] Without the spark of *prajñā, upāya* is dormant and ineffective. Ultimate reality or buddhahood was described as the union of wisdom and means. In the ritual and meditational practices, *prajñā* was symbolized by a bell, lotus, or sun as well as by the vowels of the Sanskrit alphabet *āli*.[19] *Upāya* was symbolized by a *vajra*, moon, or the Sanskrit consonants *Kāli*. In yogic ritual practices involving a female partner, *prajñā* was identified with a *yoginī*.[20]

The *Hevajratantra*, one of the earliest *yoginī* tantras, describes how the Adamantine Lord "remains in the void" until roused from slumber by the female energies of his *yoginīs*. Entreaties used by the females to awaken Hevajra include: "Arise, O Hevajra. Leave this condition of voidness . . ." and "O Lord of Bliss . . . Why do you remain in this void?" It is only through "the goddesses with the offering of various songs" that Hevajra "arises from his trance, spreading his feet upon the ground, and threatening gods and titans."[21]

In the union of *prajñā* and *upāya*, it was *prajñā* that played the dominant role, for even though the state of buddhahood was unattainable without special *upāya*, it was *prajñā* that embraced the highest reality of emptiness (*śūnyatā*) or in buddha-vision. In the tantric texts, a synonym for the feminine *prajñā* was *nairātmyā* (*anatman*, or she who has no selfhood), and it was with the female *prajñā* that a tantric practitioner, as *upāya*, was united.[22] In tantric meditational practices, deities such as Prajñāpāramitā were evoked from seed mantras (*bīja*) and were mentally or visually cultivated. One could dissolve one's individuality into essencelessness and reconstitute one's identity as a visualized form of the deity, empowered with the qualities and characteristics of the deity. Such deity yoga practices of Prajñāpāramitā are mainly preserved in the *Sādhanamāla*.[23]

Besides cultivating the presence of Prajñāpāramitā by the means of the *sādhanās*, the ethos of the tantric literature represents Prajñāpāramitā with an attitude of respect and veneration of the feminine in human form. In this practice, all women were considered embodiments of Prajñāpāramitā, being emanations of her divine qualities. This form of reverence is found in Lakṣmīṅkarā's 9th-century *Advyasiddhī*:

> One must not denigrate women,
> In whatever social class they are born,
> For they are Lady Perfection Wisdom (Prajñāpāramitā),
> Embodied in the phenomenal realm.[24]

Although Prajñāpāramitā was personified as a mother, teacher, and guide for giving rise to buddhahood, her iconographic forms did not develop, according to the epigraphic and archaeological evidence, until the 7th century. Conze's study of Prajñāpāramitā and her iconography across Asia is an outstanding and still almost the only single work of scholarship on this major deity.[25]

PRAJÑĀPĀRAMITĀ AND 10TH- TO 12TH-CENTURY KHMER EPIGRAPHY

Buddhism was well established in Cambodia from the 5th century and Mahāyāna Buddhism came to the forefront in the 7th and 8th centuries, mainly seen in the production of Avalokiteśvara images. The bulk of the royal patronage supported Śaivism and to some extent Vaiṣṇavism. Epigraphic records indicate that Prajñāpāramitā was worshiped in Cambodia from at least the 8th century, as is evident in the Sambor Prei Kuk inscription (K. 132), which mentions the installation of Śrī Vidyādhāraṇī (construed as Prajñāpāramitā) in an image erected by a physician.[26] But it was not until a revival of Buddhism in the 10th century that Avalokiteśvara and Prajñāpāramitā truly garnered widespread support.[27]

The characteristics of 10th-century Buddhist traditions and practices in Angkor are thus summarized by Phillip Green:

> "(1) They revolved primarily around the activity of merit making and merit transference, (2) they involved ritual practices surrounding Buddhist images, as well as the donation and construction of other structures, and (3) they included engagement in apotropaic tantric ritual activities, and these activities allowed Buddhists to compete within the socio-political realm alongside other sectarian rivals [Śaivas and Vaiṣṇavas] who offered aesthetically and functionally similar rites."[28]

This period saw the popularity of texts such as *Kāraṇḍavyūha Sūtra* and *Ekādaśamukhadhāraṇī*, which focus on the virtues of Avalokiteśvara in Campā and Cambodia. Along with these texts, *Mahāvairocanābhisaṃbodhi Tantra* (or *Mahāvairocanā Sūtra*) was also known in the region.[29]

During the late 9th and early 10th centuries, in Campā, as seen at the temple of Đồng Dương, new forms of Buddhism emerged and gained importance in which Avalokiteśvara played an important role.[30] King Jaya Indravarman II (r. 875–899 CE) made Buddhism the official religion. Inscriptions of Prasat Chikreng (K. 417), Prasat Ta An (K. 240), an inscribed eight-armed Avalokiteśvara stele kept at Walters Art Museum, and the *caitya* pillar (see figure 6), kept at the National Museum Bangkok, provide evidence for the presence of the *Kāraṇḍavyūha Sūtra* and *Mahāvairocanā Sūtra* in the Khmer domain during the 10th century.[31]

Khmer king Rājendravarman (r. 944–*c.* 968) and his son Jayavarman V (r. *c.* 968–1000/1) recognized the growing popularity of the Buddhist texts and accommodated the new Buddhist currents into the Khmer political realm. King Rājendravarman made donations to the vihara at Wat Kdei Car to house double images of Avalokiteśvara and a *devī* (Prajñāparamitā?).[32] State-supported Buddhism must have been a clear factor behind the growth of the religion during their reigns. In the 10th century, the first instance of recording important Buddhist officials such as Kavīndrārimathana (K. 266, K. 267. K. 268), Kīrtipaṇḍita (K. 111), Kīrttivara (K. 173), and Viīrendravikhyāta (K. 157) took place.[33] The list of deities worshiped by the Buddhists became more extensive than before in this period.[34] The Khmer epigraphy of the period repeatedly mentions "Prajñāpāramitā" to denote the supreme wisdom and links her name directly with such epithets as Jinamātṛ (mother of Jina) or Jinasantānakāriṇī (begetter of the series of buddhas) to mark the erection of an image in a temple. This plurality of concepts may denote the difference of nature between a supreme entity and its material manifestation.[35]

In fact, Kīrtipaṇḍita's efforts were specifically connected with (re)institutionalizing foundational doctrinal principles found in Prajñāpāramitā literature and Yogācāra sources. He is said to have actively disseminated the tantric texts.[36]

The inscriptional record mentions foundations of Buddhist triads of Avalokiteśvara, central buddha, and Vajrapāṇī, but sometime during the 10th century, Prajñāpāramitā replaces Vajrapāṇī as attested in the inscriptions of Banteay Neang (K. 214) and Beng Vien (K. 872).[37] Though it is not easy to understand the relationship among these triadic configurations, the pairing of Prajñāpāramitā and Avalokiteśvara demonstrates the widespread concept of wisdom, or *prajñā*, and means, or *upāya*, together leading to enlightenment as seen in the figure 3 stele (see figure 3). In the *Kāraṇḍavyūha Sūtra*, the mandala that is identified with the mantra *oṃ maṇi padme hūṃ* consists of a central buddha, flanked by a bodhisattva and by the female personification of the spell. Given the Khmer pattern of buddha–bodhisattva–female deity, Woodward argues for the possibility of this text as the source for the Khmer triad.[38] Alternately, reinforcement of the triadic thinking could have also come from the *Mahāvairocanā Sūtra* that defines the three buddha families.[39]

Three epigraphic documents critical for scholars' understanding of Khmer Prajñāpāramitā in the 10th through 11th centuries are the inscriptions of (a) Bat Cum temple, (b) Wat Sithor, and (c) Sab Bāk.

Bat Cum: The First Temple Dedicated to Prajñāpāramitā in Angkor. Early evidence of the esoteric Buddhist vehicle Vajrayāna in Angkor can be found at Bat Cum temple K. 266 (south tower), K. 267 (central tower), and K. 268 (north tower), inscribed on the doorjambs of the three towers built around 953 CE.[40]

Built by Kavīndrārimathana, the Buddhist minister of King Rājendravarman, Bat Cum celebrated a Khmer military victory over the Cam polities along the coast of what is now central and southern Vietnam. The military success was credited to the spiritual help of Vajrapāṇī, the

Figure 3. Khmer Buddhist triad depicting Avalokiteśvara–buddha–Prajñāpāramitā. Cambodia, 10th century, sandstone (h: 71 cm), Honolulu Academy of Art, Honolulu, no. 6691.1.

tantric warrior deity. Originally the site would have had a Buddhist monastery and other dwellings located near the sanctuaries, but these would have been constructed in wood and have since vanished. Bat Cum is one of the few Buddhist temples, with a sanctuary dedicated to Prajñāpāramitā/Divyadevī, within Angkor prior to the reign of Jayavarman VII.

The three sanctuaries of the temple were consecrated to buddha, Divyadevī (Prajñāpāramitā), and Vajrapāṇī. The inscription on the south tower invokes buddha, Lokeśvara, and Vajrapāṇī, respectively; the inscriptions on the central and north tower invoke buddha, Vajrapāṇī, and Prajñāpāramitā, respectively. Prajñāpāramitā takes precedence at Bat Cum by replacing Avalokiteśvara in the central and northern towers.

Inscription K. 267 (st. I) refers to the doctrine of *nairātmyā*:
vuddho vodhīṃ vidaddhyād vo yena nairātmyadarśanam
viruddhasyāpi sādhūktaṃ sādhanaṃ paramātmanaḥ

Cœdès's translation reads: "Que le Buddha vous donne la Bodhi, lui par qui a été enseignée la doctrine excellente niant l'existence de l'âme individuelle et permettant de s'identifier avec l'âme universelle qui est cependant contradictoire à cette doctrine."[41] Green translates it as: "Although it opposes [the view of] *paramātmana*, the Buddha teaches *Bodhī* (i.e., enlightenment) by means of the doctrine of *nairātmya*, which is well-said (and) leads straight to the goal."[42]

Here, wisdom (*Bodhī*) or Prajñāpāramitā is linked to the doctrine of *nairātmya*. Green argues: "Although the first verse praising the Buddha does not employ vocabulary that means to protect or defend, it does emphasize that he is responsible for making known the doctrine of *nairātmya*, which leads to the goal of liberation."[43]

The Bat Cum inscriptions do not disclose anything of the iconography of the lost Prajñāpāramitā image within, but they reveal a great deal about her character—a helpful, merciful savior goddess called Divyadevī (Prajñā) who has the ability to bestow fortune, destroy the darkness caused by ignorance, and illuminate the path of nirvana.[44] She is compared with the full moon (st. III of the central tower) and then to the sun (st. III of the north tower). This appears to highlight the dual aspect of Prajñāpāramitā as the actual source of wisdom (the full moon) and the illuminating path that leads the practitioner to attain the very same wisdom (the sun).[45]

Even though the inscription makes it clear that Kavīndrārimathana's family was also involved in Avalokiteśvara and Prajñāpāramitā rituals, little is said about their exact nature.[46] The main Bat Cum images of Vajrapāṇī, Prajñāpāramitā, and the buddha of Bat Cum are all lost.

Another unique feature of Bat Cum is a square-shaped yantra subdivided into forty-nine parts of which the central one is blank and the other forty-eight are a series of lotus petals: each inscribed with Sanskrit *akṣara*.[47] Such diagrams are known as *prastāra* and are in Woodward's words "like computer keyboards but useful only with instructions providing the specific location in the diagram of phonemes constituting a *mantra*. This was an elaborate way of keeping a *mantra* secret."[48] The deity is phonetically expressed through the seed syllables contained within the mantra. Woodward has associated the diagram with two texts: first is a Hindu *Vīṇaśikhatantra*, which was used in the ceremony of 802 CE as recorded in the 11th-century Sdok Kok Thom inscription (K. 235), and second is the now lost Buddhist *Sarvabuddh asamāyogaḍākinījālasaṃvara*, which serves as a bridge between *Adhrdyaśatikā Prajñāpāramitā* and the later Mother tantras in Tibetan Buddhism.[49]

The Bat Cum diagram shows many similarities with *Vīṇaśikhatantra*, which was surely known in Cambodia at the construction time of Bat Cum. But whether the Buddhist text or both would have been the source for the Bat Cum *prastāra* are the questions that remain unknown.

In the tantric Buddhist ritual and meditational practice, *prajñā* was symbolized by lotus and *upāya* was symbolized by a *vajra*. There were two slabs with an engraved *vajra* excavated from Bat Cum and considered to be pairs with the alphabet diagram.[50] Thus, the *prastāra* diagram with lotus petals marked on each tile and engraved *vajras* together stand for the wisdom and means that engender enlightenment.[51] A fragmentary inscription K. 772 of Prasat Beng appears to refer to the bell and *vajra* held in the hands of an adept as the two deities, Prajñāpāramitā and Vajrapāṇī.[52]

The Case of Wat Sithor. The Wat Sithor inscription records an order of Jayavarman V concerning the establishment of a Buddhist monastery.[53] It praises the highly honored Buddhist teacher Kīrtipaṇḍita, establishing the good law in its exoteric and esoteric form. In fact, Wat Sithor even redefines the role of the *purohita* (sacerdotal minister) as one who is familiar with both traditional practices and tantric Buddhist practices involving, among other things, the use of the *vajra* and the bell, iconic ritual implements of the tantric traditions.[54] Kīrtipaṇḍita was known for his special rites within the palace that were believed to ensure the pacification and prosperity of the kingdom.[55]

The opening stanzas of the inscription praise three bodies of the buddha. In addition to *Trikāya*, the opening section also praises the excellent dharma of the buddha and bodhisattvas as well as those practitioners who grasp and follow the teachings, which leads to the liberation.

Side B, verse XVII of the inscription, refers to the doctrines of *nairātmya* (no selfhood) and *cittamātra* (mind only):

nairātmyacittmātrādi
darśanārkkas tiraskṛtaḥ
mithyādṛṣtiniśā yasmin
bhūyodina ivāvabhhau||

Green's translation reads: "The sun of doctrines such as *cittamātra* and *nairātmya*, eclipsed by the night of false doctrines, once again shone in the day."[56]

Prajñāpāramitā is mentioned on side B, XLIV:

Tatsthāne sthāpitā sthityai
sarvvavidvaṅśabhāsvataḥ
prajñāpāramitā tārī
janani yena tāyinām||

Green's translation reads: "In that place the protector Prajñāpāramitā, the mother of protectors, was established by him for the sake of continuing the luminous lineage of the Omniscient [Sarvavid- Buddha Vairocana?] one."[57]

Green argues that Sarvavid is an epithet of all knowing and omniscient, and it is often used to refer to the buddha, a buddha, or even a bodhisattva. However, it is also an epithet often specifically used for Mahāvairocana, a possibility that would not be out of context in this inscription.

The question arises whether Prajñāpāramitā as mentioned in the stanza has the status of the consort of Vairocana. With the development of tantric philosophy and the fostering of mandalas as an essential component of means, the intermediate positions of the mandalas came to be occupied by four Buddhist goddesses—Locanā, Māmakī, Paṇḍaravāsinī, and Tārā. In a further evolution, they became consorts of Jina buddhas. In fact *Kālacakratantra* introduced six buddha mothers with the addition of Vajradhātviśvari and Prajñāpāramitā.[58] Collectively, the buddha-goddesses may be known by several terms such as *tārā, vidyā,* mudrā, or *prajñā,* the latter term springing from their connection with Prajñāpāramitā, understanding of which is consistent throughout Buddhist tantric literature.[59] The reference to Prajñāpāramitā as the "Mother of the Buddhas" in the inscription indicates her role in fostering buddhahood and not really as an earthly mother goddess.[60] It is perhaps in this position that she is referred to in Khmer inscriptions as "Mother of all the Buddhas," a prime deity on a par with Vairocana, the supreme buddha.

The inscription describes the *purohita* (Kīrtipaṇḍita) as being learned in the rite of the fire (*homa*) sacrifice, *vidyā,* mantra, mudrā, and heart syllables and secrets of the *vajra* and *ghaṇṭa* (bell).[61] This is strong evidence for tantric practices in 10th-century Cambodia.

Side B, stanza XXIX:

Lakṣagraṇṭham abhiprajñaṃ
yo nveṣya pararāṣṭr ataḥ

tattvasaṅgrahaṭīkādi-
tantrañ cādhyāpayad yamī ||

Green's translation reads: "Having obtained the *Lakṣagrantham Abhiprajñam* from another kingdom, he—subdued in his sense—taught *tantra* including the commentary on the *Tattvasaṅgraha*."[62]

The *Lakṣagrantham Abhiprajñaṃ* (100,000 verses on higher wisdom) may refer to the *Prajñāpāramitā Sūtra,* which is one hundred thousand verses,[63] and *Tattvasaṃgraha* to *Sarvat athāgatatattvasaṃgraha,* a key text of the *yogatantra* and other tantras.[64] The inscription also makes it clear that both exoteric (*Vāhya* = *bāhya*) and esoteric (*gūhya*) forms of Buddhism were taught and propagated during this period (st. 42) and that Cambodian priests were familiar with the concept of emptiness, which was the essence of Mahāyāna and Vajrayāna Buddhism. Based on the epigraphy and the knowledge of Buddhist *yogatantra* texts available to the Khmers by the time of Jayavarman V, Sanderson concludes that the Vairocana-centered Mantrayāna of the *yogatantra* was in vogue among the Khmers.[65] Wat Sithor temple has been rebuilt in the current Theravādin tradition beside an old stūpa like the laterite brick *prāsada,* where the Prajñāpāramitā icon would presumably have been erected.

The full extent of the Prajñāpāramitā texts Kīrtipaṇḍita was interested in is not known.

Tanaka has argued that *Adhyārdhaśatika Prajñāpāramitā* was the earliest text among the *yogatantras* that influenced the evolution of *Sarvatathāgatatattvasaṃgraha* and played an important role in the history of esoteric Buddhism.[66] There surely are common themes between the two texts, especially the esoteric transformation of the doctrine of emptiness. This reformulation is most strongly seen in the teachings of Great Bliss, which defines the process of striving toward and finally experiencing enlightenment in terms often blatantly sexual. The fundamental humanly sexual passions are boldly stated in the text and these desires are transformed into Great Bliss.[67]

As in the *Sarvatathāgatatattvasaṃgraha,* in the text *Adhyārdhaśatika Prajñāpāramitā,* Vajrapāṇī plays an important role. He takes the form of Trailokyavijaya, a wrathful deity with joined eyebrows and sword-like fangs. Vajrapāṇī is mentioned in the Bat Cum and the Wat Sithor inscriptions. K. 240 of 979 CE mentions gifts to an image of Vajrapāṇī and Trailokyavijaya.[68] A century later, Trailokyavijaya is mentioned again in the inscription K. 397 found near Phimai and dated to 1109 CE.[69] A small bronze of the deity was found at Phimai and is now kept at the National Museum of Bangkok (no. 2.271).

Banteay Neang mentions offerings of two rice fields, slaves, and water buffalos to Prajñāpāramitā under the strange but tantric-sounding name of Trailokyavijayagisvarī and to Trailokyanāthā—either Lokeśvara, Vajrapāṇī, or Trailokyavijaya at a ceremony attended by all the family members, the leaders of whom all bear names ending with *vajra* (Somavajra, Tribhūvanavajra), indicating the tantric nature of the ritual.[70]

Sab Bāk Inscription and 11th-Century Khmer Buddhism. Along with these 10th-century documents, there is another piece of evidence from the 11th century that is relevant to Khmer esoteric Buddhism. Inscription K. 1158 of 1066 CE was found near Phimai in Khorat (modern northeast Thailand) at the village of Sab Bāk.[71] The inscription begins with Vraḥ

Dhanus, the author bowing down to five Jinas and praising Vajrasattva, the sixth buddha presiding over the five Jinas.[72] It mentions a very important Buddhist center called Chpār Rānsi, which has not yet been located with certainty but was an important tantric Buddhist place in the Angkor region.[73] The inscription records Dhanus as following the path and practices of the tantric school for a long time. Reference to the *Guhya[samāja]tantra* (Scripture of esoteric assembly) and Vajrasattva in the inscription are indicators of the knowledge of strictly esoteric Buddhist rituals in the Khmer Empire. *Guhyasamāja tantra* is one of the principal texts of *yoginītantras* that deals with the various types of esoteric meditation and visualization practices, for example, the initiation rites called *guhyābhiṣeka* (secret empowerment) and *prajñājñānābhiṣeka* (empowerment of knowledge of wisdom), which involve sexual union with a female consort.[74] Much of the tantra is concerned with rituals of peace, prosperity, subjugation, and the fierce acts and demonstrates a close connection to the Wat Sithor inscription in spite of the geographical distance between their find spots.

Prajñāpāramitā is mentioned as the path that leads the practitioner to attain the Buddhahood.

> X. prajñāpāramitānīkātarkabhāṣyādivāridhim
> uttīryya gūhyavṛkṣe te śrāntās tattvaphalāśinaḥ ||

Estève's translation reads: "Après avoir traversé l'océan des commentaires, etc., du Prajñāpāramitānīkātarka, ces (guru), épuisés, dégustent (enfin) le fruit qui est l'essence des choses sur l'arbre des secrets" (After having crossed the ocean of commentaries, etc., of the Prajñāpāramitānīkātarka, the exhausted [gurus], [at last] taste the fruit of the essence of things on the tree of secrets).[75]

The Khmer portion of the text gives scholars a fairly extensive account of the presence of tantric Buddhism in the western part of the Khmer Empire and mentions a lineage of tantric adepts and the imagery they erected. Sab Bāk is one of the first explicit proofs of the presence of mature, post-10th-century Vajrayāna in the Khmer Empire.[76]

NEWLY FOUND INSCRIPTION K. 1297 AND 12TH-CENTURY KHMER BUDDHISM

Like Sab Bāk, inscription K. 1297, which was auctioned in Paris in before 2011 and being translated by a team of scholars, begins with an invocation to Buddha Vajrasattva and mentions a high central tower dedicated to Prajñāpāramitā.[77] It describes how the king Dharaṇīndravarman I (1107–1113) was not just a follower of Buddhism, like his brother Jayavarman VI (1080–1107), but venerated a female deity in the central sanctuary. Until the early 21st century, these kings were believed to be Śaiva. The inscription is an important piece of evidence for scholars' understanding of the Khmer tantric Buddhism that continued in the 11th through 13th centuries.

KHMER PRAJÑĀPĀRAMITĀ: TEMPLES AND ICONS BEFORE JAYAVARMAN VII

In spite of the rich epigraphy, no major temple complexes display images of Prajñāpāramitā. Very few Buddhist monuments dating from the 10th century have so far been found.[78] Tenth-century

Figure 4. *Prasat* Phnom Trap central sanctuary relief of four-armed Avalokiteśvara flanked by two Devis (or possible aspects of Prajñāpāramitā), Cambodia, 10th century, Kompong Cham Province.

reliefs at Phnom Trap depicting four- and eight-armed Avalokiteśvaras accompanied by two four-armed devīs or possible aspects of Prajñāpāramitā and four-armed Vajrapāṇī might be the only extant example of her imagery within the Khmer temples prior to the reign of Jayavarman VII (see figure 4).[79] Freestanding Buddhist images are also rare. No Prajñāpāramitā images have been recovered from Bat Cum, Wat Sithor, or Prasat Bang Temple in spite of the epigraphic references to her.

Several Prajñāpāramitā images that appear during this period constitute parts of Avalokiteśvara–buddha–Prajñāpāramitā triads and are not independent sculptures (see figure 3). Along with the triads, Prajñāpāramitā is depicted on six small towers or *caitya* pillars found near Thmà Puok from the village of Phnom Srok.[80] Besides these, there is one from Ta Muen, now kept at the Ashmolean Museum (see figure 5); another on from Angor Thom, kept at the Angkor National Museum, Siem Reap (Ka. 049, N. 127, 5690); and two of unknown provenance, kept at the National Museum, Bangkok (see figures 6 and 7). Her representations on these *caitya* pillars depict her as multiheaded and multiarmed.[81]

Finot argues that the female images depicted on the *caitya* pillars are all representations of Prajñāpāramitā, in spite of the significant iconographic differences.[82] The differences in iconography might denote her diverse forms and manifestations. For example, on the Ashmolean *caitya* she carries two Amitābha Buddhas above her head on one side and one Amitābha Buddha on the other. The buddhas are placed under *nāga*-hoods on both sides. Her crown, too, differs significantly on three sides of the *caitya*. On the Bangkok *caitya* (figure 6), she accompanies the dancing Vajrapāṇī. This *caitya* displays mix Buddhist–Viṣṇuite iconography.[83]

Figure 5. Khmer Buddhist *caitya* pillar depicting four-armed Prajñāpāramitās with Amitābha Buddha on the top and on the three sides and four-armed Avalokiteśvara on one side. Cambodia, 10th century, found at *Prasat* Ta Muen in Surin Province on the border between Cambodia and Thailand. Sandstone (h: 110 cm), Ashmolean Museum, Oxford. EA1999.102.
Source: Photo courtesy Pia Conti

On the other Bangkok *caitya* (figure 7) four female figures are paired with the four male deities on four sides. The *caitya* houses two aspects of Avalokiteśvara—one eight-armed belonging to the *Kāraṇḍavyūha Sūtra* and the other four-armed. The ten-armed female figure placed below eight-armed Avalokiteśvara is Prajñāpāramitā based on her similar Khmer depictions, but it is difficult to know the identity of the two-armed female figure in *varada* and *abhaya mudrā*, placed below four-armed Avalokiteśvara.[84] It could possibly be Tārā, an extension of Avalokiteśvara's compassion as argued by Woodward.[85] *Varadamudrā* is indeed a marker of Tārā, but it is equally possible that the *caitya* displays another (Tārā?) aspect of Prajñāpāramitā. During the late 11th century in India, Prajñāpāramitā's iconography appropriated that of Tārā and possibly in Cambodia, too.[86] The identity of the four-armed female figure placed below Vajrapāṇī is difficult to interpret. Where Prajñāpāramitā is clearly represented, her privileged position in 10th-century Cambodia is signaled but so is her strong link with Avalokiteśvara, for they alone appear on all six *caityas*. Prajñāpāramitā bronzes are very rare in this period, and only three or possibly four from the 10th to the 11th century are known.[87]

In the neighboring Campā kingdom to the east, 9th- to 10th-century Đại Hữu images of female deities, which are more than three feet tall and identical, were once housed in the three towers of the temple.[88] Two of these images carry Amitābha Buddha in their chignons. Based on the Khmer iconographic evidence and popularity of the Prajñāpāramitā cult, Pia Conti has

Figure 6. Khmer Buddhist *caitya* pillar depicting from left to right Prajñāpāramitā (bottom left figure), dancing Vajrapāṇī (bottom right figure), and *nāga*-enthroned buddha (top central figure) accompanied by Vajrapāṇī and Amitabha, *nāga*-enthroned buddha in the center accompanied by two flying male figures, reclining Visnu, and kneeling Vajrapāṇī (bottom central figure) accompanied by two seated female figures; *nāga*-enthroned buddha (top central figure) accompanied by two buddhas in a double *vitarkamudrā*. Cambodia or Thailand, 10th century. Sandstone (h: 72cm), Bangkok National Museum, Bangkok, no. 2.276.
Source: Photo courtesy Pia Conti

Figure 7. Khmer Buddhist *caitya* pillar depicting from left to right and top to bottom, *nāga*-enthroned buddha, a female figure placed on the coils of *nāga*, four-armed Avalokiteśvara, two-armed female deity, eight-armed Avalokiteśvara, ten-armed Prajñāpāramitā, four-armed Vajrapāṇī, and four-armed female deity. Cambodia or Thailand, 10th century, Sandstone (h: 119 cm) Bangkok National Museum, Bangkok, no. 12.2475.
Source: Photo courtesy Pia Conti

interpreted them as Prajñāpāramitā.[89] If this is the case, then the cult images of Đại Hữu show the importance of Prajñāpāramitā in the Cam domain (see figures 8 and 9).

Đồng Dương, the major Buddhist monastery of King Jaya Indravarman in Campā, was established at the end of the 9th century and was dedicated to "Lakṣmīndra Lokeśvara" in the form of a beautiful female bronze statue.[90] The identity of the statue depicted in figure 10 has sparked debate among scholars who have identified her as Tārā, Prajñāpāramitā, and a female Lokeśvara—the main deity of the inscription, which includes the king's name.[91] But the presence of a female deity in the central sanctuary of the royal Buddhist monastery indicates the presence of some form of tantric Buddhism that venerated female deities in the strong matrilineal Cam society (see figure 10).[92]

Given the Cam-Khmer royal connections from the 7th century onward, it is not unreasonable to assume that there was a related development pattern for Prajñāpāramitā in the neighboring cultures, which also shared much in architecture, even though there are few surviving images of the goddess. It is remarkable to note that in the late 10th or early 11th century, she appears as a fully developed Khmer tantric goddess based on the available examples of her multiarmed and multiheaded depictions on the *caitya* pillars.

Figure 8. Cam Prajñāpāramitā, Vietnam, 9th–10th century, found at Đại Hữu Temple, sandstone (h: 102 cm), Đà Nẵng Museum, Đà Nẵng, no. BTC 188-14.3.
Source: Photo by Trần Kỳ Phương

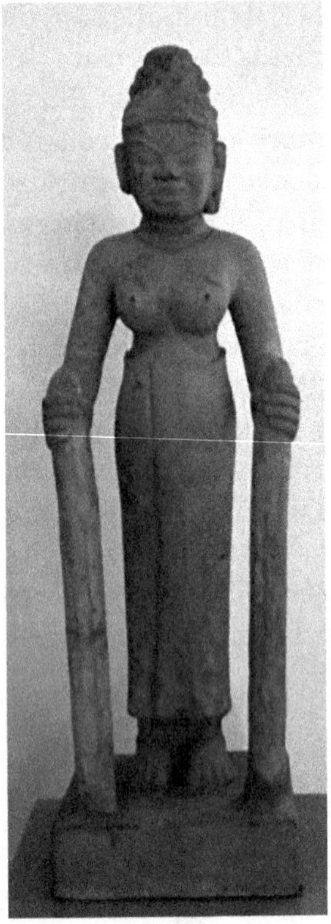

Figure 9. Cam Prajñāpāramitā, Vietnam, 9th–10th century, found at Đại Hữu Temple, sandstone (h: 97 cm), Hanoi Museum of History, Hanoi, no. LSb. 21192.
Source: Photo by Trần Kỳ Phương

The 12th-century *Sādhanamāla* text does not record a multiheaded Prajñāpāramitā, but the Khmer images of Prajñāpāramitā are far removed from her Indian models.[93] The *Sādhanamāla* indicates that in Vajrayāna, Prajñāpāramitā either carries Buddha Akṣobhya (the eastern Jina and head of the *Vajra* family) or images of five *tathāgatas* in her crown.[94] In Cambodia, she carries Amitābha Buddha in her hair, an iconographic marker of Avalokiteśvara. A Jina in the hair and a book can be markers for Tārā as well as Prajñāpāramitā. The distinction between the two is blurred as at times both share common features.[95] Tārā is generally regarded as the consort of Avalokiteśvara, born from his compassionate tear, while in contrast Prajñāpāramitā is an independent deity representing supreme wisdom.

Even though the standard iconography of Prajñāpāramitā depicts her with two, four, or six arms, in Cambodia there are eleven-headed, twenty-two-armed depictions of the goddess that are described in no known surviving text. The 11th- to 12th-century text *Niṣpanayogāvalī* (NSP 21) mentions the lower two hands of Prajñāpāramitā are in *dharmacakramudrā* or *abhayamudrā* and the upper two are holding a lotus and a book. Usually her attributes are the lotus, book, *vajra*, sword, rosary, and flask.[96] But the Khmer cult of Prajñāpāramitā has shown more varied iconography than anywhere else in the Buddhist world.[97]

Figure 10. Lakṣmīndralokeśvara, Vietnam, 9th century, main deity of Đồng Dương Monastery, bronze (h: 115 cm). Attributes: lotus (lower right hand) and conch (broken at the time of discovery). Đà Nẵng Museum, Đà Nẵng, BTC 1651-BTĐN.
Source: Photo by Trần Kỳ Phương

KHMER PRAJÑĀPĀRAMITĀ: TEMPLES AND ICONS DURING JAYAVARMAN VII'S REIGN (1180–*C.* 1218)

Unlike the 10th-century inscriptional records, the extant epigraphy of Jayavarman VII's reign reveals frustratingly little about the practices related to Prajñāpāramitā despite her diverse and innovative iconographic forms and evident popularity.

The epigraphy of the period drops the name "Prajñāpāramitā," which was commonly used in the earlier inscriptions with the exception of Banteay Chhmar, and instead uses different epithets such as Jinamātṛ, or Jinānān jananīn, emphasizing her nature as the "Mother of Buddha."[98] It seems that her nature as the root of enlightenment like a mother to her son was possibly appropriated by the king to fit into his tantric Buddhism. *Guhyasamāja tantra*, which was known to Khmers, comments on the "Mother of the Buddha":

> The sādhaka who desires his mother, sister, and daughter, attains entire siddhi, the Dharma-nature of the supreme Māhayāna; enjoying the Mother of the Lord Buddha, he is not defiled, but that wise one, free from dualistic thought, attains the Buddha-nature.[99]

Even though Jayavarman VII installed Prajñāpāramitā as the mother of buddhas (Jinamātṛ) in the central sanctuary of Ta Prohm Temple in Angkor, dedicated to his mother, Jayarājacūḍāmaṇi, no in-the-round sculpture has been found that could be identified with the inscription. Prajñāpāramitā is truly celebrated at Ta Prohm as she appears in a variety of iconographic forms in the temple reliefs. The ongoing restoration work of the Archaeological Survey of India (ASI) team has shed some light on the goddess.

Standard Depiction of Prajñāpāramitā as a Two-Armed Goddess. Prajñāpāramitā appears in reliefs on the pediments of all the south, west, north, and east *gopura* of the outermost enclosure of Ta Prohm (see figure 11).[100] She appears again on all the three pediments of the main entrance of the hall with dancers (now partially restored), a structure placed on the main axis of the temple after crossing the outermost enclosure (see figure 12). All along the walls of the temple's second enclosure, she appears in a triad with Avalokiteśvara and *nāga*-enthroned buddha (see figure 13). But unlike the earlier triads, she is now, given her size and positioning, depicted on a par with Avalokiteśvara. Along with two-armed depictions of her on the temple walls, freestanding images of her are common under Jayavarman VII, but there is one image that has posed questions of iconography that still await answers. Indradevī, Jayavarman VII's second wife, raised posthumous statues of her younger sister and the king's previous wife, Jayarājadevī, along with images of the king as per the Phimeanakas inscription (see figure 14).[101] There are two conflicting hypotheses regarding this image and other similar images. The kneeling woman was first identified as a Prajñāpāramitā on the basis of the usual Khmer marker of the goddess—Buddha Amitābha in her chignon and on the presumption that she might have once held a book in her now absent hands.[102] The second hypothesis suggested that the hands were once joined at the chest in *anjalī mūdra*, or praying gesture, or perhaps holding a lotus and thus more likely to be a representation of

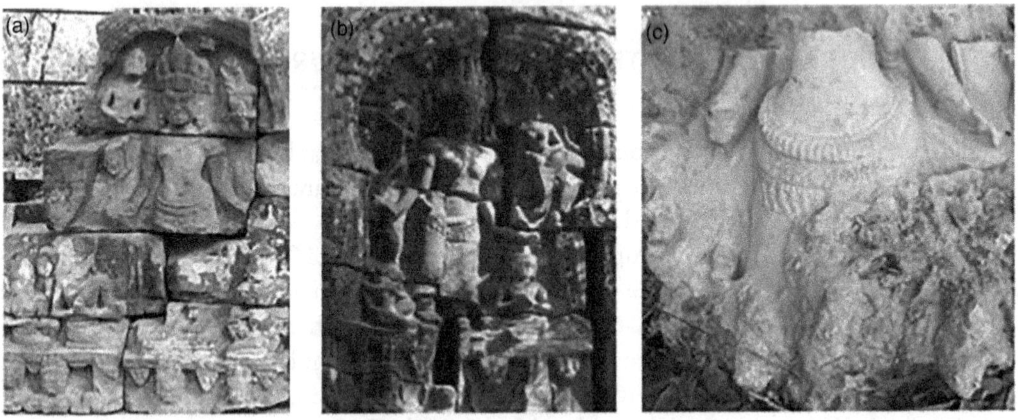

Figure 11. Two-armed depictions of Prajñāpāramitā on the pediments of the outermost enclosure of Ta Prohm, Cambodia, 12th–13th century, from left: (a) pediment from eastern *gopura*—assembled by the Archaeological Survey of India (ASI) and kept at the main entrance, (b) south pediment of the eastern *gopura*, and (c) north pediment of the north *gopura*. Sandstone.
Source: Photo by Olivier Cunin

Figure 12. Prajñāpāramitā on the eastern side pediments of "hall with dancers" at Ta Prohm, Cambodia, 12th–13th century, from left: (a) southeast pediment, (b) central pediment (multiple arms are visible but the original head was replaced by the Archaeological Survey of India [ASI]), (c) northeast pediment. Sandstone.

Figure 13. A triad Avalokiteśvara–*nāga*-enthroned buddha–Prajñāpāramitā is repeated all along the second enclosure wall of Ta Prohm, Cambodia, 12th–13th century. Sandstone.

Tārā.[103] The kneeling feminine statue with the head titled downward was correctly identified as the portrait statue of Jayarājadevī in the likeliness of Prajñāpāramitā similar to the Singosari statue of the queen Ken Dedes in Indonesia, popularly known as Leiden or Jakarta Prajñāpāramitā.[104] A portrait pair of the queen and the king was erected at Phimai, Preah Khan of Angkor, and the Bayon state temple.[105] Several short inscriptions engraved on the doorjambs of small chapels of the Bayon and other temples of Jayavarman VII mention prominent individuals and their association or identification with deities. There must have been statues of Prajñāpāramitā in these chapels but whether she is understood as the goddess or deified queen is difficult to know.[106]

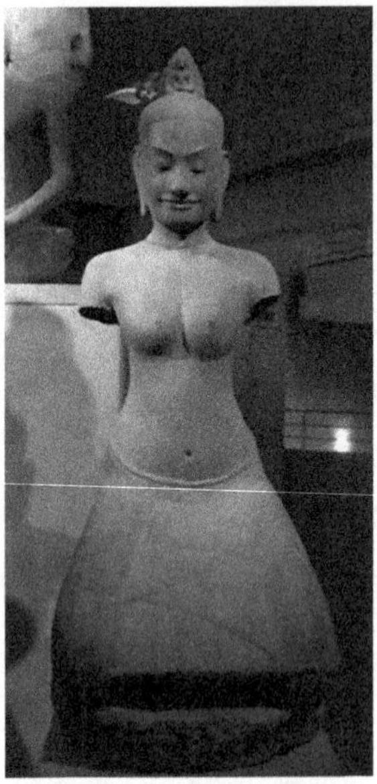

Figure 14. Portrait statue of Jayarājadevī, Preah Khan of Angkor, Siem Reap Province, Cambodia, 12th–13th century, sandstone (h: 125 cm), Musée national des arts asiatiques, Guimet, MG18043.

Prajñāpāramitā as an Eleven-Headed, Twenty-Two-Armed Goddess. Along with her standard representations, Prajñāpāramitā also appears as an eleven-headed, twenty-two-armed goddess either seated or standing, in stone, bronze, and in terra cotta tablets. This constitutes one of the most important artistic innovations of the "Bayon style." The key attestation for this form of Prajñāpāramitā is a bronze kept at the National Museum of Cambodia Phnom Penh (NMCPP), which bears the inscription "Vraḥ rūpa, vraḥ Prajñāpāramitā" that unquestionably identifies the goddess.[107] Buddha Amitābha sits in mediation mudra above the top tier of her heads (see figure 15). There are a few other examples of this form of Prajñāpāramitā in bronze.[108] Earlier in the 10th century, the Prāsat Chikreng inscription (K. 968) had contained an opening invocation to an Ekādaśamukha, or eleven-headed Avalokiteśvara, and Bhagavatī (possibly an eleven-headed Prajñāpāramitā), indicating her role as a female counterpart of the tantric Avalokiteśvara.[109] The ongoing restoration work at Ta Prohm has confirmed her place on the main *gopura* of the outer enclosure of the temple as a multiarmed and multiheaded standing goddess.[110] The central pediment of the "hall with dancers" also depicts her as a twenty-two-armed and possibly multiheaded standing deity (see figure 12b).[111] Finally at Banteay Chhmar, she appears on the pediment of the western *gopura* of the first enclosure leading to the central sanctuary as an eleven-headed, twenty-two-armed goddess in seated position (see figure 16). The entire south wing of the western gallery at Banteay Chhmar bears a renowned series of eight life-sized reliefs of the tantric Avalokiteśvara.[112]

Prajñāpāramitā Carved on the Torsos of Radiating Lokeśvaras. Along with the "Bayon style" innovation discussed in the section "Prajñāpāramitā as an Eleven-Headed, Twenty-Two-Armed Goddess," she also appears on the "radiating" Avalokiteśvara statues and

Figure 15. Khmer Prajñāpāramitā, Cambodia, 12th–13th century, exact provenance unknown. Bronze (h: 15 cm), National Museum of Cambodia Phnom Penh. Ga.5333.
Source: Photo by the late Emma Bunker

Figure 16. Prajñāpāramitā on the western pediment of the western pediment of the tower BC 32 leading to the central sanctuary of Banteay Chhmar, Cambodia, 12th–13th century. Sandstone.
Source: Photo by Philippe Stern 1936. ©EFEO Archive, Paris.

bronzes that were distributed in 1191 by Jayavarman VII to many sites throughout his realm.[113] Small buddhas cover the chest and hair of these radiating Lokeśvara statues, demonstrating a concept outlined in *Kāraṇḍavyūha Sūtra,* in which the skin pores are buddha universes, trances, and the seats of divine beings.[114] Prajñāpāramitā is placed on the chest of Avalokiteśvara, and he also carries eight of them as a belt. Woodward sees an esoteric aspect of Khmer art here—the bodhisattva can call up the goddess within his own body and through meditative exercise unite wisdom and compassion, achieving a state equivalent to buddhahood or the non-duality between *prajñā* and *upāya,* which sparks the generative prowess essential for progress (see figure 17).[115] On one of the radiating Lokeśvara bronzes kept at the Royal Palace, in the modern capital Phnom Penh, Prajñāpāramitā is replaced by dancing figures at the chest and around the waist. These dancing figures are identical to the dancers dancing around Avalokiteśvara on the reliefs seen at the Bayon and Banteay Chhmar or the *yoginīs* accompanying Hevajra. They possibly contain a symbolical reference to that of Hevajra's *yoginīs,* or her manifestation as a Prajñā of the male deity (see figure 18).[116] The Prajñāpāramitā pediments at Ta Prohm also depict *yoginīs* encircling the goddess.

Prajñāpāramitā on the Votive Tablets. Several votive tablets from Jayavarman VII's reign include Prajñāpāramitā in an assemblage comprising buddha–Lokeśvara–Vajrapāṇī. She also occupies a place in the universe of Hevajra, a Phase III deity of the Vajrayāna. The cult of the deity must have been of considerable importance under Jayavarman VII given the available material evidence. A huge 3.6-m cult statue of the deity was erected at the Bayon's eastern entrance and another one possibly at Ta Prohm, the temple dedicated to the king's mother as Prajñāpāramitā.[117]

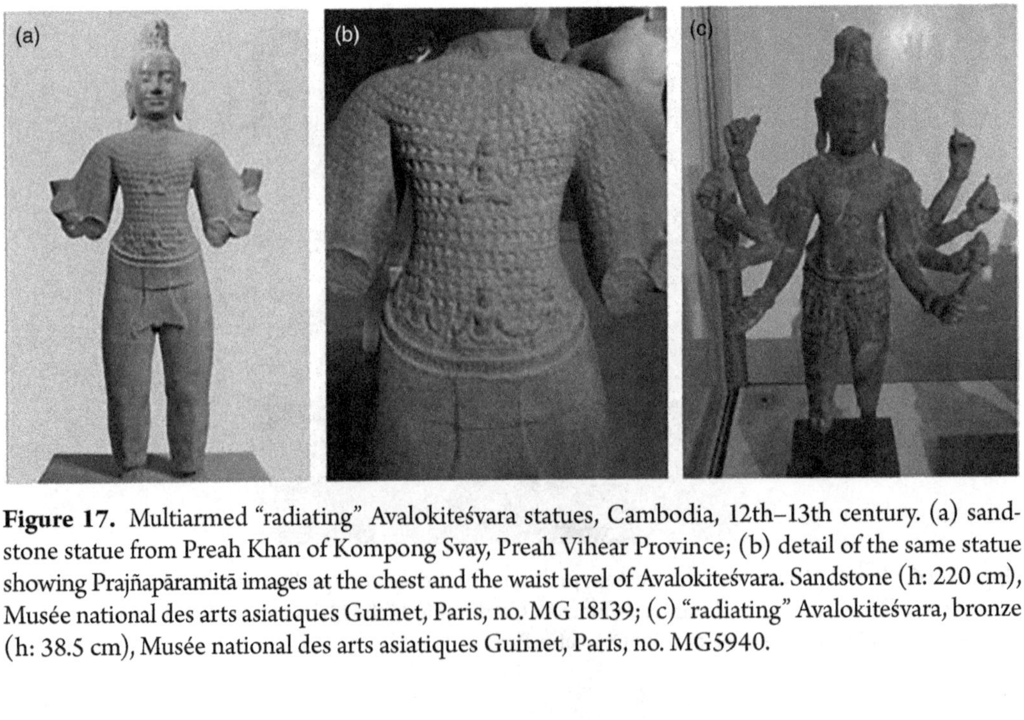

Figure 17. Multiarmed "radiating" Avalokiteśvara statues, Cambodia, 12th–13th century. (a) sandstone statue from Preah Khan of Kompong Svay, Preah Vihear Province; (b) detail of the same statue showing Prajñapāramitā images at the chest and the waist level of Avalokiteśvara. Sandstone (h: 220 cm), Musée national des arts asiatiques Guimet, Paris, no. MG 18139; (c) "radiating" Avalokiteśvara, bronze (h: 38.5 cm), Musée national des arts asiatiques Guimet, Paris, no. MG5940.

Figure 18. Multiarmed radiating Avalokiteśvara from Royal Palace, Phnom Penh, Cambodia, 12th–13th century, bronze (h: 72 cm). Left, front view, dancing female figures similar to *yoginīs* instead of Prajñāpāramitā are seen at the chest and waist level; right, rear view. First published by George Cœdès, *Bronzes Khmèrs*, Ars Asiatica V (Paris: G. van Oest, 1923), XXXII.

A bronze mold, used for making clay tablets, kept at the NMCPP positions Hevajra in the palace with his eight *yoginīs* in the center. The third story of the palace, just below a *nāga*-enthroned buddha, is occupied by a female divinity in the center, flanked by two worshipers. Based on J. J. Boeles's interpretation of a similar mold kept at the National Museum, Bangkok, Bunker and Latchford have identified the image as Prajñāpāramitā (see figure 19).[118] Another bronze mold found at Poipet shows a *nāga*-enthroned buddha on the top and Hevajra, Vajrasattva, and Saṃvara across the center. A triad at the bottom could be of six-armed Lokeśvara–bodhisattva–Vajrapāṇī (see figure 20).[119] Prajñāpāramitā possibly does not feature on this tablet, but she appears in a similar assemblage as the left bottom figure and as part of a triad next to Hevajra on the terra cotta tablets from Museum Rietberg, Zurich (see figures 21 and 22). The visual details of the figure in question on some of the molds are worn, and few attributes can be discerned. Assuming the goddess has been correctly identified in all these cases, reading the tablet as a cosmic map shows how Prajñāpāramitā ranks high in the universe of the Khmer Hevajra, alongside Saṃvara and Vajrasattva.

Prajñāpāramitā on *Caitya* Pillars: Her Apparent Esoteric Transformation. In a rare combination, on a *caitya* pillar from Preah Khan of Kompong Svay, Prajñāpāramitā is

Figure 19. Khmer Hevajra mandala, plaster cast from bronze mold, Cambodia, 12th–13th century. The figure seated directly below the *nāga*-enthroned buddha at the top is Prajñāpāramitā according to Emma Bunker and Douglas Latchford, *Khmer Bronzes: New Ineterpretations of the Past* (Chicago: Art Media Resources, 2011), 375. National Museum of Cambodia Phnom Penh, Ga. 5633.

Figure 20. Khmer mandala mold of Jayavarman VII's Buddhist pantheon, Cambodia, 12th–13th century, found at Poipet, Banteay Meanchey Province, with *nāga*-enthroned buddha at the top, Saṃvara, Vajrasattva, and Hevajra in the middle row, and Vajrapāṇī, Bodhisattva, and Avalokiteśvara in the bottom row. National Museum of Cambodia, Phnom Penh, Ga. 5657.

located on the pillar face axially opposite Avalokiteśvara; on the other two sides are dancing Hevajra and a *nāga*-enthroned buddha. All four figures are of the same size, suggesting equal rank (see figure 23).[120] There are two more examples of such pillars from Preah Khan of Kompong Svay with a possibility of a similar configuration of Buddhist deities.[121] Even though these Buddhist pillars appear in Khmer art from the end of the 10th century, the iconographic

Figure 21. Khmer mandala mold of Jayavarman VII's Buddhist pantheon, 12th–14th century, found at Lopburi, Thailand, with *nāga*-enthroned buddha at the top, Hevajra, Vajrasattva, and Saṃvara in the middle row, and Prajñāpāramitā, Avalokiteśvara, Bodhisattva, and Vajrapāṇī in the bottom row (h: 9.5 cm), Toni Gerber Collection, Rietberg Museum, Zurich, no. TG312. (For similar tablets see TG36 and TG37.)

Figure 22. Khmer Hevajra along with *nāga*-enthroned buddha and Prajñāpāramitā, 12th–14th century, found at Lopburi, Thailand (h: 7 cm), Toni Gerber Collection, Rietberg Museum, Zurich, no. TG32.

program on these *caityas* gets more complex in the 11th through 13th centuries with the advancement of esoteric Buddhism as seen on a *caitya* from Angkor National Museum (see figure 24). A dancing figure is depicted on the opposite side of a *nāga*-enthroned buddha, a Khmer substitute for Supreme Buddha—Mahāvairocana.[122] The dancing figure is similar to the Wat Pô Veal *caitya* figure discussed in the section "The Wat Pô Veal *Caitya* Pillar" and *yoginīs* of the Hevajra mandala. On the other two sides stand a female figure holding a lotus

Figure 23. Khmer Buddhist *caitya* pillar in Bayon style depicting, from left to right, four-armed Avalokiteśvara, Hevajra, two-armed Prajñāpāramitā, and *nāga*-enthroned buddha (understood as Supreme Buddha Vairocana in Khmer Buddhism during Jayavarman VII) on its four sides, found at Preah Khan of Kompong Svay, Preah Vihear Province, Cambodia, 12th–13th century, sandstone (h: 48 cm), Musée national des arts asiatiques Guimet MG18117. Also see MG18119.

Figure 24. Khmer Buddhist *caitya* pillar with *nāga*-enthroned buddha (understood as Supreme Buddha Vairocana in Khmer Buddhism under Jayavarman VII) on the left and two-armed dancing female figure on the right who is placed axially opposite the supreme buddha on the *caitya*. The other two sides depict a praying figure and a female figure holding a lotus in one hand. Cambodia, 11th–13th century, sandstone (h: 87.5 cm), Angkor National Museum, Siem Reap. DCA. 6304-No 119.
Source: Photo by EFEO fonds Cambodge, ref. CAM19196. ©EFEO Archive, Paris.

and a male figure in praying posture. Khmer esoteric Buddhist imagery never displays buddhas embracing their consorts as in Tibet or Nepal. The pairing of Prajñāpāramitā with Avalokiteśvara or *nāga*-enthroned buddha may convey the Khmer equivalent of the consort.[123] In Java, Vairocana and Prajñāpāramitā formed a couple as per the 10th-century art historical evidence.[124]

A terra cotta tablet acquired by the Museum Rietberg has an eleven-headed, twenty-two-armed Prajñāpāramitā along with a *nāga*-enthroned buddha and possibly a Śākyamuni.[125] Here she is placed in the center on a pedestal higher than that of the others (see figure 25). Another Rietberg tablet places her at the center of a mandala-type assemblage of deities that accords her ultimate rank above the *nāga*-enthroned buddha that was the main image of Jayavarman VII's Bayon state temple (see figure 26).[126]

A small 12th-century eleven-headed, six-armed female image from Phnom Kambot—is possibly a tantric manifestation of Prajñāpāramitā (see figure 27).[127] The fan-shaped arrangements of her eleven heads differ from the other eleven-headed, twenty-two-armed Prajñāpāramitā statues of the Bayon style but are very similar to the eleven-headed tantric Avalokiteśvara bronzes of Cambodia.[128] The presence of Buddha Amitābha (broken) in her head, a marker of Khmer Prajñāpāramitā, indicates her status as Prajñāpāramitā even though the praying position is unusual.[129]

ESOTERIC BUDDHIST PRAJÑĀPĀRAMITĀ: EVIDENCE FROM PĀLA INDIA

Jayavarman's court revived Sanskrit and the royal family composed long poetic inscriptions. Presumably, there was an important Khmer text or commentary on Prajñāpāramitā, which is now lost. A number of early-12th-century Indian manuscripts of *Aṣṭasāhasrikā Prajñāpāramitā*

Figure 25. Standing Khmer Prajñāpāramitā with eleven heads and twenty-two arms along with *nāga*-enthroned buddha and possibly Śākyamunī, 12th–14th century, Lopburi, Thailand, (h: 8 cm), Toni Gerber Collection, Rietberg Museum, Zurich, no. TG31.

Figure 26. Mandala of seated Khmer Prajñāpāramitā with eleven heads and twenty-two arms along with *nāga*-enthroned buddha and other deities, 12th–14th century, Lopburi, Thailand, (h: 9 cm), Toni Gerber Collection, Rietberg Museum, Zurich, no. TG35.

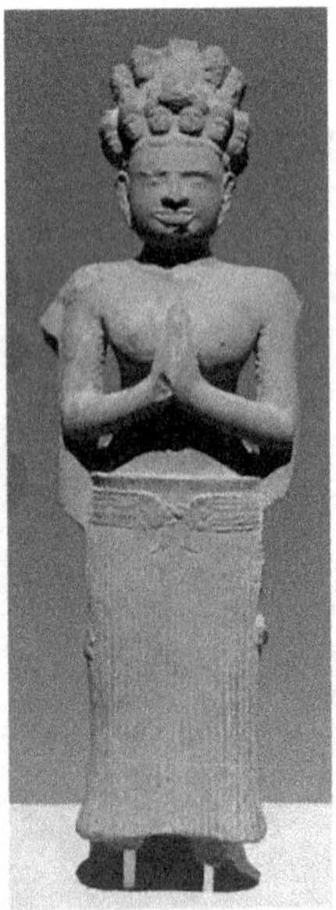

Figure 27. A possible depiction of standing Khmer Prajñāpāramitā with six arms and eleven heads and an image of Amitābha Buddha among her heads, 12th century, Prasat Kambot, Siem Reap Province, Cambodia, sandstone (h: 62 cm), Musée national des arts asiatiques Guimet MG14908. The Guimet consider it in the "Angkor Wat style" because of the sarong and belt and open, staring eyes. This could indicate an icon of the Buddhist king Tribhuvanādityavarman, younger brother of the Vaiṣṇava king Suryavarman II, who reigned from 1149 to *c.* 1180 according to K.1297.

Figure 28. Indian miniature votive stūpa, 11th century, eastern India, bronze with inlay of semiprecious stone (h: 29.2 cm), the Cleveland Museum of Art, John L. Severance Fund 1982.132.

include deities from the *Yoginī* and *Anuttarayoga tantras* such as Hevajra and Cakrasaṃvara with their respective consorts. In the late 12th and the early 13th centuries, these deities were paired with their consorts on the facing panels in the center of the manuscript so they would come together in an embrace in the closed book.[130] Kim argues: "The inclusion of the esoteric Buddhist deities in sexual embrace in a manuscript of the *AsP* not only transforms a book of the Mahayana sutra into a suitable cultic object of phase III esoteric Buddhism but also locates the esoteric Buddhist practices and theology within the age-old tradition of Prajñāpāramitā."[131]

On a miniature Pāla period votive bronze stūpa inlaid with precious stones from 11th-century India, Prajñāpāramitā is placed on the side axially opposite Akṣobhya, possibly indicating her pairing as his consort Locanā in her esoteric manifestation. On the other two sides are seated Supreme Buddha Vajrasattva holding a *vajra* on his chest and bell on his left hip—the Adibuddha or ultimate teacher of a Buddhist practitioner and the preceptor of the five *tathāgatas* in tantric Buddhist practices—and possibly a siddha figure (see figure 28).

Prajñāpāramitā was highly venerated by Indian Pāla rulers in India. Multitudes of her illustrated manuscripts and statuaries speak to her importance there from the 9th to the 12th century. East Java produced several bronzes of the goddess in the 10th century, indicating her supreme position there at the same time as the Pālas.

While the Indian or Indonesian examples are not directly connected to the Khmer ones, they appear to indicate the transformation of Khmer Prajñāpāramitā as an esoteric Buddhist deity under Jayavarman VII as in the Pāla domain.

CONCLUSION

Prajñāpāramitā made her debut in Khmer Buddhist triads during the 10th century and in the succeeding centuries was transformed into a major political icon of Jayavarman VII's esoteric Buddhist court. She was placed among his highest ranked deities with the Buddha of Phimai and the Eastern Buddha for the kings' great annual *Phālguna* circumambulation ceremony held at Preah Khan.[132] Chuttiwongs holds that in the entire Buddhist pantheon, Prajñāpāramitā was the only goddess worshiped among the Khmers, standing for the female energy in both its benevolent and destructive forms.[133] While it is true that Prajñāpāramitā often appears in

Cambodian inscriptions and is the only Buddhist goddess invoked, given her diverse iconographic forms, it is quite possible that she may have simultaneously represented other female Buddhist deities.

She was elevated under Jayavarman VII to occupy a place within the esoteric Buddhist pantheon of Supreme Buddha, Hevajra, Saṃvara, and Vajrapāṇī. The Wat Pô Veal *caitya*, discussed in the section "The Wat Pô Veal *Caitya* Pillar" (see figure 1), represents her multiple esoteric manifestations. Side B may be a rare disclosure of Hevajra's Prajñā—Nairātmya. In the sexual imagery of *Anuttarayoga tantra*, "the feminine partner is in every case a form of Prajñāpāramitā."[134] Side B of the *caitya* does display the dance posture of Hevajra and Prajñāpāramitā's twenty-two arms, possibly uniting the two in unique Khmer iconographic embrace. Along with examples of Prajñāpāramitā, a substantial body of esoteric Buddhist female images have survived from Jayavarman VII's period, which would call for further research based on a firmer understanding of the goddess.[135]

REVIEW OF LITERATURE

Study of the Prajñāpāramitā literature has focused on the buddhological approaches to texts and philosophical traditions. Edward Conze's pioneering work *The Prajñāpāramitā Literature* remains the most comprehensive and provides bibliographical information on each text and its commentaries.[136] A substantial part of Prajñāpāramitā literature survives in Sanskrit, Tibetan, and Chinese translations as well as in Indian, Chinese, Tibetan, Japanese, and Khotanese commentaries. Some of these works have been critically edited and studied and translated into English.

Studies of illustrated Buddhist manuscripts from South Asia drew the attention of scholars in the early 20th century and brought systematic publications of the illustrations with identifications. Jinah Kim's 21st-century work has taken this further by examining the material culture of Mahāyāna sutra literature of the 9th to the 13th century in India and Nepal, including several *Aṣṭasāhasrikā Prajñāpāramitā* manuscripts. This brings detailed historical and art historical analysis of the patronage, production, use, and sociocultural role of these manuscripts in society.[137] Her research highlights the way in which Phase III Buddhist esoteric deities hold central positions in the important texts of later Mahāyāna.

Though textual studies are important, a multidisciplinary approach is needed to include cultures like the Khmer, where architecture and statuary are abundant but epigraphy and text sparse because of the tropical climate. For example, the Angkor material record shows a powerful cult of a Khmer Hevajra, a Phase III Buddhist deity, in the 11th through 13th centuries, yet there is only one epigraphic mention of him in neighboring Campā and two brief inscriptional references to the related Supreme Buddha Vajrasattva in Angkor and Phimai. In addition, Khmer Buddhism turned definitively to the Theravada in the late 13th century, so there is no present-day Khmer equivalent of Hevajra in sexual union with his consort Nairātmya, as defined in the texts that remain recurrent in Tibetan and Nepalese Buddhist art. The primary ancient Khmer evidence is a large number of ritual bronze statues, libation conches, ritual instruments, and terra cotta tablets, which indicate that the Hevajra consecrations formed a significant part of the royal cult.[138] The discovery of a 3.6-m stone image of the deity, which scholars believe was erected at the main eastern entrance to Jayavarman VII's Bayon Buddhist state temple, affirms a central place for this esoteric Buddhist deity in the kingdom.[139]

The textual silence is mirrored in the large Khmer Prajñāpāramitā cult. In considering the iconography of the Khmer Prajñāpāramitā, Conze finds that "Cambodia stands outside the main stream."[140] For reasons that still need further researching, her cult there indeed went beyond the others. One of the common characteristics of Khmer images is the presence of the Amitābha Buddha on the headdress, which is attested in no known Buddhist text. Likewise, the Khmer Prajñāpāramitā–buddha–Avalokiteśvara triad that became popular from the 10th century onward has not been identified in any text but is nevertheless well known in Khmer epigraphy. The Khmer inscriptions record priests constructing temples and consecrating Prajñāpāramitā images, making offerings to her, and carrying her image in festivals. There is a further thread in understanding the Khmer Prajñāpāramitā during the 12th and 13th centuries, when she appears multiarmed and multiheaded in the universe of Hevajra, Samvara, Vairocana, and Vajrasattva.

At the time of Conze's solitary amassing of the Prajñāpāramitā literature, there was a dearth of Khmer examples, but this no longer remains the case. Emma Bunker's study of Khmer bronzes has dealt with multiple images of Prajñāpāramitā and other esoteric Buddhist female images and more have come to light since.[141] Given her diverse Khmer depictions, it seems that the prominence of the goddess in Angkor in the 10th through 13th centuries went unequaled in the medieval Buddhist world.

ACKNOWLEDGMENTS

I have been fortunate to have Olivier Cunin as a true bodhisattva, whose attention to detail and sharp eyes have given me opportunity not only to learn even more on my article but also save me from embarrassing mistakes. I am grateful to him for his help and all the useful discussions on the Ta Prohm and other Jayavarman VII temple Prajñāpāramitā images. Special thanks to Christian Luczanits for patiently going through all my Khmer images of esoteric female deities and giving his inputs on them, to Peter Sharrock for the useful discussions on the Khmer esoteric Buddhism of Jayavarman VII and tirelessly dealing with all my queries. Many thanks to Hiram Woodward for pointing out some of the Khmer images and sharing his views on them. Thanks to Johannes Beltz for generously providing the Rietberg Museum votive tablet images, to the late Emma Bunker for being really big-hearted and letting me use whatever I needed from her books, and finally to Shivani Kapoor and Andrea Acri for their interest in the subject, reading the drafts, and all the useful comments.

NOTES

1. Hewidge Multzer o'Naghten, "Prajñāpāramitā Dans Le Bouddhisme Du Cambodge Ancien," *Arts Asiatiques* 71 (2016): 31–54.
2. Emma Bunker and Douglas Latchford, *Adoration and Glory: The Golden Age of Khmer Art* (Chicago: Art Media Resources, 2004); and *Khmer Bronzes: New Interpretation of the Past* (Chicago: Art Media Resources, 2011). In earlier scholarship, the Khmer goddess and her multifaceted role in the society has been touched on briefly in studies by George Cœdès, "notes sur une statuette cambodgienne de la

Prajñā Pâramitâ," *Bulletin de l'École Française d'Extrême-Orient (BEFEO)* 20, no. 4 (1920): 59–60; Nancy Dowling, "Honolulu Academy of Art Tenth-Century Khmer Buddhist Trinity," *Artibus Asiae* 56, no. ¾ (1996): 325–341; and Hiram Woodward, "The Jayabuddhamahānātha Images of Cambodia," *Journal of the Walters Art Gallery* 52, no. 53 (1994–1995): 105–111; and Hiram Woodward, "Aspects of Buddhism in Tenth-Century Cambodia," in *Buddhist Dynamics in Premodern and Early Modern Southeast Asia*, ed. D. Christian Lammerts (Singapore: ISEAS, 2015), 218–260.

3. Hiram Woodward, "Tantric Buddhism at Angkor Thom," *Ars Orientalis* 12 (1981): 57–67, "Review: Esoteric Buddhism in Southeast Asia in the Light of Recent Scholarship," *Journal of Southeast Asian Studies* 35, no. 2 (2004): 329–354, and 2015; Wibke Lobo, "The Figure of Hevajra and Tantric Buddhism," in *Sculpture of Angkor and Ancient Cambodia: Millennium Glory*, ed. Helen Jessup and Theirry Zéphir (New York: Thames & Hudson, 1997), 71–78; and Wibke Lobo, "Adorned Buddha Protected by the Nāga," in *Sculpture of Angkor and Ancient Cambodia: Millennium Glory*, ed. Helen Jessup and Theirry Zéphir (New York: Thames & Hudson, 1997), 272–273; Peter Sharrock, "The Buddhist Pantheon of the Bàyon of Angkor: An Historical and Art Historical Reconstruction of the Bàyon Temple and Its Religious and Political Roots" (PhD diss., School of Oriental and African Studies, London University, 2006); Peter Sharrock, "Garuḍa, Vajrapāṇi and Religious Change in Jayavarman VII's Angkor," *Journal of Southeast Asian Studies* 40, no. 1 (2009): 111–151; Peter Sharrock, "Kīrtipaṇḍita and the Tantras," *UDAYA: Journal of Khmer Studies* 10 (2012): 203–237; Julia Estève and Brice Vincent, "L'about inscrit du musée national du Cambodge (K.943): Nouveaux éléments sur le bouddhisme tantrique à l'époque angkorienne," *Arts Asiatiques* 65 (2010): 133–158; and Phillip Green, "The Vat Sithor Inscription: Translation, Commentary, and Reflections on Buddhist Traditions in Tenth-Century Cambodia" (PhD diss., University of Florida, 2014).
4. Edward Conze, "The Iconography of the Prajñāpāramitā-Part 1," *Oriental Art* 1 (1949): 51; and Edward Conze, "The Iconography of the Prajñāpāramitā," in *Thirty Years of Buddhist Studies: Selected Essays*, ed. Edward Conze (Oxford: Bruno Cassirer, 1967), 250.
5. Louis Finot first coined the term *caitya* pillar for the lack of a better term for these pillar-like objects that signaled the public restoration of Buddhism in Angkor and surrounding areas. See Louis Finot, "Lokesvara en Indochine," in *Études Asiatiques publiées à l'occasion du vingt-cinquième anniversaire de l'EFEO par ses membres et collaborateurs*, 2 vols. (Paris: G. Van Oest, 1925), 227–256.
6. This buddha is commonly referred to as Mucalinda or *nāga*-protected buddha, linking it to a minor narrative in the buddha biographies about a *nāga* called Muchalinda, who left his lake or river to enwrap the meditating Śakyamuni and protect him from an unseasonal storm in the fifth or sixth week of his enlightenment. Refuting this identification, since the "*nāga*-protected" epithet risks recalling the Muchalinda episode, Peter Sharrock has coined the term "*nāga*-enthroned buddha" for the principal Khmer Buddha icon that would eventually be erected in the Bayon state temple. See Sharrock, "Garuḍa, Vajrapāṇi"; and Peter Sharrock, "Appendix: Naga Enthroned Buddha of Angkor," in *Khmer Bronzes: New Interpretations of the Past*, ed. Emma Bunker and Douglas Latchford (Chicago: Art Media Resources, 2011), 481–491. Hiram Woodward identified this buddha as the supreme Khmer Buddha in "The Bàyon-Period Buddha Image in the Kimbell Art Museum," *Archives of Asian Art* 32 (1979): 72–83, and was supported by Wibke Lobo in "Buddha paré protégé par le naga," in *Angkor et dix siècles d'art khmer*, ed. Helen Jessup and Thierry Zéphir (Paris: Réunion de Musées Nationaux, 1997), 272–273.
7. See image no. CAM00595 on the École française d'Extrême-Orient's website.
8. Bruno Bruguier, *Banteay Chhmar et les Provinces occidentales*, vol. 3, *Guide archeologique du Cambodge* (Paris: École française d'Extrême-Orient, 2009), 17.
9. Edward Conze, *The Prajñāparamitā Literature*, Indo-Iranian Monograph (Gravenhage: Mouton, 1960); Lewis Lancaster, "The Oldest Mahayana Sutra," *Eastern Buddhist* 8 (1975): 30–41.
10. The doctrinal content of the text is the letter *A*. See Edward Conze, "Text, Sources, and Bibliography of the Prajñāpāramitā- hṛdaya," *Journal of the Royal Asiatic Society* 80 (new series) (1948): 33–51.

11. Xuanzang's 7th-century translation is the first reliable dating of the text. Amoghvajra's late-8th-century translation and commentary on the Prajñāpāramitā in 150 verses establishes that it drew on the model of the *Sarvatathāgatatattvasaṃgraha*, the principal scripture of *yogatantras*. The key element in this was the esoteric transformation of the doctrine of emptiness. This reformulation is most strongly seen in the teaching of *mahāsukha*, or Great Bliss, which defines a process of striving toward and finally experiencing enlightenment in terms that often have blatantly sexual reference. See Edward Conze, "Tantric Prajñāpāramitā Texts," *Sino Indian Studies* 5, no. 2 (1956): 100–122; Ian Astley Kristensen, "The Rishukyō: A Translation and Commentary in the Light of Modern Japanese Scholarship" (PhD diss., University of Leeds, 1987), 35; and Kimiaki Tanaka, *An Illustrated History of the Maṇḍala: From Its Genesis to the Kālacakratantra* (Somerville, MA: Wisdom Publications, 2018), 85–123. Rob Linrothe argues that *Svalpākṣara Prajñāpāramitā Sūtra* is also considered tantric by some due to its emphasis on *dhāraṇī*. See Rob Linrothe, *Ruthless Compassion: Wrathful Deities in Early Indo-Tibetan Esoteric Buddhist Art* (Boston: Shambhala, 1999), 158–159.
12. Tanaka, Illustrated History of the Maṇḍala, 87.
13. Prajñāpāramitā is the central figure of the few mandalas described in Chinese and Tibetan texts. See Conze, "Iconography of the Prajñāpāramitā," 257.
14. David Snellgrove, *Buddhist Himalaya* (New York: Philosophical Library, 1957), 81; and Alex Wayman, "Female Energy and Symbolism in Buddhist Tantras," *History of Religions* 2, no. 1 (1962): 75.
15. For analysis of esoteric Buddhist deities in several Prajñāpāramitā manuscripts, see Jinah Kim, *Receptacle of the Sacred: Illustrated Manuscripts and the Buddhist Book Cult in South Asia* (Berkeley: University of California Press, 2013), 149–209. Linrothe's analysis (*Ruthless Compassion*, 158–159) of wrathful deities categorizes them into phases. Wrathful deities in Phase I serve as attendant or protective deities to peaceful bodhisattvas whereas in Phase II and III these wrathful deities come out of the shadow of their bodhisattvas and become independent and powerful deities. In Phase III, these deities are typically seen embracing their consorts. Traditionally these are known as *yogatantra* and *yoginītantra* deities.
16. Kim, *Receptacle of the Sacred*, 9.
17. Kim, *Receptacle of the Sacred*, 9.
18. James Apple, "Prajñāpāramitā," in *Buddhism and Jainism: Encyclopedia of Indian Religions*, ed. Karam Tej Singh Sarao and Jeffery D. Long (Dordrecht, The Netherlands: Springer, 2017), 928.
19. Apple, "Prajñāpāramitā," 929.
20. Apple, "Prajñāpāramita," 929.
21. David Snellgrove, *The Hevajra Tantra: A Critical Study*, London Oriental Series 6 (London: Oxford University Press, 1959), part II, v, 110–111.
22. Snellgrove, *Hevajra Tantra*, part II, iv, 40–47, 24, 104–105.
23. *Sādhanamāla* (*SM*) is a collection of instructions for meditation practice. It contains more than three hundred instructions of varying length. The earliest surviving manuscript of the text dates to 1164 CE. See Benoytosh Bhattacharya, *The Indian Buddhist Iconography, Mainly Based on the Sādhanamālā and Cognate Tantric Texts of Rituals*, 2nd rev. ed. (1925; Calcutta: Firma K.L. Mukhopadhyay, 1968).
24. *Advyyasiddhī*, verse 21: *sarvavarṇasamudbhūtā jugupsā naiva yoṣita/śaiva bhagavatī prajñā* sa(ṃ)vṛtyā rūpamāśritā. See the critically edited and translated version by Malati Shendge, *Advaya-siddhi of Laksminkara (A Study)*, M. S. University Oriental Series no. 8 (Reprinted from the *Journal of the Oriental Institute*; Baroda, India: Oriental Institute, 1964), 15. For the dating issues of the text, see 11:n18. Miranda Shaw, *Passionate Enlightenment: Women in Tantric Buddhism* (Princeton, NJ: Princeton University Press, 1994), 39.
25. Conze, "Texts, Sources and Bibliography," 47–52.
26. George Cœdès, *Inscriptions du Cambodge (IC)*, vols. 1–8 (Hanoi, Vietnam: École française d'Extrême-Orient [EFEO], 1937–1966). Inscription K. 132 (*IC*, 2:85) is incised on a buddha image: an image of

Lokeśvara entitled Jagadīśvara and a *devī*, Vidyādhāraṇī, possibly representing Prajñāpāramitā, given the context. Also see Kamaleswar Bhattacharya, "Les religious brahmaniques dans I'ancien Cambodge d'après I'epigraphie et I'iconographie," *BEFEO* 49 (1961): 18, for the identification of the inscription as Buddhist. However, o'Naghten has refuted the identification of Vidyādhāraṇī as Prajñāpāramita in "Prajñāpāramitā Dans Le Bouddhisme," 71:39.

27. Phillip Green records only two references to the Bodhisattva Avalokiteśvara prior to the mid-10th century in "Vat Sithor Inscription," 72. See inscriptions (K. 872) of 944 CE in *IC*, 5:97 and (K. 238) of 949 CE in *IC*, 6:119.
28. Green, "Vat Sithor Inscription," 169.
29. Although these texts predate the 10th century by several years, it is around this time the concepts and figures presented in these texts are attested in Cambodia. The tentative date of the *Kāraṇḍavyūha Sūtra* is the 5th to 6th century. See Alexander Studholme, *The Origins of Oṃ Maṇipadme Hūṃ: A Study of the Kāraṇḍavyūha Sūtra* (Albany: State University of New York Press, 2002), 9–17. For an art historical evidence of these texts in Cambodia, see Hiram Woodward, "The Karandavyuha Sutra and Buddhist Art in 10th-Century Cambodia," in *Buddhist Art: Form and Meaning*, ed. Pratapaditya Pal (Mumbai: Marg Publications, 2007), 70–83.
30. The inscription at the Cam temple of Đồng Dương of 875 CE alludes to the *Kāraṇḍavyūhasūtra*, and, quite remarkably, the different gestures of guardian figures at the temple are enactments of passages in the text. For the inscription (C. 66, B, st. VIII), see Karl-Heinz Golzio, *Inscriptions of Campā Based on the Editions and Translations of Abel Bergaigne, Étienne Aymonier, Louis Finot, Édouard Huber and Other French Scholars and of the Work of R. C. Majumdar: Newly Presented, with Minor Corrections of Texts and Translations, Together with Calculations of Given Dates* (Aachen, Germany: Shaker Verlag, 2004), 66, 71. For its connection to *Kāraṇḍavyūha Sūtra*, see Hiram Woodward, "Esoteric Buddhism in Southeast Asia in the Light of Recent Scholarship," *Journal of Southeast Asian Studies (JSEAS)* 35, no. 2 (2004): 348–349; and Woodward, "The Karandavyuha Sutra," 72–73. The An-Thai inscription of 902 CE (C. 138, st. VII-X) propagates the three Buddhist families around Mahāvairocana. For the inscription, see Golzio, *Inscriptions of Campā*, 89–92; and Ian Mabbett, "Buddhism in Campa," in *Southeast Asia in the 9th to 14th Centuries*, ed. David G. Marr and Anthony C. Milner (Singapore: Institute of Southeast Asian Studies, 1986). For the discussion on the inscription, see Nandana Chuttiwongs, "Le Bouddhisme du Champa," in *Trésors d'art du Vietnam: La sculpture du Champa Ve-XVe siècles*, ed. Pierre Baptiste and Thierry Zéphir (Paris: Réunion des musees nationaux, 2005), 80–81; Anne-Valérie Schweyer, "Buddhism in Čampā," *Moussons* 13–14 (2009): 315–316; and Hiram Woodward, "Aspects of Buddhism in Tenth Century Cambodia," in *Buddhist Dynamics in Premodern and Early Modern Southeast Asia*, ed. Christian Lammerts (Singapore: ISEAS, 2015), 222. For *Mahāvairocana Sūtra*, see Rolf Giebel, *The Vairocanābhisaṃbodhi Sutra* (Berkeley, CA: Numata Centre for Buddhist Translation and Research, 2005); and Stephen Hodge, *The Mahā-Vairocana-Abhisaṃbodhi Tantra with Buddhaguhya's Commentary* (New York: Routledge-Curzon, 2003).
31. (K. 417): Louis Finot, "Notes d'épigraphie," *Bulletin de I'École Française d'Extrême-Orient* 15, no. 1 (1915): 19; and *IC*, 2:48. (K. 240), *IC*, 3:76. The role of *Kāraṇḍavyūha Sūtra* in Cambodia was earlier recognized by Jean Boisselier, "Précisions sur quelques images khmères d'Avalokiteśvara: Les bas-reliefs de Bantãy Čhmmàr," *Arts Asiatiques* 11 (1964): 73–89. Translated as "Identification of Some Khmer Images of Avalokiteśvara: The Bantãy Čhhmàr Bas-reliefs," in *Studies on the Art of Ancient Cambodia: Ten Articles by Jean Boisselier*, trans. and ed. Natasha Eilenberg and Robert Brown (Phnom Penh, Cambodia: Reyum, 2008), 305–340; and Max Nihom, *Studies in Indian and Indoe-Indonesian Tantrism: The Kuñjarakarṇadharmakathana and the Yogatantra* (Vienna: Sammlung De Nobili, 1994), 137–141. The inscribed stele has added a new dimension. For (K. 1154) inscribed on the rear side of the stele that includes the words "*Om maṇipadme hūm*," which first appeared in the *Kāraṇḍavyūhasūtra*, see Saveros Pou, *Nouvelles inscriptions du Cambodge*, vol. 2–3 (Paris: École francaise d'Extrême-Orient, 2001), 129.

The stele depicts the Avalokiteśvara in a *pretasantarpita* mudra referring to an event in the sutra. The spell is translated in Studholme, *Origins of Oṃ Maṇipadme Hūm*, 129. For this stele, see Nandana Chuttiwongs, "The Iconography of Avalokiteśvara in Mainland Southeast Asia," (PhD diss., Leiden University, 1984), 380, 117; and Woodward, "Esoteric Buddhism," 348.

32. (K. 157, B, st. XIV), *IC*, 6:123–125.
33. For Vīrendravikhyāta who served under Harśavarman II (941–944 CE) and Rājendravarman II (945–968 CE), see Inscription (K. 157) of Kdei Car in *IC*, 6:123–127.
34. See (K. 225) of Thma Puok in *IC*, 3:66–69; and (K. 168) of Prasat Chikreng in *IC*, 6:168–169.
35. o'Naghten, "Prajñāpāramitā Dans Le Bouddhisme," 34–35.
36. For an English translation of the Wat Sithor inscription (K. 111, st. XXIX and XLII), see Green, "Vat Sithor Inscription," 26, 30, 69; and Tadeusz Skorupski in Sharrock, "Kīrtipaṇḍita and the Tantras," 205.
37. Vajrapāṇī appears for the first time during this period alongside the figures of Prajñāpāramitā, buddha, and Lokeśvara. See Green, "Vat Sithor Inscription," 86. Inscription (K. 214), *IC*, 2:202 refers to the three embodiments of the buddha while (K. 432), *IC*, 2:119; (K. 806), *IC*, 1:73; (K. 239), *IC*, 3:79; and (K. 339), *IC*, 5:164 praise the three jewels of Buddhism.
38. Woodward, "Esoteric Buddhism," 349.
39. Woodward, "Aspects of Buddhism," 222–225.
40. Bat Cum inscriptions were first edited and translated by George Cœdès, "Les inscriptions de Bàt Čuṃ (Cambodge)," *Journal Asiatique* 12 (1908): 213–252. For the English translation, see Green, "Vat Sithor Inscription," 291–315; and cf. Julia Estève, "Étude Critique des Phénomènes de Syncrétisme Religieux dans le Cambodge Angkorien" (PhD diss., Université Paris-Sorbonne, 2009), 377–391.
41. For (K. 266, 267, and 268), see Cœdès, "Les inscriptions de Bàt Čuṃ," 230, 241. Translation: "That the buddha gives you the bodhi [awakening], he by whom was taught the excellent doctrine denying the existence of the individual soul [i.e., *ātman*] and self-identification with the universal soul [i.e., Brahman], which is contradictory to this doctrine [i.e., a*nātamn* of the buddha]."
42. Green, "Vat Sithor Inscription," 297.
43. Green, "Vat Sithor Inscription," 301.
44. (K. 267 st. iii) and (K. 268 st. xxxvi) in Cœdès, "Les inscriptions de Bàt Čuṃ," 230, 236, 241, 251. Cf. Green, "Vat Sithor Inscription," 297; and Estéve, "Étude Critique des Phénomènes de Syncrétisme Religieux," 379, 387.
45. Cœdès, "Les inscriptions de Bàt Čuṃ," 230; and cf. Green, "Vat Sithor Inscription," 237.
46. (K. 157) Wat Kdei Car, *IC*, 6:123–125 mentions Vīrendravikhyāta and his niece Kontī, who was married to Kavīndrārimathana. Vīrendravikhyāta was himself possibly Buddhist. King Rājendravarman had gifted him bronze images of Avalokiteśvara and *devī* [Prajñāpāramitā?].
47. Seven fragments were found from the central sanctuary and the eighth was found from the north tower, together with a fragment bearing an engraved *vajra*. See George Cœdès, "Un yantra récemment découvert à Angkor," *Journal Asiatique* 240, no. 4 (1952): 465–477. François Bizot correctly identified its significance as a cosmogram. See 'Notes sur les yantra bouddhiques d'Indochine,' in *Tantric and Taoist Studies in Honour of R. A. Stein*, vol. 1, ed. Michel Strickmann (Brussels: Institut belge des hautes etudes chinoises, 1981), 155–191. There were at least two such *yantras* of the same period but belonging to two different places. See Julia Estève, "Results of the Archaeological Campaign 2011–2012 at Prasat Komnap South and Prasat Ong Mong" (Paper presented at Religious Studies in Cambodia: Understanding the Old and Tracing the New organized by APSARA, EFEO, CKS, and the University of Sydney with the help of the Friends of Khmer Culture, Siem Reap, Cambodia, June 10, 2012).
48. Woodward, "Aspects of Buddhism," 233.
49. For an English translation of *Vīṇaśikhatantra*, see Teun Goudriaan, *The Vīṇāśikhatantra: A Śaiva Tantra of the Left Current* (Delhi: Motilal Banarsidass, 1985). The Sdok Kok Thom inscription (K. 235) was dated to 1052 CE, Louis Finot, "l'Inscription de Sdok Kok Thom," *BEFEO* 15, no. 2 (1915): 53; George

Cœdès and Pierre Dupont, "Les stèles de Sdok kok Thom, Phnom Sandak et Prah Vihar," *BEFEO* (1943): 56–134; and Kamaleswar Bhattacharya, *A Selection of Sanskrit Inscriptions from Cambodia* (Siem Reap, Cambodia: Center for Khmer Studies, 2009), 123.

SBS is briefly described by Amoghavajra as the ninth assembly of his Introduction to the Yoga of the Eighteen Sections of the *Vajraśekharatantra* (T. 869). For the English translation of the text from Chinese, see Rolf Giebel, "The Chin-kang-ting ching yü-che'ieh shih-pa-hui chih-kuei: An Annotated Translation," *Journal of Naritisan Institute for Buddhist Studies* 18 (1995): 179–182. On the basis of the Tibetan text of the *Uttarottaratantra* of the *SBS*, Toru Tomabechi reconstructed the *prastāra* described in the text. See "The Extraction of Mantra (Mantroddhāra) in the Sarvabuddhasamāyogatantra," *Pramāṇakīrtiḥ: Papers Dedicated to Ernst Steinkellner on the Occasion of His 70th Birthday*, Wiener Studien zur Tibetologie und Buddhismuskunde 70, part 2, ed. Birgit Kellner, Horst Lasic, Michael T. Much, and Helmut Tauscher (Vienna: Arbeitskreis für tibetische und buddhistische Studein, Universität Wien, 2007), 903–923. This diagram shows striking similarities to the one that is attached to *Viīṇaśikatantra*. For the discussion of these texts and their association with Bat Cum *prastāra*, see Woodward, "Aspects of Buddhism," 234–235. One of the notable features of the *Sarvabuddhasamāyogaḍākinījālasaṃvara* is the introduction of the cult of Heruka and other tutelary deities deriving from Hevajra and Saṃvara. See Tanaka, *Illustrated History of the Maṇḍala*, 205–206. These deities were surely known in Cambodia by the 11th century.

50. See image nos. CAM10772 and CAM19209_2 on the École française d'Extrême-Orient's website.
51. Woodward, "Aspects of Buddhism," 236.
52. (K. 772), *IC*, 7:104–105. Cf. Woodward, "Aspects of Buddhism," 236.
53. (K. 111), *IC*, 6:195. For the inscription and translation, the author has followed Green, "Vat Sithor Inscription," Appendix, 2014 267–2014 276. Cf. Skorupski in Sharrock, "Kīrtipaṇḍita," 231–237.
54. (K. 111, st. LXIX), "The *purohita* who is learned in the rite of the fire sacrifice, *vidyā*, *mantra*, *mudra*, and heart [-syllables], and who is familiar with the secrets of the *vajra* and the bell (*ghaṇṭā*), is worthy of donations," Green, "Vat Sithor Inscription," 51, 81. Cf. Skorupski in Sharrock, "Kīrtipaṇḍita," 233.
55. (K. 111, st. XXXVI–XLIX), Green, "Vat Sithor Inscription," 149:n2.
56. Green, "Vat Sithor Inscription," 167. Cf. Skorupski in Sharrock, "Kīrtipaṇḍita," 232.
57. Green, "Vat Sithor Inscription," 76n44, 189. Cf. Cœdès's translation (*IC*, 6:206–207); and Skorupski in Sharrock, "Kīrtipaṇḍita," 233. Some Tibetan renditions of Sarvavid Vairocana depict him in female aspect (Prajñāpāramitā) as seen at Alchi temple complex in Ladakh. See Pratapaditya Pal, *A Buddhist Paradise: The Murals of Alchi* (Basel, Switzerland: Ravi Kumar, 1982), 51, 55, 66.
58. Vajradhātvīśvarī is the female form of Vajradhātu-Vairocana in the text *STTS*, but in the later tantric Buddhism she is considered to symbolize a fifth element. *Kālacakratantra* assigns Prajñāpāramitā to the Wisdom family over which Vajrasattva presides. See Tanaka, *Illustrated History of the Maṇḍala*, 252.
59. Snellgrove, *Buddhist Himalaya*, 81.
60. Probably from the time the Wisdom sutras came to be personified as the goddess Prajñāpāramitā, Wisdom in this deified form was revered as the "Mother of all Buddhas"—not really as a loving earthly mother but as fundamental theological principles in Mahāyāna and Vajrayāna. In Tibetan iconography, when Wisdom is shown in sexual embrace with her lord, as the father–mother posture—the buddha is depicted as the "son." See Conze, *Thirty Years of Buddhist Studies*, 188–189.
61. (K. 111 st. LXIX), Green, "Vat Sithor Inscription," 81. Cf. Skorupski in Sharrock, "Kīrtipaṇḍita," 235.
62. Green, "Vat Sithor Inscription," 72.
63. In the Chinese canon, the *Prajñāpāramitā Sūtras* are said to have consisted of one hundred thousand *gāthās* or *ślokas* of thirty-two syllables. See Do-Kyun Kwon, "Sarva Tathāgata Tattva Saṃgraha: Compendium of All the Tathāgatas" (PhD diss., School of Oriental and African Studies, London University, 2002), 4, 15. An 8th-century manuscript of *Śatasāhasrika Prajñāpāramitā Sūtra* is kept in the

British Library that was found in cave 17 of the Mogao Buddhist cave complex in the Gansu Province of China. See *Sutra of the Perfection of Wisdom in 100,000 Lines*. Whether the manuscript was also recognized by the name "*Lakṣagrantham Abhiprajñam*" is not known. According to Alexis Sanderson, *Lakṣagrantham Abhiprajñam* may refer to the *Prajñāpāramitā Sūtra*. See Alexis Sanderson, "The Śaiva Religion among the Khmers: Part I," *BEFEO* 90–91 (2003–2004): 427n284. While expressing his inability to source the primary reference that identifies *Lakṣagrantham Abhiprajñam* with the *Prajñāpāramitā Sūtra*, Green follows Sanderson. See "Vat Sithor Inscription," 72. Cf. Skorupski in Sharrock, "Kīrtipaṇḍita," 233, for the alternative translation of the word "Abhiprajñam."

64. (K. 111 st. XXIX) in Cœdès, *IC*, 6:205n3) suggested that the *Tattvasaṃgrahaṭīka* mentioned here was Kamalaśīla's commentary of Śāntarakṣita's *Tattvasaṃgraha*. Sanderson, "Śaiva Religion," 427n284, has argued that it is more probable that the text referenced here is the *STTS*, the principal text of the *yogatantras*. Peter Sharrock is also convinced of this position. See "Buddhist Pantheon of the Bayon of Angkor,": 16–27, 300. Skorupski in Sharrock, "Kīrtipaṇḍita," 234, suggests the text as *Kosalāmkāra-Tattvasaṃgrahaṭīka* by Śākyamitra. Cf. Green, "Vat Sithor Inscription," 72, 270.
65. Sanderson, "Śaiva Religion," 424n277.
66. Tanaka, *Illustrated History of the Maṇḍala*, 87.
67. Kristensen, "Rishukyō," 35, 164.
68. (K. 240, st. 2), *IC*, 3:76–77.
69. The fragment K. 397 dated to 1108 found on the pedestal of the southern *gopura* of the second enclosure states that an image of Trailokyavijaya was erected at the temple of Phimai in today's Thailand. See George Cœdès, "Études cambodgiennes," *BEFEO* 4 (1924): 354–358. For the discussion on the deity, see Pia Conti, "Tantric Buddhism at Prasat hin Phimai: A New Reading of Its Iconographic Message," in *Before Siam: Essays in Art and Archaeology*, ed. Nicolas Revire and Stephen A. Murphy (Bangkok: River Books, 2014), 374–396.
70. (K. 214), *IC*, 2:202. Buddhist inscription (K. 230) of Prasat Beng in *IC*, 6:241 also mentions installation of an image of Trailokyānātha along with Buddha, Lokeśvara, and Vajrapāṇī. Support for identifying Trailokyānātha as Lokeśvara in this inscription is based on the invocation to the embodiments of the Buddha, Trailokyānātha, and Vajrapani. The Khmer section of the inscription specifically says that the casted image of Lokeśvara is named Trailokyānātha. (K. 238), *IC*, 6:119, also mentions establishment of Trailokyānātha by Bajrendrācārya. Based on the Chandil inscription from Jharkhand, India, S. Chattopadhyaya discusses a female deity Trailokyavijayā, presumably Trailokyavijā's consort. See "Trailokyavijayā," in *The Śakti Cult and Tārā*, ed. Dinesh Chandra Sircar (Calcutta: University of Calcutta, 1967), 147–151.
71. Prapandvidya Chirapat, "The Sab Bāk Inscription: Evidence of an Early Vajrayāna Buddhist Presence in Thailand [K. 1158]," *Journal of the Siam Society* 78, no. 2 (1990): 11–14. See also Estève, "Étude Critique des Phénomènes de Syncrétisme Religieux," 442–453, 541–546; and Tadeusz Skorupski in Conti, "Tantric Buddhism," 381–383.
72. (st. I and II) in Estève, "Étude Critique des Phénomènes de Syncrétisme Religieux," 442.
73. Chpār Rānsi is mentioned fourteen times in the corpus of Khmer inscriptions between 924 and 1190 CE. Estève has gone over all the inscriptions in the Khmer corpus. See Julia Estève and Brice Vincent, "L'about inscrit du muse national du Cambodge (K. 943): Nouveaux elements sur le bouddhisme tantrique à l'époque angkorienne," *Arts Asiatiques* 65 (2010): 150. It may be the major Khmer temple of Preah Kahn of Kompong Svay, for Sab Bāk links it with a place called Sthalāsvāy, as noted by Chirapat, "Sab Bāk Inscription."
74. See chapter 17 (122–140) in Francesca Fremantle, "A Critical Study of the Guhyasamāja Tantra" (PhD diss., School of Oriental and African Studies, London University, 1971). Cf. Yukei Matsunaga, *The Guhyasamāja Tantra: A New Critical Edition* (Osaka, Japan: Toho Shuppan, 1978).

75. (st. X) in Estève, "Étude Critique des Phénomènes de Syncrétisme Religieux," 543, 545. Cf. Skorupski in Conti, "Tantric Buddhism," 49.
76. Kamaleswar Bhattacharya, "The Religion of Ancient Cambodia," in *Sculpture of Angkor and Ancient Cambodia: Millennium Glory*, ed. Helen Jessup and Thierry Zephir (New York: Thames & Hudson, 1997), 46.
77. The late Professor Claude Jacques of École Pratique des Hautes Études lectured on his draft translation of the stone in April 2016 at the École française d'Extrême-Orient. A team of scholars (Julia Estève, Dominic Goodall, Arlo Griffiths, Ian Lowman, Louise Roche, and Brice Vincent) is currently preparing the publication of this inscription along with the inscription K. 1222 with extensive historical commentary. Face A st. I: śrivuddham bhagavantaṁ śrivajrasa[tva] dvayadvayaṁ. Face A st. XXXIII: tuṅgaprāsādakam madhye sanmātṛpratimānvitam, sage[ha]ṁ yaḥ pariṣkuryād daśaprāsādakam punaḥ. Prajñāpāramita is mentioned in st. XIII-Prajñāpāramitābhaktir and LIII-Prajñāpāramitābhuk. Claude Jacques, 2016.
78. Jean Boisselier, *Le Cambodge* (Paris: Picard-Manuel d'archéologie d'Extrême-Orient, 1, 1966), 94.
79. In the context of the Bat Cum inscription, Prajñāpāramitā is understood as the actual source of wisdom and the illuminating path that leads to the attainment of the wisdom. Based on this, Green argues that the female figures were either understood as accompanying *devīs* (goddesses) or as a dual aspect of Prajñāpāramitā. See Green, "Vat Sithor Inscription," 226–252.
80. Two *caityas* are in Battambang Museum including figure 1; two are in the National Museum of Cambodia, Phnom Penh (Ga 1734 and Ga 1735); one in Musèe Guimet, Paris (MG 17487); and one in the conservation depot, Siem Reap. Some of these are discussed by o'Naghten, "Prajñāpāramitā Dans Le Bouddhisme," 37–39.
81. The depiction of Prajñāpāramitā from Angkor Thom, kept at the Angkor National Museum, Siem Reap, is published by Woodward in "Aspects of Buddhism," 229, fig. 7.6.
82. Finot, "Lokesvara en Indochine," 253. It is worth exploring the identity of these female images.
83. For the dating and interpretation of fig. 6, see Piriya Krairiksh, *The Roots of Thai Art* (Bangkok: River Books, 2012), 301; and Conti, "Tantric Buddhism," 376–377. Given the mix religious character of the *caitya* and double *vitarkamudra* of buddhas, similar to Phimai style, the pillar might be from the 11th century.
84. See Ka. 1735, National Museum of Cambodia, Phnom Penh; and MG 17487, Musée national des arts asiatiques, Guimet.
85. Based on the single possible appearance of Tārā in Khmer epigraphy (see Prajñāpāramitātārī in Green, "Vat Sithor inscription," st. XLIV, p. 272), Woodward questions whether it indicates the savior nature of Prajñāpāramitā or refers to a joint deity—Prajñāpāramitā and Tārā—or is a name of a goddess that could have traits of either Prajñāpāramitā or Tārā. For the analysis of female figures on the *caitya* pillar, see Woodward, "Karandavyuha Sutra," 76–77; and Woodward, "Aspects of Buddhism," 224, 231.
86. Eva Allinger, "Mahāmāyūrī and Jāṅgulī as Attendants of Prajñāpāramitā: Investigation of an Unusual Iconographic Feature Based on Bihari *Aṣṭasāhasrikā Prajñāpāramitā* Manuscripts from the 11th Century," in *Prajñādhāra: Essays on Asian History, Epigraphy and Culture, in Honour of Gouriswar Bhattacharya*, ed. Gerd J. R. Mevissen and Arundhati Banerjee (New Delhi: Kaveri, 2009), 253–261. Several steles kept at the Wat Pô Veal Museum in Battambang bear images of Avalokiteśvara along with two identical female figures. For example, see EFEO archive image no. CAM03818. It is difficult to ascertain the identity of these figures. Both could be Prajñāpāramitā or two aspects of her or one could be Tārā.
87. Emma Bunker and Douglas Latchford, *Adoration and Glory: The Golden Age of Khmer Art* (Chicago: Art Media Resources, 2004), ca. no. 40: p. 138; ca. no. 64: pp.196–197; ca. no. 67: pp. 204–205; and Emma Bunker and Douglas Latchford, *Khmer Bronzes: New Interpretations of the Past* (Chicago: Art Media Resources, 2011), fig. 5.8: p. 149.

88. The temple is unique as it featured two almost complete female deities, one discovered in the northern tower now kept at Hanoi Museum of History, one behind the southern tower now kept at Da Nang Museum, and the fragments of the third were found from the front tower. All the three towers once housed the bronzes of Vajrapāṇī-Buddha-Avalokiteśvara. Were the stone images of Prajñāpāramitā partners of the bronzes? The Bronze Avalokiteśvara statue is displayed at the History Museum of Ho Chi Minh City (no. BTLS 1289). For Đại Hữu excavations, see Louis Finot and Victor Goloubew, "Fouilles de Đại-hưu (Quảng Bình, Annam)," *BEFEO* 25 (1925): 472–474; and Schweyer, "Buddhism in Čampā," 321.
89. Conti, "Tantric Buddhism," 152–153. Tārā or Prajñāpāramitā are never mentioned in Cam inscriptions but Prajñāpāramitā often appears in Khmer inscriptions.
90. (C 66 face D, 1 10–1 16), Schweyer, "Buddhism in Čampā," 317.
91. Jean Boisselier first identified her as Tārā. See Jean Boisselier, "Un bronze de Tārā du Musée de Đà Nẵng et son importance pour l'histoire de l'art du Campa," *BEFEO* 73 (1984): 34–336. Baptiste and Zéphir identified it as Prajñāpāramitā (Thierry Zéphir and Pierre Baptiste, *Trésors d'art du Vietnam: La sculpture du Champa Ve-XVe siècles* [Paris: Réunion des Musées Nationaux, 2005], 86, 210–211). For the first time, Trần Kỳ Phương connected the image with the deity of the inscription; see Trần Kỳ Phương, "Tượng Bồ tát mới phát hiện tại Đồng Dương, Quảng Nam-Đà Nẵng" [A newly discovered sculpture of Bodhisattva at Dong Duong, Quang Nam-Da Nang], *Khảo Cổ Học* (*Journal of Archaeology*) 2 (1979): 61–63. This identification is supported by Trian Nguyễn, "Lakśmīndralokeśvara, Main Deity of the Đồng Dương Monastery: A Masterpiece of Cham Art and a New Interpretation," *Artibus Asiae* 65, no. 1 (2005): 5–38.
92. Schweyer, "Buddhism in Čampā," 319.
93. *The Sādhanamālā* has nine *sādhanas*, which describe the procedure of Prajñāpāramitā worship. Out of the nine, eight *sādhanas*—151–155, 157–159—give the description of the two-armed Prajñāpāramitā and no. 158 mentions four-armed Prajñāpāramitā. A six-armed form of Prajñāpāramitā is preserved only in Japan. See Bhattacharya, *Indian Buddhist Iconography*, 310–321; and Conze, "The Iconography of Prajñāpāramitā," 47–52.
94. *Sādhana* 151 (*SM*: 310–311) and 153 (*SM*: 313) indicate the presence of Akṣobhya, *Sādhana* 152 (*SM*: 312) and 159 (*SM*: 324) mention the image of five buddhas in her crown. Cf. Bhattacharya, *Indian Buddhist Iconography*, 197–198; and Conze, "Iconography of Prajñāpāramitā," 47–52. The Metropolitan Museum, New York, possibly has one example of her wearing a five-buddha crown. See the bronze, acc. no.1979.510.2 at the Met. Given her Thai–Khmer–Javanese mix of features, the identification as a Khmer Prajñāpāramitā is tentative.
95. Both Prajñāpāramitā and Dhanadatārā (*Sādhana* 107 of Bhattacharya, *Indian Buddhist Iconography*, 218) are depicted with the book and Jina Akṣobhya (*sādhana* 116 and 154 of Bhattacharya, *Indian Buddhist Iconography*, 244, 313). At Alchi, the distinction between Prajñāpāramitā and Tārā is at times not obvious because they both are depicted with a book. See Rob Linrothe, "Mapping the Iconographic Programme of the Sumstek," in *Alchi Ladakh's Hidden Buddhist Sanctuary: The Sumstek*, ed. Christian Luczanits, text by Rogers Goepper and photographs by Jaroslav Poncar (London: Serindia, 2023), 2:735–745. Occasionally, Tārā, too, is called a "mother of all Buddhas" as observed by Christian Luczanits, *An Exceptional and Magnificent Bronze Alloy Figure of Prajnaparamita—Prajnaparamita, Alchi and Kashmir, On the Cultural Background of a Unique Bronz* (Bejing: Poly Auction, 2016).
96. *Niṣpanayogāvalī* contains twenty-six mandalas and describes iconographic details of the several deities. See Benoytosh Bhattacharya, *Niṣpannayogāvalī of Mahapaṇḍita Abhayākaragupta*, Gaekwad's Oriental Series 109 (Baroda, India: Oriental Institute, 1949). See also Marie-Thérèse de Mallmann, *Introduction à l'iconographie du tântrisme bouddhique* (Paris: Centre de recherches sur l'Asie centrale et la Haute Asie-Bibliothèque du Centre de recherches sur l'Asie centrale et la Haute Asie, 1, 1975), 306.

97. Only the Khmer examples of the goddess have as many as twenty-two arms, the highest number of arms known in the corpus of surviving Prajñāpāramitā images. See Conze, "Iconography of Prajñāpāramitā," 51.
98. South *gopura*, east face (K. 696) in George Cœdès, "Études cambodgiennes XXXIX-L'épigraphie des monuments de Jayavarman VII," *BEFEO* 44, no. 1 (1944): 118. See foundation stele inscriptions of Ta Prohm (K. 273-st. XXXVI) in George Cœdès, 'La stele de Ta-Prohm,' *BEFEO* 6 (1906): 44–82; and Preah Khan (K. 908-A9-A10) in George Cœdès, "La Stèle du Prah Khan d'Angkor," *BEFEO* 41 (1942): 296, 255–301. For Preah Khan inscription, see Thomas Maxwell, "The Stele Inscription of Preah Khan, Angkor: Text with Translation and Commentary," *UDAYA: The Journal of Khmer Studies* 8 (2009): 73, 1–113.
99. Chapter 5, verses 2–8, of the *Guhyasamāja tantra* in Fremantle, "Critical Study of the Guhyasamāja," 41.
100. Many fragments are arranged by the Archaeological Survey of India in front of the main entrance near the eastern *gopura* of Ta Prohm.
101. Phimeanakas inscription- (K. 485), (*IC*, 2: side C-st. LXXV), 170, 178. The inscription indicates there were numerous images. So far eight kneeling statues are known from the world museums and private collection. See Olivier Cunin, "The Images of Jayavarman VII and His Queens" (Lecture given at the Royal Academy of Cambodia, Phnom Penh, June 2019).
102. George Cœdès, "Le portrait dans I'art khmer," *Arts Asiatiques*, EFEO (1960): 179–198.
103. Helen Jessup and Thierry Zéphir, eds., *Sculpture of Angkor and Ancient Cambodia: Millennium Glory* (New York: Thames & Hudson, 1997), 304–305.
104. Pierre Baptiste and Thierry Zéphir, *L'Art khmer dans les collections du muse Guimet* (Paris: RMN, 2008), 267–270. An Indonesian statue depicts the figure in a teaching gesture with a book atop a lotus bloom next to her shoulder and lowered glance. For the Indonesian statue, see Natasha Reichle, *Violence and Serenity: Late Buddhist Sculpture for Indonesia* (Honolulu: University of Hawai'i Press, 2007), 51–85.
105. A portrait statue of the king Jayavarman VII and a torso of his queen found from Prang Brahmadatta of Prasat Phimai would be one such example as argued by o'Naghten, "Prajñāpāramitā Dans Le Bouddhisme," 44. See also Cunin, "Images of Jayavarman VII and His Queens."
106. See inscription nos. 6 (L), 7(M), 28 (12) 40 (10) in Thomas Maxwell, "The Short Inscriptions of the Bayon and Contemporary Temples," in *Bayon: New Perspectives*, ed. Joyce Clark (Bangkok: River Books, 2007), 122–135. For the discussion on some adorant statues, see Woodward, "Jayabuddhamahānātha," 108, 105–111.
107. First published by George Cœdès, "Bronzes khmèrs," *Ars Asiatica* 5 (Paris: van Oest, 1923), XXXV.
108. Three are published by Cœdès, "Bronzes Khmèrs," XXXV in the collection of the Bangkok National Museum. Other examples include a beautiful and fragile bronze at the Musée des arts asiatiques de Nice (MAA no. 003.2.1), a Hoxton collection bronze, and one held in the Skanda Trust and published by Bunker and Latchford, *Khmer Bronzes*, 395, fig. 9.27, 396–397, fig. 9.28 a–b; Christie's New York, 2nd September auction; Dallas Museum of Art (no. 1952.52.3); Freer Sackler bronze (no. S2015-26); one Bayon style bronze found in Surin Province, Thailand, now at the National Museum of Bangkok (no. ThR.T26); another in Bayon style from Buriram Province at the Jim Thompson Collection, Bangkok, and one in the Ann Kinney Collection, New York. Some of these have been published by Brice Vincent, "Rapport provisoire sur six statues khmères en bronze en vue de leur authentification" (Report prepared for Centre for Khmer Studies, 2013), 14–15, fig. 6.2, 6.4, and 6.5, 1–15.
109. (K. 968), *IC*, 7:150. Jñānamitrā's commentary on Perfection Wisdom Sutra expresses the name of the sutra as "Heart of the Bhagavatī Perfection Wisdom Sutra." See Donald Lopez, *Elaborations on Emptiness: Uses of the Heart Sūtra* (Princeton, NJ: Princeton University Press, 1996), 141.
110. Olivier Cunin has confirmed this from the close examination of scattered fragments around the eastern *gopura* pediment (personal communication).

111. It is difficult to ascertain the original number of her heads because of the Archaeological Survey of India (ASI) replacement/restoration of the head, but she surely has four faces.
112. Boisselier connected the huge Avalokiteśvara reliefs with *Kāraṇḍavyūhasūtra* known to contain tantric characteristics in "Précisions sur quelques images," 73–89.
113. The name "radiating Lokeśvara" was coined by Finot in 1925 in his study "Lokeśvara en Indochine." The Preah Khan inscription of 1191 CE proclaims that the twenty-three images of Jayabuddhamahānātha had been sent to various towns in the kingdom. See George Cœdès, "La Stèle du Prah Khan d'Angkor," *BEFEO* 41 (1942): 296, 255–301. He identified the images of the inscription to the portrait statues of Jayavarman VII. Hiram Woodward has proposed scholars identify these statues with the group of radiating Lokeśvara statues despite the fact they are called buddhas—Great Lord Buddha of Victory. See Woodward, "Jayabuddhamahānātha," 106, 105–111.
114. Marie-Thérèse de Mallmann, *Introduction à l'Étude d'Avalokiteçvara*, Annales du Musée Guimet: Bibliothèque d'Études 57 (Paris: Civilisations du Sud, 1967), 43–45.
115. Woodward, "Jayabuddhamahānātha," 107.
116. The 72-cm-tall bronze was first published by Cœdès, "Bronze Khmèrs," XXXII; then by Chuttiwongs, *Iconography of Avalokiteśvara*, 346, 154A; and lastly by Bunker and Latchford, *Khmer Bronzes*, 390–391, fig. 9.25a, b.
117. The French archaeological archive (EFEO) holds photographs of most parts of the dismembered Hevajra statue excavated in 1925. The torso is at the Metropolitan Museum, New York. In 2009, Sharrock found the legs, which are now in the storeroom of the Norodom Sihanouk Museum in Siem Reap. In 2011, Japan-Apsara Safeguarding Angkor (JASA) expert suggested that it would have been placed in the eastern entrance. In 2013, the JASA group found a large stone base with a tenon outside the main eastern entrance that Cunin correctly identified as the feet of Hevajra and also concluded that the statue was placed in BY55, a large pavilion at the main entrance of the Bayon. From all the scattered pieces, Cunin produced 3D computer simulation of the whole statue and its location in the Bayon temple, which he presented at the "Exploring Angkor Symposium" at Asian Civilizations Museum in 2018. The team of the Archaeological Survey of India had uncovered two hands from the area close to the "Hall with Dancers" that houses several Prajñāpāramitā pediments. Cunin ("Exploring Angkor Symposium" presentation) identified them as "Hevajra hands" and based on his vast database of thousands of Angkor stones argued that there was possibly another Hevajra statue erected at Ta Prohm.
118. Bunker and Latchford, *Khmer Bronzes*, 375; Jan Jetso Boeles, "Two Yoginīs from Thailand," in *Essays Offered to G. H. Luce*, vol. 2, ed. Ba Shin (Ascona, Switzerland: Artibus Asiae Supplementum, 1966), 24–5, 14–29; and Hiram Woodward, "Bronze Sculptures of Ancient Cambodia," in *Gods of Angkor: Bronzes from the National Museum of Cambodia*, ed. Louise Allison and Paul Jett (Washington, DC: Arthur M. Sackler Gallery, Smithsonian Institution, 2010), 29–75.
119. Based on the identical assemblage seen on the plaster impression kept at the Bangkok Museum, Woodward identifies the figures as a *nāga*-protected buddha on the top; Saṃvara, Vajrasattva, Hevajra in the middle; and Hevajra and Lokeśvara–bodhisattva–Vajrapāṇī in the lower row in "Tantric Buddhism at Angkor Thom," *Ars Orientalis* 12 (1981): 61, 57–67. See Sharrock's identification of the deities on the Poipet mold in "Buddhist Pantheon of the Bayon," 269. In "Tantric Buddhism," 376, Conti identifies the central figure of the Poipet mold as Akṣobhya and bottom row as Vajrapāṇī–Lokeśvara–Padmapāṇī.
120. Finot had observed this rare grouping, see "Lokesvara en Indochine," 55. Louis Delaporte published his drawing of the Hevajra side in *Voyage au Cambodge* (Paris: Delagrave, 1880), 358. Lucien Fournereau in *Les ruines khmères, Cambodge et Siam* (Paris: E. Leroux, 1890), 79, published the *nāga*-enthroned buddha and Avalokiteśvara sides. The Hevajra side is published in Pierre Baptiste and

Thierry Zéphir in *L'art Khmer dans les collections du Musee Guimet* (Paris: Réunion des Musées Nationaux, 2008), 441; and Pierre Baptiste and Thierry Zéphir, *Angkor: Naissance d'un Mythe, Louis Delaporte et le Cambodge* (Paris: Gallimard, Musée national des arts asiatiques Guimet, 2013), 236. All the sides of this pillar have never been published.

121. See Musée Guimet, acc. no. MG18119 and MG 23586. The second one has been desecrated. For the discussion on these *caityas*, see Baptiste and Zéphir, *L'art Khmer*, 183–185, 441; and Baptiste and Zéphir, *Angkor*, 236.
122. Sharrock, "Appendix: Naga Enthroned Buddha of Angkor."
123. The overtly violent aspect of the Tibetan Hevajra is also absent in Khmer art. In the Khmer convention, open eyes are enough to indicate ferocity, as pointed out by Woodward in "Tantric Buddhism at Angkor," 57.
124. Pauline Lunsingh Scheurleer and Marijke Klokke, *Divine Bronze: Ancient Indonesian Bronzes from* A.D. *600 to 1600* (Leiden, The Netherlands: Brill, 1988), 92, 99.
125. An identical one from the National Museum of Bangkok was published by George Cœdès, "Études cambodgiennes XXXIX- L'épigraphie des monuments de Jayavarman VII," *BEFEO* 44, no. 1 (1951): XXXVI, 97–120.
126. Fragments of a 3.6-m-high *nāga*-enthroned buddha were retrieved from the central well under the Bayon central sanctuary in 1933 by George Trouvé.
127. Baptiste and Zéphir's hypothesis of eleven heads as *pāramitās*, or virtues, is based on the text *Niṣpannayogāvalī*. See Baptiste and Zéphir, "L'Art khmer," cat. no. 185, 430.
128. Phillip Green, "The Many Faces of Lokeśvara: Tantric Connections in Cambodia and Campā between the Tenth and Thirteenth Centuries," *History of Religions* 54, no. 1 (2014): 85–87. For some discussion on the image, see o'Naghten, "Prajñāpāramitā Dans Le Bouddhisme," 42.
129. The eleven-headed Prajñāpāramitā is possibly invoked along with eleven-headed Avalokiteśvara in the Prasat Chikreng inscription. See note 35.
130. The *Aṣṭasāhasrikā Prajñāpāramitā* manuscript kept at the Varendra Research Institute (folio 141v and folio 142r) bears a sixteen-armed, four-legged dancing Hevajra facing his consort Nairātmya. See Kim, *Receptacle of the Sacred*, 196, 201.
131. Kim, *Receptacle of the Sacred*, 197.
132. Alexis Sanderson, "The Śaiva Religion among the Khmers (part 1)," *BEFEO* 90–91 (2003–2004): 425, 349–462; and Thomas Maxwell, "The Stele Inscription of Preah Khan, Angkor: Text with Translation and Commentary," *UDAYA* 8 (2009): 73, 1–113.
133. Chuttiwongs, "Iconography of Avalokiteśvara," 333.
134. Snellgrove, *Buddhist Himalaya*, 81.
135. For a brief discussion on these images, see Bunker and Latchford, *Adoration and Glory*; and Bunker and Latchford, *Khmer Bronzes*.
136. Edward Conze, *The Prajñāpāramitā Literature, Indo-Iranian Monograph* (The Hague: Mouton, 1960); and Conze, *Thirty Years of Buddhist Studies*.
137. Kim, *Receptacle of the Sacred*.
138. Peter Sharrock, "The Mystery of the Face Towers," in *Bayon: New Perspectives*, ed. Joyce Clark (Bangkok: River Books, 2007), 265.
139. Cunin, "Exploring Angkor Symposium" presentation; and Andrea Acri and Peter D. Sharrock, *The Creative South* (Singapore: ISEAS, forthcoming 2021).
140. Conze, "Iconography of Prajñāpāramitā," 50, 51.
141. Bunker and Latchford, *Adoration and Glory*; and Bunker and Latchford, *Khmer Bronzes*.

Swati Chemburkar

PSYCHOLOGICAL INTERPRETERS OF BUDDHISM

THE DISCOVERY OF THE PSYCHOLOGICAL BUDDHISM

The term *Buddhism* is a relatively new addition to the English language. Prior to the first half of the 19th century, the word did not exist at all when, as explained by Philip Almond and others, it was coined to name novel phenomena that had been only relatively recently "discovered."[1] By the mid-19th century, a small cadre of English-speaking scholars and philologists were publishing papers, books, and translations that would ultimately serve to explain to readers what the term Buddhism meant, what the word referred to exactly. And these first individuals all held particular assumptions that remain embedded within the word Buddhism. Some of these assumptions may seem so obvious to its definition as to not require mention. Among them are that Buddhism refers to a "world religion," founded on the teachings of a religious leader—"the historical Buddha," the Shakyamuni Siddhārtha Gautama—and first practiced by peoples throughout the continent of Asia.[2]

Many of "the British discoverers of Buddhism" held an additional assumption that was equally central to their definition of the new construct: that the term Buddhism referred to a set of teachings best understood as an "ethical psychology," that the word referred to a uniquely psychological religion. One such figure, Thomas Rhys Davids, founded and chaired the Pāli Text Society to provide curious English-reading audiences with translations of "the Pāli Canon," a set of writings they believed formed the basis of Buddhism as a religion (comparable to Christian biblical texts).[3] Any reader who picked up the first publication for the Society from Thomas's wife, the important translator and commentator Caroline Rhys Davids, would find this point announced clearly in its title on the cover: "*A Buddhist Manual of Psychological Ethics of the Fourth Century* BC."[4]

At times, Thomas Rhys Davids collaborated with counterparts in continental Europe such as Hermann Oldenberg who were engaged in the same exercise for readers of their own languages.[5] While the Rhys Davids toiled away in England, figures such as Oldenberg and, importantly, Eugène Burnouf helped popularize the terms *Buddhismus* and *Bouddhisme*, respectively.[6] They, too, introduced and translated Buddhism as a religion via Buddhist texts for German and French audiences. To varying degrees, these figures all shared the presumption that Buddhism or Bouddhisme referred to a religion that was eminently psychological and in which the practitioner plumbed the depths of the interior mind.

Scholars such as Donald Lopez have long described a "psychologization" of Buddhism traditions.[7] When they use this term, they mean that, first, the actual communities, teachings, and practices that are commonly referred to as Buddhist have been (mis)interpreted using theories that are typically referred to as psychological and, as a result, reconstructed into something new: a *psychologized* Buddhism. David McMahan and others have suggested that such transformations contributed to the creation of new, larger contemporary forms that they have named *modern Buddhism* or *Buddhist modernism*.[8] However, the term Buddhism has always been used to designate a religion that was, at its very core, psychological. The construct was ready-made to be interpreted by psychologists and psychotherapists.

As Luiz Gomez has observed, scholars such as the Rhys Davids and the Sanskritist Monier Monier-Williams may have had reason to describe the texts they read as investigations of "psychological" matters.[9] While emphasizing that "it would be imprudent to accept uncritically the accuracy of this parallelism" and to miss the ways in which it can be "misleading," Gomez explains that "the parallel is not totally spurious or devoid of heuristic value: Important aspects of Buddhist doctrine and practice may be construed as efforts at understanding human psychology."[10] There are copious Buddhist textual sources throughout history that engage in deep explications of the nature of cognition and the workings of the human mind. Buddhist thinkers have engaged in debates across continents and over the course of centuries—from the Yogācāra of Indian Mahāyāna traditions to the Tiantai communities of medieval China to the Kagyü teachings of 11th-century Tibetan Buddhists—over how to categorize various forms of mentation, whether "appearance" is purely an invention of cognition, and which states of consciousness are more or less desirable and thus worth cultivating.

Scholars such as the Rhys Davids believed that the texts containing these discussions laid out the essential thought—the essential belief system, as religions were understood to be defined by inner beliefs—that comprised the new construct Buddhism. At the same time, a growing number of the early European discoverers of Buddhism also observed that the communities across Asia they called *Buddhists* appeared far more interested in practices of merit-making, propitiation of divinities, and visualizations of Pure Lands than in settling philosophical debates between Svatantrika and Prasaṅgika views on the relationship between the mind and reality. These observers largely resolved this seeming contradiction by positing that followers of the buddha had strayed from his original teachings very quickly following his death. Even the ancient Sanskrit and Pāli texts that contained the closest approximation of these original teachings were still written many years after the buddha's death and, consequently, contained "perversions" of "supernatural interferences."[11] For most early scholars of Buddhist traditions, whatever so-called "lay" or "popular Buddhism" consisted of, the term Buddhism itself, unadorned with qualifiers, should be defined (and introduced to communities in Europe and the United States) as fundamentally rational and, importantly, centered on inner psychology. The Buddhist path was an intrapsychic exploration of "self-absorption."

Meanwhile, when Caroline Rhys Davids published *A Buddhist Manual of Psychological Ethics*, "psychology" was itself still a relatively new term and very much a nascent academic discipline, often signaled by proponents referring to it as "the new psychology." To a growing community in Europe and the United States, psychology was an exciting innovation of modern science that promised to reveal the true interior workings of human beings. To declare that Buddhism was an "ethical psychology" then was not only to make a descriptive statement; it was intended as a high compliment, an endorsement of the religion's value. To introduce Buddhism as "the first psychology," the buddha as "the first psychologist," was to announce that the cultural productions of the Pāli Text Society held not only esoteric ancient wisdom but an esoteric ancient wisdom with vital insights for moderns. And announce this the Pāli Text Society did.

Caroline Rhys Davids's volume, for example, was a translation of *Dhammasaṅgaṇi*, the first book of the Abhidhamma pitaka, but the opening words of her introduction inform the reader that the work is as important in "the history of psychology" as if "a copy of some manual" belonging to "the young Socrates" had been discovered in "the ruins of Greece."[12] Rhys Davids had been a student of psychology as well as Asian religious traditions, and she presents her translation as deserving of attention because "even a superficial inspection of the Manual should yield great promise to anyone interested in the history of psychology."[13] The volume becomes but a single piece of evidence for Rhys Davids's larger contention that "early psychological thought in the East" should be "assigned its due place."[14]

When speaking before new audiences, Buddhist popularizers—Asian as well as European—seized upon the idea that Buddhist doctrine held psychological truths. Many scholars have pinpointed the 1893 World Parliament of Religions in Chicago as a watershed moment when listeners in the United States were first introduced to prominent figures they believed were representative of Buddhist communities throughout Asia.[15] Though the Japanese monk Shaku Soen led a very different community of Buddhists than the Sri Lankan/Ceylonese Anagārika Dharmapāla did, both drew upon the language of the psychological when they spoke at the event. In their efforts to legitimate Buddhist teachings and practices, figures such as Dharmapāla built upon the notion that Buddhism could stand alongside Christianity as a world religion and suggested that, more than that, it could offer an alternative for the age of science. It may have come as a surprise to Dharmapāla's listeners to hear that Buddhist thought anticipated the then-revolutionary theory of evolution, but its association with the science of psychology often needed little explanation.

Dharmapāla and Soen's interlocutors in Europe and the United States, such as the theosophist Henry Steel Olcott and the author Paul Carus, further advanced the idea that Buddhism was a scientific religion par excellence. It was a religion of the mind in its intellectualism and logical, rational, philosophical discourse and, moreover, abundant with a wealth of practices for inner exploration previously unparalleled until their recent unveiling by brave travelers in the mysterious "East." Most of this was already implicit in the texts that figures such as Carus and Olcott first read in order to learn that Buddhism existed at all. Both Carus and Olcott held the putative assumption that Buddhism was a fully developed ethical philosophy of the mind. When they encountered Buddhist practice that diverged from an adherence to the purely rational "original teachings" of the buddha, they became determined to offer correction.

Living in British colonial Ceylon, Olcott attempted to clear away the mass of superstition that he perceived had grown up in indigenous Buddhist communities there. He penned his *Buddhist Catechism* as a distillation of true Buddhist psychological wisdom of the mind and an accessible source so that this wisdom could proliferate.[16] Carus's *The Gospel of the Buddha*, meanwhile, was a more widely influential text that collected passages from a variety of Buddhist translations produced by the Rhys Davids and others. Carus had long been interested in the "new psychology" as a primary epistemological tool for devising the belief system of his "Religion of Science."[17] (One of his first publications, *The Soul of Man: An Investigation of the Facts of Physiological and Experimental Psychology*, was an attempt to recover a concept of the soul by using the latest psychological scientific research of the day.[18]) Carus believed that Buddhist thought held powerful resources for the refinement and dissemination of the Religion of Science in no small measure because it held such rarified knowledge of the psychological. Carus is also famous for his interaction and influence not only on US and European communities but on important Japanese Buddhist figures such as D. T. Suzuki (discussed further in "Psychologists of Religion") who studied with and worked for Carus at his Open Court Publishing Company for over a decade. It is likely that Suzuki's own beliefs about the relationship between Buddhist traditions and psychology have their seeds in his relationship with Carus.

PSYCHOLOGISTS OF RELIGION

Contextualized in the activities of early translators and popularizers of Buddhist traditions, it becomes clear why psychologists and psychotherapists would begin their analyses of Buddhism holding the a priori assumption that the object of this study was itself a psychological religion. During the early years of psychology and psychotherapy—throughout the 19th century—there were few who gave Buddhist teachings and practices sustained attention. Nonetheless, the construct Buddhism held a significant position in the general theories of religion of figures such as William James and James Henry Leuba. Those first clinicians and psychologists to take a stronger interest in Buddhist traditions accepted the presumption that the way to learn about those traditions was to study certain ancient texts. Most did not do this, however, but instead read the publications of those who had, texts written by translators and comparative religionists such as Olcott, or, importantly if reading in German, Leopold Ziegler and Friedrich Heiler.[19] In these texts, psychologists and psychotherapists read that the Buddhist's path was an exploration of the inner mind, a turning inward summarized by the oft-used phrase "self-absorption."

The first academic psychologists of religion attended to the topic of Buddhism to lesser or greater degrees. To an observer such as James, Buddhist traditions were important because they represented a possible complication in efforts to define the category of religion.[20] The dominant understanding of James's day was that Buddhism was an "atheistic religion." It was often cited, then, as the exception that disproved the commonly held rule that religion should be defined based on belief in a deity or deities. At the least, Buddhist traditions required explanation in surveys of the budding field of comparative religion. But it was useful for the project of a thinker such as James. James raises the topic of Buddhism while presenting his own redefinition of religion. He cites Buddhism as evidence that religion should no longer be defined by faith in metaphysical realities but instead by inner religious experience, "*the feelings, acts, and experiences of individual men in their solitude so far as they apprehend themselves to stand in relation to whatever they may consider the divine*."[21] This divine may not be a deity at all but a numinous transcendence he calls the "More." Leuba similarly turned to Buddhist traditions as "a famous example of the independence of religious experience from those intellectual concepts" of "belief in a beneficent personal divinity."[22] Buddhism served as source of encouragement to Leuba in his search for a "religion of the few bred in the atmosphere of intellectual freedom and scientific thought, whose strong faith in nature boldly discards the ragged garments inherited from the past."[23]

Another of the first psychologists of religion, James Bissett Pratt also highlighted Buddhism as "that great stumbling block to most definitions"[24] of religion, but he engaged in a more intensive investigation of Buddhist teachings and practices (and Asian religious traditions in general). Furthermore, unlike many who were interested in the topic, Pratt traveled extensively throughout Asia and interacted with living Buddhist communities. These travels produced books such as *The Pilgrimage of Buddhism and a Buddhist Pilgrimage* and *India and Its Faiths*, works in which he displayed a curiosity about Buddhist traditions as more than only a historical artifact.[25] Pratt had a desire to understand contemporaneous Buddhist practice, and he reflectively speculated about the future of Asian Buddhist communities—communities that he implicitly acknowledged were being shaped by interactions with foreign observers such as himself.

Pratt, like his colleagues, helped solidify some key prevailing assumptions about what defines Buddhist traditions. He, too, recapitulated the already-dominant understanding that a Buddhist path is defined by practitioners' investigation of their inner psychology. But from his position as an esteemed psychologist, Pratt more persuasively argued for what Caroline Rhys Davids had also sought: a recognition that "not only in physics but in psychology, also, the early Buddhists anticipated by two thousand years or more the general analytic methods of Western science."[26] Pratt and his cohort forwarded the then-common construction of the historical buddha as both the "great man" founder of a religion and an inimitably scientific thinker. But Pratt emphasized that "Gotama Buddha was probably the greatest psychologist of his age."[27]

The concept that the buddha both was a protopsychologist and had the mind of what Pratt called a "scientific physician"[28] remains fundamental to contemporary understandings of Buddhist traditions. Such sentiments from Pratt and his cohort served to increase the stature of Buddhist teachings by associating them with their new discipline of psychology. In fact, the story is often told that when William James saw Dharmapāla visiting one of his classroom lectures (given in conjunction with the monk's participation in the 1893 World Parliament), he insisted that the monk "take my chair. You are better equipped to lecture on psychology than I. This is the psychology everybody will be studying twenty-five years from now."[29]

Perhaps James's prophesy is still coming to fruition today; the claims that Buddhism was not only created by "the first psychologist" but is also uniquely psychological and anticipates psychological truths are certainly still evoked on a regular basis. There are aspects of Buddhist traditions, however, that early psychologists of religion such as Pratt also attended to that are far less audible at present. The first psychologists and psychotherapists to study and interpret Buddhist teachings believed that the goal of Buddhist practice was the achievement of nirvana, liberation from the cycle of rebirth. Dismissing them as metaphysical realities, they used psychological and psychotherapeutic theories to explain the origins of belief in nirvana, rebirth, and other Buddhist truths. Another topic that is often de-emphasized by later psychological interpreters of Buddhist traditions but that was a fundamental assumption of the first psychologists to examine them is the ethical system that these thinkers believed Buddhist teachings and practices were intended to inculcate in followers. For example, the moral psychology of Buddhist doctrine (the sorting of wholesome from unwholesome cognition) was, to Pratt, part of what distinguished Buddhist thought from the new psychology. It seemed to him that, although he and his contemporaries strived to maintain the scientific value of total objectivity, "Buddhist psychology is badly mixed up with moral concepts."[30] The highly developed ethical system of Buddhist doctrine created some confusion, meanwhile, for the early psychoanalyst Franz Alexander.

EARLY PSYCHOANALYSTS

In a 1922 lecture that he later published as the paper "Buddhistic Training as an Artificial Catatonia," Franz Alexander expressed some consternation that "nowhere in the Buddhistic literature"—that is, nowhere in the German-language commentaries that Alexander read—"has sufficient account been taken of the deep contradiction between the absorption doctrine and

Buddha's practical ethics. . . . The goal of absorption, Nirvāṇa, is a completely asocial condition and is difficult to combine with ethical precepts."[31] Alexander's interpretation of Buddhist traditions is often portrayed as representative of the general response from early psychotherapists to Buddhist traditions. Psychotherapy or "talk therapy," as such, was invented in the late 19th century by Sigmund Freud, a strident atheist who believed that his new scientific biomedical modality, psychoanalysis, would help dispel the illusions of religious belief by revealing their true psychodynamic origins. The religion and psychology scholar William Parsons has elucidated a possible Freudian perspective on Buddhist practice by studying Freud's famous dialogue with Romain Rolland on Hindu-associated meditative states.[32] Nonetheless, Freud himself never took up the subject of Buddhist traditions directly. It was left to a follower such as Alexander to apply Freud's analysis of religion more generally to Buddhist teachings and practices.

Around the same time that Alexander gave his talk at the Eighth International Psycho-Analytical Congress, a short paper titled "Psychology in Primitive Buddhism," ascribed to the pseudonymous Joe Tom Sun, was published in the journal *Psychoanalytic Review*.[33] It may be telling that the little-known analyst Joseph Thompson would have used a pseudonym for his article (one that today would be recognized as offensive). He offers a positive assessment of Buddhist teachings and practices to a community taught that religious adherence originates in pathological, obsessional patterns of behavior. Thompson, however, examines Buddhist concepts such as nirvana, karma, and *taṇhā* (desire, Skt. *tṛṣṇa*) and suggests that they are consistent with psychoanalytic theory. He goes so far as to quote psychoanalysis's founder, Freud, and then simply to insert parenthetical Buddhist equivalents for each psychoanalytic concept that Freud mentions: "The teachings of Buddha and Freud," Thompson begins, "are absolutely identical upon the subject of determinism as it applies to the individual personality. . . . Freud, in speaking to Putnam, said: 'We are what we are because we have been what we have been (the Law of Karma). And what is needed to solve the problem of human life is not moral estimates (*maya*, illusion) but more knowledge' (*vijja*, wisdom)."[34]

Thompson's short essay demonstrates that there was not a universal dismissal of Buddhist traditions by early psychoanalysts. Nonetheless, the pathologizing critique of Buddhist practice by Alexander, the far more influential figure, is likely typical of psychotherapists of this period. In "Buddhistic Training," Alexander also sought to raise Freud to the level of the buddha for having created a comparable new movement destined to change the world. He, too, catalogs a series of "striking similari[ties] between the analytical method [of Freud] and the doctrine of Buddha" but concludes that "there remains an insurmountable difference between the two doctrines, deeply founded within the difference between Indian and European culture."[35]

In Alexander's view, the central failing of the Buddhistic doctrine is that it is essentially asocial. He acquires this understanding that the Buddhist path is one of self-absorption and world renunciation from the sources he relies on: German translations and commentaries by figures such as Ziegler and Oldenberg. Whatever these "Neobuddhists,"[36] as Alexander calls them, might believe about Buddhist teachings, however, "the central core of Buddhism can be understood in its deepest meaning only in the light of psycho-analytical interpretation."[37] As Parsons has explained,[38] to Alexander, the "central core," revealed by the psychoanalytic method, was the Buddhists' wish to return to a state of narcissistic union with the mother. "Buddhistic regression," Alexander finally concludes, even "goes back to the beginning of embryonic development."[39] Buddhist practices were intended to achieve this aim, an aim that Buddhists called *nirvana*.

Despite concluding that Buddhist practice developed out of a pathological wish to return to an immature, infantile state, Alexander acknowledged that Buddhist traditions seemed to have a growing appeal in Europe and the United States. He watched as an interest in Buddhist teachings increased over his lifetime until, in the 1960s, then-popular Zen Buddhist teachings eventually took in even colleagues and friends such as the important psychoanalysts Karen Horney and Erich Fromm. Alexander advanced a psychosocial explanation for the attraction of Buddhist traditions to communities in the United States and Europe.[40] He believed that such communities were increasingly unable to adhere to their traditional religious beliefs in the face of scientific advancement (such as that offered by psychoanalysis). Religious traditions, however, had once offered individuals methods for meaning-making and self-exploration. With their loss, communities sought replacements, and the putatively atheistic Buddhist practice of turning inward would understandably appear attractive.

Perhaps the most famous psychological interpreter of Buddhist traditions, Carl Jung, had a similar explanation for what led communities in Europe and the United States to Buddhist teachings and practices.[41] Jung also anticipated an imminent secularization of society that left people bereft of their traditional means for an inner exploration of the self. In Jung's theories, this loss is of dire consequence, as he believed that psychological health depended on the individual's ability to turn inward. Only through a process of self-exploration could human beings achieve their full self-actualization, a phenomenon he often referred to as *individuation*. Jung posited that all human beings have an irrepressible drive toward this self-actualization, and without traditional religious institutions, societies in Europe would inevitably turn to new methods for the self-exploration necessary to attain it. Buddhism would understandably have an appeal, defined as it was as a psychological religion that was equipped with tools for investigating the psyche. More than only compensatory, Jung envisioned the introduction of Buddhist and other Asian religious traditions to communities in Europe as the result of a displacement of psychic energy. With the waning of traditional (i.e., traditional Christian) religious belief, new avenues for investigating the interior were destined to arise.

Jung played a singular role in the introduction of Buddhist teachings and practices to Europe and the United States. In fact, as Gomez has observed, Jung wrote prefaces and "introductions to some of the most popular and influential books on Asian religions by European authors or by Asian authors publishing in English," including a commentary to W. Y. Evans-Wentz's influential edition of *The Tibetan Book of the Dead*.[42] Often, the first words that the curious read when they took up one of these texts to learn more about the nature of Buddhist doctrine were from Jung. He explained to readers that they were about to hear teachings from a religion that contained superior means for exploring the hidden recesses of the human mind. Furthermore, Jung would introduce Buddhist texts as ancient exotic wisdom that, again, anticipated the latest findings of his analytical psychology. For instance, Jung states that if one reads *The Tibetan Book of the Dead* backward, one discovers that the text's stages of death and rebirth are an exquisite rendering of a deepening journey into the interior, a "penetration into the groundlayers of consciousness[,] . . . a bringing forth of psychic contents that are still germinal, subliminal, and as yet unborn."[43]

In 1939, when preparing his *Introduction to Zen Buddhism* for translation in Germany, D. T. Suzuki wrote Jung to solicit a foreword for his volume.[44] This foreword was included in the work's translation into English a decade later. Large audiences of readers in Europe and the United States were thus introduced to a Zen Buddhism that was defined as fundamentally concerned with individual psychology. After concerted study of psychologists such as William James and having served as a translator for enthusiasts such as Paul Carus, Suzuki contacted Jung and convinced him that Zen teachings could offer unprecedented resources for understanding and accessing the human psyche. In his foreword, Jung endorses Suzuki's presentation of Zen, declaring that "the psychotherapist who is seriously concerned with the question of the aim of his therapy cannot remain unmoved when he sees the end towards which this Eastern method of psychic 'healing'—i.e., 'making whole'—is striving."[45] Jung explains that the "satori" that Suzuki positions as the ultimate goal of the Zen path is a form of self-actualization, "the individuation process—which is my term for 'becoming whole.'"[46]

Jung is often portrayed as an unabashedly romantic advocate of Buddhist wisdom. However, he consistently emphasized his firm belief that only Asians should take up Buddhist practice. Regarding Suzuki's Zen, for example, Jung asserted that as "great as is the value of Zen Buddhism for understanding the religious transformation process, its use among Western people is very problematical."[47] Throughout his writings, Jung cites a number of reasons that direct Buddhist practice is "neither commendable nor even possible" for non-Asians, but his position may ultimately have been based on what Gomez calls a "psychology of race . . . [wherein] the so-called Indian mind seems to have no regard for external, empirical reality, but directs its eyes inward . . . an organization of the mind that places the Asian both beyond and below the limits of European normality."[48]

Jung's interpretations of Buddhist teachings thus reinforced a definition of Buddhism as psychological religion with a set of practices for inward-facing self-absorption. And yet, although previous commentators often portrayed the turn inward of self-absorption to be world-denying narcissism, Jung shifted the conversation by asserting that it has a highly positive purpose. And, even while maintaining that it should go untouched by communities in Europe and the United States, he helped solidify the notion that Buddhism was therapeutic. Going even further, when writing of the Zen described by Suzuki, Jung stated that there was no exact equivalent for it in "Western" culture and that "the only movement inside our civilization which has, or should have, some understanding of these endeavours is psychotherapy. It is therefore no accident that it is a psychotherapist who is writing [the] foreword" to Suzuki's book.[49] The ultimate aims of Buddhist practice were more than only the achievement of an enlightenment that meant the ethical transformation that Pratt and others had previously emphasized. Instead, Jung meant to reveal that the seemingly "transcendent" and "mystical" processes of Buddhist enlightenment were actually a psychotherapeutic attainment of self-actualization. Subsequent generations of psychological and psychotherapeutic interpreters of Buddhist traditions advanced highly similar theories. And some of these interpreters worked in direct concert with D. T. Suzuki.

THE POSTWAR PERIOD

D. T. Suzuki is likely the most famous Japanese Buddhist of the post–World War II period to examine how Buddhist teachings could be compatible with contemporaneous psychological theory. Around this time, however, entire communities of Japanese psychologists came together with the intention of integrating Buddhist and psychotherapeutic frames. One prominent product of the cross-cultural conversation between psychoanalytic therapists in the United States and figures within the newly burgeoning psychotherapeutic communities in Japan was the journal *Psychologia,* first published in 1957. Founded by the Japanese analyst Koji Sato, the notably English-language journal contained numerous articles comparing psychoanalytic and Buddhist concepts alongside scientific research on, for example, "The Prediction Validity of Seven Manual Dexterity tests."[50] In the pages of *Psychologia,* one found comparative analyses of "Hypnotism and Samadhi" and exchanges on "The Art of Ambiguity" between the formative psychologist and cognitive learning theorist Jerome Bruner and the "Zen Master Hisamatsu"—the professor and Nishida philosopher Shin'ichi Hisamatsu.[51]

The Japanese participants in these conversations tended to go beyond what, for their colleagues in the States, were largely theoretical exercises of comparative metapsychology. These Japanese clinicians developed new therapeutic modalities that combined Buddhist and psychotherapeutic ideas and techniques. The groundwork for such integrative approaches had previously been laid back in the 1920s with the appearance of Morita Shoma's Morita therapy. Both Morita therapy and later successors such as Naikan (inner-reflection) therapy, which was developed by retired businessman Yoshimoto Ishin in 1953, remain in use in Japan. These therapies were not only intended to achieve symptom reduction for psychiatric disorders; they were also intended to assist individuals in attaining forms of self-realization and self-actualization.

During this period, psychotherapists in the United States were drawn to similar theories from the more prominent Suzuki. In fact, the 1960s saw a more general fascination in the United States not only with the writings of Suzuki but with other popular representations of Zen, ranging from Eugen Herrigel's *Zen and the Art of Archery* to the countercultural poetry of the beat generation.[52] Convert Buddhists of European descent assisted in the establishment of their own Zendos and meditation groups based on these modern Zen forms. Texts such as Jung's commentary on Zen were commonplace in Philip Kapleau's Rochester Zen Center or Shunryu Suzuki's San Francisco Zen Center, and the communities that practiced at these institutions largely accepted psychologically attuned Zen teachings such as those of Suzuki. Suzuki had asserted that Zen practices were uniquely suited to access unconscious material and bring an awareness about one's place in the world. Whatever the appeal that such claims had to the descendants of the "the Dharma bums," they were naturally of special interest to psychologists and psychotherapists.

Psychoanalytic and humanistic therapists such as Karen Horney, her protégé Harold Kelman, and, most prominently, Erich Fromm all investigated whether Buddhist teachings could inform psychotherapeutic models of the self.[53] Suzuki had once reached out to a psychologist, Jung, in hopes that the association would grant him both entrée and an air of authenticity within new communities in Europe. Now, it was clinicians such as Fromm who sought out Suzuki on their own initiative, believing they could have common cause.

The relationship between Fromm and Suzuki ultimately had a significant effect on the way that psychologists approached Buddhist traditions for decades to come. Fromm arranged a now-famous meeting between Suzuki and nearly fifty psychoanalysts in 1957 at the University of Mexico. The edited volume that resulted from that meeting, a collection of a handful of the papers delivered at this gathering, remains highly influential today. Similarly to the articles of *Psychologia,* the essays of the now-seminal *Zen and Psychoanalysis* were a performance of comparative exercises between psychoanalytic and Zen Buddhist concepts, in which points of compatibility and, in some cases, even identity are found.[54] For example, as Parsons has explained at length, Suzuki's contribution delved deeply into Freud's concept of the unconscious, asserting that Zen practice uncovered multiple layers of unconsciousness beneath that of the personal unconscious.[55] In the relationship between teacher and student in Zen, Fromm detected a helpful analog for that of the analyst and analysand, and useful lessons about therapeutic presence for training analysts. But Fromm went beyond only detecting such areas of similarity between psychotherapies and Suzuki's Zen. He posited that both Buddhist traditions and an authentic psychotherapy were aimed at the same goal.

Such claims were unusual among psychoanalysts who followed Freud in believing that religious practice was intrinsically pathological. Though his own psychotherapeutic orientation differed in important ways, Fromm always presented himself as fundamentally aligned with the work of Freud despite the forerunner's critique of religion. Fromm believed that his intellectual hero would have embraced Buddhist traditions if he had been properly introduced to them. Fromm explained that Freud's concern about religious adherence stemmed from the thinker's contention that religions inculcate a submissive and, ultimately, dehumanizing way of being. As a Jewish refugee from the Nazi menace and a dangerously close observer of the rise of totalitarianism across Europe, Fromm was highly sympathetic to such concerns. He was, however, especially attracted to Suzuki's Zen Buddhist teachings precisely because he perceived them to be a guide to a self-actualization that meant liberation from the psychic structures that perpetuated authoritarianism.

Jung perceived prescriptions for achieving the religious experience of a Zen *satori*—as he had read it explained by Suzuki—as unhealthy for Europeans for whom, he thought, self-actualization required what Fromm described as a "surrender."[56] (However it had previously been understood by religious practitioners, this was a surrender to, an opening up to and integration of, the universal cultural wisdom contained in what Jung called the *collective unconscious.*) For Fromm, meanwhile, it was precisely Zen's seeming emphasis on human autonomy that made it so appealing. In fact, the "religious transformation" or religious experience of surrender that Jung described was, in Fromm's view, at the core of "authoritarian religions" that fostered a submissiveness that could be equally transferred to oppressive state entities. Buddhist traditions, on the other hand, seemed to him to be "one of the best examples of humanistic religion," religious traditions that raise up and exalt humanity's capacity for love and creativity.[57]

Fromm's treatment of Buddhist teachings and practices can be understood as a logical extension of the first constructions of Buddhism as a category. Thinkers such as Ziegler and Heiler, authors whom Fromm would have read while still in secondary school, had introduced Buddhist doctrine as based in self-absorption. Jung believed that this self-absorption was generated by a basic biological human instinct toward the ultimate in health, individuation, or self-actualization. The Buddhists, however, had erred in their path toward it, or, at the least, Europeans err by attempting to follow them. Where Jung saw error, Fromm detected a model. Buddhist practice appeared to be aimed toward the same ends as an authentic psychotherapy, a cultivation in which the individual culls those conscious and unconscious barriers to self-liberation, including a self-liberation that would allow people to resist politico-economic oppression. For some of Fromm's contemporaries, however, self-realization or self-actualization meant an attainment still grander.

HUMANISTIC PSYCHOTHERAPISTS

While Fromm was developing his humanistic psychoanalysis, a number of his contemporaries were theorizing new approaches to clinical practice that have come to be grouped under the larger heading of humanistic psychotherapy. Clinicians such as Carl Rogers and Abraham Maslow challenged psychotherapies that were patterned off a medical model.[58] Conceptualizing the purpose of the therapist as focused on curing illness and reducing symptomology was, to these clinicians, a kind of dehumanization. The psychotherapist should no longer place an emphasis on people's brokenness but instead their innate goodness, their inherent capabilities for growth. The true purpose of the psychotherapeutic healer was to assist people in reaching their full human potential. For some, particularly the therapists Richard Price and Michael Murphy, Asian religious traditions in general and Buddhist traditions in particular held special resources for this task.

The Esalen Institute that Price and Murphy founded in Big Sur, California, was a central site for psychotherapists' experimentation with Asian religious teachings and practices. The religion and psychology scholar Jeffrey J. Kripal called Esalen "one of America's most sophisticated mystical expressions," a center where visitors could participate in therapeutic "encounter groups" alongside classes on yoga and Zen Buddhist meditation practices.[59] Along with Rogers and Maslow, the important gestalt therapist, Fritz Perl—who, while dismissing meditation practice, extolled listeners to "be here now"—was among the invited speakers to teach classes at Esalen.[60] But Price and Murphy also welcomed lectures from scholars of "comparative religion" such as Joseph Campbell. One such lecturer—Alan Watts—was a major influence on this cohort's understanding of Buddhist teachings.

Ordained as an Episcopalian minister, Watts had been writing about his interpretation of Buddhist doctrine since 1936, when he published *The Spirit of Zen* (a book that, as Donald Lopez notes, is "largely a summary of the writings of D. T. Suzuki").[61] Price and Murphy studied with Watts in their own investigation of Asian religious traditions. Though not a therapist himself, Watts's conversations with clinicians helped shape his culturally significant volume, *Psychotherapy East and West*, published in 1961.[62] In many ways, the text carries forward assumptions that originated in the European "discovery" of Buddhism. Watts grouped a wide swath of Buddhist and Asian traditions together under the monolithic construct *the East* and sought points of connection between "Eastern" and "Western" cultural elements. His thesis was that "if we look deeply into such ways of life as Buddhism and Taoism, Vedanta and Yoga, we do not find either philosophy or religion as these are understood in the West. We find something more nearly resembling psychotherapy."[63] Watts's assertion relies on specific understandings of the constructs Buddhism and Taoism as well as psychotherapy, all of which, he believed, were, in essence, practical guides for the transformation of human consciousness.

As with the perspectives of most of the earliest psychologists and psychotherapists, Watts's views were heavily shaped by evolutionary and developmental theories. His ideas relied on a vision of an ever-evolving, ever-progressing humanity. In Watt's own universalist version of this theory, humanity's development is discernable across cultures from East to West. Humanistic psychotherapists such as Price, Murphy, and, perhaps most significantly, Maslow all held comparable beliefs about the evolution of humankind. Later clinicians in this lineage, communities of transpersonal psychotherapists, went further by formulating fully synthetic psychologies that weaved together widely disparate historico-cultural elements. The popular writer Ken Wilber, a major source of inspiration for this group, sought a "perennial psychology"—as psychological equivalent to Aldous Huxley's "perennial philosophy"—that would be a universal psychology applicable to all humanity across space and time.[64] Wilber makes frequent special reference in his writings to Asian and Buddhist religious traditions (he makes little distinction between these two categories) for offering especially useful descriptions of the "spectrum of consciousness" that he intended to map in his own writings.

From the humanist and humanistic psychotherapists of the 1960s to the later "fourth force" transpersonal psychologists and therapists, a marked shift had occurred among certain communities of psychotherapists in their views of religious teachings and practices. Whereas other communities of clinicians often remained suspicious, therapists such as Maslow perceived resources in religious traditions that could be incorporated into their clinical work. However, decades earlier, even a psychoanalyst such as Franz Alexander, who had pathologized Buddhist experience, had pronounced what Watts made into a thesis statement: Buddhism was a therapeutic ("The aims of Buddhistic teaching are therapeutic, the conquest of age, sickness, and death").[65]

The idea that Buddhist traditions offered a "therapeutic" may have been quite old, but it gained considerable strength in the 1960s and 1970s in the United States, both within and outside Buddhist communities. In the course of creating his Naropa Institute (which ultimately became the contemporary Naropa University), the Tibetan Buddhist teacher Chögyam Trungpa declared that psychology and psychotherapy would be a primary means by which Buddhist doctrine would take hold in these new communities.[66] Trungpa was a key figure for furthering an interpretation of Buddhism that saw it as repository of wisdom for exploring the realm of the intrapsychic and declared that the Buddhist practitioner could activate their own intrinsic "brilliant sanity." He developed *maitri* retreats, which incorporated Buddhist practices such as *metta* compassion cultivation into a psychotherapeutic group-therapy structure.

An acceptance of blending religious-identified elements—like those found in Buddhist traditions—with psychotherapy was thus gaining ground, but communities of clinicians did not lack for the cautious and the critical. Those psychotherapists who struggled with such activities initiated new sorts of approaches to Buddhist traditions.

"THE MINDFULNESS MOVEMENT" AND THE NEUROPSYCHOLOGICAL STUDY OF BUDDHIST TRADITIONS

In the early 1980s, John Teasdale, a psychologist researching depression-relapse prevention techniques, heard a lecture from the US-born Buddhist monk Ajahn Sumedho (né Robert Jackman) offered by the Oxford University Buddhist Society. Teasdale later recalled that he was "struck by the parallels between the core ideas of the Buddhist analysis of suffering, as described by Sumedho, and the basic assumptions of cognitive therapy."[67] That Teasdale found these parallels may be understandable. The traces of earlier psychotherapeutic interpretations of Buddhist thought are easily detectible in the teachings of Sumedho, as a leading convert voice in the Thai Forest tradition, a modern(ist) meditation revival movement whose participants often employed psychological frames in their teachings. Perhaps unsurprisingly, then, the discourse of teachers in the Thai Forest tradition such as Sumedho especially resonated within new, psychologically inflected European and US Buddhist communities such as the Insight Meditation Society in Barre, Massachusetts. It also strongly resonated with Teasdale. As a cognitive therapist, Teasdale believed that psychological distress originates in the mind, in the individual's cognitive distortions. Buddhist practices such as meditation seemed to train people to have a new relationship to cognition that could be compatible with his therapeutic approach. The difficulty, however, was that Buddhist traditions were religious and, for Teasdale, should consequently not be incorporated into secular psychotherapy.

The curiosity of Teasdale and the rest of his research team, Zindel V. Segal and J. Mark G. Williams, was therefore piqued when they learned of the work of Jon Kabat-Zinn. A researcher who had earned a PhD in molecular biology from MIT, Kabat-Zinn believed he had translated Buddhist meditation into secular, scientific terms. He was convinced that this meditation practice could have clinical benefit for stress reduction and pain management. In collaboration with Kabat-Zinn, Teasdale, Segal, and Williams designed a new psychotherapeutic modality called mindfulness-based cognitive therapy (MBCT). They acquired the word *mindfulness* from Kabat-Zinn, who explained that it refers to a particular experiential state long sought by Buddhists practitioners and cultivated through meditation. Kabat-Zinn titled his therapeutic program mindfulness-based stress reduction (MBSR) because he believed the word *mindfulness* would not betray a Buddhist association with biomedical authorities who prohibit religious practice in mainstream secular-designated institutions such as hospitals. For the team that developed MBCT, even the word *meditation* had too much of a religious tenor, and they instead labeled the new mindfulness practices they used as "attentional control training."[68]

The MBCT team consisted of cognitive therapists and communities of cognitive and behavioral therapists, who are especially invested in their status as biomedical, scientific practitioners. These communities intend to use exclusively what they call "evidence-based treatment interventions." This is in part intended to assure individuals coming to see these therapists for care that they will be provided with methodologies that are research-tested and proven to be effective for symptom reduction. Therapeutic mindfulness practices, particularly meditation practices, are some of the most frequently studied Buddhist elements in the United States, Europe, and beyond. However, researchers have employed scientific means to investigate Buddhist traditions dating back to the early psychologists of religion who sought to explain Buddhist experience using what were the high technologies of their day. The latest iteration of such efforts is the neuropsychological study of Buddhist meditation practices.

The Fourteenth Tibetan Dalai Lama, Tenzin Gyatso, has been an active supporter of these endeavors. He has worked with neuroscientists such as Francisco Varela and Richie Davidson since the 1980s, sending monks to be attached to fMRI machines to study, for example, the neuropsychology of experiential states of lovingkindness. The Dalai Lama's conversations with neuroscientists, called the "Mind and Life Dialogues," ultimately spurred the creation of the Mind and Life Institute, a key site for the development of contemplative studies. Carrying forward the tradition of the earliest psychologists of religion, the neuroscientific study of Buddhist traditions has further solidified understandings of Buddhist traditions as fundamentally psychological. Contemporary observers such as Donald Lopez express some of the same concerns as those early psychologists of religion (e.g., William James) who warned against interpreting religious experience through the lenses of medical materialism.[69] Whether the true function of Buddhist meditative experiences can be elucidated by tracking gamma and alpha waves or not, researchers herald scientific research for demonstrating the positive health effects of Buddhist practice. To a collaborator at the Mind and Life Institute such as psychiatrist and interpersonal-neurobiology researcher Dan Siegel, scientific studies that purportedly prove the health benefits of Buddhist practices legitimate their use in secular-designated psychotherapy.[70]

Cognitive behavioral therapists have translated multiple items from Buddhist traditions, items they believed to be religious, for use in clinical settings. Although their originators each came to the term *mindfulness* in remarkably different ways, enough clinicians had created mindfulness-based psychotherapies by the 1990s that one such practitioner, Steven Hayes, declared the period to be a "third wave" of cognitive behavioral therapy.[71] Alongside MBCT, the two other main mindfulness methodologies that Hayes includes in this third wave were his own acceptance and commitment therapy (ACT) (initially developed out of Hayes's desire for more effective means to decrease anxiety symptoms) and dialectical behavior therapy (DBT), which was developed by the psychologist Marsha Linehan as a treatment for people struggling with borderline personality disorder.

Despite the fact that many decades earlier, Fromm had explicitly declared that Suzuki's Zen Buddhist practice should not be treated as technique, Linehan sought—in developing DBT—to make a "Zen without the Buddhism."[72] Her use of mindfulness skills in DBT was based on the premise that certain practices and concepts can be detached from what their originators believed were Buddhist frameworks and reconstructed into treatment interventions. Ironically, late in his life, Fromm came to believe that a Buddhist practice that would likely be recognized by many today as mindfulness meditation was superior to Suzuki's Zen precisely because it seemed to him to resist, among other ills, such instrumentalization. And he learned this practice directly from the German-born monk Nyanaponika Thera (né Siegmund Feniger), a figure recognized by many to be one of the most significant influences on current dominant understandings of mindfulness.

Nyanaponika's 1954 publication, *The Heart of Buddhist Meditation: A Handbook of Mental Training Based on the Buddha's Way of Mindfulness*, popularized a version of the Burmese Mahāsī method and was read widely by Kabat-Zinn and many others of his generation.[73] In this regard, Nyanaponika's psychological interpretation of Buddhist traditions can be considered one of the more significant of the last half century. He helped solidify the common understanding that Buddhism refers to a religion defined by meditation practice for the cultivation of a particular psychological attainment that transcends tradition and is effective as a treatment not only for the ills of the individual but of society at large.

More than half a century since Nyanaponika published his seminal text, the use of therapeutic mindfulness practices has boomed into what is commonly referred to as "the mindfulness movement." Responding uneasily to this intense popular interest, clinicians have themselves increasingly voiced concerns about the effects of decontextualizing teaching and practices from Buddhist frameworks. Linehan, for example, has argued that the training and competency of mindfulness practitioners could suffer without the collective wisdom and teaching traditions of Buddhist communities.[74] Therapists such as Christopher Germer and Ron Siegel have suggested that the way to prevent misuse in corporate or military settings is to teach what they call "right mindfulness," which is *re*contextualized back into the Eight-Fold Path.[75] Others, including Jon Kabat-Zinn, have recently claimed that such a move is unnecessary.[76] This contingent suggests that mindfulness practices will always evoke deep insights into reality if preformed properly and diligently; it will always bring a complete ethical transformation equivalent to what they define as a Buddhist enlightenment, regardless of the initial motives that drive the practitioner.

Debates about whether therapeutic mindfulness practices are authentically Buddhist or whether their use results in unwholesome ends continue. Their use is so ubiquitous that today they can sometimes appear to be the only manner in which psychologists and psychotherapists have approached Buddhist traditions, though this has clearly not been the case throughout history. Furthermore, even as mindfulness practitioners were designing their methodologies, other clinicians and researchers were relating to Buddhist teachings and practices in different ways.

SELF/NON-SELF/INTERRELATED SELF

MBCT was initially created in a search for new methods of preventing people from relapsing into depressive episodes. However, following in the footsteps of Carl Rogers and others, many contemporaries of the MBCT team saw their role as healers to go beyond symptom reduction. A number continued to believe, as Carl Rogers did (and, more dramatically, as participants in the antipsychiatry movement claimed in the 1970s), that the medical model was not only counter to an authentic psychotherapy but harmful to the patients who had it inflicted on them. A growing number of psychotherapists became convinced that Buddhist teachings offered a useful counterpoint for theorizing the true purpose of human being and that this alternative model could help guide their clinical practice.

The idea dated back to the interpretations of Jung. Analysts such as Kelman had encouraged psychoanalysts to study Buddhist metapsychologies.[77] Others such as Fromm had further believed that Buddhist practice could be a useful parallel adjunct to psychotherapy.[78] It was later clinicians, however, who began to theorize how Buddhist and psychotherapeutic frames could be integrated. Some were convinced that a common essence enabled nearly all religio-cultural elements to be integrated with each other (and into their psychologies). Others sought approaches that were less fully synthetic. They often began by conducting the same sort of comparative analyses that the earliest psychological interpreters of Buddhist traditions had previously. Now, however, similarity was intended to demonstrate compatibility, to demonstrate that Buddhist and psychotherapeutic elements could be mixed together. And yet the vast majority always found significant differences between Buddhist and psychotherapeutic traditions. At times, they described such differences as incommensurable.

Fromm had believed that Buddhist and psychoanalytic paths were aimed toward the same goal of liberating self-actualization but had very distinct means to achieve that goal. For a group of therapists into the 1980s and 1990s, it was the ends that Buddhists and psychotherapists were attempting to achieve that were radically different. In one of the first book-length studies of this topic, *Psychotherapy and Buddhism: Toward an Integration*, the psychotherapist Jeffrey Rubin went so far as to suggest that Buddhist and psychotherapeutic goals were "antithetical."[79] His view has roots that stretch back to the European "discovery" of Buddhism. The first individuals to use the word Buddhism believed that Buddhist adherents engage in an immersive psychological exploration of the interior mind—which they called "self-absorption."

Later interpreters perceived this self-absorption to be a practice for achieving variations of self-actualization or self-realization. For psychotherapists in the United States through the 1970s, this self-actualization became a self-liberation and, increasingly, a liberation from certain views of the self. To Rubin and others, such a self-liberation was a liberation *from* the self, an ego dissolution they identified with a word they read in English-language explications of Buddhist doctrine: *non-self.*

In the decades that followed, psychological interpreters of Buddhist doctrine debated how exactly psychodynamically to explain reported experiences of awakening to the illusory nature of the permanent self. But for those seeking to integrate Buddhist and psychological frames, the doctrine of non-self—as they understood it—seemed completely incompatible with the goals of most psychotherapies. Psychotherapy, by and large, was directed toward assisting people to restore a whole, healthy self, not toward teaching that the self is a delusion at the root of all suffering. Whereas the first psychological interpreters of Buddhist traditions strived to explain concepts such as karma, nirvana, and rebirth in psychological terms, clinicians such as Rubin barely mentioned terms such as *rebirth*. Instead, psychological theorists have often focused on a concept such as non-self and debate how, or whether, it can be integrated with psychotherapy, whether this seeming irreconcilability between Buddhist and psychotherapeutic aims can be resolved, though there would seem to be no goal more incommensurable with those of psychotherapists than striving for release from samsara as a literal cycle of rebirth.[80]

A number of psychologies have been developed as solutions to the self/non-self question. The most famous came from the humanistic psychotherapist Jack Engler, who suggested a stage or developmental model for organizing the seemingly opposing ideals. Engler's approach can be summarized by the now-often quoted phrase "You have to be somebody before you can be nobody."[81] In his schema, psychological health, defined as a secure sense of self, is necessary before one can strive for release from the illusion of a permanent self. Psychotherapists seeking to integrate Buddhist traditions would still first seek to heal the self in those coming to see them for care. Only when the individual is sufficiently healthy and, for example, no longer feels an emotional emptiness, would the clinician begin to introduce a Buddhist understanding of the emptiness of all apparent reality.

Following Engler, a number of other psychotherapists have innovated additional methods for mixing the Buddhist and the psychotherapeutic. Some have suggested that, rather than simply creating a hierarchy between Buddhist and psychotherapeutic conceptions of the self, the former should replace the latter. The Buddhist self, as understood by these clinicians, seems far superior to dominant psychological models of the autonomous individuating self. Feminist and relational-cultural therapists such as Jan Surrey have long critiqued the "self" at the center of dominant psychologies.[82] They noted that this self had been theorized almost exclusively by men based on research employing largely male subjects. The Buddhist texts that Surrey read seemed to offer an alternative to the individual(ized) self. They described a relational self that seemed far more accurate to human beings.

As journalist and author Christina Robb has written, "Surrey psychologizes the Buddhist notion of 'dependent co-arising,' the idea that everything comes to be in relationship with everything else."[83] Of course, as has been explained by McMahan, such an understanding of "interrelatedness" is highly divergent from those conveyed in most Buddhist doctrine throughout history.[84] Buddhist communities had perceived interdependence as a fundamental aspect of samsara, a web one sought to escape rather than become more deeply enmeshed within. But, to Surrey, Buddhist teachings reveal that the true aim of psychotherapy should be to assist people in achieving what she understands to be the equivalent of Buddhist enlightenment, awakening to one's fundamental interconnectedness.

Other clinicians have emphasized the need not only to highlight differences transparently between Buddhist and psychotherapeutic frames but to preserve those differences actively, even while seeking integration between them. Clinician Pilar Jennings, for example, also draws on relational psychoanalysis to explain that it is essential to maintain differentiation and healthy boundaries in all relationships, including the "relationship between Buddhism and psychoanalysis."[85] Contemporary therapists, such as analyst and Zen Buddhist teacher Magid, go so far as to critique the explicit insertion of Buddhist teachings or practices into clinical sessions, even as he publishes multiple books with titles such as *Ordinary Mind: Exploring the Common Ground of Zen and Psychoanalysis*.[86] Magid believes that the transformative Buddhist experiences he has had in his personal life fundamentally influence his therapeutic practice, but he argues that directly incorporating Buddhist elements into psychotherapy means an instrumentalization that compromises the integrity of Buddhist truths.

Rubin, meanwhile, believes that integration is possible, but it must be conducted based on an "egalitarian relationship . . . between Buddhism and psychoanalysis."[87] He critiques the hierarchy in formulations such as Engler's assertion "You have to be somebody before you can be nobody" and worries that, while psychotherapists once held a "Eurocentric" attitude, they now overenthusiastically adopt what he calls a "Orientocentric" idealization of Buddhist teachings and practices. Therapists, indeed, do continue to critique aspects of Buddhist doctrine, for instance, for purportedly teaching disconnection from the healthy emotional experiences of anger or sexual desire. Some believe that their psychotherapies can, in this regard, provide helpful resources to Buddhists communities.

BEYOND INFLUENCE

As has been shown throughout this article, Buddhist communities in the United States and beyond have been shaped by psychological interpretation for nearly two centuries. Leading Asian Buddhist figures and leaders of Asian Buddhist communities used psychological theories to legitimate and explain their teachings—from Dharmapāla and Soen in the 19th century to Suzuki and Nyanaponika in the 20th century and to the Dalai Lama in the 21st century. US "convert" Buddhist communities, from the Zen Centers of the 1950s and 1960s to the so-called insight meditation groups of the 1990s, often simply assumed without discussion that Buddhist concepts such as rebirth should be viewed as psychological metaphors. These communities may not have always consciously drawn on psychological frames in their practice of a Buddhism that was understood to be, by definition, fundamentally psychological (as discussed in "Discovery of the Psychological Buddhism"). However, a marked turn was taken through the 1990s as a growing number of voices began to advocate *explicitly* for the active use of psychotherapeutic insights and practices within Buddhist communities.

Contemporary psychoanalytic clinician Paul Cooper suggests that the psychotherapeutic process can help unblock unconscious material that can otherwise thwart Buddhist meditators.[88]

Meanwhile, as Ann Gleig has discussed, "teacher scandals" are often cited as a prime example of how psychotherapeutic, and specifically psychoanalytic, theories can be essential for Buddhist communities.[89] Psychoanalytic teachings, it is suggested, can help these communities work through the idealization of authority figures and transform an unhealthy repression of sexual desire into creative sublimation. Claims that psychodynamic concepts could be of benefit have not only come from psychologists who may be inclined to think their work has utility. Figures such as Cooper belong to communities of both Buddhists and psychotherapists. Aside from his practice as a clinician, Cooper holds the dual role of leader of Buddhist community, serving as the head teacher of the Two Rivers Zen Community in Honesdale, Pennsylvania.

Meanwhile, prior to becoming a psychotherapist, Harvey Aronson was a Buddhist studies scholar and translator and cofounded the Dawn Mountain Community Center in Houston, Texas. A lama in the Nyingma lineage, Aronson has stressed that monks or teachers from "traditional Buddhist cultures" often do not possess the same psychotherapeutic norms and values of "modern" audiences in the United States.[90] Convert Buddhists raised in contemporary US culture, for instance, may expect a Buddhist teacher to offer relational support, and they may feel disillusioned when it is not forthcoming. Drawing on intercultural psychology and comparative religious studies, Aronson has formulated an approach to reconciling Buddhist and psychotherapeutic theories not for clinical practice but for the betterment of contemporary Buddhist communities.

Aronson and Cooper are representative of a striking feature of the state of Buddhist practice. Beyond only being influenced by psychological and psychotherapeutic frames, Buddhist communities have increasingly been founded and led by psychologists and psychotherapists. Some of the most prominent convert Buddhist figures in the United States—perhaps most visibly, Jack Kornfield—have doubled as both psychologist/psychotherapist and Buddhist teacher, and their leadership of Buddhist communities is inevitably shaped by these multiple identities.[91] Future psychological interpreters of Buddhist traditions will analyze Buddhist doctrine that is not only informed by psychotherapists but is written by them.

FURTHER READING

Gleig, Ann. "Wedding the Personal and Impersonal in West Coast Vipassana: A Dialogical Encounter between Buddhism and Psychotherapy." *Journal of Global Buddhism* 13 (2012): 129–146.

Gleig, Ann. "External Mindfulness, Secure (Non)-Attachment, and Healing Relational Trauma: Emerging Models of Wellness for Modern Buddhists and Buddhist Modernism." *Journal of Global Buddhism* 17 (2016): 1–21.

Gleig, Ann. *American Dharma: Buddhism beyond Modernity*. New Haven, CT: Yale University Press, 2019.

Gomez, Luis. "Oriental Wisdom and the Cure of Souls: Jung and the Indian East." In *Curators of the Buddha: The Study of Buddhism under Colonialism*. Edited by Donald Lopez, 197–251. Chicago: University of Chicago Press, 1995.

Gomez, Luis. "Psychology." In *Encyclopedia of Buddhism*. Edited by Robert Buswell, 678–692. New York: Macmillan Reference, 2003.

Helderman, Ira. "'The Conversion of the Barbarians': Comparison and Psychotherapists' Approaches to Buddhist Traditions in the United States." *Buddhist Studies Review* 32, no. 1 (2015): 63–97.

Helderman, Ira. "Drawing the Boundaries between 'Religion' and 'Secular' in Psychotherapists' Approaches to Buddhist Traditions in the United States." *Journal of the American Academy of Religion* 84, no. 4 (2016): 937–972.

Helderman, Ira. *Prescribing the Dharma: Psychotherapists, Buddhist Traditions, and Defining Religion.* Chapel Hill: University of North Carolina Press, 2019.

Imamura, Ryo. "Buddhist and Western Psychotherapies: An Asian American Perspective." In *The Faces of Buddhism in America.* Edited by Charles Prebish and Kenneth Tanaka, 228–238. Berkeley: University of California Press, 1998.

Kripal, Jeffrey. *Esalen: America and the Religion of No Religion.* Chicago: University of Chicago Press, 2007.

Metcalf, Franz Aubrey. "Buddhism and Psychology: A Perspective at the Millennium." *Religious Studies Review* 27, no. 4 (2001): 349–354.

Metcalf, Franz Aubrey. "The Encounter of Buddhism and Psychology." In *Westward Dharma Buddhism beyond Asia.* Edited by Charles Prebish and Martin Baumann, 348–365. Berkeley: University of California Press, 2002.

Parsons, William B. "Psychoanalysis Meets Buddhism: The Development of a Dialogue." In *Changing the Scientific Study of Religion: Beyond Freud?* Edited by Jacob A. Belzen, 179–209. New York: Springer, 2009.

Parsons, William B. "Of Chariots, Navels, and Winged Steeds: The Dialogue between Psychoanalysis and Buddhism." In *Disciplining Freud on Religion: Perspectives from the Humanities and Social Sciences.* Edited by Gregory Kaplan and William B. Parsons, 107–146. Lanham, MD: Lexington Books, 2010.

Unno, Mark, ed. *Buddhism and Psychotherapy across Cultures.* Somerville, MA: Wisdom Publications, 2006.

NOTES

1. Philip Almond, *The British Discovery of Buddhism* (Cambridge, UK: Cambridge University Press, 1988).
2. Tomoko Masuzawa, *The Invention of World Religions, or, How European Universalism Was Preserved in the Language of Pluralism* (Chicago: University of Chicago Press, 2005), 121–147.
3. For example, T. W. Rhys Davids, trans., *The Questions of King Milinda* (Oxford, UK: Clarendon Press, 1890), 58n2.
4. Caroline Rhys Davids, trans., *A Buddhist Manual of Psychological Ethics of the Fourth Century* BC (London: Royal Asiatic Society, 1900).
5. Hermann Oldenberg, *Buddha: sein Leben, seine Lehre, seine Gemeinde* (Berlin: W. Hertz, 1881).
6. Eugène Burnouf, *Introduction à l'histoire du Bouddhisme Indien* (Paris: Imprimerie Royale, 1844).
7. See, for example, Donald Lopez, *Prisoners of Shangri-La: Tibetan Buddhism and the West* (Chicago: University of Chicago Press, 1998).
8. David McMahan, *The Making of Buddhist Modernism* (Oxford, UK: Oxford University Press, 2008).
9. Luis Gomez, "Psychology," in *Encyclopedia of Buddhism*, ed. Robert Buswell (New York: Macmillan Reference, 2003), 678–692; and Monier Monier-Williams, *Buddhism: In Its Connection with Brahmanism and Hinduism, and in Its Contrast with Christianity* (New York: Macmillan, 1889).
10. Gomez, "Psychology," 679.
11. R. Spence Hardy, *Eastern Monachism* (London: Williams and Norgate, 1850), 173. See also R. Spence Hardy, *Manual of Buddhism* (London: Partridge and Oakey, 1853); and R. Spence Hardy, *The Legends and Theories of the Buddhists, Compared with History and Science: With Introductory Notices of the Life and System of Gotama Buddha* (London: Williams and Norgate, 1881).
12. Rhys Davids, *Dhammasaṅgaṇi*, xv.
13. Rhys Davids, *Dhammasaṅgaṇi*, xvi.
14. Rhys Davids, *Dhammasaṅgaṇi*, xviii.
15. See, for example, Judith Snodgrass, *Presenting Japanese Buddhism to the West: Orientalism, Occidentalism, and the Columbian Exposition* (Chapel Hill: University of North Carolina Press, 2003).
16. Henry Steel Olcott, *The Buddhist Catechism*, 44th ed. (Madras: Theosophical Publishing House, 1915).
17. Paul Carus, *The Gospel of the Buddha Compiled from Ancient Records* (Chicago: Open Court, 1917).

18. Paul Carus, *The Soul of Man: An Investigation of the Facts of Physiological and Experimental Psychology* (Chicago: Open Court, 1891).
19. Leopold Ziegler, *Der ewige Buddho: Ein Tempelschriftwerk in vier Unterweisungen*, vol. 4 (Würzburg, Germany: Königshausen and Neumann, 2004); and Friedrich Heiler, *Die buddhistische Versenkung: Eine religionsgeschichtliche Untersuchung* (Munich: Verlag Von Ernst Reinhardt, 1922).
20. William James, *The Varieties of Religious Experience: A Study of Human Nature (Being the Gifford Lectures on Natural Religion Delivered at Edinburgh in 1901–1902)*, First Library of America ed. (New York: Penguin, 2010), 36.
21. James, *Varieties*, 36.
22. James Henry Leuba, "A Study in the Psychology of Religious Phenomena," *American Journal of Psychology* 7, no. 3 (1896): 314.
23. Leuba, "Study," 314.
24. James Bissett Pratt, *The Religious Consciousness* (New York: Macmillan, 1920), 4.
25. James Bissett Pratt, *India and Its Faiths: A Traveler's Record* (New York: Houghton Mifflin, 1915); and James Bissett Pratt, *The Pilgrimage of Buddhism and a Buddhist Pilgrimage* (New York: Macmillan, 1928).
26. James Bissett Pratt, "Buddhism and Scientific Thinking," *Journal of Religion* 14, no. 1 (1934): 21.
27. Pratt, "Buddhism," 21.
28. Pratt, "Buddhism," 22.
29. For the genealogy of this tale, see Ira Helderman, *Prescribing the Dharma: Psychotherapists, Buddhist Traditions, and Defining Religion* (Chapel Hill: University of North Carolina Press, 2019).
30. Pratt, "Buddhism," 21.
31. Franz Alexander, "Buddhistic Training as an Artificial Catatonia (the Biological Meaning of Psychic Occurrences)," *Psychoanalytic Review* 18 (1931): 145n11.
32. William Parsons, "Psychoanalysis Meets Buddhism: The Development of a Dialogue," in *Changing the Scientific Study of Religion: Beyond Freud?*, ed. Jacob Belzen (New York: Springer, 2009), 179–209; and William Parsons, "Of Chariots, Navels, and Winged Steeds: The Dialogue between Psychoanalysis and Buddhism," in *Disciplining Freud on Religion: Perspectives from the Humanities and Social Sciences*, ed. Gregory Kaplan and William Parsons (Lanham, MD: Lexington Books, 2010), 107–146.
33. Joe Tom Sun, "Psychology in Primitive Buddhism," *Psychoanalytic Review* 11 (1924): 38–47.
34. Tom Sun, "Primitive Buddhism," 40.
35. Alexander, "Buddhistic Training," 144.
36. Alexander, "Buddhistic Training," 144.
37. Alexander, "Buddhistic Training," 138.
38. Parsons, "Psychoanalysis"; and Parsons, "Chariots."
39. Alexander, "Buddhistic Training," 140.
40. See, for example, Franz Alexander and Sheldon Selesnick, *The History of Psychiatry: An Evaluation of Psychiatric Thought and Practice from Prehistoric Times to the Present* (New York: Harper, 1966), 26.
41. See, for example, C. G. Jung, "The Spiritual Problem of Modern Man," in *Civilization in Transition*, vol. 10 of *Collected Works of C. G. Jung*, trans. R. F. C. Hull, Bollingen Series, no. 20 (Princeton, NJ: Princeton University Press, 1964), 86.
42. Luis Gomez, "Oriental Wisdom and the Cure of Souls: Jung and the Indian East," in *Curators of the Buddha: The Study of Buddhism under Colonialism*, ed. Donald Lopez (Chicago: University of Chicago Press, 1995), 242n46; C. G. Jung, "Psychological Commentary on *The Tibetan Book of the Dead*," in *Psychology and Religion: West and East*, vol. 11 of *Collected Works of C. G. Jung*, trans. R. F. C. Hull, Bollingen Series, no. 20 (Princeton, NJ: Princeton University Press, 1969), 509–529; and W. Y. Evans-Wentz, *The Tibetan Book of the Dead or the After-Death Experiences on the Bardo Plane, According to Lama Kazi Dawa-Samdup's English Rendering* (London: Oxford University Press, 1960).
43. Jung, "Commentary," 515.

44. D. T. Suzuki, *Introduction to Zen Buddhism* (New York: Grove Press, 1964) and C. G. Jung, foreword to Suzuki's "Introduction to Zen Buddhism," in *Psychology and Religion: West and East*, vol. 11 of *Collected Works of C. G. Jung*, trans. R. F. C. Hull, Bollingen Series, no. 20 (Princeton, NJ: Princeton University Press, 1969), 538–558.
45. Jung, foreword, 554.
46. Jung, foreword, 556.
47. Jung, foreword, 553.
48. Jung, foreword, 553; and Gomez, "Oriental Wisdom," 210.
49. Jung, foreword, 553–554.
50. Y. Rim, "The Prediction Validity of Seven Manual Dexterity Tests," *Psychologia: An International Journal of Psychological Sciences* 5, no. 1 (1962): 52–55.
51. K. Sasamoto, "Hypnotism and Samadhi," *Psychologia: An International Journal of Psychological Sciences* 5, no. 2 (1962): 73–74; and Jerome Bruner, "The Art of Ambiguity: A Conversation with Zen Master Hisamatsu," *Psychologia: An International Journal of Psychological Sciences* 2, no. 2 (1959): 101–104.
52. Eugen Herrigel, *Zen and the Art of Archery* (New York: Pantheon Books, 1953).
53. Karen Horney, *Our Inner Conflicts: A Constructive Theory of Neurosis* (New York: W. W. Norton: 1945); and Harold Kelman, "Eastern Influences on Psychoanalytic Thinking," *Psychologia* 2, no. 2 (1959): 73–75.
54. Erich Fromm, D. T. Suzuki, and Richard DeMartino, eds., *Zen Buddhism and Psychoanalysis* (New York: HarperCollins, 1960).
55. Parsons, "Psychoanalysis"; and Parsons, "Chariots."; and D. T. Suzuki, "Lectures on Zen Buddhism," in *Zen Buddhism and Psychoanalysis*, ed. Erich Fromm, D. T. Suzuki, and Richard DeMartino (New York: HarperCollins, 1960), 77–141.
56. Erich Fromm, *Psychoanalysis and Religion* (New Haven, CT: Yale University Press, 1950), 19.
57. Jung, foreword, 553; Fromm, *Psychoanalysis and Religion*, 35; Fromm, *Psychoanalysis and Religion*, 37.
58. Carl Ransom Rogers, *On Becoming a Person: A Therapist's View of Psychotherapy* (New York: Houghton Mifflin, 1961); and Abraham H. Maslow, *Religions, Values, and Peak-Experiences* (Columbus: Ohio State University Press, 1964).
59. Jeffrey Kripal, *Esalen: America and the Religion of No Religion* (Chicago: University of Chicago Press, 2007), 24.
60. Frederick Perls, *The Gestalt Approach and Eye Witness to Therapy* (Ben Lomond, CA: Science and Behavior Books, 1973).
61. Donald Lopez, ed., *A Modern Buddhist Bible: Essential Readings from East and West* (Boston: Beacon Press, 2002), 159.
62. Alan Watts, *Psychotherapy: East and West* (New York: Pantheon Books, 1961).
63. Watts, *Psychotherapy*, 3.
64. Ken Wilber, *Integral Psychology: Consciousness, Spirit, Psychology, Therapy* (Boston: Shambhala, 2000).
65. Alexander, "Buddhistic Training," 136.
66. Chögyam Trungpa, *The Sanity We Are Born With: A Buddhist Approach to Psychology*, ed. Carolyn Rose Gilman (Boston: Shambhala, 2005).
67. Zindel V. Segal, J. Mark G. Williams, and John Teasdale. *Mindfulness-Based Cognitive Therapy for Depression: A New Approach to Preventing Relapse*, 2nd ed. (New York: Guilford Press, 2001), 37.
68. Segal, Williams, and Teasdale, *Mindfulness-Based*, 41–42.
69. Donald Lopez, *Buddhism and Science: A Guide for the Perplexed* (Chicago: University of Chicago Press, 2008); and Donald Lopez, *The Scientific Buddha: His Short and Happy Life* (New Haven, CT: Yale University Press, 2012).
70. See, for example, Dan Siegel, *The Mindful Therapist: A Clinician's Guide to Mindsight and Neural Integration* (New York: W. W. Norton, 2010), 239.

71. See, for example, Steven Hayes, "Acceptance and Commitment Therapy and the New Behavior Therapies: Mindfulness, Acceptance, and Relationship," in *Mindfulness and Acceptance: Expanding the Cognitive-Behavioral Tradition*, ed. Steven Hayes, Victoria M. Follette, and Marshal Linehan (New York: Guilford Press, 2004), 1–30.
72. Erich Fromm, "Psychoanalysis and Zen Buddhism," in *Zen Buddhism and Psychoanalysis*, ed. Daisetz Teitaro Suzuki, Erich Fromm, and Richard De Martino (New York: HarperCollins, 1960), 138; and Marsha Linehan, interview by David Van Nuys, *Wise Counsel*, October 20, 2007.
73. Nyanaponika Thera, *The Heart of Buddhist Meditation: A Handbook of Mental Training Based on the Buddha's Way of Mindfulness* (Colombo, Sri Lanka: The Word of the Buddha, 1954).
74. Sona Dimidjian and Marsha Linehan, "Defining an Agenda for Future Research on the Clinical Application of Mindfulness Practice," *Clinical Psychology: Science and Practice* 10 (2003): 166–171.
75. Ira Helderman, *Prescribing the Dharma: Psychotherapists, Buddhist Traditions, and Defining Religion* (Chapel Hill: University of North Carolina Press, 2019).
76. Jon Kabat-Zinn, "Some Reflections on the Origins of MBSR, Skillful Means, and the Trouble with Maps," *Contemporary Buddhism* 12, no. 1 (2011): 290.
77. Kelman, "Eastern Influences."
78. Fromm, "Psychoanalysis."
79. Jeffrey Rubin, *Psychotherapy and Buddhism: Toward an Integration* (New York: Plenum Press, 1996), 51.
80. Helderman, *Prescribing.*
81. Jack Engler, "Vicissitudes of the Self According to Psychoanalysis and Buddhism: A Spectrum Model of Object Relations Development," *Psychoanalysis and Contemporary Thought* 6 (1983): 29–72.
82. Jan Surrey, "Relational Psychotherapy, Relational Mindfulness," in *Mindfulness and Psychotherapy*, ed. Christopher K. Germer, Ronald D. Siegel, Paul R. Fulton (New York: Guilford Press, 2005), 91–110.
83. Christina Robb, *This Changes Everything: The Relational Revolution in Psychology* (New York: Picador, 2006), 206.
84. McMahan, *Making*, 149–180.
85. Pilar Jennings, *Mixing Minds: The Power of Relationship in Psychoanalysis and Buddhism* (Boston: Wisdom Publications, 2010), viii.
86. Barry Magid, *Ordinary Mind: Exploring the Common Ground of Zen and Psychoanalysis* (Somerville, MA: Wisdom Publications, 2002).
87. Rubin, *Psychotherapy*, 41.
88. Paul Cooper, *The Zen Impulse and the Psychoanalytic Encounter* (New York: Routledge, 2010).
89. Ann Gleig, *American Dharma: Buddhism beyond Modernity* (New Haven, CT: Yale University Press, 2019).
90. Harvey Aronson, *Buddhist Practice on Western Ground: Reconciling Eastern Ideals and Western Psychology* (Boston: Shambala, 2004), 17.
91. Jack Kornfield, *The Wise Heart: A Guide to the Universal Teachings of Buddhist Psychology* (New York: Bantam Books, 2008).

Ira Helderman

PURE LAND BUDDHISM IN TIBETAN CONTEXTS

THE DAWN OF A SOLAR DEITY

A survey of the different kinds of pure land orientations in Tibetan contexts is beyond the scope of this article. The study will focus exclusively on Amitābha and his western *Blissful Land* given their prominence in Tibetan religious history, culture, and imagination. "Pure Land Buddhism" is not limited to the cult of Amitābha and to the three canonical "Pure Land texts" that grant him scriptural authority in East Asia and describe various practices connected with him. Nattier has long noted that pure land Buddhism is a movement well entrenched in Indian Mahāyāna that developed "ideas and practices related to Buddhas who are presently living in world-systems other than our own." This includes buddhas other than Amitābha, such as Akṣobhya, the Medicine Buddha, and "countless Buddha figures described in Mahāyāna texts as presiding over world-systems in all of the ten directions."[1] In Tibetan Buddhism, a variety of esoteric and exoteric practices associated with exalted destinations other than Sukhāvatī can be found. These include Śambhala, Avalokiteśvara's Mount Potalaka, Padmasambhava's Copper Colored Mountain, Vajrayoginī's Kechara, and a number of hidden terrestrial lands, the *bëyul* (*sbas yul*), located in the Himalayan valleys and made accessible only to those endowed with pure vision. Furthermore, these "terrestrial pure lands" resemble Sukhāvatī in their wholesomeness and may even function as secret portals to the pure land itself.

The obscure origins of the deity Amitābha-Amitāyus and his solar symbolism are suggestive of non-Buddhist influences from religious traditions that were prevalent in the cosmopolitan regions where his scriptures made their first appearance and during the historical milieu of the Kuṣāṇa Empire (30–375 CE)—a remarkable period in Indian history marked by foreign trade, cross-cultural contacts, and religious tolerance. The solar calendar has been observed by people across the world engaged with agriculture, farming, and livestock, since the force of the sun is vital and nourishing for the growth of all life on earth that depends upon it. Amitābha's name, which translates in Tibetan as "measureless light" or "infinite luminosity" ('Od dpag med or Snang ba mtha yas), betrays his association with the beneficent qualities of the sun. His pure land Sukhāvatī, a celestial location for the fortunate dead, is situated to the west where the setting of the sun heralds the end of day and denotes the metaphorical passage of the sun god to the underworld. Following the interval of darkness that symbolizes death, the sun re-emerges the next day victorious, shinning warmth and heat upon the living. The archetypical symbol assuages the fear of death and offers the promise of eternal life in his form as Buddha Amitāyus ("unending life" or Tshe dpag med). As noted by Tucci,

> unending life and infinite light, ζωή and φῶς, have too great an importance for religious history, in India and outside India, for us to exclude that under this myth may be hidden an extremely complex history and two originally independent cycles.[2]

There is no scholarly consensus whether the names Amitābha and Amitāyus were originally referring to two independent deities that later merged into one, or if they were two epithets highlighting different qualities of the same deity.[3] What is clear is that by the 3rd century CE the cult of Amitābha and Sukhāvatī spread from northwest India across Central Asia to China. Although there are no archaeological records to substantiate the formation of an independent pure land cult in India, literary references to Sukhāvatī abound in Indian Mahāyāna scriptures, with the earliest translation of the long *Sukhāvatīvyūha-sūtra* into Chinese by Lokakṣema in the late 2nd century CE and the short *Sukhāvatīvyūha* in the early 5th century by Kumārajīva.[4] In fact, these two canonical pure land sutras of the earliest date are available in Chinese and they were probably composed in "Greater Gandhāra," a term coined by Salomon to articulate a broad cultural zone that contributed to the rise of Gandhārī civilization.[5] Willemen proposed that Akṣobhya's Pure Land Abhirati to the east is of Gandhāran origin and of

Mahāsāṅghika affiliation. He further contended that Amitābha's paradise to the west is of Bactrian origin and of Sautrāntika-Sarvāstivāda affiliation and seems to have been an immediate reaction to this development.[6]

Nattier argued that the earlier and later versions of the long *Sukhāvatīvyūha* reveal the rise of gradual devotion to Amitābha within Indian Buddhism and support a process of doctrinal development based on the earlier *Akṣobhyavyūha-sūtra*.[7] While the cult of Buddha Amitābha and his Pure Land can be adequately explained as an endemic evolution of Indian Buddhism, this does not preclude the incorporation of solar elements embodied in the articulation of the figure of Amitābha.[8] We discern comparable descriptions that resemble Middle Eastern heavens and a more general compatibility of Amitābha with solar cults devoted to Sūrya, Ahura Mazdā, Zrvanakarana, and Apollo, worshipped by Indian, Greek, Iranian, and Central Asians present in the northwestern regions of the Indian subcontinent. For Lokesh Chandra the regal and heliocentric themes in Mahāyāna art and literature suggest the cultic progression of Mithra into Maitreya and the Bactrian transformation of Śākyamuni whose regal descent from the Solar Dynasty of the affluent Ikṣvākus heralds the emergence of Buddha Amitābha.[9] Theological innovation and religious syncretism are not incompatible processes, and as I have argued elsewhere, "the solar character and astral attributes of Amitābha suggests the domestication of non-Buddhist material that was assimilated doctrinally within an indisputably Buddhist framework."[10]

It is to this Buddhist framework that it is advisable to now briefly turn to in order to situate the Buddhist past of Amitābha as it is fully staged in the long *Sukhāvatīvyūha-sūtra*. It relates how, many years previously, he was born as the *bhikṣu* Dharmākara (Chos kyi 'byung gnas) who pursued the spiritual vocation of a bodhisattva and made forty-eight resolutions (Skt. *praṇidhāna*; Tib. *smon lam*) before the Buddha Lokeśvararāja that deal primarily with the features of his future buddha field (Skt. *buddhakṣetra*; Tib. *sangs rgyas kyi zhing*). At the time of his enlightenment, his Pure Land (*dag pa'i zhing*) Sukhāvatī arose for the benefit of all beings who may take rebirth after death in order to receive teachings, practice in the presence of a buddha, and advance along the path toward awakening. While the various versions of the long *Sukhāvatīvyūha* in Sanskrit, Tibetan, and Chinese make it clear that women must be reborn as men in Sukhāvatī,[11] for many contemporary commentators buddha fields are extensions of the bodhisattva's great compassion and the manifest fulfilment of his vows that pertain to all beings regardless of their gender. The edifying aspects of Dharmākara's Jātaka-styled narrative appeal to the devotion of believers and hint at a practical course of action for those whose aim is to embody the bodhisattva ideal for themselves. Amitābha's past lives are concocted in other Jātaka stories that differ from the long *Sukhāvatīvyūha* and with each other in substantial ways,[12] suggesting that the worship of Amitābha may not have originated with the appearance of the *Sukhāvatīvyūha* scriptures, but it may very well predate them.

TIBETAN TRANSLATIONS OF PURE LAND SCRIPTURES

The Pure Land Sutras. Pure land orientations in East Asia are indebted to three "Pure Land texts" (*jingtu sanbu ching*), but only the long and short *Sukhāvatīvyūha* sutras have been translated from Sanskrit to Tibetan. The *Meditation on Amitāyus* (Skt. **Amitāyur-dhyāna-sūtra* or **Amitāyur-buddhānusmṛti-sūtra*) attained considerable prestige in Central Asia and China, but it is not found in Sanskrit or Tibetan. The long and short *Sukhāvatīvyūha* sutras, though they are commonly referred to by the same name and are distinguished by their length, are in fact two distinct works dealing with differing subject matter. When it comes to the Tibetan titles for these works they are faithfully descriptive of their contents. The short sutra focuses on Sukhāvatī (Bde ba can) and is titled *Sukhāvatīvyūha-sūtra* (*Bde ba can gyi bkod pa'i mdo*). The long sutra centers on the past life of Buddha Amitābha and the vows he made as the bodhisattva Dharmākara and bears the title **Amitābhavyūha-sūtra* (*'Od dpag med kyi bkod pa'i mdo*).

The *Sukhāvatīvyūha* and *Amitābhavyūha* sutras are included in all known collections of the Tibetan Buddhist canon, the Kangyur. They were translated sometime in the late 8th and early 9th century during the first propagation of Buddhism to Tibet (*bstan pa nga dar*). During the time of the Tibetan Empire (*c*.608–866 CE), the prodigious Tibetan translator Yeshe Dé (Yes shes sde), whose name appears in the colophons of no less than 347 texts, is mentioned in relation to both the long and short sutras, but there is some inconsistency as to the names of the other translators among different editions of the Kangyur.[13] The earliest records for their translation from Sanskrit to Tibetan are found in two imperial registers that take their names from the places of their composition: the *Denkarma* (*Dkar chag Ldan dkar ma*), compiled in the early 9th century, followed by the *Phangthangma* (*Dkar chag 'Phang thang ma*).[14] The sutras were probably translated not long before the compilation of the *Denkarma Catalogue* in the early 9th century, which lists them both. There is no record of the Sanskrit texts that formed the basis for the Tibetan translations and we can surmise that they were procured either from India, Nepal, or Khotan. From the colophons of the sutras we learn that they were revised later during the so-called Great Revision (*zhu chen*). They were made to conform to the official standards for translating Sanskrit Buddhist texts into Tibetan as decreed by the Buddhist Council (*bcom ldan 'das kyi ring lugs kyi 'dun sa*)[15] and in accordance with the guidelines set out in the *Mahāvyutpati* lexicon and a two-volume treatise, the *Drajor Bambo Nyipa* (*Sgra sbyor bam po gnyis pa*).

In the *Denkarma Catalogue*, the long *Sukhāvatīvyūha-sūtra* is listed under the section *Mahāyāna Sūtra of the Ratnakūṭa Class* with the title *'Od dpag med kyi bkod pa* (Skt. **Amitābhavyūha-sūtra*).[16] In the *Phangthangma Catalogue* the listing is a slightly different size and bears the title *De bzhin gshegs pa 'od dpag med kyi zhing gi bkod pa* (Skt. **Tathāgata-amitābha-kṣetravyūha-sūtra*) under the section *Mahāsūtra according to Size*. The variation in title and length in the catalogs suggests that different Sanskrit texts were consulted for the translation.

In the *Denkarma*, the short *Sukhāvatīvyūha* is itemized in the section *Miscellaneous Mahāyāna Sūtra Less Than One Bam-Po* with the name *Bde ba can gyi bkod pa* (Skt. *Sukhāvatīvyūha*). The *Phangthangma* provides the same title and length, placing the sutra under the section *Small Sutra Less Than One Bam-Po Long*. There is also a Chinese-Tibetan translation of the short *Sukhāvatīvyūha* entitled *Amituo jing* (T. 12, no. 366), which, according to Akamatsu Kōshō, is based on Kumārajīva's Sanskrit-Chinese translation. Pelliot Tibétain 758 is kept in fragmentary condition in the Bibliothèque nationale in Paris. It dates, in all likelihood, to the times of the Tibetan occupation of Dunhuang (786–848),[17] which had a profound influence on the social and cultural life of its Chinese residents and contributed to the formation of a "Tibeto-Chinese" community as attested by Chinese texts written in Tibetan script and Tibetan texts used by the Chinese community.[18]

Dhāraṇī. In addition to the long and short pure land sutras, the Kangyur includes *dhāraṇī* dedicated to Amitābha, Amitāyus, and Aparimitāyurjñāna. In the Chinese and Tibetan pure land orientations all three refer to the same deity. The *Dhāraṇī of the Heart of Ārya-Aparimitāyurjñāna* (Skt. *Ārya-aparimitāyur-jñāna-hṛdaya-nāma-dhāraṇī; 'Phags pa tshe dang ye shes dpag tu med pa'i snying po shes bya ba'i gzungs*) is a an early-12th-century Sanskrit to Tibetan translation by the Indian scholar Puṇyasambhava and the Tibetan translator-cum-scholar Patsap Nyima Drak (Pa tshab Nyi ma grags; *c.*1055–1140). This text is extant in Sanskrit and Chinese and its *dhāraṇī* varies considerably from the one given in the early *Ārya-Aparimitāyur-jñāna-nāma-mahāyāna-sūtra*. Other canonical *dhāraṇī* include the *Bhagavān-amitābha-dhāraṇī-mantra* (*Bcom ldan 'das snang ba mtha' yas kyi gzungs sngags*), a very short mantra-text composed for the purpose of recollecting the buddha (Skt. *buddhānusmṛti; sangs rgyas rjes su dran pa*) and purifying obscurations and downfalls. It is nearly identical with the *Recollecting Amitābha* (*Snang ba mtha' yas rjes su dran pa*) that has no Sanskrit title and makes no mention of a Tibetan translator. It starts with a brief praise to *Bhagavān, Tathāgata, Arhat and Perfectly Enlightened Buddha Amitābha* and proceeds with a *dhāraṇī* whose recitation twenty-one times has the power to purify negativities and moral downfalls: *tadya thā/a mi te/a mi to tabha be/a mi ta saṃ bha be/a mi ta bi krānta gā mi nī/ga ga na kīrti ka re/sarba kle sha kṣa oṃ ka ri svā hā*. Other undated texts include *The Dhāraṇī for Seeing Amitābha* (*'Od dpag med mthong bar gyur ba'i gzungs*), a short but intriguing text whose recitation allows Buddha Amitābha and countless other buddhas and bodhisattvas to be perceived at the moment of death. There is also the *Two Short Dhāraṇī of Aparimitāyurjñāna* (*Tshe dang ye shes dpag tu med pa'i gzungs thung ngu gnyis*), also listed by the title *The Heart of Amitāyus* (*Tshe dpag med kyi snying po*), a pithy text that includes the *dhāraṇī*: *oṃ bajra ā yu she huṃ ya*, meant to be recited continually, and the *mantra* (*sngags*) *oṃ pu ṇyae pu ṇyae ma hā pu ṇyae/a pa ri mi twa ā yur pu ṇya jnyā na soṃ bha ro pa tsi te svā hā* to be rehearsed during long-life initiations involving water.[19] These incantations are meant to be delivered for the purpose of recollecting (*buddhānusmṛti*) Amitābha and for purifying harmful dispositions.

Dunhuang Texts. There is a large number of Tibetan manuscripts from the Tarim Basin listed in the catalogs of the Pelliot Tibétain and Stein collections.[20] Scriptures, from roughly the times of the Tibetan occupation of Dunhuang (780–850) or later, which are devoted to Amitābha-Amitāyus and Sukhāvatī include sutras, eulogies, mantra, *dhāraṇī*, and ritual texts. Few of these have received scholarly attention.[21] As noted, an early text dated to the end of the 8th century, Pelliot Tibétain 758, has been of special interest to readers because it is a Tibetan translation of Kumārajīva's Chinese translation of the Sanskrit short *Sukhāvatīvyūha* (T. 366). There are also two popular *dhāraṇī-sūtra* associated with Buddha Amitābha/Amitāyus and his buddha field listed in both collections: the *Ārya-Aparimitāyur-jñāna-nāma-mahāyāna-sūtra* (*'Phags pa tshe dang yes shes dpag du myed pa zhes bya ba theg pa chen po'i mdo*) and the *Ārya-Anantamukha-nirhāra-nāma-dhāraṇī* (*'Phags pa sgo mtha yas pas bgrub pa zhes bya ba'i gzungs*). The *Aparimitāyur-nāma-mahāyāna-sūtra* deserves special attention because it survives in nearly 1,000 Tibetan copies and it is linked with mortuary rites and the Mahāyāna cult of the book in Central Asia.[22] According to Pelliot Tibétain 999, it was donated in Chinese and Tibetan scrolls to the Linghongsi *vihāra* for the commemoration of Ösrung's ('Od srung, 842 or 843–*c.* 890) ascension to the Tibetan throne by the Chinese and Tibetan residents of Dunhuang.[23]

Another pertinent text for discussion is cataloged in the Paris National Library (Pelliot Tibétain 16) and in the British Library (IOL Tib J 751). It mentions the inauguration of Buddhist statues, including a statue of Amitābha installed during the consecration of the Dega Yutsel Temple (De ga g.yu tshal) in the early 9th century. Inspired by the *Sukhāvatīvyūha* sutras, it recommends the recitation of Amitābha's name for the purification of all negative deeds (*sdig pa*)—a meritorious act that leads one to be reborn in Amitābha's buddha field. The interesting passage reads:

> Installed, too, is the bodily image of Buddha Amitābha, whose field is best among those of all buddhas, where even the names of the three evil destinies and eight obstacles are unknown. Dwelling there, adorned with all the ornaments of divine enjoyment, so that there cannot be even the name of nirvana, in that field adorned with all perfect, world-transcending happiness, he acts on behalf of sentient beings. Because his compassion is especially great, just by calling his name all sins are purified and one is blessed to be born in that buddha field (27b2–27b4).[24]

This is not the only statue of Amitābha dating to the times of the Tibetan Empire. Songtsen Gampo designed the ground floor of the Jokhang Temple in Lhasa with five inner chapels with the assistance of the royal lady Khri btsun (Bhrikuti Devi) from Nepal, who later completed the task. According to *The Scholar's Feast* (*Mkhas pa'i dga' ston*), each chapel contained various statues of Buddhist deities, with a statue of Amitābha with eight bodhisattvas and two guardians placed to the north of the central chapel (*gtsang khang dbus ma*). None of the original wall images dating to the times of the foundation of the Jokhang survive, but Pawo Tsuglag Trengwa (Dpa' bo gtsug lag phreng ba, 1504–1566) describes the lost murals of the ground floor featuring a representation of Sukhāvatī between the south and west corners and depictions of the paradises of Kasarpani and that of Mañjuśrī.[25]

Amitābha's reception in imperial Tibet and its colonies should not be overemphasized but measured in relation to other popular Mahāyāna deities and their sutras, as, for example, Vairocana, whose cult is attested in religious art of this period. Kapstein rightly noted that "to the extent that rebirth in Sukhāvatī was emerging as a soteriological goal for Tibetan Buddhists, it was by no means an exclusive goal or one that was decisively preeminent in relation to other important Buddhist ends."[26] That being said, it would appear that the Buddha of Immeasurable Light gained wide acceptance by Tibetans of the imperial period who not only longed for his Pure Land and relied on his salvific powers, but actively contributed to the spread and development of mainstream pure land practices across the Tibetan plateau and Central Asia.

EXOTERIC SCRIPTURES

Aspiration Prayers. Aspiration prayers for achieving rebirth in Amitābha's Pure Land are so abundant in Tibetan Buddhist literature that they rightly form a unique genre known as the *demön* (*bde smon*; an abbreviation of *bde ba can gyi smon lam*, "aspiration prayers" (*smon lam*) to Sukhāvatī (*bde ba can*). The *demön* is broadly defined as a particular class of religious compositions that articulate the intention and methods to realize Sukhāvatī. They often conclude with a dedication of one's merit directed toward rebirth in his realm. There are numerous aspiration prayers to Sukhāvatī composed by eminent masters from all schools of Tibetan Buddhism. Those composed by leading Tibetan scholars are often obligatory prayer texts for memorization by monks and nuns in their respective orders.

Along with a considerable number of "hymns of praise," or "eulogies" (Skt. *stotra*; *bstod pa*) to Amitābha and his Pure Land, aspiration prayers are for the most part exoteric works. References to tantric visualizations in works belonging to the *demön* genre challenge a strict division between exoteric and esoteric literature and point to their blending, a distinct feature of Buddhist soteriology in Tibetan contexts. The inclusion of a *sādhana* titled *Prayer to Sukhāvatī* (*Bde ba can gyi smon lam*), said to have been composed by Padmasambhava's Tibetan consort Yeshe Tsogyal, and revealed by Tagsham Nuden Dorje (Stag sham nus ldan rdo rje, *c.*1655–1708), serves as an example of the union between exoteric and esoteric pure land works.

Some of the better-known prayers of the Tibetan tradition include *Prayer for Rebirth in Sukhāvatī: Opening the Door to the Supreme Field* by the founder of the Gelug school, Tsongkhapa (Tsong kha pa, 1357–1419); *The Swift and Unobstructed Path to Sukhāvatī* by Panchen Lobsang Chökyi Gyaltsen (Paṇchen Blo bzang chos kyi rgyal mtshan, 1567–1662); *An Aspiration Prayer to Sukhāvatī* by the Fifth Karmapa Dezhin Shekpa (De bzhin gshegs pa, 1384–1415); *A Sukhāvatī Prayer* by Padma Karpo (Pad ma dkar po, 1527–1592), the systematizer of the Drugpa Kagyü school; *An Aspiration Prayer for the Pure Land Sukhāvatī* by Karma Chagme (Karma chags med, 1613–1678); *Opening an Unlimited Door: An Aspiration Prayer to Sukhāvatī* by Ratna Lingpa (Ratna gling pa, 1403–1478) the compiler of the *Collected Tantras of the Nyingma*; *An Aspiration Prayer* by the Nyingma treasure-revealer Jigme Lingpa ('Jigs med gling pa, 1730–1798); *An Aspiration Prayer to Sukhāvatī* by Taranātha (1575–1634); *An Aspiration Prayer* by the astute Sakya philosopher Gorampa Sonam Senge (Go rams pa bsod nams seng ge, 1428–1489); and the *Condensed Sleeping Meditation for (Beholding) Amitābha* by Jamyang Khyentse Chökyi Lodrö ('Jam dbyangs mkhyen brtse chos kyi blo gros, 1893–1959).[27] This list is by no means exhaustive, but indicative of the fact that Sukhāvatī has long been the focal point of devotional writing by well-known scholars from all Tibetan schools. Even the instigator of the controversial *zhentong* (*gzhan stong*) teachings on extrinsic emptiness of the Jonangpa school, Dolpopa Sherab Gyaltsen (Dol po pa Shes rab rgyal mtshan, 1292–1361), was not indifferent to Amitābha's field. He authored two aspiration prayers for rebirth in Sukhāvatī and a commentary to the long *Sukhāvatīyūha-sūtra*.[28]

The most widely recited prayers in Tibetan monastic settings feature Tsongkhapa's prayer, whose shorter version was rehearsed annually in the Great Prayer festival that he initiated in Lhasa in 1409, and Karma Chagme's renown *Aspiration Prayer*.[29] Chagme's prayer for rebirth in Sukhāvatī moves beyond formulaic pure land themes, introducing distinct Tibetan elements relating to the cult of Tārā and Padmasambhava. Another popular prayer recited today derives from the pure-vision revelation of his most gifted disciple, Namchö Mingyur Dorje (1645–1667), entitled *The Brief Sukhāvatī Aspiration Prayer* (*Smon lam bsdus pa*):[30]

Emaho!
In that field-realm of immeasurable wonder, bliss, and happiness known as Sukhāvatī,
Is the remarkable Buddha Amitābha with the Great Lord Avalokiteśvara to his right,
and the heroic Vajrapāṇi to his left, surrounded by a retinue of incalculable buddhas and bodhisattvas.
When my time comes to pass away from this present life,
May I take rebirth there right away without going elsewhere along the way,
And having being born there, may I behold the face of Amitābha.
Blessed by the buddhas and bodhisattvas of the ten directions
May this aspiration prayer uttered by me
Be fulfilled without any hindrance.
Tadhya tā pañca dri ya ā va bo dha nā ye svā hā

Commentaries. Aspiration prayers served as a platform for the composition of elaborate commentaries (*'grel ba*) that drew inspiration and legitimation from the short and long *Sukhāvatīvūha* sutras and served as elucidations on aspiration prayers for rebirth in Sukhāvatī. Eminent Tibetan scholars payed particular importance to Dharmākara's nineteenth vow, in the Tibetan version of long sutra,[31] where four causes are stated for achieving rebirth in the pure land. The relevant passage reads:

> Ānanda, any sentient being who recollects again and again the Tathāgata and his aspects, generates immeasurable roots of virtue, completely dedicates [his merits for that cause with the mind of enlightenment], and prays to be born in the Land [of Bliss], when the time of death nears he will face the Tathāgata, Arhat, Perfectly Enlightened Amitābha, surrounded by an assembly of monks.

The four causes can be outlined as follows: (a) repeatedly recollecting the Tathāgata Amitābha and his qualities; (b) generating immeasurable roots of virtue (merit); (c) developing the mind of enlightenment; and (d) completely dedicating one's merits for rebirth in Sukhāvatī. Though not all commentators agree as to which of the four causes is the most important, they all emphasize the merit of fulfilling all four conditions. In fact, the intimate relation of these stages of practice allowed commentators to discourse on the entire Mahāyāna path, offering detailed instructions on how to integrate pure land contemplation in daily Buddhist practice. In *The Lotus Garland: Commentary to the Aspirational Prayer* (*Bde smon 'grel ba padma'i phreng ba*) Karma Chagme explains that the second cause can be accomplished by enacting the seven-branch practice outlined in *The King of Aspiration Prayers: The Noble Aspiration for Excellent Conduct* (*Ārya-bhadracaryā-praṇidhāna-rāja*)[32] located in the *Gaṇḍavyūha*, the thirty-ninth chapter of the *Avataṃsaka-sūtra*. In respect to this, whatever merits one has gained by: (a) prostrating to Amitābha and his retinue; (b) presenting material (i.e., water, flowers, incense, light, perfume, and food) or visualized offerings to him; (c) confessing all nonvirtuous actions; (d) rejoicing at the wholesome deeds of others; (e) requesting from the buddhas to turn the wheel of dharma; and (f) beseeching them (the buddhas) not to pass into nirvana, ought to be dedicated to the benefit of all beings that they may attain perfect enlightenment. *The King of Aspiration Prayers* has been widely cited and commented upon by pure land enthusiasts given its direct references to the aspiration of encountering Buddha Amitābha at the time of death, being born in his Pure Land Sukhāvatī from a beautiful lotus, and receiving a prophesy (*lung bstan pa*) from Amitābha foretelling one's future enlightenment.

Other notable commentaries include a drawn-out commentary by Lala Sonam Chödrup (Glag bla bsod nam chos 'grup, 1862–1944) on Karma Chagme's *Aspiration Prayer*, titled *Illuminating the Path of Liberation: Explanatory Commentary on Karma Chagme's Aspiration Prayer for the Pure Land Sukhāvatī* and divided according to the four causes for rebirth in the pure land;[33] Patrul Orgyen Jigme Chökyi Wangmo's (Dpal sprul o rgyan 'jigs med chos kyi dbang po, 1808–1887) commentaries on the Tsongkhapa's and Karma Chagme's *Aspiration Prayers*; two commentaries dedicated to the correct understanding and practice of Sukhāvatī by Mipham Jamyang Namgyal (Mi pham 'jam dbyangs rnam rgyal, 1846–1912); Dolpopa's commentary to the long *Sukhāvatīvūha-sūtra* entitled *The Expedient Means for Oneself and Others to Attain Birth in Sukhāvatī*; and Dodrupchen Jigme Tenpa Nyima's (Rdo grub chen 'jigs med bstan pa'i nyi ma, 1865–1926) commentary on the long *Sukhāvatīvyūha-sūtra*.[34]

ESOTERIC SCRIPTURES

Buddha Amitābha is commonly linked with an entire complex of esoteric associations related to one of the five buddhas (Skt. *pañcatathāgata*) and the unique characteristics of his lotus family (see table 1). In this context, he figures in a number of tantric works and he is regularly associated with enlightened speech and the capacity to bestow consecration on words, letters,

Table 1. Buddha Amitābha and the Correspondences of His Family

Buddha Family	**Padma**
Wisdom-Buddha	Amitābha
Consort	Pāṇḍarāvasinī
Bodhisattva	Avalokiteśvara
Wisdom	Discrimination/discernment
Skandha	Perception
Kleśa	Desire
Color/light	Red
Element	Fire/heat
Direction	West
Symbol	Lotus (padma)
Initiation	Third initiation
Animal	Peacock
Seed syllable	*Hrīh*

Buddha Family	**Padma**
Season	Summer
Sense	Smell
Temperature	Hot
Mudrā	*Dhyāna*
Chakra	Throat
Organ	Liver
Time	Sunset
Day	Fifteenth of the lunar month
Wind	Upward-moving
Nectars	Semen
Fingers	Ring finger
Sense offerings	Incense or conch
Ornaments	Earrings
Bardo visions	Fourth day
Realm	Hungry ghosts

and texts. The consecration (*rab gnas*) is commonly performed by visualizing him in union (*yab yum*) with his consort Pāṇḍarāvasinī (Gos dkar mo), the personification of his wisdom aspect (Skt. *prajñā*), and dissolving them both into light as they undergo transformation into the form of letters. Sukhāvatī does not gain an esoteric description per se but it is associated for the first time in Tibet with the tantric technique of mind transference, or *phowa* (Skt. *utkrānti*; Tib. *'pho ba*),[35] a tantric method that belongs to the *Six Dharmas of Nāropā* (*Na ro chos drug*) taught by the *mahāsiddha* Nāropā to his Tibetan disciple Marpa. During the practice of transferring one's awareness to a buddha field the yogi visualizes his subtle awareness in the shape of a tiny sphere of light ascending through the central subtle channel (Skt. *avadhūti*; Tib. *dbu ma rtsa*) and exiting from the crown of the head to merge with the buddha residing in Sukhāvatī. The continuous and successful practice of *phowa* ensures that the practitioner will circumvent the *bardo*, or intermediate state following death, and have rebirth in Amitābha's Pure Land.[36]

There are also several guru-yoga manuals in Tibetan literature that entreat the root teacher in the form of Buddha Amitāyus or Amitābha to descend in the form of light from the crown of one's head and merge with the supplicant. These practices are conceptually and technically paired with *phowa sādhanas* where the inverse process is enacted during meditation. In the devotional songs of the famous *mahāsiddha* Zabkar (Zabs dkar, 1789–1851), Buddha Amitābha is conflated with the lama, the unexcelled guide to Sukhāvatī.

> When the time comes for me to die, may you, my guru, come to lead me without hindrance to the Blissful Buddhafield. May we then travel to many Pure Realms, make offerings to all the Buddhas, and return to this impure world to guide all beings![37]

Sukhāvatī features in funeral rites and scriptures dedicated to the ritual care of the dead (*'das-mchod*). The structure and performance of Tibetan death ceremonies varies according to a set sequence of events. Traditionally these may include: (a) gaining the attention of the deceased and alerting them to the fact that they are dead and caught in the intermediate state between death and birth; (b) dispelling negative forces and obstacles that may hinder self-awareness when the *bardo* visions flood the consciousness of the departed; and (c) transforming the five root delusions (Skt. *kleśa*) into five pure elements represented by the five buddha families. For the duration of these funereal rites, the consciousness of the deceased is coaxed into increasing levels of clarity until the time for the ritual transference to Sukhāvatī. Following this, the ritual specialist performs the cremation ceremony that incorporates the basic elements of *homa* (*sbyin sreg*) and the disposal of the corpse or effigy in a fire. According to the *Tibetan Book of the Dead,* or rather the *Liberation by Hearing in the Intermediate States* (*Bar do thos grol*), Buddha Amitābha is visualized in union with his consort in the western channel branch of one's heart. In the fourth day after death, he will appear before the deceased as the purified element of fire and the aggregate of perception accompanied by two male bodhisattvas, Avalokiteśvara and Mañjuśrī, and two female bodhisattvas, Gītā and Ālokā.

Amitābha's Pure Land features also as the subject of dream-yoga meditations (*rmi lam*) whose aim is the cultivation of lucid awareness during sleep for the purpose of meeting Amitābha and receiving transmissions directly from him in one's dreams. A short dream-yoga work authored by Karma Chagme details instructions for merging one's awareness with Amitābha during dream time and space. This work is reminiscent of Sakya Paṇḍita's composition that outlines tantric visualizations with the objective of visiting Sukhāvatī during one's sleep.[38]

In both the Sarma and Nyingma lineages, Amitāyus is one of three main long-life deities and is associated exclusively with tantric *sādhanas* aimed at extending one's life span (*tshe sgrub*). In the Nyingma school, he is also linked with *karmamudrā* practices said to have been performed by Padmasambhava and Mandāravā at the Māratika cave in Nepal where they attained the long-life siddhi. In tantric contexts, both Amitābha and his reflex Amitāyus undergo an eventual interiorization visualized in terms of subtle-body anatomy and the manipulation of subtle winds (Tib. *rlung*; Skt. *prāṇa*) while the pure land Sukhāvatī is no longer perceived as a reality external to the practitioner but as the outcome of gaining realization of and mastery over the mind's most subtle movements. It is not uncommon for the teachings of Dzogchen to equate the pure land with the enlightened nature of one's mind.

The Revelations of Amitābha. Undoubtedly the most well-known revealed texts that belong to the *demön* genre come from the pure visions of Namchö Mingyur Dorje redacted by Karma Chagme. There are several treasure-texts (*gter ma*) that extoll the virtues of Amitābha's Pure Land and prescribe esoteric methods for realizing it. Pure land treasure texts by well-known masters include *From the Heart Essence of Mitra: A Spoken Aspiration Prayer to Sukhāvatī*, by the Indian Mitrayogin (mid-12th century/early 13th century); *Aspiration Prayer to Sukhāvatī* by Rigzin Gödem (Rig 'dzin rgod ldem, 1337–1408), the founder of the Jangter (*byang gter*) tradition; Yeshe Tsogyal's *Aspiration Prayer to Sukhāvatī* revealed by Tagsham Nüden Dorje (Stag sham nus ldan rdo rje, 1655–1708); *Aspiration Prayer to Sukhāvatī* by the Thirteenth Karmapa Dudül Dorje (Karma pa Bdud 'dul rdo rje, 1733–1797); *Aspiration Prayer to Sukhāvatī* by Chogyur Dechen Lingpa (Mchog gyur bde chen gling pa, 1829–1870); *Aspiration Prayer to Sukhāvatī* by Tragthung Dudjom Dorje (Khrag 'thung Bdud 'joms rdo rje, 1835–1904) also known as Dudjom Lingpa; and *From the Treasury of Mantras: A Sādhana of the Speech of Vajra Amitābha* by Dorje Dechen Lingpa (Rdo rje bde chen gling pa, 1857–1928).[39] This list is by no means exhaustive of Amitābha's popularity in treasure literature. Kongtrul Lodro Taye (Kong sprul Blo gros mtha' yas, 1813–1899), elucidating on the revelations by Chogyur Dechen Lingpa, composed a short text on eleven modes of liberation. In his section on liberation through cultivation (*sgom*), he details mainstream exoteric practices for attaining liberation through rebirth in Amitābha's Pure Land that include visualization of Sukhāvatī, prostrations, offerings, and prayers to Amitābha, recollection of the buddha and recitation of his mantra, concluding with a dedication of merit for attaining rebirth in the pure land.[40] His function as one of the three and later five buddhas in the *maṇḍala* of cardinal directions has earned him a place in the *imaginair* of tertons, ensuring continuity between "Tibetan tantric Treasure practices and the pure land–related practices of mainstream Mahāyāna Buddhism."[41]

ELEMENTS OF ICONOGRAPHY

Mythological accounts relate how Amitābha, out of compassion for the land of Tibet, sent Avalokiteśvara in the form of primordial man, the ape, to tame and mate with a native ogress (*srin mo*) representing the lower instincts, the titanic nature of man relying on blood sacrifices. From their union the Tibetan race was born—half-celestial and half-chthonic. This allegorical episode with a Buddhist flavor became central to Tibetan literary tropes in nation-building sagas. It is, however, rarely represented in art. The most common iconographic configuration of Amitābha's Pure Land in Tibetan and Himalayan art is a triadic arrangement sanctioned in the long *Sukhāvatīvyūha-sūtra* and the Chinese *Amitāyurdhyāna-sūtra* (T365). Thangka paintings and temple murals commonly depict Amitābha in the center of his palace or in front of a large bodhi tree seated on a lotus or a peacock throne. He has a peaceful countenance, is dressed in three monastic robes, and is flanked on either side by the Bodhisattva of Compassion, a standing white Avalokiteśvara to his right, and the Bodhisattva Mahāsthāmaprapta (who gets conflated with Vajrapāṇi in the Tibetan tradition), in blue, standing to his left (figure 1). Amitābha's color is commonly deep red and in his hands, held in the *dhyāna-mudrā* gesture, is an alms bowl.[42] It is not unusual for Amitābha to be accompanied by the eight great bodhisattvas and be surrounded by buddhas, bodhisattvas, monks, deities, offering goddesses, and fortunate beings being birthed from lotus blossoms in a pool of water at the bottom of the composition. A unique variation on Sukhāvatī iconography incorporates elements from the sky-dharma collection revealed by Namchö Mingyur Dorje where various tantric forms of deities, depictions of Tibetan teachers, and the five buddha families (Skt. *pañcakula*; Tib. *rigs lnga*) are found. In another illustration, faithful to Karma Chagme's *sādhana, Invoking the Guardians of Sukhāvatī* (*Bde chen zhing sgrub kyi bka' srung gsol mchod*), male and female lion-faced *dharmapālas* are portrayed riding on horses and their two *bam-ro* assistants hold ritual

Figure 1. Buddha Amitābha with attendants. Erdenzu Monastery, Mongolia.

cakes (*torma*) on their monkey feet ready to thrust them against the enemies of the pure land teachings.[43]

The Tibetan majority of Sukhāvatī depictions portray Amitābha as iconographically distinct from Amitāyus. While they are generally held to be two names of the same buddha following Mahāyāna sutra conventions, their functions and imagery differ in Tibetan contexts. Considering that in Indian and later Chinese scriptures their names are used interchangeably, it would seem that this differentiation came about with the advent of tantric Buddhism where Amitāyus is specifically invoked in conjunction with alchemical practices associated with long life and immortality. The 12th-century biography of Padmsambhava, the *Kathang Zanglingma* (*Bka' thang zangs gling ma*) attributed to the treasure-discoverer Nyangräl Nyima Özer (Nyang ral nyi ma 'od zer, 1124–1192), relates how Padmasambhava set out with Princess Mandāravā of the kingdom of Zahor to the Maratika Caves. After three months of practice, master and consort received a vision of Amitāyus who bestowed upon them the *siddhi* of power over life. For the new schools, lineages of the long-life deity Amitāyus can be traced to the *sādhana* of the *Amitāyus Nine Deity Maṇḍala* (*Tshe dpag med lha dgu dkyil 'khor*)[44] composed by the Indian Acārya Jetāri, and to the Queen of Siddhas (Grub pa'i rgyal mo) who taught Milarepa's disciple Rechungpa (Ras chung rdo rje grags pa, 1083/84–1161). Thus, it is conventional for Amitābha to serve as the reigning buddha over mortuary rites and the transfer of the dead to Sukhāvatī. Amitāyus, principally a long-life deity, is represented also in the color red, wearing a crown, jewel ornaments, and silk garments, and holding his special emblem, a "long-life vase" filled with ambrosia (*tshe bum pa*). Both can be shown in their respective *maṇḍalas* with or without consorts, though it is more common to find depictions of Amitāyus in sexual union (*yab yum*) with his female principal Pāṇḍaravāsinī.

Amitābha is the presiding lord of the lotus family (Skt. *padmakula*; *pad ma'i rigs*) and therefore it is not uncommon to find depictions of him accompanied by Buddhist deities assigned to his family, like Tārā, Avalokiteśvara, Hayagrīva, and so forth. The popular Tibetan convention of 1,000 armed Avalokiteśvara, and Songtsen Gampo, who is considered an emanation of the latter, appearing with Amitābha in his headdress, finds precedent in the *Kāraṇḍavyūha-sūtra* translated into Tibetan in the 9th century (figure 2). There are many legendary associations between Amitābha and his emanation Avalokiteśvara, whose six-syllable mantra (*oṃ maṇi padme hūṃ*) purifies lower rebirths and causes one to be born in Sukhāvatī.[45] For the Nyingma school, Padmasambhava, the Lotus-Born Guru, is considered an emanation of Buddha Amitābha and is strongly associated with Tibet's imperial glory. He iconographically figures in a vertical or horizontal arrangement formation where Amitābha, situated in the center or above, represents the *dharmakāya*, Avalokiteśvara situated in the middle or the right stands for the *shaṃbogakāya* body, and Padmasambhava, to the bottom or the left, represents the *nirmāṇakāya*. The substitution of Padmasambhava in place of

Figure 2. Songtsen Gampo. Shenzhen Museum, special exhibition of Tibetan art, 2017.

Vajrapāṇi in the Sukhāvatī triad is both unmistakable and understandable given that, like Vajrapāṇi, the lord of esoteric lore, Padmasambhava is heralded as the tantric master of Uḍḍiyāna that brought the Vajrayāna teachings to Tibet. This is a postimperial artistic convention that finds literary precedent in the opening homage to the *Zanglingma* that reads: "I prostrate to the divine *trikāya, dharmakāya* Amitābha, *shaṃbogakāya* Avalokiteśvara, and the *nirmāṇakāya* Padmasambhava."[46]

REVIEW OF LITERATURE

Western commentators have noted the importance of pure land literature in Tibetan Buddhism, as signaled in the pioneer works of Peter Schwieger, *Ein Tibetisches Wunschgebet um Wiedergeburt in der Sukhāvatī* (1978), Tadeusz Skorupski, "A Prayer for Rebirth in Sukhavati" (1995), and Matthew Kapstein, "Pure Land Buddhism in Tibet? From Sukhāvatī to the Field of Great Bliss" (2003). There has also been a significant body of Japanese scholarship devoted to Tibetan pure land literature including studies by Ryōshun Kajihama, Akamatsu Kōshō, Nakamura Hajime, Onoda Shunzō, and others.[47] To date, the most substantial English monograph on the topic of Tibetan pure land Buddhism is Halkias's *Luminous Bliss: A Religious History of Pure Land Literature in Tibet* (2013). His survey of pertinent literature includes a wide selection and translation of important Tibetan canonical and paracanonical Buddhist texts centered on Amitābha and the soteriological import of his Pure Land. His work begins with an introductory discussion of the development of pure land ideology within Mahāyāna Buddhism and its spread across imperial Tibet and the Tibetan-occupied areas of Central Asia, followed by a Tibetan–English translation of the short *Sukhāvatīvyūha-sūtra* and a lengthy discussion of the Tibetan pure land genre, the *demön*. Having covered the exoteric material, Halkias dedicates two chapters to the unique esoteric literature of Tibetan tantric practices associated with Buddha Amitābha and his Pure Land. Despite a sizable corpus of Tibetan pure land literature upheld by regimes of clerical power, the author has shown that there has never been a sectarian, self-conscious movement of pure land Buddhism in Tibet. Another work by the same author, "Ascending to Heaven after Death: Karma Chags med's Commentary on Mind Transference" (2019), contains a detailed study of an important Tibetan commentary on the most important pure land tantric technique, the practice of *phowa*.

PRIMARY SOURCES

This survey draws from my own research on pure land Buddhism in Tibetan contexts and is based on a wide selection of Tibetans sources, which, for the most part, have not been translated into English. Specific references have been given throughout this article, and for a substantial introduction to the variety of pure land sources in Tibetan Buddhism the interested reader may consult the *Anthology of Pure Land Texts* (*Bde smon phyogs bsgrigs*) in two volumes—the first volume containing root texts and *dhāraṇī* (*rtsa gzhung skor*), and the second volume, pure land commentaries (*'grel ba'i skor*). The anthology is attributed to Karma Chagme and others and was published by Si khron mi rigs dpe skrun khang in Chengdu in 1994. This work and many related sources are accessible online from the Buddhist Digital Resource Centre (https://www.tbrc.org/).

DIGITAL MATERIALS

84000: Translating the Words of the Buddha: An ongoing digital database for providing high-quality English translations of Tibetan texts from the Kangyur and Tengyur.

Buddhist Digital Resource Centre: A comprehensive and essential site for accessing Tibetan Buddhist texts from a number of Tibetan canons and collections (https://www.tbrc.org).

Himalayan Art Resources: An invaluable and impressive searchable resource for accessing Tibetan and Himalayan Buddhist art from Tibet, Bhutan, India, China, Mongolia, and Nepal (https://www.himalayanart.org).

The Treasury of Lives: A Biographical Encyclopedia of Tibet, Inner Asia, and the Himalaya: An encyclopedic resource for reading biographies of important Tibetan and Indian Buddhist masters, translators, royalty, doctors, clans, abbots, and so forth (https://treasuryoflives.org).

FURTHER READING

Chen, Shu-Chen. *Cultural Change of Indian Pure Land Buddhist Teaching in Chinese and Tibetan Buddhism.* PhD diss., University of Virginia, 2007.

Cook, Lowell. *'Ju Mi pham on Pure Land Doctrine and Practice.* MA thesis, Kathmandu University, 2016.

Ducor, Jérôme. *Le Sûtra d'Amida prêché par le Buddha.* Schweizer Asiatische Studien Études Asiatiques Suisses, Monograph 29. Bern: Peter Lang, 1988.

Gómez, Luis. *The Land of Bliss: The Paradise of the Buddha of Measureless Light: Sanskrit and Chinese Versions of the Sukhāvatīvyūha Sutras.* Honolulu: University of Hawaii Press, 1996.

Halkias, Georgios T. "Pure-Lands and other Visions in Seventeenth-Century Tibet: A *Gnam-chos sādhana* for the Pure-Land Sukhāvatī Revealed in 1658 by Gnam-chos Mi-'gyur- rdo-rje (1645–1667)." In *Power, Politics and the Reinvention of Tradition: Tibet in the Seventeenth and Eighteenth Century.* Edited by Brian Cuevas and Kurtis Schaeffer, 121–151. Leiden, The Netherlands: Brill, 2006.

Halkias, Georgios T. "Compassionate Aspirations and Their Fulfilment: Dol-po-pa's A Prayer for Birth in Sukhāvatī." In *As Long as Space Endures: Essays on the Kālachakra Tantra in Honor of H.H. the Dalai Lama.* Edited by Edward A. Arnold, 259–275. Ithaca, NY: Snow Lion, 2009.

Halkias, Georgios T. *Luminous Bliss: A Religious History of Pure Land Literature in Tibet. With an Annotated Translation and Critical Analysis of the Orgyen-ling Golden Short Sukhāvatīvyūha-sūtra.* Honolulu: University of Hawaii Press, 2013.

Halkias, Georgios T. "Ascending to Heaven after Death: Karma Chags med's Commentary on Mind Transference." *Revue d'Etudes Tibétaines* 52 (2019): 70–89.

Halkias, Georgios T., and Richard K. Payne, eds. *Pure Lands in Asian Texts and Contexts: An Anthology.* Honolulu: University of Hawaii Press, 2019.

Imaeda, Yoshiro. "À propos du manuscrit Pelliot tibétain 999." In *Sūryacandrāya: Essays in Honour of Akira Yuyama on the Occasion of His 65th Birthday.* Edited by Paul Harrison and Gregory Schopen, 87–94. Swisttal-Odendorf, Germany: Indica et Tibetica Verlag, 1998.

Kajihama, Ryōshun. "A Study of a Prayer Book on Rebirth in the Land of Bliss (Sukhāvatī) Written by Tsong kha pa." *Monograph Published by the Faculty of International Language and Culture, Setsunan University* 23, no. 3 (1991): 293–322.

Kajihama, Ryōshun. "3rd rDo Gruchen Rinpoche's Pure Land Thought (I)." *Journal of Indian and Buddhist Studies* 43, no. 1 (1994): 492–498.

Kajihama, Ryōshun. "3rd rDo Gruchen Rinpoche's Pure Land Thought (II)." *Journal of Indian and Buddhist Studies* 44, no. 2 (1996): 948–952.

Kajihama, Ryōshun. "3rd rDo Gruchen Rinpoche's Pure Land Thought (III)." *Journal of Indian and Buddhist Studies* 50, no. 2 (2002): 984–987.

Kajihama, Ryōshun. *Tibet no Jyōdo Shisō no Kenkyū* (*The Study of Pure Land in Tibet*). Kyoto, Japan: Nagata Bunshōdō, 2002.

Kapstein, Matthew. "Pure Land Buddhism in Tibet? From Sukhāvatī to the Field of Great Bliss." In *Approaching the Land of Bliss: Religious Praxis in the Cult of Amitābha*. Edited by Richard Payne and Kenneth Tanaka, 1–16. Honolulu: University of Hawaii Press, 2003.

Neumaier, Eva. "The Cult of Amitābha and the Apotheosis of the Tibetan Ruler." *Pacific World* 9 (2007): 231–244.

Payne, Richard K. "Aparimitāyus: 'Tantra' and 'Pure Land' in Late Medieval Indian Buddhism?" *Pacific World* 3, no. 9 (2007): 273–308.

Payne, Richard K. "How Not to Talk about Pure Land Buddhism: A Critique of Huston Smith's (Mis) Representations." In *Path of No Path: Contemporary Studies in Pure Land Buddhism Honoring Roger Corless*. Edited by Richard K. Payne, 147–174. Berkeley, CA: Numata Centre for Buddhist Translation and Research, 2009.

Payne, Richard K., and Kenneth Tanaka, eds. *Approaching the Land of Bliss: Religious Praxis in the Cult of Amitabha*. Honolulu: University of Hawaii Press, 2003.

Schopen, Gregory. "Sukhāvatī as a Generalized Religious Goal in Sanskrit Mahāyāna Sūtra Literature." *Indo-Iranian Journal* 19 (1977): 177–210.

Schwieger, Peter. *Ein Tibetisches Wunschgebet um Wiedergeburt in der Sukhāvatī*. St. Augustin, Germany: VGH Wissenschaftsverlag, 1978.

Silk, Jonathan. "The Virtues of Amitābha: A Tibetan Poem from Dunhuang." *Būkkyo Bunka Kenkyūjo Kiyō* 32 (1993): 1–109.

Skorupski, Tadeusz. "A Prayer for Rebirth in Sukhavati." In *The Buddhist Forum III*. Edited by Tadeusz Skorupski, 375–409. London: School of Oriental and African Studies, 1994.

Skorupski, Tadeusz. "Funeral Rites for Rebirth in the Sukhāvatī Abode." In *The Buddhist Forum VI*. Edited by Tadeusz Skorupski, 137–178. Tring, UK: Institute of Buddhist Studies, 2001.

NOTES

1. Jan Nattier, "The Realm of Akṣobhya: A Missing Piece in the History of Pure Land Buddhism," *Journal of the International Association of Buddhist Studies* 23, no. 1 (2000): 71–102, quote at 74.
2. Giuseppe Tucci, *Tibetan Painted Scrolls* (Bangkok: SDI, 1999), 349. This text was originally published in 1949.
3. For a discussion on the occurrence and etymology of these names, see Seishi Karashima, "On Amitābha, Amitāyu(s), Sukhāvatī and the Amitābhavyūha*," *Bulletin of the Asia Institute* 23 (2009): 121–130; Jan Nattier, "The Names of Amitābha/Amitāyus in Early Chinese Buddhist Traditions," *Annual Report of the International Research Institute for Advanced Buddhology at Soka University for the Year 2005* 9 (2006): 183–199; and Jan Nattier, "The Names of Amitābha/Amitāyus in Early Chinese Buddhist Traditions," *Annual Report of the International Research Institute for Advanced Buddhology at Soka University for the Year 2006* 10 (2007): 359–394.
4. Jan Nattier, "The Indian Roots of Pure Land Buddhism: Insights from the Oldest Chinese Versions of the Larger *Sukhāvatīvyūha*," *Pacific World: Journal of the Institute of Buddhist Studies* 5 (2003): 179–201, esp. 189.
5. Richard Salomon, *Ancient Buddhist Scrolls from Gandhāra* (London: The British Library, 1999), 3.
6. Charles Willemen, "Early Yogācāra and Visualization (Bhāvanā)," in *Wading into the Stream of Wisdom: Essays in Honor of Leslie Kawamura*, ed. Sarah F. Haynes and Michelle J. Sorensen, Contemporary Issues in Buddhist Studies Series (Honolulu: University of Hawaii Press, 2013), 211–382.
7. Nattier, "The Indian Roots."

8. For a discussion on how pure land Buddhism utilizes doctrines from the Pāli canon, see Robert Szuksztul, "Possible Roots of the Pure Land Buddhist Notion of Practice in Light of Some Early Buddhist Sources," *Polish Journal of the Arts and Culture* 16, no. 4 (2015): 155–177.
9. Lokesh Chandra, "Royal Attributes of the Nirmāṇakāya Śākyamuni and the Dharmakāya Buddhas," in *Sanskrit Vimarśaḥ*, Special Issue Vol. 6, ed. Radhavallabh Tripathi et al. (New Delhi: Rashtriya Sanskrit Sansthan, 2012), 355–368.
10. For an examination of evidence, see Georgios T. Halkias, *Luminous Bliss: A Religious History of Pure Land Literature in Tibet. With an Annotated Translation and Critical Analysis of the Orgyen-ling Golden Short Sukhāvatīvyūha-sūtra* (Honolulu: University of Hawaii Press, 2013), 20–32, quote at 23.
11. See vow thirty-six in the Tibetan version of the long *Sukhāvatīvyūha-sūtra*. As shown by Paul Harrison, "Women in the Pure Land: Some Reflections on the Textual Sources," *Journal of Indian Philosophy* 26 (1998): 553–572, Sukhāvatī was understood to have been paradigmatically single-sex (i.e., male), while the widespread belief that the inhabitants of the western realm are neither male nor female finds no clear support in the Sanskrit, Tibetan, and Chinese versions of the long sutra. While the textual sources are unambiguous in this respect, there are Chinese and Japanese "birth accounts" (Jp. *ōjōden*; Ch. *wangshengzhuan*) of women who were allegedly born in Sukhāvatī; see Christophe Kleine, "Portraits of Pious Women in East Asian Buddhist Hagiography: A Study of Accounts of Women Who Attained Birth in Amida's Pure Land," *Bulletin de l'Ecole Française d'Extrême-Orient* 85 (1998): 325–361.
12. See Hisao Inagaki, *Amida Dhāraṇī Sūtra and Jñānagarbha's Commentary: An Annotated Translation from Tibetan of the Anantamukha-nirhāra-dhāraṇī Sūtra and Ṭikā*, Kyoto Ryukoku Literature Series 7 (Kyoto, Japan: Ryukoku Gakkai, 1999), 12.
13. For a discussion, see Halkias, *Luminous Bliss*, 64–65.
14. For an introduction on the history and contents of these catalogs, see Georgios T. Halkias, "Tibetan Buddhism Registered: An Imperial Catalogue from the Palace Temple of 'Phang-thang," *The Eastern Buddhist* 36, nos. 1–2 (2004): 46–105.
15. See Nils Simonsson, *Indo-tibetische studien: die Methoden der tibetischen Übersetzer, untersucht im Hinblick auf die Bedeutung ihrer Übersetzungen für die Sanskritphilologie*, vol. 1 (Uppsala, Sweden: Almqvist & Wiksells, 1957), 259–260.
16. The contents of this section draw on Halkias, *Luminous Bliss*, 63–65.
17. Akamatsu Kōshō, "Chibetto-yaku Amidakyō no ihon: Tonkō shahon P tib 758 ni tsuite," *Indogaku Bukkyōgaku Kenkyū* 33, no. 1 (1984): 150–151.
18. For an informative discussion on the formation of a Tibeto-Chinese community based on textual evidence see Tokio Takata, "Tibetan Dominion over Dunhuang and the Formation of a Tibeto-Chinese Community," *Buddhist Road Paper*. Special issue: *Central Asian Networks. Rethinking the Interplay of Religions, Art and Politics across the Tarim Basin (5th–10th c.)*, ed. Erika Forte, 6, no. 1 (2019): 85–106.
19. See Georgios T. Halkias, "With and Without Titles in Sanskrit: Indo-Tibetan Pure Land Texts in the Kangyur," *Journal of the Centre for Buddhist Studies (Sri Lanka)* 11 (2012): 195–206.
20. For pertinent catalogs for further research see Marcelle Lalou, *Inventaire des Manuscrits tibétains de Touen-huang conservés à la Bibliothèque Nationale*, 3 vols. (Paris: Bibliothèque Nationale, 1939–1961); Tsuguhito Takeuchi, *Old Tibetan Manuscripts from East Turkestan in the Stein Collection of the British Library*, 3 vols. (London: The British Library, 1997–2000); Louis de la Vallée Poussin, *Catalogue of the Tibetan Manuscripts from Tun-Huang in the India Office Library*. (Oxford: Oxford University Press, 1962); and Zuihō Yamaguchi et al., eds., *Sutain Shushu Chibetto-go Bunken Kaidai Mokuroku (A Catalogue of the Tibetan Manuscripts Collected by Sir Aurel Stein)*, 12 vols. (Tokyo: Toyo Bunko, 1977–1988).
21. See, for example, Jonathan A. Silk, "The Virtues of Amitābha: A Tibetan Poem from Dunhuang," *Bukkyô Bunka Kenkyûjo Kiyô* 32 (1993): 1–109, and a new reading of IOL Tib J 724 by the same author, "The Ten Virtues of Loudly Invoking the Name of Amitābha: Stein Tibetan 724 and an Aspect of Chinese

Nianfo Practice in Tibetan Dunhuang," *Journal of the American Oriental Society* 137, no. 3 (2017): 473–482.

22. For a discussion and a Tibetan–English translation of the *Aparimitāyur-nāma-mahāyāna-sūtra,* see Halkias, *Luminous Bliss,* 67–75.
23. See Yoshiro Imaeda, "À propos du manuscrit Pelliot tibétain 999," in *Sūryacandrāya: Essays in Honour of Akira Yuyama on the Occasion of His 65th Birthday,* ed. Paul Harrison and Gregory Schopen (Swisttal-Odendorf, Germany: Indica et Tibetica Verlag, 1998), 87–94.
24. Mathew T. Kapstein, "The Treaty Temple of the Turquoise Grove," in *Buddhism between Tibet and China,* ed. Matthew T. Kapstein (Boston: Wisdom, 2014), 21–72, quote at 46.
25. Roberto Vitali, *Early Temples of Central Tibet* (London: Serindia, 1990), 75–76.
26. Mathew T. Kapstein, "Pure Land Buddhism in Tibet? From Sukhāvatī to the Field of Great Bliss," in *Approaching the Land of Bliss: Religious Praxis in the Cult of Amitābha,* ed. Richard K. Payne and Kenneth K. Tanaka (Honolulu: University of Hawaii Press, 2004), 16–51.
27. *Bde smon phyogs bsgrigs,* vol. 1 (Khreng tu'u: Si khron mi rigs dpe skrun khang, 1994).
28. Georgios T. Halkias, "Compassionate Aspirations and their Fulfilment: Dol-po-pa's A Prayer for Birth in Sukhāvatī," in *As Long as Space Endures: Essays on the Kālacakra Tantra in Honor of H.H. the Dalai Lama,* ed. Edward A. Arnold (Ithaca, NY: Snow Lion, 2009), 259–275.
29. For a German translation and introduction to the *Rnam dag bde chen zhing gi smon lam,* see Peter Schwieger, *Ein Tibetisches Wunschgebet um Wiedergeburt in der Sukhāvatī* (St. Augustin, Germany: VGH Wissenschaftsverlag, 1978). For an English translation, see Tadeusz Skorupski, "A Prayer for Rebirth in Sukhavati," in *The Buddhist Forum III,* ed. Tadeusz Skorupski (London: School of Oriental and African Studies, 1994), 375–409.
30. *Bde smon phyogs bsgrigs,* vol. 1, 215–216.
31. Peking, vol. 22, 5.9.119. The Tibetan version lists forty-nine vows. For a comparative table of the vows between the Sanskrit version and Chinese translation attributed to Saṃghavarman, refer to Luis Gómez, *The Land of Bliss: The Paradise of the Buddha Measureless Light* (Honolulu: University of Hawaii Press, 1996), 264–265.
32. *'Phags pa bzang po spyod pa'i smon lam gyi rgyal po,* Dpe bsdur ma, vol. 13, 898–906.
33. *Rnam dag bde chen zhing gi smon lam gyi 'grel bzhad thar lam snang byed* in Gla bla bsod nam chos 'grup *Gsung 'bum,* vol. 5, 25–562 (Delhi: dkon mchog lha bris).
34. The commentaries are found in the *Bde smon phyogs bsgrigs,* vol. 2. (Khreng tu'u: Si khron mi rigs dpe skrun khang, 1994).
35. There are no references to *phowa* practices to Sukhāvatī in India and East Asia and their appearance in Tibet are traced to treasure literature of the 14th century; see Halkias, *Luminous Bliss,* 154–163.
36. For a detailed study of Karma Chagme's commentary on the different kinds of *phowa,* see Georgios T. Halkias, "Ascending to Heaven after Death: Karma Chags med's Commentary on Mind Transference," *Revue d'Etudes Tibétaines* 52 (2019): 70–89.
37. See *The Life of Shabkar: The Autobiography of a Tibetan Yogi,* trans. Matthieu Ricard (New York: State University of New York Press, 1994), 488.
38. Halkias, *Luminous Bliss,* 134–136, 148.
39. See *Bde smon phyogs bsgrigs,* vol. 1.
40. James D. Gentry, "Liberation through Sensory Encounters in Tibetan Buddhist Practice," *Revue d'Etudes Tibétaines* 50 (2019): 73–131.
41. See Gentry, "Liberation through Sensory Encounters," 100.
42. For Tucci, Amitābha is commonly portrayed in red in his *maṇḍala,* though the use of the golden color is justified by the literary tradition: *Tibetan Painted Scrolls,* 288.
43. For an introduction and translation of Karma Chags med's *Invoking the Guardians of Sukhāvatī,* see Halkias, *Luminous Bliss,* 179–185.

44. For a 15th-century thangka of the Amitāyus Nine Deity Maṇḍala, see HAR: Himalayan Art Resources.
45. Avalokiteśvara's mantra has remained linked in the Tibetan consciousness to the idea of rebirth in Sukhāvatī due to an appreciation of the close relationship between Avalokiteśvara and Amitābha; see Alexander Studholme, *Origins of Oṃ Maṇipadme Hūṃ: A Study of the Kāraṇḍavyūha Sūtra* (New York: State University of New York, 2002), 118.
46. *Bka' thang zangs gling ma* (Khreng tu'u: Si khron mi rigs dpe skrun khang, 1989).
47. For a comprehensive list of Japanese authors and their works pertaining to Tibetan pure land devotion see Jonathan A. Silk, "In Praise of His Mighty Name: A Tibetan Poem on Amitābha from Dunhuang," in *Pure Lands in Asian Texts and Contexts: An Anthology*, ed. Georgios T. Halkias and Richard K. Payne (Honolulu: University of Hawaii Press, 2019), 496–539.

Georgios Halkias